Praise for *God's Bankers*

"*God's Bankers* is often fascinating reading, full of international intrigue. . . . *God's Bankers* is meticulously researched. Almost 200 pages of end notes indicate the care Posner took in nine years spent researching his subject. . . . The book tells a compelling story, but never at the expense of journalistic principles. Posner might speculate, but he is always careful to mark it as such, and to point out the facts and primary sources that support or undermine the speculation. . . . His work pulls together existing scholarship and massive amounts of original research to present the closest thing to a definitive account of the workings of money and finance within the Vatican that could be produced without cooperation from the Vatican itself." —*Washington Independent Review of Books*

"Posner . . . uses his superlative investigative skills to craft a fascinating and comprehensive look at the dark side of the Catholic Church. . . . Accessible and well written, Posner's is the definitive history of the topic to date."
—*Publishers Weekly* (starred review)

"The Vatican began trying to reform its bank, but with only modest success. Now there's a new sheriff in town, Pope Francis, and he has made significant progress. Posner's compelling book provides a benchmark for measuring his success." —*The Philadelphia Inquirer*

"A dogged reporter exhaustively pursues the nefarious enrichment of the Vatican, from the Borgias to Pope Francis. . . . A meticulous work that cracks wide open the Vatican's legendary, enabling secrecy." —*Kirkus Reviews*

"Why all this reform? Wall Street–lawyer-turned-author Gerald Posner lays it out in his deeply researched, passionately argued book, *God's Bankers: A History of Money and Power at the Vatican.* Posner . . . is a merciless pit bull of an investigator, marshaling mountains of evidence to make his arguments. . . . The heart of *God's Bankers* lies in chapters devoted to the church's actions during and immediately after World War II. In these chapters, Posner dissects the church's
—*Chicago Tribune*

"A fast-paced read that brings history alive on every page. The book will captivate those who prefer their historical nonfiction spiked with real-life tales of murder, power, and intrigue." —*Booklist*

"A highly anticipated book, the result of a nine-year investigation by author Gerald Posner. It reads like Robert Ludlow's fiction [and] paints a picture of murder, double-dealing, and fraud surrounding the bank. . . . It is the nonfiction version of *The Da Vinci Code*." —Michael Smerconish, CNN

"Expertly shows that theory and conjecture aren't necessary when the real-life narrative is compelling enough. . . . Posner's history of the institution reads like a sprawling novel, full of complex characters and surprising twists. . . . Readers interested in issues involving religion and international finance will find Posner's work a compelling read." —*Library Journal*

"A stunning exposé by investigative reporter Gerald Posner. As exciting as a mystery thriller." —*Providence Journal*

"An outstanding book." —John L. Allen, journalist for *The Boston Globe*

"An exhaustive history of the financial machinations at the center of the church in Rome. . . . Posner weaves an extraordinarily intricate tale of intrigue, corruption, and organized criminality. . . . Posner's gifts as a reporter and storyteller are most vividly displayed in a series of lurid chapters on the American archbishop Paul Marcinkus, the arch-Machiavellian who ran the Vatican Bank from 1971 to 1989." —*The New York Times Book Review*

"Right out of the gate this book fascinated and intrigued me. . . .This is the first time that an account of church history has seemed unfiltered—reduced to its blemished and often ugly truth. Utilizing his skills in investigative journalism, Posner thoroughly details and lays out the facts for readers. It is an uncomfortable read that includes murder, money laundering, corruption, and genocide. . . . The tangled tapestry that Posner unravels between the Vatican and its bank is a twisted tale—but *God's Bankers* is a must read!"

—*Rational Doubt*

Also by Gerald Posner

Mengele

Warlords of Crime

The Bio-Assassins

Hitler's Children

Case Closed

Citizen Perot

Killing the Dream

Motown

Why America Slept

Secrets of the Kingdom

Miami Babylon

GOD'S BANKERS

A History of Money and Power at the Vatican

GERALD POSNER

Simon & Schuster Paperbacks
New York London Toronto Sydney New Delhi

Simon & Schuster Paperbacks
An Imprint of Simon & Schuster, Inc.
1230 Avenue of the Americas
New York, NY 10020

First Simon & Schuster trade paperback edition September 2015

Illustration credits are on page 733.

Interior design by Robert E. Ettlin

Manufactured in the United States of America

10 9 8 7 6 5 4 3 2

The Library of Congress has cataloged the hardcover edition as follows:

Posner, Gerald L.
God's bankers : a history of money and power at the Vatican / By Gerald Posner.
pages cm
1. Catholic Church—Finance. 2. Catholic Church—Corrupt practices. 3. Istituto per le opere di religione—Corrupt practices. 4. Banks and banking—Vatican City. 5. Catholic Church—History—20th century. 6. Catholic Church—History—21st century. 7. Catholic Church—Controversial literature. I. Title.
BX1950.P68 2015
364.16'8—dc23 2014021061

ISBN 978-1-4165-7659-4
ISBN 978-1-4391-0986-1 (ebook)

To Trisha, my muse and eternal love

Contents

Preface

In 1984, I traveled to Buenos Aires as part of my research for a biography of Auschwitz's "Angel of Death," Nazi Dr. Josef Mengele. I petitioned Argentina's first democratically elected president, Raúl Alfonsin, for access to the country's secret files on Mengele. There was no response for several weeks. Then, one night, at nearly 11:00 p.m., several uniformed police knocked on the door of my downtown hotel. I was put into the back seat of a blue Falcon, the very type of unmarked car that had become notorious under the military junta for taking away thousands of dissidents, many of whom were killed. But my trip ended at the main headquarters of the Federal Police. A grim-looking colonel informed me that he had been ordered to produce some documents. The folder I soon reviewed in an adjacent room contained a treasure trove of information about Josef Mengele and his decade as a fugitive in Argentina, everything from the original International Red Cross passport under an alias on which he had arrived from Europe to details of how he stayed one step ahead of Nazi hunters. A few of those papers raised broader questions about whether Nazi war criminals had reached safe haven in South America after World War II with the assistance of a few ranking Catholic prelates in Rome.

A few weeks later, I was in Asunción. There, I toured the country with Colonel Alejandro von Eckstein, a military officer who was not only a good friend of the country's dictator, Alfredo Stroessner, but who had personally cosponsored Mengele's application for Paraguayan citizenship. With von Eckstein in tow, I reviewed a small part of that country's sealed Mengele file. And I met a contingent of diehard neo-Nazis in Nueva Bavaria (New Bavaria), in the south of the country. Mengele had found safe haven there in 1960. Feeling safe to talk openly because of von Eckstein's introduction, they regaled me with stories about how a local hotel in the rain forest had served decades earlier as a clearinghouse for some of the most notorious Nazis. And mixed in those stories were references once again to clerics in Rome to whom those South American National Socialists were grateful.

After that book, *Mengele*, was published in 1986, I moved on to other subjects. But the story about the church and its possible ties to the Third Reich had captured my attention and I tried staying abreast of it. In 1989, *The New York Times* published my long letter, "Why the Vatican Kept Silent on Nazi Atrocities; The Failure to Act." That was a response to an editorial by conservative commentator Patrick Buchanan absolving the church of any moral responsibility for the Holocaust. Two years later the *Times* published my op-ed, "The Bormann File," in which I castigated Argentina for not releasing a secret dossier about Hitler's deputy that I had seen when I was inside the country's Federal Police headquarters.

The last paragraph of my 1989 *Times* letter explained that I approached the question of any role the church might have played during World War II both as a reporter and a Catholic: "Although my father was Jewish, my mother was Catholic, and I was educated by Jesuits. I consider myself as much a Catholic as Mr. Buchanan. But I am embarrassed by his need to defend the church on every historical issue. The church has been involved in terrible undertakings, and they cannot be denied. That many individual nuns and priests exhibited great bravery during World War II to save many victims does not diminish the silence or acts of the church's hierarchy."

My focus, I would discover in the coming years, was far too narrow. I had thought the story was about a volatile mixture: institutional anti-Semitism and a fear of communism exacerbated by church leaders who failed to act forcefully when confronted with one of history's greatest horrors in the Holocaust. What I discovered instead was that what happened within the church during World War II was part of a much more complex saga. The truth could be found only by following the trail of money.

As Elliot Welles, an Auschwitz survivor and a Nazi hunter for the Anti-Defamation League, told me, "Profits. They matter as much in the church as they do inside IBM. Don't forget it."

Even in 2005, when I started this book in earnest, I still underestimated its scope. Then I envisioned reporting only the story of the scandal-ridden Vatican Bank, founded in the middle of World War II. It has operated for seventy years as a hybrid between a central bank of a sovereign government and an aggressive investment banking house. While the Vatican Bank is at the center of this modern chronicle, it is impossible to fully understand the finances of the Vatican without going back in church history.

This story is a classic investigative tale about the political intrigue and secretive inner workings of the world's largest religion. It is not about faith, belief in God, or questions about the existence of a higher power. Instead, *God's Bankers* is about how money, and accumulating and fighting over it, has been a dominant theme in the history of the Catholic Church and often in shaping its divine mission. "You can't run the church on Hail Marys," said one bishop who ran the Vatican Bank.

God's Bankers lays bare how over centuries the church went from surviving on donations from the faithful and taxes levied in its vast earthly kingdom to a Lilliputian country that hesitatingly embraced capitalism and modern finance. During the 1800s, Catholics were barred from even making loans that charged interest. A century later the Vatican Bank orchestrated complex schemes involving dozens of offshore shell companies as well as businessmen who often ended up in jail or dead. How and why that remarkable transformation took place is in part the tale of *God's Bankers*.

The challenge in this project was to follow the money from the Borgias to Pope Francis, all the while prying into an institution that guards its secrets and keeps massive documentation sealed in its self-described Secret Archives. Compounding the problem, as one author wrote in 1996, "Vatican officials would sooner talk about sex than money." The story that Rome preferred I not tell had to be pieced together from documents scattered in private and public archives, information gleaned from litigation files and court records, and dozens of interviews. A handful of clerics and lay officials in Rome—who, fearing retribution, spoke only on the condition of anonymity—provided an unprecedented insight into the cutthroat infighting that has often crippled the modern Papacy. Those interviews laid out the considerable challenge confronting Pope Francis when it comes to reforming the finances of the Vatican.

As I assembled my reporting, I realized a crucial part of the mix was missing: the inexorable quest for power that is tied to the pursuit of money. In the Vatican, it is a volatile brew. There are nearly a thousand men, most celibate, who live and work together, and wield not only great earthly power but who believe for the most part that they have inherited divine rights in safeguarding the "one and true" church. In the end, they are human, hobbled by the same frailties and shortcomings common to the rest of us. Little wonder that despite their best intentions they have often ended up in internecine wars and stunning scandals that rival those of any secular government.

A public mythology in books, articles, and movies has grown around the church and its money. Freemasons, the Illuminati, mobsters protected by priests, murdered Popes, hoards of Nazi gold in the Vatican's basement—the wildest theories might be entertaining but they poorly serve history. *God's Bankers* cuts through the masses of misinformation to present an unvarnished account of the quest for money and power in the Roman Catholic Church. No embellishment is needed. That real tale is shocking enough.

GOD'S BANKERS

1

Murder in London

London, June 18, 1982, 7:30 a.m. Anthony Huntley, a young postal clerk at the *Daily Express*, was walking to work along the footpath under Blackfriars Bridge. His daily commute had become so routine that he paid little attention to the bridge's distinctive pale blue and white wrought iron arches. But a yellowish orange rope tied to a pipe at the far end of the north arch caught his attention. Curious, he leaned over the parapet and froze. A body hung from the rope, a thick knot tied around its neck. The dead man's eyes were partially open. The river lapped at his feet. Huntley rubbed his eyes in disbelief and then walked to a nearby terrace with an unobstructed view over the Thames: he wanted to confirm what he had seen. The shock of his grisly discovery sank in.[1] By the time Huntley made his way to his newspaper office, he was pale and felt ill. He was so distressed that a colleague had to make the emergency call to Scotland Yard.[2]

In thirty minutes the Thames River Police anchored one of their boats beneath Blackfriars' Number One arch. There they got a close-up of the dead man. He appeared to be about sixty, average height, slightly overweight, and his receding hair was dyed jet black. His expensive gray suit was lumpy and distorted. After cutting him down, they laid the body on the boat deck. It was then they discovered the reason his suit was so misshapen. He had stones stuffed in his trouser pockets, and half a brick inside his jacket and another half crammed in his pants.[3] The River Police thought it a likely suicide. They took no crime scene photos before moving the body to nearby Waterloo Pier, where murder squad detectives were waiting.[4]

There the first pictures were taken of the corpse and clothing. The stones and brick weighed nearly twelve pounds. The name in his Italian passport was Gian Roberto Calvini.[5] He had $13,700 in British, Swiss, and Italian currency. The $15,000 gold Patek Philippe on his wrist had stopped at 1:52 a.m. and a pocket watch was frozen at 5:49 a.m. Sandwiched between the rocks in his pockets were two wallets, a ring, cuff links, some papers, four eyeglasses, three eyeglass cases, a few photographs, and a pencil.[6] Among the papers was an address book page with the contact details for a former official at the Banca Nazionale del Lavoro; Italy's Socialist Finance Minister; a prominent London solicitor; and Monsignor Hilary Franco, who held the honorary title of Prelate of the Pope.[7] Police never found the rest of the book.

A city coroner arrived at 9:30, two hours after the body's discovery, and took it to London's Milton Court morgue.[8] There they stripped the corpse, took his fingerprints, and prepared for an autopsy. Their notes reflect that the dead man oddly wore two pairs of underwear.[9]

London police quickly learned from the Italian embassy that the passport was a fake. And it took only a day to discover the false name was simply a variation of the dead man's real one: he was sixty-two-year-old Italian banker Roberto Calvi, chairman and managing director of Milan's Banco Ambrosiano, one of Italy's largest private banks. He had been missing for a week. A judge there had issued a fugitive warrant because Calvi had jumped bail pending the appeal of a criminal fraud conviction the previous year.

A Roman magistrate and four Italian detectives flew to London to help British police cobble together a personal dossier.[10] Calvi had risen from a middle-class family to become the chief of the Ambrosiano. He had turned a sleepy provincial bank into an aggressive international merchant bank. The magistrate informed his British counterpart that Calvi was no ordinary banker. He was involved with some of Italy's greatest power brokers in a secret Masonic lodge and he was a confidant of the Vatican's top moneymen.[11]

Despite his criminal conviction, the Ambrosiano's board had allowed him to remain at the helm of the bank. Although Calvi publicly promised to rescue his financial empire and restore its reputation, he knew that the Ambrosiano was near collapse under the weight of enormous debts and bad investments.[12] The bank's board of directors had fired him only the day before his body swung from Blackfriars.[13]

The police began patching together how Calvi ended up in London. His odyssey had begun a week earlier when he had flown from Rome to Venice.

From there he went by car to Trieste, where a fishing trawler took him on the short journey across the Gulf of Trieste to the tiny Yugoslavian fishing village of Muggia.[14] The moment he left Italy's territorial waters he became a fugitive. From Muggia, an Italian smuggler arranged for him to be driven overnight to Austria, where he shuttled between several cities for a few days before boarding a private charter in Innsbruck for a flight to London. He spent the last three days of his life in flat 881, a tiny room at the Chelsea Cloisters, a dreary guesthouse in the capital's posh South Kensington district.[15]

The number of unanswered questions grew as the investigation continued. They were not even certain how Calvi got to Blackfriars. It was four and a half miles from his guesthouse. On a walk he would have passed half a dozen other bridges, any of which would have been just as suitable for a flashy suicide. Calvi was well known for his entourage of bodyguards. But British investigators found none. Nor could they locate a black briefcase supposedly crammed with sensitive documents.[16] Calvi's waistcoat was buttoned incorrectly, which friends and family told the police was out of character for the compulsive banker.[17] He had shaved his trademark mustache the day before his death, but police interpreted that not as a sign of a suicidal man but evidence that he was altering his appearance to successfully stay on the run.[18]

Two men had been with Calvi in London. Silvano Vittor, a small-time smuggler, had flown with him on the charter. The other, Flavio Carboni, was a flashy Sardinian with diverse business interests and much rumored mob connections.[19] They had fled London before detectives could interview them.

The police had also to cope with a flood of false sightings. Many thought they had seen Calvi in his final days, everywhere from the Tower of London to a sex parlor to a nightclub in the company of a cocaine trafficker.[20]

Police soon confirmed that Calvi had a $3 million life insurance policy that named his family as the only beneficiaries.[21] In his spartan hotel room investigators found a bottle of barbiturates, more than enough for a painless suicide. But toxicology reports revealed no trace of any drug. When police interviewed Calvi's wife, Clara, she said that in one recent telephone call he told her, "I don't trust the people I'm with anymore."[22] Anna, Calvi's daughter, told the inspectors that she had spoken to her father three times the day before he died. He seemed agitated and urged her to leave her Zurich home and join her mother in Washington, D.C. "Something really important is happening, and today and tomorrow all hell is going to break loose."[23]

Another complication was that Calvi suffered from mild vertigo. The police calculated that he had to be acrobatic to reach his hanging spot. It required climbing over the parapet, descending a narrow twenty-five-foot ladder attached to the side of the bridge, rolling over a three-foot gap in construction scaffolding, and then tying one end of the rope around a pipe and the other around his throat, all the while balancing himself with twelve pounds of rocks and a brick crammed into his pockets, suit, and crotch. Not likely, thought the lead detective.[24] Moreover, the police matched the stones to a construction site some three hundred yards east of the Thames. Calvi would have had to pick up the rocks there and return to Blackfriars before putting them into his clothing. But lab tests found no residue on his hands. Also, since the ladder he would have descended was heavily rusted, police expected some trace on his hands, suit, or polished dress shoes. There was none.

The London coroner, Dr. David Paul, expressed no doubts that the cause of death was suicide. He relied on the opinion of Professor Keith Simpson, the dean of British medical examiners, who had performed the autopsy.[25] A month after Calvi's body was found, an inquest was held in the Coroner's Court. Paul presented the details of the police investigation and autopsy to a nine-person jury. Simpson testified that in his postmortem exam he found no signs of foul play and "there was no evidence to suggest that the hanging was other than a self-suspension in the absence of marks of violence."[26] Thirty-seven others testified, mostly police officers.[27] Calvi's brother, Lorenzo, surprised the inquest with a written statement that revealed that Roberto had tried killing himself a year earlier. Carboni and Vittor, the duo with Calvi in London, refused to return to England but submitted affidavits. When they last saw Calvi late on the night he died, he was relaxed. Nothing seemed out of the ordinary. Police would not discover for another decade that Carboni had left London with Calvi's briefcase packed with important documents.[28]

Paul admitted that it was difficult for Calvi to kill himself at Blackfriars. But it would have been just as tough for someone to murder him and leave no trace evidence or injuries on the body.[29] Paul took ten hours to set forth his case. He allowed only a twenty-minute lunch break. It was Friday evening and the jury seemed restless to go home. But the coroner insisted they start deliberations.

The six men and three women reported back in under an hour. They were having trouble reaching a verdict. Dr. Paul instructed them that their decision did not have to be unanimous. Seven of nine jurors would suffice for a verdict.[30] After another hour, at 10 p.m., they returned with a majority finding that Calvi had killed himself.[31]

The Calvi family instantly rejected the finding.[32] Clara told an Italian newspaper that her husband was murdered and his death was connected to "ferocious struggles for power in the Vatican."[33] Some questioned whether she was motivated by money in pushing a murder theory since Calvi's life insurance was voided if he killed himself.[34] But the Calvis were not the only ones skeptical about the suicide ruling. Italian investigators who had assisted the British police believed there was foul play.[35] And businessmen and government officials who knew Calvi were startled by the finding. "Why bother to go to London to do that," a senior bank director said. The British and Italian press were unanimous that the British inquest seemed a surprisingly incompetent rush to judgment.[36] That verdict would probably have been greeted with even greater derision had it then been public knowledge that only days before his death Calvi had written a personal letter—part confessional, part a plea for help—to Pope John Paul II.[37] In the letter, Calvi declared he had been a strategic front man for the Vatican in fighting Marxism from Eastern Europe to South America.[38] And he warned that upcoming events would "provoke a catastrophe of unimaginable proportions in which the Church will suffer the gravest damage."[39] He pleaded for an immediate meeting with the Pontiff so that he could explain everything. He also claimed to have "important documents" for the Pope.[40]

The catastrophe Calvi wrote about might have been the Ambrosiano's collapse, which took place within weeks of his death.[41] Early news reports said the bank had a debt of $1.8 billion, much of it guaranteed by the Istituto per le Opere di Religione (the Institute for Works of Religion, or more simply, the Vatican Bank).[42] Investigators soon learned the Vatican Bank was the Ambrosiano's largest shareholder. Did the Vatican itself play a role in the Ambrosiano's failure? British tabloids quickly dubbed Calvi "God's Banker."[43] A veritable conspiracy industry in "Who killed Calvi?" sprang up, complete with TV documentaries, books, and even walking tours of Blackfriars Bridge.

Nine months after the coroner's verdict, three Italian forensics experts conducted a second autopsy but could not resolve whether the death was suicide or murder.[44] The Calvis pushed for a new inquest.[45] A British appellate court ordered one almost a year to the date after the original hearing.[46]

A different coroner, Dr. Arthur Gordon Davies, impaneled another jury of nine. This time there was no crammed single day of testimony and deliberations. Instead, the "what's-the-rush" pacing translated into a nearly two-week hearing. When the jurors got the case they deliberated for three hours before settling unanimously on an "open verdict," a British bureaucratic loophole that essentially means "we don't know." The original suicide finding was vacated. The case was reclassified unsolved and there was no official cause of death.[47]

The Calvis then petitioned Italian prosecutors to get a new investigation of the death.[48] The family hired U.S.-based Kroll Security Group—a preeminent private investigative company—to conduct a fresh probe.[49] Kroll concluded that both British inquests were "incomplete at best and potentially flawed at worst," as they had glossed over evidence that indicated Calvi might have been drugged and murdered.[50] The following year, the Calvis retained two former Scotland Yard forensic scientists to utilize a laser test not available in 1982 to reexamine the clothing. They discovered water staining on Calvi's suit and unexplained marks on the back of his jacket. It was "almost inconceivable," they concluded, that Calvi alone had climbed to the spot on the bridge's scaffolding from which he was hanged.[51]

In 1998, sixteen years after his death, the Calvi family convinced a Roman judge to order the body exhumed. Pathologists at Milan's respected Institute of Forensic Medicine conducted a thorough autopsy.[52] They cited suspicious circumstantial evidence, including possible bruises on the banker's wrist and foot. They also identified traces of another person's DNA on Calvi's underwear.[53] The team offered a complicated explanation of how water stains on the clothing—read against a table of the tides on the fateful night—suggested it was likely murder. But there still was not enough compelling evidence to move the case forward.

Meanwhile, Italian prosecutors had a problem. Too many people were either confessing to killing Calvi or trying to cut deals on their own criminal cases by asserting they knew who had done it. So many claimed to have "the inside story" that after a while an offer to solve the Calvi case became the quickest way for a plea-bargaining defendant to lose credibility.

In 2002, when movers were packing up the Institute of Forensic Medicine in preparation for a cross-town move, they stumbled across some mislaid evidence—Calvi's tongue, part of his intestines and neck, and some fabric from his suit and shirt—in the back of a cupboard. Three Roman investigating magistrates ordered the evidence be turned over for yet another examination.

Scientists applied the latest forensic techniques, some of which had not existed just a couple of years earlier. If Calvi had climbed into place over the bridge's scaffolding, reenactments demonstrated that he would have had microscopic iron filings under his nails or on his shoes and socks. There were none. And markings on his upper vertebrae indicated two points of strangulation. Calvi was strangled *before* the cord was placed around his neck.[54]

The Calvis cited those findings in demanding the criminal investigation move faster. But prosecutors were in no hurry, hoping to avoid any mistakes in a case already marked by many missteps. It took another three years before they had enough evidence to issue murder indictments against five people, including the former chief of the secret Masonic lodge of which Calvi was a member and also Flavio Carboni, who was with Calvi in London over the fateful days in 1982.[55]

A high security courtroom in Rome's Rebibbia Prison was built for the sensational televised trial, which got under way on October 6, 2005.[56] The murder case was circumstantial. And the motive was a convoluted one involving embezzlement and blackmail. Still, many legal observers expected a guilty verdict. The jury got the trial after twenty months but deliberated only a day and a half. Almost two years to the date of their arrest, the defendants received the verdict: not guilty on all charges.[57]

"It [the acquittal] has killed Calvi all over again," a stunned prosecutor told the press.[58] In 2010 and 2011 two Italian appellate courts upheld the acquittals.[59]

What did Calvi know that was so important that someone killed him and disguised it as an elaborate public suicide? That cannot be answered without pointing a spotlight on the corridors of power and money inside the Vatican. The underlying tale is how for centuries the clerics in Rome, trusted with guarding the spiritual heritage of the Catholic faithful, have fought an internecine war over who controls the enormous profits and far-flung businesses of the world's biggest religion. Only by examining the Catholic Church's often contentious and uneasy history with money is it possible to expose the forces behind Calvi's death. Ultimately, Calvi's murder is a prequel to understanding the modern-day scandals from St. Peter's and fully appreciating the challenges faced by Pope Francis in trying to reform an institution in which money has so often been at the center of its most notorious scandals.

2

The Last Pope King

Long before the church became a capitalist holding company in which men like Calvi flourished, the Vatican was a semifeudal secular empire.[1] For more than a thousand years popes were unchallenged monarchs as well as the supreme leaders of the Roman church. Their kingdom was the Papal States. During the Renaissance, Popes were feared rivals to Europe's most powerful monarchies. And at its height in the eighteenth century the church controlled most of central Italy. Popes believed that God had put them on earth to reign above all other worldly rulers.[2]

The Popes of the Middle Ages had an entourage of hundreds of Italian clerics and dozens of lay deputies. In time, they became known as the Curia, referring to the court of a Roman emperor. They assisted the Pope in running the church's spiritual and temporal kingdoms. Those outside the Vatican thought of the Curia simply as the bureaucracy that administered the Papal States. But that simplistic view minimized the Ladon-like network of intrigue and deceit composed largely of celibate single men who lived and worked together at the same time they competed with each other for influence with the Pope.[3]

The cost of running the church's kingdom while maintaining the profligate lifestyle of one of Europe's grandest courts pressured the Vatican always to look for ways to bring in more money.[4] Taxes and fees levied on the Papal States paid most of the empire's basic expenses. The sales of produce from its agriculturally rich northern land as well as rents collected from its properties throughout Europe brought in extra cash. But over time that was not enough to fuel the lavish lifestyles of the Pope and his top clerics. The church found the money it needed in the selling of so-called indulgences, a sixth-century invention whereby the faithful paid for a piece of paper that promised that God would forgo any earthly punishment for the buyer's sins. The early church's penances were often severe, including flogging, imprisonment, or even death. Although some indulgences were free, the best ones—promising the most redemption for the gravest sins—were expensive.[5] The Vatican set prices according to the severity of the sin and they were initially available only to those who made a pilgrimage to Rome.[6]

Indulgences helped Urban II in the eleventh century offset the church's enormous costs in subsidizing the first Crusades. He offered full absolution to anyone who volunteered to fight in "God's army" and partial forgiveness for simply helping the Crusaders. Successive Popes became ever more creative in liberalizing the scope of indulgences and the ease with which devout Catholics could pay for them. By the early 1400s, Boniface IX—whose decadent spending kept the church under relentless financial pressure—extended indulgences to encompass sacraments, ordinations, and consecrations.[7] A few decades later, Pope Paul II waived the need for sinners to make a pilgrimage to Rome. He authorized local bishops to collect the money and dispense the indulgences and also cleared them for sale at pilgrimage sites that had relics of saints.[8] Sextus IV had an inspired idea: apply them to souls stuck in Purgatory. Any Catholic could pay so that souls trapped in Purgatory could get on a fast track to Heaven. The assurance that money alone could cut the afterlife in Purgatory was such a powerful inducement that many families sent their life savings to Rome. So much money flooded to Sextus that he was able to build the Sistine Chapel.[9] Alexander VI—the Spanish Borgia whose Papacy was marked by nepotism and brutal infighting for power—created an indulgence for simply reciting the Rosary in public. The new sales pitch promised the faithful that a generous contribution multiplied the Rosary's prayer power.[10]*

Each Pontiff understood that tax revenues from the Papal States paid most of the day-to-day bills, while indulgences paid for everything else. The church overlooked the widespread corruption and graft inherent in collecting so much cash and instead grew ever more dependent on indulgences.[12] And as they got

* Historians credit Johann Tetzel, a popular sixteenth-century Dominican priest and dispenser of indulgences, with the first advertising jingle: "As soon as the coin in the coffer rings, a soul from Purgatory springs."[11]

ever easier to buy and promised more forgiveness, they became wildly popular among ordinary Catholics.[13]

Indulgences were, however, more than a financial lifeline. They also helped medieval Roman Popes withstand challenges to their secular power. So-called antipopes—usually from other Italian cities—claimed they, rather than the pope elected in Rome, had the political or divine right to rule the Catholic Church.[14]* Although some antipopes raised their own armies and had popular backing, they never mustered the moral authority to issue indulgences. Repeated efforts over centuries by pretenders to the Papacy to package and sell forgiveness for sins failed. Few Catholics believed that anyone but the Roman Pope had the direct connection with God to offer a real indulgence.[16] And when the Pope's armies were called upon to sometimes crush an antipope, it was usually the flood of cash from indulgences that paid for the war.

By the reign of Leo X—the last nonpriest elected Pope in 1513—a growing chorus of critics condemned indulgences as a shameless ecclesiastical dependence. Leo, a prince from Florence's powerful Medici family, was a cardinal since he was thirteen. He was accustomed to an extravagant lifestyle by the time he became Pope at thirty-eight. Leo made the Papal Court the grandest in Europe, commissioning Raphael to decorate the majestic loggias. The Vatican's servants nearly doubled to seven hundred. Assuming the role of a clerical aristocracy, cardinals were called Princes of the Church.[17] Leo had no patience for critics who demanded he curb the sale of indulgences. He tried silencing his detractors by threatening excommunication.[18] When that failed, he pressed ahead with a futures market by which diminution was available for sins not yet committed.[19] So much cash flooded in that he could build St. Peter's cathedral.[20]

Pope-Kings unvaryingly were scions of a handful of powerful Italian families. When one of their sons became Pope, the by-products of a Papacy often included rampant corruption, pervasive nepotism, and unbridled debauchery.[21] The cash from indulgences mostly became a bottomless pit.[22]

The licentious lifestyle of the Papal Court and the widespread abuses in

---

* The Holy See's official directory lists thirty-nine antipopes and 265 Popes. Other sources list as many as forty-seven antipopes. An accurate count is difficult because standards for electing Popes changed frequently for more than a thousand years. Some Pontiffs were later classified as dissidents. The antipopes peaked during the twelfth to fifteenth centuries, with two or more antipopes sometimes claiming the Papacy.[15]

selling indulgences became a rallying cry for Martin Luther and the Reformation.[23] Pope Leo responded by excommunicating Luther.[24] One of the few benefits from the schism was that since Protestants condemned indulgences, the Holy See remained unopposed when it came to selling forgiveness to believers in Christ.

The steady flow of cash became ever more important as the Vatican suffered from the repercussions of the liberal political and social upheaval that swept Western Europe in the late eighteenth century, climaxing in the 1789 French Revolution. Monarchies friendly to the church were either toppled or greatly weakened. When Napoleon came to power in France in 1796 he demanded the Vatican pay millions a year in tribute to him. When the church could not afford to do so, he dispatched troops to Italy to strip many churches and cathedrals of anything of value and return the plunder to France. Worse, Rome's real estate income in post-revolution France was extinguished as the nascent republic nationalized many church properties.[25] The new National Assembly banned French bishops from sending to Rome any of the money they raised. It was not much better in other countries. In Austria, cash-strapped Emperor Joseph II undercut Papal authority by diverting the Vatican-bound money to his own treasury. Revenue from Britain, Scandinavia, and Germany slowed.[26] Even Italy's Prime Minister—personally approved for the office by Pope Pius VI—imposed a tax on church properties in a bid to stem the country's financial crisis. Pius VI denounced the new tax as "the work of the devil."[27]

The fallout continued as political unrest in Europe spilled over into the first half of the nineteenth century: Papal income fell in a remarkable forty of the century's first fifty years.[28] A few lay advisors worried that the social instability that wreaked havoc with church finances would not pass quickly. They recommended exploring ways by which the church might become less dependent on donations from the faithful. But such suggestions were invariably dismissed. Most ranking clerics believed that modern economic theory was a pernicious and reprehensible component of the liberal secular movement that had infected Europe. The Vatican had consigned to the inviolable Index of Prohibited Books John Stuart Mill's seminal *Principles of Political Economy*.[29] Pope Benedict XIV, in a much heralded encyclical, *Vix Pervenit* (On Usury and Other Dishonest Profit), reiterated the long-standing church ban on loaning money with interest. By condemning interest-bearing loans as "illicit," "evil," and a "sin," Benedict ended any internal debate.[30]

The Vatican's antiquated view about money meant that it did nothing to encourage fiscal growth or industrial development in the Papal States. The economy stagnated, and over decades tax revenues steadily declined.[31]

By the time Gregory XVI, the son of a lawyer, became Pope in 1831, the situation was so dire that he felt compelled to do something remarkable: he borrowed money from the Rothschilds, Europe's preeminent Jewish banking dynasty.[32] The £400,000 loan ($43,000,000 in 2014) was a lifeline to the church.[33] The Rothschilds had a solid reputation when it came to bailing out distressed governments. They had steadied Austria's finances after the Napoleonic Wars and provided enough money to squash two rebellions in Sicily.[34]

James de Rothschild, head of the family's Paris-based headquarters, became the official Papal banker.[35] One of his brothers, Carl, who ran the family's Naples branch, began traveling to Rome to consult with the Pope. Their financial empire prompted a mixture of envy and resentment among church officials. Most traditionalists, who referred to James as the leader of "international Jewry," were appalled that the church had resorted to "Christ-killers" for financial succor.[36] French Poet Alfred de Vigny wrote that "a Jew now reigns over the Pope and Christianity. He pays monarchs and buys nations."[37] German political writer Karl Ludwig Börne—born Loeb Baruch but changed his name upon becoming a Lutheran—thought that Gregory had demeaned the Vatican by giving Carl Rothschild an audience. Börne noted that "a wealthy Jew kisses his [the Pope's] hand" whereas "a poor Christian kisses the Pope's feet." He fanned the distrust among many of the faithful: "The Rothschilds are assuredly nobler than their ancestor Judas Iscariot. He sold Christ for 30 small pieces of silver; the Rothschilds would buy Him, if He were for sale."[38]

It had been only thirty-five years since the destabilizing aftershocks from the French Revolution had led to the easing of harsh, discriminatory laws against Jews in Western Europe. It was then that Mayer Amschel, the Rothschild family patriarch, had walked out of the Frankfurt ghetto with his five sons and established a fledgling bank. Little wonder the Rothschilds sparked such envy. By the time Pope Gregory asked for a loan they had created the world's biggest bank, ten times larger than their closest rival.[39]

Church leaders may not have liked the Rothschilds but they did like their cash. Shortly after the first loan, the Pope bestowed on Carl the medal of the Sacred Military Constantinian Order of St. George. For their part, the Rothschilds thought the Vatican was the most disorganized and chaotic mess they had ever encountered. They were startled to discover the church had no budgets or balance sheets. The prelates who controlled the money had no financial training. There were no independent reviews or audits. The combination of secrecy and disorder was ripe for abuse. When the Papal States fell into debt, the Pope sometimes simply repudiated the obligation and refused to pay. It was little wonder that the number of countries or banks willing to loan to the church had shrunk. Still, the Vatican rebuffed all financial reforms the Rothschilds suggested. Pope Gregory was suspicious of modernity, thought democracy was dangerous and destabilizing, and condemned even railroads as the work of the devil.[40]

Gregory died in 1846. His successor was Pius IX. Pius, the fourth son of a count, confronted a new problem: a surging tide of Italian nationalism that threatened the church's control of the Papal States.[41] Since the eighth century, the Papal States had been the earthly symbol of the church's power. By the time Pius became Pope, the Vatican's land spread east from Rome in a broad swath that split Italy in half. It was sandwiched between two colonial powers, the Hapsburgs to the north and the French to the south. Pius was barely on the Papal throne when popular uprisings erupted across Italy. A loosely knit federation of anticlerical anarchists and intellectuals hoped to expel the colonial powers and establish a unified Italian republic with Rome as its capital. In their vision there was no room for the Papal States. Pius viewed the nationalists with alarm and disdain.[42]

Determined not to lose the church's empire and all its income, Pius tried dampening the widespread nationalist fervor with a conciliatory step: he introduced some reforms in the Papal States.[43] His decrees established the first ever city and state councils and lifted some restrictions on speech. He freed more than a thousand political prisoners and created a Consultative Assembly composed of twenty-four elected lay representatives.[44] The standing gallows in the center of each city were demolished, and the Pope loosened the censorship on newspapers. The changes were popular. But they were a decade too late.

Sicily exploded in full rebellion in January 1848. There was a revolt in Palermo that same month.[45] Pius scrambled to stay ahead of the deteriorating situation by making more concessions. He set forth the outlines for a constitution that alluded vaguely to limiting his own secular power.[46] But the compromises from Rome got lost in the escalating violence. The nationalists drove the Austrians from Milan that spring. Fearing the Austrians might try to seize some of the church's lands in retaliation, Pius dispatched ten thousand troops. Word spread fast that the church's army was on the march. Ordinary Italians were enthusiastic. But almost as quickly as Pius had sent them, he reversed himself, declaring that he did not think the church should be at war with a devoutly Catholic nation such as Austria.[47]

Popular sentiment boiled when Pius wavered. Romans, in particular, were furious and condemned the Pope as a reactionary posing as a reformer. Large crowds protested daily outside St. Peter's and breakaway gangs clashed frequently with the Vatican's Swiss Guards. On November 15, 1848, a mob surged into the Palace of the Chancellery and chased down Count Pellegrino Rossi, the Papal Prime Minister. They cornered him on a staircase and slit his throat.[48] The next day an armed gang swarmed near the Palazzo del Quirinale and killed several Swiss Guards as well as the Pope's personal secretary.[49] Some in the mob insisted the Pope be taken prisoner. A few days later, disguised as a common priest—and with his face partially concealed by a large scarf and dark glasses—Pius fled Rome in a carriage for the remote sea fortress at Gaeta in southern Italy. The king of Naples guaranteed his safety.

France's Louis Napoleon (later Napoleon III) commissioned an expeditionary force of nine thousand troops and sent them to battle the Italian nationalists so Pius could return to Rome. The fighting was bitter and it took eight months before the French retook Rome and toppled the fledgling Republic. French army officers and three senior cardinals (the so-called Red Triumvirate) ran the city while the Pope was in exile. The French would not allow Pius to return until they were confident all the nationalist cells were eliminated.[50]

Pius returned to the Vatican nine months later. He was now the reactionary that people mistakenly thought he was before the fighting had forced him to flee for his life. The Pope would never again consider any reforms nor would there be any more compromises. The disarray he witnessed upon his return to Rome further convinced him that modern thought caused disorder. Crime was rampant. Price gouging over food exacerbated widespread hunger. Jews, a favorite scapegoat, received most of the blame, especially since some had worked with the nationalists.[51] Pius even made Rome's Jews pay the cost of his return since he contended they must have somehow been the agitators responsible for his exile in the first place.[52]

Worries about the chaos in Rome were soon replaced by concerns over the dire condition of the church's finances. The bedlam meant sales of indulgences had plummeted. Collection of taxes in the Papal States had been badly affected. There was an enormous pile of two years of unpaid bills as well as new obligations to pay for the French garrison that now protected Rome. The Vatican desperately needed an infusion of cash. The Catholic bank to which Pius hoped to go for help, Paris-based Delahante and Company, had collapsed from the fallout of the Third French Revolution.[53] Although the aristocratic Pius was an unrepentant advocate of a medieval view of Jews as the evil architects of everything from rationalism to Freemasonry to socialism, he reluctantly agreed that only the Rothschilds could again keep the Church afloat.[54]

The new Rothschild loan was 50 million francs—more than $10,000,000. That was more than the Vatican's entire budget for a year. Two additional loans were soon forthcoming, totaling another 54 million francs.[55]*

The Rothschilds, meanwhile, were criticized by some Jewish leaders who felt as though the family simply profited from the church without making any effort to change its harsh policies toward Jews. So the Rothschilds tried leveraging their influence to beseech the Holy See to improve conditions for the fifteen thousand Jews in the Papal States.[57] They asked that the Pope cancel extra taxes levied solely on Jews, the prohibition on taking property from the ghetto, and the ban on working in professions, and that he abolish onerous evidentiary standards that put them at tremendous disadvantage in court cases. Pius sent a written assurance to the Rothschilds through the Papal Nuncio in Paris that he would help.[58] Privately, he told some of his aides that he preferred martyrdom to acceding to the Rothschild requests.[59] Pius ultimately made only a single concession: he tore down the walls and chained gates that ringed Rome's notorious Jewish ghetto, the last in Europe set apart by a physical boundary.[60] But it had no practical effect, as Jews were prohibited from moving anywhere else.[61] When Carl Rothschild visited Rome four months later and complained that little had changed, Pius mollified the family by lifting a long-standing requirement that Jews attend proselytizing sermons every week on their Sabbath.

---

* The Vatican issued the equivalent of bonds that paid between 5 and 8 percent interest. The Rothschilds bought the commercial paper from the church at a 75 percent discount. What they paid the Vatican constituted the loan. The Rothschilds then resold the paper as bonds to the public, with their profit being the difference between what they paid the church and the final sales price. The interest to the buyer was in the form of a discount from the full face value. That arrangement allowed the Vatican to maintain the farce that it followed scripture and did not earn or pay interest on its investments.[56]

Pius bristled at the church's dependency on the Rothschilds. So did prominent Catholic bankers, like the Belgian André Langrand-Dumonceau, who declared it "shameful" to borrow money from Jews.[62] Church leaders believed Jewish financiers were Freemasons, part of a larger international effort to destabilize the Vatican and push a secular philosophy in which worship of money replaced that of God.[63] To make the church less reliant, Pius appointed a deacon, Giacomo Antonelli, as his Cardinal Secretary of State (roughly the Pope's Prime Minister) as well as chief of the Papal Treasury.* Antonelli, who came from a prosperous Napolitano family, had been one of Pius's few trusted aides in exile.[65] It was a controversial selection. According to Antonelli's biographer, Frank Coppa, "In pride he was considered a match for Lucifer, in politics a disciple of Machiavelli."[66] But he had the backing of Pius, the only person who mattered. The Pope gave him broad leeway to make the church self-sufficient.[67]

Antonelli began by ending the Vatican's financial subsidies for clerical orders such as the Jesuits and Franciscans. They had historically been a costly drain.[68] Although it caused a furor among the religious orders that relied on getting money from Rome, Pius refused any entreaty to reverse the decision. And as part of an ambitious restructuring of the church's debt—and against the advice of a majority in the Curia—Antonelli raised taxes and introduced new tariffs in the Papal States. He negotiated with the Rothschilds to consolidate some of the Vatican's outstanding debts into a single forty-year loan.[69] It was for a then staggering 142,525,000 francs (around $30,000,000, some 40 percent of the church's outstanding debt) at a 5 percent interest rate.[70] Antonelli proved as tough a negotiator as James Rothschild. He resisted the bankers' demands that the Vatican's extensive real estate serve as collateral. In 1859, with the new loan in place, Antonelli balanced the Papal budget for the first time since the start of the century.[71]

Antonelli soon devised a plan to entirely bypass the Rothschilds: the church would sell interest-bearing debt directly to the faithful without using an investment bank. Two Catholic newspapers offered the chance to test his do-it-alone proposal. In 1861, the Vatican brought the Jesuits' fortnightly *La Civiltà Cattolica* (Catholic Civilization) to Rome. And it purchased *L'Osserva-*

---

* Antonelli was one of the last deacons to become a cardinal. Benedict XV, in 1917, ruled that only ordained priests could be cardinals. Many clerics never fully trusted Antonelli since he was not a priest, and many believed he was secretly a Freemason.[64]

tore Romano (The Roman Observer), a paper that became required reading in far-flung Catholic communities.[72] Besides generic articles about faith, Antonelli crammed both papers with appeals for donations. The cash that came in was double his target.[73] The Pope approved the sale of future debt without the Rothschilds.

In 1860, the church issued 60 million lire in Vatican "bonds." Priests urged the faithful to buy them as their "religious duty." Bishops collected the money and sent it to Rome.[74] And when the church eventually needed help managing its debt, Antonelli and Pius ushered in two Paris-based Catholic bankers, the Marquis de la Bouillerie and Edward Blount.[75] Free of the Rothschilds, it was not long before Pius rebuilt some of the wall around Rome's Jewish ghetto.[76]

Catholics gave money to the church despite Pius's unpopularity. Italians longed for a unified Italy. They knew the Papal States were an obstacle to achieving that. The Pope's likability quotient had also suffered after a widely publicized incident in 1858 in which the Papal police in Bologna forcibly seized a six-year-old boy, Edgardo Mortara, from his Jewish parents after a Catholic housekeeper told friends she had secretly baptized the child years earlier when he had been gravely ill as an infant.[77] Once children were baptized the church considered them to be Catholic and therefore Jewish parents could not be trusted to raise them. For centuries, children allegedly baptized in the Papal States had been taken from their birth parents and raised either by a Catholic family or placed into a church-run institution dedicated to the conversion of Jews.[78]

What made the Mortara case different was that the youngster's confinement to a Rome conversion center had sparked appeals to Pius personally to intervene and order the boy returned to his parents. Pius instead directed the boy be brought regularly to the Vatican's Esquiline Palace, where he promised to personally raise him as a Catholic.[79]

The boy was, of course, awed by the splendor of the Papal Court, and Pius steadfastly ignored many appeals for his release. Napoleon III, who found it galling that the French garrison made it possible for the youngster to be held, condemned the kidnapping, as did his devout and popular wife, Empress Eugénie. The Prime Minister of the Italian state of Piedmont—seeing this as an opportunity to weaken the Papacy—promised to return the boy to his parents.[80] And Catholics in America and Britain denounced the boy's taking. Pius dismissed the outcry as a conspiracy of "freethinkers, the disciples of Rousseau and Malthus."[81] Later, in a reference often used about Jews, Pius chided his critics as "dogs" and complained there were too many in Rome.[82]

When a delegation of Roman Jews visited Pius and pleaded for the boy's release, the Pope erupted in anger, accusing them of stirring up popular sentiment against the Papacy. Personal appeals from the Rothschilds went unanswered. *La Civiltà Cattolica* fed the widely held belief that Jews murdered Christian children in order to use their blood in rituals. It reported Eastern European Jews had kidnapped and crucified children and suggested that the child's parents wanted him back only so they could torture him since he was now a Catholic.[83] The paper also published a story about Edgardo's early months in Rome, claiming that "he begged to be raised in a Christian home," and that, supposedly, without any coaxing, he said, "I am baptized and my father is the Pope."[84]

Antonelli knew the impassioned controversy was bad for business. Contributions from the faithful had plummeted due to the international outrage. Antonelli asked the Pope to reconsider. But Pius would not budge. "I have the blessed Virgin on my side," he told his Secretary of State.[85] And as for those who might not want to give money to the church because they were alienated by the taking of the boy, Pius told Antonelli that was his job to fix it.[86]*

The Pope had picked a bad time to test the limits of his secular power. Although the French had returned Pius to Rome, the nationalists had not abandoned their quest to unite Italy. A new wave of bloody insurrections kicked off across the peninsula in 1859. The resurgent instability caused distress inside St. Peter's. Napoleon's armies joined Sardinian militias in fighting Austrian troops and soon all of Italy was engulfed in civil war. The Hapsburgs eventually lost Lombardy. And the Bourbons relinquished control of Naples. Venice and Sardinia fell into the nascent unified Italian Republic. In 1861, the nationalist army annexed most of the Papal States. The Pope was now the secular king only of Rome.

Antonelli beseeched Pius to liberalize the Vatican's investments. Having lost the Papal States' income, the church would either have to downsize the

* In 1864, as the pressure on Rome increased, Pius defended the seizure of another Jewish boy. This time it was nine-year-old Giuseppe Coen, who lived in Rome's ghetto. The church claimed the boy wanted to become a Catholic and had voluntarily sought out a priest. The public outcry was again fierce. European Catholics led by the French beseeched Pius to release Coen. He again ignored them.[87]

Pope's court and Curia or find creative ways to bring in more cash. Approving Vatican "bonds" as he had the previous year was only the first step, Antonelli told the Pope. Antonelli confided to a colleague that he thought Pius would give him more leeway over the finances so long as the Pope did "not consult the Holy Spirit."[88]

Pius gave his answer later that year in an encyclical, *Quanta Cura (Condemning Current Errors)* and an attached *Syllabus of Errors.* The *Syllabus* caused an uproar.[89] It relied on edicts of previous Popes to denounce eighty tenets of modern life, including freedom of speech, divorce, the right to rebel against a lawful government, and the choice of people to practice religions other than Catholicism. *Syllabus* deplored materialism, science, liberalism, and democracy. Its eightieth statement declared there was no reason any "Roman Pope" should ever have to "harmonize himself with progress . . . [or] recent civilization."[90]

Syllabus was an unrelenting broadside condemning the modern world and held stubbornly to the notion that the church could thrive according to the standards of a bygone century.[91] Its harsh tone was particularly startling since Pius understood the church's history better than many of his predecessors. Some had hoped that Pius might revert to the reformer traits that marked his early Papacy. But *Syllabus* crushed such expectations. Antonelli knew that Western governments were dumbstruck by the denunciations of freedom of thought and of conscience.[92] In private, he tried explaining away Pius's anti-intellectual diatribe.[93] But much in the same way that the kidnappings of the Jewish children had undermined the Pope's moral standing, *Syllabus* undercut his intellectual integrity. Italian university students burned copies in protest. A few priests left their orders citing *Syllabus.* Secular newspapers trashed it.

As with the kidnappings, Pius dismissed all criticism. He boasted that *Syllabus* was a seminal pronouncement and the attacks only reinforced his view that he alone had been divinely selected to guide the church. Eventually, to settle any simmering internal dissent, he ordered all bishops and cardinals to Rome in 1869 to debate the church's role in opposing rationalism. Seven hundred ninety-two made the journey.[94] The First Vatican Council—held in the acoustically dreadful St. Peter's—focused instead on whether a Pope's authority had limits. After seven months of raucous debate a majority of the bishops voted in favor of a declaration that on all issues of faith the Pope could unilaterally invoke infallibility.[95]

But there was little time inside Pius's inner circle to celebrate. The day after the infallibility vote France declared war on Prussia.[96] The war was the ideal pretext for Napoleon to withdraw his garrison and leave Rome undefended.[97] Pius pleaded in vain to other Catholic countries for help. None did. Appalled by the two kidnappings and convinced that the Pope was an obstructionist, no leaders had any incentive to risk the lives of their troops to save a Pontiff who was so incredibly at odds with modern society.

The Vatican was defended now by Zuavi Pontifici—Papal light infantry—several thousand young, unmarried Catholic volunteers from more than two dozen countries. Few thought the ragtag force could withstand a sustained assault. The Italian king sent an emissary who offered to spare the church a humiliating military defeat by pretending the nationalist army took control of Rome under the guise of protecting the Pontiff. The nationalists even offered to recognize Papal sovereignty, the right of the Vatican to have ambassadors, and to pay some money to offset the income the church had lost from the Papal States. Pius would hear none of it. Instead, he let loose with a vicious verbal assault. The King's envoy was so shaken that in his rush to get away from Pius he almost walked out a third-story window instead of a door.[98]

Rebuffed by the Pope, Italian troops massed outside Rome. Pius could not be dissuaded of his delusion that no Italian army would dare attack Rome—a sacred city—so long as he was there.[99] When nationalist troops breached the city's outer perimeter, the Pope urged his garrison to resist the "vipers."[100] Rome fell in a day. The Pope ordered the white flag raised over St. Peter's at 9:00 a.m. on September 20. For the first time in a millennium, the church had no sovereign seat of power. Its sixteen thousand square miles of feudal empire had been reduced to a tiny parcel of land.

To soften the blow, the new republic offered the Pope the Leonine City, a large Roman district around which the ninth-century Pope Leo IV commissioned the Leonine Wall. But Pius worried that if he agreed to anything it would imply he endorsed the legitimacy of Italy's rule over his former kingdom.

Some cardinals and the Father Superior of the Jesuits advised that he flee and establish a Papacy in exile. Antonelli advised against abandoning Rome.[101] Pius needed little persuasion. He quickly refused. His exile in Gaeta had been too unsettling. He felt too old at seventy-eight to leave Italy. And he had a different plan. Although Italian officials assured him he was free to come and go as he wanted, Pius declared himself the "prisoner of the

Vatican"—a victim Pope—and remained shuttered inside St. Peter's.[102] He excommunicated those who had played key roles in the conquest of Rome. And when the new government wanted to move into the Quirinale—built in the sixteenth century as a Papal summer palace—Pius petulantly refused to hand over the keys.[103]

Pius and his advisors had every reason to resort to high theatrics: Italy's unification was disastrous for the church. And to their great frustration, there was little they could do about it. As Antonelli feared, the seizure was more than just a blow to the Vatican's prestige. The Papal States had included the Vatican's wealthiest regions and almost all its population.[104] Antonelli knew the loss meant the church was teetering on the verge of bankruptcy, some 20 million lire in debt.[105] The situation would have been worse had Antonelli not secretly met with an Italian aristocrat, Baron Alberto Blanc, and through his efforts got Italy to return 5 million lire belonging to the Holy See, all in bank accounts seized by the secular government.[106]

Pius seemed oblivious to the bad news.* He wanted money for a new militia of mercenaries to counter the nonexistent threat that Italian armies might appropriate the Vatican itself.[108] He also thought it important to preserve the spectacle of the sumptuous Papal monarchy. Pius refused to dismiss any workers. And he insisted on paying salaries and pensions for officials who had been fired by the new Italian government, as well as for those who resigned out of loyalty to the Vatican. In less than a year, 15 percent of the church's budget went to salaries of ex-employees of the Papal States.[109]

Antonelli knew it would take too long to raise money with another debt issue. After much debate, Pius and his advisors settled on an unexpected solution: to rekindle Peter's Pence. *"Obolo di San Pietro"* in Italian, "offerings from the faithful," was a fundraising practice that had been popular a thousand years earlier with the Saxons in England (before Henry VIII had banned it). Peter's Pence started as only donations, but expanded over time to include some fees paid by loyal Catholics for services such as weddings, funerals, and confirmations.[110] Special taxes levied during the Crusades were tallied as part of Peter's Pence.[111]

In better times, the Vatican set aside money raised from Peter's Pence

---

* Corrado Pallenberg, in a 1971 book, *Vatican Finances*, reported that Pius quipped, "Sarò forse infallibile, ma sono certamente fallito (I may be infallible, but I am certainly bankrupt)." There is no citation, however, and the author cannot find it in any previous history.[107]

only for extraordinary costs.[112] Now it was needed to pay day-to-day operating expenses. Catholic journals, local churches, and even Catholic politicians throughout Europe, South America, and the United States pleaded to bail out the Pope. Not only did Pius need money to survive, the pitch went, but the church also required a professional army to protect what little it had left. Cash poured in. Austrian Archduke Maximilian and most of the French aristocracy gave generously. The poor and uneducated were induced to donate by tales that Italian inquisitors had chained the Pope to a prison wall. One fraud even sold samples of "Holy straw" from the nonexistent cell's floor.[113] Catholics in different countries competed with one another to see who could raise the most.[114]

The revival of Peter's Pence was the first time ordinary Catholics felt as though they individually could help the "imprisoned" Pope. Pius adopted the unfamiliar mantle as a popular fundraiser. He acknowledged the most generous donations. The advent of photography allowed key contributors to receive signed pictures. And he doled out framed letters, personal benedictions, Papal titles of nobility, and knighthoods. The Italian ambassador to the United States noted, "Because they have no aristocracy, the Americans are particularly susceptible to this form of flattery."[115] Pittsburgh's Protestant Mellon family gave a large enough contribution to earn a Papal Marquis. Still, Antonelli knew it was not wise to fund the church on the hope that the faithful would steadily send in a lot of money. For the first three years of the reinstituted Peter's Pence, the annual receipts covered on average just four months of the church's annual deficit.[116] Another of Antonelli's ideas was to have European bishops appeal to Catholic worshippers for separate contributions—dubbed loan subscriptions—to pay down the Vatican's outstanding debt. The bishop of Autun assured his congregants "The Pope is a good risk."[117]

In Rome, Catholic financiers pitched more money-raising proposals to the Pope. Pius rejected one for a worldwide lottery to supplement Peter's Pence. He judged it a volatile mixture of capitalism and gambling.[118] And he also said no to the idea of capitalizing the remaining Papal properties throughout Europe so they could be leveraged to produce more revenue. Pius thought that violated Catholic doctrine forbidding business speculation.

Some of the Vatican resistance to capitalism was a leftover of Middle Age ideologies, a belief that the church alone was empowered by God to fight Mammon, a satanic deity of greed. And some doctrine, such as its ban on usury—earning interest on money loaned or invested—was based on a literal biblical interpretation.[119]*

Pius was especially distrustful of capitalism since he thought secular activists used it as a wedge to separate the church from its integrated role with the state. In some countries, the "capitalist bourgeoisie," as the Vatican dubbed it, had even confiscated church land for public use.[121] When leading Catholic banker André Langrand-Dumonceau went bankrupt in 1870 under the weight of too much debt, it further confirmed to the Pope that free market concepts were dangerous.[122] Also behind the resistance to change was the church's traditional view that capitalism was mostly the province of Jews. *La Civiltà Cattolica* regularly denounced the financial business as the evil dominion of Jews. Typical was this: "It [international Jewry] is the giant octopus that with its oversized tentacles envelops everything. It has its stomachs in the banks . . . and its suction cups everywhere. . . . It represents the kingdom of capital . . . the aristocracy of gold. . . . It reigns unopposed."[123]

Running parallel with the ingrained anti-Semitism was a vituperative anti-Protestantism. Protestants did not promote capitalist principles, but certain Lutheran and Calvinist doctrines were receptive to the activities that collectively emerged as capitalism. Protestants embraced private ownership of property and the right to earn profits, and allowed borrowing and lending money as well as earning interest on it. German sociologist Max Weber contended that the surge of capitalism in northern Europe was a direct result of the tenets of Protestant Christianity. He tracked how the growth of Calvinism and Methodism ran parallel to the rise of capitalism in those countries.[124] Protestants encouraged workers to find well-paying jobs and contended that employers should endeavor to provide decent working conditions.[125] They invested in ventures for profit and then used those earnings for more investments.[126] Catholic theology, in contrast, downplayed the rights of individuals, contending instead that workers should consider that one benefit of low paying work was that it contributed to the common good of fellow worshippers and the church. Vatican traditionalists condemned the capitalism that took hold in Protestant countries.[127]

---

* The ban on earning interest was not relaxed until the mid-1800s and not lifted entirely until the middle of World War I. As late as 1903, when Pius X became Pope, the anticapitalist theme continued in *Sacrorum Antistitum* (The Oath Against Modernism). That decree required all priests to swear an oath denouncing "Americanism," something Pius considered an insidious slide toward modernism.[120]

But capitalism was only a financial philosophy. The more fundamental struggle among many nineteenth-century church philosophers was whether the Vatican should even be part of the modern world. The internal debate was fierce and long. Pius led the traditionalist camp. But in 1871, a new temporal crisis overshadowed that divisive argument. In May, under pressure from Italy's enormous Catholic population, a divided parliament passed the Law of Papal Guarantees.[128] It recognized the Pope as a "sovereign Pontiff," granting him the same privileges as an Italian King; extended special territorial status to the Vatican and the Papal summer villa; and issued Vatican envoys immunities and honors. The law also exempted all church property from taxation and set aside an annual subsidy of 3,225,000 lire to help offset the income lost from the Papal States.[129]

The Pope detested the law, telling aides that it was a shameless effort to leave him a denuded figurehead with only a "royal palace."[130] It was not a treaty between equal partners, he contended, but a unilateral act that any future parliament could undo. Pius issued a hastily drafted encyclical repudiating the law and reiterating his demand that Italy instead restore the Papal States to the Vatican's control.[131] He warned the faithful that "wickedness" was afoot and that the guarantees were "unholy" and the government leaders who offered it were "stigmatized [by] their absurdity, cunning and mockery."[132] The Pope excommunicated more Italian officials he labeled as antichurch and even refused the annual subsidy—money the church needed desperately and for which Antonelli lobbied hard.[133]

Italy pressured the church. It seized dozens of monasteries and nunneries and converted them to government offices. In 1874, Italy banned mandatory religious classes in schools. It eliminated the exemption for the clergy serving in the military as well as abolishing the religious oath in courtrooms. And much to the Vatican's fury, the state recognized civil marriages, an institution over which all Popes had insisted the Catholic Church alone had authority.[134] Every time Pius lashed out with more invectives—he denigrated government ministers as everything from "monsters of hell" to "satellites of Satan in human flesh"—the state pushed back with more restrictive legislation. In 1876, parliament came short by only a few votes from passing a statute of Clerical Abuses that would have banned all political statements from the pulpit as well as abolishing the inviolable secrecy of the confessional.

Still, Pius refused to recognize the Italian state. Nor would the Pope allow

Catholics to vote in national elections. Without a Catholic counterweight at the polls, the most anticlerical politicians were elected.

By the time the eighty-five-year-old Pius died in 1878, after a record thirty-two-year reign, devout Catholics revered him as an uncompromising Pope. And most of Italy's leaders reviled him. Even his funeral was not free of drama. Hundreds of thousands turned out for his memorial procession. Army troops had to forcibly stop some in the crowd from snatching the coffin and tossing it into the Tiber River.[135]

Spies had penetrated the Vatican and reported back that some hard-line prelates were talking about boycotting "occupied Rome" for the Conclave of Cardinals to elect the new Pope. If they convened in another country, officials fretted it could lead to the first non-Italian Pope, someone who might be more aggressive than even Pius in challenging Italy's sovereign claim to the Papal States. Italy sent a message to the senior cardinals: the government guaranteed not to meddle in the conclave, but if the cardinals held it elsewhere, they could never again gather in Rome. The clerics decided to stay in the Eternal City.[136]

3

Enter the Black Nobles

Pius's replacement, Perugia's Cardinal Vincenzo Gioacchino Pecci, took the name Leo XIII. The sixty-eight-year-old Leo had none of Pius's irascible and often volatile charisma. Even his longtime advisors considered him utterly uninspiring. Some insiders speculated that Leo prevailed on the conclave's third ballot because he was the antithesis of his hot-tempered predecessor. Others thought he was a stopgap choice since he was reportedly in poor health and unlikely to be Pope long. Leo himself averred when elected that he was too old and feeble to handle the pressures of the Papacy.[1]

His reputation as a cardinal was a moderately conservative traditionalist. Leo had been born into an upper-middle-class family with some claim to nobility. He gave conflicting signals early on about whether he shared Pius's taste for grandiose pomp. On the one hand, he was the first Pope to deem the traditional Papal apartment, adjacent to the throne room, too grand. He slept instead in a cavernous but spartan ground-floor room.[2] But he also insisted that all visitors, including secular officials, kneel throughout any audience. Even top clerics were forbidden from sitting when addressing him.[3]

Leo was not long Pope before he learned that Pius had bequeathed to the Vatican about 30 million lire (the Popes from wealthy families often left the church their personal fortunes).[4] It consisted of some gold, bank deposits, and unfortunately many uncollectible IOUs. As a result, Pius's bequest did not make a dent in the church's ravaged finances: Leo had inherited a 45 million lire deficit. Although Peter's Pence had paid many operating expenses for a decade, nothing had been done to trim costs or reduce the staggering debt.[5] And even more startling was that the mess seemed the fault of the unassailable late Secretary of State and chief of the Treasury, Giacomo Antonelli.[6] He had passed away two years before Pius. It was only now that Leo learned of the grim consequences of the unfettered autonomy Cardinal Antonelli had wielded. Antonelli had accumulated great personal wealth while the Vatican's assets plunged. He had ennobled his middle-class family. His four brothers had been made Papal Counts. One, Luigi, was the administrator of the Pontifical Railroads. Gregorio attended to church affairs outside the Vatican. And his eldest brother, Filippo, made a sizable fortune after he was nominated as a governor of the reorganized state-owned Banca Romana, the capital's first savings bank.[7] Antonelli had directed many of the sixty families of the Black Nobles—aristocratic Catholics who stayed loyal to the Pope when Italian troops seized Rome in 1870—to his brother's bank.[8] With Antonelli dead, Italian aristocrats and businessmen disclosed that he had rebuffed their pleas to invest Peter's Pence in conservative ventures.[9] Instead, he had deployed a network of Papal nuncios to sell precious collectibles donated by the faithful and smuggled the money out of Italy.[10] His final will left the bulk of his estate—623,341 gold francs—to his brothers and nephews. Some gems were bequeathed to the Vatican museum, and as for the Pope, Antonelli left him only his own desk crucifix.[11] The coup de grâce came when a young countess, Loreta Lambertini, stepped forward and claimed she was the cardinal's illegitimate daughter and was entitled to a share of the property, palaces, and gold he had amassed.[12]

Leo felt compelled to entertain bold measures to strengthen the church's anemic balance sheet. It was not long before he approved the church's first ever, albeit limited, interest-bearing loans. The Pope soon learned that simply changing the rules did not guarantee success. His unsophisticated clerical advisors—without any financial training—did not insist on collateral for the first round of loans they issued. Instead they based their decisions solely on the name of the penurious aristocrat borrowing the money. In the first year of Leo's reign more than a million lire in loans were written off as worthless debts.[13]

The bad results prompted the Pope to immerse himself in the basics of lending. He insisted that, going forward, he review each loan. And he reserved final approval for all real estate deals, soliciting Peter's Pence, and raising cash from pilgrimages. Leo's advisors considered his micromanagement unnecessary and his incessant meddling time-consuming. But his fear they were incompetent kept him from giving them more authority. Leo also worried about thievery. He kept much of the church's spare cash, jewelry, and gold in large trunks stacked in his enormous bedroom.[14]

The Pope flirted with buying a small newspaper network dedicated to battling Freemasonry.[15] But before the deal closed, the Catholic bank and financiers who had pitched the proposal went bust. That convinced him that instead of putting the church's money at risk in a business venture, it was safer in real estate. Starting in the 1880s, he ordered that most of Peter's Pence be invested through silent partnerships into Roman property. Leo caught the early stages of a massive speculative building boom.[16] The spiraling property prices brought tremendous profits. Many Black Nobles became rich just by investing their own money into the same projects the church chose.[17] A handful of those men used their wealth to fund the start-up Banco di Roma (Bank of Rome).[18] They then convinced the risk-averse Pontiff to make a sizable investment in the bank. The Vatican also followed the bank's lead in buying shares in Rome's trolley system as well as a controlling stake of a British-owned company that supplied water to the capital.[19] Subsequently, when Italian aristocrats took loans from the church, they often provided their shares in the Bank of Rome as collateral, further binding the church and the bank.

Leo turned out to be more successful at stabilizing the church's finances than he was at quelling the deteriorating political turmoil between the church and Italy. A succession of left-wing, anticlerical administrations passed laws hostile to the Vatican, exacerbating Leo's mistrust of secular government. One statute abolished an obligation that Italian farmers pay the Vatican a tithe. Another authorized the confiscation of some church assets. The tension between church and state grew so fierce that Leo decided to abandon Rome and govern the church in exile from France. But just as Italian officials had been warned eight years earlier when the cardinals considered moving the conclave from Rome, informants tipped them off about Leo's plans. Italy gave the Pope an ultimatum: if he left he could never return. Leo and his advisors stayed put. The episode caused great concern inside the Papal Court that secular spies had penetrated it. So Leo consolidated authority in an ever-smaller group of longstanding clerical aides.[20]

The decision to stay in Rome meant the Pope was there to witness firsthand the great property crash of 1887. The Bank of Rome, in which the Vatican was a major investor, suffered huge losses. The church itself was badly damaged, losing about a third of its capital in less than a year.[21] Leo disclaimed any responsibility for the debacle. Monsignor Enrico Folchi, who held a senior position in the Vatican's finances for eleven years, got blamed. The Pontiff unceremoniously dismissed him. Many inside the Papal Court, however, felt as though Folchi was a convenient scapegoat.

Folchi's replacement was Monsignor (later Cardinal) Mario Mocenni, a cleric with a reputation as a fiscal conservative.[22] Soon after taking office he indicated that he might be more willing than his predecessors to experiment with modern financial techniques: "If money had a religion, it would be Jewish, but fortunately it doesn't have one, as a result of which it can be venerated by everybody."[23] Mocenni sent some of the church's gold and cash to the Rothschilds for safekeeping in Paris, the first time they were again involved with the Vatican since Pius IX had unceremoniously cut them off in 1860.[24]

Monsignor Mocenni was soon overshadowed by a layman, Ernesto Pacelli.* Pacelli had become the president of the Bank of Rome in the aftermath of the real estate bust. His sage and conservative stewardship stopped the bank's hemorrhaging and led quickly to a profitable resurgence. As the property crash played out, Pacelli and Leo had met regularly and developed a good friendship. By 1891, Leo had overcome enough of his anxiety about possible government spies to allow Pacelli to become his most trusted lay confidant. Pacelli was wise to the Machiavellian politics of the Papal Court. He assiduously doled out favors—ranging from generous Bank of Rome loans to prestigious directorships in private companies—to dozens in the Pope's entourage. As the bank's president, Pacelli also counted as friends many senior Italian government ministers. That allowed him the opportunity to act as an unofficial mediator between the Vatican and the often belligerent Italian state. Pacelli managed to persuade Italy's officials to refrain from passing more punitive laws against the church while convincing Leo to dial back his antigovernment rhetoric and threats of excommunication.

Most European governments wanted some assurance that Leo would distance himself from the reactionary tone set by his predecessor's *Syllabus*. They were tired of the standoff between church and state. During the early years of his Papacy Leo had taken small but encouraging steps that raised the expectations of reformers. He reopened the Vatican's abandoned observatory and

---

* Ernesto's cousin Eugenio joined the priesthood. He rose to become the Vatican's Undersecretary of State, then in 1920 the Papal Nuncio to Germany, before being elevated to Cardinal Secretary of State in 1930. In 1939, Eugenio Pacelli was elected Pope Pius XII.

appointed an astronomer, not a priest, to run it. With a single decree he eliminated the eunuchs who for centuries had sung in the Sistine Chapel.[25] And he surprised academics and historians by opening some of the Vatican archives, even to non-Catholics.[26]

Those small reforms were soon forgotten when Leo reaffirmed Pius's ban on Catholics participating in Italian elections. Pacelli had failed to convince Leo that the ban was counterproductive since it sacrificed any influence the church might have in the new Italy. Allowing Catholics to vote, the Pope feared, would implicitly acknowledge the legitimacy of the secular government. Leo demanded, as had Pius, nothing short of a full restoration of the Papal States. And he naively thought he could convince Germany, Austria, and France to support his bid. Pacelli, who had far more real-world experience than the cloistered Leo, told him that was unrealistic. That did not dissuade the Pope, who tried escalating the restoration of the Papal States into a pressing international issue. Leo tried putting what by then was called the "Roman Question" on the agenda at a conference of Western countries in The Hague. After ten months of aggressive lobbying, the Vatican could not even get an invitation.

Pacelli cited the diplomatic missteps to argue that the church's strength was not in secular diplomacy but instead in the power and independence of its finances. He urged the Pontiff to be more open-minded about free enterprise. The Pope initially seemed resistant when he condemned unrestrained capitalism in several encyclicals. But Pacelli influenced Leo's most famous edict, *Rerum Novarum* (On the New Things), a not very subtle effort to stem the surge of socialism and militant Marxism. In that encyclical—for the first time—although the church condemned capitalism's exploitation of workers, it backed the right to a decent wage, better working conditions, and even trade unions. (*Rerum* earned Leo the nickname "the worker's Pope.")[27]

Pacelli also asked the Pontiff to make some modest investments in banks, construction firms, and utility companies. He argued that it did not constitute capitalist behavior since those were essential industries that allowed average Catholics to live comfortably. Whether the Pope believed that or simply needed a credible justification for saying yes, he agreed.[28] By the start of the twentieth century, the Vatican had gone so far as to open forty-four small Catholic banks throughout Italy, all dedicated to providing Catholic workers a trusted place in which to deposit their earnings. Those church-owned banks even offered a few limited loans to the faithful.[29] And in keeping with his encyclical trumpeting workers' rights, Leo opened the first of what would become a national network of social and economic cooperatives to help Italy's poorest workers. There were soon Catholic-sponsored peasant leagues, workers' unions, and food cooperatives.[30]

Those tentative steps toward embracing modern financial practices made Leo stand out from the regressive isolation of his predecessor. But in the final years of his Papacy, Leo reversed course and became increasingly intolerant, destroying whatever goodwill he had earned. Over a dark eighteen-month stretch he reaffirmed *Syllabus*, spoke out against the separation of church and state, condemned freedom of the press and religious tolerance, and reiterated the medieval philosophy of Thomas Aquinas that only those who accepted Catholicism could be productive.[31] He rebuffed all appeals to reverse the Papal ban on Catholics serving in government.[32]

Leo even questioned whether there was any intrinsic value in democracy. He bitterly denounced so-called Americanism, the U.S.-based movement to modernize Catholicism.[33] In just over a century, the number of Catholics in America had soared from thirty thousand to more than six million, largely because of a surge in Italian and Irish immigrants. There was great promise for the church in the New World. But Leo and many Roman clerics opposed pluralism. America's separation of church and state, combined with its embrace of personal liberty and unfettered individual capitalism, rankled the Vatican. It was heresy, concluded Leo, to allow any secular state to develop without the integral involvement of the church at every stage.[34] The best form of government, concluded the Pope, was a benevolent monarchy (which conveniently included a Papal empire).[35]

By the end of his Papacy, Leo was every bit as reactionary as Pius.

The "frail" Leo, elected in part because some cardinals considered him a stopgap Pontiff who would have a short reign, died in 1903 at the age of ninety-three. During his quarter century as Pope, he had outlived many of the cardinals who had voted for him. Inside the Vatican, there was almost a palpable relief at Leo's passing. He seemed, even to those who liked him, too old and out of touch. The church was just a few years into a new century. And as the cardinals began arriving in Rome to elect a new Pope, there was widespread consensus that the next Pontiff should be different. The problem was that no one could agree on which quality was most important. That promised a wide-open conclave.

4

"Merely a Palace, Not a State"

The selection of every Pope has meant behind-the-scenes intrigue and heavy politicking. Up until the sixth century, the horse-trading began before the sitting Pope was even dead. And during the Middle Ages, a few aristocratic Italian families got together and ate and drank until they had agreed on a new Pontiff. The gathering after Leo's death was not marked by any of the fistfights, threats, and bribes that had been a hallmark of some notorious conclaves.[1] But it turned out to be the last assembly of cardinals in which Catholic European powers affected the outcome. France, Spain, and Austria had wielded an effective veto power for more than a hundred years. After Leo's death, Vienna blacklisted the odds-on favorite, the dead Pope's powerful Secretary of State, Cardinal Rampolla del Tindaro.[2] They considered him too cozy with the French. That opened the door to Venetian Cardinal Giuseppe Sarto, whose best quality seemed to be that he was not closely identified with any of Leo's mostly unpopular policies. After ten ballots, he emerged as the Pope and chose the name Pius X.[3]

The new Pius had served nearly twenty years as a parish priest before beginning his ascent to the Papacy. He had a well-deserved reputation as ultraconservative, humble, and disciplined. His longtime aides warned others that he was also a great pessimist. Pius's Papal motto—"to restore all things in Christ"—indicated he considered that religious obligations always trumped secular ones.[4] Black Nobles worried that as the first modern Pope from a simple working-class family, he might not appreciate the pomp of the grand Papacy. They were right. He was not inclined to dole out lavish favors and princely gifts to either his friends or those serving in the Papal Court. When one aristocrat suggested he elevate his own sisters to Papal Countesses, he dismissed him. "They are sisters of the Pope, what more can I do for them?"[5]

Other small changes signaled a populist touch. For the first time, the Pope's secretaries dined with him. And he permitted lay Catholics to sit in his presence, changing the centuries-old imperative that they kneel. Kissing his slipper was no longer allowed. He claimed that the sedia gestatoria—an ornate, portable ceremonial throne—made him dizzy. The new Pius ended the requirement that everyone applaud whenever he entered St. Peter's. And he took strolls in the Vatican gardens on his own instead of being surrounded, as had Leo, with a retinue of Noble Guards.[6]

Besides stripping away some of the gilded obsequiousness attached to the Papacy, he also tried to streamline the chaotic web of the Roman Curia. The Vatican's bureaucracy had grown over centuries to consist of often redundant congregations, offices, and tribunals, many of them tainted by huge financial waste and nepotism.[7] Although the church was international, the Curia was almost entirely Italian. To outsiders it seemed oppressively complex and marked by a lethargic work ethic.[8] After the loss of the Papal States, the Curia defied logic by expanding instead of shrinking. Pius ordered it to reduce its thirty-seven departments to nineteen.[9] Reforming the Curia however was not as simple as issuing a few directives. Those with entrenched power resented that Pius was one of the first Popes never to have worked in the Curia. They were determined from the outset to undermine any major reorganization. "Popes come and go," was the unofficial motto inside the Curia, "but we go on forever."[10] Their resistance took the form of pretending to undertake most of the reductions. The career bureaucrats shuffled jobs between various offices and also folded some small departments into larger ones. Only insiders knew that the window dressing belied the fact that little had changed.[11]

Believing that the Curia was reforming itself, Pius turned his attention elsewhere: how best to stem the growing popularity of a movement of clerics and lay philosophers who challenged traditional Catholic dogma on everything from interpreting the Old Testament to whether the church should embrace democracy. So-called modernists—dubbed that since they collectively wanted the church to adapt itself to the changes of a new world—urged widespread reform and liberalization.[12] The modernist movement had gained momentum while Leo was still Pope, but he had rebuffed it by reaffirming the reactionary *Syllabus*. Now, some modernists appealed to the new Pontiff, hoping he might be more receptive. But those familiar with his tenure as Venice's cardinal knew it was unlikely. Pius was a conservative pastor, without any formal education. He was not in the least sympathetic to modernism.

"These people expect to be treated with oil, soap and embraces," Pius said. "What they need—and what they will get—is a good fist."[13] He gave them a "good fist" by releasing an encyclical, *Lamentabili Sane* (Lamentable Certainly), a rambling condemnation of the liberalization movement.[14] Pius followed that by creating a clerical committee in every diocese across Europe to guard against the perversion of the faith. For the first time in its history, the church deployed the equivalent of a secret police, relying on informers to uncover modernists and those who secretly supported them.[15] Anonymous denunciations were encouraged. No one was spared. The cardinals of Vienna and Paris as well as the rectors of several top Catholic universities were denounced among the hundreds who were purged (even Archbishop Giacomo Della Chiesa—who would become the next Pope—was investigated for suspicion of "doctrinal deviance").[16] Pius required that all priests take an antimodernist oath (it was in place until Pope Paul VI eliminated it in 1967).[17] He lowered to seven from twelve as the age at which children made their first confession and received communion. That would help priests monitor any youngster who might be entertaining modern thoughts.[18]

Beyond ferreting out suspected sympathizers, the crackdown expanded to net scholars whose work the simple Pius viewed with suspicion. Encouraged by the Pope, the church moved more aggressively than ever to ban books it considered dangerous. The works of acclaimed modernist scholars such as Ernesto Buonaiuti and Alfred Loisy were transferred to the Index Librorum Prohibitorum (Index of Prohibited Books). Writers who refused to be silenced, like George Tyrell, were excommunicated.* And the Pope stacked the Vatican's Biblical Commission with regressive prelates who recommended the suspen-

---

* The Index Librorum Prohibitorum was active from 1559 until Pope Paul VI eliminated it in 1966. Catholics could be excommunicated for owning or reading the banned books. The Koran and Talmud were prohibited. More than 3,000 authors and 5,200 books were banned over the centuries. The writers ranged from ancient ones such as Aristotle and Plato to philosophers such as Voltaire and Kant to novelists such as Hugo and Balzac. Sometimes, seemingly objectionable books never got listed, such as Charles Darwin's work about evolution, *The Origin of Species*, and Adolf Hitler's *Mein Kampf.*[19]

sion of the entire theological faculties at leading Swiss and French institutes and universities.[20]

A Pope with such a backward view of the world did little to modernize how the Vatican's financial advisors operated.[21] He relied on Pacelli, who told him that the church was solvent although money was tight. Yet the Pope's innate pessimism meant that no matter how many times Pacelli reassured him, he fretted about being short of money. In his first year, he even shuttered the tiny zoo in the Vatican's gardens as he feared it too great a financial drain.

Pius's dark mood lifted somewhat when early in his tenure Pacelli informed him that Peter's Pence contributions had set a record.[22] The upsurge in cash was an unintended consequence of the Pope's unyielding rejection of secularism and his refusal to cooperate with other faiths. It seemed that ordinary Catholics loved when the Pontiff brooked no compromise in those high-profile squabbles. In France, Prime Minister Émile Combes, a lapsed Catholic who had become a Freemason, was instrumental in passing the Law of Separation. It removed Catholicism as the country's official religion. Pius responded by suspending diplomatic relations with France, which had long been the church's closest ally.[23] When the Portuguese also separated church and state, Pius castigated them. Much to the irritation of Britain, he backed Ireland's Catholics. He angered Germans by issuing an encyclical praising a saint who had fought against the Protestant Reformation. And Russia was miffed by his aggressive efforts to energize Catholics there.[24] He even once refused to grant an audience to Teddy Roosevelt because he thought the ex-President had insulted Catholicism by visiting Methodist and Masonic groups in Rome. The widespread press coverage of his slight to Roosevelt caused contributions to spike again.[25]

The flood of cash had a liberating effect on the miserly Pontiff. Cardinal Pietro Gasparri, Secretary of State to two Popes, had once said, "The Vatican, even with its gardens, is merely a palace, not a state."[26] Although Pius shared with his predecessors the unrealistic desire to restore the Papal States, he felt that the church had to make the mini-state it called home grander. He was confident he had sufficient resources from the surge in Peter's Pence. Pius nearly doubled the Vatican's size by purchasing adjacent properties, including the Italian Mint. A single building to house the new Pontifical Biblical Institute cost a then record 400,000 lire.[27] Having given up on streamlining the bureaucracy, Pius added three Roman palaces for more office space for the Curia.[28]

Physical expansion was only one way the Pope intended to enhance the church's stature. He spent millions more building churches throughout Italy to accommodate the growing Catholic population.[29] And when a major earthquake ravaged some Italian towns in 1908, Pius used the disaster to demonstrate that the church was as effective as the state in helping the victims.[30] The faithful rewarded his activism with more than 6 million lire in additional contributions.[31]

Pius had a tremendous mistrust of secular politicians. Those misgivings were amplified as Italy's socialists gained popular support. They were a hodgepodge of disparate groups, inspired partly by Karl Marx, and consisting of a loose affiliation of peasant leagues, worker's cooperatives, trade unions, and political activists. Many were allied with anarchists. Their movement had little room for God and none for organized religion.[32] As the cardinal of Venice, Pius had rallied the city's Catholics to form an alliance with political liberals to oppose the socialists. Now, as Pope, socialism's surge so alarmed him that it trumped his antiquated opposition to modernity. He lifted the church's ban on Catholics voting in and running for public office.[33] The result was dramatic. Catholics were elected to the Italian parliament in 1904 and 1909. And so many were victorious in 1913 that they blocked a socialist takeover of the Italian legislature.[34]

Pius also reached an arrangement with Italy to give the church an unrestricted right to buy and sell property.[35] Before then Black Nobles helped the Vatican circumvent complicated Italian laws about the acquisition and inheritance of real estate and other assets. Pius now agreed the church would no longer hide its investments through proxies.[36]

Bankers like Pacelli became ever more important as the laws about the church's role in business became less restrictive. Besides being the president of the Banco di Roma, Pacelli was also a Roman city councilor and on the board of some of Italy's most successful companies. And he had forged strong relationships with prelates inside the Curia. Pius trusted him, as did powerful cardinals, such as Merry del Val and Vives y Tuto, the respective Secretaries of State, and the Inquisition.[37] Pacelli convinced Pius to invest millions to help the Bank of Rome expand its operations to Egypt, then a British colony.[38] By 1913, half of the Vatican's income came from interest earned on its giant stake in Pacelli's bank.

The banker diversified the Vatican's holdings, making small investments in Italian gas and electric companies, French banks, Swiss railways, and even a few stocks in Italy, Germany, and Spain.[39] Pacelli was the president of Italy's only film producer. Although the Pope was suspicious of the new medium and had issued several decrees banning priests from seeing films, no church official complained when Pacelli invested some Vatican money in the new technology.[40]

But there was a limit to what Pius would do for Pacelli. One of the Bank of Rome's directors, Marchese Alberto Theodoli, was also a Black Noble. He asked Pius to transfer whatever money the Vatican still had on deposit with the Rothschilds to the Bank of Rome. Pius refused. The Pope told Theodoli and Pacelli that whenever previous Popes had moved the Church's money away from the safekeeping of Jews to the control of Christians, it turned into a disaster.[41] But that was a minor disagreement compared to the quarrel they had about Italy's invasion to expand its African empire by seizing Libya from Turkey in 1911. The Bank of Rome provided the money for a consortium of Italian companies that hoped to exploit Libya's rich oil and mineral deposits by converting the country into Italy's colonial "fourth shore." The bank financed everything from uniforms to supplies for the army.[42] Pacelli also poured money into the country, investments that would only flourish in the wake of an Italian military victory.[43] He lobbied Pius to endorse Italy's fight for the colony as justified. And he did persuade a few cardinals to ratify the campaign as a battle of civilizations between Christianity and Islam. But Pius refused. He told Pacelli that he would not abandon the Vatican's long-standing policy of neutrality. The church's strength, Pius argued, was its impartiality. "In ancient times," Pius lamented, "the Pope with a word might have stopped the slaughter, but now I am powerless."[44]

But Pacelli was persistent. He beseeched the Pope for a Vatican endorsement of the Libyan expedition. Since patriotic Italians facing war flooded the Vatican with contributions, Pacelli cited that as evidence of the war's popularity and that it had unintended benefits for the church.[45] Pacelli never shared with the Pontiff that the church was at significant risk should the Bank of Rome stumble in its Libyan venture.[46] Eventually, so irritated by Pacelli's refusal to accept a simple no, the Holy See began distancing itself from him. Pacelli was surprised to discover that he suddenly had to make an appointment through Pius's private secretary. Next, their weekly meeting was canceled. The harder

Pacelli tried recouping his influence, the more Pius pushed him further away. Pacelli's entrenched foes, jealous of his friendship with the Pope and covetous of his power, began a whisper campaign attacking his character. Leading cardinals who had been his friends did nothing to help him. After twenty years as the chief lay advisor to two Pontiffs, Pacelli was finally without influence. His fall was so great that when Pius was on his deathbed in a couple of years, a Papal chamberlain turned him away.

5

An Unholy Alliance

The seventy-nine-year-old Pius died on August 20, 1914, having lived just long enough to see the outbreak of World War I. By the time the cardinals began gathering for their conclave, the Germans had captured Brussels and were within thirty miles of Paris. The Russians had advanced into East Prussia. Thousands had died in major battles. Pressured by their own governments and spurred by nationalism, the French, German, and Austrian cardinals arrived in Rome each promoting their own partisan as the next Pope. They also had compiled short lists of cardinals they intended to oppose at all costs.

After ten rancorous ballots Bologna's Cardinal della Chiesa, a long shot, emerged to become Benedict XV.[1] After deadlocking on more partisan choices, a majority overcame the German and Austrian objections and coalesced around the moderate della Chiesa. Having endured Pius's brutal modernist purge, the cardinals settled on a leader they hoped could guide the church through the war without becoming mired in the often debilitating internal theological battles waged by traditionalists on reformers. The diminutive, thin Genovese aristocrat—his nickname was Picoletto (tiny one)—not only had a reputation as a Francophile but he had been a cardinal for only three months.[2]

Judging by his appearance, it did not seem that Benedict could match Pius's unrelenting fire. A childhood accident had left him with only one working eye and ear. His voice was high-pitched. One shoulder was noticeably higher than the other, and he had a halting limp and an ashen complexion. "I am but an ugly gargoyle on the beauties of Rome," he commented once about his demeanor.[3]

Benedict promptly set to mark the Papacy as his own. He dismissed his strongest rival, the British-educated Spaniard Cardinal Merry del Val, giving the Secretary of State just enough time to clean out his desk.[4] And he kept Pacelli ostracized but also shunned the advice of other senior advisors he inherited. A fresh start appealed to Benedict—especially since he faced navigating the church through the uncertainty of a worldwide war. The conflict battered the church's balance sheet. Peter's Pence contributions from warring nations like France and Belgium plummeted.[5] After Italy declared war against Germany in 1916, donations from German Catholics also tumbled.

The crisis created by the plunging revenues was exacerbated by Benedict, who turned out to be a spendthrift.[6] He yearned for the days of a majestic Papacy. Some of his directives—such as reinstalling the right of lay Catholics to kiss his slippers and again banning anyone from eating with the Pope—came at no cost. But to restore the pomp that predecessors had eliminated was expensive.[7] And since he relied on the mediocre advice of a few handpicked cardinals who had little better business sense than he, the Vatican had trouble figuring out how to stem the hemorrhaging.[8] Compounding the problem was that the church's fixed costs had soared as the buying power of the lira had nose-dived due to hyperinflation.[9] Only a year after becoming Pope, Benedict had trouble paying even the salaries of his court.[10]

Unaware of the church's own dismal finances, when the Bank of Rome got squeezed in a credit crunch, its chairman, Count Carlo Santucci, a devout Black Noble, beseeched Benedict for a bailout. Santucci was the Pope's own pick to replace Pacelli as the bank's chief. He convinced the cash-strapped Benedict that the best way to protect the church's stake in the bank was to invest more money. The Vatican scrounged up 9 million lire, with which it could ill afford to part.[11] But the infusion was not enough. Halfway through the war, the Vatican's 42.5 million lire equity in the Bank of Rome was worth less than 15 million.[12] And it lost millions more in trying to save several regional Catholic banks.

Benedict had no better luck in misguided efforts to bolster five leading Italian Catholic dailies.[13] They had lost advertisers during the war and the cost of paper and ink had risen steeply. During peacetime, they had eked out small profits, but the war brought debt of some 8 million lire. A couple teetered on the verge of bankruptcy. The Vatican did not want to use its own money, instead asking American bishops for a long-term, low-interest-rate loan of $500,000. But since the U.S. church was in the middle of its own financial crunch, the American bishops declined.[14] Benedict had no choice but to dissolve the centralized financial hierarchy that ran the newspapers. The Pope reluctantly approved a long-term loan of nearly 2 million lire and also convinced another Black Noble, Count Giovanni Grosoli, to forgive some remaining debts he had previously advanced.[15]

Benedict fared little better politically than he did financially. He lobbied through intermediaries to prevent Italy from joining the Allies (Britain, France, and Russia). Catholic newspapers argued that joining the war was bad for the country (those "stay neutral" pleas were covertly subsidized by a German diplomat based in Rome).[16] At one stage the Pope thought he had brokered a deal by which Austria would abandon its claim to its former Italian territories in return for Italy staying neutral. That deal fell through.[17]

Benedict knew he had few good options. Italy and the Austro-Hungarian Empire were crucial Catholic bastions. That they might fight each other was distressing enough. Benedict agonized publicly about "the monstrous spectacle of this war with its streams of Christian blood."[18] But equally sobering was the thought that only one could be victorious. A loss by the Austrians could weaken their role as a wall against Russian Orthodoxy. And if Italy joined the Allies and lost, social instability might spread throughout the country. Although Benedict had no love for Rome's secular government, he realized the possibility of widespread civil unrest in the wake of a defeat would be terrible for the Vatican.

Benedict failed to get Italy to stay neutral. The Italians declared war on Germany and joined the Allies in 1915. That did not change the Allied view that the Pope was unabashedly pro-German.[19] British intelligence had confirmed that Benedict had authorized purchases of so-called Italian War Loans that raised money for the war.[20] And the Allies had also learned that Benedict believed that Germany and Austria-Hungary—the Central Powers—would prevail. His conviction was so strong that he approved a substantial Vatican investment in Austrian stocks, a decision that resulted in sharp losses.[21] The Allies also knew that the Vatican rented one of its Roman properties to an arms manufacturer that supplied the Germans (when the British eventually leaked that to the press, the church feigned shock, claiming it was not aware of its tenant's business).[22]

Even the Allies did not know the extent of the Vatican's secret connection to the Central Powers. Germany was covertly funneling cash to the church through Swiss banks and labeling it "Peter's Pence."[23] That helped stabilize the church's finances. The German Foreign Ministry separately sent the Vatican cash from a propaganda slush fund. And the Austrians joined with a clandestine subsidy to Benedict.[24] Besides the secret payments, Matthias Erzberger, the head of Germany's Catholic Center Party, raised money for the Vatican from German businesses and wealthy industrialists. So pleased was the Pope with the large donation Erzberger presented to him in 1915 that the Pontiff thanked him with special gifts and a Papal decoration.[25]

In January 1917, Italian authorities charged Monsignor Rudolf Gerlach, a Papal chamberlain, as a German spy.[26] The Vatican, tipped off to Gerlach's imminent arrest, whisked him from Italy to Switzerland. Several lay co-conspirators were put on trial and found guilty, while Gerlach was convicted in absentia and sentenced to life.[27] Benedict was shocked, by all accounts, that someone he trusted had acted both as a German paymaster for covert operations as well as passing secret communications through the Vatican's diplomatic pouches.[28]* The Gerlach episode fueled rumors across Italy that the Pope had struck a secret deal with the Central Powers to return to the church most of the Papal States after the war.[30]

The Pontiff released a seven-point peace plan on August 1, 1917, three years into the war.[31] Benedict and his Secretary of State, Cardinal Gasparri, thought it would make the church a key mediator for peace. But the Allies ignored it, having long ago decided to snub any Papal entreaties for ceasing hostilities. America had entered the conflict only four months before Benedict released his plan. With the United States in the war, the Allies felt even more confident to disregard the Vatican. Some mocked the plan's generalities: "We have never ceased to urge the belligerent peoples and Governments to become brothers once more." Even the Central Powers derided as naive and impractical Benedict's call for countries to disarm after the war.[32] The Papal peace overture was such a flop that it only further weakened the church's influence.[33]

Although the Allies ignored the Pope, since they considered him pro-German, many Catholics in war-torn Europe thought he had abandoned them by failing to endorse either side (a French priest in Paris reflected a com-

---

* Despite Gerlach's conviction for espionage, the Vatican continued through the war to seek his advice on matters concerning Germany. When Gerlach left the priesthood after the war, Germany, Austria, and Turkey awarded him military service decorations.[29]

mon sentiment, "Holy Father we do not want your peace").[34] When Italy's army was routed at Caporetto in November 1917, Italians blamed the Pontiff for spreading "defeatism."[35] As the war stretched on, donations to the church kept declining. The annual pilgrimages to St. Peter's dried up and large-scale Papal audiences—used by the Vatican as fundraising events—disappeared.

The nadir for Benedict's diplomatic influence came when the Allies refused to allow the Vatican to be included in the 1919 Paris Peace Conference.[36] When the war had begun, Benedict's main worry was that Russian Orthodoxy might seep westward. The Bolshevik Revolution during the middle of the war meant now that hostilities were over, the threat from Russia had dramatically changed. The hard-line Russian communists were equal-opportunity atheists, zealously eradicating temples, churches, and synagogues and promising to export their godless revolution around the globe.[37]

Not long after the war ended a small cadre of clerical advisors insisted to Benedict that finances, not politics, be paramount. Since he had become Pope, the church had lost almost 60 million lire—about 40 percent of its capital—on a broad range of soured investments.[38] Years of war had left much of Europe ravaged and millions of Catholics faced high unemployment and a great recession.[39] Distressed congregants in Germany, Austria, and Hungary were clamoring for financial aid from the Vatican.[40]

The only positive glimmer was that French Catholics somehow managed to increase their donations in the run-up to Joan of Arc's highly publicized canonization. Forty thousand French pilgrims came to Rome for the ceremony.[41] But it was not enough. The Vatican's crisis forced it to open its books in 1919 to the Italian government to avoid cash-strapped bureaucrats from taxing the church's income.[42]

To avert an even worse financial crunch, Benedict dispatched Monsignor (later Cardinal) Bonaventura Cerretti to America to plead for a million-dollar loan from the American branch of the church.[43] The secretary of the United States Conference of Catholic Bishops dubbed Cerretti's trip a "begging mission."[44] The U.S. bishops again refused, but they arranged for the Knights of Columbus—an influential Catholic men's service society—to give the Pope a substantial gift of $250,000.[45] American dollars were especially valuable as they had appreciated nearly 90 percent against the lira during the war.[46]

Money problems continued front and present when the sixty-eight-year-old Benedict unexpectedly died from complications from influenza in January

1922. The church was in such dire straits that Secretary of State Gasparri had to arrange another Rothschild loan to pay for Benedict's lavish funeral, the ensuing Conclave of Cardinals, and the coronation of the next Pope.[47]

It took a grueling fourteen ballots at the ensuing conclave before the cardinals settled on another compromise, Milan's sixty-five-year-old Cardinal Achille Ratti. He became Pius XI. Ratti was the son of a Milanese factory manager. An ex-archivist in the Vatican Library, the bookish Ratti had dual doctorates in theology and canon law. As a voracious reader and scholar, he likely had a better appreciation of the historical and political significance of the Papacy than most of his predecessors.[48]

Pius was short, thickset, softly spoken, and charming. He also had a well-deserved reputation for a volatile temper.[49] His aides knew he demanded absolute obedience. In meetings his intense questioning at times made him seem like a prosecutor. Once apprised of the church's fiscal mess, he ordered its first-ever internal audit. He slashed the size of the Papal Court and cut some of what he deemed unnecessary pomp that Benedict had reinstituted. Pius appointed Signora Linda, his longtime maid, to supervise the Vatican's large housekeeping staff. When told that no Pope had ever allowed a woman to work or live inside the Vatican, he replied: "Then I shall be the first."[50]

Money woes weren't the only matters occupying his early tenure. Political upheaval gripped Italy. The country's parliamentary coalition was in trouble, with the traditional liberal and conservative blocs deadlocked. Leftist militants were gaining momentum, and there was an upsurge from the radical right's National Fascist Party. Fascist paramilitary squads had targeted Catholic social institutions in central and northern Italy and had also besieged the powerful Catholic Partito Popolare Italiano (Italian People's Party) with a venomous propaganda campaign. All the chaos culminated only eight months after Pius's election with the "March on Rome." Tens of thousands of armed fascists converged on the capital to demonstrate their political clout. After a tense one-week standoff with the King and the elected government, the fascist leader, Benito Mussolini, was sworn in as Prime Minister.[51]

Before Mussolini's unexpected ascent, Pius had rejected any accommodation with fascism. There seemed to be little room for compromise with a man who was an avowed atheist, had written a pamphlet titled *God Does Not Exist*, and had once suggested to a newspaper that the Pope should leave Rome.[52]

Il Duce (the leader)—the name Mussolini preferred—climbed to power on the back of a strong anticlerical platform that called for confiscating church property. He had once described priests "as black microbes who are as deadly to mankind as tuberculosis germs."[53]

Pius, a political realist, was not in the least sympathetic to fascism. Nevertheless he felt that appeasing Mussolini might be the best way to ensure peace between the church and state.[54] The Pope believed that an autocrat was necessary to check embedded government corruption as well as to control the political instability fueled since the end of World War I by record unemployment, mass strikes, and a growing anarchist movement.[55] Pius dispatched a trusted cleric, Father Pietro Tacchi Venturi, to convince Mussolini that the church was not an enemy. A self-described "good Jesuit and good fascist," Venturi believed the church's most dangerous enemy was the "worldwide Jewish-Masonic plutocracy."[56]

The Pope's outreach to Il Duce came at the right moment. Although the Pontiff had lost much of his temporal power, he still carried great moral influence inside Italy.[57] Mussolini, a savvy politician, knew that while his anticlerical rhetoric was popular inside his party, now that he was prime minister he needed the Vatican's endorsement to consolidate broader support in a country that was 98 percent Catholic.[58] So he decided to forge a temporary peace with the church and then move against the Vatican in later years when he was in absolute control. Only a handful of his top ministers knew about his long-term strategy.[59] For public consumption, Mussolini appeared to court the Vatican.[60] Not long after taking power he reintroduced religious studies into state primary schools, provided some money for restoring churches, and even allowed crucifixes into public buildings from which they had been banned since 1870.[61]

One of the first tests for the budding alliance happened early in Pius's reign. The Bank of Rome, entangled in another financial crisis, needed cash. The Vatican was still the bank's major investor. Pius did not have any spare money so he dispatched Secretary of State Gasparri to meet with Mussolini. Carlo Santucci, the president of the bank, allowed the pair to meet at his central Roman palace. It was the first direct contact between the Vatican and the Italian state since the loss of the Papal States.[62]

Il Duce agreed to bail out the bank.[63] The price for the Vatican was that Mussolini personally selected fascist directors to replace the church's trustees on the bank's board. The bank's payments to the Catholic press and political parties were terminated.[64] Also, Mussolini required the Vatican to stop its subsidy of the main Catholic party, the Partito Popolare Italiano, and to cut off all support for Confederazione Generale Italiana del Lavoro, the enormous Catholic trade union, as well as its agrarian cooperatives and credit unions.[65]

By 1928, the internal audit Pius had ordered was ready. It had taken six years to complete and concluded what many suspected: the Vatican was down to its last dollars.[66] The Pope authorized the church's first-ever bookkeeping system and ordered a rudimentary budget. But not even the first official confirmation of the frightful state of the Vatican's finances was enough to compel Pius to loosen the church's restrictions on commercial investments. Instead, that same year he banned bishops and priests from any involvement in banking, even with Catholic institutions, unless they agreed to be personally liable to the faithful for any losses.[67] Rather than looking for ways to revive the Vatican's failing investments, the Pope seemingly put his faith in fascism. Mussolini's Blackshirts would not allow the church to go under, Pius reasoned, so long as they considered the church an ally. Pius had no idea that Mussolini had barely enough money to fuel his own visions of grandeur, much less help bail out the Vatican.

When Mussolini unveiled an ambitious and expensive redesign of Rome as a triumphant celebration of fascist power and architecture, Pius worried that such a grandiose capital might overshadow the Vatican. The Pope countered with his own impressive building plans.[68] Pius's projects were unrealistic, given the state of the church's treasury.[69] While Pius talked incessantly about his impressive vision, many Vatican employees grumbled about low salaries and a decade without any pay raise. Instead of constructing new buildings, some wondered aloud: Why not take better care of the existing ones? Large swaths of Vatican City were crumbling. Mold and mildew threatened some of the church's priceless art collection, there were leaks in St. Peter's, and vermin infestation was rampant.

Even when Pius realized that his plans were impossible, he refused to allow his advisors to embrace modern finances. Pius had a better idea: the Vatican should tap simply its rich new relative in America. There was widespread disdain inside the Vatican toward Americans. But the Pope believed the American church might prove to be the Vatican's economic salvation, as its followers were rich.[70] In 1928, the Chicago Archdiocese arranged a $300,000 loan and also allowed its property to be used as collateral so the Vatican could borrow 3 million lire.[71] Since the middle of the Roaring Twenties, American Catholics were the largest contributors to Peter's Pence.[72] To show his appreciation, Pius made a Chicago seminary a pontifical university, an elite status that eluded many long-established and prestigious institutions.[73] The British Minister to the Holy See told London that Pius's elevation of archbishops Mundelein of Chicago and Hayes of New York as cardinals was prompted by "American gold," and that "it is not so much of an exaggeration to say that the United States is now looked up to as if it were the leading Catholic nation."[74] Before their promotion, there had been only four American-born cardinals. And within a few years Pius would confer the high honor of Papal Orders on more than one hundred U.S. citizens. Seven were given noble titles.[75]

The financial aid from America alleviated the Vatican's money woes, so much so that Pius and his top clerics had by the late 1920s shifted their focus from finances to national politics. The prominent internal debate was about whether the Vatican should sign a formal agreement with Mussolini's fascists, one that would officially acknowledge the rights of both to exist and flourish. Mussolini had created the climate for such a deal. In addition to soft-pedaling his anticlerical vitriol and reinstituting elements of religious life into Italian society, his wife, Rachele, and their two sons and daughter were baptized in a public rite in 1923.[76] In 1926, although he and his wife had married in a civil union eleven years earlier, they renewed their vows in a religious ceremony. And in 1927, the man who used to boast that he had never been to a Mass was himself baptized. Although all of those moves were symbolic, Mussolini's instincts were good. Such theater defused much of the opposition from the country's devout Catholics. While courting Catholics, Mussolini also had to quell opposition in his own party. Many hard-core fascists hoped for the demise of the church. They contended that any alliance with the Pope would not only violate their core principles but would lead to the "Vaticanization" of Italy.[77]

Pius knew there was some resistance in the Curia to such a deal. He was the first Pope since the church had lost the Papal States even to consider restoring relations with the Italian state. His four predecessors had labeled themselves prisoners in the Vatican and refused any direct communication with the government. Ultimately, instead of trying to gauge popular sentiment inside the church, the Pope followed his intuition. Father Pietro Tacchi Venturi, Pius's liaison to Il Duce, encouraged Pius to make an agreement. Tacchi Venturi assured him that Mussolini, notwithstanding any shortcomings, could be trusted to keep his word.[78]

What followed was nearly two years of intense talks.[79] Tacchi Venturi and Francesco Pacelli, an attorney, shared the role as the church's negotiators.[80] (There was increasing talk that Francesco's brother, Eugenio Pacelli—later Pius XII—might soon be the Cardinal Secretary of State.[81]) On February 11, 1929, the Vatican and the fascists signed the Lateran Pacts, sometimes referred to as the Lateran Accords, consisting of three parts: a political treaty, a concordat that set forth the terms of the relationship between the Holy See and the state, and a financial convention.[82] The Accords—named after the Vatican's sixteenth-century Lateran Palace, built on the site from which the Crusades were launched—gave the church the most power it held since the height of its temporal kingdom.[83]

The political treaty set aside 108.7 acres as Vatican City and fifty-two scattered "heritage" properties as an autonomous neutral state. It reinstated Papal sovereignty and ended the Pope's boycott of the Italian state that had been in place since the Papal States were lost.[84]* The Pope was declared "sacred and inviolable," the equivalent of a secular monarch, but invested with divine right. A new Code of Canon Law was established, which included two of Pius's key demands: that the Italian government recognize the validity of church marriages and that Catholic religious education be obligatory in both primary and secondary state schools.[86] Cardinals had the same rights as princes by blood.

The concordat granted the church immense privilege. Most important was its declaration that Catholicism was fascist Italy's only religion. Freemasonry was outlawed, evangelical meetings in private homes banned, and Protestant Bibles forbidden. Marriage was acknowledged as a sacrament. All church holidays became state holidays. Priests were exempted from military and jury duty.[87]

The three-article financial convention—the Conciliazione—granted "ecclesiastical corporations" a tax exemption. It also compensated the Vatican for the confiscation of the Papal States with 750 million lire in cash and a billion

---

* The Vatican is the world's smallest sovereign nation, only two-thirds of a mile wide and half a mile north to south. Its perimeter can be walked at a leisurely pace in about forty minutes. Tiny Monaco is six times larger. And a third of the Vatican is set aside for lush manicured gardens and ornate grottoes. It has no natural resources and must import all food, energy, and labor. At the time of the Lateran Pacts, the new country had only 973 citizens, the overwhelming majority of whom were celibate priests.[85]

lire in government bonds that paid 5 percent interest.[88] The settlement—worth about $1.3 billion in 2014 dollars—was approximately a third of Italy's entire annual budget and an enormous windfall for the cash-starved church.[89] The Vatican wanted double that, but Mussolini persuaded the Pope and his negotiators that the government was itself in precarious shape. It could ill afford anything more.[90] As an extra inducement, Italy agreed to pay the meager salaries of all 25,000 parish priests in the country.[91]

"Italy has been given back to God," the Pope told the Vatican newspaper *L'Osservatore Romano*, "and God to Italy."[92] The church threw its full power behind the fascists.[93] The Vatican disbanded its influential Partito Popolare Italiano and exiled its leader from Italy.[94] Italian bishops swore an oath of allegiance to the fascist government and clerics were prohibited from encouraging the faithful to oppose it.[95] Priests began offering prayers at Sunday Masses for Mussolini and for fascism. Some clergy joined the National Fascist Party and a few even served as officers.

The Lateran Pacts converted Mussolini into a hero for devout Italians. Many homes soon had a picture of Il Duce hanging next to one of the Pope or a crucifix.[96] Even Hitler hailed the church for "making its peace with Fascism."[97] The influential Cardinal Merry del Val said Mussolini was "visibly protected by God."[98]

National elections were held only a month after the Lateran Pacts were signed. The Vatican knew it needed Mussolini's government in power to ensure that parliament approved the agreement. So priests used their pulpits to urge Catholics to vote for the fascists. In those elections—the first time women were allowed to vote—the National Fascist Party won an astonishing 98 percent of parliamentary seats.

On July 25, 1929, for the first time since Pius IX declared himself a "prisoner Pope" in 1870, a Pontiff ventured outside the Vatican. Mussolini told his followers in parliament that their Fascist Party "had the good fortune to be dealing with a truly Italian Pope."[99] Milan's archbishop called Il Duce "the new Constantine." Pius declared him a "man sent by providence."[100] The partnership between the Vatican and Mussolini was in full bloom.[101]

6

"The Pope Banker"

The Lateran Pacts settlement left the church with more cash than it had had at any time since it lost its empire. Pius was troubled that he had no competent financial advisor to fill the gap left by Ernesto Pacelli's fall from grace fifteen years earlier. As he made inquiries, one name topped everyone's list: Bernardino Nogara.

Pius ordered a background report. The information that came back was good. A devout Catholic who never missed a morning Mass or afternoon devotional, the fifty-nine-year-old Nogara came from a middle-class farming family in a small village near Lake Como.[1] He had graduated with honors in industrial and electrical engineering from one of Italy's premier schools, Politecnico di Milano. In his first overseas job in 1894, he oversaw mining operations in south Wales. That is where he became fluent in English, as well as where two years later he met and married his wife, Ester Martelli.[2]

After returning to Italy in 1901, he reached out to an acquaintance, Giuseppe Volpi, a Venetian seven years his junior who was in the early stages of a career that would bring him to the pinnacle of Italian business and political power. Volpi was part of a well-connected group of financiers, politicians, and aristocrats, all of whom worked in league with Italy's largest bank, Banca Commerciale Italiana (BCI).[3] He arranged a five-year contract for Nogara to serve as a general manager for a Bulgarian-based mining venture that was planning to expand throughout Asia Minor. In 1907, Volpi tapped Nogara to direct the Constantinople branch of his expanding empire. It was there Nogara learned Turkish and discovered a natural talent for mastering the cutthroat political intrigue that was the hallmark of the Ottoman capital.[4] Through his work with Volpi, Pius learned, Nogara earned a reputation for his financial acumen.[5]

After the Italo-Turkish War—a one-year conflict between Italy and Turkey in 1911 over control of Libya—the Rome Chamber of Commerce selected Nogara as the Italian delegate to the Ottoman Public Debt Council. It was a European-run organization of some five thousand employees whose brief was to pay off the enormous Ottoman Empire debt to Western countries by managing its monopoly and customs revenues in receivership.[6]

After World War I, Nogara was chosen as the Turkish expert to Italy's economic delegation at the Versailles Peace Conference, a forum to which the Vatican was denied a role. Nogara impressed his colleagues with his business savvy. Then in 1924, he began a five-year stint in charge of the industry division of the Inter-Allied Commission responsible for rebuilding war-ravaged Germany. There he met many of the same men who now urged the Vatican to hire him to handle the Lateran settlement and remake the church's finances.[7]

It was to his favor that Nogara was friendly with the Pope's family.[8] As a layman, his religious credentials were also important. Among his twelve siblings, four brothers had become priests. Two were archbishops, Giuseppe in the northern city of Udine and Roberto in Cosenza, in the south. Luigi was a rector at the Seminary of Molfetta. Pope Benedict had appointed another brother, Bartolomeo, a noted archaeologist, as the general director of the Vatican Museums and Monuments. Bernardino's only sister was the mother superior of a convent.[9] Entrenched rumors that Nogara was secretly a practicing Jew made their way to Pius.[10] The Vatican directed parish priests to produce his baptismal records. Nogara came from a Venetian family that had been Jewish before converting during the 1500s when Pius IV expelled all Jews from the Papal States, confiscated their property, and imprisoned and tortured those who stayed and did not convert. Although Pius was satisfied about the matter, the "he's really a Jew" gossip dogged Nogara during his long tenure.

On June 2, 1929, the Pope met privately with Nogara. That meeting was one of the few not recorded on the Vatican calendar.[11] "I know that by asking you [to work here] I am interrupting a brilliant career as a private financier," the Pope reportedly told him.[12] The Pontiff's solicitous approach won Nogara over and Pius meanwhile was convinced by their meeting that Nogara was right for the job.[13]

Nogara's selection required Mussolini's approval since the church's investments could have major repercussions for Italy. Though Nogara was not a Fascist Party member, he casually knew Mussolini. Il Duce gave his consent.[14]

Pius created a new division—the Amministrazione Speciale della Santa Sede (Special Administration of the Holy See, or ASSS)—and put Nogara in charge. The ASSS, or simply Special Administration, was responsible for investing the huge settlement from the Lateran Pacts. Nogara moved into a sprawling apartment in the just-constructed Governor's Palace, adjacent to the Pope's private residence. Pius made it clear that not even cardinals had the authority to interfere with his work.[15] Nogara met only with the Pope, and his one obligation was to provide Pius an annual written report that was then stored in the Pope's private safe.[16] No copies remain.

The cliquish old guard of Black Nobles and senior clerics were wary of the newcomer.[17] They were incensed that Pius had picked a lay commoner and were confident they could undermine him since he was a neophyte. Nogara's Curial antagonists underestimated him.[18] Between his service on large government commissions and also at BCI, a bank known for its brutal infighting, the Milanese banker had learned adeptly how to battle political foes. He moved quickly to fortify his power by hiring several private industry colleagues. Traditionalists were horrified, for instance, when a Credit Suisse banker, Henri de Maillardoz, visited the Vatican to meet with Nogara. The influential Monsignor Domenico Tardini fretted that the mere arrival of Maillardoz—as well as some other bankers from Société de Banque Suisse and Union de Banques Suisses—was a sign that Nogara was contemplating prohibited financial speculation. Tardini thought there were "quieter, safer more stable" ways of guarding the church's money, and if Nogara and his new team were "wrong, then the Holy See would suffer the consequences of the mistakes."[19] But Tardini protested in vain. Maillardoz left Credit Suisse to become the Secretary to the Special Administration.[20] Nogara's new aides reported to him and he in turn only to the Pope, reinforcing the buffer between him and the old guard.

And to keep his rivals busy on other matters, he ordered that every Vatican department prepare an annual budget and issue monthly income and expense statements.[21] He insisted that traditional Curia power brokers produce rudimentary reports that made them accountable for how they spent their money.

No longer could cardinals hide the mismanagement in their departments with the excuse that the Vatican itself was in awful fiscal shape. Although such rules seemed elementary accounting, they were new to an institution that had no history of fiscal oversight.[22]

Nogara decided that the Vatican's investments were too concentrated in bonds and in the Bank of Rome.[23] Any financial problems at that bank would translate into trouble for the Vatican. He boldly diversified the church's risk, transferring some of the Bank of Rome deposits to Swiss, French, and other Italian banks.[24] Next, Nogara invested some of the Lateran Pacts settlement into French and Hungarian railroads as well as German industry.[25] From his tenure on the Allied Commission tasked to rebuild German manufacturing, he was convinced Germany was poised for resurgence after its World War I pounding.[26] He was friendly with Bertha Krupp, one of the heirs to the eponymously named industrial giant. She reinforced his belief that business investments there would yield large returns. Nogara shied from German stocks, however, judging them too unstable.[27] That was fortuitous. In October, only months after he had assumed his Vatican posting, the U.S. stock market crashed. Equities worldwide were hammered. Nogara pivoted from determining how to invest the church's Lateran Pacts money to trying to safeguard its finances from calamity.

Nogara cited the Wall Street crash in advising Pius to reconsider the timing for his transformative redesign of Vatican City. The church, under a secret side deal with Mussolini, was already on the line for a 50 million lire contribution to a new fascist banking institution—the Istituto Centrale di Credito—dedicated to helping distressed Catholic credit unions and banks.[28] But Pius was not persuaded by Nogara's austerity pitch.[29] So despite the stock market crash, the Pope approved the Vatican's largest modern-day construction boom, what historians dub the "Imperial Papacy."[30]

Nogara managed to get himself appointed to the committee responsible for overseeing the construction, hoping that he might be able to control the costs. It proved impossible. Nearly a third of the Lateran Pacts cash went to a mail and telegraph office, a train station, a power plant, and an industrial quarter composed of garages, shops, and factories.[31] Courts and a prison were erected, the Catholic press got its own printing facility and offices, and a radio station opened.[32] A two-year binge commenced of ripping out the small gardens and laying miles of pipes to irrigate lavish formal gardens planted with trees and exotic plants imported from five continents. A replica of the grotto of Lourdes was built. Small, centuries-old houses were demolished and replaced by extravagant new palazzos to house church officials, visiting dignitaries, and foreign diplomats.[33]

Pius also expanded the Vatican museums, adding a picture gallery and extending the library. The Pope built a wall around Vatican City, the first time it was physically separated from the rest of Rome. And when the Vatican announced it would abandon horse-drawn carriages, American auto companies stumbled over each other to see who could get free cars to Pius.[34]

Many of the new buildings—all prominently adorned with Pius's personal coat of arms—were designed in the then popular neoclassical style.[35] They seemed even more grandiose than the contemporary fascist buildings built as part of Mussolini's plans for a majestic Rome. Some observers thought that Pius was competing with the fascist government's imposing display of power. The British ambassador to the Holy See described the church's new architecture as "disfiguring."[36]

The Imperial Papacy was building more than simply a grander Vatican City. Over five hundred new positions were added to the Curia in the two years following the Lateran Pacts.[37] None of this came cheaply. Nogara's concerns about the possible fallout from Wall Street were prescient. The malaise that had started with the American stock exchange crash spread worldwide and infected far more than equities. Unemployment rates zoomed in industrial countries and manufacturing production plummeted. Mussolini grappled with Italy's worsening financial crisis. He no longer had spare money with which to help the church. Moreover, as Italians grew increasingly concerned about the financial crunch, Mussolini sometimes distracted them by allowing his top officials to ramp up the polemics against the church, blaming Catholic trade associations for favoring their friends instead of pitching in to help ordinary Italians. An angry crowd torched a bishop's palace in Verona. At least one fascist rally was punctuated with calls of "death to the traitor Ratti," Pius's name before he ascended to the Papacy.[38]

Pius was furious at the agitation caused by Mussolini. He considered it a breach of their treaty. The Pope had put his own reputation on the line inside the Vatican when he had assured critics that Mussolini was a trustworthy man. Pius issued a prominent 1931 encyclical, *Non Abbiamo Bisogno* (We Do Not

Need), in which he censured the fascists for their cult of violence and veneration of the state.[39]* "We do not fear," he wrote about the bullying from Mussolini. But Pius avoided condemning the fascist state. He agonized over whether Mussolini might retaliate by reinstituting taxes against the church to make up for Italy's fiscal shortfall.[41] The public spat between the Pope and Il Duce was settled in another deal—this one secret—that further denuded the power of the Azione Cattolica (Catholic Action), the huge lay social organization founded by Pius X in 1905. The fascists feared its independence and unpredictability. It made no difference that the Lateran Pacts had promised to protect Catholic Action.[42] In return, Mussolini pledged to tone down the attacks on the church.

The squabble between the Pope and Il Duce accelerated a precipitous drop in Peter's Pence.[43] Pius asked some well-off American dioceses, such as Chicago and New York, to advance Rome a loan against its future collections. They demurred. The request demonstrated how little the Pope appreciated the depth of the U.S. economic malaise. When Pius asked for money in 1932, unemployment in the United States was nearing an unprecedented 23.1 percent. Fear had frozen American Catholics from contributing to their own dioceses. There was no spare money.

In Britain, that same year, hundreds of thousands demonstrated in Hunger Marches, demanding work and food. Vatican documents reveal that instead of being concerned about the humanitarian crisis that forced so many to protest, church officials were oblivious to the dire state of affairs. Instead they fretted about whether the unrest might further cut the flow of funds from British Catholics to Rome.[44]

Nogara was so troubled about the impact of the church's tumbling income that he persuaded Pius to cut employee salaries between 10 and 15 percent.[45] And to raise extra cash, the Vatican christened 1933 a "Holy Year," the twenty-fourth since Pope Boniface announced the first one in 1300. It resulted in a brief spike in pilgrims and donations.[46]

---

* After World War I, Italian intelligence had penetrated the Vatican with clerical informants and lay agents, ranging from cooks to footmen to policemen. They focused not just on politically significant information, but also on compiling compromising dossiers on the sexual predilections of top clerics. Such dirt was also useful as blackmail. One of the few matters about which the informants failed to provide advance notice was Pius's 1931 antigovernment encyclical. Mussolini shook up his intelligence agency's leadership so he would not again be surprised.[40]

Nogara's worst-case warnings about the consequences of the international financial downturn were realized.[47] Another precipitous drop in the value of the British pound meant big losses for Vatican holdings there.[48] Defaults on interest payments by Peru, Chile, Brazil, Greece, Hungary, Austria, and Bulgaria—all countries to which the Vatican had issued loans—meant more red ink. Even the huge international banking firm Kreuger & Toll failed to pay any return on the money the church had invested there.[49]* In 1933, the Vatican lost its investment in the Missouri Pacific Railroad when that firm went bust. And the slide in the dollar further damaged its American holdings.[51] By the end of 1933—the height of the Great Depression—the Vatican tallied losses of more than 100 million lire. Its annual revenues had slumped dramatically.[52] The church did not have the money to help Catholic institutions stay afloat. By the end of the decade, seventy-four Catholic community banks had failed. It cost tens of thousands of ordinary Catholics more than a billion lire in lost deposits.[53]

The financial maelstrom did not cause Pius to lose faith in Nogara. He knew that without Nogara the church could be in worse shape. The grim international forecast convinced Pius to give Nogara autonomy he was unlikely to have ever had in more stable times. The Pope agreed not to exercise his traditional veto over money matters so long as Nogara was in place. It was an unequivocal signal not only about the frightening depths of the crisis but also evidence of the unrivaled scope of Nogara's authority. Some in the Curia mocked Pius as "the Pope banker."[54] Even Nogara's most entrenched opponents concluded that so long as Pius was Pope, he was untouchable.[55]

Nogara embarked on an investment strategy—radical by Vatican standards—intended to reverse the church's downward spiral. He first turned to gold. Giuseppe Volpi, his longtime business colleague and friend, had just finished a three-year tenure as Mussolini's Finance Minister. Volpi had returned the lira to the gold standard. He encouraged Nogara to accumulate the precious metal as a hedge for bad times.[56] Over just a few months, Bernardino

---

* Kreuger & Toll collapsed when it was exposed for having perpetrated one of the largest twentieth-century frauds. The Vatican was merely one of hundreds of institutions swindled. The company's Swedish chairman, Ivar Kreuger, known as the "Match King," killed himself after his company's deceptions were revealed. (The Kreuger family, and some subsequent authors, have contended the suicide was, in fact, murder.)[50]

added $4 million in gold bars to the Vatican's reserves.[57] Next, he invested in real estate, something he thought less susceptible to the fluctuations of securities and currencies. The Depression had caused real estate prices to plunge, so there were many attractive deals for cash buyers. Nogara bought prime properties in France, Britain, and Switzerland.[58] And he was at the forefront of a new strategy—arbitrage—in which he purchased government bonds from one country while selling a different batch in another nation, hoping to profit on the price fluctuations between them.[59] It was risky and speculative, a practice still in its infancy, but promised significant profits if his hunches on price movements were right.[60]

The Vatican did not like to advertise its financial moves. Nogara hid the purchases. He put them through a network of holding companies. The chief one was Groupement Financier Luxembourgeois (Grolux S.A.), headquartered in Luxembourg.[61] His choice of that country was no mistake.[62] Just two years earlier Luxembourg had passed laws and regulations that made it an even more attractive investment haven than neighboring Switzerland and Liechtenstein. Funneling much of the money through Grolux meant that Nogara was assured inviolable confidentiality.[63] Under Grolux Nogara established other foreign firms. Paris-based Sopridex managed the ASSS's real estate in France. Lausanne Immobilier was his Swiss firm, and British Grolux ran the UK properties. To assuage the Papal financial advisors he had displaced, he stocked the boards of his holding companies with handpicked French, British, and Italian aristocratic Catholics.[64]

His foreign operations required special attention. Nogara established a small unit inside the ASSS to concentrate solely on those ventures. Each new person hired in that section had to be fluent in German, Italian, French, and English.[65]

Nogara was a longtime director of BCI, Italy's largest bank, and also was on the board of a Swiss bank, Sudameris. He created another holding company so the Vatican could invest in those, and other, banks.[66] And instead of relying just on Italian banks to move money, he used Maillardoz's Union de Banques Suisses in Switzerland; Enskilda in Sweden; and Mees & Hope in the Netherlands.[67] He tapped the House of Morgan in New York, London, and Paris to hold some of the church's gold reserves, as well as hundreds of thousands of dollars in securities. Giovanni Fummi, a Morgan executive from a patrician Italian family, and an avid Mussolini supporter, became Nogara's man on Wall Street.

Pius was pleased to learn of the Morgan involvement. Before he became Pope he had spent seven years directing the Vatican Library. One of his projects was restoring sixty Coptic fragments recovered from a thousand-year-old monastery. The Morgan Collection in New York had sent the fragments to Rome for restoration. Pius—then Monsignor Ratti—met repeatedly with J. P. Morgan, the patriarch of the New York banking dynasty. He liked the garrulous American, having no idea that the Episcopalian Morgan had once lobbied hard to keep a Catholic off Harvard's board.[68] When Nogara told him about the new relationship, Pius considered it a providential sign (Pius later bestowed on Morgan, and his CEO, Tom Lamont, the Grand Cross of Saint Gregory the Great for their extraordinary service to the church).[69]

While Nogara's Vatican investments were international, he concentrated on Italy, the market he knew best. The Depression had battered many Italian firms. By the mid-1930s he had invested in Italian financial, utility, mining, textile, and property companies.[70] And to watch over the investments, Nogara often served as a director for the acquired companies. He cultivated friendships with an expanding circle of business associates and politicians.[71] Among others, he befriended Fiat's founder, Giovanni Agnelli; Alberto Pirelli, heir to the country's rubber monopoly; and the chairmen of two Italian insurance giants, Edgardo Morpurgo of Assicurazioni Generali and Arnoldo Frigessi di Rattalma of Riunione Adriatica di Sicurtà (RAS).[72]

Aftershocks of the Depression had caused an Italian credit crisis. The share prices of banks, including the Bank of Rome, Sardinian Land Credit, Banco di Santo Spirito, Credito Italiano, and even Nogara's BCI, got hammered. The church's long-standing investments turned into deep losses. So Nogara joined other bankers and businessmen and lobbied Mussolini to create the Industrial Reconstruction Institute (IRI), a government agency that would seize the shares of the ailing institutions and institute strict regulations to stave off a collapse of Italy's banking system.[73] Mussolini's version of nationalization was to carve out a small role for private capital. He established the IRI—a hybrid of state nationalization with a private sector.

Nogara had his own plan for how the IRI might benefit the Vatican.[74] He convinced the IRI to allow the church to redeem its shares in some of the nationalized banks at the full value for which the Vatican had purchased them.[75] This allowed the church to avoid millions in losses and transferred the debt to the Italian Treasury.[76] Nogara found other ways to capitalize on the banks' hard times. As a director at many of them, and as a friend of the IRI's fascist directors, he often knew in advance which banks would get the government's biggest capital injections. Armed with that insider knowledge, Nogara invested Vatican money in those few that managed to emerge from state control.[77]*

Nogara also found opportunity in a fascist holding company for the distressed oil and gas industry. He managed to get the inside track on the one major private firm, Italgas, a leading natural gas conglomerate, in which the fascists decided to sell a majority stake. As a BCI director, Nogara had taken part in Italgas's bailout and he served on the government holding company in which the company's shares were held. When Mussolini finally approved the sale, Nogara and his Black Noble partners—led by Marquis Francesco Pacelli (the brother of the future Pius XII)—managed to take a majority stake for less than a quarter of its market value.[79] Italgas turned into one of the church's most profitable investments.[80]

And as he had done before with Grolux, Nogara selected prominent Catholic laymen to serve on the boards of the rescued banks and companies, all of whom eventually received Papal titles and decorations.[81] Over several years, those handpicked directors expanded their influence as they served on interlocking boards for many of Italy's largest firms.

Nogara later swapped some of the Vatican's ownership in a few of the reconstituted banks for IRI bonds paying 5 percent interest.[82] The investment in fascist-issued bonds was not only a good deal for the Vatican, but it further tied the church's economic health to the Italian state. By 1935, with the exception of farming, there was no sector of the Italian economy in which the Vatican did not have a significant investment or ownership interest.[83] Only Mussolini's government owned more than the Vatican.

Fascist politicians and businessmen served on many of the company boards in which the Vatican had a stake, putting fascist and church representatives at the same decision-making table in key industries. This commingling meant

---

* In the 1930s, Italy had the largest state ownership of companies other than the Soviet Union. At the end of Mussolini's reign in 1943, 80 percent of all Italian banks were still under IRI control.[78]

the Vatican had every reason to maintain at the minimum a benign political tolerance for Mussolini's regime. In many respects that was not difficult. Il Duce was refreshing compared to the anticlerical mixture of socialists and free-thinkers who—to the church's great detriment—had played significant roles in Italian politics since the late nineteenth century.[84] And the church did not have to make any compromises when it came to fascist social policies. Mussolini's insistence on public morality, belief in the inferior role of women, and the ban on contraception and abortion made the fascists palatable to the church.[85]

Equally important was that Mussolini's anticommunist stance was comforting. The Vatican feared godless bolshevism far more than it detested fascism. Pius had come to despise communism during his tenure as Poland's Nuncio.[86] And his Cardinal Secretary of State, Eugenio Pacelli, had been the target of an unsuccessful assassination by a communist cell when he was Germany's Nuncio. Pacelli had an equally hard-line view.[87] Both men knew that the Soviets had not just declared a rhetorical war on organized religion. In Russia the state waged a bloody war against all faiths, jailing or murdering the clergy, destroying churches or turning them into atheist museums, and banning any teaching of God to children under the age of sixteen.[88]

While the Vatican and Mussolini were cementing their de facto partnership, Pius issued three encyclicals on economic and social issues.[89] Each reiterated a condemnation of unbridled capitalism and the accumulation of great wealth by a few, as well as decrying as "deadly" international finance and its focus on profits. He denounced capitalists "addicted to excessive gain."[90] Medieval dogma declared money itself was an unproductive pursuit. Loaning money at interest was immoral. Pius was the first Pope in decades to restate that dogma so forcefully: "The desire for money is the root of all evil."[91]

Those encyclicals puzzled Italians in the private sector who were doing business with the church. What the Pope said would have precluded many of Nogara's investments. But only a handful of ranking clerics knew that before Nogara had accepted Pius's appointment at the Vatican, he had made it clear he would do so only if his work was not restricted by religious doctrine. Nogara had also insisted he should be free to invest anywhere in the world, no matter what the country's politics.[92] And while some in the Curia grumbled that Nogara's financial speculation violated the church's core values, so long as the balance sheets showed surpluses, Pius and his chief advisors were pleased.[93] It was also somewhat easier for officials to give wide latitude to Nogara since he was a layman.[94]

Nogara's freedom paid off. His diversification stabilized the church through the Great Depression. An unintended consequence of his investments was that as the worldwide financial crisis began easing, the Vatican and Mussolini were thoroughly entwined.

7

Prelude to War

The Vatican-Mussolini partnership was set against the backdrop of Italy's flourishing alliance with Germany's Third Reich, the so-called Rome-Berlin Axis. The church had good reason to monitor that political union. A third of Germans were Catholic. Despite the godless ideology promoted by Adolf Hitler's National Socialist Party, the church realized it had to work with the Nazis if it meant safeguarding the rights of Catholics.

The Vatican saw in the Nazis the same fervent anticommunism that was an integral element of Mussolini's fascism. Pius knew, however, that deciding how best to deal with Germany was not as simple as concluding that Hitler was less evil than Soviet dictator Joseph Stalin. The Vatican feared that Hitler was more passionate about his anticlerical rhetoric than was Mussolini. Nazi policy was that the state alone should be revered. Since Hitler was raised Catholic and a few Third Reich ministers occasionally spoke of "positive Christianity," some church officials hoped Hitler might soften his antichurch theme over time. The Führer gave conflicting signals. Once he declared that churches should be an integrated element of German national life. Another time he said: "You are either a Christian or a German. You cannot be both." [1] Privately, however, Hitler promised colleagues that he would "eradicate" Christianity from Germany.[2]

If anyone had faith that the Germans could be trusted despite the harshness of their rhetoric, it was Secretary of State Eugenio Pacelli. An admitted Teutophile, he had been the Papal Nuncio to Germany for twelve years. Within weeks of Hitler's 1933 appointment as Chancellor, Pacelli sent the Führer a private letter in which he obliquely endorsed the Nazi's strong anticommunist policies.[3] At the time, no European country yet had recognized Hitler's government. Hitler saw an opening in Pacelli's note. He reasoned that if the Vatican conferred the stamp of its moral authority on the Third Reich, it might encourage other nations to follow. The same impetus had propelled Mussolini into a pact with the Vatican. And although Hitler wanted to crush the church, he did not want to repeat the mistake of his predecessor, Bismarck, by taking on so early a widely popular faith.[4] The Nazi hierarchy knew that Pacelli was as likely as any church official to be receptive to a deal. During his tenure as Nuncio, Pacelli had hammered out concordats with Bavaria (1924), Prussia (1929), and Baden-Württemberg (1932).[5]

Hitler dispatched to Rome Vice Chancellor Franz von Papen—a Papal Knight—to determine whether the Holy See might entertain a formal treaty with the Third Reich.[6] Hermann Göring, a decorated chief of the Luftwaffe and one of Hitler's closest aides, accompanied Papen to emphasize to the Vatican that the Germans were serious. Starting in April 1933, Pacelli and Papen began secret negotiations.[7] That was the same month that the Nazis ratcheted up their war against the Jews. On April 1, the National Socialists launched a nationwide boycott of Jewish businesses.[8] Nazi storm troopers burned Jewish shops and assaulted Jews.[9] Three days after the start of the hooliganism, the Third Reich passed its first decree directed at Jews—the Law Regarding the Admission to the Bar—banning Jewish attorneys.[10] It was the start of what some historians have called "plunder by decree."[11] A few days later a law dismissed Jews from the civil service since they were not "Aryan." A week later another law prohibited them from serving as teachers and judges.[12] The number of Jews allowed to study in universities was set at a fixed quota of one percent. Jewish war veterans and their families—more than 32,000 Jewish German soldiers had died in World War I—were cut off from benefits. On April 11, for the first time the Nazis defined Jews by blood: one Jewish grandparent marked someone as "non-Aryan."[13] Thousands of instructional charts were distributed to help average Germans distinguish Jews from Aryans.[14] In May, the Nazis celebrated the first in a series of public-spectacle book burnings. They were meant to expunge from public libraries the literary and scientific contributions of Jewish intellectuals and scholars, including books by Kafka, Hesse, Brecht, Einstein, and Freud.[15]

The violent national boycott, the exclusionary law, and the book burnings were all an early test for the church. Would it tolerate the Nazis' unrelenting anti-Semitism? During those first seminal months—while negotiations with the Nazis were under way—no Vatican official or German bishop condemned what was happening to Germany's Jews.[16] Breslau's Cardinal Adolf Bertram instead dismissed a plea for intervention by averring that the Nazi "measures [were] directed against an interest group which has no very close bond with the Church." In any case, said Bertram, "The press, which is overwhelmingly in Jewish hands, has steadfastly remained consistently silent about the persecution of Catholics."[17] Munich's Cardinal Michael von Faulhaber, one of the most influential clerics, distributed an order directing German clergy to support the Nazi state. He reiterated his full "confidence" in the Third Reich.[18] Faulhaber later wrote a letter to Pacelli: "We bishops are being asked why the Catholic Church, as often in its history, does not intervene on behalf of the Jews. This is not possible at this time because the struggle against the Jews would then, at the same time, become a struggle against the Catholics, and because the Jews can help themselves. . . ."[19]

On April 25, thousands of German priests became part of what historian John Cornwell calls an "anti-Semitic attestation bureaucracy," by surrendering their parish marriage and baptism records.[20] The Nazis used those documents to verify blood purity. In less than two months, on July 14, the Nazis enacted the Law for the Prevention of Genetically Diseased Offspring. It institutionalized sterilization for people determined to have one of nine supposedly hereditary conditions, including deafness and blindness, bipolar and schizophrenia, "feeblemindedness," physical deformity, and even alcoholism. Vatican officials discussed what to do since such mandatory sterilization was a gross violation of church teachings and a 1930 encyclical Pius had issued, *Casti Connubii* (Of Chaste Wedlock).[21] The Pope feared, however, that any criticism might jeopardize the ongoing negotiations with the Third Reich. The Vatican stayed silent.[22] Pius privately told his bishops not to rule out a future campaign against the sterilization decree, but neither did he encourage them to start one. Eventually 400,000 Germans were sterilized, and the Vatican did not issue a Pastoral Letter against it for another decade, only after the tide of the war had begun to turn against the Nazis).[23]*

---

* While church officials remained quiet about forced sterilization, another controversy in Germany had them in a frenzy: *Freikörperkultur Entwicklung*, the nudism movement. Shedding clothes in public was a popular avant-garde trend at some bohemian camps during the 1920s and 1930s. Ranking clerics held dozens of meetings about how the church might best battle it. The Vatican condemned it as a "fetish of the flesh." Pacelli considered nudity "perverse," and judged it a contributing factor to the declining

Less than a week later, on July 20, Papen and Cardinal Pacelli signed a thirty-three-article pact—a Reichskonkordat—that was the result of nearly three months of negotiations. Pacelli was reportedly not pleased with the final agreement, feeling it was rushed and that the Germans had more leverage.[25] Still, Hitler granted, at least on paper, many of the safeguards the church wanted. The National Socialists guaranteed the right of Catholics to practice their faith as well as the freedom to express it publicly without retribution. Catholics were "protected in their establishments and their activity." Religious orders were exempted from paying taxes on stipends they received from the church. The right to operate Catholic schools was reaffirmed.[26] Government workers were forbidden from criticizing the church.[27] And there was a formal acknowledgment of "the right of the Church to levy" the Kirchensteuer, its tax on German Catholics that had been in effect since 1919. The church often had trouble getting the faithful to pay it voluntarily, so the Third Reich later agreed to collect the 8 to 10 percent tariff through automatic payroll deductions of Catholic wage earners.[28] That would mark the first time that any country had agreed to provide the Vatican a share of government-collected tax money. It uniquely tied the church to the Third Reich.[29]*

In return, the Vatican gave Hitler the formal endorsement he wanted. Article 16 of the Reichskonkordat required German bishops and cardinals to swear an oath of loyalty to the Third Reich. It was a dramatic reversal from 1932 when a German bishops' conference had banned membership in the Nazi Party and forbade anyone wearing a swastika from receiving the sacra-

---

birth rate among "purely Catholic marriages." He convinced Mussolini to confiscate and destroy all copies of a book by a Dutch author that encouraged nudity. Germany was the epicenter, said Pacelli, with some five million "mentally imbalanced" adherents. Cardinal Merry del Val called nudism one of the "most detestable and pernicious aberrations of our times. . . . An attack on Christian morality." The church never issued such unequivocally condemnatory language to address Hitler's and Mussolini's anti-Semitic race policies.[24]

* The Reichskonkordat never stopped some high-ranking Nazis from attacking the church. In a 1938 speech, Hitler's military secretary, Martin Bormann, said, "We Germans are the first to be appointed by destiny to break with Christianity. It will be an honor for us." Bormann reminded Nazi provincial governors in a confidential memo that the German church "must absolutely and finally be broken." In his book—*The Myth of the Twentieth Century*—Alfred Rosenberg, the Nazi Party's philosopher and ideologue, attacked Jews and also launched an unmitigated assault on Christianity, particularly Catholicism. When the Vatican added Rosenberg's book to its banned list, Hitler responded by promoting him as overseer of the Nazi Party's "world view."[30]

ments.[31] The agreement also decreed that a "special prayer . . . for the welfare of the German Reich" be inserted into every Sunday and Holy Day Mass.

The Germans also prevailed on the most contested provision, Article 32: it banned all clergy from joining any political party. That accelerated the demise of the Catholic Center Party, forcing the resignation of priests who had been elected to the Reichstag.[32] And all church organizations and orders were prohibited from expressing any political opinions. The definition of "political" was left to the discretion of the Nazis. The Reichskonkordat was clear: anything that was not about "the dogmatic and moral teachings and principles of the Church" was suspect.[33]

And to ensure the purity of the priesthood, the Nazis required all priests practicing in Germany to be natural-born citizens who had a German education. They would answer only to German superiors. Religious instruction had to encourage patriotism and devotion to the state.[34]

Pacelli had tried inserting a sentence to protect Catholics who had converted from Judaism, what the Nazis dubbed "non-Aryan Catholics." Under the Third Reich's race laws, such converts were considered Jews. Even children and grandchildren of converts, of whom there were some 300,000 in Germany, were still Jews according to the Nazis.[35] Church officials fretted that if only blood controlled Jewish identity, there would be no further inducement for Jews to convert to Catholicism.[36] In the worst historical persecutions against Jews—even the bloody Spanish Inquisition—converting was enough to avoid torture or death. Pius XI had made conversion one of the central tenets of his Papacy.

But the Germans rejected any protection for "non-Aryan Catholics." Nazi theorists considered converted Jews dangerous. By adopting Catholicism they might be able to mask their Jewishness and become sleeper agents spreading corruption inside Germany.[37] (Five years later Pacelli issued an appeal to bishops to help obtain up to 200,000 exit visas for non-Aryan Catholics.)[38]

A delighted Hitler boasted that the "treaty with the new Germany means the acknowledgment of the National Socialist State by the Catholic Church."[39] The Reichskonkordat convinced ordinary Germans that the Vatican approved of the Third Reich. German Catholics embraced the Nazis without any lingering reservations. In the months following the agreement, a record number of Catholics became Nazi Party members (some clergy also joined, with one bishop entering the SS).[40]

That September (1933), after the German Reichstag ratified the agreement, the Papal Nuncio to Germany, Archbishop Cesare Orsenigo, celebrated with a Pontifical High Mass at Berlin's grand eighteenth-century St. Hedwig's cathedral. Catholic SS members received special invitations. The cathedral's vaulted dome was festooned with Papal flags that hung next to those emblazoned with swastikas. In his sermon, Orsenigo praised Hitler as "a man marked by his devotion to God, and sincerely concerned for the well-being of the German people." Since the crowd was so large—thousands could not squeeze into the standing-room-only cathedral—loudspeakers broadcast the service to enthusiastic throngs outside.

The Reichskonkordat was important for the Nazis.[41] It gave them the parliamentary votes of the Catholic Center Party, further tightening their grip on government.[42] And Hitler was right. His first treaty with a foreign power—even one as Lilliputian as the Vatican—polished his image.[43] In a Sunday sermon, Cardinal von Faulhaber, who came to regret the deal, praised the Führer: "This handshake with the papacy, the greatest moral power in the history of the world, is a feat of immeasurable blessing. . . . May God protect our Chancellor for our people."[44]

The Nazis were proud the Vatican stayed the course through the negotiations during the first major escalation of their campaign against Jews. Hitler told other Nazis that the treaty had created a political tone that was "especially significant in the urgent struggle against international Jewry."[45] The Führer boasted privately: "I shall be one of the few men in history to have deceived the Vatican."[46]

Two weeks after the Pontifical High Mass in Berlin, the Nazis issued new race orders that excluded Jews from all artistic, dramatic, literary, film, and news enterprises. The following day, Jewish farmers were banned from owning farmland and were denied inheritance rights to family property.

Just a month after the agreement, Pope Pius XI told a British diplomat that he knew about "German persecutions of the Jews."[47] But he gave no indication that he intended to say anything in protest. The Pope had been raised and educated in a church theology steeped in anti-Semitism.[48] Moreover, he had demonstrated he was no reformer when it came to relations between the church and Jews. Five years before the Reichskonkordat, Pius had rejected the efforts of a reformist Catholic movement, the Friends of Israel, to remove Holy Week references to the "perfidy of Jews" and "perfidious Jews."[49] He thought the protesting Jews were attempting to promote Zionism and create a homeland in Palestine.[50] That was taboo. His predecessor, Pius X, had made that clear in a 1904 meeting with the father of Zionism, Theodor Herzl. The Pope told Herzl: "We cannot prevent the Jews from going to Jerusalem, but [we] could never sanction it. . . . The Jews have not recognized our Lord. Therefore, we cannot recognize the Jewish people, and so, if you come to Palestine and settle your people there, we will be ready with churches and priests to baptize all of you."[51] In accord with that rhetoric, Pius XI disbanded the Friends of Israel.[52]

Church officials did not speak out against the November 1933 Nazi legislation that provided for the internment in concentration camps of the homeless, beggars, and the unemployed. Nor when the Third Reich enacted a law in June 1935 introducing compulsory abortions to prevent the passing of hereditary diseases. More silence ensued in September 1935 with the passage of two so-called Nuremberg Laws. The first, the Law for the Protection of German Blood and German Honor, criminalized sexual relations and marriage between Jews and Aryans. The second, the Reich Citizenship Law, stripped Jews of their citizenship.

Germany was not the only Vatican concordat partner that gave the church discomfort with its policies. The same was true for Italy. In 1935 the Vatican had to choose between the moralities it preached and the hunt for profits that had become a part of Nogara's investment strategy.

On October 3, 100,000 Italian soldiers swept over the border from Italian Somaliland and invaded Ethiopia. There was no declaration of war. In less than two weeks, Italy's troops had routed Emperor Haile Selassie's half-million-man army, many primitively armed with spears, bows, or in some cases outdated nineteenth-century rifles. The Italians swept through the holy capital of Axum (sending a sacred obelisk back to Rome as a trophy for capturing the city).*

The Ethiopian campaign was an essential part of Mussolini's grand ambition to re-create an Italian empire that stretched without interruption from southern Europe through central and east Africa. Ethiopia—then Abyssinia—was a prime candidate for Il Duce's expansionist policies. It was one of the few African nations not already a European colony. France and Britain had large empires and several other European countries boasted African colonies.[54]

---

* The Obelisk of Axum was placed in a central Roman square, in front of what would become the United Nations Food and Agriculture Organization. Italy resisted returning it for decades, but finally did so in 2005.[53]

Mineral-rich Ethiopia was a natural extension of Italy's Eritrean colony to the northwest and Italian Somaliland on the east. And finally, Mussolini was in part avenging Italy's defeat during the First Italian-Abyssinian War thirty-nine years earlier.

The invasion was brutal. Although Italy had signed the 1925 Geneva Protocol governing the acceptable conduct of war, Mussolini's troops ignored those rules. In artillery and aerial bombardments, they used between four and five hundred tons of prohibited mustard gas, terrorized civilians by firebombing the city of Harar, and even used the gas on Red Cross ambulances and camps.[55]

The mostly ineffective League of Nations—the predecessor to the United Nations—condemned Italy as the aggressor, but member countries could not agree on what to do. Nogara monitored the League's efforts since he hoped to derail any effort to pass sanctions that might damage Italy's economy. The League moved so slowly it gave time to some of Nogara's Italian friends to transfer their assets to Vatican holding companies. The Vatican would be untouched by anything the League did since the Holy See was an independent country not involved in the conflict.[56] But all the worrying was unnecessary. The sanctions had no bite and Italy blithely ignored them.[57]

The war caused little anxiety inside the Vatican. In fact, the church had no reason to take on Mussolini. Most Italians supported the invasion. Pius had himself blessed some of the troops as they left for the fighting.[58] And the Pope made no attempt to dampen the clerical enthusiasm evident from church pulpits. He was even silent when Milan's Cardinal Alfredo Ildefonso Schuster declared the war a crusade for Catholicism.[59] Popular archbishops in Amalfi, Brindisi, and Sorrento rebuked the League of Nations as godless hypocrites.[60] Mussolini bragged to Nazi officials, "Why they [the Vatican] even declared the Abyssinian war a Holy War!"[61]

Britain and France were upset with Pius's tacit support of the Italian campaign and his refusal to speak out either against the aggression or about the plight of civilians. And the same criticism extended to Secretary of State Pacelli, who maintained a strict diplomatic silence about the invasion. Some observers thought that the Pontiff's reluctance to wield his moral authority was because Ethiopia was mostly Muslim and had few Catholics.

But the Pope was motivated not so much by Ethiopian demographics as by what was best for business. The church had stakes in Breda, Reggiane, and

Compagnia Nazionale Aeronautica, manufacturers of munitions and weapons.[62] Nogara had made it clear to the Pontiff that the Vatican's huge investments in Italian stocks and Mussolini's state-issued bonds meant that the church's interests were best served by a brief and successful campaign. With Nogara as middleman, the Vatican made a substantial wartime loan to the fascist government (it stayed secret for decades).[63] In exchange, Mussolini gave the church "ecclesiastical dispensations" from special levies of corporate, real estate, and sales taxes that he imposed to raise money to fund the offensive.[64]

Nogara was concerned about intensifying British and American opposition to the invasion. He briefed the Pope, as well as Raffaele Guariglia, chief of Italy's Bureau of Ethiopian Affairs and a strong advocate of colonial expansion.[65] The message from Nogara to both was the same: a prolonged conflict would burden Italy's resources and budget, create widespread pessimism among ordinary Italians, and potentially lead to an economic downturn that might spur the growth of extremist political parties.[66]

The Vatican shared Nogara's concerns. Pius was delighted that the brutal combat ended on May 7, 1936, when Italy annexed the country and named the Italian King, Victor Emmanuel III, as Emperor. Mussolini merged the three contiguous colonies—Ethiopia, Eritrea, and Somaliland—into Italian East Africa. Two thousand five hundred Italian troops had been killed during the brief war. But an estimated 275,000 Ethiopians—soldiers and civilians—had been massacred. Reports of the bloodbath got lost in Italy's jubilation over its conquest. Even the Pope joined leading Italian dignitaries in celebrating the war's end and offering Mussolini his heartfelt congratulations.

Exiled Ethiopian Emperor Haile Selassie gave a rousing speech in Geneva before the League of Nations the following month. He warned, "It is us today. It will be you tomorrow." The League passed another ineffective condemnation. Mussolini, emboldened by his victory, had withdrawn Italy from the League of Nations weeks earlier.

In the new colony, the fascists imposed anti-miscegenation laws, banning interracial marriage, cohabitation, and sexual relations. Residential segregation, in the formerly liberal country, was instituted and strictly enforced. The Vatican was silent.

There was money to be made from the conquered colony. Mussolini announced a new agency—Regia Azienda Monopolio Banane (the Royal Banana Monopoly Business)—to control the lucrative banana trade from all its African colonies. The agency doled out exclusive concessions to forty-eight businessmen, all of them ranking fascists or handpicked by the Vatican.[67]*

When Ethiopian insurgents failed in a 1937 assassination attempt on the colony's military commander, Mussolini ordered mass executions as punishment. An estimated thirty thousand Ethiopians, including half of the younger educated class, were killed. Again, there was no public protest from Pius or any ranking cleric. In the British Foreign Office, a flurry of cables between officials reflected the now widespread Western view that the "Church has proved that it is purely Italian and far from 'Catholic'" and that "the Church is in Mussolini's pocket."[69]

In 1937, Nogara accelerated the pace of the church's investments beyond Europe.[70] He traveled to America and stopped in the wealthy dioceses, including New York, Chicago, Washington, Philadelphia, and Cleveland. He met influential businessmen in each city. In New York, he spent much of his time with Giovanni Fummi and his fellow investment bankers at the House of Morgan.[71] Relying on their advice, he put $3.5 million into the stocks of manufacturing companies, some electrical utilities, and U.S. Treasury bonds.[72] Under Nogara's cautious guidance, the Vatican now had an economic toehold in the New World.

Nogara's decision to diversify further was prompted by his concern over Hitler's increasingly confrontational rhetoric about Germany's claim to the Sudetenland, a portion of northern and western Czechoslovakia with mostly German-speaking residents. The Czech military, worried that Hitler might forcibly reclaim it, had begun building fortifications and moving troops to the border.

Nogara was not the only one inside the Vatican who thought that Germany

---

* When Pacelli visited the United States that November, he met with seventy-nine bishops in twelve of the sixteen American church's Ecclesiastical Provinces. And the day after President Franklin Roosevelt's reelection, Pacelli met the president at his Hyde Park home. There is no indication that the Ethiopian invasion was discussed. Instead, Roosevelt was concerned with the wildly popular but bigoted radio broadcasts of an American priest, Charles Coughlin. And Pacelli wanted to encourage the United States to reestablish relations with the Vatican (the last American diplomat was withdrawn in 1867). Although the substance of those talks was never disclosed, the results were evident. Two days after the meeting, Coughlin announced the last broadcast of his provocative show that reached thirty million listeners. And Roosevelt eventually bypassed resistance in Congress to restoring diplomatic relations with the Holy See by dispatching industrialist Myron Taylor as his personal envoy.[68]

was ratcheting up tensions. The Nazis were also flagrantly violating the Reichskonkordat. As part of a coordinated effort by the Third Reich to diminish the church's moral sway over ordinary Germans, the Nazis had begun holding public "morality trials" at which priests and nuns were prosecuted for concocted financial corruptions or sexual crimes.[73] Catholic weeklies were subjected to ever stricter censorship.[74] Nazis even spread the rumor that the Pope's grandmother was a "Dutch Jewess." Pius wanted to confront the Nazis, but Pacelli counseled moderation.[75] Drafts of an encyclical were passed around to senior prelates and its language was tempered during an intense internal debate.[76] The compromise was Pius's encyclical *Mit brennender Sorge* (With Burning Sorrow).[77] By the obtuse standards of encyclicals, it included some remarkably direct language, such as the Pope's condemnation of how the Nazis had repeatedly broken the treaty. In other instances it more indirectly chastised the Third Reich for encouraging a growing worship of the German state to the exclusion of religion.[78] Pius distanced the church from the "so-called myth of blood and race."[79] Jews were not mentioned, although the encyclical obliquely offered "consolation and strength" to those who had converted to Catholicism.[80]

Third Reich officials took little satisfaction that the encyclical did not mention the persecution of Jews or condemn Germany's institutionalized anti-Semitism. They were instead furious with its overall theme that cast the church as indispensable as the state.[81] The German companies that had printed it were shuttered and their employees jailed. The Foreign Office rebuked ranking German bishops for having read it from their pulpits.[82] Some Nazi officials urged annulling the Reichskonkordat.[83] But Hitler wanted to keep the agreement in place. Although he did not mind upsetting the church, he did not intend to move against it with the full power of the state until after the war.[84] Moreover, notes from Germany's ambassador to the Vatican, Diego von Bergen, reveal that in a meeting with Cardinal Pacelli, after the encyclical was released, Pacelli offered appeasement. He was solicitous, expressing his own sympathy for the plight of the German people. Pacelli even proposed meeting Field Marshal Göring if it would help temper any Third Reich indignation.[85] Göring responded by accelerating the pace of the morality trials intended to humiliate German priests and nuns.[86]

By the following year (1938), the Pope was uneasy about the militant anti-Semitism in both the Third Reich and fascist Italy.[87] In a turnabout, he even suggested that the Sacred Congregation for Seminaries and Universities find Italian theology professors who might challenge the Nazi racial pseudo-science.[88]

When the Führer visited Rome in May on a state visit, he did not stop by the Vatican. Pius went to Castel Gandolfo, the Papal summer residence. Both sides claimed they snubbed the other but there was little doubt that neither tried very hard to set up a meeting.[89]

In July, the Pope directed his frustration to Mussolini. Pius was furious when Il Duce issued his Manifesto of Race, signed by a hodgepodge of fascist academics. It concluded that Italians were a "pure Aryan race" and that "Jews do not belong to the Italian race."[90] Pius told his aides that the manifesto and the subsequent race laws were "contrary to Catholic doctrine."[91] But as was the Pope's style, the Vatican said nothing publicly. Only in a private audience with the British Minister to the Vatican, Sir D'Arcy Godolphin Osborne, did Pius share his frank fear that Europe's new fascists had replaced communism as the church's most dangerous enemy.[92]

A couple of months later, at an audience with Belgian pilgrims, Pius turned teary-eyed after the visitors presented him with a gift of an ancient missal. The Pontiff flipped the pages to a section about Abraham. "We recognize that everyone has the right to self-defense and may take the necessary means for protecting legitimate interests," he said. "But anti-Semitism is inadmissible. Spiritually, we are all Semites."[93]

Pius had reached his breaking point. Only a few aides knew that in late June he had summoned John LaFarge, an American Jesuit, to Castel Gandolfo. The Pontiff asked LaFarge to draft an encyclical addressing anti-Semitism and racism. It signaled a momentous shift in the Vatican's policy of silent observance. The choice of LaFarge meant Pius was serious. As an editor of the Jesuit magazine *America,* LaFarge had a well-deserved reputation as one of the strongest editorial voices against Southern segregation. The previous year, LaFarge had published a book, *Interracial Justice as a Principle of Order,* which was a well-received broadside against American racism.[94] LaFarge, sworn to secrecy, picked two fellow Jesuits to help him, both of whom had collaborated on previous encyclicals.[95] They worked steadily for three months in Paris.

The Third Reich had compromised the German church with double agents and informants, even obtaining a source—likely a German bishop—who provided inside information at the highest level.[96] He warned the Nazis that Pius was at long last focusing on an encyclical that would assault the Germans for their war on the Jews.

That September, LaFarge submitted a draft titled *Humani Generis Unitas* (The Unity of the Human Race). As required by church protocol, the trio turned in versions in English, Latin, French, and German, to Father Wladimir Ledochowski, the patrician Polish Father General of the Jesuits (a man called the "black pope," after the color of his vestment and the power he wielded; American intelligence secretly concluded he was "a tireless supporter of Fascist political movements in every country including Italy").[97] Ledochowski passed it in turn for trimming to Father Enrico Rosa, editor of the Jesuit journal *La Civiltà Cattolica*. That was a seemingly odd choice for what Pius intended to be a groundbreaking encyclical. *La Civiltà Cattolica* had a storied history of virulent anti-Semitism. Father Rosa himself had written about Jews as "presumptuous and powerful" and "as the actual leaders of occult sects, they are forging plans for world hegemony" and were working in partnership with Freemasons to "persecute the Catholic Church."[98]

The eighty-one-year-old Pius was in poor health. Riddled with diabetes, heart disease, and ulcerated legs, he had been declining for a couple of years.[99] Still, Ledochowski and Rosa did not seem in any rush. The three Jesuits who drafted *Humani Generis Unitas* feared that their Father General might be "bent on sabotaging the encyclical" by delaying it.[100] Ledochowski would have recognized that it ventured far beyond the normal church boundaries for intervention and discourse. And the Father General of the Jesuits was a close friend of Cardinal Pacelli. The two had worked together on previous encyclicals. Both knew that as Secretary of State, Pacelli would be on any shortlist to replace Pius. Would such a bold proclamation hamper Pacelli if he became the next Pope? Ledochowski had no doubt that *Humani Generis Unitas* was far too audacious for the more cautious Pacelli. He also knew that some senior clerics were irked that the Pope had tapped an unproven American cleric to be the lead author on such a critical subject.

Events outside the Vatican should have given impetus to the encyclical. The same month that LaFarge submitted the first draft, Mussolini copied the Nazi race laws for Italy. The statutes purged Jews from the civil service, barred Jewish children from public schools, and gave all foreign Jews six months to leave the country.[101] Pius was particularly incensed that the law banned marriages between Italians of the "Aryan race" and anyone "belonging to another race." Father Pietro Tacchi Venturi had lobbied Mussolini in vain, contending it infringed on the rights of the church as set forth in the Lateran Pacts to be the final arbiter of all marriages.[102]

But Italy's race laws did not hasten the review of the encyclical. The Jesuit hierarchy was still passing around the draft on November 9, 1938—Kristallnacht, the Night of Broken Glass—when Nazis attacked Jews throughout Germany, killing dozens and destroying thousands of businesses and synagogues. Although Kristallnacht was condemned worldwide, the Vatican stayed silent.[103] Several German bishops spoke out through sermons, but it was to incite further animus. They talked about the "murderous hatred" that Jews had toward Jesus.[104] The provost of Berlin's St. Hedwig's cathedral, Bernhard Lichtenberg, was one of the few who condemned the frenzy of violence. The Nazis made an example of his public dissent, sentencing him to two years in prison (he later died while being transferred to Dachau).[105]

The start of 1939 marked a further deterioration in Pius's health. He was well enough, however, on January 13, to welcome the British Prime Minister, Neville Chamberlain, for a state visit.[106] During a formal luncheon packed with dignitaries, a frail Pius told Chamberlain that he prayed daily for "the many million Catholics in Germany, whose most grievous tribulations we follow and we share each day." The Prime Minister reminded Pius that the abuses in Germany affected far more than just Catholics and that England "deplored the sufferings inflicted" on Protestants and Jews as well.[107] Pius did not answer.

A few weeks after Chamberlain's visit, in early February, the Pope fell seriously ill. He had prepared a condemnation of fascism—a condensed version of his encyclical—that he wanted to personally deliver on February 11, the tenth anniversary of the signing of the Lateran Pacts. But he was bedridden. Although a team of doctors and his closest clerics attended to him, he died of a heart attack on February 10.[108] *

No one can say with certainty whether *Humani Generis Unitas* got to Pius

---

* That Pius was old and sick did not stop some inside the Vatican from embracing conspiracy theories about his passing. French Cardinal Eugène Tisserant believed that he had been murdered. According to Tisserant, one of Pius's chief doctors—who happened to be the father of Mussolini's film star mistress—had injected him with poison on orders from Il Duce. Tisserant even thought that Pacelli might be an accomplice. The motive was supposedly to prevent the bedridden Pius from releasing to all the bishops a Papal letter in which he savaged fascism. No such letter has ever been found.[109]

before he died. After his death, Secretary of State Pacelli ensured that all drafts of the encyclical as well as all personal papers on Pius's desk were sealed in the Vatican's Secret Archives.[110] No one who worked on the encyclical spoke about it again and the memory of it was soon lost in the great turmoil of World War II. It remained mostly forgotten until 1972, when the *National Catholic Reporter* related the story in a front-page article.[111] By that time, the English and French drafts were missing. A German draft was tracked to the personal papers of one of the priests who had assisted LaFarge, but the Jesuits refused to release it. After much prodding the Vatican admitted it had the Latin draft—which some believe was the original prepared for Pius's signature—but the church denied historians access. A former Jesuit finally passed along a French version on microfilm that had been entrusted to him by LaFarge.[112]

Considering that the encyclical was in the editing domain of Father Rosa and drafted during an era in which the church still referred to "perfidious Jews" in its liturgy, not all its language was friendly to Jews.[113] It said "Jewish people . . . promote revolutionary movements [bolshevism] which aim to destroy society and to obliterate . . . the knowledge, reverence and love of God."[114] As a result of being "blinded by their dream of worldly gain and material success" they deserved the "worldly and spiritual ruin" that had befallen them.[115] Some of LaFarge's pioneering work against segregation in America was cited as an argument *for* the segregation of Jews and Christians.[116]

Yet all the antiquated prejudices seemed insignificant compared to the overriding theme that condemned any government that pursued racist and anti-Semitic policies. They were "totally at variance with the true spirit of the Catholic Church." Anti-Semitism and racism were linked for the first time, since "the struggle for racial purity ends by being uniquely the struggle against the Jews." Moreover, the encyclical castigated governments that treated "innocent persons . . . as outlaws by the very fact of their parentage."[117]

Historians are split over whether the Holocaust might have been averted had the encyclical been released. Some consider it a tragic missed opportunity that would have forced Hitler to at least postpone the Final Solution until after the war. Others counter that it would not have slowed Hitler in his war against the Jews but would only have guaranteed that the Nazis sent every German bishop to the concentration camps.[118]

What is not in dispute is that Secretary of State Pacelli prevented the church from taking any public position condemning the Nazi reign of terror on the Jews. Not only did he keep the church from exercising its moral authority, he ensured that the remarkably direct language of *Humani Generis Unitas* was buried in the archives. That reaffirmed the Nazi confidence that Pacelli would insist at all costs the church maintain strict neutrality through the war.

8

A Policy of Silence

As war clouds built in Europe, national political allegiances added an element of uncertainty to the conclave to select a new Pope. Vaticanisti, knowledgeable observers of the church, tried hard to handicap which cardinals tilted toward the Germans or the Allies.[1]*

The question of who would be the next Pope made its way even to Hitler. An unidentified intelligence source inside the Vatican approached the Gestapo with a tantalizing offer: the election could be fixed for 3 million gold reichsmarks. Once the secret tariff was paid, the Germans could pick the cardinal they wanted and he would win on the first ballot. Only a handful of top Nazis were let in on the secret proposal, and it ignited a furious debate at the highest level of the Third Reich. Hitler was tempted to approve the bribe but at the last moment he passed, worried the offer was too good to be true and might be a setup to embarrass the Nazis.[2]

Among the cardinals who would pick the next Pope, the front-runners were the pragmatic Secretary of State, Eugenio Pacelli, and Florence's Cardinal Elia dalla Costa, a pious scholar. The British and French prelates assumed that because of Pacelli's extensive diplomatic background he would stand for the democracies and resist the totalitarian governments.[3] It is a testament to Pacelli's accomplishments that he was even on the short list, given that he was an acknowledged Germanophile.[4] He made no secret that his happiest years

* In the twentieth century, the term *Vaticanologists* also came into wide use. It is most commonly used to refer to journalists who cover the Vatican.

were his dozen serving as Papal Nuncio to Germany. He was fluent in German, surrounded himself with German advisors and housekeepers, and expressed a "special love" for all things German.[5]

Unknown to the British and French cardinals, the Italian and German ambassadors to the Vatican also encouraged their country's cardinals to vote for Pacelli.[6] They were convinced that his admiration of Teutonic culture and history would tilt him toward the Axis powers. But assuming that Pius would align himself with the Third Reich because he loved its culture and people was too simplistic. Having lived there during the rise of Hitler, he was wary of the Führer's anticlerical sentiments. In 1935, he had interceded to help Jewish refugees abused by the Nazis in the Saar, a small territory returned to German control that year by the League of Nations. In 1937, Pacelli confided to an American diplomat he "did not believe Hitler capable of moderation." The following year he told U.S. ambassador Joseph Kennedy that the church was "at times powerless and isolated in its daily struggle against all sorts of political excesses from the Bolsheviks to the new pagans arising from the 'Aryan' generations." Still, Pacelli thought the Nazis were preferable to the communists. As Papal Nuncio, he dispatched regular reports to the Pope about "ferocious Bolshevism." Ultimately, as a pragmatist, he concluded that since the Nazis were in power, he had no choice but to work with them.[7]

The Roman-born Pacelli descended from a long line of Black Nobles. His great grandfather had been Gregory XVI's Minister of Finance. His grandfather had founded the *L'Osservatore Romano* newspaper and Pius IX had tapped him to serve as Undersecretary of the Interior for the Papal States. Pacelli's father was the chief of Catholic Action as well as the dean of the Consistorial College of Advocates, which prepared cases for beatification. His brother Francesco was a key church negotiator for the 1929 Lateran Pacts. By the time of the conclave, Francesco was a Papal Marquis, and Mussolini had crowned him a prince. Even Pacelli's two sisters had married ranking Vatican officials.[8]

Pacelli had begun studying for the priesthood when he was only fifteen. There was no doubt that he was smart and that his family name opened doors.[9] By the time he was twenty-two he had doctorates of philosophy, canon law, and theology.[10]

At six feet and a featherweight 125 pounds—with an ash-gray complexion and a high-pitched, nasal voice—the sixty-three-year-old was delicate. When he had been appointed the Nuncio to Germany, he arranged at considerable cost a private rail car for the trip to Berlin. Baron Carlo Monti, a Black Noble, complained personally to Pope Benedict that Pacelli also had an additional car packed with dozens of cases of groceries that would not trouble his stomach.[11] An otherwise glowing 1939 profile in *Life* noted that his doctors were "very severe with him" because he "suffers from liver trouble and neuralgic headaches."[12]

Pacelli was an avid reader and classical music enthusiast, and a moderately talented pianist and violinist. The cardinals who backed him cited his intelligence and his extraordinary memory. He showed it off once by reading twenty verses of Homer just twice and then reciting them.[13] He was also not afflicted with Pius's tremendous rage.[14] No one could recall a single incident in which Pacelli had lost his temper. Even during the tensest stages of the Reichskonkordat negotiations, no matter how many times the Nazis provoked him, he maintained an unflappable expression and never raised his voice. That same steely discipline, combined with his insistence that those who spoke to him did so only in soft tones, made him often seem distant and aloof.

He was the most modern frontrunner ever, the first to have flown in an airplane, shaved with an electric razor, embraced daily exercise, used a typewriter and a telephone.[15] To his supporters in the College of Cardinals, he seemed well suited to lead the church.

As a high-profile Secretary of State, he had earned his share of entrenched enemies and jealous rivals over the years. His opponents spread unsubstantiated gossip in the hope it might slow his momentum.[16] At the start of his clerical career, Pacelli had lobbied for a special Vatican dispensation to live at home with his mother. He stayed there until he was thirty-eight, an unusual accommodation for an ambitious cleric who wanted to rise in the church hierarchy.[17] In the all-men's world of the Vatican, that gave him a "mother's boy" rap. Combined with his refined and what some deemed effeminate mannerisms (one writer said he "move[d] with almost feminine grace"), he was the subject of salacious rumors inside the gossip-obsessed Curia.[18]

Pacelli once told Sister Pascalina Lehnert—a fiercely loyal Bavarian nun who had been his confidant since becoming his chief housekeeper in 1917—that they could not go on a skiing vacation alone lest they spark unwarranted backroom chatter.[19] There were raised eyebrows and whispered stories about her role as his unofficial gatekeeper. Despite his warning, she accompanied him sometimes on holidays, cooked his food, prepared his clerical robes, and even advised him on whether he was too tired to hold an audience.[20] (When he was later Pope, she stood near him after every general Mass to disinfect his right hand since hundreds of the faithful had kissed his fisherman's ring during the service. Skeptical Curia officials eventually gave her the irreverent nickname of "La Popessa," the female Pope, and historians rank her as one of a handful of the most influential women who ever lived inside the city-state).[21]

The gossipmongers even tried raising untoward inferences over Pacelli's close personal friendship he had while a Nuncio with Francis Spellman, then a young American priest serving in the Secretary of State's office.[22] The two had vacationed in the Swiss Alps and spent so much time together that Pascalina reportedly intervened to separate them. But Spellman, whom Pacelli called "Spelly," won the nun over.[23] Pacelli sent the Curia rumor mill into overdrive when in the summer of 1930 he took both the priest and the nun on a one-month private holiday through Germany, Switzerland, and Austria.[24]

Most of Pacelli's critics, however, were not worried about salacious gossip. They were concerned instead about more fundamental shortcomings. He had no pastoral experience since he had spent his career as a diplomat.[25] Without having managed his own diocese, there were doubts about whether he had the skills to control the unruly Curia. There was also considerable pre-conclave debate about whether he was too cautious to be a decisive Pontiff. One of Pacelli's closest aides, Monsignor Domenico Tardini, had said he "was not born with the temperament of a fighter."[26] Diplomats who had worked with him did not think he had a strong enough character.[27] "Devoid of will and character," concluded the Spanish ambassador to the Vatican. Osborne, the British Minister, noted that he was "not devoid of intelligence, but essentially there to obey."[28] The small contingent of foreign diplomats assigned to the Vatican all agreed that while in meetings he was charming, he often seemed uncomfortable. Conversations were frequently reduced to trivial issues and banal niceties. When pressed on any contentious matter, Pacelli would repeat his last sentence several times and then fall silent, hoping that somehow the conversation might change course. In cables to London, Osborne warned British ministers that Pacelli despised a fight and would refuse—even when he thought he was right—to overrule anyone.[29]

The concerted effort to stop him failed. The fear of war worked in his favor. His years as Nuncio and then Secretary of State convinced most of the cardinals that he was qualified to lead the church during a period of secular strife. On March 2, 1939, in the fastest conclave in three hundred years, Pacelli was selected as the 261st Pope after only three ballots.[30] He was the first Secretary of State chosen in more than three centuries.[31] He too chose the name Pius.

Only three days after he had become Pope, Nazi troops marched into Czechoslovakia and divided it into two states. The next day Pius convened a meeting with four leading German cardinals. He had not called them together to chastise the Führer for the armed aggression. Instead, Pius—who had chosen a dove carrying an olive branch as his coat of arms—believed that a condemnation would only worsen the tension.[32] He told the bishops that his election presented the Third Reich and the Vatican with an unprecedented opportunity to repair the fraying relationship he had inherited.[33] He assured them he would personally oversee German affairs and insisted he wanted excellent relations with the country he considered his second home. It was a complete break from the harsh rebuke of Nazi policy that his predecessor had proposed in *Humani Generis Unitas*. After debating whether he should address the Führer as "Illustrious" or "Most Illustrious," he gave the cardinals a personal affirmation, in German, to take back to the Reich.[34]

"To the Illustrious Herr Adolf Hitler, Führer and Chancellor of the German Reich! Here at the beginning of Our Pontificate We wish to assure you that We remain devoted to the spiritual welfare of the German people entrusted to your leadership. . . . May the prosperity of the German people and their progress in every domain come, with God's help, to fruition!"[35] (The next month he directed Archbishop Orsenigo, his Papal Nuncio to Germany, to host a grand reception for Hitler's fiftieth birthday.)[36]

Pius, who started every day punctually at 6:00 a.m., immersed himself in the minutiae of the Vatican's daily operations. Every bishop worldwide was instructed to send him regular written reports. He insisted on being kept up-to-date on all political developments. Papal Nuncios sent daily dispatches from their capitals. And the new Pope sent back instructions to them by shortwave radio.[37] After reinstating the discarded Papal tradition of dining alone, and ordering his three Franciscan servers to remain silent, he used mealtimes for an uninterrupted review of his huge pile of daily paperwork.[38] One cardinal who later had to rewrite a letter sixteen times before Pius approved it said that "An audience with Pope Pius XII was like a university examination."[39]

When it came to the church's financial wizard, Bernardino Nogara, Pius did not immediately embrace him. While Pacelli was still Secretary of State, Nogara had passed a letter from the CEO of the House of Morgan to Mussolini, warning Il Duce that the United States would resist German—and therefore implicitly Italian—aggression.[40] Pacelli regarded it a breach of protocol, since he considered diplomacy his exclusive domain; Nogara should stick to finances. Now, as Pope, he announced there would be no further overtures to any government unless he signed off.

But there were other problems when it came to Nogara. Some of those in Pius's kitchen cabinet did not like Bernardino. Pascalina, for instance, distrusted him.[41] So did the Pope's cousin, Ernesto Pacelli, who had been the first president of the Black Noble–founded Bank of Rome. Nogara had been a trusted advisor since 1925 for Ernesto's direct competition, Banca Commerciale Italiana (BCI).[42] Ernesto warned his Papal cousin that Nogara's loyalty was to foreigners, not to the Pope.[43]

Since Nogara had reported directly to the late Pope for a decade, no one in the Vatican was quite sure what he did. In an institution where gossip sometimes seemed an avocation, the secrecy surrounding his work resulted in several scurrilous rumors. Some believed he had squandered or stolen the multimillion-dollar settlement from the 1929 Lateran Treaty.[44] Others thought he was conspiring with an ultrasecret Masonic lodge against the church.[45]

Pius XII appointed three cardinals to investigate whether there was truth to the malicious whispers.[46] While that probe was under way, the Pope canceled Nogara's standing weekly meeting.[47] The cardinals grilled Nogara as well as all the employees in his Special Administration. They pried into his private life, questioned his friends, and compiled a thick dossier about his personal habits.

The new Pope wanted a fast resolution. Pius remembered all too well the bedlam caused by World War I and the debilitating economic fallout that followed the peace. If the cardinals uncovered evidence of malfeasance, there would be little time to find Nogara's replacement.[48]

All the fretting ended when the cardinals returned in two months with their report. It concluded that the Vatican was far better off under Nogara's guidance than at any time in its history. Nogara had invested Mussolini's $92 million and it had grown over a decade to nearly $1 billion.[49] Nogara lived in a modest apartment and supported himself mostly from his private savings. Once a week he went to the movies, preferring American films. There was no evidence of anything disreputable in his personal life. He took only a nominal salary of less than $2,000 annually (about $27,000 in 2014 dollars).

Pius marveled, asking the prelates how Nogara did it. "From point A to point B, we have understood it all," one of the cardinals reportedly replied. "But, your Holiness, Nogara has gone through the entire alphabet. And we are just simple cardinals."[50]

The report flipped Pius from a Nogara skeptic to an avid supporter. The Pontiff now saw Nogara as a reflection of himself, a loyal servant of God who put service to church above personal and financial gain. He restarted his weekly meetings with Nogara. The only change was that Nogara no longer maintained his notes of those one-on-one briefings.[51]

Having resolved any questions about Nogara, Pius turned his attention to the politics roiling Europe.[52] In the months following his election, there had been a rush of new anti-Semitic decrees passed across the continent. In Italy, Jews were further banned from public employment. The Third Reich ordered them to carry special identity cards (a precursor to a later decree that would force them to wear a yellow star).[53] Given his trademark cautious approach, Pius avoided any public comment.[54]

But in some countries, the Pope unwittingly sent the wrong message about anti-Semitism.[55] He lifted Pius XI's ban that prevented French Catholics from joining the anticommunist Action Française party. But Action Française was fiercely anti-Semitic. Pius was willing to ignore its anti-Jewish hatred as an inevitable element of its commitment to fighting bolshevism. None outside his senior advisors knew what prompted his decision, and it was instead widely interpreted as a tacit approval of the party's venomous platform.[56]

In Hungary, the priests who served in parliament had voted for the country's 1938 race laws. Some bishops and priests supported the Hungarian knockoff of the Nazi Party, the Arrow Cross.[57] Not only did the Pope fail to urge restraint for any clerical support of the fiercely anti-Semitic party, but Pius again sent mixed signals by promoting József Grösz—a key Arrow Cross backer—as Hungary's second ranking bishop.

In Slovakia, a country that resulted from the Nazi appropriation of western Czechoslovakia, the Catholic clergy were at the forefront of a national effort to bar Jews from the country's business and social life.[58] Priests had founded the principal political party, the unflinchingly anti-Semitic Slovak People's Party. Jozef Tiso, the President, and Vojtech Tuka, the Prime Minister, were both priests. Pius was Pope only a month when Monsignor Tiso introduced Slovakia's first race law (eventually thirty-eight race decrees were passed). The Third

Reich expressed its "undisguised gratification" that such harsh anti-Semitic statutes "had been enacted in a state headed by a member of the Catholic clergy."[59] In line with Nazi racial doctrines, blood triumphed over religion. Anyone who converted to Catholicism after October 30, 1918, was deemed Jewish. Tiso, a theology professor, noted support for the laws in the contemporaneous writings of a Slovakian Jesuit theologian who concluded, "The Church advocates the elimination of the Jews."[60] Pius's reaction to the events in Slovakia was to send Tiso an Apostolic Blessing.[61] He did not do so to ratify its race laws but rather because the Vatican was pleased to have a new Catholic-run country in Eastern Europe. But many Catholic Slovaks interpreted the special blessing as a Papal endorsement.*

To his credit, Pius reached out to Britain, France, Italy, and Germany to gauge if they were interested in him mediating a peace. But no country took him up on it. Although they all liked Pacelli as a conclave front-runner, now that he was Pope they were uncertain of his loyalties. British intelligence speculated Pius might be an agent for Mussolini. The French Foreign Ministry went one step further, thinking it possible that his pick as Secretary of State, Cardinal Luigi Maglione, was a fascist spy.[63] Any role Pius hoped to play as a mediator was crushed in August when the Third Reich and the Soviet Union announced a nonaggression pact. Pius had long tolerated the more thuggish aspects of the German Reich in part because he thought there was no better buffer to Stalin's red menace. The new alliance seemed to many Vaticanisti a catastrophic development.

The news worsened the next month when the Nazi blitzkrieg into Poland marked the start of World War II. Ninety-eight percent of Poland's thirty million residents were Catholic, making it one of the church's largest congregations. Sixteen days after the Nazi invasion, the Soviets attacked from the East. Poland fell on October 6. The Nazis and communists split the country in half.[64]

Pius mistakenly believed that a fast conquest of Poland satisfied Hitler. He assured Cardinal Tisserant—who had been a French army intelligence officer during World War I—that there would be a peace within days.[65] It was quickly evident that the Pope had greatly underestimated the scope of Hitler's ambi-

* A year later, Tiso passed new laws banning marriage between converted Jews and Catholics. Pius understood that unless Jews were assured that conversion spared them from discrimination and punishment, the church would have a tough time getting converts. Since Tiso was a priest, Pius expected him to be receptive to that argument. But Tiso was unmoved. The Pope stripped Tiso of his monsignor's title, demoting him to merely a priest.[62]

tion. The German-occupied half of the country became ground zero for the war on Europe's Jews, and an Italian consul who had fled told church officials early on about "unbelievable atrocities."[66] The American envoy to the Vatican later reported that Pius feared that a "forthright denunciation of Nazi atrocities, at least in so far as Poland is concerned, would only result in the violent deaths of many more people."[67]

Pius knew there was particular reason to be vigilant about any upsurge in anti-Semitic violence in Poland. The country had a troubled and often violent history with its three million native Jews. When vicious pogroms swept the country in 1938 and 1939, the Catholic press said they were "understandable."[68] Top Polish prelates touted blood libel, the belief that Jews murdered Christian infants and used their blood either to make unleavened bread or Passover wine.[69] The Vatican issued no reprimand a few years earlier when the country's ranking cardinal, August Hlond, contended "that the Jews are fighting against the Catholic Church, persisting in free thinking, and are the vanguard of godlessness, Bolshevism and subversion."[70]

Some Polish bishops were alarmed not by German moves against Jews but rather by Nazi-ordered closings of dozens of churches and arrests of hundreds of priests. A few were so frustrated by Pius's passivity that they even talked about severing their allegiance to Rome in protest.[71] There was more anger among Polish clerics when on March 11, 1940—seven months after the Nazi invasion—Pius received German Foreign Minister Joachim von Ribbentrop for a state visit at the Vatican.[72] When the Pope learned of the mutiny talk, he ordered his Nuncio to Germany to intercede with the Third Reich to ask for kinder treatment of Polish priests and lay Catholics.[73] The Germans turned the Nuncio away.[74]*

Poland was only the first moral challenge Pius faced now that a war was under way. Starting in 1941, Monsignor Giuseppe Burzio, the Nuncio to Slovakia, sent Pius the first of several reports that Jews were being rounded up and executed.[76] Nuncios in Hungary and Switzerland confirmed the grim account.[77] When Pius responded the following year it was in two polite, private

---

* The best the activist clerics mustered from their repeated entreaties was a private letter by Pius nearly two years later. He authorized five thousand copies be distributed through the church's underground. In that letter, the Pope expressed his solidarity with Polish Catholics. Even then, he did not mention Jews or criticize the Nazi violence against both Jews and the church.[75]

dissents about the deportations to Karol Sidor, the Slovak delegate to the Vatican. The protests seemed focused on baptized Jews and in any case were too genteel an intervention to give the Slovakian perpetrators any pause.[78] Since Prime Minister Tiso was still a priest, Slovakia presented Pius with unique leverage. Monsignor Domenico Tardini—one of the Pope's closest aides—thought it was a mistake not to keep Tiso in check. "It is a great misfortune," he wrote, "that the President of Slovakia is a priest. Everyone knows that the Holy See cannot bring Hitler to heel. But who will understand that we cannot even control a priest?"[79] (The Vatican waited until after the war to condemn Tiso, when the Allies hanged him for war crimes.)

Slovakia was no exception. Other countries with large Catholic populations were swept up into Hitler's killing machine as the Nazi aggression expanded. The conservative Catholic majorities of the conquered nations could have been expected to pay heed to strong leadership from the Vatican. And none better than Croatia, a country that only came into being after Germany conquered and dismembered Yugoslavia in 1941. Members of the lay Croatian Catholic Movement and priests dominated the governing political party, the Ustaša (Rise Up). It was rabidly anti-Semitic, anti-Serb, and anticommunist.[80] Zagreb's Archbishop Alojzije Stepinac was head of the Croatian church and also the Supreme Apostolic Vicar General of the Ustašan Army.[81] The Ustašan leader, Ante Pavelić, a devout Catholic, boasted he never missed daily Mass. Pavelić declared fascist Croatia as Europe's first fundamentalist Catholic nation. The man called the Poglavnik (Führer) considered a good relationship with the Vatican as key as the one he had with the Third Reich.[82]

Archbishop Stepinac had direct access to the Pope, meeting him in February 1941.[83] He lobbied for a Papal audience for Pavelić. When the Yugoslavian government in exile learned that Pius might meet Pavelić, it protested.[84] Pavelić had been convicted and sentenced to death in absentia by French and Yugoslavian courts for assassinating French Foreign Minister Louis Barthou and Yugoslavia's King Alexander. Mussolini had provided Pavelić safe haven during the 1930s. He was now the leader of an occupied nation and an illegitimate government.[85] The British Foreign Office also tried dissuading the Pope from meeting Pavelić, calling the Croat leader "a notorious terrorist and murderer."[86] The head of the Catholic Slovene People's Party petitioned the Pope: "In this moment of urgent danger and necessity, we appeal to Your Holiness and most humbly beg for your intervention."[87]

Pius, however, considered Pavelić "a much maligned man." The church had wanted a Catholic state in the Balkans since the Crusades, so it was difficult for the Vatican to turn him away.[88] Monsignor Tardini told the Ustašan envoy to the Vatican, "Croatia is a young state. . . . Youngsters often err because of their age. It is therefore not surprising that Croatia has also erred."[89] The Pontiff agreed to see Pavelić, but in a nod to his critics did not mark it as a state visit.[90]

The Pope and Croatian leader met at the Vatican on May 18, 1941, the same day the Ustaša passed copycat versions of the Nazi's Nuremberg Laws (Croats were exempt since they claimed to have Nordic origins that somehow tangentially related them to Aryans, the racial subgroup of Caucasians that the Nazis had proclaimed the superior race).[91] The Vatican maintains that no notes or journal entries were kept of that meeting. Whatever the conversation, Pavelić returned home and soon unleashed a bloodbath against the country's Jews and Orthodox Christian Serbs.

The massacres in Croatia did not begin until the German army withdrew to the east in June to join in Operation Barbarossa, Hitler's surprise invasion of the Soviet Union. Inside the Vatican, the German offensive into Russia reaffirmed for Pius that he was right for placing his faith in National Socialism as a bulwark against communism. Pius now concluded that Hitler's 1939 nonaggression pact with Stalin had been only a ploy to buy the Germans time to find the right moment to take on the Russians. A successful German offensive would alter the political face of Europe, removing the most powerful and antagonistic philosophy the Vatican had faced in centuries.

That the Third Reich was now involved in what some clerics considered a holy war against godless Bolsheviks meant there was little chance Pius would say anything that might inflame the Germans.[92] Both the church and the Nazis shared a common goal, the complete destruction of the Stalinist state.[93] Just three months after the start of the Russian campaign, Dr. Fritz Menshausen, the diplomatic counselor at the German embassy in Rome, told the Foreign Ministry in Berlin that well-informed officials in the Vatican had repeatedly assured him the Pope privately stood with the Axis forces.[94]

Even if Pius had decided to give the Germans leeway because of their fight against Stalin, there was no reason why he could not intervene to stop the bloodletting when it involved only Catholic Croatians. Pavelić started the first widescale killings in July, only two months after meeting with the Pope.[95] In Croatia, there was no bureaucracy of mass murder as with the Germans, no systematic march of trainloads of emaciated prisoners to the gas chambers. There was instead brutal and chaotic ethnic cleansing. Many Jews, Serbs, Gypsies, and communists were burned alive. Roving fascist gangs went on mutilation frenzies, cutting off the breasts of women and the genitals of men, and in some cases collecting the eyes of victims as gruesome trophies. The killers put thousands of others onto hanging meat hooks or chopped them up with butcher knives and axes. Pavelić created an exemption to his own race laws to protect his half-Jewish wife.[96]

In contrast to the Nazis who tried to keep victims from learning about their deadly fate until they arrived at a concentration camp, the Croats let word of the terror spread across the tiny country.[97] Pavelić figured that if he murdered half of all the Serbs, the survivors would either flee or convert to Catholicism.[98] He intended to kill all of the Jews.

The Vatican faced a unique challenge in Croatia since priests partly ran the murder machinery. Sarajevo's Bishop Ivan Sarić—later dubbed the "Hangman of the Serbs"—told the faithful that the elimination of Jews was a "renewal of human dignity."[99] Catholic priests served in Pavelić's private bodyguard.[100] A Franciscan monk, Miroslav Filipović-Majstorović, earned the moniker the "Devil of Jasenovac," a concentration camp where forty thousand Jews and Serbs were slaughtered.[101] Three Franciscan monks—also Ustašan officers—served as the Devil's deputies.[102] Father Bozidas Bralo, Sarajevo's chief of security, was responsible for enforcing the country's anti-Semitic legislation. And a popular priest, Father Dyonisy Juricev, wrote in a leading newspaper that it was no longer a sin to kill Serbs or Jews so long as they were at least seven years old.[103] The role played by clerics in the killings helped absolve ordinary Catholics from being afflicted by a troubled conscience.[104]

Branko Bokun was a young ex–Foreign Office worker who had joined the International Red Cross at the start of the war. At twenty-one, the Red Cross gave him a file packed with blood-curdling details about the Croatian massacres. His mission was to get to Rome and to petition the Pope to intervene. Before Bokun left Zagreb, the local head of the Red Cross—and a former chief of Yugoslav counterintelligence—explained why a public condemnation by the Vatican was critical. Bokun recorded it in his diary entry for June 26, 1941, only a month after Pius welcomed Pavelić to the Vatican: "These Catholics are killing Serbs and Jews, because in their primitive minds they are convinced that it will please the Vatican. If the Vatican does not intervene immediately, the fight between Serbs and Croats will reach such proportions it will take centuries to die down."[105]

The Pope and his advisors were probably better informed about what was happening in Croatia than any other country.[106] Every Ustašan military unit had a priest as a field chaplain. The Pontiff's Undersecretary of State, Monsignor Giovanni Battista Montini—later Pope Paul VI—was in charge of collecting reports from both Croatia and Poland. Aggrieved clerics sent Montini chilling accounts of the atrocities. Every day he briefed Pius, who had a reputation as a Pope who wanted the details.[107] In December 1941, on a state visit to Venice, Pavelić boasted to the Italian Foreign Minister as well as Nogara's good friend, Giuseppe Volpi, that Croatia's Jewish population had been reduced by a third.[108]

Hitler gave his seminal speech on the fate of European Jewry on February 9, 1942. That was just twenty days after the Wannsee Conference, named for the Berlin suburb where Nazi leaders met and approved the Final Solution, a plan to exterminate the continent's Jews. In his talk, Hitler promised: "The Jews will be liquidated at least for a thousand years!" The most inflammatory passages were reprinted in Roman newspapers and the Vatican Secretary of State discussed it with Western diplomats. Pius ignored all entreaties that the church publicly distance itself from Hitler's hateful rhetoric.

The frustrated British Minister to the Vatican, D'Arcy Osborne, told his colleagues that Pius was hedging his bets on a Nazi victory.[109] The Allies sensed that the turning point had been the Nazi invasion of Russia the previous summer.[110] Now in the wake of Hitler's promise to "liquidate" Europe's Jews, the judgment that the Pope was partisan was reinforced when the Vatican opened diplomatic relations with Japan, the third Axis partner. The United States and Britain had pressed Pius not to formalize ties with Japan, but the church claimed it did not have "sufficient elements of proof" about Japanese atrocities. In any case, the Vatican argued it had a duty to the eighteen million Catholics in the Far East.[111] Further evidence of the Vatican's skewed allegiance came in a classified report by Viscount Oliver Lyttelton, Winston Churchill's Minister of State in the Middle East. Issued the same month as Hitler's speech, it was passed around a handful of senior British ministers with "to be kept under lock and key" stamped across the top. Based on extensive British intelligence data, Lyttelton concluded that throughout a dozen Middle Eastern countries, "the Roman Catholic Church has developed Fascist and pro-Axis tendencies, which dominate its spiritual functions." The report revealed that the church helped distribute fascist "political propaganda, and since the war it has lent encouragement to espionage, sabotage and the escape of prisoners of war." Lyttelton recommended replacing partisan Italian clerics with "non-enemy nationals." That never happened. When the British reached out to the Vatican, the church shelved the findings.[112]

Only a month after Hitler's speech, SS officer Kurt Gerstein walked into the Berlin office of the Nuncio, Cesare Orsenigo, wanting to confess his first-hand account of the killing of eight hundred Jews at the death camp Bełżec.[113] Because a diesel engine that produced the gas kept malfunctioning, it had taken a torturous stop-and-start three hours to kill the naked victims, packed into four tiny rooms of a crude gas chamber. Gerstein could not shake the gruesome images. But Orsenigo's personal assistant, a priest who was a secret Nazi Party member, intercepted him.[114] No one knows what the assistant told Orsenigo, but it was enough for him to turn away the SS officer. Gerstein went next to Berlin's auxiliary bishop, Otto Dibelius. That bishop sent the first-ever confirmations of the mass murder by an SS officer in both coded cables and diplomatic pouches to the Vatican. It was buried in Rome. Nothing was shared with other countries.[115] When Berlin's Bishop Konrad von Preysing later tried mobilizing his fellow bishops to condemn the ongoing deportation of Jews and even warned they would be answerable before God for their silence, no one supported him. His colleagues argued that the deportation of non-Catholics was troubling but not their duty to address. They refused to tell German Catholics that it was a mortal sin to kill Jews. Preysing concluded that the moral deadlock could not be broken without the Pope's forceful intervention. Pius did not get involved, allowing those who wanted to do nothing to prevail.[116]

The Pontiff summoned Croatia's Archbishop Stepinac to the Vatican the month after the Gerstein report arrived.[117] Soon after arranging the meeting the previous year between Pius and Pavelić, Stepinac had begun vocally turning against the bloodlust.[118] He had even tried in vain to encourage his fellow Croatian clerics to distance themselves from the slaughter.[119] By the time he met with Pius, Nazi mobile killing squads—the Einsatzgruppen—had murdered about 1.5 million Jews in Poland and Russia. Stepinac's Croatia was on its way to eliminating 85 percent of its Jewish population.[120]

The archbishop returned to Croatia more outspoken than ever against the slaughter. But Pius declined even a Papal letter that Stepinac could share with other church officials.[121]

Pius seemed frozen, incapable of decisive action. It was the character weakness that those who had opposed his selection as Pope most feared. Compounding the problem, the Nazis misinterpreted his silence.[122] The Third Reich had penetrated the Vatican with well-placed informants.[123] The Germans had also managed to break the simple codes employed by the church's diplomatic corps. It was possible Hitler inferred that Pius stayed quiet because he did not object to the killing of Jews so long as the perpetrators were Catholic.[124]

That summer, on the heels of Gerstein and Stepinac, the archbishop of Léopol in Ruthenia (southern Ukraine) reported to the Vatican "the number of Jews massacred in our small region has certainly exceeded 200,000."[125] Soon after, an Italian priest, an abbot, and a Latvian archbishop passed along separate accounts of the murder of Jews in Poland and Latvia.[126] The Polish government in exile released a report estimating that 700,000 Jews had been killed since the Nazi invasion and even cited the existence of gas vans at the Chelmno death camp.[127] This news, combined with the Pope's inaction, prompted British Foreign Office officials to complain, "Papal timidity becomes ever more blatantly despicable."[128]

Franklin Delano Roosevelt dispatched his personal envoy, Myron Taylor, to meet Pius that September.[129] The goal was to convince the Pope that his moral duty as head of the world's largest faith trumped the Vatican's insistence on neutrality. On the day Taylor arrived, in a coordinated effort, Britain, Brazil, Poland, Belgium, and Uruguay appealed to the church, warning that its "policy of silence" likely meant "a renunciation of moral leadership and a consequent atrophy of the influence and authority of the Vatican."[130] Two days after his arrival, Taylor received an urgent cable from Washington. The Geneva office of the Jewish Agency for Palestine had passed along an account of German war crimes from two surviving eyewitnesses: "Liquidation of the Warsaw Ghetto is taking place. Without any distinction all Jews, irrespective of age or sex, are being removed from the ghetto in groups and shot. Their corpses are utilized for making fats and their bones for the manufacture of fertilizer." The report went on to detail mass executions in Lwów and Bełżec.[131]

Taylor and Pius met privately three times. The American envoy, the former head of U.S. Steel, was an adept negotiator. He knew it would not be easy to convince the Pontiff to take action. He had earlier failed to persuade him to excommunicate Hitler and Mussolini.[132] Now Taylor suggested that if the Pope did not want to specifically condemn Hitler and the Nazis, he might issue, at a minimum, a more general denunciation of the atrocities themselves.[133] He warned Pius that the Nazi crimes were part of a "vile and anti-Christian code of conduct" and should they prevail it "would destroy all semblance of a Christian Europe."[134] The Pope averred that he felt as though he had spoken out enough about "the aggressions of war" and the "sufferings of civilians," but complained that his "appeal was little heeded."[135]

Before leaving Rome, a frustrated Taylor met with other ranking clerics.[136] Monsignor Domenico Tardini told him that Pius could not concentrate on the war on the Jews since his priority was to stop communist attacks in the East on Catholics.[137] When Taylor met with Cardinal Maglione, he pleaded with the Secretary of State.[138] People of all faiths, not just Catholics, said Taylor, were anxious for the Pope "to denounce the inhuman treatment of refugees, hostages, and above all the Jews in the occupied countries."[139]

Maglione assured Taylor that the Pope at his first chance "would not fail to express anew his thought with clarity."[140] As for the report from the Geneva office of the Jewish Agency for Palestine, Maglione later scribbled in the margin: "I do not believe we have the information which can confirm—in particular—this terrible news. Is this not so?"[141] Weeks after Taylor left, Maglione gave the Americans an unsigned statement that acknowledged the Vatican had received from other sources "reports of severe measures taken against non-Aryans," but claimed the church could not "verify the[ir] accuracy . . . and [t]he Holy See is taking advantage of every opportunity offered in order to mitigate the sufferings of non-Aryans."[142]

That was not true. By then, the Vatican had accumulated chilling evidence of the ongoing civilian carnage in nine countries. Because the church had hundreds of local parishes where the atrocities were taking place, it was uniquely situated to become a repository of eyewitness accounts long before the Allies could confirm the mass murder.[143]

It cannot be determined how much Pius fretted about the fate of Europe's Jews during 1942. Pius's personal secretary, Father Robert Leiber, a German Jesuit who met daily with the Pope and kept a diary of their meetings, burned all his papers after the war.[144] What is indisputable is that a good portion of the Pope's summer was consumed not by concerns about how to stop the civilian massacre but instead on a film he had commissioned about himself. *Pastor Angelicus* (Angelic Shepherd) was a narcissistic hour-long look at Pius's life, from his birth to his reign at the Vatican.[145]* Part documentary, part reality show, it focused on the Pontiff's daily routine. Among other scenes, Pius was filmed getting into his limousine as his driver dropped to his knees and crossed himself, greeting the Italian royal family, visiting a class of First Communion girls, and working late into the night in his grand office.[147] *Pastor Angelicus* gave no hint that Europe was in the middle of its greatest war or that Pius was under siege to intervene to stop history's largest civilian slaughter.[148]

Pius's attention was also diverted from the grim war news by a secret project he had authorized soon after becoming Pope. Three years earlier he had appointed a former aide and chief of the German Catholic Party, Monsignor Ludwig Kaas, to direct four members of the Papal Institute for Christian Archaeology to hunt in the underground Vatican Grottoes for the body of St. Peter, one of Jesus's original twelve apostles and the founder of the Catholic Church.[149] The small team was sworn to secrecy. The quest for St. Peter's corpse had long been a Catholic equivalent of the mythical hunt for the Holy Grail. Catholics based their claim to be the one and only true church in part on the belief that Peter had come to Rome from the Middle East, became the first Pope, and was then crucified for his faith. Emperor Constantine in 333 built the original St. Peter's Basilica over what was thought to be Peter's gravesite. All Popes descended in a straight line from Peter. Non-Catholics dismissed the story as a fairy tale. Protestant scholars contended that Peter never reached Rome. The Vatican had long sought to find Peter's tomb to settle the matter. When Pius approved the dig, it was the first time in 350 years that one had been undertaken.[150] To keep it secret, Pius paid for the archaeological hunt from his personal bank account.[151]

In late May, Kaas reported excitedly to Pius that they had reached a promising spot—almost directly underground from the high altar in St. Peter's—

---

* "Pastor Angelicus" came from supposed prophecies by St. Malachy O'Morgair, a twelfth-century monk, to describe a future Papacy that Pius believed was his. Although some Catholic scholars have dismissed the "prophecies" as a sixteenth-century forgery, Pius wholeheartedly embraced them, believing they forecast that he had a divine destiny.[146]

precisely where an ancient map had plotted the burial monument. With Pius often sitting in a chair just above the opening to the underground pit, the team spent weeks retrieving 250 bone fragments that filled three small lead boxes.[152] Some nights, long after the workers had left, Monsignor Giovanni Montini joined Pius, and the two stood at the opening to the pit and prayed that the bones belonged to Peter.[153] When the excavation was done, the Pope directed the remains be locked, sealed, and stored in his private apartment.[154] The only person allowed access to what had been found was Pius's personal physician, Riccardo Galeazzi-Lisi. The general practitioner, with no training in anthropology or forensics, told the Pope that the bones appeared to belong to a single person, probably a man somewhere between sixty and seventy years old. It was a broad-enough description to include Peter.[155]*

By the fall of 1942, Pius refocused on the war. In October the United States created the investigatory War Crimes Commission. On December 17, the Allies for the first time condemned the Nazi extermination of the Jews.[157] On December 21, Kazimierz Papée, the Polish ambassador in exile to the Holy See, handed Monsignor Tardini the most detailed report to date about atrocities.[158] It was the first confirmation of the existence of gas chambers and "as for the number of Polish Jews exterminated by the Germans, it is estimated it has passed a million."[159]

Pius's reaction was to ask the Allies to agree to a unilateral two-day truce for Christmas Eve and Day so Christians could celebrate the holiday in peace. The United States and Britain said no. To Washington and London, Pius seemed even more detached from the realities on the ground.[160]

The Allies had begun a bombing campaign against Italy's industrial north with major air raids against Genoa and Turin. The month prior, Field Marshal Bernard Montgomery's decisive victories at El Alamein over Field Marshal

---

* It was eight years, 1950, before Pius announced that he believed St. Peter's grave had likely been found. He did not mention any bones. They were still in his apartment. There they remained for another fourteen years until an Italian anthropologist examined them and concluded they belonged to several people and even some animals. That same year, 1964, Margherita Guarducci, a professor of Greek epigraphy at the University of Rome, published a book asserting that some of the bones were indeed those of the apostle. She based her case on a questionable translation of Greek graffiti at the excavation site. Although leading anthropologists ridiculed her conclusion, it carried much weight inside the Vatican. On June 26, 1968, Pope Paul VI (who, as Monsignor Montini, had joined Pius at St. Peter's during the dig) declared that the church had recovered the bones of St. Peter. In November 2013, Pope Francis concluded a Year of Faith by displaying the bones publicly for the first time since their discovery.[156]

Erwin Rommel had put the Germans in full retreat and marked a turning point in the battle for North Africa. And although the Nazis had boasted they would take Stalingrad in days, it had held firm for five months. The Germans showed signs of buckling under the severe Russian winter. If the Pope had been banking on a quick Axis victory, it was far from assured.

On December 17, the Allies approved a declaration condemning German-led genocide in Europe.[161] It was blunt, citing "numerous reports" of "this bestial policy of cold-blooded extermination." From the occupied countries, "Jews are being transported, in conditions of appalling horror and brutality to Eastern Europe." Poland was "the principal Nazi slaughterhouse" and Jews were either being "slowly worked to death in labour camps" or "deliberately massacred in mass executions." The Allies promised "that those responsible for these crimes shall not escape retribution."

That resolution finally fired up Pius to say something about the civilian slaughter. The Pope worried that if he did not, the Vatican might become irrelevant and not play any postwar peace-making role. Pius, who had been trained during his diplomatic service to never confront a matter directly, hesitantly touched on the Holocaust in his 1942 Christmas radio address. In a five-thousand-word, twenty-six-page prepared statement, the Pope devoted several dozen words to it. He condemned "arbitrary attacks" and said that no nation had the right to "herd people around as if they were a lifeless thing." Near the end, he talked about "hundreds of thousands, who without any fault of their own, sometimes only by reason of their nationality or race, are marked down for death or gradual extinction."[162] Pius never uttered the words "Jew" or "German" or "Nazi."[163] He had reduced the number of victims from the million cited in the report delivered from the Polish ambassador to "hundreds of thousands."

The Allied envoys at the Vatican thought that Pius had squandered his chance to make a substantive difference. A Papal aide defended the ambiguous statement to the British envoy: "The Pope could not take sides."[164] When the French ambassador asked Pius why he omitted the Nazis, the Pope said that would have required him to talk about the communists.[165] Mussolini mocked the address to his colleagues, saying it's "a speech of platitudes" and that any parish priest could have done a better job.[166] Even some of the Pope's strong defenders, such as American Jesuit Vincent McCormick, admitted the talk was "much too heavy, ideas not clean-cut, and obscurely expressed."[167] Berlin's Bishop von Preysing thought it was too abstract to have any impact.[168]

A week after the Christmas talk, the Pope met with Myron Taylor's assistant, chargé d'affaires Harold Tittmann. Pius declined to sign an Allied declaration expressly condemning the Nazi crimes.[169] Tittmann reported to Washington that Pius sincerely believed he had spoken "clearly enough to satisfy all those who had been insisting in the past that he utter some word of condemnation of the Nazi atrocities." The Pope seemed surprised when Tittmann told him he did not agree.[170] Tittmann thought Pius's reluctance to be more direct was because he feared that German Catholics, "in the bitterness of their defeat, will reproach him later for having contributed, if only indirectly to its defeat."[171]

The year 1943 began with more bishops and lay officials urging the Pontiff to more forcefully use the power of his bully pulpit. In March, Bishop von Preysing informed Pius about more roundups and deportations of Berlin's Jews and pleaded with the Pope to intervene. But Pius told Preysing he had said all he intended in his Christmas address, that it "was brief but it has been well understood." All he could do now, he said, was to pray.[172] Those Jews were gassed at Auschwitz.

In a personal audience, the Hungarian Catholic activist Margit Slachta appealed to the Pope to intercede on behalf of the remaining Slovakian Jews—twenty thousand of the original population of ninety thousand. Many of the survivors had converted to Christianity.[173] Pius "expressed his shock," she later noted, "[but] he listened to me and said very little."[174] Vatican records show he seemed more upset that young Jewish girls were being used as prostitutes than by the pending death camp deportations.[175] It took Pius more than a year before he sent a private letter to the Slovak government asking that "Jews who are still . . . [alive] may not be subjected to even more severe sufferings."[176] The Germans killed fifteen thousand of the remaining Slovakian Jews before the war ended.

Bratislava's chargé d'affaires, Monsignor Giuseppe Burzio, sent Secretary of State Maglione a letter with details about the killings. He included a note from a parish priest: "A German officer confirmed this coldly and cynically in the presence of a person I know. Jews are killed with poison gas or guns or other means. The girls and women, after suffering every kind of humiliation and violence, are stripped and coldly murdered. Soap is made from the corpses."[177]

That letter was filed in the Secret Archives. The same thing happened to an unsparing nine-page report describing the horrors in Croatia that Archbishop Stepinac presented to Pius in May 1943, his third wartime visit to the Vatican and the Pope.[178]*

A few months later in July, a French priest, Père Marie-Benoît, met with Pius and implored him to help Jews trapped in the Italian occupation zone in southeastern France.[180] The Pope listened and the Vatican Secretary of State's office later told the priest that it would work on a rescue plan with the Italian government. Nothing happened. Many of those Jews ended up at Auschwitz.[181]

Marie-Benoît's plea came when Pius was otherwise preoccupied. The Allies had landed in Sicily on July 10 and established a beachhead. Their aggressive offensive exacerbated his worries that they might carpet-bomb Rome as had earlier been done to many German cities. The Pope had made an impassioned plea to the British ambassador as far back as 1940, arguing that Rome should be off limits. The city was filled with historical monuments and important religious relics, contended Pius, and loved by people around the globe. Most important, it was home to the Vatican.[182] The Pope warned that any attack on the spiritual center of Catholicism would result in an unequivocal public protest, the very condemnation he refused to make about the Holocaust.[183] Roosevelt assured Pius that "aviators . . . have been specifically instructed to prevent bombs falling within the Vatican City." But the British refused to give the same assurance. Anthony Eden, the War Secretary, told Parliament in January 1943, "We have as much right to bomb Rome as the Italians had to bomb

---

* As for Stepinac's nine-page document, not only did the Vatican lock it inside the Secret Archives, it is still sealed, "accidentally" withheld from a postwar Vatican production of documents. The Secret Archives are estimated to contain fifty-two miles of shelving packed with documents, some dating back to the seventh century. The collection is stored today in temperature-controlled, fireproof underground chambers dubbed the "Bunker." Over the centuries important files were lost. Much of the Inquisition's history was burned in 1559. Part of the archive was lost in 1810 when it was transported to Paris by Napoleon's troops. Some documents were lost in transit or later sold in bulk for the value of the paper itself. Most files about Pius XII were sealed for seventy-five years from the beginning of his pontificate. The date upon which they would have been made public was March 12, 2014. It passed without any documents released by the Vatican.

It was during this time—May 1943—that Ante Pavelić, the murderous head of Croatia, wanted to again visit the Pope. Although the Vatican had by then been inundated with firsthand accounts of the slaughter in Croatia, Secretary of State Maglione inexplicably assured Pavelić there would be no problem, but reminded Pavelić that he could not "be received as a sovereign." And Pius promised Pavelić another Apostolic Blessing. Only the deteriorating conditions on the battlefield caused Pavelić to cancel the trip.[179]

London. We shall not hesitate to do so . . . [if] such bombing [is] convenient and helpful."[184]

D'Arcy Osborne reflected a commonly held British government opinion when he later wrote in his diary: "The more I think of it, the more I am revolted by Hitler's massacre of the Jewish race on the one hand, and, on the other, the Vatican's apparently exclusive preoccupation with the effects of the war on Italy and the possibilities of the bombardments of Rome."[185]

To the Pope's distress, as the Allies advanced from Sicily, they began regular bombing runs on northern Italian cities. Pius often stood at the east wing windows of the Apostolic Palace watching through his binoculars as the planes flew over Rome. On July 19, hundreds of Allied planes bombed Rome's train yards. Stray bombs hit residential neighborhoods as well as damaging the Basilica di San Lorenzo fuori le Mura (Basilica of St. Lawrence outside the Walls). That news was the only time Vatican officials ever saw Pius cry. Cardinal Maglione had never seen him so "deeply saddened."[186] Pius and Monsignor Montini drove to San Lorenzo that afternoon and prayed with the enormous crowds, handed out money, and announced an extraordinary plenary indulgence for all sins for the victims of air raids.[187] That evening, the Pope dashed off a furious letter to Roosevelt, expressing horror at "witness[ing] the harrowing scene of death leaping from the skies and stalking pitilessly through unsuspecting homes, striking down women and children."[188]

Only a week after the San Lorenzo bombing, King Emmanuel III shocked Italy by arresting Mussolini.[189] The previous day the Grand Council of Fascism voted no confidence in Il Duce's government. Mussolini's successor, Marshal Pietro Badoglio, a decorated military officer and tough ex-Viceroy of Italian East Africa, had little zeal for fascism. Badoglio disbanded the Fascist Party two days after assuming power. Within a week he had begun secret armistice talks with the Allies. Badoglio also considered annulling Mussolini's race laws. He did not, in part, because of mixed signals from the Vatican. The Pope had dispatched Father Pietro Tacchi Venturi to inform the new government that the church did not want to abrogate the law.[190] Tacchi Venturi lobbied *only* for a repeal of the ban on marriages between Jews and Aryans, so that the church could again regain control over the sanctity of all Italian nuptials.

Any debate between the new Italian government and the Vatican over who controlled mixed marriages seemed unimportant when on September 8 Badoglio announced Italy's unconditional surrender to the Allies. The Nazis took advantage of the resulting civil strife to seize the northern half of the country. German troops marched into Rome September 10. The next day Hitler topped off the high drama with his first radio address in six months. He threatened Italians for the poor way the nation had treated Il Duce.[191] The day after Hitler's talk, a small squad of elite Nazi commandos freed Mussolini from his mountaintop jail in central Italy and brought him to Germany, from where he announced he would soon return to occupied Italy and form a fascist government in exile.[192]

During two decades the church had become comfortable and familiar with Il Duce and his ministers. Although at times there was considerable friction between the church and Mussolini's state, the Pope and ranking clerics never felt threatened by the fascists. The Germans, however, were another matter. The Allies stoked the Pope's anxiety by passing along a succession of rumors that Hitler planned to occupy the Vatican and take the Pope to Germany in shackles.[193] On the day the Nazis occupied Rome, German troops were visible from the windows of Vatican City. Pius doubled his personal bodyguard and ordered the gates to Vatican City and the giant doors to St. Peter's to be locked. The Swiss Guards replaced their ornamental pikes with firearms.[194] The Pope's personal papers were buried under a slab of marble flooring in the palace.[195] The Allied diplomats residing inside the city-state also began burning their more sensitive documents. Cardinals packed their suitcases in case they had to flee.[196]

After several days, German ambassador Ernst von Weizsäcker pulled up to the Vatican accompanied by a military vehicle. Weizsäcker, a German aristocrat, was lukewarm in his dedication to National Socialism. He passed along the comforting news that the Germans would "protect Vatican City from the fighting."[197]

While that assurance was earnest, Pius had no idea that the Vatican's continued sovereignty in the middle of occupied Rome would bring the Nazi war against Europe's Jews to his very doorstep. Two weeks after the German occupation, SS Obersturmbannführer Herbert Kappler—who the following year would earn the moniker "The Butcher of the Ardeatine Caves" for his massacre of 335 Roman civilians in retaliation for Italian resistance attacks—informed Rome's Jewish community that unless it delivered 50 kilograms of gold, two hundred residents would be deported to concentration camps.[198] These were the descendants of the oldest Jewish community in Western Europe, predating even the arrival of Christians. Their ancestors had seen Popes build, tear down, and then rebuild the walls of the ghetto in which they lived and worked.

Word of the Nazi extortion spread fast. Rome's Jews started gathering the gold. The Chief Rabbi, Israel Zolli, was acquainted with the Vatican's moneyman, Bernardino Nogara. Disguised as a Catholic engineer, Zolli made his way into Vatican City, where he met with Nogara.[199] The Rabbi had wisely selected the ideal person to lobby. Nogara, more than anyone else at the Vatican, was someone to whom everything was filtered as a business transaction. After checking with Secretary of State Maglione, Nogara agreed to help raise the gold. Rome's Jews would have four years to repay it.[200]

It is unlikely that Maglione and Nogara would commit to something so sensitive without Pius's approval.* Pius's inaction throughout the war was mostly in instances in which he thought speaking out might worsen conditions for the church, Catholics, or the victims. There were no such risks when it came to the gold demanded by the Nazis. At most, the church risked the nonpayment of the loan. The Nazis simply wanted their tribute; they did not care how Rome's Jews got it. It was even possible that Hitler and his top officials might like that they were able to wrest away even a small amount of the church's wealth.

On September 28, Zolli again visited Nogara. This time it was to inform him that the Vatican gold was no longer needed since the Roman Jews had raised it themselves.[202]

On October 16, the stakes changed dramatically. Despite receiving the gold, the Nazis still decided to move against the Rome ghetto. The Pope be-

---

* Some historians have thought any offer of help in gathering the gold was out of character for the risk-averse Pius. Defenders of Pius have often distorted the offer of a loan by converting it instead into an outright gift. Some have Zolli skipping Nogara entirely and appealing directly to the Pontiff. Others claim Pius added a million lire as a gift on top of the gold. On the other hand, hard critics of Pius refuse to credit the Vatican with any role. That is because the story relating the Vatican's offer of assistance was not told until 1954, eleven years after the incident, in a book by the former Chief Rabbi. By then, Zolli and his wife had made a stunning 1945 conversion to Catholicism, and he had taken the Pope's given name, Eugenio. He even had a job in the church's Pontifical Biblical Institute. Zolli was simply concocting the story, some claimed, to buttress the church's philo-Semitism during the war. But a contemporaneous letter from Nogara to Secretary of State Maglione leaves no doubt that Zolli's recollection is fact based. In that September 29, 1943, letter, Nogara confirmed that the Vatican had completed accumulating the gold Zolli had requested.[201]

came an eyewitness to the Holocaust: the Nazis rounded up 1,200 Jews.[203] The operation was directed by Obersturmbannführer Kappler. Although the ghetto was about a mile from the Vatican, the Nazis transported the Jews along the outer perimeter of a piazza a mere 250 yards from Pius's windows.[204] The Nazis locked the Jews into the Italian Military College in Via della Lungara, only a few hundred yards from the Vatican.[205] Two days later, trucks transferred one thousand of them—896 women and children—to Rome's main rail station. There they were jammed into freight cars with little food and water and no toilets.

Pius said not a public word in support of Rome's Jews. No one then knew that Ambassador Weizsäcker had told the Pope a week earlier of an impending "resettlement."[206] The Vatican never warned Jewish leaders, evidently fearing that it might put both Rome's Jews and the church at risk of Nazi reprisal.[207]

On the day of the roundup, Weizsäcker asked Secretary of State Maglione whether the Vatican intended to issue any statement. Third Reich officials privately worried that the deportations could spark strong opposition from war-weary Italians who did not share the German fervor for eliminating Jews. If the Pope weighed in against the deportations, Nazi leaders in Berlin had discussed scrapping their plans.[208] According to Maglione's notes, he told Weizsäcker, "It is sad for the Holy See, sad beyond telling that right in Rome, under the eyes of the Common Father, so many people have been made to suffer only because they belong to a particular race."

Weizsäcker again asked if the Pope intended to say anything.

"The Holy See would not want to be put into the necessity of uttering a word of disapproval," Maglione said.[209]

Pius feared that any squabble with the Nazis over the plight of Rome's Jews might only benefit the communists. If he castigated the Germans in public, Hitler might use that as a pretext to turn Rome into a military garrison and convert it into a barrier against the advancing Allied armies. That, of course, would destroy much of the city, something Pius feared.[210]

The same day as the roundup, the Vatican appointed Alois Hudal, an Austrian bishop based in Rome, to continue any further talks with Weizsäcker.[211] Hudal was the leading bishop urging the Aryanization of Catholicism, in which Christ was an "intellectual Führer."[212] He was friendly with dozens of high-ranking Nazis and in 1936 had written *The Foundations of National Socialism,* a virulently pro-Nazi treatise.[213] Pius and his advisors evidently thought Hudal might carry more gravitas with Nazi officials than the Pope's Italian Secretary of State.[214] It had been Pius who appointed Hudal as the rector of the Pontificio Santa Maria dell'Anima, Rome's theological school for German seminarians.[215] The two were friendly (a friendship from which the church tried hard after the war to distance itself).

At near midnight on that same day, Weizsäcker sent two telegrams to the Foreign Office in Berlin. He summarized what he had learned from Hudal, whom the ambassador referred to as "an authoritative Vatican dignitary, who is close to the Holy Father."

"I can confirm that this represents the Vatican's reaction to the deportation of the Jews of Rome," wrote Weizsäcker. "The Curia is especially upset considering the action took place, in a manner of speaking, under the Pope's own windows. The reaction could be dampened somewhat if the Jews were to be employed in labor service here in Italy."[216]

That was a great relief to the Nazis in Berlin. It confirmed the Pope would not stir up Catholic Rome against the deportation of the Jews. The contingency plans prepared in case any Papal condemnation ignited civilian unrest were shelved.[217]

The day after the roundup, Secretary of State Maglione privately requested that the Germans release any baptized Jews, what the Vatican called "Aryanized Jews." The Nazis initially refused. Later that day they set free nearly 250 prisoners, but those were non-Jews, foreigners, one Vatican official, and some "Aryan servants" who had been visiting the ghetto and swept up in the raid.[218]

The Nazis did not want to keep the Jews in Rome long. Just two days after they were detained, a train left packed with a thousand Jews. The next day, in a remarkable showing of the degree to which Vatican officials failed to understand the moral and historical significance of the events unfolding around them, the church formally thanked Hitler's Foreign Minister, Joachim von Ribbentrop, for the German military's respectful wartime behavior to the city-state.[219] And the Vatican asked for *more* Nazi forces to keep Rome's communists under control.

Five days after the boxcars left Rome, the log at Auschwitz marked their arrival at the Third Reich's largest extermination center: "Transport, Jews from Rome. After the selection 149 men registered with numbers 158451–158639 and 47 women with numbers 66172–66218 have been admitted to the detention camp. The rest have been gassed."[220] Only fifteen survived the war.[221]*

After the war, Pius wrote in his personal journal about which single day he believed would "be known in history as the most sorrowful for the Eternal City during the Second World War."[223] For Pius it was the Allied bombing raid that accidentally damaged the Basilica di San Lorenzo fuori le Mura. He did not mention anything about the roundup and deportation of Rome's Jews.

Sir D'Arcy Osborne had an hour-long private audience with Pius the day after the Nazis transported the Roman Jews to Auschwitz.[224] Osborne asked under what conditions the Pope might consider abandoning Rome. Never, said Pius, unless he was forcibly removed. He had no complaints, he told a surprised Osborne, about the Nazi occupation of the city.[225] When Osborne raised the matter of the deported Jews, the Pope did not answer. He had decided that silence would be his response to any direct questions about them.[226]

Osborne watched in dismay only a few weeks later when a stray "British" bomb hit a mosaic workshop in Vatican City. Pius was furious. Two members of the Pope's kitchen cabinet, his nephew, Prince Carlo Pacelli, and Count Enrico Galeazzi, asked the German ambassador to deploy antiaircraft artillery inside the Vatican. That never happened. The Allies convinced Pius and his aides that the so-called bombing raid was a Nazi-sponsored propaganda mission.[227]

Within two months of the Rome deportations, the Nazis seized another 7,345 Jews in northern Italy. Most went to Auschwitz, where 6,746 were

---

* Defenders of Pius XII claim that there were no more roundups of Rome's Jews because the Pope covertly intervened. Gary Krupp claims that after October 16, the Germans did not capture a "single Jew in Rome." Outside the Italian capital, however, another thousand Jews were seized after that date, with not a single word of protest by Pius. Another 2,500 to 3,000 Roman Jews not found by the Nazis went into hiding, many finding safety in monasteries and nunneries. A diary from the Augustinian nuns of the Roman convent of the Santa Quattro Coronati—leaked by the church in 2006 from the Secret Archives—claims that Pius ordered "hospitality be given in the convents" to "his children, also the Jews." In 2013, Jerusalem's Yad Vashem Holocaust Memorial softened the text in an exhibit to acknowledge that "the lack of overt and unequivocal guidance by the Vatican left the decision to initiate rescue of Jews to the heads of Catholic institutions. Some superiors of convents, monasteries and other institutions opened their doors to Jewish fugitives, sometimes with the knowledge of the Vatican." Contemporaneous wartime documents reveal that the Curia was divided over whether Catholic institutions should shelter Jews. The credit for saving many Roman Jews belongs to Père Marie-Benoît, the priest who had beseeched Pius three months earlier to intervene on behalf of Jews in the Italian-occupied French zone. Israel honored him in 1966 as one of the Righteous Among Nations for his brave work. A mostly spontaneous network of lay Italians and parish priests helped those on the run.[222]

gassed. At a detention camp near Trieste, SS and Ukrainian guards murdered 620 Jews, many by vicious beatings, others by execution.[228]

The massacres in neighboring European countries dwarfed the number of victims in Italy. Only a couple of months after the roundup in Rome, Maglione noted that Poland's Jewish population had been decimated from 4.5 million before the war to 100,000. The Cardinal Secretary got some details wrong, but his notes serve as a contemporaneous marker about how much was known inside the Vatican about the Holocaust. Maglione wrote about the "horrendous situation" and how Jews were "finished off under the action of gas" at "special death camps at Lublin [Treblinka] and near Brest Litovsk [Sobibor]."[229] That coincided with a letter to Pius from a Warsaw parish priest, Monsignor Antoni Czarnecki, providing jaw-dropping details of gassings at Treblinka.

Some ranking prelates ignored Pius's policy of silence and bravely tried to slow the Nazi murder machinery. The Hungarian Papal Nuncio, Angelo Rotta, repeatedly risked his life to counter Nazi directives and help Jews by providing baptismal certificates and passports. Now, from April through May 1944, he told Pius that the Nazis—who had occupied Hungary and shoved aside the puppet government only that March—had begun deporting the country's Jews to Auschwitz.[230] With the enthusiastic help of the Hungarian fascist Arrow Cross, Germans began a feverish conclusion to years of genocide, as nearly half a million Jews were sent to Auschwitz over several months.

Rotta asked once again for Pius to issue a directive to stand against the Nazi deportations. The second-highest-ranking Hungarian prelate, Archbishop Gyula Czapik, had earlier advised his colleagues "not [to] make public what is happening to the Jews; what is happening to the Jews at the present time is nothing but appropriate punishment for their misdeeds in the past."[231] In a religion where Pius's predecessor had established Papal infallibility, administrators of the Hungarian church—as did the leading clerics in most European countries—looked to the Pope for direction. Priests, likes those in Croatia who ran the death camps, were free to do as they wished since the Pope never issued a decree prohibiting their role in murdering Jews.[232]

Most frustrating about Pius's silence is that there was less reason than at any time during the war for the Pope to have feared German retaliation for speaking out against the mass murder. By the time of Rotta's warnings, it was evident the Germans were losing the war. The successful Allied invasion at Normandy on June 6 added to the growing battlefield momentum of Allied and Soviet troops. Diplomatic rumors had reached the Vatican that some high-ranking Nazis were angling for a negotiated truce.

By now the Allies knew precisely what was happening at Auschwitz, from a bone-chilling account told by two escapees (the so-called Auschwitz Protocols).[233] Slovakian Nuncio Monsignor Burzio summarized the information from the two escapees into a grim, single-spaced, twenty-nine-page report that he sent to the Pope that May. The Papal Nuncio to Turkey—Bishop Angelo Giuseppe Roncalli, later Pope John XXIII—received the Auschwitz Protocols from a friend, a delegate to the Jewish Agency, a humanitarian aid organization. The future Pope cried as he read it. Roncalli expressed his frustration and anger about the inaction of his Vatican superiors.[234]

With their worst fears realized in the closing phase of the war, the Western governments, Protestant leaders, and neutral countries such as Switzerland bombarded Pius with urgent pleas for him to invoke his moral authority to try to save Hungary's Jews. The Pope's trusted apostolic delegate to the United States, Archbishop Amleto Cicognani, sent a direct appeal from four prominent rabbis who warned that the lives of possibly a million Jews were at stake. A strong appeal by Pius might shame the Nazis into sparing them. Palestine's chief rabbi made a similar plea.[235]

But during the spring of 1944 Pius again appeared to be more fixated on averting any Allied bombing of the Vatican than he was about the frenzied end of the Holocaust. When Allied bombers mistakenly flattened the sixth-century St. Benedict Abbey at Monte Cassino, eighty miles south of Rome, pictures of German troops risking their lives to save precious objects from the smoldering ruins scored the Nazis a major propaganda coup.[236] Pius told the Americans and British that they would "stand guilty of matricide before the civilized world and in the eternal judgment of God" if they bombed Rome.[237] Unknown to Pius, Roosevelt was determined to take the capital before the presidential elections that November, even if it meant bombing sorties.[238] The Germans played off of Pius's obsessive fears by moving their command operations in the shadow of the Vatican, assuming that the city-state afforded them protection from Allied airpower.

Pius knew it was only a matter of time before the Americans liberated the city. The Pontiff directed his Secretary of State to formally request of Osborne that "no Allied colored [nonwhite] troops would be among the small number that might be garrisoned at Rome after the occupation." The Pope thought black troops were more prone to raping civilians than white soldiers.[239] When he was Nuncio to Germany, he accepted as fact the often repeated tales that French African troops had committed terrible assaults on women and children in the post–World War I occupation of the Rhineland.[240] Pius also repeated his opposition to the Allies' insistence on an unconditional Nazi surrender. He feared it would devastate Germany and advance communism.[241] The Pope's comments about "colored troops" and his desire that the Allies not force the Nazis to fully surrender added to the Western perception that Pius was out of touch.[242]

On June 5, 1944, Allied troops liberated Rome. The Vatican had fretted that Hitler might order his army to mount a destructive door-to-door battle to hold the city, but German troops simply retreated north. Although relieved the Germans were gone, Pius spent his first day calling his Secretary of State to insist the Americans move a tank that he could see from his window. He thought its proximity to the Vatican showed a lack of respect for the church's sovereignty.[243]

With the battle for Rome over, Pius basked in the unabashed adoration of Romans, most of whom hailed his role in saving the city from destruction. Newspapers bestowed on Pius a medieval title, *Defensor Civitatis* (Defender of the Citizenry), and it stuck.[244] But it did not take long before Allied representatives at the Vatican brought Pius back to earth, turning his attention again to the mass deportations under way in Hungary. Pius told Osborne that he was not sure why everyone seemed so agitated only about the Jews in Hungary. What about Soviet atrocities against Catholics in Poland? Even Osborne, accustomed to the many ways by which Pius avoided taking any responsible action over the mass murder of Jews, was surprised at this latest canard. He told the Pope that the British had seen no evidence of Russian crimes, and whatever might have been done to Catholics did not compare to the systematic slaughter of the Jews.[245]

Pius consulted with Cardinal Maglione, Monsignor Montini, and some other aides. He would not, Osborne was told, criticize the Nazis. On June 25, the Pope instead sent a short telegram to the Hungarian Regent, Admiral Miklós Horthy: "We personally address Your Royal Highness, appealing to your noble sentiments and being fully confident that you wish to do all in your power in order that so many unfortunate people be spared further afflictions and sorrows."[246]

Western governments sent their own warnings to Horthy alluding to criminal consequences for helping the Nazis move against the country's Jews.[247]

Horthy dithered for several weeks before he stopped cooperating with the German deportations. By that time, half of Hungary's Jews had been murdered. The hiatus was short lived. That October, a hard-line Arrow Cross government shoved Horthy aside and resumed the transports to Auschwitz. The Allies asked the Pope for another note since the Arrow Cross leadership was mostly Catholic. Pius refused. He resented that he felt pressured into his first plea to Horthy. Once was enough he decided. Although the Papal Nuncio, Angelo Rotta, continued to send a steady stream of ghastly details to the Vatican, Pius did not again react.[248]*

Other than his short and generic telegram over the Hungarian deportations, there is no journal entry or other contemporaneous account of Pius or any of his top advisors anguishing over what else they might do to stem the genocide. Pius's public silence and inaction in the face of such barbarity has sparked for decades a fierce debate among historians and theologians as to why he did not do more. The extremes are on the one hand the depiction by British historian John Cornwell of Pius as "Hitler's Pope," and the other is the Vatican's move to anoint Pius a saint (in 2009 Benedict XVI bestowed on him the title of "Venerable," meaning the church has officially acknowledged his Heroic Virtue, the first step in Pius becoming a saint).[250]

Most historians search for the truth somewhere between those two poles. Those less partisan than the Vatican, but still sympathetic to the Pope, contend that he was convinced his cautious approach spared the Jews even greater atrocities. In 1940, Pius had told the Italian ambassador to the Vatican that if he had forcefully spoken out, he feared "making the plight of the victims even worse."[251] And he worried—with some justification—that the Nazis might use such a Pontifical statement to declare him an enemy and to wage a war against the church, arresting clergy, limiting the rights of Catholics to worship, bombing or seizing Vatican City, and possibly imprisoning him.[252]

Some explain away Pius's wartime actions by noting that his great love for

---

* When Secretary of State Maglione died in August 1944, Pius considered his old friend Cardinal Spellman for the role. An internal FBI memo dated April 12, 1945, reported a "persistent rumor" that Spellman was at the top of a short list. But the opposition to Spellman inside the Curia was furious. Pius was so confident of his own diplomatic capabilities that he decided not to appoint anyone, instead assuming the duties, assisted by Maglione's two undersecretaries, Monsignors Domenico Tardini and Giovanni Montini. "I don't want advisers," Pius told Tardini. "I want people who do as I say." Pius left the Secretary of State office empty for the rest of his tenure, another fourteen years.[249]

Germany made him resistant to believing the gory details that filtered into the Vatican, and then reticent to act. The public silence of Pius was no worse, others assert, than that of the Allied governments, which before the end of the war knew as much as the Vatican about the atrocities. The Allies still said little publicly and refused to bomb the railway lines on which the packed deportation trains kept running on schedule to Auschwitz.

But the Vatican had a unique power to influence events compared to the Allies. As the head of the world's then largest religion, Pius wielded a moral authority far beyond the scope of any Western government. The church counted millions of loyal worshippers inside Nazi Germany and the occupied countries. They had become accustomed to Popes setting policy on critical and often divisive issues. Catholics dominated the leadership of every puppet government allied with the Nazis. Many devout Catholics maintained their faith at the same time they worked at concentration camps and ran the Third Reich's bureaucracy of mass murder. Some priests were involved in both fascist politics and the civilian slaughter. The Pope's passive behavior did nothing to disabuse them of that contradiction. In an era in which the faithful were more likely to follow Pontifical decrees, an unequivocal declaration from Pius that it was a mortal sin for any Catholic to aid in the killing of Jews might have dealt a serious blow to Hitler's Final Solution.

The justifications offered for Pius's silence seem insufficient to explain why he failed in his spiritual and moral duty to condemn in public a genocide that unfolded during his Papacy. Pius did not symbolically excommunicate Hitler and Mussolini or banish *Mein Kampf* to the Vatican's list of disapproved books. He did not publicly renounce the Reichskonkordat even after it was evident the Nazis had violated every substantive article. The best Pius could do was muster vague appeals against the oppression of unnamed victims.

There is little doubt that Pius's diplomatic training taught him to write and speak in periphrases and so as not to offend anyone.[253] He might have better served the church during the war as the Vatican's Secretary of State rather than as the leader of hundreds of millions of Catholics who considered him the Vicar of Christ. The tool he knew—diplomacy—was useless when dealing with Hitler and institutionalized mass murder.

Pius believed—as had all Popes before him—that his first obligation was to protect Catholics. He would do nothing that might heighten the risks for the church in Germany, Austria, and the occupied countries. Western diplomats privately dubbed this "the faith of a long perspective." It was the idea that the church had survived nearly two thousand years of wars, horrendous Popes, the persecutions by unfriendly Kings, and the sacking of Rome by foreign armies. "The Vatican thinks in centuries and they regard Fascism as a transitory interlude," concluded British envoy D'Arcy Osborne.[254]

A further consideration that likely pushed the Pope to stay silent was rooted in the church's own tortured history of anti-Semitism. Pius and his top advisors had been raised and inculcated with a religious bias against Jews that was an integral part of Catholic theology and liturgy. Centuries of Catholic traditions had helped sow the seeds of Hitler's hatred toward Jews. It was a Pope, Paul IV, who had in the sixteenth century issued a decree that ordered all Jews under Papal control into ghettos, ruling they were condemned to "eternal slavery" for crucifying Jesus.[255] Pius XII—when still a cardinal—had written and talked at length about how Jews were the masterminds of Russia's godless Bolshevik Revolution, and that their main goal was to destroy Christian civilization.[256] That learned anti-Semitism meant there was little urgency to help the Jews.[257] And it might even have contributed to a sense that the horrible events unfolding in Europe were somehow God's will—what Catholics called *divine law*—against the people who had rejected Christ.[258]

There is another factor, however, that likely influenced Pius to remain silent in the face of overwhelming evidence of mass murder: money. A similar dynamic had played out in 1935 when Pius XI remained quiet during Italy's brutal aggression into Ethiopia. The church then had investments in munitions companies and was inextricably bound with Mussolini's government. Any moral duty for the Pontiff was lost in the pursuit of profits.

In World War II, Pius XII's silence helped protect a complex web of interlocking business interests with the Third Reich, relationships that yielded significant profits for the Vatican. In some cases they are dealings the Church has denied to this day. And some of the biggest returns came from Nazi-occupied countries, the same ones in which the Pope mostly turned a blind eye to mass murder. It was in the killing fields of Eastern Europe that Bernardino Nogara created a labyrinth of multijurisdictional shell companies that kept profits, bloody and not, flowing into the Vatican's coffers.

9

The Blacklist

A fast-thinking financial savant like Bernardino Nogara was tailor-made for the violent chess game that became World War II. An Italian patriot, he recognized that Mussolini had inalterably bound the nation's fate to Germany. And Nogara knew firsthand about Pius's special affection for Germany. But he was unsentimental when it came to money. He did not make his investments based on which army he hoped would prevail. His loyalty was to the church and to accumulating and protecting its wealth.

In the early spring of 1939, after the commission of cardinals cleared him and Pius restored his full authority as head of the Special Administration, Nogara scrambled to safeguard the Vatican's money. Not only would the war complicate successful investments and steady profits, he knew that armed conflicts had historically caused a drop-off in Peter's Pence. The fighting might disrupt income from his commercial real estate ventures in France and England, two countries certain to be combatants. All the uncertainty highlighted the importance of the money the church got from the Kirchensteuer, the 8 to 10 percent tax imposed on every German Catholic. The revenue to the church had risen sharply since the Nazis had made it mandatory and collected it on behalf of the church. Just before the 1939 Nazi invasion of Poland, Nogara checked the amount: that tax alone returned enough money to Rome to pay for most of the church-state's operating expenses.[1]*

---

* Without the Kirchensteuer, Nogara would have been far more pressed to juggle the church's finances. The Nazis collected and paid the Kirchensteuer to the Vatican throughout the war. In 1943, the tax revenue hit a then record, just over $100 million (a 2014 equivalent of $1.7 billion). Files still sealed in

The start of the war in September only heightened Nogara's sense of urgency. He feared that Germany would repeat its World War I strategy and claim neutral Luxembourg as an early victim. So he closed Grolux S.A., the holding company he had established there in 1933 to invest some of the Lateran Pacts millions in Paris, London, and Lausanne real estate.[3] Six months later Nogara began consolidating some at-risk assets in neutral countries. He put Société Privée d'Exploration Immobilière, a successful Paris-based real estate firm he had created in 1932, under the control of Profima, one of his Swiss holding companies (under Swiss law there was no requirement for any public accounting, and when the Allies later suspected that the Vatican might be laundering some Aryanized Jewish assets from Paris through Société Privée, its closed books stymied the investigation).[4] And in May, Nogara moved some other scattered European operations under Profima's umbrella, as well as to one of his early Swiss holding companies, Lausanne Immobilier.[5]

Nogara's hunch was right. Germany invaded Luxembourg as part of a broad offensive that overran the neutrals Norway, Belgium, and the Netherlands. Hitler's divisions then swept into France. The breadth of Nazi aggression prompted Nogara to protect the church's movable assets, mostly gold and stock certificates. America seemed safe. It was solidly neutral, with most Americans thinking the country's interests were best served by staying out of "Europe's war" (the United States had not yet even condemned the Nazi annexation of Czechoslovakia or the invasion of Poland).[6] Nogara traveled to London with the House of Morgan's Roman representative, Giovanni Fummi. They arranged to transfer to the United States $7.7 million—the 2014 equivalent of $126 million—of the Vatican's gold held by Morgan's British affiliate, Morgan Grenfell.[7] Nogara also soon sent a "sizable amount" of the church's Italian gold reserves to America. He consolidated most of the Vatican's smaller stocks of gold scattered around Europe to Switzerland's Credit Suisse.[8] Tens of millions of U.S. and Canadian stock certificates were transferred from Lausanne to Rome, where Nogara directed they be locked inside the Vatican vaults.[9]

---

the Secret Archives might answer whether Pius XII's muted response to the Nazi atrocities was in part prompted by the fear that any condemnation might cause Hitler to refuse to collect the tax, or instead to collect it and keep it for the Third Reich. The Vatican's dependence on this income might also explain its steadfast opposition to Allied and Russian demands later in the war for Germany's unconditional surrender. There was no guarantee that the Kirchensteuer would survive in a Germany occupied by foreign powers (it did).[2]

Nogara knew, however, that protecting the church's money required far more than shuffling its hard assets to safe havens. He had learned through his BCI work during World War I that governments fought wars beyond the military battlefield, waging a broad economic battle to defeat the enemy. The Axis powers and the Allies imposed a series of draconian decrees restricting many international business deals, banning trading with the enemy, prohibiting the sale of critical natural resources, and freezing the bank accounts and assets of enemy nationals. A month before Nogara had sent the first shipment of the church's gold to the Federal Reserve, Franklin Roosevelt issued Executive Order 8389—dubbed the freezing order or block list—forbidding any financial transactions relating to any nationals or property of two early victims of Nazi aggression, Norway and Denmark.[10] Roosevelt wanted to be certain that the Third Reich could not get any of the money belonging to the countries it conquered. Only the Secretary of the Treasury had the authority to issue limited hardship and humanitarian exemptions.[11]

Roosevelt's block list was amended repeatedly to eventually encompass almost all of Europe.[12] On June 14, 1941, FDR's list was modified with an Economic Defense amendment. It expanded the power of the United States to prohibit trade with any country, company, or person when the Treasury Department considered the action "necessary in the interest of national defense and security."[13] Sixteen new countries were listed, not only obvious belligerents such as Germany and Italy, but neutral nations such as Switzerland, and the tiny principalities of Monaco, San Marino, Liechtenstein, and Andorra.[14]

Only the Vatican and Turkey were left off. Turkey was still then aligned with the Allies because of a 1939 agreement it had signed with Britain and France. The Vatican was the only European country that proclaimed neutrality not placed on the block list.[15] Instead, Treasury issued a general trading and business license to "the Roman Curia of the Vatican City State."[16] Nogara was relieved. Despite the Vatican's declaration of neutrality, he had worried the United States might list the church-state. He knew if that happened it would close off his critical pipeline of dollars for lines of credit, currency exchange, investments, and bill payment. There was good reason for his concern. Some American officials wanted to place the Vatican on the block list since they contended that its neutrality was a fiction. The Vatican was, after all, only a small parcel of land in the capital of an enemy nation. It was indebted to Mussolini for its sovereignty granted just a decade earlier under the Lateran Pacts. The fascists could squeeze the Vatican at any time since it depended on Italy for all its energy, food, water, and communications, and also relied on a stable Italian lira as its currency. But the strongest argument in favor of putting the Vatican on the block list was the likelihood that those who ran the church could not put aside their own nationalism. Popes had been Italian since Hadrian VI died in 1523. The Curia was 90 percent Italian, men who were bound together through a network of lay friends with whom they had grown up, attended school, and still socialized. The families of those clerics were just on the other side of the church's territorial boundaries. In many cases, they had brothers in the military or relatives whose livelihoods depended on the war effort. The most important cardinals heralded from patrician lineage, and counted relatives who were titans of Italian industry. The nephew of the former Pope, Pius XI, was a decorated military officer who ran a Milanese bank at the same time he served as the civil chief of Vatican City.[17] Pius XII's cousin had been president of the Bank of Rome.

By the start of the war, American intelligence relied on "workable contacts" to compile a dossier on forty-eight cardinals who wielded influence both with Pius and inside the Vatican. The conclusion: the most powerful cardinals were either fascist or pro-Nazi.[18] Failing to freeze the Vatican, some argued, would create a major loophole by which Italians could bypass Allied regulations.[19]

Working in the church's favor was that the hard-line opinion about the church was confined to a small group in Treasury. In contrast, the White House had little stomach for a confrontation with America's large and politically powerful Catholic community. The Pope had earned FDR's enduring loyalty by breaking precedent and backing Roosevelt's 1936 reelection bid (an endorsement engineered by Cardinal Spellman).[20] A strong Catholic vote helped put Roosevelt back into office in 1940. Moreover, the State Department encouraged FDR not to do anything that might alienate the Pontiff. The President wanted Pius as an ally, hoping he might assist the United States through silent diplomacy.[21] Those sympathetic to the church argued that the Vatican could always be added to the list later.

Five days after the Economic Defense amendment, Pius XII summoned the American chargé d'affaires, Harold Tittmann, to a "strictly confidential" meeting in the Pontiff's private residence on the top floor of the ocher-tinted Vatican Palace.[22] It was the only time in six years of service there that Tittmann walked up the long staircase, past the relics of the Medici and Borgia Popes, and entered the apartment that the Pope reserved only for his closest friends and family. The private gathering turned out to be about money, which surprised Tittmann as much as the invitation had. Pius had never shown any public interest in finances. The Pope thanked Tittmann for the American decision to leave the Vatican off the block list.[23] There was, however, another concern. The Pontiff gave the details about several private bank accounts in New York. Pius claimed that although they were Vatican property, they were listed under different, unrelated names. And he confided that he maintained his own personal account at a New York bank (according to an FBI report issued later that year, it had a balance of $60,999, the 2014 equivalent of $1,009,577). The Pope asked for Tittmann's help in safeguarding all those accounts from any American wartime regulations. The chargé d'affaires sent a cable to Myron Taylor. As a result of their intervention, the Treasury protected those accounts without asking any further questions about why the Vatican had claimed ownership in the names of different people and companies.[24]

Less than a month after that meeting, in July 1941, FDR created the Proclaimed List of Certain Blocked Nationals, referred to as the "blacklist." It required a lower threshold of proof and allowed Treasury, the State Department, and the attorney general to list all foreign businesses and nationals merely *suspected* of being pro-Axis. Fifteen thousand businesses and persons, many in neutral countries, were eventually blacklisted.[25] And anyone who did business with a banned company or firm was himself subject to blacklisting.[26]

Just as U.S. officials responsible for economic warfare argued whether the Vatican should be blocked or blacklisted, a similar debate played out in Great Britain. The Trading with the Enemy Branch of the Foreign Office (TEB), like its American counterpart at Treasury, thought some Vatican money movements were suspicious.[27] Early in the war, TEB intercepts revealed the accounts at Nogara's British Grolux had been pledged by the Italian government as collateral for lira credit lines at different banks. It raised the specter that Italy was partially funding its war machine by using Vatican assets to circumvent Allied restrictions. When questioned, church representatives claimed they had violated no wartime rules since no money had ever left church-controlled accounts or gone to Italy.[28] When Nogara caught wind of the TEB queries, he transferred the shares in British Grolux to the Morgan Bank.[29] The TEB investigators had to stand down.[30]

The Ministry of Economic Warfare, another British enforcement division, believed that Nogara was "up to some dirty" schemes to help the Axis powers exchange reichsmarks and lire for hard unblocked currency.[31] Since 1925 Nogara had been a director of BCI, Italy's largest bank.[32] The Allies had targeted BCI as an enemy financial institution and closed its U.S. operations.[33] He was also a director of a Swiss-based BCI subsidiary, Banca della Svizzera Italiana, a firm the British had blacklisted for doing business with Nazi allies in Romania and Bulgaria.[34] And one of Nogara's Swiss holding companies, Profima, had a troubling stake in a BCI South American subsidiary, Banque Française et Italienne pours l'Amérique du Sud (Sudameris).[35] The British and Americans had both blacklisted Sudameris as a "willing [Nazi] collaborator."[36] The Americans pressured South American governments to close the bank's operations. Nogara and his good friend, Giovanni Malagodi, another BCI director, tried an end run around the efforts by transferring most of the bank's assets to Profima.[37] They gambled that no Catholic-dominated South American country would move against the company if the Vatican claimed ownership.[38] That worked in Argentina, but Brazil shuttered Sudameris's branches and seized its assets.[39]

Both the Americans and British were furious that Nogara so brazenly chased profits through a bank whose management was pro-fascist. But instead of freezing Vatican assets and accounts, the governments merely complained through their envoys to the Vatican's Secretary of State.[40] Cardinal Maglione—who was not a financial insider—assured the envoys that if he had known all the details beforehand, he would have opposed the Sudameris investment. The Vatican was neutral, he reminded them. Nogara's brief was to focus only on investments, not politics.[41]*

It was not just Nogara's shuffling and masking of holding companies in multiple banking jurisdictions throughout Europe and South America that Washington and London considered suspicious. Treasury investigators were

* Nogara battled in vain to get the British and United States to reverse their Sudameris blacklisting. His offer to appoint two Rome-based receivers to run the company failed. Tom Lamont, a J. P. Morgan director, lobbied Roosevelt administration officials with whom he was friendly. When Lamont made no headway, Nogara turned to Myron Taylor and offered to sell half of Profima's holding in return for a removal from the blacklist. That effort was also rebuffed. It was not until four months after the end of the European war that Nogara could transfer half of Profima's shares to J. P. Morgan in New York. When Sudameris was removed from the blacklist in November 1945, Nogara wrote an effusive letter of gratitude to Myron Taylor.[42]

uneasy over stock and bond securities that had been registered in blocked countries before Nogara forwarded them to the church's correspondent bank accounts at J. P. Morgan and City Bank in New York.[43] Trading in those securities would have been banned since they originated from blocked nations.[44] No interest or dividends could be earned. But Nogara sought a Treasury exemption citing humanitarian and religious needs.[45] A few American officials suspected the Vatican might be laundering the securities, claiming they belonged to the church when the real owner was a blocked person or company. The Vatican could earn a generous fee for taking the risk of bringing them to the United States under the cover of church property. But without conclusive evidence, no Treasury investigator dared brand the church representations a lie. The Treasury Department—possibly concerned about political fallout—did not even ask the Vatican to supply "evidence of beneficial ownership [that] is clear beyond a doubt," a routine request in such cases.[46] Treasury granted the Vatican a special license to trade in and profit from the securities.[47] That meant Nogara was uniquely positioned. When the war turned against the Axis powers, he could run much of the Vatican's business from safe dollar accounts in the United States.

Nogara's good fortune continued in April 1942, when Secretary of the Treasury Henry Morgenthau granted the church yet another dispensation. The Vatican wanted to spend money inside Italy and also in Nazi-occupied countries without running afoul of U.S. regulations. The Pope said it was the only way the church could maintain its many missions in those nations. Morgenthau approved the exemption, making the Vatican the only country permitted to operate in both Allied and Axis zones without fear of retribution from either side.[48]

Nogara knew that the Allies tracked all the church's financial dealings since the Vatican used Western banks. Every transaction left a paper trail. The ability to conduct more of its business in secret would give him the latitude to be more aggressive and creative with the church's money. He had a trump card to play. The June 27, 1942, formation of the Istituto per le Opere di Religione (IOR)—the Vatican Bank—was heaven-sent.[49] Nogara drafted a *chirografo* (a handwritten declaration), a six-point charter for the bank, and Pius signed it.[50] Since its only branch was inside Vatican City—which was not on any block or blacklist—the IOR was free of any wartime regulations. The Vatican Bank could operate anywhere worldwide, did not pay taxes, have to show a profit, produce annual reports, disclose balance sheets, or account to any shareholders.[51] Located in a former dungeon in the Torrione di Nicolò V (Tower of Nicholas V), it certainly did not look like any other bank.*

The Vatican Bank, created as an autonomous institution, with no corporate or ecclesiastical ties to any other church division or lay agency, had only one shareholder: the Pope. Nogara ran it subject only to Pius's veto.[53] Its charter said it was "to take charge of, and to administer, capital assets destined for religious agencies."[54] Nogara interpreted that liberally to mean the IOR could accept deposits of cash, real estate, or stock shares (that expanded later during the war to include patent royalty and reinsurance policy payments).

Many nervous Europeans wanted a safe haven for their money. Italians in particular were anxious to get cash out of the country. Mussolini had decreed the death penalty for anyone exporting lire from Italian banks.[55] Of the six countries that bordered Italy, the Vatican was the only sovereign not subject to Italy's border checks.[56] Now that it had its own bank, Italians needed only a willing cleric to deposit their suitcases of cash without leaving any trail. And unlike other sovereign banks, the IOR was free of all independent audit requirements. It was required—supposedly to streamline recordkeeping—to destroy all its files every decade (a practice it followed until 2000).[57] The IOR left virtually nothing by which postwar investigators could determine if it was a conduit for shuffling wartime plunder or held accounts or money that should be repatriated to victims.

Nogara tapped Monsignor Alberto di Jorio to be the IOR's senior cleric (by 1944 he held the title president).[58] The fifty-eight-year-old di Jorio had worked for the IOR's predecessor—the Pontifical Commission for Works of Religion—since 1920. During the 1930s, he adapted well to Nogara's more aggressive financial style and showed a talent for investing. It was not long before the IOR became a way station for capital fleeing Italy and other European countries. The bank's instant popularity surprised even Nogara.

The mid-war creation of the Vatican Bank served another important purpose: it made it much more difficult for the Allies to track Nogara's movement of church money. The FBI and the Office of Strategic Services (OSS—the

---

* "In Italy, everybody considers us to be a bank," Bishop Paul Marcinkus, the chief of the IOR in the 1970s and 1980s, told *Il Sabato*, a Catholic weekly. "In reality we are an institute which operates with its own procedures."[52]

predecessor to the CIA) tried hard, but the IOR complicated their efforts. Allied investigators struggled to keep up with Nogara's aggressive back-and-forth transfers of Swiss francs, lira, dollars, sterling, and even gold bullion, through a slew of holding companies in a dozen countries on several continents.[59]

In its June 1941 amendment to the block list, the U.S. had included tiny countries that had well-deserved reputations as offshore havens, such as Monaco, San Marino, Liechtenstein, and Andorra.[60] One of the chief reasons the Vatican had been left off was because it was the *only* sovereign European country that did not have its own banking system. The creation of the Vatican Bank changed that. But it did not, for reasons still unclear, prompt Treasury to revive discussions about whether the church-state should be blocked.

Mussolini was also worried that the IOR would help the church hide its financial moves. Il Duce asked Pius XII to allow Domenico Pellegrini Giampietro, an academic and economist who worked for the Minister of Finance, to visit the Vatican to stay informed about the IOR's work. The Pope agreed.[61]

The best evidence of how little the Allies knew about the IOR's activities is the dearth of information about the Vatican Bank in U.S. and British government files. It took the OSS nearly two years after the IOR's formation before it stumbled across intelligence that Hitler's Reichsbank was transferring money to the Vatican and disguising its origin by using a Swiss bank as an intermediary.[62] But by then the OSS had far more pressing wartime matters than running down the details of whatever scheme the Reichsbank and Vatican had concocted. That information ended up in a confidential file but there was no apparent follow-up. Just before Germany's 1945 surrender, U.S. intelligence uncovered Vatican Bank instructions to Switzerland's Union Bank to pay 100,000 Swiss francs to the Bank Suisse Italienne of Lugano, which had been on the Allied blacklist since June 1940.[63] Another closing war intercept found the IOR directing a Portuguese bank to "forward 2500 large dollar notes in a sealed packet to the Vatican through the medium of the Papal nuncio in Lisbon."[64] In other instances, such as the Vatican's five cash accounts at Third Reich banks, FBI agents would not discover their existence until after the war.[65]

Throughout the war, the IOR operated in what the FBI called *black*, off the radar for Western investigators.

10

Blood Money

The church will not disclose whether the IOR later destroyed its wartime records or they remain sealed inside the Vatican.[1] Eastern European countries occupied by the Nazis have shown little enthusiasm to search for documents that might expose their own dubious collaboration. Complicating the quest for answers is that files of some major companies that did business with the IOR remain inaccessible to private researchers and historians. A few firms did not preserve their wartime records.[2] Bombing raids demolished the archives of others, such as the giant German insurer Allianz. Russian troops seized truckloads of paperwork in the closing days of the war, and sometimes burned them or in other instances shipped them to Moscow, where they remained undiscovered for decades. Some Third Reich business documentation ended up in Polish government archives, most of it damaged in a 1997 flood, before any historian had reviewed it.[3] Argentina's Juan Perón destroyed most of his country's wartime state banking records, closing the door to tracking the IOR through its primary South American trading partner. And the largest Italian insurance firm, Assicurazioni Generali, claimed for decades that important files were destroyed at the end of the war, but in 1996 two private detectives found them on the top floor of a waterfront warehouse in Trieste, Italy.[4]

Despite all those obstacles, there are scattered remnants of information in accessible private files of companies with whom the IOR did business, as well as in the national archives of several countries. That diverse information provides a broad picture of what the Vatican Bank did during the war.[5] Much of it leads back to Nogara's close friend Count Giuseppe Volpi di Misurata, one of Italy's most celebrated industrial titans. U.S. intelligence described Volpi as "an unscrupulous man, absolutely unreliable," who wielded "great[er] power than J. P. Morgan, John D. Rockefeller and Bernard M. Baruch, plus a dozen other magnates."[6] Volpi and Nogara had become friends in 1902 and business colleagues shortly after. Serendipitous events aligned their financial interests. During World War II Nogara felt safe investing Vatican money in Volpi's companies while Volpi wanted the IOR's cash since it came with the church's implied moral sanction.

Volpi was a self-confident promoter. Long before the war he was involved in ambitious private projects throughout the Balkans, Constantinople, and his native Venice.[7] Nogara had started his career as an electrical and mining engineer for a company owned by an investment group that included Volpi.[8] The efficient and low-key Nogara was the perfect foil for the flamboyant and garrulous Volpi. Volpi engineered Nogara's appointment as a director to BCI, Italy's largest bank.[9] Nogara worked with Società Commerciale d'Orientale in Constantinople. The Società was BCI's Ottoman financial syndicate.[10] From there, Nogara became Volpi's indispensable insider, managing a coterie of informants in the Turkish capital.[11] And he helped Volpi arrange enormous loans to establish beachheads in steel and shipping, a seaport development, Italy's largest electrical utility, and a transnational railroad. The pair even managed to secure a personal stake in Montenegro's lucrative tobacco monopoly.[12]

As ardent Italian nationalists, both men saw Mussolini as a bulwark against encroaching communism. His goal of expanding the Italian empire, they believed, was good for business.[13] While Nogara advanced at Società Commerciale d'Orientale and BCI, Volpi served four years as Il Duce's Governor of Libya and another three as Italy's Finance Minister.[14] After Volpi stepped down as Finance Minister in 1928, Mussolini tapped him the following year to be a key negotiator in talks with the church over the Lateran Pacts.[15]

When Nogara moved to the Vatican to invest the $92 million settlement that Volpi had helped negotiate, Volpi flourished in the private sector.[16] He was elected president of the country's most powerful trade group, Confindustria.[17] As Nogara carved out his power base at the Vatican, Volpi boasted that his goal was to build Italy Inc., a diversified Italian-based business empire that would rival the country's great industrialists, the Pirelli and Agnelli families.[18] Nogara and Volpi were back in business. Nogara used his BCI connections to arrange the financing for Volpi to take control of Wagons-Lits, a travel conglomerate that ran the Orient Express and also owned the international travel agency Thomas Cook (Nogara had earlier tried and failed to buy the grand Wagons-Lits Parisian headquarters).[19] He also convinced BCI to finance more Volpi deals for electrical utilities in Greece and Dalmatia, a banking network in Croatia, and a newly formed insurance consortium, The Group, in Romania.[20] In return, Volpi offered Nogara preferred terms on deals involving the church. The Vatican invested in SADE, Volpi's Italian and Balkan-based electric utility, as well as Bastogi, the country's oldest holding company, which Volpi had recently purchased.[21] It was the insurance industry, particularly Italy's largest insurer, Assicurazioni Generali, that Nogara judged as the best business opportunity for the Vatican.

The small Jewish communities in Venice and Trieste had founded Generali in 1831.[22] By the mid-1930s, Nogara had bought a stake in Generali for the Vatican and was friendly with all its directors.[23] Mussolini's 1938 anti-Semitic laws crushed Generali and other Jewish-owned insurers such as Riunione Adriatica di Sicurtà (RAS).[24] At Generali alone, twenty Jewish directors were forced to resign and sixty-six top ranking employees were dismissed. All the Italian insurers appointed fascist directors. A government decree converted Generali into an Italian company and relocated its headquarters to Rome. Generali's Jewish chairman—the son of the company's founder—had to stand down.[25] His replacement? Volpi.[26]*

Nogara was one of the Generali investors who supported Volpi's appointment to fill the vacancy created as a result of the race laws.[28] Men like Nogara and Volpi likely viewed the removal of Jewish executives as the price of doing business in fascist Italy.[29] The great irony was that Generali was primarily successful because of its Jewish roots. Generali's founder, Giuseppe Lazzaro Morpurgo, had set about in the nineteenth century to target the nascent insurance trade among Eastern European Jews. He believed that the poor Jewish populations in the East would welcome a Jewish insurer who offered them life insurance policies that doubled as annuities. The policies—often called a poor man's Swiss bank account—guaranteed a payout at the end of a fixed term and were marketed as an easy and safe way for families to save money.[30] They

---

* When Baron Robert Snoy, the aristocratic president of Wagons-Lits, later sent Volpi a new order further restricting Jews in any form of commerce, Volpi was required to declare his race and religion. On December 1, 1940, he wrote: "I hereby declare that I am . . . of the Aryan race, as are my ancestors since time immemorial, and I have always professed the Catholic faith."[27]

also offered an immediate payout to the families if the policyholder died early. Morpurgo knew the untapped market was huge. Generali started by setting up small information tables at marketplaces popular with Jewish families.[31] In those early decades, Jews showed up in person, paid their premiums in cash, and left with a tiny chit of paper as proof of their policy. Eventually Generali established formal offices in all Eastern European capitals.[32] Its success fed on itself. As it grew, Generali branded itself as the most reputable and safest of insurance companies.[33] The result of Morpurgo's singular focus was that by the start of the twentieth century, Generali dominated the Eastern European Jewish insurance market.

Generali's Jewish roots and success did not bother Volpi, an opportunist who was concerned about profits far more than he was about anti-Semitism.[34] The Italian insurance industry accounted for a remarkable quarter of Italy's gross national product. And Generali was far and away the most successful company, claiming a third of Italy's insurance trade.[35]

Some Generali executives had fresh memories of how badly World War I had hurt their business. They warned Volpi about the pitfalls of any new European conflict. Increased death rates for soldiers and civilians translated into punishing early payouts on life insurance policies.[36] The damage from bombing raids in the transport of commercial goods meant huge losses. Writing fire insurance on industrial facilities put enormous capital at risk. Generali's assets during World War I had plummeted by a third.[37] But none of that worried Volpi. His natural confidence set him apart from his colleagues and he demonstrated that early on. He had taken charge at Generali at the same time Hitler announced the Anschluss between Germany and Austria. Two dominant German firms, Allianz and Munich Re, planned to subsume the Austrian insurance industry. But Volpi objected and lobbied German executives as well as Italian government ministers.[38] The result was an extraordinary assurance from the Reich Economics Ministry that going forward Generali would be treated as a German insurance company.[39] Volpi took personal control of Generali's Austrian subsidiary, Erste Allgemeine, and ended up with a solid share of business in the new order.[40] In return, Generali reiterated its loyalty to the Axis powers. And Volpi led the effort to establish Roma, a well-funded Italian reinsurance syndicate that became an integrated partner with its German counterparts.[41]

Volpi wanted to expand his interests in many countries. He and other Italian businessmen knew that high returns were available only beyond Italian borders. At the same time, Nogara was investing heavily in British, French, and Swiss real estate through his shell companies.[42] Mussolini had forced those men to look abroad as Italian profits were squeezed between crippling regulations and high taxes. Most risk takers favored the Balkans and Eastern Europe, a region still developing in the wake of its post–World War I independence from the Ottoman and Austro-Hungarian empires.[43]

Once the war began, Germans and Italians rushed to scoop up the enormous business left behind by the British, who were cut off from their continental insurance trade. Sometimes, as in Poland, they split the business. Munich Re and Generali ended up controlling about half of Poland's insurance, using local companies to mask the true extent of ownership.[44] Concerns about the magnitude of the new risks across Europe prompted the competitors to form the Association for the Coverage of Large Risks, with Munich Re and Swiss Re each owning 25 percent, and Generali and RAS each with 10 percent. Smaller German and Swiss insurers divided the rest.[45]

More often they could not agree on how to divide the spoils. Volpi was willing to fight the Germans and others for business share in the conquered Eastern territories.[46] Austrian insurer Wiener Allianz, for instance, was rejected in its bid to sell insurance in bloody Slovakia and the German protectorates of Moravia and Bohemia. German and Swiss firms tried monopolizing the lucrative opportunities there but Generali and RAS muscled in.[47] In Greece and the succession states of Yugoslavia, Volpi pushed Generali's marketing, undercutting German pricing by using holding companies to avoid heavy regulatory costs.[48] And in Croatia he took advantage of lax rules about capital requirements for reinsurance and currency exchange to best the Germans in a struggle to control the insurance trade.[49] The profits he shared with Nogara—who oversaw the Vatican's extensive stake in Generali—were enormous.

Neither man objected when some of Generali's local subsidiaries in the occupied territories eliminated their Jewish directors. Nor was there any protest when the Gestapo later sometimes seized Jewish insurance assets and converted the cash value of policies.[50] Instead, Volpi, as chairman, and Nogara, as the largest investor, focused on the bottom line: Generali retained on average about twice as much business as its German competitors.[51]

As a neutral sovereign, the Vatican was not supposed to do business with any blocked or blacklisted company or person. Generali was itself blacklisted, as were all other Italian insurance companies. The Treasury Department had closed and liquidated Generali's American branch in 1941 (it remained shuttered until 1952).[52] The Allies were stymied, however, in efforts to prove the Vatican retained any ownership in Generali. Not only did Nogara keep that stake, but not long after the war started he invested in most top Italian insurers.[53]

In 1940, Nogara extended the Vatican's role in Italy's insurance industry. The fascists seized the assets of a British insurer, Norwich Union, which had been doing business in Italy since the turn of the century. Mussolini assigned Norwich's complete portfolio to Fondiaria, Italy's fourth largest firm.[54] Just before that news became public, Nogara—who was a director of Fondiaria's credit union—bought a controlling interest for the church.[55] The insider tip likely came from Volpi.[56] Adding to the incestuousness, the Pope's cousin, Ernesto Pacelli, served as president of a Fondiaria real estate subsidiary in Rome.[57] The Vatican's purchase of Fondiaria came only two months after it finished purging its Jewish executives.[58] When the Norwich asset transfer was announced, the Vatican's stake multiplied in value. The Allies would not find out about the church's ownership of Fondiaria until its president was arrested after the war.[59] *

Fondiaria continued to do business with German insurers in Nazi-occupied countries throughout the war. And many of those Italian firms owned shares of successful midsized German and Austrian insurers, all of which were on the Allied blacklists.[61] (After the war when Allied investigators pressed the Italian insurers for copies of their contracts with German companies, the Italians claimed many had been destroyed during the fighting.)[62]

Although Nogara's Generali and other insurance investments were profitable for the Vatican, the stakes came with moral consequences. Volpi, for instance, did a lucrative business under Poland's General Government, the Nazi military administration that ran the country as ground zero in the murder machine against European Jews.[63] In Romania, where the fascist Iron Guard eliminated the country's Jews and Gypsies, Volpi split the profitable transport

---

* The venture with Fondiaria was one of Nogara's riskiest. The following year, when the U.S. expanded its block list to cover Italy and most of Europe, the Vatican's controlling interest in Fondiaria would have meant instant freezing of the church's U.S. bank accounts. An even riskier venture is discussed by Professor Michael Phayer in his book *Pius XII, the Holocaust, and the Cold War*. Phayer makes a provocative case suggesting that Nogara might have used money—cleared by the U.S. Treasury for "food exports" in Spain and Portugal—to buy tungsten carbide. Prices for that metal had spiked because of low supply and widespread use in military hardware and steel production. Phayer's case is suggestive, but pending release of still classified documents, it is not yet conclusive.[60]

insurance business with Germany's Munich Re and Jauch and Hübener.[64] Volpi allowed Albula, a small Swiss-based financing firm owned by Generali, to act as a proxy so Jauch and Hübener could secretly buy the shares of a Romanian insurance company.[65] Even in supposedly neutral Latin and South American countries, Generali, RAS, and the German insurers used local agents and multiple layers of reinsurance and phantom trustees to mask their ownership.[66] Reinsurance allowed blacklisted companies to redeem policies in neutral countries, creating another way of moving around cash that would otherwise have been blocked.

U.S. and British intelligence tried unmasking the identities of the companies behind each proxy.[67] It was, according to Britain's Trading with the Enemy Branch, "extraordinarily difficult."[68] Generali alone used up to eighty international subsidiaries—which U.S. agents considered "as an intelligence organization of no small efficiency"—to hide the real ownership as well as the distribution of profits.[69] But the Americans and British had little doubt that firms like Generali were often directing the insurance trade in foreign countries.[70] The insurers sometimes sent information through Italian diplomatic pouches (the Allies suspected, but could never prove, that Generali and others might have also had occasional access to Vatican diplomatic bags).[71] At least one of those off-shelf partnerships, through which Generali participated in profitable reinsurance of industrial facilities, utilized slave labor. And others wrote insurance for rail transports, some of which were the trains that carried Jews to the death camps.[72]

Volpi emphasized to Nogara that since Italy was at war with the Allies, nothing precipitous should be done to rupture Vatican-Italian business ventures. One day the conflict would be over. Mutual friends, including Giuseppe Ferrario, the chairman of the fascist Confederation of Employees of Credit and Insurance Institutes, and Giovanni Dall'Orto, President of the fascist Confederation of Traders, said the same.[73] It was unlikely Nogara needed the advice that he should continue the Vatican's business ventures with Italians. In fact, since he was unsure who would prevail in the conflict, he made certain the Vatican was invested in both sides. British historian Patricia McGoldrick, in her 2012 study of Vatican financial transactions during World War II, concluded that by 1941, Nogara's "investments in Great Britain were focused on the heavy industrials, Rolls-Royce, United Steel Corporation, Dow Chemical,

Westinghouse Electric, Union Carbide, and General Electric, all of which were being actively accumulated."[74] And Nogara was no less focused on maintaining business interests in America. By the middle of the war, 1942, the Vatican was generating considerable income from its investments in U.S. Treasury bills, as well as shares of publicly traded companies, including among others AT&T, Sears and Roebuck, Procter & Gamble, Southern Pacific Railway, General Motors, Standard Oil, Chrysler, Ingersoll Rand, Goodyear Tire, National Lead Company, and E. I. du Pont.[75] It also owned income-producing bonds issued by Humble Oil and Refining, the Aviation Corporation, and ASARCO (American Smelting and Refining).[76]

In February 1942, American intelligence learned that Generali was negotiating to buy the Argentine company La Immobiliaria.[77] The U.S. did not know that Immobiliaria was the Argentine proxy for one of Nogara's Swiss holding companies, Lausanne Immobilier. Generali needed real estate outside Europe to convert some wartime reinsurance business into more liquid assets.[78] An equity stake by the Vatican would complicate Allied efforts to determine the real owners, just as it had when Nogara and the IOR took a majority stake in Sudameris.[79]

That same year, an unidentified American banker passed along information to U.S. authorities that a Mexican firm, America Latina Insurance Company, was an Axis front. According to the informant, one of Mexico's largest banks, Banamex, controlled the suspect company's stock as a proxy for Volpi's Generali. Volpi had a secret agreement to buy the shares after the war.[80] Nogara and the IOR also used Banamex. Some in Treasury wondered if the Vatican Bank had a stake in the front company. But a probe went nowhere since the layers of multiple cover companies proved too difficult to penetrate.[81]

The Allies failed to notice that Volpi used a BCI-owned Swiss private bank, Banca della Svizzera Italiana, to earn enormous profits by facilitating gold sales in countries such as Turkey, where the metal commanded a huge premium.[82] Nogara was a Svizzera director despite the British blacklisting of the bank for doing business with Nazi puppet governments in Romania and Bulgaria.[83]

In 1943, any Vatican investments in Italian insurance companies, especially Generali, developed into stakes that profited from the ongoing murder of Europe's Jews.[84] German giant Allianz had set the precedent several years earlier by escheating life insurance policies of Jewish policyholders and refusing to pay accumulated annuities to those alive.[85] What started off as small-time and unorganized looting developed into one of the largest thefts of the Holocaust. Postwar investigators estimated that between the illegally retained premiums and the unpaid benefits that upward of $200 billion was stolen (notices of nonpayment and evidence of the looting scheme appear in U.S. intelligence files as early as 1946).[86] Although most of the money was made after the war, when families of survivors tried to collect on their policies, there were also wartime profits.

Generali's paperwork on this matter is missing. Allied intelligence concluded, however, that Generali began escheating some policies as early as 1942 in occupied Eastern European countries, where the company held more Jewish policies than all other firms combined.[87] Other Italian insurance companies soon followed. Postwar investigators believe Generali cloaked the income from the misappropriation of Jewish annuities into reinsurance issued by subsidiaries, such as Romania's Generali Asigurari.[88]

All the insurers must have realized this opportunity for theft was possible only during the confusion of war. Is it merely a coincidence that Generali and others began escheating Jewish life insurance policies only after Nogara had formed the IOR? The Vatican Bank was critical from its inception to business titans such as Volpi, men who recognized that since the IOR was not answerable to any country's central banking authority, it was the world's best offshore bank.

Did Volpi and Nogara strike such a deal? Did the IOR provide that service for its own insurance company, Fondiaria? The answers, if any, are likely inside the sealed archives of the Vatican. But the church has refused even to acknowledge that it maintains any relevant financial and business records for those years. (In response to a request from the author to access the files, Bishop Sergio Pagano, the Prefect of the Secret Archives, said that a researcher "would not find material" in the Secret Archives about "the financial dimension of the Holy See." That documentation, said the bishop, might be at "the Institute for Works of Religion [IOR] which, of course, by its very nature excludes outside public access." The Vatican is the only European nation that denies historians general access to its archives.)[89]

What is undeniable is that the Vatican's stakes in Generali, RAS, Fondiaria, and other insurance firms provided a high rate of return in part because some of the profits were from the escheatment and nonpayment of life insurance and annuities to Jewish policyholders. Since the Vatican itself was not a direct insurer, however, it was never included in any postwar restitution paid by the insurers to the victims. After the war, the U.S. military office in charge of Operation Safehaven—the Allied program to retrieve plundered assets and illegally obtained profits—admitted that when it came to the Italian insurers and their strategic partners, "we know absolutely nothing."[90]

When Mussolini was forced from office in July 1943, the web of interlocking business directorates and cloaked companies that Italian businessmen had carefully created began disintegrating. The new Prime Minister, Pietro Badoglio, dissolved the Fascist Party only a couple of days after assuming power. Nogara cut all ties with Generali. Croatia, Hungary, Romania, and Bulgaria moved to seize the insurance business for themselves.[91]

Volpi, ever the survivor, denounced fascism and donated to socialist and republican political parties.[92] But events turned against him when the Nazis occupied northern Italy in September 1943, and reinstated Mussolini as the titular head of a puppet government. Il Duce wanted payback for Volpi's flip-flop. The Nazis were agreeable since they accused Volpi of deploying dirty tactics when competing against German industrialists in the Nazi-occupied territories (his real "crime" was that he often beat the Germans for the business). Volpi beseeched Nogara for protection, but his Vatican friend could not help. The church-state was still fretting about its own security and independence in the wake of the Nazi occupation.[93]

On September 23, 1943, SS Obersturmbannführer Herbert Kappler—who the following month would round up the Jews of Rome—arrested Volpi at his Roman palazzo. In one of the great ironies of the war, the Nazis detained him on generic charges that he was "an agent of the Jews" and that Generali was a Jewish company that had been instrumental in spreading "the worst news . . . over Germany, on its internal situation and the military."[94] Volpi in fact had implored Mussolini to protect Michele Sulfina, a Jewish Generali executive who survived the war in Rome.[96]* That race charge allowed the Nazis

* During the war, Sulfina and his family were designated "undiscriminated," meaning the race laws were not enforced against them. While Sulfina trained a new general manager to take his place at Generali, he lived at a Vatican-owned Roman property. After the war, there was a heated internal debate between U.S. intelligence and the State Department about whether Sulfina was a collaborator or merely the recipient of Volpi's kindness. The same debate raged over several other Jewish businessmen, including the former RAS chairman. The consensus was that Sulfina was a likely Nazi collaborator, but the United States ultimately failed to convince the Italians to remove him from postwar Generali. He effectively ran Generali from 1948 to 1953 together with a well-connected ex-fascist, Gino Baroncini.[95]

to plunder Volpi's personal accounts, even seizing his wife's jewelry. His important collection of art and furniture—and even some collectible tombstones from the family cemetery—went by train to Field Marshal Hermann Göring.[97]

There is no written record of the two-day SS interrogation of Volpi, or of his months in a Nazi-run prison in northern Italy. But to friends and family who later saw him, he seemed broken. Once the Vatican was confident the Germans would not move against the Pope, Nogara intervened and with the help of the Papal Nuncio in Switzerland, the Swiss agreed to patriate the Volpi family. The Germans, convinced they had gotten all they could from him, allowed them to go to Switzerland in 1944. Volpi spent most of the rest of the war in a Lausanne hospital where he was treated for exhaustion. He died in 1947 at the age of sixty-nine from a heart attack, shortly after returning to Italy.[98] Knowing by then that a new history was being written about the Vatican and its wartime role, Nogara did not attend his friend's funeral.

11

A Nazi Spy in the Vatican?

In addition to his labyrinthine business web with Volpi, Nogara's other wartime safe haven had been gold. Bullion was the first hard asset Nogara had protected at the brink of war when he transferred much of the Vatican's British and Italian gold reserves to America. The metal had a stable value (then about $35 an ounce), was not as volatile as national currencies, was universally accepted, and could be transformed easily to disguise its origin. By the middle of the war, the Allies had recognized that the Axis powers were not only looting the gold reserves of occupied countries, but that the metal was critical in financing their war effort.[1] The vast amount of plundered bullion and the shady ways it was often disposed of meant that Nogara's concentration on it proved as morally problematic for the church as the Vatican's insurance stakes.

The gold reserves of most Nazi-occupied countries were relocated during the war, often with the crucial help of the Swiss-based Bank for International Settlements (BIS). BIS was almost as much a financial outlier as the IOR. Formed in 1930 through an intergovernmental arrangement between the Rothschilds and eight countries, BIS was a facilitator between Western central banks, an analogous predecessor to the IMF. It was the one organization on whose board British and German directors served together throughout the war.[2] As a multinational consortium, BIS, like the Vatican Bank, had no accountability to any national government. Notwithstanding its mix of international delegates, and even though it boasted an American president, it was firmly under Nazi control from 1940 on.[3]

The German BIS representatives were Baron Kurt von Schröder, a leading banker and Gestapo officer; Hermann Schmitz, the chief of the industrial conglomerate I. G. Farben; Walter Funk, Reichsbank president; and Emil Puhl, an economist and vice president of the Reichsbank.[4] Under their influence, BIS became a central clearinghouse for emptying gold reserves from countries such as Austria, Belgium, and Czechoslovakia.[5]

"Washing gold" was the euphemism for how BIS described bringing bullion covertly into Switzerland and converting it into untraceable cash, usually Swiss francs.[6] About 80 percent of all Reichsbank gold sent abroad was laundered through Switzerland.[7] In early 1942, Puhl—who oversaw BIS's gold program—shared with Funk that the Gestapo had begun depositing gold from concentration camps into the Reichsbank.[8] By that November, an internal Reichsbank report noted that it had received an "unusually great" amount of smelted dental gold.[9] In 1943, the Reichsbank received the first packets of gold stamped "Auschwitz" (it is impossible to determine precisely how much gold the SS sent to the Reichsbank since the records of those shipments that were seized by the U.S. military later disappeared; the United States failed to make copies before returning the documents to the predecessor of the Bundesbank, where the files were destroyed, allegedly as part of routine maintenance).[10]*

BIS was involved in far more than washing gold. Once it purchased $4 billion in gold from the Nazis, a fair amount of which was looted from the national reserves of Belgium and the Netherlands.[12] And in 1942 it received advance intelligence about the November 8 Allied invasion of North Africa.[13] That information proved profitable. BIS bet on a Nazi defeat and used Vichy-controlled banks to pledge billions in gold reserves to Algeria's Central Bank. BIS used its gold as collateral to take an enormous stake against the Reichsmark. After the invasion and the Allied battlefield successes, BIS pocketed $175 million (the 2014 equivalent of $2.4 billion).[14] The leaked intelligence about the Allied invasion came from the Vatican's espionage unit, clerics working under the cover of a peace delegation.[15]

It is little wonder that the Vatican played an intelligence role with BIS.[16] The glue between the two was Allen Dulles, a senior partner in the Wall Street law firm of Sullivan and Cromwell, who had moved to Switzerland during the war to run the OSS. Dulles employed a network of agents, including

---

* In 1997, the World Jewish Conference released a study that some five tons of central bank gold recovered by the Allies was from concentration camp victims and had never been redistributed to the victims or their families.[11]

Hans Bernd Gisevius, a Nazi operative who worked at the Reichsbank.[17]* An integral part of Dulles's wartime financial operations involved the Vatican Bank. Clerics protected by diplomatic immunity and a bank that answered only to Pius and Nogara was tailor-made for Dulles. Allen's brother, John Foster, who remained in the United States, was the American lawyer for BIS.

"Sullivan and Cromwell's investors [clients] needed the Vatican bank to launder their profits under the watchful eyes of both the Nazis and their own governments," according to John Loftus, a former Justice Department prosecutor in the Office of Special Investigations, "while the Vatican needed the Dulles brothers to protect its own investments in Hitler's Germany."[19]

Was this nebulous juncture of intelligence and business—where espionage was utilized as much for outsized profits as it was for strategic military or political advantages—the Vatican domain of Bernardino Nogara? Historians have mostly judged Nogara as an apolitical financial manager who did not choose sides during the war. However, a 1945 OSS intelligence report discovered by this author in the U. S. National Archives lists someone with the surname Nogara as a wartime spy for the Germans. James Jesus Angleton, then chief of the Rome desk for the OSS's elite X-2 Counter Espionage Branch, compiled the intel report, which is marked *Secret* on every page.[20]

Angleton, the report's author, would become one of America's most storied spymasters. At the time he was responsible for eradicating foreign intelligence agents in Italy and recruiting the better ones for the Allies.[21] The looming Cold War with the Soviet Union meant that any Italians or Germans who had valuable information, or themselves might prove useful, were a priority for Angleton and other OSS warriors. Germany had surrendered just weeks before Angleton wrote his report. Many Nazi officers, including top intelligence agents, were still underground. Angleton and X-2 agents unsparingly believed that Allied interests trumped justice for wartime crimes.

The possibility that Nogara was more partisan than widely accepted is raised in an attached one-page appendix to a summary of an interrogation of Reinhard Karl Wilhelm Reme, a German intelligence (Abwehr) officer who

---

* In 1945, the Treasury Department charged that Gisevius—who worked for the Reich Security Main Office—had laundered German money to Switzerland, and that Dulles was instrumental in moving much of the Hungarian Treasury through Nazi banks to Switzerland. Dulles denied the charges and the Treasury probe stalled amidst the confusion of the war's aftermath.[18]

disguised his wartime spying under a cover job as a partner at the German insurer Jauch and Hübener.[22] Angleton included a chart displaying the Abwehr hierarchy in Italy as of October 1944. By that time, the Allies had liberated most of the country. The Nazis, still entrenched in the north, were desperate to slow the war's momentum by directing sabotage cells in Allied-occupied central Italy.[23] The Abwehr used Vicenza as its headquarters and ran four divisions from other cities, including one from Slovenia. Beneath Reme's Milan-based außenstelle (remote branch) was a cell under the control of someone named Nogara. Angleton did not include a first name.[24]*

Reme admitted to being an Abwehr recruiter. He tried downplaying his role, averring that he had been drafted into the army only in the spring of 1943 and after some basic training sent to Milan for German intelligence. Angleton was skeptical, noting that Reme had a law degree, spoke German, English, and Italian, and had traveled extensively before the war to Spain, Greece, and England.[25] To Angleton, that meant it was "possible Reme was working for the Abwehr before the war."[26]

After his first interrogation Angleton concluded that Reme was "head of the recruiting center in Milan for [the] Abwehr."[27] Reme had arrived in Milan pretending to be simply a supply officer for the German army, when in fact he ran the local intelligence effort from his Piazzale Cadorna office.[28]

Angleton realized Reme's position meant he was familiar with the identity not only of German agents in the country but also the civilian informant network still in place. Through Abwehr surveillance on partisans in Italy, Reme might even be able to identify many of the Soviet agents operating there.

Reme's 1943 arrival in Milan coincided with the height of a brutal internal power struggle between the Abwehr and the SD (Sicherheitsdienst), the SS's intelligence service. Hitler had sided with the SS and began to dissolve

* Subsequent to the publication of the hardcover (February 3, 2015), the author uncovered a second OSS document from the U.S. National Archives referring again to an Abwehr-related *Nogara* only by surname. An undated four-page document, marked *Top Secret,* and titled "German Intelligence HQs, Schools etc in Northern Italy," lists *Nogara* as one of twenty-six names. The document has additional information about some named on that list, including their German intelligence contacts, addresses, even a few cover names. The *Nogara* listing has only "Abwehr HQ: Dienststelle KEISER," a reference to the command group in Germany to which he answered. ("German Intelligence HQs, Schools etc. in Northern ITALY," Top Secret, Copy No. 4, undated, records of the Office of Strategic Services, RG 226, File 174, Box 4, NND 917114).

the Abwehr in February 1944.[29] By July, its operations and agents had been transferred almost entirely to the control of the SD's Ämter VI (Group 6), SD-Ausland (intelligence outside of Germany) division.[30] The only exceptions to this transfer of power were the Abwehr's Italian operations.[31] Those cells, such as Reme's unit, retained their independence and operated covertly, since they did not want to risk any intercept of their communications to SD's German headquarters.[32] After the war, the chief of Ämter VI, SS-Brigadeführer Walther Schellenberg, bemoaned to his British captors that his own office had "sparse" contacts in the Vatican. But Schellenberg admitted that the Abwehr "had many men in the Vatican."[33] He told Angleton that he knew the Abwehr had recruited a network of foreigners from Constantinople—including the butler to the British ambassador—during the years Nogara lived there. An unnamed Italian was a key "link" during World War II. But Schellenberg was adamant he did not know his name.[34]

Angleton knew that the unusual nature of the Abwehr meant that by the late stages of the war its ranks included anti-Nazi agents. Some had even passed information to the Allies. Admiral Wilhelm Canaris, a devout Catholic, was its passionately pro-German but anti-Nazi wartime chief. Diehard Nazis like SS chief Heinrich Himmler challenged Canaris's commitment to National Socialism. Canaris provided false data to Hitler to persuade the Führer not to invade Switzerland, and he did the same with Generalissimo Francisco Franco so the Spanish dictator would not allow the Nazis to use Spain for transit. To Hitler's great rage, Canaris occasionally used Jews as agents and other times helped some escape from Germany. He appreciated the importance of recruiting agents at the Vatican, men capable of traveling with sacrosanct consular pouches, using the diplomatic passports of their own sovereign state. Canaris had appointed Munich lawyer Josef Müller to run Rome's Abwehr office largely because Müller was good friends with Pius's personal secretary, Father Robert Leiber.[35] Vatican agents, in conjunction with a handful of German cardinals and bishops, could be useful to Canaris's sub-rosa plans to undermine Hitler. It was Canaris's support of the unsuccessful July 20, 1944, assassination attempt on Hitler that ended in the spy chief's arrest, trial, and execution.

Angleton had cultivated his own low-level OSS agents inside the Vatican and had kept abreast of the city-state's political intrigue.[36] And the Yale-trained Angleton likely had a more personal understanding for what was transpiring in Italy than most of his OSS colleagues. He had been partly raised in Milan, where his father owned the Italian franchise for National Cash Register.*

In defeat, Schellenberg, Reme, and other Nazis knew that information was their only bargaining leverage. They needed ways to trade intelligence for leniency. Reme gave his interrogators the names of fifty-eight agents he and his Italian-based spy unit had recruited during the war. Nogara is not among them.[38] But he provided the name to Angleton on the supplementary Abwehr chart, meaning the Nogara on that chart was almost certainly recruited before 1943, and likely before the war.

Is the Nogara on the chart Bernardino? He had two prewar opportunities to strike up a relationship with German spies. When he was with BCI before World War I, he lived in Constantinople. The Turkish capital swarmed with spies, informants, and double agents working for European powers and their spy agencies.[39] Nogara had directed a loose-knit web of informers that helped Italian companies gain an upper hand in the race against Germany and the Austro-Hungarian Empire to capture some of the enormous business opportunities in the crumbling Ottoman Empire.[40]

Another opportunity for the Germans to have recruited Nogara was during the late 1920s, just before he began working at the Vatican. As the Italian representative running the division of the Inter-Allied Commission charged with rebuilding German industry, he spent considerable time in Germany over a five-year stretch beginning in 1924.

Could the *Nogara* listed be one of Bernardino's relatives? His siblings did not have intelligence value for the Abwehr. One was a museum superintendent at the Vatican. Two were provincial archbishops. None would have been as important a coup for the Germans as Bernardino. And none had such clear prewar opportunities for connecting to German intelligence.

---

* While serving as the OSS chief of the Rome desk, Angleton forged several documents purporting to be secret Vatican telegrams. He planted them inside government files under the code name JVX. The "Vatican telegrams"—shifting responsibility away from the OSS for later helping Nazi fugitives—landed in the National Archives and journalists and historians sometimes relied on them before they were unmasked as fakes forty years later. Did Angleton insert *Nogara* onto Reme's command chart to realize some unknown intelligence aim? It is highly unlikely. Although Angleton knew few boundaries when it came to what he thought were the best interests of the United States, he survived for decades in the CIA, serving under four presidents. Concocting information that could be easily disproved would have imperiled him. If *Nogara* was Angleton's invention, the fabrication would be unmasked by only a single question to Reme from another American or British interrogator. Not even an intelligence school recruit would be so reckless.[37]

As for unrelated *Nogaras*, after the hardcover publication some researchers claimed a twenty-five-page file in the British National Archives showed the name on Reme's chart was Bruno Nogara, a twenty-four-year-old junior officer in an Italian naval reconnaissance and sabotage unit that was also under Abwehr direction.[41]* The young Nogara was captured while on a patrol near the Adriatic coastline on April 11, 1945.

The problem with that conclusion is that Bruno Nogara's squad—Abwehr unit 257—was based in the northern Italian city of Treviso and commanded by Reichsstatthalter Hubert Pfannenstiel.[42] The *Branch Nogara* listed by Angleton, however, was an autonomous cell operating in another city (Milan), and under a separate unit (Abwehr 254), and directed by a different commander (Reichsstatthalter Ernst Schmidt-Burck).[43] Schmidt-Burck reported directly to Wilhelm Reme, the source of Angleton's information.[44]

Bruno Nogara was a Venetian native with no apparent family, school, or professional connections to Milan, the city from which Reme's *Nogara* ran a cell. And the younger Nogara's final motorboat reconnaissance launched from Sant' Angelo, which was under the jurisdiction of Pfannenstiel's Abwehr unit 257, not the Milan unit from which Reme's *Nogara* ran a branch.[45]

For Bruno Nogara to be the same as the one Reme divulged, Angleton would have had to not only put the *Branch Nogara* under the wrong Abwehr unit, with an incorrect commanding officer, but also in a mistaken city. While such an error cannot be excluded, nor can the possibility that the document in the British National Archives shows only that two men named Nogara had Abwehr connections in October 1944.

In the world of realpolitik in which Angleton excelled, he would not have been surprised that the layperson responsible for the church's purse strings might watch out for the Vatican's interests by being in touch with German intelligence. As a spymaster he would also have recognized the ramifications.

---

* The question of "unrelated Nogaras" was addressed in the hardcover: "Given that there are millions of files in the national archives of the three countries, and an equally large amount in private archives of companies, banks, and independent international charities and political associations, it is not possible for a single author to have reviewed every wartime document. All major government archives have finding tools, although there is no universal name search since no government has fully digitized all its files. Still, excluding someone—such as how many Nogaras are mentioned—is easier than finding a specific document on a particular subject. While it is not possible to say with absolute certainty that there was no unrelated Nogara who might have been an Abwehr agent in Italy during World War II, the author has not found evidence of one."

What could a German spy at Nogara's level do to sabotage the Allied war effort and at the same time find ways to help finance the Axis powers? Or what could he have done to sabotage the Nazi war effort by supplying the Germans false information?

Why would Bernardino Nogara still be in touch with the Germans as late as October 1944, when the Axis defeat was a certainty to all but fanatics? Unless, of course, Nogara was working with the Abwehr's Milan cell as an intermediary between the Germans and neutral governments in Madrid and Lisbon. Spain and Portugal were still trying to broker a peace deal that did not require an unconditional Axis surrender. And Nogara had financial interests to protect for the Vatican there since his interlocking joint ventures ran through Madrid and Lisbon on the way to Buenos Aires.

Angleton's response to Reme's intelligence was to recommend that Reme be sent to the Combined Services Detailed Interrogation Centre (CSDIC) for "further interrogation."[46] CSDIC was a secret prison in Bad Nenndorf in Germany run by British military intelligence, MI5. This author has found no follow-up in the files of the OSS, Counter Intelligence Corps, or Military Intelligence.[47]

By the account of his contemporaries, Nogara was a shrewd businessman who approached war as he did his investments: diversify and reduce the risk. During World War II that would have meant not banking on only one side to prevail, but instead developing relationships with both that facilitated the church's ventures during the hostilities and bought it goodwill from the victors after the conflict. It is the only reasonable explanation if Angleton stumbled across the report pointing to Nogara and then buried the information. Short of revelations about an Allied connection in still unsealed government files, all that can be derived definitively from the Reme/Angleton memo is that the business of the Vatican during World War II ends with a question: was the church's long-serving financial wizard, Bernardino Nogara, a Nazi spy?[48]

12

The Ratline

The official end of the European war in May 1945 was only a technicality on a calendar for Nazi officials and leaders of the German puppet governments. They had work to do: hiding billions in stolen loot. Pilfered assets were scattered all over Europe, everything from plundered museum art and real estate to missing gold reserves.[1] Many saw the Vatican as a secure repository since no country would dare violate the church's sovereignty by demanding an inspection or accounting.

Sturmbannführer Friedrich Schwend had directed Operation Bernhard, an ambitious wartime counterfeiting operation of British pounds (most of the fake money was made on printing presses by inmates at the Sachsenhausen concentration camp).[2] The plan was to raise hard currency for the Reich as well as to sink British sterling by flooding the market with phony bills. In early 1945, Schwend set the groundwork for his eventual escape to South America by volunteering to become an informant for Allen Dulles's OSS.[3] To safeguard millions stashed in Swiss banks, he moved it all to the Vatican Bank. He avoided any possibility the Allies might track a wire transfer by sending the cash packed into several trucks (there are unconfirmed reports Red Cross ambulances made the journey through the war-torn countryside). Schwend's Swiss drivers brought the money to a castle in Merano, an Italian town just over the Swiss border. Italians then drove it the rest of the way to the Vatican, where the cash disappeared. Shortly after the Schwend shipment to Rome, OSS intercepts revealed that the Vatican was exchanging large amounts of old five- and ten-pound British notes for new ones through "agents in England" (the Vatican dismisses such charges as having "no basis in reality").[4]

As the war ended, the flow of suspect gold turned from a trickle to a flood. The Vatican did nothing to discourage it. U.S. intelligence had early reports after the formal truce that Ustašan leader Ante Pavelić and many of his henchmen had fled blood-soaked Croatia only after looting most of Zagreb's banks, the Croatian state mint, and the National Bank. An American intelligence memo reported the Ustašan fugitives had stolen upwards of 350 million Swiss francs of gold, most of it coins, "some of which were plundered from the victims of the Croatian Holocaust."[5] In the weeks after the war, British troops seized about 150 million of the plunder at the Swiss-Austrian border.* According to the memo about $47 million (the 2014 equivalent of $125 million) entered the Vatican "for safe-keeping," with unconfirmed rumors that it had "been sent to Spain and Argentina through the Vatican's 'pipeline.'"[7] Giving credence to the possibility that the gold had been transferred to South America was a separate U.S. intelligence report. It concluded that German companies and banks such as the IOR may have moved upward of a stunning $450 million to Argentina.[8] Emerson Bigelow, the investigating agent, suspected the Vatican was still somehow involved. He noted that the stories of the transfer to other countries might "merely [be] a smokescreen to cover the fact that the treasure remains in its original repository [the Vatican]."[9]

William Gowen, a Counter Intelligence Corps (CIC) officer based in Rome, monitored the Vatican to see if he could develop leads on Pavelić's whereabouts.[10] Gowen was one of the CIC's best agents. A former Ustašan colonel told Gowen that in 1946 up to ten truckloads packed with gold traveled from Switzerland to Rome, where the precious metal was unloaded at the College of San Girolamo degli Illirici, the Croatian seminary, only a mile from the Vatican. The convoy reportedly arrived with Vatican license plates, accompanied by some men wearing stolen British military uniforms and others dressed as priests.[11]

Although several U.S. intelligence reports differ about the amount of gold that arrived in Rome, they agreed on a critical issue: any looted precious metal

---

* When a U.S. Army Counter Intelligence Corps (CIC) agent later questioned Pavelić, the Croatian leader admitted the British had detained him and his gang when they had crossed into Austria. The British threatened to turn them over to the new Yugoslavian communist government, where the gang was wanted for war crimes. Instead, Pavelić claimed they were set free after turning over two truckloads of gold to the British soldiers. The CIC officer thought Pavelić was lying to hide "where this money was." There was also some suspicion inside the CIC that Angleton might have been the author of that Pavelić "admission," to hide the real trail of the money.[6]

that came from Croatia ended eventually with an Ustašan Croatian priest, Krunoslav Draganović. When Gowen later interviewed Draganović, the priest admitted that the looted gold convoy had arrived in Rome under the control of an Ustašan lieutenant colonel.[12]

During the war Draganović had been a senior official of the Ustašan commission dedicated to the forced conversion of Serbs.[13] In 1943, Pavelić had dispatched him to Rome as the secretary of San Girolamo. In addition to being a school for Croatian seminarians, San Girolamo was the center of Ustašan intelligence operations in Rome.[14] Draganović was the highest-ranking Ustašan cleric in Rome and he was informally liaison to the Vatican. He cultivated connections with both Italian and Vatican intelligence agents.[15]

Josip Broz Tito and his communist rebels had come to power in a unified Yugoslavia a month before the war ended. Without a church-friendly government in Belgrade, the Vatican appointed Draganović as the Apostolic Visitator for Pontifical Assistance for Croatians. That made him a Vatican official who reported directly to Monsignor Giovanni Montini (later Pope Paul VI) in the Secretary of State's office.[16] Draganović met frequently with Montini, and the Vatican's Pontifical Assistance Commission ensured that the Croatian had plenty of identity papers.[17] When Montini learned that Gowen was snooping around looking for Pavelić and also asking about the Monsignor's own connections to Draganović, Montini complained to Angleton about the nosy American CIC officer. The result was a CIC order by which Gowen's team was told "hands off" when it came to Pavelić and the Croatian priests.[18]

An American Foreign Service officer privately told Gowen that his probe was ordered closed because he had "violated Vatican extraterritoriality."[19] (Much later, when Gowen learned that his operation was shut down the same month that Draganović began helping U.S. intelligence, Gowen came to believe that Angleton had engineered it all as a favor to Montini).[20]

Despite that directive, Gowen continued accumulating intelligence. He eventually concluded that Draganović had turned the Croatian gold and other loot over to the Vatican Bank, even driving some of it in a convoy to St. Peter's Square.[21] Before he shut down his probe, Gowen had interviewed not only Draganović but also half a dozen other top Ustašan officials. The IOR, he concluded, had accepted the Croatian gold since the church classified it conveniently as "a contribution from a religious organization," and then hid its existence by "convert[ing] this without creating a record."[22]

At the same time U.S. intelligence was trying to determine if the Ustašan gold might still be inside the Vatican, it also was probing whether the church had received gold of questionable provenance from a prominent Italian family. Dr. Francesco Saverio Petacci had been Pius XI's personal physician. Petacci's daughter, Clara, was Mussolini's longtime mistress. And Petacci's son, Marcello, was a fascist official who was murdered in 1945 as he tried crossing into Switzerland with crates of cash (neither the killer nor the money was ever found). Allied investigators discovered that Marcello had been the middleman brokering large deals between foreign companies and Mussolini's fascist state. The younger Petacci had earned commissions in Spain alone that totaled a then staggering 50 million pesetas (the 2014 equivalent of $340 million).[23] A substantial amount of gold that Petacci had evidently accumulated was missing. American investigators followed leads to Spain to see if the family had moved the gold there, but determined it was "not likely." Instead, Vincent La Vista, a senior Rome-based officer in the U.S. Division of Foreign Activity Correlation, concluded, "if the Petacci family had any vast hoard of gold, it would have been, and in all probability is, put away for safekeeping in Vatican City."[24] La Vista directed Operation Safehaven, the ambitious U.S. multiagency effort to retrieve looted assets. He ran into a solid roadblock of noncooperation when he tried pushing his inquiry. An informant told him why: "Petacci had, and still has, very dear and close friends high in the inner councils of the Vatican. . . . He is personally held in very high regard by influential personages close to the Holy See."[25] La Vista closed the Petacci investigation without any resolution about the missing gold.

After the war, the Vatican and its Roman properties served as far more than a repository for wartime loot. The war was not long over before the church got swept into the frenzy of its next secular political fight, this one against communism. If Pius XII had in part stayed silent about Nazi atrocities because he considered the Germans a bulwark against godless communism, the unintended consequences of Allied victory fueled his worst fears. On their march to topple the Third Reich, Stalin's armies had swept over half of Europe. Instead of returning to Russia when the war ended, the Soviets stayed put and replaced the Nazi puppet governments with their own lackeys. The new regimes took orders from Moscow. The Soviets were in firm control of Catholic bastions such as Poland, Hungary, Romania, Czechoslovakia, and Bulgaria. Six

Catholic-dominated nations that had won a temporary independence between the world wars—Croatia, Macedonia, Montenegro, Serbia, Slovenia, and Bosnia and Herzegovina—were united under the banner of Yugoslavia and the iron-fisted rule of its communist leader, Tito. Over time, Pius worried, the Catholic populations of those countries might lose their faith under the aegis of atheistic regimes. And Germany itself, the country for which Pius had so much affection and affinity, was sliced in two. The Soviets occupied the eastern half.

Stalin had taunted the Pope in 1944 and early 1945 by sentencing a dozen priests to death and imprisoning hundreds in Siberia. In response to being told by Churchill that the Vatican opposed Soviet policies, Stalin shrugged and asked, "How many divisions has the Pope?"[26] Pius told Myron Taylor in 1945 that he feared the Russians were infiltrating the Italian army "so it could join with the Russian army in overtaking all of Europe."[27] (As late as 1947, Pius and Monsignors Tardini and Montini believed the Soviets were about to invade northern Italy. They often asked incredulous American diplomats about whether there was news of any Russian troop movements and a pending invasion.)

Italy was home to Europe's largest postwar communist movement, led by a charismatic leader who Pius believed was a Soviet agent.[28] When Mussolini had outlawed the Bolsheviks they went underground, and many fought with the resistance. Italy had paid a price for being on the losing side of the war. Most ordinary Italians were sick of a system they blamed for creating such a terrible mess, and were willing at least to consider what the communists offered. They were the only political party that had stood firmly against fascism. Only three months after the end of the war (and six months after FDR's death), the OSS intercepted Pius's order to Father Norbert de Boynes, the Vicar General of the Jesuits, to dispatch his priests to uncover "documentary proof of orders given by and financial aid furnished by the Soviet Union to Italian Communists."[29] Pius watched with alarm as some Italian Catholics spoke of developing a Christian leftist government.[30]

Adding to the Vatican's high agitation, Western Europe was flooded with millions of refugees. Most were displaced from ravaged Eastern Europe. A million streamed into Italy alone.[31] The Vatican had prepared itself since late 1943 for what it knew would be a human tidal wave.[32] Most, as expected, were innocent civilians forced to abandon their homes in the war's violent closing months. Pius gave Monsignor Montini full authority to run the Pontificia Commissione di Assistenza (Pontifical Commission for Assistance), which oversaw all the Vatican's humanitarian efforts. And the Pope appointed Monsignor Ferdinando Baldelli, Sister Pascalina, and Otto Faller, a German Jesuit, to help Montini cope with the enormous numbers who clamored for shelter, food, and other assistance.[33]

Blending in anonymously in the swarm of refugees were some Nazi fugitives. Some had either worked in the extermination camps, others had run the bureaucracy of the Holocaust, and a few were high-ranking officials responsible for the Third Reich's ruinous war. They had shed their military uniforms, donned civilian clothes, and were frantically trying to avoid the American and British military police searching for them.[34] The Allied Nazi hunters had no idea then that a handful of Catholic clerics in Rome anxiously awaited the Nazis. The church provided those fugitives not only a place to sleep and some food, but something far more valuable: false travel documents as well as a ticket by boat to a welcoming foreign country.[35]

Helping fleeing Nazis was not a policy established by Pius XII. The Vatican became a mandatory postwar stop for many war criminals fleeing Europe for a hodgepodge of reasons. Some prelates believed that the new communist regimes—particularly Yugoslavia with its demands for the return of all Ustašan leaders—were incapable of providing fair trials. Church officials felt that returning the wanted men was as good as killing them. Others were deluded by a notion that the fugitives might reunite and rally in a war to drive out the communists. And still others were fascist sympathizers or even dedicated National Socialists who wanted to do whatever they could to help the Nazis escape.[36]

Since the church had been silent during the Holocaust, on which there was a flood of grisly evidence since the end of the war, it was reasonable to wonder if Pius and his advisors felt any moral duty to unequivocally prohibit clerics from assisting criminals involved in that mass killing. There was no such policy. Pius, Montini, and Tardini never uttered a word in opposition to the priests who helped the fugitives. If the Pope's silence during the war had fostered an environment in which otherwise dutiful Catholics could participate in mass murder and not fear excommunication or eternal damnation, after the war his approach to Nazi criminals created an atmosphere in which Catholics were free of any responsibility for the Holocaust. Instead, sympathetic prelates were emboldened to help murderers evade justice.

Pius stubbornly resisted any effort to apologize for the Vatican's wartime inaction (such an apology would not come for nearly fifty years, under Pope John Paul II).[37] He expressed public anger over the convictions of half a dozen Croatian Catholic priests by the Yugoslav War Crimes Commission.[38] The Pope believed those trials were not about delivering justice for wartime atrocities but were propaganda intended to embarrass the church. The same tribunal convicted Bishop Stepinac, but only after he had refused Yugoslavia's offer of safe passage to Rome. Pius was so infuriated that he made the imprisoned Stepinac a cardinal (John Paul II beatified him in 1998, the first step toward sainthood).[39]

The Pope's passion—more than he ever demonstrated over wartime reports of the massacres of Jews—did not stop with a handful of Croatian Catholic prelates. He urged the commutation of death sentences for some of the most notorious Catholic Nazi criminals. U.S. Military Governor of Germany General Lucius Clay rejected Pius's personal plea for clemency for SS officer Otto Ohlendorf, an infamous chief of an Einsatzgruppen (mobile killing) squad in Russia.[40] The Pope's request for leniency for Obergruppenführer Arthur Greiser, who earned a reputation as a merciless ethnic cleanser, raised a fury in Poland, the country where Greiser had been a regional governor. Polish officials rejected the Pope's appeal and newspapers condemned the Pontiff's "flirtation . . . and defense [of] Germany."[41] That did not stop Pius from also asking for clemency for Hans Frank, the lawyer turned Governor General who oversaw the Holocaust in occupied Poland, as well as Oswald Pohl, one of the chief administrators for all Nazi concentration camps.[42] Despite Pius's interventions, all the men were hanged.

The Pope's clemency appeals encouraged a similar outpouring of pleas from German priests.[43] Cardinal von Faulhaber decried denazification—the Allied effort to prevent hard-core Nazis from returning to postwar German industry and politics—as "unnecessary." Other bishops denounced the Nuremberg trials as illegal, and even managed to win a commutation of death sentences for some of the Catholic defendants in the "doctors' trials," including the debauched concentration camp physician Hans Eisele.[44] In December 1945, Bishop Aloisius Muench, the Vatican emissary to the U.S. Military Governor in Germany, wrote a pastoral letter that compared the Nazi murder of millions to the Allied rationing of food after the war. Other bishops used their pulpits to mythologize Catholic resistance to the war and to assure German Catholics that "collective guilt" was not applicable to Germans and the Holocaust. Pius thought that if ordinary Germans were burdened with too much guilt over what happened to the Jews, they might be distracted from concentrating on the Russian red menace.[45]

Given this atmosphere, some inside the church felt secure enough to help the fugitive Nazis by using some of the questionable gold that had arrived at the Vatican. Part of that gold may have paid for food and board for the fugitives, fake paperwork, travel money, and sometimes even work in a foreign safe haven.[46] Some money might have even come from the Pope.[47] The Vatican classified large untraceable payments as "information services" to Vilo Pečnikar, Pavelić's son-in-law. U.S. intelligence had numerous reports that Papal payments funded the Croatian escape network, with Franciscan priest Dominic Mandić acting as the official liaison between the Vatican and the ratline.[48]* In April 1947, the British detained suspected Vatican-ratline middleman, Croatian General Ante Moskov. He had 3,200 plundered gold coins and seventy-five diamonds. The Pope personally appealed to the British, in vain, to release Moskov and fourteen other Ustašan officers.[49]

Pavelić, the number-one-wanted Croatian, stayed in Rome and evaded a CIC manhunt for more than two years.[50] Even before U.S. authorities ordered Gowen to stand down in his search, the former Croat leader had moved between several Vatican-owned properties to avoid detection, including St. Anselmo's, a Benedictine seminary, and Santa Sabina, a Dominican basilica.[51] Most of the time, however, he was in San Girolamo under Draganović's protection.[52] By that time, San Girolamo had become a seminary like no other. All visitors were searched for weapons. Casual callers were questioned about how they had learned about it. Passwords were required to enter any locked room.[53]

A 1947 British Foreign Office report concluded that Pavelić had left San Girolamo and might instead be living "within Vatican City."[54] Gowen thought that the Vatican's protection of Pavelić was so strong that the only way to get him might be to seize him from the church properties, but the idea of violating Vatican sovereignty was a nonstarter in Washington.[55] The Vatican ended the

* Ratline is a sixteenth-century nautical word referring to crude ladders on the sides of ships made from strips of rope. Sailors on sinking ships climbed down the ratlines in the hope of reaching a lifeboat. As used in reference to World War II, it refers to the last escape routes for the Nazis.

debate over what to do about Pavelić in 1947 when it sent him through its ratline to Argentina. A group of Franciscan priests greeted him on his arrival at the port of Buenos Aires.[56] The former Croatian henchman became a security advisor to Argentine dictator Juan Perón.[57]*

Draganović concentrated on his fellow Croatians. Other clerics helped the Germans. None was more energetic than Bishop Alois Hudal, the rector of the Pontificio Santa Maria dell'Anima. The Vatican picked him as the intermediary with the German ambassador during the 1943 roundup of Rome's Jews.[59] After the war, Hudal dropped his emphasis on all things German, referring to himself instead as "the Austrian bishop in Rome," and establishing the Austrian Liberation Committee.[60]

Franz Stangl was the commandant of the notorious Sobibor and Treblinka death camps, where an estimated 1,000,000 to 1,250,000 Jews and Gypsies were gassed. In the closing days of the war, he had fled westward from Poland and by the time he reached Austria, "I heard of a Bishop Hudal at the Vatican in Rome who was helping Catholic SS officers, so that's where we went." Stangl, like many other fleeing Nazis, recalled, "I had no idea how one went about finding a bishop at the Vatican."[61]

While walking across a bridge in Rome, Stangl ran into an SS intelligence officer whom he knew.

"Are you on the way to Hudal?" asked the SS officer, who was himself on the run.

A half hour later Stangl was in a room at a nearby rectory. Bishop Hudal walked in and put out both his hands to welcome him. "You must be Franz Stangl," Hudal said in German. "I was expecting you."[62]

Hudal put Stangl at the Germanikum, a Jesuit hostel for German theological students. He remained there until his Red Cross passport arrived, at which time Hudal gave him some money and sent him packing to Syria. Not far behind Stangl was another Sobibor death camp commandant, Gustav Wag-

* Pavelić was badly wounded in a 1957 assassination attempt in Buenos Aires, and died from complications from his wounds two years later in the German Hospital in Madrid, Spain. As for Draganović, he stunned everyone by turning up at a Belgrade press conference in 1967 and praising Tito's communist government. He lived there until his 1983 death. The debate over whether he voluntarily defected, or had possibly always been a communist double agent, or even whether he was kidnapped by Yugoslavian intelligence, remains heated among historians.[58]

ner, "The Beast." He had earned a dreaded reputation for his extreme sadism. (Stangl was captured in Brazil in 1967 and died in a West German prison of a heart attack in 1971. Hudal sent Wagner to Brazil, where he was arrested in 1978. A Brazilian court freed him, ruling that the German extradition request had "inaccuracies."[63] In October 1980, he was found dead in his São Paulo apartment with a knife in his chest. Wagner's attorney said it was a suicide, which Brazilian authorities accepted, but many suspected revenge by Nazi hunters.[64])

Hudal relied on several German-affiliated seminaries and rectories to house the crowd of Nazis. Some of the fugitives arrived disguised as monks.[65] As recounted by Stangl, every day they were woken at dawn and had to leave their safe houses. They got daily meal tickets for lunch at a kitchen run by nuns. And their only instruction was not to draw any attention to themselves until they returned each evening.[66]

SS Standartenführer Walter Rauff, who engineered the mobile gas vans that killed 97,000 Jews before the Nazis developed more efficient gas chambers, played OSS and church cards to escape justice. Rauff had represented the SS in secret 1944 negotiations (Operation Sunrise) with Dulles's OSS and the Wehrmacht to ensure that the German surrender in Italy would be orderly and not marked by victor's vengeance. When U.S. counterintelligence detained him after the war in northern Italy, Rauff threw about Dulles's name as if it alone would set him free. But his CIC investigators were unimpressed. The chief of the CIC concluded Rauff was "most uncooperative during interrogation . . . his contempt and everlasting malice toward the Allies [is] but lightly concealed. [Rauff] is considered a menace if ever set free, and failing actual elimination, is recommended for lifelong internment."[67] Rauff escaped. He later boasted, "I was helped by a Catholic priest to go to Rome."[68] Some historians believe Angleton sprang Rauff, through S-Force Verona, a joint American-British elite counterintelligence cell based in Italy.[69] Once free Rauff went underground, relying on Hudal's protection, and stayed ahead of his pursuers through the "convents of the Holy See" before fleeing for Syria.[70] In Syria, he served as an intelligence advisor to the country's military dictator. (Rauff ended up in Chile as an unofficial advisor to strongman Augusto Pinochet. He died there in 1984.)

Father Anton Weber, a Palatine priest in the St. Raphael Society, worked with Hudal. He processed the paperwork for Adolf Eichmann, the SS officer in charge of all the trains that carried Jews to Poland's extermination centers. While Weber prepared the paperwork, Eichmann was sheltered at a monastery under the jurisdiction of Genoa's Archbishop Giuseppe Siri.[71]

During the war, Pius had charged Weber with responsibility for saving Rome's baptized Jews. He estimated that of the twenty thousand Jews in wartime Rome, about three thousand were baptized. The Vatican saved only two to three hundred.[72] In contrast, after the war, Weber, Hudal, and others saved many more Nazis.[73] When confronted decades later by a journalist, Weber admitted the difference was that he tried to filter out the Jews who pretended to be converts. He did not even do a cursory exam to spot the Nazis. "They [Jews] were all claiming to be Catholics. . . . I made them recite the Lord's Prayer, and the Ave Maria; that proved in a hurry who was genuine and who wasn't."[74] As for the fugitives he helped, "We really didn't know the people we aided. At least, we knew nothing beyond what they themselves told us. . . . How on earth could I know that he was someone else?"[75]

"It was curious that Catholic priests kept helping me on my journey," Eichmann recalled years later. "They helped me without asking any questions."[76]*

Were priests such as Draganović, Hudal, and Weber lone wolves who took advantage of the Vatican's humanitarian postwar bureaucracy and abused it for their own perverted motivations, or did the church's effort to save war criminals proceed with the blessing of its highest officials, including Pius?

Draganović was in fact aided by some of the church's top prelates. His benefactors included Monsignor Montini and Cardinal Angelo dell'Acqua, in the Secretariat of State; Cardinal Pietro Fumasoni-Biondi, who ran the Vatican's intelligence service as Prefect of the Congregazione de Propaganda Fide; and Genoa's powerful Archbishop Giuseppe Siri, an avid anticommunist who considered the Ustašans reliable allies in the fight against bolshevism. Those clerics, as did Pius, embraced the prospect that one day a revived Ustaša might topple Tito and return Catholicism to power in Croatia.[78]

From 1945 to 1947, while Draganović ran his ratline, Pius and his Secretary of State's office peppered the Allies to reclassify detained Ustašans from their status as hostile prisoners of war to something more benign. The church

* Weber and other clerical helpers for Hudal did sometimes baptize Protestant SS fugitives as Catholics. Although that was in violation of canon law, the priests liked that the men they saved were now members of the Roman church.[77]

hoped that a milder classification might result in their freedom or at least prevent their extradition to Tito's Yugoslavia.[79] At Draganović's urging, Pius appealed to release some Croatians from a POW camp under British control. The British Foreign Office bristled at the Vatican's interference and rejected the church's request.[80]

In January 1947, Yugoslavia insisted the British arrest five ranking Croatian fugitives hiding in the Pontifical Institute of Oriental Studies. Although the institute was outside the territorial walls of Vatican City, Article 16 of the 1929 Lateran Treaty specifically gave it full extraterritoriality.[81] In a flurry of urgent cables, the British debated what to do. "We would arrest and surrender these men if they were anywhere else in Italy than the Vatican," wrote one Foreign Office official.[82] Having spent the war inside the Vatican, British envoy Sir D'Arcy Osborne knew the Pope and top clerics as well as any other Western diplomat. He knew that Pius would be outraged at any hint of infringing on the church's territorial status. Osborne convinced the Yugoslavians to ask the Vatican directly for the men's extradition. He also tried to persuade the church that the British had "no doubt" about the guilt of the five men, and warned that should Pius refuse to return the Croatians it would reinforce a growing international perception that Vatican officials were the "deliberate protectors of Hitler's and Mussolini's ex-minions."[83] Papal officials ignored the Yugoslavian extradition requests.

Monsignor Tardini tried placating the Allies. He told Osborne, "the Pope had recently issued strict orders to all ecclesiastical institutions in Rome that they were not to entertain guests, i.e. harbour fugitives, without higher authority."[84] Instead of soothing the Allies' irritation, Tardini's response prompted concerns that the micromanaging Pius might have taken personal control of which fugitives received safe haven.

"I do not believe for a moment," wrote Osborne to the Foreign Office, "that the Pope would give the order for their surrender."[85]

Three weeks later when Tardini again met with Osborne, he informed the British envoy that there was nothing the church could do. He claimed the five wanted Ustašans were no longer at the Pontifical Institute. A frustrated Osborne addressed Yugoslavian complaints that Draganović—with the assistance of Monsignor Montini's Pontifical Commission of Assistance—was flagrantly using the San Girolamo seminary as a way station to send war criminals to Argentina.[86]

Tardini was nonplussed. Monsignor Montini's Pontifical Commission had "nothing to do with the Secretariat of State" so unfortunately the monsignor could be of no assistance.[87]

Beyond the Ustašan criminals, did the Pope know about Hudal's energetic work to save Nazis? Decades later, when the revelations about Hudal's ratline came tumbling out in declassified government files, the Vatican tried distancing Pius from Hudal.

There is no question that Hudal and Pius knew each other from when Pius was the Nuncio to Germany. Pius performed the celebratory Mass to mark Hudal's appointment as a bishop in 1933. One cleric dates their friendship as far back as 1924 when the two were at a Vatican celebration for the Austrian ambassador.[88] Pius's key German advisors—Father Robert Leiber, Augustin Bea, and Monsignor Bruno Wüstenberg—were unquestionably friends with Hudal.

Still, Pius's defenders say there is no evidence that Hudal ever told the Pope about the ratline. In 1977, in its only public statement on the matter, a deputy spokesman for the Vatican said about Hudal, "Generally the Vatican leaves this problem to the historians, because much time has passed and it's difficult to say what happened."[89]

It is uncontested that the indefatigable Monsignor Montini, who met with the Pontiff daily about all refugees' matters, supervised Hudal.[90] According to contemporaneous U.S. intelligence, Hudal gave "large compensation" to Draganović, further evidence the ratlines the two men ran symbiotically used many of the same sources for obtaining Red Cross passports, arranging travel, and even setting up jobs in safe haven countries.[91]

In 1947, when Eva Perón, the wife of Argentine strongman Juan Perón, arrived in Rome as part of a European tour, Pius XII gave her a state reception. "Evita" also met with Bishop Hudal, and with Draganović at a reception hosted by the Italian government at the Rome Golf Club. An informant later reported to CIC officer William Gowen that Draganović and Perón discussed visas and Croatian emigration to Argentina.[92] Buenos Aires was the port of choice for war criminals processed through both ratlines. U.S. intelligence had concluded that Buenos Aires's archbishop, Antonio Caggiano—a close Perón ally—was a conduit between the Italian escape networks and the South American church.[93]

The same year as the Perón visit, American counterintelligence concluded that the Vatican as an institution—not merely as a group of scattered, rogue clerics—was helping high-ranking Nazis escape justice.[94] The report singled out Hudal, named twenty-one Vatican relief organizations suspected of assisting fugitives, and even exposed how easy it was for them to get fake travel papers. That explosive document kicked off a heated debate inside the U.S. State Department about how best to respond.[95]

Unknown to State Department officials, by the time of that classified report, the Cold Warriors in charge of U.S. and British intelligence had struck a secret deal with the church to share its ratlines.[96] The Americans and British were racing against the Soviets to scoop up the best Nazi intelligence agents and rocket scientists.[97] The partnership with the Vatican worked well. SS officer Klaus Barbie—nicknamed the "Butcher of Lyon"—gave the British and Americans crucial information about the network of informants he had developed in occupied France. Once they had what they needed, the OSS handed Barbie over to Draganović at a Genoa railway station and paid the Croatian priest to get Barbie to South America.[98] By putting Barbie and others into the Vatican's ratline, the intelligence services created an additional layer of deniability for their own postwar utilization of the Nazis. And the church benefited. Both British and American intelligence promised to protect the Vatican in case any other Allied government division started an investigation. The OSS, for instance, ensured that the report like the one that arrived at the State Department was shelved. And it kept from the diplomats any knowledge of Bishop Hudal's 1948 request to Juan Perón for five thousand visas for "anti-Bolshevik" German soldiers.[99] The CIA picked up the costs for running Draganović's ratline through 1951.[100]

Pius's obsession with communism made the Vatican a predictable Cold War ally. In men like Winston Churchill, Harry Truman, J. Edgar Hoover, and the Dulles brothers, Pius XII found that the British and American leadership embraced his anticommunist worldview.[101] Pius printed and distributed copies of Churchill's 1946 Iron Curtain speech. The Pope used the same hard-line rhetoric during some of his own talks to the faithful, referring to Catholics as "soldiers prepared for battle" with international communism.[102] In June 1947, the U.S. announced the Marshall Plan, the massive American financial commitment to rebuild Europe. The Soviets condemned it as a blatant attempt to spread U.S. hegemony over Western Europe. The Vatican's support was unqualified.[103] No one but a handful of insiders knew that hidden inside the Marshall Plan was what New York's Cardinal Spellman dubbed "black currency," covert funds—some of which came from captured Nazi assets—to help the church offset anything it spent to help defeat the communists in the Italian national elections set for 1948.[104]

The dominant role the United States played in the Allied victory tilted the political balance of power away from Europe and toward America. A similar dynamic played out inside the church. The Vatican's core theological and political conservatives aligned themselves with America. Church leaders believed that the U.S. shared Christian values and that the war victory confirmed a new American century. The American branch of the church had an unparalleled fundraising capability. It raised more donations for the Pope than the next dozen countries combined. Preeminent among the U.S. prelates was New York's Cardinal Spellman. Friendly with almost every key U.S. political power broker, Spellman was anticommunist and worked hard to arrange support among U.S. institutions for the church's covert role in the first postwar Italian balloting. Upon returning from a visit to Rome, Spellman shared with friends that Pius was "extremely worried about the election results, and in fact had little hope of a success for anti-Communist parties."[105] The Curia dreaded a "disastrous failure at the polls which will put Italy behind the Iron Curtain," noted a Vatican emissary, Bishop James Griffiths.[106]

In the year leading up to Italy's elections, Pius and President Harry Truman exchanged a series of letters, some of which leaked to the press before the election. Those letters cemented the Washington-Vatican alliance. Over domestic Protestant protests, Truman dispatched Myron Taylor back to the Vatican as the President's personal representative. And Spellman—mocked as "the American Pope" by some Italian clerics—arranged a series of fall visits to the Vatican for eighteen U.S. senators and forty-eight congressmen.[107] Some Vatican diplomats, such as France's Jacques Maritain, resigned, protesting that Pius's obsession with communism and his alignment with the United States had made him far too partisan.

Pius ignored that critique as well as the Lateran Pacts' prohibition against the church being involved in politics. He hoped that the relationships formed then put into play elements that would safeguard the Vatican for decades to come. If the communists won the election, Pius had decided to emulate Pius IX and become a prisoner Pope, never venturing outside Vatican City so long as the reds were in power.[108]

The church revived Catholic Action—the lay social organization that Mussolini had shuttered—and it organized Italian voters across the country. The CIA sent in millions in covert aid and used the fear inside the Vatican to cement a firmer relationship with the ranking prelates who ran the city-state.[109]* James Angleton, William Colby, and a support team (the Special Procedures Group) handpicked by Allen Dulles, orchestrated a campaign that mixed together propaganda and political sabotage (the lessons learned in that election became the template for helping handpicked candidates win in other countries).[111] With some of the U.S. money, Monsignor Montini directed a campaign slush fund through the Vatican Bank.[112] And the Vatican encouraged priests to condemn bolshevism from their pulpits and to remind worshippers that Catholicism and communism were incompatible. The Pope even gave a remarkably partisan pre-election speech, calling the vote "the great hour of Christian conscience."[113]

It marked the church's greatest role in secular politics since the mid-nineteenth century when it controlled the Papal States.[114] In April 1948, 90 percent of eligible Italians went to the polls.[115] The Pope had backed the right side. The conservative Christian Democrats crushed the left-wing Popular Democratic Front.[116]

The new Prime Minister, Alcide De Gasperi, an antifascist who had hidden inside the Vatican during the war while working as a librarian, embraced the country's concordat with the church.[117] The communists had vowed to repudiate all the church's special treatment. De Gasperi reaffirmed Mussolini's financial pact with the Vatican, including its tax-free status and complete independence from any Italian scrutiny regarding its financial affairs.

In May 1949, *Look* asked Spellman to write a cover story titled "The Pope's War on Communism." He wrote that Pius had "embarked on a spiritual crusade against the atheistic philosophies of Communist Russia. . . . [the Pope's] armies are the God-loving peoples of the earth."[118] Two months later, Pius announced that he would excommunicate any Catholic who "defend[ed] and

---

* During the run-up to the 1948 election, the CIA laid the groundwork for its alliance with Intermarium (Between the Seas), a strong Catholic lay organization composed primarily of Eastern European exiles. At least half a dozen of Intermarium's chief officers were later identified as former Nazi collaborators. Draganović was the Croatian representative on its ruling council. With the help of the CIA, Intermarium morphed into Radio Free Europe. MI6, the British equivalent of the CIA, funneled money through the Vatican Bank to a related anticommunist group, the Anti-Bolshevik Bloc of Nations.[110]

spread the materialistic and anti-Christian doctrine of Communism." The church's harshest punishment now applied to anyone who even read communist newspapers or literature. The Holy See insisted the notice be posted in churches worldwide.[119] Other Vatican officials followed Pius's lead. Cardinal Tisserant decreed that communists could no longer receive Christian burials. And the cardinals of Milan and Palermo banned communists from confession or receiving absolution. In contrast to Pius's laissez-faire attitude during the war, when it came to whether Catholicism was incompatible with Nazi Party membership, in the postwar the Pope was unequivocal: it was not possible to be a Catholic and a communist.

13

"He's No Pope"

As Draganović and Hudal ran the Vatican ratlines and Pius and his cardinals waged war on communism, Nogara fine-tuned the IOR. The church was poised to benefit from the emerging new order of the Cold War. Many of Nogara's worst fears had been realized by the ravaged conditions in postwar Europe. Industrial production had plummeted. Unemployment had soared. There were more than eight million displaced persons.[1] A quarter of all German urban housing was destroyed, and the country's gross domestic product had dropped off by an astonishing 70 percent.[2]

The 1948 Christian Democrat election victory did lift Nogara's mood since it put a stop to the communist threat to nationalize many industries. That would have wiped out huge Vatican investments and committed leftists would have replaced the church's proxies on the boards of major firms.[3] Although Nogara was confident the IOR could have survived nationalization, he knew it would have resulted in stunning short-term losses.

Nogara turned seventy-eight a couple of months after the election. That his health was good and mind sharp had not prevented him from preparing for the day he was no longer at the Vatican. He had assembled a small team of trusted clerics and laymen. Monsignor Alberto di Jorio had worked with him longer than any other cleric. Di Jorio was the secretary to the IOR's three-cardinal oversight commission (which did little more than review annually a single-page summary of the bank's activities).[4] Its chief was Nicola Canali, one of the prelates who had investigated Nogara when Pius XII first became Pope. Canali was also tasked with oversight of the Special Administration, responsible for the property the church received from the Lateran Pacts. Unofficially called the Minister of Finances, he was an adept Curia politician.[5] Nogara liked Canali because he was a strict disciplinarian. Bernardino felt he would ensure that the IOR and Special Administration never veered far from their profitable course.[6] Nogara did not, however, pin his hope for the future of Vatican finances on the clerics. He put his faith in a handful of younger laymen.

Papal Count Carlo Pacelli was one of three of Pius XII's nephews at the Vatican. He was the city-state's General Counsel. During the war Nogara had relied on him for nuanced advice about the IOR's international deals.[7] Not only did Pacelli have Bernardino's ear, but he was one of the few lay officials with whom the Pope met regularly.[8]

Nogara had personally asked Massimo Spada to join the Vatican's financial department in 1929. Spada, who was then a stockbroker, had never heard of the Administration of the Works of Religion. Nogara told him it acted as a quasi-bank in administering the deposits of religious institutes and ecclesiastical charities.[9] That was enough for Spada, whose pedigree was sterling. His great-grandfather had been the private banker to a leading Black Noble, Prince di Civitella-Cesi Torlonia. Spada's grandfather was a Bank of Italy director, and his father had been the chief of a foreign exchange agency that did business with the church. With his trademark charcoal gray double-breasted suits and high-waisted trousers, Spada was a familiar sight around the Vatican. He had become a favorite of senior prelates after he led the fight to fend off an unfriendly takeover of the IOR-controlled Banca Cattolica del Veneto.[10] By the end of the war, he was the IOR's Administrative Secretary, the highest ranking layman behind Nogara.[11]

Luigi Mennini, the father of fourteen children, was a savvy private banker whom Nogara had also asked to work at the IOR.[12] He had become Spada's most trusted advisor.[13] Raffaele Quadrani, who had spent a couple of years at banks in Paris and London, was another early hire by Nogara. Bernardino's brother, Bartolomeo, the director of the Vatican Museum, had recommended him.[14]

Geneva-based Credit Suisse banker Henri de Maillardoz was another of the first foreign bankers Nogara had trusted with church investments.[15] The urbane and aloof Maillardoz had known Nogara since 1925.[16] He was responsible for the decision to consolidate some of the church's European gold reserves at his former employer Credit Suisse. When Nogara battled the Allies over their blacklisting of Sudameris, he dispatched Maillardoz to Washington in November 1942 to appeal to Treasury officials.[17] By the end of the war, Pius had given him an honorary noble rank, Marquis, and he had become the Secretary to the Special Administration and a special consultant to Bernardino.[18] Maillardoz was the banker whose visit to the Vatican in the early 1930s caused alarm for Cardinal Domenico Tardini. Tardini had feared that the mere presence of a Swiss banker presaged that Nogara was about to engage in prohibited financial speculation.[19]

The battles over the permissible scope of Nogara's work were now distant memories. There were few restraints on where to invest except any that the IOR might place on itself. Nogara and his team knew the Balkans and Eastern Europe were off-limits so long as Soviet puppet governments controlled them. Western Europe—cloaked under the American nuclear umbrella—was as safe as it had ever been. But they reached a consensus that the best investment was into the country they knew best—Italy. In light of the Christian Democrat victory, and the country's firm alliance with America, they concluded it was a rare opportunity. Italy, without doubt, was in the same poor state as the rest of Europe, mired in recession, inflation, and unemployment. But the Vatican team was confident that the Marshall Plan's massive influx of billions would fuel a reconstruction boom and kick-start the stagnant economy. Many good Italian companies were available at fire-sale prices, their stock prices having been battered.

Nogara's first significant postwar investments were in the construction industry, which he thought would be first to rebound since ravaged cities and demolished infrastructure needed rebuilding. In 1949, the church bought 15 percent of Società Generale Immobiliare (SGI), one of the country's oldest construction and real estate holding companies (it would acquire a controlling share over several years).[20] The IOR next took a stake in an ailing cement maker, Italcementi.[21]

Widespread hunger coupled with agricultural disruptions had led to food shortages and dramatic spikes in the prices of basic commodities. The Vatican invested in the food processing and farming industries.[22] Nogara became chairman of one of Italy's largest agrarian societies and the church bought stakes in expansive communes and four dominant agricultural companies. The communists would later charge that the church had a monopoly control of fertilizer and had used it to exploit Italy's farmers and reap outsized profits.[23]

The IOR expanded beyond those sectors with investments in Italian blue-chip companies, including Italgas (natural gas), Società Finanziaria Telefonica (telecommunications), Finelettrica (electric utility), Finmeccanica (defense contractor), and Montecatini (chemicals).[24] Nogara also scooped up four failing textile companies at bargain prices (Volpi, from his Swiss exile in 1947, had recommended the companies to Monsignor di Jorio as good long-term prospects).[25] Nogara merged the four companies into a new firm, SNIA Viscosa.[26]

Confident that any recovery would include the financial sector, Nogara's team went on a buying binge of Italian banks. By 1950 the IOR owned a share or had a majority interest in seventy-nine of the country's banks, ranging from enormous holding companies like the Allied-backed Mediobanca to small regional credit unions.[27] No other investor owned a more significant postwar share in Italian finance than the church. Some of Nogara's investments, such as Italcementi, turned into additional equity in the financial sector as it formed its own holding company and acquired banks starting in the 1960s.

But Nogara wanted more than investments.[28] He also sought a say in how the companies were run. Sizable investments were conditioned on obtaining at least one seat on the board of directors. Enrico Galeazzi (later a Papal Count) was the Vatican's chief architect, a close friend of Cardinal Spellman, and part of Pius XII's kitchen cabinet. Nogara tapped Galeazzi to be one of the Vatican's directors at SGI, the Bank of Rome, Credito Italiano, and insurance giant RAS. Marcantonio Pacelli, another Pius XII nephew, was on the board of many companies, including SGI. Giulio Pacelli, yet another nephew, was also on numerous boards, including Italgas and BCI bank. Carlo Presenti, president of two important banks, became the church's director at Italcementi. And in return, Presenti picked Massimo Spada to be a director and vice president for his banks. Nogara asked to be a director on those companies he either considered challenging turnaround candidates or those with which he had long relationships, among them chemical giant Montecatini, hydroelectric conglomerate SIP, real estate consortium Generale Immobiliare, and the water pipeline supplier, Società Italiana per Condotte d'Acqua.[29] Those placements on top corporate boards meant the Vatican played a historic role in commercial businesses that would have been unthinkable just a few decades earlier.

By 1950, Spada was emblematic of the tangled relationship between the Vatican and Italy's private sector. He was a chairman or director of more than thirty companies, including insurance giants Generali and RAS (the Vatican had reinvested in both), Banco di Roma, Mediobanca, Finelettrica, Italmobiliare, Finmeccanica, and Italcementi.[30] "The Italian stock market is controlled by about 20 financial companies of such interwoven ownership that their directors answer mainly to themselves," noted *Time* in a story about Italy's incestuous finances.[31]*

The guessing game at the Vatican was which of the men who had worked for Nogara would succeed him. Before the war, there had been widespread speculation that the House of Morgan's Giovanni Fummi would be his replacement. The patrician Fummi had represented Volpi, the Vatican, and most of Italy's aristocrats. But Nogara had lived long enough that Fummi, only a year younger, was now himself too old.

Laying the groundwork for his eventual successor, starting in the early 1950s, Nogara formed a trust of Catholic financial advisors. The new consultants were informally dubbed *uomini di fiducia*, men of confidence.[33] Popes had long used Black Nobles to assist them in business. Bernardino had for decades relied on his own close circle of confidants, men like Fummi and Volpi, trusted advisors and sometimes partners. Nogara envisioned that the men of confidence would meld the best traits from the Black Nobles and his own clique of advisors. He decreed they should be top bankers or financiers, selected for their loyalty and ability. And he thought it important that they did not work for the church, hoping their independence might free them of the stifling Curia bureaucracy and crippling power wars. Nogara's first selections were two of Pius's nephews, Giulio and Marcantonio Pacelli.[34]

Despite his advanced age and a promise to curtail his workload, Nogara was still a director or managing director at a dozen of Italy's largest companies.[35] And when challenged inside the Curia by another power broker, he demonstrated he was adept at protecting his turf. In 1953, he clashed with Monsignor Giovanni Montini.[36] The two had tangled since the war. Montini had lobbied Pius to get the Vatican Bank—the only accessible source of foreign

* Volpi had thought it would take a generation to rebuild the war-ravaged Italian insurance industry. But the Allies wanted all of the industries, including insurance, revived faster because of the Cold War. Restarting the private sector in Italy and Germany was the best way to ensure that the communist parties in those countries could not make gains by exploiting terrible tales of postwar poverty and economic paralysis. The Allies relinquished oversight of private industry to the Italians in 1947; Generali was up and running just months later, with all of its assets reinsured by American companies. Although the U.S. military command complained that the new Generali leadership consisted of some hard-core fascists, it no longer had the jurisdiction to do anything about it.[32]

currency—to aid his huge refugee efforts.[37] Bernardino did not like the IOR playing a passive role in programs over which it did not have full control. Now, decades later, what had been a simmering enmity broke into the open. Montini complained to colleagues that it was an error to allow a layman—even such a talented one—to gain so much power. And he asked why Nogara did not just concentrate on the IOR and his Special Administration instead of meddling elsewhere in the Curia. The monsignor also charged that the rising stature of Pius's nephews, under Nogara's sponsorship, smacked of nepotism.[38]

Nogara, and others—chiefly Sister Pascalina—who were not fans of Montini, made their rebuttal directly to Pius.[39] In a 1953 consistory, the Pope appointed twenty-one new cardinals.[40] Montini was on everyone's shortlist. But Pius stunned Vaticanologists by not giving Montini a red hat.[41] And the following year, the Pope settled the increasing backbiting between Montini and Nogara by elevating Montini as an archbishop and dispatching him to run Milan. Since Milan was the largest archdiocese in Italy, a cardinal was traditionally in charge.[42] The slight was clear. The seventy-eight-year-old Pope had ensured that Montini would not be his successor.[43]

In 1954, the same year Montini was sent to Milan, Nogara selected Henri de Maillardoz as the IOR's Delegato.[44] It was the position that only Nogara had held since the bank's 1942 inception. Maillardoz, who had in his private career overseen Credit Suisse's industrial portfolio, felt at home in his new role. Bernardino remained at the Vatican during the transition. It took two years, until 1956, before Nogara felt his hand-selected team was ready to move forward. He retired at the age of eighty-six, but reminded his colleagues that he lived in a nearby Vatican-owned home and would be pleased to consult.[45]

During his twenty-seven-year tenure Nogara had revolutionized the world of Vatican finances. With the full backing of two Popes, he had successively defeated the entrenched Curia traditionalists and transformed the church from a primitive financial institution into a savvy international holding company with its own central bank. By the time of his departure, the intense arguments about whether the Bible prevented the church from playing any role in financial speculation seemed archaic. Nogara's Special Administration was as capitalist as any Wall Street investment bank. In the eleven years since the end of World War II, his postwar concentration in Italian industry had proven an inspired investment. SNIA Viscosa was now Italy's largest and most profitable textile company. SGI had become an international conglomerate with gigantic construction projects on five continents, and had taken ownership interests in dozens of related companies. Montecatini had tripled in size and expanded into electric power and pharmaceuticals. Italgas had gone from a small regional utility to the country's largest natural gas provider.[46]

Nogara had also tended to his two sons, Paolo and Giovanni. Paolo was the chairman of two Vatican-owned companies, the Montefluoro mining firm, and later Ceramica Pozzi, a ceramics firm.[47] Giovanni ran an IOR-controlled metals firm, Pertusola, and was a director of the Tarvisio travel conglomerate.[48] Like his father, Giovanni was an engineer and also served as the director general of the mining company, Predil, in which the IOR had also invested.[49]

The eighty-year-old Pius was himself frail by the time of Nogara's departure. Pius had never seemed robust so it was sometimes difficult to be certain whether the Pontiff was as sick as he appeared. A bad gastrointestinal infection—"constant vomiting and nausea," recalled Sister Pascalina—over the Christmas holidays in 1954 had taken its toll.[50] Now Vaticanologists debated the state of his health. Ricardo Galeazzi-Lisi, an eye specialist, had been Pius's chief physician since 1939. He was the doctor Pius trusted to examine the "bones of St. Peter" in 1942. Aside from Pascalina, many insiders were wary of Galeazzi-Lisi and his self-made tonics and herbal remedies.[51] His botched treatment of Pius's gum problems with chromic acid—used in tanning hides—led to esophageal complications that now plagued the Pope with chronic hiccups.[52]* And it was Galeazzi-Lisi, and Pascalina, who had vouched for Paul Niehans, a Swiss physician who administered "living cell therapy," injections that consisted of chopped fetuses from freshly slaughtered ewes. Many in the Vatican did not like that Niehans was an ordained Protestant minister, and traditionalists objected to his use of animal fetuses for his injectable tonic. But Pius liked him and dismissed accounts that some Niehans patients had suffered seizures after the injections. Pius even appointed him to the prestigious Pontifical Academy of Sciences.[54]

---

* No one inside the Vatican knew that Galeazzi-Lisi was a secret source of information about the Pope's health and sometimes even some general church gossip for newspapers and magazines. Many had him on a regular retainer. Paul Hoffman, then a junior reporter at *The New York Times* Rome desk, dropped off the doctor's "retainer fee in an envelope" at his central Rome office. "On the phone he always introduced himself as 'Dick' . . . because the Vatican phones were being tapped by the papal police," Hoffman later wrote. The *Times* "didn't know at the time that he was receiving more such envelopes from other clients."[53]

During one particularly bad bout of sickness, Pius asked Niehans: "Tell me the truth, do you seriously believe that I shall recover completely and be able to fulfill my duties fully? If not, I shall not hesitate to resign." Niehans assured Pius he would get better.[55] It was not until 1955, after Pius almost died from an infection, that two Italian doctors gathered enough evidence challenging Niehans's claims and safety record to convince Pius to bar him from further visiting the Vatican.[56] But as his health worsened, Pius changed his mind, and by 1958 Niehans had returned to the Pope's private chambers.[57]

Pius now said he "was ready to go to heaven."[58] Italian newspapers added to the sense that something was amiss when they reported about Pius's self-described hallucinations. In one he saw a Fatima-like replica of the sun spinning in the sky, and in another Jesus appeared in his bedroom to assure him that his reign was not yet over.[59] The declaration to have seen the Son of God was the first by a Pope in a thousand years.[60] Some skeptics thought by claiming divine visions, Pius was campaigning for his posthumous ascent to sainthood. Others thought it was further evidence that illness and age had taken their toll.

The laymen who had inherited the IOR and Special Administration steered clear of any backroom chatter about the Pope. They knew that whatever the state of Pius's health, given his advanced age it was only a matter of time until there was a new Pope. Since most of them had never worked under any other Pontiff, that prospect alone created considerable angst.[61]

Despite all the grim speculation about Pius's health, many insiders were still surprised and saddened when they learned that the Pope had suffered a massive stroke on October 6, 1958. His shortcomings and peculiarities aside, he had led the church through difficult times. During his nineteen-year reign, he had promoted the Papacy as a position of unrivaled central power, a divine monarch who was a throwback to the boldest Popes from earlier generations. Three days after his stroke, the Pontiff died of what the Vatican called a "circulatory phenomenon."[62]

The conclave that began gathering was different from the one that had elected Pius in 1939. Pacelli had then been the odds-on favorite. The vote that made him Pope was the fastest in three hundred years. There was no frontrunner now. And much to the consternation of the Vatican, the press for the first time speculated about the conclave as if it were a secular political campaign. Even Spellman was mentioned as a leading candidate. He had no chance. He had far too many enemies in the Curia, who coined *Spellmanism* to refer to a condition in which someone had too large an ego and too obvious an ambition.[63]

Once the conclave began, the eighty cardinals—twenty-nine of whom were Italian—split into ideological camps. Pius's successors were the conservatives, strong anticommunists and authoritarians who believed in an all-powerful Papacy. They coalesced around Genoa's Cardinal Giuseppe Siri, the prelate whose archdiocese was where the Croatian priest Draganović had run one of his ratlines. The progressives wanted to reduce the church's partisan Cold War role and were amenable to some modernist reforms. They were split among several candidates, with Bologna's Cardinal Giacomo Lercaro having the seeming momentum.[64]

The divisions among the cardinals became evident to the crowds packing St. Peter's Square. Over three days, black smoke—indicating no Pope had been selected—poured ten times from the smokestack erected over their meeting hall. White smoke followed on the eleventh ballot. The divided conclave's compromise? Venetian Patriarch Angelo Roncalli, one month shy of his seventy-seventh birthday.[65] No one over seventy had been selected Pope in more than two hundred years.[66] They had coalesced around him as a short-term caretaker.

The congenial, pudgy Roncalli was the physical antithesis to his reserved and isolated predecessor. Although Roncalli had been on no one's shortlist, he believed he was a serious contender. When his election was announced inside the conclave, he pulled from the pocket of his vestment a long acceptance speech he had written in Latin.[67] As for his Papal name, he surprised his colleagues by announcing without any hesitation it would be John, a name all Popes had avoided since the last John had been a divisive antipope in 1410 (Roncalli was fond of it because it was the name of the parish church in which he was baptized).[68]

In the first twenty-four hours of his Papacy Roncalli demonstrated that he did not intend to be a caretaker only. At the end of the conclave he had placed the red hat on Monsignor Alberto di Jorio, the chief prelate responsible for the IOR. Di Jorio had been the conclave's secretary, and by elevating him to cardinal, Roncalli reinstated the practice that two Popes had abandoned. And no sooner had he donned his Papal vestments than he announced that Monsignor Domenico Tardini would be his Secretary of State, filling a position left open by Pius for fourteen years.[69]

Roncalli was the third of thirteen children—the eldest son—from a poor sharecropper family in the northern Italian village of Sotto Il Monte. His parents enrolled him in a local seminary when he was only eleven. A priest added some prestige to a family. It also meant one fewer mouth to feed. At nineteen, he won a scholarship to study at Rome's Accademia dei Nobili, a seminary that was a recruiting ground for the Curia. The Bishop of Bergamo picked him to be his personal secretary, a ten-year period that was broken when Roncalli was drafted as a chaplain into the Italian army during World War I. By 1925, Pius XI appointed him an archbishop and he got the first of his assignments, to Turkey, as a Nuncio. Greece and France followed.*

When it came to World War II and the question of the Holocaust, he was different from his predecessor. Roncalli had so often urged Secretary of State Maglione to convince the Pope to speak out about the Nazi atrocities that Maglione complained to his colleagues in Rome about Roncalli's persistence.[71] In 1944, Franz von Papen, the German ambassador to Turkey, approached Roncalli, who was then the Nuncio in Istanbul. Papen said that if the Pope condemned Hitler, a group of German patriots would negotiate a truce with the Allies. When the Nuncio sent Papen's offer to the Vatican, Pius and Maglione dismissed it, believing that Roncalli was unsophisticated and easily duped by the Germans, who might be setting a trap for the Pope.[72]

The moment of truth came in late spring of 1944. Roncalli was the first ranking church official to receive a copy of the Auschwitz Protocols, the bone-chilling May report of two Slovak Jews who had escaped the death camp. That document left little doubt the Nazis were preparing their largest death camp to receive Hungary's Jews.[73] He sent it by diplomatic pouch to the Vatican. When Ira Hirschmann, the War Refugee Board's representative, approached Roncalli that summer, the Nazis had started the massive Hungarian deportations. He asked Hirschmann whether the Hungarian Jews might be willing to be baptized, "only to save their lives . . . not really to convert, you understand."[74] Hirschmann said yes. Two weeks later Roncalli confirmed that he had sent "thousands of baptismal certificates" to the Papal Nuncio in Buda-

* In 1944, Roncalli received a coded cable in Istanbul informing him of his appointment as the Nuncio to liberated Paris. Incredulous, he rushed to Rome. He met with Monsignor Tardini in the Secretary of State's office. "Are you mad?" he asked. "How could you think of asking me to take such a difficult post?" The normally voluble Tardini looked at him quietly for a moment before responding: "You may be sure all of us here were more surprised than you."[70]

pest. That simple act saved more Jews over a couple of months than all of Pius's dithering during six years of war.

When Pius XII finally made him a cardinal in 1953, most had thought his red hat was an award for longevity and loyalty, not because his career was distinguished. As opposed to Montini or Siri, Roncalli had no powerful Curial backers nor had he formed any alliances that promoted his candidacy. No one thought of him as predestined for the Papacy.[75] What did stand out throughout his earlier service was that he had earned a reputation as being likable. Wherever he served, the jocund, grandfatherly Roncalli was popular with ordinary Catholics.[76] Although no one then realized the significance of it, he was assuming the Papacy during the early days of television. Roncalli would be the first Pope seen by tens of millions of the faithful through their TV sets. It was an ideal medium for his personality.

Although Roncalli had mustered the necessary votes to become Pope, some questioned his ability to lead the church. Sister Pascalina groused he was not worthy of succeeding Pius. The new Pope responded the day after his election by barring Pascalina from entering her apartment, which adjoined his quarters. She was told to leave the Vatican. Before she departed, a longtime Curial foe, Cardinal Tisserant, confronted her and demanded to know why she had burned three overstuffed hampers filled with documents belonging to Pius XII. "The Holy Father ordered everything to be burned and it has been."[77] Some of the papers had been drafts of speeches he had written over his two decades as Pope. She did not know, however, all the contents and she did not think it her place to look inside.

Tisserant was furious. "Do you realize that you have burned a great treasure?"

"We know that better than anyone, but it was an order of the Holy Father's, who was sacrosanct to us throughout his life and is no less so after his death."[78]

No one besides Tisserant seemed too concerned that Pascalina had destroyed thousands of pages of Pius's personal papers. Everyone was instead focused on Roncalli. "He's no Pope," the outspoken Spellman told some colleagues upon returning to New York. "He should be selling bananas."[79] Spellman failed to see in Roncalli the talent necessary to be a great sovereign. The New York cardinal and other traditionalists believed ordinary Catholics wanted a royal Papacy. Pius's reign marked the zenith of that monarchal power. Roncalli would strip away much of the imperial Papacy, ending everything from the five-hour-long coronation to the requirement that lay Catholics kneel in his presence or that his staff remain mostly silent when around him.[80] Those who liked the new simplicity referred to the dramatic change in styles as "de-Stalinization in the Vatican."[81] But a Black Noble reflected the view of those who thought the reforms denigrated the office: "It looks as if this Pope is trying to introduce into the church some of that democracy which has been such a disaster everywhere else."[82]

Genoa's Cardinal Siri—the leading traditionalist candidate at the conclave—shared Spellman's concern that the congenial Roncalli did not have their passion as a Cold Warrior. The CIA had the same worries, concluding that Pope John was "politically naive and unduly influenced by the handful of 'liberal' clerics with whom he is in close contact."[83] The new Pope believed that the church should stay out of secular politics.[84] It was a sea change from Pius XII, who had played the tipping role in the 1948 national elections, allowing Catholic Action to mobilize votes, even personally attending to on-the-ground details such as busloads of nuns making their way on election day from convents to polling stations. John XXIII instead pulled the church back from its full partnership with the Christian Democrats. The new Pontiff did not see communism as a mortal threat. Spellman and Siri fretted that a passive role by the church created an opportunity for the Italian left to gain power.[85]

But before there was any chance to test John XXIII's credentials as a Cold Warrior, on November 15, only eleven days after his coronation, the eighty-eight-year-old Bernardino Nogara died of an apparent heart attack.[86] The news of his passing was mostly lost in the wake of the election of a new Pope, and rated only a few lines in a handful of newspapers.[87] Nogara's death was a watershed moment, however, for Maillardoz, Spada, and Mennini, who now ran the church's finances according to the template he had created.[88] They were apprehensive about Roncalli's election. Speculation was rampant about whether Roncalli would bring in his own loyalists for key positions (it did not help that when asked how many people worked in the Curia, the new Pope said, "About half").[89]

Only three months after taking office, John XXIII stunned everyone by calling for only the second Vatican Council in the church's two thousand–year history.[90] All its cardinals, scholars, and 2,500 bishops had to trek to Rome for wide-ranging discussions about possibly changing everything, including the liturgy, how bishops were selected, and streamlining and reducing the power of the Curia.[91] Although it would not start for three years, it confirmed the fear of Spellman, Siri, and others that the congenial John was at best unpredictable.[92]

But to the relief of Maillardoz, Spada, and Mennini, the new Pope did not tinker with the IOR and Special Administration. Vaticanologists interpreted di Jorio's elevation to cardinal as an endorsement of his oversight of the Vatican Bank. Even Pius's titled nephews retained their positions.

In sharp contrast to Pius, Pope John did not have a reputation as a micromanager. During his tenure as the cardinal of Venice he was known as an easygoing, hands-off overseer who had an aversion to administration and instead let capable assistants run the diocese's bureaucracy.[93] He was uncomfortable with finances and even in discussing money.[94] Maillardoz, Spada, and Mennini were on their own.

One of the first steps they took was to boost the IOR's reserves by taking advantage of Italy's need for land to host the 1960 summer Olympics. They sold some of the church's Roman real estate to the Italian National Olympic Committee. The church owned about 102 million square feet of property around Rome, making it not only the largest nongovernmental landowner, but also the only sovereign state on the planet that owned more property outside its borders than within.[95] The Vatican sold enough at premium prices so that Italy could build fifteen stadiums and complete the work on the Leonardo da Vinci–Fiumicino International Airport. There was criticism from the political left that the prices were too high. So when the government needed more land to build the Olympic Highway to connect the split sports complexes, the Vatican again profited but this time used a front company to provide the property.[96]

But the successors to Nogara were under no illusion. They realized the outsized gains earned from the frenzied Olympics preparations were a one-off event. They would have to apply Nogara's principles about steadily accumulating profits through conservative investments. They embraced Bernardino's belief that the future of the Vatican's finances lay with men of confidence. It was a decision that would lead Nogara's successful creation to the edge of ruin and in the process tarnish the Vatican itself.

14

The Men of Confidence

A few months before he died, Nogara met thirty-eight-year-old Michele Sindona, one of the country's preeminent tax attorneys. The lean, five-foot-ten Sindona had a widespread reputation for a rare combination of smarts and charm (a business colleague called him a "snake charmer in the business of seduction").[1] The Sicilian-born Sindona had made his reputation in Nogara's hometown of Milan, one of the few southern Italians to carve out such success in the country's elitist north. The eldest of two brothers born into a dirt-poor family in 1920, Sindona was a gifted student who won a full scholarship that helped lift him out of grinding poverty.[2] During World War II he learned enough English to work as a translator for the U.S. Command.[3] He also earned a law degree at the University of Messina and after a few years in the legal unit of Sicily's tax department, he moved north with his wife and daughter.[4] He boasted he spoke Italian without any accent that betrayed his southern roots, a plus in Milan, which offered business opportunities that matched the scope of his ambition.[5] It was there in 1950 that Sindona met Monsignor Amleto Tondini. Sindona's cousin Anna Rosa was married to the priest's younger brother.[6] Tondini was an admired Latinist, running the Secretariat of Briefs to Princes and of Latin Letters, a small Curia department responsible for Latin editions of Papal encyclicals and correspondence. He was also a close friend of Monsignor Montini, then still running the church's refugee efforts in Rome. Sindona and Tondini instantly liked each other.[7] To help the unassuming thirty-year-old attorney, who had a seemingly conservative approach to business, the monsignor suggested he consider doing some legal work for the Vatican.[8] Sindona was agreeable. Tondini wrote to Massimo Spada, by then titled a Prince by Pius XII, asking that Sindona be put on Spada's list for any legal services the IOR might require in Milan.[9]

When Spada met Sindona he thought the attorney was "young, skinny and nervous" but also "a stimulating conversationalist." He called the owners of Italy's largest textile industrial group and a giant electrical utility, both of which the Vatican had stakes in, and asked them to send some business to Sindona. The work did not turn out to be that much. But on occasional visits to Rome, Sindona stopped by the IOR and developed a good relationship with the men in charge. His break came in 1954 from outside the IOR. Soon after Pius surprised everyone by dispatching Montini to Milan, Monsignor Tondini introduced the new archbishop to the young lawyer. They had more in common than either might have expected. They shared conservative views on a broad range of social and political issues and were pleasantly surprised to discover a mutual dislike for fascism. Montini's father, a lawyer and journalist who had been elected to parliament three times, was known for his distaste for Mussolini.[10] When Sindona was attending university, he had refused to wear the military-style uniform Il Duce mandated for students. The school lowered his grade point average in punishment.[11] It was not long before Sindona boasted to friends and family about the bond the two men had formed.[12]

Montini told Sindona about his disappointment that the Milan to which he returned was an urban bastion of Italy's communist movement. The city was one of the few that had voted for the red ticket in the 1948 elections. And it had tilted even further left since then, with a remarkable 40 percent of its 3.5 million residents registered as communists.

Montini wanted to rally the working class for the church and its candidates. He decided to visit the area's mines, celebrate Mass in the city's blue-collar neighborhoods, and tour local factories. Pietro Secchia, a communist labor leader whose agenda had no room for an archbishop who might strike a populist chord, tried blocking him from offering Mass at the city's plants.[13] Montini turned to Sindona, whose fervent capitalism made him a natural anticommunist ally. Among his clients, Sindona counted owners of the city's major mills and factories. He and Montini soon stopped daily at the factories. Sindona and the archbishop tried convincing the workers that their best future was to be had by embracing capitalism and faith in God. Those visits had an impact. In a decisive vote the following year, Secchia lost control of his union to a conservative Christian Democrat rival.[14] Montini owed Sindona for having proven a well-connected and effective ally.[15]

The result for Sindona was a flurry of work from the IOR. His new services extended beyond Milan. He established more complicated legal structures for some of the church's foreign transactions. Spada also arranged for Sindona some work at two Vatican-controlled firms, Società Generale Immobiliare and SNIA Viscosa.[16]

In early 1959, shortly after Nogara's death, Montini—John XXIII had made him a cardinal just a few months earlier—summoned Sindona to Milan's lavish cathedral.[17] A priest who sat a few pews behind later recounted that the men prayed before discussing business. Montini needed $2 million to build Casa Madonnina, a Catholic retirement home. Sindona said it was no problem. As he stood to leave, Sindona leaned over and assured Montini, "Don't worry. I won't abandon you."[18]

Sindona reportedly raised the money in a single day.[19] Whether or not that was true it was an accepted fact inside Milanese business circles and Montini bragged about the young attorney's miraculous fundraising to Spada and others at the IOR.* Italy was halfway through the postwar economic boom that Nogara had predicted. It was a founding member of the European Economic Community, a two-year-old organization of half a dozen European countries that hoped economic integration might better allow them to compete with the United States. Italians called the two decades that started in 1950 an "Economic Miracle," a period during which the country led all European nations in per capita income (it had been a terrible laggard before the war).[21] The country had a newfound confidence and no city reflected that more than Milan, the nation's business capital. A story like Sindona raising a couple of million dollars so quickly for Montini no longer seemed improbable, but rather fit with the hubris that fueled the financial boom.

In 1960 the Vatican and Sindona became partners. Massimo Spada had

---

* Some unsourced published reports cite the CIA as the source of Sindona's retirement home money. Victor Marchetti, a controversial former CIA officer who has promoted the theory that American intelligence killed John F. Kennedy, speculated it "is possible" the money was from the CIA. Although Marchetti's unproven conjecture received considerable coverage in the Italian press, the author has found no credible evidence to support it. In the 1970s Marchetti reported that the CIA had sent secret payments to Pope Paul VI to influence his Papacy, something the church dismissed as "completely false."[20]

introduced Sindona to a client who wanted to sell his small Milanese bank, Banca Privata Finanziaria (BPF).[22] BPF was unique since it operated as both a normal credit bank and offered services usually found only in boutique Swiss banks. BPF counted among its clients some of Italy's leading patrician families and industrialists.[23] The Vatican bought BPF through a proxy account at the Credito Lombardo and retained 60 percent while distributing the remainder to Sindona and his partners.[24] At Spada's request, Sindona arranged a front company so the IOR's ownership remained secret.[25]

Soon after that deal, the IOR started using BPF as its chief correspondent bank by which to conduct the church's business in Milan. That October (1960), Cardinal di Jorio—who sometimes clashed with Spada over the direction of the IOR—insisted that the Vatican would be better served with only a minority stake in BPF. Sindona used his own interlocking web of Liechtenstein holding companies to become the majority owner.[26] He then appointed Spada as a director.[27] And no sooner had Sindona taken charge of the bank than he began buying Canadian real estate for himself and the Vatican through two Liechtenstein shells controlled by the church.[28] When he sold those properties, the proceeds went to Swiss banks under the name of one of Sindona's holding companies (Fasco). The IOR then instructed him how to reinvest the profits.[29] Sindona's legal background, plus the several years he had worked in the government tax office in Sicily, meant he knew how to thread the loopholes in Italy's tax and money exchange laws, always minimizing the levy on any profits.[30]

The following year, Sindona convinced Fidia—a holding company consisting of the IOR, FIAT, Pirelli, Generali, and the giant investment bank Mediobanca—to take an 80 percent stake in a resort development he planned along the Adriatic Riviera.[31] He bought a controlling share of Geneva's prestigious Banque de Financement. The IOR became a one-third partner.[32] That became the model Sindona and the Vatican used for future bank takeovers.[33]

The fast rise of a Sicilian in Milanese business circles led to backroom gossip that Sindona was Mafia sponsored.[34] He dismissed it as the inevitable by-product of envy.[35] Maillardoz, Spada, and Mennini knew Sindona's record was unblemished when it came to serving the IOR. They gave no credence to the unsubstantiated rumors that found their way back to the Vatican. He had earned the right to be a man of confidence.

When Cardinal Nicola Canali died in 1961, John XXIII was so consumed with preparations for the Second Vatican Council that he did not even initially replace him. Cardinal di Jorio was left as the chief prelate responsible for oversight of both the IOR and the Special Administration.[36] Canali's death had no effect on Sindona's cozy relationship with the IOR.

But another death in the Vatican did have an unintended impact on his standing with the church. On June 3, 1963, the Vatican announced the death of the eighty-one-year-old John XXIII. For months he had fought a losing battle against cancer.[37] According to canon law, the Pope's passing meant the Second Vatican Council, which had been under way for eight months, was suspended. The next Pope would have to bring it to a successful end. "It is notoriously easier to begin a Council than to conclude one," wrote Peter Hebblethwaite, a former Jesuit turned author.[38] Traditional and reformist cliques had staked out firm positions on divisive issues. The challenge was to wrap up the Council without splintering the church. The new Pontiff would also have to deal with a confrontational tone from Italy's left-center political coalition, from proposals to tax the church to legalizing contraception to introducing sex education in schools.

The news of John XXIII's death was barely public when the backdoor bargaining began among the cardinals. Before Spellman left for Rome, a CIA officer who wanted to know if it were possible to elect a committed anticommunist, someone more in the style of Pius XII, visited him. The CIA thought John had undone much of Pius's Cold War work. Soviet Premier Nikita Khrushchev felt comfortable enough in 1961 to send the Pontiff personal greetings on his eightieth birthday. The Pope replied in kind. Many at the CIA believed a rapprochement with the Eastern Bloc would unravel years of anti-red progress. In Italy's 1962 national elections, the Pope had ignored entreaties for the church to mobilize votes for the Christian Democrats. Leftist parties surged at the polls, pulling in nearly a million more popular votes than during the previous election. CIA Director John McCone made a rare trip to the Vatican, where he met with the Pontiff.[39] McCone, who was authorized to speak for President Kennedy, told the Pope that the United States worried about what it perceived as the Vatican's turn to the left. John was amiable, as always, but not persuaded by McCone's argument. McCone went home without the commitment to fight communism for which he had hoped.[40]

Spellman told the CIA officer he would try to promote a cardinal with conservative credentials, but noted that his own influence in Rome had waned during the previous four years.[41] Before their meeting ended, the officer left Spellman with the CIA's only imperative: anyone but Milan's Cardinal Montini.[42]

When he arrived in Rome, Spellman was not surprised to learn that the conservatives had again rallied behind Giuseppe Siri, Genoa's fifty-seven-year-old cardinal. Siri told fellow traditionalists that "it will take the Church fifty years to recover from his [John XXIII] pontificate."[43] But once Spellman had a chance to speak to other cardinals, he concluded that Siri's chances were dim. A bloc of northern European cardinals had aligned against him.[44] The bad news, at least for the CIA, was that the progressives had coalesced around Montini. This development was due to a spreading rumor: on his deathbed, Pope John had supposedly said, "Cardinal Montini would make a good Pope."[45] Some cardinal electors thought they should honor the Pontiff's last wish. Montini, of course, was the same prelate whom Pius XII had passed over as a cardinal to ensure he would not be eligible to become Pope upon Pius's death. Having achieved the red hat from John XXIII, the humiliation from Pius seemed a distant memory now that he was a surprising frontrunner.*

Spellman and Montini had strained relations. Spellman criticized Montini for lack of zeal when it came to fighting communism. Montini's personal

---

* Both inside and outside the Curia, an oft-repeated rumor was that Montini was gay. It was not the type of salacious gossip that had spread inside the Curia thirty years earlier about then Cardinal Pacelli, but it was a persistent story. Those who passed it along claimed to know details about dates and places and said that Montini's longtime lover was an Italian actor, Paolo Carlini. Some clerics even suspected he took the Pontifical name Paul as a secret tribute to Carlini, who was subsequently a frequent visitor to the Papal apartment. In 1976, Montini—then Pope Paul VI—angered both traditionalists and gay rights proponents when he approved a "Declaration on Certain Questions Concerning Sexual Ethics," in which the church distinguished between "transitory" and "incurable homosexuals." Bestselling French novelist Roger Peyrefitte, a gay activist, was so angry that he told an Italian magazine that the Pope "had as a boyfriend a movie actor whose name I am not going to mention but whom I recall very well." Although Peyrefitte did not name Carlini, the public airing of the rumor caused such an uproar that Montini addressed it in his April 18, 1976, Sunday sermon. The Pontiff, in unprecedented direct language, dismissed Peyrefitte's charge as "horrible and slanderous insinuations." The Italian police confiscated and destroyed copies of the newsweekly with the Peyrefitte interview, and the Vatican set aside a "day of consolation" for the Pope. There was less public drama the following year when a more expansive charge was leveled against Paul VI in a self-published book, *Nichita Roncalli: Controvita di un papa*. Franco Bellegrandi, a Chamberlain of the Cape and the Sword of His Holiness (a Papal Chamberlain), disclosed what he claimed were intimate details about Montini's closeted life. Financier Michele Sindona had heard a charge that Montini's lover until 1960 was a young protégé, Sergio Pegnedoli (later a cardinal). But he thought there was no truth to the gay rumors. A police commander, General Giorgio Manes, disagreed. Much later Manes told *L'Espresso* that when Montini was blackmailed over his secret life he had sought the help of Italy's Prime Minister Aldo Moro. Whatever the veracity of the rumors, the long-standing gossip about Montini's private life did not pose a barrier to his 1963 election as Pope.[46]

assistant, Father Pasquale Macchi—dubbed "Montini's Mother Pascalina" by some Curialists—was an avowed socialist and Spellman worried that Macchi carried more influence with Montini than he should given his administrative position.[47] The Cold War was on Spellman's mind. It had only been eight months since the Cuban Missile standoff. But in Montini's favor, Spellman felt he would not lead the church too far from its centuries-old dogma. If anything, Montini was known for tormenting himself with indecision. After weighing both sides of an argument, he often vacillated long after most people had made up their minds. John XXIII once called him "our Hamlet cardinal."[48]

Spellman, ever the politician, saw a chance to refurbish his standing at the Vatican by helping put Montini over the top. The two cardinals met the day before the conclave. At the end of their three-hour caucus, Spellman had committed not only his own vote but also those of the four other American cardinals.[49]

The conclave started on June 19, 1963. Montini was only a few votes from sealing the election by the fourth ballot. But according to accounts later provided by several cardinals, a few hard-liners tried hard to rally votes in opposition. Cardinal Gustavo Testa broke the conclave's rule of silence, stood up, and announced that he wished that the cardinals sitting near him should stop their obstruction and vote instead for Montini.[50] On the sixth ballot, just over two days into the conclave, the sixty-five-year-old Montini had the necessary votes.[51] He took the name Paul VI.

Even Montini's most avid supporters knew it was impossible for the new Pope to be as popular with the faithful as John. He lacked his predecessor's charisma. Catholics had embraced John as a grandfatherly figure. He had built an enthusiastic following among the faithful. From the start of John's reign he had gone out of his way to disabuse anyone of the idea that the Papacy was a "self-imposed imprisonment." In contrast to Pius XII, John invited reporters to follow him everywhere, from visiting the malodorous "Queen of Heaven" prison (where he kissed and blessed a convicted murderer) to a wildly popular sixteen-hour whistle-stop train tour across Italy to pray at shrines from Assisi to Loreto (the first time a Pope left Rome since 1857).[52] In an era where personal security was not yet stifling, he often visited schools and hospitals. The Vatican's old guard thought his casual mingling was unseemly for a Pope and a diminution of the office's regal power.[53] They cringed when on Holy Thursday in 1960, at a ceremony meant to recall Christ washing the feet of his apostles at the Last Supper, he included black, Japanese, Polynesian, and West Indian seminarians.[54]

In contrast, most who met Montini described him as detached, somber, and brooding. He carried out his duties but seemed joyless about doing so. When he redecorated the Pontiff's private quarters in a sleek "Milan modern" style, some thought that the cool design matched his personality.[55] Montini seemed to disdain even mixing with others inside the Vatican.[56] The effect of the change in personalities from outsized to restrained was evident in the drop-off in contributions to Peter's Pence. In the last year of John XXIII's tenure, the donations peaked at $15 million. In the first year of Montini's reign they plunged to $4 million.[57]

Montini—the third son of an upper-middle-class family from the Lombardian village of Concesio—was a career prelate whose ambition had long been obvious to his colleagues. While few could have guessed that he could rebound from Pius XII passing him over as a cardinal, none doubted he long believed he was what insiders dubbed *papabile*, having the qualities necessary to become Pope.[58] Montini, who had a doctorate in canon law, had a fast career in the Secretary of State's office. And he long chafed at what he thought was the lack of appreciation that Pius and others showed for his decades of service. He was not overwhelmed by the challenge of being the Pope but was instead eager to make his mark on the church. One of his first acts was to reconvene the Second Vatican Council.

There were few people happier at the news of Montini's election than Sindona. Having the Pope as a friend meant that Sindona's Vatican credentials were now unimpeachable. Some newspaper reports included him as part of what was dubbed "the Milan Mafia" that Paul VI brought with him to Rome.[59]

Inside the IOR, Spada was the biggest beneficiary since Montini was a longtime friend. He knew that the new Pope, who had a reputation for "taking a personal interest in budgetary matters," would be much more involved than his predecessor when it came to administering the church's finances.[60]

A few months after his coronation, the Christian Democrats formed a ruling coalition with the country's two largest socialist parties. It was Italy's most left leaning postwar government.[61] Aldo Moro became Prime Minister. When Sindona spoke to the new Pope, he shared his fear that fresh government proposals for increased state ownership of public utilities and some financial institutions would likely stop the long Italian economic expansion. Since Nogara had so intertwined the Vatican with Italian industry, any fallout from an economic downturn could be disastrous for the church. Montini directed Maillardoz and Spada to work with Sindona to develop a strategy to protect and diversify the Vatican's vast Italian holdings.*

Sindona was tailor-made for such work. By the time of Montini's election, Sindona was attracting name-brand partners for his diverse ventures. Switzerland's Nestlé and France's Paribas Bank worked with him to acquire the Chicago-based food-processing firm Libby, McNeil & Libby.[63] General Foods became his partner in an Italian candy company. Sindona convinced Bank of America to help him obtain a stake in a premier luggage manufacturer. With strong bank financing, the forty-three-year-old attorney had become a key figure in dissimilar industries from publishing to petrochemicals to textiles. He was president at seven companies and on the board of several dozen. Except for the Italian branch of Condé Nast, on which the Vatican did not have a director, he served on those boards with an IOR director.[64]

That same year, Sindona used his Luxembourg holding company, Fasco, to buy a controlling interest in Brown Company, a major American-based pulp and paper producer. Over the next couple of years Sindona went on to buy interests in Crucible Steel; a chemical company, Pachetti; a real estate firm, Sviluppo; the largest Italian luxury hotel chain, Ciga; Paris's luxe Hotel Meurice (Nazi headquarters during World War II), and Rome's opulent The Grand.[65]

One of his most ambitious launches was an international currency brokerage firm, Moneyrex.[66] Sindona thought there was an undeveloped market for a private clearinghouse to service banks. He envisioned balancing the currency accounts of financial institutions around the world—locating, for instance, a bank with excess deposits of dollars and then matching it with another bank short of dollars. The banks already did this themselves. But given the enormous size of the international currency market, Sindona was confident that a private company would be far more effective. And he proposed that Moneyrex's fee

---

* Although the Vatican was concerned about the growing extent of the new government's interference in private enterprise, the church remained the largest investor in IRI bonds, the debt issued by Italy's quasi-nationalized banking authority. The IOR also owned a share of the country's state-run telephone monopoly, STET (Società Finanziaria Telefonica).[62]

would only be $\frac{1}{32}$ of 1 percent of the money it handled. It took a couple of years before most banks saw the benefits in outsourcing the work. To make certain that Moneyrex had enough capital to survive, Sindona had large partners, including America's Continental Illinois National Bank, British-based Hambros Bank, and the IOR.* Moneyrex would become the largest company of its kind, eventually serving some 850 banks worldwide, and handling about $200 billion annually in revenues.[68]

With the Pope's blessing, Sindona further intertwined himself in Vatican finances. He expanded his banking empire by acquiring some of Italy's healthiest regional banks.[69] The IOR took a substantial minority stake in each.[70] Sindona appointed Spada as the president of BPF, the first bank he had acquired in 1960. In 1962, Spada had retired from the IOR, at the time telling *L'Espresso* that he had "reached[ed] the limits of age," although he was only fifty-seven.[71] To most Vatican insiders it seemed as if Spada was merely changing the technical status of his employment as he moved across town and started working at the Sindona Group, involved in many of the same projects that consumed his time at the Vatican Bank.[72] Pope Paul VI tapped Luigi Mennini to serve as Maillardoz's deputy. Sindona's business with the church continued uninterrupted.

It was a heady time for the church in which the Vatican Bank and its finances had always been far in the background. Father Richard Ginder, the American editor of a prominent Catholic weekly, captured the excitement in one of his 1963 columns: "The Catholic Church must be the biggest corporation in the United States. We have a branch office in almost every neighborhood. Our assets and real estate holdings must exceed those of Standard Oil, A.T.&T. and U.S. Steel combined. And our roster of dues-paying members be second only to the tax rolls of the United States Government."[73]

By this time Sindona was getting great international press coverage. Dubbed "the Shark" for his aggressive take-no-prisoners business style, *Time* called him a "dedicated free trader" and noted that few Italian businessmen "have had

---

* Hambros Bank, founded in 1848, was one of a handful of British merchant banks on which Nogara had relied starting in the 1930s. Hambros retained its close ties with the IOR after Nogara's retirement. Spada had introduced Sindona to Jocelyn Hambro, the bank's chairman, and the two became friends. Hambros became an indispensable part of many of Sindona's early deals, as was National City Bank (now Citibank), Chase National Bank (now JPMorgan Chase), N. M. Rothschild & Sons, Lazard Frères, and Credit Suisse.[67]

more spectacular success than Milan Financier Michele Sindona, who founded and heads a corporate complex of manufacturing firms in nine countries and real estate firms in five."[74] *Business Week* dubbed Sindona "Italy's most successful and feared financier." He is "one of the world's most talented traders," noted *Fortune,* while *The New York Times* said he was a "Milanese version of a Texas tycoon."[75] *The Economist* proclaimed him "a financial wizard."[76]

A test of his investing philosophy came in 1966 when he met Licio Gelli, a wealthy businessman who had a widespread reputation as a fixer. To outsiders, the forty-five-year-old Gelli, with dual Italian and Argentine citizenship, enjoyed the pampered life of the country's super-rich, splitting his time at grand villas in Milan, Monaco, and Buenos Aires. Gelli's opulent parties were covered in the social pages.[77] But few knew that his real role was as the chief of an underground Masonic lodge, Propaganda Due (P2).[78] By the time police ultimately disbanded it in 1981 over suspicions it was plotting a coup, its nearly 1,000 members included four sitting cabinet ministers, more than fifty generals and admirals, and some of Italy's most important industrialists, financiers, journalists, public prosecutors and judges, and even intelligence operatives.[79] That membership roster was such a stunning collection of who's-who that Italian journalists dubbed it a "parallel state within a state."[80] In many countries a Masonic lodge such as P2 might have been considered just an exclusive club. But in Italy, starting in 1738, eight successive Popes had condemned Freemasonry and tried eliminating any vestige of it. The church was suspicious of everything, from the rituals of the Masonic initiation ceremony to its promotion of naturalism and religious tolerance. Italy's nineteenth-century republicans and anticlerics who wrested away the Papal States were themselves Freemasons. Masonic flags flew in the streets when Garibaldi marched into Rome to liberate the city from Papal rule.[81] Mussolini shared a distrust of Masons. Il Duce outlawed all lodges in 1925 and even removed their symbols from public buildings and monuments.[82] Postwar Italy had few Freemasons.[83]

There was considerable personal risk for Gelli in running such a lodge. The titans who joined knew that public disclosure would be at the very least embarrassing. Since almost all who joined were Catholic, they were subject to automatic excommunication under Canon Law 2335.[84] But the risks seemed small compared to the potential benefits of being part of such a powerful clique. Gelli spoke to new recruits about his dream that one day a right-wing, authoritarian government—composed of the P2 men—might replace the never-ending stream of weak coalition governments that had become a depressing staple of postwar Italy.

Gelli raised the subject of P2 when he thanked Sindona for having helped "a dear and important fellow Mason," General Vito Miceli, a senior officer in the army's intelligence service.* "Until then I hadn't known that General Miceli was a Mason," Sindona later recounted.[86] Gelli talked to Sindona about issues important to the Sicilian businessman, emphasizing P2's anticommunist credentials, and touching on shared matters of interest, including free trade and too powerful trade unions. Sindona realized from just a sampling of names mentioned by Gelli that being aligned with such men could only be good for his business.[87] Gelli was confident he could trust Sindona. The attorney had bragged to a group of American businessmen, "Ninety-five-percent of my clients come to me because they know I can keep a secret."[88]

At Gelli's request, Sindona drafted proposals for reenergizing Italy's economy and for improving its currency and credit status abroad. Gelli distributed them to some other P2 members, with Sindona's name redacted.[89] And he introduced Sindona to a few of his fellow Masons, most of whom were anxious to do business with him.

When Sindona turned his attention back to the Vatican in 1967, it was for more than another joint venture with the IOR. Henri de Maillardoz had announced his retirement as the Vatican Bank's Delegato. The former Credit Suisse banker had benefited by staying the course with Nogara's postwar investments in the expanding Italian economy. By the time he stepped down, he was on a remarkable winning streak. SGI, the moribund construction company in which the IOR had invested in the late 1940s, was now run by Count Enrico Galeazzi. It had become an international conglomerate with significant or controlling stakes in more than fifty real estate and urban development companies.[90] The Vatican had four seats on the board.[91] A major SGI subsidiary, SOGENE (Società Generale per Lavori di Pubblica Utilità), had become the country's largest public works contractor. During Maillardoz's tenure, SGI had

---

* In 1970, Miceli became the director of all military intelligence (Servizio per le Informazioni e la Sicurezza Militare—SISMI). A U.S. House Select Committee on Intelligence investigation later disclosed that over the objections of the CIA station chief in Rome, the then U.S. ambassador gave Miceli $800,000 in cash in 1972. The payment, which came without any preconditions, had been approved by National Security Advisor Henry Kissinger. The hope was that Miceli would use it for anticommunist propaganda efforts. Instead, the money disappeared and was never accounted for.[85]

won the bid to build the Watergate residential and office complex in Washington, D.C., the largest luxury apartment tower in Canada, and a planned city of 100,000 people on 1,300 acres outside Mexico City.[92]

One of Nogara's early favorites was Montecatini/Edison. It had expanded beyond electric power into pharmaceuticals and mining, and its annual revenues had reached nearly a billion dollars. Italcementi had grown to 6,500 workers and had become Europe's second largest cement producer. SNIA Viscosa now produced 70 percent of Italy's textile fabrics. Italgas had become the exclusive gas supplier for thirty-six Italian cities, including Rome, Venice, Florence, and Turin.[93] Maillardoz had ensured that Vatican investments tied the church to a postwar alliance with America as great as any it had during World War II with Germany and Italy. Beginning in the mid-1960s, the Vatican purchased stock in IBM, General Motors, General Electric, Shell, Gulf Oil, Chase Manhattan, Procter & Gamble, and Bethlehem Steel, among other blue chips.[94]

Luigi Mennini, by then given the honorary title Gentleman of His Holiness, replaced Maillardoz.[95] Mennini formalized Sindona's relationship as the Holy See's special financial consultant. Sindona was pleased that the men who ran the church's finances had such unfettered faith in him. But he also shared with some confidants that he was somewhat disappointed that Montini had taken a liberal turn since becoming Pope.

Montini had reconvened the Second Vatican Council only three months after his election. A month later, twelve fundamental changes to the liturgy, the largest revision in church history, were approved. The most notable to lay Catholics was the end of the Latin Mass.* Traditionalists were irate. Genoa's conservative Cardinal Siri said it was "the greatest disaster in recent ecclesiastical history."[97] Many in the Curia were incensed at moves they viewed as diluting their powers. Decisions that used to be the exclusive province of Rome were delegated to the countries where the issues originated. Local dioceses would now decide contested marriage court cases that previously went straight to Rome. Moreover, foreign bishops joined the boards of directors of most Curial agencies. The Curia now sent its proposals to local bishops for re-

---

* It was during the Second Vatican Council that the church finally renounced the belief that all Jews bore collective historical guilt for the death of Jesus. In *Nostra Aetate* (In Our Time), the church declared that "Jews should not be presented as rejected or accursed by God." It also renounced its centuries-old policy that it was a duty of Catholics to convert Jews.[96]

view before making any final directive. And regional meetings of those bishops meant more could be accomplished independent of the Vatican.[98]

Beyond controversy over the Council there had been a noticeable political shift to the left by the Pope. Paul increasingly criticized the American bombing of North Vietnam that had started in 1965. In 1966, Cardinal Spellman and other conservative clerics were incensed when the church announced $15 million in aid for North Vietnam at the same time it dispatched two Vatican officials to visit Vietnam (Pope Paul had himself wanted to go as a symbol of support, but it was deemed too dangerous).[99] His 1967 reception for Soviet President Nikolai Podgorny marked the first state reception for a communist official at the Vatican, and it sent a chill through entrenched anticommunist warriors in the Curia.[100] That same year, Paul issued an encyclical, *Populorum Progressio.* It was a clarion call for economic and social justice and set a goal of "just distribution" of wealth in Third World countries to help bridge the gap between rich and poor.[101] The *Wall Street Journal* scorned that Papal decree as "souped-up Marxism," but it would become the rallying cry for a generation of activist priests in Central and Latin America who advocated liberation theology, a volatile mixture of left-wing politics and Catholicism.[102]*

Populorum Progressio at first concerned Sindona since it also attacked unrestrained capitalism: "Free market competition, however, should not be abolished, but simply maintained within moral limits." The Pope, however, did not intend that his message about economic equality in any way limit a buying binge that Sindona had planned with the IOR. Mennini, Spada, and Sindona rolled out their expansion plan in early 1967. The church increased its investments in the country's largest passenger shipping line (Finmare), Italian insurers Generali and RAS, and more regional banks and credit unions.[104]†

But the IOR-Sindona strategy would be forced later that year to take a sharp detour from its Italian-centric focus. It would result from a long-simmering

---

* A few Curialists later came to believe that a handful of right-wing cardinals engineered a coup against Pope Paul because they could no longer tolerate his leftist politics. He was replaced with an almost identical impostor, according to the conspiracy theorists, who later published photos they claimed illustrated the distinctive differences over time for his ears and eyes, proving the "two-Pope theory." In 1983, five years after Pope Paul VI's death, a British Catholic paper (*The Universe*) reported that only the impostor had died and the real Paul was living in a Rome suburb.[103]

† That same year the Banco di Sicilia's president was arrested and charged with fraud. Over eight years, he had hired about a hundred relatives, some of whom had never shown up for a single day of work. The public did not know that the IOR had a controlling stake in the bank.[105]

political row between the Vatican and Italy's government over investments and dividend taxes. Four years earlier, in 1963, a socialist minister of Italy's Treasury had first questioned why the Vatican was not subject to a new government dividend tax.[106] It was a 15 percent levy so long as the owner registered the shares with the tax office, or 30 percent if the owner did not disclose them and the government found out about it. It was thought that all taxpayers would gladly disclose their stock ownership to avoid the much higher tariff for secrecy.[107]

Under Clauses 29, 30, and 31 of the 1929 Lateran Treaty, Mussolini had exempted the church from paying taxes for "ecclesiastical corporations." Nogara lobbied the fascist government to interpret *ecclesiastical* so broadly that over time the exemption included everything done by the Special Administration and the IOR. Even when Mussolini levied two special taxes (corporate and real estate) in 1936 to offset the enormous costs of the Ethiopian war, a special decree excluded the Vatican.[108]

The church also got a special exemption in 1937 when Italian companies had to pay a new tax on common stock. When a national sales tax went into effect in 1940, Italy's finance minister announced it did not apply to the church. In 1942, just four months after the IOR's founding, the fascist government waived any money the Vatican would have owed under another dividend tax. That December, the Finance Minister published a list of all exempt Vatican organizations. The IOR and Special Administration were free from any tax.

Now Prime Minister Aldo Moro tried appeasing his socialist coalition partners by requesting that the Vatican at least demonstrate good faith. As a first step toward possibly obtaining a further exemption, Moro asked the church to provide the government a list of all its stock holdings. Secretary of State Cardinal Amleto Cicognani refused, asserting that Italy had no authority to ask for such information or to impose any tax because the Vatican was a sovereign country. Any tax violated the Lateran Pacts.[109] *

---

* Another new tax—15 percent of the interest earned on individual bank accounts—brought a surge of deposits to the Vatican Bank. Even under Nogara, the IOR had profited by assisting wealthy Italians avoid taxes and currency regulations with so-called *in nero* (in black) transfers. Sindona noted that "most people confuse hiding and laundering." Money moved *in nero* was all right, Sindona later told author Nick Tosches, since it "belongs to respectable people . . . [and is] legitimately accounted wealth." The church moved *in nero* only "for the purpose of avoiding taxes." On the other hand, "dirty money is money made through crime." The church's intermediary *in nero* role was lucrative, up to a commission

Despite the efforts of the Moro government, the push to apply the tax to the Vatican lost steam. A series of investigative stories in 1967 by the leftist *L'Espresso* revived the dispute and even amplified it with rhetoric that dubbed the Vatican as "the biggest tax evader in postwar Italy."[111] Published guesstimates of what the Vatican owed on just the dividend tax ranged as high as $720 million annually (the equivalent of $4.8 billion in 2014).[112] The ruling coalition pledged to apply the tax to the church.[113] The Vatican had, by coincidence, only recently established a press office.[114] The tax issue was addressed first by its spokesman, Monsignor Fausto Vallainc (*New York Times* reporter Paul Hoffman said about Vallainc that "in addition to being uninformed, he was a bungler").[115] Besides reiterating that the church was exempt because of the Lateran Pacts, he put forth a novel argument: since the Vatican was a world-renowned attraction, it should be given a credit for some of the money tourists spent in Italy.[116] Vallainc's plea was not successful. The government stripped the church of its exemption for the special dividend tax (although remarkably the leftist coalition did not end the hundreds of millions given annually to the church in direct subsidies, another practice begun by Mussolini and not terminated until 1990).[117]

Sindona told the Pope and his colleagues in the IOR and the Special Administration that although Italy was on weak legal ground when it came to the dividend tax, the Vatican could not prevail. The issue had become entangled in politics. The concern now was whether it might become a precedent prompting the revenue-hungry government to pass even more taxes. And since the state collected the tax at its source—the companies paid what was owed to the government before distributing the rest to the shareholder—it did not matter if the Vatican continued protesting. Merely allowing its collection would damage the credibility of the church's claim of independent sovereignty.

Sindona urged the creation of a separate division inside the Curia to focus primarily on real estate. That department, he said, should also be responsible for fully funding the Curia. Sindona contended that such a move would allow the church to benefit from its tax-free status on all income from its enormous property holdings, while freeing the IOR to concentrate on other investments.

---

of 10 percent of principal. Much of the money moved was for Black Nobles, their personal friends, and leading Christian Democrats.[110]

On August 15, 1967, Pope Paul established the Administration of the Patrimony of the Holy See (Amministrazione del Patrimonio della Sede Apostolica, APSA), and appointed his Secretary of State, Cardinal Amleto Cicognani, as its first chief.[118] It had, as Sindona urged, responsibility for the church's real estate as well as raising money for the Curia's budget and paying the Vatican payroll.[119] The Special Administration, which had been established in 1929 to deal with the money given to the Vatican by Mussolini as part of the Lateran Pacts, was dissolved and folded into APSA.[120]

Paul VI also created the Prefettura degli Affari Economici della Santa Sede (the Prefecture for the Economic Affairs of the Holy See), responsible for the oversight of all Vatican finances, with the notable exception of the IOR, which was left independent and self-regulating.[121] As part of its duties, the Prefecture produced an annual report of all budgets (except the IOR).[122] Any construction project in Vatican City now had to be run past the Prefecture. The Pope had considered putting the Vatican Bank under the new Prefecture, but Mennini argued successfully that because of Pius XII's intent, if the bank was put under the control of another entity, it would sacrifice its essential independence that made it both unique and so useful.[123]

Paul VI hoped that a central administrator might illuminate the obscure thicket of church finances.[124] And Sindona may have been right that creating APSA as a tax strategy was a good idea. But invariably it overlapped with the Vatican Bank as well as the asset-rich Congregation for the Evangelization of Peoples (Propaganda Fide).[125] There was trouble integrating the new bureaucracies.[126] Compounding the problems, Cicognani and the other clerics in charge of APSA had little background in finance. Most of them had difficulty even reading a balance sheet.[127] The same was true at the Prefecture. Paul VI appointed Cardinal Egidio Vagnozzi, who had been the Apostolic Delegate to the United States and whose career specialized in diplomacy.[128] Vagnozzi's claim to any business sense was that his family ran the largest confectionary in Rome.[129] His two assistants were seventy-nine-year-old Cardinal Joseph Beran and seventy-year-old Cardinal Cesare Zerba. Beran had returned to the Vatican after sixteen years in prison in Czechoslovakia, and Zerba was a theologian who ran the Congregation of the Sacraments.[130] They had no financial expertise or realistic expectation about what awaited them in the splintered world of Vatican finances.[131] Vagnozzi was not long in his new post before he told a colleague that it would take a "combined effort of the CIA, KGB, Interpol, and the Holy Spirit" to make sense of the Vatican's financial ledgers.[132]

APSA and Prefecture for the Economic Affairs of the Holy See ultimately added to the confusion and lack of transparency over Vatican finances.[133] But at the time of their creation, they were a testament to the influence of Sindona in the Papacy of Paul VI.

Sindona knew, however, that creating APSA was only one part of a comprehensive response to the government's imposition of the dividend tax. He urged the Vatican Bank to sell many of its Italian stock and corporate holdings. Those sales would not only spare the Vatican from paying any tax under the new law, but would constitute a public rebuke to the secular government. Without a significant stake in Italy's private sector, the church would not be affected if future governments levied new taxes on dividends, capital gains, or even so-called intangibles taxes (a fixed levy on the total value of an investor's portfolio). Sindona assured IOR director Mennini that if the church freed up the money it had tied up in Italian companies, he would help invest the funds abroad. But there was considerable resistance inside the IOR to unraveling the portfolio that Nogara had so meticulously compiled, especially given that its components were performing so well.

The tipping point in favor of Sindona's argument came in early 1968. Italian reporters uncovered evidence that the Vatican had invested in Istituto Farmacologico Serono, a pharmaceutical company that made birth control pills, as well as Udine, a military weapons manufacturer (there were also unconfirmed newspaper reports of church money in gunmaker Beretta, a Monte Carlo casino, and a printing firm that published pornographic magazines).[134] Nogara's son Giovanni was on Udine's board. Serono's chairman was none other than Pius XII's nephew Prince Giulio Pacelli.[135] Former IOR chief Massimo Spada ran a wholly owned Serono pharmaceutical subsidiary, Salifera Siciliana.[136] The embarrassment over the Serono holding was intense. It was the same year Paul VI issued *Humanae Vitae* (Human Life), his most controversial encyclical, in which he banned all artificial birth control.[137]

That spring, in the rococo Apostolic Palace, four men assembled late at night in the Pontiff's private third-floor study to discuss what to do about the church's finances.[138] The Pope was joined by Sindona, and Cardinals Cicognani and Vagnozzi. Sindona had once had dinner with the Pope and his private secretary, Macchi, but this evening was not a social visit. No official entry was made in the Pope's diary about the meeting.[139] Sindona made his case for why the Vatican should divest itself of all holdings in Italian companies. He explained that so long as the church owned stocks in Italian firms, the government would continue to roll out more taxes.

Sindona argued that the Vatican's ownership in so many firms was as much a political and social liability as it was an economic asset. Nineteen sixty-eight was a year in which social unrest in Italy was peaking between student sit-ins and massive street demonstrations. Public opinion polls showed a remarkable two thirds of the country thought the nation's future was bleaker than its present.[140] Mixed into this cauldron of pessimism was increasing criticism directed at the church for its corporate holdings. Every time one of its companies took a hard line during negotiations with trade unions or cut back on the number of workers at an unproductive plant, leftist politicians and newspapers slammed the church for not protecting working-class Catholics. Sindona reminded them that when Italy had created the Olympic Highway in 1960, critics had charged that SGI had gouged the Roman government. The previous year, leftist newspapers accused the Vatican of manipulating local zoning regulations to help Hilton build a new hotel.[141] And just a few months before the late night meeting, workers had occupied the church-owned flour mill, Pantanella, after the Vatican had slashed the mill's book value to stay solvent.[142]

Those headaches were problems the church did not need, contended Sindona. They would only grow over time, especially as the press became increasingly alarmist and intrusive.[143] Moreover, by maintaining majority positions in companies, the church was on the line for business failures, putting it at risk for having to use its own money to shore up firms that hit hard times due to bad management or an uncontrollable turn in the economy or marketplace.[144] Finally, he assured them, he would reinvest the money from the stock sales into new and better investments abroad, ones that would free the church from worrying about taxation or social criticisms. It would also provide a layer of confidentiality difficult to maintain with Italian stocks.

The Pope liked the idea that Sindona might be able to increase the church's return on its money. It needed more income. Paul VI was overseeing an institution with 600 million followers, five million lay employees, twenty million children in parochial schools, a million nuns, 250,000 priests, and a charity that was the world's largest (thirteen million people were receiving some type of assistance).[145] Although religious orders and all dioceses were responsible for their own finances, since the Second Vatican Council the Vatican had assumed broad new responsibilities that had increased its employment by a third.

Paul VI, as was his style, had agonized for months over what to do. But he had reached the conclusion that Sindona's plan was in the best interests of the Vatican. The two cardinals agreed. Paul turned to Sindona. With the cardinals as witnesses, the Pontiff informed Sindona that he had earned the title *Mercator Senesis Romanam Curiam sequens,* Latin for "the leading banker of the Roman Curia," or informally, "the Pope's banker."[146] The personal involvement of a Pope at this intimate level of decision making was unprecedented, as was the notable absence at the meeting of any IOR or APSA official.

The press later dubbed the radical shift as the "Pauline Policy." Adding to Sindona's allure, *The New York Times* reported, "There are rumors in Italy . . . that Mr. Sindona had signed the final agreement with Pope Paul VI" (he had not, but the Pope had conferred on Sindona his elite advisory status).[147] When *Time* confirmed the meeting a year later, it noted it was "almost unheard of for a Pope personally to conduct the church's business affairs, but this was no ordinary occasion. Sindona and Pope Paul closed a deal that started a shift of profound consequence in the Holy See's management of its vast temporal wealth."[148]

The first sale was the holding in the SGI conglomerate and the resignation of its president, a former Governor of Vatican City, and four Vatican financial advisors on its board.[149] APSA was technically responsible for the sale but the IOR—with Spada as the key advisor—set the terms and handled all the money.[150] The church had always managed its investments so as not to attract any attention, yet somehow the information was leaked to the media.[151] *The New York Times* noted that the SGI sale was "the beginning of a sweeping plan to sell the Vatican's Italian stocks and buy investments abroad."[152] Many reports warned that if the Vatican dumped hundreds of millions in its stock holdings it would punish a weak Italian stock market. The SGI sale did cause a temporary swoon in the prices of the Milan indexes. Sindona, meanwhile, received widespread and positive credit for having arranged the sale.[153]

Mennini, and the IOR's chief internal accountant, Pellegrino de Strobel (a director of a joint Sindona-IOR–owned Geneva bank), and ex-chief Spada as a consultant, worked to dissolve most of the church's domestic holdings.[154] The IOR would no longer take any controlling interests in Italy's private sector.

Within a year, Cardinal Vagnozzi, the chief of the Prefecture for the Economic Affairs of the Holy See, gave a first-ever, broad-ranging interview to *Institutional Investor*. He announced that the process was complete: "Today there are no more companies controlled by the Vatican."[155] In addition to disclosing that the Vatican had divested all its majority stock positions, the Pope also tasked Vagnozzi with downplaying the size of the church's wealth. The cardinal dismissed as "wild" the press reports that the Vatican had nearly $13 billion in liquid investments. It was probably closer to $500 million, he claimed.[156] Vagnozzi's estimate was unrealistically low since he had no information from the IOR.[157]

The Vatican still owned some stocks in Italian companies.[158] But by significantly reducing them, the church had given up much of its private sector control, and the IOR had become a passive investor. It marked a momentous change. And it presaged an unparalleled era for Sindona and other men of confidence.[159]

15

"You Can't Run the Church on Hail Marys"

During this frenzied stretch of work, Sindona had a fateful meeting with Paul Casimir Marcinkus, a Catholic priest.[1] Two years older than Sindona, the six-foot-three American-born Marcinkus seemed more like a football lineman than a low-ranking clerical bureaucrat assigned to the Secretary of State's office. The youngest of four sons of Lithuanian working-class immigrants (his father was a window washer), he grew up in Cicero, a rough Chicago suburb best known as Al Capone's hometown.[2] Marcinkus later recalled, "We were poor. . . . This was [the] time of the Depression. I had twenty-five cents a day for food and travel to school, and I was always figuring out ways to make it stretch so I could afford a ball game or take in a movie."[3] The family was one of the few without a car.[4] A solid student and competitive athlete, he surprised most of his friends when at eighteen he entered St. Mary of the Lake, a seminary in Mundelein, Illinois.[5] He had been thinking "this was the kind of life I'd like" since he was thirteen.[6]

Although America was soon at war with the Nazis and Japanese, his seminary enrollment gave him an automatic draft exemption.[7] He studied theology for four years and philosophy for another three before his ordination as a priest in 1947. After two years of pastoral work at St. Christina's, a working-class Chicago parish, he later said he "must have shown some proclivity for the law" since he was moved to the matrimonial tribunal in the diocese's chancery office.[8] Within a year he went to Rome to study canon law at the Gregorian University.[9] It was a career move made by ambitious priests who hoped someday to have a shot at becoming a bishop.* Marcinkus joined the English Section of the Secretariat of State in 1952, earning $90 a month plus room and board. He earned a doctorate in divinity the following year.[11] In 1954, after graduating from the Vatican's diplomatic school, he was dispatched for assignments in Bolivia and Canada. His energetic work in both postings won the admiration of his superiors and he was promoted to monsignor.[12] In 1959, he returned to Rome and what he later described as "rather mundane" work in the Secretary of State's office.[13]

His colleagues thought the gruff Marcinkus was quintessentially American. Most of them had never been to America, but there was little doubt from all they had read and the movies they had seen that Paul Marcinkus was the epitome of whatever that meant. When he drank whiskey he did not hide the bottle when a senior cleric walked into the room. He smoked cigars and did not ask permission before lighting one. A large borrowed Chevrolet was his trademark as he navigated the chaotic Roman traffic, offering to take a visiting group of pilgrims to Castel Gandolfo or a few kids to a local soccer match. A rough-and-tumble amateur sportsman who enjoyed boxing and tennis, he had founded the Vatican's first baseball team, and starred on its intramural rugby squad.[14] He was also an avid golfer—with a reputed five handicap—and one of the few priests who could talk his way into playing a round at the SGI-owned luxury country club, Oligata Romana.[15] (He later told a journalist that he "loved physical work because it got the badness out of me.")[16]

Full of energy, he talked as loudly and as animatedly as any native Italian.[17] Some at the Vatican found him amusing and his lack of piety refreshing. But most disliked his apparent lack of self-doubt. His love of sports was thought by many to be inappropriate for a Vatican-based prelate.[18] They bristled whenever he told newcomers, "just call me Chink for short" (in Italian, his surname was pronounced Mar-chink-us). When they discovered that he liked reading West-

---

* Thirty-five years later, in the middle of an unfolding scandal, Marcinkus claimed somewhat disingenuously to a *Chicago Tribune* reporter, "I can assure you that a career here [at the Vatican] wasn't what I wanted. All I ever really wanted was to be a parish priest. But at my ordination, when I promised to obey, I felt that what happened to me after that was in my superiors' hands. I've never asked for a specific task, but I've also never refused a job that was given to me. I guess you'd call me a team player. I play whatever position the coach puts me in."[10]

erns, it fit with the caricature they had of him, and made it easier to dismiss the perennially tan Marcinkus as a cowboy priest who would likely soon be back in America.[19]

Marcinkus knew that he was hard to miss. A *Chicago Tribune* reporter who knew him said he "possessed the tact of a trailer truck."[20] But Marcinkus had decided when he first arrived in Rome not to change his style. He observed that in the Vatican, "with Italians you have to be careful. It's kind of Oriental. . . . There is subterfuge."[21] Inside the Curia, he was wise to the pitfall of falling into the back-and-forth gossip that often derailed promising careers. "I don't want to work like a Hoover, pick up dirt, pass it on."[22] He thought that Vatican City was like a "village of washerwomen" who spent every day "squeezing all the old dirt out. In normal life people get away and have other interests, but here what else is there to talk about?"[23]

It did not take Marcinkus long to learn that the Curia was a bureaucratic nightmare. "The way they do things around here," he later said, "annoys me at times. You can send a memo and not get an answer for months. Your memo just gets ignored. That's the way they deal with things: ignore them and hope they just go away on their own."[24] The Italians considered him naive.

"The careerists were in awe of him," said Peter Murphy, years later the Deputy Chief of Mission for the U.S. embassy to the Vatican. Murphy, who became a good friend with Marcinkus, recalled, "He was so unlike any Italian. They just didn't know what to make of him. Even his sense of humor rubbed them the wrong way, they were so serious."[25]

Marcinkus got his first break in 1962 when John XXIII picked him as an interpreter for a visit to the Vatican by America's Catholic First Lady, Jacqueline Kennedy.[26] The Pope and the First Lady mostly spoke French during their thirty-two-minute meeting, but Marcinkus used the opportunity to ingratiate himself with some of the U.S. clerics who had traveled with Mrs. Kennedy, including Scranton's influential Archbishop Martin O'Connor and the future cardinal of New York Edward Egan. The U.S. delegation left Rome with a good impression of the gregarious young priest. And John XXIII—who had himself been criticized for so sharply breaking from the stiff formality of Pius—liked the brash American.

Marcinkus had picked a good time to make an impression on the Pope. John XXIII's Second Vatican Council was about to begin that October. Some three hundred American bishops—most unfamiliar with Rome—would soon arrive. Ernest Primeau, an American bishop living in Rome, recommended to the Pope that the young American monsignor with a reputation for orderliness and punctuality be put in charge of helping the U.S. bishops.[27] Pope John agreed and made Marcinkus a one-person service bureau.[28] Soon, he was everywhere, flitting around Vatican City from dawn until late at night. Marcinkus did everything for the bishops, keeping minutes for key meetings, arranging flights, smoothing out problems during their long stay, tending to them like a five-star-hotel concierge. By the time the Second Vatican Council finished, almost all U.S bishops knew him and had a good impression. They left Rome trading their personal favorite stories of "the Pope's man."[29]

His status was much grander than would have been expected if someone knew only his lowly rank in the Secretary of State's office. That alone irked many contemporaries. One of them leaked to Italian newspapers gossip that Marcinkus was pocketing money from a charter business that handled the travel for most of the bishops at the Council, as well as for groups of pilgrims. Marcinkus went out of his way to deny it. "I didn't want to see all our cardinals and bishops getting fleeced by all these airlines, so I got ahold of this friend who ran pilgrim deals. . . . I didn't make anything out of it."[30] After four years in Rome, Pope John understood how rumors in the Curia developed from the tiniest germ of truth. He dismissed the reports as baseless.[31]

Marcinkus's ascent as a can-do administrator was not derailed when John died in 1963. Giovanni Montini had been friends with Marcinkus since the early 1950s when they were stationed in Rome.[32] Both then served in the Secretary of State's office. Marcinkus was a newly arrived junior priest and Montini a monsignor then directing the Vatican's refugee programs. "I used to see him [Montini] walking around the grounds," Marcinkus later told a reporter from the *Chicago Tribune*, "and I'd give him a lift in my car."[33] Marcinkus had made an impression on Montini. The future Pope, who at first found him overbearing, admired his organizational skills, hard work, and take-charge attitude.[34]

On the day Montini was elected Pope, all the clerics in the Secretary of State's office paid respects to him. When it was Marcinkus's turn to kneel before the Pontiff and kiss his ring, the new Pope greeted him affectionately and said, "I'll see you tomorrow."[35] Marcinkus became his private secretary for English affairs.[36] In 1964, after a chaotic trip to Jerusalem, Paul VI promoted Marcinkus to the honorary grade of Domestic Prelate and christened him as his advance man for other Eucharistic Congresses (they traveled eventually to nine cities on five continents).[37] Marcinkus was aggressive when it came to protecting the Pope while ensuring that the trip went well. In India, when police tried blocking him from following the Pope onto an altar platform, he lifted one of them to the side so he could stay astride Paul VI. At the airport tarmac in Bogotá, when Archbishop Giovanni Benelli, the Deputy Secretary of State, arrived and questioned some security arrangements at the last moment, Marcinkus shut him down in front of the entire Papal delegation.[38] It earned him the lasting enmity of Benelli, a powerful Curial official.[39] (Years later in Britain, Anglican officials almost banned Marcinkus from the Canterbury Cathedral after a contentious argument over the extent of protective services.)[40] But his talent was more than organizing the logistics and watching out for the Pope's safety. On each trip, local church officials fought to see who would sit closest to the Pontiff, and each submitted long lists of contributors and friends with whom they insisted the Pope meet. A prelate told Marcinkus he was the "only man I know who will say *no* to a cardinal."[41] That made him irreplaceable.[42] It also earned him, as he later recalled, "an enemy or two among our own people."[43]

Papal watchers soon noticed that at the Vatican, every time an English-speaking dignitary had a Papal audience—from Chicago Mayor Richard Daley to Martin Luther King Jr. to British Prime Minister Harold Wilson to Robert Kennedy—Marcinkus was there.[44]

In his roles as private interpreter and advance man, Marcinkus had earned a place inside the Pope's inner circle. Marcinkus realized he was more than a literal translator. Paul trusted that when they met with American politicians such as Richard Nixon or Hubert Humphrey, Marcinkus knew what was important to emphasize.[45]

In the following year, 1965, Marcinkus accompanied the Pope for a much anticipated visit to the United States, the first ever North American visit by a Pontiff.[46] He was again the translator when Paul VI met Lyndon Johnson in a suite at New York's Waldorf Towers.[47] In 1966, the Pope dispatched Marcinkus back to the U.S. so he could deliver a Papal letter to LBJ at his Texas ranch. It carried Paul VI's unsuccessful plea that Johnson stop bombing North Vietnam and that America unilaterally declare a cease-fire.[48]

When Cardinal Spellman died on December 2, 1967, Marcinkus let it be widely known in the Curia that he had wealthy patrons in Chicago and New York. Spellman had been an incredible fundraiser.[49] Some leading American clerics disliked that the U.S. church's main strength in Rome was its ability to raise money, and thought it was insulting that Italian clerics nicknamed Spellman "Moneybags."[50] But the Italian-dominated Curia needed American dollars. The U.S. economy was growing at a robust 10 percent a year. In Europe, the postwar expansion was winding down. National economies were struggling under fast rising inflation. Many in the Vatican admired the American model. Even without Spellman's contributions, U.S. Catholics were far and away the largest contributors.

Marcinkus hailed from the largest American diocese, and he had good relationships with every key cardinal in the United States. Two weeks after Spellman's death the Pope transferred Marcinkus from the Secretary of State's office to the Vatican Bank. Soon after that he became the secretary to the three-cardinal Commission of Vigilance that oversaw the IOR.[51]

Marcinkus was a financial neophyte. He later tried to downplay that. He told one journalist he had spent several days picking up tips by visiting banks in New York and Chicago. "That was it. What kind of training you need?"[52] To another he claimed to have taken several weeks of business administration classes at Harvard.[53] There is no evidence he ever took any.[54] He later admitted, "I didn't do a course because I didn't have any time."[55]

As for the history of the IOR and Special Administration, Marcinkus figured that he did not need to know it since Mennini and de Strobel—the "technicians" as he called them—had worked there for decades and could answer any questions.[56] He bought some books about international banking and business. After he talked to the two senior IOR laymen for some additional background, he told Chicago's Cardinal John Cody that from 1940 on "[the IOR] has been a gravy train."[57] His new bank colleagues were not so sure he was the right choice. One noted that he "couldn't even read a balance sheet."[58]

Marcinkus met Sindona only a month after his promotion. It took Sindona little time to discover that the monsignor's widespread reputation as frank and outspoken was well deserved.

Marcinkus asked Sindona what he thought about Mennini and de Strobel. Without waiting for an answer, Marcinkus volunteered that he thought little of them. He surprised Sindona by saying if he ran the IOR he might start his tenure by dismissing Mennini. Sindona thought that Mennini—who had been with the IOR since its inception—was "the only competent man there."[59] He told Marcinkus that he greatly underestimated the talent of those laymen.[60]

In subsequent meetings Sindona concluded that it was in fact Marcinkus who was in over his head, inept in financial matters, yet had the "pretensions to be a financier."[61]

"He was not very smart," Sindona told a reporter years later, "[and he] thought a free meal in a good restaurant was a big deal."[62] Marcinkus's borderline incompetence was made only worse by his unrestrained overconfidence on matters about which he knew nothing.[63] But since Marcinkus had the unconditional backing of the Pope, Sindona had no choice but to learn as best he could to live with the American monsignor.

At the same time that Marcinkus arrived at the IOR, another newcomer appeared on the periphery of the church's financial web, someone who would prove every bit as important as Sindona. At first glance Roberto Calvi seemed just another smart Milanese banker. But Calvi's ambition was grander, his focus sharper, and his persistence unyielding. He would win over Sindona and every key official in the Vatican Bank, even the newcomer Marcinkus.

Calvi, the eldest of four children from a middle-class Milanese family, was born in 1920, a month before Sindona. His father was a midlevel BCI bank manager. Calvi studied economics at Bocconi University before joining an aristocratic cavalry unit in which he served honorably on the Eastern Front during the war.[64] After the Germans occupied northern Italy in 1943, he went to work as a clerk for a small BCI branch in Bari.[65] Although not blessed with Sindona's charm, he was as determined to become a banking titan.

In 1946, Calvi thought he might have a better chance of reaching his goal if he worked at a Catholic bank. Friends at Catholic Action helped him land a job at the "bank of priests," Milan's Ambrosiano, which had been founded in 1896 to counter the influence of lay banks.[66] Monsignor Giuseppe Tovini, the Ambrosiano's founder, had named it after St. Ambrose, the city's patron saint.[67] Its bylaws required that anyone opening an account should first produce a baptismal certificate (that let in Protestants but barred Jews).[68] Only "good Catholics" could work there, although obtaining a letter of recommendation from a parish priest normally sufficed. Tovini—beatified in 1998 by Pope John Paul II—required that the bank's work be "moral and pious" and that its profits be distributed "for charitable purposes and Catholic schools."[69] (Through the 1980s, every annual report expressly thanked "Divine Providence" for guiding the bank to greater profits.)[70]

When the twenty-six-year-old Calvi joined the staid Ambrosiano, the bank managed the investment portfolios of most Catholic religious orders. His colleagues thought Calvi a humorless workaholic who wore formal dark suits and matching fedoras to appear he held a more important post than he did.[71] And the prematurely bald, mustached man was socially awkward. But his reserved appearance and personality made him popular with the bank's many conservative clients.[72] Having refined his school-taught French and German, he soon handled many of its Swiss, German, and French customers.[73]

In 1956, when Sindona and Montini had celebrated the end of communist control at Milan's largest trade union, Calvi toasted his own appointment as a joint manager at the Ambrosiano. Although it was only a midlevel position, it marked a milestone. It was the highest rank his father had achieved over a fifty-two-year career. Two years later, one of the Ambrosiano's senior executives, Carlo Alessandro Canesi, became Calvi's mentor and promoted him as his private deputy.[74]

In 1960, while Sindona and the Vatican were negotiating the terms of their joint venture in Banca Privata Finanziaria (BPF), the forty-year-old Calvi was devising a way to bypass Italy's ban on banks offering mutual funds. Calvi encouraged the Ambrosiano to take stakes in a Swiss bank and two in Luxembourg, through which he devised a rudimentary mutual fund, offering Italian investors the opportunity to invest in foreign stock funds.[75] A smashing success, the Ambrosiano had the market pretty much to itself. With the exception of a couple of Vatican-owned institutions, other Italian banks did not follow with competing products for nearly a decade.[76] Calvi was ecstatic.[77] When Canesi became the Ambrosiano's chairman in 1963, he promoted the forty-five-year-old Calvi to the post of *direttore centrale*, making him one of the bank's six most powerful officers.[78] Calvi did not try hiding his ambition. "He lived for power," another longtime colleague, Roberto Rosone, recalled. "There was only one woman for him, and that was power."[79]

Just after the New Year in 1969, Sindona's son-in-law—a college friend of Calvi—told Sindona that the Ambrosiano banker wanted to meet him.[80] When they got together, Sindona was amused that instead of talking about business, Calvi regaled him with stories about his family and a small retreat he owned near the Swiss border. At one point, he showed Sindona a badly scarred right index finger and then launched into a long account about how he mishandled an ax while killing a turkey at his country getaway. Only at the end of their meeting did Calvi briefly mention that he considered the Ambrosiano an antiquated bank. He hoped to modernize it with Sindona's help.[81]

When Sindona asked Calvi's Ambrosiano boss for his judgment about the young banker, he was told to dismiss whatever Calvi said. The advice to disregard Calvi had the opposite effect on Sindona. His second meeting with Calvi a few days later was all about business. Calvi was direct. He said that the Ambrosiano held large sums of money in safe but dull money market accounts. He would like to use that cash in more aggressive ventures with Sindona. The problem was that the bank's conservative board of directors was certain to reject it as too risky. Did Sindona, he asked, have any ideas about how to get the Ambrosiano's cumbersome bureaucracy to free up that money?

Sindona knew that if anyone had influence at the Banco Ambrosiano, it would be the lay officials at the IOR. The Vatican could always use an eager new colleague. If Calvi could gain more power at the Ambrosiano, he might become an integral partner.

Calvi liked the idea. "You must help me. Introduce me to Massimo Spada and ask him to speak on my behalf to the board and the general manager of the Ambrosiano."[82]

Sindona introduced Calvi to Spada. Although Spada now worked for Sindona, he had been at the IOR for more than three decades and was still involved on many projects with his former colleagues there. Spada judged Calvi as sincere and eager, and assured him he would try to help. A few weeks later, Calvi went to the IOR and met Luigi Mennini, Pellegrino de Strobel, and Monsignor Marcinkus.[83] They all liked the young Ambrosiano banker. Calvi soon ingratiated himself further by hiring one of Mennini's sons, Alessandro, as an assistant manager in the Ambrosiano's international division.[84]

A month before Calvi's arrival, Pope Paul VI had consecrated the forty-six-year-old Marcinkus as a bishop.[85] He also elevated him to be Secretary of the Administrative Office of the IOR, the Vatican Bank's first non-Italian director.[86] Although eighty-four-year-old Cardinal di Jorio was still the highest-ranking prelate on the oversight committee, his role was now an honorary one. Everyone realized that the outspoken American bishop was effectively running the Vatican Bank.[87] The ultimate sign of his new power: Marcinkus requested direct access to the Pontiff. Paul VI agreed. Marcinkus was the first cleric inside the IOR to have a straight reporting line to the Pope. Many envied this accommodation.[88] Making matters worse for Marcinkus's enemies, he retained his role as the Pope's advance man for foreign trips, which gave him a chance to stay personally close to Paul.

Two weeks after his promotion, a *Time* magazine profile of Marcinkus noted he "is now the key man in Vatican finances," controlling assets that "run into the billions." As for his lack of financial experience, "By his own admission, Marcinkus needs all the help he can get. . . . He is a first class organizer, but readily confesses: 'I have no banking experience.' "[89] *

The question *why appoint him?* dominated the gossipy Curia. Cardinals John Wright of Pittsburgh and Michele Pellegrino of Turin expressed to the Pope their concerns about Marcinkus's inexperience. But Paul VI's private secretary, Monsignor Pasquale Macchi, told him to ignore the naysayers. Macchi was sick of the imperious di Jorio and he liked Marcinkus, who he thought would learn quickly on the job.[91]

Some thought that the Pope had selected Marcinkus hoping that his take-command style might shake up the church's staid finances. But most believed Paul VI wanted to know the details of what was happening inside the opaque IOR. Marcinkus was a trustworthy guard dog who would report honestly.[92] Since Marcinkus was tough, the Pope figured he could withstand the IOR's intensely competitive environment.[93] A few even speculated Marcinkus was a stalking horse for the American church, laying the foundation for the future election of a U.S. cardinal as Pope. That theory had legs. Cardinal John Cody, from Marcinkus's hometown of Chicago, seemed to be the new Spellman. Cody flew to Rome for Marcinkus's consecration. When boarding his plane, Cody had told a reporter, "Although Bishop-elect Marcinkus has served for many years in important tasks outside the archdiocese, we still consider him one of our own."[94] In the Machiavellian world of the Curia, with ever-shifting allegiances in quests for power, some interpreted that to mean that Marcinkus had dual loyalties that made him untrustworthy. The Pope evidently paid no heed to the chatter.

Mennini and de Strobel were disturbed that the Pope had not weighed financial qualifications as a prerequisite for appointing someone as the overseer of an institution as important and powerful as the IOR. They now had to re-

---

* *Time* noted that Marcinkus's annual salary was $6,000, "about a teller's salary in a New York City bank." As for the value of the church's stocks under his control, *Time* estimated the value between $10 billion and $15 billion ($94 billion and $153 billion in 2014 dollars).[90]

port to Marcinkus. Their hope was that he might follow in the tradition that the clerics who oversaw the IOR did so passively. That was quickly dashed. Although Marcinkus did not dismiss Mennini, as he had once told Sindona he might, he let it be known he intended to be a hands-on manager.[95]

Not long after his appointment, Marcinkus summoned Sindona to his office in the squat fifteenth-century Tower of Nicholas V.[96] When Sindona arrived, Vittoria Marigonda, Marcinkus's secretary for a decade, greeted him. Sindona knew Marigonda because she worked briefly at an investment bank at Group Sindona before she moved to the Vatican.[97] He also noted several new, young Italian secretaries, prettier than any women Sindona had ever seen working at the Vatican.[98] Once he walked inside the bishop's office, he noticed that di Jorio's traditional décor had been replaced with modern black leather sofas and chairs, a low-rise glass coffee table, and some large metal sculptures. A golf bag was in the corner, with a tag from Acquasanta (Holy Water), Rome's most exclusive country club. Marcinkus had moved up from his days of having to sweet-talk his way into playing a round of golf at the SGI-owned Oligata Romana.[99] The archbishop had also gotten an "honorary membership" at one of Rome's oldest and most prestigious clubs, the Circolo della Caccia (The Hunting Club).[100]

Marcinkus was smoking a pipe and sitting in an overstuffed leather chair. A large pewter ashtray overflowed with Marlboro butts and cigar stubs. The bishop beckoned Sindona to sit in an adjoining chaise.

"I asked for full powers as the condition *sina qua non* for my accepting the presidency," Marcinkus told Sindona. He paused for dramatic effect. "And the Holy Father granted them to me."*

Sindona said nothing but felt Marcinkus was exaggerating.[102]

Both men knew they had the Pope's unquestioned backing. Marcinkus's showy display confirmed to Sindona that the path to business at the IOR was

---

* Fifteen years later, when embroiled in a great scandal, Marcinkus told author John Cornwell just the opposite: "I said four times, 'You must be out of your minds!' I said, 'Why don't you get somebody else? I have no experience in banking!' And they said, 'You have to kind of watch over things.' I said, 'I'm incompetent for that!' That's the way they do things around here!" He told *Il Sabato*, the Catholic weekly, "I have never been a businessman. I would not know where to begin." But Marcinkus said he felt he had no choice but to accept the posting. "I've never asked for a job and I've never refused one. I don't believe I have a right to refuse."

"He's never ever technically run the bank," claimed his private secretary, Vittoria Marigonda. "The bank has been run by Luigi Mennini for nearly forty years."[101]

now through the bishop. As for Sindona, he hoped that Marcinkus might stumble and make a mistake that could shake Paul VI's faith in him. But instead of making an error that sidelined his career, events unrelated to the Vatican Bank boosted the Pope's confidence in him. When Nixon came to the Vatican in 1969, tens of thousands of students protesting the Vietnam War rioted in Rome's streets.* Marcinkus personally took control of security arrangements for the church, directing Nixon's helicopter to land in St. Peter's Square. He then stood down the Secret Service in a tense argument and barred them from a private meeting with the Pope, at which Marcinkus was the translator. As the police battled huge running crowds, the President and the Pope met. A couple of months later Marcinkus used a body block to free the seventy-one-year-old Pontiff from a crowd that besieged him in Switzerland.[104] In July, Marcinkus played a key role on a trip to Nigeria where the Pope tried in vain to promote a peace conference between the Nigerians and the secessionist state of Biafra.[105] The following year, he helped get the Pope to safety in Sardinia when a left-wing mob stoned the motorcade, as well as at Castel Gandolfo when a heckler just missed the Pope's head with a brick. In a visit to the Philippines, a man wielding a butcher knife jumped out from a Manila crowd and lunged at the Pontiff.[106] Marcinkus's quick reaction proved a *Boston Globe* article from the previous year correct that his unofficial role on foreign trips was to be "a one-man squad of bodyguards."[107] Paul VI gave him a special commendation when they returned to Rome. In the Curia some now dubbed him *il gorilla* (he disliked that nickname because, "A gorilla at home in the States is like . . . a hood").[108]

Leading prelates in the Curia knew that Marcinkus provided far more than

---

* The riots that greeted Nixon were just another sign to the members of the P2 Masonic lodge that Italy was under siege by militant leftists. In April, Milan's main railway station was bombed. In August, explosions hit several trains. Just before the 1969 Christmas holidays, bombs exploded at the National Bank of Agriculture in Rome's Piazza Fontana, the National Bank of Labor, and a national monument to King Victor Emmanuel II. Seventeen innocent bystanders were killed and nearly one hundred maimed. The following month marked the formation of the Red Brigades, a radical Marxist group whose goal was the violent overthrow of the government. Sindona and many other P2 members considered themselves the last line between order and chaos. The turn to violence, coupled with a rapidly declining lira, brought the IOR a new flood of rich Italians seeking a safe haven. As for the Piazza Fontana bombings, police thought they were the work of leftists and anarchists. But eventually investigators believed right-wing fanatics were responsible. In 1995, after twenty-six years of multiple arrests, indictments, trials, and appeals, the police and prosecutors admitted defeat. No one was ever convicted of the bombings. Conspiracy theories about it are as popular in Italy as JFK assassination theories are in the United States.[103]

just good security and planning. The Pope had come to completely trust his instincts and judgment. In 1971 the Pope elevated Marcinkus to president at the IOR to more accurately reflect his full authority there.[109]

In February, Roberto Calvi was promoted to general manager at the Ambrosiano, the bank's third-ranking position. When the CEO retired that December, Calvi became its *consigliere delegato*, its president. With Sindona's help, he set about to transform the sleepy Ambrosiano into an international merchant financial institution that traded stocks, invested in real estate, and even took stakes in private companies. To bypass restrictive Italian banking laws that limited the permissible scope of activities for a bank, Sindona had shown Calvi how to establish a web of holding companies in offshore banking havens such as Luxembourg, the Bahamas, Panama, and Costa Rica. Those jurisdictions prided themselves on the strictest client secrecy, allowing local attorneys and bankers to serve as proxies so that the true ownership of companies and banks was hidden from Italian tax authorities. On March 23, 1971, Calvi used Compendium, a Luxembourg holding company that he later renamed Banco Ambrosiano Holding, to register the Cisalpine Overseas Bank in Nassau, Bahamas.[110] It was impossible on paper to track it back to the Ambrosiano, much less to discover that the Vatican Bank and Sindona held minority shares (the bank was capitalized for just $2.5 million, but in a few months would boast about $100 million in equity, most of it redirected Ambrosiano deposits, and $16.5 million in Swiss francs and German marks from the IOR).[111] The maze of offshore holding companies was so effective in hiding the real owners that an official from Italy's central bank would later admit they only found out the details of the Ambrosiano's Bahamian operations when "we . . . read it in the newspapers."[112]

A huge unregulated business dubbed the Eurocurrency Market had boomed in the island nation. It was a $65 billion industry in funds loaned by U.S. and European banks outside their country of origin.[113] The banks avoided domestic disclosure about the details of loans, and in some cases, such as British banks, they avoided a tax on earnings connected to interest on the loans. It would take a decade before British and U.S. authorities managed to close most of the Eurocurrency loopholes. But in 1971, when Calvi first visited the Bahamas with a handful of other Ambrosiano executives, it was an ideal place to establish the bank's most distant offshore subsidiary.

Calvi asked Marcinkus to become a member of the Bahamian bank's board of directors. Sindona had told Calvi it was a good idea because wherever "I put him in . . . it helps me get money."[114] The bishop accepted. On August 5, 1971, a letter from Cisalpine informed the Bahamian registry of companies that a "Mr. Paul C. Marcinkus" was a new director. "The Most Reverend" was left off. Nogara's unofficial rule had been that only IOR laymen or Black Nobles should join the boards of companies into which the Vatican invested. Nogara thought it would be untoward to have one of the cardinals from the oversight committee serve as a corporate director. The clerical garb carried too great a symbolic moral approval from the church. But there was no Nogara to persuade Marcinkus that it was a bad idea. Instead, when Calvi asked him, Marcinkus thought, "Why not?"[115] As a director of Ambrosiano's Bahamian branch, he was the first bishop in church history to serve on any board of any bank.*

Sindona suggested Pierre Siegenthaler, a Swiss thirty-four-year-old world-class yachtsman who also had some New York banking experience, become Cisalpine's managing director. Calvi agreed.[117] Siegenthaler, with a penchant for Gucci shoes and oversized Rolexes, ran Cisalpine from his Nassau home.[118] Calvi liked the Bahamas so much that he bought a villa in a new luxury development in Lyford Cay. When Calvi and his wife, Clara, and their two teenage children spent their first holiday there that year, Marcinkus joined them.[119] When Clara saw Marcinkus, she recalled that "he threw his arms around me and sang 'Arrivederci Roma.'"[120] The men spent the holiday discussing their bold new ventures while tuna fishing.[121]

In the following months, Calvi used his Luxembourg holding company Compendium to establish more offshore banks, not only in traditional European havens such as Luxembourg, Switzerland, and Liechtenstein, but also in less savory asylums like Panama, Nicaragua, and Peru. Calvi formed so many shell companies in Panama that he soon ran out of people to name as directors, resorting on the last one to naming the Ambrosiano's switchboard operator.[122]

---

* Much later, when the IOR faced embarrassing questions over the extent of the church's relationship with Calvi and his complex business network, Marcinkus tried downplaying his Cisalpine role. He told the BBC's *Panorama* television program that he seldom saw Calvi and that when it came to Cisalpine, "I am not even present [at board meetings] because of commitments elsewhere." In fact, records reveal that over eleven years, Marcinkus only missed one of twenty-two board meetings, traveling to attend them in Paris, London, New York, Geneva, Zurich, and Nassau.[116]

Calvi soon had a new deal to pitch to Marcinkus. He wanted the IOR to help the Ambrosiano move large sums out of Italy, in excess of what was permitted by Italian currency regulations. To help disguise the money moves, Calvi proposed *conto deposito*, so-called back-to-back operations in which the Ambrosiano would make deposits with the IOR, who would then pass the money to Cisalpine and other Calvi-controlled offshore companies. For Italian banking regulators, it would appear that the Ambrosiano's money was merely parked at the IOR, when it had actually been moved to little-regulated foreign shells. At times, the IOR could direct the money to companies that needed it temporarily to boost their balance sheets. For its role, the IOR would earn one quarter of one percent of all the money that passed through it (that was later reduced to one sixteenth).[123] Marcinkus thought it sounded like easy profits. By the end of December, the IOR had opened a $37 million five-year Cisalpine certificate of deposit, at an above-market rate of 8.5 percent interest.[124]

At the Vatican Bank, Mennini was one of the few who knew about Marcinkus's decision to join Cisalpine's board. He did not think it wise for the IOR to become further entwined in offshore deals. But Marcinkus dismissed him as well intentioned but old-fashioned. The IOR had to adapt to new and more sophisticated times. "You can't run the church on Hail Marys," he said.[125]

16

Operation Fraulein

Only months after helping Calvi incorporate Cisalpine in the Bahamas, Sindona embarked on a period of aggressive expansion. In Italy, he and Calvi bought La Centrale Finanziaria, a financial holding company that had long been on his wish list.[1] And at the behest of Graham Martin, the American ambassador to Italy, Sindona purchased an influential Rome-based English-language newspaper, *The Daily American*. Martin wanted to keep the paper—in which the CIA had a covert 40 percent share—out of the hands of a socialist publisher.[2] At a lavish reception at Rome's Grand Hotel to celebrate the acquisition, Martin joined the city's mayor, several cabinet ministers, and Marcinkus in toasting Sindona.[3] An article two days later in *The Wall Street Journal* dubbed Sindona "Italy's Howard Hughes," noting, "Bishop Marcinkus' attendance at the reception was taken as proof of Mr. Sindona's strong ties with the Roman Catholic Church."[4] The *Journal* also predicted that it was likely only a matter of time before Sindona would "make a substantial increase in his American investments."[5]

Five months later Sindona proved the *Journal* right when he made a successful $40 million bid to buy a controlling stake in America's eighteenth largest bank, the Long Island–based Franklin National.[6] *The New York Times* noted that while Sindona "was a substantial investor in a variety of American enterprises," the Franklin purchase meant "he [had] moved into the big time in the United States."[7]

Laurence Tisch, a principal in Loews Corporation, sold Sindona his shares in the $3.4 billion bank. Franklin was under earnings pressure for nearly a year. Arthur Roth, its former chairman, had been trying to buy back the bank he had founded. But Sindona, using his Luxembourg holding company, Fasco, outbid Roth by $8.25 a share, a 25 percent premium to the stock's trading price.[8] He raised the cash by selling two successful holding companies to Calvi. Sindona dismissed some critics who thought he overpaid: "I have never lost money on the stock exchange."[9] (Later, when Franklin turned out to have financial problems, he'd complain that he had "trusted the American system . . . I [should] have done an audit myself.")[10]

Roth challenged the Tisch-Sindona sale. He asked New York's Superintendent of Banks to withhold approval until the state was fully satisfied that Sindona's character was "above reproach."[11] And as part of a public relations campaign to reverse the sale, Roth released an open letter to Tisch in which he asked: "Do you know enough about Michele Sindona to unconditionally recommend him as a person who will be good for the bank? Will there be a full disclosure of his finances, his backers, and detailed biographies?"[12]

Roth, who had been ousted in 1970 in what he called a "palace revolution," cited a *Wall Street Journal* investigation the previous year into Sindona's purchase of two American companies, Interphoto and Oxford Electric. The *Journal* reported that the deals were marked by a clear "conflict of interest." The paper concluded that Sindona's maze of Liechtenstein holding companies was "a tangled web of interlocking ownerships, directorships and debt."[13] But that incident proved of little help to Roth's effort to discredit Sindona. The SEC cleared those purchases and dismissed any concerns after a two-day hearing.[14]

In challenging the Franklin acquisition, Roth also complained to federal officials, asking they bar Sindona from taking a controlling interest since his Liechtenstein-based Fasco had previously purchased shares in other U.S. industrial firms. Federal law then prohibited companies from holding banks at the same time they had stakes in other commercial businesses. Sindona, however, turned out to be exempt as he was buying Franklin as an "individual purchaser."[15]

A month after the successful bid, Franklin appointed Sindona, and one of his top executives, Carlo Bordoni, to its board.[16] Sindona encouraged Calvi to join him in the American market. The Ambrosiano bought $16 million of convertible bonds in Cleveland's Union Commerce Bank.[17] The two developed solid business connections, counting ex–Texas Governor John Connally as a friend and advisor. Calvi became a frequent guest at Connally's sprawling Texas ranch.[18] David Kennedy, Nixon's Secretary of Treasury, was a close Sindona friend and had done business with him when Kennedy had been chairman of Continental Illinois Bank.[19]

Sindona retained the Wall Street law firm of Mudge, Rose, Guthrie & Alexander. It was there he had met Richard Nixon, one of the firm's partners, in April 1965.[20] Now, only a few days before Election Day, flush with the success of his Franklin buyout, Sindona called Maurice Stans, the chairman of Nixon's 1972 reelection campaign. He offered a stunning million-dollar personal contribution ($5.4 million in 2014 dollars). Sindona asked only for anonymity. Stans reluctantly said no. The deadline for disclosing contributions had passed. (When the secret offer became public a couple of years later, it kicked off congressional and IRS investigations to determine whether the mere offer and the failure to disclose it might have broken any laws; it had not.)[21]

Although Sindona was focused on opportunities in the United States, he kept making deals in Italy. That summer he sold to Calvi—in a convoluted $119 million deal—most of his stake in La Centrale Finanziaria.[22] At the same time, the two used Suprafin S.p.A., a company partly owned by the IOR, plus two offshore companies and accounts at three Swiss banks, to accumulate shares of the Ambrosiano. Neither of them seemed bothered that it was illegal in Italy for a bank to buy its own shares on the open market.[23] Their goal was to acquire control of the bank, but to do so in small enough increments that no government regulator or Ambrosiano official would notice.[24]

But the matter that most consumed their time was a year-long deal over whether to buy one of the church's most prestigious holdings, the Banca Cattolica del Veneto. It was Sindona's idea. He discussed it first with Massimo Spada, before encouraging Calvi to make a formal bid.[25] The Cattolica was the Ambrosiano's sister bank in Venice, one of Italy's most important Catholic institutions since its 1878 opening, and intertwined historically with the Venetian clergy and Black Nobles.[26] Sindona and Spada thought Banca Cattolica was a natural fit with the Ambrosiano's expanding empire. But they also knew that the two banks were fierce competitors.[27]

Calvi thought it unlikely that the church would part with the Cattolica. Albino Luciani, Venice's Patriarch, whose archdiocese owned a minority share, was almost certain to object. Nevertheless Calvi pitched the idea to Marcinkus in 1971. In a letter, Calvi offered to purchase up to 50 percent of the bank at a hefty premium.[28] The offer posed little downside risk. If the Vatican was receptive, Calvi's prestige at the Ambrosiano would be enhanced. If Marcinkus declined because such a move would cause too much of an uproar inside the Curia, no one at the Ambrosiano would blame Calvi since it was a long shot in the first place.

Marcinkus, however, liked the idea and raised it with Paul VI. The Pope was hesitant. The bank was one of the church's crown jewels. As was his style, for months he vacillated between okaying or prohibiting the sale. Marcinkus arranged a private meeting between Calvi and the Pope.[29] It was there that Calvi was his most persuasive, arguing that the Ambrosiano would be not only a superb caretaker for the church by maintaining Cattolica's traditions and integrity, but that the bank's outdated methods would be modernized, leading to higher profits. Calvi told the Pontiff that he wanted a large enough share so he controlled the bank, and the Vatican would own the rest, thereby benefiting from any surge in earnings.

A week later Marcinkus met Calvi and shared the news that the deal was approved.

"Are you sure," Calvi asked. "Is it available to you? Is the boss [the Pope] in agreement with it?"[30]

Marcinkus assured him Paul VI had personally given his consent.

In March 1972, the IOR announced the transfer to the Ambrosiano of a 37.5 percent interest of Banca Cattolica for $46.5 million.[31] The executed contract between the church and Calvi was top secret even by IOR standards. Few officials saw it. Marcinkus did not want anyone outside the Vatican Bank to know he had unilaterally decided to sell Calvi a 50 percent stake, 18,060,000 shares, not the 37.5 percent, or 13,500,000 shares of the announced deal.[32] And to address the Pope's concerns about the integrity of the bank, the contract contained a clause that the new owners must preserve the Cattolica's "high social, moral and Catholic aims."[33]

The parties followed Sindona's advice to complete the deal. The Vatican Bank's shares went to a Sindona-owned Liechtenstein holding company, which held them as a fiduciary for the Ambrosiano. The money was paid in five installments, in a convoluted back-and-forth of offshore transfers that had become a hallmark of Calvi, Sindona, and Marcinkus deals (the IOR put all its proceeds into Calvi's Bahamian bank, bringing Marcinkus's deposits in Cisalpine to a dizzying $112.5 million).[34]

Not everyone was happy with the sale of a controlling block of Banca Cattolica. Venice's Luciani complained to Pope Paul and to the influential deputy

1

2

From the sixth century, much of the money to run the Catholic Church's lavish Papal Court came from the sale of indulgences, promises that God would forgo earthly punishment for the buyer's sins. By Gregory XVI's papacy (1831–1846), overspending, abysmal management, and antiquated views about investments forced the Pope (*left*)—to borrow money from James de Rothschild (*right*), the patriarch of Europe's preeminent Jewish banking dynasty.

3

For more than a thousand years, along with leading the church, Popes were monarchs of the Papal States, a temporal kingdom that at its height in the late eighteenth century included much of central Italy. A succession of Popes condemned the popular uprisings that toppled European monarchies as a destabilizing modernist movement. Here, two Italian nationalists are beheaded in Rome in 1868.

As the rebellion to unify Italy gained momentum, the Vatican paid for its own army—Zuavi Pontifici (Papal Infantry)—of mostly young, unmarried Catholic volunteers from many countries. However, when in 1870, nationalist troops massed outside Rome, Pius IX (1846–1878) realized his militia was outnumbered, and ordered the white flag raised over St. Peter's Basilica. That surrender reduced the church's 16,000-square-mile empire to a tiny parcel of land.

4

5

For Pius IX, the loss of the Papal States—the church's earthly symbol of power—also deprived it of huge income. Pius, the first Pope to be photographed, declared himself a prisoner in the Vatican and steadfastly refused to recognize the new Italian state.

6 

Pius X (1903–1914), the first modern Pope from a working-class family, was an ultraconservative who encouraged anonymous denunciations of so-called freethinkers and modernists. And while he condemned unrestrained capitalism and reinforced the church's backward view of finances, he also spent liberally, doubling the size of Vatican City.

7 

Bologna's Cardinal Giacomo Paolo Giovanni Battista della Chiesa became Pope on Pius's death in 1914. He took the Pontifical name Benedict XV (1914–1922). All countries rejected his efforts at peacemaking during World War I. By the time he died in 1922, the Vatican was reeling from a 40 percent loss of its capital caused by a series of bad investments.

8

The son of a Milanese factory worker, the hot-tempered Pius XI (1922–1939) ordered the Vatican's first internal audit. It took six years to complete and revealed that the church was down to its last dollars. Yet the Pope still refused to loosen the restrictions on commercial investments or to modernize its finances.

9

Benito Mussolini (*center*) led the radical right-wing National Fascist Party. Only eight months after Pius's election, Mussolini led tens of thousands of fascists in a "March on Rome." A week later he was sworn in as prime minister. His ascent seemed ominous for the church. An avowed atheist, he had once described priests "as black microbes who are as deadly to mankind as tuberculosis germs."

10

Pius feared godless bolshevism more than Italy's fascists. Eugenio Pacelli, the Papal Nuncio to Germany, reinforced the Pope's fear. Pacelli, who descended from Catholic aristocrats, had faced off against an armed gang of communist revolutionaries in Munich in 1925. Although he escaped unhurt, the confrontation reaffirmed his belief that communism was the greatest threat to the church.

11

In 1929, Pius XI was the first Pope since the 1870 loss of the Papal States to recognize the Italian state. The Februrary 24, 1929, cover of *La Domenica del Corriere* shows Benito Mussolini (*far right*) signing the treaty with Papal Secretary of State Cardinal Pietro Gasparri. It recognized the Vatican as a sovereign nation and gave the church its greatest power in centuries.

12

As part of the 1929 pact, Italy paid the Vatican for confiscating the Papal States. The Pope hired Bernardino Nogara (*left*), a well-connected businessman and banker, to invest the windfall. Giuseppe Volpi (*right*), a business tycoon, was Nogara's close friend and mentor.

13

Despite Wall Street's 1929 stock market crash, Pius XI embarked on the "Imperial Papacy," Vatican City's largest modern-day construction boom. He approved a telegraph office, train station, power plant, an industrial quarter, and a printing facility. Here, Cardinal Pacelli (*left*) and Pius XI attend the opening of Vatican Radio in 1931.

Secretary of State Cardinal Pacelli (*seated, center*), signing an agreement with German Vice Chancellor Franz von Papen (*far left*). In a historic 1933 accord, the Vatican was the first sovereign state to sign a bilateral treaty with Adolf Hitler's Third Reich. The Nazis promised to protect Catholics inside Germany in return for the church endorsing Hitler's government.

In October 1935, 100,000 Italian troops invaded Ethiopia, part of Mussolini's vision for a vast East African empire. The Vatican had investments in manufacturers of wartime munitions and weapons. At left, a priest celebrates mass on the front line. Mussolini was so pleased that he told Nazi officials, "Why they [Vatican officials] even declared the Abyssinian war a Holy War!"

By 1938, Pius XI picked an American Jesuit, John LaFarge, to lead a small team in drafting a Papal Encyclical—*Humani Generis Unitas* (The Unity of the Human Race)—condemning anti-Semitism and racism. Pius died the following year before the decree was finished. His successor, Pius XII, buried the encyclical in the Vatican's Secret Archives. LaFarge is far right, during a 1963 presentation of the St. Francis Peace Medal to the Rev. Martin Luther King Jr.

17

Cardinal Pacelli, who became Pope in March 1939, took the name Pius XII. He was an acknowledged Teutonophile. In 1931, the number two Nazi, Field Marshall Hermann Göring—who had instituted so-called morality trials intended to embarrass Catholic priests and nuns—visited the Vatican. Here, Göring (*second from left*) is with Angelo Giuseppe Roncalli, the Papal Nuncio to Bulgaria, and later Pope John XXIII. Göring sent a wire to Hitler: "Mission accomplished. Pope unfrocked. Tiara and pontifical vestments are a perfect fit."

18

Three days after Pacelli became Pope, Germany invaded Czechoslovakia. High-ranking Nazis and church officials met frequently despite the aggression. At a Berlin reception, Papal Nuncio Cesare Orsenigo (*left*) greets Hitler and his foreign minister Joachim von Ribbentrop. In 1942, Orsenigo turned away an SS officer who wanted to confess a firsthand account of the massacre of Jews.

19

The war presented the church with great business risks and opportunities. A central figure was Giuseppe Volpi, a former finance minister for Mussolini, and one of Italy's most successful businessmen. With Volpi often acting as a proxy, the Vatican invested money in profitable ventures, many of which were in the killing fields of Eastern Europe.

20

SS-Brigadeführer Walther Schellenberg directed Nazi foreign intelligence operations from July 1944. After the war he told U.S. interrogators that the Nazis "had many men in the Vatican." Another German intelligence officer, Reinhard Karl Wilhelm Reme, disclosed the network of Third Reich agents he had recruited in Italy. That list included the name Nogara. That revelation, reported in this book for the first time, raises the question of whether the Vatican's chief moneyman was a Nazi wartime spy.

21

A Croatian priest based in Rome, Krunoslav Draganović, was a member of the Ustaša, an anti-Semitic, anti-Serb, and anti-communist party in power in wartime Croatia. Draganović ran one of several postwar escape networks—sanctioned by high-ranking Vatican clerics and ultimately U.S. and British intelligence—through which hundreds of criminals found safe haven in South America and the Middle East.

22

The Vatican used gold as its chief hard asset. Since the Nazis looted the gold reserves of the countries they conquered, the church's accumulation of the metal proved as morally problematic as did many of its business stakes. Here, an American soldier holds wedding rings from Holocaust victims. The Vatican later denied that it was the repository for the rings and gold coins from 28,000 gypsies murdered in Croatia.

Secretary of State, Archbishop Giovanni Benelli, that the deal was against the church's long-term interests. Luciani reminded Benelli that not only was he the chief prelate of the diocese that owned part of the bank, but that the Cattolica was also headquartered in Venice. He felt he should have been more involved in the decision over whether to sell. Luciani was also upset since Calvi canceled the bank's preferred interest rates to Catholic institutions.[35]

Benelli tried palming Luciani off to Marcinkus. During the one time they talked about it, the IOR chief listened to Luciani's plea that the deal be undone.

Marcinkus told him it was too late. Luciani persisted.

"Eminence, don't you have anything better to do?" Marcinkus asked.[36]

The discussion was over. Luciani returned to Venice simmering at the cavalier way in which Marcinkus had dismissed him. All he could do to protest the sale was to move the accounts of the Venetian diocese from Banca Cattolica to the tiny Banco San Marco. The entire affair meant Luciani became yet another in a growing list of ranking prelates now hoping that Marcinkus would trip up.[37] And much to the horror of those who detested Marcinkus, that summer some American newspapers speculated not only that Pope Paul might retire when he turned seventy-five in September, but that Marcinkus "was an outside possibility for election to the papacy."[38] While Vaticanologists thought that was laughable and revealed the extent to which the American press did not understand church politics, that Marcinkus could even be mentioned publicly as the next Pontiff infuriated his foes. That October, at a Cisalpine director's meeting held at London's tony Claridge's Hotel, Marcinkus joked with Calvi that he was accumulating enemies faster than the IOR was gaining depositors.[39]

In March 1973 some of his opponents thought there might be an opportunity to bring Marcinkus down a couple of notches when the Vatican Bank got embroiled in a spat with the U.S. Securities and Exchange Commission. The SEC obtained an injunction against an unregistered California-based investment advisor who had acquired options to buy 27 percent of an American oil and gas equipment firm, Vetco Offshore Industries. The disclosure statements mandated by the SEC for such a large holding had not been filed.[40] After some further investigation, the American Stock Exchange suspended trading in the company because "unusual activity in Vetco stock raised questions as to whether the market in the stock may have been artificially influenced."[41]

The Vatican's secret role came to light when the SEC discovered that the unlicensed California investment advisor, a former liquor salesman, Irving Eisenberger, was acting on behalf of Liechtenstein-based Fiduciary Investment Services A.G. Its only client turned out to be the IOR.[42] Before that disclosure, Vetco was unaware it was the Vatican that had benefited in the $35 million in option trades and some short swing profits.[43] The company's share price had doubled as a result of Eisenberger churning the stock since the previous summer. Under U.S. securities regulations, insiders—defined as anyone controlling 10 percent or more of a company—were banned from excessive trading. Vetco demanded the Vatican return its improperly earned profits.[44]

Marcinkus reached out to Sindona for help since he had ten years of investing experience in the United States. Sindona advised Marcinkus to resolve the dispute immediately to keep it off the media's radar. Marcinkus reached a fast agreement with the Vetco directors. There was not a lot of money involved (the IOR turned over $320,000 it had earned in profits).[45] Eisenberger signed a consent decree with the SEC.[46] The story got little traction in the Italian press and it did not prove useful to the bishop's enemies.

Marcinkus had another close call that same year, one that at first seemed to have the potential to put a stop to his career momentum.[47] A few months after the Vetco news, U.S. Justice Department investigators met with Marcinkus in Rome as part of a criminal probe into an international counterfeiting ring involving the Mafia and stolen or counterfeit American securities.[48] They had questions about whether the IOR—and possibly even Marcinkus himself—had played a role.

The Justice Department visit to the Vatican was the culmination of a broad eighteen-month racketeering investigation into the Genovese crime family that had started in the Manhattan District Attorney's office. In its early stages, the DA's probe had focused on Vincent Rizzo, a Genovese soldier thought to be a middleman in a South American drug cartel that fed the Northeast (soldiers are the lowest-ranking mobsters in a crime family).[49] Rizzo lived on Avenue A, not far from a Little Italy social hall that served as a hangout for a lot of New York mobsters. Joe Coffey, the lead Rackets Bureau detective, obtained court-ordered wiretaps for some of Rizzo's regular haunts, including the social hall.[50] When the police learned that Rizzo was planning a trip to Germany in February 1972, Coffey got permission to follow him. Through Interpol, German police agreed to bug Rizzo's Munich hotel room.[51] Rizzo met two men there: Alfred Barg, an apparently legitimate German director of a

Swiss investment firm, and Winfried Ense, a self-described "facilitator" whom Interpol had investigated a year earlier for a possible role in the sale of stolen U.S. Treasury certificates.

The trip had nothing to do with narcotics. Over a couple of days, Coffey learned that Rizzo had somehow come into a large cache of Triple-A corporate bonds, stock certificates, and some U.S. Treasury bonds. Included among the companies were AT&T, Coca-Cola, Chrysler, and Pan Am.[52] It was not clear from what Coffey heard whether the securities were stolen or counterfeit.* Rizzo had come to Barg and Ense because a Philadelphia-based mobster had vouched that the two Germans could move an enormous quantity of black-market securities.[54] At one point, Ense said that they knew an Austrian, Leopold Ledl, with contacts in the Vatican. "They [the Vatican] want all they can get," he told Rizzo.

Coffey would soon discover that Ledl was a con man and swindler with a thick Interpol dossier.[55] He owned a multimillion-dollar estate outside Vienna and ran an Austrian-based construction firm and a Liberian shipping company. He also had two Liechtenstein holding companies. Interpol suspected he had earned his fortune in everything from arms trafficking to stolen securities to narcotics. In legit business circles he used the title "Honorary Consul," something he falsely claimed Michel Micombero, the President of the African Republic of Burundi, had bestowed on him (investigators later learned Ledl had sold at least three hundred "Honorary Consul" titles, for up to $100,000 each, throughout Europe).[56]

As a veteran New York City detective, Coffey liked running his own investigation. He knew that by bringing in federal authorities he would lose control. But he had no choice. He had stumbled across an international conspiracy about fake or stolen securities that included U.S. Treasuries, plus a possible link to the Vatican.[57]

"Coffey came and asked us to work the investigation with them," recalls William Aronwald, then deputy chief prosecutor for the Justice Department's Organized Crime and Racketeering Strike Force. "I had been in the Rackets

---

* A congressional committee at the time estimated the size of the black market in counterfeit and stolen U.S. securities to be about $50 billion. Large blocks of Coca-Cola stock were stolen in late 1970 in New York and Los Angeles. Two years later, around the time of Rizzo's German meeting, some of the missing Coke stock started surfacing in Europe, Lebanon, and Panama.[53]

Bureau in the DA's office so the New York detectives felt comfortable with me. We entered into a joint venture consisting of the District Attorney, their Detective Squad, as well as the FBI."[58] Aronwald dubbed the strike team Operation Fraulein because of the German connection.

Based on additional wiretaps, the investigators suspected that Rizzo was only a front man for Matteo de Lorenzo, a Genovese captain. And the conspiracy to sell the illegal securities was widespread, including mobsters from Buffalo to Beverly Hills as well as a group of swindlers, and even a few crooked stock and options traders.[59]

In May 1972, de Lorenzo joined Rizzo on another trip to Munich. This time, a New York detective, Mario Trapani, accompanied Coffey. The German police again bugged the phones in the mobsters' suite at the Bayerischer Hof Hotel, and also placed a bug in the bedroom lamp. But the mobsters met with Barg and Ense in the suite's living room, frustrating the detectives, who were unable to decipher anything on the muffled recordings.[60]

Shortly after returning from that trip, the strike team arrested in the U.S. a British con man and swindler, Hyman Grant. In return for leniency on possible drug charges, he provided details about the still evolving scheme.[61] Grant tied Ledl to Rome's Mario Foligni, an extraordinary poseur who claimed to be a count and an owner of half a dozen successful businesses. Although many were skeptical of Foligni's claims to nobility and his boasts of great wealth, he had sterling contacts inside the Vatican, including passing friendships with ranking prelates like Archbishop Benelli and Bishop Marcinkus.[62]

That November, Coffey, this time accompanied by an FBI agent, Richard Tamarro, flew to Munich (the first time the FBI had ever sent an operational agent overseas to investigate an open case).[63] Their assignment was to convince Barg and Ense to cooperate. They first met with Barg. Over a couple of bottles of Chivas Regal in their hotel room, the two strike team members pressed him hard. Since he was the only legitimate businessman among the conspirators, they were confident he would be the most likely to fear the consequences of not cooperating. It took ten hours before Barg reluctantly agreed to become a government informant in return for a grant of full immunity. Tamarro and Coffey next took Barg to meet with Ense. After another half day of heated negotiations, Ense also agreed to help the American investigators.[64]

Both Germans swore they were victims of the American mobsters, who they claimed were blackmailing them to sell counterfeit bonds and common stocks. But the real story, according to them, was what Ledl and the gangsters had been up to.[65] The corporate bond and stock certificates held by the New Yorkers were near-perfect copies. Ledl had arranged a buyer: the Vatican. According to Ense, some high-ranking prelates in Rome—in partnership with crooked officials at Italy's central bank—had agreed to pay $650 million for $950 million of the phony paper. The New York mobsters agreed to later kick back $150 million as a "commission" to the Vatican, still leaving the American mob with a profit of nearly half a billion dollars.[66]

As best the FBI could later determine, someone in the Vatican Bank intended to use the fraudulent securities as collateral for obtaining dollar-for-dollar financing (banks might finance $950 million or more for the church so long as $950 million in cash equivalents—the bonds and stock certificates—were pledged as escrow). Rizzo had already used stolen Coca-Cola and Chrysler securities as collateral to finance a luxury residential development in the South of France.[67] Ledl later said that the IOR wanted to help fund Sindona's ultimately unsuccessful hostile takeover of Bastogi, Italy's largest holding company (a bid supported by both Calvi and P2's Gelli, among others).[68]

The banks making the loans against the phony paper would have no idea the collateral was worthless. If the IOR's investments were profitable, it would pay off the loans and no one would ever discover the bonds and stock certificates were fake.[69] But if the IOR's investments went sour, the lenders would demand the collateral to cover any unpaid balance. Only then would the counterfeits be unmasked and the entire plot collapse. The IOR could then claim that it had itself been an innocent victim of a complex fraud.[70]

When pressed for specifics, Barg and Ense claimed that during a telephone call, Ledl said the recently deceased Cardinal Eugène Tisserant knew the details and approved of the scheme.[71] The previous July, Ledl went to Rome with $14.5 million in counterfeit AT&T, GE, Pan Am, and Chrysler bonds. Ense met him and was present when Ledl telephoned Tisserant's private secretary to say they had samples of the securities for the cardinal's approval (Vatican logs showed Ledl had signed in on several occasions, listing Tisserant as the person he was visiting).[72]

Ense also described a trip he took with Ledl to Turin. They drove to a monastery on the edge of the city limits. Ledl went inside while Ense waited in their rental car. A BMW soon pulled up, and a tall priest, wearing a long black coat, went inside the monastery. Aronwald's strike team later came to believe the priest was Marcinkus, matching the car described by Ense to one used by the bishop. Ense also picked Marcinkus from a photo lineup.[73]

Back in the States, Aronwald's squad worked to confirm whether the Austrian con man and the late Cardinal Tisserant had known each other. The U.S. investigators discovered that Ledl had frequently traveled to Rome, stayed in room 338 of the Vatican-owned Hotel Columbus, and met not only with Tisserant, but also with Cardinals Egidio Vagnozzi, chief of the Prefecture for the Economic Affairs of the Holy See, as well as Giovanni Cicognani, Dean of the College of Cardinals.[74]

Aronson dispatched Coffey and Tamarro to Vienna to offer Ledl the same immunity deal to which Ense and Barg had agreed. They stopped in Frankfurt on the way to convince Rudolf Guschall, a Frankfurt attorney they suspected of providing notary stamps for the securities, to cooperate. When they started questioning Guschall, he panicked, began crying, and yelled that he wished he were dead. He then ran to a large window and tried opening it before Tamarro restrained him. Once calm, he began talking, filling in some missing details for the investigators.[75]

Before getting to Vienna, the two Americans made one more detour, this time to Luxembourg. There, Ernest Shinwell, the black sheep son of a British lord, was in jail for having defrauded some banks in the duchy.[76] Shinwell, it turned out, knew other elements of the plan. He talked to them for hours.[77]

In Vienna, Tamarro and Coffey discovered that Ledl was not at his turn-of-the-century office but instead at a local prison. Austrian police had arrested him, not for his role in any grand scheme, but on fraud charges related to the sales of the fake Burundi Honorary Counsel titles. When the Austrians had searched his office and home they found, among other incriminating items, stock certificates that turned out to have been stolen from a Petaluma, California, doctor two years earlier. They also learned that Ledl had been in possession of counterfeit IBM common stock.[78]

Gathered in a small interview room, Ledl asked that the Austrians not monitor the conversation, afraid that what he shared with the Americans might add to his legal problems in his native country. After the Austrians left, Ledl began talking. In his July 1971 visit to Rome, he said he met with Tisserant inside the Vatican. Tisserant directed him to bring the $14.5 million in the fake securities as a deposit for the overall deal to a monastery in Turin.[79]

There, Tisserant's private secretary, and Monsignor Alberto Barbieri, a writer and lecturer for the Vatican's publishing house, greeted him.[80]* When Bishop Marcinkus soon arrived, said Ledl, they discussed the quality of the counterfeits and the next steps.[82]

Ledl refused the offer of immunity to testify in the United States about what he knew. He had told them enough, he said, and wanted to be left alone.[83]

Possibly the most important evidence Ledl directed them to were two letters, dated June 29, 1971, on original letterhead for the Vatican's Sacra Congregazione dei Religiosi (the Sacred Congregation for Religion, a little known Curia division responsible for setting guidelines so bishops kept separate their religious and secular duties). The letters confirmed the IOR's intent to buy the securities in five installments over several months.†

"These were very powerful charges," says Aronwald. "We knew Ledl had a record for one con after another, so we weren't going to rely on him unless we could independently corroborate everything he told us. And as for Ledl meeting with Marcinkus, we had only him and Ense vouching for it."[85]

Aronwald wanted his two investigators to head to Italy to interview "Count" Mario Foligni. But the Italian police did not cooperate. Instead of just having them wait in Austria while the paperwork churned through the Italian bureaucracy, Aronwald called Coffey and Tamarro home.[86]

The FBI, meanwhile, confirmed that Marcinkus was in Turin the day that Ledl claimed to have met him in the monastery.

Aronwald had to get approval for the next stage of his investigation at the highest level of the Justice Department. The Attorney General, Richard Kleindienst, was preoccupied with the unfolding Watergate scandal. Kleindienst still

* Barbieri was well known around Rome for his vintage Maserati and tailor-made vestments. He also kept a secret mistress. The Vatican later defrocked him.[81]

† The FBI later compared the signature in the letter to that of Marcinkus. While it was similar, it was too illegible for a conclusive match. The bureau did not ask for signature samples of anyone inside the Sacra Congregazione dei Religiosi. Nor did the FBI ask for permission to test typewriters to see if they could locate the one used to type the letters. The name of the congregation on the letters had been modified in 1968 to Sacra Congregazione per I Religiosi e gli Istituti Secolari. But Curia departments sometimes used existing supplies of letterhead until they were exhausted, even after a name change. This congregation produced so little paper correspondence that investigators concluded the letters could be authentic.[84]

had jurisdiction over the investigation into the just reelected president (a Special Prosecutor would be appointed the following May).

"It was time to approach the Vatican," says Aronwald. "This was all very unusual, and highly sensitive, and especially since Marcinkus had become a target in the investigation."[87]

Aronwald was worried that the case might stall at the swamped Justice Department. To his great relief, after a couple of weeks they got permission to move forward.

Aronwald and Whitney North Seymour Jr., the U.S. Attorney for the Southern District of New York, arranged a meeting with New York's Cardinal Terence Cooke.[88] Because it was so sensitive—its details are set forth here for the first time—the government investigators and church officials did not meet at the archdiocese headquarters nor any government building, but at a private conference room inside the New York Public Library's main research branch at 42nd Street and Fifth Avenue.

"We explained some of the details of our investigation to Cardinal Cooke," recalls Aronwald. "It was very awkward because he was friendly with Marcinkus."[89]

Cardinal Cooke agreed to contact the Papal Delegation in Washington, D.C. A few weeks later, the Papal Nuncio, Archbishop Jean Jadot, told the American investigators that he had arranged an off-the-record meeting with officials at the Vatican.

The Justice Department, relying on advice from the FBI, selected as its team Aronwald, Tamarro, and William Lynch, the Washington, D.C.-based chief of the Justice Department's Organized Crime and Racketeering Division. Coffey was furious he was left out. New York police detectives had started the investigation. Coffey knew it as well as anyone. But the order from the Justice Department was unequivocal.[90]

On April 25, 1973, Tom Biamonte, the FBI liaison officer at the American embassy in Rome, and a good friend of Marcinkus, brought the men to the Vatican. Archbishop Benelli, the martinet Deputy Secretary of State, greeted them.

"It was my first time ever to Europe," recalls Aronwald, "and it was a little unnerving since I was a Jewish kid from Brooklyn."[91]

"First, he told us the Cardinal Secretary of State was busy," recalls Tamarro.

"And although we were in a big chamber, we were all told to sit on one small couch, no table, nothing to spread out our documents."[92]

Benelli introduced them to three monsignors on his staff. Eduardo Martínez Somalo, the assessor in the Secretary of State's office (later a cardinal), led the Vatican delegation. The interpreters were Monsignor Justin Rigali (currently the cardinal emeritus of Philadelphia) and Karl Josef Rauber (later an archbishop and Nuncio to both Liechtenstein and Luxembourg).

"We started off by setting out the broad parameters of the investigation," says Aronwald, "and what we were looking for. It pretty quickly became a contentious meeting. It was awkward in some ways because Bill Lynch—a great guy—is a Catholic in every sense of the word. And he did not seem very comfortable."

Tamarro had the least seniority. But he was the one tapped to explain the details of the probe.

"I laid out some file folders on my lap," he says. "Whenever I would say, 'We need to know this or that,' they would not really answer."[93]

Tamarro asked Martínez to authenticate or debunk the letters on Vatican letterhead that Ledl had provided. He refused. When shown a list of some counterfeit bonds and securities, and asked if he had ever heard of any of them, Martínez demurred.[94]

"At one point," says Tamarro, "I said we need to know something specific. Because we were there to get some help, but it seemed they had just come to listen. And this time he answered and I could make it out because it was so short and succinct. He said, 'Absolutely no.' And the translator told us, 'We are here to assist you in any way we can.' I was so fucking pissed. I slammed my folders and papers shut and started to get up to leave. But Lynch ordered me to stay put."[95]

The standoff continued for only a few minutes.

"Then we were told very curtly that the meeting was over," remembers Aronwald. "We could tell they were not at all happy because they knew this entire matter could be a great embarrassment to the Vatican. But the good news was that we were told we could meet the next day directly with Marcinkus."[96]

"They had simply kissed us off," says Tamarro. "And just as we were about to leave that room, Lynch said to them that he couldn't go back to his kids unless he had a rosary blessed by the Pope. Rigali said that was no problem and asked Aronwald and me if we wanted one. Aronwald said, 'Sure, I'll have one.' I said, 'Absolutely not!' I was so pissed off I didn't want anything from them. That night, when we were back at our hotel, we all had a little too much to drink. I said to Lynch and Aronwald, 'How could you take anything from them when they gave it to us up the ass today?' "[97]

The trio had to wait three days before they were summoned back to the Vatican. This time they were escorted past the Church of Sant'Anna dei Palafrenieri and the Swiss Guard barracks, toward the Apostolic Palace, and into the Tower of Nicholas V that housed the IOR. Vittoria Marigonda, Marcinkus's secretary, led them into his large office. Marcinkus came around from his desk to greet each of them with a hearty handshake.

In their first descriptions ever of that encounter, Aronwald and Tamarro told the author they found the bishop "disarming, totally charming," "a regular guy," and "very cool" about why they were there.[98] They thought he looked more like a "bodyguard than a bishop," and one of the first things he did was offer them a drink. He talked nostalgically about America. And he regaled them with stories about Rome and the Vatican. But when the talk got to the criminal investigation, Marcinkus became guarded. For a moment he changed his congenial tone: "Look, I don't have to tell you anything!" Then, after a long pause, he again smiled. "But I will, because I want to cooperate with the FBI."[99] He dismissed the charges as "wild" and said those who had instigated them were likely enemies inside the Curia who were jealous that he, an American at that, had risen to run the IOR and had such a close personal relationship with the Pope. He told them that Ledl's friend, "Count" Mario Foligni, and Monsignor Mario Fornasari had tried to interest the IOR in two large deals.[100] After he passed, Marcinkus claimed, Foligni had started spreading rumors about corruption inside the Vatican Bank.[101] As for Sindona, Marcinkus admitted knowing him and told the U.S. investigators that he thought the Sicilian financier was "ahead of his time as far as financial matters were concerned."[102] The bishop denied ever meeting Ledl.[103]

Marcinkus answered many questions with a general denial, dodged pointed ones, and at times claimed he could not provide any information because of banking secrecy laws and fiduciary obligations. When asked about specific securities, he produced a list he had prepared, purporting to show those owned by the church. Of course, it included none that were on the Justice Department list, which had been shown just a few days earlier to the uncooperative monsignors from the Secretary of State's office.[104] Near the end of the meeting, he leaned forward and assured the trio that he would never be part of a conspiracy to deposit counterfeit securities into the IOR.[105]*

"We left without any conviction whether there was truth to the allegation or the other way around," Aronwald told me. "We didn't leave the Vatican with evidence that added to our case, and we didn't have any exculpatory material either. All we had was Marcinkus's protestation of innocence. We had laid out to him a lot of what we knew, wanting to judge his reaction. Our hope was that he might be able to explain things or that he would slip and say something that would help us. He didn't do either."[107]

The men knew the investigation was stalled. There was little they could discover without Marcinkus's cooperation. The bishop was not willing to let the American investigators have access to the IOR's records. Tamarro felt that Marcinkus had done what he set out to: charm the investigators without providing any information that would help them.[108]

Back in the States, the prosecutors put the finishing touches to their probe. Aronwald presented the government's case to the grand jury.† On July 11, 1973, sixteen defendants (nine Americans and seven Europeans) were charged in a twenty-page indictment with conspiring in "a pattern of racketeering activity" to distribute stolen and counterfeit securities in Italy, Switzerland, Germany, Belgium, Panama, and California.[110] Ledl, Rizzo, and "Count" Foligni were all named (by the time the indictment was issued, Rizzo had been sentenced to twenty years on an unrelated cocaine-trafficking case).[111]

---

* When the story of the Justice Department's meeting with Marcinkus broke nine years later in 1982, the archbishop was much firmer, telling a *Wall Street Journal* reporter, "I had never heard of any of the names. I never met or talked to them in my life. There is no foundation to this in any way." Of course, by then he had the benefit of hindsight to know that he had never been charged with a crime and others had gone to prison for the counterfeit conspiracy. He was also embroiled in a new scandal over Calvi's Ambrosiano, so he had additional incentive to try to quickly quash the counterfeiting story when it became public.[106]

† Ense and Barg came to the United States as part of their immunity deal and testified before the grand jury. "Their testimony was critical," recalls Aronwald. German prosecutors later asked U.S. authorities for a copy of that sealed testimony. "I took the position we should not betray them," says Aronwald. The Justice Department, however, complied with the German request, concluding that the grant of immunity covered only American prosecutions. Barg was convicted in Germany of crimes based on his statements before the U.S. grand jury. "That was disgraceful," says Aronwald. "We had given him our word. That decision is much to the federal government's everlasting discredit."[109]

Conspicuous by his absence was Matteo de Lorenzo, the Genovese crime captain. The investigators did not produce enough evidence to charge him. The same was true of Marcinkus.[112] On background, Aronwald told a *Wall Street Journal* reporter that an unindicted and unnamed "man of the cloth" inside the Vatican was suspected of having a material role in the illegal scheme.[113]

"In the end, we just didn't have enough to indict Marcinkus," says Aronwald. "Our investigation never cleared him, but it also never proved it. The allegations were just left hanging out there. . . . We could never give Marcinkus a clean bill of health."[114]

Inside the Vatican, Marcinkus's detractors used the investigation's potential embarrassment to lobby for his ouster as the IOR chief. The Pope refused even to contemplate it, instead assuming that since he was not indicted, the Americans had cleared him of all the scurrilous rumors.

17

Il Crack Sindona

Marcinkus's 1973 problems with the Security and Exchange Commission and his close call with the American Justice Department played out against a chaotic backdrop in Italy. Domestic terrorism and financial instability seemed at times to push the country toward the edge of anarchy. Although Italians had gotten accustomed to the musical-chair nature of the country's politics—seventeen governments since World War II—most were not prepared for the increasing violence that shook the nation's confidence and destabilized its financial markets. Anti-American sentiment over the U.S. bombing of North Vietnam had fueled a militant left-wing movement. In communist-led Bologna, the city council voted to greet the New Year by burning "Father Napalm," an oversized Uncle Sam effigy.[1] Extremists bombed the Milan offices of the right-wing National Vanguard Movement two weeks later.[2] In March, an anarchist group claimed credit for the public execution of a forty-six-year-old Milanese industrialist. In April, rising Middle East tensions spilled over into the country when a Palestinian radical shot dead an employee of the Israeli airline El Al in front of a large crowd at a central department store.[3] Neo-fascists followed that up by torching a synagogue in Padua.[4] The following month, a bomb in a Milan bank killed two. A few days later an anarchist threw a hand grenade into a crowd of mourners paying respects to an assassinated police officer. Two were killed and forty-five were wounded.[5]

Interspersed between the bombings were running street battles in the nation's largest cities between neo-fascists and communists; a surge in kidnappings of wealthy Italians (the July abduction of John Paul Getty III from the busy Piazza Farnese, in the heart of Rome, added to the growing sentiment that no one was safe); and a spike in Mafia-related violence, including a brazen assassination of a prominent police investigator in front of his Roman home.[6]

Adding to the gloomy national mood, the police had made few arrests. Italians judged law enforcement as either incompetent or compromised. After the Milan grenade attack, the government was so flummoxed that it asked for assistance from police in the United States, Britain, France, Switzerland, and Israel.[7]

The loss of public confidence forced Prime Minister Giulio Andreotti's resignation in July.[8] The next ruling coalition did little to restore faith in government. To many it seemed the same politicians responsible for the slide had just shuffled positions. Giovanni Leone was back for his third time as President. Mariano Rumor became Premier for the fourth time.[9] A right-wing faction called the Mussolini Action Squad greeted the new regime with two bombs at Milan's Mondadori publishing headquarters.[10]

International tensions did not help. That September, Colonel Muammar Gaddafi's air force attacked an Italian warship that veered too close to the Libyan coast.[11] Only a few weeks later, Egypt and Syria launched a surprise attack on Israel, the start of the Yom Kippur War. When Nixon refused the Saudi King's request not to resupply Israel with American fighter jets in the middle of the conflict, Arab states announced their first-ever oil boycott of the United States, Japan, and most of Western Europe including Italy.[12] Oil prices doubled within a week, on their way to what would become a tenfold increase over several years.[13]

The oil shortage caused serious problems for all the countries on the boycott list. Italy had to cut private gasoline sales by 10 percent in November causing long lines at gas stations. It also began to ration oil deliveries.[14] And the oil shock destabilized the already weak Italian economy. Fears of a deep recession combined with high inflation pummeled Italy's stock indices.[15] Due to the oil shortage, the Italians endured their worst winter since World War II. *The New York Times* noted, "In Italy they are talking about the end of 'la dolce vita.'"[16]

Just before Christmas, a bloody attack on Rome's airport by the Palestinian Liberation Organization seemed a grim year-end note to the sour state of affairs. Thirty-two were killed in a gun and grenade assault that made security forces look particularly inept.[17]

Pope Paul VI's holiday message was his most sober since assuming the Papacy. He pleaded with Italians to unite in stopping the country's slide into further violence and disorder, and urged them to reject a "mafia-style mentality."[18]

In the midst of such widespread pessimism, many leading Italian businessmen looked abroad for stability. Sindona and Calvi thought Argentina presented such an opportunity in the spring of 1973. As Italy's bedlam played out, Juan Perón returned to power in Buenos Aires after an eighteen-year exile. Licio Gelli, who ran the underground Masonic P2 chapter that counted Sindona and most of Italy's top businessmen and politicians as members, had been helping Perón behind the scenes. The two had met in 1971 while the Argentine was in exile in Spain. The day after his proxies had won the national election, Perón, accompanied by Gelli, flew into Buenos Aires on an Alitalia jet.[19] Perón had barely settled back into Casa Rosada, the presidential palace, when Sindona talked to Gelli about establishing a consortium to oversee Argentina's enormous, but largely underutilized, natural resources.[20] Gelli—whom Perón soon named an Honorary Consul General—and Sindona thought they could help Argentina halt the widespread Latin American tilt to the left. Calvi also suggested that the Ambrosiano establish a large Argentine presence in the hope that the Italians might parlay their special status with Perón into enormous profits. Sindona arranged for Calvi and Gelli to meet.[21]

"Calvi . . . was ever eager to believe in the occult powers of others," Sindona later told a journalist, "[and he] was quite swept away by Gelli at their first meeting. He believed that Gelli and P2 could be of inestimable help to him in Italy and abroad."[22] And he liked the "sense of protection" that Gelli and his powerful comrades offered.[23] For his part, Gelli judged Calvi as "serious . . . intelligent, complicated."[24] Calvi joined P2.[25]

Sindona called Marcinkus to see if the IOR would also commit to the new venture. Marcinkus liked the idea and offered the IOR as a fiduciary bank in support of any of the Ambrosiano's business in Argentina.[26] And Sindona and Marcinkus compiled a list of offshore companies the new endeavor should use to operate free of Italy's currency exchange restrictions.

"I told Marcinkus to get in touch with the lawyers in Costa Rica who had organized similar operations for Citicorp of New York or Barclay's Bank of London," Sindona later recalled.[27]

The plans for the grand expansion hit early headwinds. Perón was frustrated by political infighting that matched or exceeded that in Italy. The back-scenes battle for power meant that Sindona, Calvi, and Marcinkus had to wait for the ailing seventy-seven-year-old Perón to approve their new undertaking.

Sindona was impatient. He had worked hard on the Argentine venture and the delay was infuriating. He complained to colleagues that his native Italy was beset by instability that made it difficult for businessmen to make long-term plans. Adding to his bad mood was that he had recently failed in a highly publicized hostile takeover of Bastogi, a storied Italian holding company.[28] For nearly a year, Sindona had debated whether to move out of Italy. Switzerland seemed his most likely choice. Not only was it close to Milan, but he already had a fifth-floor apartment in Geneva, in the Rue de la Bourse building that served as the Swiss headquarters for his Finabank. But Nixon's reelection the previous November pushed him toward America. By early 1973, Sindona had bought a $300,000 apartment at New York's Pierre Hotel, with a grand view overlooking Central Park.[29] *

When Sindona told Marcinkus about his pending move, the bishop said, "Hey! You operate over there like you operate here in Italy, you will end up in jail. See? Different laws, different standards."[31] Marcinkus's warning did not give Sindona any second thoughts. He opened business headquarters at 450 Park Avenue.

America welcomed Sindona as a financial whiz. Harvard Business School, the University of Chicago, and Carnegie Mellon invited him to lecture. In January 1974, the U.S. ambassador to Italy, John Volpe, presented him with the *Man of the Year* award.[32]

What Sindona did not say publicly was something that only he and a handful of his top lieutenants knew: his Italian banking empire was under great pressure. The man that *Fortune* had pegged the previous year with a $450 million net worth was holding some huge paper losses on foreign currency trades.[33] Plummeting stock prices and an international credit squeeze meant he could not raise enough money to cover his bad investments. Without any progress on the Argentine project, Sindona merged Banca Privata Finanziaria—in which Marcinkus and the IOR had a minority stake—and his Banca Unione into a

* Another reason Sindona may have left Italy is that he had lost faith that a strong, pro-capitalist, pro-American government would be in power anytime soon. John McCaffrey, Hambros Bank's Italian representative and a wartime British espionage agent, was a close Sindona business colleague. In a sworn 1981 statement, McCaffrey said that Sindona had approached him "with his plan for a coup" to install a conservative government and purge all socialist and communist parliamentarians and ministers. "It was clear to me from these conversations with Sindona," said McCaffrey, "that he was the key to the entire operation." According to McCaffrey, the coup failed in large part due to "the lack of know-how, courage, and conviction on the part of Italian politicians . . . [and the] lack of courage on the Italian military leaders."[30]

new financial institute, the Banca Privata Italiana. He hoped the merger might keep Italian regulators from discovering the extent to which the banks were in trouble.[34] But Guido Carli, the Bank of Italy's governor, had already authorized a broad review of Sindona's complex financial empire.[35] Despite the pressure on his business, Pope Paul VI and some leading Christian Democrat politicians asked Sindona to contribute to fight a national referendum to block the right to divorce; he gave $2 million. The church and conservative politicians lost the referendum that May, when 60 percent of the electorate sided with the idea that civil divorce should be legal.[36]*

In May 1974, Sindona's American ventures showed their first cracks. Franklin National reported a foreign exchange trading loss of nearly $39 million.[38] The bank's traders had shorted the lira and bought large dollar positions just before the markets moved in opposite directions.[39] Such trading had become much more volatile since central banks no longer supported their national currencies at fixed rates. Few banks had yet developed sufficient safeguards in their trading departments to manage the risk.[40]

Sindona seemed furious. When Franklin president Harold Gleason met with him, just after the board had learned about the loss, Sindona "paced[d] back and forth like a caged animal," yelling profanities and demanding answers.[41] But his display of anger was mostly for show. It was Sindona himself who had approved the bank's bold lira trade against the dollar.[42]

Following three consecutive quarters of losses at Franklin, the Federal Reserve's Board of Governors cited its underperformance and weak internal controls in rejecting the bank's merger with Talcott National, a large American finance firm in which Sindona had accumulated a 50 percent share. Although the New York Federal Reserve had recommended an approval, the full Fed feared that Franklin would siphon off the assets and reserves from the healthier Talcott.[43]

Senior Franklin officials claimed the bank's problems were a temporary blip

---

* Sindona did more than just help his friend Paul VI by contributing to political referendums. That same May, a French cardinal, Jean Daniélou, was found dead in the apartment of a twenty-four-year-old nightclub stripper whose husband had a criminal record as a pimp. Police discovered that the cardinal, appointed by Paul VI five years earlier, had about $10,000 in cash on him. The Pope sent a clandestine message to Sindona to ask if his French business contacts might prevent the story from becoming a scandal. Sindona called on banking colleagues who evidently convinced the Parisian detectives that their dossier was best kept secret.[37]

caused by a combination of a rogue trader, high interest rates, a weak economy, and exorbitant Manhattan rents.[44] But regulators did not buy it. Representatives from the SEC, the Federal Reserve, and the Comptroller of the Currency met with Sindona and the bank's chief officers over the weekend of May 11 and 12.[45] They insisted that Sindona guarantee a $50 million recapitalization to stabilize the bank.[46] He agreed, although none of the regulators knew he did not have the money.

The dire warnings that Franklin's founder, Arthur Roth, had raised about Sindona's lack of expertise seemed prescient. That Monday, Franklin's board dismissed the bank's president and executive vice chairman and suspended the stock dividend. It was the first time since the Great Depression that an American bank had canceled a quarterly dividend payment.[47] The Federal Reserve tried calming markets by announcing it would make advances to Franklin as needed; the bank borrowed $110 million, more than any Fed official had anticipated.[48] That same afternoon, the SEC halted trading in the company's stock until the firm refigured its first quarter losses.[49]

Sindona could not catch a break. Rumors that he was in a serious cash crunch prompted some large New York banks to warn against conducting business with any of his companies.[50] Earlier that year, San Diego's U.S. National had become the country's first billion-dollar bank failure. It had frayed nerves throughout the American financial industry.[51]

Sindona's problems were compounded because he was unable to reassure the markets by injecting some of his own considerable wealth. His $40 million Franklin investment was worth only $8 million since the stock had plummeted 80 percent during his ten months of ownership.[52] And many more millions of dollars were tied up in ventures with Calvi and Marcinkus.

Sindona called Calvi. He had $18 million in a joint venture with the Ambrosiano chief.[53] Calvi claimed he could not help because the money was committed to business deals with other firms, including the Vatican.[54] Sindona was furious. When he visited Italy that June, Calvi's secretary ran interference every time Sindona called. Sindona was not surprised that Calvi avoided him. He knew that the Ambrosiano chairman "was frightened by my plight. He was afraid that he, as my partner, might be dragged down as well."[55]

Similar distancing played out between Sindona and Marcinkus. "He, like Calvi, had run scared," Sindona later recalled, "washing his hands of me. On his visits to New York, he didn't even telephone to ask after my well-being."[56]

Sindona's Mercedes was no longer listed as one of a handful of cars that the Swiss Guards waved through the front gates of the Vatican without any questions.[57] What Sindona did not know was that Marcinkus had no spare money with which to bail him out. By that time, the IOR had committed so much cash to ventures with Calvi that the church had little left for a cushion in case of an investment downturn.[58]

That same month, Sindona approached the Banco di Roma and asked to borrow $100 million, acknowledging to the bank's chairman, Mario Barone, that his Italian banks were in trouble.[59] Barone gave him the $100 million credit line, with the restriction that the money could only be used to stabilize Sindona's Italian operations, not bail out Franklin.[60] Sindona had to pledge his Italian bank shares as collateral, as well as 100 million shares of his construction conglomerate, SGI.[61] As an additional condition of lending the money, Banco di Roma got the right to appoint its own SGI management team. It forced the resignation of Carlo Bordoni, the chairman, a longtime Sindona confidant.[62]

Sindona was back to Barone in just two weeks, asking for another $100 million.[63] This time he said there was a run on deposits at his banks. Their failure could infect the entire Italian banking system.[64] Sindona's timing was bad. German regulators had just liquidated one of Cologne's premier private banks, Bankhaus I. D. Herstatt, because it had racked up $500 million in foreign exchange losses. The Herstatt collapse had made all European banking regulators more vigilant.[65] To get the second loan, Italy's central bank had to give its approval. This time Sindona had to pledge the rest of his controlling stake in SGI.[66] And the Banco di Roma joined the Bank of Italy in developing contingency plans to protect depositors and creditors while searching for ways to move Sindona out of SGI.[67]

Back in the States, Franklin's reconfigured quarterly earnings revealed it had lost $63 million in the first five months of 1974, some $25 million more than when the bank had provided guidance just six weeks earlier.[68] Joseph Barr, a respected former chairman at the FDIC—the Federal Deposit Insurance Corporation, the U.S. government agency tasked with insuring bank deposits—agreed on June 20 to become Franklin's CEO and chairman. As Barr moved in, Carlo Bordoni stepped down from the board.[69] Franklin had used its open window at the Federal Reserve to borrow $1.2 billion in just over a month.[70] Barr began working in Washington to find a way to keep Franklin out of receivership. He knew it would not be simple. The SEC had complicated matters by opening a broad investigation into Franklin's foreign currency transactions. It was trying to determine if the trades were legitimate, or merely represented the shuffling of assets between Franklin and a Sindona-owned Swiss bank, Amincor, all intended to artificially boost the bank's balance sheet.[71] If the SEC concluded the trading was bogus, the losses reported by Franklin would grow significantly.[72]

Sindona's frustration boiled over in an interview with a journalist from Milan's daily, *Corriere della Sera.* Declaring that "finance is the passion of my existence," he lambasted his critics in Italy for having "sought to mount a propaganda campaign that, being unable to formulate specific charges, has given rise to the image of the mystery man, which in the States, certainly is not appreciated." Sindona had come to realize that the lack of transparency over how he created his great wealth had turned from simple curiosity to more sinister speculation.[73]

Sindona was desperate for cash. In July, he sold one of his prized Italian banks, Banca Generale de Credito, at a fire-sale price to Roman and Milanese financiers who had been his competitors.[74] He wanted instead to merge the profitable SGI with one of his other financial holding companies, Edilcentro Sviluppo, and then use an initial public offering to raise large funds. People would line up to own a piece of SGI. But to Sindona's dismay, the left-of-center Treasury Minister, Ugo La Malfa, rejected his application.[75] In August, he tried cashing out his 50 percent stake in a small Hamburg-based bank, Bankhaus Wolff. Since it would not have had enough capital to stay in business without Sindona's investment, West German regulators forced it to close, tying up his money in receivership court.[76]

The failure of Bankhaus Wolff was the first time during Sindona's travails that the Vatican came up publicly. The West German press reported that the IOR had suffered "substantial financial losses" in the bank's collapse. The persistent stories prompted a statement from a Vatican spokesman, Father Paul Hashim. He said the IOR had a "very limited interest" in Sindona's Banca Unione, which had owned the German bank's shares.[77]

That September, Sindona was so cash-strapped that he sold his Talcott shares for $5.6 million. They cost him $27 million the previous year.[78] It had only been five months after the first cracks had appeared in his business empire, but he was undoubtedly now under broad attack. The first of what would soon be a flood of shareholder lawsuits alleging negligence or mismanagement for the bank's downturn were filed in the United States. In Italy, the central bank announced it was liquidating Banca Privata Italiana.[79] Giorgio Ambrosoli, a corporate lawyer with a reputation for scrupulous honesty, was appointed as the liquidator.[80] (Some legal observers thought the thirty-six-year-old Ambrosoli was too inexperienced for such a complex case, but his diligence and smarts soon proved them wrong.) Sindona's 51 percent stake became worthless overnight.

The liquidation order by the Bank of Italy was also bad news for Marcinkus. He had made substantial IOR investments not only in Banca Privata Italiana but also in the soon-to-be-shut Finabank.[81] Marcinkus was a silent partner with Sindona in Liberfinco (Liberian Financial Company), a Finabank subsidiary used almost exclusively for foreign currency trading.[82] Both banks had increased their capital in the months leading up to their receivership, allowing Marcinkus to reduce the extent of the church's exposure by selling some option rights to the new debt.[83] Still, Marcinkus knew those failures resulted in the IOR's biggest ever losses in private company investments. He assigned de Strobel and Mennini to determine the extent of the damage.

By that time, Italian regulators had uncovered evidence that the losses at Sindona's banks were not just from bad currency speculation but wrong bets on the price of silver, trades executed mostly through his Bahamian and Cayman holding companies.[84] Investigators at first pinpointed upward of $200 million in losses, and later settled it at $386 million.[85] Separately, Italy's equivalent of the Securities and Exchange Commission discovered that Sindona had accumulated another $50 million in bad currency trades at SGI.

In mid-September a Milanese magistrate sent Sindona a notification that he was under investigation about whether his financial dealings had broken any laws. The magistrate advised Sindona to retain counsel.[86] That news caused great consternation at the IOR and the Ambrosiano since both were heavily intertwined with Sindona's offshore businesses.[87]

The flattering press coverage of Sindona's business acumen had reversed itself. The Banco di Roma's Barone told reporters, "When you gamble with other people's money, you have to realize what you were doing." "I say he's dead financially," an anonymous "former associate in Switzerland" told *The New York Times*. An unidentified "Rome banker" told the same paper, "The empire has collapsed, and there will be business for lawyers over the next 10 years in picking up the pieces."[88]

Sindona resigned as a Franklin director on September 22, saying he instead wanted to "devote my attention to my other personal affairs."[89] He hoped his resignation might relieve some of the pressure from federal regulators.[90] But it was too little too late. During October, what was left of his empire imploded. On October 3, the FDIC rejected Barr's eleventh-hour plan to keep Franklin independent, citing the proposal as too costly a bailout.[91] Sindona knew it was the end of Franklin. News on both sides of the Atlantic was grim. Six days later, Milanese prosecutors issued an arrest warrant, charging Sindona with falsifying accounts and fraudulent bankruptcy connected with Banca Unione three years earlier.[92] The indictment carried a possible fifteen-year sentence.[93]

The following Monday, the Comptroller of the Currency declared Franklin insolvent, making the $2 billion failure the then largest bankruptcy in U.S. banking history.[94] (The next month, in unusually blunt comments, Federal Reserve Chairman Arthur Burns told reporters that when it came to Franklin, the United States and foreign countries had been "sitting on a volcano" and "luck more than anything" averted "a real panic, here and abroad.")[95] The Bank of Italy meanwhile had started liquidating Sindona's remaining assets and seized what personal property it could find.[96] A group of Italian construction firms eventually made the highest bid to buy SGI from the Banco di Roma (later they discovered that bad currency and commodity trades had resulted in nearly $100 million in losses at SGI).[97]

Within a week, the district attorney's office in Rome disclosed it was also investigating whether Sindona violated any laws with large contributions to the country's main political party, the Christian Democrats.[98] Sindona told a reporter that "If they tried me, half of Italy, people who matter, would end up in jail."[99]

A week after the criminal indictment, the SEC capped off its own five-month investigation by filing fraud charges against nine former directors and officers of Franklin, including Sindona.[100] The SEC laid bare in particular how Sindona used Swiss and Liechtenstein holding companies to "manufacture profits" at Franklin while also diverting money from that bank to some of his offshore shells.[101]

Sindona was on the run by the time of the SEC charges. He had flown to Geneva since he thought Switzerland was less likely to extradite him to Italy to stand trial for white-collar crimes.[102] Bordoni and his wife fled to Venezuela, where he used some of the stolen money to buy a $3 million home and citizenship.[103] P2's Licio Gelli called Sindona in Geneva to warn him that the Italians were close to striking a deal with Swiss Interpol for his arrest.[104] Sindona left his wife and family and flew to Jamaica with his Swedish-born mistress fifteen years his junior. There he gave her an envelope containing information about some of his secret bank accounts. She flew alone to Buenos Aires, where Licio Gelli awaited her.[105] Although Perón had died the past July, his wife, Isabelita, had taken control of the government. Gelli maintained his influence in Buenos Aires and Rome. Sindona hoped that the P2 chief might persuade Italian prosecutors to back off.

Sindona's next destination was Hong Kong. The British colony did not have an extradition treaty with Italy. The flight from Jamaica to Hong Kong included a stopover in Bangkok. Although Sindona knew the Thais had an extradition treaty with Italy, he expected no problem as his itinerary did not require a change of planes. But his flight landed just before a typhoon shut down Don Mueang International Airport. The grounded passengers had to clear customs, which made Sindona fear arrest. But to his surprise, Interpol and the Italians had not passed along the information. He cleared Thai authorities. He checked into a Hyatt and did not venture outside on the off chance that someone might recognize him from the newspaper coverage, particularly the *International Herald Tribune,* which had carried his photo. For four days he stayed locked in his room, ordering room service and making a few calls to his family.[106] To his great relief, his departure from Bangkok proved as uneventful as his arrival.

Sindona's family visited once he was safely in Hong Kong. But after a week in the British colony, he was off again, this time to Taiwan. Sindona was friendly with Chiang Kai-shek, the eighty-seven-year-old nationalist ruler of the island nation. Taiwan granted Sindona temporary political asylum and named him a financial advisor to the president.

Although he was insulated against extradition to Italy, Sindona knew he was vulnerable to a U.S. indictment and extradition request. While both Chiang Kai-shek and the British in Hong Kong might ignore Italian requests for Sindona's return, being so cavalier with the United States would be a different matter. His American lawyers had told him that a federal investigation was under way in New York, and that Italian investigators had met with the U.S. Attorney to share information.

After mulling his options for a month, he told one of his sons, Nino, that he had decided to return to the United States and fight extradition to Italy from there. That December, U.S. customs agents escorted Sindona through John F. Kennedy Airport. He, and his legal team at Mudge, Rose, Guthrie & Alexander, prepared his defense to Italy's request. Sindona moved back into the Pierre. He later told *The New York Times* that he had "not one dollar in assets" and that his friends in Italy had sent him money to pay for his suite at the Pierre, Park Avenue office, and Mudge Rose lawyers.[107]

"America will protect me against Italy because I have always protected the American interest in New York," Sindona told his son. "I have many friends there. I will win in America."[108]

Halfway around the world, Marcinkus was left to handle some of the fallout in Italy from what the Italian press dubbed *il crack Sindona* (the broken Sindona). It was widely accepted that Sindona and the Vatican did business together, but no one knew fully to what extent. The IOR had a minority interest in most of Sindona's Swiss and Italian banks, with its largest stake in Banca Unione. Marcinkus had also allowed Sindona to invest several million dollars in foreign currency trades. When the Swiss shuttered Sindona's Geneva-based Banque de Financement—considered one of the financier's safest—because of heavy losses in precisely those trades, *The New York Times* noted that a "sizable block of [the] bank's stock is reportedly held by the Vatican."[109] The church had a one-third share.

In the wake of Sindona's collapse, the Italians indulged in a guessing game of how much money the church had lost. Some put it as high as $750 million ($3.9 billion in 2014 dollars). The Vatican said only that it was hurt to a "limited extent."[110] The Pope established a commission of five cardinals to investigate how much damage had been incurred. The commission was in place only a couple of months when one of Italy's most prominent newsweeklies, *Panorama*, reported that the cardinals had recommended that Paul VI replace Marcinkus.[111] Citing anonymous sources, the magazine said the Pope had met with Marcinkus that September and told him that he would retain his title without power until he was moved to another position.[112] It was not true. Marcinkus believed the story was planted by one of his many enemies. He tried to stem any damage by issuing a brief denial the day after Panorama hit the newsstands: "The magazine article is all imagination and fantasy with no foundation in fact. I do not foresee any transfer for me for a long time."[113] He also dismissed reports that the IOR had lost several hundred million dollars in Sindona's implosion, contending that there were only some "paper losses."[114]

In January 1975, the Pope vetoed the church's proposed annual budget, concluding that the IOR losses had created "a grave burden, too grave a burden for the Holy See to bear."[115] The new budget included severe cutbacks.[116]

On January 30, Massimo Spada, who had been at the IOR under Nogara and Maillardoz before leaving to work for Sindona, gave an interview to the newsweekly *L'Espresso*, in which he estimated the Vatican had lost $56 million, or 10 percent of its liquid assets.[117] Spada's guesstimate was given wide credence because he worked with many of his former IOR colleagues on joint ventures for Group Sindona. He added to the public pressure on the Vatican by disclosing that one of the IOR's top currency experts had developed a fondness for trading the dollar against the lira, and that his new avocation had cost the church about $10 million (Spada did not reveal the name).[118] Inside the IOR, even Marcinkus, Mennini, and de Strobel struggled to figure out how much they had lost.[119]

Sindona wanted the bishop to know that he would not say anything to make matters worse for the church. So he used the press to send a message to Marcinkus. He told *Business Week*, "I acted morally, ethically, and in the correct way. I'm fighting for the principle and for my family. I want to show my friends that they were right when they placed their trust in me."[120] And he hired Fred Rosen, a New York publicist, to try and reverse the damage to his savaged reputation. He chose Rosen because the publicist was friendly with A. M. Rosenthal, *The New York Times* executive editor. Sindona naively thought that by hiring Rosen he might favorably influence the paper's coverage.[121] With Rosen's help, Sindona started a rehabilitation tour in mid-April, with an address to Wharton graduate students titled "The Phantom Petrodollar."[122] It was his first public appearance since Franklin's collapse and attracted widespread media coverage. He drew some nervous laughter when he was introduced as a "tax expert," but used his thirty-five-minute speech to emphasize a new theme: what *The New York Times* called "a ringing defense of the strength of the American economy."[123] Some thought it ironic that Sindona castigated Chase Manhattan, UBS, and Lloyd's of London for "cooking their books" and "reckless gambling" when it came to foreign exchange trading.[124] Wharton was the first in a series of lectures that spring and summer, including among others Harvard, the University of Chicago, Columbia, and UCLA.[125] At New York University in June, he condemned government bailouts as destabilizing the national economy, and said it was a mistake "when a country takes on itself the errors of its entrepreneurs."[126] He managed to keep his talks focused on international economics and took no questions about his legal problems.

But instead of mollifying Marcinkus, Sindona's refusal to keep a low profile as he battled extradition caused considerable dismay.[127] The fugitive financier stayed in the news. There were rumors that he had fed information to the Milan district attorney in the hope that the head of the Italian central bank—whom Sindona blamed for liquidating his own banks—might himself be indicted.[128] And in April, a seventy-six-count federal indictment charging conspiracy to obstruct justice and fraud among eight of his ex-Franklin colleagues, including his right-hand man, Carlo Bordoni, insured that Sindona would not drop off the front pages anytime soon.[129]

Many of the stories regurgitated speculation about the extent of the Vatican's dealings with him as well as raising questions about the size of the church's business empire. Reports of the city-state's great wealth caused a drop-off in Peter's Pence contributions. Paul VI, after reading one newspaper account about the Vatican's supposed riches, complained that such guesswork was costing the Papacy millions of dollars in donations. Many Catholics thought the church was so well off that it did not need their money.[130] Although the Pope, bolstered by Marcinkus, would not broker any suggestion for more transparency of the church's investments, the Pontiff did dispatch Cardinal Egidio Vagnozzi, the chief of the Prefecture for Economic Affairs, to talk to a small group of hand-selected journalists. Vagnozzi was the spokesman when the Vatican last tried to quell rumors with a 1971 *Institutional Investor* interview.[131]

The cardinal emphasized two related themes: that the church was not nearly as wealthy as most people believed, and that the Pope could not survive without the generosity of the faithful. He dismissed reports that the Pope oversaw a $10 billion investment portfolio ($43 billion in 2014 dollars) as "totally untrue." The Archdiocese of Chicago, he claimed, took in twice as much annual income—$170 million—as the Holy See. As for the Vatican, Vagnozzi said its income came mostly from Peter's Pence, trusts, last testament gifts from the faithful, and sales of stamps, gasoline, and religious artifacts. Although he claimed not to know the precise size of its investment portfolio, he said it probably contributed "less than 5%" to the church's annual income. He not only refused any questions about Sindona, but tried to distance the church from the financier by asserting that when it came to investments, "the Vatican as such does not speculate."[132]

Vagnozzi reminded the reporters that he was addressing only the finances of the city-state itself, and that he was not speaking for all the congregations and dioceses around the world that managed their own budgets. As for the Holy See, he highlighted escalating costs for the upkeep of Vatican City, increased salaries and pension requirements for an ever-expanding lay component of the Curia, as well as funds needed to maintain diplomatic missions in dozens of countries.[133] Overall "the Vatican is rather poor . . . [and] it is only the voluntary help which the Pope receives from the faithful year after year that we manage—not without difficulty—to close the constant deficit in the Vatican's relatively small budget."[134]

In November 1975, Milan's public prosecutor and its investigating magistrate visited the U.S. Attorney and the SEC, hoping their American counterparts might expedite Sindona's extradition.[135] They presented evidence they had uncovered no fewer than forty-three Sindona-controlled offshore companies.[136] Their visit prompted the financier to launch another round of PR, telling reporters that his "enemies" were Italy's "leftists" and that his own problems were the result of his vigorous defense of the country's free enterprise system. "They want to put me in jail and brainwash me," he said. "They talk to me about suicide as the best thing."[137] Gelli had already assured Sindona that he was marshaling some important public figures in Italy—supporting the theme that the charges against him were a leftist vendetta—to make a personal appeal to the U.S. government to reject the Italian extradition efforts. But Gelli also confided to Sindona that his enemies wanted his head. One of Italy's most prestigious bankers, Enrico Cuccia, had privately told some colleagues, "Sindona should not only be destroyed, but his ashes scattered to the winds."[138]

As Sindona continued proclaiming his innocence from his Manhattan perch, there were signs that American probes into his activities were accelerating. In December, Peter Shaddick, one of the key defendants in the federal indictment of Franklin executives, struck a deal with prosecutors to plead guilty to participating in a scheme that cost the bank more than $30 million. He also agreed to cooperate with the U.S. Attorney in return for a reduced sentence. That prompted speculation that Shaddick was ready to buy his freedom by implicating Sindona. And the slow U.S. response to the Italian extradition request made sense if the New York prosecutors wanted instead to indict and try him in America.[139]

Calvi saw Sindona's problems as an opportunity for the Ambrosiano. His bank's shares at first had suffered because of the perception that the men were close, but they stabilized as details emerged revealing that the Ambrosiano was not damaged by Sindona's failure.[140]* The same month Italian prosecutors visited the U.S. to press for Sindona's extradition, the Ambrosiano's board elected Calvi as president (he had effectively been running the bank from his number two position as director). He had by then even received from the President of Italy a distinguished title, Cavaliere del Lavoro (Knight of Labor).[142] And the Italian press had "discovered" Calvi, covering him often in the same glowing manner in which they had once treated Sindona.

The general social instability in Italy made Calvi conscious—some say paranoid—about business secrecy and personal security.[143] Calvi now ordered scrambler telephones installed in his office and homes so his conversations could not be intercepted, and he had the bank's executive headquarters swept weekly for listening devices. He installed separate telephone lines to talk with P2 chief Licio Gelli, as well as for another P2 member, attorney Umberto Ortolani, who had become Calvi's trusted consigliere.[144]† His fourth-floor executive suite was separated from the rest of the office with an imposing pair of bombproof doors. Later, at his Rome and Milan apartments, as well as the family's country house, he deployed multiple alarm systems. He even carried a personal panic button that alerted the bodyguards that patrolled the buildings or the property's perimeter. And he chose a bulletproof Mercedes as his company car. Calvi's security bill eventually topped $1 million annually.[146]

Calvi was now ready to take advantage of his former partner's downfall: to

---

* In fact, the Ambrosiano did lose some $9 million in failed Cisalpine loans to a Sindona shell company, but Calvi wisely did not write that off for more than a year, long after the initial fear in the markets over the Sindona fallout had passed.[141]

† Sindona thought Ortolani "was an excellent lawyer, but not much of a banker." In October 1975, Calvi used Swiss-based United Trading (in which the IOR had a stake), to pay $3.25 million to an account at Geneva's Union Bank of Switzerland in the name of Ortolani's daughter-in-law. Calvi also sent another $3 million later that year to an account in the name of Ortolani's son Piero. Over the next six years, Calvi sent some $250 million to Ortolani-controlled bank accounts. Italian investigators believe that Ortolani served as a conduit to other powerful Italians, even kicking some money back to Calvi and possibly even to the IOR. "If it did, I never saw it," Marcinkus later declaimed to author John Cornwell.[145]

get all of Sindona's business with the Vatican for the Ambrosiano. He met with Marcinkus and urged him to protect the church from further losses. He said the IOR's problems were not the result of bad trades and excessive speculation, but rather matters specific to Sindona: investing too much in America, a country about which he knew too little; spreading his money too thin and acquiring too much debt; and not monitoring his operations carefully enough.

Calvi told Marcinkus that the church's best option was to obscure its trail of investments and arrange for companies without significant assets to be responsible in case its investments turned sour. This conversation was possibly an inflection point when it came to the IOR's reliance on so-called men of confidence.

Did the financial losses and public embarrassment over Sindona make Marcinkus skittish about further relying on men like Sindona and Calvi? There is no evidence it did. Marcinkus later said he had "no reason . . . to question [Calvi's] honesty, integrity," since he still had "a tremendous reputation . . . was well respected in the banking community . . . [and] was a decent fellow."[147] (Only years later Marcinkus would say that although he had "nothing to apologize for . . . I might be ashamed of one thing, if you want to call it that. Maybe I trusted Calvi, maybe, too much."[148])

Marcinkus was simply too intertwined with Calvi to consider distancing the IOR. Under his tenure thus far at the IOR, the Vatican had loaned tens of millions of dollars to Cisalpine, the Calvi-owned Bahamian bank of which Marcinkus was a director. Marcinkus had already informally given Calvi a three-year extension on the first $45 million due.[149] By the close of 1975, the church had active banking relationships with almost a dozen Calvi-controlled shell companies in Panama, the Bahamas, Liechtenstein, Luxembourg, and Switzerland.[150] One of the Luxembourg-based shells that had been created with the approval of the IOR, Manic, had borrowed $35 million from Calvi's Nassau bank.[151] When a Swiss banker—at Calvi's direction—sent the IOR's Luigi Mennini a copy of Manic's balance sheet and asked for a written "agreement and ratification of our actions," Marcinkus ordered Mennini not to respond. The IOR chief instead convinced Calvi to write a letter to the Vatican Bank guaranteeing that Cisalpine "assumed full responsibility, exonerating the Institute from each and every charge and responsibility."[152]

In the middle of the year, the IOR bought its first public stake in the Ambrosiano. The Vatican paid $16.8 million, a 30 percent premium to the market, for 4.6 percent of the bank. Marcinkus was acting as a proxy for Calvi, who had promised to eventually buy back the shares from the church at an even higher price.[153]

For nearly two years, the IOR had earned a tidy profit for running questionable back-to-back operations in which it "loaned" tens of millions in U.S. dollars and Swiss francs to Calvi's banks and companies to bolster their balance sheets when private and government audits came due. In those instances, the companies passed the financial inspections since they had enormous cash deposits. None of the auditors knew that most of that cash would be wired out of the firm usually the same day the review finished. The money was returned to the IOR, through a maze of offshore banks to mask its trail. For its efforts, the Vatican took a tiny percentage of the total sums moved as a commission, or sometimes made its profit by inflating the exchange rate at which it swapped the currencies.[154] Ethics and banking regulations aside, it was easy money for the church. Moreover, Marcinkus was so stung by the financial beating the IOR had suffered in the Sindona debacle that he made a mistake common to many inexperienced investors: he had little patience in recovering the church's losses. Consequently his appetite for risk was increased. He doubled down with Calvi.[155]

That decision would prove far more disastrous for the Vatican Bank than any of the fallout from *il crack Sindona.*

18

The Battle of Two Scorpions

On February 4, 1976, Marcinkus flew to Geneva to attend his tenth Cisalpine board of directors meeting. The IOR by this time had loaned or invested $175 million in Calvi-backed offshore companies.[1] Marcinkus knew that Cisalpine was reporting the Vatican's loans as deposits from independent banks. He was also aware the IOR money accounted for more than three quarters of the Bahamian-based company's cash balance. As the minutes reflect, he said nothing at the Geneva board meeting. Nor did he object to a proposal to increase Cisalpine's stake in yet another Ortolani-controlled bank, Bafisud.[2] Instead, he agreed to provide 10 percent of the new venture's money.[3]

The Ambrosiano and the Vatican Bank were shuffling back and forth tens of millions of dollars between their many offshore companies. Typical was a transfer made just two weeks after Geneva. The IOR opened its fourth account at the Ambrosiano's Milan branch, and transferred from it another $2.5 million to one of its accounts at Rome's Banco di Santo Spirito. It then moved the money to a new Ortolani company in Switzerland.[4] Calvi increasingly relied on the IOR's help with the furious transfers between accounts, which were used to cover losses at some of the firms and to hide the money trail from Italian tax inspectors and banking regulators.

In late March, Calvi took advantage of a 20 percent increase in the price of the Ambrosiano's stock and solicited shareholder approval to raise another $46 million in capital. By April, the Bank of Italy gave Calvi permission to double to $50 million the Banca Cattolica's line of credit to Cisalpine. Within just two months of the Geneva directors meeting, the IOR had funneled another $20 million to Calvi.

An Italian law enacted on April 30 encouraged the duo to believe they were poised for even greater profits. Since the lira had fallen by more than 30 percent during the first four months of the year, Italy stiffened its currency export penalties, including for the first time jail sentences.[5] Wealthy Italians who wanted to move money out of their unstable country looked to the IOR. Since it was the central bank of a sovereign it was not subject to the tough new regulations. The Vatican's role was more important than ever in the convoluted Ambrosiano network. And it allowed Marcinkus to negotiate a higher commission for moving Calvi's money around the globe.[6]

Whatever the two men did, they were incapable of doing it simply. In April, the Ambrosiano agreed to buy for $32 million a Vatican-controlled property company, Società Immobiliare XX Settembre. The transaction took a mind-numbing eleven months to complete, and at different times involved byzantine bank transfers, inflated currency conversions, phantom loans, questionable back-to-back financial arrangements, the use of escrowed funds to manipulate a tiny Florentine bank, and the last-minute replacement of the Ambrosiano as the buyer with Pantanella, a former Vatican company that went bankrupt after stepping into the contract.[7] When the Bank of Italy inspectors eventually investigated the XX Settembre sale, they were utterly bewildered.

That summer, Calvi renamed Compendium—the Luxembourg shell that he originally used to register Cisalpine—to Banco Ambrosiano Holding (BAH). The Bank of Italy approved a transfer of more than $100 million from the Ambrosiano to BAH. He also got the approval to swap his 40 percent stake in the Banca del Gottardo (worth another $100 million) for BAH's share in La Centrale Finanziaria, an ex-Sindona holding company. There was a purpose beyond just obfuscation in the flurry of activity: although it was not obvious, Calvi was trying to streamline his labyrinthine financial web by directing all his foreign operations through a single company, BAH. Even he sometimes had trouble keeping track of the multitude of transactions on hundreds of pieces of hastily scribbled notepaper that he carried inside his locked attaché case.

It was not, however, in Calvi's DNA to do things straightforward. The following July (1977), Cisalpine transferred $30 million to the IOR, under an agreement by which the Vatican Bank used that money to buy a stake in BAH. Marcinkus agreed to hold the shares in trust since Cisalpine did not want to be the on-the-record buyer (none of this activity was ever recorded, as legally required, in Cisalpine's books or discussed at subsequent board meetings attended by Calvi and Marcinkus).[8] Calvi also convinced Marcinkus to put into the IOR's name "as a fiduciary" all the shares of the Panamanian United Trading Corporation, Cisalpine's parent. In return, Calvi sent him a July 26 letter, on the Ambrosiano's letterhead, in which he assured the Vatican Bank that United Trading was operating legally and swore to indemnify it from any liability.[9]*

That same day, Calvi sent a second letter, this time on Cisalpine's letterhead, offering similar assurances about Intermax, another shell for which the IOR had a management contract and was also the apparent owner.[11] For helping Calvi manage his maze of companies, the IOR earned on these deals only one thousandth of the monies transferred, about $100,000 annually.[12] It was not much, but it seemed to Marcinkus to be safe and easy. That was further evidence that he had learned nothing about managing risk from his troubled experience with Sindona. Marcinkus later told author John Cornwell that when the IOR invested its money with Calvi, he did not want to know the details.[13]

For Marcinkus, his frenetic work with Calvi helped the IOR scandal with Sindona recede into memory. Italy's extradition request for Sindona had languished for over a year at the State Department before it was sent to Justice, which also seemed in no rush to do much about it. Milan's prosecutor visited the U.S. Attorney to encourage him to hurry along the process.[14] And Italy hoped the United States might take the charges more seriously after a Milanese court sentenced Sindona in absentia to three and a half years in prison on twenty-five counts of bankruptcy fraud.[15]

Marcinkus and Calvi had no idea that Sindona was growing restless in America. As the Franklin denouement had played out, Richard Nixon had resigned because of Watergate. When Democrat Jimmy Carter became presi-

---

* There later came to be a furious finger-pointing disagreement between Marcinkus and Calvi about whether the contract including the United Trading bearer stock certificates was fraudulently backdated to November 21, 1974 (which is what Marcinkus claimed), or whether it was really signed in 1974 and merely confirmed in Calvi's letter three years later (Calvi's assertion). Donato De Bonis, an IOR monsignor who worked closely with Marcinkus, and Pellegrino de Strobel, the Vatican Bank's secretary and chief accountant, admitted they had signed the document, but claimed they left it undated. When the Vatican later tried to draw distance from Calvi's business network, it contended it did not control United Trading as early as 1974, a date that marked the start of highly questionable financial maneuvering. Italian prosecutors and investigators with two parliamentary commissions concluded that the IOR was the effective owner as of 1974 and that Marcinkus agreed to the backdating as a favor to Calvi. Marcinkus could never explain why, when Calvi had sent him a copy of the "backdated" agreement in 1977, the archbishop did not complain about the supposedly wrong date.[10]

dent in 1976, Sindona's Republican power connections seemed useless.[16] Italian communists had also made strong electoral gains in 1976 and Italy's ruling coalition soon ratcheted up the campaign for Sindona's return. Carter's Justice Department was more receptive and persuaded a court to issue an arrest warrant.

Sindona surrendered in September 1976 at the federal courthouse in downtown Manhattan. On the witness stand he swore that he had only $800,000 in assets. The judge allowed him to stay free pending a $3 million bail (he secured it with $150,000 in cash and Treasury bills as well as the deed to his Pierre co-op).[17] Sindona's defense team soon filed a motion to dismiss the extradition request. In their seventy-two-page brief they argued that Sindona's leftist enemies wholly concocted the charges. His life was in danger, they contended, if he were extradited to Italy. The Chief Justice of the Italian Supreme Court, Carmelo Spagnuolo (a P2 member), submitted an affidavit in support of the notion that Sindona might be killed if he returned to Italy.[18]

The Sicilian financier considered the extradition battle a sideshow to his chief concern: a possible American criminal indictment. In March, the same judge who presided over the extradition hearing sentenced six former midlevel Franklin executives on fraud charges.[19] When they received reduced sentences in return for their cooperation, many legal observers assumed that meant a U.S. indictment against Sindona was imminent.[20] But nothing had happened by the fall of 1977.

Meanwhile, some of Sindona's family and friends thought he might be better off simply returning to Italy. Investigators there charged he had looted $225 million from these banks.[21] If Sindona could somehow pay it back, he could void his absentia guilty verdict. To raise the cash, Sindona sued the Bank of Rome claiming he had a verbal agreement by which the bank had promised to cover up to $254 million of his debts in exchange for a lien on his interest in SGI. Marcinkus cringed when that suit was filed. It pitted Sindona against the Bank of Rome's Mario Barone, a banker with a close working relationship with the IOR.[22] To Marcinkus's relief, it did not take long before a Roman judge tossed the case, declaring it "inconceivable" that there would not be a written record of a commitment for such an enormous sum.[23] Sindona reached out in desperation to Gelli and the P2. Gelli worked frantically, even raising the matter with Prime Minister Giulio Andreotti, hoping to convince Italy's central bank to bail out Sindona.[24]

As far as Sindona was concerned, a central bank rescue was the only option left for a business comeback.[25] But Giorgio Ambrosoli, the court-appointed liquidator of his Italian banks, frustrated every effort by Gelli and his well-placed cohorts. Ambrosoli was opposed to using any public money to rescue Sindona from his misdeeds. In heated exchanges he threatened more than once to go public if the government reached a deal to pay off the debts. Two Bank of Italy directors sided with Ambrosoli and resisted any P2 strong-arm lobbying.[26]

Sindona told colleagues he was frustrated that Ambrosoli had thwarted his appeal to Italy's central bank. However, his friends thought he seemed more preoccupied with an all-consuming jealousy he had developed about Calvi's flourishing relationship with the Vatican Bank.[27] Calvi was ungrateful for all he had done for him, Sindona complained to colleagues, and he often groused that Calvi owed him millions of dollars for the Ambrosiano shares Sindona had secretly bought for him.[28] In the early fall of 1977, Rodolfo Guzzi, Sindona's chief Milanese attorney, called on Calvi. Sindona needed money for his spiraling legal bills. Sindona wanted Calvi to buy one of his villas for $500,000. There would be no change in title. It was just a means by which Calvi could send his beleaguered friend half a million dollars.

Calvi wanted to stay as far away from Sindona as possible, but he also did not want to turn him into an enemy. So he vacillated. Guzzi called daily looking for a yes. Calvi dodged him.[29] After a couple of weeks, one morning as Calvi drove to work, he was stunned to see bright white and blue posters plastered across the pale yellow-fronted Ambrosiano headquarters and several adjoining buildings along the narrow Via Clerici.[30] In bold, large print Calvi was accused of "fraud, issuing false accounts, unjustified appropriation, export of currency and tax swindles." The posters declared that Calvi "has transferred tens of millions of dollars into the following Swiss accounts." They even listed the correct names in which he held two Swiss bank accounts.[31] Someone had tipped off *L'Espresso,* which got a photographer there to snap pictures before Calvi's security team ripped down the posters.[32]

Calvi had no doubt that Sindona was behind the smear, his desperation causing him to become reckless and more dangerous. A few days later, Calvi got a call from Luigi Cavallo. Calvi knew him, not from his former job as a U.N. translator, but as a renowned freelance agitator best known for his acquittal in a left-wing coup against Italy's government.[33] He also published a small quarterly, *Agenzia A,* a broadsheet devoured by journalists and politicians for its torrid mixture of offbeat news and blind gossip.* Cavallo told Calvi that unless he honored promises he supposedly made to Sindona years earlier, more mud would come. Calvi was noncommittal.

Everything was quiet for a few weeks. Calvi hoped that Sindona had called off his attack dog. But over the Christmas holidays Cavallo wrote Calvi a letter about a Ugandan parable of two scorpions in a bottle and how they "embark on a battle to the death which inevitably has a lethal outcome for both contenders."[35]

Just after the New Year, Cavallo published an edition of *Agenzia A* in which he set forth a blistering, fictional indictment against Calvi, charging him with knowingly publishing false balance sheets for the Ambrosiano. More salacious posters appeared.[36] Business associates urged Calvi to go to the police. But he could not publicly charge that Sindona was extorting money without possibly admitting that the charges were true. Calvi reached out to Gelli for help. The P2 chief told Calvi to pay the money, which he did that March, wiring $500,000 from United Trading to a numbered Sindona account at Union Bank in Chiasso, Switzerland.[37]

Calvi had much more on his mind, however, than just Sindona's blackmail as 1978 got under way. Cisalpine's accountant, Price Waterhouse, was insisting on answers about the bank's confidential accounts. When he no longer could delay replying, Calvi dismissed them. Their replacement, Coopers & Lybrand, were only on the job a few months before they began peppering Calvi with queries about the IOR. They also complained about their "difficulty in obtaining any specific financial information" about the Vatican Bank. Calvi assured them that all the dealings between Cisalpine and the IOR were "on normal commercial terms."[38]

Although none of Calvi's regular colleagues noticed any change in his demeanor, the Coopers & Lybrand interest in the IOR agitated him. On top of that, a $20 million loan to the Vatican was due at the end of January. Calvi

* When it comes to Sindona, Calvi, and Marcinkus, even the simplest matters are often more complicated than they first appear. Was Cavallo working for Sindona? Guzzi, Sindona's attorney, later claimed that he had hired Cavallo at Sindona's direction. And Guzzi was later found guilty of extortion over this matter. Sindona denied having anything to do with Cavallo, telling author Nick Tosches that the provocateur was most likely working for the Italian government. And as for Cavallo? In an unsworn statement, he told prosecutors that Sindona retained him to squeeze as much money as possible out of Calvi. But later, under oath and threat of perjury, Cavallo told an Assize court that he had done it on his own and that Sindona had tried repeatedly to stop him.[34]

did not have the money. For months he had been trying to find new investors, pitching proposals to money managers on three continents. His efforts paid off with only days to spare. Calvi received the first of four loans totaling $160 million from Banca Nazionale del Lavoro and Ente Nazionale Idrocarburi (ENI), a state-owned bank and multinational run by two P2 members.[39]

Marcinkus, meanwhile, was so pleased with his mushrooming dealings with Calvi that he kicked off 1978 by renewing or expanding loans to the usual suspects—including Manic, Zitroppo, and Banco Ambrosiano Holding (BAH)—as well as giving fresh infusions of church money to new Panamanian-based firms, Astolfine and Belrosa. Despite the repayment of the $20 million loan, the Vatican Bank's cash invested in Calvi's labyrinthine global businesses in 1978 soared from $200 million to a dizzying $330 million ($1.2 billion in 2014 dollars).[40]*

With Marcinkus confident that the Ambrosiano's businesses were solid, Calvi concentrated on Sindona, who had continued to threaten him. Sindona had considered the $500,000 a down payment on what he believed was owed him. In April 1978—the same month that a dozen Bank of Italy inspectors showed up unexpectedly at the Ambrosiano's headquarters—Sindona and Calvi met in Washington.[42] Father Philip Guarino, a director of the Senior Citizens Division of the Republican National Committee, hosted a party for Sindona at the Capitol Hill Club.[43] Calvi went to tell Sindona that he could not help him further. Sindona demanded more money and refused to back off. In the coming months, Calvi diverted upward of $5 million through Gelli to Sindona (the following spring, when Sindona learned that Calvi was a guest at New York's Carlyle Hotel, he showed up and would not leave until Calvi agreed to accelerate the payments).[44] Calvi at the time had no idea that it was a tip provided by Sindona about some of Calvi's secret Swiss bank accounts that prompted the Bank of Italy investigators to swarm over the Ambrosiano.[45] When Calvi called Gelli to fix the results of the probe, Gelli was powerless to help. None of the Bank of Italy inspectors were P2 members.[46]

The month after their Washington meeting, three years after the Italian government had asked for Sindona's return, a federal judge approved the extra-

---

* Another sign of the depth of Calvi's involvement with the IOR was evident in January 1978, when the Vatican Bank gave Calvi letters falsely describing all its loans as Ambrosiano deposits at the IOR. Calvi stored the letters in case he needed them later to deflect Italian investigators.[41]

dition.[47] His lawyers appealed. As that worked its way through the legal system during the summer, the U.S. Attorney in New York announced indictments against three top ex–Franklin National executives. Sindona, and his former right-hand aide, Carlo Bordoni, were unindicted co-conspirators.[48] The U.S. Attorney told reporters that the investigation into Franklin was continuing. For Sindona it was a dilemma: return to Italy and the fraudulent bankruptcy charges or stay in the United States and face a likely criminal indictment.

19

"A Psychopathic Paranoid"

While Sindona obsessed about where to make his best legal stand, his two former business partners had their own problems. Calvi fretted about finding more financing to prevent any single part of his empire from cracking and setting off a calamitous chain reaction. Marcinkus was absorbed not with the IOR's business dealings, but rather with pending changes inside the Vatican that might threaten his power.

Pope Paul VI, Marcinkus's great patron, had since 1977 become increasingly withdrawn. There was speculation that he might be the first Pope in centuries to resign. In the early part of his Pontificate, Paul had taken more international trips than the previous thirty Popes combined. Now, debilitating arthritis left him mostly confined to the city-state. He occasionally mustered enough strength to travel the seventeen miles to Castel Gandolfo, his summer residence. A combination of persistent pain and little rest took its toll, sending him spiraling into a depression.[1] "He looks frail and often sounds mournful," noted *The New York Times*.[2]

During a 1974 synod of bishops, Paul told the cleric sitting next to him, "Old age itself is the illness" (an open microphone picked up his softly spoken Latin, *senectus ipsa est morbus*).[3] "I see the threshold of the hereafter approaching," an emotional and almost wistful Paul VI told pilgrims near his eightieth birthday in 1977.[4] As he spent more time locked away in his private quarters, there seemed to be a rumor du jour about one medical malady or another. Unconfirmed accounts from insiders about "occasional lapses of memory" found their way into the press.[5]

Ironically, it was Paul VI who mandated that all bishops offer their resignations when they reached seventy-five. And he had directed that no cardinal older than eighty could vote in any conclave. Many Vaticanologists had expected that he might establish a precedent for the Roman church by stepping down on either his seventy-fifth or eightieth birthday.[6] But both birthdays passed uneventfully. There was a synod of bishops four days after his eightieth birthday, and many speculated that Paul had waited to announce it there.[7] But again nothing. Now, in 1978, with the Pope eighty-one years old, the resignation rumors had a renewed urgency.[8]

The infirm Paul was under siege on many fronts. Fresh efforts to overturn his encyclical banning all artificial birth control had gathered momentum, especially in America. British scientists had conceived the world's first test-tube baby. The development rattled the Vatican. And French scientists had created a fly from a test tube after ten years of research. What did it mean when life could come from a laboratory? A modern Protestant reformation that allowed priests to marry and liberalized previously orthodox views of homosexuality put pressure on the Roman church to loosen its rules.[9] Some of the impetus to modify the centuries-old mandatory clerical celibacy came from polls that showed that 40 percent of Italian clerics thought it should be abolished, and a third of Spanish priests wanted it optional.[10] A new study showed that record numbers of priests and nuns were leaving their orders.[11]

The church itself seemed in revolt, with priests contesting orders from their bishops, and bishops in turn resisting directives from Rome. The Pope struggled to maintain a monolithic faith in which all direction came from Rome. Traditionalists blamed Paul VI for misguided and heterodox reforms. They demanded a return to the church as it existed before the Second Vatican Council. A tad more reasonable were so-called conservatives, who were open to some modernization. Those conservatives also castigated Paul VI, not as a heretic, but as someone who went too far in his zeal to update the church. Yet another group, modern theologians, represented by the Swiss priest Hans Küng, questioned all conventional thinking, on everything from Papal infallibility to homosexuality and abortion to even limits on the divinity of Christ (Küng's 1971 bestseller, *Infallible? An Inquiry*, challenged the heart of whether a Pope spoke for God on matters of faith). The Charismatics believed that the church needed to return to its early roots by emphasizing the power of the Holy Spirit. The progressives, a fast growing subset, believed Paul had not gone far enough in his reforms and that the ideal future was in a loose partnership with leftist secular governments who followed the teachings of Jesus by redistributing wealth to the poor and underclass.

The threats the church had faced during World War II and the early Cold War seemed lost in the confusion of the social revolution that had kicked off in the mid-1960s. It showed little signs of abating.

A steady stream of bad news also left Paul emotionally exhausted. The brutal murder of Congolese Cardinal Émilie Biayenda, to whom he had personally given the red hat in 1973, put him into a funk.[12] But no event affected him more than when the radical left-wing Red Brigades killed five bodyguards and kidnapped Aldo Moro, a two-time Italian Prime Minister, from a busy Rome street. The Pope, who had long known Moro and had great affection for him, led the appeals for his release. For two months, starting in March 1978, the kidnappers managed to keep one step ahead of a massive security hunt. The captive Moro wrote personal letters to his political colleagues and to Paul, begging them to do whatever was needed to free him. And the Pontiff in turn pleaded with Italy to strike any necessary compromise. Against the advice of his advisors, he even made a dramatic public offer to trade places with Moro.[13] The Red Brigades ignored his appeal. Instead, that May, Moro was shot ten times in a circle around his heart and left to bleed to death, stuffed into the trunk of an abandoned car in central Rome.[14]

Pope Paul was inconsolable.[15] He joined the nation in heartfelt mourning. Despite his pain, he insisted that he personally say the funeral Mass for the assassinated leader. On a cold spring day that May, Paul VI crossed Rome to preside over the funeral at a packed Basilica of St. John Lateran. It was the first time Vaticanologists could recall a Pope saying a requiem Mass for anyone other than a cardinal.[16] And a few days after Moro's murder, the normally taciturn Paul fought back tears as he addressed a group of children at St. Peter's.[17] Both the church and his beloved Italy, he later dejectedly told his personal secretary, Monsignor Macchi, seemed under attack.

Macchi had witnessed for several years the bitter resignation with which Paul observed the secular violence and instability in Italy. All the leading Red Brigades were Catholics who had abandoned their faith to embrace a violent strain of communism that now engulfed Italian cities. And it was not just Italy. The grim news continued to pour in that summer. A Spanish general and his aide were assassinated in broad daylight by left-wing terrorists in Madrid.[18] Twelve white teachers and children were butchered by guerrillas in Rhodesia.[19]

A grenade nearly killed Iraq's ambassador in London, and a terror attack on the Iraqi embassy in Paris left two dead.[20] PLO bombs killed five and wounded dozens of Israelis on a Jerusalem bus.[21]

The spiraling violence played to Paul's natural pessimism. The Pope had lost interest in the more mundane aspects of overseeing the Curia. For nearly a year, day-to-day administrative duties had been split between Archbishop Giovanni Benelli, the powerful Substitute Secretary of State, and Macchi. The two often clashed.[22] That was resolved when the Pope elevated Benelli to the rank of cardinal and dispatched him to Florence. But removing Benelli did not help. Benelli may have irritated many with his abrupt Tuscan ways, but even his detractors knew he was capable of making quick decisions and sticking to them. Cardinal Jean-Marie Villot, who had been Secretary of State for a decade, wielded tremendous influence with Paul, but the aloof Frenchman was himself challenged when it came to the Curial bureaucracy. And Macchi seemed exhausted, unable to prevent Paul from indulging in interminable vacillation.

In the spring, Malachi Martin, a former Jesuit professor at Rome's Pontifical Biblical Institute, told *The Boston Globe* that the only reason Paul VI had not yet resigned was because he had not succeeded in rallying enough support for a radical plan to allow some limited participation in the next conclave by non-Catholic Christian faiths.[23] By appointing many Third World cardinals among twenty-nine red hats in 1973, Paul had eliminated the possibility that a European-only bloc could elect the next Pope. And in 1976, when he elevated another twenty-one bishops to become cardinals, most were from outside Europe. Only two were Italians, the smallest percentage from Italy in the church's history.[24] Still, according to Martin, the demographics of the cardinals were too conservative to guarantee the Pope he would get the progressive successor he wanted. As a result, claimed Martin, Paul clung to the Papacy.[25]

A resignation by Paul would have a more deleterious effect on Marcinkus than most Curia power brokers. Marcinkus's frankness and no-frills manner had inspired confidence in the Pope for over fifteen years. Paul relied on the American bishop's fearlessness, a trait he admired but could never emulate. The unique dynamic of their friendship meant that Paul never hobbled the IOR through the fog of indecision and equivocation that was a trademark of his Papacy. He allowed Marcinkus to run the Vatican Bank.

When *il crack Sindona* had exploded three years earlier, the Pope could have silenced any criticism over the IOR's role by transferring Marcinkus to Curial Siberia. Some prominent cardinals and bishops had demanded just that. But Paul had proven decisive and firm in sticking by his beleaguered IOR chief.

The Pope's resignation would also end the tenure of Monsignor Macchi. Many Curialists resented Macchi for the outsized power he wielded as Paul's alter ego. Macchi and Marcinkus ranked as the two most unpopular officials at the Vatican. An unnamed monsignor in the Curia told author John Cornwell that "Maachi had the Pope's ear and Marcinkus had the purse-strings."[26] Persistent gossip accused the duo of plotting to get their pet projects rubber-stamped by the infirm Pontiff.[27]

Marcinkus was not only concerned about losing his patrons at the top of the Vatican. Developments in the United States also threatened his strongest ally there, Chicago Cardinal John Cody. The two had been friends since the 1950s. For several years there had been some published reports critical of Cody's authoritarian governance. As head of America's largest Catholic diocese, Cody wielded tremendous power. And after New York's Cardinal Spellman died in 1967, he had become the biggest American fundraiser for Rome. Through the 1970s, Cody had seemed untouchable. This despite the energetic efforts of Father Andrew Greeley, a liberal American priest and professor of sociology much admired by the American media, who was on a mission to prove that Cody was guilty of financial improprieties.[28] Greeley used his syndicated national newspaper column to press his case.[29] And privately, and later in print, Greeley often became an armchair psychologist, diagnosing Cody with "a borderline personality disorder" or speculating that he was even "a psychopathic paranoid."[30] According to Greeley, Cody was a binge drinker who checked into a handful of southwest Chicago hotels so he could go on all-night benders. And Greeley accused the Chicago police of suppressing several drunk-driving arrests.[31] Rome judged Greeley an unreliable, attention-hungry gadfly, dismissing his wild charges without paying them much heed.

But now Macchi shared with Marcinkus that some damning information independent of Greeley had filtered into the Vatican about how Cody might be running America's largest diocese into the ground. In July (1978), a two-inch-thick dossier made its way from the United States to Rome. It was the result of a detailed probe Paul VI had ordered.

As he reviewed the dossier, Paul dismissed much of it as inevitable jealous infighting, including the stories that Cody was a bigot, had a vindictive streak, that he espoused neo-fascist military views, and that he was in regular contact with the right-wing John Birch Society. He was more concerned about the complaint that he had alienated Chicago's clergy and top laymen with his heavy-handed ways. The file included a remarkable public condemnation of Cody by the Association of Chicago Priests. They charged that the cardinal had lied to them and that he employed a network of informants to maintain his authoritarian rule through fear and intimidation.[32] There was even information that Cody might have too close a personal relationship with a Chicago area woman.*

But the accusations that got Pope Paul's full attention were about money. One marked Cody as a bad financial manager. While treasurer of the National Conference of Catholic Bishops, he had invested millions in Penn Central shortly before its insolvency. The other more troubling charge was that he had refused to account for millions more in diocesan funds. Cody had blocked access to the accounts to both prelates and accountants and there were suggestions that he might have diverted some of the money to a lavish lifestyle.[34]

The file did not include a recommendation as to what the Pope should do. On such a sensitive matter, Paul would ordinarily weigh his options for months. But not only was the evidence presented strong, but the complaints from many of the Chicago prelates dated back to 1976. All of Paul's trusted advisors—including his Secretary of State, Cardinal Villot; Monsignor Agostino Casaroli, secretary of the Council of the Public Affairs of the Church; and Cardinal Sebastiano Baggio, the take-no-nonsense Prefect of the Sacred Congregation for Bishops—thought Cody should go. Paul even reached out to Florence's Cardinal Benelli, who had looked into some of the charges when he was still in the Secretary of State's office. He also thought Cody should resign.

Who to replace him? Baggio thought the natural choice was Cincinnati's Archbishop Joseph Bernardin, whom Paul had made the youngest American

* Compared to the many other charges of impropriety, the suggestion that Cody might have broken his celibacy vows did not then seem important. But in a couple of years it was that relationship—with Helen Dolan Wilson—that would be the basis for a federal grand jury investigation of Cody and whether he had diverted more than $1 million in church funds to the sixty-six-year-old divorcée. At the time, the Pope did not know that Cody had brought Wilson—who was the cardinal's step-cousin—to Rome for his coronation as a cardinal; loaned her money to buy a vacation home in Boca Raton, Florida; put her on the payroll of the archdiocese; padded her work records so she got a larger pension; and steered the life insurance business of many Chicago priests to Wilson's insurance-agent son.[33]

bishop ever in 1966. The Pontiff liked Bernardin. The bishop had an unblemished reputation as an efficient and decent administrator of the Cincinnati church. While Bernardin shared Paul's liberal political views, he was also a traditionalist on core theological matters such as clerical celibacy and ensuring that women were not eligible for the priesthood.

What about Marcinkus, wondered the Pope? He was a Chicagoan and had a strong working relationship with the chief clerics in that diocese. It would seem the ideal way to give Marcinkus a red hat and to ensure that his move from the IOR was a promotion. Baggio advised against it. The Chicago church was a mess in part because it had been directed so poorly. As Marcinkus had never run a diocese, suggested Baggio, this would not be the time for him to learn on the job. The Pope took it under consideration.[35]

Paul settled on a plan that would move Cody out in a face-saving way. Baggio—known as "the Pope's fixer"—flew to Chicago to inform the cardinal that the Pontiff wanted the appointment of a bishop as coadjutor, someone who would be responsible for the diocese's day-to-day operations. The press release would cite Cody's poor health as the reason a new bishop was assisting him. And Cody would remain as the cardinal until he reached retirement age in 1982, at which point Bernardin would fully take charge.

In early August at Cody's villa in Mundelein, Baggio confronted the Chicago cardinal with the evidence and the Pope's directive. Cody was not contrite, nor did he agree to a coadjutor. Baggio stormed out after a contentious hour. Baggio's report to Rome: the cardinal was defiant and in violation of Canon Law for failing to follow a Papal order.[36] Monsignor Macchi intercepted Baggio's report. It arrived at an inopportune time. The Pope was not feeling well, and Mario Fontana, his chief physician, had just placed him on antibiotics because of a suspected urinary tract infection. Paul was running a fever and his hands were shaking. Seventy-four-year-old Fontana told Macchi he should wait a few days before discussing church matters. Macchi held back the news about Cody.[37]

By Saturday, August 5, the Pope was not feeling better. Macchi canceled the Pontiff's Sunday benediction. He was disappointed not to make it. It marked not only the Feast of the Transfiguration, a celebration of Christ's resurrection, but was the thirty-third anniversary of the bombing of Hiroshima. Paul had prepared a special blessing for world peace.[38]

That Saturday night, the Pope felt strong enough to join Macchi and another personal secretary, Monsignor John Magee for dinner. Afterward they prayed for the dozens of Israelis killed and injured earlier that day when a PLO bomb tore apart Tel Aviv's popular Carmel Market.[39] But the Pope cut the prayers short, complaining of intense pain.[40] Macchi called Fontana, who ordered more rest. The antibiotics needed more time to be effective, said the physician.

On Sunday morning, August 6, when Fontana and Macchi walked into the bedroom, the Pontiff was sweating and complaining about pain. This time Fontana was more concerned. The Pope's temperature had spiked and his blood pressure was low.[41]

Fontana telephoned a specialist at Rome's Agostino Gemelli Hospital. What about transferring the Pontiff by helicopter to Gemelli, asked the specialist? No, Fontana had discussed it with Macchi and the other secretaries. They agreed that Paul should stay at Castel Gandolfo. Taking him to a hospital would be unprecedented. When Paul had his prostate surgery a few years earlier, a surgeon had done it in a makeshift operating room in the Apostolic Palace. What about dispatching Gemelli's renowned mobile intensive care unit to Castel Gandolfo? The problem, said Fontana, was that their arrival on an otherwise quiet Sunday would alert the press corps. If the Pope's condition worsened, Fontana assured the Gemelli specialist that he would summon the emergency crew.

Fontana then told the grim-faced household staff that if Paul survived the next twelve hours, he would pull through.[42]

Around 5 p.m. the Pope's condition worsened. He was still lucid but his blood pressure was more erratic. Paul asked Macchi to summon his brother and his favorite nephew.[43] Secretary of State Villot soon arrived. He had brought with him a small silver hammer that had been handed down for more than a thousand years. It was the hammer used in church tradition to determine if a Pontiff was dead.[44] Villot was prepared for the worst. The tall French cardinal paced along the edge of the bedroom chamber, as much from anxiety over the Pope's condition as from being unable to light up one of his trademark Gauloises. No smoking, Fontana politely told the chain-smoking Secretary of State when he arrived at Castel Gandolfo.

At 6 p.m., Macchi asked the small group to join him in a Mass in the chapel adjoining Paul's bedroom. In the pew closest to the open door between the rooms, Magee and Fontana kept an eye on the Pope. A few minutes into the Mass, Paul had trouble breathing. Fontana detected a rapid and irregular heartbeat. It was likely a heart attack. He told Macchi the time was short. Rome's AP bureau got the word and flashed the first wire service story only a few minutes later at 6:15 p.m. that "Pope Paul VI suffered a heart attack. He is semi-conscious."[45]

A grim silence settled over the small gathering. Macchi gave Paul a Communion wafer. Villot administered last rites.[46] For the next three hours Paul lapsed in and out of consciousness. At 9:40, it seemed he had stopped breathing. Fontana again put a stethoscope to his chest. "It's over."[47]

That medical opinion did not suffice by church protocol. Villot retrieved the silver hammer. He tapped the Pontiff in the middle of his forehead with the flat head of the hammer. "Giovanni Battista Enrico Antonio Maria, are you dead?" Silence. A minute later Villot repeated the ritual. Again silence. And then he did it a third time. The Pope did not move.

Villot turned to those in the room. "Pope Paul is truly dead."[48]*

Villot was now Camerlengo, the cardinal responsible for running the church until the next Pope was elected.[50] Clerics in the Secretary of State's office began sending telegrams in Italian and French to all the cardinals. They said: "THE POPE IS DEAD. COME AT ONCE. VILLOT."[51]

The politicking to select the 263rd Pontiff in the church's history would soon begin.

---

* Part of Villot's duties was to take custody of the Fisherman's Ring that is custom-made for each Pope. During the upcoming Conclave of Cardinals, the Secretary of State was required to smash that ring with other cardinals as witnesses. In ancient times, when wax seals were the mark of authenticity on official documents, it was important to destroy the deceased Pope's ring and all his seals to guarantee that no one could impersonate the dead Pontiff. Villot was stunned to see the ring missing from Paul's right hand. Villot ordered Macchi to find it before the conclave. He did, four days later, stuffed under some papers in the back of a desk drawer in the Pope's study.[49]

20

The Year of Three Popes*

Paul VI had been Pope for fifteen years. Only eleven cardinals who were at the 1963 conclave were still alive. Genoa's Giuseppe Siri was still a darling of conservatives. A few months before the Pope's death, Siri had turned seventy-two but that did not prevent traditionalists from promoting him. After the liberal slide for which they blamed Paul VI, the church needed a turn to the right, even if Siri's age meant it would be a short one. The progressives were enthusiastic about another veteran, seventy-three-year-old Vienna's Franz König. He had polished his reformer reputation at the Second Vatican Council. In recent years he had established a dialogue between the church and Eastern European communist regimes.[1] And although Secretary of State Jean-Marie Villot was just short of his seventy-third birthday, nobody counted him out.

Vaticanologists handicapping the race knew that a slate of younger cardinals was as papabile as any of the veterans. There was plenty of time for speculating. That is because Villot set a slow schedule, picking August 25 for the conclave, nineteen days after the Pope's passing. It was the last possible date allowed under rules Paul VI set for the selection of his successor.[2]

The Italians grumbled that Villot had stretched out the process to allow the foreign cardinals enough time to build a coalition to elect the first non-Italian since Hadrian VI had died in 1523.[3] The foreign cardinals on the other hand had the opposite worry, that Villot's leisurely pace was crafted to allow the

* This phrase was first used by the Catholic press in 1978, and subsequently by the mainstream media. It was also the title of a book by the late Vaticanologist Peter Hebblethwaite.

Italian prelates extra time to consolidate their support for a single, unbeatable candidate.[4]

Pope Paul had expanded the College of Cardinals to an unprecedented 130. Fifteen were barred from voting since they were older than eighty (although they could still be elected Pope themselves).[5] Four others were too ill to attend. Of the remaining 111 elector-cardinals, a bare majority (fifty-seven) were European.[6]

Villot methodically set about protecting Paul's legacy. When he learned that Paul's executor, Monsignor Macchi, was about to destroy the late Pontiff's private papers, he intervened. Villot dispatched many of the documents to the Secret Archives. As for the Pope's file about Cardinal Cody, Villot told Macchi, that must go to the next Pontiff.[7]

Villot wanted to ensure that the upcoming conclave was free from prying eyes. A few months earlier a sweep by Camilio Cibin—Inspector General of the Corpo della Gendarmeria, the Vatican security and police force—had uncovered eleven American- and Russian-made bugs.[8] A 1973 bestselling book by two Italian journalists, *Sex in the Confessional,* based on bugged confessionals, fanned Villot's apprehension. So Villot directed Cibin to ensure that there were no listening devices in the conclave. Cibin returned in a day with alarming news: the church-run Vatican Radio planned to bug the conclave so it could get the scoop on the Pope's election. There might be other such plans afoot, Cibin warned.[9]*

Since there had not been a Papal election in fifteen years, there was a more intense press scrutiny. As the conclave's opening date drew near, the speculation about the supposed frontrunners ramped up. That the published reports usually selected different candidates was good evidence that it was a guessing game.

Although some thought that Giovanni Benelli was too young at fifty-seven, the brusque Tuscan, who had been a Curial powerhouse before Paul dispatched him to Florence, seemed to be on most shortlists.[11] Many supported him since

---

* Vatican Radio succeeded in planting a rudimentary transmitter disguised as a shirt button on one of the lay attendants in the Sistine Chapel. It was not capable of picking up voices but instead sent a low-pitched ping to a receiver hidden inside the Vatican Radio office. The attendant was instructed to press it three times when a Pope was elected.[10]

they thought he was the most electable progressive. A German newspaper ran a large front-page photo of Benelli, under the headline "The Next Pope?"

If a favorite were determined just by the number of press mentions, it was probably sixty-eight-year-old Sergio Pignedoli, the influential Chief of Secretariat for Non-Christians.[12] The Paul VI protégé had enough Curial experience, combined with a widespread reputation as a moderate not afraid to make tough decisions, to attract a solid centrist following. The Curial rumor was that Pignedoli was so confident of winning that he had gone on a crash diet to look his best in the ceremonial white cassock he would don when elected.[13]

The New York Times relied on "Vatican sources" to name four cardinals who the paper claimed had pulled away from other contenders: Florence's Benelli; the conservative Pericle Felici; and progressives Sebastiano Baggio and Turin's Anastasio Ballestrero.[14] The night before the conclave, an Italian newspaper published the results of a first ever computer forecast: Cardinal Baggio would be the next Pontiff.[15] In London, Ladbrokes, the betting syndicate, irritated the Vatican by allowing gamblers to bet on the outcome for the first time.[16] The British odds? Sergio Pignedoli—missed entirely by *The New York Times* and the Italian computer program—was the favorite at 5–2; Baggio and Ugo Poletti, the Vicar of Rome, 7–2; Florence's Benelli, 4–1; Dutch Cardinal Johannes Willebrands, 8–1; Argentine Eduardo Pironio, 12–1; Austrian Cardinal König, 16–1; Basil Hume of England, 25–1; and the long shots were Brazil's Aloísio Lorscheider, Pakistani Cardinal Joseph Cordeiro, and the progressive Cardinal of Brussels, Leo Josef Suenens, 33–1.[17]

If Marcinkus had a favorite, he never shared it with anyone. One of the few issues on which many progressives and conservatives found common ground was the belief that the unchecked Vatican Bank had grown too powerful and that the next Pope needed to make it more accountable. Malachi Martin, the former Jesuit and Vatican insider, had published a widely cited book only a few months earlier (*The Final Conclave*), which discussed Sindona at length. It revived many of the unpleasant questions still lingering over that scandal and the IOR.

All the cardinal-electors were aware that nine months earlier a U.S. federal judge had ordered Sindona extradited to Italy. Although Sindona's top-flight legal team had appealed that decision, it was only a matter of time before the Sicilian financier stood in the docket of an Italian courtroom. His Vatican dealings would again be grist for salacious media coverage. Marcinkus realized a new Pope might well consider his continued tenure at the IOR an unnecessary distraction from the business of running the rest of the Roman church. Even Cardinal Cody, clinging to power in Chicago, had backed off his unwavering support for Marcinkus by suggesting the next Pope should clean up the IOR's financial morass.[18]

As the conclave got under way, Siri polled the most votes on the first ballot.[19] The Genovese cardinal had been in the same spot in 1958 and 1963. And once again he was unable to build any momentum. Siri faded during four ballots over two days, as did the original progressive frontrunners discussed most often before the voting started.[20] To everyone's surprise, the Papacy went to the sixty-five-year-old Patriarch of Venice, Cardinal Albino Luciani. He had been on few shortlists (British bookmakers had not even listed him).[21] Vaticanologists had not considered him since he had dropped in the church's power hierarchy in 1972 after Paul VI, Benelli, and Marcinkus rebuffed his last-minute appeals to reverse the sale of Venice's revered Banca Cattolica to Calvi.

Luciani's winning coalition appreciated his reputation as someone who trimmed the fat of the Venetian curia.[22] In the last years of his Papacy, Paul VI had bemoaned his own failure to streamline the Curia or to curtail its power. His 1967 efforts at simplifying the Vatican's finances had the unintended consequence of creating more bureaucracy and leading to two parallel financial fiefdoms, APSA and the IOR. Every time Paul pushed for change, entrenched Curialists pushed back harder. Maybe an outsider could do better. Another plus for Luciani was that his warm, personal style harked back to the friendlier, charismatic John XXIII, the type of leader many cardinals believed could energize the faithful following fifteen years of Paul's cool remoteness.[23]

After his election, Luciani's first words were, "God will forgive you for what you have done to me."[24] If he was surprised by his selection, it was not evident by how quickly he announced his Papal name when Villot asked.

"I will be called Gianpaolo One." (John Paul I, in a tribute to the influence of John XXIII, who had made him a bishop, and to Paul VI, who had given him the red hat; it was the first original name chosen since 913 when a short-lived Pope had chosen Lando.)[25]

Luciani had made it clear even before the conclave that he thought the church should emphasize spiritual obligations over politicking.[26] Bishops, priests, and even laymen worldwide were demanding a more decentralized church, one in which the Curia no longer held the Pope hostage to its byzantine ways. And that fit with Luciani's view that the Pope should be less a monarch and more a pastor.

His background offered a sharp contrast to his predecessor. As opposed to Paul, who had spent decades in the Curia, Luciani's career was mostly free of Rome. The eldest of four children from his father's second marriage, he was born on October 17, 1912, in the remote northern Italian village of Canale d'Agordo.[27] The family was poor even by the standards of a region devastated by World War I. His father, a bricklayer, spent years as a migrant worker in Switzerland and Germany before getting a regular job as a glassblower on the Island of Murano in the Venetian lagoon.[28] Luciani was only eleven when his devout mother entered him into a minor seminary at Feltre.[29] Ordained a priest on July 7, 1935, the twenty-two-year-old Luciani spent two years as a chaplain and teacher at Agordo's Technical Mining Institute.[30] In 1937 he received his doctorate in theology from Rome's Gregorian University.[31] And that year he became the vice rector at the Seminary of Belluno, where for the next decade he taught everything from canon law to philosophy.[32] In 1958, John XXIII consecrated him bishop of Vittorio Veneto, a small city south of Belluno. It was another eleven years, December 15, 1969, before Paul VI appointed him the Patriarch of Venice, in part because he was a likable administrator not hobbled by too great an ego and ambition.[33] After three and a half uneventful years as Venice's Patriarch, Pope Paul gave him his red hat in 1973.[34]

The man who once told a friend, "Had I not become a priest, I would have liked to have been a journalist," was a traditionalist when it came to church dogma.[35] He agreed with his predecessor on every major issue except for the ban on all artificial birth control. Luciani had been on the Pontifical commission that had recommended an exception be made for the pill, but had been overruled by Paul VI in his much-debated encyclical *Humanae Vitae*.[36] The mere suggestion that the new Pope might liberalize that core doctrine alarmed traditionalists.[37]

Luciani left no doubt from the outset which clerics had his ear. Cardinal Benelli had made the difference in the conclave by throwing his support to Luciani.[38] Now it was clear that the hardworking Benelli had a direct line to John Paul. It was odd to some that the Pope who spoke about reforming the

Curia might rely on the Florentine cardinal who had been a martinet Deputy Secretary of State and general administrator, sometimes even called the "Vatican's Kissinger." But once he left the Curia, Benelli had begun talking about reforming it. Some feared that for Benelli *reform* was a code word for revenge. But while a debate over his motivation raged, it was acknowledged that if anyone knew how to trim the Vatican's redundant bureaucracy, and had the will to fight the Curialists, it was Benelli.[39]

For Marcinkus, it was hard to imagine a worse combination of news than Luciani's election and Benelli's resurging influence. Luciani was the cardinal whom Marcinkus had dismissed in 1972 when the Venetian Patriarch contested the IOR's sale of Banca Cattolica to Calvi and the Ambrosiano. "Eminence, don't you have anything better to do?" Marcinkus had asked him at the time, ending the conversation and sending Luciani back to Venice in a fury.[40] Their chilly relationship had not improved during the ensuing six years. Calvi had reneged on his promise to maintain all of Banca Cattolica's preferences for Venice's Catholics and the diocese. And when the Sindona scandal tarred the Vatican it further convinced Luciani that Marcinkus's judgment was poor.

Benelli, meanwhile, had met in 1973 with FBI agents who visited the Vatican in their investigation into counterfeit securities and the IOR. Benelli counseled Paul VI that Marcinkus was involved in too many questionable ventures and that he required more oversight. He had even offered to monitor the IOR and Marcinkus. But the Pope had sided with Marcinkus and dispatched Benelli out of the Vatican to Florence.

On September 5, only two days after John Paul became Pope at a simple outdoor ceremony without much pomp, the new Pontiff read *Il Mondo*, a weekly news magazine of Italy's preeminent *Il Corriere della Sera*, Italy's preeminent financial newspaper. There was a damning front-page story about the Vatican Bank that highlighted the uncertainty and danger over Sindona's eventual extradition to and trial in Italy. That morning, after an early breakfast, John Paul assembled a thin manila folder with his notes about what Benelli and another career Curialist, Cardinal Pericle Felici, had shared with him about the church's finances (the Vatican will not disclose to the author if those notes are preserved, but if so, they would likely be in the Secret Archives and not available for review until at least 2063).[41]

The information passed along by the two cardinals was not good. Peter's

Pence had dropped precipitously during the entire fifteen years of Paul VI's Papacy.[42] Bequests to the church from well-to-do worshippers had slumped by 30 percent in just five years. After adjusting for inflation, the church was collecting just over half of what it took in a decade earlier.[43]

As for Marcinkus, his secrecy and arrogance was a poor combination for the chief of the Vatican Bank. Benelli and Felici contended the IOR was not fulfilling its charter's primary directive to "provide for the custody and administration of capital destined for religious works."[44] The Vatican Bank had more than eleven thousand accounts, but only a thousand belonged to Catholic organizations and religious orders, and another five hundred to parishes worldwide. The rest belonged to individual prelates, Black Nobles and some of their wealthy friends, a few diplomats, and even possibly some foreign companies who did business with the church. Marcinkus was the problem, they told John Paul, not the solution. After spending ninety minutes reviewing the notes, the Pope informed Benelli that Marcinkus's position as the chief of the IOR was under review.

Later that day, which was packed with audiences by visiting dignitaries and church officials, the new Pope met with Leningrad's archbishop, Metropolitan Nikodim, the second-ranking prelate of the Russian Orthodox Church. At six feet and three hundred pounds, with an enormous long beard, Nikodim attracted attention, even inside the Vatican. Nikodim and John Paul met in the Pope's private study. The Pontiff later shared with his private secretaries what happened next. Nikodim sipped coffee from a cup the Pope had just poured. Then the bishop dropped his cup and saucer. He clenched at his throat as he gasped for air, and fell over backward, smashing a small table as he slammed into the floor.[45] Luciani called for help and dropped to his knees to administer the last rites. By the time Dr. Renato Buzzonetti, the deputy chief of the Vatican medical service, arrived a few minutes later, the forty-eight-year-old Nikodim was dead.[46]

No autopsy was performed. Given that Nikodim had suffered several previous heart attacks, few were surprised in a few days when a massive heart attack was listed as the official cause of death.[47] But even before that announcement, a conspiracy theory swept through the Vatican: a poisonous brew that had been intended for the new Pope had killed Nikodim.[48] Some Russian Orthodox prelates thought instead that Nikodim, a strong advocate of Christian unity, was the real target and the murderers were Catholic traditionalists who opposed the increased interfaith dialogue that Paul VI had begun. Some anticommunists thought it was the work of the KGB, a not subtle signal from Soviet Premier Leonid Brezhnev, who had resisted any effort to legalize the Catholic Church and had waged a relentless war of attrition against it.[49]

Nikodim's death, although personally unsettling for John Paul, did not distract him from focusing on the work at hand during his transition. He made solid progress that first month. And what stood out was how ordinary Catholics embraced him. After just a couple of weeks there was considerable talk about the large crowds and exuberance Luciani attracted. "St. Peter's Square was jammed to the brim for the noon blessing the past two Sundays, something that has occurred only very seldom previously," said eighty-five-year-old Carlo Confalonieri, the Dean of the College of Cardinals.

John Paul's natural warmth and willingness to talk to anyone in the Vatican, no matter how lowly their rank, was refreshing in an institution in which his predecessor's chronic illnesses and depression had added a grim mixture to his innate detachment. When John Paul left the Vatican on September 23 to say Mass at the nearby Lateran Basilica, mobs swarmed his entourage in a frenzy not seen since John XXIII was Pope twenty years earlier.[50] Four days later, fifteen thousand worshippers crammed into the Sala Nervi to hear his sermon.

Not all Curialists were as enthusiastic about the new Pope as the average Catholic. His common touch generated the same snide commentary that had greeted the likable John XXIII. Some sarcastically dubbed him *the smiling Pope* because of his seemingly perpetual grin. Others were dismissive of what they judged his "*Reader's Digest* mentality," a tendency to simplify complex issues.[51]

Luciani had no time for Curia gossip. He was instead immersed in learning as much as possible about several pressing matters that demanded his early attention. As part of that, he met with Marcinkus for an hour. It was awkward. They traded niceties and John Paul asked few pointed questions. Since the new Pope had not been a career Curialist, Marcinkus knew he had latitude to press some denials for which the Pontiff would have to take his word. And it was also common knowledge that John Paul did not like confrontations. Marcinkus felt it unlikely he would find a hostile reception.

Sindona was on everyone's mind because of his pending extradition. Marcinkus tried to distance himself from the Sicilian financier. He claimed to have met Sindona maybe a dozen times, once at a baptism, and another time for only a minute. What was most important, said Marcinkus, was that he did not do business with him. "The ones that had a dealing with him were APSA. They sold him the shares for Immobiliare. . . . I had nothing to do with it."[52]

John Paul did not have to work in the Curia to know that Paul VI's 1967 creation of APSA, the Administration of the Patrimony of the Holy See, was at Sindona's urging. Moreover, while APSA might have been the department responsible for divesting the church's interest in SGI Immobiliare and other companies, the Vatican Bank executed the decision.

Marcinkus tried deflecting John Paul away from Sindona by talking about how much money was available to the Pope from different Vatican foundations. But according to Marcinkus, John Paul "couldn't care less. He didn't want to know. And he talked about the Secretariat of State reports that they bring him, and what a burden it was."[53] Monsignor Magee, one of John Paul's trusted personal secretaries, thought the number and complexity of the IOR issues were too much to grasp for a Pontiff whose primary financial concern during his first month was whether he might lose his state pension since he was now head of a sovereign state (in fact, the pension ends for any Italian elected Pope).[54]

It was an unofficial custom that word about what transpired in a Pope's private meeting spread around the halls of the Vatican as soon as the door to the Papal study reopened. Sometimes a Pope instructed his aides to say something sub rosa to prepare the Curia for an upcoming decision. The person who had met with the Pontiff might leak his own version to try to get ahead of any pending Vatican action. And at other times, Curialists who had no idea of what had transpired spread rumors as if they had been present, all to further their own interests. The source for the persistent gossip that started after Marcinkus and John Paul's meeting ended is not known. But what is not in dispute is that a glum Marcinkus returned to the IOR offices and announced to no one in particular, "I won't be around much longer."[55] (Ten years later, Marcinkus denied saying he thought John Paul was about to let him go, claiming that instead back at the IOR he said only, "Gee, he [the Pope] looks tired." When he later heard that John Paul had intended to let him go, he said, "I said that's the funniest way to fire a guy. He couldn't have been nicer.")[56]

Marcinkus and the IOR were not the only problems the new Pope faced. Cardinal Baggio had presented him with the Cody file and the news the Chicago prelate had rebuffed his predecessor's effort to ease him out of office. A plan that Paul VI had long considered to internationalize the Curia was also waiting for a ruling.[57] Approving it would cause a minor revolt among the dominant Italians inside the church's bureaucracy. And there was the question of what to do about the prominent Swiss theologian, Hans Küng, whose teachings and writings served as the intellectual sustenance for a growing movement challenging many core church doctrines. Paul VI had dithered for years and had died without censuring Küng. John Paul would have to decide if Küng could carry on without incurring the wrath of the Vatican (on December 18, 1979, the church revoked Küng's *missio canonica*, his license to teach as a Catholic theologian).

John Paul had expected to be briefed about Cody, Küng, and the pending Curia reform. One matter, however, took him by surprise: the severity of a spat between the Jesuits and Paul VI. Jesuit theologians had ignored Paul's many requests to refrain from intense political activism. The sight of the black-uniformed prelates being dragged away by police at the front lines of massive protests over the war in Vietnam or efforts to ban the bomb were too frequent as far as the Vatican was concerned. Even worse was their enthusiastic dissemination of liberation theology, the combination of Catholicism and Marxism that fueled communist movements in El Salvador and Guatemala. The Jesuits' Superior General, Pedro Arrupe, was an avowed political leftist and had resisted all requests for moderation from Rome. If John Paul did not bring the Jesuits into line, Arrupe might well judge the new Pope as indecisive as his predecessor.[58]

It is little wonder that with so many critical matters pending, John Paul sometimes seemed frazzled. He joked with one of his aides, Monsignor Giuseppe Bosa, that he wished there was a machine that could help him do all the reading that piled up daily.[59] *"Une charge très lourde"*—it is a heavy burden—the Pope conceded to Cardinal Villot.[60] Marcinkus later recounted, "This poor man . . . comes out from Venice; it's a small, aging diocese, 90,000 people in the city, old priests. Then all of a sudden he's thrown into a place and he doesn't even know where the offices are. He doesn't know what the Secretary of State does. They called him the '*smiling* Pope.' But let me tell you something . . . that was a very nervous smile. So, he takes over. He sits down; the Secretary of State brings into him a pile of papers, says, 'Go through these!' He doesn't even know where to start."[61]

Much of the progress John Paul made during this tough transition was a result of his sixteen-hour workdays. The new Pope was a man with a reputation for little sleep. He was also someone who liked to adhere to a schedule.[62] Every morning, Sister Vincenza Taffarel, the head of his household who had been with him for twenty years, brought him coffee no later than 5:00.[63] In Venice, she brought it into his bedroom and put it on a side table. But in the Vatican, since many thought it improper for a nun to enter the Pope's bedroom unannounced, she had left a small tray in front of his bedroom door. John Paul put the tray back into the hallway when he was finished and Sister Vincenza retrieved it.[64] He was in the chapel by 6:00, where Monsignor Magee joined him for prayer. By 7:00, Monsignor Diego Lorenzi, his other private secretary, arrived and the three celebrated Mass, after which they had a light breakfast.[65]

On Thursday morning, September 28, Sister Vincenza left the tray a few minutes before 5:00.[66] It was untouched when she went to collect it thirty minutes later. She never knew the Pope to oversleep. She put her ear against the door but heard nothing. Vincenza knocked softly. Silence. She knocked louder. Still nothing.[67] She knelt and peered through the keyhole, but could not see him. If he was awake, why was he not answering? She decided to enter the room. John Paul was sitting upright in bed. An open file was clutched in his right hand and some papers were strewn across the bed and floor.* His reading glasses were resting on the tip of his nose and his eyes were open.[69]

"Santissimo Padre? Albino?"[70]

When he did not respond she ran out of the room to Magee's bedroom one floor above and roused him from a deep sleep. "Santissimo Padre. Something's happened!"[71]

Magee sprinted to John Paul's private chamber. He put his hand on the Pontiff's cheek. It was cold. Rigor mortis had begun to set in. Magee telephoned Villot, whose residence was two floors below. He worried about calling the seventy-two-year-old Secretary of State because he knew Villot had a heart condition. Nevertheless, he was blunt.[72]

"The Holy Father is dead."

"No, no, no, no . . . he couldn't be dead. I was with him last night!"

---

* Monsignor Lorenzi, who arrived after only a few minutes, recalled much later, "The sheets of paper were quite upright. They had not slipped out of his hands and fallen on the floor. I myself took the sheets out of his hand. I did!" Unknown to Lorenzi, Sister Vincenza had picked up the scattered papers and put them back in the folder before he had arrived.[68]

"Listen, he's stone-cold dead."[73]

The normally unflappable Villot sounded more agitated than the monsignor had ever heard him.[74] Magee then telephoned Dr. Renato Buzzonetti, who lived only minutes away.[75] Lorenzi, meanwhile, who was well acquainted with John Paul's longtime Venetian doctor, Giuseppe da Ros, called with the news. "He had seen the Pope the previous Sunday afternoon," Lorenzi later recalled, "and he found him in very good health."[76] (One of Dr. da Ros's few subsequent comments about that physical was that he had concluded John Paul was "very well.")[77]*

By the time Villot rushed into the room, Monsignor Lorenzi was leading a Rosary at the foot of the bed together with Sister Vincenza and several nuns.[79] When Dr. Buzzonetti arrived he inspected the body. He had never treated the Pope and knew nothing about his medical history: "The first time I saw him in a doctor-patient relationship, he was dead."[80] After a few minutes, Buzzonetti stepped away from the bed and announced that the Pontiff had died of an "acute myocardial infarction" (an arterial blockage that quickly causes the heart muscle to die).[81]† As for the time of death, he estimated it was between 10:30 and 11:00 the previous night. His conclusion was based on the Pope's just-from-the-crypt ashen complexion, a sign that the skin had been starved of blood, consistent with a myocardial infarction. He did not know that John

---

* The only flight to Rome from Venice that morning was completely booked, so da Ros jumped in his car for what turned out to be a nine-hour drive to Rome. The corpse was off limits by the time da Ros arrived. In an interview with an Associated Press reporter a few days later, da Ros admitted that when he examined his longtime patient the week before his death, "the stress of his new post was great. . . . He was not prepared, accustomed to that responsibility. I told him that he could not continue at that pace and he replied he could not do anything about it."[78]

† The question of whether John Paul had a heart condition was later hotly debated. Initial information from the Vatican was that he "was not known to have had any chronic heart trouble." Subsequent unconfirmed press reports were that Luciani had suffered four heart attacks, but there is no confirmation of that based on interviews with his family and information provided later by his doctors. Monsignor Petri Lina (Pia) Luciani, John Paul's physician niece, told the Associated Press in 1978 that he had no history of heart disease: "He is delicate, but, I advise you, he is not a traveling hospital." A decade later she said that her uncle had been hospitalized in 1975 for a thrombosis of the retinal artery at Rome's Gemelli Hospital. But that has never been confirmed. Also a decade after the Pope's death, Monsignor Lorenzi told an Italian reporter that he remembered that the evening before John Paul died, he had "a dreadful pain" in his chest, but he "absolutely forbade" Lorenzi from calling a doctor. "And I obeyed, because one should obey the Pope." Lorenzi never told anyone of his refreshed memory, he claimed, because "I didn't connect this [the heart pain] with a round-the-corner heart attack, because I'd never studied these things." Monsignor Magee a decade later told author John Cornwell that the Pope "was constantly talking of death." The night John Paul died Magee supposedly said to Sister Vincenza, "It would be terrible to lose a Pope now after losing Paul VI. How many days is it now? Thirty-three?"[82]

Paul suffered from chronic low blood pressure, making it less probable—but not impossible—that he was a victim of a massive coronary. Nor did he ever review any of the medications the Pope took or talk to Dr. da Ros, John Paul's personal physician.[83]

Villot's hands were trembling as he walked over to the body.[84] The French cardinal used the same silver mallet by which he confirmed the death of Paul VI a month earlier. After tapping John Paul's forehead three times, saying his name aloud, and getting no answer, he pronounced the 263rd Pope of the Roman church dead. Once again, Villot was the Camerlengo.[85]

Villot summoned Sister Vincenza and the other aides. After learning what had happened, he was immediately concerned about the public perception of an unaccompanied nun discovering the Pontiff's corpse. The mere fact that a woman had the authority to enter on her own volition the Pope's private bedroom might spark gossip, or as Villot dubbed it, "unfortunate misunderstandings."[86] So the Cardinal Secretary of State made a critical decision, one that would set the groundwork for conspiracy theories to flourish in the wake of the sixty-five-year-old John Paul's untimely death.

"I can't put that the sister found him dead," an exasperated Villot told Magee.[87] All of them were to keep what had really happened a secret. Villot ordered Sister Vincenza to move to a convent outside Vatican City as soon as it was feasible. She was to avoid any public comment for the rest of her service to the church.[88]

Magee would instead say that he had discovered the body upon entering the chamber to check on why the Pope was late for morning prayers. No mention would be made of any file of papers.[89] Instead, when Father Francesco Farusi, Vatican Radio's chief reporter, learned from a "Vatican source" that on the Pope's nightstand there was a copy of *De Imitatione Christi* (The Imitation of Christ), a fifteenth-century devotional handbook, he put out the story that the Pope had been reading that at the time of his death.[90] The tip was false. "[That book] was in the chapel, not by his bedside," Farusi later recounted. "I suppose it [the tip] was to avoid anyone saying he was reading a pornographic magazine . . . or, you never know what they'll say, a cowboy story." (Only four days later, Vatican Radio retracted that story as "inaccurate," but by then it had been repeated so many times that it was a widely accepted fact.)[91]

Sometime after 7 a.m., two glum-looking men, dressed in black raincoats,

23

New York's Cardinal Francis Spellman had been a friend of Pius XII since the 1920s, when the Pope was a Nuncio to Germany and Spellman was an ambitious monsignor. Spellman was a great asset as the Vatican's chief American fundraiser. He was also a vehement anticommunist who ensured that the church and the CIA worked together to elect a conservative government in Italy's first postwar election (1948). In October 1960, a month before they faced off in a presidential election, Spellman hosted Senator John Kennedy and Vice President Richard Nixon at New York's Alfred E. Smith memorial dinner.

24

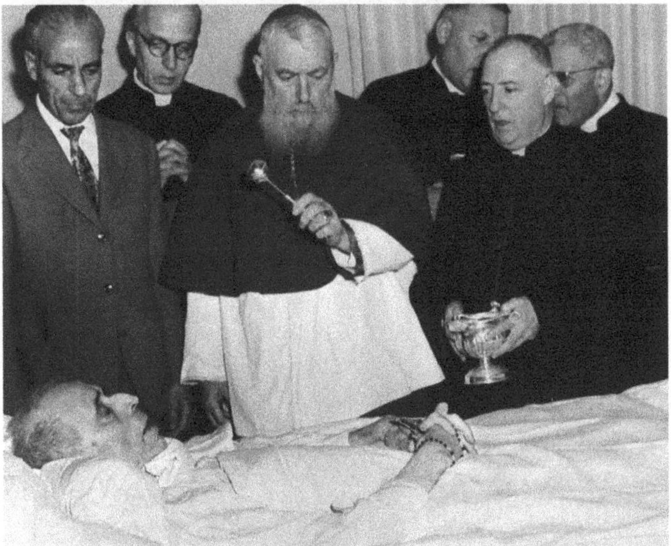

The death of Pius XII in 1958 was a watershed moment for the Vatican. French Cardinal Eugène Tisserant (*center*) is blessing the Pope's corpse. For more than nineteen years Pius had wielded the power of the Papacy as a divine monarch, a throwback to the boldest Popes from early centuries.

It took three days and eleven ballots in 1958 before the divided cardinals settled on a compromise, Venetian Patriarch Angelo Roncalli. One month shy of his seventy-seventh birthday, he was the first Pope over seventy in more than two hundred years. His choice of John as his Papal name was a surprise: no Pope had taken it for five hundred years because the last John was a divisive anti-Pope. Although some colleagues questioned his capability, he proved wildly popular with ordinary Catholics. During his five years as Pope, John XXIII stripped away much of the pomp his predecessors had carefully guarded. In 1958 he visited Rome's largest prison at Christmas.

25

26

Paul VI (1963–1978) oversaw a revolution in how the church managed its money and investments. He relied on so-called men of confidence, lay Catholic financiers who not only advised the Pontiff about how to invest the church's money, but also became partners with the Vatican on many speculative ventures. American Monsignor Paul Marcinkus (*left*) coordinated the logistics and security for the Pontiff's foreign trips, and served as translator for U.S. dignitaries. In this 1964 audience, the Pope met with civil rights leaders Dr. Martin Luther King Jr. and the Rev. Ralph Abernathy.

In the late 1950s, Michele Sindona (*left*), an aggressive tax attorney in Milan, started doing some legal work for the Vatican Bank. His influence grew exponentially but ended in 1974 with the then record $2 billion failure of his Franklin National Bank. For the next twelve years he battled criminal charges in Italy and the United States. In 1986, Sindona was convicted in the assassination of Giorgio Ambrosoli (*right*), the court-appointed liquidator of his banking empire. Two days later Sindona died in his high-security Italian jail cell after drinking cyanide-laced espresso. The coroner ruled it suicide.

29

Many people who met the six-foot-three Chicago-area native Paul Marcinkus thought he seemed more likely to be a football lineman than a Catholic priest. His rise in the church started in 1971, when Pope Paul VI promoted him to bishop and appointed him as the chief cleric at the Vatican Bank. Marcinkus had a healthy appetite for risk, one that eventually put the Vatican Bank at the center of half a dozen international criminal and government investigations.

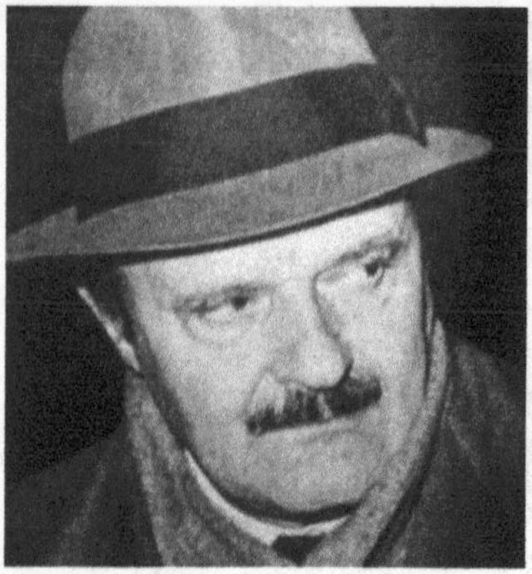

Roberto Calvi was an ambitious banker who replaced Sindona as the leading Italian financier working with the Vatican Bank. When his overextended empire collapsed, it almost took the Vatican Bank with it. In 1982, while on the run from Italian police, Calvi turned up dead, hanging from Blackfriars Bridge in London. Ruled at first a suicide, it took the Calvi family twenty-five years to convince authorities that he was murdered. In 2010, five men were tried and acquitted in Italy. Calvi's murder remains unsolved.

30

31

32

Luigi Mennini (*left*), the father of fourteen children, was a savvy private banker who started working in a Vatican financial department in 1930. Massimo Spada (*above, center left*) was a stockbroker who began working there in 1929. Over several decades they became the most powerful lay executives at the Vatican Bank and were key advisors to Marcinkus. Italian prosecutors unsuccessfully tried bringing both men to trial—with Marcinkus—for fraud.

Licio Gelli was a wealthy businessman with a reputation as a fixer. He also led a secret, underground Masonic lodge, Propagande Due (P2). By the time police disbanded it in 1981 over suspicions it was plotting a coup, its 953 members were such a stunning collection of "who's who" that Italian journalists dubbed P2 a "parallel state within a state." Sindona and Calvi were members, and Gelli did business with Marcinkus and the Vatican Bank.

33

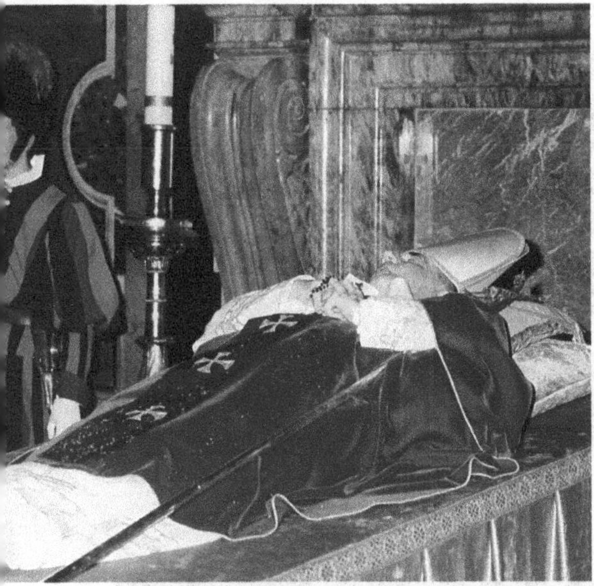

34

Albino Luciani, the Patriarch of Venice, was elected Pope in 1978. He took the Papal name John Paul I. Three days later a nun found the sixty-five-year-old John Paul dead in his bed. The cardinals voted not to conduct an autopsy (*at left, his body on display*). Unfounded but popular conspiracy theories that the Pope was murdered to prevent him from reforming the Vatican Bank have since flourished.

35

It took three days for the cardinals to select Kraków's Karol Jósef Wojtyla. At fifty-eight, he was the youngest Pope since 1846 and the first non-Italian selected in more than four centuries. He took the name John Paul II. His fierce anticommunism made him a natural ally of Ronald Reagan, shown here with Nancy Reagan meeting John Paul for the first time in 1982.

36

CIA director William Casey met with John Paul II frequently, and the Vatican and the United States shared intelligence about the Eastern Bloc. With the Pope's approval, millions of dollars of covert U.S. aid passed through the Vatican Bank to Solidarity, the Polish trade union at the heart of resistance to the Communist government. On May 13, 1981, at St. Peter's Square (*right*), a Turkish gunman shot and almost killed John Paul. To this day, many believe that the anticommunist Pope was the target of a plot hatched by Bulgarian intelligence.

37

In 1994, President Bill Clinton signed an executive order declassifying wartime files from eleven key government agencies, including the CIA, NSA, and State Department. One 1946 memo from a Treasury agent reported that about $225 million in stolen gold had ended up at the Vatican. Edgar Bronfman Sr., the influential head of the World Jewish Congress (*right*), spearheaded an international restitution effort that relied in part on lawsuits from survivors, as well as pressure from Western governments. Only the Vatican refused to open its files or make any contribution to a Holocaust compensation fund.

38

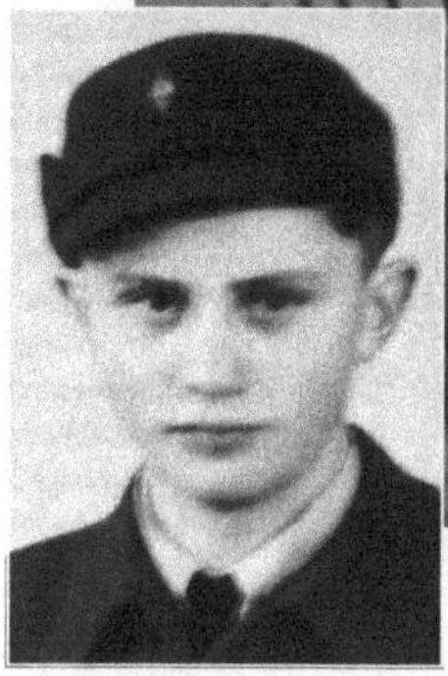

39

The last decade of John Paul's Papacy was defined in part by his personal battle with Parkinson's disease. Upon his 2005 death, many Vatican observers expected the cardinals to select a younger Pontiff. But their choice was seventy-eight-year-old Cardinal Joseph Aloisius Ratzinger. A hard-line conservative, Ratzinger was the first German elected Pope in a thousand years. His Papal name was Benedict XVI. His selection sparked controversy in part because he had served as a teen in the Hitler Youth (*left, at sixteen*, in 1943, drafted into a German antiaircraft unit). In 2006 (*right*) he visited the Nazi death camp Auschwitz.

40

41

Benedict selected Genoa's Cardinal Tarcisio Bertone (*center*) in June 2005 as his Secretary of State. Bertone stocked the Vatican's bureaucracy with loyalists and resisted financial reforms. Benedict's unprecedented resignation in 2013 stunned insiders and ordinary Catholics alike. On the far left is German Monsignor Georg Gänswein, Benedict's personal secretary. When Gänswein appeared on the cover of the Italian edition of *Vanity Fair* in 2013, it kicked off a firestorm of backbiting and jealousy about him inside the Vatican.

42

In 2009, Benedict appointed Ettore Gotti Tedeschi, a conservative economist and chief of Italian operations for Spain's Banco Santander, as the president of the Vatican Bank. The outspoken Gotti Tedeschi irritated many senior clerics. What little headway he made in reforming the Vatican Bank was stopped cold by a 2012 Italian criminal investigation into money laundering. Gotti Tedeschi was dismissed after a "no confidence" vote by the Vatican Bank's directors.

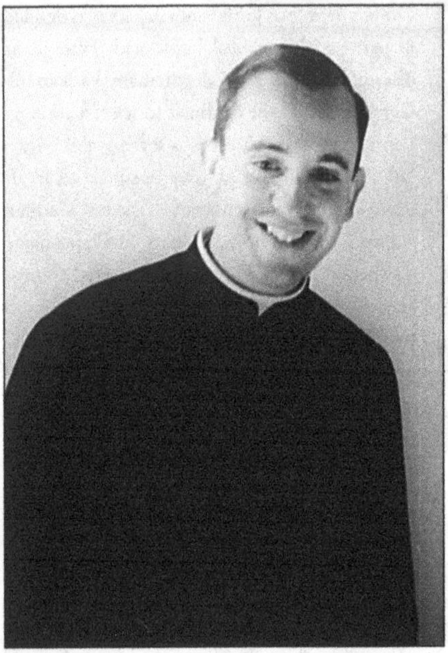

43

44

At the conclave of cardinals in March 2013 that selected Benedict's replacement, most church observers wrote off Buenos Aires' Cardinal Jorge Bergoglio (*left*, in 1966, as a seminarian). Although he had finished second in the 2005 vote, at seventy-six he was thought too old. But it took only five votes to put him over the top. Pope Francis emerged from the conclave as a likable and humble populist who was instantly popular with both Catholics and non-Catholics. Pope Francis (*right*) as "Man of the Year" for 2013 on the cover of *Time* magazine.

45

Pope Francis has backed the reformers when it comes to the finances of the Vatican. One of the key arrivals is René Brülhart. He is a forty-two-year-old Swiss anti-money-laundering expert who for eight years ran Liechtenstein's Financial Intelligence Unit. At the Vatican, he has earned the full support of Pope Francis. When Brülhart complained that five directors on his regulatory authority were slowing his progress, Francis fired them all in May 2014. Two months later the Pope hired a trio from Wall Street to fix the Vatican's wayward finances.

arrived. They were brothers, Arnaldo and Ernesto Signoracci, respected morticians from a family firm founded in 1870 ("We've fixed up three dead Popes," Arnaldo later told a journalist. "When they're dead, they're all the same to us.")[92]* Villot had telephoned Professor Cesare Gerin, a renowned University of Rome professor and director of Italy's Institute of Legal Medicine. Gerin in turn called the Signoraccis.[94] But Villot had not summoned them to remove the body. Instead, they took out a rope from a small canvas bag. They tied some around the corpse's ankles and knees. Then they straightened his legs and secured the rope to each end of the bed's frame. The Signoraccis looped it around John Paul's chest, and both pulled his arms and torso until the corpse was flat (a false rumor later made its way around the Vatican that the morticians had broken the Pope's back when straightening the body).[95] They closed his eyes and pulled the bedsheet just under his chin.[96]

The Signoraccis left for a Vatican guesthouse where they spent the next few days.[97] (When they returned a few hours later to get the body ready for public viewing, they began embalming the corpse. That meant opening the femoral arteries and injecting an anti-putrefaction liquid. Ernesto had trouble getting the injection in since there had been some clotting around the Pope's neck.)[98]

By 7:30 that morning, Villot had collected the Pope's personal papers and disposed of his prescription pills (it is not known if the Pontiff had filled any medications from the Vatican pharmacy during his month in office, since the pages that cover that time are missing from the dispensary's records).[99] Villot had also prepared the official press statement. Father Romeo Panciroli, the chief of the press office, began telephoning the major Italian and foreign wire services. The first wire story of the Associated Press carried the sanctioned version:

> Today Sept. 29 around 0530 the Rev. John Magee, the pope's private secretary, entered the bedroom of His Holiness John Paul I; since he

---

* An ANSA wire service story incorrectly reported that on the morning of the death an unidentified person had telephoned the Signoraccis at 5 a.m.—before the Pope's body was discovered—and dispatched a Vatican car to bring them to the Apostolic Palace. That was incorrect. Mario di Francesco, the journalist who wrote the story, got the wrong time from Renato Signoracci, yet another brother in the family business, but one who did not go to the Vatican. Conspiracy theorists nevertheless continue to cite this as proof of foul play in John Paul's death.[93]

> had failed to see him in the chapel as usual, he looked for him in the room and he found him dead in the bed with the light on as with a person who had been reading.
>
> The doctor, immediately summoned, ascertained his death, presumably occurred around 2300 hours yesterday Thursday because of sudden death from acute myocardial infarction. The venerated body will be placed on display around noon in a hall of the Apostolic Palace.[100]

The cover-up that Villot had engineered, mostly to hide the fact that a woman—albeit a nun—might be alone with the Pontiff in his bedroom in the early morning, was poorly thought out and certain to unravel. The Secretary of State, raised and steeped in the church's cult of secrecy, had made a bad situation far worse.[101] But it all came apart sooner than might have been expected. Shortly after the official statement was released, an unidentified insider with knowledge of what happened got in touch with Civiltà Cristiana (Christian Civilization), a bellicose right-wing Catholic group that boasted some fifty thousand members in dozens of countries. At the start of the conclave that elected John Paul a month earlier, Civiltà Cristiana had plastered Rome with brightly colored posters sarcastically insisting: "Elect a Catholic Pope." Now, when the group's Secretary General, Franco Antico, answered the telephone at its Rome headquarters, the anonymous person on the other end told a remarkable story that exposed the Vatican's version as a lie.

Antico, no stranger to the press, was on the phone by 8 a.m. with ANSA, Italy's wire service. Villot and John Paul's aides were lying, Antico claimed. He demanded an autopsy for the just deceased Pope. ANSA sent Antico's demand worldwide.[102] When reporters clamored for a comment from Panciroli, he checked with Villot. The Secretary of State ordered him to issue a "no further comment." Meanwhile, by mid-morning, Antico had gotten more information from his source. He now told reporters they should interview Sister Vincenza and Monsignor Magee. When Villot heard that, he compounded his run of bad decisions by ordering Magee and Lorenzi to promptly leave for a private seminary outside Rome. Villot told them he would call when it was safe to return.[103] (Sister Vincenza had already been driven away a couple of hours earlier.)

Monsignor Magee moved into the Maria Bambina Institute adjacent to St.

Peter's Square, but he was increasingly distraught and wanted "to stay with my sister Kathleen, who lives outside Liverpool."[104] Villot's office was slow to help him, so Magee went to Marcinkus. The IOR chief got him airline tickets in twenty minutes, and ordered a car and driver to take him to the airport. Two days after John Paul's death, while reporters were still badgering the Vatican switchboard asking for Magee, the monsignor was a thousand miles away in England.[105]

But Antico's source knew not just many details about how the dead Pontiff was discovered, but he also had the scoop on Villot's cover-up. Antico next told reporters they should ask where Vincenza and Magee had moved. On Villot's orders, Panciroli told reporters that Sister Vincenza was "inaccessible" and Monsignor Magee had "left the country."[106]

The problem was made worse because the journalists covering the Vatican had little faith in the accuracy of anything Father Panciroli told them. Since assuming control of the press office a couple of years earlier, his dismissive ways and frequent misstatements and obfuscations had earned him the nickname "Padre Non Mi Risulta" (Father I Don't Have Anything on That).[107]

Villot called an emergency meeting for the following morning of all cardinals in Rome. By that time, Villot had cleared the nineteen rooms of the Papal residence of all of John Paul's goods, and the Pontiff's apartment was sealed pending the conclave.

At 11 a.m. on Saturday, the thirty-four cardinals who had already arrived in Rome gathered in the enormous, gilded Sala Bologna, built in 1575 as a Papal dining room befitting a grand Pope-Monarch. None of them, other than Villot, knew the real story. Most speculated that Antico and Civiltà Cristiana were being duped by someone who wanted to plant a fake story to tarnish the church. A few, including Vienna's Franz König, thought the false reports were part of a Soviet disinformation plot.[108]

Villot first addressed the burial date. The cardinals agreed on a funeral in five days, on the Feast of Italy's patron saint, Francis. Then Cardinal Confalonieri brought up all the sinister whispers about John Paul's death. Although he understood it violated church protocol, Confalonieri suggested an autopsy might best settle all suspicions. Some cardinals gasped.[109] Cardinal König said he thought at the very least all the cardinals should be in Rome before voting to break such long-standing precedent. Moreover, König suggested that the autopsy would be difficult to keep secret. Conducting a historic postmortem exam, he averred, might further fuel the gossip that something untoward ended John Paul's life.

The problem with waiting until all the cardinals had arrived was that some from distant countries would likely not be in Rome until after the funeral. An autopsy would have to be done before that. Cardinal Felici suggested that a Rome pathologist and two doctors examine the Pope's body. Within forty-eight hours they would report back on whether or not they recommended an autopsy. That compromise was approved by a 29–5 vote.[110]

Two days later, Monday, October 2, eighty-five cardinals gathered in the Sala Bologna. The public clamor about John Paul's death had picked up momentum. German, British, and Spanish papers suggested the cardinals should order an autopsy since the Vatican constitution did not explicitly forbid it.[111] Respected Catholic writer Carlo Bo wrote a front-page editorial for *Corriere della Sera,* arguing that given the church's long history of murders and intrigue surrounding medieval popes, they could best eliminate any doubts about this death by embracing modern science.[112]

By the time of their new gathering, the cardinals knew that Villot and Buzzonetti had directed the Signoracci brothers to embalm the deceased Pope. "The reason they embalmed him on the first evening was because of Paul VI," Monsignor Lorenzi later recalled, "who had begun to swell up and smell unpleasantly."[113] "It's a problem because they go on view for four days, the heat and all that" admitted Ernesto Signoracci, one of the morticians who prepped the body.[114]

Despite having been there early on the morning the body was discovered, the Signoraccis knew the corpse was unattended for at least several hours after the death. It might deteriorate faster than they hoped. A contemporaneous Associated Press report about the first day the body was on public display noted: "The pope's face looked gray and waxen, and the basilica was shut down periodically Monday so morticians could retouch it."[115]

The cardinals were not familiar with the science of postmortems. They did not pay attention to the recommendation of some forensic pathologists that they preserve samples of John Paul's blood and tissue before the embalming so it might be possible to test in the future for foreign substances, poisons, or drugs. They did not know that the chemicals used by the morticians reacted with bodily fluids, making it difficult if not impossible to spot poisons since they would be masked or washed out during the embalming.*

While the mainstream press urged an autopsy, Franco Antico and his Civiltà Cristiana gained an ally inside the church. Blas Piñar, president of a prominent Spanish lay organization, Fuerza Nueva (New Force), noted the Pope's death had "raised so much suspicion." Piñar cited a speech Paul VI gave before his death in which he cryptically said, "From some fissure the smoke of Satan has entered the temple of God." Piñar insisted, "An autopsy must be carried out."[117]

At their Monday meeting, Villot presented the recommendations and findings of the three doctors who had examined the body at the cardinals' request. Two concluded the cause of death was a massive heart attack. They based their conclusion on their interviews with the Vatican's deputy chief of medicine, Dr. Buzzonetti, and on a summary that Villot had ordered created about John Paul's health history. As far as they were concerned, no autopsy was necessary. The pathologist disagreed. While he also thought a heart attack the most likely cause of death, he could not be certain without an autopsy.[118]

When Villot asked if there was any objection to accepting the majority medical opinion, most cardinals turned to Felici, who a couple of days earlier was the chief proponent of an autopsy. Felici scowled, his arms folded in front of him. But he did not say a word (later, he claimed he felt it was useless to protest since two of the doctors had decided no).[119]

Villot called for a vote. The cardinals agreed by unanimous acclamation that no autopsy should be conducted. The consensus was that the rumors and gossip about the sudden death would blow over with the election of a new Pope in just twelve days. The cardinals were otherwise preoccupied with their unprecedented second conclave in just six weeks.[120] †

---

* Italian law barred embalming within the first twenty-four hours of death. The Signoraccis were not concerned about violating Italian law. "We did the same with Pope John," Ernesto later told author John Cornwell. "We began the same day that he died. There's no problem, because the Vatican is a foreign country. . . . They're not bound by the Italian magistrates . . . especially with sudden-death."[116]

† In 1984, the rumors of foul play in the death of John Paul I were at the center of a salacious nonfiction book, *In God's Name,* by British author David Yallop. He mixed suspicions about Marcinkus and Cody into a convoluted murder plot masterminded by none other than Sindona, Calvi, Cardinal Villot, and P2's Gelli. John Paul was most likely poisoned, contended Yallop, by an overdose of digitalis, a heart medication. Villot's cover-up after the Pope's death, combined with the failure to do an autopsy—actions that Father Andrew Greeley called "just plain stupid"—was grist for Yallop. *In God's Name* was

Villot lit a cigarette first thing in the morning. And it was the last thing he did before turning in for the night. He smoked three packs a day. But during this time of great stress he was up to four. The Italian press had questioned whether all the cardinals who were papabile should be required to undergo a full physical before the first ballot. Not only was it ludicrous, thought Villot, but the church was already straining under the weight of costly back-to-back conclaves. Sending all 111 cardinals for expedited comprehensive exams was an expense he had no intention of incurring.[122] In any case, there was no time. The cardinals had a tight schedule for burying the Pope and starting the conclave. It all had to be accomplished in half the leisurely pace Villot had set after the death of Paul VI.

The press began its guessing game of who would be the next Pontiff. Father Andrew Greeley got wide coverage when he announced that a previously unknown Chicago group called the National Opinion Research Center used a "complex decision-making model" to pick the likely winner: Corrado Ursi, the moderate seventy-year-old cardinal of Naples. Church insiders were as dismissive of Greeley's model as they were of Ladbrokes bookmaking odds.

This time the politicking for the Papacy seemed more brazen, even among the most reserved cardinals. There was a widespread sentiment that the modern church was at a crucial juncture. The death of Paul VI, followed by the sudden start-stop nature of John Paul's brief Papacy, only added impetus to the sense that the next selection was important.

Conservatives, as they had just a month earlier, rallied behind Genoa's Siri. It was the fourth conclave at which the seventy-two-year-old cardinal was embraced by the Curia's traditional wing as the rightful heir to Pius XII. Some of

---

criticized by many, who deemed it a speculative theory unsupported by credible evidence. The Vatican, which normally ignored such books, issued multiple condemnations, calling it "infamous rubbish," "absurd fantasies," and "shocking and deplorable." The more the Vatican damned it, the more the book sold, an estimated six million copies. Elton John and his partner David Furnish added ultimately to the church's angst by buying its film rights.

In 1989, author John Cornwell published *A Thief in the Night*, in which he demolished Yallop's assumptions. Cornwell offered his own tantalizing theory that rested instead on negligence. In his account, one of John Paul's secretaries, Monsignor Magee, discovered the Pope was dead at 11 p.m. the previous night. Magee convinced Monsignor Lorenzi to help him put the Pope into his bed and fix him so Sister Vincenza would discover him the next morning.

By 1988, a decade after the Pope's death, a new theory had gained momentum: the CIA had murdered John Paul because he was about to reveal the identity of the American-backed assassins of Aldo Moro. In this plot, Marcinkus worked for the CIA.[121]

them interpreted John Paul's untimely death as a providential sign to redouble their efforts for the autocratic Siri.

But Siri had plenty of competition. Many thought that if John Paul were alive, he might well select someone who reflected his pastoral emphasis and charismatic temperament, possibly Pericle Felici. What better way to honor the late Pontiff's memory than by putting into the Papacy the man considered his closest copy? Of course, John Paul had relied on the advice of Florence's Benelli. Although Benelli's curt ways irritated many in the Curia, even his detractors admitted that he managed to get work done in an institution where delay and equivocation seemed unyielding. When Benelli arrived at the conclave carrying a portable typewriter, some colleagues joked that he was preparing to type a long acceptance speech.[123]

There was also talk about whether—after 455 years—it was time for a non-Italian Pope. That was unlikely. Although some foreign cardinals had substantial prestige inside the church, and ran populous foreign dioceses that had more Catholics than any Italian city, they carried no weight inside the Curia. If anything, their outsider status meant that most church officials considered them powers to be appeased from a distance, but never to be embraced to sit on the throne of St. Peter.

In the last conclave, the Italians had cut enough deals to keep the support of the chief foreign cardinals. There were only a handful strong enough to persuade others to follow their endorsement. A diverse group, they were from England, Brazil, Spain, Argentina, Samoa, and Austria.[124] The problem for Siri and the traditionalists was that Pope Paul VI had appointed almost all of them as cardinals, and he had picked them because they were among the most progressive bishops in their countries. Some press reports even touted Cardinal Bernardin Gantin as a long shot. The Benin native had worked in the Curia since Paul VI put him there after the Second Vatican Council. His reputation as a moderate pragmatist did not upset the traditionalists, but few seemed ready to make history by electing the first black Pope.

The non-Italians had a different view of the church than those who worked inside the closeted Curia. Kinshasa's cardinal, Joseph Malula, told Gantin, "All that imperial paraphernalia, all that isolation of the Pope, all that medieval remoteness and inheritance that makes Europeans think that the church is only Western—all that tightness makes them fail to understand that young countries like mine want something different."[125]

The unquestioned dean of the non-Italian cardinals was Vienna's seventy-three-year-old Franz König. He feared nothing more than heading into the eighty-third conclave with the possibility that Siri, whom he considered an unyielding reactionary, might at long last become Pope and reverse two decades of reforms. Siri tried repositioning himself as a centrist but few electors believed he had moderated his hard-line positions.

Some press reports and Vaticanologists speculated before the conclave about whether even König could become Pope. But he confided in a few of his closest colleagues that he had no interest in the Papacy. However, König allowed the speculation to build in the hope that it might give him more influence at the conclave.

The first ballot on October 14 put Siri at the top with twenty-three votes, an unprecedented fourth time in twenty years he had gathered the largest bloc of support at the conclave's outset. But it was a poor showing for a man whose pre-conclave expectations were at least fifty first-ballot votes.[126] Only one vote behind was Florence's Benelli. Three other Italian cardinals were next, Felici, Ursi of Naples, and Palermo's Salvatore Pappalardo (famous for being the first Sicilian cardinal ever to condemn the Mafia). Those five Italians had pulled ninety-five votes, twenty more than required to be elected Pontiff. König worried that the conclave might have already turned into an Italian-only fight. If the Italians struck a deal and consolidated their support behind one candidate, the conclave would be over. The Viennese cardinal thought however that it was just as likely the intense dislike each had for one another might make it difficult for them to reach a consensus.

Kraków's Karol Józef Wojtyla had gotten the votes of five cardinals. Besides being a pastor of one of Poland's biggest cities, Wojtyla was a prolific theological author. König liked him and reflected the view of many others that Wojtyla's humility and low-key approach was a welcome respite from the frenetic narcissism of some of the more flamboyant Italians. American cardinals Cody and Cooke also liked Wojtyla. Both the Americans oversaw large Polish American congregations. (Cody had sent more than a million dollars to Wojtyla to support the Polish church.) But Poland's senior cardinal, Warsaw's Stefan Wyszyński, told König before the voting that he thought his fellow Pole was "too young [58], he's unknown, he could never be Pope."[127]

Nevertheless, König and the Americans started lobbying for Wojtyla, suggesting to some colleagues that at the very least they should vote for him to slow the Italians. "They were planning a palace coup, but no one believed they could pull it off," according to Father Andrew Greeley.[128]

Siri faded by the second ballot. His supporters had moved to Benelli, who now had forty votes, and Felici followed with thirty.[129] The top five were the same Italian cardinals, but this time they had 107 votes. König's and Cody's efforts on behalf of Wojtyla had almost doubled his support to nine. To the Italian frontrunners, he was too far behind to matter.

After that second ballot, König brought in a major ally for Wojtyla: Madrid's Vicente Enrique y Tarancón threw his support to the quiet Polish prelate. That opened the door to the Latin and South American cardinals, who had so far shown little desire to look beyond Italy.

The third ballot narrowed the field. Benelli pulled away from the other Italians, now corraling forty-five votes. Wojtyla was still stuck at nine. During a break between votes, Benelli met with some of the other first-ballot contenders. On the fourth ballot, he surged to sixty-five votes, only ten short of victory. Benelli had momentum. One more ballot might put him over the top.[130] Many of the cardinals were tired, having made the trek to Rome for their second pressure-filled conclave in less than two months. A quick resolution would demonstrate to the faithful that they were in sync about the future of the church. But on the fourth ballot Wojtyla had jumped from nine votes to twenty-four. That indicated Benelli's supporters might not be firm. If that was the case, König intended to politick during the next break to build support for the cardinal from Kraków.[131]

On the third day, Monday, October 16, the Benelli camp seemed confident during breakfast. They boisterously dominated the center dining table. Some Italians had decided that as much as they disliked Benelli, he was preferable to a non-Italian.

In the next vote, Benelli scored seventy votes, just five short of becoming Pope. Villot ordered an hour between ballots. Can you live with Benelli and his imperious ways, König asked his colleagues? The next ballot changed the race. Benelli lost eleven cardinals. Wojtyla was now at fifty-two. Although Benelli's table was downhearted, Wojtyla also seemed glum, simply staring at his food. More than once he had told his Polish colleague Wyszyński, as well as König, that he did not want to be Pope.

"You simply must face the truth," König told him. "This is what the Holy Spirit wishes."

"It's a mistake," Wojtyla whispered.[132]

The first ballot of the afternoon confirmed that the momentum belonged to Wojtyla. He pulled seventy-three votes, just two short of winning. Benelli had dropped almost in half to thirty-eight. The eighth ballot, taken at 5 p.m., put Wojtyla over the top with ninety-seven votes.[133] Wojtyla looked so grim that Cardinal Hume felt "desperately sad for the man."[134]

With his white hair and weathered face he seemed the contemporary of Benelli and Felici, men a decade older. At fifty-eight he was the youngest Pope since the fifty-four-year-old Pius IX in 1846. He was the first non-Italian since the Dutch Adrian VI in 1522. And Wojtyla also had the fewest connections to the Curia of any Pope in centuries.

When it came to doctrines of faith, Wojtyla had a reputation as a moderate with an open mind. He had been a firm and popular leader of Kraków's two million Catholics.[135] And although he had distinguished himself for developing a productive church-communist dialogue in Poland, he also maintained a hard line when it came to the godless political philosophy that ruled his homeland. In his writings, he condemned persecution against Catholics by those who see it as "the opiate of the people," a reference to the slogan made popular by Karl Marx.[136]

Standing in front of the cardinals who had just elected him, Wojtyla suddenly seemed energized. Because of his respect for his two predecessors, he had settled on the Papal name John Paul II.[137]

As word spread into the packed crowd at St. Peter's, there were cries of "E il Polcacco" (It's the Pole). That the College of Cardinals had done the truly unexpected was settling in fast.

21

The Backdoor Deal

The cardinal they picked, Karol Józef Wojtyla, was the youngest of three children born into a devoutly Catholic household in Wadowice, a small town thirty miles outside Kraków. His father was a noncommissioned army soldier, and his mother, a schoolteacher, died during childbirth when he was eight.[1] In 1938, a year before the start of World War II, Wojtyla enrolled in Kraków's Jagiellonian University where he studied Polish literature, was an avid member of the drama club, and played as goalkeeper on the soccer team.[2] When the Nazis and Soviets divided Poland, he avoided deportation to Germany by working at menial jobs the Germans assigned him, including at a limestone quarry, then a chemical plant, and even as a messenger for a restaurant.[3] After his father died in 1941, the twenty-one-year-old entered an underground theological seminary and spent the last year of the war studying for the priesthood.[4] On August 6, 1944, the so-called Black Sunday on which the Nazis rounded up more than eight thousand young men, he escaped to safety in the palace of Kraków's cardinal.[5]*

After the war, Wojtyla studied for a doctorate at Rome's Pontifical Athenaeum Angelicum, and he returned to Poland in 1948 as a parish priest in a small town just outside Kraków. He remained in Poland when the country became a full-fledged Soviet satellite in 1952. Wojtyla was a prodigious writer

---

* Just after the war, the twenty-six-year-old priest faced an unusual situation. A Catholic family had hidden a Jewish boy from the Nazis, and had learned that the Germans had murdered the child's parents. They brought the youngster to Wojtyla and asked him to baptize the child. In contrast to Pope Pius IX and his abductions and forced baptisms of two Jewish boys, Wojtyla refused. The boy should be raised Jewish in the tradition of his parents, Wojtyla told the parents.[6]

about church history and canon law. As a popular teacher of moral philosophy at Lublin's Catholic University and at the Kraków seminary, he had a reputation far beyond Poland.[7] At thirty-eight, he became the second youngest bishop in the world, and five years later Pope Paul VI elevated him to an archbishop.[8] Most parishioners in Kraków thought he was smart and likable.[9] And although he was undoubtedly spiritual and a serious scholar, his strong character was forged by his experience as a Polish prelate living under a communist government. To do something in his own diocese, he had to apply for permission to a special government ministry that oversaw all church matters. The freedom of religion taken for granted in America and many Western European countries was still a distant dream for him.

By selecting a cleric from Soviet-dominated Eastern Europe, the cardinals had selected the most fervently anticommunist Pope since Pius XII. Just three days after Wojtyla's election, the CIA's National Foreign Assessment Center circulated a four-page confidential memo that concluded that the election of a Polish Pontiff would complicate matters for the Soviet Union and would "undoubtedly prove extremely worrisome to Moscow."[10] And just as Pius XII's zeal about fighting communism was shared by contemporaneous, secular Western leaders like Harry Truman and Winston Churchill, similarly like-minded heads of state would soon join Wojtyla. Margaret Thatcher began her eleven-year tenure as Britain's Prime Minister just five months after he became Pope.[11] And Ronald Reagan came into office two years later. Reagan and Thatcher would lead the fight to break the Soviet empire. They had Wojtyla's full support.

As he settled into the Papacy, John Paul II met with CIA analysts, who briefed him on American efforts to destabilize communist governments behind the Iron Curtain. Egyptian intelligence agents gave him a better understanding of events in the Middle East. Italy sent security service officers to update him on the fight against the Red Brigades.[12] The message from the new Pope was clear: he was not going to rely only on the traditional channels of information filtered first by the Curia.

Inevitably, John Paul II would revive Pius XII's policy that the church had a duty to be involved in secular politics when it came to standing against communism. Covert money would be needed for anticommunist cells in Eastern Europe. The Vatican Bank was proven to be as instrumental in this new phase as it was in safeguarding the church's fortune during World War II.

On December 1, 1978, less than two months after assuming the Papacy,

John Paul summoned Marcinkus for a meeting at the Apostolic Palace. It was the first time since his election that the two met alone. Six weeks earlier, Cardinals Benelli and Felici had given his predecessor a damning file about the IOR chief and the unchecked manner in which he ran the Vatican Bank. They worried that John Paul might not give it the attention it deserved. Although Kraków was a large, cash-poor diocese that he managed well, he was known not to like money matters. He did not even have his own bank account.[13] Before the Pope met with Marcinkus that day, Felici checked to make sure the Pope had read the file. He had.[14]

When Marcinkus arrived, he sat on the far side of a large desk, across from the Pontiff. Marcinkus remembered enough of his parents' Lithuanian dialect that they made some small talk in Polish.[15] It was a good start. The duo had in common their outsider status, and the Pope knew that Cody and Marcinkus had facilitated contributions from American Poles in Chicago that had helped support his Kraków diocese.

Instead of talking about finances, John Paul surprised Marcinkus by discussing his plans for a foreign trip. Mexico would be his first stop, John Paul told him, since the church was challenged on many fronts there, from ingrained poverty, corruption, a power surge by leftists, and even the growth of rival Pentecostals. Would Marcinkus organize the trip and accompany him? The fifty-six-year-old IOR chief must have felt great relief. He had gone from almost certain banishment a couple of months earlier under Luciani to being offered a chance by the new Pope to reprise his insider's role on foreign trips.

And there was something else addressed—revealed here for the first time. For several years there had been a simmering financial scandal about a group of Pauline monks that ran a Philadelphia-area shrine to Our Lady of Czestochowa, the "Black Madonna" revered by Polish Catholics for having spared a holy monastery from a seventeenth-century Swedish siege.[16] A month before John Paul became Pope, the scandal about the Polish monastic order went public in the United States when Gannett News Service published an investigative series.[17] The Vatican, with assistance from U.S. cardinals, had appointed in 1975 two hard-nosed prelates—Camden, New Jersey's, Bishop George Guilfoyle and the Reverend Paul Boyle, the provincial chief of Chicago's Passionist Fathers—to look into possible financial mismanagement at the shrine and monastery.[18]

What they discovered shocked church officials. The Pauline Fathers had not only squandered nearly $20 million in charitable contributions, but there was evidence of "mismanagement, dubious business practices and what Vatican investigators described as 'chaotic' and 'immoral' life styles."[19] Guilfoyle and Boyle compiled a long list of problems. The Paulines had raised $400,000 for bronze plaques for the shrine but never made a single one. Donors gave $250,000 for Masses that the priests never celebrated. Sixty-four thousand dollars went to cemetery upkeep that was never performed. Making matters worse, the monks had violated their poverty vows. Although the order had defaulted on $4.3 million in church bonds bought mostly by Polish American Catholics, Guilfoyle and Boyle concluded the Paulines ran their 130-acre hill-top monastery "more like a resort hotel than a monastic institution." A majority of the thirty monks had their own cars, paid for by contributions from the faithful, and all had credit cards that were charged against donations.[20]

The wayward Paulines had retained the services of a disbarred attorney—who had served jail time for federal tax evasion—as their chief financial advisor. The Vatican auditors also uncovered a trail of secret investments in private companies in five states, all designed as "tax-avoidance schemes."[21]

Guilfoyle and Boyle found the monks' accounting so convoluted that they retained Peat, Marwick & Mitchell to make sense of it. Typical of what they discovered was the monks' purchase of the local Westminster Cemetery at a "grossly inflated price" from the order's attorney.[22] In less than a year, the monks had emptied the cemetery's legally mandated $500,000 perpetual care fund, improperly withdrawn $120,000 of its operating revenue, pledged its ninety-seven acres to borrow another $660,000, and even padded its payroll with friends.[23] To the anger of local parishioners, the Paulines took another $100,000 to allow Sun Oil to build a gas station at the cemetery's entrance, although it meant relocating many existing graves.[24] The monks had appointed two friends of their disbarred advisor at $1,000 a week each to manage the graveyard. When Guilfoyle and Boyle interviewed the managers, they claimed they were forced to kick back half their salaries to Father Michael Zembrzuski, the shrine's seventy-year-old vicar-general. Zembrzuski kept a mistress with church money (one of the managers later told reporters Zembrzuski avoided criminal charges only by threatening to go public with what he knew).[25]

When Guilfoyle and Boyle ordered the Paulines to turn in their televisions, high-end stereos, credit cards, and car keys, half the monks left the order.[26] The report that made its way to the Vatican was several hundred pages and crammed with supporting details.* The unwavering recommendation from Guilfoyle and Boyle—backed by Philadelphia's Cardinal John Krol—was that Zembrzuski tender his resignation and that the offending priests be "severely disciplined."[27]

Before any news broke, Zembrzuski had traveled to Poland to discuss with his close friends—the country's top prelate, Cardinal Stefan Wyszyński, and Kraków's cardinal, Karol Wojtyla—what he should do. Wyszyński oversaw the entire Pauline order. The meetings took place by coincidence just before John Paul I died. With his death, and the ensuing focus on the conclave, any action on the Pauline scandal was postponed.

Once Wojtyla became Pope, the Paulines appealed directly to him. Only seventeen days after assuming the Papacy, John Paul reversed the recommendations of the investigating committee. The following May he issued a Papal Decree ending all investigation into the Paulines and vacating the original findings.[28]

The problem facing John Paul was that most of the Polish American faithful who had loaned money to the monks had resisted efforts by the church to forgive the debt and write it off as a donation. Many were elderly parishioners. In some instances they had put their entire savings into the low-interest bonds issued by the Paulines. Since the bonds were unsecured, they were last on the list for repayment. Some devout Catholics were so furious with the loose operations by the monks that they consulted attorneys about suing. There was even talk of possible criminal charges, and the SEC was probing whether there was fraud in the sale of bonds to build a 1,700-seat cathedral that never got off the drawing board.[29]

Only one thing could put the mess to rest. Money. John Paul knew the American church had already spent considerably on cleaning up after the Paulines. Cardinal Krol of Philadelphia had used emergency diocese funds to pay off $722,000 in bank loans.[30] But individual bondholders clamored for another $4 million, far more than Krol could spare. So, John Paul raised the matter with Marcinkus at their December 1 meeting. The beleaguered IOR chief saw it as a chance to ingratiate himself further with the new Pontiff. Over the next several months, Marcinkus directed more than $5 million to

---

* The Vatican has never released the complete report, and this author's requests to review it went unanswered.

Cardinal Krol, all of which paid creditors—from additional banks to most of the faithful—as well as to reimburse the Philadelphia diocese for much of the money it had spent.[31]

The backdoor deal over the Paulines was the initial glue in the John Paul–Marcinkus friendship.[32] In the coming months, as they prepared for the Mexico trip, Marcinkus spent hours alone with John Paul. Marcinkus then had no idea of just how dramatic a turn his fortunes had taken. John Paul II saw in him a trustworthy ally capable of finding the money to bolster nascent pro-democracy movements. And he knew from Marcinkus's service to Pope Paul VI that the American prelate prided himself on loyalty and secrecy. His help in resolving the Pauline payments without garnering any additional publicity was a good sign, indicating how quietly he could operate. The new Pope knew he would need those traits as a buffer against the undercutting Italians that dominated the Curia.*

Three months after assuming the Papacy (January 1979), John Paul II flew to Mexico. Marcinkus handled all logistics and security. During that trip, Marcinkus told the new Pope who he believed had planted the rumors about foul play in the death of John Paul I: the KGB, to create mischief in the church.[34] For John Paul, a prelate who had fought for decades the communist efforts to destabilize the Polish church, it made sense. Had the KGB also fanned the rumors about the Vatican Bank and Sindona in order to hurt the church further? The two men had little doubt it was possible. John Paul assured Marcinkus that under no circumstances would he allow the KGB or any other disinformation effort to ruin the reputation of the IOR or Marcinkus.[35]

By the time they returned to Rome, Marcinkus was joking with the Pope, about how the Curia would soon punish him for not being servile enough.

---

* Wojtyla's election was as fortuitous for Cardinal Cody as it was for Marcinkus. After reading the Cody file, the new Pope decided not to do anything until he visited Chicago, a trip planned for October 1979. Ultimately, when John Paul got there, Cody presented him with a reputed $1 million gift and lobbied hard to defend himself. Although John Paul repeatedly told his aides he intended to move Cody out, he never did. Instead, a lay insider from the Chicago diocese got in touch with the U.S. Attorney the following year. The tales of financial impropriety were enough for a grand jury to be impaneled. And the *Chicago Sun-Times* soon assigned a team of investigative reporters to chase the many Cody rumors. In 1981, that resulted in one of the most carefully vetted investigations in the paper's 137-year history. It was a devastating tell-all that showed that Paul VI and John Paul II were wrong when they did not insist Cody step down.[33]

Marcinkus's long-entrenched enemies were disappointed at the obvious friendship. The bishop from Cicero had lived to serve another day.[36]

His foes did not know that in March, Marcinkus received an inquiry from the FBI about the possible criminal misuse of a Vatican Bank account. The author has discovered that the U.S. Deputy Presidential Envoy to the Holy See delivered a three-page telex to Marcinkus from Benjamin Civiletti, the Deputy Attorney General. It provided details about a Justice Department probe into whether "a United States corporation appears to have defrauded the United States Government and others, by concealing millions of dollars in the Institute of Religious Works."[37] According to Civiletti, a federal contractor, American Training Services, had gone bankrupt owing the government more than $1 million. That debt was settled for 10 cents on the dollar before the government learned "ATS concealed millions of dollars in foreign bank accounts" including that "$7.7 million is in two accounts in the Institute Per Le Opera di Religione." Those had been opened five years earlier by American officers of ATS or its subsidiaries.

Civiletti was straightforward: "There is evidence indicating that much of the money may originally have been obtained by fraud." Civiletti wanted Marcinkus to provide "any assistance you could render to temporarily immobilize these funds."

It would seem a simple matter. Bank officials routinely work with law enforcement to freeze funds while a criminal probe is under way. It was not clear why the two IOR accounts listed by Civiletti even existed at the Vatican. Neither had a cleric or religious order as an account signatory, and neither had as its stated purpose religious philanthropy or service.[38]

Marcinkus replied a month later about what he called "the deplorable situation created by American Training Services," but claimed he could not help since he had gone through all the relevant records and could not find any of the names or companies listed in Civiletti's letter. Marcinkus said with considerable understatement: "First of all, let me explain our organization to you. The Institute for Religious Works is not a bank in the ordinary sense of the word."[39] Marcinkus disingenuously said he was confident that such accounts did not exist at the IOR, since the $7 million of deposits pinpointed by the Justice Department were such "large sums . . . we would have been very much aware of any such operation. Ours is a modest organization and any operation involving large sums would not go unnoticed." That statement was contradicted by the tens of millions of dollars that had transferred back and forth with Sindona and Calvi. But Marcinkus said "to be on the safe side" he had checked to see if he could match the "sums of the size you mention coming from the U.S. in the period indicated in your letter." He found nothing. "I am at a loss to know how I can be of assistance to you on this matter."[40]

Blocked by Marcinkus from examining the records at the Vatican Bank, Civiletti had no choice but to accept the bishop's denial as the final word.[41] Justice Department officials complained privately about the IOR's failure to conduct a more thorough search for records and transactions. When word of their displeasure reached Marcinkus several weeks later, he sent off a missive to Civiletti in which he said he was "perplexed." But most of his two-page, typewritten letter was a rebuke—revealed here for the first time—of how the FBI handled sensitive information it gathered as part of the bureau's 1973 investigation into counterfeit bonds and securities that had climaxed when two federal prosecutors and an FBI agent visited Marcinkus at the Vatican.

"Now I come to the point," Marcinkus wrote before launching into his diatribe. He set the background with the origin of the "investigations concerning a gigantic fraud, which involved the sale of some $900,000,000 worth of stocks and bonds, made up of stolen and counterfeit denominations." The IOR got swept into it, he said, because of the stories told by some "confidence people."[42]

He emphasized that he had voluntarily met with the American investigators and answered their questions to the "best of my ability." The reason Marcinkus was so furious is that he had learned that in the German trial of one of the defendants, an FBI memo summarizing the agents' talk with Marcinkus had been submitted into evidence.

"Much to my surprise and stupefaction," he wrote, "the memorandum . . . was inaccurate in many respects, [and] it seemed to me to be even tendentious. I feel if good relations are going to exist, confidence must be respected and above all accuracy of statements must be maintained. I feel injured by this testimony and I wish to be assured that the F.B.I. will make amends."[43]

The Justice Department ignored Marcinkus's outburst. No one had any intention of apologizing to the IOR prelate. Those who ran the 1973 probe felt he was somehow involved, but they simply never found the evidence to charge him.[44]

22

"The Vatican Has Abandoned Me"

Marcinkus quickly solidified his position at the IOR with the new Pontiff. He not only fended off tales of scandal over the Sindona affair, but he managed John Paul—Pope only a month—when a new government probe put the Vatican Bank on the defensive. In November 1978, after seven months of examining Ambrosiano's records, Bank of Italy investigators finished a five-hundred-page report that raised troubling questions about Calvi and whether the Ambrosiano was capitalized properly.[1] After Sindona's collapse, the Bank of Italy was risk-averse. But the inspectors could not gather enough information to determine if their concerns were justified. Calvi's multiple layers of foreign shell companies did what he intended: prevented the authorities from figuring out who controlled which entities and where the money went.[2] The report—named after its chief inspector, Giulio Padalino—devoted twenty-five pages to questionable dealings between Ambrosiano and the Vatican Bank.[3] It chided Calvi for failing to disclose the details of his business with the Vatican.[4]

A few copies of the Padalino Report leaked to reporters.[5] Fortunately for the Vatican, it was written in the dense language of government bureaucrats and was hobbled by numerous caveats about missing evidence. The inspectors did not seem to understand fully the relationship among the Ambrosiano, Calvi, and his spider's web of offshore companies.[6] Its convoluted dissertations fell far short of a persuasive case.[7] Many reporters did not read much further than the obtuse summary.

Milan's criminal prosecutors, however, carefully read the Padalino Report. Although they recognized it asked far more questions than it answered, they also realized it made a strong circumstantial case that Calvi had profited by violating Italy's currency control laws. That December (1978), one of the office's most aggressive prosecuting magistrates, Emilio Alessandrini, opened a criminal probe into Calvi and the Ambrosiano. He enlisted the help of the Guardia di Finanza, an Italian law enforcement division that specialized in white-collar crimes.[8] The goal, Alessandrini instructed them, was to develop enough evidence to charge Calvi with manipulating the share prices of public companies and passing any profits through different countries to circumvent taxes and restrictions on the export of the lira.[9] Calvi was stunned to learn he was under criminal investigation when a few weeks later he flipped open a January 21, 1979, issue of *L'Espresso.* Prosecutors had leaked news of the probe instead of giving Calvi and his lawyers a heads-up.[10]

Eight days after *L'Espresso*'s scoop, five masked men walked up to an orange Renault stopped at a traffic light in the center of Milan. The prosecuting magistrate, Alessandrini, was inside. As part of his daily routine, he had dropped off his son at a school a few blocks away just minutes earlier. The masked men dragged him from his car, forced him onto his knees, and executed him in front of horrified witnesses. They escaped in a small car, throwing smoke bombs as they sped away.[11]

Calvi was not the only major investigation on which Alessandrini had been working. He also was responsible for building a case against a suspect in the assassination of former Prime Minister Aldo Moro. Alessandrini's gunmen later turned out to be from Prima Linea (Front Line), an even more violent offshoot of the Red Brigades. But in the weeks before that became clear, there was speculation the murder was tied to Calvi.[12]

The government's Christian Democratic coalition, headed by Prime Minister Giulio Andreotti, had been criticized for having failed to stop domestic terrorism. Now, it collapsed two days after the assassination. It was the fortieth government in thirty-four years.[13] Luca Mucci, an earnest white-collar crime specialist, took over the Calvi probe. He lacked Alessandrini's ability to cut through the judicial bureaucracy. It would take six months before the Guardia di Finanza returned his calls. And even then it was to inform Mucci they could find no evidence of criminal wrongdoing. No one then knew that Raffaele Giudice, the Guardia di Finanza's chief, was a P2 member whom Gelli had lobbied on Calvi's behalf.[14] Uncertain about what to do next, Mucci reached out to the Ufficio Italiano dei Cambi, the Italian government department responsible for enforcing currency laws.[15]

None of this gave Calvi any pause in his frenetic deal making. Despite the questions raised by the Padalino Report, Calvi persuaded four prominent Catholic businessmen—all with close Vatican ties—to serve on the board of La Centrale, his Italian holding company. And to a few colleagues he seemed more distracted by events affecting his empire in Latin America than he was about the Bank of Italy report. The civil war in Nicaragua had taken a turn against strongman Anastasio Somoza's government forces. The Marxist Sandinista National Liberation Front was on the verge of capturing the capital. Calvi worked to move the core of his Latin American operations from Managua to Lima.[16] He renamed his new venture Banco Ambrosiano Andino and promised in the Italian press that the new firm would become partners with leading South American banks in offering financial services throughout the Southern Hemisphere.[17] In fact, the Ambrosiano owned Banco Andino. When South American banks did buy small stakes in the new company, Calvi supplied the funds for those investments.[18] Calvi transferred to Andino more than $100 million in back-to-back loans that the Vatican Bank had made with United Trading and Cisalpine.[19] The following year, emboldened by the lax banking regulations prevalent throughout Latin America, Calvi launched Banco Ambrosiano de America del Sud, headquartered in Buenos Aires.[20]

While Marcinkus did not know all the details of Calvi's South American deals, he thought the expansion was a good idea. Sindona later told reporters: "I had told Calvi to tell Marcinkus that if they [the IOR] can help, it is in their own interest. South America is Catholic. They don't want to lose this big a part of their account."[21]

Even in Italy, where one might have expected that the Padalino Report was a flashing yellow light, Calvi was as aggressive as ever with the Ambrosiano. Some of his decisions were terrible, as when he approved a large loan to a P2 colleague, Mario Genghini, whose business empire was in serious trouble. The Ambrosiano lost more that $42 million when Genghini's businesses collapsed.[22] But as fast as he lost money, Calvi used his Vatican connections to bail out the Ambrosiano. Marcinkus persuaded some big Vatican customers to loan Calvi money, including Italy's largest nationalized financial institution, Banca Nazionale del Lavoro, as well as Ente Nazionale Idrocarburi, the country's state-owned energy holding company, in which the Vatican had investments.[23]

• • •

As Calvi expanded the Ambrosiano network, Sindona fended off an increasingly aggressive legal assault in the United States. His problems had expanded far beyond Italy's extradition efforts. In January, the same month the Calvi criminal investigation went public in Italy, U.S. prosecutors leaked to *The New York Times* that a grand jury was investigating former Nixon Secretary of the Treasury David Kennedy over a $200,000 personal loan from Sindona.[24] The day after that story, a federal jury in New York capped an eight-week trial by returning guilty verdicts against Franklin National's former chairman, president, and senior vice president.[25] The three were convicted of falsifying the bank's records to cover up the extent of its losses. Sindona, one of several unindicted co-conspirators, had been subpoenaed to testify during the trial. He avoided answering any questions by invoking his Fifth Amendment rights.

The long-awaited U.S. criminal move against Sindona came less than two months later, on March 19, when a grand jury returned a sweeping ninety-nine-count indictment against him and his former top aide, Carlo Bordoni.[26] The charges included fraud, conspiracy, and misappropriation of $45 million from Franklin.[27] The detailed indictment was strong proof that two and a half years after the collapse of Franklin National, federal prosecutors had seemingly solved the riddle of how Sindona shuffled millions between his Italian banks and offshore shells, all intended to boost the paper value of his companies while running Franklin into the ground.[28]

Sindona promptly issued a statement: "I am innocent of any wrongdoing. I will plead not guilty to the charges and expect to be vindicated at trial. In any case, according to my understanding, all charges rest on false documents and information originating from Italian sources." He added: "I was the principal victim of [Franklin's] collapse."[29]

Sindona's indictment dominated the news in Italy. Marcinkus was not surprised that because of the American criminal charges most of Sindona's Italian friends had further distanced themselves from him. "Everybody was calling Sindona a very close friend [during his zenith at] the Banco d'Italia," a sarcastic Marcinkus later told author John Cornwell. "But it's strange, that now I'm the only one who has ever known Sindona in Italy. It's like they said right after the war, 'There's not a Fascist in Italy.' Where did they all go?"[30]

Marcinkus was not able to rewrite history, as had many of Sindona's less high profile friends. Sindona's close affiliation with Pope Paul VI and the IOR was too well documented. Instead, the bishop hoped that Sindona would not try to deflect attention from his own problems by creating headaches for the church.

More bad news came a couple of weeks after the Sindona indictment. Giorgio Ambrosoli, the attorney who had been appointed by the Bank of Italy to liquidate Sindona's $200 million bankrupt Banca Privata Italiana, released a ten-pound, two thousand–page report based on his five-year probe.[31] Although Ambrosoli recycled some unfounded conjecture about Mafia connections, much of his report was a compelling indictment of the shady ways Sindona had run his business empire.[32] Ambrosoli had overcome significant hurdles to gain rare access to the records of two Swiss banks Sindona controlled.[33] And he demonstrated that Sindona had violated Italian laws when he used money from Banca Privata's depositors to purchase Franklin National.[34] The report exposed how Sindona looted seven banks in Italy, Switzerland, West Germany, and the United States. Two hundred and seventy million dollars had disappeared through dubious loans, vanishing interbank deposits, and questionable fiduciary contracts (the 2014 equivalent of $854 million).[35]

But the most explosive charge—and the worst for the Vatican—centered on Sindona's role in Calvi's purchase of the Banca Cattolica del Veneto. Ambrosoli had uncovered that in August 1972, Sindona had transferred $6,557,377.04 into Radowal, one of Calvi's offshore shells. That $6.5 million, charged Ambrosoli, was "probably paid as a commission to an American bishop and a Milanese banker."[36] The unnamed American bishop was clearly Marcinkus and the Milanese banker was Calvi.[37] Due to the sensitivity of naming the sitting head of a sovereign central bank—Marcinkus—as the recipient of a multimillion-dollar payoff, Ambrosoli had deferred to the wishes of others in the Italian judiciary and the Bank of Italy who thought his public report should only identify Marcinkus by his position, not name. At the time the report was released, Marcinkus did not say a word publicly.

Starting in December 1978, unidentified men with Sicilian accents began calling Ambrosoli, sometimes offering bribes and other times threatening to kill him for his "lies."[38] He taped a call on January 12 in which a muffled voice said, *Devi morire come un cano* (You should die like a dog).[39] Ambrosoli did not take the threats lightly. In one of his diary entries he wrote, "I will pay a very high price for this job. I knew this before I took it on, and I am not complaining at all because this is a unique chance for me to do something for my country."[40]

Ambrosoli visited New York that June. He shared his findings with American prosecutors, including the evidence about the $6.5 million payoff split between Calvi and Marcinkus.[41] A few weeks later Ambrosoli visited Boris Giuliano, the superintendent of Palermo's noted Flying Squad, an elite anti-racketeering police unit with a storied record of success against the Mafia. They compared notes on mobsters who might have banked with Sindona as well as those who could have links to Calvi.[42] Giuliano also confided he was pursuing credible leads about tens of millions laundered by Sicilian heroin traffickers and disguised as legal transfers through Sindona-owned banks in Italy and Switzerland.[43]

Sindona was in a fury when he learned about Ambrosoli's cooperation with the American prosecutors and Italian racketeering squad. For five years Ambrosoli had been chasing Sindona. And it was Ambrosoli who had repeatedly blocked Gelli's efforts to convince the Bank of Italy to bail out Sindona's banks and give the Sicilian a second chance. Now, with his damning report, Ambrosoli was in the spotlight as the man not only capable of finishing off Sindona but also exposing the full extent of the Sicilian financier's ties to the Vatican Bank and Roberto Calvi.

That the young prosecutor could not be bought or scared off frustrated Sindona. According to banker Enrico Cuccia, a fierce business competitor, he overheard Sindona at a meeting in New York supposedly threatening that "he wanted everyone who had done him harm killed, in particular Giorgio Ambrosoli."[44]

On the evening of July 11, after a long day of depositions Ambrosoli left his office and drove to his Milan apartment.[45] After parking his car in its normal spot, he crossed the dark street. Three men came around the corner and ran toward him.

"Are you Doctor Ambrosoli?"

"Yes."

"Excuse me," one stranger said. He pulled out a .357 Magnum and fired five bullets into Ambrosoli's chest.[46] Ambrosoli's wife ran outside and stayed with her husband until paramedics arrived. Notwithstanding their frantic efforts, he died on the way to the hospital, but not before he managed to say that the men who killed him spoke with Italian American accents.[47]

The FBI and Italian police were immediately suspicious that Sindona had played a role. He certainly had the motive. Italy, however, was racked by violence against judicial officials. Since leftists and mobsters had killed eight judges, police officials, and prosecuting magistrates over several years, it was possible that someone else wanted the incorruptible Ambrosoli dead.[48] When asked by reporters if he had anything to do with the murder, Sindona was outraged at the suggestion.[49]

Two days later, police Lieutenant Colonel Antonio Varisco, who was responsible for investigating P2 and its money laundering, was killed during the morning rush hour in central Rome. And ten days after Ambrosoli was gunned down, a hit man went after Boris Giuliano, the chief of the Flying Squad, who had just finished breakfast at his regular Palermo café. As he went to pay the cashier, a man ran up and emptied his pistol, hitting Giuliano twice in the back of the head. He died instantly.[50]

One result of the triple killings was that the official investigation into Sindona's looting of Banca Privata Italiana, and the charge about the $6.5 million commission that Calvi and Marcinkus might have split, downshifted to slow motion. It was impossible for any Ambrosoli replacement to quickly master five years of files about a complex case.[51] And probable suspects for the murders such as mobsters or the Red Brigades spooked some investigators. A team of five financial forensics police inspectors abandoned plans to trace lost funds transferred abroad by Banca Privata. At least one of them received death threats. Giuliano's successor, Emanuele Basile, was killed the following year, shot repeatedly in the back while walking with his four-year-old daughter, who was not harmed.

On August 2, 1979, just three weeks after Ambrosoli's murder, Sindona's family reported the startling news that the Sicilian financier was missing. Eyewitnesses last spotted him wearing a light beige suit, blue shirt, and a club tie walking south along Fifth Avenue around 7:15 p.m.[52] A few hours after he failed to show up for a business meeting the following morning, a man who refused to identify himself called Sindona's secretary. In heavily accented English, he said, "We now have Michele Sindona as our prisoner. You will be hearing from us."[53]

Because it was only five weeks before the start of his criminal trial, the FBI and police suspected Sindona had fled. But his family feared he was the victim of foul play.[54]

One of Sindona's lead attorneys, former federal judge Marvin Frankel, received a letter from an unidentified group claiming it had Sindona and would subject him to "proletarian justice."[55] The New York bureau of ANSA, the Italian news agency, got a call from a man who spoke Italian with an American accent: "Here is proletarian justice. Michele Sindona will be executed by firing squad at dawn tomorrow."[56] A few days later Sindona's family received a handwritten letter from him, assuring his wife, Katerina, that he was "not afraid" although the kidnappers were "interrogating me at length every day."[57] Another packet, postmarked from New York, arrived the following week. It contained short notes from Sindona mostly trying to calm his family.[58]

The FBI resisted changing the case from a missing person to a kidnapping. But it placed the prosecution's key witness, codefendant Carlo Bordoni, into protective custody and issued calls for public assistance.[59] By that time—two weeks after the disappearance—Interpol, and dozens of detectives and FBI agents, were working leads.[60]

Three weeks passed. No one knew if Sindona was alive or dead.[61] His trial, scheduled to start on Monday, September 10, was adjourned indefinitely. The next day Sindona's son-in-law, Pier Sandro Magnoni, received a letter asking for details about Sindona's businesses, and warning, "If you value his life, you will provide all the facts in your possession." Sindona's Rome attorney, Rodolfo Guzzi, got an envelope postmarked from Brooklyn. It included ten handwritten questions about senior Italian politicians, prominent businessmen including Fiat's Agnelli family, and even the Vatican. A notation after the last one said, "All written by me on precise orders, Sindona."[62] An enclosed photo showed Sindona thin and haggard and sporting an unkempt beard. Around his neck hung a sign with the hand-scrawled words, *Il giusto processo lo faremo noi* (The fair trial will be done by us). The note was signed by the Cornitato Proletario di Eversione per una Giutizia Migliore (the Proletarian Committee of Subversion for Better Justice).[63]

A few days later the first letter asking for money arrived. The kidnappers boasted that Sindona had given up incriminating information about some noted Italians and the Vatican.[64] But this time the Italian police got lucky and arrested the messenger who delivered the letter. He was Vincenzo Spatola, a thirty-one-year-old Palermo contractor with solid ties to New York's Gambino family (the Gambinos were one of New York's original five Mafia families).[65]

Just a few days after Spatola's arrest, on October 16, 1979, Sindona's attorney, Marvin Frankel, picked up the telephone at his office. Sindona was on the other end. He sounded exhausted, his voice barely audible: "I was kidnapped but I am free now." He was at a pay phone in Manhattan at 42nd Street and Tenth Avenue. It had been seventy-six days since his disappearance.

When his son-in-law and psychiatrist picked him up, Sindona seemed almost hallucinatory. He was recovering from a poorly stitched-up bullet wound on the back of his left thigh.[66]* They checked him into Manhattan's Doctors Hospital with two federal marshals posted outside his private room.[68]

Eight days after his return, a still weak Sindona appeared before Judge Thomas Griesa. Claiming his memory was poor as the kidnappers had kept him drugged, he gave a brief and vague account of what had happened, "Leftists" took him at gunpoint from midtown Manhattan. They demanded information they could use against the rich and threatened to try him for "economic crimes" against the people.[69] His captors wore masks so he could not identify them, and they all spoke perfect Italian.[70] He was blindfolded and moved four times, each trip taking at least an hour. His wound came when a guard shot him during a failed escape. And, Sindona said—speaking in a voice so low that the judge often had to ask him to speak up—he was shocked when the kidnappers set him free in Manhattan.

Although the prosecutors wanted Sindona remanded to jail, Judge Griesa allowed him to stay free on bail and ordered around-the-clock security for him and his family.[71] The judge, concerned that speculation about Sindona's disappearance might prejudice the jury pool, imposed a gag order on the lawyers.[72]

Unknown to Sindona and his legal team, Italian police had detained John Gambino, a senior captain in the Brooklyn-based crime family, during a visit to Italy. Stopped for a passport irregularity, when they searched him

---

* Sindona had been treated by several psychiatrists for more than a decade, and was at different times prescribed a combination of anti–depressant/psychotic/anxiety medications. Side effects caused him to stop taking some antipsychotics. He also had at times a dependence on narcotic painkillers, and then laxatives to counter the constipating effects of the opiates. Although none of his psychiatrists ever disclosed the clinical diagnosis, business colleagues and some family members speculated it might have been bipolar disorder. Some of his worst business decisions coincided with stretches of little sleep but tremendous energy, what psychiatrists consider the manifestations of the manic phase of that mental illness.[67]

they found a slip of paper containing the notation in Italian, "741, Saturday, Frankfurt." It seemed unimportant. But the FBI discovered that a TWA flight with that number had left Frankfurt for New York's Kennedy Airport on October 13, three days before Sindona turned up.[73] Gambino was a cousin of Vincenzo Spatola, the man arrested in Rome on October 9 for delivering hostage letters.

In a pre-9/11 era, airlines never maintained passenger lists after flights were completed. FBI agents had to examine every customs declaration filled out at JFK the day TWA 741 arrived. One bore the name Joseph Bonamico of Brooklyn. The street address did not exist, so the agents sent it to the bureau's forensics lab. Near the same time, Luigi Cavallo, the provocateur who had blackmailed Calvi on Sindona's behalf was detained by the FBI at JFK. He was traveling on a false passport. And in Italy, police arrested two brothers with ties to the Gambino family, suspects they thought might help answer what happened to Sindona during the ten weeks he was missing.[74] Meanwhile, the FBI lab's results were startling: not only did the handwriting belong to Sindona but his fingerprints were on the customs declaration card in the name Bonamico.

What the FBI could not yet prove was whether Sindona had planned his "kidnapping."[75]

When FBI agents confronted Sindona about the TWA flight, he seemed nonplussed. Some in the U.S. Attorney's office thought he had used his "kidnapping" to raise money in Sicily for his expensive legal defense. But they could not trace the money paid to his attorneys.[76]

Sindona, meanwhile, was focused again on his upcoming criminal trial. He reached out through Guzzi, his Roman attorney, to the Vatican. Sindona needed strong witnesses willing to testify about his good character. None of his business colleagues were willing to come forward and vouch for his honesty and integrity. What better character witnesses than bishops or cardinals from the Vatican? Guzzi telephoned Marcinkus.

It is difficult to imagine that after all the terrible fallout from the Vatican's relationship with Sindona, that Marcinkus—or any other ranking prelate for that matter—would consider doing anything publicly to help Sindona. At an extraordinary special congress, John Paul II called all of the church's 123 cardinals to Rome a few months earlier. They addressed a series of important issues at the one-year point of his Papacy. And Vatican finances, which were in the red by $20 million, were a priority (the deficit marked the first time the church had ever announced a year-end profit or loss).[77] News stories about how "the Vatican has been plagued by money worries" and "serious financial problems" often mentioned the still-undetermined losses from the Sindona affair.[78] John Paul had closed the congress and "painted a gloomy picture." The Associated Press reported, "No Pope has ever spoken so openly on the Vatican's finances."[79] Some top prelates, including the Pope's close friend, Warsaw Cardinal Stefan Wyszyński, suggested that the IOR's profits be used to erase the Church's deficit. That idea never gained any traction.[80]

On December 5, 1979, Marcinkus met in his IOR office with Graham Garner, a partner of the accounting firm Coopers & Lybrand. For more than a year Calvi had foiled Garner's inquiries about the Vatican Bank and the Nassau-based Cisalpine. Since Marcinkus was still a Cisalpine director, Garner had badgered him for a couple of months before getting the December meeting.[81]

Marcinkus introduced Garner to Mennini and de Strobel, and then for an hour gave him a broad description of how the IOR functioned. He tried addressing Garner's confusion over the Vatican Bank's dual role as borrower and depositor at the Cisalpine. Every time Garner asked for specifics, Marcinkus either dodged the question or claimed that the IOR's governing rules prevented him from providing details.[82] Garner left that meeting still in the dark that some $228 million in transfers from the Cisalpine to the IOR were in fact back-to-back loans. Most of that money was ending up in a tiny Panamanian firm.[83] It was the IOR that stood to lose more than $137 million if Cisalpine and the rest of Calvi's network collapsed. So while it might be understandable as to why Marcinkus would cover for Calvi, doing so created tremendous liability that would haunt the church in a few years.*

Given the spotlight on the church's finances, it would have seemed natural for Marcinkus to pull away from Calvi and Sindona. But he did the opposite.

* Ten weeks later, on February 21, at Claridge's Hotel in London, the full Cisalpine board met with Garner and another accountant: the directors approved financial statements that confirmed that the IOR owed Cisalpine $228 million. Only Calvi and Marcinkus knew that was not true, but neither objected. The Coopers & Lybrand accountants submitted a management letter stating in part: "It is our understanding that none of the directors of Cisalpine, other than Bishop Marcinkus, are aware of the current financial condition of this entity." Marcinkus evidently objected to being listed as the sole official with full knowledge of what was taking place at the IOR. Garner modified the letter to say instead that the full information was "only available to a very limited number of individuals in the Vatican."[84]

December 1980 marked the first time in several years that Marcinkus approved the Vatican Bank's purchase of another $65 million in promissory notes issued by some of the Ambrosiano's offshore companies.[85]

And incredibly, as for Sindona's request made through his Italian attorney for Vatican assistance, Marcinkus agreed to help. The bishop also lobbied two cardinals, Giuseppe Caprio and Sergio Guerri—both familiar with Sindona from his APSA dealings—to testify that Sindona was a stalwart, decent, and hardworking businessman. They agreed.[86] Sindona's legal team was so pleased that on January 24, lead counsel Marvin Frankel informed Judge Thomas Griesa that the high-ranking church trio would testify.[87] Frankel said that under the policies of the city-state, the clerics could not appear in person at the New York trial. Griesa allowed their testimony to be videotaped at the American embassy in Rome on February 1.[88]

The Vatican's new Secretary of State, Cardinal Agostino Casaroli, was enraged when he learned about it.[89] He knew that supporting Sindona would be a public relations nightmare. Casaroli banned the three clerics from making the depositions.

When Frankel arrived at the Vatican to prepare Marcinkus, Caprio, and Guerri for their testimony, they informed him that they had no choice but to decline. Frankel pressed hard to change their minds. Marcinkus spoke for the trio, unswerving in his no.[90]

Sindona, upon hearing about the reversal, told Frankel that "the Vatican has abandoned me."[91] He blamed Marcinkus for the change, not knowing that Marcinkus had battled Casaroli over the ban, at one stage threatening to still go public for Sindona.[92]

What Casaroli did next is disclosed here for the first time. He was so upset with Marcinkus that he asked a close aide, Monsignor Luigi Celata—now an archbishop—to enlist the help of General Giuseppe Santovito, Italy's Military and Security Service chief, to obtain compromising information about Marcinkus. Santovito appointed Francesco Pazienza, an ambitious young intelligence officer, to the matter.[93] Pazienza did not uncover any straightforward blackmail. But in Switzerland, he unearthed documents that revealed how Marcinkus was the conduit for funneling church money to key conservative politicians. It would create a firestorm in the Italian press and add to the pressure for Marcinkus to resign.[94]

Instead of handing the information to Casaroli, Pazienza decided that

Marcinkus was a more important Vatican power broker than the Secretary of State. "So I arranged a meeting with Marcinkus," Pazienza revealed to the author. "I knew he loved power. He would not want to lose it."[95]

"I have been hired to fuck you," Pazienza told the IOR chief. Marcinkus did not show any visible sign of surprise.

"What do you intend to do?" Marcinkus asked.

"Nothing."[96]

Pazienza got what he wanted: a bond of loyalty.

While Marcinkus had dodged a possible bullet with Pazienza, Casaroli had demonstrated his power by prevailing in the standoff over the Sindona character testimony. In withdrawing Marcinkus and the cardinals from the witness list, Frankel informed Judge Griesa that his trip to the Vatican was a "catastrophe."[97]

The day before the trial got under way, on February 6, the U.S. Attorney's office asked for a closed hearing in the judge's chambers. There the FBI presented the evidence that instead of being ferried around blindfolded by kidnappers in New York and New Jersey, Sindona had engineered his own disappearance and spent it in Europe, mostly Sicily.[98] The fake abduction was intended to generate sympathy, but it had turned into a tragi-comedy. The Sicilian mobsters who afforded him safe haven decided they could make more money by extorting information from him and threatening his family.[99] The bullet wound was the result of a deliberate shot from an Italian doctor, Joseph Miceli Crimi, who knew where to aim the gun so it inflicted the least damage.[100] When the gangsters had released Sindona, they swore him to silence lest his wife and children became targets.[101]

The judge later called it "the blackest day of my life in a courthouse." He revoked the $3 million bail. A dozen federal marshals descended on the courtroom and hustled Sindona to jail.[102]

The trial started on February 7, 1980. Sindona's ex-friend and Franklin colleague, Carlo Bordoni, was the prosecution's star witness.[103] And the government used evidence of the fake kidnapping to demonstrate to the jury a "consciousness of guilt."[104] Much of the testimony and legal arguments centered on financial minutiae. Although no one from the Vatican was on trial, and the indictment did not list the IOR as an unindicted co-conspirator, the lead prosecutor, John Kenney, repeatedly linked the Vatican Bank to the case. He told the court that the IOR had worked with Sindona to help "prominent

Italian depositors" engage in financial dealings "which would not comply with the religious tenets of the Vatican or the Roman Catholic Church."[105]

The end of the trial could not come quickly enough for Marcinkus. It took seven weeks for the case to go to the sequestered jury. The six men and six women deliberated for six days before reaching a verdict: guilty on sixty-five counts of fraud, misappropriation of bank funds, and perjury.[106]

In June, two days before he was to be sentenced, Sindona—who said later that the verdict made him "believe only in injustice . . . the government is the real Mafia"—slashed one wrist and took a pharmaceutical cocktail he had somehow smuggled into prison (a mixture of digitalis, a heart stimulant; Darvon, a painkiller; and Librium, an antianxiety medication).[107] But he was quickly resuscitated, and after a few days in the hospital the judge ordered him to appear for his sentencing.[108] Griesa meted out the maximum to the unrepentant defendant, four twenty-five-year sentences to be served concurrently.[109]

Sindona soon got more bad news. The FBI was hunting for a low-level American hoodlum, forty-five-year-old William Arico. The charge: being the hit man in the 1979 execution-style murder of Giorgio Ambrosoli, the Milanese magistrate who had been investigating Sindona. The break came through an unlikely source, Henry Hill. He was a convicted extortionist later made famous in Nicholas Pileggi's book *Wiseguy*, and played by Ray Liotta in Martin Scorsese's 1990 film *Goodfellas*.[110] At the time of Ambrosoli's murder, Hill and his family were only months away from entering the U.S. witness protection program.[111] The gangster told the FBI that during the mid-1970s he had served time at a federal prison with two New York Gambino-connected hoodlums, Billy "The Exterminator" Arico, and a convicted heroin trafficker, Robert Venetucci. In the fall of 1978, according to Hill, after all three were released and living near one another on Long Island, Hill sold Arico five pistols and a machine gun with a silencer. "The Exterminator" bragged that Sindona hired him for a contract murder in Italy. Hill next ran into Arico in 1979, just after Ambrosoli was killed in Milan. Arico pointed to an Italian newspaper clipping about the murder and bragged: "This is the fellow I whacked out over there."[112]

The FBI did not then know that since 1978 Sindona had been Venetucci's silent partner in Ace Pizza, a cheese and olive oil importing company in Queens.[113] Venetucci had hired Arico after Sindona asked him to handle his problem with Ambrosoli. At Sindona's direction, his son was wiring money from the Union Bank of Switzerland to Ace Pizza's account at New York's Bank Leumi (some investigators suspected that was how Venetucci got the $40,000 he paid Arico).[114]*

At the time the FBI got the tip from Hill, Arico was serving a four-year sentence on an unrelated jewelry heist in Manhattan's diamond district. But before the bureau questioned him, Arico escaped from New York's Rikers Island in June 1980, the same month Sindona was sentenced on the Franklin case.[116] It was two years before the FBI ran him to ground in Philadelphia.[117]

When the Arico news went public, the Italians insisted Sindona be extradited to stand trial for Ambrosoli's murder. But under the existing U.S.-Italy extradition treaty, Sindona had to finish at least five years of his jail sentence for his American conviction.[118]

Three months after Sindona's sentencing, Luca Mucci, the Italian prosecutor in charge of the Ambrosiano investigation, ordered Calvi to surrender his passport. Mucci based his decision on a fresh June 12, 1980, report from the Guardia di Finanza that concluded Calvi likely violated currency laws, falsified bank records, and even committed fraud.[119]

Calvi reached out to Marcinkus for help. Much of his work at the Ambrosiano had been in partnership with the IOR. He thought the two of them could fend off the prosecutors. But Marcinkus and the IOR had their own problems. On February 5, 1981, Milan prosecutors had stunned the Vatican by arresting Luigi Mennini, the bank's long-serving chief administrator, and Marcinkus's most trusted deputy.[120] The seventy-one-year-old Mennini had served as the IOR's director at Sindona's Banca Unione, and prosecutors thought he might be complicit in illegal currency trading there.[121] Mennini was an iconic figure inside the Vatican, having been hand-selected in 1930 by Bernardino Nogara.[122] And in 1967, when Henri de Maillardoz left as the chief layman at the IOR, Mennini took his position.

---

* Sindona's son, Nino, then a thirty-five-year-old businessman who had worked with his father, demonstrated the extent to which the Sindona family detested Ambrosoli, in a contemporaneous interview with journalist Luigi DiFonzo. In discussing the deceased Ambrosoli, Nino said: "I have no compassion for the fucking guy. [He] deserves to die—and this is not enough for a son-of-a-bitch like him. I'm sorry he dies without suffering. Let's make sure on this point . . . Ambrosoli doesn't deserve to be on this earth." (Nino Sindona refused requests by the author for an interview.)[115]

Italian police had arrested Mennini when he left the Vatican after work one day. John Paul II and Marcinkus raised a howl. After spending a few weeks in jail, Mennini was given "provisional liberty."[123]

The arrest caused great concern at the Vatican. Were former or current IOR officials so involved with Sindona that they may have broken the law? What trouble could Sindona cause when he was extradited to Italy to stand trial over charges similar to those brought against Mennini?

No one outside of a few executives knew what was going on inside the secretive IOR. Marcinkus had developed a defense: Mennini was a political target for leftists as payback for all the church's work over the years on behalf of the Christian Democrats. That sounded reasonable since a left-leaning coalition was in power. Combined with Mennini's proclamations of innocence, it was enough to calm jittery nerves in the Vatican.

Since Marcinkus was consumed with his own problems, Calvi sought help elsewhere. He again turned to Licio Gelli. But the P2 chief, who had earned millions by working his extensive contacts for Sindona and Calvi, was himself about to come undone. The break came in February 1981. Two Italian magistrates were investigating whether the Mafia had helped Sindona during his fake kidnapping. They noticed that when Sindona was in Palermo, Joseph Miceli Crimi, the financier's physician, had taken a two-day trip to the small northern village of Arezzo, a six-hundred-mile journey. The magistrates questioned Dr. Crimi, who claimed the trip was because he had had a toothache and his dentist lived there. But the investigators were skeptical. Crimi ultimately admitted he went to Arezzo to visit Licio Gelli. "Gelli is my Masonic brother," the physician confessed. "And a close friend of Michele Sindona."[124]

The magistrates applied for a search warrant for Gelli's villa and an office he maintained at a local textile factory.[125] One of Gelli's nicknames was *Il Cartofilo* (the Paper Lover), a tribute to his obsessive collection and organization of paperwork.[126] Although the search of his house yielded nothing, when the police executed the warrant at his office on March 17, 1981, they discovered a brown leather attaché inside a safe.[127] It contained a treasure trove of documents and membership applications detailing 953 of P2's members and its convoluted activities.[128] There were thirty-two sealed manila envelopes with photocopies of bank transfers and cash receipts attached to names of ranking politicians, judges, and private industry titans. In the seized files police found inciminating information about oil bribes and the state-run petroleum agency, arms discussions with Argentine military officers, illegal payments to political parties, and tax evasion by top businessmen.[129] One of the folders was labeled *Roberto Calvi* and detailed the many times Gelli had intervened to derail official investigations into the Ambrosiano chairman.[130] And the police discovered a cache of startling photographs, including embarrassing ones of prominent Italians.[131] The investigators ultimately concluded that Gelli had obtained many of the most salacious pictures from P2's intelligence members. Most were never used as blackmail, but Gelli seemed a compulsive collector of information that one day might prove useful.[132] One of the photos was of a naked Pope John Paul II sunning himself by a pool. The police did not then know that Gelli had sometimes shown that photo to others, using it as an example of how poor the personal security was around the Pontiff: "If it's possible to take these pictures of the Pope, imagine how easy it is to shoot him."[133]

Gelli got a tip about the search warrant too late to empty his safe, but before customs had received an all points bulletin to detain him, he fled to Uruguay via Switzerland on an Argentine passport.[134] Umberto Ortolani, Gelli's deputy, who was also involved as a middleman for many Sindona and Marcinkus money transfers, fled to Brazil.[135]

The public was stunned when the names of the P2 members were released that May. The list was a who's-who of leading businessmen, prominent judges and prosecutors, top-ranking military and intelligence officers, and respected journalists (one of the less well-known names was Silvio Berlusconi, the founder of a new television channel, and later three times a Prime Minister). A report from the investigating magistrate to Prime Minister Arnaldo Forlani concluded, "P-2 is a secret sect that has combined business and politics with the intention of destroying the constitutional order of the country and of transforming the parliamentary system into a presidential system."[136] Authorities had also found evidence of P2's role in right-wing terror plots.[137] It had not helped that three cabinet ministers, including the country's Attorney General, were P2 members. Speculation was rampant that there were more P2 members than those whose names were seized in Gelli's files. Many thought that Marcinkus was part of P2, disguised with a secret code name. Three years earlier *L'Osservatore Politico*, a muckraking weekly, named Marcinkus—with 120 cardinals, bishops, and influential monsignors—as Freemasons. Marcinkus later denied any role in P2 member or that he was a Mason: "I don't even know what a lodge looks like. . . . I was brought up to believe it was a mortal sin."[138] *

The days when Calvi could reach out to Gelli and his P2 colleagues were over. An aggressive new investigating magistrate was now in charge of the criminal probe. Only the Vatican might be able to help the Ambrosiano banker retain his power. Calvi was about to test the limits of his relationship with the church.

* The journalist behind the story of the Freemason-Vatican connection, Carmine "Mino" Pecorelli, was shot to death the following year by a hit man armed with a silencer-equipped pistol. Sixteen years later, Giulio Andreotti, the seven-time Italian Prime Minister, went on trial along with dozens of top mobsters for ordering Pecorelli's murder to cover up a pending bribery story. When Andreotti, a devout Catholic and daily-Mass attendee, was later acquitted of all charges, a Vatican spokesman, Joaquín Navarro-Valls, issued a statement that John Paul II learned of the verdict with "satisfaction."[139]

23

"You Have to Kill the Pope"

On Wednesday afternoon, May 13, 1981, Pope John Paul II was standing in an open-air car circling St. Peter's Square as he greeted some ten thousand worshippers. He shook hands, held and kissed babies and small children, and smiled and waved at the throngs. At about 5:20, there were several loud pops near the Vatican's large bronze gate. Some people, even those in the Pope's small entourage, thought it was firecrackers or the backfire of a nearby car. But a few police and security personnel recognized them instantly as gunshots. They looked to the sixty-year-old Pope. A small red stain appeared on his crisp, white cassock and started to spread. His hands had flown up toward his face. Then he fell backward into the arms of his private secretary, Father Stanislaw Dziwisz, and his chamberlain, Angelo Gugel.

Two bullets tore into John Paul, hitting him in the stomach, right arm, and left hand. Within minutes, the semiconscious, seriously wounded Pontiff was in a wailing ambulance speeding the two miles to Rome's Gemelli Hospital where he underwent five and a half hours of surgery to stem the blood loss and internal damage.[1] By midnight, the hospital issued its first official status report that the Pontiff was in "guarded and serious condition."[2]

The olive-skinned man tackled at the scene with a Browning 9mm semi-automatic pistol was thirty-three-year-old Mehmet Ali Ağca, a convicted murderer who had escaped two years earlier from a prison in his native Turkey. Ağca had written to newspapers threatening to kill John Paul II in the name of Islam.[3] Not everyone was convinced it was quite so straightforward. A BBC documentary only months after the shooting fingered the KGB as the mastermind behind the attempted assassination.[4] The official Soviet newspaper

Pravda ran a series accusing the CIA of having concocted the conspiracy.[5] NBC followed up with a persuasive program that put the blame on Bulgaria's secret service.[6]

Ağca had been on the periphery of the Gray Wolves (Bozkurtlar), an ultranationalist Turkish cell for which he had carried out the 1979 assassination of Abdi İpekçi, an editor of a prominent left-wing newspaper. Six months after a court sentenced him to life for that murder, he somehow donned an army uniform and walked through eight normally locked doors at a high-security military prison and found safe haven in neighboring Bulgaria.[7] That country was under the iron-fisted control of Todor Zhivkov, a Stalinist-styled autocrat who had been in power since 1954. It was unlikely that a fugitive Turkish political murderer could stay there without coming to the attention of the National Intelligence Service, Bulgaria's equivalent of the CIA. The National Intelligence Service's intimate working alliance with the KGB later served as the foundation for the conspiracy theories that identified those agencies as the ones likely to have wanted John Paul II, the most stridently anticommunist Pope since Pius XII, dead.[8]*

Vladimir Zhirinovsky, the deputy speaker of the Russian State Duma, later told Russian Radio: "There is no direct evidence of necessarily a Russian connection here, but it was not to our liking that a Pole became the Pope of Rome, inasmuch as it was done specially by the CIA special services and by the USA to influence the situation in Poland through a Pole, the Pope of Rome, and this succeeded. A movement began there for real, akin to what we now regard as an orange revolution."[10]

The "orange revolution" to which Zhirinovsky referred was the beginning of Pope John Paul's activism against the communist regime that controlled his native Poland. Encouraged by Margaret Thatcher and Ronald Reagan (who himself had survived an assassination attempt only six weeks before John Paul

---

* Ağca later added to the frenzied speculation when he picked from a photo lineup three Bulgarian state officials and intelligence agents as accomplices. Italian prosecutors charged the three Bulgarians and four others, including Turkish ultranationalists, but failed to convict any. Ağca was mentally unstable, often claiming he was the world's messiah. Later he dropped the Bulgarians from his story and said instead he got weapons training in Syria at a Soviet-sponsored camp for the terror group the Popular Front for the Liberation of Palestine. After his release from a Turkish prison in 2010, he announced that he shot the Pope because Ayatollah Ruhollah Khomeini, the father of Iran's fundamentalist revolution, had told him, "You have to kill the Pope in the name of Allah. You have to kill the devil's mouthpiece on earth."[9]

was shot), the Pontiff embarked in early 1981 on a policy of covertly supporting anticommunist movements throughout Eastern Europe.[11]

John Paul had been Pope less than a year when Polish shipyard workers in Gdańsk, led by Lech Walesa, a young union activist, had a standoff with the communist authorities. That resulted in the formation of a worker's trade union, Solidarity. It eventually claimed nearly ten million members, about a quarter of Poland's population.[12] CIA Director William Casey considered Solidarity the ideal vehicle through which to rattle Poland's communist leaders and the Soviets. At Casey's encouragement, Poland became the U.S. administration's first target by which to undermine the Soviet Bloc, which Reagan would in a couple of years dub the "Evil Empire."[13]

As Walesa stood up to the communists, there were rumors that the Soviets might crack down on the trade unionists, just as they had crushed incipient democracy movements in Hungary in 1956 and Czechoslovakia in 1968. Pope John Paul dispatched Marcinkus on a secret trip in August 1980, sending a handwritten note to Soviet premier Leonid Brezhnev.[14]* In the letter, John Paul threatened to spearhead the Polish resistance if Soviet troops invaded.[15] Once the Vatican leaked word of the Pope's letter to the Polish clergy, it spread like wildfire through the ranks of Solidarity.[16]

In a pre–glasnost and perestroika era, it seemed natural that the Reagan administration would want a partnership with a Polish Pope who had repeatedly demonstrated his commitment to his native country's small pro-democracy movement. All of the top American national security and intelligence officials—CIA Director Casey, National Security Advisor William Clark, Secretary of State Alexander Haig, and roving ambassador and ex-CIA Director General Vernon Walters—were devout Catholics.[17] U.S. officials also turned to Philadelphia's archbishop, Cardinal John Krol, a Polish American and a close friend of John Paul II, as well as Archbishop Pio Laghi, the just-appointed Nuncio to the United States. Krol and Laghi became the original go-betweens for the Americans and the Vatican.[18] Casey and Clark soon began dropping by the Nuncio's Washington residence on Massachusetts Avenue for a briefing

---

* John Paul believed that delivering the note to Brezhnev was a critical intervention in the standoff over Solidarity. The Pope considered several emissaries, including Secretary of State Cardinal Casaroli, Vienna's Cardinal König, and John Paul's private secretary, Monsignor Stanislaw Dziwisz. Casaroli had the advantage of speaking Russian. Marcinkus, who also spoke some Russian, was chosen because the Pope was convinced that he was the least likely to be intimidated by the Soviets or Brezhnev.

and breakfast. Laghi visited them—at least half a dozen times—at the White House.[19]

By the spring of 1981, Casey and General Walters began traveling to the Vatican every six months to brief the Pope, often with Secretary of State Cardinal Casaroli present. They met with John Paul fifteen times over the next six years.[20] The American consul to the Vatican at the time, Michael Hornblow, was at the first meeting between Casey and John Paul. "Anyone expecting a 'holy alliance' in their first get-together would have been disappointed," Hornblow told the author. "It was a simple twenty minutes mostly of small talk, with the Pope having a hard time understanding Casey because of his thick New York accent."[21] But in subsequent meetings, the work began in earnest. The CIA shared classified intelligence with the Pontiff, everything from satellite photos of Soviet troop movements and missile sites—the Pope was fascinated by them—to data about communist efforts to undermine Solidarity.[22] And Casey asked the church's assistance in transporting to the resistance everything from communications equipment to printing presses.[23]

There was little doubt about the importance of their meetings given the events unfolding at the same time. On March 27, 1981, Poland had the largest demonstrations against a communist government since World War II. It was a movement that the United States and the Papacy were doing their best to encourage.

Reagan, who would have a private fifty-minute meeting with John Paul the following year at the Vatican, later told journalist Carl Bernstein: "We [Reagan and the Pope] both felt that a great mistake had been made at Yalta and something should be done. Solidarity was the very weapon for bringing this about."[24] The President confided to his National Security Advisor, William Clark, that he intended to make the Vatican a loyal ally, even if that meant breaking precedent and recognizing the church-state (Reagan did that in 1984, ending more than a century of U.S. opposition to such relations. The Supreme Court declined to hear the case brought by those opposed to diplomatic relations).[25]

"This was one of the great secret alliances of all time," says former National Security Advisor Richard Allen.[26] There was "considerable sharing of information about developments in Poland with the Vatican," by Casey, Walters, and "sometimes our ambassador to the Vatican" (that was William A. Wilson, one of Reagan's closest friends and a member of the president's small kitchen cabinet of closest advisors).[27] Lech Walesa and Solidarity leaders got steady intelligence from both U.S. agents as well as Catholic priests.[28]

The KGB took a dim view of the new alliance between Washington and the Vatican. A four-page top secret KGB assessment in early 1981warned about the church's aggressive campaign to influence events inside the Pope's native country.[29] In April, KGB chief Yuri Andropov prepared a top secret dossier that concluded the Polish communist leadership was "inept" and suggested massive military maneuvers near the Polish border, leaving open the possibility of sending Soviet "troops into Poland."[30] In June, Hungarian intelligence distributed a report to the KGB and East Germans, titled "The Role of Zionists and the Catholic Church in the Activities of Solidarity." The Hungarians concluded that the church was allied not only with the U.S. government, but also with "Italian Jews" and "Israel, as well as Polish emigrants in Western Europe."[31]

The Vatican's partnership with U.S. intelligence meant that Marcinkus's help was sometimes required. Early on, he served as an informal conduit between Washington and the Vatican. His ability to brief the Pope, and to pass along intelligence during Papal travels, was considered indispensable. CIA Director Casey liked that in addition to his high rank inside the Vatican, Marcinkus was an American citizen.

John Paul, in return, had something to trade with the CIA. Just as the church's army of clerics native to every country had provided Pius XII with grisly accounts of the Nazi Holocaust before any Western leader knew the details, John Paul provided the CIA with useful intelligence gathered from Polish priests. The information was so good that Reagan himself began awaiting the Pope's summaries.[32]

The Pope gave Marcinkus the approval to create a secret conduit to send church money to Solidarity. That became an even greater priority after December 13, 1981, when Poland's military ruler, General Wojciech Jaruzelski, declared martial law, outlawed Solidarity, detained six thousand members, charged hundreds with treason, and cut the telephone lines between Poland and Vatican City.[33] For the next eight years, Marcinkus diverted an undetermined amount of money to what had become an underground movement to overthrow the communist regime.[34] It is not clear where Marcinkus obtained the cash, but it likely came from a slush fund, either provided covertly by U.S. intelligence or through spare funds that Marcinkus had accumulated through his Calvi and Sindona dealings. Marcinkus never admitted to accepting half of the $6.5 million commission that Ambrosoli had charged that Sindona paid to the IOR chief and Calvi. But even his most ardent foes seldom accused him of profiting from any of the IOR's questionable dealings.[35] Instead, if money like that "commission" from the Banca Cattolica sale ended up in a special fund used at the direction of the Pope, it would be understandable how John Paul became such a strong defender of Marcinkus. Sindona later concluded that Marcinkus "was greedy because he wanted to give the money to the Pope because he wanted to become a cardinal."[36]

And Calvi, who still needed the backing of the church as his own problems mounted in Italy, was ready to also assist. An Italian government investigation into the Ambrosiano years later raised questions about whether Calvi had paid Marcinkus extra cash for his refusal to disclose their convoluted business relationship even to Cisalpine's accountant, Coopers & Lybrand. Investigators were suspicious about a $500,000 payment from a special Banco Ambrosiano Holding account at the IOR. It was paid out in 1980 at Calvi's direction to an anonymous Vatican City recipient. The IOR has refused to open its records to show who received the money.[37]

Although Calvi later denied playing any role in the church's covert money pipeline to Solidarity, he told a journalist that he warned Marcinkus the entire matter was a dangerous game that could lead to World War III: "If it comes out that you're giving money to Solidarity, there won't be a stone left of St. Peters." And once, when secretly taped by Flavio Carboni, Calvi warned that if Marcinkus's secret network and slush funds to funnel money to Solidarity were exposed, "the Vatican would collapse."[38]

Italian intelligence agent Francesco Pazienza told the author that Marcinkus tapped him to convert $3.5 million of Vatican cash into physical gold from Credit Suisse. "They were the only Swiss bank at the time offering 99.99 percent pure gold ingots in small sizes," Pazienza recalls. The gold was put in a Lada Niva SUV, hidden in a custom-built double bottom as well as inside its doors. "And a priest from Gdańsk drove it from Italy back to Poland."[39]

A less comprehensive and dramatic political dynamic played out between the U.S. and the Vatican in Latin and Central America. In 1979, Nicaragua's Marxist Sandinista revolutionaries overturned the U.S.-backed dictator, Anastasio Somoza. In a country where 89 percent of the population was Catholic, an atheist government that linked itself with godless Soviets caused great consternation at the Vatican. Other Latin American countries confronted the same fate from leftist insurgency movements. In Peru, the establishment was under assault by the Shining Path, violent Maoist guerrillas. El Salvador was in the midst of a civil war, with the Farabundo Martí National Liberation Front, an umbrella military wing of four left-wing guerrilla organizations and the Salvadoran Communist Party, gaining ground. Colombia's government was having a tough time fighting the Revolutionary Armed Forces, FARC, a Marxist-Socialist paramilitary force. And on the horizon was the Guatemalan National Revolutionary Unity, another hard-core band of Marxist revolutionaries.

It was not a stretch for Bill Casey and Vernon Walters to convince John Paul that the church's best interests in Latin and Central America were the same as those of the United States: supporting authoritarian regimes that were at least nominally Catholic.

Although John Paul condemned "savage capitalism," and even told a reporter that there were "kernels or seeds of truth" in Marxism, he nevertheless dramatically changed course from Paul VI when it came to liberation theology, a twentieth-century mixture of Catholicism and left-wing ideologies that emphasized a redistribution of wealth to help the poor, particularly through political activism.[40] Marcinkus, from his work with Sindona and Calvi, was more familiar than any other Vatican official with how to move money around Central and Latin America. The money arrangements among U.S. intelligence agencies, covert operatives, and Marcinkus left few footprints.[41]*

John Paul rewarded Marcinkus for his service in September 1981 by appointing him as the city-state's pro-president of the Pontifical Commission for Vatican City State, the church's chief administrator. The position automatically made Marcinkus an archbishop. In his new post, he oversaw the management of Vatican City's day-to-day affairs. It encompassed everything from the rela-

---

* The fall of communism that began in 1989 across Eastern Europe and the Soviet Union made the Washington-Vatican alliance less urgent. In Poland, Solidarity was again legal, and the following year Lech Walesa was elected the country's president. Signs of some strain in the partnership were evident that year. In December, Panama's strongman, Manuel Noriega, took refuge in the Vatican's embassy in Panama City. The previous year the church and Reagan administration had discussed finding a Latin American or European nation willing to grant Noriega asylum. The church had worked hard to get Spain to take Noriega. But under President George H. W. Bush, the Associated Press reported, the Americans had dressed down the Pope and his diplomatic staff in "extraordinarily tough terms." The Vatican allowed U.S. authorities to take Noriega back to America to stand trial. The partnership between the United States and the Vatican was never again the same.[42]

tions with its 3,200 employees to all construction and maintenance projects, to the rules affecting its museums, radio station, post office, and newspaper.[43] It was a remarkable turnaround even by the nine-lives standards of the Vatican. Marcinkus had weathered public scandal. He had emerged from assured banishment when John Paul I was elected to having not only reinforced his grip on the Vatican Bank, but expanded his influence. Curial gossip was that Marcinkus would return soon to America as a cardinal.

A wire service story by UPI agreed: "One of the most active prelates in the Vatican, Marcinkus will most probably be made a cardinal when the pope calls the next consistory. Traditionally, presidents of pontifical commissions are cardinals. Vatican observers said the new appointment and the fact that Marcinkus will maintain the presidency of the Vatican Bank, are clear indications that John Paul has full confidence in the prelate."[44]

But while events played out in Marcinkus's favor during 1981, matters beyond his control would soon trip him up.

24

"Tell Your Father to Be Quiet"

Gerardo D'Ambrosio, Milan's chief investigating magistrate, had taken charge of the Calvi probe in April 1981.[1] The following month, on May 20, Calvi was arrested at his Via Frau apartment.[2] It was only a week after the attempted assassination on John Paul, and six days before Italy's fortieth coalition government since World War II collapsed because of fallout from the P2 scandal.

Calvi and six directors of La Centrale Finanziaria, a financial company at which he was also president, were indicted for violating the country's currency statutes by improperly exporting up to $50 million of lire through a web of offshore operations.[3] News of Calvi's arrest kicked off a tumble on Milan's stock exchange, the beginning of a 40 percent slide over several weeks.[4] The central bank drafted six major Italian banks into a consortium to stabilize the Ambrosiano with a line of credit.[5]

To his family and friends Calvi insisted that he had only carried out the actions at the heart of the indictment on behalf of the Vatican Bank. Marcinkus, Mennini, and the IOR's chief accountant, Pellegrino de Strobel, were aware of every transaction. The evidence he said, was in the files of one of the Ambrosiano's Swiss banks, the Banca del Gottardo. Papers there proved the deals were actually masked transactions for the IOR. Swiss privacy laws, however, barred releasing documents about a third party without their consent.

"My father really wanted the Swiss bank to disclose the IOR information," Carlo Calvi told the author, "because he knew it would immediately shift the responsibility for the offshore deals from him to the Vatican. But they wanted none of it."[6]

What was at the Banca del Gottardo showed that the Vatican Bank—through its secret ownership of United Trading and Manic—owned all the offshore companies named in the indictment.[7] Key Gottardo executives had played more than just an intermediary role; they had in some cases assumed director's positions on companies like United Trading.[8]

Calvi could not do much as he was in jail since the court had refused him bail.[9] One day after visiting him in prison, his wife, Clara, and daughter, Anna, got into a waiting car to return home. Calvi had given Clara some papers on which he had written: "This trial is about the IOR." He had told her to go to Marcinkus and ask for his help.[10] Clara later claimed that Luigi Mennini's son Alessandro jumped into the car before they drove off and warned her: "You must not mention this name [IOR] even in confession."[11]

Calvi, meanwhile, had hired Francesco Pazienza as a "special consultant" for a huge retainer of 600 million lire (about $500,000).[12] The thirty-four-year-old ex-intelligence officer was a nonpracticing physician and adventurer who boasted contacts in Italian and American politics as well as good ties to U.S. and French spy agencies.[13] He was also close with Marcinkus. Although he was not a P2 member, he was a top Gelli ally and a friend to many others in the Masonic lodge.[14]

Pazienza had a reputation for digging up dirt. That was why Secretary of State Casaroli had tapped him the previous year to look for any scandal about Marcinkus. And in 1980, conservative Republicans had hired him as a free-lancer to investigate President Jimmy Carter's brother, Billy. "I uncovered everything," Pazienza told the author.[15] He discovered that the "first brother" had taken $50,000 from Libya's Muammar Gaddafi, and had also visited Yasir Arafat of the Palestinian Liberation Organization as well as wanted terrorist George Habash, of the Popular Front for the Liberation of Palestine.[16] Pazienza's findings became a 1980 presidential campaign issue after the explosive story was published that October in *The New Republic*.[17] And Pazienza had added to his own allure with a series of dramatic and ever-changing claims. At times he said he had given the Vatican a six-month advance warning about the attempted assassination of the Pope; and that he was the founder of Gran Italia, a group headquartered on New York's Park Avenue whose stated goal was to unite all 120 million Italians worldwide for a "second Risorgimento."

Pazienza later claimed Gran Italia was a cover for an intelligence operation to nab Italians linked to terrorism.[18]*

"My father had personally hired Pazienza," recalls Carlo, "because he was recommended by the former Secretary of the Christian Democratic Party. He was close to military intelligence officials and top industrialists as well as other men my father respected. He was one of those people who acted as a fixer."[20]

Pazienza's ambitious brief from Calvi was to work to resolve the Ambrosiano's mounting problems.[21] "I start all my work diplomatically," he told the author, "but if you want to get destroyed, okay, then I can destroy you." But he also had another goal: to use his connections with Middle Eastern oil sheiks and Western investors to find a buyer willing to pay up to $1.2 billion for 12 percent of Ambrosiano. The deal seemed tantalizingly close at times but ultimately never happened.[22]

With Pazienza working in the background, Calvi requested that his son, Carlo, then living in Washington, D.C., fly to the Bahamas to look for any exculpatory evidence. The senior Calvi had arranged for his son to access his personal safe deposit box at the Nassau bank Roywest.[23]

"When I opened the safe box," recalled the younger Calvi, "there were lots of papers, most of them hard to figure out. But one that seemed clear was on the letterhead of the accounting firm Coopers & Lybrand. It asked whether the Vatican was good for the money behind the deals, whether the money was recoverable from the IOR.

"And here I was, caught between my father wanting the Vatican to release the Swiss files, and the church saying no. I was excited because I thought I finally had found a document to force the Vatican's hand."[24]

In a pre–cell phone and email business era, telexes were often used for fast

---

* Italian criminal prosecutors later investigated Pazienza as the "mastermind" of an intelligence plot to coach the Pope's would-be assassin into incriminating the Bulgarian secret service (no charges were ever filed). He was subsequently charged with fraud over Calvi's Ambrosiano and extradited in 1986 from the United States, where he had been arrested in 1984 (Pazienza told the author he had helped the U.S. Marshals and FBI on key cases and considered the extradition "a complete betrayal by the Americans"). Although he was acquitted of the Ambrosiano charge, he was convicted in a subsequent case of trying to derail the massive investigation into the 1980 terrorist train bombing in Bologna that had killed eighty-five. Prosecutors said Pazienza had laid a trail of false evidence putting the blame on foreign extremists. Licio Gelli was convicted in absentia. Both men received ten-year sentences. An appeals court overturned the convictions in 1990, but Pazienza's conviction was reinstated four years later. He was paroled in 2009. This author located him through an Italian priest, Father Lorenzo Zorza.[19]

and reliable international communications. An afternoon storm had knocked the bank's telex machine out of order. So Carlo walked through a tropical downpour to a public station next to the courthouse. From there he sent a telex to Marcinkus: "Call me after 3 p.m. Carlo."

Back at his hotel, he took a nap. At 3 p.m. when the phone woke him he was so groggy that he had forgotten who was calling until he heard Marcinkus's voice.

"Why are you bringing up our problems with the bank?" Marcinkus asked. "Our problems are also your problems."[25]

Marcinkus called Pazienza and told him that the young Calvi was trying to pressure the church. Pazienza got on the next flight to Nassau. "I put a stop to Carlo's craziness," he told the author. "I told him if he tried to use any telex machine again, I would personally smash it with my fists."[26]

Carlo thought that the Banca del Gottardo should issue a statement about his father's innocence.[27] "They agreed to answer some interrogatories," says Carlo, "and promised they would help. But in the end, they released almost no information. It all stayed in Switzerland." The Italian court rejected the Gottardo proclamation about Calvi because it was so generic, and crippled by too many caveats and legal disclaimers.[28]

Pazienza called the younger Calvi and said he was "authorized" to arrange a personal meeting between Carlo and Archbishop Giovanni Cheli, the president of the Vatican's Council for Migrants and Travelers and also its United Nations observer in New York.[29] Calvi had no idea that Cheli had secretly been angling to replace Marcinkus as chief of the IOR.[30] At a predetermined time, the young Calvi flew to New York and took a taxi to a Manhattan address supplied by Pazienza.

Two men were waiting inside an Upper East Side apartment. One was Sebastiano Lustrissimi, a businessman who worked for Italy's largest construction company, Condotte d'Acqua (a company in which the Vatican had sold its controlling interest to Sindona in 1969).[31] He was a friend of Pazienza (the young Calvi mistakenly thought he was either a mobster or an Italian intelligence agent).[32] The other man was Lorenzo Zorza, a middle-aged priest. Zorza was living at Manhattan's St. Agnes parish and was an energetic volunteer to the Vatican's Permanent Observer Mission to the United Nations.[33]

"When I met him—Zorza—he was dressed like a priest," Carlo Calvi recalled, "but he did not behave like one. I can't really explain it, but I had doubts about him right away."[34]

Zorza had a nervous habit of twitching his head from side to side. And Calvi's instincts about having some "doubts" were good. Zorza was no ordinary priest. A favorite with parishoners, the voluble Zorza always seemed to be part of some grandiose scheme that promised to blend religion and commerce. At Pazienza's urging, Zorza had asked the senior Calvi for $5 million from the Ambrosiano to develop a huge project in Brazil. Half of that loan would have been a kickback split between Pazienza and "the people at the Banca."[35]*

That early summer evening in 1981, Calvi sat between Lustrissimi and Zorza. They did almost all the talking. "Be polite to Monsignor Cheli," Zorza cautioned Calvi. "And listen carefully. And be certain to pay attention to his advice."[37]

Lustrissimi drove Zorza and Calvi to the United Nations. There they met Archbishop Cheli in a hallway. Cheli talked to Calvi in a hushed tone so no one nearby might overhear. He said, "Tell your father to be quiet, not to reveal any secrets, and to continue to believe in providence."

"Unfortunately," recalls Calvi, "providence was not something I could then believe in."[38]

---

* The following March, the forty-two-year-old Zorza was arrested on federal charges of smuggling stolen Italian Renaissance paintings into the United States. An informant testified at the trial that Zorza carried a two-foot-square diplomatic pouch, and told his customers he preferred that when it came to stolen canvasses, "It's better if it can fold." He pled guilty and got three years probation. Five years later, New York City detectives arrested Zorza for trying to sell $40,000 in stolen Broadway tickets. The case never went to trial.

In April 1988, Zorza was charged in the U.S. for using a New Jersey home for runaway girls as a cover for shipping millions of dollars in Sicilian heroin to the U.S. The New York press dubbed Zorza the "Pizza Priest." Italian police arrested him in Bologna and charged him with "associating with organized crime, criminal association for drug trafficking, importation of drugs, counterfeiting and illegal exportation of art works." The U.S. charges were dismissed—his lawyer was high-priced, Miami-based criminal defense attorney Frank Rubino, who later represented Panama's strongman Manuel Noriega. In Italy, Zorza was ultimately convicted and served eighteen months. As the only inmate-priest, he was treated very well, enjoying his spare time refereeing prison soccer matches. When the author located Zorza in 2013, he was traveling between Europe, America, and Brazil. He still boasted solid Curial connections, some of which the author confirmed. The man who asked me to call him Father Larry was promoting an Amazon-based herb company as well as seeking investors for a mammoth rainforest shrine to Popes Benedict and Francis. "I have made some mistakes in my past," he admitted. "They have made me a better server to God."[36]

Carlo Calvi called Marcinkus several more times. "He kept brushing me off."[39]

After the senior Calvi's indictment, Pazienza could not derail his trial. It got under way in a Milan courtroom that June. On the stand Calvi was hesitant, speaking in broad generalities. He tried shifting the blame for any wrongdoing to one of his codefendants, Alessandro Canesi, the bank's ex-chairman and his longtime mentor. Canesi was also a former chief of La Centrale Finanziaria, now headed by Calvi, which was allegedly behind the entire illegal export operation. Conveniently, Canesi was unable to answer the charges since the eighty-four-year-old had died at his villa near Lake Como on June 15, a few days after the trial started.[40]

While the courtroom drama played out, on June 30, at Calvi's insistence, two senior Ambrosiano executives, Filippo Leoni and Carlo Olgiati, met at the Vatican with Marcinkus, Mennini, and de Strobel. They were frustrated that the Vatican officials refused to tell them what the IOR might do if questions arose about its ownership of the ghost companies.[41]

On July 9, a defense attorney told a stunned courtroom that Calvi had failed to show up for the trial that morning because he had tried killing himself by swallowing ninety barbiturate pills and cutting one of his wrists.[42] Calvi's family cited it as startling evidence of his melancholy. His prison warden cast doubts on it, claiming that the wrist wound was superficial and that Calvi had not taken a lethal dose. "We're dealing with a suicide attempt that failed at birth," he told the press.[43]

Carlo Calvi thought his father's botched suicide was a sign of his desperation over the Vatican's refusal of the Ambrosiano's pleas for help.[44] The next day, the Ambrosiano's Leoni Olgiati and deputy chairman Roberto Rosone met again at the Vatican with Marcinkus and his top two deputies. They all later gave slightly different accounts of what transpired but agreed the discussion was about whether the IOR would continue cooperating with the Ambrosiano.[45] By this time, the Vatican officials worried that the fallout from the Calvi affair might result in their own criminal problems. Only five days before that meeting, de Strobel had traveled to Lugano, Switzerland, to review files at the Banca del Gottardo. Marcinkus needed some documents there. But de Strobel was concerned that if he returned with photocopies, he might be stopped and searched by Italian authorities. Instead, the Papal Nuncio in Berne later forwarded the Gottardo papers by diplomatic pouch.[46]

Meanwhile, Calvi's suicide attempt was serious enough to land him in the prison hospital. There he developed pneumonia and was too ill to attend the trial that continued while he recovered. He was still in the infirmary when the three-judge panel issued its verdict on July 20, 1981: guilty as the mastermind of illegally exporting $26.4 million to Switzerland. His sentence was four years in prison—more than the prosecutors requested—plus an $11.7 million fine.[47] Calvi was released on bail pending his appeal. His wife picked him up from the hospital in their armored Mercedes. The security motorcade—two cars with bodyguards—took the convicted banker home.[48] To Calvi's detriment, word leaked that before his release, he had met with prosecutors and discussed possibly cooperating in return for vacating his sentence.[49] Nothing was firm, but such news was a potentially ominous sign for those who had profited from Calvi's many ventures.

Only eight days after his conviction Calvi chaired a meeting of the Ambrosiano's board of directors. The Bank of Italy thought he should resign but was powerless to remove him. And the Ambrosiano's directors voted unanimously to keep him as chairman, saying there had been no suggestion at the trial that Calvi ever profited from his wrongdoing.[50]

Maybe even more surprising was that Calvi's felony conviction did not scare off Marcinkus. When asked why a few years later, Marcinkus offered a weak justification: "When Calvi was in jail, I asked somebody, 'Hey! What's going on?' And the fellow says, 'Nah, if you're not caught, you're not worth anything.'"[51]

For the remainder of 1981, the Ambrosiano's stock price climbed.[52] Some market analysts suggested that investors were voicing their confidence in Calvi's savvy running of the bank and a widespread belief that his talented legal team would prevail on appeal.[53] Others concluded that between the P2 revelations and the string of powerful politicians who had testified to his good character, small investors believed they were investing in a company protected by the so-called *sottogoverno* (the secret government).[54]

No investor then knew that the Ambrosiano's foreign subsidiaries in Peru, Nicaragua, Panama, the Bahamas, and Luxembourg had borrowed over a billion dollars from other banks and the IOR, much of which Calvi had recycled to buy the Ambrosiano shares, thereby inflating the stock price. The IOR was still on the line for about $140 million.[55]

The greatest problem facing Calvi by the end of 1981 was that the Ambrosiano's many offshore subsidiaries had fallen behind on servicing its back-to-back loans and accumulated debt.[56] He was desperate because if he could not raise money his convoluted ghost company network would unravel.[57] So Calvi turned to Marcinkus, the only person he trusted.

Calvi broke his holiday in the Costa Smeralda and flew to Rome on a Learjet owned by United Trading.[58] On August 26, he met with Marcinkus at the IOR headquarters and pleaded for help. Marcinkus agreed to give Calvi two official IOR letters, known in the banking industry as "letters of patronage" or "letters of comfort," documents meant to assure third parties that the Vatican stood behind the Ambrosiano. Written in English on Vatican Bank stationery and dated September 1, 1981, the letters read, "This is to confirm that we directly or indirectly control"—it then listed ten of the Panamanian, Luxembourg, and Liechtenstein ghost companies. "We also confirm our awareness of their indebtedness towards yourselves as of 10 June 1981 as per attached statement of accounts."[59] One letter was addressed to Nicaragua's Banco Comercial and the other to Peru's Banco Andino.[60] The language was vague, not constituting an express guarantee of the debt, but rather intended to convey the impression that the IOR was somehow endorsing the $1.4 billion in unsecured debt the Ambrosiano had issued to the ghost companies. Read with a lawyer's eye, the letters did not represent that the IOR had any intention of honoring the debts. Luigi Mennini, as the IOR's chief administrator, and Pellegrino de Strobel, the Vatican Bank's chief accountant, signed for the Vatican.[61]

Attached to the letters was a purported assets and liability summary for seven of the ten companies. According to that eight-page document, the companies owed $867 million to the Nicaraguan and Peruvian banks, but had assets of $1.21 billion. This balancing act was accomplished by inflating the value of the Ambrosiano shares and also omitting $217 million of back-to-back debts between the Cisalpine and Banco Andino (or, as a *Wall Street Journal* investigation concluded six years later, "In essence, the Vatican bank had borrowed money . . . and lent it to itself").[62] Marcinkus would have known the figures on Calvi's attachment were wrong. The financial statements he had just received from Switzerland's Banca del Gottardo showed the true and far more sobering numbers.[63]

As a condition of giving the letters of patronage, Marcinkus insisted that Calvi give the IOR a secret counter-letter—backdated to August 26—absolving the Vatican of *any* obligation to repay the loans. Calvi agreed that no matter what the patronage letters said, the IOR would incur "no further damage or loss."[64] A one-page attachment listed all the outstanding back-to-back loans and stated that $300 million was owed to the Vatican.[65] That Calvi letter also had an important clause upon which Marcinkus had insisted: the IOR's role in the ghost companies would terminate in another ten months, no later than June 30, 1982.[66] Marcinkus had belatedly concluded that it was time for the Vatican to extricate itself from Calvi's offshore empire. The best the IOR chief could do was to start the clock running.

Calvi assured Marcinkus he would only share the patronage letters inside the Ambrosiano with his fellow directors. He did not keep that promise. Calvi needed the letters to calm the Ambrosiano's jittery foreign lenders.[67] Marcinkus would later aver that he gave Calvi those letters as an "assistance to a friend" because "Calvi comes out of jail . . . and he says, 'I'm having trouble and I've got to get this thing all set up.'"[68] Sindona told author Nick Tosches, "Calvi—no one knew this, but it is true—paid the Vatican through Marcinkus, $20 million for those two letters of comfort."[69] (Two parliamentary investigations failed to find evidence of such a payoff.) What was proven was that the day after Calvi got the patronage letters, Mennini transferred $3.5 million from an IOR subsidiary in Lugano to a Swiss lawyer, who in turn sent it along to an account in Lausanne controlled by Pazienza, Calvi's crisis manager.[70]

The following month, October 26, Mennini and de Strobel—with Marcinkus's approval—signed revised patronage letters to the Banco Comercial and the Banco Andino.[71] The new language suggested that any money raised from the sale of assets would not necessarily be used to reduce the debt of the ghost companies. Most incredibly the letter appointed Calvi as the "attorney in fact" for "all relevant purposes" under the agreements.[72] (Lawyers for the IOR subsequently contended that the power of attorney had been given to Calvi only at his "express request, to formally empower him to manage the companies which the IOR de facto controls, though unwittingly so." In essence, the church's unlikely explanation was that once it discovered it was the unknowing owner of the ghost companies, rather than protesting, it recorded a power of attorney appointing Calvi as the administrator of the ten shells.)[73]

The day after the Vatican gave Calvi that authority over the ghost companies, Marcinkus and Calvi were in Zurich for another Cisalpine board meeting. According to the minutes, Marcinkus asked far more questions than usual, but neither he nor Calvi disclosed to their fellow directors anything about the patronage or indemnity letters.[74]

Pope John Paul II had created a special commission of fifteen cardinals to study Vatican finances and devise safeguards to prevent future Sindona-like scandals.[75] The panel included American cardinals John Krol of Philadelphia and New York's Terence Cooke.[76] But few inside the Vatican thought that the Polish-born Pope intended the investigation to be hard-hitting. Marcinkus, meanwhile, did not tell the cardinals about the patronage letters. When they later learned about them they were enraged. Cardinal Pietro Palazzini's reaction was typical: it "was crazy."[77] German Cardinal Joseph Höffner, another committee member, was so furious at Marcinkus's deception that he insisted to John Paul that the IOR chief promptly resign.[78] The Pope refused.[79]

During this time, Calvi made a critical acquaintance separate from the Vatican. He spent his August holiday on Pazienza's yacht, off Costa Smeralda. They chanced upon another yacht, owned by Flavio Carboni, a forty-nine-year-old Sardinian property developer. Carboni also happened to be the partner of Carlo Caracciolo, the publisher of *La Repubblica* and *L'Espresso*.[80] Italy's Secretary of the Treasury was on the boat that day. The flashy Carboni, with his fleet of fast cars, a plane, and two mistresses in addition to his wife, was a well-known personality in southern Italy.[81] His solid connections, Calvi hoped, might allow him to offset Gelli's lost influence.[82]

Although Calvi was not the most personable man, Carboni got along with him from the moment they met.[83] The Sardinian wanted something from the Ambrosiano too, a $500 million loan for an ambitious seaside resort project. Though short of money, Calvi nevertheless agreed.[84] It took only a couple of months for the relationship to go beyond lender and borrower, to friendship, and then to confidants. Carboni visited Calvi at his home and was often at the Ambrosiano's headquarters. Knowing of Calvi's pending prison sentence, Carboni offered to lobby important politicians on his behalf.

Some close to Calvi were unsure about Carboni's intentions. Carlo Calvi did not like him. Nor did Calvi's Ambrosiano deputy, Roberto Rosone, who warned others there was something sinister about him.

As 1981 drew to a close, Calvi also got involved with one of Italy's leading businessmen, Carlo De Benedetti, a former ranking executive at Fiat. In 1976, De Benedetti had taken control of office equipment firm Olivetti. Acclaimed for turning the company around, much as Lee Iacocca was later for his 1980s turnaround of Chrysler, he thought the Ambrosiano was a bargain.[85] In November, Calvi and De Benedetti announced that the Olivetti chief had invested $45 million to buy a 2 percent stake. De Benedetti became an Ambrosiano director and its deputy chairman.[86]

The financial world was astonished at the union between Calvi, the convicted felon, and De Benedetti, whose reputation was flawless.[87] It was a moment of personal triumph for Calvi. "He considered it maybe a last opportunity to really revitalize himself and the bank," recalls Carlo Calvi. "He was so proud when he introduced me to De Benedetti."[88]

Sixty-five days later the honeymoon was over. Once De Benedetti had full access to the bank's records, he was "appalled" to discover its finances were utterly dismal.[89] The Ambrosiano's Peruvian unit had accumulated a massive $800 million in debt in just over a year. De Benedetti was stunned that most of the borrowers were unknown foreign companies whose creditworthiness he could not verify. He wanted out. Calvi was resistant but when De Benedetti threatened to go public, he had no choice. Within two months, their brief "marriage" was annulled. De Benedetti got back his original investment with interest.[90] (When he met the following month with the Vatican's Secretary of State Casaroli, De Benedetti warned him that there were grave problems at the Ambrosiano.)[91]

The Ambrosiano was desperate for cash. Calvi again approached the Vatican Bank but this time Marcinkus turned him away. He warned Calvi that the IOR expected to be "made whole." Calvi was more concerned about finding a financial lifeline than figuring out how to repay the Vatican. But the IOR chief did do one last favor for him. According to the byzantine paperwork between the IOR and the Ambrosiano, the Vatican owed about $18 million on some phantom loans used to boost the balance sheets of Banco Andino and the Cisalpine. With Marcinkus's approval, Calvi used an old holding company, Zitropo, to pay $18 million to IOR accounts at Chase Manhattan and the Banca di Roma per la Svizzera. The Vatican Bank then passed that money back as payments it supposedly owed on the outstanding loans. The problem was that Zitropo was essentially bankrupt. Although it tapped lines of credit to pay the IOR, it was eventually liquidated with $46 million in debt (for allowing Calvi to use its accounts for the questionable trading, the IOR collected a small percentage of the transferred monies, a profit of $267,492).[92]

Although Marcinkus deemed any further investment into the Ambrosiano as too perilous, a few businessmen with a healthy appetite for risk thought the distressed bank offered an opportunity for fast, huge gains. Only days after De Benedetti's departure, Orazio Bagnasco, a wealthy Genovese property developer and owner of the luxury hotel group Ciga, invested $20 million in the Ambrosiano.[93] Bagnasco became the bank's deputy chairman.[94] And not long after he came aboard, in January 1982, his faith seemed justified when the bank announced that its prior year's profits had tripled. The financial press heralded the results as proof that the Ambrosiano was intrinsically sound and thriving despite Calvi's legal problems.[95]

The Bank of Italy, meanwhile, was still pursuing a probe into possible criminal wrongdoing. In February, only a month after Bagnasco's investment, the central bank sent investigators to Peru to follow up on suspicious Banco Andino transactions. But Peruvian banking officials refused to cooperate.

A small circle within the Ambrosiano knew that the stellar earnings meant nothing. The debt through its foreign subsidiaries was staggering. Marcinkus was increasingly concerned about having provided the patronage letters. He confided in Calvi that he was having difficulties inside the Curia maintaining a unified front for the beleaguered banker. Still, in March, Marcinkus went public with his support. He gave an interview to the Italian newsweekly *Panorama*. "Calvi merits our trust," he said. Some of the investments with Calvi, claimed Marcinkus, "are going very well." As a result, he said, the Vatican did not intend to sell its stake in the Ambrosiano.[96]

That interview set off stormy arguments and accusations inside the Vatican between the IOR's boosters and those who thought Marcinkus had again tarnished the church's reputation. At the Ambrosiano, when executives like the deputy chairman, Roberto Rosone, questioned some of the immense Panamanian loans, Calvi dismissed them by citing the *Panorama* interview: "Behind those loans is the Vatican, the Pope," Calvi told his fellow directors. "Do you have the slightest doubt about the Vatican bank?"[97]

Calvi was, of course, aware that the Bank of Italy was investigating his foreign subsidiaries. In a display of bluster (or possibly denial), he directed Coopers & Lybrand to prepare the documents so the Ambrosiano could offer a new class of preferred stock to raise millions of dollars (the bank had already issued additional shares earlier in the year, increasing the number of shareholders by 30 percent and nearly doubling its available capital).[98]

By the spring of 1982, Calvi warned his family that he feared for their safety. He told his wife, Clara, that the Vatican and Sindona were all his enemies. Calvi started carrying a pistol in his black attaché. He showed the handgun to his daughter, Anna: "If they come, I will kill them."[99] She also overheard one day a telephone conversation that her father had with Carboni. Calvi told him: "I'm just tired . . . I've had enough and if I have to, I will speak and tell everything about everyone."[100]

A few minutes before 8 a.m., on April 27, a gunman ran up to Roberto Rosone on a quiet side street in central Milan. Rosone, who had just left his apartment, was shot twice. An accomplice was waiting on a motor scooter and the would-be assassin jumped on and sped away. A security guard rushed toward the fleeing bike and put two deadly bullets into the shooter's head.[101] The man turned out to be the boss of a local drug syndicate, Danilo Abbruciati.[102]

Not many outside the bank knew that Rosone—who survived—had encouraged a small group of the bank's investors to write a personal appeal to Pope John Paul II. The note, which was translated into Polish before being sent to the Vatican by messenger, warned about serious problems at the Ambrosiano. It asked whether the Pontiff knew about the many dealings between Calvi and Marcinkus. (It cannot be confirmed that John Paul ever saw the note.)[103]

Calvi commiserated with the recuperating Rosone, contending that the failed hit was meant to intimidate the bank's directors. "Madonna, what a mad world!" Calvi told his wounded colleague.[104] It would be another couple of months before investigators tracked a $150,000 payment from Calvi to the hit man.[105] In the wake of the shootings, most marveled at Calvi's composure and apparent coolness. At home, however, stripped of his public bravado, his wife and family saw that he was increasingly glum.[106]

Adding to his angst, Marcinkus reminded him that the IOR's patronage letters were set to expire at the end of June. Carboni had been lobbying Marcinkus for an extension. He now appealed to Luigi D'Agostini, a Rome lawyer with solid Vatican connections. D'Agostini enlisted the help of Cardinal Pietro Palazzini, another Marcinkus friend.[107] Calvi and Carboni met with the cardinal, and Calvi even sent a pleading letter, in which he complained about how "Marcinkus and Mennini refuse" to be reasonable. He also wrote about the "many loans and bribes . . . to political parties and politicians."[108] Palazzini tried intervening on Calvi's behalf but later informed the beleaguered banker that there was nothing he could do since the IOR was "impenetrable."[109] Marcinkus could not be swayed. By then, he was intently focused on limiting the Vatican Bank's exposure.

When Marcinkus traveled with the Pope to the United Kingdom in May, Carboni took the opportunity to meet with Mennini at the Vatican.[110] The Sardinian developer had made a bold proposal to Calvi: if he could repair the relationship between the IOR and the Ambrosiano and bring fresh money into the partnership, his reward would be a staggering $100 million. Enticed by that supersized commission, Carboni made an all-out effort. But he made little headway with the IOR's number two man. When Marcinkus returned to Rome and learned Carboni had tried circumventing him, he telephoned Calvi and angrily demanded he stop looking to the Vatican for assistance.[111]

Calvi was more desperate than ever to find a white knight. Two back-to-back loans to the IOR, totaling $124 million, were due on May 15 (Marcinkus reluctantly gave him a one-month extension just before the deadline).[112] Calvi claimed to his family that he was working on a Vatican-approved rescue plan involving Opus Dei, the secretive Catholic organization founded in 1928. For nearly twenty years, Opus Dei had wanted its status as a religious order upgraded from a secular institute, under the bureaucratic supervision of the Vatican, to a personal prelature that reported directly to the Pope.[113] In the deal Calvi spoke about, Opus Dei would somehow assume the Ambrosiano's debt and shield the church from financial losses and public fallout.[114] In return, John Paul would elevate Opus Dei to a personal prelature. Even if Calvi hoped to broker such an accord, it is doubtful it went beyond a few initial conversations. In May, he stopped talking about Opus Dei (later, when the story went public, the order issued a formal denial).[115]

Calvi switched his attention to his Coopers & Lybrand accountants, who suggested an eleventh-hour deal with another of its clients, Bahamian-based Artoc Bank & Trust. Peter de Savary, Artoc's British-born chairman, had invested in a Kuwaiti oil company. He and his Arab partners had opened Artoc in Nassau. The Ambrosiano already owned 20 percent of Artoc, and the accountants suggested the companies merge to form Artoc Ambrosiano.[116]

Since the Ambrosiano was headquartered in Italy, the Italian central bank had to approve the merger. Any chance that might happen was dashed on May 31 when the Bank of Italy's Milan branch sent a four-page, single-spaced, typed letter to Calvi, demanding that the Ambrosiano explain in detail its $1.4 billion in loans to subsidiaries in the Bahamas, Peru, and Nicaragua.[117]

The central bankers insisted that their letter of inquiry be read at the next Ambrosiano board meeting, and that each director state publicly whether or not they had approved the massive foreign loans.[118] That letter kicked off a raucous clash when the board met a week later, on June 7. Calvi refused the requests of several directors to produce the underlying loan documents to the ghost companies. For the first time during his seven-year tenure as chairman, the board voted 11 to 3 against him, passing a resolution authorizing the Ambrosiano to gather all the necessary financial documents requested by the Bank of Italy.[119]

The next morning, Calvi again told his family he thought they should leave Italy. And he met a final time with Marcinkus at the Vatican, asking his longtime friend to help him buy a large block of Ambrosiano shares at a significant premium to the market price. Calvi promised to repay the IOR, and hoped the purchase might rally its battered shares. Marcinkus again passed.[120]

Calvi brought a letter he had written a few days earlier, addressed to Pope John Paul. In it, he pleaded that the Pontiff was his "last hope."[121] Calvi boasted of having been a strategic front man for the Vatican in fighting Marxism around the globe.[122] And he warned that upcoming events would "provoke a catastrophe of unimaginable proportions in which the Church will suffer the gravest damage."[123] He implored John Paul for an immediate meeting so he could explain everything, and "put at your disposal important documents in my possession."[124]

That letter was a few days old by the time Calvi met with Marcinkus. If he had any thought of asking the IOR chief to pass it to the Pope, Marcinkus's chilly reception was enough to change his mind. When Calvi left he gave it instead to Carboni, who in turn handed it to a Czechoslovakian bishop working inside the Vatican.[125] (It is not known if the Pope ever received the letter, as the Vatican will not confirm or deny anything about it. Its existence was not known for another decade, when it turned up as part of yet another Italian government investigation into the Ambrosiano.)

Three days later, Friday, June 11, when Calvi's driver arrived to take the banker to work, he was not there. Aided by Carboni, Calvi had begun his circuitous journey to reach London, flying from Milan to Rome the night before. News that he had disappeared spread fast, and many colleagues feared for his safety. Later that same day he called his daughter, Anna, and Graziella Teresa Corrocher, his private secretary, to assure them he was safe.[126] "Stay calm," he said.[127] Since Calvi's real passport was in the custody of the court pending the appeal of his conviction, Carboni had used his underworld contacts to obtain a false travel document.[128]*

Calvi was now a fugitive. On the first working Monday after he had fled the country, the Bank of Italy dispatched six inspectors to the Ambrosiano's headquarters with court orders providing access to all the bank's records.[129] Its stock price fell 12 percent that day. That was the same day that $250 million in back-to-back IOR loans came due.[130] Panic began setting in at the Vatican Bank. Late that afternoon, Marcinkus wrote to Cisalpine chairman Pierre Siegenthaler saying that because of his "many other commitments," he had to resign his director's post at the Nassau-based bank.[131] It is difficult to imagine why it had taken Marcinkus so long to draw some distance between himself and that offshore bank. (He would later disingenuously claim that the resignation "had been in the works for a couple of years.")[132]

Secretary of State Agostino Casaroli again confronted Marcinkus.[133] John Paul had entrusted Casaroli with oversight of all the Vatican's finances with the notable exception of the IOR.[134] Casaroli and Marcinkus had worked together on some of John Paul's first foreign trips and had a good early bond but it had deteriorated. They now often scrapped over money and power.[135] Marcinkus was in no mood to be castigated. "I've done my best and if it's not good enough you can always get someone else."[136] Casaroli did not then know that only a day after Calvi disappeared, forensics investigators for Italy's central bank discovered that the Ambrosiano's biggest debtor was the Vatican Bank.

Rosone, the Ambrosiano's acting chairman, requested an urgent meeting with Marcinkus. The Vatican Bank chief was in Switzerland and suggested Rosone caucus instead with Mennini and de Strobel. On Wednesday, June 16, Rosone flew to Rome and met with the two IOR officials. He emphasized the patronage letters the duo had signed. Mennini then pulled out his "trump card," the indemnity letter in which Calvi assured the Vatican that it was not responsible for any of the Ambrosiano's debts.[137] Rosone was stunned. It was the first anyone at the Ambrosiano knew that Calvi had secretly indemnified

---

* Pazienza told the author that he was not surprised at Calvi's flight from Italy. A few months earlier Pazienza had made initial preparations for an elaborate escape plan involving a Calvi double, a Hollywood makeup artist, a speedboat with a champion powerboat driver, and stops in Corsica and a military airfield in Morocco before a final destination in Panama. The plan was a contingency in case Calvi had no other way to get out of Italy.

the Vatican. He asked if Michel Leemans, the managing director of the Ambrosiano's holding company, La Centrale, could join them. Mennini agreed.[138]

When Leemans arrived and learned about Calvi's secret indemnity letter, he contended that the Ambrosiano had been as duped by Calvi as was the Vatican Bank. They should share the risk. If the IOR accepted responsibility for all the debt, Leemans would help them raise a billion-dollar loan at 5 percent (he thought Olivetti owner De Benedetti might be interested in such a deal). Mennini said no. It put all the risk on the Vatican. Why should the Vatican accept responsibility for any debt? As far as the IOR executives were concerned, Calvi's indemnity letter cleared the church of any responsibility.[139]

Leemans was totally exasperated. "Don't you realize that this is a fraud. This will be a worldwide scandal."[140]

The two IOR officials appeared unfazed.

What about the shares the IOR owned of the Ambrosiano, asked Rosone?

Take them back, the Vatican duo offered.[141]

Rebuffed by the Vatican Bank, Rosone returned the following day to Milan and convened an emergency meeting of the bank's board. Nearly a year after Calvi's conviction for fraud, the directors finally passed a resolution removing him as chairman and appointing Rosone as his replacement. The stock price was getting hammered. Nervous depositors might make a run on the bank. During the middle of the meeting, Rosone returned to his private office to take a telephone call. It was Leemans who had managed to get a meeting with Marcinkus soon after the archbishop had returned to Rome. Leemans had again insisted that the IOR live up to the promises in its patronage letters and guarantee the repayment of the ghost companies' debt. Again he had floated the idea of a one-billion-dollar bailout loan. Marcinkus proved no more receptive than Mennini and de Strobel. The IOR would not consider any deal in which the church accepted responsibility for even a dime of the ghost company loans.

"You realize what this means?" asked Leemans. "When I leave this room I go straight to the telephone, and let the Ambrosiano board know there's nothing else for it; they'll have to call in the Bank of Italy. That means everything about the letters of patronage will have to come out."

"I realize I'm going to have to pay a high price for that, personally," replied Marcinkus.[142]

Rosone and Leemans agreed that without any help from the Vatican they had no alternative but to ask the Bank of Italy to take control of the Ambrosiano. By six that night, Bank of Italy regulators swarmed into the bank's headquarters. Rosone stayed in his office to give some press interviews over the phone, trying to spin the day's developments and to calm the nerves of 39,000 depositors and 4,200 employees. He repeatedly told reporters that it was only a temporary arrangement to help the bank stabilize itself amid a torrent of contradictory rumors. Around 7:15 p.m., while Rosone talked to a journalist from the weekly *L'Espresso*, someone ran in yelling, "Oh my God, she's killed herself!" The "she" was fifty-five-year-old Graziella Teresa Corrocher, Calvi's personal secretary, and an Ambrosiano employee for thirty years. She had evidently leapt out a fourth-floor window.[143] A handwritten note scribbled in a red felt marker was found on her desk. In it, she apologized for any "disturbance I give," but she also castigated Calvi, saying about him, "What a disgrace to run away. May he be cursed a thousand times for the harm he has done to everyone at the bank."[144] Milan's coroner ruled her death a suicide.

That same night, Roberto Calvi died in London. His body hanged from Blackfriars Bridge until its discovery the next morning. The news of his death sent the Ambrosiano's shares tumbling 18 percent before regulators suspended the stock (it never traded again).[145] And the news was barely public when Father Lorenzo Zorza, the priest who had met Carlo Calvi in New York with the Vatican's U.N. envoy, called the Calvi family to offer his services. "I thought maybe they needed my help," Zorza recalled. "I might be able to assist them in some way. We knew a lot of the same people."[146] They refused.[147]

25

"Protect the Source"

The Calvis braced for what they expected would be the complete unraveling of the Ambrosiano and its role with the Vatican. They had enough problems without getting involved further with Father Zorza.

The man on the spot, however, after Calvi's death, was Archbishop Marcinkus. Even the *Chicago Tribune*, normally friendly to the hometown boy, reported, "The plot would do credit to a paperback thriller, but it is less than entertaining to key men in the Vatican who are deeply worried by Archbishop Marcinkus's latest brush with the shadier side of Italy's financial world."[1]

There was little doubt that Marcinkus's long list of Curial enemies, as well as those who resented the IOR's unmatched autonomy, would demand full answers and real reforms.

Il Mondo, a financial weekly, broke the story that Marcinkus and the IOR had given Calvi "guarantees of some of its dealings in South America" (the patronage letters).[2] When the Italian Bankers' Association held its annual meeting in Rome on June 22, 1982, it seemed that everyone was trading gossip about the rumored comfort letters. That same day the parliamentary committee investigating the P2 scandal expanded its probe to encompass Calvi and his businesses (a second committee would soon focus solely on the Ambrosiano). The Calvi family added to the drama by announcing they believed that Roberto Calvi had been murdered.[3]

On Friday, July 2, Beniamino Andreatta, Italy's Treasury Minister, told parliament that he expected no less than "a clear assumption of responsibility on the part of IOR, which appears to have played the part of a de facto partner in certain operations with Banco Ambrosiano."[4] Andreatta, a committed leftist, was not about to allow the church to shirk its responsibilities, as he believed it had done when the Sindona affair had unraveled.[5] He realized there was "practically no way to confront the IOR because of the autonomy it enjoys."[6] So he instead urged the Pope to voluntarily acknowledge the church's responsibility for the $1.2 billion in debt that had led to the Ambrosiano's collapse.

That same day, two Bank of Italy investigators met informally with Marcinkus at the Vatican.[7] The issue was again the patronage letters. Marcinkus repeatedly refused to answer direct questions.[8] But he repeated what Mennini and de Strobel had told the Ambrosiano's Rosone: the secret letter from Calvi absolved the Vatican of any responsibility for the debts listed in those letters. As far as the investigators were concerned, that counter-letter meant that Marcinkus and Calvi had conspired to pull off the scam. Calvi had written his indemnity while serving as the chairman of Ambrosiano Overseas in Nassau, the very company on which Marcinkus sat on the board.[9]

To assuage their obvious irritation, Marcinkus suggested that the Vatican Bank might accept responsibility for a single loan—for an undetermined amount—to the Banco Andino branch in Peru.[10] That was an offer he soon might have wanted back. The following day, a senator, Franco Calamandrei, announced from the floor of Italy's parliament, "A traffic in sophisticated arms to Argentina through the Banco Andino seems to be the last link in the chain of events that led to Mr. Calvi's death beneath Blackfriars Bridge."[11]

The Italian press was in a feeding frenzy, mixing solid reporting with a hodgepodge of anonymously sourced rumors. Milan's *Corriere della Sera* and Turin's daily, *La Stampa*, reported that Secretary of State Casaroli had prevailed on John Paul to convince Marcinkus to resign.[12] According to Milan's *Il Giornale Nuovo* "the pope would appoint Marcinkus as archbishop of Chicago to fill the position left empty since Cardinal John Cody died last April."[13] A Rome tabloid claimed Italian prosecutors were weighing fraud charges against the IOR chief.[14]

"Every day there were more bad headlines in the Italian press," recalled former U.S. Deputy Chief of Mission Michael Hornblow, who was stationed at the Vatican from 1980 to 1983.[15] "It was such a big deal. It was hard to know what was true or not, but there's no doubt that a lot people blamed Marcinkus for the scandal. And there were plenty who were asking why the Pope did not get rid of him."[16]

Marcinkus was not aware that Italy's Treasury Ministry was lobbying hard behind the scenes to get him booted. The Bank of Italy officials who had interviewed him just days earlier had sent John Paul a blunt memo, contending that in order "to avert further embarrassment. . . . It is in the best interests of the Holy See that the Archbishop not remain in a position of suspicion."[17] The recommendation was unofficial since Italy could not advise the Pope, a sovereign head of state, to fire Marcinkus.

On July 7, Marcinkus gave his first public statement since Calvi's death, a few sentences to his hometown newspaper, the *Chicago Tribune*: "I don't resign under these circumstances. I have not been involved in anything that could be considered fraud . . . I am completely unaware of any move by the Holy Father to get rid of me."[18]

A few days later, on July 11, the Vatican announced the appointment of Cincinnati's Archbishop Joseph Bernardin as the acting head of the Chicago diocese (the Pope would give Bernardin a red hat the following year). Church officials hoped that made it clear "that Marcinkus would remain at the Vatican."[19] But it was too subtle a message to slow the media speculation. For the rest of the year there was a steady stream of press stories that Marcinkus was either about to resign or be fired. In November, he again dismissed the rumors as "unfounded," and said, "I don't intend to tender a resignation. I intend to see this thing through to the end."[20]

Secretary of State Casaroli wanted to demonstrate the Vatican was doing more than just being reactive.[21] So his office announced that the church had taken the unusual step of calling in three outside financial experts to examine the Vatican Bank–Ambrosiano dealings.[22] The three laymen were Joseph Brennan, former chairman of New York's Emigrant Savings Bank; Carlo Cerutti, the vice chairman of STET, the communications subsidiary of a large Italian conglomerate; and Philippe de Weck, the former chairman of Union des Banques Suisses.[23] Soon, Hermann Josef Abs, Deutsche Bank's ex-chairman, came on. Their assignment, according to the Vatican's press release, was to "examine the situation" and then to provide "suggestions and advice."

All members of the independent committee were devout Catholics. Vaticanologists had little expectation they might be given adequate investigating powers or that their final report might be made public.[24] Italy's Treasury noted that the committee was "a positive thing."[25] Even those words had been intensely debated, some wanting instead to push openly for Marcinkus to be relieved of his duties.

The first in a series of defaults began in mid-July on a Midland Bank $40 million loan to Luxembourg's Banco Ambrosiano Holdings.[26] That caused a chain reaction of cross-defaults with dozens of other banks.[27] Later that same day the Bahamian government suspended the banking license of the Ambrosiano Overseas and began an official investigation.[28] Eventually, the so-called Gang of 88, the creditor banks to Banco Ambrosiano Holdings, demanded payments of upward of $500 million in bad loans just from that single Calvi offshore subsidiary.[29] The Bank of Italy resisted calls to bail out the Ambrosiano's foreign subsidiaries, even though there were fears it might devolve into an international banking crisis. Instead, on August 6, the Treasury Minister shuttered the Ambrosiano, making the $1.4 billion dollar failure the largest in the country's history.[30]

As Marcinkus and the IOR prepared for what they knew would be intense scrutiny, pressure built about P2 and Sindona. After executing another search warrant, prosecutors found evidence the Masons had been planning a coup.[31] Was it possible that Marcinkus, so closely involved with top P2 members, knew nothing about it? Carlo Calvi told the press that Poland's Solidarity had received money through his father and P2. Marcinkus knew it was only a matter of time until the IOR got dragged into "the money to Solidarity" story.*

On July 22, more bad news broke on a new front. A Milanese judge, Bruno Apicella, indicted Luigi Mennini and Pellegrino de Strobel and twenty-two other defendants for fraudulent bankruptcy and illegal currency trading related to the 1974 collapse of Sindona's Banca Privata.[33] Sindona was among those charged, as was Massimo Spada, the former IOR official and top Sindona aide.[34] Before the month was finished, Luigi D'Osso, an investigating magistrate, sent comunicati giudiziari (judicial communiqués) to the Vatican informing Marcinkus, Mennini, and de Strobel that they were material witnesses in the criminal probe into the Ambrosiano's collapse.[35] The Vatican refused to accept that notice since the Italians had not sent it through diplomatic channels.[36]

With all the bad press and flurry of charges and countercharges, even some of Marcinkus's best friends sometimes worried about whether he might

---

* "[Calvi] never talked to me about Solidarity," Marcinkus later claimed. "I never sat down and talked specifics with him in any sense. He never mentioned Solidarity to me at all. If he gave something to Solidarity, okay, but I don't know anything about it."[32]

have crossed some legal line. One of them, William Wilson, then Ronald Reagan's personal envoy to the Vatican, was a convert to Catholicism who was—according to his deputy, Michael Hornblow—"more Catholic than the Pope."[37] Wilson was one of Reagan's closest friends, the head of his informal kitchen cabinet, and a co-trustee of Nancy and Ronald Reagan's living trust.[38] He had lobbied hard to get the Vatican assignment even though he could have chosen a far more prestigious foreign service posting. Although he was a businessman and not a politician or diplomat, Wilson's instincts were good. He was convinced that with the first Pope ever from an Iron Curtain country, the Vatican might be a far more important ally to Cold Warrior Reagan than anyone imagined.[39]

Wilson settled into Rome in February 1981. Before long he described Marcinkus as "a very good friend."[40] "We saw Marcinkus a lot," Hornblow, the Deputy Chief of the U.S. Mission, recalled. "Marcinkus was number one on our list of people to whom we wanted to talk as much as possible. He saw the Pope the most often. He was a great gossip and storyteller."[41]

Disclosed here for the first time, soon after Wilson's arrival in Rome, Marcinkus became a confidential source of information to the U.S. mission at the Vatican.* State Department files declassified to the author reveal that Marcinkus even provided U.S. officials with personal details about the Pope. The documents lay out plans by Marcinkus—at the behest of embassy officials—to encourage John Paul to publicly endorse American positions on a broad range of political issues, including: the war on drugs; the guerrilla fighting in El Salvador; bigger defense budgets; the Soviet invasion of Afghanistan; and even Reagan's ambitious missile defense shield.[42]

Although Vatican finances dominated the public news, U.S. embassy officials did not ask the archbishop about that since Washington was not inter-

---

* The secret relationship between Marcinkus and the ambassador's office was revealed as part of this author's Freedom of Information request to the State Department, in which forty-two documents constituting 160 pages were released on August 15, 2007. Among those documents, for instance, is an October 1, 1980, cable from Ambassador Wilson's assistant, the embassy's Deputy Chief, Michael Hornblow, to State Department headquarters, in which Marcinkus provided private details about the Pope's upcoming East Asia trip. Near the top of the document, marked "Secret," Hornblow wrote, "He [Marcinkus] revealed the following information to me in strict confidence and it is of the utmost importance that Marcinkus as the source of the information be strictly protected." The State Department never had a higher-ranking confidential source of information inside the Vatican than the American-born bishop.

ested. The focus was only politics. Marcinkus discussed with them the Vatican's take on Eastern Europe, Lebanon, the Philippines, and a territorial dispute between Argentina and Chile. And he shared his belief that America should encourage Italy's socialists to break their alliance with the communists and move toward the political center. He warned Wilson and Hornblow that the Christian Democrats had lost "credibility with the people" and would only regain it if they got "rid of scandal and corruption."[43] Marcinkus even agreed on one occasion—the Pope's major 1981 address at Hiroshima about the danger of a nuclear holocaust—to review the speech in advance and try to influence it in a way the Americans desired.[44] When some of Marcinkus's private information was passed along to ambassadors at other U.S. embassies, the cables admonished in bold letters: "Please be sure to protect the source."[45] "The bottom line is he trusted us and we had a good relationship with him," recalls Hornblow.*

The good relationship meant that Wilson widely shared with diplomats, politicians, and prominent Catholics his opinion "that both he [Marcinkus] and the Vatican Bank are innocent of any wrongdoing."[47] Their friendship also helps to explain why Wilson was prepared to make a remarkable intervention in mid-1982, on Marcinkus's behalf, to the Justice Department (a move that would in a couple of years come back to haunt both men). In a three-page typewritten letter dated July 15, 1982, Wilson wrote to his good friend, William French Smith, Reagan's Attorney General. New York publishers Holt Rinehart were about to release a book by Richard Hammer, a true crime author, with the first ever account of the 1973 fraud and counterfeit investigation that prompted the FBI to interview Marcinkus at the Vatican.[48] Wilson told the Attorney General that Marcinkus was "very concerned about the book" since it "will contain large amounts of untrue material concerning him."[49] According to Wilson, Marcinkus was "thinking of filing a lawsuit," but "it would be much better for the Vatican and everyone concerned if the book were not published

* The special relationship between the American embassy and Marcinkus was not always limited to matters of politics and national security. The diplomat who replaced Hornblow, Peter Murphy, got a call once from pop star Michael Jackson, who wanted a private audience with the Pope when he visited Rome as part of a European concert tour. "If I had asked one of the Italians, they would have just said no. So I went to Marcinkus." The IOR chief did not think it a good idea to have the Pope meet with Jackson, but he did arrange for an early morning private tour of the Sistine Chapel. Marcinkus accompanied Jackson and his entourage around Vatican City. When he left the city-state, Jackson gave Marcinkus a sealed envelope. It contained a check for $1 million for Ospedale Pediatrico Bambino Gesù, Rome's best known church-affiliated children's hospital.[46]

at all if it does contain false information." New York's ex-Mayor Robert Wagner was Wilson's predecessor at the Vatican. Wilson informed Smith that he had already urged Marcinkus to also discuss his options with Wagner.

Wilson's letter included an extraordinary eight-page attachment that purported to summarize the charges against Marcinkus. On the first page of his letter, Wilson wrote that the attachment "was handed to me in London last week." On the next page he stated that Marcinkus "has given me the enclosed letter and its attachments." If it were Marcinkus who gave him the attachment in London it would be noteworthy since Calvi had been found dead in the British capital only a few weeks earlier. (Wilson wrote to Smith, "More lately, you will recall, a Mr. Calvi was found hanging from the Black Friars [*sic*] Bridge in London.")[50]

Wilson assured the Attorney General that the accusations against Marcinkus were based on "innuendo and, possibly, even by association" since the IOR owns "1.5% of the common stock of Banco Ambrosiano" and Marcinkus served as a director of a Nassau-based subsidiary.

"It is my personal opinion and certainly my sincere hope that Marcinkus will, again, survive this."[51]

Then Wilson got to the reason for his letter: a hope that the archbishop be allowed to "review the FBI files for any information they might contain concerning discussions between the FBI agents and Marcinkus." Wilson asked the Attorney General to "supply him with a summary of what the files contain" and that "would be helpful to him and appreciated by both him and myself." The ambassador suggested he "would prefer not to be involved in the matter." It should be resolved between Marcinkus and the Justice Department.

Wilson's direct intervention with a sitting U.S. Attorney General over a possible target of a Justice Department criminal investigation was unprecedented. If made public, it put Wilson at the risk of an obstruction-of-justice charge. Attorney General Smith directed his special assistant, John Roberts, to respond to Wilson the following month. Roberts made it clear that Justice would not entertain any special accommodation for Marcinkus "in such a sensitive area." If the archbishop hoped to see anything in the bureau's files about himself, Roberts suggested that Marcinkus follow the same procedure as any other American citizen and submit a Freedom of Information request.[52]

Wilson was not finished. He wrote to the IOR chief one day after receiving the Roberts brushoff, and tried to make light of the need for Marcinkus to make a FOIA request: "Thank heavens we still have some privacy privileges left in this country." He went on to describe the three conversations he had with former New York mayor and Vatican envoy Robert Wagner. In each instance, Wilson pushed Wagner to use his influence to stop the publication of Hammer's book. Wagner had sent a letter from his New York law firm—Finley, Kumble, Wagner—demanding that Marcinkus have an opportunity to review the manuscript prior to publication.[53] He also spoke to Holt Rinehart's president about possibly delaying the publication. Wagner was rebuffed in both instances.[54] That had not dissuaded Wagner, who planned to meet with the Holt Rinehart president "to try to really get down to business to see what the implications would be for the publishing company if they went ahead with the book or what could be done to modify its contents."[55]

Wilson assured Marcinkus: "Bob's desire is to try to settle this matter in a friendly fashion rather than to become involved in litigation, however, from the way he spoke I get the feeling he is ready to put on the gloves if need be."

After the next meeting Holt Rinehart accelerated the book's debut by a month from October to September.[56] As part of its publicity campaign it ran national newspaper ads describing *The Vatican Connection* as "The astonishing account of a billion-dollar counterfeit stock deal between the Mafia and the Church." *The Vatican Connection* added to the perception that Marcinkus was up to no good in his Vatican post. *Newsweek*'s review: "If the charges that Archbishop Paul Marcinkus oversaw a decade-old scheme to obtain millions of dollars worth of counterfeit securities for the Vatican . . . are true, they can only add to the controversy surrounding the archbishop."[57] As far as Wilson was concerned, he remained convinced that Marcinkus would emerge from his problems "without any long-term bruises" but that "it may take a little longer."[58]

26

"A Heck of a Lot of Money"

The bad news kept coming the rest of 1982. Eight days after the notice that the lay IOR officials were under criminal investigation, Flavio Carboni was arrested in Switzerland. There was an outstanding warrant for him because of his role in aiding Calvi's flight to London. When the Swiss police searched his car they found documents in his briefcase revealing that the Ambrosiano had paid Carboni some $20 million in less than a year. Most of that had ended up in Swiss bank accounts controlled by Carboni and a few business associates.[1]

On Monday, September 13, Licio Gelli was arrested at the main Geneva branch of Union Bank. He was trying to transfer $55 million.[2] It was such a large amount that the bank had insisted he come in person. Two policemen were waiting. He presented them with an Argentine passport in a different name. By now, the fugitive Gelli had dyed his silver hair brown, grown a bushy mustache, and abandoned his trademark glasses. But once the police began questioning him at the local station, he admitted his identity.[3] When the Swiss announced his capture that evening, the Italian news was captivated with a new round of speculation about P2, Calvi's corpse, and the Vatican's silence.

As 1982 closed, Pope John Paul told a gathering of the Sacred College of Cardinals that the church's trust had been abused. He pledged that the Vatican would do whatever was necessary to bring the entire truth about the Ambrosiano to light.[4] What no one then knew was that the prestigious panel of four financiers already had a preliminary report. They concluded that the IOR had owned or controlled ten of Calvi's ghost companies, but absolved Marcinkus of any blame and instead put the responsibility on Calvi, determining that he had exploited his less sophisticated Vatican Bank colleagues.[5] It was because of

Calvi's chicanery, they contended, that the IOR did not realize it had become the owner of the ghost companies now at the crux of the scandal.[6] Marcinkus himself would have been hard pressed to write a better report. (Soon he had a new stock answer to deflect questions about the $1.2 billion in loans listed in the patronage letters: "All I can say is that it's a heck of a lot of money.")[7]

The Vatican Bank chief seemed unbowed when questioned by the panel of fifteen cardinals appointed by John Paul. The IOR was only an intermediary, not a real owner of anything, he insisted. Some of the cardinals criticized him for running the Vatican Bank without adequate checks and balances. And there were heated discussions about what to recommend to the Pope. Ultimately the clerics backed the IOR's beleaguered chief and deputies.[8] They did urge that the Vatican Bank curtail its financial speculation, and that it also introduce balance sheets that could be distributed to other Curial divisions.[9]

The Vatican needed to demonstrate it was serious about addressing whatever shortfalls had led to the Ambrosiano mess. The idea had taken hold in some of Italy's leftist press that Marcinkus was merely the chief of "an offshore bank in the center of Rome."[10] A nine-member parliamentary panel investigating P2, directed by Senator Tina Anselmi, had expanded into the Calvi and Sindona affairs because both financiers were Masons. They had questions for the IOR. So did separate parallel parliamentary investigations into Calvi and Sindona that were under way.[11] *

On Christmas Eve, a joint Italian-Vatican commission composed of lawyers and bankers was established. To most outsiders, it appeared to be yet another in a growing number of competing probes to find out what had happened. But Marcinkus and other insiders knew its real purpose was to start negotiations over how much the Vatican might have to pay to settle the mess.[13]

On December 29, the Los Angeles–based center named after famed Nazi hunter Simon Wiesenthal charged that Hermann Abs, the Deutsche Bank chairman appointed to the special advisory panel, had been a high-level Nazi collaborator. Rabbi Marvin Heir, head of the Wiesenthal Center, issued a press release in which he asked the Vatican to remove Abs from the committee.[14]

---

* In early December, Italian newspapers ran front-page stories about Clara Calvi's charge that her husband's "murder" was "to hide the fact" that the IOR "was bankrupt." A few months earlier she had said the motive was to hide the "risky operation" her husband had undertaken to arrange "the assumption of the IOR debts by Opus Dei."[12]

The charge hit the church unawares. No one inside the city-state had done a background check on someone with such solidly Catholic credentials and respected standing inside Germany's business sector.

Abs told the Vatican that he had not been a Nazi Party member. In 1972, he claimed, a Stuttgart court awarded him $8,400 from an East German author and a Cologne publisher who charged he had seized Jewish property during World War II and given it to the Nazis. A spokesman for Deutsche Bank also dismissed the charges, saying "Hermann Abs does not respond to slander."[15] But Heir was not dissuaded. He released to the press, and mailed to the Vatican, a 360-page, 1946 U.S. Military Government report that listed Abs on the board of "26 important industrial companies and 14 banking institutions" during the war.[16]

It was evident that despite being on the defensive for a year over the Sindona, P2, and Calvi scandals, the Vatican had learned little about crisis management and handling the media. It took the church more than a week to respond, and then it was only a telephone call from Monsignor Jorge Mejía, the secretary of the poorly named Secretariat of Relations with Jews. He asked the Wiesenthal Center to produce more evidence. The press-savvy Heir on the other hand had barely gotten off the phone with Monsignor Mejía before calling reporters and complaining about the Vatican delay.[17]

The Wiesenthal Center had by now leveled more charges, including that Abs had personally benefited from expropriation of Polish and Jewish property and that he had attended I. G. Farben director's meetings at which both slave labor and Auschwitz were discussed. Father John Pawlikowski, a prominent American theologian, urged the Vatican to "fully investigate" the "accusations against Mr. Abs."[18] As with the major financial probes under way in Italy, the Vatican was hesitant to provide any fresh information, engage its critics, or address issues as they became public.

The church did not like playing by the Wiesenthal Center rules that everything that went on between them also went to the press. After Monsignor Mejía's request for more evidence was leaked to reporters, the Vatican stayed silent. That also did not work well. On January 11, almost two weeks after the story broke, the Wiesenthal Center announced that a research group had pieced together testimony before a 1945 Senate subcommittee, as well as information from a 1979 biography of Pope John Paul II, to conclude that Abs had been an executive at the company that ran the stone quarry where the Nazis had forced Polish prisoners, including the future Pope, to work breaking rocks during the war.[19]

As with Marcinkus, the worse the news, the more the church seemingly rallied around Abs. That outsiders wanted him out was more reason for the Vatican to resist. Reporters were not certain whether Pope John Paul was referring to Marcinkus, Abs, or both, when he told them in February that "Your faith must be stronger than what you read in the newspapers, especially in this difficult age. . . . I too read the newspapers. You can read many incredible things in newspapers that have no truth in them."[20] That April, John Paul visited Los Angeles as part of his North American tour. He met with Rabbi Heir and twenty-nine other members of the Wiesenthal Center.

"I made a direct appeal to him, both to remove Abs," Heir recalled, "as well as to issue an unequivocal message condemning anti-Semitism. It was long overdue, and this was the right time."[21] John Paul had spoken out about anti-Semitism during a 1979 visit to Auschwitz and again after the terrorist bombing of a Rome synagogue in 1982.[22] But both fell short of what many Jews thought was necessary to make up for centuries of abusive treatment at the hands of Roman Catholics.

The Pope declined to remove Abs.

"That is a moral travesty," said Heir. And Heir was "disappointed" that while the Pope said Jews and Christians should work together "to deepen their bonds of friendship," he did not issue a clear denunciation of anti-Semitism.[23]

All of the missed opportunities merely amplified that—as one journalist later called it—the Vatican's "public relations operation [was in] the dark ages."[24]

Marcinkus and the IOR, desperate for a top-grade crisis manager, unfortunately knew that better than most.

27

"I've Been Poisoned!"

Whether the scandal swirling around the IOR would kill a red hat for Marcinkus was answered that January (1983). John Paul appointed eighteen cardinals from six continents, including five from Communist-controlled countries.[1] Among the high-profile selections were Chicago's well-liked Archbishop Joseph Bernardin; the Patriarch of Lebanon's Maronite Christians; and a Parisian bishop who was born a Polish Jew but raised a Catholic after the Nazis killed his mother at Auschwitz.[2] The *Chicago Tribune* said of Marcinkus that "a year ago [he was] to be almost sure of promotion" and that as "the governor of Vatican City . . . [his] job virtually assures cardinal rank."[3] "Archbishop Marcinkus may have been passed over because of his administration of the Vatican Bank," noted *The New York Times*, "which has been a subject of controversy."[4]

John Paul had not passed over Marcinkus because of all the bad ink. He believed the IOR chief had made mistakes only from good intentions and that the press had unfairly mauled him. But he could not give Marcinkus a red hat since the run of bad news about the Vatican Bank was not over. Only a handful of insiders knew that the Vatican was a few weeks into intense negotiations with Italian officials and a consortium of international banks about possibly settling its liability in the Ambrosiano debacle. The church had appointed three men that past Christmas Eve—Agostino Gambino, a prominent lawyer who had represented Sindona; Pellegrino Capaldo, a university professor; and Father Renato Dardozzi, a cleric who worked in the Secretariat of State—to represent the Vatican.[5] The trio hashed out the broad outlines of a palatable settlement.[6] It was clear that the church would have to write a large check to make its problems go away. Worse, the Vatican had just clocked a $30 million budget deficit.[7] To raise cash, John Paul declared that an extraordinary Holy Year Jubilee would start on Ash Wednesday (February 16) and run for fourteen months. Millions of the faithful would flock to Rome hoping for special indulgences and the chance of an audience with the Pope.[8] The Jubilee also meant that tens of millions of dollars would flow into Vatican coffers, donations for everything from the sale of souvenirs to "pilgrim's packets" complete with maps and walking tours. The Pontiff's designation of a Holy Year caught many by surprise. The last one had been only eight years earlier. For more than six centuries, the church held them only every twenty-five or fifty years.[9] But John Paul followed the precedent set by some early Pontiffs who called Jubilees out of sequence whenever the church was in dire financial straits.[10]

Not even the excitement over the Holy Year, however, could obscure the continuing bad news about the IOR. Only a few days before the Jubilee's opening ceremonies, prosecutors in Turin announced that Monsignor Donato De Bonis, the IOR's secretary and second-ranking prelate, was under investigation in a multimillion-dollar gasoline tax-avoidance scheme. By the time De Bonis's name entered the scandal, dozens of Italian businessmen and government tax officials had pled guilty.[11] A judge took the unprecedented step of blocking the cleric from using his Vatican passport at any Italian airport or seaport.[12]

De Bonis was a trusted aide to Marcinkus. He had started working at the Vatican Bank in 1954 when he was only twenty-nine years old, and spent the first sixteen years of his career as the protégé of the IOR's chief prelate, Cardinal Alberto di Jorio. When Marcinkus rose to power in 1970, he relied on veterans like De Bonis.[13]

De Bonis so enjoyed working at the Vatican Bank that he passed on an appointment as an auxiliary bishop to Genoa so that he could instead remain inside the Tower of Nicholas V.[14] As the bank's secretary, he had cosigned some key documents for Calvi's companies, including Intermax, United Trading, and Suprafin. He and the IOR's accountant, Pellegrino de Strobel, had signed off on most of the questionable Calvi transactions, including an inflated $60 million partial sale of Vianini, a Vatican-owned company. Italian prosecutors later heatedly debated indicting De Bonis as an accessory to fraudulent bankruptcy in the Ambrosiano collapse. They concluded, however, he was a mere functionary and not a substantive decision maker.[15]

But now that De Bonis was under investigation in the fuel tax scheme, it added to the perception that the Vatican Bank had systematic problems.[16] Marcinkus's image was further under siege in "God's Banker," a *Frontline* documentary that aired to huge audiences in the United States and Britain in February 1983. It introduced millions of viewers to the scandal.[17] It was not long before the top-rated U.S. TV news program, *60 Minutes*, investigated the unfolding crisis. Reporter Mike Wallace spent several on-air minutes telephoning Marcinkus's office, only to be given an ever-changing, evasive runaround by the archbishop's secretary.[18] (Some credited *Frontline* with encouraging a British court the following month to overturn the suicide finding in Calvi's death and order a new inquest.)[19]

Top clerics worried that the steady drumbeat of scandal had begun souring the public about the church. When Italy forced the Ambrosiano into compulsory liquidation, it transferred the bank's remaining good assets to a new bank (Nuovo Banco Ambrosiano). Since the government underwrote the venture, taxpayers were furious they got stuck with a $700 million bill.[20] Opinion polls showed many Italians blamed the church.

In March, the IOR responded to the joint commission's many requests for records and financial ledgers by releasing eleven thin files of internal documents that addressed in the vaguest terms its relationship to the ghost companies in the letters of patronage. It was the first time the Vatican Bank ever produced private files for the investigators of another sovereign. And that was the result of a hard-fought compromise to an Italian demand that forensic accountants be allowed direct access to the IOR archives.[21] The Vatican's limited cooperation did not prove helpful to the joint commission, whose work was already hobbled by resistance from some major banks entangled with the Ambrosiano, including the Gottardo, Cisalpine, and Kredietbank. The commission was also stymied in accessing 1,500 pages of Calvi's working papers as a Bahamian court had frozen a safe deposit box in Nassau's Roywest Bank.

The biggest obstacle confronting the joint commission, however, was that the Vatican had refused to allow Italian investigators to question Marcinkus, Mennini, and de Strobel.[22] Hoping the church might change its mind, the commission twice postponed its original March 31 deadline. An intense struggle inside the Vatican about whether the three officials should cooperate played out during the spring of 1983.[23] The compromise was a July 1, twenty-two-page memorandum signed by Marcinkus that claimed to be a "detailed description of the relationships at issue."[24] To the great disappointment of investigators, the Marcinkus memo—prepared under the close supervision of

Vatican attorneys—provided little new information. It was mostly a defiant reargument of his long-standing contention that the bank did not have any responsibility for the Ambrosiano collapse.*

The joint commission hoped that Licio Gelli, the former P2 chief who was under arrest in a Swiss prison, might help unravel the mess in return for leniency on charges he faced in Italy. That was dashed on August 9 when several prison guards Gelli had bribed helped him escape. He was driven to Monte Carlo hidden in the back of a van. From there, he traveled on a fake passport to South America, taking with him many of the documents on the commission's wish list.[26]†

The joint commission was frustrated at every turn. In the preamble to its subsequent report, the members agreed, "What has emerged is a complicated web of facts, documents and opinions, from which it was extremely difficult to distinguish truth from falsehood."[28] Compounding the problem, by late summer 1983, Italian and Vatican negotiators were sharply divided. The church-appointed commissioners were unwavering that there was no evidence proving the IOR was the real owner of the ghost companies. The Vatican Bank, they argued, was an innocent "intermediary." Their position was summarized in an August memo to Secretary of State Casaroli, concluding that Calvi had taken advantage of Marcinkus.[29]

The Italians meanwhile thought that the Vatican Bank and its top officials were knowing partners in the scheme. Two—lawyer Alberto Santa Maria and corporate finance professor Mario Cattaneo—were hard-liners, contending that the "IOR's knowledge of the decisions and arrangements adopted . . . was both continuous and constant."[30] The duo admitted there was no smoking gun, but they were convinced a preponderance of the evidence buttressed that

---

* In June, a fifteen-year-old girl, Emanuela Orlandi, disappeared after leaving her family's Vatican City apartment for a music class. She was never found and theories about her disappearance have gripped Italy for decades. In 2008, a mistress of a deceased Mafia don stunned authorities by claiming that her former lover's gang had kidnapped the girl. According to this account, the mobster had been procuring young girls for sadistic sex parties at Marcinkus's request. Since police could not substantiate her claim, her story serves as an odd footnote to the Marcinkus tale.[25]

† Gelli evaded capture for four years before being nabbed and returned to Italy. There, tried on numerous charges, he was convicted of fraud in the Ambrosiano collapse. He again disappeared in 1998 from the confines of house arrest. He was returned to Italy the following year after being tracked down to the South of France. Incredibly, a judge ordered him returned to house arrest.[27]

conclusion. The third, Christian Democrat chief Pasquale Chiomenti, feared that too hard a stance against the church might prevent the two sides from ever reaching a deal. He moderated his colleagues' view of the Vatican Bank's role.[31]

Chiomenti had a well-deserved reputation as an adept mediator. He feared that any deal struck by Italy with the creditor banks—clamoring for some $600 million—would fail if it did not include the Vatican. The banks had indicated that if they could not get a decent offer from the Vatican, they would sue the church in multiple jurisdictions.[32] Through most of the summer of 1983, Chiomenti was crestfallen that the negotiations had stalled in a nasty round of mutual recrimination.[33]

On August 10, at a country house near Lucca, Chiomenti met with Ted Sturmer, a senior partner at the British law firm that represented National Westminster, one of the lead creditors. After several intense hours they had agreed that the banks should be repaid 70 percent of their losses.[34] In return, both men decided to work on persuading the Vatican to pay as much of that as possible. They knew it would not be easy, but the carrot they offered the church was freedom from all lawsuits as well as no need to be publicly contrite or to admit any responsibility for the Ambrosiano affair.

Inside the Curia a fiery debate raged about how much, if anything, the church should offer to end the scandal. Marcinkus was firm that it should not pay a single cent. "You're crazy!" he said. "Don't even open up that conversation. If we're not guilty, we don't pay. And we're not guilty. . . . If you're preaching the truth, you've got to fight for it."[35]

Although the IOR chief was not fazed by the possibility of years of costly litigation, at times in jurisdictions that might subject the church to embarrassing discovery, it frightened many top clerics. Marcinkus, it seemed, was the only one in a fighting mood.

The following month, when Secretary of State Casaroli met with the leaders of Italy's newly elected socialist-led coalition, he made the church's first settlement offer. Casaroli said that even if the church sold some assets, the most it could pay was $140 million. Although it was a huge amount for an institution that had long insisted it owed nothing, it was also far less than what the creditors demanded. That offer was rejected. Casaroli dispatched more firepower into the negotiations with his committee of "wise money men": ex–Emigrant

Savings Bank CEO Joseph Brennan; Carlo Cerutti, the vice chairman of the telecommunications giant STET; and Philippe De Weck, a Union des Banques Suisses director (the controversial Hermann Josef Abs had resigned by then).

After several meetings with the creditors, the trio advised the church to bump its figure by $10 million and insist it was "not negotiable."[36] The no-more-negotiating stance crumbled within a couple of weeks when the church raised its offer to $160 million. The creditors did not budge. Despite pressure from Italy, the Vatican fell silent. Delay was second nature to a bureaucracy that thought in terms of centuries instead of years.

The following March the stakes became much higher. Milan's State Prosecutor, Maurizio Grigo, sent letters to Marcinkus, Mennini, and de Strobel, notifying them they were formal targets of a criminal investigation into an $86 million 1972 Vatican Bank loan to Milanese holding company Italmobiliare.[37] Prosecutors contended the loan was designed to hide illegal kickbacks between church officials and financier Carlo Pesenti, who was Italmobiliare's president as well as the Ambrosiano's largest shareholder.[38] To avoid the problem they had confronted the previous year when the Vatican refused to accept judicial communiqués for Marcinkus and his two lay assistants, this time prosecutors submitted their "notice of investigation" through formal diplomatic channels at the Italian Foreign Ministry.[39]

The day it arrived at the Vatican, Marcinkus told reporters, "I will have nothing to hide from the Italian judges, especially because the operation [loan] was carried out in the most absolute normality."[40] But no matter how brave a front Marcinkus put on, the criminal probe was a terrible turn of events.

The prosecutors were weighing fraudulent bankruptcy charges against the archbishop and his top aides. Italian law allowed those who suffered damages in civil matters to attach themselves as additional parties to the criminal proceedings. The creditors had so far declined to do that. They feared it might hurt their chances of reaching an out-of-court settlement with the IOR. If those negotiations failed, however, the creditors had unanimously decided to hitch their fortunes to any criminal prosecution and immediately move to obtain court orders freezing all Vatican Bank assets inside Italy.

The news kicked off a new round of speculation about whether Marcinkus could hold on to his Vatican Bank post. In April, John Paul announced seventeen significant Curial reforms, a shake-up that Italian newspapers called *il terremoto* (the earthquake).[41] By shuffling some of the bureaucracy's top prelates and appointing reformers, the Pope hoped to weaken the Curia's stranglehold on power and to make it less Italian.[42] The reorganization was the first signal that Marcinkus's power was on the decline. In the reworked Curia, he no longer had unchecked administrative powers as governor of Vatican City.[43]

Possible fallout from the criminal probe dominated the church's internal debate over how much money to offer the Ambrosiano creditors. If Marcinkus and his top aides were found criminally liable, it would open the floodgates to huge civil liability. Marcinkus still tried rallying his colleagues. He contended that it was hypocritical for them to say the church was short of money and plead for contributions during the Holy Jubilee, and then at the same time make a massive payout to settle the Ambrosiano. "How is it you're telling everybody you've got no money [but] you're paying out money you don't owe?" he argued. If the church paid anything, he charged, it would be "just throwing it out the window" and create a permanent "stigma."[44] As for proposed settlement language that would require the church accept only moral responsibility, Marcinkus was incensed. It would fool no one, he said, but simply mean "we must be guilty."[45]

Marcinkus was outvoted. Pope John Paul personally overrode his objections.[46] In early May, the Vatican and 120 creditor banks announced a deal. The church agreed to pay a stunning $244 million as a "voluntary contribution" to acknowledge its "moral involvement" with the Ambrosiano.[47] The paperwork was executed on May 25 in Rome, with De Bonis and a glum Marcinkus signing on behalf of the IOR.[48] The 161-page agreement absolved the Vatican Bank of all culpability.[49] It also granted Italian courts exclusive jurisdiction for resolving any disputes over its terms. It was the first time the Vatican had allowed the Italian judiciary to have control over any of its affairs.[50]

Although the quarter-billion-dollar payoff was only a fifth of what the IOR was committed to by the letters of patronage, it was a body blow to the city-state. It came on top of what some investigators believed were tens of millions in losses from worthless investments in the wake of the Ambrosiano's collapse.[51] The settlement consumed half of all the Vatican's cash, forcing it to sell its remaining $35 million stake in Vianini, one of Italy's premier construction conglomerates, as well as to borrow heavily from London banks, and to unload some stocks and real estate in France and America.[52] In exchange for some wide-ranging modifications demanded by the socialist government to the church's 1929 concordat, Italy agreed to underwrite the remainder of the $406 million settlement.[53]

The changes to the concordat would have once been unthinkable. The church dropped its insistence that Roman Catholicism be the state religion. Moving forward, the state had to confirm church-annulled marriages. Parents were given the right to opt their children out of formerly mandatory religious education classes. And Rome was no longer considered a "sacred city," a classification that had allowed the Vatican to keep out strip clubs and the porn industry. Italy even managed to get the church to relinquish control of the Jewish catacombs. "The new concordat is another example of the diminishing hold of the Roman Catholic church in civil life in Italy," noted *The New York Times*.[54]

In return, Italy instituted an"eight-per-thousand" tax, in which 0.8 percent of the income tax paid by ordinary Italians was distributed to one of twelve religious organizations recognized by the state. During its early years, nearly 90 percent of the tax went to the Catholic Church (by 2010, the church received less than 50 percent as the tax was more equitably distributed). Not only did the tax relieve Italy of its responsibility for the $135 million annual subsidy it paid for the country's 35,000 priests, it meant the church had a steady and reliable source of much needed income.[55]

The eight-per-thousand tax was the only glimmer of good news for the Vatican. Despite the massive Ambrosiano settlement, Marcinkus and the IOR continued getting bad ink. On June 9, just weeks after the Vatican had struck its historic deal, the press was consumed by a prepublication leak about David Yallop's book *In God's Name*, charging that a six-man clerical cabal that included Marcinkus had murdered John Paul I. Although the church believed the book was nonsense, Yallop's front-page disclosures—about the purported reasons some might have wanted John Paul I out of the way—seemed credible to casual readers.[56] *In God's Name* changed in part the lay perception of Marcinkus from a wayward IOR director with shady friends to someone now thought capable of murdering a Pope to preserve his power.

The following month a leak from the Justice Department fueled headlines about Ambassador William Wilson's two-year-old intervention for Marcinkus with U.S. Attorney General William French Smith. A few months earlier, Ronald Reagan had overcome political opposition to establish formal relations with the Holy See and upgrade the U.S. legation to the Vatican into a small but full-fledged embassy. Now it was caught in its first firestorm.[57] Reagan stood firm and resisted calls to relieve Wilson of his post.[58]

Although it was Wilson who took the public heat for misusing his influence, that the American ambassador to the Vatican thought Marcinkus might be under a U.S. criminal investigation was strong evidence of how low the IOR chief's stock had fallen.*

In late August, about a month after the Wilson news broke, an Associated Press wire service story titled "Career of Once Powerful American Prelate in Decline" was widely picked up.[60] It noted that just two years earlier Marcinkus had been "the most powerful American in the Vatican." An unidentified archbishop was quoted saying that the Pope was "reluctant to slap him down." Instead, church officials had "applied the typical Roman solution" of isolating him and limiting his power.[61]

It seemed possible that the Pope might "slap him down" the following month when rumors swirled that Italmobiliare's president, Carlo Pesenti, struck a deal with Italian prosecutors to tell a court about the hidden details of an $86 million IOR loan that Pesenti had repaid at a staggering 300 percent interest. The persistent gossip was that in exchange for his cooperation, prosecutors had agreed to drop a probe into whether Pesenti had illegally obtained some of his enormous Ambrosiano stake. But Marcinkus's luck had not run out. The day before the seventy-seven-year-old Pesenti was to appear in court, he collapsed while meeting with his attorney. He was pronounced dead of a heart attack a few hours later at a hospital.[62]

No matter how low a profile Marcinkus adopted, he could not manage to stay out of the news. The month after Pesenti's death, after years of high-stakes legal wrangling, Michele Sindona was extradited to Italy.[63] His return, under heavy guard, was major news in Italy. Since there was little new to initially report, newspapers and magazines filled space by rehashing stale stories about the Sicilian financier and his unprecedented role as Pope Paul VI's hand-selected banker.[64]

At Sindona's sensational trial, the Vatican seemed to be a missing unindicted co-conspirator. There were weeks of uncomfortable testimony about how the IOR lost millions through its Banca Unione investments. The following March (1985), Sindona's conviction for fraud and his fifteen-year sentence prompted many legal analysts to wonder why no one else, especially Mar-

---

* Wilson resigned in 1986 after it was disclosed that he had an unauthorized secret meeting with Libyan leader Colonel Muammar Gaddafi.[59]

cinkus, had paid a price for the more than $200 million in financial misdeeds exposed at the trial.[65]

The extradition treaty by which the United States sent Sindona to Italy required that he finish his prison term in America before starting his Italian sentence. But Italy wanted to keep him so they could file charges in the 1979 murder of Giorgio Ambrosoli, the court-appointed liquidator of his Italian banking empire. The U.S. Justice Department agreed. Another widely covered trial and more unwanted coverage of the salacious history of the Vatican Bank–Sindona partnership ensued. In 1986, almost a year after his fraud conviction, a panel of six jurors and two judges returned a guilty verdict on the murder charge. Sindona got a life sentence.[66] The drama was not yet over. Just two days later, after he was served breakfast in his private cell in a specially constructed high-security prison wing, Sindona stumbled from the bathroom and staggered toward the front of the cell, gasping, *"Sono stato avvelenato, Sono stato avvelenato!"* (I've been poisoned, I've been poisoned).[67] He collapsed. By the time doctors arrived a few minutes later he had slipped into an irreversible coma. He died two days later.[68]

The police lab pinpointed a lethal dose of cyanide as the cause of death. Investigators later determined that nearly a gram of the poison was in his espresso.[69] Many thought his death suspicious, especially legal insiders who knew that prosecutors had secretly offered a significant reduction in Sindona's life sentence in return for his cooperation on everything from P2 to Calvi to Mafia money laundering. To prevent suicide or foul play, his jailers had monitored him by video around the clock, as well as deploying twelve guards who worked in shifts (three on duty at all times). Sindona's meals were prepared in a special section of the prison's kitchen, watched over by a guard, and then delivered in sealed metal containers opened only inside his cell.[70] It took eight months for an investigating magistrate to reach a much contested but never disproven conclusion: the jailhouse poisoning was suicide.[71]*

Even the debate over whether Sindona had been murdered became yesterday's news by the following February, 1987. Italian magistrates Antonio Pizzi

---

* Ivan Fisher, the prominent New York criminal defense counsel who had been one of Sindona's attorneys, told the author: "Given what I knew about Michele, I believe that he arranged to have himself poisoned. My entire sense of him, of how his head worked, was that he honestly believed he would beat the fraud and murder charges in Italy and get back his reputation. Once that did not happen, once he realized he was going to just die in prison, I think he decided to take control of his own exit."[72]

and Renato Bricchetti issued a stunning twenty-six-page arrest warrant for Marcinkus, Mennini, and de Strobel, charging them as accessories to fraudulent bankruptcy related to the Ambrosiano's collapse five years earlier.[73] The warrants were based on evidence discovered in a safe deposit box in Lugano's Banca del Gottardo. The incriminating papers revealed the extent to which the IOR and the Ambrosiano had operated the ghost companies. The documents convinced prosecutors that the Vatican was far from the unwitting dupe in the Ambrosiano's demise that it had tried hard to project.[74] The magistrates believed the contents of the safe deposit box were enough to prove that the three Vatican officials had "full knowledge" they had helped Calvi divert the Ambrosiano's funds to worthless foreign shells.

The arrest warrants dominated the news.[75] To the mortification of many inside the Vatican, with the death of Sindona, the press now referred to Marcinkus as "God's banker."[76] Some tabloids ran pictures of him with the banner: "Wanted: Monsignor Marcinkus."[77] The French edition of *Penthouse* ran a salacious story sandwiched between racy photos of naked women. Inside the city-state there was tremendous anger that the Italians had gone so far as to issue criminal indictments. The charges against the archbishop, who held dual American and Vatican passports, put a spotlight on whether Italy had a right to pursue church officials it accused of breaking Italian laws. Mennini and de Strobel were both Italian citizens who lived inside the Vatican.[78] As for Marcinkus, just a couple of days earlier police had shown up at Rome's Villa Stritch, outside the walls of the Vatican. The IOR chief kept a small apartment there and had visited only a couple of hours earlier.[79]

Since there was no extradition treaty between the countries, the Ministry of Justice cited Article 22 of the Lateran Treaties requiring the Vatican turn over those accused of committing crimes inside Italy.[80] Some Justice officials even talked about the remarkable if unlikely scenario of requesting the United States to order the extradition of the American Marcinkus from the Vatican.[81] No one in the church wanted to push the limits of its sovereignty by allowing Marcinkus, Mennini, or de Strobel to leave the city-state and risk an arrest. The three were safe only so long as they stayed inside the walls of the Vatican.[82] The Italians realized that meant they would only get the men if the Pope said yes.

The church's first public response to the indictments was "profound astonishment."[83] Within a few days it adopted an unequivocal position: it had "absolutely no intention" of ever handing over to Italy any cleric or lay official.

"A tough reply from the Vatican to the arrest warrants: Marcinkus will never go to Italian prison," noted *Corriere della Sera.*[84]

Unidentified Vatican officials condemned the warrants as politically motivated by Italy's socialists to embarrass the church.[85] The Vatican contended the prosecutors were powerless, since Article 11 of the Lateran Treaty stated, "Central organs of the Catholic Church are free from every interference on the part of the Italian state."[86] Moreover, the church added that Marcinkus had given "substantial and loyal collaboration" by "producing copious documents and notes" during the five-year probe (although it made no mention that he had refused any interviews or sworn declarations).

John Paul's intuition that Italy's left-of-center coalition would capitalize on the standoff to humiliate the Vatican at every opportunity was right. Police leaked to reporters innovative ways they might arrest the trio. Rome's hospitals were put on notice to summon the carabinieri if any of the wanted men turned up at an ER. Tourists took pictures of a police car parked at the front of the exclusive Aqua Santa country club, just in case Marcinkus tried sneaking in a round of golf. And a policeman checked in regularly at one of the archbishop's favorite Roman restaurants, where the owner got a lot of free publicity by keeping a table vacant for his return.

In the beginning of his self-imposed exile, Marcinkus went daily to a corner of the Vatican gardens and converted it into a makeshift putting green. "And soon one of the Italian cardinals sent him a letter instructing him to 'stop ruining the grass,'" recalls Peter Murphy, the U.S. Deputy Chief of Mission. "There were some of his Italian colleagues who had been waiting a long time to revel in his misfortune."[87]

The media coverage went into overdrive with leaks from more than four hundred pages of "confessions" by Calvi's former fixer, Francesco Pazienza, now dubbed "Deep Throat" by the Italian media.[88] Unsubstantiated stories tied the IOR to everything from millions of dollars spent on phantom consultants to an overpriced Costa Rican farm on which Nicaragua's leftist Sandinistas trained guerrillas.

Fourteen cardinals convened an emergency meeting only a few weeks after the news broke. They had no material say over the standoff with Italy's judiciary. Instead, their task was to find ways to cope with the largest ever Vatican City budget deficit (a $56 million shortfall in 1986, increasing to nearly $80 million in 1987).[89] The $244 million payout to the Ambrosiano creditors had not only left the church with few reserves but the controversy had caused a 75 percent plunge in Peter's Pence.[90] Plus, the dollar's steep slide against the lira meant the church took in even less by the time its American dollar contributions got converted in Italy.[91]

"For all its splendor, the Vatican is nearly broke," noted *Fortune* in a special investigation published that December.[92] A "deep financial squeeze" had resulted from skyrocketing operating expenses and a growing bureaucracy: "The Holy See spent nearly twice as much as its income."[93] In just five years, spending had doubled. Nearly 60 percent of that was labor costs. Pensions were an increasing drain.[94] The normally passive Association of Lay Vatican Employees was griping about abysmally low wages and meager benefits. The Vatican's newspaper, *L'Osservatore Romano*, and its radio station, were hemorrhaging money. One underlying problem highlighted by *Fortune* was that "financial management is practically an act of faith" since the church relied heavily on contributions for its income.

The cardinals reported back to John Paul that restoring the Vatican's tattered image was a priority if there was any chance of encouraging ordinary Catholics to be more generous.[95] If that meant making concessions about Marcinkus, the Pope let them know it was off the table.[96]

Marcinkus continued frustrating the cardinals since he refused to provide them with the IOR's basic operating figures. "The institute never publishes its balance sheets," one anonymous Vatican official told *The New York Times*. "The cardinals have repeatedly asked to see them, but Marcinkus was able to refuse because he enjoyed the confidence and trust of the Pope. . . . When it [the IOR] paid out $240 million, was that half or three-quarters or what percentage of its capital?"[97]

Still, they managed a small breakthrough by Vatican standards. Moving forward from 1987, the Holy See agreed to send out twice-a-year financial statements to the approximately three thousand bishops and heads of religious orders. They were rudimentary and did not include any data from the Vatican Bank. Yet they marked the first time that Rome revealed *any* of its finances to so many clerics. The cardinals thought that since the statements were dismal, those who received them could use the numbers to rally contributions to help the Pope.[98]

The struggle over the degree to which the Vatican Bank would assist the commission of cardinals seemed less pressing at the end of March when Italy made history again in its relations with the church, this time by formally petitioning the Foreign Ministry to request the extradition of the three bank officials.[99] A few days later, John Paul made his first public comments about the matter. During a flight to South America for the start of a two-week tour, the Pontiff walked to the rear of the cabin and held an impromptu news conference with the press corps. He said that the church had studied the case with "competent authorities," taken the matter "seriously," and had determined that it was wrong for Marcinkus to be "attacked . . . in such an exclusive and brutal manner."[100] The Pope's strong words left no doubt that he still believed that Marcinkus, Mennini, and de Strobel were the victims of a media witch-hunt.

As far as the Pope was concerned, Marcinkus was a decent man whose many years of solid work at the IOR had been lost in a deluge of muckraking. There was little doubt that those who worked with him saw a gentler side than the calculating bank chief portrayed in the press. His friends liked to tell how Marcinkus would climb onto scaffolding on scorching summer days to offer water to the construction workers. Or how when Munich's Cardinal Joseph Ratzinger moved to Rome to take charge of the Congregation for the Doctrine of the Faith, Marcinkus surprised him with an entire wardrobe.[101] John Paul sometimes liked retelling a story about the time when an assistant had interrupted a meeting between Marcinkus and American Bishop Robert Lynch. Mother Teresa had arrived unexpectedly at the Vatican Bank and wanted to see Marcinkus. The IOR chief looked to Lynch and smiled: "This visit will cost us a minimum of $1 million." And it almost did. A mattress company wanted to donate twenty thousand mattresses to her Calcutta charity, but she needed money to ship them.[102] It was a shame, thought John Paul, that what he judged as Marcinkus's well-intentioned mistakes had obscured his many good deeds.

"The Pope was not alone in that view," recalls Peter Murphy, the American embassy's number two official at the Vatican during that time. "I, for instance, never thought Marcinkus had made a dime off any of the dealings. The problem was that he had ended up in the wrong job and he did not have the background or ability to cope with some of the sharks with whom he had to swim." Murphy said that he and many of Marcinkus's supporters recognized that it was Mennini who had responsibility for the bank's day-to-day operations. If anyone might be responsible for the IOR's problems, it was likely its senior lay executive. "Marcinkus was not the type of man," Murphy said, "to be anything less than loyal and to take full responsibility for everything that happened under him. But there is no doubt that Mennini was very, very clever. He dealt with all the Italian and international banks and knew everyone in business and politics. Marcinkus was too trusting and just never really understood how that world worked."[103]*

The Pontiff decided to quash the Italian extradition effort with a legal assault challenging Italy's power to make such a request. The church's lawyers petitioned the Tribunale della Libertà, a specialized branch of the judiciary that dealt with such issues. In mid-April, the court stunned Vaticanisti by upholding the warrants.[105]

Any residual hope that the worst might be over was dashed in early May when Milanese prosecutors issued companion arrest warrants for twenty-five former Ambrosiano officers and board members. Nothing better illustrated the low state of Vatican-Italian relations. In the new round of warrants, the magistrates went out of their way to exempt all the accused from being arrested and enduring the humiliation of a perp walk in front of news photographers. Instead, those who lived in Italy had to check in weekly at a police station, and those abroad had to telephone regularly. Italy noted that the new defendants were "not socially dangerous nor possible fugitives."[106] Yet prosecutors offered no such accommodation for Marcinkus, Mennini, and de Strobel. The Italians insisted they were "dangerous" and should be arrested and jailed pending their trial.[107]

The Vatican appealed the adverse ruling to Italy's court of last resort, the Corte Suprema di Cassazione. The church also submitted the question of whether the arrest warrants were valid to its own courts. In mid-June—to no one's surprise—the Vatican judiciary rejected the warrants as groundless and concluded that Italy lacked the authority to issue them.[108]

Some commentators thought the Vatican was hypocritical by resisting Italian jurisdiction in the Ambrosiano case. "When Ali Agca, a Turk, shot Pope

---

* Murphy was sitting with Marcinkus one day when the IOR chief took a call. Marcinkus got angry quickly. "He's a jailbird. What were you thinking? Why did you recommend him?" Within a minute he slammed down the phone. Murphy asked what had happened. An Italian cardinal had recommended a young accountant to take the number two position in the Governorate. Marcinkus had learned that he had a criminal record and had just been released from prison. He demanded to know from the cardinal why he suggested the youngster. "Because he is my sister's son, my nephew," was the answer. "That is so typical of the Italians who made up most of the Curia," Murphy told me. "And there were a lot of them who did not like that Marcinkus applied his American standard of morality when it came to doling out favors, especially to family."[104]

John Paul II in 1981, both the target and the would-be killer were well within Vatican territory," wrote George Armstrong, the respected Rome correspondent for London's *Guardian*. "The Vatican was happy to have him arrested, tried and sentenced in Italy, and under Italian law, and his life sentence will be at the expense of the Italian taxpayer. The Vatican becomes another country only when it chooses to be."[109] Armstrong even put into print a question many were asking privately: "Does the Vatican, or the Holy See, or the Pope, really need a bank of its very own? The Vatican could do its banking anywhere, including in Italy."

During a consistory of cardinals that began on June 28, 1988, there was another heated debate over the IOR. Agostino Gambino, the chairman of the three-person committee who had led the negotiations for the $244 million settlement with the Ambrosiano's creditors, presented a hearty defense of Marcinkus and his tenure. There had been serious blunders, admitted Gambino, but no bad intent. Secretary of State Casaroli thought the mismanagement was so great that the consistory should recommend that the Pope replace his IOR chief.

The cardinals sided with Gambino.[110] The church tapped Monsignor De Bonis to counter some of the terrible press. De Bonis seemed an odd choice since he had been Marcinkus's shadow on many of the questionable IOR transactions with Calvi and Sindona. And he was himself under investigation in a complex tax fraud.[111] Whatever his shortcomings, however, De Bonis made colorful copy. He told *La Repubblica* that the three indicted IOR officials had been framed, "victims of an obscure and complicated situation in which someone, in bad faith, wanted to put the blame on their shoulders and without their knowledge." He assured the reporter that the three had no idea what happened to millions of missing Ambrosiano funds. "It did not end up here [the IOR]."[112] And when pressed about who might have set them up, he offered that "the real culprits are in another place and far from here."[113]

When De Bonis was asked if Vatican officials had confidence that the Italian courts would resolve the standoff over the arrest warrants, he was unwavering. The church had "complete faith" in Italy's highest tribunal.[114] That seemed prescient a few days later when that court concluded that Italy had no jurisdiction since the three IOR officials were members of a "central entity" of the Vatican. It reversed the lower tribunal's verdict and invalidated the arrest warrants.[115] That unequivocal and unappealable decision left the Ambrosiano prosecutors powerless to pursue the trio.[116] Monsignor De Bonis reflected a widely held sentiment inside the Curia: "We've finished a nightmare."[117] When a reporter reached Marcinkus for comment, the beleaguered IOR chief said, "I'm happy. My faith in Italian justice has been restored."[118] And he told a conservative Spanish church daily, *Ya*, that whatever he had done with Calvi had been "a simple error of judgment, but not a crime."[119] Within a week he celebrated by playing a round of golf at the Aqua Santa country club.[120]*

But the Milanese prosecutors were not yet done. In December, they broadsided the church by filing a brief with Italy's Constitutional Court contending that the ruling to exclude Vatican officials from their jurisdiction violated constitutional guarantees of equal justice under law. Antonio Pizzi, the chief prosecutor, advanced a clever argument: the concordat provision invoked by the church was unconstitutional since it created a class of people—high-ranking Vatican officials—who were beyond the reach of the law.[122] Pizzi noted that Italy had recently enacted a series of statutes that gave prosecutors beefed-up powers to seize illicit narcotics proceeds in Italian banks. But under the high court decision, if that same illegal money was deposited by Mafia bosses into Vatican Bank accounts, although it was physically in the heart of Rome, the dirty cash would be off limits to any forfeiture. As a result of the high court ruling, any criminal racketeering probe would go cold once it reached the door of the IOR. The Vatican Bank could not be served with a search warrant or an order to produce documents. Its phones were not subject to legal wiretaps. Court-ordered mail intercepts were forbidden. None of its employees could be required to testify. It was a loophole so large, argued Pizzi, that it made a mockery of Italian law enforcement.[123]

The Constitutional Court took five months before dismissing the prosecutor's appeal.[124] It dodged the central issue of whether the Vatican's concordat exemption from Italy's judicial oversight violated the country's constitution. Instead, it concluded that the Corte Suprema di Cassazione, which had decided the case the previous year, had the final say. Moreover, it noted that the challenge by the Milanese magistrates was too late in the process.

---

* A month after the good news from Italy's highest court, Marcinkus sought an injunction against Doubleday and author A. J. Quinnell to stop the publication in the U.S. of an espionage novel that put him at the center of a conspiracy to assassinate the Soviet Premier. Marcinkus also asked the court to order that 77,000 copies of the novel, stored in a Long Island warehouse, be destroyed. A New York Supreme Court justice rejected both requests.[121]

That final chapter in the criminal investigation was only a couple of weeks old when the Pope introduced his next round of Curial reforms, many focused on finances. In 1981 John Paul had appointed a commission of cardinals to look for ways to increase the Vatican's income.[125] Now, among the changes addressed in a 111-page document, he expanded their scope to monitor the Vatican Bank and its thirteen employees.[126] Part of their brief was to try to stem some of the large deficits. Simultaneous with the changes at the IOR, the Vatican disclosed that it had suffered another record operating loss (about $78 million, prompting a new worldwide plea for more Peter's Pence contributions).[127]* The church was still spending far more than it took in and had almost depleted its Peter's Pence reserves.[129] Dioceses around the world, covering thousands of parishes, struggled to keep up with their own expenses, and had little extra money to send to Rome.[130] The Kirchensteuer, the German tax on Catholics that helped fuel the Vatican's coffers during World War II, was generating more than $3 billion annually, but was now consumed mostly by the German dioceses.[131] Italy's eight-per-thousand tax was bringing in a lot of money, but not enough to pull the church into the black. Although some religious orders were financially comfortable, they did not have large enough surpluses to bail out the Vatican.

Several proposals to cut the deficit were floated but rejected. Some of the oversight cardinals thought Peter's Pence would produce more money if it got a new name that did not imply small change. "I don't like names that don't reflect what's happening," said Toronto's Cardinal Gerald Carter. Some of the names floated included Papal Charity, Aid to the Holy Father, and Papal Support.[132] None stuck. Other proposals that got serious consideration included selling some of the IOR gold Nogara had accumulated or streamlining the Curia's lay employees (when the Vatican did sell some of its gold four years later, its timing was bad since bullion prices had dropped almost 40 percent).[133] There was also

* In 1985, the faithful contributed $28 million to Peter's Pence. That increased to $32 million in 1986, but produced less money for the Vatican since so many donations were from the United States, and the lira had strengthened against the dollar. It resulted in an exchange rate of 5 billion less lire. In 1987, Peter's Pence donations jumped to $50 million, but it was not enough to stop the hemorrhaging. It was after that collection, before the 1988 and 1989 deficits, that the Vatican issued a dire warning: "Reserves have now been almost completely exhausted." The Vatican was so stressed by its finances that in 1989 it struck a controversial deal for $4.175 million with Japan's Nippon Television to film the renovation of Michelangelo's Sistine Chapel frescoes. That money bought Nippon the exclusive rights to exploit the images for three years.[128]

a debate about renting some of the nearly 2,000 church-owned apartments in prime Roman neighborhoods at market rates instead of subsidizing rents of lay workers and clerics. Italy's rent control law—widely ignored by ordinary Italians—prohibited such a move by the church. So that idea was shelved.[134]

Beyond the question of how to best cut the deficit, Philadelphia's Cardinal Krol was the first to suggest it was time to retain an internationally recognized accounting firm to perform an annual audit of all the church's finances.[135]*

Not everyone was impressed by the Pope's reforms. Some critics had hoped he would fold the Vatican Bank into the Curia. A new commission of cardinals seemed only to add another layer of bureaucracy. Nothing diminished the bank's power, made it more transparent, or put in place autonomous lay experts who might transform it into a compliant central bank. Compounding the problem, none of the oversight cardinals had the financial training to figure out how to break free of the Vatican Bank's morass. Giuseppe Caprio, the cardinal who ran the Prefecture for the Economic Affairs of the Holy See, told a journalist, "The changes provided are more formal than substantive."[137]

To the satisfaction of the reformers, however, the restructuring did spark another round of press speculation about whether Marcinkus might be finished.[138] But his staying power, and the Pope's lasting faith in him, confounded the Vaticanologists who had half a dozen times incorrectly predicted his imminent ouster. The fifty-nine-year-old Monsignor Donato De Bonis, whose father was a successful banker, was instead elevated as a prelate of equal rank to Marcinkus.[139] De Bonis, whose career had been boosted by his reputation for discretion, had emerged from the shadows. He was now the link between the supervisory committee of cardinals and the Vatican Bank.[140]

Massimo Spada, the IOR's chief before leaving in the 1960s to work with Sindona, took notice of the power shift. "De Bonis is clever compared to Marcinkus," Spada told author Benny Lai. "Marcinkus has been downgraded. . . . His power in the IOR is almost dried up."[141]

---

* Local dioceses still got stuck with bills they thought Rome should cover. The Vatican, for instance, paid the cost for the chartered plane for the Pope and a dozen in his entourage for a ten-day trip to the United States in September 1987. The U.S. government and the American church covered the rest. While the American taxpayer bore $6 million in extra Secret Service and police security costs, dioceses covered everything from stadium rentals to cleanup expenses, to the tune of some $20 million. It took them a couple of years to pay off those expenses.[136]

28

White Finance

Elevating De Bonis was not the clean sweep for which some had hoped. Vaticanologists did not know that Secretary of State Casaroli wanted an outsider to run the bank. The man on whom Casaroli had his eye was forty-nine-year-old Angelo Caloia, an economics professor at a Catholic university, as well as the CEO of Mediocredito Lombardo, a merchant bank. Caloia was a top Milanese Catholic financier, part of an elite group who had formed the Group for Culture, Ethics, and Finance. Their goal was to create an informal consortium of Catholic-dominated banks that earned profits without sacrificing their "Christian identity." Together they were known as *finanza bianca* (white finance).[1]

Casaroli dispatched Monsignor Renato Dardozzi to see if Caloia might like the challenge of straightening out the IOR. Dardozzi, dressed in lay clothes, showed up one day at Caloia's Milan office. He was so effusive in praising the Group for Culture, Ethics, and Finance that Caloia initially thought all the flattery was setting the groundwork to solicit a large donation. Instead, as the meeting drew to a close, Dardozzi surprised Caloia. "I came to tell you that we consider you the most suitable person to hold the office of the director general of the IOR. Even if I had any doubts, this meeting has dispelled them."[2]

Caloia had no interest in the IOR posting. His professional and personal life revolved around Milan, where he lived with his wife and four children. He had no desire to move to Rome.

"The meeting ended rather coldly," Caloia later recalled. "What I knew about the IOR I had only read in the newspapers. Did I have to be an instrument of God or the Devil to work there? In any case, I thought the matter was settled."[3]

A few months later Dardozzi again showed up at Caloia's office. This time he wore his clerical garb.[4] There was no small talk.

"Professor, you are the man we need. There is no need to move to Rome, just help us to give a new structure to the IOR."

Dardozzi explained that it had taken five difficult years to reach the point where the Pope was ready to replace Marcinkus. Casaroli had twice almost resigned over the standoff.[5] Caloia would be the chairman of a small board of directors and the Vatican would provide any support he required.[6] And he could commute between Milan and Rome, as his full-time presence at the Vatican was not required.

Caloia accepted in principle. "You have to obey the Holy Roman Church," he later said. "I had a priest in front of me, who spoke to me as a priest. Personal problems had to fade into the background."[7]

That kicked off a series of secret meetings at the Vatican between Caloia and Casaroli. "I went in disguise so no one would know about it," recalls Caloia.[8] Their discussions about the daunting task ahead were "frank." Caloia said he even hoped to redraft the IOR's charter drawn by Pius XII and Bernardino Nogara. He thought the bank's scope and authority were too broad. Casaroli knew that would be no easy task since no church institution gave up power unless ordered to do so by the Pope.

By March 1989, Casaroli privately informed Marcinkus that he would remain at his post only until a replacement arrived.[9] Somehow word leaked to reporters. Still, there was no formal announcement, leaving Vaticanologists puzzled. The bank seemed to be in limbo.[10]

The following month events in Italy gave some impetus to hurry Marcinkus's exit. A public prosecutor, Pierluigi Dell'Osso, announced a new round of wide-ranging indictments against dozens of former Ambrosiano executives and associates. P2 chief Licio Gelli was among those charged. And Dell'Osso made it clear that he would have indicted Marcinkus if it were not for the previous court rulings that declared the archbishop exempt.[11] Marcinkus had again proven what he told *Fortune* a couple of years earlier: "I may be a lousy banker but at least I'm not in jail."[12]

To speed Caloia's arrival, Cardinal Casaroli called the banker to his private study. Three other laymen were there: Theodor Pietzcker, a Deutsche Bank director; former UBS chairman Philippe de Weck; and Thomas Macioce, president of the U.S. retail chain Allied Stores, and a prominent member of the

Order of the Knights of Malta.[13] Casaroli proposed they all be part of an extraordinary supervisory panel of laymen empowered to supervise the IOR. Within a week, José Ángel Sánchez Asiaín, cochairman of the Banco Bilbao Vizcaya, was added as the fifth member (Caloia later noted that Sánchez Asiaín was selected as a nod to the growing influence of Hispanics in the church. "He was a very nice Basque, but his English was bizarre and I had to struggle hard to understand him.")[14]

For the first time in the IOR's history, a lay board—chaired by Caloia and with de Weck as vice president—oversaw the bank's financial operations.[15] Meanwhile, Marcinkus was still at the Vatican Bank. The transition was a stop-and-start affair. It took Caloia until March of the following year (1990) to get Giovanni Bodio, the number three executive at Caloia's Mediocredito Lombardo, appointed as the IOR's first lay director since Henri de Maillardoz in the 1960s.[16]

In late May, questions about how to speed up the transfer of power were again overshadowed by news of past bank scandals. The long-awaited criminal trial against thirty-five Ambrosiano defendants had started in Milan. Although the prosecutors had been blocked from charging Marcinkus, Mennini, and de Strobel, that did not prevent them from presenting extensive evidence about the Vatican Bank's role. The IOR was treated as if it was as culpable as any of the accused in the defendant's dock.[17] (To the great consternation of the church, Francis Ford Coppola's *Godfather III*, released later that year, had a storyline based on the bank's role in the Ambrosiano collapse; in the film, an archbishop in league with the Mafia is murdered in a Vatican stairwell, with his corpse replicating sixteenth-century Protestant images of the defeat of the Antichrist.)

Five months into the trial, Mennini and de Strobel resigned their bank postings and moved out of Vatican City. And to the relief of almost everyone, Marcinkus submitted his formal resignation to John Paul.

"I am very grateful to the Holy Father for having granted my request to retire from Vatican service and to return to the United States. The forty years that I have spent away from my diocese—in diplomatic service, working with the preparation and performance of Papal trips, serving the Institute for Works of Religion and the Governorate—have enriched my priesthood and given me a keener perception and deeper appreciation of the unity and universality of the Church. They have also confirmed my conviction about the necessity of pastoral work in the life of every priest. The ministry of the parish has always been my ambition and day after day I tried to be faithful to this vocation addressing every aspect of my work with pastoral spirit. Now that I am free from administrative responsibilities and returning to the U.S., I will be useful in those pastoral services that I will be given to perform, as are many other elderly priests of my diocese."[18]

A few days later, Marcinkus told a reporter: "I have never done anything wrong. I would like to set the record straight."[19] Marcinkus's exile was as an ordinary priest in the rather unremarkable parish of a retirement community in Sun City, Arizona. In his new diocese, no one was quite certain of why such a high-ranking Curia official had become their pastor. There was no dearth of misinformation. Marcinkus was "wanted in Rome for being associated with a bank robbery," one local detective answered an Interpol inquiry in 2003.[20]

"He was a broken man but would never give his enemies the satisfaction of revealing that," his friend U.S. diplomat Peter Murphy said.[21]

To *The New York Times,* Marcinkus said, "I think they were surprised when I told them I was leaving."[22] Many Vaticanologists had trouble believing that. "I have no doubt that I will be remembered as the villain in the Calvi affair." That was something on which most agreed.*

---

* Marcinkus died in 2006 at the age of eighty-four from complications from emphysema. He never gave a wide-ranging interview about his Vatican tenure once he returned to the States. When the author reached him by phone in November 2005, he said, "I have no interest in revisiting that time." The author was not successful in finding Marcinkus's personal papers and journals. In particular, the Chicago diocese never responded to written requests as to whether a published report that Marcinkus had left his personal diaries and papers to that diocese was correct. As for Marcinkus's two lay colleagues, they also died without addressing the controversies that had tarnished the final years of their service. Mennini's son Paolo is currently the chief of the Extraordinary Division at the Vatican's APSA.[23]

29

Suitcases of Cash

With Marcinkus gone from Rome, Angelo Caloia was unchallenged in his energetic oversight of the Vatican Bank. It seemed a much tamer institution. Under Caloia's direction there was hope that the bank might morph into something pedestrian rather than rogue.

Although Caloia was a devout Catholic and avid member of Opus Dei, he did not have the patrician heritage that was the hallmark of the Black Nobles.* Born in 1939 into a working-class family in the small northern village of Castano Primo, his mother was a seamstress and his father a carpenter. When Caloia was eight, he fell ill with typhoid, and a burst appendix that led to peritonitis complicated his recovery. During months of difficult recuperation, he listened to the "Microphone of God," jarring radio broadcasts by Riccardo Lombardi, a provocative politician who was a committed socialist and advocate for a "working man's Catholic Leftist party." Those broadcasts made an indelible impression on the youngster, so much so that in later years he was politically left of most Catholic financiers.[2] Although he had worked his way to a position of privilege, he rejected the elitism that often accompanied such standing. The Italian press began referring to him as Italy's *Catholic banker*. He told a colleague the only thing worse would be to be called the *Pope's banker*.[3]

---

* Members of Opus Dei dominated the lay selections for prominent Vatican positions under Pope John Paul II. The Pontiff reduced the influence wielded by the Jesuits, an order that had long opposed elevating Opus Dei to a personal prelature of the Pope. Fifteen years earlier, Pope Paul VI had rejected Opus Dei's application for such a special status. John Paul II granted it in 1982. That was precisely what Roberto Calvi had told his family Opus Dei had wanted in failed discussions he had with it about bailing out the Ambrosiano.[1]

Caloia preached transparency and strict ethics. A handful of IOR officials, however, realized that no matter how pure his intentions, he faced great obstacles in reforming the Vatican Bank. His appointment marked a sea change in the personal relationship between the Pontiff and the head of the bank. Marcinkus had regular access to John Paul. It took Caloia two years before he met with the Pope. And that was only a quick greeting after a morning Mass, in which Caloia brought along his wife and children. That was a strike against him, especially since many in the Curia measured power and influence by easy and frequent access to the Pope. Caloia's distance led some to believe he was only a temporary place holder for some other, yet undetermined, bank chief.

Monsignor Renato Dardozzi, who had convinced Caloia to take the job, thought he was a good pick. Dardozzi's concern was that some long-serving IOR officials acted as though Caloia wielded no authority over them. Dardozzi was on the three-person panel that helped negotiate the $244 million payment to the Ambrosiano's creditors. He had been a senior engineer at STET, the state-owned telecommunications company, before becoming a priest at fifty-one.[4] Secretary of State Casaroli asked Dardozzi to keep an eye on the goings-on at the bank. Now, his frustration mounted as he watched everything from phantom charities to illicit political donations flourish despite Marcinkus's departure.[5]

Dardozzi was particularly bothered by an account opened at the Vatican Bank on June 15, 1987. That was at the height of the debate over whether Italy's arrest warrants could be executed against Marcinkus, Mennini, and de Strobel. It was the Fondazione Cardinale Francis Spellman (Cardinal Francis Spellman Foundation—no such entity existed outside of the Vatican Bank).[6] The two signatories were Monsignor Donato De Bonis, the bank's secretary, and Italy's leading Christian Democrat politician, Giulio Andreotti (before Andreotti died in 2013, he was the nation's most dominant postwar public figure, leading seven governments as prime minister and having served thirty-four times as a minister, eight times in charge of the Defense Department).[7] The IOR required all account holders to maintain a copy of their wills on file so the bank would know what to do in case of death. De Bonis's will provided that upon his death any funds went to "His Excellency Giulio Andreotti for charitable works and assistance according to his discretion."[8]

In the six years that followed the opening of the Cardinal Francis Spellman Foundation account—during which Andreotti again became Italy's prime minister—about $60 million passed through.[9] Evidence that the church knew the account was sensitive is in internal correspondence in which senior officials referred to De Bonis by the pseudonym *Roma* and Andreotti as *Omissis* (other pseudonyms used, such as Ancona and Siena, have never been decoded).[10] The reason for the subterfuge was the bank's awareness that the disclosure of such an account—millions of dollars in a veritable slush fund run by the IOR's top prelate together with the country's most powerful Christian Democrat politician—would have sparked a great scandal.

While some of the money that passed through the Spellman Foundation found its way to religious orders, monasteries, and convents, much of it was scattered to Andreotti's friends and associates, including one of his attorneys and a Florentine jewelry designer.[11] And De Bonis sent millions more through untraceable wire transfers to Swiss and Luxembourg banks. Sometimes Dardozzi spotted De Bonis leaving the Vatican with suitcases of cash and later returning empty-handed.[12]

In 1992, a prominent socialist politician, Mario Chiesa, was charged with accepting a bribe in return for granting a political favor. Chiesa's arrest kicked off a broad judicial investigation dubbed *Mani Pulite* (Clean Hands) that eventually toppled the coalition government. The *Mani Pulite* probe—dubbed by *The New York Times* as "one of the most extraordinary scandals of postwar Europe"—continued for three years, ensnaring five thousand defendants and leading to hundreds of convictions of politicians and businessmen, including a breathtaking half of parliament.[13]

Although *Mani Pulite* was then in its earliest stages, it nevertheless caused considerable concern in the Vatican. Just a month after Chiesa's arrest, Caloia received a preliminary report raising questions about the Spellman Foundation account. That prompted the IOR's Board of Superintendence, chaired by Caloia, to issue an April 1, 1992, edict that no one—"whether it be as an employee, active or retired, a manager, an auditor or accountant, [or] a prelate"—could trade or manage the accounts they did not personally own.[14]

De Bonis ignored that directive. And Caloia was frustrated he had few tools by which to force De Bonis to comply. "All [IOR] controls were internal," Caloia later recalled. "It was not monitored. The cardinals knew little and the Holy Father was kept in the dark."[15]

Although Caloia was De Bonis's superior, it seemed that inside the Vatican a cleric had more standing and respect than a layman.[16] A sign of De Bonis's continuing power was that he retained the IOR's "most beautiful office" and was in contact "with everyone in Rome who mattered, politically and otherwise. Francesco Cossiga [a former Italian president] called him by the affectionate nickname 'Donatino,' and Giulio Andreotti held him in high esteem, as did prominent aristocrats, financiers, and artists, like Sophia Loren."[17]

It did not take long before Caloia discovered that the Spellman Foundation was not his only problem. He began compiling a list of questionable accounts ostensibly opened for everything from Catholic community associations to Trappist monks to Carmelite nuns. What appeared suspicious in each was outsized financial activity. Some—such as Assisi for the Amazon, Adorers of the Eucharist, Holy House of Loreto, and St. Seraphim Fund—were seemingly for nonexistent groups.[18]

On July 7 Caloia distributed to his fellow lay commissioners a report stamped *Classified*. It concluded that the situation inside the IOR was "very serious" and that the Vatican Bank was possibly on the verge of a new Marcinkus-styled scandal.[19] Caloia wanted to better control the so-called numbered foundation accounts. Veterans like De Bonis were naturally resistant to anything that might limit their broad discretion.

Instead De Bonis did his best to undermine Caloia. In back halls, he ridiculed Caloia's inexperience and warned that as a layman he would never understand the reasons why the IOR had to sometimes operate as it did. Caloia had a British wife and he had lived and studied for several years in London. That was evidence, contended De Bonis, that Caloia was not fully *Italian*, not in a way by which he could be trusted. Was Caloia truly loyal to the Pope or was he instead serving his own private career?[20]

Caloia was so concerned that he decided to appeal directly to John Paul. But the Pope had just been operated on for a malignant intestinal tumor and his doctors had ordered a lighter schedule. Caloia thought the matter too important to wait. He was worried that De Bonis and others were running the equivalent of a "laundry in the center of Rome," protected by the Vatican's sovereignty.[21] So on August 5 he sent a memo to John Paul's secretary, Stanislaw Dziwisz. Caloia included details about several foundations De Bonis managed. Also included were seventeen other dubious accounts on which De Bonis was the signatory. [They were pledged to never-heard-of congregations, religious shrines, and purported charities.[22]] One held the estate bequeathed to the IOR by Cardinal Alberto di Jorio, the bank's former chief prelate. Di Jorio had left a villa, bonds, and cash, naming the bank as the sole beneficiary. But he also appointed De Bonis as his executor. De Bonis had never transferred any money to the IOR but instead managed the account as his own.[23]

One foundation accepted contributions from the faithful for Masses to be offered for the dead; ten thousand Masses had been paid for but there was no evidence that a single one was performed.[24] Another account hid over $30 million belonging to a senior police commander and a bishop, both of whom were directors at Italy's largest psychiatric hospital in Bari, an eight-hundred-bed facility that had been built on the site of property that previously belonged to the Ancelle della divina Provvidenza-Bisceglie (Sisters of Divine Providence-Bisceglie).[25]

Although Caloia did not yet know the full extent of the IOR's secret network, he delivered a blunt recommendation: the Pope must act to extinguish the parallel bank flourishing inside the Vatican.[26]

Caloia thought it unlikely that all the money passing through the foundations was donations and inheritances. He was right. When the psychiatric hospital in Bari later became embroiled in scandal—a case of inflated public contracts and stolen funds from the Ministry of Health, resulting in multiple embezzlement and money laundering indictments—a nun from a nearby convent told prosecutors she had seen the police commander cram shoeboxes of cash into his car and drive off to the Vatican.[27] Worse yet, in a related case the prosecutors wanted to indict Cardinal Fiorenzo Angelini, the head of the Vatican's Pontifical Council for the Pastoral Care of Health Care Workers, on charges he extorted money from a pharmaceutical company.[28] But the same defense of absolute sovereignty that had protected Marcinkus prevented any move against Angelini.

Two of the accounts he tagged for their frenetic money transfers were for the Santa Casa di Loreto (Holy House of Loreto), a charity based in the popular eponymously named pilgrimage town. In 1988, John Paul had appointed Monsignor Pasquale Macchi, Pope Paul VI's closest personal aide, as Loreto's bishop. It was Macchi, a trusted Marcinkus ally, who now helped De Bonis administer two off-shelf accounts.[29] Caloia was learning a sobering lesson: "Even in priests' robes there lurk human weaknesses," he later said.[30]

Most of the troublesome accounts had opened under Marcinkus. It was not much of a secret that for decades Italy's elite had used the IOR to hide their money. In 1981, not long after Marcinkus had taken charge, one internal review estimated there were approximately 9,300 accounts belonging to "privileged citizens of Italy" compared to only 2,500 that met the bank's strict rules. Some accounts were rumored to be proxies for the Spatola and Inzerillo crime families. Marcinkus's departure had not slowed the flow of untracked cash. And it was not difficult to understand why the accounts were so valued—the IOR not only paid on average about 9 percent interest on the deposits but it was tax free.[31]

"They really had no effective internal controls in place," Peter Murphy, the U.S. Deputy Chief of Mission at the U.S. embassy at the Vatican, said. "There were accounts that remained active long after they should have been closed." (After Murphy left in 1989 as an accredited diplomat appointed to the Holy See, he was no longer entitled to the IOR account that had been opened as a courtesy during his posting; it took twenty-two years before the bank closed it.)

Caloia would ultimately discover that upward of $400 million moved through seventeen *in nero* (in black) accounts during the first four years after Marcinkus's departure (1989–93).[32] Although that cash came almost entirely from undetermined sources, it was invariably listed on the IOR ledgers as contributions from the faithful. Much of it disappeared in a flurry of transfers to Switzerland and Luxembourg, jurisdictions where banking secrecy stopped any inquiries cold.

The Vatican bureaucracy, much to Caloia's frustration, moved at a glacial pace.[33] So it was not surprising he had not heard from the Pope. But he did not even know if Dziwisz had shown the memo to John Paul, or whether the Pontiff had not been persuaded it was urgent.

While waiting for the Pope, something unexpected added to Caloia's sense of unease about the IOR accounts. In 1992 prosecutors indicted Pavel Hnilica, a Slovak bishop living in Rome, together with Calvi's former colleague, Sardinian developer Flavio Carboni, over a convoluted shakedown of the Vatican concerning the contents of Calvi's long-missing attaché case.[34] Also charged was a convicted forger and reputed mobster, Giulio Lena.[35] Police had raided Lena's house in a separate counterfeiting investigation, and had stumbled across unsigned checks from Hnilica's Vatican Bank account.[36] Investigators believed the seventy-two-year-old bishop had written Carboni $2.8 million in checks from his IOR account, hoping to buy Calvi's briefcase.[37] Rome's Public Prosecutor, Francesco De Leo, said that Lena and Carboni hoped to get upwards of $40 million from the Vatican for Calvi's case.[38]

Bishop Hnilica, who became an instant paparazzi favorite with his 24/7 dark glasses and thick gold neck chain around his priest's collar, initially insisted that someone had forged his signature on the checks. In any case, he did not want the attaché case, but thought he was simply helping Carboni launch a publicity campaign to bolster the Vatican Bank's battered image.[39] Later he changed his story to say he wanted Calvi's documents because Carboni assured him they would clear the IOR of any wrongdoing in the Ambrosiano collapse.[40] Hnilica maintained he was "inexperienced, foolish and ignorant of Italian law" but was nevertheless ready "to give my life for the Holy Father and the Church."[41]

The involvement of Hnilica, a Rome-based bishop who worked with Eastern European refugees, raised more questions than it answered. It turned out that Hnilica had met Calvi shortly before the banker died. They had discussed the covert transfer of money to Poland to help the incipient pro-democracy movement. The church made no public response about the flurry of charges and countercharges, sticking instead to a policy of silence.[42] The Hnilica episode further concerned Caloia, who feared that what he did not know about the inner workings of the IOR might come to haunt him.

In the spring of 1993, Caloia thought he had prevailed. De Bonis was transferred from the IOR. But it was a short-lived victory. Instead of rebuking De Bonis, the Pope elevated him from monsignor to bishop and appointed him the chaplain of the Sovereign Military Order of Malta, a position with diplomatic immunity.[43] De Bonis no longer worked inside the IOR; he continued exercising influence at the bank through a handful of friends and colleagues.[44] The Cardinal Spellman account and others were frozen but not closed.

Caloia soon appealed to Cardinal Rosalio José Castillo Lara, president of APSA and the chairman of the IOR's cardinal oversight committee. Cardinal Castillo Lara was a powerhouse in the church's money departments and a personal favorite of John Paul.[45] Maybe, Caloia thought, Castillo Lara might make headway with the Pontiff. But the Venezuelan-born cardinal, who had a well-deserved Curial reputation as a masterful political infighter, was allied with De Bonis.[46]

Next Caloia went to the new Secretary of State, Angelo Sodano, who had replaced Cardinal Casaroli in 1990. Sodano was different from his predecessor.* He was loud, confrontational, and often struck newcomers as brash. Combined with a well-deserved reputation as a Machiavellian Curialist who had an appetite for power and a habit of doling out favors to friends, the lifelong diplomat was in the style of princes of the church from a bygone era.[48] Caloia knew that one of Sodano's brothers, Alessandro, had been arrested and charged with fraud in the sweeping *Mani Pulite* probe.[49]

Caloia wrote Sodano a six-page handwritten letter that July. He did not mince words. "It is increasingly clear that criminal activity is being conducted deliberately by those who, according to their chosen way of life and the role they fulfill, should instead have provided a strict critical conscience. It is becoming more and more difficult to understand the continuation of a situation such that the person in question [De Bonis] continues, from a no less privileged position, to manage indirectly the activities of the IOR."[50]

The IOR chief soon learned that Sodano's view of damage control was keeping any news that might be embarrassing sealed inside the Vatican. The Secretary of State once told a Papal aide that bad information could only harm the church if it became public.[51]

In October, Caloia's worst fears were realized. Once again some of Italy's top industrialists were under indictment in the so-called Enimont scandal, for having paid outsized bribes to dozens of leading politicians. The difference this time was the amount of money, a staggering $100 million in illegal payoffs resulting from a multibillion-dollar joint venture between ENI, a state-owned oil company, and Montedison, a privately owned chemical firm.[52] On October 4, Milan's chief prosecutor, Francesco Saverio Borelli, telephoned Caloia.

"Hello, nice to hear from you," Caloia said. "What do I owe the pleasure of this call?"

Borelli was not in the mood for small talk. "Dear Professor. There are problems concerning the IOR, contacts with Enimont . . ."

---

* Author Jason Berry wrote about Sodano in his seminal book *Render Unto Rome* and noted that he was a "committed anti-leftist" who had been close to Chilean strongman Augusto Pinochet when he had served as Nuncio there. According to Berry, Pope John Paul II was "famously bored by Curial politics, [and] had in Sodano a firewall from the inner wrangles." Berry also broke the story that Sodano had pressured German Cardinal Joseph Ratzinger (later Pope Benedict XVI) to scuttle investigations into appalling charges of sex abuse in two high-profile cases: Vienna's archbishop Hans Hermann Groër and Marcial Maciel Degollado, the founder of the religious order Legion of Christ. Repeated entreaties to the Vatican Press Office to interview Cardinal Sodano went unanswered.[47]

Just the word *Enimont* chilled Caloia. "We are in the middle of the Tangentopoli scandal, and it is defined by Enimont, the 'mother of all bribes,'" Caloia later recounted to author Giancarlo Galli. "The President of ENI, Gabriele Cagliari, had taken his own life in jail a few months before [Cagliari had suffocated himself in prison while awaiting trial by tying a plastic bag around his head]. The exuberant Raul Gardini, owner of the Ferruzzi Group, fearing for his arrest, had shot himself in the head on a summer morning."[53]

Borelli invited Caloia to visit with his investigative unit "so that we could clarify some things, without the press or TV." When Caloia arrived the next day he learned some sobering details. About $4 million in the tainted Enimont cash had landed in De Bonis's Spellman Foundation.[54] And worse, more than half of *all* the bribes ($75 million) had passed through an IOR account held for Luigi Bisignani, a former P2 member and chief publicist for Montedison as well as a novelist and editor-in-chief of the Italian news wire service ANSA (De Bonis had performed Bisignani's 1990 wedding Mass).[55] The most active Bisignani account was titled the Louis Augustus Jonas Foundation (USA), supposedly organized to collect money to "help poor children." There was in fact such an organization with headquarters in New York City, but Caloia could not determine if the eponymously named IOR account had anything to do with it.[56]*

The Milanese prosecutors asked Caloia to take some interrogatories back to the Vatican. He declined. He was savvy enough to know that if he took the questions with him it would have spared the prosecutors the difficult task of trying to serve legal papers on the Vatican. But he assured them that he would do all he could to ensure that the IOR cooperated.[58] (The prosecutors submitted their interrogatories through official diplomatic channels).[59]

Caloia sent off two letters to Sodano with the grim news. By this time the Secretary of State had retained Franzo Grande Stevens, one of Italy's most prominent and well-connected attorneys.[60] Stevens, he hoped, might provide advice on how to deal with the parallel IOR that seemed beyond the control of Caloia and his lay colleagues. Giovanni Bodio, who had been the number

---

* The Manhattan foundation was a nonprofit organization that ran a full-scholarship, invitation-only leadership camp in Rhinebeck, New York, for boys aged fourteen to sixteen. George Edward (Freddie) Jonas, a former OSS officer during World War II and also the heir to a felt hat manufacturing fortune, established the foundation in 1930. According to Bisignani, Jonas and Marcinkus had set up the account at the IOR in the early 1970s and they later passed it to De Bonis.[57]

three banker at Caloia's Mediocredito Lombardo before coming to the Vatican, had proven a disappointment. Bodio and his two assistants, Pietro Ciocci and Antonio Chiminello, had failed to move aggressively against the IOR's proxy foundation accounts. Instead of closing suspicious ones, they opened new ones that were often just as questionable. Caloia thought Bodio was "a very good, generous and exemplary person," but that he paid too much deference to clerical power. "All it took him to allow an investment was to be invited for breakfast by someone with a red tunic."[61]

Caloia later discovered Bodio was not only liberal when it came to opening accounts for cardinals, but that he continued the IOR's long history of doing it for rich Italians as well. Relying on Article 2 of the Vatican Bank's governing statutes, which allows the IOR to accept "goods with a purpose at least partially set for the future works of religion," Bodio helped open multimillion-dollar accounts for Italian tycoons, such as industrialist Domenico Bonifaci.[62] Since Italy's highest tax rate on earned interest and stock dividends was 30 percent, Bonifaci thought the Vatican Bank was a bargain: a 10 percent fee for the cash and 7 percent for any securities and stocks, all paid to the church as a fixed annual donation. Incredibly the church lost money on Bonifaci's account since the IOR agreed somehow to pay him 11.75 percent interest on his deposits, a rate the Vatican Bank only guaranteed monks, friars, and a handful of religious organizations.[63] (Bonifaci had thoroughly ingratiated himself in the power corridors at the Vatican, helping APSA's Cardinal Castillo Lara purchase for the church a historic luxury estate just outside Rome.)*

A frantic internal debate played out during the fall of 1993 about whether the church should cooperate with Milanese prosecutors. Caloia and the reformers wanted to help but they were staunchly opposed by reactionary prelates who thought the church had no obligation to do anything. The charismatic Cardinal Castillo Lara made a persuasive argument against any accommodation that might weaken the church's inviolable sovereignty. It owed no duty, he contended, to assist Italy's criminal probe.[65]

---

* Caloia replaced Bodio with Andrea Gibellini, a sixty-three-year-old banker and director from Banca Popolare di Bergamo. Gibellini had a reputation as a tough disciplinarian. And Caloia sometimes began relying for advice on Vincenzo Perrone, a Milanese friend and professor of business management. Sodano, meanwhile, assigned his personal secretary, a forty-two-year-old American monsignor, Timothy Broglio, to assist Stevens and Caloia.[64]

Castillo Lara believed it might not be possible to demolish the parallel IOR without making the Vatican Bank crash in on itself. At every turn, he adeptly blocked Caloia's efforts to make the bank more transparent.[66] Some reformers meanwhile suspected that the cardinal was more than just an obstacle to reform. They thought the powerful APSA boss was the source of press leaks that made it appear that it was Caloia's team that had failed to rein in the bank's questionable activities.[67]

The Vatican's resistance to cooperating with Italian prosecutors did not surprise Italy's leading politicians. Former Prime Minister Emilio Colombo—the Minister of Foreign Affairs—later told colleagues that the Vatican did whatever it wanted and there was "nothing more we could do. When there are treaties for mutual legal assistance, the relationships are based on reciprocity. I was almost certain it would be impossible to obtain their cooperation."[68] (For that matter, not many Italian politicians had much enthusiasm about aiding the "Clean Hands" prosecutors. When Prime Minister Bettino Craxi and four top ministers resigned in April 1993, the next Prime Minister, Silvio Berlusconi, himself under investigation for possible illegal payments from one of his companies, slowed the anticorruption crusade by issuing an executive decree that severely limited the use of preventive incarceration. It had been one of the prosecutors' most effective tools).[69]

By the late fall (1993), Sodano updated the Pope about the bank. The situation, he told John Paul, was much more complicated than simply identifying and closing abused proxy accounts. Disclosing information to Italian prosecutors, Sodano counseled, might set off a chain reaction of events beyond the church's control.[70] That briefing left John Paul convinced that the IOR was a minefield better left undisturbed.[71]

Late that autumn a Venezuelan attorney, Alberto Jaime Berti, cooperated with Italian magistrates in return for immunity from prosecution on charges that the IOR was at the center of laundering several hundred million dollars through Swiss and Panamanian banks on behalf of a handful of senior Opus Dei officials.[72] The Italian media reported that Berti fingered De Bonis as his Vatican Bank connection and produced dozens of documents with the monsignor's signature. Prosecutors believed that De Bonis had the key to a safe deposit box at Geneva's Banque de Paris et des Pays-Bas. It was in that box, said Berti, that a cache of documents laid out exactly how the IOR laundered the money. De Bonis, cloaked by immunity in his Knights of Malta position, denied even knowing Berti.[73] The prosecutors, unable to move against him, had to stand down.

On November 13, 1993, Caloia was driving back to Rome from Padua when he swerved to avoid hitting a truck stuck in the motorway and lost control of his car. He was badly injured. A helicopter took him to a nearby hospital, and he was soon transferred to Gemelli's trauma unit in Rome.

"In the state of unconsciousness, I had a flash of lucidity." He believed that God had saved him so he could do the right thing when it came to the Vatican Bank. If he recovered, he promised, he would redouble his reform efforts.[74]

The Curia, meanwhile, was awash in malicious rumors that the wreck was the result of foul play.[75] During Caloia's nearly one-month hospital recuperation, the bank garnered more bad headlines. At the trial of Sergio Cusani, a leading socialist politician and the financier charged with engineering the kickbacks at the heart of *mani pulite*, prosecutors presented evidence that much of the dirty money was deposited at the Vatican Bank. Worse, the church had earned an $8 million fee for cashing the Treasury bills used as bribes to then ex–Prime Minister Bettino Craxi.[76]* The former journalist Luigi Bisignani, the holder of the account through which most of the money had passed, gave a gripping account of how he brought millions in Treasury notes in large, unmarked envelopes into the IOR, where they were deposited into his slush fund.[78] Bisignani received $2.6 million in cash for his services, money he used to buy a house in Venice and fuel a luxurious lifestyle.

Carlo Sama, a former top executive at Ferruzzi—Italy's second largest private company after Fiat—told the court about how De Bonis helped him and his wife, Alessandra, open an account titled the San Serafino Foundation, named after a seventeenth-century Capuchin friar. In eighteen months, through mid-1992, about $38 million passed through it. That money went to two Swiss banks and one in Luxembourg, where it was exchanged into nontraceable bearer bonds.[79] Sama testified that the IOR was his bank of choice for any clandestine money transfers as it provided "absolute confidentiality."[80]

Cusani's trial presented Caloia another opportunity to lobby Sodano for

---

* After Cusani's 1994 conviction, he served nearly six years in prison. The Vatican inexplicably petitioned the government to pardon him.[77]

better cooperation with Italian investigators.[81] But the Vatican steadfastly rebuffed all efforts by Italian investigators to open the IOR's books.[82] Prime Minister Andreotti was never charged in the Enimont scandal because the IOR remarkably kept his identity from Italian authorities (the link to Andreotti would only become public in 2009).[83] Even appeals from the financiers on the supervisory lay commission—an angry letter with eighteen pointed questions for Sodano—were buried in a slow-moving internal investigation that went nowhere. Cardinal Castillo Lara again championed the theory that the latest instance was just another unfortunate example where unscrupulous laymen had taken advantage of the IOR.[84]

As the Enimont scandal played out, Italy oddly lost enthusiasm in pursuing any possible crimes at the Vatican Bank. There was not even a serious effort to get the IOR to return the profits it reaped from the accounts at the center of the bribery scandal. The magistrates instead accepted the church's excuse that the Vatican Bank could not have known the final destination of the millions that flowed through its accounts, and therefore had no responsibility for how it was used.[85]

Italy's lack of zeal when it came to investigating the Vatican also spared the church further embarrassment a year later when a high-ranking Mafia snitch, Francesco Marino Mannoia, told investigators about how P2's Licio Gelli used the IOR to deposit illegal money belonging to Palermo's godfather, Salvatore Riina.[86] And in 1994, during a police interrogation, mobster Vincenzo Calcara claimed that he personally knew that under Marcinkus the IOR helped launder $6.5 million in Mafia cash. In a sworn statement, Calcara said he had flown from Sicily to Rome carrying two large suitcases stuffed with 100,000-lire banknotes. Two politicians had tagged along. At Rome's Fiumicino airport, Marcinkus and a cardinal to whom they were not introduced were waiting. The group drove to a lawyer's office on the Via Cassia in the north of Rome.[87] Calcara turned over the cash. He claimed not to know how Marcinkus did it, but in a month it was available as clean money, less the IOR's service fee. Another ranking mobster and courtroom witness, Rosario Spatola, testified that he heard Marcinkus "bragging" about his Mafia influence.[88]

"We are 100 percent sure that this is pure invention," Cardinal Castillo Lara told a reporter, perhaps sounding as hopeful as he did convincing.[89]

What did Italy's Justice Ministry do with the well-placed tips that the mob had found safe haven inside the IOR? Top prosecutors decided not to pursue the leads. "Go after the Vatican?" asked one magistrate of the Palermo court. "Haven't we made enough enemies already?"[90]

In 1994, the Pope and Cardinal Sodano discussed whether it was finally time to select a cleric to replace De Bonis at the Vatican Bank. Monsignor Dardozzi let it be known that he might be interested. But Sodano wanted the position left unfilled. He tasked one of his assistants in the Secretary of State's office, Monsignor Gianfranco Piovano, a career diplomat responsible for Peter's Pence, to familiarize himself with the bank's operation.[91] On the rise at the same time as Piovano was Lelio Scaletti, a nondescript sixty-five-year-old layman who had worked his way up the IOR ranks since starting at the church when Pius XII was Pope. It was doubtful that Scaletti, a traditionalist who would remain at the Vatican Bank for another fifteen years, would back bold changes.[92]

Meanwhile, Caloia and his fellow director, Philippe de Weck, persuaded the IOR's supervisory cardinals to hire outside auditors. Their choice was Switzerland's Revisuisse, a Price Waterhouse subsidiary. Cardinal Casimir Szoka, the chief of the Prefecture of Economic Affairs, and former treasurer of the American Bishops' Conference, soon heralded Revisuisse's work as providing the Vatican's first ever "consolidated balance sheet."[93]

Dardozzi, who by now had decided that reporting wrongdoing was essentially a waste of time since no one seemed to do anything about it, watched as the Revisuisse auditors failed repeatedly to uncover information that might unmask the bank's proxy account problems. The one department to which Revisuisse did not have access to any books or ledgers was the IOR.

At a mid-June 1994 press conference, Cardinal Szoka presented the "audited" figures confirming an annual surplus for the Vatican. It was strong evidence that at least the church had turned a financial corner. A reporter asked what was so revolutionary about retaining outside accountants so long as the IOR's financial statements were still secret. The question irritated Szoka. The IOR is not part of the Holy See, he answered; it is a separate department, unique inside the Vatican.[94] That belied that all IOR profits belonged only to the Pope, who distributed them at his own discretion. Just three months before, Caloia had written a private letter to John Paul, passing along the news that the IOR had earned $70 million in profit the previous year.[95]

In 1995, Caloia broke nearly five years of silence as the IOR's director. "We've tried to move on by tapping the transparency button," he told a reporter from *Corriere della Sera.* "Unfortunately, recently, in the past months [the Enimont scandal], we ended up in the newspapers, but through no fault of our own."[96]

Caloia was well aware that his "transparency button" was not working well. That year an Italian lawyer arranged a meeting with Dardozzi and Scaletti. He represented the heirs of one of Italy's deceased property tycoons, Alessandro Gerini, who had been dubbed "God's Builder" in Italy because of the dominant role he played on many Vatican construction projects. Gerini had created an eponymously named foundation to benefit the Salesians of Don Bosco, a religious order.[97] Now, the heirs—Gerini's grandchildren—wanted to claw back some of the nearly $175 million that Gerini had bequeathed. During the talks, the Vatican learned about a multimillion-dollar bank account in Uruguay that supposedly had some money that had gone missing during the frenetic final days of Calvi and the Ambrosiano.[98]

Monsignor Dardozzi feared that the Ambrosiano tip might be some sort of trap and passed it along to Secretary of State Sodano. It soon made its way to the Pope. And Sodano again sought the advice of Franzo Grande Stevens, the elite attorney retained for special consulting. The church decided it was too risky to pursue any Uruguayan account. The clerics feared it might prompt Italy to take a second look at the Vatican's $244 million settlement over the Ambrosiano. If any money related to the Calvi affair was recovered, Italian officials might contend the Vatican should contribute more to the Ambrosiano creditors.[99] *

That some IOR-Calvi money might be sitting in an abandoned account in South America was simply another vivid reminder to Caloia of the bank's hidden landmines. And just when he thought he had heard the worst of it, there was a new setback. An account belonging to the religious movement Lumen Christi, run by a charismatic Argentine priest, Domingo Izzi, emerged as problematic. Upon opening it in 1991, Izzi had requested an IOR loan for disparate

* It took another twelve years to resolve the dispute with Gerini's heirs. The succeeding Secretary of State, Tarcisio Bertone, himself a Salesian, negotiated and signed the settlement. But five years after that, the Salesians were fighting hard to stay out of bankruptcy after losing a court case in which Bertone claimed he had been misled into signing an agreement that upon closer inspection was actually against the best interests of the Salesian Order. In July 2014, Rome magistrates announced charges against a Syrian businessman, an Italian lawyer, and the priest who had been the chief financial officer for the Salesians, for falsifying documents and inflating the value of Gerini's estate so they could get a commission of more than $100 million.[100]

Argentine ventures including livestock, a helicopter service, and organizing a national lottery.[101] All of that, promised Izzi, would "provide for the needs resulting from the activities of the movement in the Lumen Christi and the propagation of the Faith" in South America and Italy. Six million dollars went from the IOR to Father Izzi and Lumen Christi less than twenty-four hours after he applied for a loan. Repayment was due in two years. Izzi did not repay a cent. When Caloia instructed the IOR to collect, it got the title instead to the Lumen Christi share of two Rome apartments. But those were so encumbered with mortgages that they were worth less than what was owed. Caloia was nothing if not persistent. Despite appeals to Cardinal Castillo Lara and the Papal Nuncio to Argentina, and personal calls to Father Izzi urging him to repay the money, Caloia could not collect any of the loan. It had ballooned by 1995 to $8.2 million with interest and penalties.[102] (Although Caloia would chase it for several more frustrating years, the IOR had to ultimately write it off.)[103]

The following year, 1996, the Vatican bragged that the Enimont scandal had prompted the IOR to adopt "the principles laid down by the FATF [Financial Action Task Force] regarding measures to prevent money laundering."[104] That sounded good at first pass. The FATF was an intergovernmental body established in 1989 by sixteen European countries to "set standards and promote effective implementation of legal, regulatory and operational measures for combating money laundering, terrorist financing and other related threats to the integrity of the international financial system."[105] Yet, despite the Vatican's claim, it had not subjected itself to any FATF supervision or regulation. Other FATF-member countries with dodgy reputations when it came to money laundering—including Luxembourg, Switzerland, Singapore, and Hong Kong—had by then taken more concrete steps than the Vatican toward opening their banking systems to independent regulators.[106]

Vatican Bank insiders knew that the announcement about the FATF guidelines changed nothing.

30

Burying the Trail on Nazi Gold

To the considerable relief of Pope John Paul and the Curia's hierarchy, after the Enimont scandal the IOR managed to mostly stay out of the news. Stories about anonymous accounts, political bribes fueled with church funds, money laundering, and the financing of illicit empires like those of Sindona and Calvi seemed matters of the past. When a Sicilian archbishop, for instance, was charged with extorting money from the contractors he chose to renovate a twelfth-century cathedral, it did not tarnish the bank. Although investigators found a million dollars hidden in an IOR account, Vaticanologists considered the archbishop a rogue prelate, not an instance in which Vatican officials were themselves suspected of wrongdoing.[1]

The reduced amount of bad ink was good news for Caloia, whose five-year term had been renewed in 1995. Cardinal Castillo Lara and De Bonis wanted to replace him with an American, Virgil Dechant, the Supreme Knight of the Knights of Columbus. Dechant was a smart alternative. John Paul liked the garrulous American who had raised a lot of money for Solidarity. But Caloia had the support of all his lay colleagues on the supervisory panel as well as the key endorsement of Secretary of State Sodano.

Caloia began his second term with a list of goals. At every opportunity, he reaffirmed that the IOR's purpose was to serve the spiritual needs of the church "while excluding speculation and unethical financial transactions."[2] He urged the bank's employees to "better select their customers" before opening accounts. Even in small ways—such as ending the unwritten rule that barred women from working in managerial positions—he tried modernizing the IOR (one press report said the ban on female executives was "apparently on the unspoken assumption that sooner or later, they would put family first").[3]

One challenge that carried over from his first five years was how to stop the abuse of the bank's accounts. He knew there was no quick fix. Many customers legitimately handled enormous amounts of cash. Charities and ecclesiastical missions relied largely on cash donations and then disbursed it in wire transfers around the globe. Putting too many restrictions on the flow of cash would generate a pushback from genuine account holders. Better monitoring would require the IOR to be fully digital. But many records were still kept by hand.

A couple of months after his reappointment, Caloia got a clear reminder of the hurdles he faced when it came to the bank's accounts. A former CIA officer living in Italy, Roger D'Onofrio, was charged as a central figure in an international smuggling ring of arms, drugs, and plutonium.[4] In a stunning declaration he fingered Barcelona's cardinal, Ricardo María Carles Gordó, as the intermediary with the gangsters. D'Onofrio claimed the duo had run nearly $100 million through an IOR account.[5] The money was traced to D'Onofrio's Swiss business partner. The Italians wanted to determine why Cardinal Carles Gordó's name was on the Vatican account and if he knew anything about money laundering.[6] Thirty-six indictments had already been issued by the time Italian prosecutors notified Carles Gordó that he was under investigation.[7] The archconservative Carles Gordó dismissed the inquiry as politically motivated by leftists. He had "no relations" with the motley crew of ex-spooks, mercenaries, and mobsters. The Spanish government backed the church on the question of sovereignty and blocked Italian investigators from even questioning him.[8] (Carles Gordó was never charged with any crime; the following year Pope John Paul promoted him to the Prefecture for Economic Affairs of the Holy See, and he remained as Barcelona's chief prelate until his 2004 retirement.)[9]

What most bothered Caloia about the Carlos Gordó episode was that $100 million could pass through the bank without anyone asking questions. Another baffling episode soon followed. Italian police announced they were investigating the cardinal of Naples, Michele Giordano, for extortion and usury and hiding his ill-gotten gains in an IOR account. Police unearthed a trove of incriminating documents when they raided the home of the cardinal's brother, a captain in the Camorra crime family. That evidence suggested the cardinal had used the IOR for moving mafia money. When detectives raided the cardinal's office, the

Vatican lodged a formal complaint with Italy.[10] Ultimately, the Church took the unprecedented step of standing back and allowing prosecutors to bring the seventy-year-old prelate to trial as part of his brother's loan-sharking ring (a magistrate acquitted him in 2000; in 2002 he was convicted of illegaly converting real estate bequeathed to his diocese, but that conviction was reversed in 2005).[11] More important to Caloia than whether the cardinal was guilty, was why no one inside the IOR noticed that his account had quickly gone from a long-standing small balance to millions of dollars. It again heightened Caloia's fear that what would land him and the IOR back on the front pages was something hidden in an account about which he knew nothing.

But what soon put the IOR back on the defensive had nothing to do with the flood of cash that flowed through it. Instead, the Vatican and its bank were about to become the focus of Holocaust survivors' groups and the World Jewish Congress, which had begun insisting on an accounting from Swiss banks and Allied countries about stolen victims' assets.

By 1996, the media's attention and the public's sympathy had been captured by the children of Holocaust survivors—who had traveled to Switzerland to collect the money left in the bank accounts of their murdered parents—only to be turned away because they could not produce death certificates. "Nazi gold" was coined to describe the wartime loot that disappeared into Swiss banks, never to be seen again (the World Jewish Congress called it "victim's gold"). Growing pressure had pushed Switzerland to cooperate with a commission headed by Paul Volcker, former chairman of the U.S. Federal Reserve. Volcker planned a series of forensic audits of top Swiss banks to determine how much money might be missing.[12] New York Senator Alfonse D'Amato held the first of five hearings before the Senate Banking Committee in which Swiss bankers were grilled about victims' money.[13]

The Swiss estimated there was about $40 million in dormant accounts; some Jewish organizations put that amount, with accrued interest, at $7 billion.[14] Many Swiss banks privately considered the restitution effort a shakedown.[15] They stonewalled. Their intransigence eventually prompted a threat by New York's comptroller to divest the city's pension funds of Swiss bank holdings and to prevent them from underwriting future city debt.[16]

In October 1996 a Holocaust survivor filed a $20 billion class action lawsuit in Brooklyn federal court against one hundred Swiss banks. The suit claimed the banks had "acquired and transferred gold which the Nazis plundered from

Jewish victims, including gold removed from victims' teeth."[17] It opened the litigation floodgates, kicking off class action suits not only against the Swiss, but also banks in Austria, Germany, and France; German companies for having profited from slave labor; and museums that had art stolen by the Nazis.[18]

The Vatican had initially been left out of the bruising sparring over wartime loot and missing gold. It had not been the subject of any claims for restitution by victims or their families. But its luck ran out in the summer of 1997, when the church and the Vatican Bank's conduct during World War II came under new scrutiny. The U.S. State Department declassified an October 21, 1946, one-page memo from Treasury agent Emerson Bigelow, in which he wrote about the enormous booty that Croatia's Ustašan fugitives had stolen during the chaos of the closing days of the war. Bigelow concluded "approximately 200 million Swiss francs was originally held in the Vatican for safe-keeping" (about $225 million in 2014 dollars).[19] He said that the Vatican had either sent the loot to Spain and Argentina through its "pipeline" or used that story as a "smokescreen to cover the fact that the treasure remains in its original repository [inside the Vatican]."[20]*

The Bigelow memo put a spotlight on the Vatican and the IOR. And that memo was only the first in what the U.S. government estimated were some fifteen million still classified documents relating to the "safekeeping of Nazi-plundered gold."[22]

Two days after the Bigelow memo was made public, Rabbi Marvin Heir, the director of the Simon Wiesenthal Center, told reporters that the gold deposited at the IOR was likely used to fund "the Vatican rat line [where] basically many leading Nazi war criminals escaped to South America with Vatican passports."[23]

Heir's charge kicked off a frenzy of reporting about the long-forgotten alliance between the church and the Nazi-puppet government in Croatia.[24] Some commentators used it to reevaluate Pope John Paul's controversial decision the

* The Bigelow memo was released on the heels of the 212-page Eizenstat Report, named after Stuart Eizenstat, the Assistant Secretary of State whom President Bill Clinton had chosen to coordinate a review of still-classified wartime files in the archives of eleven government agencies, including the CIA, NSA, Defense, State, and Treasury. That report was a bombshell. It blasted Switzerland for its wartime business with the Nazis and laid bare the extent to which that neutral nation had profited. It concluded that the Nazis stole about $580 million in gold alone ($7.6 billion in 2014 dollars) and sent about half to Switzerland. Beyond the gold, the Eizenstat Report estimated that the Swiss hid an equivalent amount in non-gold-looted assets.[21]

previous year to be the first Pontiff to pray at the tomb of Alojzije Stepinac, Zagreb's wartime cardinal. Stepinac had led the Croatian church during the war and was later convicted of war crimes.[25]

The church's early response to the Bigelow memo was terse. "These reports have no basis in reality," claimed Joaquín Navarro-Valls, the Vatican's chief press spokesman. "The information, which is without any documentation, is only based on a *reliable source* [emphasis added] in Italy which, even if it existed, remains unidentified and of dubious authority."[26]

Edgar Bronfman, an heir to the Seagram's liquor and real estate fortune, was the volunteer head of the World Jewish Congress. He requested a personal meeting with the Pope. "Everybody is going to have to get involved in answering the questions of what happened to the property of the Jews who were killed during the Holocaust," Bronfman told reporters. "That includes the Vatican."[27] Another press release from Rabbi Heir charged that the Vatican had set up twenty-two committees after the war to help spirit wanted Nazis out of Europe.

That May, survivors filed a class action suit against seven major European insurers for escheating life insurance policies and failing to pay claims.[28] To the few Vatican insiders familiar with the IOR's profitable and integrated partnership with Italian insurance companies that operated in Nazi-occupied Eastern Europe during World War II, there was temporary relief the church was not named as defendant. But there was no dearth of bad news about the IOR and the war. Reuters obtained newly declassified U.S. intelligence documents from the National Archives that revealed the Vatican Bank had used Swiss middlemen at least three times during World War II either to get money from the Reichsbank or to transfer funds through blacklisted companies.[29] And the Holocaust Educational Trust, a British-based charity, issued a twenty-five-page report that cited new state archival documents revealing that while the Allies had returned more than three hundred tons of central bank gold to ten countries plundered by the Nazis, about 5.5 tons from concentration camp victims had never been redistributed to the victims or their families.[30] In the wake of that report, the United States and a dozen European countries contributed to a Holocaust compensation fund. The Vatican refused to cooperate.

On September 10, 1997, Shimon Samuels, the European director of the Simon Wiesenthal Center, had an audience with the Pope. Samuels was in

Rome to attend an annual conference of the International Council of Christians and Jews. He was aware the Vatican had a long-planned "millennium examination of conscience" scheduled for the following month, and that its focus was the church's history of injustice against Jews. He thought it an ideal time to ask the Pontiff to open the church's archives to resolve the charges that the Vatican Bank had collaborated with Croatian fascists and that Nazi gold helped war criminals reach South America. Most Western countries had statutes by which documents in their archives were opened to the public after a set number of years had passed. For the Vatican and the IOR, opening such sensitive files required a sovereign decision by the Pope.

When Samuels made the request, the Pope sat silently, refusing even to answer. When he later put the question to Monsignor Remi Hoeckman, the Secretary of the Vatican's Commission for Religious Relations with the Jews, Hoeckman was blunt: the church would "not address the issue; it is out of the question."[31]

Samuels told reporters about the rebuff. What church leaders failed to realize was that they were in the middle of a public relations battle they could not win. Within a week, an Auschwitz survivor protested at St. Peter's Square, wearing a striped prisoner's uniform and carrying a placard that read: "Pius XII and the Vatican are also guilty of the Holocaust." He collected signatures for a petition demanding an international investigation about the extent to which Pius XII remained silent during the Holocaust, tolerated Nazi atrocities, and ignored actions of pro-Nazi Catholic clergy.[32]

When a Vatican symposium to address anti-Semitism in Christian society opened that November, the news was dominated not by the Pope's address to the attendees, but by a public letter addressed to John Paul from the Wiesenthal Center calling again for the opening of the secret archives and the IOR's wartime ledgers: "In this age of transparency, the Vatican is among the last hold-outs in not sharing its full documentation on the period of the Holocaust, thus hampering its contribution to a universal pedagogy in drawing its lessons from, and even in its practical co-operation in, the search for Nazi criminals."[33]

The international pressure built on the city-state. At the end of that month, forty-one countries gathered in London to discuss what to do about the 5.5 tons of concentration camp gold repatriated by the Tripartite Gold Commission, a body set up after the war to settle the issue of stolen assets. The Vatican initially refused to attend. There was no reason to be part of it, said a spokesman, since the church had revealed all there was to tell.[34]

Few believed that. And under strong behind-the-scenes lobbying from the United States, France, and Germany, the Pope sent two representatives, Giovanni d'Anello, a diplomatic advisor to the Secretariat of State, and a Jesuit priest and history professor, Marcel Chappin.[35] Other countries balked, however, when they learned the Pope sent the duo only as silent observers. Under more pressure, the Pontiff upgraded their status to full delegates.

A day into the conference Donald Kenrick, the chief of the International Romani Union delegation, charged that gold coins and rings worth nearly $2 million were taken from 28,000 Gypsies killed in the Croatian concentration camp Jasenovac. That money, said Kenrick, was sent to the Vatican at the end of the war and deposited into the IOR.[36] Although Kenrick did not provide much evidence for his shocking accusation, it was international front-page news.[37]

The Vatican representatives said nothing over three days. Privately they informed the other delegates they would not be part of any joint closing statement. They refused also to discuss opening the secret archives to historians or to allow auditors into the IOR.[38] At one point they almost stormed out in protest when the Americans broached the idea of expanding every country's obligation to include hunting for stolen artworks, escheated insurance policies, and seized bank accounts, bonds, and securities.[39]

The conference finished with a promise by forty-one countries to meet again the following year for a progress report. Only the Vatican and Russia refused to agree to the next meeting or to offer any interim help.[40] The Vatican also rebuffed a personal entreaty from Undersecretary of State Stuart Eizenstat to "examine their documents and make them available."[41] The church's representatives would not even commit to a deadline of December 31, 1999, to which all other countries had agreed, to submit their own historical report on any role it might have had with missing victims' assets.[42]

All the Vatican intransigence made the church seem an outlier on what appeared to be a clear-cut moral issue. It promoted banner headlines such as the one in London's *Telegraph*: "Vatican Comes Under Heavy Flak. World: 'Archives Hold Key to Nazi Gold.'"[43]

"Everyone left London just shaking their heads in disbelief," recalled Elan

Steinberg, the World Jewish Congress's representative. "Two hundred tons of gold from the pro-Nazi Croatian government found its way to the Vatican. Here they were, one of the world's great moral institutions, and they refused to tell us what their view was, much less to lift a finger to help recover any looted assets. It was terribly disappointing."[44]

Five days after stonewalling at the London conference, Vatican spokesman Joaquín Navarro-Valls surprised everyone by claiming that the church had performed an "exhaustive perusal of the pertinent documents and could affirm that there is nothing to add to what has already been published." Moreover, he declared: "Regarding the gold looted by the Nazis in Croatia, searches done in the Vatican archives confirm the inexistence of documents related to the subject and thus ruling out any kind of supposed transaction attributed to the Holy See. Thus the Holy See can look to the past with serenity."[45] As for the many calls that the Vatican open its archives and those of the IOR, Navarro-Valls was clear it would not happen.[46]

No one thought it likely that the Vatican had really conducted a thorough archival search. Speed was against the church's ingrained centuries-old trait of operating at a snail's pace. The general skepticism about Navarro-Valls's adamant denial of wrongdoing was reinforced within a week from a new batch of declassified documents. They identified the Vatican as one of four countries that had illegally received and stored gold bars emblazoned with swastikas (those bars usually included gold from the dental fillings of death camp victims).[47]

By early 1998, however, the British government was optimistic that months of secret talks with church officials had paid off in an agreement by which its investigators could access the Vatican's archives (although the IOR was still off limits). But even that promise turned out to be empty. In March, the church's Commission for Religious Relations with the Jews released a document, "We Remember: A Reflection on the Shoah."[48] It was further evidence of how poorly the Vatican understood the sensitivities of the controversy in which it was enmeshed. It said, "During and after the war, Jewish communities and Jewish leaders expressed their thanks for all that had been done for them, including what Pope Pius XII did personally or through his representatives to save hundreds of thousands of Jewish lives. Many Catholic bishops, priests, religious and laity have been honored for this reason by the State of Israel." Some survivors' groups were particularly incensed by the defense of Pius.[49]

A supplementary 180-page U.S. government report issued that spring (June 2, 1998) provided more evidence that neutral countries, including the Vatican, had profited by hiding Nazi gold in their central banks.[50] In addressing the church, the report noted that since "the postwar disposal of the wartime Croatian treasury remains obscure. . . . There are questions about aspects of the Vatican's record during and immediately after the war, to which the answers may only exist in Vatican archives."[51]

During a press conference at which the report was released, Stuart Eizenstat urged the church and the IOR to open its archives.[52] The Clinton administration gave the Vatican yet another chance that month to contribute to a fund for Holocaust victims, not because it was legally obligated to do so, but as a "moral gesture."[53] That was in keeping with the vague language—"moral involvement"—that had been acceptable to the church when it settled the Ambrosiano case. The Vatican, however, was dismissive. "I don't have anything to add to what was said in the past," said Joaquín Navarro-Valls.[54] By the end of that month, several dozen nations launched a collaborative initiative to identify the size of missing Nazi gold, ascertain the amount of unpaid life and property insurance claims, as well as catalogue artworks.[55]

By late August, a consortium of nations released a progress report. Thirty-one countries had declassified documents. New information came from private banks as well as the Allies' postwar gold commission. There was a joint call for further international cooperation to locate and distribute money to aging Holocaust victims by the end of the century, only eighteen months away. Britain's Lord James Mackay singled out the Vatican and castigated it for not opening its files or providing any assistance about what its bank did with the loot it received.[56] The theme of "Vatican Under Fire over Nazi Gold" dominated the news cycle.[57]

In August 1998—on the eve of the first class-action trial—the Swiss banks settled all pending litigation for $1.25 billion.[58] It was the then largest human rights settlement in history. With the Swiss banks out of the line of media fire, the Vatican moved front and center.

"The Swiss very reluctantly worked with us, kicking and screaming all the way to the negotiating table," said the World Jewish Congress's Steinberg. "But in comparison, when we later tried to get information from the Vatican, the Swiss were an open door. The Vatican told us to get lost."[59]

At the end of September, the World War II–era Tripartite Gold Commission disbanded after more than five decades. Its remaining archives were made public. They revealed that the commission had been unable to account for a stunning 177 tons of gold that went missing from Nazi-occupied territories. And it could not estimate how much privately held gold from victims had been mixed in with bullion it had returned at the end of the war to the central banks of eleven nations. Undersecretary of State Stuart Eizenstat cited that report to implore again the Vatican to open its records.[60]

Seemingly oblivious to the controversy, the ailing seventy-eight-year-old Pope John Paul visited Croatia again and this time beatified Zagreb's wartime archbishop, Aloysius Stepinac. The Pope rebuffed last-minute appeals from the Simon Wiesenthal Center to postpone the beatification "until the completion of an exhaustive study of Stepinac's wartime record based on full access to Vatican archives."[61] Instead, a source identified only as a "Croat inside the Vatican" was quoted in press reports dismissing questions over Stepinac's wartime role as "old claims that had since been disproved" and that "these untruths continue to be recycled by the media."[62] (That Christmas when Croatian prelates offered two special requiem Masses to honor the Ustaša's murderous leader, Ante Pavelić, the Pope did not issue any criticism or rebuke.)[63]

Pressure built on the Vatican that November when Argentina, which had long refused to open its World War II archives, began making them public. It was the final stage of a multiyear review by an international commission of historians.[64]* In the United States, work conducted by the Holocaust Assets Presidential Advisory Commission, combined with more aggressive intervention by the Clinton administration over the continuing declassification of American intelligence records, rewrote the history about the extent to which neutral countries had aided the Nazis in the wholesale theft of billions in victims' assets.[66] It was a watershed moment for historians.[67]

Even the Swiss had gotten into the spirit of transparency over their unsa-

---

* This author played an indirect role in the opening of Argentina's Nazi files. In a *New York Times* op-ed, "The Bormann File," on November 13, 1991—timed to coincide with a visit by Argentine President Carlos Menem to President George H. W. Bush—I wrote about my failed efforts over seven years to get Argentina to release a file about Hitler's secretary Martin Bormann. I had seen that folder when I was in the secret archives of the Federal Police in 1984 while researching a biography of Auschwitz's Dr. Josef Mengele. At the time, the Argentines denied my request to examine the file. In *The New York Times*, I called on Argentina to "release the Bormann papers. There should be no safe haven for the files of mass murderers." Argentine officials initially denied having any such documentation but after several years of stonewalling, they admitted its existence. It took until 1997 for Argentina to establish the Commission for the Clarification of Nazi Activities.[65]

vory past. Switzerland formed an Independent Commission of Experts not only to release their own files, but to shine a light on what other neutral nations like the Vatican did through Switzerland during the war.

In November 1998, Israel published a list of a dozen Holocaust-era archival collections that it charged "have refused or have been uncooperative in sharing information."[68] They included the national archives of the Vatican, France, Russia, and Poland's State Archives, as well as smaller, more targeted collections such as Britain's MI5, the British Custodian of Enemy Property, and documents held by Prague's Jewish Museum.

"We appeal to each institution listed to open their files so that we may learn why civilized society failed in its basic commitment to ensure the safety, lives, liberty and property of our people," the Israelis appealed.[69]

The Vatican ignored the request.

In December, forty-four nations gathered as they had promised a year earlier for a four-day conference in Washington, D.C., to "redress unjust confiscation" by the Nazis and "ways to find prewar owners and make restitution, whether or not heirs are found." The first day marked a breakthrough when Russia announced that it would at long last cooperate with historians and Holocaust organizations in finding looted assets and releasing its files. U.S. Secretary of State Madeleine Albright, who was raised a Catholic but learned only the previous year that her Czech grandparents were Jewish victims of the Nazis, made an emotional appeal to the Vatican representatives. "We cannot restore life nor rewrite history," she said, her voice at times cracking. "But we can make the ledger slightly less out of balance by devoting our time, energy and resources to the search for answers, the return of property and the payment of just claims."[70] Albright's plea ended in another dead end. Navarro-Valls reminded reporters that the church had no relevant files about the Holocaust and nothing at all about Croatian gold.[71]

By now the church had extra motivation to stay mum. The previous month a class action lawsuit filed in San Francisco federal district court named the Vatican Bank and the Franciscan religious order with having enriched themselves from the Ustašan gold.[72] That lawsuit was the first to name the IOR. Jonathan Levy, a solo practitioner with a PhD in political science, filed the complaint. It relied on declassified wartime State Department reports that linked the IOR to the disappearance of hundreds of millions of dollars of cash, gold, and silver looted by the Ustašans from Serbian and Jewish victims.

"I had submitted hundreds of Freedom of Information requests to every government and military department I could think of," Levy said.[73] He was initially uncertain whether he could even serve the Vatican Bank. He mailed a copy of the complaint to Angelo Caloia. "It was a Hail Mary of sorts," Levy confided. "After a couple of weeks he [Caloia] wrote back telling us to cancel our lawsuit, and in the margin of the complaint he had written notes about what he claimed we supposedly had wrong. So we argued to the court that his marked-up version constituted the proof of service. The judge agreed."[74]

Some of the early Freedom of Information documents prompted Levy to amend his complaint to include Swiss banks as defendants. Levy's expanded lawsuit charged that the IOR, together with a Chicago-based Croatian Franciscan group (Croatian Franciscan Custody of the Holy Family), had knowingly sent Nazi gold and cash through Swiss banks to Ustašan war criminals in Argentina.[75] A 1948 U.S. Army Intelligence report confirmed that 2,400 kilos of Ustašan gold were covertly transferred from the Vatican Bank to one of the church's secret Swiss bank accounts. The CIA tracked 5 million Swiss francs from Switzerland to Argentina in 1952. That likely included, contended Levy, the Vatican's Ustašan gold. That blood money ended up with war criminal Ante Pavelić in Buenos Aires.

In December 1999, the German government and private industry reached a $5 billion deal with the plaintiffs over slave labor claims. It eclipsed as the largest human rights legal settlement the $1.25 billion settlement of the previous year by Swiss Banks.[76] A highly critical final report from the Volcker Committee and the Independent Commission of Experts prompted the Swiss to take additional measures to compensate victims.[77] The London Conference on Nazi Gold raised $61 million in contributions. Former Secretary of State Lawrence Eagleburger led the International Commission on Holocaust-Era Insurance Claims (ICHEIC). It had made substantive progress on relaxing the standards of proof required for claims filed by victims' families.[78]

The Vatican was the only nation that still refused to do anything. Church officials had even less incentive to cooperate since the IOR had been named as the chief defendant in a class action. Caloia steered clear of expressing any opinion about whether the IOR should examine its old records and ledgers. It was history in which he had played no role, and although he was generally sympathetic to the request for open archives, he could not afford to waste any political capital in fighting for it.

The church did not even budge when newly declassified American documents revealed that priests at the Portuguese Shrine of Our Lady of Fatima, where hundreds of thousands of the Catholic faithful make an annual pilgrimage, had hidden 110 pounds of Nazi gold. Each bar had been stamped with a swastika and the words *Preußen Staatsmünze—Berlin—1942* (the Prussian State Mint in Berlin). They were smelted from gold stolen from Dutch Jews (the 2014 equivalent of $2.8 million).[79] The Fatima clerics had stored their Nazi gold in safe deposit boxes at a local bank. The church's initial response to the news was silence. A Portuguese bishop, Januário Torgal Ferreira, tried to shift the blame when he told local reporters that while the Fatima gold "had a savage past" it was "money [that] is the true devil."[80] The Vatican, on background only, assured reporters that whatever happened with the Nazi gold at Fatima, none of the swastika-emblazoned bars had found their way to the IOR. The Fatima bishops tried quelling the story by announcing they had sold all their Third Reich bullion a decade earlier to pay for an expansion of the shrine's sanctuary. There were no records since the bank was out of business. In response to an outcry from Holocaust survivors and the World Jewish Congress, the bishop of Leiria promised to donate some unspecified amount of money to "social causes in order to purify the memory of those Nazi ingots." (The author has not been able to confirm what, if any, contribution the local church made.)

Ultimately, all the Vatican gave to survivors and Jewish groups was John Paul's personal statement of regret over the church's long role in fostering anti-Semitism. In March 2000, at Yad Vashem, Israel's Holocaust Memorial, the Pope said: "As bishop of Rome and successor of the Apostle Peter, I assure the Jewish people that the Catholic Church, motivated by the Gospel law of truth and love, and by no political considerations, is deeply saddened by the hatred, acts of persecution and displays of anti-Semitism directed against the Jews by Christians at any time and in any place."[81]

"What it was not was an apology," Elan Steinberg, who had spearheaded much of the restitution campaign for the World Jewish Congress, told the author. "He was very careful not to say he was sorry for anything the church had done or failed to do when it came to the deaths of millions of Jews and other innocent victims during World War II."[82]

Despite more diplomatic pressure, the Pope left Israel without even so much as a promise to consider opening Vatican archives (in 2003 it released documents about its assistance to prisoners of war, and in 2005 some files about Pius XII's time as a Nuncio to Berlin).[83] Measured by the notable progress of other nations both in assisting historians as well as helping victims and their families, the Pope's remarks rang hollow. By the time of John Paul's statement, the large class actions had been settled against the Swiss banks and German companies. French banks had reached a settlement in their litigation at the beginning of that year, as had Austria's banks and private companies.[84] The two major remaining lawsuits were Levy's class action against the Vatican Bank and another filed against Italian and German insurers. When Germany soon signed a broad agreement to address outstanding restitution complaints, German insurance firms were removed from that lawsuit.*

In November 2000, the IOR's American attorneys asked a federal court to dismiss Levy's lawsuit for lack of jurisdiction. "Plaintiffs lack standing to bring a general challenge to the wartime political decisions of a foreign sovereign," the church's lawyers argued in their forty-one-page motion.[86]

"It was clear to us," recalls Levy, "that the Vatican did not want to have to go through any discovery. The idea of discovery really scared them. They would not even entertain having a U.S. government representative act as an intermediary to determine whether or not we could reach a settlement."[87]

In the interim, Levy had launched an effort to get more evidence about the IOR and its role with looted assets by filing lawsuits against a dozen U.S. government agencies, including the CIA. He hoped to force the release of documents that the agencies had either withheld or heavily redacted in answering his earlier Freedom of Information requests. And over the Vatican's objections, Levy convinced the District Court to permit some preliminary discovery to assist in determining the question of whether the court had proper jurisdiction.

The court would not rule on the question of whether the Vatican Bank was immune from the claims of victims for another decade.

* Austrian and Swiss insurers also got their lawsuits dismissed or settled. Only Italy's Generali—which had contributed $100 million to the International Commission for Holocaust-Era Insurance Claims—litigated for nearly another decade. Generali ultimately settled by paying another $35 million to the victims, bringing its total payment for 5,500 claims to $135 million. "They got off lightly," Elan Steinberg told the author. "They made billions and they paid back pennies on the dollar sixty years after the war. For those insurance companies, crime did pay."[85]

31

"A Criminal Underground in the Priesthood"

All the attention on Holocaust restitution claims distracted many Vaticanologists who might have otherwise kept a better watch on what was happening inside the IOR. But for those paying close attention, there were warning signs that the bank was still plagued by systemic problems. In 1999, the $232 million fraudulent empire of American financier Martin Frankel unraveled. The FBI tracked down Frankel and arrested him in Germany. Prosecutors discovered a troublesome IOR link. Frankel had established the St. Francis of Assisi Foundation to Serve and Help the Poor and Alleviate Suffering, a British Virgin Islands company through which he ran millions of offshore dollars, much of it stolen from clients. A seventy-nine-year-old monsignor, Emilio Colagiovanni, had allowed Frankel to use his separate foundation at the Vatican Bank so that Frankel's money transfers stayed off the radar of financial watchdogs.[1]

That Colagiovanni had any connection to a swindler like Frankel surprised prosecutors. The elderly monsignor was a scholar who edited a Vatican-approved canonical law quarterly and served as an emeritus judge on the Roman Rota, the Pope's prestigious court of appeals. Seventy-three-year-old Peter Jacobs was another priest dragged into the scandal. Father Jacobs was president of Frankel's offshore foundation, and had himself been suspended from his priestly duties for having earlier defied his archbishop by running a popular Manhattan restaurant that was supposed to send its profits to the poor, but was the subject of press stories about how it fueled lavish lifestyles for shady characters.[2]

Frankel had promised the Vatican a $55 million contribution. The terms of the "contribution" meant that the Vatican would have kept only $5 million and the other $50 million would stay under Frankel's control in a Vatican Bank–linked foundation.[3] But Frankel never gave a cent. Prosecutors had trouble believing that no one at the bank spotted that the Frankel foundation had unrestricted use of a third-party IOR account through which millions in cash passed regularly. And their suspicions were heightened when they discovered that Colagiovanni had consulted with the Vatican's third-ranking prelate, Cardinal Giovanni Battista Re, the Sostituto for General Affairs of the Secretariat of State, as well as the Papal Nuncio to the United States, Cardinal Pio Laghi.[4] Soon questions led back to Gianfranco Piovano, the Vatican Bank's chief prelate. Piovano, it turned out, had met several times with Colagiovanni, Jacobs, and their attorney, Tom Bolan, a former partner of legendary New York lawyer Roy Cohn.[5]

The media loved the Frankel case. A search of his Greenwich home had uncovered an enormous stash of pornography, a Ouija board, and printed reminders to shred documents and to check on jurisdictions that did not have extradition treaties with the U.S.[6] Still, the Vatican Bank ultimately deflected inquiries about its own civil liability. The IOR instead blamed any wrongdoing on the two American priests, claiming as Marcinkus had a decade earlier, that it was the unwitting victim of sophisticated con men. In one of its most impolitic defenses, Vatican spokesman Joaquín Navarro-Valls downplayed Colagiovanni's status by saying he was merely a "pensioner" and dismissed Jacobs as an "ex-Jew." Father Jacobs had a Jewish father, although his mother was Catholic; he converted to Catholicism in his twenties, was baptized, and ordained a priest in 1955.[7] As for the wayward foundation, Navarro-Valls said it "does not have any relationship with it [the Vatican] whatsoever."

The Frankel probe was another reminder to Caloia that even after nine years he did not have full control of the bank's numbered foundation accounts. It was the same issue that had frustrated him with Monsignor De Bonis and the Cardinal Francis Spellman Foundation. Whenever Caloia thought he had made improvements, something like the Frankel scandal mocked his lack of progress.

Even though Caloia drilled down inside the IOR to find out what had gone wrong with Frankel, his focus in 1999 was on ensuring that the Pope appoint him for another five-year tenure. His term was set to expire that October, and his opponents were anxious to find a replacement.

American Cardinal Casimir Szoka was no Caloia friend.[8] Szoka carried weight inside the Curia. John Paul had picked him in 1990 to run the Prefecture for the Economic Affairs of the Holy See, and in 1997 he was appointed the President of the city-state's Governorate, one of Marcinkus's old posts. Before arriving at the Curia in 1990, Szoka was the treasurer of the American Bishop's Conference as well as Detroit's archbishop. During ten difficult years in Detroit, he oversaw that diocese's considerable downsizing. Even his critics acknowledged he was a tough decision maker who ran a lean administration (he had to close thirty parishes due to lack of money).[9] And, as the son of a Polish émigré who himself spoke fluent Polish, he had influence with John Paul.[10] Szoka wanted Hans Tietmeyer, the outgoing president of Germany's central bank, to be the IOR chief.[11]

The anti-Caloia contingent even planted stories attributed to "Vatican sources" that the church was wooing Tietmeyer.[12] While the German banker had an impressive résumé, his sponsors underestimated the enmity that John Paul and his private secretary, Stanislaw Dziwisz, had toward Germans due to what the Nazis had done to Poland.[13] Although John Paul had no special affection for Caloia, the IOR chief's gray countenance worked to his benefit: neither had he made an enemy of the Pontiff during nearly a decade of service. Ultimately, the Pope was not persuaded that Tietmeyer—who did not even speak Italian—was a better replacement. Not even Szoka could change John Paul's mind. All the jockeying for power ended when the Pontiff vowed publicly, "As long as I'm alive, there will never be a German in charge of the Vatican's finances."[14] The Pope confirmed Caloia for a third term.

During his first decade, Caloia had discovered that the religious community often had a terrible view of the Vatican Bank. "There was a wall of distrust," Caloia said, "at least not much enthusiasm. For them, the IOR was intent on 'profiteering' and 'speculation.'" Many clerics were conflicted about money. They realized it was necessary to run the parishes and dispense help to the needy, but at the same time, "Holy monks consider money the shit of the devil."[15] As far as Caloia was concerned, "the challenge is if money is the devil's shit, then we Christians must be able to turn it into a good fertilizer."[16]

By 2000 Caloia had come to see his role as that of a "financial advisor" who had "customers" with different needs and wants. Some were rich religious orders "with custodians who speak ten languages and play the stock market." Others were poor and only worried about not losing money in a swindle or fraud. And he tended to those differences in ways Marcinkus and Nogara had never contemplated. Under his guidance there were only a few clerics left inside the IOR. The bank had three times as many employees as just twenty years earlier. His easy-going stewardship meant morale had lifted.[17]

On the cusp of his third term, the seasoned Caloia knew that unforeseen crises from some hidden shadows in the bank might prevent him from accomplishing his informal to-do list. "The Devil is always lurking, multifaceted, and treacherous," he told friend and author Giancarlo Galli.[18] He could not then have imagined that just as the all-consuming fight over Holocaust restitution had distracted top clerics from focusing on his reform proposals, a shocking problem—priests and child sex abuse—would derail his efforts this time around. The sex abuse scandal had captured the interest of inquisitive Vaticanologists, diverting their attention from the IOR. It soon centered on money issues as billions of dollars were paid out for decades of crimes of pedophilic priests. It meant that Caloia's substantive plans for remaking the bank got lost in a deluge of sordid crimes and disturbing charges of cover-up at the highest levels of the church.

For decades, the Vatican and dioceses dismissed occasional cases of sexual abuse of minors by clergy as aberrations unique to the individual priest accused of wrongdoing. Among clerics, just as in the general population, it was expected that there might be some sexual deviancy. There were, according to the church, few such cases. But some insiders knew that was a lie. A priest assigned to a rural Louisiana parish, Gilbert Gauthe, was arrested in 1984 on multiple counts of forced sex on boys as young as seven. When parents discovered that Gauthe had a predatory history and that instead of alerting civil authorities his superiors had transferred him around to different parishes, they sued.[19] That attracted the attention of a dogged Louisiana-based investigative journalist, Jason Berry. During his early reporting, Berry cultivated a Deep Throat source he code-named Chalice. And in reviewing a court file Berry came across the deposition of a local bishop who admitted that he then knew about a second pedophile in his parish. But he refused to identify him to the lawyers for the parents.[20]

While reporting the story Berry also pitched his article to national outlets. *Vanity Fair*, *Rolling Stone*, *Mother Jones*, *The Nation*, and *The New York Times Magazine* all passed. Berry's groundbreaking three-part investigation began running in May 1985 in a free Louisiana alternative newsweekly, *The Times of Acadiana.*[21] The editors, in a preface to Berry's first part, noted "incest and molestation by caretakers of young people are on the rise. It is also a problem of the Catholic Church outside of Louisiana. Other cases involving priests who molested youngsters in California, Oregon, Idaho and Wisconsin have recently been reported."[22]

Berry's investigation was a searing indictment of how church officials in Louisiana buried reports of sexual abuse of minors and did their best to pay off victims to keep them silent. By the time his story ran, the tiny Lafayette diocese in which Gauthe had committed his crimes was deeply in the red from $4.2 million in confidential settlements to the families of nine victims, and $114 million in pending claims in another eleven lawsuits.

The Times of Acadiana had a circulation of 25,000. Berry had struck a deal with the *National Catholic Reporter* to run a condensed version of his series in June. In an editorial note to a companion piece, NCR publisher Thomas Fox wrote, "In cases throughout the nation, the Catholic Church is facing scandals and being forced to pay millions of dollars in claims to families whose sons have been molested by Catholic priests." But the national press mostly ignored the story. "There was no popular sense back then that sexual child abuse in the church was an issue," Berry later said.[23] (Berry won a Catholic Press Association Award and was nominated for a Pulitzer for his work.)

There were some exceptions. Berry's hard-nosed reporting motivated Carl Cannon at the *San Jose Mercury News* and Karen Henderson at the Cleveland *Plain Dealer* to start their own investigations.[24] A small group of American victims formed Survivors Network of Those Abused by Priests (SNAP) in 1988.[25] That same year Berry told the *National Law Journal,* "There is a whole string of little sexual Watergates laced out across the map of America."[26] And Berry and Cannon discussed it on the *Phil Donahue Show*. A few in the clergy's hierarchy realized there was a serious problem. Canadian bishops issued guidelines in 1992 for better screening of abusive priests after sordid revelations about abuse at a Newfoundland orphanage emerged.[27] But that stirred little interest in America media. That same year, 1992, Berry published *Lead Us Not into Temptation: Catholic Priests and the Sexual Abuse of Children*, a seminal book about the American clergy and the hidden problem of child sex abuse (despite Berry's high profile, more than a dozen publishers passed on it before a former seminarian who was the religious editor at Doubleday said yes to the finished manuscript).[28]

Despite the book's critically sound reception, the topic of sex abuse and the clergy largely remained off the front pages.[29] As Frank Bruni wrote a decade later in *The New York Times*, "Catholic leaders insisted that child sexual abuse by priests was an aberrant horror, expertly quelling any significant protest among American Catholics and containing a debate about the need to reform church traditions. Cases of priests' preying on children came and went, and though some of them badly embarrassed the church, none ultimately shook it."[30] That was true until the beginning of 2002 when the issue exploded in the United States.[31] Pedophilia revelations and lawsuits over several months broke in Dallas; Pittsburgh; Manchester, New Hampshire; Boston; Tucson; and Philadelphia.[32] In the wake of a criminal conviction of a defrocked priest, John Geoghan, for molesting a ten-year-old boy, *The Boston Globe* sued for the release of sealed church files. The documents revealed that the Boston diocese had ignored dozens of horrific abuse reports over thirty years, tried unsuccessfully to rehabilitate Geoghan, and when that failed began transferring him from parish to parish. Cardinal Bernard Law, then America's senior prelate, had approved some of the transfers, as well as authorizing $15 million in confidential settlements to victims and their families. The files documented sexual abuse charges against eighty other Boston-area priests, some dating back to the 1960s.[33]

By January 2002, the Catholic Church in Ireland settled abuse claims that extended back twenty years with a then record payment of $175 million. By then, priest sex abuse cases had been reported from Australia to France to England.[34]

When Pope John Paul spoke out the first time that March, it was to say that the sexual abuse charges were casting a "dark shadow of suspicion" over all clergy. "As priests," he said, "we are personally and profoundly afflicted by the sins of some of our brothers who have betrayed the grace of ordination in succumbing even to the most grievous forms of the mystery of evil at work in the world."[35]

That fell far short of the language for which many had hoped. John Paul did not apologize to the victims. He did not order all bishops to contact local police in instances in which sex abuse was uncovered. The Pope thought it was the responsibility of the dioceses, instead of the Vatican, to rid the priesthood of abusers. That is because in appreciating the extent to which sexual abuse of minors was a church-wide cancer, there was in the Vatican a sense that the problem was confined to a few Western countries, particularly America. John L. Allen, Jr., the *National Catholic Reporter*'s chief Vatican correspondent, told the *Boston Globe* that inside the Vatican, top clerics did not believe that "sexual abuse of kids is unique to the States, but they do think that the reporting on it is uniquely American, fueled by anti-Catholicism and shyster lawyers hustling to tap the deep pockets of the church. And that thinking is tied to the larger perception about American culture, which is that there is a hysteria when it comes to anything sexual, and an incomprehension of the Catholic Church."[36] Secretary of State Sodano later told reporters that "the [sex abuse] scandals in the United States received disproportionate attention from the media. . . . It is fair to condemn evil, but one must keep it in proportion."[37] The Pope made it clear he did not think Rome had to intervene.

Meanwhile a survey commissioned by the American bishops had revealed that sex abuse was a bigger problem among U.S. priests than had been thought (the first report in 2002 identified 850 priests that had been accused since the 1960s, with 350 of those having been defrocked). Victims' groups contended the number was much larger. The likelihood they were right was buttressed later that year when Australian church records revealed that one in ten priests there had been accused at some point of sexual abuse of a minor.[38] (It was not then widely known that some clerics had returned to their priestly duties *after* serving prison sentences for sex crimes with minors.)

The Pope summoned twelve American cardinals and two senior bishops to Rome for an emergency meeting in April 2002.[39] In prepared remarks he thanked them for keeping him "informed regarding the complex and difficult situation which has arisen in your country in recent months." That caused much consternation since it again cast clerical sex abuse as if it were a recent American phenomenon. While he condemned sexual abuse of minors by priests as "an appalling sin in the eyes of God," he also seemed to absolve the failure of some bishops to root out the predators. He claimed they had come up short because of "a generalized lack of knowledge of the nature of the problem and also at times the advice of clinical experts." Instead of apologizing to the victims, the Pope said only, "I express my profound sense of solidarity and concern." And he infuriated many by seemingly dismissing the overall impact of the crisis and its effect on the priesthood: "A great work of art may be blemished, but its beauty remains."[40]

Before returning to the United States, the American cardinals issued their own statement. It called for better training in seminaries as well as a national day of repentance and prayer but fell short of promising the expulsion of abusive clerics or providing a framework by which sex abuse crimes could be reported to civil authorities.[41] The cardinals did not address whether to inform local police about abusers. They also refused to embrace a "one strike and you're out" standard.[42] As for defrocking priests, they would act only against those clerics who had become "notorious and [are] guilty of the serial predatory sexual abuse of minors." In cases that were not notorious, the bishops said that individual dioceses would handle them.[43]

Los Angeles' Cardinal Roger Mahoney expounded on the collective statement to reporters. When it came to priests guilty of sexually abusing minors, but the incidents were decades old and there were no recent complaints, he said they should be left alone. What purpose was there in punishing them after so many years, asked Mahoney.[44]

The cardinals were not long back in the United States when Archbishop Julián Herranz Casado, the president of the prestigious Pontifical Council for Legislative Texts, gave a talk at the Catholic University of Milan. Herranz Casado castigated the U.S. media for "sully[ing] the image of the church and the Catholic priesthood." He condemned large financial settlements as "unwarranted" and accused the American bishops of falling prey to a climate of "exaggeration, financial exploitation, and nervousness." The records of sexually abusive priests should not be turned over to civil authorities, he warned, lest the church's sovereignty be weakened. Finally, Herranz Casado noted that to the extent there was any sexual abuse crisis, it was a result of gay men who had become priests. Child abuse, said Herranz, was a "concrete form of homosexuality."[45]*

---

* Archbishop Herranz repeated the view of other top Vatican officials who had publicly linked clerical sexual abuse of minors *only* to homosexuality. That is demonstrably false. In society as a whole, most pedophiles are heterosexual. That is not surprising since heterosexuals are the large majority of the population. But it was different in the all-male priesthood, where 80 percent of the abuse cases were men to boys. Cardinal Joseph Ratzinger had written a much cited October 1, 1986, letter to all bishops "on the pastoral care of homosexual persons." In it, Ratzinger wrote that "homosexual persons . . . [have] a disordered sexual inclination which is essentially self-indulgent." Simply being gay exhibited a "strong tendency ordered towards an intrinsic moral evil." Ratzinger's conclusion—that the "practice of homosexuality [that] may seriously threaten the lives and well-being of a large number of people"—was

The following month, one of the Vatican's most influential canon lawyers, Father Gianfranco Ghirlanda, dean of the canon law faculty at Rome's Gregorian University, weighed in. In a Vatican-approved article for *La Civiltà Cattolica,* he wrote, "From a canonical point of view, the bishop or religious superior is neither morally nor legally responsible for a criminal act committed by one of his clerics." Moreover, Ghirlanda, widely reported to be passing along the private feelings of the Pope, said that any priest transferred to another parish after being "treated because of a history of sexual abuse" should not have any "good reputation" ruined by having his sexual misconduct against minors revealed to his new parish.[47]

The U.S. Conference of Bishops tackled the subject directly in a three-day heated conference in Dallas that June. They voted 239 to 13 for what most of them considered a beefed-up policy on clerical molesters. The bishops vowed to administratively remove sex offenders from any job where they were in regular contact with children but not to defrock them.[48] "From this day forward, no one known to have sexually abused a child will work in the Catholic Church," confidently predicted the conference chair, Illinois Bishop Wilton D. Gregory.[49]

Not everyone agreed the new rules were tough enough. Victims' advocates thought they were riddled with loopholes that allowed abuse to go unpunished.[50] "It isn't zero tolerance," said Peter Isely, a member of SNAP. "It is simply not what Catholics wanted."[51]

In August, at a meeting of 125 top Catholic orders in Philadelphia, the delegates agreed that sexually abusive priests could not be stripped of their right to wear religious habits nor could they be expelled from their orders. The Reverend Canice Connors, a Franciscan priest who was the conference president, told the assembly that the media's coverage of predator priests was slanted to

---

often cited by traditionalists for the facile argument that the church's sex abuse problems resulted simply from too many gay priests. Such gay bashing only hastened a public debate that played out in the media about "how widespread is homosexuality among priests?" A report that studied death certificates from the mid-1980s concluded that "The death rate of priests from AIDS is at least four times that of the general population." As late as 2011, Bill Donahue, president of the influential Catholic League for Religious and Civil Rights, continued to dismiss the sex abuse crisis as caused primarily by gay priests. In the *National Catholic Reporter*, Donahue wrote, "While it is true that most homosexual priests are not molesters, most of the molesters have been priests who are homosexual," and that abuse cases among priests had increased because "there was an exodus of heterosexual priests after Vatican II. . . . And there was a surge in homosexuals in the seminaries."[46]

create a "vengeful atmosphere" and he rejected calls by victims to adopt a zero tolerance policy for abusers. Zero tolerance, Connors said, was a "war slogan" that was not right for the Catholic Church (American bishops had approved such a policy a couple of months earlier, but it lacked any effective enforcement mechanism).[52]

No one then knew that the "transfer and don't tell" policy adopted by Boston's Cardinal Law was far more widespread than imagined.[53] New York's Cardinal Edward Egan startled even stalwart Catholics when he told reporters that the church would decide on its own if and when to pass along information about sex crimes to police and prosecutors. It was under no obligation to do so, Egan said.[54] Despite much public outcry, the New York legislature failed to pass a law that would have added the church to a roster of professional groups, which included doctors and teachers, legally obligated to report all child abuse cases. The Catholic Church argued that such a law would be an undue state interference with its sovereign affairs and the sanctity of the confessional box.

America's bishops in fact had ignored warnings about a sex abuse epidemic in the clergy for at least seventeen years. In 1985, two clerics had drafted a report about pedophiles in the priesthood—"The Problem of Sexual Molestation by Roman Catholic Clergy: Meeting the Problem in a Comprehensive and Responsible Manner"—and submitted it to the bishops.[55] One of the authors was Father Thomas Doyle, a canonical lawyer at the Vatican's embassy in Washington, D.C., who was considered on a fast track to becoming a bishop.[56] Doyle was helped by Ray Mouton, the lawyer in the Gauthe case, and by Father Michael Peterson, an openly gay man who converted from Mormonism to Catholicism and founded a medical clinic with the sole mission to treat clerics with sexual compulsions and disorders.[57] That ninety-three-page "eyes only" report warned that sexual abuse of minors by priests was "the single most serious and far-reaching problem facing our church today." In a prescient warning, the authors said, "Those presumed to be guilty of sexual misconduct, especially if it involves child molestation, must never be transferred to another parish or post as the isolated remedy for the situation."[58]

The authors predicted that even if the bishops acted with determination to address the problem, the church could still have to pay more than $1 billion in victims' settlements. "If church leaders persist in cover-up rather than succoring the faithful, the world's largest Christian institution would fall into a slough of financial and spiritual despair."[59] It urged that "clerics suspected of abuse" not be permitted to be parish priests in contact with children.

Not only did the American bishops dismiss that unsolicited report as alarmist, but it put a stop to Doyle's promising career.[60] He lost his position at Catholic University and was transferred from his embassy posting, first to the Grissom Air Force station in Indiana, and later to the remote Thule base in Greenland.[61] (The Nuncio at the time who took the punitive action against Doyle was Archbishop Pio Laghi. Pope John Paul subsequently gave Laghi a red hat.) Peterson, meanwhile, was criticized for overhyping the report to drive more "business" to his medical clinic, where he treated priests with sexual addictions. By 1987, Peterson had died of AIDS.[62]

That there was such resistance to the report was evidence that the church's top officials hoped to manage the problem rather than confront and root it out. Implementing what the report had suggested—it included a manual with guidelines for a national "crisis control team" to reach out to victims—would have meant admitting the seriousness of the crisis. Now, in the summer of 2002, and faced with an onslaught of media coverage, the bishops could no longer ignore it.[63]

Many victims who thought that the American bishops were responding too hesitantly looked to the Vatican and Pope John Paul for help. They found none. The Pope was quiet when accused pedophile priests threatened litigation against their bishops for violating their employment rights by defrocking them.[64] And the Pontiff also did not respond publicly when a support group for sex abuse victims beseeched him to prevent priests from filing malicious defamation lawsuits against their accusers. John Paul was a bystander as the American church quietly approved an aggressive new legal strategy that included, as *The Washington Post* uncovered, "hiring high-powered law firms and private detectives to examine the personal lives of the church's accusers, fighting to keep documents secret and engaging in new tactics to minimize settlements."[65]

To the great dismay of victims' rights groups, what did prompt the Pope and Vatican to intervene was when the American bishops were told that they did not have the authority to administratively remove a priest charged with sexual abuse. Instead, the Vatican decreed that canon law demanded a full church trial for accused priests.[66]

The previous December, John Paul had consolidated authority over the church's often baffling and arcane rules that governed when and how a priest could be defrocked into the Congregation for the Doctrine of the Faith (the Supreme Sacred Congregation of the Roman and Universal Inquisition until it was given a less inflammatory name in 1965).[67] German cardinal Joseph Ratzinger—later Pope Benedict XVI—was the Congregation's chief. American bishops had for years recognized that the cumbersome rules governing that office worked to the benefit of child molesters. Thirteen years earlier (1989), U.S. bishops had sent some canonical law scholars to the Vatican to argue in vain for a streamlined process. In any case, the byzantine rules of Ratzinger's office only applied to defrocking ordinary priests. No one could touch bishops, so when Palm Beach's Bishop Anthony O'Connell admitted he had molested a seminarian, the only recourse was to ask for his resignation.[68]

What was not evident to most outsiders was that the Vatican's reactionary policy about sexual abuse by priests was driven largely by worries over financial ramifications. The Pope's failure to apologize to victims was the direct result of fear that with thousands of lawsuits filed against dozens of dioceses around the world, plaintiffs would use a Pontifical mea culpa as an "admission against interests" by the church.[69] The Vatican was also concerned that the church's powerful American branch and its large payouts were setting a bad precedent that might soon have dire consequences for dioceses internationally.[70]

By the spring there were nearly a thousand lawsuits filed in the United States. Some of the dioceses had put aside tens of millions in contingency funds for settlements.[71] It was evident to the church's top moneymen like Caloia that the American parishes—the biggest contributor to Peter's Pence—were going to be constrained for money between the litigation and settlement costs. They would be tapping their own parishioners for contributions to replenish those funds, and that would slash what they could send to Rome. The Vatican had to prepare for reduced income.

During intense backroom strategy sessions in 2002, the Vatican decided that no matter how the abuse scandal played out, it had to inoculate itself as much as possible against financial exposure. Although the Vatican controlled many aspects of local church life, even including the words used in liturgical prayers, it wanted to make certain that individual dioceses had the full responsibility for managing the sex abuse scandal.[72] The church's policy would last through all further shockwaves of sexual abuse in any country: each diocese was its own separate legal entity, responsible for its own liability. The financial problems in one diocese were insulated so they did not affect a wealthy neighboring diocese. Each was its own non-profit corporation, usually with trusts for its real estate holdings, so that any bills and judgments against it could not be collected against any other diocese, and particularly not from the Vatican itself. Some of the largest, like Chicago, had a long-established separate banking system that added another layer of complexity to its financial relationship with Rome.[73] To further insulate the individual dioceses, the American bishops had voted to double to $10 million how much a diocese could liquidate of its own assets without seeking Vatican approval (Rome approved the higher limit and even suggested the American church tie it to an inflation index so it automatically increased over time).[74]

Attorneys retained by the church double-checked to ensure that all 2,864 Catholic dioceses and 412,886 parishes worldwide—even Rome itself—were legally independent from the Vatican and that any financial fallout from the sex abuse litigation would not affect the city-state.[75] Putting all the pressure on the individual dioceses had predictable consequences. After a large 1985 jury award, insurance companies in the United States began excluding coverage for sex abuse from their liability policies.[76] That meant many dioceses had to self-insure when it came to the costs of litigating and settling abuse cases. The following year Boston paid $85 million to settle cases with 552 victims.[77] Boston had about $14 billion in just property holdings, and $160 million worth of that property was unused.[78] Still, since it was cash poor, it had to close schools to raise the settlement money, a move that embittered many loyal Catholics.[79] Portland, Oregon, on the other hand, did not have any cushion. Facing a $53 million settlement, it was the first archdiocese to declare bankruptcy in 2004 (two religious orders and eleven other dioceses have since filed bankruptcy).[80]

Even that first insolvency could not have prepared the church for the coming flood of litigation and criminal probes: more than $3 billion and still counting as of 2014 in settlements and awards *just* on American abuse cases; the ransacking of clergy pension and retirement funds; the shuttering of churches, schools, and in some instances entire parishes; and special assessments that have strained the purses of ordinary parishioners to keep some dioceses afloat.[81] Sometimes the struggle for survival led to bitter fights when bishops relied on canon law to "suppress a parish"—the equivalent of a civil eminent domain action—and thereby gain control over the property and money.[82] *

Even the parish bankruptcy filings got mired in millions of dollars of litigation. Portland's archbishop, for instance, argued that he had "bare legal title" to the diocese's assets and properties and therefore contended he could not sell anything to satisfy the claims of victims. Moreover, his lawyers cited the U.S. Constitution's separation of church and state as a financial shield, saying it prevented any court from interfering with its church-granted powers.[84] "Neither the bishop nor the diocese is the owner of parish property under Canon Law," Nicholas Cafardi, the dean of Duquesne Law School and himself a canon law scholar, said in a sworn statement.[85]

Notwithstanding all its careful planning to keep a legal moat around the Vatican, in 2003 the church was caught by surprise when a Louisville, Kentucky, gun-slinging medical malpractice attorney, William McMurray, filed a federal class action and named the Holy See. Three Louisville men claimed they were abused by priests for decades and sought damages on behalf of all American victims of clerical abuse. McMurray based his suit on a 1962 document uncovered in the discovery of another case, signed by Pope John XXIII, directing that sex abuse complaints against priests should be "pursued in a most secretive way."[86] Top church officials were furious about the Kentucky suit and moved to dismiss it on well-established grounds that the Pope was immune as a foreign sovereign from civil litigation in U.S. courts. Secretary of State Sodano, in a meeting with Condoleezza Rice, his American counterpart, urged her to convince the administration of George W. Bush to intervene to get the case dismissed. According to WikiLeaks cables in which State Department officials recorded the back-and-forth between Sodano and Rice, he complained about "aggressive attorneys" and told her, "It is one thing for them to sue bishops but

---

* Resentment built in the United States when it became public that Cardinal Sodano's nephew, Andrea Sodano, was in business with Raffaello Follieri, a flashy young Italian businessman—known best in America for dating actress Anne Hathaway and living in a $37,000-a-month Fifth Avenue Manhattan penthouse—who boasted he had insider information and Vatican contracts to buy $100 million in the distressed American church properties. Follieri, who was friends with Bill Clinton and bragged of meeting Pope Benedict, pled guilty to fourteen counts of wire fraud in 2008 and was sentenced to fifty-four months in federal prison. Upon his 2012 release he was deported to his native Italy. As for Andrea Sodano, the FBI considered him an unindicted co-conspirator. "It helps to have an uncle in robes," wrote author Jason Berry.[83]

another thing entirely to sue the Holy See."[87] Secretary Rice explained that his request was impossible because of America's separation of powers.[88] Sodano believed that her failure to stop the litigation against the Pope demonstrated "a lack of respect for Vatican sovereignty."[89]

Sodano's extraordinary plea to Rice was evidence that Rome was very worried that the U.S. court system was unpredictable and that eventually a jury inflamed by the sordid details of an abuse case might decide to hold the church's CEO—the Pope—responsible for the actions of his wayward priests and the connivance of cardinals and bishops in protecting the abusers.[90] To the Vatican's great frustration, not only did it fail to get a dismissal, but the Kentucky filing encouraged similar lawsuits against the Pope in other American jurisdictions.*

The full extent of the sex abuse scandal was made clear in a February 2004 145-page research report about the crisis undertaken by New York's John Jay College of Criminal Justice.[91] The U.S. Conference of Catholic Bishops had authorized the study.[92] It concluded that 95 percent of American dioceses had at least one complaint of a sexual assault by a priest against a minor (the authors did not count incidents before 1950).[93] During the five-plus decades, 4,392 priests had been accused of abusing 10,667 children, a figure that in some years was as high as 10 percent of all priests.[94] At least 143 were serial molesters who carried out their attacks in multiple dioceses.[95] Four out of five victims were minor boys.[96]

"Few incidents [less than 5 percent] were reported to the police," the study concluded. The authors speculated it was because so many victims were children that they often did not report the crime until after the statute of limitations had passed. Even when the police were notified about abuse in a timely

---

* Some cases in which the Holy See was named as a defendant—such as a 2005 Houston case—were dismissed based on sovereign immunity. But that defense did not always work. In the Louisville case, for instance, in 2007, U.S. District Judge John G. Heyburn III ruled a suit could proceed; in 2008 the Sixth Circuit Court of Appeals decided that while the Vatican was immune from most litigation, the case could move forward on the narrow question of whether top Curial prelates had engaged in a deliberate cover-up of sex abuse by American priests. In 2009, the Ninth Circuit U.S. Court of Appeals ruled that another lawsuit—*Doe* v. *Holy See*—could proceed under an exception to the Sovereign Immunities Act. In 2011, a federal judge allowed a Portland case to advance, ruling that the plaintiff had produced "evidence that tends to show the Holy See knew of [the abusing priest's] propensities and that in some cases, the Holy See exercised direct control over the conduct, placement, and removal of individual priests accused of similar sexual misconduct." The Supreme Court refused to hear the appeal of the Portland case. It was not until 2012 that a U.S. District judge put an effective end to the claims against the Pope with a ruling that the Holy See is not the employer of molesting priests.

manner, only one in three priests were charged with a crime. Fewer than 3 percent of those served any prison time. And astonishingly, "the priests with *many* allegations of abuse were *not* more likely than other priests to be charged and serve prison sentences."[97]

The study determined that significant numbers of abusive priests had themselves been abused as children, and as clerics they often battled substance abuse problems—overwhelmingly alcohol—or untreated mental illness. Yet, only a quarter were ever referred for any treatment by their clerical superiors.[98] To try to cure offenders of their sexual compulsion, they were often sent to "spiritual counseling."[99] And to the church's embarrassment, it had spent more on attorney fees in defending the abuse litigation ($38.4 million) than it did on treating all its problem priests over fifty years ($33.3 million).[100] Only much later was it discovered that millions more had been spent on attorneys who lobbied state legislatures to block efforts to extend the statute of limitations when it came to child sex abuse claims.[101]

Many victims and their families felt betrayed by their own church. So did many ordinary Catholics who sensed the church only reacted when there was another story or lawsuit. Author Jason Berry wrote that Pope John Paul II "responded to continuing allegations of clergy abuse with denial and inertia." Berry noted that the Pontiff was "a commanding figure" in dealing with major international and political issues, but that when it came to "the greatest internal crisis facing the church, the pope failed, time and again, to take decisive action in response to clear evidence of a criminal underground in the priesthood, a subculture that sexually traumatized tens of thousands of youngsters."[102]

Father Richard McBrien, a Notre Dame theology professor, called the clerical sexual abuse scandal "the greatest crisis to confront the Catholic Church since the Reformation of the 16th century." Regarding rooting out the abusers, McBrien later concluded that John Paul "had a terrible record, full of denial and foot-dragging."[103] In one of the highest-profile cases, John Paul had sent out a dreadful message to the highest echelons of the church. He had failed even to consider the evidence of sexual abuse charged by nine respected seminarians against Marcial Maciel Degollado, the powerful Mexican priest who founded the Legion of Christ and Regnum Christi movements.[104] Maciel shared the Pontiff's ultraconservative political philosophy and was, according to Jason Berry, "the greatest fundraiser of the modern church."[105] Maciel spread his money around to build good will for his order, everything from grand parties for Secretary of State Sodano to cash gifts to the Vatican. In 1999, the Pope intervened to close an internal case in which two of the abused seminarians sought Maciel's excommunication in a proceeding before the Congregation of the Doctrine of the Faith.[106] When Father Rafael Moreno, Maciel's personal assistant for nearly two decades, tried warning the Pontiff in 2003, John Paul "didn't listen, didn't believe." When Moreno tried getting an audience with the Secretary of State, Sodano refused to meet him.[107]

Maciel was ultimately unmasked for having not only abused boys, but for having sexual relationships with at least two women, and fathered up to six children. One of the boys Maciel had fathered with a domestic servant thirty-seven years his junior claimed that the bishop repeatedly had raped him.[108] When news became public of John Paul's protection of the influential insider, it seemed to represent on a larger scale what had happened with many far less powerful and well-known child-molesting priests in local parishes.[109]

32

"His Inbox Was a Disaster"

By 2005, John Paul was battling persistent rumors that he was seriously ill. His private doctors had diagnosed him with Parkinson's disease in 1994, but in keeping with its centuries-old tradition that any public discussion about the Pope's health was inappropriate, the Vatican swore the physicians to secrecy. A decade earlier, the only manifestation of the degenerative neurological disease was a slight tremor in John Paul's left arm and hand.[1] Parkinson's would over time prove a tremendous challenge. But John Paul insisted that his struggle stay private, even though performing his duties had become increasingly difficult, especially when it came to his trips abroad and demanding public appearances at the Vatican.[2]

Whenever he was not seen in public for a while, rumors swirled that he was gravely ill. The previous year an announcement that the eighty-three-year-old Pontiff had canceled his traditional Ash Wednesday service at the Basilica of St. Sabina to instead preside over a simpler Mass at St. Peter's prompted two British bookmakers to offer odds on his likely successor. The favorite was Milan's Cardinal Dionigi Tettamanzi.[3] Not until it was clear that John Paul had survived the Easter services did the betting stop.

Few knew that John Paul considered his affliction the will of God. Since he was convinced that God had guided his fellow cardinals to select him as the Vicar of Christ, he thought himself Pope for life. There was no room in the Catholic Church, he told colleagues, for an honorary Pope.[4] And resignation was unthinkable. Most Catholics agreed. "The idea of a pope retiring really has no precedent, and the continuity of the papacy depends upon the election of a new pope on the death of another," wrote journalist James Murray.[5] Sixty-five percent of Italians polled said the Pontiff should never resign, no matter how debilitating any end-of-life illness.[6]

Although his deteriorating health had not stopped him from sitting on the throne of St. Peter, it affected what happened inside the Vatican. Parkinson's, coupled with chronic pain from other ailments, made it difficult for him to spend long hours in meetings or reading reports. U.S. diplomat Michael Hornblow said, "He was very energetic, but not a great administrator. I was told his inbox was a disaster."[7] Even as a bishop in Poland he never had a reputation as a micromanager. His illnesses meant that during the last decade of his Papacy he concentrated only on what mattered most to him. He spent tremendous time on his extraordinary international pilgrimages. After his Parkinson's diagnosis, each trip out of Italy was more difficult. They required far more logistical planning (by the end of his Papacy, he tallied 104 foreign trips, more than *all* his predecessors combined). From 1994 until 2005, he made sixty foreign trips, including demanding ones to India, the Middle East, Africa, and two visits to the United States. For weeks before each one, John Paul prepared by studying up on the clerics and influential Catholics whom he would meet.

One of the things for which he no longer had time was any oversight of the Vatican Bank. Angelo Caloia was left alone to run the bank subject to the loose supervision of the IOR's commission of cardinals and some advice from its lay directors. Caloia's own ideas for bank reform were occasionally discussed, but there was no crisis that gave any urgency to convert them from the drawing board to practice. Despite Caloia's good intentions, during the decade of John Paul's declining health, the bank had yet to undergo any of the core institutional reforms that would mark the end of its role as an offshore banking haven.

There were some warning signs that the IOR's apparent tranquillity was an illusion. In 2000, Italian police arrested twenty-one mobsters who were part of one of the first-ever online banking frauds, an electronic scheme to steal up to $900 million from Sicily's central bank using pilfered computer files and passwords. Legal wiretaps had caught the mobsters boasting of accomplices inside the Vatican Bank. Police made the arrests before the theft was pulled off since "it would have been impossible for the Italian state to recover [the money]" if it had gotten inside the IOR.[8] But as result of acting so fast, prosecutors could not determine who inside the Vatican Bank had been part of the conspiracy.

That same year, the Institute of Applied Economic and Social Research at the University of Melbourne published the results of an extensive study of international money laundering.[9] The authors compared the banking systems of two hundred countries. The Vatican ranked in the top ten money laundering havens, behind Luxembourg, Switzerland, the Cayman Islands, and Liechtenstein, but ahead of Singapore.[10] Also, in 2000, the Vatican finished in the top ten "most attractive countries for money launderers" in another report, this time by the United Nations' Congress on Economic and Social Issues.[11] The following year, 2001, a report by the *London Telegraph* and the *Inside Fraud Bulletin* rated the Vatican as a top cutout country along with such offshore banking sanctuaries as Nauru, Macao, and Mauritius. A cutout was a nation in which banking secrecy made it all but impossible to trace laundered funds back to their source. The IOR, concluded the report, was the primary conduit for $55 billion annually just in illegal Italian money. And for the third time in a year, the Vatican Bank had the dubious distinction of getting tagged as a top offshore shelter, the eighth most popular bank for money launderers and the fourth-best cutout. The IOR beat out Liechtenstein, Switzerland, and the Bahamas.[12]

Despite its high rankings on those unsavory lists, the announcements garnered little more than shrugs from the media, long accustomed to assuming the worst about the Vatican Bank. If the reports concerned Caloia and his associates running the bank, they did not do anything to address the structural shortcomings that allowed the IOR to flourish as a popular destination for illegal cash. (John Walker, the chief investigator on the Melbourne and U.N. reports, told the author in 2014 that the Vatican "remains up there with the best places to launder money.")[13]*

What did attract press attention, though, were new developments in old scandals. In the United States, insurance commissioners in five states used racketeering statutes (RICO) to file civil lawsuits totaling $600 million, nam-

* In 2005, a Mexican bishop said that donating money to the church "purified" it. Some Vaticanologists thought that was a not subtle pitch to get narco-traffickers to be more generous with their religious contributions. A Mexican monsignor addressed the matter more directly: "It is immaterial where the donations from drug trafficking originate and it's not up to us to investigate the source of the money." Such donations are called *narco limosnas* (narco-alms) in Mexico. No money laundering laws are violated so long as the Mexican clerics do not kick some of the cash back to the traffickers. But the U.S. Drug Enforcement Administration believes the Mexican church's willingness not to ask questions about large cash gifts is a significant reason why the Catholic church's wealth there has multiplied in recent years.[14]

ing the IOR and the Pope as two of the defendants, to recover money in the 1999 fraud of financier Marty Frankel.[15] Each state claimed the Vatican Bank knew and failed to stop Frankel from swindling investors by using Catholic charities as fronts.[16] The church managed to ultimately get the litigation dismissed, arguing that the Vatican was exempt from the proceedings since Frankel's foundation "did not have Vatican juridical character" and had "always acted outside of any Vatican context."[17] But to Rome's consternation, the cases drew a lot of attention while they were pending. (Frankel, and the two priests who helped him, Fathers Colagiovanni and Jacobs, pled guilty to counts of racketeering, conspiracy, wire fraud, and money laundering. Because of their advanced age, the clerics each got probation; Frankel is still serving a seventeen-year prison sentence.)

Beyond Frankel, the Ambrosiano and the never-ending investigation into Roberto Calvi's death returned to the headlines. A film about the case premiered in Italy in 2002, but an Italian judge ordered it removed from theaters after Flavio Carboni, the Sardinian property developer and Calvi associate, filed a defamation suit.[18] That year new forensic tests suggested that Calvi had been murdered. By 2003, the headlines asking "Who Killed God's Banker?" were replaced by new ones announcing that Italian prosecutors were investigating four mobsters as murder suspects.[19] The formal declaration that foul play was involved came almost twenty-one years to the day after Calvi's body had been found swinging from Blackfriars Bridge. It kicked off stories speculating about who might be behind the murder: the Mafia, Masons, or even the Vatican.[20] Starting in 2000, more than half of all English language news stories about the Vatican Bank in a five-year period were about Calvi's murder and included a reprise of at least some aspect of the Ambrosiano scandal.[21]

As far as John Paul was concerned, he was likely pleased that the bank was not involved in any new imbroglios. Caloia's deliberate low profile seemed the perfect antidote to the otherwise salacious Italian tabloid press. In 2005, Caloia was up for yet another five-year term. Most Vaticanologists expected the Pontiff to rubber-stamp the extension. But before John Paul extended his IOR director's tenure, the eighty-four-year-old Pontiff died on April 2, 2005. Although he had soldiered through years of chronic illnesses, his passing still surprised most Catholics.[22] His Papacy had lasted twenty-seven years. A young generation of the faithful had known no other leader.

33

The Kingmaker Becomes King

In the days after his death, the frenzied attention about funeral details and the speculation over who might next assume the throne of St. Peter pushed some news about the Vatican Bank into the back pages of newspapers. Although the public may not have paid much attention, it was on the minds of the arriving cardinals. The same day that Pope John Paul died, an anonymous "church banker" told a U.S. journalist that the Vatican Bank had accumulated a record $5 billion in cash reserves (an earlier estimate by *The Financial Times* concluded the IOR and APSA separately controlled about a $60 billion real estate and stock portfolio, a figure the Vatican said was inflated).[1]

But not all the economic news awaiting the next Pontiff was good. Only days after John Paul's passing, there were press reports that after a decade of surpluses that had lasted until 2003, the Vatican was expecting its third consecutive year in the red. Cardinal Sergio Sebastiani, the chief of the Holy See's economic affairs office, blamed it on unexpected currency losses from a near 20 percent surge in the value of the dollar, a tough investment climate, and stagnant European economies. John Paul's expansion of the church's diplomatic presence in dozens of countries had resulted in hundreds of new lay employees.[2] Cardinal Edmund Szoka, Sebastiani's predecessor for more than a decade, told reporters that the slide was due to low returns on the church's investments—since all its money was managed so conservatively. "If it were my own money," Szoka told *The Wall Street Journal*, "I would be much more aggressive."[3]

Although no official acknowledged it, there was little doubt that the sex abuse crisis had caused a sharp drop-off in contributions to Rome, particularly from Americans. By the time of John Paul's death, the U.S. church had paid $840 million in out-of-court settlements to victims, and three dioceses, Tucson, Spokane, and Portland, had declared bankruptcy.[4] Professor John Pollard, author of sober histories about early Papal finances, told reporters, "The impact of the priest pedophile scandal of the U.S. could impact anywhere between one-third and 40 percent of Peter's Pence."[5]

No matter the underlying cause of the turnaround from profit machine to money loser, it suggested the cardinals who had demonstrated they were adept at managing finances might have an advantage at the conclave.[6] John Paul's successor would also confront whether or not to make substantive reform at the Vatican Bank a priority. Some Vatican observers speculated that poor investments at the IOR might be the reason behind the flip from profits to losses. Since all of the Vatican Bank's business was secret, it was not possible to know whether the Pope's distanced role had allowed the bank to fall into old habits of excessive speculation.[7] Its checkered history meant even the simplest questions caused anxiety. In providing a shortlist of what attributes were required of the next Pope, one commentator suggested: "He's going to have to avoid Vatican bank scandals."[8]

The 2005 conclave took place in a different world than the one that selected John Paul in 1978. Back then, Jimmy Carter was president and Margaret Thatcher was not yet England's prime minister. The Cold War and communism's oppression of tens of millions of Catholics, factors that may have led to selecting a strong anticommunist from an Eastern Bloc country, was now history. And the makeup of the electors in the conclave itself had radically changed. Just three of the 117 eligible cardinals for the upcoming conclave had been at the last one. John Paul appointed all the rest. That led most Vaticanologists to believe that the race was wide open. The only certainty, wrote one commentator, was that it was "highly uncertain."[9]

One cardinal omitted from all the early speculation was Joseph Aloisius Ratzinger, the powerful head of the Dean of the College of Cardinals and Prefect of the Congregation for the Doctrine of the Faith. "His role and his 'fame' as John Paul II's rigorous guardian of doctrinal orthodoxy was said to rule him right out of the contest," wrote one Vaticanologist.[10] No one doubted that Ratzinger was John Paul's ideological soul mate. But that appeared a weakness in a church seemingly overdue for a fresh direction. Although some respected Italian journalists, with good Curial contacts, wrote only a few months before the Pope's death that Ratzinger was papabile, most dismissed that as unfounded gossip.[11] As the cardinals gathered in Rome, the conventional wisdom remained that Ratzinger's senior status and intellectual rigor on church doctrine made him the indisputable *grande elettore* (the kingmaker) but not a candidate. And in any case, at seventy-seven, his day had passed.[12] Poland's Zeon Grocholewski even broke the unwritten rule of not commenting about other cardinals when he told reporters that Ratzinger was intelligent but "too old."[13]

Since it had been twenty-seven years since the last conclave, the media seemed initially a little rusty in its coverage. They had to find a new batch of talking heads for the now omnipresent television coverage. And they covered it like a political election with a veritable torrent of speculation about which frontrunner might be the next Pontiff and what it meant for the world's 1.1 billion Catholics. Since the Pope is also the Bishop of Rome, some Curialists leaked word that it was time again for an Italian. One of the most frequently mentioned was Milan's seventy-two-year-old Dionigi Tettamanzi, an esteemed theologian and ardent opponent of euthanasia and abortion. Venice's sixty-three-year-old Cardinal Angelo Scola was high on the popularity meter. And Genoa's Cardinal Tarcisio Bertone worked hard to ensure he was not left behind. Bertone was the only cardinal to stand in the long line with lay mourners to pay respect to John Paul while his body lay in state inside St. Peter's. He brought along a camera crew to record his shaking hands and blessing babies during his hours of waiting.[14] And Bertone ensured he stayed in the news by renewing a campaign to ban Dan Brown's bestselling *The Da Vinci Code.*

But the media wanted stories beyond the usual suspects. Had the time come for a Pope from Africa or Latin America?[15] A theological hard-liner, Cardinal Francis Arinze, a Nigerian who had been at the Vatican for twenty years, was on some shortlists. He had good credentials, the equivalent of two cabinet-level posts under John Paul, head of the Pontifical Council for Interreligious Dialogue, and the chief of the Congregation of Divine Worship. The idea of the first black Pope sent the press speculation about Arinze into overdrive. And seventy-year-old Brazilian Cardinal Claudio Hummes seemed the favorite if the time was right to acknowledge the increasing power and growth of Catholicism's Hispanic base.[16]

The press focused on the personalities of the frontrunners. Inside the College of Cardinals, however, the underlying struggle was the same one that confronted each conclave since the 1958 death of Pius XII: would the church select a progressive committed to reform or preserve John Paul's conservative orthodoxy? Many progressives liked Jesuit Cardinal Carlo Maria Martini, Milan's former archbishop. The problem was that Martini was seventy-eight, had been retired for several years in Jerusalem, suffered himself from what appeared to be early stages of Parkinson's, and had said repeatedly he had no desire to be Pope. Some thought he was simply a stalking horse to test the extent of the progressives' strength in the early balloting. If he did well, they planned to consolidate around a real candidate, likely another Jesuit, Buenos Aires's outspoken Cardinal Jorge Mario Bergoglio (to quash any momentum for Bergoglio, someone spread the rumor that he was not strong enough to cope with the strains of the job since he had lost a lung as a teenager).[17]

As for the conservatives, Secretary of State Sodano was mentioned a lot, but at seventy-seven many thought him too old. And some foes tried diminishing his chances by reminding their colleagues that he had once lavished praise on the theologian Hans Küng, who had subsequently had his license to teach as a Catholic theologian revoked.[18]

The seventy-one-year-old cardinal of Brussels, Godfried Danneels, was a reliable moderate, and his backers hoped that the progressives and conservatives might deadlock. If so, Danneels might emerge as a compromise.[19]

Only as the cardinals arrived in Rome was there some chatter that Ratzinger might be a contender after all. But any such talk was always tempered by the commentary that he was so divisive it was unlikely that two thirds of the cardinals would ever agree to bow before him and kiss his ring. In a discussion of frontrunners, London's *Daily Mail* noted that Ratzinger had entrenched enemies since he had risen "to prominence as something of a reformer, but has come to embody 'radical orthodoxy.' Liberals hate him."[20] It was not hard to understand why. On every major issue he was a reactionary advocate. He would neither brook a discussion about ending celibacy, nor consider the ordination of women as priests. Ratzinger championed still the excommunication of dissident theologians. Gays, he said, were afflicted with an "objective disorder." Jews deplored his "theological anti-Semitism," his view that they could only be fulfilled if they accepted Christ. Protestants bristled at his description that they were "gravely deficient" and the suggestion that their houses of worship were not worthy of being called churches.[21]

That Ratzinger might be considered as the next Pope scared his adversaries, many of whom spoke anonymously to reporters.[22] A "church source" was quoted saying, "Cardinal Ratzinger doesn't want a pope as right wing as Pope John Paul II. He wants a Pope more right wing than Pope John Paul II." Another "church source" said, "Cardinal Ratzinger wants a church which is pure and disciplined. He would focus so much on the dogma and on the purity of the church that he would drive people away, and although that would not please him, it wouldn't bother him that much either."[23] "He has too many enemies due to his heavy-handed, centralized and arrogant approach to theology," one widely quoted "Vatican insider" said.[24] "A German Rottweiler," said an unnamed Italian cardinal.[25] "It fills me with horror," said one unidentified theologian. "He would probably be a great Pope," one nameless Western cardinal was quoted as saying. "But I have no idea how I would explain his election back home."[26]

Some worried that Ratzinger would disappoint ordinary Catholics. He might seem a bland successor to the personable and captivating John Paul. Ratzinger had little sense of humor, never lost control of his emotions, was devoid of sentimentality, and prided himself on rigorous discipline and ecclesiastical purity. John Paul realized that a successful Pope is measured in part by the same standards as a popular political leader, a dash of charisma and an occasional sense of the showman. Ratzinger had none of that.

Camillo Ruini, the Cardinal Vicar General of Rome, in remarks widely interpreted as criticizing Ratzinger, told reporters that Catholics needed a *people's pope*, someone who cared more about "ministering to the faithful rather than for bureaucratic credentials."[27] John Paul had broken ground by mixing with everyone from rock stars to top athletes to aboriginal dancers. Not only did it endear him to the faithful, but it humanized a Papacy that had seemed remote with every modern predecessor except for the short tenure of John XXIII more than forty years earlier. John Paul seemed the real headliner at a 1997 Bob Dylan concert in Bologna, with 300,000 fans cheering the Pontiff to Dylan's "Knockin' on Heaven's Door."[28] That concert, broadcast live on Italian television, sealed the Pope's image as a modern icon. Only inside the Vatican were top officials aware that the chief opponent to the Dylan concert had been Ratzinger.[29] Mixing with popular culture was unseemly for a Pontiff, he contended, and in any case, Dylan was the wrong type of "prophet."[30] It might, argued Ratzinger, even be interpreted as an endorsement by the church of the often loose morals expressed both in the songs and personal lives of pop stars. John Paul ignored similar warnings from Ratzinger when he attended a rock concert in 2000 to raise money to relieve the crushing debts of Third World countries (he greeted the Eurythmics and Alanis Morrisette, but passed on meeting Lou Reed, whose drug-saturated lyrics were considered too risqué). Even John Paul's annual Christmas parties were unprecedented. Over the years he shared the stage with Lionel Richie, Tom Jones, Lauryn Hill, Gloria Gaynor, Dionne Warwick, John Denver, and Whitney Houston. (After Ratzinger became the next Pope, he refused that first Christmas to meet with any of the performers who had already been invited while John Paul was alive; he canceled the event after that.)[31]

It had taken years for John Paul's proactive populism to infuse Catholics with a personal enthusiasm about the church. Now some fretted that Ratzinger could cause all that to dissipate. The *National Catholic Reporter*'s John Allen, who five years earlier had written a biography of Ratzinger, was not surprised. "Many observers see Ratzinger as more Catholic than Jesus," Allen wrote about the devout German.[32]

The conclave was set to start April 18. The 115 voting cardinals were well aware that a record-breaking two million mourners had crammed St. Peter's to pay respect to John Paul (two cardinals, Mexico's Adolfo Suárez Rivera and Jaime Sin of the Philippines were too ill to attend). The wait to pass by the deceased Pontiff's casket was sometimes eight hours.* Certainly none of the cardinals was accustomed to the media horde. During the twenty-seven years of John Paul's Papacy, CNN had created the 24/7 cycle. There was now the Internet, with its attendant minute-by-minute scrutiny. Determined to stop anonymous mudslinging, the Vatican had ordered even cleaners, cooks, and elevator operators servicing the conclave to sign an oath that threatened instant excommunication for any leaks.[34] And three times the Sistine Chapel was swept for electronic listening devices (none evidently were found).

On the eve of the first session, London's *Sunday Times* ran a startling headline: "Papal Hopeful Is a former Hitler Youth." Ratzinger had never hidden that he had joined the Hitler Youth when he was fourteen, in 1941, shortly after it was made compulsory. He had addressed it in his own autobiography.[35] The

---

* American sex abuse victims were outraged that the disgraced Cardinal Bernard Law, who had resigned as the chief of Boston's diocese after the firestorm over disclosures of how he shuffled about pedophile priests rather than discipline them, led one of the nine official funeral Masses in Rome. Just as infuriating, since he was under eighty, he was one of the conclave's voting cardinals.[33]

timid child who preferred solitude to company with other children was only six when Hitler had become Chancellor. His great-uncle on his father's side, Georg Ratzinger, was one of Bavaria's most noted authors and politicians, as well as a leading anti-Semite.[36] His parents—father a police officer and mother a cook in local bed-and-breakfasts—had determined his future for him when he was only twelve by entering him and his older brother, Georg, into a minor seminary. It took him six years after World War II before he was ordained a priest. And fitting with his loner personality, as a new prelate he wanted nothing of parish life. He became a theology professor instead at the southern German University of Tübingen, and delved with considerable success into a secluded world of books and philosophy. When the student riots and protests of the late 1960s hit Tübingen, it convinced Ratzinger that the outside world was a dangerous and unstable place. He moved to the backwater University of Regensburg, a place free from all the political discord he found so upsetting.[37] His loyal service as the theological advisor to the German Bishops' Conference was rewarded with an appointment in 1977 as Munich's archbishop. For the man who preferred his days studying ancient texts and discussing church doctrine, he had trouble adapting to his administrative duties. He struggled for five years running that diocese. Few who worked with him in Munich thought he had the natural talent of an administrator or leader, traits about which the best archbishops and cardinals usually boasted.[38] After his Munich service, he reentered the world of academia and the Curia when John Paul appointed him the chief of the church's powerful doctrinal congregation. He never again tried his hand at running a diocese.

John Allen, Ratzinger's biographer, had written that he "was only briefly a member of the Hitler Youth and not an enthusiastic one."[39] Since Hitler Youth was intended by the Nazis to break the church's early influence on youngsters, new recruits were barraged with anti-Catholic propaganda. Was that sharp contrast to his education at a minor seminary the reason for his less than keen embrace of the Nazi youth group? It was not clear. But what was undisputed was that his membership had never been widely covered. And the *Sunday Times* declared that despite Ratzinger having disclosed it himself seven years earlier in his autobiography, not even many members of the church knew about it. The *Times* predicted it "may return to haunt him as cardinals begin voting in the Sistine Chapel tomorrow."[40]

It was in fact news to millions of people. After finishing two years with the Hitler Youth, at sixteen, Ratzinger enrolled in a German army antiaircraft unit posted to guard a BMW factory that manufactured aircraft engines. That factory used forced labor consisting of inmates from the nearby Dachau concentration camp. Ratzinger long insisted he never had any combat role. When he later transferred to Hungary, and saw Jews sent to death camps, he deserted in April 1944.[41]

Just a few years earlier the Vatican and the Holy See had been named—and dismissed—in a series of lawsuits about restitution to Nazi victims. There were still unanswered questions about looted gold and the possible role of the Vatican Bank. Would Ratzinger's conclave support dissipate because the cardinals might shy away from selecting not only a German, but one with youthful ties to the Third Reich?

Ratzinger offered no last-minute defense. Instead, in the final pre-conclave Mass, he told his fellow cardinals, "We are moving toward a dictatorship of relativism that has at its highest goal one's own ego and one's own desires. . . . Adult faith is not one that follows tides of trends and the latest novelties."[42]

A final snapshot of all the guesswork about who would be the next Pope was set by three British bookmakers who laid odds for gamblers. It is also a testament to how little the lay public understood about Vatican politics. Italy's Tettamanzi and Nigeria's Arinze led the pack at 4 to 1. Right behind was Honduras's Óscar Rodríguez Maradiaga (9 to 2). Ratzinger was back at 7 to 1, with Brazil's Hummes at 9 to 1 and a recent surge of betting on Austria's Christoph von Schönborn bringing him up to 14 to 1.[43]

On the first day of the conclave, Monday, April 18, the cardinals took only one late afternoon vote. Ratzinger and Martini were expected to end in a dead heat, setting the stage for the hand-to-hand battle between the ideologically divided camps. The surprise was that while Ratzinger got forty-seven votes, far short of the seventy-seven needed to become Pope, the progressives were splintered. Buenos Aires's Bergoglio pulled ten votes while Cardinals Martini and Ruini got only six each.[44] Could Ratzinger build on his first-ballot momentum, or would the progressives rally behind one candidate? As a result of politicking that night, Martini threw his support to Bergoglio. Eighty-one-year-old Cardinal Achille Silvestrini, too old to vote in the conclave, encouraged his fellow liberals at least to band together to block Ratzinger.[45]

The next morning, the cardinals took an early vote to see where they stood after a night of reflection. Ratzinger had added to his support, now tallying sixty-five. Bergoglio had more than tripled to thirty-five. The next highest vote getter was Cardinal Sodano far back with four votes. Just a day into the conclave, it was a two-man race. Bergoglio's ascent was something of a surprise. His enemies had tried scuttling his chances three days before the conclave, publicizing the filing of a lawsuit that claimed Bergoglio was complicit in the 1976 kidnapping of two left-wing Jesuits by the then ruling Argentine military junta. The cardinal dismissed the charge.[46]

Australia's Cardinal George Pell, himself talked about before the conclave as a possible contender, threw his support to Ratzinger after that vote. Cardinal Sodano gave up any hope of emerging as Pope and begun lobbying the Italians to line up behind Ratzinger. He was old, said Sodano, so he would only be a temporary place holder for the Papacy, and the fears of his polarizing the faithful were overblown.[47] Angelo Scola overcame his own misgivings and also supported Ratzinger.

The cardinals were working fast. Just before lunch they took a third ballot. It almost put Ratzinger over the top with seventy-two votes (five short of becoming Pope). Bergoglio had added five but seemed stuck far back with forty. After breaking for lunch, the prelates returned and took the final ballot of that afternoon. It was decisive. Ratzinger got eighty-four votes, seven more than needed. Most came from Bergoglio defectors who evidently decided that a fast and unified front to the world was better for the church than a prolonged battle.[48] Other than the conclave that had selected Pius XII on the eve of World War II, it was the fastest election in more than a century.[49]

The man at the center of so much controversy became Benedict XVI (in tribute to the fifth-century monk who was the patriarch of Western monasticism and Benedict XV, who had tried to prevent World War I). The exuberant crowd that greeted him when he made his first appearance as Pope sounded as if it were a soccer crowd shouting "Ben-e-detto! Ben-e-detto!"[50]

Ratzinger was the first German elected Pope in a thousand years and the oldest Pope in three centuries. His ascension felt as historic a change as when the cardinals had selected a Polish Pope twenty-seven years earlier. There was little doubt that to the lay public his selection was as controversial as that of any modern Pope. "From Hitler Youth to the Vatican" was the jarring banner headline in London's *Guardian*; "White Smoke, Black Past," declared Israel's *Yedi'ot Aharonot.*

At a Mass he celebrated two days later for the cardinals before they left

Rome, Benedict told them, "I welcome everybody with simplicity and love to assure them that the Church wants to continue in open and sincere dialogue with them, in search of the true good of man and society. . . . I have a sense of inadequacy and human turmoil at the responsibility entrusted to me."[51]

For at least one moment, friends and foes alike found solace in his conciliatory tone. They hoped that the man whose motto was "truth is not determined by a majority vote" might become as Pope the church's compassionate father.

34

"As Flat as Stale Beer"

A week before Ratzinger was elected Pope, a split U.S. Circuit Court of Appeals panel in San Francisco rejected the Vatican Bank's dismissal motion from the Nazi gold class action.[1] Writing for the majority, Judge Margaret McKeown said: "In the landscape before us, this lawsuit is the only game in town with respect to claimed looting and profiteering by the Vatican Bank." The majority noted that little was known about the IOR: "The exact relationship between the Vatican and the Vatican Bank is less than clear at this stage of the proceedings. . . . The actual dealings of the bank, however, are murky. . . . Indeed, the Vatican Bank's holdings and its specific transactions are opaque."[2]

Those Curialists who had lived through the $244 million settlement with the Ambrosiano were alarmed not only that the church's reputation and finances were at risk, but worse that it was subject to unpredictable American courts. Benedict, however, showed no discernible concern. Nor did he discuss it with others in the Curia.[3]

In a classified cable sent to State Department headquarters in Washington—made public later through WikiLeaks—the U.S. embassy at the Vatican concluded only a month after Benedict's election that he was a religious hardliner with no political skills, and that he was too old to acquire any.[4] As a result, U.S. officials warned that made it doubtful that he could effectively control or streamline the unruly Curia. In his style of governing he ignored the advice of most officials and "only a handful of experts are aware of imminent decisions."[5]

Within a couple of months, that same embassy staff had determined that Benedict was not even an effective autocrat. They noted he not only avoided difficult decisions but he did not authorize anyone else to address problems.

That July, less than three months after he had assumed the Papacy, the chief United Nations war crimes prosecutor at The Hague, Carla Del Ponte, visited the Vatican (she had started her career in 1982 in her native Switzerland investigating the Sicilian Mafia and Roberto Calvi).[6]* She met with Archbishop Giovanni Lajolo, the Secretary for Relations with States (the church's Foreign Minister). Del Ponte had a lead indicating that a former Croatian general wanted for war crimes might be hiding in Franciscan monasteries in Croatia.[8] The Croatian Bishops' Conference had been "voicing defiant expressions of support" for the fugitive, she told Lajolo. He gave her the brush-off by claiming the "Vatican is not a state, so it could do nothing."[9] Del Ponte was skeptical when Lajolo claimed Rome had no authority over the Croatian bishops.

Del Ponte insisted on meeting with Benedict. The Pope, not sure what to do, simply refused. U.S. diplomats later learned that Benedict did not want to have to choose between ordering the Franciscans to turn over the Croat general or seeming less than cooperative with the U.N. when it came to a war crimes investigation.[10] Del Ponte persisted. She was finally told that if she wanted to meet Benedict, she should just join the public any Saturday in St. Peter's Square. She might be lucky enough to be selected to kiss the Pontiff's fisherman's ring.[11]

That September, London's *Daily Telegraph* ran a jarring headline: "Vatican Accused of Shielding 'War Criminal.'" "One of the most wanted war criminals is being shielded by the Roman Catholic Church and the Vatican hierarchy, the United Nations' chief prosecutor for former Yugoslavia said yesterday," the paper reported.[12]

The American diplomats appointed to the city-state watched as Benedict and his team fumbled changing the public narrative that cast the church as an obstructionist in the pursuit of justice. Vatican spokesman Joaquín Navarro-Valls claimed at first that Del Ponte had not provided enough details for the church to act. And, in any case, said Navarro-Valls, the lack of action was Del Ponte's fault. She had contacted the wrong department.[13]

Those cavalier responses fueled the controversy. The bad press continued

---

* In 2001, Del Ponte had worked a genocide investigation against four Rwandans, two of them Catholic priests, one living under a false name in Italy and the other hiding under an alias in Switzerland. After appealing to the Vatican for help in persuading the priest in Italy to turn himself in, she later discovered that "church officials sent him into hiding." "I was," she wrote in her book, *Madame Prosecutor*, "to put it mildly, furious."[7]

until that December when the fugitive Croat general was arrested in Spain. In his four years on the run, it turned out he had been to Argentina, China, Chile, Russia, the Czech Republic, Mauritius, and even Tahiti. So if the Vatican had not been shielding him, why did it so badly handle the accusation that it was protecting a wanted war criminal? Was it a rookie mistake or a sign that Benedict's administration had a more serious problem?

The answer, soon in coming, was not good. Another confidential State Department memo (also a WikiLeaks release) highlighted more of what was wrong in the new Pontificate. There was, according to the cable, a "lack of generational or geographical diversity in the Pope's inner circle. Most of the top ranks of the Vatican—all men, generally in their seventies—do not understand modern media and new information technologies. . . . A culture in which many officials do not even have official email accounts." It noted "the Italo-centric nature of the Pope's closest advisors. Other than Archbishop James Harvey, an American and head of the Papal household, there is no one from an Anglophone country in the Pope's inner circle. . . . This meant few had exposure to the American—or, indeed, global—rough and tumble of media communications." Whenever the Pope's advisors wrote something for public release, their style was so "old-fashioned [and] inwardly focused" that "no one outside their tight circles can decipher [it]." As far as the U.S. diplomats were concerned, there was even an unanswered question about "who, if anyone, brings dissenting views to the Pope's attention."[14]

The failure of Benedict and his team to master modern spin control meant that the Vatican invariably played defense whenever problems arose. Instead of delivering and controlling its own message, it seemed only to react—often poorly—to stories that angered or provoked it. The church's historic view that all things could wait no longer seemed viable. Additionally, the Pope kept missing opportunities to humanize himself and thereby engender populist goodwill. Even when his coterie announced with great fanfare that Benedict had his own email and Twitter accounts, as well as a Facebook page, it was only window dressing. The Pontiff still wrote everything by hand. Although he received hundreds of thousands of emails and tweets, he never looked at a single one. Through his tenure Vatican landlines did not have voice mail; the favored means of correspondence was fax.[15]

If Benedict did not have a charismatic connection with the faithful would he at least prove his worth with an unwavering and an undiluted vision of the church and his role? That would be a prerequisite for reforming the Curia. Every Pontiff since Pius XII had promised to tackle the Roman behemoth that at times seemed to run Popes more than they ran it. Was it possible that the church's "hard-knuckled intellect" might be the right man for the task?[16] Hope ran high with Benedict.[17]

There was little measurable progress, though, in the first year of his Papacy. Benedict held endless meetings but they resulted in little concrete action. He issued no hoped-for decrees streamlining the overlapping responsibilities and powers between Curial departments.

Angelo Sodano, the blustery Secretary of State, was past the customary retirement age of seventy-five when Benedict was elected.[18] But the Pontiff had allowed him to remain in office. Besides the Pope, no person inside the Vatican wields as much power as the Secretary of State. So Vaticanologists expected that to be one of Benedict's first appointments. But when he did announce a replacement the following June, more than a year into his Papacy, the pick surprised many.[19] The Pope tapped Tarcisio Bertone, Genoa's cardinal.[20] Bertone had no diplomatic experience and had never worked a day in the Secretariat of State. But Benedict knew, admired, and trusted him. He had been Benedict's deputy for seven years at the Congregation for the Doctrine of the Faith.[21] The Pope—insisting on absolute loyalty—did not want a Secretary of State whom he had to worry might undermine him.

Sodano, who would become the Dean of the Sacred College of Cardinals, evidently found it galling to hand off the keys to someone who would be learning on the job. No matter what one thought of Sodano's haughty and often dismissive ways, everyone agreed that he and his small cadre of advisors were seasoned veterans. When John Paul was increasingly hobbled by illnesses during the later years of his Papacy, Sodano and his team had directed much of the church's day-to-day administration.

Since Bertone's promotion did not become effective until mid-September, Sodano had time to consolidate his power.[22] He wanted to ensure that top aides were rewarded with prestigious postings.[23] One slot of particular interest was that of the chief prelate at the IOR, a position that had been empty for thirteen years since De Bonis's transfer to the Knights of Malta.[24] Sodano was the chairman of the committee of cardinals with oversight of the Vatican Bank. Under John Paul, he knew it was not possible to push through such a key appointment without the Pope's express approval. But Benedict was more pliable.

Sodano's pick as the Vatican Bank's chief cleric? He appointed forty-five-year-old Monsignor Piero Pioppo, his longtime personal secretary.[25]

Some senior prelates griped to Benedict that Pioppo's selection smacked of favoritism and might not be in the IOR's best interests. That long-empty Vatican Bank position should be the proper province of the incoming Secretary of State, they contended. But Benedict declined reversing it. Instead, he simply instructed his private secretary, Monsignor Georg Gänswein—a noted theologian and canon law professor—to keep an eye on Pioppo.[26]

It was bad that Benedict had a reputation as someone who could be pushed around by a strong cardinal. Worse was that Bertone turned out to be the wrong man to serve as Secretary of State. Not only did he not have the respect of key Curialists whose support he needed, but he was heavy-handed in throwing around his newfound power.

Secret State Department cables reveal that American officials concluded quickly that Bertone was a disaster. The American embassy to the Vatican informed Washington the Curia was "more disorganized than before under Bertone's leadership." That was a rather remarkable judgment given the Curia had long been considered an unadulterated mess.[27] In language particularly blunt, the American diplomats warned, "Bertone's lack of diplomatic experience (he speaks only Italian, for example), and a personal style that elevates 'pastoral' work—with frequent foreign travel focusing on the spiritual needs of Catholics around the world—over foreign policy and management" meant that the Pope was poorly served by his top Curial pick.[28]

If there was one area in which some Vaticanologists predicted Benedict might make bold steps, it was with church finances. The Pope's aides had spread the word that he intended to make the arcane Vatican money world more transparent. "The target of Benedict's [reform] strategy is the Vatican Bank," said one press report.[29] There was even news that he might make the bold move of merging the IOR and APSA.[30]

Benedict had allowed Sodano to get his way when it came to Monsignor Pioppo becoming the Vatican Bank's chief cleric. Now Vaticanologists waited to see what the Pope might do about the IOR's top layman, Angelo Caloia? John Paul had been expected to reappoint him. Caloia boosters pointed out that, to his credit, he stayed out of Vatican politics. There was little question that under his leadership the IOR was certainly attracting less bad press than when Marcinkus was in charge. Caloia's low-key approach had prevented him from making too many enemies inside the Curia. It also meant he had few strong backers.

But according to press reports, Caloia would soon be history.*

"Angelo Caloia, an Italian Catholic banker who is its long-serving governor, was provisionally reappointed this year, but the Pope has yet to confirm this. . . . Almost unnoticed, the Pope has moved to end the Caloia era," wrote Richard Owen in London's *Times*.[31] "Signor Caloia is respected for his discretion and rectitude, but he is identified with the previous regime and the succession battle to be the new 'God's Banker' is on."

Other reports said that the Pope's advisors had urged him to replace not only Caloia but also two other parallel powerhouses of Vatican finance: Cardinal Sergio Sebastiani, of the Prefecture for the Economic Affairs of the Holy See, and Cardinal Attilio Nicora, APSA's chief. It was clear, claimed many reports without attribution, that Benedict favored "a fellow German with international credentials" to run the IOR.[32]

Despite all the high expectation for big changes at the Vatican Bank, Benedict did virtually nothing. He renewed Caloia's term for another five years. Those who had been banking on the man the *Daily Telegraph* had once dubbed the Panzercardinal to reorganize the IOR were disappointed. But given his shortcomings as an administrator, it is not that surprising that he shied away from playing too aggressive a hand when it came to the church's money matters. A warning sign to those expecting reform should have been that shortly after Benedict became Pope, he tabled the Vatican's annual budgets from the Governorate and APSA.[33] Some interpreted that to mean he was tearing apart the figures and preparing to come back to both departments with tough questions. But it turned out he simply had not found the time to sign off on the final drafts, delaying their distribution to the cardinals and bishops for the first time since the policy was adopted in 1987. Although it had no material impact on how the church raised money and paid its bills, it reinforced Benedict's image as someone disconnected from finances.

And it was not just the Pontiff's failure to tackle reform; his supporters were just as disheartened by his remote approach to seemingly every major issue.[34]

---

* Just before John Paul's death there were rumors that he was considering banker Roberto Mazzotta, president of Caripio, a Milan-based bank and charitable foundation, as Caloia's replacement. Mazzotta was a respected member of the white finance movement, of which Caloia had been a founder.

"One year after his election, Benedict has hardly begun to define his papacy," wrote author Michael Valpy. "As a nervous Vatican watches . . . just one thing is sure: He's not John Paul."[35]

Benedict had trouble connecting with ordinary Catholics, making the church and the Papacy once again seem less relevant. A September 2006 trip to Germany, thought most Vaticanologists, presented his team a prime opportunity to soften his image and boost his popularity.[36] Instead, the trip highlighted Benedict's emotional detachment. Victor Simpson, a veteran AP reporter, thought the Pope appeared to be "going through the motions."[37] In the village of Marktl am Inn, when he walked past his birth home, he barely glanced at it, instead fretting about staying on a tight schedule. "The photographers and camera operators who had waited for hours outside the house for a poignant visual came away empty handed," recalls Catholic News Service bureau chief John Thavis, who was part of the traveling press corps.[38] "At a southern German sanctuary that had been a favorite of his as a youngster, he did not even mention his personal connection during his talk.[39] "This was a pope who didn't feel obligated to emote in public, and whose speeches and sermons in Bavaria were as flat as stale beer," Thavis concluded.[40]

For an address at the University of Regensburg, he had prepared a long discourse about the gap between Europe's secularism and Islam's rigid orthodoxy. He quoted a fourteenth-century Byzantine emperor: "Show me just what Muhammed brought that was new, and there you will find things only evil and inhuman, such as his command to spread by the sword the faith he preached."[41] Reporters traveling with the Pope had received an advance copy and before his talk some had pointed out the offending language to the new press secretary, Father Federico Lombardi. But Lombardi "seemed disinclined to run interference for Benedict."[42]* As the journalists predicted, Benedict's speech prompted a firestorm.[43] Riots erupted in a dozen countries.[44] There were threats of revenge and calls for Benedict's death from Middle Eastern al Qaeda offshoots to radical imams at an anti-Pope rally outside London's Westminster Cathedral.[45] The Pope was burned in effigy during massive demonstrations in leading Arab capitals. He apologized four times, each more effusive than the last. But the story had a life of its own. Six churches in the Palestinian

* Lombardi is the same press spokesman who ignored more than a dozen requests from the author for comments and interviews inside the Vatican, as late as 2014.

territories were torched, a sixty-six-year-old nun in Somalia was executed, an Italian priest was shot to death on the steps of his parish church in Turkey, and an EU diplomat was stabbed to death in Morocco.[46] Even John Paul's recently paroled wannabe assassin, Mehmet Ali Ağca, told reporters that if he could talk to Benedict, he would say: "As someone who knows these matters well, I say your life is in danger."[47] The violent response meant that when the Pope made public appearances, marksmen now took positions on rooftops. When the Pontiff visited Turkey that November, he wore a bulletproof vest under his clerical robe. Three thousand elite army troops guarded him.[48]

The church later offered a series of excuses as to why none of Benedict's aides warned him that his language about Muslims was likely to be misinterpreted: Secretary of State Bertone was in transition; it was press secretary Lombardi's first foreign trip; and no one had yet replaced the outgoing chief responsible for relations with Muslims.[49] Vaticanologists knew, of course, that the underlying reason was that those who had influence over Benedict—including his ambitious personal secretary, German Monsignor Georg Gänswein, and a medieval music scholar turned nun, Ingrid Stampa—had little understanding of how every utterance by the Pope was dissected. No one appreciated the ramifications if something was taken out of context and went viral.[50]

The Islamic calamity was to prove to be the template for the rest of Benedict's papacy. The Pope and those around him showed time and again they were inept when it came to public relations. In a talk explaining his Muslim comments he angered Jews when he described the crucifixion of Jesus as a "scandal for the Jews."[51] He ticked off South Americans and indigenous groups in Brazil when he omitted any mention of crimes the colonizers had committed. The natives, he said, had been "silently longing" for the Catholic faith the conquistadors brought.[52]

Nor did the Pontiff and his advisors do a better job of handling their perceived response to one of the most critical issues of his Papacy, the unfolding sex abuse scandal. Whether deserved or not, the public had a poor perception of Benedict, judging him as less than enthusiastic in pursuing pedophile priests when he ran the Congregation for the Doctrine of the Faith. That dicastery had been responsible since 2001 for the oversight of all reported abuse cases. (By 2010, a U.S. public opinion poll showed only 12 percent of Americans thought Benedict was doing a good job in dealing with the scandal.)[53] That view was reinforced by the slow probe into sex abuse charges over Marcial Maciel Degollado, the founder of the Legion of Christ (the investigations were still under way when Maciel died in 2008).[54] Although ex–Secretary of State Sodano had been Maciel's main defender and responsible largely for delaying his prosecution, it was John Paul and then Benedict who got blamed (Benedict at least forced Maciel from his active ministry for "a life of prayer and penance," a disciplinary action John Paul had refused).

When a slew of decades-old sex abuse accusations in Switzerland, the Netherlands, Germany, Ireland, Belgium, and Austria hit the press, Benedict and his team defensively explained why the church still did not favor reporting the crimes to civil authorities. They were unskilled at getting out the word about what steps Benedict had taken, such as streamlining the process to defrock abusing priests (it would not be until January 2014 that news broke that a record number of 384 priests had been defrocked during just two years of Benedict's reign, 2011–12).[55]

Given the bungling of those charged with burnishing the Pope's reputation, it was little wonder the Vatican often seemed under siege. When a *New York Times* story claimed that while he was a cardinal, Benedict had failed to order the removal of a Milwaukee priest accused of abusing up to two hundred deaf boys, his enraged aides seemingly stumbled over each other to prove who was the most incompetent.[56] In one Sunday sermon at St. Peter's, with Benedict in the front pew, a priest compared the church's bad press over the sex abuse scandal to what Holocaust victims had endured. Cardinal Sodano tried putting out that fire with a lecture to the press corps, but he set off another uproar by dismissing the sex abuse charges as "idle gossip." A couple of weeks later Vienna's Cardinal Christoph von Schönborn, in what he mistakenly thought was an off-the-record chat with reporters, revealed how Sodano had forced Ratzinger in 1995 to back off a sex abuse probe of Schönborn's predecessor, Cardinal Hans Hermann Groër.[57]

Even mundane public relations events often turned into problems. When the Pope attended a Vatican Christmas, the press focused on an embarrassing moment when four male acrobats stripped off their shirts in front of the red-faced Benedict. "Strippers in Vatican" went viral on YouTube and led to another round of finger pointing among his advisors about who should have previewed the act.[58] A few weeks later, at a Christmas fest in Cologne, photographers snapped photos of the Pope greeted by the *Jungfrau*, a traditional blond maiden. Papal aides were seemingly aware that the maiden at the Cologne Carnival was always a man dressed as a woman. Pictures of Benedict cavorting with a drag queen were the last thing the Vatican's inexperienced public relations team wanted.[59]

As this fiasco played out, Curial officials appealed to Bertone as the Secretary of State to take charge of the Pontiff's public image. Bertone assured his colleagues he would help the Holy See avoid further embarrassments. But the Secretary of State was not up to the job.

When a Polish weekly published the accusation that Benedict's top choice to become archbishop of Warsaw had cooperated with Poland's communist-era secret police, Bertone did not believe it. Then—only a couple of days before Stanislaw Wielgus's investiture—a historical panel in the Vatican informed Bertone that the charges were true. He underestimated the impact of such a disclosure in the former communist bloc country so he did not advise Benedict to stop the appointment. Instead, the affair played out to the church's humiliation when Wielgus resigned within hours of becoming the Warsaw archbishop, admitting that a slew of fresh reports about his communist-era collaboration were true.[60]

In 2009, Benedict faced a firestorm after he lifted the excommunication of Richard Williamson, a British bishop based in Buenos Aires.[61] Bertone, who oversaw Williamson's vetting, had apparently not even Googled him. If he had, he would have discovered an interview the bishop gave only three days before to Swedish television, in which he said about the Holocaust: "I believe that the historical evidence is hugely against six million Jews having been deliberately gassed in gas chambers as a deliberate policy of Adolf Hitler. I believe there were no gas chambers."[62] The U.S. embassy later sent a confidential cable to the State Department reporting that Bertone had lost even more respect when—during the middle of the scandal over the Holocaust-denying cleric—he "referred to the offending bishop by the wrong name, then denounced the media for 'inventing' a problem where there was none."[63]

Bertone's missteps did not shake the confidence of the most important person at the Vatican, Benedict. The Pope was not even upset with the abysmal performance by his press office. The war with the media was proof that secular powers were intent on waging a campaign of vilification against the church.[64] That Catholicism was in a war with secularists was shared by at least one of his closest unofficial advisors, the nun Ingrid Stampa.[65] Instead of making Benedict angry with those who had let him down, the public farces made him bitter and turned him away from what he saw as a hostile world.[66] It reinforced his suspicious and conspiratorial view that there was no such thing as balanced reporting and that the news served a hidden agenda to somehow shake the faith of loyal Catholics.

35

Chasing the White List

The bursting of the American housing bubble in 2006, and the collapse of a secondary investment market based on subprime mortgages, kicked off what turned into a devastating two-year global financial recession. The Vatican always moved in tandem with the booms and busts of neighboring countries. Italy, which had one of the weakest European economies going into the crisis, affected the church more than any other nation.[1] Unemployment and bankruptcies soared while GDP and industrial production plummeted to levels not seen in forty years.[2] The Vatican experienced a drop-off in contributions, including a sharp downturn in Peter's Pence (it fell by a third in 2006).[3]

The straight numbers reveal the impact. The Vatican turned from a budget surplus of $3.1 million in 2006 to a $13.5 million deficit in 2007, its worst performance in years.[4] The international financial plunge rekindled inside the church fears over the risks inherent in unrestrained capitalism. "Money vanishes," Pope Benedict said in a speech during the free fall. "The only solid reality is the word of God."[5]

Even the church's money men, who knew that Marcinkus was right when he once said, "You can't run the church on Hail Marys," were pressured to find ways to cushion the church against the fallout. Two financial experts wrote in the Vatican's newspaper, *L'Osservatore Romano*, that Islamic finance might be a model for Western banks. In theory, it was similar to the white finance Angelo Caloia and his Catholic economists advocated.[6]

At the nadir of the crash, October 2008, the press-shy Caloia gave a rare interview. After the bankruptcy of New York investment giant Lehman Brothers, and with some enormous French and Spanish banks reportedly battling for survival in the face of enormous losses, some of Caloia's colleagues urged him to calm jitters at the IOR's partner banks about the secretive institution's solvency.

In keeping his well-known distance from the mainstream media, he gave an exclusive interview to *Famiglia Cristiana*, a Catholic family magazine. His message was not only reassuring. It was the envy of central bankers everywhere: "Our assets are solid and we don't have any shortage of liquidity. We've always been very prudent, I would dare to say conservative, in managing our resources. We've always invested defensively."

The IOR's assets were not at risk, Caloia said, because under his nearly nineteen-year tenure the bank had never participated in stock options, much less derivatives (highly leveraged financial instruments). He did not disclose precise numbers, but indicated a recent press report concluding that the IOR's unadventurous investment philosophy meant 80 percent of its assets were in low-yield AAA government bonds and the rest in a mixture of gold and dividend-yielding stocks, sounded about right.[7]

The Vatican Bank did not issue loans so it was not facing customers unable to make repayments.* Instead, Caloia noted the bank adhered to conservative investments that were "clear, simple and ethically based." The IOR did not profit, he emphasized, from any dishonorable endeavor such as trading in international armaments.

Caloia, who believed the crisis was largely the result of greed, also took a swipe at those international banks that were in distress, saying that their "behavior [was] improper to the point of fraud" and that it was little wonder that "today, in world finance, no one trusts anyone else."[9] Privately, and away from earshot of any reporter, Caloia said he thought that some top American clerics were "too enamored with Wall Street."[10]

The philosophy of white finance was the backbone of a major policy paper Benedict issued that December about the meltdown. In direct language, he castigated Western countries for not responding more forcefully and faster to cope with the crisis, especially since the credit crunch disproportionally hammered

* Caloia thought the name *bank* was a misnomer for the IOR since it was not in the business of lending money. It did, while he was there, "give grants to a mission in the Amazon, a small church in Kampala, but loans in the classical sense are excluded." The reason for the "no loans" policy, said Caloia, was that "it would rain down requests from every corner of the planet, and we would not be able to rank the priorities."[8]

the world's poorest.[11] In calling for reform, Benedict urged that a "necessary first step" was closing all international tax havens, which he said had "given support to imprudent economic and financial practices and have also played a significant role in the imbalances of development, allowing a gigantic flight of capital linked to tax evasion. Offshore markets could also be linked to the recycling of profits from illegal activities."[12] The Pontiff's statement even listed some of the worst offending "offshore centers" such as "the Channel Islands." It was not clear if Benedict fully realized the extent to which the super rich had used the Vatican Bank as a tax haven since its inception.

But that December policy statement was only a warm-up for a Papal encyclical released the following July (2009). It was a dense thirty-thousand-word treatise about social injustice that included swipes at the excesses of capitalism, especially the robust American variation. The theme was that "The economy needs ethics in order to function correctly, not any ethics, but an ethics which is people-centered."[13] It reinforced the widespread view that Benedict was better suited as an academic and philosopher than a hands-on administrator.

That highly promoted encyclical about what was wrong with Western capitalism had the misfortune of getting released at the same time as the publication of *Vaticano S.p.A.*, a book by Italian journalist Gianluigi Nuzzi, that was filled with electrifying disclosures of decades of abuse inside the Vatican Bank. Nuzzi's tell-all was based on thousands of internal documents stolen over several decades by the IOR insider Monsignor Renato Dardozzi. How Nuzzi got the secret documents was a riveting story in itself. Dardozzi, who had died in 2003 at the age of eighty-one, had never given an interview, and there are only a couple of known photos of him. The reclusive monsignor seemed an unlikely whistleblower. It turned out that Dardozzi had been frustrated and upset by the ongoing abuses at the IOR under De Bonis.[14] Over time he became determined that the wrongdoing he witnessed not go forever unreported. In the late 1990s he had begun secreting away copies of confidential files, notes from private meetings, and sensitive correspondence between key IOR and Curial officials. And he had stored the purloined documents with friends—who remain anonymous to this day—in Ticio, Switzerland, just over the Italian border. When Dardozzi died, his executors contacted Nuzzi. Dardozzi's last will and testament directed: "These documents should be published so that everyone can learn what has happened here." It took Nuzzi months to scan the paperwork, make CD-ROMs of the notes, and download the larger files.

When Nuzzi returned to Italy on his final trip, he carried two large Samsonite suitcases, each crammed with forty pounds of the damning copies.[15]

In a preview of *Vaticano S.p.A.* in the Italian weekly *Panorama,* Nuzzi wrote that Marcinkus had "simply passed the baton" to De Bonis, ensuring that "a river of money, including cash and government bonds, was conveyed in a kind of parallel IOR, a web of offshore deposits disguised with charities that did not exist."[16]

Vaticano S.p.A. exposed everything from Prime Minister Giulio Andreotti's political slush fund disguised as the Cardinal Francis Spellman Foundation to revealing how putative charities used the bank to move about millions of dollars beyond the reach of law enforcement and financial regulators. Nuzzi revealed in detail that political bribes were doled out from fake IOR accounts; how money deposited by the faithful for Masses for the dead went missing; the millions that had passed through an account owned by an order of nuns had simply disappeared; even cash that had been sent to genuine charities sometimes got misappropriated by crooked clerics.

Although most of Nuzzi's disclosures involved abuses during the early to mid-1990s, the cumulative impact of seeing it spelled out in the bank's own documents had a tremendous impact. Journalist and author Philip Willan summarized a widespread feeling among both ordinary Catholics and Vaticanologists when he wrote in Britain's *Guardian* newspaper that such revelations were disheartening given that the "political and financial scandals" of Marcinkus, Sindona, and Calvi had "brought lasting discredit on the Catholic church three decades ago. . . . We were led to believe that a new broom, wielded by the lay banker Angelo Caloia, had since swept the premises of the IOR. . . . Despite the best efforts of Caloia, a cavalier attitude to financial ethics appears to have continued."[17]

Nuzzi's book made it abundantly clear that during Caloia's nineteen-year tenure as the IOR director, veteran clerics had repeatedly outwitted him and his efforts at reform. Worse, Nuzzi concluded that he trusted no one at Vatican Bank: "Despite the full collaboration promised and publicized in the press, they [the IOR] limit themselves to referring only what can no longer be concealed."[18]

The Vatican's response to the Nuzzi onslaught? Nothing. Although there were evidently more than a dozen attempts to craft a comprehensive defense, none got past the drafting stage. Nuzzi had made his case relying on the Vatican Bank's own documents, so efforts to explain it away seemed lame and defensive.[19] De Bonis had died in 2001. When Andreotti, who in 2006 had failed in a bid for the presidency of the Italian Senate, was confronted about the Cardinal Spellman Foundation and the millions distributed from it to his family and friends, he quipped: "I do not remember this account."[20]

Overnight the public perception of Caloia changed from a well-intentioned advocate of white finance who had burnished the Vatican Bank's reputation to someone either incapable of controlling what was going on in his own bank or clueless about the breadth of the illicit operation thriving beneath him. Nuzzi's revelations made clear that Caloia "was suspicious about the parallel bank" just two years after he became the IOR's director. But despite his efforts, "nothing happened."[21] The press turned on Caloia, picking up a theme that at best his oversight of the bank was lackadaisical.

Nuzzi's exposé sparked a desperate power struggle inside the Vatican for control of the bank. Should Caloia and his team of laymen finish the remaining two years of their term or should a new director immediately take control?[22] Cardinal Attilio Nicora, chief of APSA, fought for his friend Caloia. Nicora had helped the professorial banker survive less potent threats to his tenure in early years. But Caloia had lost Bertone's critical support. The Secretary of State told the Pontiff that Nuzzi's book was not only a terrible embarrassment but that its disclosures showed that the church must concentrate on cleaning its own financial house before lecturing nations about their offshore banking havens and the pitfalls of capitalism. Bertone thought it was time to purge the last remnants of John Paul's old guard, and the disclosures that Monsignor De Bonis and others had run circles around the hapless Caloia was the perfect pretext.[23] As the chairman of the five-cardinal panel that oversaw the IOR, Bertone suggested it was time for Caloia to go.[24]

Benedict, of course, could have ended any effort to remove Caloia by stating his support for his long-serving IOR chief. In this case, however, Benedict's inherent indecisiveness was made worse. He had never developed a personal relationship with Caloia. Even the IOR chief said as much just six months earlier when he admitted he did "not have a functional relationship" with the Holy See.[25]

The winner of the Curial tug-of-war was clear September 23 when Cardinal Bertone issued a brief statement announcing Caloia's resignation. Bertone thanked him for his "generous services" but gave no explanation for the exit.[26]

Privately, Bertone's aides leaked their own spin to selected journalists: Caloia's departure was not a sign of discord but rather a move toward reform. That seemed possible since simultaneously Bertone disclosed that the IOR had its first new director in nearly twenty years, sixty-five-year-old Ettore Gotti Tedeschi, a conservative economist and chief of Italian operations for Spain's Banco Santander. Gotti Tedeschi had never been inside the IOR but Bertone knew him. Earlier that year the Secretary of State had sought his advice in helping the Pope craft his *Caritas in Veritate* encyclical about finances and social justice (Gotti Tedeschi was so enthusiastic about that encyclical that he cited it in nominating Benedict for a Nobel Prize in economics).[27] Gotti Tedeschi kept his Santander job, believing he could carry out his Vatican Bank obligations part-time.

Caloia declined any comment, allowing the Vatican for once to control the public narrative. Typical was *The Wall Street Journal*'s front-page coverage calling the changes "a sweeping overhaul." The paper cited "senior Vatican officials" for the proposition that Bertone "has long sought to shake up the bank's management in a bid to modernize its operations." Moreover, the *Journal* quoted "one Vatican official" as saying that while reforming the IOR would be difficult, "We expect deep change." Gotti Tedeschi's arrival meant the Vatican Bank was "moving in the direction of more transparency."[28] The *National Catholic Reporter*'s John Allen wrote that the change was "a move towards greater transparency and better business practices at the Vatican Bank."[29]

To add to the impression that the moves were part of a coordinated clean sweep, the church also announced that the four other lay directors of the IOR's supervisory board had resigned along with Caloia. The newcomers who now joined Gotti Tedeschi were Carl Anderson, the American head of the Knights of Columbus; ex–Deutsche Bank chairman Ronaldo Hermann Schmitz; the president of Credito Valtellinese, Giovanni De Censi; and Spanish banker Manuel Soto Serrano.[30]*

---

* In subsequent media coverage, Caloia's inability to rein in De Bonis and others in the 1990s turned into something more nefarious. "Monsignor Angelo Caloia had expanded money laundering and keeping secret accounts for favored politicians for which the bank became notorious." "Under Monsignor Angelo Caloia, Marcinkus' successor as head of the bank, the Vatican consistently expanded its money-laundering activities." It appears in those reports journalists confused Monsignor Donato De Bonis and Angelo Caloia. However, Caloia evidently made no effort to correct the record, and for those unfamiliar with the IOR's past, those press reports made him responsible for behavior that is not supported by any credible evidence.[31]

What did Gotti Tedeschi's unexpected appointment augur for the IOR? Besides his Santander role, he boasted an impressive résumé. He taught financial ethics at Milan's Catholic University, was a director of Cassa Depositi e Prestiti (the Deposits and Loans Fund), the operational wing of Italy's Treasury Ministry, a board member of Turin's Banca San Paolo, and a chairman of the government created Infrastructure Fund.[32] It was a plus that he was a devout Catholic, daily communicant, and Opus Dei member.

Gotti Tedeschi boasted that he was "a concrete and practical economist" with decades of business experience, "not an academic, a theorist."[33] He shared Caloia's concern about the need for more ethical behavior in financing and championed the theories of other leading Catholic free-market thinkers.[34] But the comparison to his predecessor ended there. Gotti Tedeschi was far more provocative than the soft-pedaling Caloia. In a 2004 book, he had argued that Protestantism was responsible for some of capitalism's "defects," including an obsession with turning profits.[35] Nine months before becoming the IOR chief, he had proposed in *L'Osservatore Romano* that wealthy Western countries form a "good bank" from which massive investments could be made into developing nations. Even English Prime Minister Gordon Brown took note, endorsing Gotti Tedeschi's grand Marshall Plan–styled bank. It had little chance of ever happening, but it was evidence that Gotti Tedeschi did not shy from broad, bold initiatives.[36]

Besides his economic philosophy, he prided himself as a strict moralist. When he told strangers he had five children, he often added "and all from the same mother." It was his subtle dig at Italy's rising divorce rate and out-of-wedlock births.[37] Just before the Vatican picked him for the IOR post, he had given a much discussed talk in which he contended that while America's "debt addiction" was a primary cause of the global financial crisis, a contributing factor was that people did not follow the church's ban on birth control, which he said led to "the rejection of life and the suppression of childbirth."[38] Between his provocative writings, outspoken lectures, and opinionated involvement in economic proposals for Italy's politicians, he seemed in many ways the opposite of the reserved Caloia.

Gotti Tedeschi walked into a firestorm at the IOR. In December 2000, the Vatican had signed a Monetary Convention with the European Union so that the church could issue its own euro coins (distinctively stamped with *Città del*

Vaticano) as well as commemorative coins that it marked up significantly to sell to collectors.[39] That agreement did not bind the Vatican, or two other non-EU nations that had accepted the euro—Monaco and Andorra—to abide by strict European statutes regarding money laundering, terrorism financing, fraud, and counterfeiting.[40]

That lack of compliance had become a sticking point for EU officials in Brussels who contended that the city-state reaped the benefits of a one-way relationship that allowed it to use the euro without having to follow the rules that applied to member nations. The EU's unease went as far back as 1998, when the Vatican had agreed in principle to use the common currency.* That was the same year the Organisation for Economic Co-operation and Development (OECD), a thirty-four-nation economics and trade group that tracks openness in the sharing of tax information between countries, had begun investigating tax havens. Those nations that shared financial data and had in place adequate safeguards against money laundering were put on a so-called white list. Those that had not acted but promised to do so were slotted onto the OECD's gray list, and those resistant to reforming their banking secrecy laws were relegated to a black list. The OECD could not force the Vatican to cooperate since it was not a member of the European Union. So it held off putting the city-state on any list.[41]

Meanwhile, at the Vatican, a powerful contingent of senior clerics resisted the principles of transparency preached by the EU and argued that the IOR's inviolable secrecy was one of its greatest attributes. Just because the modern world had moved in the direction of openness was no reason why the church should follow, they contended. If the EU got its way and the Vatican had to conform to Europe's money laundering and terrorism financing laws, the IOR would be subject to independent secular oversight. Many veteran clerics shuddered at the prospect of European financial regulators accessing the records and files of the Vatican Bank.

The standoff between European representatives and IOR officials had

* The Vatican had been forced to adopt the euro because Italy had decided to do so. Italy was one of twelve European nations that made the euro its currency. The much loved lira, in use since 1472, was history. Lost in the widespread coverage of that historic move was that Italy's decision meant the Vatican—which used the lira—had to follow suit or develop its own currency.

boiled over at a luncheon at the Vatican shortly before Gotti Tedeschi arrived at the IOR. One of the EU regulators asked if it were possible to get some information about what controls the bank had in place to guard against money laundering?

"How can you ask us such questions?" one of the Vatican Bank officials shouted.[42]

The European officials returned to Brussels.

As Gotti Tedeschi discovered, the Vatican was in a tough quandary. The Monetary Convention the church signed in 2000 restricted how many coins it could mint annually.[43] The Vatican wanted a higher limit. Brussels saw this request as leverage by which to push the clerics in Rome to comply with European money laundering and anti-terrorism statutes.

Gotti Tedeschi threw his weight with the pragmatists who contended that as distasteful as it was to contemplate any European oversight of the IOR, the Vatican's future was undoubtedly with the euro. Opting out of the euro and creating its own currency seemed an unrealistic dream.

Just three months after Gotti Tedeschi had become the bank's director, the church and the EU signed a new Monetary Convention. It allowed the city-state to mint €2.3 million annually, up from €1.4 million. In return, the Vatican agreed to start taking all steps necessary to adhere to the tough post-9/11 financing laws that Brussels had promulgated.[44] The city-state—which remarkably had no laws against money laundering—was now committed to develop and implement its own finance statutes.[45] It was also obligated to create an independent watchdog agency empowered with certifying that all Vatican financial departments complied with any new laws. These were not simply promises the Vatican could make and shelve. The agreement put real obligations on the church to perform, and the EU was set to monitor its progress. The Vatican's long-term goal was to qualify for the OECD's white list.[46]

Almost lost in the final hectic debate over the new Monetary Convention was that on December 29, the Ninth Circuit Court of Appeals in San Francisco delivered some unexpected good news to Gotti Tedeschi and his colleagues at the bank. That court affirmed the IOR's dismissal from the Nazi gold class action lawsuit filed in 1999. The Vatican's attorneys had prevailed that the Sovereign Immunities Act, which shields foreign countries from being sued in American courts, was a complete bar to any civil action against the bank.[47] The concerns of a decade earlier about whether the Nazi gold claims might result in a settlement as devastating as the Vatican's $244 million payment to the Ambrosiano now seemed distant. Gotti Tedeschi had no history with any of that. But he was pleased the lawsuit was over. He had a clean slate going forward to build a bank that adapted to the political and financial realities of modern-day Europe.

36

The World Has Changed

The Vatican approached its obligations under the December 2009 Monetary Convention in its typical unhurried manner, in no rush to begin the hard work of qualifying for the white list. The IOR had performed well for decades without outside interference. Few in the church believed that getting the OECD's formal blessing would make much of a difference in its bottom line. Officials in Brussels, meanwhile, were not accustomed to the slow shuffle. The EU was focused on a promise they had secured during the negotiations: Pope Benedict was to issue a decree by which he acknowledged the church's willingness to comply with Europe's money laundering and antiterrorism laws. For several months, EU officials bristled as queries went unanswered or came back with unresponsive information. In the late spring, the IOR and OECD met twice. But according to Jeffrey Owens, the OECD's director of the Center for Tax Policy and Administration, the discussions were so generic as to be nothing more than a primer about how the church might one day get on the white list. "They know what the standards are," said Owens. "Do they want to advance the dialogue with the aim of committing to the standards?"[1]

The EU believed that the Holy See had no incentive to live up to its Monetary Convention obligations, in part since its sweetheart relationship with Italy meant there was little strict enforcement of rules and regulations against IOR accounts held at Italian banks. So in the summer of 2010, Brussels nudged Italy's central bank to tighten its controls when dealing with the Vatican Bank.

There was soon evidence that the pressure was working. On September 9, the Bank of Italy distributed an internal notice advising Italian banks to more aggressively scrutinize their business with the IOR. The memo emphasized that the Vatican Bank was a non–European Union bank and that it was not on the OECD's white list.[2] Italy had recently ruled that the Vatican itself was a "non-equivalent extracommunitarian country."[3] That meant it was subject to tougher standards.[4] It was the clearest sign to date that the incestuous relationship between the Vatican and Italy was ending. Still, the church did not pick up its pace in addressing its duties under its new Monetary Convention. Gotti Tedeschi and his crew did not seem particularly concerned.

They should have been. In mid-September 2010, Italian state television (RAI), citing unnamed "judicial sources," reported that Gotti Tedeschi and the bank's director general, Paolo Cipriani, were under investigation in a criminal investigation of possible violations of Italy's beefed-up 2007 money laundering law.[5] Some in the Vatican dismissed the report as baseless. On September 20 Italian prosecutors froze $30 million at an IOR account held at a Rome branch of Credito Artigiano S.p.A. The IOR had wanted to transfer most of that money to J. P. Morgan's Frankfurt branch, and the rest to the Rome-based Banca del Fucino.[6] Credito Artigiano had followed the letter of the law by asking the IOR the identity of the account holder and the reasons for the transfer. The Vatican Bank ignored those requests. That had prompted Credito Artigiano to inform Italy's central bank that there were "irregularities."[7] The Bank of Italy's financial intelligence unit in turn tipped off Rome's prosecutors.*

The day after the $30 million was frozen, all Benedict's public relations team could muster was to buy some time with a note published in its newspaper, *L'Osservatore Romano*: "The Holy See, therefore, is perplexed and astonished by the initiative of the Prosecutor of Rome, especially since the information necessary is already available from the relevant offices of the Bank of Italy. . . ." Gotti Tedeschi had been on the job only a year. "The Holy See expresses its maximum confidence in the president and director general of the IOR."[9]

Two days later, press spokesman Father Federico Lombardi released a longer statement to the *Financial Times*. Now he claimed it was all "a misunderstanding" and "could have been clarified with great simplicity." Lombardi raised

* To relieve some of the pressure on the Vatican, an unidentified Bank of Italy official confided to reporters, "This is not another Banco Ambrosiano or Enimont." But that was not as reassuring as it was intended. Longtime Vatican Bank watchers knew that neither the Banco Ambrosiano nor Enimont scandals seemed so grand when the news first broke.[8]

eyebrows in Brussels and Rome when he claimed, "The IOR is located within the territory of Vatican City State, beyond the jurisdiction and surveillance of various national banks." That seemed a throwback to the defense the church employed to avert the service of arrest warrants on Archbishop Marcinkus. But everyone seemed to agree with Lombardi's conclusion: "The IOR is not a bank in the normal definition of the term." [10]

Bank of Italy officials thought the expressions of surprise were feigned. Their pervasive view was that the Vatican had deliberately failed to answer Credito Artigiano's queries about the $30 million. Maybe, contended some, the IOR wanted to test what would trigger Italy's enforcement mechanism. "A well-placed Italian official, who asks not to be named," told the *Financial Times*, "Perhaps they want to go back to their past special status. But the world is more complicated these days. Perhaps it is just their culture of secrecy. Who knows?" [11]

The following month Rome prosecutors widened their money laundering probe to include $1.3 million in withdrawals from IOR accounts at two of Italy's largest banks, UniCredit and Intesa Sanpaolo.[12] In a separate case, police arrested six people in Sicily on fraud and money laundering charges. One of them was an Italian priest who helped his father launder $350,000 in European Union grant money for a nonexistent fish farm development through an IOR account. The Vatican Bank distributed the money to a mobster uncle of the cleric.[13] It highlighted the fear in Brussels that the IOR accounts held in Italian banks were still easily disguised to hide the flow of illicit cash. "IOR cannot work like this anymore," an unidentified Italian official told the *Financial Times*. "People have used the IOR as a screen." [14]*

It had only taken a year for Gotti Tedeschi to find himself in the uncomfortable public spotlight of scandal that had plagued his predecessors. Behind the scenes he worked frenetically to get Italian authorities to release the $30 million. Vatican attorneys had filed emergency motions to free the funds but two judges upheld the seizure, citing the IOR's failure to adequately ex-

* By coincidence, Jonathan Levy, the plaintiff's attorney in the Nazi gold class action against the IOR that had been dismissed the previous December, had written two months earlier to the European Central Bank in Frankfurt. Levy raised new questions about whether stolen wartime gold from IOR deposits may have been used to mint gold Vatican euros. Levy told reporters that the Italian money laundering probe into the IOR added to the credibility of survivors' claims that the bank misused the Croatian gold it received in 1945.[15]

plain the money's provenance.[16] Prosecutors provided the judges with additional documentation raising questions about a 2009 IOR transfer under a false name, and a million-dollar withdrawal in 2010 from an Italian bank in which the Vatican refused to provide the cash's destination.[17] The next step for the IOR was to appeal to Italy's highest court but a decision there might not be quick.

Few knew that Gotti Tedeschi was struggling inside the Vatican Bank. Its records had been in much worse shape than he expected and he was having a tough time getting the Curia to understand what he meant by transparency.[18] He decided to use the crisis to push the Vatican into the financial modern age.

Gotti Tedeschi sent a letter to the Paris-based Financial Action Task Force (FATF), the intergovernmental body set up by the G7 to combat terrorist financing and money laundering.[19] The FATF was the group whose principles the Vatican had promised in 1996 to emulate in the wake of the Enimont scandal. Gotti Tedeschi now assured the FATF that the IOR was ready to strictly adhere to the group's standards. That would subject the IOR to peer review by FATF's European arm, the Committee of Experts on the Evaluation of Anti–Money Laundering Measures and the Financing of Terrorism (Moneyval).[20] When Italian prosecutors heard about Gotti Tedeschi's representations, they thought he was simply trying to burnish the church's image in the legal battle over the frozen $30 million.[21] But European officials were less cynical and sensed that Gotti Tedeschi was sincere. Their only question was whether he was capable of delivering on his promise.

A few weeks later, on October 15, IOR and EU officials met and this time agreed that Pope Benedict would do whatever was necessary to bring the Vatican's laws in sync with the tough European regulations.[22] When an anonymous "senior FATF official familiar with the negotiations" told the Associated Press that Gotti Tedeschi had also personally vouched for the IOR's willingness to conform to the EU's strict statutes, it put the Vatican Bank chief into the middle of the church's long-fought debate about the breadth of its sovereignty.[23] Since the restoration of independent statehood through Mussolini's Lateran Pacts, it was hard to think of a more explosive political issue inside the church. Many clerics had personal memories of the brutal court battles that had gone to Italy's highest tribunal over the Marcinkus arrest warrants.

Some top financial clerics—such as Archbishop Carlo Maria Viganò, who had become the General Secretary of the Governorate the previous year—thought the crisis so great that the church should withdraw from the euro and mint its own Vatican lira, which would float in value against other currencies.[24] Viganò and several others argued that any downside risks for the Vatican launching its own currency were preferable to allowing EU officials—many of whom were entrenched secularists with outright disdain for the church—to enter Vatican City and have unprecedented access to the IOR.

Although many of Viganò's colleagues were sympathetic to his rallying cry to preserve the bank's sovereignty at all costs, few thought it feasible.[25] If it wanted to develop its own currency, it should have started years earlier. Such a radical response to intense pressure from Brussels might lead other countries to brand the city-state a rogue outlier when it came to money laundering and antiterrorist financing laws.[26] American and European banks might stop doing business with it. That would not boost the value of any currency it rolled out. With some significant undercurrent of dismay, Viganò's proposal to leave the EU failed to get any traction. A handful of the Pope's closest aides instead began drafting the Papal declaration that the church had promised Brussels.

The result was a remarkable December 30 decree that gave the Vatican its first ever anti–money laundering law, set to go into effect the following April 1.[27] "The Prevention and Countering of Illegal Activities in the Area of Monetary and Financial Dealings" was issued as a *motu proprio*, a document historically signed personally by the Pope. Benedict took full responsibility for the decision. At 501 words it was short by the standards of apostolic letters and Papal decrees. The Pope deemed money laundering and terrorist financing a "phenomena" and referred to the Vatican's pledge made with the EU in its Monetary Convention the previous December. Most important, he rolled out the Vatican's first-ever internal oversight and enforcement authority, the Autorità di Informazione Finanziaria, AIF (literally, Financial Information Authority, but the Vatican translates it as the Financial Intelligence Authority).[28]

Rather than operating as a dicastery run by a cardinal, the five-member AIF—described by *Fortune* as "the Vatican equivalent of the Securities and Exchange Commission"—had both a religious president and a lay director.[29] The Pope gave it expansive powers to investigate all suspicious money activity in every Vatican department connected to money, from the IOR to APSA to the Governorate.[30] The AIF would answer only to Benedict, and he emphasized its "full autonomy and independence." Not only did the AIF have the right to audit all the Vatican's financial divisions, it had the authority to punish violators with stiff fines (set soon at a limit of €2 million).

APSA's no-nonsense Cardinal Attilio Nicora was appointed president and Francesco De Pasquale, an attorney with the Bank of Italy and Italy's Exchange Office, was tapped as its first lay director.[31] Three academics filled out the rest of the directors' seats.[32]

The same day as Benedict issued his *motu proprio*, press spokesman Federico Lombardi released a prepared statement noting that "international solidarity" was critical since criminals had become more "ingenious" and "increasingly insidious."[33]

That statement was as close as the church would ever come to admitting that its informal financial monitoring in place for decades had been woefully inadequate. "The implementation of the new norms will certainly require great commitment. . . . Those errors which so quickly become the cause of 'scandal' for public opinion and the faithful will be avoided. In the final analysis the Church will be more 'credible' before the members of the international community, and this is of vital importance for her evangelical mission. . . . This is a good way to conclude the year: with a step towards transparency and credibility!"[34]

The OECD's Jeffrey Owens told reporters that establishing AIF was "clearly a step in the right direction."[35] Gianluigi Nuzzi, the author of the 2009 book that precipitated the string of events from Caloia's exit to the *motu proprio*, expressed the feelings of many Vaticanologists: "A few years ago, an anti-money-laundering law in the Vatican and the Holy See would have been unthinkable. They used to say, 'We're a sovereign state; these are our affairs.' The important thing is that they created an anti-money-laundering law and an authority to enforce it. Without that, the Vatican Bank will remain an offshore bank."[36]

The New York Times best summarized the promise and challenge inherent in Benedict's historic declaration: "It was also seen as a victory by Benedict over factions in the hierarchy who would prefer to defend the Vatican's sovereignty, versus those who wanted more openness. But the test will be how the new law is put into practice—especially by the Vatican bank, which has periodically come under sharp scrutiny and is now the target of a money laundering investigation."[37]

37

The Powerbroker

Even those clerics who opposed Benedict's *motu proprio* did not criticize the Pontiff. The man they blamed for the capitulation to Brussels and its secularist regulators was the cleric everyone considered the power behind Benedict's throne, Secretary of State Tarcisio Bertone. As the head of the Vatican's diplomatic corps, contended some critics, Bertone more than anyone should have been sensitive to how the *motu proprio* might restrict the church's ability to operate under authoritarian governments like those in Myanmar, Iran, Cuba, and China. What might happen to the church's "independent missions" in offshore financial havens such as the Turks and Caicos and the Cayman Islands? How could Bertone allow the church's missionary arm to be subject to the stringent new financial oversight?

Bertone's strong support for the *motu proprio* reenergized an effort to force him from the Curia. Influential clerics had been trying to oust Bertone since 2009. That year a senior archbishop, Cardinal Angelo Bagnasco, representing a group of ranking prelates, met with Benedict at Castel Gandolfo. He had laid out what he thought was a damning case of incompetence and overreaching against Bertone and pleaded with the Pontiff to dismiss him. Benedict waved Bagnasco away, saying *enough* in German and Italian.[1]

Something as significant as a cardinal asking the Pope to fire his Secretary of State did not long stay secret inside the Vatican. When Bertone learned about that failed effort his response was to further consolidate his power. He had already begun the previous year to punish some on his enemies list. Most prominent had been Archbishop Piero Pioppo, whom his predecessor, Sodano, had appointed as the chief prelate of the IOR just before Bertone took power.

At the time it had been interpreted not only as a slight to Bertone but evidence of Benedict's weakness since the Pope ignored appeals from cardinals to void the appointment. At Bertone's direction, Pioppo was dispatched to become Papal Nuncio to Equatorial Guinea and Cameroon (where he still is, as of 2014).[2]

In the wake of the dustup over the *motu proprio* Bertone moved to solidify a loyal team. The Secretary of State favored clerics from the Salesians, his own religious order.[3]*

In February 2011, Bertone moved against the popular Cardinal Dionigi Tettamanzi, Milan's former archbishop and the chief of the Istituto Toniolo, a wealthy religious foundation that controlled the prestigious Cattolica University. During a dispute over Tettamanzi's management of the Cattolica, Bertone sent the cardinal a brusque fax telling him to resign. Tettamanzi appealed to the Pope, who agreed to see both cardinals that April at Castel Gandolfo. After that meeting Benedict gave Tettamanzi two months to step down. But the message was clear: Bertone had prevailed.[5] As Tettamanzi confided to others what had transpired it reinforced the images of both Benedict and Bertone, one as a man too weak to be Pope and the other as too ambitious to be Secretary of State.

In May, Bertone lobbied Gotti Tedeschi to make a $260 million bid for a controlling share of Milan's San Raffaele Hospital, founded by a priest who was a Berlusconi confidant. By the time Gotti Tedeschi got around to checking the hospital's books, there were millions in outstanding debts. San Raffaele's administrator killed himself that October in his own office with a Smith and Wesson revolver. "The Mysterious Suicide That Has Rocked the Vatican" was the headline in London's *Independent*.[6] Local prosecutors had begun a fraud investigation. Much to Bertone's fury, Gotti Tedeschi balked. "We do not know how big the deficit is," he told some colleagues. "There are no accounting records at all. We are walking in the dark."[7]

The San Raffaele marked one of the few setbacks for Bertone. Overall, he

---

* Among some of Bertone's foes whom he transferred out of the Vatican over a two-year purge were Monsignor Vincenzo Di Mauro, the Secretary of the Prefecture for the Economic Affairs of the Holy See; Archbishop Carlo Maria Viganò, the powerful Secretary General of the Governorate; and Monsignor Ettore Balestrero, the Undersecretary for Relations with States. Bertone had also helped block Cardinal Angelo Scola from becoming the president of the Italian episcopal conference. And he replaced Cardinal Fernando Filoni, who held the key position of the Sosistuto in the Secretariat of State, with fifty-two-year-old Archbishop Giovanni Becciu, the Apostolic Nuncio to Angola, and someone who notably had never in his career served inside the Vatican.[4]

was leaving his mark inside the Curia. The Italians—many of his choosing—were again on the ascendancy.[8] By 2011 they were more than half (thirteen of twenty-five) of Benedict's top appointments. When the Pope next picked twenty-two new red hats, for the first time in decades the European cardinals had a slight majority for the next conclave (sixty-seven out of 125).[9] The Italians were back to thirty, boosting their chance of either retaking the Papacy or at least playing a kingmaker role.[10] Some Vatican watchers were uneasy that with all the maneuvering, "one could think with some certainty that Bertone may be a shoo-in for the next pope."[11]

A few tried at least slowing Bertone's power grab. Adolfo Nicolás, the Superior General of the Jesuits, wrote to Benedict enclosing a letter he had received warning of "paralyzing fear" inside the Vatican over Bertone's leadership.[12] An anonymous "Vatican analyst" told Britain's *Guardian*, "I don't think Bertone is a thief, he is just not up to the job."[13]

But Benedict was committed to the man who had served him as a deputy for seven years when they served in the Congregation for the Doctrine of the Faith.[14]

Given a free hand by Benedict, and as the cardinal to whom the IOR oversight committee reported, Bertone exercised broad authority when it came to finances. He had settled the aborted debate the previous year over whether the Vatican should withdraw from the euro. In February, two months after the Pope's historic *motu proprio*, Bertone sent a letter to the Secretary General of the Council of Europe. In that letter he requested that Moneyval, the EU's primary monitoring division in fighting money laundering and the financing of terrorism, evaluate the Holy See and the Vatican city-state.[15] This is precisely what Gotti Tedeschi had been urging since his 2009 arrival at the IOR. Bertone reckoned that there was no use in further delaying the inevitable. If the church had any chance of qualifying for OECD's white list, it needed a good Moneyval report.

Some in the IOR and the Curia who agreed in principle with Bertone thought it was premature. What if the Moneyval examiners found so much wrongdoing once they got inside the bank that the Vatican got slotted onto the gray, or possibly even black, list?

In early April, Brussels sent word that it had agreed to evaluate the city-state.[16] That was only a few days after the Vatican announced, as a further sign of good faith, that anyone entering Vatican City with more than €10,000

($14,000) in cash had to declare it.[17] It was a dramatic departure from the days when clerics working at the Vatican Bank watched Monsignor Donato De Bonis carrying suitcases stuffed with cash.

Representatives from Moneyval and the IOR had to work out the details of any evaluation. It could not be done remotely. The inspectors required access inside the Vatican to IOR files and ledgers that had never before been shared even with other Curial departments. Moneyval would need to conduct evaluations over several years.

On June 1, 2011, the Italians freed the IOR's $30 million that prosecutors had frozen at Credito Artigiano. It was released only after the Vatican struck an agreement to allow Moneyval to have full access to the IOR and other Curia financial departments for a week beginning November 20.[18] A follow-up onsite visit was scheduled for the following spring.[19]

Moneyval assembled a seven-person team with impeccable credentials in criminal law, regulatory issues, and law enforcement.[20] The anxiety was high that November when Moneyval carried out its first thorough assessment inside the city-state. Its visit coincided with the worst financial crisis Italy had faced since World War II, a meltdown that was raising fears about the IOR's possible exposure to an Italian debt default.[21]

Everyone inside the church put on a brave face for the team from Brussels. They knew the results would reveal how close or far away the Vatican was from making it to OECD's white list. The church emphasized transparency for the visit. Pope Benedict met with the inspection team, as did Gotti Tedeschi and a list of who's-who related to the church's money.[22] At the IOR, the examiners faced a "unique challenge" since they were in a sovereign country that also was the seat of the Catholic Church. "An unusually large amount of documentation was seen during the course of the assessment," Moneyval's executive secretary John Ringguth later told reporters.[23]

What played out that November between Moneyval and the IOR was watched far beyond Europe. Former U.S. Treasury Department official Avi Jorisch summarized in *Forbes* what was on the minds of financial compliance officers and law enforcement personnel around the globe: "In today's interconnected financial world, instituting measures to mitigate abuse of the international financial sector is part of the cost of doing business. Unquestionably, one of the most serious public policy challenges the international community will face in the foreseeable future is how to use every tool in its arsenal to make progress against those who exploit tainted money. While the Vatican answers to a higher calling, the EU, FATF and Moneyval should insist that its earthly responsibilities are equally important."[24]

What no Moneyval inspector then knew was that Bertone had engineered the exile to America of Archbishop Carlo Maria Viganò, the industrious and outspoken Deputy Governor of Vatican City, who had led the fight for the church to withdraw from the euro instead of acceding to European inspectors entering the sovereign Vatican. Bertone had not, however, moved Viganò because of his stance on the euro. The archbishop had been transferred from Rome because during his two years as the second ranking cleric in charge of the Vatican's infrastructure, he had made powerful enemies. The brusque Viganò had dedicated himself to breaking up a web of entrenched nepotism, corruption, and cronyism when it came to awarding contracts for work inside the Vatican.[25] His unyielding stance earned him a reputation as a "ballbreaker." Viganò's crusader attitude made him someone the Vatican would seemingly want to showcase to Moneyval. Even if his work did not affect whether the IOR was in compliance when it came to money laundering and terrorism financing laws, clerics like Viganò would impress upon the examiners from Brussels that the Vatican was embracing the EU's dual themes of transparency and reform.

What happened to Viganò was a cautionary tale. Once he had pointed out that many longtime contractors had cozy relationships with the Vatican's old guard, a leak campaign was launched to discredit him. Anonymous sources in the Italian press accused him of being inefficient, overbearing, and even as someone interested only in accumulating personal power.[26] But no one could have predicted what happened behind the scenes when Bertone went to rein in Viganò.

When Bertone called the seventy-year-old archbishop to his office in March, it was to inform him that he was to be transferred nearly three years before his Governorate term was over. Viganò was "astonished" and broke protocol by going over the Secretary of State's head.[27] He wrote two extraordinary letters. One to Bertone was blunt. He said that the information relied on by the Secretary of State in reaching his decision was "falsified . . . a grave injustice . . . [and] the fruit of serious slander."[28] Viganò's second letter was a handwritten one to Benedict. He warned: "My transfer from the Governorate would, in this moment, greatly dismay and discourage all those who believed it possible to correct so many long-entrenched instances of corruption and abuse of power in the management of several departments."[29]

When Benedict did not answer, Viganò requested a private audience. At an early April meeting, Viganò passed to the Pontiff a remarkable memorandum he had prepared. Communications to the Pontiff were normally cloaked in flowery language and any criticisms were so oblique as to be practically invisible. This memo, however, detailed the "widespread corruption" Viganò had discovered when he started in the Governorate in 2009 and what he had done to fix it. He warned that significant Vatican City investments were under the control of two funds managed by a group of Italian bankers "who turned out to have put their own interests before ours." And he provided Benedict with several examples of the rampant malfeasance he had uncovered. In a single instance suppliers and contractors had overcharged the church $2.5 million. Viganò said that was to be expected since "work was always given to the same companies at costs at least double compared to those charged outside the Vatican."[30] In another case, he had shaved $1.2 million from the annual upkeep for the Vatican's gardens, and put that savings toward a renovation of the city-state's thermal power plant.

The archbishop confided that the Vatican's own maintenance workers were demoralized by how badly outside vendors ripped off the church. There were no consequences for the gouging other than getting more business. Viganò shared with Benedict that shortly after he arrived in the Governorate he discovered that the large nativity scene in St. Peter's Square had cost more than $700,000. By bidding out the project the following year, the church saved $300,000. The scene looked the same.[31] Competitive bidding had slashed in half the annual bill from electronic giant Siemens. He even had the numbers demonstrating the sharp reduction of thefts from inventory after he installed surveillance cameras in the Vatican's warehouses.

Viganò was proud that he was instrumental in turning around the Governorate from an annual deficit of more than $10 million the year he arrived to a recent surplus of more than $30 million.

"Everybody is betting on my demise," he told Benedict. If the Pope did not act, the archbishop cautioned that his transfer out of the Vatican would "be perceived by all as a verdict of condemnation of my work, and therefore as a punishment" and it would also "expose those who have assisted my renewal action to acts of revenge and humiliating retaliation."[32]

No one outside the Vatican knew that Viganò's fate was so precarious. Italy's best-connected Vaticanologists were unaware of the drama. *La Stampa*'s normally prescient "Vatican Insider" ran a long story in late May about the "musical chairs" at the Curia. It mentioned that Viganò had met with Benedict that spring. According to "Vatican Insider," the Pope "credited him for the cleaning work and the fight against waste which in two years has enabled the Governorship to transform liabilities for seven million Euro in profits for thirty." And as for what all the shuffling in the Curia meant for Viganò? "Vatican Insider" predicted that while Viganò had been "considered the natural successor of Cardinal Giovanni Lajolo, Governor of the State of Vatican City, now his name is being made as leader of the Ministry of Finance (a cardinal assignment)."[33]

As word spread throughout the Curia about Bertone's move against Viganò, others watched it as the ultimate test of Benedict's commitment to the financial reforms. Four high-ranking Italian cardinals appealed personally to Benedict, asking him to reverse Bertone.[34] The cardinals even suggested that the Pope should immediately elevate Viganò as a cardinal to conclusively demonstrate his faith both in him as well as the zealous cleanup on which he had embarked. One of Benedict's closest confidants, Sister Ingrid Stampa, met him privately and lobbied for the beleaguered Viganò.[35]

In the case of Viganò, a senior Curial cleric who had the courage to identify widespread corruption and wanted the Pontiff's backing to stop it, Benedict was frozen. Viganò did not, as "Vatican Insider" predicted, get elevated to a cardinal and put in charge of the Ministry of Finance. Only weeks before the Moneyval inspectors had arrived, he was sent four thousand miles from the Vatican to serve as the Papal Nuncio to Washington. Once again, as he had throughout his Papacy, Benedict had shied away from confronting his Secretary of State. Bertone's power seemed unchecked.

38

The Butler

In late 2011 a handful of insiders gathered at the Vatican apartment of one of Benedict's closest advisors. There was a war, they concluded, playing out for the soul of the church between reformers and the old guard. They were convinced that while Benedict's heart was solidly with the reformers he was incapable of asserting himself to change the tide of the battle. By allowing his Secretary of State to make unchallenged decisions about top Curial appointments, the Pope had abdicated his administrative powers. That evening the discussion of what to do got around to whether a coup inside the Curia was possible.* They wanted Bertone out. After all, they argued, it was Benedict who had been elected Pope, not Bertone. Sandro Magister, one of Italy's most respected Vaticanologists, captured the essence of what so rankled those gathered that evening: "There are appointments that only the pope can make, but that Bertone is in the habit of administering himself with nonchalance, as if they belonged to him."[1] If Benedict was not going to stop his Secretary of State from acting as if he ran the church, maybe they could find an unorthodox way to move against him.

This was not easy for any of them. Each was loyal to the church and to

* This chapter is largely based on extensive interviews by the author with two people in Rome during September 2013. Both of them had regular and close access to Pope Benedict during his Papacy. They are in a position to know the details of what took place behind the scenes up until Benedict's unexpected 2013 resignation. Each is still affiliated with the church, and since they fear retribution for their disclosures, they have asked that I not only omit their names but make certain that they cannot be identified by too detailed a description of their work or exact quotations about what they saw and heard. I have tried my best to deliver in full the facts while preserving their anonymity.

Pope Benedict. None wanted to do anything that hurt either. But they also realized that if they were to push Bertone from his throne, it could be messy. They knew there would likely be unintended consequences from any plot they hatched.

There were few realistic options. They could try to get a private meeting with Benedict. A few were close to him, personal friends on whom he had long relied. Arranging such a get-together would not be difficult, and it could be kept off the official calendar. Yet they knew firsthand that senior clerics had already met and pled with the Pope to restrain or dismiss Bertone, all to no effect.

Maybe they should enlist some of Bertone's fellow cardinals, and with them develop a strategy to check the Secretary of State. But the cardinals who would be instrumental were survivors through many power wars. They were unlikely to risk their own political capital in taking on Bertone at the behest of a group of lower-ranking clerics and some laymen who might be gone once Benedict was no longer Pope.

The small group of Benedict supporters gathered that night were not simply upset at money matters gone awry. There was, as they discussed that evening, something that made most of them squirm. They had seen the proof of what one called a "gay lobby." The common bond for the gay clerics at the highest positions of the Curia was that they had abandoned their celibacy vows. The problem, the small group agreed, was that they often used sex as a carrot for advancement to ambitious up-and-coming clerics. It was deplorable, they concluded, that a fast career track was within reach for any cleric willing to submit to the Vatican's equivalent of a casting couch.[2]*

They were not an old-world throwback to antigay traditionalists in the church. One had a gay sister and another a pair of brothers who had come out to their family. They did not pay attention to the sometimes salacious rumors that made the rounds at the Vatican about the sexual escapades of those clerics. "Play, don't pray" was the mantra for some, who according to the insiders included dinner parties of clerics and male prostitutes that ended in nights of

---

* Of course, to the extent that there was any casting couch inside the Vatican, it had to be gay since it is a self-contained society of men living and working together. Any chance of promotion into the hierarchy of the church is only available by men appointing other men. An equivalent form of advancement among heterosexual priests who abandoned their celibacy vows is simply not possible.

drugs and sex. Just the previous year, the press was filled with salacious stories about a Vatican choirboy who was dismissed after it was discovered that he was arranging male prostitutes for a Gentleman of His Holiness who also served as a senior consultant to the Congregation for the Evangelization of Peoples.[3]

None of those gathered that night admitted having witnessed any of it with their own eyes. Moreover, they knew that some of the clerics who were part of the gay lobby were among the Curia's most effective reformers and among Benedict's best prelates.

The small group that evening did not know that the lobby they had discovered had a long history in the Vatican. Mussolini's spies had compiled thick dossiers on the secret gay lifestyles of key Papal aides as far back as the 1920s. The police even privately concluded that a 1928 knife attack by a young man on the Vatican's fascist intermediary, Father Tacchi Venturi, was over a love affair with another man.[4] Peter Murphy, the U.S. Deputy Chief of Mission to the Vatican from 1984 to 1989, told me that while he could not verify anything about the Vatican after he left, while he was there, "I know the gay lobby was true. I know it to be absolutely true. It was discreet but I had evidence of it with some of those with whom I worked and saw socially." (Murphy raised the matter with the archbishop who was a senior official for the U.S. Conference of Bishops. "He refused to believe me," recalls Murphy. He also told Archbishop Marcinkus about it. "He did not seem that surprised, but did not say anything.")[5] In 1999, a small publishing house released a book by Luigi Marinelli, a monsignor who had worked at the Vatican for forty-five years. Fearing reprisals from the church, he wrote *Via col vento in Vaticano* (Gone with the Wind in the Vatican) under a pseudonym.[6] The seventy-two-year-old prelate who was dying of liver and bone cancer had decided to purge his conscience. In sometimes overwrought prose, Marinelli presented a hodgepodge of accusations of corruption and venality within the Vatican. One of his strongest charges was that inside the Curia, where he had worked, simply being gay "can help a hopeful candidate advance more quickly and cause a rival to lose the desire to present himself for promotion . . . the one who gives himself from the waist down has a better chance than the one who gives his heart and mind to the service of God and his brothers. For many prelates in the Curia, the beautiful boy attracts more goodwill and favor than the intelligent one." According to Marinelli, there was also widespread sexual blackmail inside the Curia, the kind that "in the national civil code . . . is punishable as a crime; in the ecclesiastical code, the demand is justified by that golden rule *promoveatur ut amoveatur,* which means, 'let it be moved forward so that it can be put aside.' "[7]*

Since that 2011 evening when those Benedict insiders discussed a "gay lobby" at their hastily called meeting, there has been some frank public talk about it. None more so than Benedict's successor, Pope Francis, who in a June 2013 meeting with representatives from CLAR (the Latin American and Caribbean Confederation of Religious Men and Women) in charge of communities of priests, monks, and nuns, startled everyone: "In the Curia, there are holy people. But there is also a stream of corruption. The 'gay lobby' is mentioned, and it is true, it is there. We need to see what we can do."[9] A month later, after advisors contended that such an admission was unnecessary and potentially damaging, Francis pulled back during an impromptu news conference on a flight to Rome from Brazil. "So much is written about the gay lobby. I have yet to find on a Vatican identity card the word 'gay.' . . . I think that when we encounter a gay person, we must make the distinction between the fact of a person being gay and the fact of a lobby, because lobbies are not good."[10]

In 2014, Elmar Mäder, the former commander of the Swiss Guard, told a Swiss newspaper about "a network of homosexuals" and said that to the extent it had "become a network or even a kind of secret society, I would not tolerate it in my sphere of decision making."[11]† Some suspected Mäder as the source of the embarrassing leak the prior year that the Vatican owned a central Rome property that served not only as housing for some cardinals but also had

---

* Marinelli's book might have gone unnoticed had not a Vatican court ordered him to appear before it to answer as to why he should not be punished. He refused to show up, and told a reporter he would not recant. The Vatican tried removing the tell-all from bookstores, which catapulted it almost overnight from unknown to a bestseller. Marinelli told *The New York Times* that he was not surprised but nevertheless disheartened by the church's campaign against him: "The book does not question the sanctity of Jesus Christ, the Eucharist or the Catholic Church. It just points out that the Vatican is made up of men, like me, who are flawed." Marinelli died in October 2000, a year after the publication.[8]

† Mäder's revelations came only a few weeks after another member of the Swiss Guard told the same newspaper that he and others in the small force regularly received many "unambiguous sexual requests" from clerics in the Curia. New arrivals to the Guard were warned about the more aggressive prelates. For Vatican veterans, Mäder's charges brought back memories to the 1998 murder-suicide in the city-state of the then commander of the Swiss Guard, his wife, and a corporal in the Guard. The official motive was that the corporal had been passed over for a promotion and sought revenge on his superior and his wife. Contemporaneous stories in the Italian press speculated that Opus Dei was involved since two of the murdered were members (Opus Dei denied that). An East German spy link was also reported but never confirmed. Publications since have suggested that the commander and corporal were having an affair. Typical is the 2011 headline in the *Daily Beast,* "Vatican Murder Mystery: Was It a Gay Love Triangle?"[12]

Europe's biggest gay bathhouse (at a weekly "bear night," a man dressed as a priest was billed as "Bruno, a hairy pastor of souls . . . [who] wants to expose his body and soul").[13]

The group that gathered that night in 2011 to decide what to do about Bertone was upset by recent headlines that had nothing to do with whether a gay lobby flourished inside the Vatican. They had been startled by the news that the church reportedly profited from pornography published by Weltbild, its wholly owned $2.3 billion German bookseller. The tabloid press reprinted some of Weltbild's more profane titles such as "Slut's Boarding School" and " 'Fuckable' Lawyer's Whore." Instead of banning the publication of such titles, the church instead threatened litigation against some of the tabloids. Such raunchy material accounted for only a tiny fraction of Weltbild's publications. The material in question was "erotica." It did not meet any legal definition of porn. Moreover, one spokesman pointed out, all such sales amounted to $391,000, not a great deal of money.[14]

One of those at the table had recently spoken to Ingrid Stampa, the German nun who had Benedict's ear. She said all the crises facing the church were so serious that anything undertaken must be bold.[15] That added to the sense that they should act even if it was messy. After four hours of sometimes heated discussions the group settled on a plan. It was fraught with danger and real risk for the person tapped to carry it out.

The coup's *il corvo* (the raven) was an unlikely choice, Paolo Gabriele, the forty-five-year-old butler to Pope Benedict, someone investigative journalist Gianluigi Nuzzi later described as "a pious Catholic so devoted to the Pontiff that he saw him as his own father."[16] The posting held by the well-liked Gabriele was one of the Vatican's most coveted lay positions. A Pope's butler attends to all the Pontiff's needs from the moment he awakes. Gabriele typically clocked twelve-hour days, seven days a week. He lived in the Vatican, close to the Apostolic Palace, with his wife, Manuela, a devout Catholic, and their three young children. Whether Benedict was meeting with a head of state, traveling abroad, receiving a personal gift or donation from a prominent visitor, or consulting with other clerics inside the Apostolic Palace, Gabriele, with his trademark array of dark suits, starched white shirts, dark ties, and spit-shined shoes, was ever present. Sometimes Gabriele was invited to sit at the Pope's table for meals.

Gabriele was not a lifelong Vatican employee. After falling out from the church as a teenager, and working with a film company, in the mid-1990s he reconnected with his Catholicism after his prayers about an important personal matter were answered by St. Faustina, a mystic Polish nun. He began doing small jobs around a local diocesan church in Rome. The pastor was Polish and knew John Paul II. He liked the energetic young man and his family and recommended him to John Paul's private secretary, Monsignor Stanislaw Dziwisz (now the Cardinal of Kraków). Not long after—around 2002—Milwaukee-born Monsignor James Harvey, who was the Prefect of the Papal Household, called on Gabriele. He was soon working as a janitor inside the Vatican.* Everyone liked the quiet, shy, hardworking newcomer. Gabriele soon moved up under the direct supervision of a legendary Papal butler, Angelo Gugel, who had cultivated a reputation for fierce loyalty. Gugel, who was a source of some of the most coveted gossip in the city-state, wielded far more power than his position would have indicated.

Pope John Paul took notice of the good-looking young apprentice with the military posture and immaculate clothes, and often made a point of acknowledging Gabriele—calling him *Paoletto* (little Paul)—when he walked past the domestic staff. Others noted that Gabriele had carved out a fast reputation as an eager go-getter.

When Ratzinger became Pope in 2005, Gugel kept the coveted butler's spot. But by 2006, Monsignor Gänswein, who was himself Benedict's jealous gatekeeper, decided it was time to get rid of Gugel. He had too lofty a view of his role as butler. Gänswein directed Monsignor Harvey to find someone who was efficient and loyal but also faded into the background, a person with no ambition to wield influence with the Pontiff.

Gugel fought for his job, but when he realized change was imminent, he pushed for his son-in-law. Harvey instead surprisingly tapped Gabriele.

As Gabriele later recounted to a colleague, he learned of the decision when Gugel called him into his apartment. The longtime butler looked grim, almost, Gabriele recalled, as "if someone had died." When Gabriele sat down, Gugel informed him that he had been selected as Benedict's butler.

---

* In conversations with friends, Gabriele indicated he was somewhat surprised that he was working only one floor underneath the Papal residence without anyone having done a background check. All it took was the right word from a well-placed prelate, in his case Monsignor Harvey, to land the job. And he was not required to sign any employment contract, nor any confidentiality form regarding what he saw during his work.[17]

"It is very, very hard work," Gugel said. "If you can't do it, say so now."

Gabriele realized that Gugel was looking for any excuse to return to Harvey and report that Gabriele was in over his head.

"No, no, it's okay," Gabriele assured him.

There were only nine people who had access to the Pope's private apartments. In record time, Gabriele was one of them.[18] For the next two months Gugel and Gabriele worked together on the transition. The relations between them were frosty, and Gugel did the minimum of what was required to bring the newcomer up to speed. Gänswein kept an eye on the duo. Always polite and humble, with never any desire to gossip, Gabriele seemed the antithesis of Gugel. Gabriele's desk was set up on the far side of the same room in which Gänswein worked. He said nothing unless he was spoken to. He was just what Gänswein had ordered.

The first sign of what Gabriele was up to came to light on January 25, 2012, on a respected Italian television program, *Gli Intoccabili* (The Untouchables). Gianluigi Nuzzi, the investigative journalist who had written the 2009 exposé of the Vatican Bank based on Dardozzi's treasure trove of IOR documents, was the host. Somehow Nuzzi had learned about Archbishop Viganò's efforts to root out corruption in Vatican City and that his transfer to America was against his will. Once again someone inside the Vatican had fed Nuzzi information. Nuzzi portrayed clerics in the Secretariat of State as well as some of Viganò's colleagues in the Governorate as if they were part of a cover-up to protect corrupt contractors.[19]

Press secretary Lombardi and his staff had picked September 26 as the day to get some good media coverage for the church's rewriting of its 2010 anti-money-laundering law. Moneyval inspectors had informed the Vatican a few months earlier that the statute did not meet the EU's stringent standards.[20] The revisions obligated the church to create a roster of terror organizations in line with those identified by the U.N., and also required it to enter into agreements with other countries by which it promised to share financial data. At the same time, the Vatican had ratified three anticrime treaties with New York, Vienna, and Palermo, to comply with standards set by the Paris-based Financial Action Task Force to help combat money laundering and terrorism financing.[21]

But Lombardi's plans to talk about the church's progress with the EU got scuttled when he woke up to front-page stories about Nuzzi's show. No one was interested in the Vatican's financial fine-tuning. By mid-morning Lombardi issued a statement blasting the program, complaining about its "questionable journalistic methods" and its "biased coverage of the Vatican and the Catholic Church."[22] But all he could offer weakly about the factual core of Nuzzi's story was that "the positive criteria of correct and transparent management which inspired Archbishop Viganò certainly continue to guide the current directors of the Governorate."[23]

How did Nuzzi obtain the embarrassing insider information? The hunt for the leaker was on. The Vatican police, under the control of General Domenico Giani, a former commander in Italy's financial police, the Guardia di Finanza, ran the investigation.[24] Giani, who had been with the gendarmes since 1999, had been in charge since 2006. The man Nuzzi dubbed the city-state's *Napoleon* was considered the most able security chief in the Vatican's modern history.[25]

A few days later, on January 31, the Italian daily *Il Fatto Quotidiano* published the contents of a confidential memo from the influential APSA chief Cardinal Nicora. In the memo he raised serious questions about whether the Vatican should fully comply with EU money laundering statutes, reigniting concerns in Brussels about whether or not the Vatican was serious when it came to reform and compliance.[26]

What no one then knew was that the secret group of Vatican insiders who had concocted a plan to oust Bertone had personally selected Nuzzi. He was accumulating an ever-growing cache of explosive documents. Every Thursday, in an unfurnished apartment in Rome's Prati district, the journalist met with Gabriele—someone he identified only as "Maria"—and at each get-together received confidential documents.[27] Nuzzi then scanned the documents and transferred them to a USB stick that he wore around his neck. It was his safety precaution to ensure that someone did not break into his home or office and take back Gabriele's papers.[28]

The leaks started to pour. On February 1, the story broke about the messy fight between Bertone and Gotti Tedeschi over the failed San Raffaele Hospital bid.[29] The documents made Bertone look as if he were reckless in trying to force the quarter-billion-dollar offer against the advice of almost everyone, including the Pope. A week later, the next episode of *The Untouchables* added fuel to what the media had dubbed "Vatileaks."[30] Italian prosecutors had opened criminal investigations against four priests whose IOR accounts were used to launder Mafia cash. On the program, Luca Tescaroli, a Roman prosecutor, said that he had submitted to the Vatican three formal requests for information relating to Roberto Calvi's death. The Vatican had not answered.[31]

Benedict's Papacy had by this point been marked by six years of inept handling of the church's public image.[32] With the advent of Vatileaks, Lombardi and his staff did not morph into a world-class public relations unit. It was admittedly not easy for them. They had no idea who was the leaker or what was coming next. Still, all they offered were reactive and often weak responses to each subsequent disclosure. In the first week they established the defensive tone that became the hallmark of their approach. As for the four priests under investigation for money laundering through IOR accounts, Lombardi dismissed the story as "recycled accusations" and "sadly defamatory."[33] Worse than the generic denials was when the Vatican tried countering the substance of the leaks. After the story about how Viganò had been transferred because of his corruption busting, his former colleagues at the Governorate issued a statement dismissing Nuzzi's account as the "fruit of erroneous evaluations or based on unproven fears." They boasted that their own quick investigation proved that the "suspicions and allegations" were "completely unfounded." Most observers thought that self-serving statement was evidence the Vatican was not serious about getting to the bottom of the charges.[34]

The next round of leaked information—an internal memo reporting what Palermo's Cardinal Paolo Romeo said during a trip to China the previous November—found its way to the front page of *Il Fatto Quotidiano.* The leakers had hoped that the press would concentrate on a portion where Romeo said the Bertone-Benedict relationship "was full of conflict." That would add to the public perception that Benedict might be better off with a different Secretary of State. But instead, the press jumped all over a different portion of Romeo's remarks in which he said that the fight for power at the top of the church had become so nasty that he predicted that Benedict would be dead within twelve months. It did not matter whether Romeo meant someone was plotting to murder the Pope or if he believed the stress would take its toll on the nearly eighty-five-year-old Pontiff. But the result of that leak was different from anything that Gabriele could have imagined. Instead of Bertone being tarnished, the entire hierarchy of the church appeared to be in the middle of internecine warfare so great that the Pope's very life was threatened.[35]

No faster did one story break and grab headlines than the next slew of documents changed the focus to another embarrassment. The attention frequently fell off of Bertone. Vatileaks dominated all other news about the city-state. At a Vatican summit held in early February about the sex abuse crisis, it was disclosed that in America alone some $2.2 billion had been spent to settle claims by nearly 100,000 victims (it was estimated that another billion had gone to lawyers).[36] The shocking figures barely got noticed. Sexual abuse was, by 2012, a story to which the media occassionally returned, but Vatileaks and its depiction of the church as a den of snakes was all encompassing.[37]

By late February, Nuzzi aired an interview with Gabriele, in which his face and voice were digitally disguised.[38] He claimed to be a whistleblower working inside the Secretariat of State: "Maybe there is a kind of omerta to prevent the truth from surfacing. Not because of a power struggle but maybe because of fear" was his ominous message.[39]

Gabriele—acting on his own, he later insisted implausibly—or the entire group that had gathered the previous November, had underestimated the difficulty of controlling a breaking news story. Many commentators concluded correctly that Bertone was the target of leaks that cast him as a poor manager who spent much of his time expanding his Curial influence. Some Vatican watchers thought that Benedict himself was the target, since his hands-off management style had fostered many of the problems. And others thought the leaks were not targeting a single person but more generally corruption and inefficiency inside the Vatican's financial institutions.

None of the leakers had foreseen how the scandal weighed on Benedict. "The secretary of state is increasingly alone, in a curia he does not govern and with a pope he does not help," wrote Sandro Magister in *L'Espresso.*[40]

Benedict gave a "Pontifical mandate" to a special committee of three cardinals to conduct their own investigation. The chairman was eighty-two-year-old Cardinal Julián Herranz, the longtime private secretary to the founder of Opus Dei. Their simple brief was to take whatever action was necessary to find the whistleblower.[41] No one at that time knew that Bertone had ordered his own secret probe and had used Vatican police commander Domenico Giani to tap the telephones of some officials in the Curia (when it later became public, press spokesman Lombardi tried minimizing it by saying there were "only a few wiretaps, possibly as few as three").[42]

As the damage built from the financial mismanagement portrayed in the leaked documents, there were Italian press reports "of political jockeying among church officials who, sensing an increasingly weak and aging pontiff, are already preparing for a conclave."[43] The idea that Benedict might not long be Pope was boosted by how frail he looked. For a February ceremony in St. Peter's Basilica in which he officially gave the twenty-two new cardinals their red hats, birettas, and rings, the Pontiff was wheeled in on a moving platform. For his upcoming trips to Cuba and Mexico, few public events were planned. When senior clerics complained to Benedict about his Secretary of State, the Pontiff's standard response was now "We are an old Pope."[44] As veteran Vatican journalist Nicole Winfield noted, that Benedict "has been slowing down recently" meant "that a conclave is very much on the minds of cardinals new and old."[45]

Benedict had appointed Bertone in 2007 as his Camerlengo, the person responsible for running the church after his death and before the selection of a new Pope. Bertone running the church unchallenged, even if briefly, was a prospect to which few of the cardinals looked forward.

39

A Vote of No Confidence

Not all the bad news came from Vatileaks. The State Department announced in early March that for the first time it had added the Vatican to a list of sixty-eight countries it considered a "concern" for money laundering.[1] And a few days later the investment bank JPMorgan Chase announced it was shuttering a Vatican Bank account in Milan since the IOR had failed to respond to multiple queries about the account for two years. That account was a so-called sweeping facility, meaning that at the end of each day any funds were transferred to a Vatican Bank account in Germany. Over some eighteen months, while JP Morgan had been waiting for answers about the origin of the money in that account, some $2.2 billion had passed through it.[2] JP Morgan was one of the IOR's correspondent banks, institutions through which it conducted its foreign transactions. All the correspondent banks had themselves been pushed hard by European regulators for strict compliance. They were in no mood to cover for any sloppiness by the Vatican Bank.[3]

That a major American investment bank had to close an active IOR account because it could not get information required by anti-money-laundering laws did not look good for an institution that was supposedly working hard to get on the OECD white list. And it did not reflect well on Gotti Tedeschi. Did he know about the JP Morgan requests and ignore them or did his management style mean he was uninvolved in the bank's details? Neither answer was comforting.

That spring, Moneyval sent a top secret draft to the Vatican with its preliminary conclusions.[4] It wanted to give the church an opportunity to comment before the report was released that July. Gotti Tedeschi told colleagues he felt he had made considerable progress in meeting the EU standards, but he was frustrated about how long it took directives he issued to become operational. Approaching three years as the bank's director, he was still surprised at the enormous divide between efficiency and performance in his private finance work and what passed for banking inside the city-state.[5]

The Moneyval draft was unequivocal: the Vatican had a long way to go before it would be transparent and compliant enough to qualify for OECD's white list. Moneyval's recommendations included reorganizing the Financial Intelligence Authority (AIF) and reducing the power of the Secretariat of State over financial affairs. The European inspectors did not like a change that Bertone had made to AIF's oversight of the Vatican Bank: any monitoring had to have the Secretary of State's express permission.

Bertone privately castigated the draft's recommendations as an undue interference with the church's sovereignty. But others, like APSA's Cardinal Nicora, felt vindicated. Nicora had opposed Bertone's power grab over money matters, and at the time had written a secret letter to the Secretary of State warning, "We are taking a step back and remaining a tax haven."[6]

Gotti Tedeschi advanced the most logical argument: since the Vatican had agreed to EU oversight, change was coming one way or the other. There was no use in postponing the inevitable.[7]

Moneyval's reorganization suggestions to further empower AIF got a boost in May when Italian prosecutors complained they had subpoenaed records for an IOR account held by a Sicilian priest. The Vatican had stonewalled for a month. That criminal investigation focused on $1.5 million that went through the cleric's IOR account over two years. The probe also centered on several real estate investments and sales both by the priest and his local bishop, all disguised to clean mob profits.

"We have made a request for information to the Vatican City State in the spirit of collaboration with regard to an investigation into sums of money in financial transactions undertaken by the Diocese of Trapani," the prosecutor said in a public statement.[8] No one from the church initially made any comment. When they did, it was to say that the paperwork the prosecutors wanted was missing.[9] (When the priest turned into a witness for the civil authorities, the Pope suspended the cleric and dismissed the bishop.)[10]

On May 19, Gianluigi Nuzzi announced the publication of his new book, *Sua Santità: Le carte segrete di Benedetto XVI* (His Holiness: The Secret Papers of Benedict XVI). It was based on the trove of information leaked to him by Gabriele since 2011. Nuzzi for the first time disclosed that his source had started collecting documents after the death of John Paul II in 2005.[11] Nuzzi reproduced dozens of personal letters, internal memos, faxes, and even personal notes in *Sua Santità*. He claimed he had omitted anything about private lives and concentrated only on matters on which he thought transparency was necessary. The book was nevertheless a titillating and mortifying look at the Vatican's dirty laundry and an instant bestseller in Italy.[12] Everyone it seemed was talking about some of its revelations: the top newsmen who gave large "donations" to the church before landing private audiences with the Pope or the prominent businessman who wangled a favor from Benedict in exchange for a $100,000 white truffle (that ended up in a soup at a Vatican-run shelter for the homeless).[13] Nuzzi revealed confidential notes about how senior clerics were perplexed and fascinated by the 1983 disappearance of fifteen-year-old Emanuela Orlandi, the daughter of a church employee who was never seen again after leaving her family's Vatican apartment to go to a music lesson.[14] And despite the assurance that he steered clear of private lives, Nuzzi disclosed the secret letters of Dino Boffo, the former editor of a Catholic newspaper, complaining to Benedict and a ranking cardinal that another Catholic newspaper editor had leaked a fake document charging that Boffo was a "known homosexual who was already known to the police" for sexual harassment. That leak had kicked off a media feeding frenzy in 2009 that cost Boffo his job. Nuzzi reprinted two private letters from Boffo to the Pope's powerful private secretary, Monsignor Georg Gänswein, in which the newspaper editor accused Bertone of engineering the character assassination.[15]

The book also set out how senior Vatican officials judged America—between the sex abuse epidemic and liberal secular policies—as a moral wasteland. An assignment to Washington, as was done with Archbishop Viganò, was unquestionably a punishment.

There was one major story playing out inside the Vatican about which Nuzzi was in the dark since Gabriele had never learned about it. Gotti Tedeschi had been methodically compiling a secret dossier about the Vatican Bank that he intended to present to Pope Benedict.[16] The IOR chief had stumbled across information that he considered so explosive about how the IOR was being misused by mobsters—sometimes family members of the clerics who worked inside—that he feared his life might be in danger if others found out before he reached Benedict.[17] *Corriere della Sera*, Italy's paper of record, later concluded that Gotti Tedeschi uncovered accounts in the names of the "politicians, shady intermediaries, contractors and senior (Italian) officials, as well as people believed to be fronts for Mafia bosses."[18] Part of what Gotti Tedeschi had discovered was linked to the IOR's inexplicable obstruction for two years about inquiries from Italian prosecutors about a bank account held by two clerics in Sicily. Gotti Tedeschi had also come across a name that sent a shiver through him—Matteo Messina Denaro, an arms and narcotics kingpin who was suspected of dozens of murders over a twenty-year reign.[19] The man nicknamed Diabolik had been on the run since 1993 (he is still a fugitive). "With the people I've killed, I could make a cemetery," he once boasted.

On at least two occasions Gotti Tedeschi told Benedict's secretary, Gänswein, that he wanted to meet with the Pope. He did not share with Gänswein the full details of what disturbed him but confided it was a matter "of the greatest urgency." The last conversation with Gänswein was on May 21. The IOR chief did not hear back.[20] Gotti Tedeschi had a paper calendar on which he kept his appointments. Listed for Friday, June 1, was a shorthand notation to nudge Gänswein. Time was of the essence.[21] By now, Gotti Tedeschi's memo had more than fifty attachments of email, notes, and copies of relevant papers.[22]

Gänswein was in no hurry to arrange for the IOR chief to see the Pope.[23] The chief of the gendarmes, Domenico Giani, had confidentially informed Gänswein that questions had been raised about Gotti Tedeschi's mental stability. A Rome psychotherapist, Dr. Pietro La Salvia, whose specialty was the psychology of workplace stress, had observed Gotti Tedeschi at the IOR's 2011 Christmas party. He was "dismayed" by what he saw and wrote a letter to the Vatican Bank's director general, Paolo Cipriani. As a result of his casual observation, the psychotherapist thought Gotti Tedeschi exhibited "traits of egocentricity, narcissism and a partial disconnection from reality that could be a psychopathological dysfunction."[24] Although La Salvia emphasized that his three-month-old opinion was not a clinical diagnosis, word spread quickly at the top of the Curia and IOR that something might be amiss with Gotti Tedeschi.

On Thursday, May 24, as all of the Vatican and Italy seemed consumed with Nuzzi's new tell-all, the Vatican Bank's supervisory board of lay directors assembled in the late afternoon for their scheduled quarterly meeting. Carl

Anderson, the American director, had stunned Gotti Tedeschi only a couple of days earlier by informing him that the board was considering a no confidence vote that could result in his dismissal. Gotti Tedeschi did not know then that his colleagues had already made up their minds. The board's vice president, ex-Deutsche Bank chairman Ronaldo Hermann Schmitz, had earlier written to Bertone with a catalogue of complaints about the IOR chief and said he would quit if Gotti Tedeschi was not sent packing.[25]

At the meeting, Gotti Tedeschi gave an impassioned defense of his three-year tenure. As far as he was concerned, the bank's problems were the results of years of mismanagement by his predecessor, Angelo Caloia (when that eventually went public, Caloia demanded in vain a Vatican apology).[26] But his fellow directors—Anderson, Schmitz, Manuel Serrano of Banco Santander, and an Italian notary, Antonio Marocco—peppered him with hostile questions. Gotti Tedeschi realized his presentation was useless. After seventy minutes he scooped up his papers and stormed out.[27] A Swiss Guard, unaware of the high drama that had just played out inside the ancient tower, saluted him as he screeched at high speed from the Vatican.[28]

The four Vatican Bank directors then unanimously passed a resolution of no-confidence in Gotti Tedeschi.[29] And they submitted a scorching internal memo setting forth nine reasons for his dismissal. Among them, he had "abandoned the premises of the Institute without notice."[30] It noted that he exhibited "progressively erratic personal behavior" and had been sacked because of "his failure to fulfill various primary functions of his office . . . to carry out basic duties . . . or to provide any formal explanation for the dissemination of documents last known to be in the president's possession."[31] It took only two days before that memo was leaked to reporters and the contents splashed across Italy's front pages.[32]

The reference to the "dissemination of documents" was a not subtle reference to their shared belief that Gotti Tedeschi might have leaked information about financial mismanagement inside other Vatican departments in order to make the IOR look better in comparison.[33] One particular leak—an email from the general director of the AIF to Gotti Tedeschi complaining about the burden imposed by the Vatican's anti-money-laundering law—could only have been leaked, they concluded, by Gotti Tedeschi.[34] The fact that most people thought the leaks cast Gotti Tedeschi in a positive light was further evidence to them that he had released only those documents that showed him as a serious financier focused on what was best for the Vatican while his Curial colleagues appeared intent only either on destroying their enemies or undermining the EU efforts to apply financial regulations to the city-state.

The IOR's lay board noted that despite its frequent warnings about the bank's "governance," under Gotti Tedeschi's tenure the "situation has deteriorated further."[35] The directors made no mention of how furious they were when they had learned he had been talking with Anna Maria Tarantola, the second in command of the Bank of Italy's Vigilance Department, seeking the central bank's help in closing some problematic Vatican accounts.[36]

The Vatican Bank's cardinals' commission, chaired by Secretary of State Bertone, announced it would meet the following day to discuss "future steps." Meanwhile, Gotti Tedeschi told ANSA, the Italian wire service, "I'm torn between a concern to tell the truth and not wanting to disturb the Holy Father. My love for the Pope is even more important than the defense of my reputation, called into question in a cowardly way."[37] He told Reuters, "I paid the price for transparency."[38]

Gotti Tedeschi was surprised that Benedict had not intervened to save him. What he did not know then was that the Pope had not even been aware of the coordinated effort to dismiss him. When Benedict later learned about his ouster, he was "surprised, very surprised."[39] That Pope Benedict did not know about the struggle for control of the Vatican Bank was another bad sign that the feud in the Curia was raging in part because there was not a strong Pontiff capable of putting an end to the fighting.

40

"A Time Bomb"

The day after Gotti Tedeschi's dismissal, Friday, May 25, Giani's gendarmes arrested Paolo Gabriele at his Vatican apartment. They found boxes of confidential documents. Giani had questioned him three days earlier as the list of suspects narrowed. It had been Gänswein who had finally turned the investigation toward Benedict's butler. When he read Nuzzi's book, Gänswein realized that only he and Gabriele had access to three of the leaked documents. With Benedict's permission, Gänswein questioned the small group that made up the "Pope's family." One of them, Sister Cristina Cernetti, had also sensed that Gabriele was the leaker. After he had been questioned, why did the shy and devout butler not dispose of any incriminating documents? He and his wife and three children lived across the street from Giani. Had someone higher promised Gabriele protection, or assured him that even if he were discovered that nothing would happen to him? Some published reports speculated that more than a dozen accomplices helped the butler while others said the conspiracy included some of the Pope's closest confidants.

The public-relations-challenged Vatican even debated whether to ask Italian prosecutors to drag in Nuzzi for interrogation since he refused to name his sources. "What crime have I committed?" Nuzzi asked when he heard about that. "I am not interested in where the letters came from, just the news they contain."[1]

Gabriele was led across the street from his flat to a twelve-foot-by-twelve-foot cell in the Vatican's seldom-used jail. By that time, the Internet and broadcast media already had "The Butler Did It" as their lead story. Those who knew him best had trouble believing that the pious butler who had dutifully served the Pontiff would do anything to hurt Benedict. Was it possible that Gabriele was only a middleman, holding the documents found in his apartment for someone who had not picked them up before the police arrived? By the end of the day of his arrest, many in the Vatican assumed it was only a matter of time before Gabriele's handler was unmasked.[2]

Between the forced departure of Gotti Tedeschi and the arrest of the Pope's butler, the church was buffeted by two major stories that, no matter how hard it tried, it could not control. The IOR's Carl Anderson was interviewed the day after Gabriele's arrest for *La Stampa*'s "Vatican Insider" column. When asked why Gotti Tedeschi had been fired, Anderson said: "He lost the esteem of the staff and of the heads of the IOR, he caused divisions."[3] Gotti Tedeschi's number two, Paolo Cipriani, later said that his former boss "didn't take things in hand. It was as if he were absent, even when he was present."[4] Cipriani claimed that Gotti Tedeschi had refused to show him the problematic accounts.[5] (Gotti Tedeschi at least gave some credence to the idea that he may not have spent enough time at the IOR, telling prosecutors that he came to the office only on weekends, spending his workweek running Spain's Banco Santander office in Milan, a position he kept when he started at the Vatican in 2009.)[6]

Anderson was adamant that he and his fellow directors had been contemplating a no-confidence vote on Gotti Tedeschi for some time, but that since the board met only quarterly, it had fallen by chance at the same time as Gabriele's arrest. "It is just a coincidence, nothing more," Anderson said, although conspiracy-loving Italians found that hard to believe.[7] As for whether Bertone had pressured the four directors, Anderson again swore it was not so. They had informed the Secretary of State of what they intended to do—"as a polite gesture"—but insisted there was "no pressure, no influence."[8]

Anderson, and the IOR's interim president, Ronaldo Hermann Schmitz, had written letters to Bertone only a couple of days before their no-confidence vote. Those were now conveniently leaked to some of the church's favorite reporters. In them, Anderson accused Gotti Tedeschi of showing a "lack of an adequate response" when JPMorgan had requested information on the IOR account they shuttered in Milan. Schmitz said the Vatican Bank was "in an extremely fragile and precarious position" and that under Gotti Tedeschi its international reputation had taken such a beating that he feared lasting and "imminent danger." Schmitz bemoaned Gotti Tedeschi's "wanting loyalty."[9]

On June 1, Pope Benedict took a needed break from the Vatican for a three-day visit to Milan. It was capped by his celebration of an outdoor Mass attended by more than a million people. To the great disappointment of those who had executed the often misguided leak campaign to dislodge Bertone, the Pontiff invited Bertone to join him on the trip. The two made a point of standing together at many of the public events. It was a strong endorsement by Benedict of his embattled Secretary of State. On Sunday, June 3, the final day of the Papal visit, *La Repubblica* ran an anonymous note it received claiming that up to twenty whistleblowers would continue to send incriminating documents to the media so long as Bertone remained Secretary of State and Monsignor Gänswein was Benedict's personal secretary.[10] No one was sure if there were additional leakers or if someone was merely taking advantage of the media's eagerness to publish almost anything connected to Vatileaks. (Evidence that the Vatican knew it was outmatched when it came to handling public relations was the hiring later that month of Greg Burke, a Fox television broadcaster, as the first-ever communications advisor to Bertone.)[11]

The Pope was not long back inside the Vatican when the outside world again seemed inhospitable. Palermo prosecutors announced they were investigating claims that a Sicilian godfather had laundered millions of mob cash through an IOR account.[12] An unnamed "church official" warned there is a "time bomb" about to engulf the IOR and dirty Mafia cash. Another anonymous cleric confided that "tainted money" was in IOR accounts and told *La Stampa*, "What has surfaced is only a splatter of lava; underneath there's a time bomb, which is ready to explode."[13] No one then knew that this information was part of what Gotti Tedeschi had accumulated and wanted to show the Pope before he was let go.

On the early morning of June 5, Friday, the high drama took an unexpected turn. Forty miles north of Milan, in the small town of Piacenza, Gotti Tedeschi was weighing whether to make the three-and-a-half-hour high-speed train trip to Rome.[14] He wanted to "put on the record" that he was still trying to sound the alarm about abuses inside the Vatican Bank.[15] What better way than trying once again to see the Pope? The odds were against him, he was realistic enough to know that. But maybe someone there might appreciate the fallout if word got out that the Vatican turned away the dismissed IOR chief with a "must see" dossier.

Gotti Tedeschi was known as a fastidious dresser. That morning he settled on a conservative ensemble, wanting to impress his former colleagues at the church that he was there on serious business. He picked a charcoal gray wool flannel, with peak lapels. He matched it with a striped shirt with a spread collar, and a solid, dark silk tie. Grabbing his leather briefcase, he stepped from his home on the quaint Via Giuseppe Verdi. Four men stood near his car. His instinctive reaction was that they were there to murder him.[16] But they were policemen from a special financial crimes unit and had been dispatched by prosecutors in Rome and Naples. They presented him with a search warrant they had obtained that morning in connection with an ongoing corruption probe of Finmeccanica, the state-run defense and aerospace firm. Finmeccanica's president was a close Gotti Tedeschi friend and prosecutors suspected that some military equipment was sold to India using a Vatican Bank account at JPMorgan. Gotti Tedeschi was not yet a target of the probe but he might have documents relevant to the investigation. They ushered him back inside his house and began rummaging through his home office. Gotti Tedeschi called his Milan attorney, Fabio Palazzo, one of Italy's most respected white-collar-crime specialists. At the same time, detectives executed another search warrant at his Santander office in Milan, around the corner from the La Scala Opera House (later that morning they also searched his country home in the village of San Paolo).

The police seized two cabinets crammed with files, paperwork, and three-ring binders, as well as a stack of notebooks, a day planner, a briefcase, and several computers. They even took a stack of memos from a wall safe, which Gotti Tedeschi opened at their request. In those papers were some Vatican Bank secrets, including emails that demonstrated how some church officials had resisted the full enforcement of EU money laundering and antiterrorism financing.[17] There was also data about a few suspicious numbered accounts.[18] In the forty-seven folders carted away from Gotti Tedeschi's house, prosecutors would discover the broad outline of how the ex-IOR chief had ran into trouble when he tried dismantling the network of clerics who still used the bank as if it was their own private trust.

Gotti Tedeschi voluntarily went to the police station, where his lawyer was waiting. Prosecutors were also there.[19] They spoke for several hours before agreeing to meet again the next day. Over the course of their discussions, Gotti Tedeschi did not tell them everything, as he later admitted to a colleague. He worried that the Vatican might have an informant inside the police or prosecutor's office, or if not an agent, then maybe a brother, nephew, or cousin to one of his clerical foes inside the Curia.[20] Gotti Tedeschi told the prosecutors that his problems at the IOR began soon after he asked to see "information about accounts that were not in the church's name."[21] And he confided something he had seen that was odd for a bank: that the IOR sent tens of millions of euros through encrypted money transfers designed to make it tough for regulators to identify who was behind the transactions (Gotti Tedeschi's deputy, Cipriani, later denied that the bank used any encrypted wire transfers).[22] In one of his memos, the police found Gotti Tedeschi's handwritten entry: "I've seen things in the Vatican that scare me."[23]

If Bertone remained in power at the Vatican, Gotti Tedeschi later told the Roman prosecutor Giuseppe Pignatone, the IOR would never get onto the OECD white list. Benedict was a holy and well-intentioned Pontiff, but he was simply incapable of issuing the clear-cut directives needed to clean up the bank.[24]

Prosecutors found Gotti Tedeschi credible.[25] But at times he came up with some theories that stretched credulity and made them question whether everything he told them was accurate. A Jewish-Masonic plot, he claimed, had targeted him since he was an Opus Dei member.[26] Two of its co-conspirators, he told Pignatone, were thirty-year-old Michele Briamonte, a partner to Franzo Grande Stevens, the lawyer who had long been one of the Vatican's chief advisors, as well as thirty-three-year-old Marco Simeon, the director of the Vatican desk at Italy's public television. And he was suspicious about Jeffrey Lena, a solo practitioner in Berkeley, California, who had, among other cases, defended the Vatican in the class action brought by Holocaust victims over the IOR and looted Nazi gold.[27]

The idea that Italian police might have confidential IOR files as a result of searching Gotti Tedeschi's home and office was of great concern at the Vatican. It issued a public statement that "we have faith that the prosecutors and Italian judicial system will respect our sovereignty—recognized internationally—with regard to these documents."[28] Behind the scenes, the Vatican had decided to further discredit Gotti Tedeschi. Beyond the internal memos and letters that had already been leaked about his "progressively erratic personal behavior," several reporters now got anonymous tips about the psychotherapist who thought Gotti Tedeschi suffered from a possible "psychopathological dysfunction."[29] Once the Italian press began repeating that story in various iterations, each seemingly more dramatic than the last, it was soon an "established fact" that Gotti Tedeschi was crazy.

But instead of stemming the torrent of terrible news between Vatileaks and the discord at the IOR, tarnishing Gotti Tedeschi's reputation seemed to only fuel the media's near-obsessive interest. There was growing frustration inside the Vatican about how to deal with the press. In mid-June, Bertone lashed out, blaming the media for the scandals. He told an Italian Catholic weekly that journalists had "a will to create division that comes from spite" and that they were "pretending to be Dan Brown [author of the fictional *Da Vinci Code*] . . . inventing stories and replaying legends."[30]

On Thursday, June 28, Lombardi arranged for what he, and Bertone, thought might take the attention off Gotti Tedeschi and Vatileaks. For the first time ever, journalists were invited inside the IOR offices in the fifteenth-century Tower of Nicholas V. The fifty-one members of the fourth estate discovered they were not entitled to do much reporting; instead, as *The Wall Street Journal* noted, it was "tightly choreographed."[31] Could they take pictures? Not allowed. Sound recordings. No. Could they see the main vault? Off limits. What about questions? Preferred in writing. Instead they sat in the ornate conference room through a particularly dull three-and-a-half-hour PowerPoint presentation by the bank's acting director, Paolo Cipriani. Gotti Tedeschi's name was never mentioned. At one stage, Cipriani draped on his lectern a T-shirt with "Anti–Money Laundering Expert" emblazoned across it.[32] He told the reporters that "we need to take away the veil, the shadow" that had settled over the IOR.

The journalists left unsold. More important, another audience—the EU's financial enforcement officials—were not convinced that all was good at the IOR. Vatileaks and its disclosures of unattended corruption and infighting among the church's leaders had revealed general chaos in the Vatican that inspired little confidence in Brussels.

41

The Swiss James Bond

The flap over Gotti Tedeschi's dismissal was temporarily pushed off the front pages on July 18 when Moneyval released its long-anticipated 241-page *Mutual Evaluation Report: Anti–Money Laundering and Combating the Financing of Terrorism—The Holy See (Including Vatican City State).*[1] For the first time in history the public had an inside look at the Vatican Bank. There were just over 33,000 accounts and some $8.3 billion in assets.[2] It was not even a midsized bank by U.S. standards.

The European observers complimented the church for having "come a long way in a very short period of time" and also for putting into place the "building blocks" for solid financial transparency and regulations. But tempering that was the news the Vatican was not compliant on half of Moneyval's forty-five recommendations. And when it came to the sixteen "key and core recommendations," on which the Vatican had to achieve a passing mark on every one to qualify for the OECD white list, it failed seven.[3]

The single most important matter was that the Vatican's all-important watchdog group, the Financial Intelligence Authority (AIF), got a failing grade. Moneyval cited the AIF's failure to define a clear mission as well as its lack of meaningful independence. The Vatican's three-year-old supervisory and oversight division was at best stuck in neutral. And Moneyval highlighted a continuing problem at the Vatican Bank: a huge number of cash transactions with few effective controls to determine the source of the money, especially when the funds were from one of the church's third-world outposts. The rules at the IOR regarding wire transfers, the reporting of suspicious transactions, and the criteria for customer due diligence were all judged deficient. The managers at the bank also needed to be selected by stricter criteria and better supervised.[4]

There was some bad news for one of the most powerful cardinals, APSA chief Attilio Nicora. Moneyval concluded that his dual role as the chief of AIF and as a director of the IOR's supervisory commission was a "serious conflict of interests" and "therefore strongly recommended that the same person not hold [both] positions."[5] (Nicora stayed on AIF's seven-person board of directors and relinquished his Vatican Bank position.)

The EU inspectors also discovered something odd: 10 percent of the cardinals holding accounts at the Vatican Bank were deceased (236 accounts, but only 213 living cardinals).

Most Vaticanologists and financial observers thought that the Vatican had done about as well as could have been expected. It fell in the middle of Moneyval's rankings for all its member countries, and was compliant in just under half of all the EU's recommendations. The same day as Moneyval released its report, the Vatican said it intended to use the recommendations so that the city-state could become "a reliable partner in the international community."[6] Toward that goal, Moneyval and the Vatican agreed to an updated evaluation the following year.

In July, Paolo Gabriele was released from his tiny Vatican City cell. He had been held for sixty days on charges of illegally possessing confidential Papal documents. In August, after having denied any role, Gabriele reversed himself and admitted being Nuzzi's whistleblower.[7] He was now adamant that he acted alone. By the end of that month, the butler's attorney asked to leave the case. His client would not heed any legal advice. At the end of September a rare event got under way in Vatican City: a criminal trial (Italy's police deal with the Vatican's common petty crimes such as pickpockets or ripping off tourists).*

In a critical decision on the eve of the trial, the three judges ruled that none of the evidence gathered by Benedict's Vatileaks investigative commission of three cardinals would be admitted into evidence. That killed any chance of answering the questions about whether Gabriele had help, and if so, how

* A codefendant, Claudio Sciarpelletti, a computer technician from the Secretariat of State, was tried separately for making a false statement to the gendarmes when asked who gave him a file folder that ended up with Nuzzi. He received a two-month suspended sentence.[8]

much and by whom. If it could not get to the entire truth, it seemed the church would be quite satisfied with simply convicting Benedict's butler.

The Vatileaks trial, covered by a pool of journalists, was around-the-clock news. It was the lead story internationally when Gabriele took the stand and complained about mistreatment in jail (his cell was too small and the lights were kept on to disrupt his sleep, causing a "psychological depression").[9] Spectators leaned forward to hear the soft-spoken butler admit to copying documents in the Pope's private apartment, but contended he did not understand why it was a crime. He loved Benedict, he said, "as a son would." The theme of Gabriele's testimony was that he alone was involved and that he had not meant any harm. "My intention was to find someone trustworthy with whom to share my state of mind and my perplexity regarding a situation that was unbearable," he testified, "not only for me but for many inside the Vatican."[10]

When he was found guilty, the judges sentenced him to thirty months, but reduced it to eighteen months since they agreed he had no bad intent. Reporters peppered the Vatican press office with questions about whether Benedict might pardon his former butler. It was too soon to discuss, said Lombardi. Although the judges had ordered Gabriele to serve his time under house arrest, after a week he was returned to the Vatican's unused jail. (In November, Lombardi announced that the Pope had indeed pardoned Gabriele and he would be released in time to rejoin his family for Christmas. The church kept him on its payroll, putting him at the Vatican-owned Bambino Gesù Hospital, on the condition that he refrain from talking to the press.)

Gabriele's trial was a sideshow to some real progress at the Vatican regarding its finances and the IOR. The same day that Gabriele's trial had gotten under way, September 30, the Vatican had hired René Brülhart to run the AIF (acting chief Francesco De Pasquale stayed on as a board member).

Brülhart was a forty-year-old Swiss anti-money-laundering expert who for eight years had directed Liechtenstein's Financial Intelligence Unit.[11] His good looks and his penchant for high-styled bespoke suits led one magazine to dub him the James Bond of the financial world. But he had the substance to go along with the slick style, credited with having cleaned up tiny Liechtenstein. When Brülhart had arrived there it had a reputation every bit as notorious a tax and money laundering haven as the Vatican. He confronted not just a banking system steeped in secrecy and resistant to change, but he also helped root out the aftereffects of an enormous 2006 Siemens bribery scandal that had infected the small principality with a culture of corruption. Among his many accomplishments in Liechtenstein he won accolades for finding assets owned by Saddam Hussein's former government and returning them to Iraq's newly elected leaders.[12]

His colleagues were so impressed that in 2010 he got a two-year appointment as the deputy chief of the Egmont Group, a storied network of national financial-intelligence agencies that share information to better fight the financing of terrorism and combat money laundering.

When he had finished in Liechtenstein, that country had moved from the OECD's black to white list, indicating its compliance with the same EU regulations that the church had now promised to satisfy.[13] Hiring Brülhart was a strong signal that the city-state was finally getting serious about cleaning up its financial house.

The Vatican liked that Brülhart had solid Catholic credentials, although unlike Gotti Tedeschi and many previous laymen who had served in the Vatican's financial divisions, he was not an Opus Dei member.[14] As a student in Fribourg he had briefly studied canon law. Brülhart made it clear when he was approached for the job that while he was Catholic, that did not mean he would give the church any leeway when it came to his enforcement role at AIF. And he insisted he be given the full power to succeed. "If not, I would not accept. And if I arrived and it were not so, I would leave. I got the assurance I needed before saying yes. I came as a free man."[15]

Before agreeing to the posting, Brülhart told Bertone that he would set out to build a financial-intelligence unit that could investigate *all* suspicious money moving through the Vatican. Although he had not yet spent a day at AIF, he had no doubt from checking its roster that while its employees might have the desire to do a good job, they lacked essential training. He knew also from the Moneyval report that AIF did not have the express right to demand access to books and ledgers or other important data. Molding it into the independent arm it was intended to be, free of interference from anyone in the Vatican, was another perquisite to coming on board. "To create something where there is nothing," he said, "that was the challenge I liked."[16]

Bertone, who had to sign off on hiring him, agreed to Brülhart's conditions.[17] During his first week on the job, he began assembling a crisis management team so AIF could better monitor accounts and track the bank's flow of money.[18] "When I started, I got a full understanding of where the vulnerabilities were," he told the author. "What did we have to do to mitigate the bank's exposures, which mostly involve cash? Some of it was merely raising the awareness of their legal obligations and giving them the tools to take protective actions to help the bank."[19]

The year 2013 got off to a bumpy start for the Vatican and Brülhart. On New Year's Day, Italy's central bank announced it was terminating all debit and credit card transactions inside the city-state. It was terrible news. Rome was still packed with holiday tourists and most of those who spent money at the Vatican's shops and museums did so with credit and debit cards. Putting the Vatican on a cash-only diet would sharply cut revenue. Church officials thought it had to be a misunderstanding. They brusquely dismissed it as a technical problem that would be resolved within twenty-four hours.[20]

According to the Italians, a routine review in 2010 had disclosed that Deutsche Bank Italia—which provided the card services for Vatican City for the past fifteen years—had never obtained the required authorization from the Bank of Italy. When the Italians informed Deutsche Bank, it applied. But the Bank of Italy surprisingly rejected the application. An unidentified "close source" to the investigation told *The New York Times,* "The Bank of Italy did not approve Deutsche Bank's request for a license because Italy does not see the Vatican as a fully compliant country under money-laundering norms."[21] An unidentified "senior banker" at a correspondent bank to the IOR told the *Financial Times*: "The message sent was simple: if you want to participate in the modern world, you have to adopt modern rules."[22]

The city-state's financial officials were blindsided by the Bank of Italy's decision. And they were angry at what they considered Italy's grandstanding. The crisis was Brülhart's public debut. In an interview with Vatican Radio he said, "I am truly surprised. The reality is that, considering the particular nature of the Vatican City State, adequate measures have been adopted for vigilance, prevention, and fighting money laundering and financing terrorism."[23]

What the AIF chief did not tell Vatican Radio was what he shared with the author months later in Rome (September 2013). He had discovered within twenty-four hours of the central bank's decision "that someone in the Vatican knew two days before Christmas what might happen to the cash machines. They knew we might have no credit cards and did not tell anyone else."[24] Brülhart considered that failure to inform him a remarkable breach of duty.

He had gotten a bumpy introduction into the arcane world of Vatican finances. But he also recognized that while the Bank of Italy had taken disciplinary action against Deutsche Bank, it was the Vatican that suffered the consequences. "Italians think that the Vatican is part of Italy, that they have jurisdiction over the Vatican," he concluded. "They must learn that it is a global institution."[25] His protective attitude about the Vatican's sovereignty instantly endeared him to veteran Curialists.

Brülhart's confidence was infectious. Others who worked inside the IOR and APSA told the author—in interviews conducted in Rome ten months after Brülhart had taken control of AIF—that his appearance had signified the start of a change in terms of the attitudes inside the Vatican's money departments. Before his arrival, there was a feeling that Cardinal Attilio Nicora's AIF was not always in sync with what secular organizations like Moneyval wanted. It was as if they spoke different languages. Another problem was that the Vatican's strictly hierarchical order meant that directives from superiors were to be followed with absolute obedience. For divisions of the Curia that had existed for hundreds of years, that was not a problem, as everyone knew precisely to whom they had to report and follow. But AIF had been in existence for less than three years, and Bertone had made a significant effort to control it. Or at least to make certain that AIF did not do anything material when it came to the Vatican Bank without first obtaining his blessing. The Secretary of State's interference with AIF was one of Moneyval's biggest complaints. Many midlevel employees were enthusiastic that Brülhart—given his tough-as-nails credentials—was now in charge of the Vatican's enforcement branch.

On January 25, Brülhart met with the Bank of Italy's Director General, Fabrizio Saccomanni, and some Deutsche Bank Italia representatives, to resolve the credit card crisis. The closure had cost the Vatican sizable lost revenue. The talks were slow, the Bank of Italy being obstinate about lifting the ban. It was Brülhart's first real test. And he soon passed it. Working with his small staff, he searched for a new company to replace Deutsche Bank as the Vatican's credit and debit card processor. He realized that the only reason the Bank of Italy had any say was because the German owners of Deutsche Bank Italia were members of the European Community. Through his banking contacts, he located a new firm, Aduno, willing to do the work for the Vatican. It was a Swiss company, fully owned by Swiss banks. Brülhart knew that since Switzerland was not an EU member that meant the Bank of Italy was no longer able to give or withhold its approval.

On February 12, six weeks after it started, the crisis was over.

"Pilgrims, as well as tourists," announced the press office's Lombardi, "who visit the church of St. Peter's every day can now use the ordinary payment service, including paying for the Vatican museums."

Everyone was impressed with Brülhart. Some cardinals stopped by that following week to introduce themselves. There was no better sign of acceptance inside the Curia.

For Brülhart, the standoff with the Bank of Italy had presented him with the opportunity to write his own script as to how others viewed him inside the church. As the lay chief of AIF, he could have easily been considered no better than the head of an internal affairs unit in a police department, someone with whom clerics and financial officials were obligated to deal, but for whom they had no trust or liking. Now they saw Brülhart's AIF role differently. By having someone in charge of financial oversight who understood how to best navigate the labyrinthine rules of the European Union and neighboring Italy, the Vatican may have found someone who could help bring the institution into the modern era.

That goodwill meant he had the leeway to craft AIF into the oversight and regulatory department he wanted. It was an important moment for the Vatican since Benedict had yet to appoint anyone to replace Gotti Tedeschi. Paolo Cipriani, the director general, was considered by most observers as competent but unlikely to get the nod. Some had incorrectly thought the Vatican Bank's vice president, Deutsche Bank's Ronaldo Hermann Schmitz, might get named the previous Christmas.

Brülhart knew that while it was important to have a capable person running the IOR, if he managed to make AIF into a strong oversight group with tough enforcement powers, the Vatican Bank chief posting was not as critical as it was in the past. The financial reputation of the Vatican would no longer rest on the head of the bank. A Brülhart-styled AIF would have flagged Marcinkus's deals with Sindona and Calvi, and the rogue IOR accounts of De Bonis and other clerics would have been cleaned up much earlier. Still, Brülhart told the author, the pick to run the Vatican Bank was one in which he had an opinion. "I wanted a cooperative and knowledgeable colleague," he said.[26] Someone with his Germanic mind-set would be quite good.

February marked nine months since Gotti Tedeschi's dismissal. Two new names had come to the forefront, both cardinals, Leonardo Sandri, Prefect of the Congregation for Oriental Churches and former Sostituto of the Secretariat of State, and Domenico Calcagno, who had succeeded Nicora as the chief of APSA. Both were nearly seventy (Sandri a few months shy), and although they were considered capable, there was no consensus that either was an inspired choice. The debate had stalled.

On February 11, 2013, all of the conjecture about who might lead the Vatican Bank was subsumed in the total shock of Benedict's historic announcement that he would be the first Pope in six hundred years to resign. His simple statement that he would leave the Papacy on February 28 belied how stunning was the news: "After having repeatedly examined my conscience before God, I have come to the certainty that my strengths, due to an advanced age, are no longer suited to an adequate exercise of the Petrine ministry. . . . In today's world, subject to so many rapid changes and shaken by questions of deep relevance for the life of faith, in order to govern the barque of Saint Peter and proclaim the Gospel, both strength of mind and body are necessary, strength which in the last few months, has deteriorated in me to the extent that I have had to recognize my incapacity to adequately fulfill the ministry entrusted to me."[27]

As would be expected, the press coverage over the Pope's historic resignation was split between speculating about why he stepped down and who might replace him. If anyone knew the answer to *why*, it was likely his personal secretary, Monsignor Georg Gänswein. But he was not talking. Everything else was guesswork. And there was plenty of that. A few theories took the lead as most popular if not necessarily most accurate. The power struggles exposed by Vatileaks had pained Benedict so much that he could not go on. No, it was the nonstop soap opera at the Vatican Bank that proved overwhelming. Not true, he was a defeated man since the church's sex abuse scandal kept going on despite his defrocking of a record number of priests. One conspiracy had Brülhart forcing the resignation after giving Benedict an ultimatum over enforcing money laundering and terrorist financing laws (when asked about that by the author, Brülhart laughed and said no).[28]

But no theory rivaled the power and prevalence that the frail Pontiff had been stunned into resigning after the three cardinals he had appointed to investigate Vatileaks gave him what was said to be a jaw-dropping three-hundred-page top secret report exposing in detail a "gay network" of ranking clerics. In that report were details about regular sex parties and the charge that as a group, not only did they exert "undue influence" in the Curia but that some of them were blackmailed by lay outsiders.[29] Adding to the smoke was *La Repubblica*'s account that the report—consisting of two volumes with red covers stamped *"Segreto Pontificio"* (Pontifical Secret)—were presented to Benedict the previous December 17, the very day on which he had decided to step down. The books were packed with notes of dozens of confidential interviews conducted by the investigating red hats. Enough, Benedict was supposed to have said after poring over the lurid details, leave it all to someone else.[30] Evidence of his anger and frustration, some contend, is that a few days later he denounced homosexuality and same sex marriage, calling it a "manipulation of nature."

Other than finding out from Benedict, no one can definitively say why he decided to control when he left the Papacy as opposed to waiting for God to let him know the "best time" through his death.* Conversations in Rome—seven months after the resignation—by the author with several well-placed Curial employees, and two advisors of Benedict, indicate that it was not prompted by a single scandal. Instead, each of the bandied-about theories had some element of truth. All of those matters weighed on a Pontiff who had always recognized that his strength was as a teaching Pope. It had been his misfortune to be selected to lead the church at a time when infighting had turned the Curia into what one senior prelate called a division of "little Borgias."[32] In this view, popular with senior officials, Benedict's resignation was a selfless act since he had come to realize he was not capable of leading the modern church and making the tough decisions that were needed. "It wasn't one thing, but a whole combination of them," concluded Paolo Rodari, *Il Foglio*'s veteran Vatican reporter. Vatileaks, said Rodari, "was a constant drumbeat on the Pope."[33]

"Ratzinger was afraid to intervene on a deadlocked Roman Curia, with reformers on one side, and the money changers on the other," wrote author Gianluigi Nuzzi. "So he decided to create a clean slate by bowing out and paving the way for the election of a strong Pope."[34]

Father Federico Lombardi, the press spokesman, alluded to something sim-

---

* Six months after he resigned, a Catholic news agency, Zenit, reported that Benedict stepped down because of a "mystical experience" in which God ordered him to do so. It was picked up as the "definitive answer" as to what was behind the resignation. A week after it broke, Monsignor Gänswein told Italian TV that it was a fake story, "made up from alpha to omega."[31]

ilar at a press conference: "The Church needed someone with more physical and spiritual energy who would be able to overcome the problems and challenges of governing the church in this ever-changing modern world."[35]

Once he broke the news of his resignation in a February 11 talk with some cardinals, everyone assumed that until he stepped off in seventeen days that he would be a caretaker Pontiff. Considering that he was not much of a firebrand during his previous eight years, it was likely that he would go out quietly. But just four days after announcing that he would resign, he surprised many Vaticanologists by ratifying the recommendation of his commission of cardinals and at long last appointed a new IOR president: fifty-three-year-old Ernst von Freyberg, a devout Catholic and German aristocrat who was a well-respected businessman and lawyer specializing in mergers and acquisitions.[36] He was also a ranking member of the Sovereign Military Order of Malta and in his spare time escorted pilgrims on tours of the healing waters at Lourdes.[37] In finding Freyberg, the Vatican had used its first-ever headhunting firm, and it had whittled down a group of forty solid finalists. Brülhart thought the choice was inspired. Freyberg had a solid reputation as the chairman of the executive board of German shipyard Blohm + Voss.*

With his IOR chief in place, Benedict set the conclave to start on March 12, just under two weeks from when he became Pope Emeritus (after some frenzied debate about what to call him) and turned over the keys to the Vatican to his Camerlengo, Secretary of State Bertone.

* News accounts reported that his company was involved in building Nazi warships eighty years earlier. Freyburg was a descendant of one of the firm's founders. He was also criticized for keeping his day job at the firm since it built modern warships for the German navy and the Vatican had steered clear of all armaments investments. The controversy petered out quickly.[38]

42

"The People's Pope"

It was a wide-open field, with more than a dozen cardinals discussed as front-runners. Benedict's resignation had caught the red hats by as much surprise as the lay public. Those who had the ambition to be Pope had not had the opportunity to politick that often arises in the final weeks of a Pope's terminal illness. Everyone was running a short race from the same starting line.

Buenos Aires's cardinal, Jorge Bergoglio, who had finished second eight years earlier to Benedict, did not seem to be a contender this time. The wide consensus was that although Latin America had more Catholics than anywhere else, it was unlikely that the College of Cardinals would select their next leader from there. Only nineteen of the 117 cardinals were Latin American, and it was not even certain that they would vote as a bloc geographically.[1] The *National Catholic Reporter*'s John Allen, who provided sober commentary as on-air CNN consultant, wrote a story about Bergoglio's second-place finish in 2005. Allen was in the know as much as any Italian Vaticanologist, with excellent Curial sources. His view was given wide credence. In summarizing Bergoglio's chances, Allen wrote that while he "at least merits a look" it was unlikely that he would emerge as Pope.

Fifty of the cardinals from the last conclave were voting again. Allen noted, "They may be skeptical that the results would be any different this time around." Although Allen set forth a long list of reasons why Bergoglio might attract some votes, in the end, he said, "there are compelling reasons to believe that Bergoglio's window of opportunity to be pope has already closed." To the extent exhaustion and age caused Benedict to resign, it was yet another strike against an older candidate like Bergoglio, who would be only two years younger than Benedict when he was selected. According to Allen, there was "the standard ambivalence about Jesuits in high offices," and the fact he had never worked inside the Vatican. The final factor working against the Buenos Aires cardinal was that "doubts that circulated about Bergoglio's toughness eight years ago may arguably be even more damaging now, given that the ability to govern, and to take control of the Vatican bureaucracy, seems to figure even more prominently on many cardinals' wish lists this time . . . there may be concerns about his capacity to take the place in hand."[2]

Bergoglio may have agreed with Allen's assessment. After he finished second to Ratzinger in the conclave, he returned to Buenos Aires and told colleagues he looked forward to retirement. An old-age home for clerics in the Buenos Aires neighborhood of Las Flores, where he was born, was where he intended to move after he stepped down. In 2010 he said, "I'm starting to consider the fact that I have to leave everything behind." He had handed his resignation letter to the Pope when he turned seventy-five in 2011, but Benedict had done nothing about it.[3]

Few of the "inside shortlists" included Bergoglio. The names that did get bandied about the most included two American cardinals, New York's glad-handing populist Timothy Dolan and his polar opposite, Boston's unassuming Sean O'Malley. The Italians seemed to be split between two powerful cardinals, Milan's Angelo Scola—who it was said had been John Paul II's personal selection to replace him—and Genoa's Angelo Bagnasco, who had benefited from his recent condemnation of Italian Prime Minister Silvio Berlusconi's poor morals. There was, as in every lead-up to each conclave since the 1960s, speculation about whether the church was ready for its first black Pope. Ladbrokes and Paddy Power had Ghana's Cardinal Peter Appiah Turkson as the frontrunner at 5 to 2. Right behind was Canada's Marc Ouellet at 3 to 1, and Nigeria's Francis Arinze was 4 to 1. The odds for the others covered a wide range, from Timothy Dolan's 25 to 1 to the semiretired eighty-year-old Cormac Murphy O'Connor, who was a long shot at 150 to 1.[4] Bergoglio was not on the list.

On Tuesday, March 12, the 115 voting cardinals met in the Sistine Chapel. They did not get under way until the afternoon, and managed only one vote. It resulted in black smoke. No one had gotten the support of two thirds of all cardinals. News reports that night said Italy's Angelo Scola and Brazil's Odilo Scherer were in a tight race. Scola was a solid favorite of many Italian cardinals who wanted the Papacy back after thirty-five years under a Pole and then a German. Scola's problem was that reformers feared he was too much a Vatican insider, while traditionalists thought he would embark on too radical a redo of the Curia. In fact, he had garnered fewer votes on the first round than most cardinals expected, ending in a virtual tie with Canada's Marc Ouellet. Bergoglio surprised everyone as a strong third.[5]

On the second day, Scola's support started peeling away.[6] The cardinals agreed that it would be a good sign to the faithful if they showed unity by settling on someone quickly. By the third ballot it was a two-person race between Ouellet and Bergoglio. On the fourth ballot Bergoglio moved ahead, and Ouellet threw his support to him (there was speculation later that the two had struck a deal by which Ouellet would become Secretary of State; in fact he received no appointment from the new Pope).[7]

So it took one more vote, the fifth ballot, to put Bergoglio over the top, making him the first non-European Pontiff since a Syrian, Gregory III, 1,300 years earlier.

"It was very moving as the names were sounding out," Ireland's Cardinal Sean Brady recounted later to reporters. "Bergoglio, Bergoglio, and suddenly the magic number of 77 was reached. The cardinals erupted into applause. "I don't think there was a dry eye in the house," said New York's Timothy Dolan.[8]

Brazil's Claudio Hummes was sitting next to Bergoglio. He leaned over, embraced his Argentine friend, and kissed him on the forehead.

"Don't forget the poor," Hummes said.

"And that struck me . . . the poor," Bergoglio later recalled. "Immediately I thought of St. Francis of Assisi. Francis was a man of peace, a man of poverty, a man who loved and protected creation. How I would love a Church that is poor and for the poor." When he was asked for his new name, he did not hesitate with Francis.[9]

When word filtered out the news wires carried headlines such as "unexpected choice" and "surprise election."[10] Some of the stories rehashed allegations from the 2005 conclave. "Already Francis's brief papacy has been touched by controversy." They were stale charges that he was somehow complicit in the kidnapping by the Argentine military junta of two leftist Jesuits. A troubling variation of this story was that in the mode of Pius XII and the Holocaust, he had remained silent during the junta's human rights abuses.[11]

The Vatican dismissed the accusations the following day as baseless and libelous. Lombardi went so far as to suggest the charges were a smear by a "left-wing, anti-clerical" plot.

Bergoglio seemed unfazed by the controversy. He had heard it before. Having run a diocese in a major urban center—with a thriving media and robust tabloids—he was accustomed to sometimes rough and tumble public treatment. While ordinary Catholics did not yet know what to make of him, inside the walls of the Vatican—even during his first week—Francis was a sharp contrast to the dour Benedict. He smiled, laughed, went out of his way to talk to even the lowliest workers, cracked jokes, and seemed genuinely interested in the lives of those he met.

Born in 1936—the eldest of five children—in Buenos Aires to Italian immigrants (his father was a railroad worker and his mother a homemaker), Bergoglio planned to be a chemist, but at twenty-one decided instead he wanted to be a Jesuit. He was motivated by a desire to serve the poor, something he did not think he could do as well in private business.[12] Among other subjects he taught philosophy and psychology, and for six years starting in 1973 he was Argentina's Jesuit provincial before becoming the rector of the seminary from which he had graduated.[13] Bergoglio was never swept up in the progressive liberation theology that flourished among many of his contemporaries. No group was more radicalized throughout Latin America than the Jesuits. But the limit of his own activism was to mix into his faith a theme of strong social justice for the underprivileged.

Twelve years later, 1992, he was named Buenos Aires's auxiliary bishop. When Cardinal Antonio Quarracino died of a heart attack in 1998, Bergoglio took his place. And John Paul gave him the red hat three years later. He had by this time earned a deserved reputation as an unwavering traditionalist on church dogma, not only in condemning homosexuality, same sex marriage, and abortion, but even giving a spirited defense of no contraception.[14] (In 2010, Argentina's President, Cristina Fernández de Kirchner, admonished him for his contention that gay adoption was a form of discrimination against children.)

What did surprise the 13.5 million Catholics in Buenos Aires was the reception Francis received at the Vatican. He had been a likable enough cardinal in Argentina but there was no indication that he would morph into such a popular Pope on the world stage. Francis benefited from the contrast to the besieged Benedict. But it was far more. He was a populist who knew how to play to the crowd. On the day he was elected, at his first appearance on the balcony of St. Peter's, he refused to wear the traditional ermine-trimmed red cape and silk slippers, nor would he carry the jewel-encrusted gold cross. He shunned the grand Papal living quarters in the Apostolic Palace and instead moved into a simple apartment at Casa Santa Marta, the city-state's modest guesthouse. He told Monsignor Georg Gänswein, who remained as his Papal Secretary, to put away all the ornate vestments, instead donning only the simplest white cassock and skull cap. The jeweled triple tiara was put in storage. There would be no trappings of an imperial Papacy so long as he was in charge.[15]

If Benedict seemed not only burdened but at times even defeated by the modern world, Francis showed he was a master of twenty-first-century tools. And he demonstrated an innate talent at managing his own public image. He hugged a man with a terribly deformed face at St. Peter's; washed the feet of female convicts; and celebrated his seventy-seventh birthday by inviting a homeless man to breakfast in his private apartment. He seemed an ordinary man, giving friends a lift in his car and even taking selfies with babies and visitors at St. Peter's Square. His first trip outside of Rome was to meet the impoverished "boat people" of the Italian island of Lampedusa. Images of him there praying with migrants went viral. He sent out his own tweets. A small plenary indulgence was offered for those who followed him on Twitter. Another indulgence was provided to Catholics who attended World Youth Day in Rio de Janeiro, where he gave a talk to a million people. Francis surprised even his aides by telephoning at random some of those who had written him letters (four nuns retold dozens of reporters how startled they were to return to their convent and have a New Year's message from the Pope on their answering machine). The unpredictability that so endeared him to the faithful at times unnerved his personal staff, who were accustomed under Benedict to strictly timed schedules from which no variation was permitted.[16]

But it was more than symbolism that so endeared him to both Catholics and non-Catholics alike. During spur-of-the-moment press conferences, or at times during a prepared speech when he tossed away the paper and spoke extemporaneously, the self-effacing Pontiff invariably said something that sounded tolerant and different. About gays, "If a homosexual person is of good will and is in search of God, who am I to judge?" Gays, he said, "feel like the church has always condemned them. But the church does not want to do this." What about women who consider abortion because they were raped? "Who can remain unmoved before such painful situations?"[17] On the divisive question of whether divorced and remarried worshippers can again take the sacraments, he held out hope for reform, saying that Communion was "not a prize for the perfect but a powerful medicine and nourishment for the weak."[18] He told the Jesuit journal *La Civiltà Cattolica* that many Catholics and social conservatives were obsessed "only on issues related to abortion, gay marriage and the use of contraceptive methods" and that instead they should focus on "a new balance . . . [a] pastoral ministry."[19]

In each of these instances Francis's words were carefully crafted. He never promised to make any substantive reforms or alter long-established doctrine, nor did he ever commit to radically change course from the traditional positions he championed for decades in Argentina. But the lay public was unaccustomed to a Pope talking frankly—much less so empathetically—on issues that under previous Pontiffs had been matters on which Catholics only got lectures and rules to follow.

Francis's openness captured people's imaginations. And the notable difference in style instilled in many a belief that a change in substance was imminent. In some ways, he became a Rorschach test. People saw in him what they wanted in a Pope. On the online world, there were thousands of blogs predicting what the church would look like in a few years under a Francis Papacy. Most were no more than wish lists by the bloggers who created them, but they reflected the promise that millions had invested in Francis. Gays believed he might soften his predecessor's condemnation of homosexuality as an "objective disorder" and open the door to same sex marriage. Women were convinced that Francis would be the first Pontiff to loosen absolute bans on contraception for the poor and the prohibition of abortion in cases of rape and incest. Some predicted that he would break tradition and consider women as priests. Every special interest group had something online dedicated to the new Pope. He would end celibacy for priests. Sex abusers would be tossed out of the priesthood and turned over to civil authorities. Catholicism would focus on lifting the poor and chastising the rich.

"I prefer a Church which is bruised, hurting and dirty because it has been out on the streets, rather than a Church which is unhealthy from being confined and from clinging to its own security," he wrote not long after assuming the Papacy.[20]

Little wonder the Pontiff dubbed "The People's Pope" was "Man of the Year" for *Time* ("The septuagenarian superstar is poised to transform a place that measures change by the century") as well as *The Advocate,* a leading LGBT magazine ("a stark change in rhetoric from his two predecessors").[21] *Rolling Stone* put him on its cover—the first time for a Pope—and titled their profile "The Times They Are A-Changing."[22] "Pope Francis Is a Liberal," gushed the online magazine *Slate.*[23] A monitor of web usage concluded that he was the most talked-about person on the Internet in 2013.[24] Francis's Twitter account, @Pontifex, had more than four million followers in ten languages. The entire Francis package was "stunning," agreed most Vaticanologists.[25]

Critically important for the church, Francis reenergized the faith for tens of millions of young Catholics who had given up hope that the clerics in Rome might ever be relevant in their lives. Priests in dozens of countries reported that Mass attendance soared. Volunteers for Catholic relief and charities zoomed. Contributions for Peter's Pence jumped.[26]

The best politicians realize there is a natural charisma, a chemistry of sorts, that allows a handful of them to connect with people in a way about which most can only dream. Despite shortcomings on promises and a failure to meet expectations, these men and women still inspire confidence and get high favorability ratings in opinion polls long after people would have soured on less magnetic personalities. Francis appeared to fall into this select group. Throughout his first year as Pope, people ignored what he did or said that they did not like.

Six months into his Papacy, in September, he gave a broad-ranging interview to *America,* a prominent Catholic magazine, in which he pedaled back on some of his most popular impromptu remarks. "On issues related to abortion, gay marriage and the use of contraceptive methods . . . the teaching of the church, for that matter, is clear, and I am a son of the church, but it is not necessary to talk about these issues all the time."[27] That same month in a talk to Catholic gynecologists he issued as harsh a condemnation of abortion as anything Benedict or John Paul ever said: "In a decisive and unhesitating 'yes' to life" he said that abortion was a product of "a widespread mentality of profit, the 'throwaway culture,' which has today enslaved the hearts of so many."[28] He later tweeted support for pro-life demonstrations, reminding Catholics that life "begins in the womb," and declaring, "This is not something subject to alleged reforms or 'modernizations.' It is not 'progressive' to try to resolve problems by eliminating a human life."[29]

He declined, when asked, to soften what he had said in 2009 when as a cardinal he opposed a gay marriage bill pending before Argentine legislators: "Let's not be naive, we're not talking about a simple political battle; it is a destructive pretension against the plan of God. We are not talking about a mere bill, but rather a machination of the Father of Lies that seeks to confuse and deceive the children of God."[30]

In July 2013, the U.N. Committee on the Rights of the Child had sent Francis a request for "detailed information" on the investigations and results of the Vatican's sex abuse cases. The U.N. wanted transparency on previous offenders, especially so that any who were defrocked under Benedict might not return to civilian society as pedophiles without anyone the wiser. The Holy See had in 1994 ratified the U.N. Convention on the Rights of the Child (CRC), a legally binding instrument that committed it to protecting children.[31] But in nineteen years, the Vatican had in 2012 only submitted a single summary, lacking any details. The U.N. thought that under Francis the church might be more forthcoming. But in November, the Vatican refused to provide the CRC the names or details it had gathered over the years about clerical sexual pedophiles.[32]

"It is not the practice of the Holy See to disclose information on the religious discipline of members of the clergy or religious according to canon law." (The next January, 2014, at a U.N. hearing in Geneva, Vatican representatives sat in silence as CRC delegates publicly castigated the church for its refusal to cooperate: "The Holy See has consistently placed the preservation of the reputation of the Church and the protection of the perpetrators above children's best interests," charged a CRC attorney. The CRC scolded the Vatican again in May, urging the church to "take effective measures." In September, the Vatican shot back, criticizing the CRC for a "grave misunderstanding" of the church's sovereignty.)[33]

Those who know the Pope best do not think there is any contradiction between the progressive and reactionary Francis. Boston's likable Cardinal Sean O'Malley, and the Pope's closest American confidant, cautioned a reporter from *The Boston Globe* that Francis had softened the church's tone but said, "I don't see the Pope as changing doctrine."[34]*

---

* Over time, many traditionalists changed their opinion and concluded that Francis was meddling in long-established doctrines of faith. At an October 2014 synod on the modern family, there was firm pushback from conservative bishops over a Francis-favored draft that proposed liberalizing rules about

And except for a few on the American political right—Rush Limbaugh condemned Francis's take on capitalism as "pure Marxism"—millions who wanted change inside the Vatican were not bothered. His socially liberal supporters seemingly tuned out any part of his message about which they did not agree, and focused instead on common ground, especially his unwavering commitment to the poor.[36] Francis had sold them that he was the real deal when it came to reform and compassion and conservative statements that echoed his predecessors did nothing to dent his extraordinary appeal. At the end of 2013, *after* he had pulled back on many of the critical social issues, a slew of public opinion polls confirmed that all the excitement and mostly laudatory media coverage had made Francis one of the most well liked religious figures of the modern era. Ninety-two percent of U.S. Catholics approved of how he ran the church, reported ABC. A similar number in a CNN poll showed his "approval rating [is] sky high"; even 75 percent of non-Catholics liked him.[37] A remarkable 85 percent thought Francis was neither too liberal nor too conservative and that he was the first Pope to be integrated with the modern world. London's *Express* tabloid asked, "Could Pope Francis be the most popular ever?"[38]

No wonder church veterans thought Francis was heaven sent. They remembered all too well that a similar poll taken in 2003, eighteen months before the end of John Paul's tenure, revealed that more than half of U.S. Catholics thought the Pontiff was out of touch with their lives and the church had less meaning and influence for them than ever.[39]

The remarkable change in the fortunes of the Vatican during the nine months of Francis's 2013 Papacy was best summed up by Kay Campbell, an American religion reporter: "In the space of my lifetime, the Catholic Church has gone from pariah to rock star."[40]

---

nonmarital relationships and the right of remarried Catholics to receive the sacraments. Ross Douthat, a *New York Times* conservative Catholic columnist, suggested that if Francis pushed too radical an agenda too quickly, it could lead to "a real schism."[35]

43

"Back from the Dead"

It is anybody's guess as to whether Francis's incredible popularity can be sustained. But his historic international reception gave him enhanced power as a new Pontiff. No clerical faction was foolish enough to take him on. No one dared criticize him. Most inside the Vatican viewed the developments as a phenomenon on which to ride along. Francis, as a result, had an unprecedented opportunity to tackle significant Curial reforms. The challenge was great. The Pope oversaw an institution with 1.2 billion followers, 6 million lay employees, 4,500 bishops, 412,000 priests, and 865,000 members of religious institutes and schools. Catholic charities were the world's largest (some twenty million people receiving some type of assistance).[1]

Near the top of his to-do list was the Vatican Bank. He knew reform there would have to be a centerpiece of his Papacy if he was going to successfully streamline the city-state's finances. Instead of repeating Benedict's first year of unfulfilled expectations, Francis did act, and often decisively. He was not long in office when he issued two Papal decrees intended to speed reviews and provide more transparent oversight. Unnamed Bank of Italy sources told the *Financial Times* that those early decrees "marked important steps toward real reform of the legal and institutional framework."[2] But they were stopgap measures. Francis was faced with a historic decision: whether to shutter the Vatican Bank and have the church rely on the banks of other countries, or undertake the systemic change that had frustrated his predecessors.[3]

René Brülhart's AIF issued its 2012 annual report in May 2013, highlighting an enhanced screening system for reporting cash transactions and boasting it had more success in spotting suspicious activity—six cases had been sent on for investigation as opposed to only one the previous year.[4] Meanwhile, the Vatican was working to meet a July deadline to submit an update to Moneyval demonstrating what progress it had made in those areas the evaluators had judged deficient.

Ernst von Freyberg went on the offensive for the IOR in his first full interview as president in May. Noting that during "the financial crisis we were never in trouble. No government had to bail us out, we are very, very safe," he boasted the banks 2012 profit was $113 million. As for the IOR's terrible reputation, he claimed it was largely the result of media "slander."

"I can tell you that I have taken all the names I have found in the newspapers and looked them up myself. I didn't find a single one of these names. This Mafia boss, this politician, Osama bin Laden. None of them have accounts here, nor are they delegates to accounts."

Since Freyberg's interview was with Vatican Radio, nobody pressed him on how secret proxies had been used for decades in the bank to hide the identities of true account owners. A simple name check would not have sufficed to uncover them then or now. But his quotes made for good copy.[5]

The real reason he had gone public was that top IOR officials had decided they needed to lobby for the bank's survival as the rumors of its pending dissolution picked up pace. Freyberg had not yet had a personal audience with Francis, raising concerns that the Pope was putting it off so as not to confer legitimacy on the bank until he had decided on its future. "If we ask the question 'should we close the IOR,' our clients have voted 99.99 percent against it," Freyberg said.[6] Director General Paolo Cipriani followed up by telling reporters off the record that the bank's Curial enemies had launched a vicious whisper campaign. On the record, he said that the IOR kept the church independent and that was not "just essential, but an obligation."[7]

On June 26, Francis created a five-person commission and invested it with broad powers to do a top-to-bottom review of the bank. It had complete authority to access all the IOR's files. That panel was tasked to provide Francis with guidance about how to bring the bank into "harmony" with its original ecclesiastical mission.[8] And it came less than two weeks after the Pope had tapped Monsignor Battista Mario Salvatore Ricca as the interim prelate, replacing Monsignor Pioppo, who had been exiled to Equatorial Guinea in 2011.[9] The pick of Ricca was a progressive choice by the Pope. In a few weeks, Ricca was under assault when *L'Espresso* reported scandalous details over his private life during his service as the Nuncio in Uruguay.[10] According to the paper, Ricca had a semipublic affair with a Swiss army captain, and it had been the subject of nonstop scandal among Rome's bishops. Once Ricca was beaten up at a gay bar. Another time, when firemen had to release him from a trapped elevator at the nunciature, he was found with a partially clothed young man.[11] Some were bitter that Francis had chosen Ricca, while others contended he was a genuine reformer and that resurrecting a seamy past chapter was no more than a smear campaign by the old guard.[12] After a few days the Vatican issued a statement that "the pope has listened to everyone and has confidence in Ricca."[13] Francis stuck by his choice.

Unknown outside of the Vatican, Francis had a newfound enthusiasm in tackling reform at the IOR. That summer he summoned to Rome six top Catholic financiers from around the globe.[14] In a day-long meeting at the his Casa Santa Marta guesthouse, Francis told the moneymen he needed their help. The Pope, speaking Italian and relying on a translator, set forth a litany of financial problems facing the church. "You are the experts," he said, "and I trust you. Now I want solutions to these problems, and I want them as soon as possible."[15] Those lay experts became directors of a new advisory council to guide the Pope in rolling out his reforms.[16]

Not even Francis, however, with all his good fortune, managed to get through 2013 without some bumps when it came to the Vatican Bank. Two days after he had appointed the special oversight commission, sixty-one-year-old Monsignor Nunzio Scarano, an APSA senior accountant, was arrested. Prosecutors charged he was the mastermind in helping friends avoid taxes on $26.2 million, some of it cash flown to Italy on a private jet from Switzerland.[17] Scarano's money flowed through two accounts at the Vatican Bank (one personal and one a charitable foundation he controlled). The IOR was back on the front pages (typical was *The New York Times* headline "Cleric Arrested in $26 Million Plot, Leaving New Blot on Vatican Bank"). And Scarano's tale had all the elements that kept it newsworthy for the rest of the year. A banker before he was ordained a priest at the age of thirty-five, Scarano had been suspended from his APSA job the previous month over an investigation by prosecutors into whether he had laundered $750,000 of Mafia funds through his own Vatican account.[18] His nickname was *Don cinquecento* (Monsignor 500) because he habitually flashed a thick wad of cash and boasted that the 500-euro note ($670) was his favorite. When he reported a multimillion-dollar art theft from his 7,500-square-foot luxury apartment in Salerno, police asked how a simple monsignor—who earned about $40,000 a year—could afford it all. "Donations from friends," he replied.[19] The millions he passed through his IOR account allegedly belonged to three brothers of a wealthy Italian shipbuilding family, close friends of then Italian Prime Minister Silvio Berlusconi. Arrested with Scarano was a suspended intelligence agent from Italy's equivalent of the FBI. (Scarano's trial started in September 2014 and he faces up to twenty years in prison if convicted.)[20]

Only a few days after Scarano's arrest, the Vatican announced a shake-up inside the IOR. Gone were Paolo Cipriani, the bank's director general, and his deputy, Massimo Tulli.[21] The Vatican said their parting was "in the best interest of the institute and the Holy See."[22] But few were buying it. Their departure seemed hasty and unplanned, especially since there was no one set to replace the director general. Two Italian bankers with broad international experience in the private sector were brought in. One filled Tulli's post while the other became the bank's newly created chief risk officer.[23] Freyberg announced that he would keep his president's job while temporarily assuming Cipriani's role.

The resignations caught Brülhart by surprise. He learned about them on his way to Sun City, South Africa, for the Egmont Group's annual meeting. Just that week he had received the good news that the Vatican had gotten a prized membership in Egmont, becoming part of a club whose goal is to freely share financial information in order to fight money laundering and terrorism financing.

What Brülhart did not know is what had prompted the abrupt departure of the IOR duo. Behind the scenes, the Scarano prosecutors had informed the Vatican that they had wiretapped phone conversations that demonstrated Scarano was in regular touch with Cipriani and Tulli to get their approval to move huge amounts of cash through his accounts.[24] When Brülhart learned about that, he pressed for full disclosure, contending to his colleagues that they should get credit for having taken swift action by dismissing the two bank officers. The old IOR would never have done that and it was to the Vatican's credit that it happened now. But he was overruled and, not being at the city-state, he was unable to forcefully argue his case. Admitting publicly errors of that magnitude was a level of transparency for which the church was not yet ready.[25] Brülhart was proven right, however. A week later Italy's financial police, led by a Rome magistrate, released a twenty-five-page report about how the IOR had for years circumvented money laundering laws. The conclusion was a familiar one: the Vatican Bank had operated as an offshore bank in the heart of Rome.[26] A few days later someone leaked documents to Reuters that revealed Roman prosecutors had concluded that Cipriani and Tulli violated Italy's money laundering statutes by failing to provide sufficient information about Scarano's transfers.[27] Soon, Michele Briamonte, an IOR legal consultant best known for his private jet and flashy lifestyle, was pulled into the criminal probe for possible insider trading (no charges were filed against Briamonte but Cipriani and Tulli were indicted with money laundering violations in March 2014 and are awaiting trial).* Once again the IOR looked as though it was only reactive, instead of jumping ahead as Brülhart had suggested.

With Brülhart back from South Africa, he and Freyberg used the scandal to press their case to hire, for the first time in Vatican history, a financial consulting firm that could assist the AIF's monitoring and enforcement. Their pick was Promontory Financial Group, a self-described "risk management and regulatory compliance consulting firm." In lay speak it is a troubleshooter for all types of financial problems. Freyberg and Brülhart lobbied hard to get the approval for a $1 million retainer.[29] When Elizabeth McCaul, a Promontory partner, met with Freyburg, the IOR chief minced no words. "You are the only bullet I have left," he told her. Within a couple of days McCaul had moved in a twenty-five-person team, setting up temporarily in what used to be the oversized director general's office. They cross-checked the voluminous paperwork against computer files to ensure there was proper documentation for each account and that the paper trail for money transactions was transparent. (Promontory's role inside the Vatican lasted nearly two years; the final bill was $9 million.)[30]

During the coming months, the IOR opened a website (www.ior.va) and published an annual report. The website did not have online banking and the annual report did not list clients. Instead it explained what the Vatican Bank was and what it did. For the IOR, which historically had not even listed its address or telephone number in the Vatican's annual yearbook, it was a modern way of demonstrating that change was under way.[31]

* That same month, March, after Italian prosecutors cleared Gotti Tedeschi in their money laundering probe, the ex-IOR chief announced that he was considering suing the Vatican because of the damage to his reputation done by his dismissal. "They have to say they're sorry," Gotti Tedeschi told reporters, "and finally explain after two years why they did what they did. . . . They ruined my life. It's a shame that it was the Italian magistrates who had to clear this up and not the Church."[28]

At the end of August, Francis replaced Secretary of State Bertone with Archbishop Pietro Parolin, the Papal Nuncio to Venezuela, the youngest man to hold the post since Eugenio Pacelli in the 1930s.[32] Peter Sutherland, Goldman Sachs International's nonexecutive chairman, briefed the Pope's most senior advisors: "Transparency is important and necessary."[33] The Pope—who had made it clear he was personally overseeing the IOR reform—continued to set the overall tone. He appointed eight cardinals that October as special advisors in restructuring the Curia. "Heads of the Church have often been narcissists, flattered and thrilled by their courtiers," Francis told them during their first meeting. "The Court is the leprosy of the Papacy."[34]

And that same month he issued a *motu proprio* against money laundering and financing terrorism, reinforcing in clear language the importance of every Curial department to adhere to the letter of the law, but also reemphasizing the oversight power of Brülhart's AIF when it came to the church's internal finances.[35] A month later Francis followed up on suggestions by Brülhart and issued a new *motu proprio* further strengthening the AIF.[36]

In comments made after the spring purge, Freyberg told reporters, "It is clear today that we need new leadership to increase the pace of this transformation process." It took almost another five months, November 28, before the public got to see what Pope Francis and his Vatican Bank team meant by "new leadership." Francis appointed his loyal private secretary, fifty-five-year-old Monsignor Alfred Xuereb, to a new supervisory IOR role.[37] The Maltese native was the Pope's eyes and ears when it came to the progress and activities of the two commissions studying the bank. Although Xuereb had no financial experience, his role was not to run the bank. Instead he had the Pope's absolute trust. With his selection Francis had sent a message that he was watching those who were watching the Vatican Bank.[38] *

One month later in December, the action-packed year ended when Moneyval released its latest report on the Vatican's progress toward complying with EU money laundering, terrorism financing, and transparency statutes. It commended the city-state on making significant headway and noted that "a very wide range of legislative and other measures have been taken in a short time by the Holy See." Nonetheless, it concluded more oversight was necessary. There

---

* Two days after Xuereb's appointment, Freyberg announced that deputy director Rolando Marranci, who had joined the IOR only in June, had been promoted to serve as the bank's director general.[39]

were still inadequate controls at both the IOR and APSA to prevent financial crimes. In a direct reference to Brülhart's AIF, Moneyval said it was "somewhat surprising" that his intelligence unit had not yet conducted any full inspections of either the bank or APSA. But AIF did get credit for closing several questionable IOR accounts and for flagging some potential money laundering.

Before the year ended, without any fanfare, Brülhart's AIF signed memorandums of understanding to share information about suspicious transactions with its counterparts in Germany, Italy, the United States, Spain, the Netherlands, Belgium, and Slovenia.[40] And he was negotiating up to twenty more.[41] Meanwhile, more big-name consulting firms had joined Promontory in trying to make the IOR bulletproof. They included EY (formerly Ernst & Young), KPMG, and Deloitte & Touche. Separately, Francis hired American-based McKinsey & Co. and Lord Christopher Patten, the ex-chief of the BBC, to overhaul the Vatican's media relations.

For observers of the Vatican Bank, such as Nigel Baker, Britain's savvy ambassador to the Holy See, the pace of reform under Francis was "unprecedented." Baker noted that when he was appointed ambassador in 2011, "It was a standing joke that whenever a journalist wrote an article about the IOR, it had to include a mention of Banco Ambrosiano and Roberto Calvi under Blackfriars Bridge. Yet that scandal happened over 30 years ago. There was a sense amongst commentators that the Holy See had in the past only paid lip service to the need to change its financial structures." The move toward reform, transparency, and modernization, he said, had begun under Benedict but Francis had made it a top priority.[42]

Two thousand and fourteen was the year when Francis proved his commitment to changing forever the culture of the Vatican Bank. On January 16, he purged the IOR's top ranks because he was not satisfied with the pace of its reforms. His target this time was the bank's traditional oversight committee of cardinals. Before he resigned, Benedict had renewed the terms for each committee member, including Cardinals Bertone, Italy's Domenico Calcagno, Brazil's Odilo Scherer, India's Telesphore Topp, and France's Jean-Louis Tauran. Less than a year into their five-year terms, Francis replaced all but Tauran. The incoming Secretary of State, Pietro Parolin, took Bertone's spot as chairman. The new slate of cardinals were known as reformists who had extensive experience in financial affairs in their own dioceses.[43]

Vatican Bank observers were again impressed. "This is an important turn in the political economy of the Vatican," noted Professor Giuseppe Di Taranto, an economist at Rome's LUISS University. "It is following the new political line of Pope Francis towards transparency for Vatican finance."[44]

Francis was not done. Two weeks later, on January 31, the Pope swept clean the last of the old financial guard. Out was AIF's president, seventy-six-year-old Cardinal Attilio Nicora. His replacement was sixty-six-year-old Bishop Giorgio Corbellini, a legal expert and president of the city-state's labor office responsible for dealing with the lay workers. Corbellini was also considered a reformer.[45] And his selection was timed to coincide with the hiring of two international firms to audit Vatican finances.[46]

There was no better reminder of the consequences of failure to all those entrusted with getting the IOR onto the OECD's white list.[47] And the deadline was in place. It was two years and counting. When Moneyval finished its evaluation the previous December, it set 2015 for the next report from the Vatican.

The Vatican was a place in flux. In February, Francis issued a *motu proprio* that established a new division, the Secretariat for the Economy. It was the same type of bold decree that his predecessor, Benedict, had used in 2010 to commit the Vatican to its first anti-money-laundering law. The Secretariat was given broad authority to govern all the city-state's money matters.[48] An oversight council of eight cardinals and seven lay financial experts were tasked with coordinating the budgets for nearly two dozen Curial divisions. And Francis put his personal stamp on the new department by picking one of his closest advisors, Australia's no-nonsense Cardinal George Pell, as its chief.[49] The *motu proprio* also made clear that moving forward, APSA would operate as the Vatican's central bank.

In April, Francis ended a year of speculation by announcing finally that he would not close the Vatican Bank. The press office issued a statement that the IOR "will continue to serve with prudence and provide specialized financial services to the [Roman] Catholic Church worldwide."[50] ("The Vatican Bank Is Back from the Dead" was the headline in *The Daily Beast.*)[51] Brülhart's AIF in late May showed how well its regulatory system was working: it had uncovered 202 suspicious transactions inside the IOR in 2013, compared to just six the previous year.[52]

According to Massimo Faggioli, an Italian theology professor who has long studied the Vatican, Francis acted decisively because he is the first Pope in the last thirty-five years to understand how important it is to achieve substantive reform. "Pope John Paul II didn't touch the bank because it served his purpose of funding Solidarity from the Vatican. Pope Benedict did not touch it because he had no interest in controlling it. Pope Francis is different because he knows the damage that has been done to the credibility of the church by this very small bank and its history of scandals."[53]

In May, the German newspaper *Bild* reported that former Secretary of State Bertone was under criminal investigation for approving a $20 million Vatican loan to a friend's television production company—over the objection of ex-IOR chief Gotti Tedeschi. Bertone's friend, an Opus Dei member, defaulted on the questionable loan.[54] According to *Bild*, there were questions about whether the ninety-three-year-old head of the company that made religiously themed films had kicked some money back to the Secretary of State's office. While reviewing records in 2013, outside auditors had discovered the loan and the IOR board subsequently had to write it off.[55]

It was the type of unexpected story that in the past had presaged a new scandal that put the church on the defensive. But Francis did not allow the report to fester, instead dispatching his spokesman, Federico Lombardi, the very next day to unequivocally deny its veracity.[56] And less than two weeks later, the Pope ensured that any lingering rumors of a Bertone probe were forgotten because of the dramatic announcement that the Pontiff had fired the entire five-man board of Brülhart's AIF.[57]

On a flight returning to Rome from Israel, Francis told reporters that he had made new appointments because "economic administration calls for honesty and transparency. . . . The key is trying to avoid that there are more [scandals]."[58]

Brülhart had successfully persuaded the Pope to replace his five "old guard" directors with independent professionals who had qualifications similar to his own.[59] And Brülhart got a new vice director, Tommaso di Ruzza, a respected jurist who had helped draft the Vatican's anti-money-laundering statutes.[60] The press coverage of the sacking and the new appointments was universally positive, casting the Pope as someone willing to make bold moves to clean up the financial morass he inherited.[61]

Francis—who once said "Money is useful to carry out many things . . . but when your heart is attached to it, it destroys you"—put the final touches on his revolution in Vatican finances in July.[62] He replaced Ernst von Freyburg, the IOR's chief, with Jean-Baptiste de Franssu, the former CEO of Investco

Europe and the founder of a firm that specialized in merger and acquisition consultations.[63] Joining him on the board were new directors who had strong experience in private finance and Wall Street. Michael Hintze had worked at Salomon Brothers, then ran all UK trading at Goldman Sachs, before becoming the chief of convertible bonds in Europe for Credit Suisse, and finally opening his own hedge fund (CQS). Another new director was Clemens Boersig, a former chairman of Deutsche Bank. And for the first time, Francis tapped a woman to serve as a director, Mary Ann Glendon, a seventy-four-year-old Harvard law professor and ex–United States ambassador to the Vatican.[64]

"Vatican Turns to Wall Street to Fix Bank" was the lead story on CNN.[65] The IOR released its annual report for 2013 on the same day as the director shuffle. It provided further evidence that a complete shakeup of the old regime was furiously under way behind the walls of the city-state. About 3,500 IOR accounts had been closed during the previous year—some because they were dormant, others because they did not qualify in the first place.[66] The private accounts held by Italy's ultra-rich and politically well connected, the source of so much scandal that had plagued the bank for decades, were under assault by the reformers.

And yet another significant restructuring was rolled out. The IOR's investment work would be moved to a newly created division, Vatican Asset Management.[67] Going forward, the Vatican Bank would primarily be a payment service and financial advisor for employees, Catholic charities, and religious orders.[68] The revamped IOR would no longer be able to trade in property and stocks as it did in its heyday under Nogara and Marcinkus.

Cardinal George Pell, the new über-cleric of the Vatican's money, has shaken up the Vatican's old guard with his insistence on sweeping reforms. He drove home the point at a 2014 press conference: "Our ambition is to become something of a model of financial management, rather than the cause for occasional scandal."[69] Pell told the *Boston Globe*, "The ambition is to be boringly successful, to get off the gossip pages. The aim is to become a model of good practice in financial administration. Along the way, we're not going to generate any less revenue for the works of the Church."[70]

As 2014 came to a close, Pell showed the depth of the problem he faced in ending the Vatican's often-cavalier approach to its finances. He found more than a billion dollars in cash that had been unaccounted for, never appearing on any balance sheet and with no oversight as to how it was spent. That cash, he said, had been "tucked away" in different departments of the Holy See.

Although Pell had not uncovered any wrongdoing, he admitted, "It was impossible to know accurately what was going on overall."

April 2015 marked the point at which it was no longer possible to reverse course on Francis's financial reforms. That is when Italy and the Vatican signed a historic tax information exchange agreement (TIEA).[71] While Italy previously signed TIEAs with Switzerland, Monaco, and Liechtenstein, there was no country more important than Italy. That deal marked the effective end of wealthy Italians using the Vatican Bank as an offshore haven to avoid taxes and bypass currency regulations. It formalized the transparency and sharing of data to insure an end to the political slush funds in the names of Italy's top politicians. The TIEA with Italy was well received in the press. "Holy See Cleans House" (AP); "A Haven for Money Laundering & Tax Evasion No More" (*International Business Times*); the end of the "last fiscal and banking wall" in Italy (*La Repubblica*); and a "new decisive step" (*Panorama*).[72]

Just eight days before the agreement was signed, this author wrote an opinion piece in a leading publication for tax professionals, concluding: "The only way it [Italy] can verify that the bad old days of the Vatican Bank are truly over is to sign a TIEA with the church. When that happens—possibly by the end of March, according to some insiders—then Italy will be one step closer to freeing itself of what many officials consider an offshore bank operating in the heart of Rome."[73]

In September 2013, the author met René Brülhart in the courtyard of a rundown Roman sixteenth-century palazzo that is now a hotel for pilgrims and visitors to nearby Vatican City. Over two hours, Brülhart provided an intensive and thorough insider's view of the massive reforms that were then under way. The Vatican was unique, said Brülhart. As opposed to Liechtenstein, or work he had performed in his native Switzerland, the city-state was not a financial center. There was no commercial activity. He had all the power and latitude he needed, he assured me, to make certain the IOR was compliant and ready to be added to the white list. He thought that "most of the difficult steps are ahead" and estimated it would take three to five years "to fully implement."[74]

"I came here with no expectations," he said. "But I can see at the end delivering a financial institution to the Holy See that is above reproach. It is certainly not simple to do, but it is achievable."

What if Marcinkus saw the bank as it operated today?

"I don't think he would recognize it. And that is a good thing."

Acknowledgments

Writing about an institution that prizes its secrecy is no easy task. The research for this book began in 2005. The Vatican was resistant to cooperating, rejecting my application for access to its Secret Archives and also ignoring many requests for interviews. The story of power and money Rome preferred I not tell was instead found scattered in the archives of governments and private companies in more than a dozen countries on three continents. Litigation files and court records over the sex abuse scandal opened a door to understanding how the church protected its assets. Documents unearthed from World War II intelligence files answered some long-standing questions about whether the Vatican profited in the killing fields of Europe during the Holocaust. Buried inside the U.S. Securities and Exchange Commission were records that helped fill in some missing parts of the puzzle about how the Vatican Bank did business through proxies. More than 150 hours of interviews supplemented the information in the archives, and in some instances led to independent revelations about the church's finances. A handful of clerics and lay officials in Rome—who, fearing retribution, spoke only on the condition of anonymity—gave me an extraordinary look into the cutthroat infighting that has often crippled the modern Papacy. Those interviews lay out clearly the challenge that faces Pope Francis when it comes to successfully reforming the finances of the Vatican.

I am indebted to many people for assistance during this investigation. I am particularly grateful once again to the now retired Robert Wolfe, whose pioneering efforts at the Independent Working Group were critical in the declassification of some of the U.S. documents necessary to understand what the Vatican Bank did during World War II. Also many thanks to Rebecca L. Collier, William Cunliffe, Greg Bradsher, and Miriam Kleiman, National Archives at College Park, Maryland, and Washington, D.C.; David Clark, Harry S. Truman Library, Independence, Missouri; Renata Martano, Historical Archives of the Bank of Italy (ASBI), Rome; Dr. Robert K. O'Neill and Justine Sundaram of the John J. Birns Library, Boston College; Karen Beach, Boston Athenaeum, Boston; Sandra Garcia-Myers, Higham Collection, USC Cinematic Arts Library, Los Angeles; Lynn Conway and Scott Taylor, J. Graham Parsons and William A. Wilson Papers, Georgetown University Library, Special Collections Research Center, Washington, D.C.

In the production of documents from Freedom of Information requests, I am indebted to Thomas McIntyre, William Stewart III, Martin Renkiewicz, Kevin Smith, GayLa D. Sessoms, Thomas Sylvia, David M. Hardy, David Mrozowski, and Katherine Myrick at various subsections of the Justice Department, most notably the National Drug Intelligence Center and the Drug Enforcement Administration; Anne Baker and Gaisha Cook at the State Department; Deborah Osinbajo and Gregory Smith at the Financial Crimes Enforcement Network and Dale Underwood at the Department of the Treasury; Scott Koch at the Central Intelligence Agency; and Louis F. Giles at the National Security Agency.

Many thanks to David Clohessy at SNAP (Survivors Network of Those Abused by Priests). My wife, Trisha, and I enjoyed the hospitality of Dr. Jonathan Levy. He was very generous with his time and provided his litigation files in his decade-long class action against the Vatican Bank. Marc Masurovsky, of the European Shoah Legacy Institute, has a remarkable knowledge of the Nazi ratlines and Allied intelligence. His groundbreaking work was a great assistance.

Jason Berry is in a small club of successful journalists. Not only has his award-winning work on the church and the clerical sex abuse crisis set the standard for investigative work in this field, but he was always remarkably willing to help. Even when he was on deadline he would somehow find the time to point me to key sources and provide information from his own voluminous research. His help was beyond the call of duty, and for that I will always be obliged. Equally helpful was Professor Michael Phayer, the author of two acclaimed books about the Vatican and World War II, who guided me principally when it came to matters of Nazi gold and the church. Professors and authors John Cornwell and John F. Pollard also were generous in assisting me on my research requests. And in Italy, many thanks to authors Philip Willan and the late Benny Lai.

Curtis Hoxter, of the Conference on Material Claims Against Germany, and Moshe Sanbar, the former governor of the Bank of Israel, helped me navigate through the mass of information about German and Italian insurance companies during World War II and opened the door to how reinsurance might be the key to money ventures with the Vatican. Thanks also in this regard to Joseph Belth of the Insurance Forum, his 1998 monograph on Holocaust-era insurance issues was elucidating.

Elan Steinberg of the World Jewish Congress helped me through many difficult stages. His untimely death in 2012 at the age of fifty-nine is a great loss to his family and to the World Jewish Congress, as well as to those of us who counted him as a friend. I am sorry he did not live to see this book.

Lorenzo Zorza and Francesco Pazienza were generous with their time in discussing events that were decades old. Their perspective proved valuable, especially since they allowed me constantly to challenge their memories with documents and accounts of others.

I am especially indebted to René Brülhart, the Director of the Vatican's enforcement division, the Financial Intelligence Authority. He demonstrated his independence inside the Vatican by being the only high-ranking official in the city-state to meet with me on the record. His perspective and firsthand account provided an invaluable look inside the church's ambitious reform efforts of the past few years.

Michael Hornblow and Peter K. Murphy are two former U.S. diplomats who served in the American embassy to the Vatican. I am very grateful for their fresh perspective of what was going on inside the church during the 1980s. Special acknowledgment should be given to former prosecutor William Aronwald and FBI agent Richard Tamarro, who patiently reconstructed for me the criminal investigation that brought them inside the Vatican. The story would have been incomplete without them.

Carlo Calvi has lived in the shadow of his father's death for decades. Nevertheless he answered my many queries without fail and shared documentation. I thank him for never losing faith that one day I would finish this book.

Some people gave assistance beyond their obligations or call of friendship. I would like to make particular mention of Mark Young in London; Michael Sanchez in Panama; Bishop Agustín Román in Miami; Father Richard J. Vigoa,

Miami; Archbishop Thomas Wenski, Miami; Archbishop Carlo Maria Viganò, Washington, D.C.; Ivan S. Fisher, New York; Jacopo Pierfederica, Rome; Claudio Sidoti, Miami; Mitchell Garabedian, Boston; Michael Schwartz, New York; David Alexander, New York; David Ness, London; Joan Lewis, Rome; Bill Cooke, Miami Beach; Elliot Welles, New York; Abraham Foxman, New York; Rabbis Marvin Heir and Abraham Cooper, Simon Wiesenthal Center, Los Angeles; Charles Higham, New York; Glenn Garvin, Miami; Dr. Curtis Slipman, Miami; Ann Froelich, New York; Stanley Wertheim, Miami; and Italo Insolera, Rome. Paola Desiderio, Eleonora d'Este, and Patrizia Melloni were super on handling a lot of translation work under tight deadlines and sometimes unusual circumstances for interviews. Many thanks to Sam Pinkus for so carefully negotiating this book contract and to Steve Goldberg, Esq., for his sage legal advice. My apologies to anyone I omitted.

And a very special thanks to those who remain anonymous, particularly a brave contingent in Rome whose perseverance and dedication to the truth made it possible for me to understand what happened inside the Vatican during the past decade. I appreciate fully that no one wants their assistance to me to jeopardize their work or their family. My wife, Trisha, and I are forever grateful for the often prodigious and selfless assistance.

Brendan Howley, a very talented Canadian investigative journalist, has long been immersed in the world of Nazis, World War II, and the church. His assistance in research at the U.S. National Archives—where he uncovered some critical documents—combined with his unerring reporter's instinct for the story, was essential. I was greatly aided by the constant debate in which he engaged me.

I was fortunate that a high school friend, Christopher Petersen, who had worked in the world of private finance, had not long ago retired. Once he said he was looking for something to do, I challenged the limits of our friendship by enlisting him in every phase of the book. Chris discovered an unknown talent for research and fact-checking. He compiled an archive of thousands of historical articles and academic papers, and created a timeline with supporting documentation that proved a valuable resource. At times an amateur editor and at other times someone simply to run an idea by, Chris was an untiring volunteer and indispensable part of this project.

Jonathan Karp, the President of Simon & Schuster, is a rarity in an industry known for taking few risks. He gave me an opportunity to pursue an ambitious two-century investigation of a behind-the-scenes look at power and money inside the Catholic Church. Few publishers would have made such a strong commitment without knowing in advance what the book would turn out to be. But Jonathan's faith empowered me to find the evidence and uncover the story. I am indebted to him for that vote of confidence. And in an age when many authors complain about the lack of support from their publishers, I count myself very fortunate. Assistant Editor Brit Hvide was gracious and helpful in handling my many requests. Associate Art Director Christopher Lin designed a super cover. Elisa Rivlin's legal vetting was meticulous. Copyeditor Fred Chase managed a comprehensive and very helpful review with little time. Senior Production Editor Mara Lurie helped me meet tight deadlines on a very demanding manuscript without creating extra anxiety. And I owe a huge debt of gratitude to Ben Loehnen, a dream of an editor. Ben believed in this ambitious project and championed it. And he turned out to be a remarkably skillful editor with a good eye for solid journalism. At times when the scope of the reporting or the breadth of the story seemed insurmountable, he somehow always had the right advice that kept me energized and focused. His ideas, comments, and edits made this an immeasurably better book.

It is not an exaggeration to say that my wife, Trisha, is a force of nature responsible for any of my success. She did far more than suffer patiently while I worked on this project. Instead, as an author in her own right, she is my incredibly resourceful partner, accompanying me on trips, sifting through archival files for days on end, and helping in every interview. The best information I uncover is often because Trisha has established a relationship of trust with an important source or somehow manages to ask just the key question at the right moment. Her judgment is unerring. Trisha's commitment to the truth and her tremendous energy inspire me. When she grew up as a Jewish Londoner, it is unlikely she thought that one day she might marry an American Catholic. And beyond her imagination was that she would spend nearly a decade of her life delving into the wonderful mysteries of the Catholic Church and the Vatican. But to my eternal gratitude, she has done both. I get the credit because my name is on the cover. But I know this book is as much hers as mine.

Although *God's Bankers* would not have been possible without the help of everyone listed above, I am ultimately responsible for what was done or left undone. I accept sole responsibility.

Selected Bibliography

Books

Aarons Mark. *Sanctuary: Nazi Fugitives in Australia.* Melbourne: William Heinemann, 1989.

———, and John Loftus. *Unholy Trinity: The Vatican, the Nazis, and the Swiss Banks.* New York: St. Martin's/Griffin, 1998.

Allen, John L. Jr. *All the Pope's Men: The Inside Story of How the Vatican Really Thinks.* New York: Doubleday, 2004.

———. *Cardinal Ratzinger: The Vatican's Enforcer of Faith.* New York: Continuum, 2000.

———. *Pope Benedict XVI: A Biography of Joseph Ratzinger.* London: Bloomsbury Academic, 2005.

Alvarez, David. *Spies in the Vatican: Espionage and Intrigue from Napoleon to the Holocaust.* Lawrence: University Press of Kansas, 2002.

Authers, John, and Richard Wolffe. *The Victim's Fortune: Inside the Epic Battle over the Debts of the Holocaust.* New York: HarperCollins, 2002.

Bazyler, Michael. *Holocaust Justice: The Battle for Restitution in America's Courts.* New York: New York University Press, 2003.

Bernstein, Carl, and Marco Politi. *His Holiness: John Paul II and the History of Our Time.* New York: Penguin, 1996.

Berry, Jason. *Lead Us Not into Temptation: Catholic Priests and the Sexual Abuse of Children.* New York: Doubleday, 1992.

———. *Render Unto Rome, The Secret Life of Money in the Catholic Church.* New York: Crown, 2011.

———, with Gerald Renner. *Vows of Silence: The Abuse of Power in the Papacy of John Paul II.* New York: Free Press, 2010.

Besier, Gerhard, with the collaboration of Francesca Piombo, translated by W. R. Ward. *The Holy See and Hitler's Germany.* New York: Palgrave Macmillan, 2007.

Binchy, Daniel A. *Church and State in Fascist Italy.* New York: Oxford University Press, 1941.

Blet, Pierre SJ. *Pius XII and the Second World War: According to the Archives of the Vatican.* New York: Paulist Press, 1997.

Bokun, Branko. *Spy in the Vatican, 1941–45.* London: Vita, 1973.

Breitman, Richard, and Norman J. W. Goda, Timothy Naftali, and Robert Wolfe. *U.S. Intelligence and the Nazis.* Cambridge: Cambridge University Press, 2005.

Carroll, James. *Constantine's Sword: The Church and the Jews.* New York: Houghton Mifflin, 2002.

Castelli, Leone. *Quel tanto di territorio: ricordi di lavori ed opera eseguiti nel Vaticano durante il Pontificato di Pio XI (1922–1939).* Rome: Edizioni Fuori Comercio, 1948.

Chadwick, Owen. *Britain and the Vatican During the Second World War.* Cambridge: Cambridge University Press, 1986.

———. *A History of the Popes, 1830–1914.* New York: Oxford University Press, 1998.

Chernow, Ron. *The House of Morgan: An American Banking Dynasty and the Rise of Modern Finance*. New York: Grove, 1990.
Chesnoff, Richard Z. *Pack of Thieves: How Hitler and Europe Plundered the Jews and Committed the Greatest Theft in History*. New York: Doubleday, 1999.
Cooney, John. *The American Pope: The Life and Times of Francis Cardinal Spellman*. New York: Crown, 1984.
Coppa, Frank J., ed. *Controversial Concordats: The Vatican's Relations with Napoleon, Mussolini, and Hitler*. Washington, DC: Catholic University of America Press, 1999.
Cornwell, John. *Hitler's Pope: The Secret History of Pius XII*. New York: Viking, 1999.
———. *A Thief in the Night: Life and Death in the Vatican*. New York: Penguin, 2001.
Cornwell, Rupert. *God's Banker*. New York: Dodd, Mead, 1983.
Cymet, David. *History vs. Apologetics: The Holocaust, the Third Reich, and the Catholic Church*. Lanham, MD: Lexington, 2010.
Dalin, David G. *The Myth of Hitler's Pope: How Pope Pius XII Rescued Jews from the Nazis*. Washington, DC: Regnery; annotated edition, 2005.
D'Antonio, Michael. *Mortal Sins: Sex, Crime, and the Era of Catholic Scandal*. New York: Thomas Dunne, 2013.
De Rosa, Luigi, and Gabriele De Rosa. *Storia del Banco Di Roma*, 3 Volumes. Rome: Banco de Roma, 1982.
DiFonzo, Luigi. *St. Peter's Banker: Michele Sindona*. New York: Franklin Watts, 1983.
Ericksen, Robert P. *Complicity in the Holocaust: Churches and Universities in Nazi Germany*. Cambridge: Cambridge University Press, 2012.
Falconi, Carlo. *The Popes in the Twentieth Century: From Pius X to John XXIII*. Boston: Little, Brown, 1968.
———. *The Silence of Pius XII*. Boston: Little, Brown, 1970.
Feldman, Gerald D. *Allianz and the German Insurance Business, 1933–1945*. Cambridge: Cambridge University Press, 2001.
Ferguson, Niall. *The House of Rothschild, Vol. 1: Money's Prophets, 1798–1848*. New York: Viking, 1998.
———. *The House of Rothschild, Vol. 2: The World's Banker, 1849–1999*. New York: Viking, 1999.
Friedländer, Saul. *Nazi Germany and the Jews, Vol. 1: The Years of Persecution, 1933–39*. New York: HarperCollins, 1998.
———. *Pius XII and the Third Reich: A Documentation*. New York: Alfred A. Knopf, 1966.
Friedman, Max Paul. *Economic Warfare, Enemy Civilians, and the Lessons of World War II Nazis and Good Neighbors: The United States Campaign Against the Germans of Latin American World War II*. Cambridge: Cambridge University Press, 2005.
Galli, Giancarlo. *Finanza bianca. La chiesa, i soldi, il potere*. Milan: Arnoldo Mondadori, 2004.
Godman, Peter. *Hitler and the Vatican: Inside the Secret Archives That Reveal the New Story of the Nazis and the Church*. New York: Free Press, 2004.
Gollin, James. *Worldly Goods: The Wealth and Power of the American Catholic Church, the Vatican, and the Men Who Control the Money*. New York: Random House, 1971.
Goñi, Uki. *The Real Odessa: How Perón Brought the Nazi War Criminals to Argentina*. London: Granta, 2002.
Grilli, Giovanni. *La finanza vaticana in Italia*. Rome: Editori Riuniti, 1961.
Gurwin, Larry. *The Calvi Affair: Death of a Banker*. London: Pan, 1983.
Hachey, Thomas E., ed. *Anglo-Vatican Relations, 1914–1939: Confidential Annual Reports of the British Ministers to the Holy See*. Boston: G. K. Hall, 1972.
Hammer, Richard. *The Vatican Connection*. New York: Charter, 1983.
Helmreich, Ernest Christian. *The German Churches Under Hitler: Background, Struggle and Epilogue*. Detroit: Wayne State University Press, 1979.
Hesemann, Michael. *Der Papst, der Hitler trotzte. Die Wahrheit über Pius XII*. Augsburg: Sankt Ulrich Verlag GmbH, 2008.
Higham, Charles. *Trading with the Enemy: An Exposé of the Nazi-American Money Plot, 1933–1949*. New York: Delacorte, 1983.
Hlond, August. *The Persecution of the Catholic Church in German-Occupied Poland. Reports Presented by H. E. Cardinal Hlond, Primate of Poland, to Pope Pius XII*. New York: Longmans, Green, 1941.
Hoffman, Paul. *Anatomy of the Vatican: An Irreverent View of the Holy See*. London: Robert Hale, 1985.

Katz, Robert. *The Battle for Rome: The Germans, the Allies, the Partisans, and the Pope, September 1943–June 1944*. New York: Simon & Schuster, 2003.

Kent, Peter C. *The Lonely Cold War of Pope Pius XII: The Roman Catholic Church and the Division of Europe, 1943–1950*. Montreal: McGill Queens University Press, 2002.

———. *The Pope and the Duce: The International Impact of the Lateran Agreements*. New York: St. Martin's, 1981.

Kertzer, David I. *The Kidnapping of Edgardo Mortara*. New York: Alfred A. Knopf, 1997.

———. *The Pope and Mussolini: The Secret History of Pius XI and the Rise of Fascism in Europe*. New York: Random House, 2014.

———. *The Popes Against the Jews: The Vatican's Role in the Rise of Modern Anti-Semitism*. New York: Alfred A. Knopf, 2001.

Koehler, John. *Spies in the Vatican: The Soviet Union's Cold War Against the Catholic Church*. New York: Pegasus, 2009.

Lai, Benny. *Finanze e finanzieri vaticani tra l'ottocento e il novecento da Pio IX a Benedetto XV*. Milan: A. Mondadori, 1979. Updated and edited as *Finanze Vaticane: Da Pio XI a Benedetto XVI*. Rome: Rubbettino Editore, 2012.

Lawler, Justus George. *Popes and Politics: Reform, Resentment, and the Holocaust*. New York: Continuum, 2002.

Lehnert, Sister M. Pascalina. *His Humble Servant: Sister M. Pascalina Lehnert's Memoirs of Her Years of Service to Eugenio Pacelli, Pope Pius XII*. South Bend, IN: St. Augustine's Press, 2014.

Lernoux, Penny. *In Banks We Trust: Bankers and Their Close Associates: The CIA, the Mafia, Drug Traders, Dictators, Politicians, and the Vatican*. New York: Anchor/Doubleday, 1984.

Lewy, Guenter. *The Catholic Church and Nazi Germany*. New York: McGraw-Hill, 1964.

Lo Bello, Nino. *The Vatican Empire*. New York: Trident, 1968.

Lukas, Richard C. *The Forgotten Holocaust: The Poles Under German Occupation, 1939–1944*. Lexington: University Press of Kentucky, 1986.

Martin, Malachi. *Rich Church, Poor Church*. New York: G. P. Putnam's Sons, 1984.

Modras, Ronald. *The Catholic Church in Poland and Anti-Semitism, 1933–1939*. Abingdon-on-Thames: Routledge, 2000.

Molony, John N. *The Emergence of Political Catholicism in Italy: Partito Popolare, 1919–1926*. London: Croom Helm, 1977.

Morgan, Thomas B. *A Reporter at the Papal Court: A Narrative of the Reign of Pope Pius XI*. New York: Longmans, Green, 1937.

Murphy, Paul I. *La Popessa: The Controversial Biography of Sister Pascalina, the Most Powerful Woman in Vatican History*. New York: Warner, 1983.

Nuzzi, Gianluigi. *Ratzinger Was Afraid: The Secret Documents, the Money and the Scandals that Overwhelmed the Pope*. Rome: Adagio, 2013.

———. *Sua Santità: Le carte segrete di Benedetto XVI*. Milan: Chiarelettere, 2012.

———. *Vaticano S.p.A.: Da un archivio segreto la verità sugli scandali finanziari e politici della Chiesa*. Milan: Chiarelettere editore, 2009.

Pacelli, Francesco. *Diario della conciliazione*. Libreria Editrice Vaticana, 1959.

Pallenberg, Corrado. *Inside the Vatican*. New York: Hawthorn, 1960.

Passelecq, Georges, and Bernard Suchecky. *The Hidden Encyclical of Pius XI*, translated by Steven Rendall. New York: Harcourt Brace, 1997.

Peters, Walter H. *Life of Benedict XV*. Milwaukee: Bruce, 1959.

Phayer, Michael. *The Catholic Church and the Holocaust, 1930–1965*. Bloomington: Indiana University Press, 2000.

———. *Pius XII, the Holocaust, and the Cold War*. Bloomington: Indiana University Press, 2008.

Piazzesi, Gianfranco. *Gelli: La carriera di un eroe di questa Italia*. Milan: Garzanti Libri, 1983.

Pollard, John F. *Benedict XV: The Unknown Pope and the Pursuit of Peace*. London: Burns & Oates, 2005.

———. *Money and the Rise of the Modern Papacy: Financing the Vatican, 1850–1950*. Cambridge: Cambridge University Press, 2005.

———. *The Vatican and Italian Fascism, 1929–32: A Study in Conflict*. Cambridge: Cambridge University Press, 2005.

Raw, Charles. *The Moneychangers: How the Vatican Bank Enabled Roberto Calvi to Steal $250 Million for the Heads of the P2 Masonic Lodge*. London: Harvill/HarperCollins, 1992.

Reese, Thomas J., SJ. *Inside the Vatican: The Politics and Organization of the Catholic Church.* Cambridge: Harvard University Press, 1996.
Rhodes, Anthony. *The Vatican in the Age of the Dictators, 1922–1945.* London: Hodder & Stoughton, 1973.
Riccards, Michael P. *Vicars of Christ: Popes, Power, and Politics in the Modern World.* New York: Crossroad, 1998.
Rickman, Gregg J. *Conquest Redemption: A History of Jewish Assets from the Holocaust.* New Brunswick, NJ: Transaction, 2007.
Romano, Sergio. *Giuseppe Volpi: Industria e finanza tra Giolitti e Mussolini.* Milan: Bompiani, 1979.
Rychlak, Ronald J. *Hitler, the War, and the Pope.* Columbus, MS: Genesis, 2000.
Sarfatti, Michele, translated by John and Anne C. Tedeschi. *The Jews in Mussolini's Italy: From Equality to Persecution.* Madison: University of Wisconsin Press, 2006.
Seldes, George. *The Vatican—Yesterday, Today and Tomorrow.* New York: Harper & Bros., 1934.
Sereny, Gitta. *Into That Darkness: An Examination of Conscience.* New York: Vintage, 1983.
Simoni, Gianni, and Giuliano Turone. *Il caffè di Sindona: Un finanzieri d'avventura tra politica, Vaticano e mafia.* Milan: Garzanti Libri, 2009.
Simpson, Christopher. *Blowback: America's Recruitment of Nazis and Its Effects on the Cold War.* New York: Weidenfeld & Nicolson, 1988.
Stourton, Edward. *John Paul II: Man of History.* London: Hodder & Stoughton, 2006.
Tannenbaum, Edward R. *The Fascist Experience: Italian Society and Culture, 1922–1945.* New York: Basic Books, 1972.
Tardini, Domenico (Cardinal). *Memories of Pius XII,* translated by Rosemary Goldie. Westminster, MD: Newman Press, 1961.
Teeling, William. *Pope Pius XI and World Affairs.* New York: Frederick A. Stokes, 1937.
Teodori, Massimo. *Vaticano rapace: Lo scandaloso finanziamento dell'Italia alla Chiesa.* Venice: Marsilio Editiori, 2013.
Thavis, John. *The Vatican Diaries: A Behind-the-Scenes Look at the Power, Personalities and Politics at the Heart of the Catholic Church.* New York: Viking, 2013.
Thomas, Gordon, and Max Morgan-Witts. *Pontiff.* Garden City, NY: Doubleday, 1983.
Tittmann, Harold. *Inside the Vatican of Pius XII: The Memoir of an American Diplomat During World War II.* New York: Doubleday Religious Publishing, 2004.
Tosches, Nick. *Power on Earth.* New York: Arbor House, 1986.
Volk, Ludwig. *Das Reichskonkordat vom 20, Juli 1933.* Ostfildern: Matthias-Grünewald-Verlag, 1972.
Walsh, John Evangelist. *Bones of St. Peter: The First Full Account of the Apostle's Tomb.* New York: Doubleday, 1982.
Webster, Richard A. *The Cross and the Fasces: Christian Democracy and Fascism in Italy.* Stanford: Stanford University Press, 1960.
———. *Industrial Imperialism in Italy, 1908–1915.* Berkeley: University of California Press, 1975.
Weigel, George. *Witness to Hope: The Biography of Pope John Paul II.* New York: Cliff Street, 1999.
Weisbord, Robert G., and Wallace P. Sillanpoa. *The Chief Rabbi, the Pope, and the Holocaust: An Era in Vatican–Jewish Relations.* New Brunswick, NJ: Transaction, 1992.
Willan, Philip. *The Last Supper: The Mafia, the Mason and the Killing of Roberto Calvi.* London: Robinson, 2007.
———. *The Vatican at War: From Blackfriars Bridge to Buenos Aires.* Bloomington, IN: iUniverse LLC, 2013.
Willey, David. *God's Politician: John Paul at the Vatican.* New York: St. Martin's, 1993.
Wills, Garry. *Papal Sin: Structures of Deceit.* New York: Doubleday, 2000.
Wynn, Wilton. *Keepers of the Keys: John XXIII, Paul VI, and John Paul II—Three Who Changed the Church.* New York: Random House, 1988.
Zuccotti, Susan. *Under His Very Windows: The Vatican and the Holocaust in Italy.* New Haven: Yale University Press, 2002.

Selected Articles, Reports, and Other Publications

Allen, John L. Jr. "Debunking Four Myths About John Paul I, the 'Smiling Pope.'" *National Catholic Reporter,* November 2, 2012.

———. "New Vatican Transparency Guru Brings Unique Pedigree." *National Catholic Reporter*, September 12, 2012.

———. "Vatican Abuse Summit: $2.2 Billion and 100,000 Victims in U.S. Alone." *National Catholic Reporter*, February 8, 2012.

Amatori, Franco. "Entrepreneurial Typologies in the History of Industrial Italy (1880–1960)." *The Business History Review* 54, no. 3 (Autumn 1980).

Anderson, Harry, Rich Thomas, and Hope Lamfert. "Inside the Vatican Bank." *Newsweek*, September 13, 1982.

Assicurazioni Generali: Source Materials on Communist Expropriations of Generali and Insurance Claims Paid to Holocaust Victims. Prepared for the National Association of Insurance Commissioners, January 15, 1998.

Bardazzi, Marco. "No Transparency. That's Why We Fired Gotti Tedeschi." "Vatican Insider," *La Stampa*, May 27, 2012.

Bazoli, Giovanni. "The Ambrosiano Failure." *The American Banker*, July 12, 1983.

Belth, Joseph. "Life Insurance and the Holocaust." *The Insurance Forum*, Special Holocaust Issue 25, no. 9 (September 1998).

Berry, Jason. "The Shame of John Paul II: How the Sex Abuse Scandal Stained His Papacy." *The Nation*, May 16, 2011.

———. "The Tragedy of Acadiana." *The Times of Acadiana*, May 23, 1985.

Blanshard, Paul. "The Roman Catholic Church and Fascism." *The Nation*, March 1948.

Burnett, Michael, Father Thomas Doyle, and Dr. James Freiburger. "Report of the Audit and Review of the Files of the Capuchin Province of St. Joseph." June 2013.

Cameron, Rondo E. "Papal Finance and the Temporal Power, 1815–1871." *Church History* 26, no. 2 (1957).

Cannon, Carl M. "The Priest Scandal: How Old News at Last Became a Dominant National Story . . . And Why It Took So Long." *American Journalism Review*, May 2002.

Chadwick, Owen. "Weizsäcker, the Vatican, and the Jews of Rome." *Journal of Ecclesiastical History* 28, no. 2 (April 1977).

Colby, Laura. "Vatican Bank Played a Central Role in Fall of Banco Ambrosiano." *The Wall Street Journal*, April 27, 1987.

DiFonzo, Luigi. "Justifiable Homicide." *New York*, April 11, 1983.

Dinmore, Guy. "Upheaval Lifts Vatican Bank's Veil of Secrecy." *Financial Times*. October 16, 2009.

Farnsworth, Clyde H. "Michele Sindona, the Outsider as Insider in Worldwide Finance." *The New York Times*, May 20, 1974.

Gallagher, Jim. "The Pope's Banker." *Chicago Tribune*, March 13, 1983.

Hametz, Maura. "Zionism, Emigration, and Anti-Semitism in Trieste: Central Europe's 'Gateway to Zion,' 1896–1943." *Jewish Social Studies*, New Series 13, no. 3 (Spring–Summer, 2007).

Hawkins, Dana, and Jason Vest. "A Vow of Silence: Did Gold Stolen by Croatian Fascists Reach the Vatican." *U.S. News & World Report*, March 22, 1998.

Hebblethwaite, Peter. "Scandal in Rome Has Buffeted the Church; Italian Political Corruption Purges." *National Catholic Reporter*, March 26, 1993.

Horne, J. Paul. "The Cardinal as a Money Manager." *Institutional Investor*, January 1971.

Hughes, John Jay. "The Reich Concordat 1933: Capitulation or Compromise?" *Australian Journal of Politics and History* 20 (1974).

Jorisch, Avi. "The Vatican Bank: The Most Secret Bank in the World." *Forbes*, June 26, 2012.

Kent, George. "Pope Pius XII and Germany: Some Aspects of German–Vatican Relations, 1933–1943." *American Historical Review* 70 (October 1964).

Kent, Peter C. "A Tale of Two Popes: Pius XI, Pius XII and the Rome-Berlin Axis." *Journal of Contemporary History* 23 (1988).

Leigh, David. "How the Vatican Built a Secret Property Empire Using Mussolini's Millions." *The Guardian*, January 21, 2013.

Lewin, Ernst A. "The Finances of the Vatican." *Journal of Contemporary History* 18, no. 2 (April 1983).

Lipscher, Ladislav. "The Jews of Slovakia: 1939–1945," in *The Jews of Czechoslovakia*, ed. Avigdor Dagan, vol. 3 of Historical Studies and Surveys (New York: Society for the History of Czechoslovak Jews, 1984).

Magister, Sandro. "All the Denarii of Peter. Vices and Virtues of the Vatican Bank." *L'Espresso*, June 15, 2009.

———. "For Peter's Cash, A Calm Amid the Storm." *L'Espresso*, January 30, 2009.
———. "No Glorious Sunset for Cardinal Bertone." *L'Espresso*, February 2, 2012.
———. "Vatican Diary/Viganò, the untouchable." *L'Espresso*, January 26, 2012.
Maltese, Curzio, and Carlo Pontesilli, Maurizio Turco, "Scandal, Intrigue and Mystery; The Secrets of the Vatican Bank." *La Repubblica*, January 26, 2008.
McGoldrick, Patricia M. "New Perspectives on Pius XII and Vatican Financial Transactions During the Second World War." *The Historical Journal* 55, no. 4, (December 2012).
Nuzzi, Gianluigi. "Ior parallelo. Conti segreti in Vaticano." *Panorama*, May 17, 2005.
Palmo, Rocco. "God's Bankers: Not Afraid." *Whispers in the Loggia*, October 14, 2008.
Pollard, John F. "Conservative Catholics and Italian Fascism: The Clerico-Fascists," in Martin Blinkhorn ed., *Fascists and Conservatives: The Radical Right and the Establishment in Twentieth Century Europe* (London: Unwin Hyman, 1990).
———. "Religion and the Formation of the Italian Working Class," in R. Halpern and J. Morris, eds., *American Exceptionalism? US Working-Class Formation in an International Context* (London: Palgrave Macmillan, 1997).
———. "The Vatican and the Wall Street Crash: Bernardino Nogara and Papal Finances in the Early 1930s." *The Historical Journal* 42, no. 4 (December 1999).
———. "The Vatican, Italy and the Cold War," in Diane Kirby, *Religion and the Cold War* (London: Palgrave Macmillan, 2002).
Popham, Peter. "The Case of God's Banker: Roberto Calvi the Trial Begins." *The Independent* (London), October 6, 2005.
Pullella, Philip. "At the Vatican Bank—Money, Mystery and Monsignors." *FaithWorld*, Reuters, June 12, 2012.
———. "Corruption Scandal Shakes Vatican as Internal Letters Leaked." Reuters, January 26, 2012.
———. "U.S. Adds Vatican to Money-Laundering 'Concern' List." Reuters, March 8, 2012.
Reeves, William Harvey. "The Control of Foreign Funds by the United States Treasury." *Law and Contemporary Problems*, Duke University Law School, 1945.
Sanderson, Rachel. "The Scandal at the Vatican Bank." *The Financial Times Magazine*, December 6, 2013.
Shelah, Menachem. "The Catholic Church in Croatia: The Vatican and the Murder of the Croatian Jews," in *Remembering for the Future: The Holocaust in an Age of Genocides*, Vol. 1 (Oxford: Pergamon, 1988).
Squires, Nick. "Division Among Cardinals Paved Way for Selection of Pope Francis." *Christian Science Monitor*, March 15, 2013.
Terry, Karen, et al. *The Nature and Scope of Sexual Abuse of Minors by Catholic Priests and Deacons in the United States, 1950–2002*, prepared by the John Jay College of Criminal Justice for the U.S. Conference of Catholic Bishops. Washington, DC: U.S. Conference of Catholic Bishops, 2004.
———. *The Nature and Scope of the Problem of Sexual Abuse of Minors by Catholic Priests and Deacons in the United States: Supplementary Data Analysis*, March 2006.
———. *The Causes and Context of Sexual Abuse of Minors by Catholic Priests in the United States, 1950–2010*, May 18, 2011.
Tornielli, Andrea. "The Vatican and Transparency: Moneyval's Objections." "Vatican Insider," *La Stampa*, May 8, 2012.
———. "The Vatican's Temptation to Exit the Euro." "Vatican Insider," *La Stampa*, July 24, 2012.
Tosatti, Marco. "The Secretariat of Mysteries and the Shadows of Accomplices." "Vatican Insider," *La Stampa*, May 29, 2012.
Trifković, Srdjan. "Rivalry Between Germany and Italy in Croatia, 1942–1943." *The Historical Journal* 36, no. 4 (December 1993).
"Vatican's Finances: Paul's Pence." *The Economist*, February 8, 1975.
Wassermann, Andreas, and Peter Wensierski. "Transparency vs. Money Laundering: Catholic Church Fears Growing Vatican Bank Scandal." *Der Spiegel*, July 2, 2012.
Webster, Richard A. "The Political and Industrial Strategies of a Mixed Investment Bank: Italian Industrial Financing and the Banca Commerciale, 1894–1915." *VSWG: Vierteljahrschrift für Sozial-und Wirtschaftsgeschichte*, 61. Bd., H. 3, 1974.
White, Elizabeth. "The Disposition of SS-Looted Victim Gold During and After World War II." *American University International Law Review* 14, no. 1, Article 15 (January 1998).
"Why the Pope Chose to Sign the Concordat." *The New York Times*, March 31, 1929.

Winfield, Nicole. "Pope Proposes New Financial Order Guided by Ethics." Business News, Vatican City, Associated Press Online, July 7, 2009.

———. "Pope Wants a Closer Look at Vatican's Finance Reform," The Big Story, Associated Press, November 28, 2013.

Government Publications

Acta Apostolicae Sedi (Acts of the Apostolic See). The official gazette of the Holy See, first issued under Pius X in 1909, and then about twelve times a year since then. Online at http://www.vatican.va/archive/aas/index_en.htm.

Administration of the Wartime Financial and Property Controls of United States Government, United States Treasury Department, Foreign Funds Control, December 1942.

Commission Inquiry Report into the Activities of Nazism in Argentina. CEANA, 1999.

Commissione Parlamentare D'inchiesta Sul Caso Sindona E Sulle Responsabilita Politiche Ed Amministrative Ad Esso Eventualmente Connesse (Parliamentary Commission of Inquiry into the Case of Sindona and Responsibilities and the Political and Administrative Connected to It), Chamber of Deputies of the Senate, VIII Legislature, Doc. XXIII, May 22, 1980 and June 23, 1980.

The Eizenstat Report and Related Issues Concerning United States and Allied Efforts to Restore Gold and Other Assets Looted by the Nazis during WWII, May 1997.

Elimination of German Resources for War, Volumes 1–9, U.S. Congress, Hearings Before a Subcommittee of the Senate Committee on Military Affairs, 79th Congress, 2nd Session, Washington, DC: U.S. Government Printing Office, 1945.

"Fate of the Wartime Ustaša Treasury." Report of U.S. State Department, June 2, 1998.

Foreign Relations of the United States, Diplomatic Papers, Europe, 1942. Washington, DC: U.S. Government Printing Office, 1964.

Foreign Relations of the United States, Diplomatic Papers, Europe 1943. Washington, DC: U.S. Government Printing Office, 1964.

Holocaust Victims Assets in Swiss Banks. Senate Banking Committee, New York City Hearing, October 16, 1996.

Independent Commission of Experts. *Switzerland and Gold Transactions in WW2*, May 25, 1998.

Interagency Task Force on Nazi Assets Directed by Under Secretary of State Stuart Eizenstat, U.S. Department of State. "U.S. and Allied Efforts to Recover and Restore Gold and Other Assets Stolen or Hidden by Germany During World War II," Preliminary Study (1997), Washington, DC: U.S. Government Printing Office.

"Klaus Barbie and the United States Government." A Report to the Attorney General of the United States, August, Office of Special Investigations, U.S. Department of Justice, 1983.

Mutual Evaluation Report. Anti-Money Laundering and Combating the Financing of Terrorism. Committee of Experts on the Evaluation of Anti-Money Laundering Measures and the Financing of Terrorism, the Holy See (Including Vatican City State) (MONEYVAL), July 4, 2012.

Papers from the London Conference on Nazi Gold, December 2–4, 1997, UK.

Plunder and Restitution: The US and Holocaust Victims' Assets. Findings and Recommendations of the Presidential Advisory Commission on Holocaust Assets in the United States and Staff Report, December 2000.

Records and Documents of the Holy See Relating to the Second World War. *Actes et documents du Saint Siège relatifs à la Seconde Guerre Mondiale*. Vatican City: Liberia Editrice Vatican, 1965–81. Editors: Pierre Blet, Angelo Martini Burkhart Schneider, and Robert A. Graham.

———Volume 1: *Le Saint Siège et la guerre en Europe Mars 1939–Août 1940.*

———Volume 2: *Lettres de Pie XII aux Évêques Allemands 1939–1944.*

———Volume 3: Two parts: *Le Saint Siège et la situation religieuse en Pologne et dans les Pays Baltes 1939–1945.*

———Volume 4: *Le Saint Siège et la guerre en Europe Juin 1940–Juin 1941.*

———Volume 5: *Le Saint Siège et la guerre en Europe Juillet 1941–Octobre 1942.*

———Volume 6: *Le Saint Siège et la guerre en Europe Mars 1939–Décembre 1940.*

———Volume 7: *Le Saint Siège et la guerre en Europe Novembre 1942–Décembre 1943.*

———Volume 8: *Le Saint Siège et la guerre en Europe Janvier 1941–Décembre 1942.*

———Volume 9: *Le Saint Siège et la guerre en Europe Janvier–Décembre 1943.*

———Volume 10: *Le Saint Siège et la guerre en Europe Janvier 1944–Juillet 1945.*
———Volume 11: *Le Saint Siège et la guerre en Europe Janvier 1944–Mai 1945.*
Relazioni di Commissioni Parlamentari di Inchiesti, Relazione conclusiva della commissione parlamentare d'inchiesta sul caso Sindona e sulle responsabilità politiche ed amministrative ad esso eventualmente connesse, VIII legislatura–Doc. XXIII n. 2-sexies, Relazione conclusiva di maggioranza, relatore on. Giuseppe Azzaro, Rome, March 24, 1982.
Report by the Attorney General: The Allegations of Sexual Abuse of Children by Priests and Other Clergy Members Associated with the Roman Catholic Church in Maine. February 24, 2004.
Report by the Attorney General. The Sexual Abuse of Children in the Roman Catholic Archdiocese of Boston. July 2003.
"Schweizerische Versicherungsgesellschaften im Machtbereich des Dritten Reich" (Swiss Insurance Companies in the Area Governed by the Third Reich). Independent Commission of Experts, Karlen, Stefan and Lucas Chocomeli, Kristin D'haemer, Stefan Laube, Daniel C. Schmid, ICE, Vol. 12. Zürich: Pendo Verlag GmbH, 2002.
Supplementary Report on Nazi Assets. Washington, DC: U.S. Government Printing Office, June 1998.
U.S. Department of the Treasury. *Documents Pertaining to Foreign Funds Control*, Roman Curia—Generally Licensed National—General License No. 44. Washington DC: U.S. Government Printing Office, 1945.

Private Papers and Archival Collections

Archives of the Archdiocese of Chicago, Mundelein Papers, 1872–1939.
Archivio Centrale dello Stato, Italian Central State Archives, Rome.
Archivio Storico della Banca Commerciale Italiana, Historical Archive of the Banca Commerciale Italiana, Milan.
Berlin Catholic Church collection, Diözesanarchiv Archiv, Berlin.
Center for Corporate History of Allianz, historical archives of the Munich Reinsurance Company, Munich.
Charles Higham Collection, University of Southern California, Cinematic Arts Library, Archives of Performing Arts, Los Angeles.
Companies House, London, File 270820, British Grolux Ltd., Annual Returns, 1932–33.
Document Archives, Laws and Legislation, NSDAP, 1933–36, Archives, National Holocaust Museum, Washington, DC.
International Committee of the Red Cross Historical Archives, Geneva, Switzerland.
Franklin D. Roosevelt Presidential Library, Hyde Park, New York.
———Henry Morgenthau III Papers.
———Myron C. Taylor Papers, 1933–52, Manuscript Collection.
Georgetown University, Special Collections, Washington, DC.
———J. Graham Parsons Papers.
———William A. Wilson Collection.
Harry S. Truman Presidential Library, Independence, Missouri.
———Oral History Interview of Giovanni Malagodi.
———Papers of Bernard Bernstein, "Documents Pertaining to Foreign Funds Control."
———Myron C. Taylor Collection.

Government Collections

Bundesarchiv, Berlin
———Records from the former Berlin Document Center
———Captured Foreign Ministry files returned from the UK
National Archives, Kew, UK
———Cabinet Papers
———Foreign Office Papers, Financial Activities of the Vatican
———German Foreign Ministry
———Government Communications Headquarters (GCHQ)

National Archives (Washington, DC/College Park, Maryland)
———Captured German and Related Records
———Department of State (including the separate record group for Foreign Service Posts)
———Interagency Working Group, FBI Secret Intercepts
———Office of Military Government (OMGUS)
———Office of Strategic Services
———Safehaven Files
———War Department Claims Board (including separate record groups for Treasury and Foreign Claims)
———World War II Crimes Records
Segreteria di Stato, Archivo Nunziatura Napoli, scatole 125–27, Archivio Segreto Vaticano, Vatican City.
Trading with the Enemy Files, Department of Trade and Industry: Enemy Property Claims Assessment Panel (EPCAP) Secretariat; Database of Seized Property, Reference Section NK 1, National Archives, Kew, UK.

Selected Trial Transcripts and Proceedings

Adolf Stern v. Assicurazioni Generali, Superior Court of Los Angeles, California, 1996.
The Catholic Bishop of Spokane Debtor, Committee of Tort Litigants v. The Catholic Bishop of Spokane et al., Eastern District of Washington, May 27, 2005.
George Dale for the State of Mississippi et al. v. Emilio Colagiovanni and The Holy See et al., United States District Court for the Southern District of Mississippi, Jackson Division, 2007.
Friedman v. Union Bank of Switzerland, Eastern District of New York, 1996 and *Weisshaus v. Union Bank of Switzerland,* Eastern District of New York, 1997, are the core cases for the so-called Swiss Bankers litigation.
SNAP v. The Holy See, Victims' Communication Pursuant to Article 15 of the Rome Statute
Requesting Investigation and Prosecution of High-Level Vatican Officials for Rape and Other Forms of Sexual Violence as Crimes Against Humanity and Torture as a Crime Against Humanity, International Criminal Court File No. OTP-CR-159/11, Submitted on Behalf of the Survivors Network of Those Abused by Priests and Individual Victims/Survivors, September 13, 2011.
William W. Gowen, Emil Alperin v. Vatican Bank, Case No. C99-04041 MMC, USDC Northern District of California, December 12, 2005.

Interviews conducted by the author and unpublished government and private documents not listed here are cited fully in the Notes.

Notes

Chapter 1: Murder in London

1 Statement of Anthony Huntley to Metropolitan Police (London), June 23, 1982, copy provided to author by Carlo Calvi. Huntley told the police, "This didn't really register at first but on taking a second and longer look, I saw there was a complete body hanging by the neck." See also Philip Willan, *The Last Supper: The Mafia, the Mason and the Killing of Roberto Calvi* (London: Robinson, 2007), 1–2.

2 Larry Gurwin, *The Calvi Affair: Death of a Banker* (London: Pan, 1983), 122; see also Willan, *The Last Supper*, 2.

3 Metropolitan Police Report on the death of Roberto Calvi, London, June 19–22, 1982, copy provided to author by Carlo Calvi; see also statement of Police Constable (PC) John Palmer, City of London Police, June 23, 1982.

4 Statement of PC Donald Bartliff, City of London Police, June 28, 1982; see also Willan, *The Last Supper*, 2.

5 Peter Popham, "The Case of God's Banker: Roberto Calvi the Trial Begins," *The Independent* (London), October 6, 2005.

6 Statement of PC John Palmer, City of London Police, June 23, 1982.

7 Rupert Cornwell, *God's Banker* (New York: Dodd, Mead, 1983), 198.

8 Metropolitan Police Report on the death of Roberto Calvi, London, June 19–22, 1982.

9 If the police had more thoroughly examined his clothing they would have known his true identity a day earlier. His name was printed on a label of his suit's breast pocket. Public Prosecutor's Office, Preliminary Hearing File, Public Prosecutor's memorandum on the murder of Roberto Calvi, Rome, December 28, 2004, 2–3. See also Willan, *The Last Supper*, 3, 5.

10 Lieutenant Colonel Francesco Delfino, an Italian military intelligence officer (Servizio per le Informazioni e la Sicurezza Militare, known by the acronym SISMI), arrived two days after Calvi's body was found. He did not assist Scotland Yard, but instead monitored the probe's progress with his British colleagues at MI5.

11 The court before which he had been tried on criminal charges had impounded Calvi's passport nearly a year before he arrived in London. Calvi's fake was good enough to fool customs agents.

12 Popham, "The Case of God's Banker."

13 Minutes of the Ambrosiano Board from June 17, 1982, published in *Il Mondo*, July 12, 1982.

14 Charles Raw, *The Moneychangers: How the Vatican Bank Enabled Roberto Calvi to Steal $250 Million for the Heads of the P2 Masonic Lodge* (London: Harvill/HarperCollins, 1992), 414–19; see also Penny Lernoux, *In Banks We Trust: Bankers and Their Close Associates: The CIA, the Mafia, Drug Traders, Dictators, Politicians, and the Vatican* (New York: Anchor/Doubleday, 1984), 192.

15 Calvi, who had a house account at London's Claridge's Hotel, detested his 120-square-foot Chelsea Cloisters room with two single beds. Testimony of Silvano Vittor and Margaret Lilley, Coroner's Inquest of June 13–27, 1983, courtesy of Carlo Calvi.

16 Author interview with Carlo Calvi, September 27, 2005.

17 A month later the police admitted they might have unbuttoned the vest when they first searched the body at the bridge, and then incorrectly rebuttoned it before taking any photos. Italy's *L'Espresso* published a front-page photo of the corpse with the incorrectly buttoned vest, sparking the first round of frenzied murder speculation. Report of Detective Inspector John White, July 20, 1982, cited in Willan, *The Last Supper*, 8.

18 Metropolitan Police Report on the death of Roberto Calvi, London, June 19–22, 1982; filed London Police investigation/case summaries dated July 1982.

19 Testimony of Fabiola Moretti, cited in Willan, *The Last Supper*, 183–84.

20 One of the sightings that has become part of the widely accepted "facts" about Calvi's whereabouts is the recollection twenty years after the event from a waiter who worked at San Lorenzo, a popular Knightsbridge trattoria. Tracked down by Italian investigators who were reexamining the case, the former waiter identified Calvi from a photo. He also picked out Umberto Ortolani, a member of a secret Masonic Lodge, as one of several of Calvi's supposed dinner mates that night. Because of the long time lapse, and since the waiter admitted he had seen photos of Calvi in the media before the investigators showed him any pictures, the San Lorenzo sighting is at best speculative. See generally Willan, *The Last Supper*, xxxi–xxxiii.

21 The policy was for 4 billion lire, approximately $3 million at the time of death.

22 Thomas T. Noguchi and Joseph DiMona, *Coroner At Large* (Coroner Series) (Premier Digital Publishing, 1985; Kindle edition, location 2756 of 2971).

23 Unfortunately for the police, the telephone system at the Chelsea Cloisters was antiquated and operated through a switchboard. The operator put incoming calls through to the rooms and no record was kept of them. As for outgoing calls, guests had to request an outside line from the operator, and rates were priced by units according to whether the call was local or international. No records were maintained of the numbers called. Records reveal that Calvi made seventeen requests for outgoing calls, although it could not be determined if all of those had been successfully completed or if in some instances they went unanswered. Calvi used 463 billing units, more than enough for the calls to which his wife and daughter testified. As for the remaining credits, police never determined whom he called. Raw, *The Moneychangers*, 431–32; Cornwell, *God's Banker*, 196; Author interview with Carlo Calvi, September 27, 2005.

24 See generally statement of Police Constable Donald Bartliff in Willan, *The Last Supper*, 6–7.

25 In handwritten notes Simpson later made about the case he indicated that during the first call he received the morning the body was discovered, the constable indicated that the death was "Nothing very unusual" and "Doesn't look like a crime, sir, but would you like to look at it?" See also Colin Evans, *A Question of Evidence: The Casebook of Great Forensic Controversies, from Napoleon to O.J.* (Hoboken, NJ: John Wiley, 2003), 191.

26 Transcript summaries from Coroner's Inquests, July 23, 1982, and June 13–27, 1983, courtesy of Carlo Calvi; see also Associated Press, International News, A.M. cycle, July 23, 1982.

27 Transcript summary from Coroner's Inquest, July 23, 1982, courtesy of Carlo Calvi.

28 "The Vatican's Business; Ambrosia Again," *The Economist*, April 25, 1992, 58 (UK edition, 56).

29 Evans, *A Question of Evidence*, 195.

30 Gurwin, *The Calvi Affair*, 147.

31 "Jury in London Declares Italian Banker a Suicide," *The New York Times*, July 25, 1982, 5.

32 Barnaby J. Feder, "Calvi's Family Asks New Inquest," *The New York Times*, Section D, March 29, 1983, 5.

33 David Willey, *God's Politician: John Paul at the Vatican* (New York: St. Martin's, 1993), 213.

34 In 1988, a Milan civil court ruled that Calvi was likely murdered and entered a judgment ordering the insurer, Assicurazioni Generali, to pay Calvi's family the full amount of the policy.

35 Lt. Colonel Francesco Delfino, who monitored the London investigation, thought that the British detectives were handling the case as if it were "the suicide of a tramp." Willan, *The Last Supper*, 9–10. See also Paul Lewis, "Italy's Mysterious, Deepening Bank Scandal," *The New York Times*, July 28, 1982, A1.

36 See generally "Banco Ambrosiano Liquidated," *Facts on File World News Digest*, Nexis, August 13, 1982.

37 Richard Owen, "Plea to Pope from 'God's Banker' Revealed as Murder Trial Begins," *The Times* (London), October 6, 2005.

38 Andrea Perry, Mark Watts, and Elena Cosentino, "Help Me. Murdered Banker Calvi's Last Desperate Plea to the Pope," *Sunday Express* (London), April 16, 2006, 39.

39 Owen, "Plea to Pope from 'God's Banker' Revealed as Murder Trial Begins."
40 Lefteris Pitarakis and Philip Willan, "So Who Did Kill Calvi?," *The Sunday Herald*, June 10, 2007, 28; Perry, Watts, and Cosentino, "Help me."
41 "Italy Liquidates Ailing Banco Ambrosiano," *The Globe and Mail* (Canada), August 10, 1982.
42 "Banco Ambrosiano: Come Again?," *The Economist*, August 14, 1982, 61.
43 In Italy, the press previously called Calvi the "Vatican's Banker" or the "Pope's Banker."
44 "Calvis Claim New Evidence Shows Banker Was Murdered," United Press International, International Section, A.M. cycle, March 28, 1983.
45 Ed Blanche, "Judge Accepts Family's Challenge to Suicide Verdict," Associated Press, A.M. cycle, January 13, 1983; Barnaby J. Feder, "Calvi's Family Asks New Inquest," *The New York Times*, Section D, March 29, 1983, 5; Michael Harvey, "Star Solicitor of Causes Celebres," Press Association, September 26, 1994.
46 "Court Orders New Inquest in 'Hanging' Italian Banker's Family Wins Reopening of Case," *Miami Herald*, March 30, 1983, A9.
47 "Inquest Jury Undecided on Calvi," *The New York Times*, Section D, June 28, 1982, 1; "Open Verdict in Italian Banker's Death," Associated Press, P.M. cycle, International Section, June 27, 1983; see also "Calvi Inquest Indecisive," *The Globe and Mail* (Canada), June 28, 1983.
48 Author interview with Carlo Calvi, September 27, 2005.
49 Chester Stern, "New Forensic Evidence May Reopen Calvi Case; 'God's Banker' Murder Probe," *Mail on Sunday* (London), October 18, 1992, 2.
50 Michael Gillard, "Calvi—The Tests That May Point to Murder," *The Observer* (London), January 31, 1993, 27; see also David Connett, "Calvi Was 'Murdered,' Tests Find," *The Independent* (London), October 18, 1992, 3; Willan, *The Last Supper*, 8–9. In 1994, Kroll sued the Calvi family in federal court in New York for the nonpayment of $3 million of its $4.5 million fee. The case was settled for an undisclosed amount. See Chris Blackhurst, "Cash-Strapped Kroll Sues Calvis for Pounds 2M," *The Observer* (London), August 7, 1994, 1.
51 Gillard, "Calvi—The Tests May Point to Murder."
52 "Italy Exhumes 'God's Banker' to Review Earlier Suicide," *The New York Times*, December 17, 1998, A19; Bob Beaty, "Mystery Extends from Alberta to Italian Mafia: Family of Roberto Calvi Allege Vatican Also Involved in Banker's Death," *Calgary Herald* (Alberta, Canada), December 31, 1998, B5.
53 Philip Willan, "DNA May Solve Banker's Murder," *The Guardian* (London), December 30, 1998, 11; "Bruising Found on Remains of Italian Banker Calvi," Agence France-Presse, English edition, International News, January 25, 1999; see also "New Evidence Supports Theory Death of 'God's Banker' Was No Suicide, Family-Hired Expert Says," Associated Press Worldstream, International News, December 10, 2000.
54 Jim McBeth, "Who Killed God's Banker," *The Scotsman*, October 1, 2002, 2; Peter Popham, " 'God's Banker' Believed Murdered; New Autopsy Rejects Suicide Theory," *Hamilton Spectator* (Ontario, Canada), February 18, 2003, 4.
55 John Phillips, "Mason Indicted over Murder of 'God's Banker,' " *The Independent* (London), July 20, 2005, 20. Four men were indicted, with a fifth added several months later. "Italy: 4 Charged in Banker's 1982 Death," World Briefing, *The New York Times*, April 19, 2005, A11. Carboni, and Pippo Calo, a reputed mob boss, had been charged in 1997 with conspiracy to murder Calvi. But the case was never prosecuted for lack of evidence. The 2002 indictments were superseding counts and included expanded charges. "Italy Exhumes 'God's Banker' to Review Earlier Suicide," *The New York Times*, December 17, 1998, A19.
56 " 'God's Banker' Murder—Five Cleared," Sky News (U.K.), June 6, 2007.
57 "Italy: 5 Acquitted in Banker's 1982 Death," World Briefing, *The New York Times*, June 7, 2007, A17; Frances D'Emilio, "Jury Acquits All 5 Defendants of Murder in Death of Italian Financier Called 'God's Banker,' " Associated Press, International News, June 7, 2007.
58 " 'God's Banker' Was Murdered, Judges Say," ANSA English Media Service, July 15, 2010.
59 Ibid.; Tony Thompson, "Mafia Boss Breaks Silence over Roberto Calvi Killing," *The Guardian*, May 12, 2012.

Chapter 2: The Last Pope King

1 The name "Vatican" comes from the ancient Roman name for the hill—*Vaticanus*—on which St. Peter's is built. Pope comes from the Greek *pappas* for "father."

2 Paul Hoffman, *Anatomy of the Vatican: An Irreverent View of the Holy See* (London: Robert Hale, 1985), 16.

3 The Roman Curia didn't officially exist until 1089 when Urban II named the bureaucracy. But it remained small until the mid-sixteenth century, when its first formal division, the Congregation of the Inquisition, was formed. It has increased forty-fold since then. The "pontifical court" was officially dropped by Pope Paul VI in the 1960s.

4 John F. Pollard, *Money and the Rise of the Modern Papacy: Financing the Vatican, 1850–1950* (Cambridge: Cambridge University Press, 2005), 22–23.

5 Robert W. Shaffern, "'Buying Back' Redemption," as part of a discussion, "Sin, and Its Indulgences," *The New York Times*, February 13, 2009.

6 "In reality, however, no one has ever purchased an indulgence, but may have made a money contribution to a pious or charitable cause that asked for donations, such as the relief of the poor or the construction of a church": ibid.

7 J. N. D. Kelly, *The Oxford Dictionary of Popes* (New York: Oxford University Press, 1986), 231–32.

8 Martin Luther condemned such pilgrimage sites, noting that although there were only twelve apostles, there were twenty-six "apostles" buried in Germany alone. Bartholomew F. Brewer, *Pilgrimage from Rome* (Greenville, South Carolina: BJU Press, 1986), 132.

9 Dominique Chivot, *Vatican* (New York, Assouline, 2009), 81.

10 The rules regarding the Rosary indulgence changed over time. According to AgeofMary.com, a website dedicated to "The Most Holy Rosary of the Blessed Virgin Mary": "Plenary Indulgence: A Plenary Indulgence may be gained (under the usual conditions) when the Rosary is prayed in a Church, in a family group, or in a religious community. The 'usual conditions' refers to (1) being in the state of grace, (2) going to confession within eight days (before or after) of performing the indulgenced act, and (3) actually intending to gain the indulgence. Additional conditions for gaining the Rosary Plenary Indulgence are the following: Five decades of the Rosary must be prayed continuously. The prayers of the Rosary must be prayed vocally and one must meditate upon the Mysteries of the Rosary. If the recitation of the Rosary is public, the Mysteries of the Rosary must be announced. Partial Indulgence—One may gain a partial indulgence for the Rosary's recitation in whole or in part in other circumstances," http://holyrosary.ageofmary.com/indulgences-of-the-rosary/.

11 Tetzel sources: James MacCaffrey, *History of the Catholic Church from the Renaissance to the French Revolution*, Vol. 1 (Maynooth, Ireland: St. Patrick's College, 2011); John Woolard, "Luther's Protest For The Ages; Stand Up: He questioned the Catholic Church, leading to a new religious direction," *Investor's Business Daily*, December 14, 2007, A3.

12 John L. Allen Jr., "Part of a Culture War? Hardly," as part of a discussion, "Sin, and Its Indulgences," *The New York Times*, February 13, 2009; see also MacCaffrey, *History of the Catholic Church from the Renaissance to the French Revolution*, 73–74.

13 John L. Allen Jr., *All the Pope's Men: The Inside Story of How the Vatican Really Thinks* (New York: Doubleday, 2004), 99: "Outlandish requests for indulgences, which was part of the landscape that led to the Protestant Reformation."

14 All the confusion over antipopes has occasionally led to the existence of two Popes with the same name (Innocent III, an antipope in 1179 and a Pope in 1198; John XXIII, a 1410 antipope and a 1958 Pope; and two antipopes named Victor IV, in 1138 and 1159). For some specific instances of challenges: Urban VI (1378–1389) and Boniface IX (1389–1404) were opposed by Robert of Geneva ("Clement VII") (1378–1394) as well as Pedro de Luna ("Benedict XIII") (1394–1417) and Baldassare Cossa ("John XXIII") (1400–1415); Innocent VII (1404–1406) was opposed by Pedro de Luna ("Benedict XIII") (1394–1417) and Baldassare Cossa ("John XXIII") (1400–1415); Gregory XII (1406–1415) was opposed in part by Pedro de Luna ("Benedict XIII") (1394–1417) and Baldassare Cossa ("John XXIII") (1400–1415), but mostly by Pietro Philarghi ("Alexander V") (1409–1410); and Eugene IV (1431–1447) was opposed by Amadeus of Savoy ("Felix V") (1439–1449); see also Kelly, *The Oxford Dictionary of Popes*. A digital chronological list of some antipopes is at http://www.philvaz.com/apologetics/a13.htm.

15 Kelly, *The Oxford Dictionary of Popes*; Owen Chadwick, *A History of the Popes, 1830–1914* (New York: Oxford University Press, 1998).
16 "Working Out the Road to Salvation: A Study of the Catholic Christian Faith," July 11, 2012, http://catholicischristian.wordpress.com/.
17 Chivot, *Vatican*, 81.
18 MacCaffrey, *History of the Catholic Church from the Renaissance to the French Revolution*, Vol. 1, 79.
19 Ibid., 72–73.
20 "For German-speakers the Basilica of St. Peter is an especially bittersweet sight, because it was the sale of indulgences to pay for its construction that helped trigger the Protestant Reformation": Allen, *All the Pope's Men*, 79.
21 The word *nepotism* had its origins in the Papal Court; the Latin *nepos* refers to both nephew and grandson. Through the Renaissance, Popes thought it normal to have a "Cardinal Nephew."
22 Joseph McCabe, "The Popes and Their Church," *Rationalist Encyclopædia*, 1948, p. 6e. McCabe was a freethinker and rationalist who had left the priesthood when he was twenty-nine years old. His subsequent writings were so critical of the church that some critics castigated him as a "Catholic basher." His biographer addressed in a separate chapter the question of whether McCabe's many writings could be dismissed as someone who was simply "an anti-Catholic bigot." His conclusion? Only "Catholic apologists" leveled that charge and a review of McCabe's many writings demonstrated he "was most certainly not bigoted. . . . If evidence of bigotry is wanted, it is to McCabe's enemies that we should turn. It is among these people where, not infrequently, bigotry and condescension mix happily." Bill Cooke, *A Rebel to His Last Breath: Joseph McCabe and Rationalism* (Amherst, NY: Prometheus Books, 2001), 211–12.
23 John Julius Norwich, *Absolute Monarchs: A History of the Papacy* (New York: Random House, 2011), Kindle edition, location 5557 of 8891.
24 Shaffern, "'Buying Back' Redemption"; McDowell, *Inside the Vatican*, 38–39.
25 Cameron, "Papal Finance"; see also "Modern Rome and the Papal Government," *Foreign Quarterly Review* 11 (1833): 661–62.
26 Pollard, *Money and the Rise of the Modern Papacy*, 23.
27 Pius VI quoted in Chivot, *Vatican*, 82.
28 Edward Elton Young Hales, *Revolution and Papacy, 1769–1846* (Garden City, NY: Hanover House, 1960), 247–54.
29 Bolton King, *A History of Italian Unity—A Political History of Italy from 1814–1871*, 2 vols. (London, 1909), Vol. 1, 75.
30 The early church made it illegal for clergy to charge any interest on loans (in 314 in the Councils of Arles and 325 at Necaea). The Council of Vienne in 1311 extended the ban to any Catholic, declaring that anyone who charged interest was a heretic. In light of that unyielding history, some contemporaneous historians thought that *Vix Pervenit* created a small loophole because Benedict defined usury as "an exorbitant rate of interest." An English translation of *Vix Pervenit* in its entirety is at http://www.papalencyclicals.net/Ben14/b14vixpe.htm.
31 Pollard, *Money and the Rise of the Modern Papacy*, 23.
32 David I. Kertzer, *The Popes Against the Jews: The Vatican's Role in the Rise of Modern Anti-Semitism* (New York: Alfred A. Knopf, 2001), 80. According to Kertzer, "Prohibited by law from owning land and kept out of trades controlled by the guilds, the Jews found in finance and money-lending the only economic path to prosperity open to them." (79). See also David Willey, *God's Politician: John Paul at the Vatican* (New York: St. Martin's, 1993), 206.
33 Niall Ferguson, *House of Rothschild: Money's Prophets 1798-1848*, Kindle edition, Vol. 1, 6419 of 14008). The Rothschilds worked with an Italian banker, Torlonia, on the Papal loan.
34 Egon Caesar Corti (Count), *The Rise of the House of Rothschild* (New York: Cosmopolitan Book Corporation, 1928), in which several instances are discussed about how the Rothschilds helped stabilize secular governments facing financial crises from the political tumult of the mid-nineteenth century; see also Virginia Cowles, *The Rothschilds: A Family of Fortune* (New York: Alfred A. Knopf, 1973); The Rothschilds' Paris-based branch served as the principal banker for Sardinia, and ultimately provided a unified Italian republic its first loan. See Rondo E. Cameron, "French Finance and Italian Unity: The Cavourian Decade," *American Historical Review*, Vol. LXII, no. 3 (April, 1957).
35 See generally Niall Ferguson, *House of Rothschild: Money's Prophets 1798-1848*, Vol. 1 (New York:

Viking, 1998); Niall Ferguson, *The House of Rothschild: The World's Banker, 1849–1999*, Vol. 2 (New York: Viking, 1999).

36 Cameron, "Papal Finance," 133.

37 Ferguson, *House of Rothschild*, Kindle edition, Vol. 1, 6419 of 14008.

38 Both quotes from Ludwig Börne are from Ferguson, *House of Rothschild*, Kindle edition, Vol. 1, 6425 of 14008.

39 Ibid., 6685 of 14008 and Vol. 2, locations 92, 195-96 of 15319.

40 Michael P. Riccards, *Vicars of Christ: Popes, Power, and Politics in the Modern World* (New York: Crossroad, 1998), 5–6; Owen Chadwick, *A History of the Popes, 1830–1914* (New York: Oxford University Press, 1998), 50.

41 For a good synopsis of Pius's life before becoming Pope at the age of fifty-four, see Jason Berry, *Render Unto Rome, The Secret Life of Money in the Catholic Church* (New York: Crown, 2011), 41–42.

42 Kelly, *The Oxford Dictionary of Popes*, 309.

43 Riccards, *Vicars of Christ*, 15; Mario Rossi, "Emancipation of the Jews in Italy," *Jewish Social Studies*, Vol. 15, No. 2, April 1953, 121.

44 Riccards, *Vicars of Christ*, 7; Chadwick, *A History of the Popes*, 64.

45 Chadwick, *A History of the Popes*, 73.

46 Edward Elton Young Hales, *Pio Nono: A Study in European Politics and Religion in the Nineteenth Century* (New York: P. J. Kenedy, 1954), 71.

47 Chadwick, *A History of the Popes*, 74–79.

48 The opulent Palazzo della Cancelleria (Palace of the Chancellery) was built for Cardinal Raffaele Riario, who was the Cardinal Chancellor for his uncle, Pope Sixtus IV. The money to build it reportedly came from a single night of high-stakes gambling by Riario with some of Europe's wealthiest aristocrats.

49 David Alvarez, *Spies in the Vatican: Espionage and Intrigue from Napoleon to the Holocaust* (Lawrence: University Press of Kansas, 2002), 11.

50 Norwich, *Absolute Monarchs*, Kindle edition, location 7162 of 8891.

51 Rossi, "Emancipation of the Jews in Italy," 131.

52 John Cornwell, *Hitler's Pope: The Secret History of Pius XII* (New York: Viking 1999), 300. Pius reinstituted medieval laws greatly limiting the professions available to Jews and punished them with special taxes. He also gave new impetus to a program of compulsory baptisms. See generally Rossi, "Emancipation of the Jews in Italy," 130.

53 *Annuaire de l'économie politique et de statistique* (Paris: Guillaumin, 1859), 279–80.

54 Pius IX canonized Pedro de Arbués for sainthood, a decision that prompted protest from Jews worldwide and even from some Catholics. That was because de Arbués was the First Inquisitor for Aragón during the Spanish Inquisition. He was personally responsible for torturing and killing thousands of Jews, and was himself killed by a Jewish merchant whose sister he had sentenced to death. Some in the church oddly defended the canonization by claiming there were worse inquisitors than de Arbués. Chadwick, *A History of the Popes*, 554–56.

55 Corti, *The Rise of the House of Rothschild*, 279; Ferguson, *The House of Rothschild*, Kindle edition, location 2337, 2341 of 15319.

56 Ferguson, *The House of Rothschild*, Kindle edition, Vol. 2, 2331–2348 of 15319.

57 The estimate on the number of Jews in the Papal States is from *Statistica della popolazione dello Stato Pontifico dell'anno 1853* (Rome: Ministerio del Commercio e Lavori Pubblici, 1857).

58 Ferguson, *The House of Rothschild*, Kindle edition, Vol. 2, location 13169 of 15319, n. 10.

59 Frank J. Coppa, *Cardinal Giacomo Antonelli and Papal Politics in European Affairs* (New York: New York University Press, 1990), 82.

60 Chadwick, *A History of the Popes*, 128–29.

61 Ferguson, *The World's Banker*, vol. 2, 27–29, 590; see also Pollard, *Money and the Rise of the Modern Papacy*, 29; Norwich, *Absolute Monarchs*, Kindle edition, location 6954 of 8891. The unwalled Rome ghetto survived through World War II.

62 Ferguson, *The House of Rothschild*, Kindle edition, Vol. 2, location 2854 of 15319.

63 Giancarlo Galli, *Finanza Bianca. La chiesa, i soldi, il potere* (Milan: Arnoldo Mondadori, 2004), 17.

64 Cameron, "Papal Finance." The portion about distrust and Masonry is from Frank J. Coppa, *Cardinal Giacomo Antonelli and Papal Politics in European Affairs* (New York: New York University Press, 1990).

65 Carlo Falconi, *Il Cardinale Antonelli: Vita e carriera del Richelieu italiano nella chiesa di Pio IX* (Milan: Mondadori 1983); Pollard, *Money and the Rise of the Modern Papacy*, 28; Riccards, *Vicars of Christ*, 18. The title Secretary of State had come into regular use at the Vatican during the Papacy of Innocent X in the mid-seventeenth century. Originally, the position was called Domestic Secretary.
66 Coppa, *Cardinal Giacomo Antonelli*, 2.
67 Chadwick, *A History of the Popes*, 92–93; see also Peter Godman, *Hitler and the Vatican: Inside the Secret Archives That Reveal the New Story of the Nazis and the Church* (New York: Free Press, 2004), 14.
68 Coppa, *Cardinal Giacomo Antonelli*, 225–29.
69 Ferguson, *The House of Rothschild*, Kindle edition, Vol. 2, location 2348 of 15319.
70 Isadore Sachs, *L'Italie, ses finances et son développement économique,1859–1884* (Paris, 1885), 456; Cameron, "Papal Finance," 134.
71 Cameron, "Papal Finance," 134–36; see also Coppa, *Cardinal Giacomo Antonelli*, 51, 85.
72 See generally *L'Osservatore Romano* in English at http://www.vatican.va/en/; and at http://www.osservatoreromano.va/it/; also see La Civiltà Cattolica at http://www.laciviltacattolica.it/it/. In the twentieth century, *L'Osservatore Romano* was sometimes mockingly referred to as *Pravda*, the Soviet Union's official newspaper. John L. Allen Jr., the Vatican reporter for the *National Catholic Reporter*, wrote that the comparison was made since *L'Osservatore Romano* "is filled with pictures and speeches by the Great Leader and because it muffles criticism." Allen cited an instance in 1914 when the paper printed a "stinging editorial" denouncing a report that Pius X had a cold. The Pope died the next day. Allen, *All the Pope's Men*, 48.
73 Pollard, *Money and the Rise of the Modern Papacy*, 8–9.
74 Cameron, "Papal Finance," 136.
75 Blount was British, but had moved to Paris as a young banker and was one of the era's most successful French-based financiers.
76 James Carroll, *Constantine's Sword: The Church and the Jews* (New York: Houghton Mifflin, 2002), 442.
77 Garry Wills, *Papal Sin: Structures of Deceit* (New York: Doubleday, 2000), 40. There were fewer than two hundred Jews living in Bologna. The Vatican had decimated the flourishing community with a series of restrictive laws during the sixteenth century. Pope Clement VIII finally expelled them from the Papal States in 1593, but some had gradually returned.

Families like the Mortoras thought they were safe since the church's policy was not to baptize a child living with his birth parents without the parents' consent. What they did not know was that the Vatican carved out an exception for children who were baptized when they were seriously ill. Even in instances without any apparent illness, church officials consistently upheld the baptisms. David I. Kertzer, *The Kidnapping of Edgardo Mortara* (New York: Alfred A. Knopf, 1997), Kindle edition, 59. The Mortara child had been baptized with tap water when he was only eleven months old. The church did not learn about it until he was nearly seven. Rossi, "Emancipation of the Jews in Italy," 130.

78 Kertzer, *The Kidnapping of Edgardo Mortara*, Kindle edition, 32-33-34, 55, 255. Kertzer writes "[t]he taking of Jewish children was a common occurrence in nineteenth-century Italy." Many of the children forcibly taken from parents, such as the 1844 case of a nineteen-month-old Jewish girl, ended up confined to the Casa dei Catecumeni (House of the Catechmen). That was a sixteenth-century Catholic organization started by Ignatius of Loyola, the founder of the Jesuits, and dedicated to converting non-Catholics. Jewish parents were barred from visiting their birth children. See also Cesare, *The Last Days of Papal Rome*, chapter XII, 176–84. In the case of Edgardo, he lived most of the time with seminarians in a Roman Catechmen and each Christmas stayed with the Pope.
79 The church dangled the possibility that if the parents converted to Catholicism their son might be returned. Without an ironclad promise that they would be reunited, they passed.
80 Chadwick, *A History of the Popes*, 130–31. A decade later, one of the most popular plays in Rome was "A Hebrew Family," a loose adaptation of the Mortara affair. The Vatican and its clerics were cast as villains. Cesare, *The Last Days of Papal Rome*, 179.
81 Kertzer, *The Kidnapping of Edgardo Mortara*, 158.
82 Kenneth Stowe, *Popes, Church, and Jews in the Middle Ages: Confrontation and Response* (Surrey, UK: Ashgate, 2007), 57–59.

83 Kertzer, *The Kidnapping of Edgardo Mortara*, 113, 136–37; Wills, *Papal Sin*, 41.
84 "Il piccolo neofito, Edgardo Mortara," *Civiltà Cattolica*, ser. 3, vol. 12 (1858), 389–90, cited in Kertzer.
85 Kertzer, *The Kidnapping of Edgardo Mortara*, 32, 81, 85, 157; see also Giacomo Martina, SJ, *Pio IX (1851–1866), Miscellanea historiae ecclesiasticae in Pontifica Universitate Gregoriana* 51 (1986).
86 When Edgardo was with Pius in the Papal Court, the boy sometimes hid under the Pontiff's clerical robe. The Pope enjoyed asking visitors, "Where is the boy?" Then he would lift his vestment to reveal the youngster. Edgardo became a priest, adding Pio to his name in honor of the Pope, whom he referred to as his "Father." Most of his life was spent as a missionary dedicated to converting Jews, and he even tried unsuccessfully to convert his own mother. Catholics in many countries became familiar with him as he regaled audiences with the tale of his conversion. He lived long enough to testify in the beatification process of Pius IX: "I greatly desire the beatification and canonization of the Servant of God." Mortara died in 1940 at an abbey in Belgium.
87 Kertzer, *The Kidnapping of Edgardo Mortara*, 257–59.
88 Coppa, *Cardinal Giacomo Antonelli*, 82.
89 Norwich, *Absolute Monarchs*, Kindle edition, location 7314 of 8891.
90 "The Catholic Church and Modern Civilization," *The Nation*, September 19, 1867, 229–30; Chadwick, *A History of the Popes*, 175–77; Wills, *Papal Sin*, 239–44.
91 For a copy of Pius IX's 1864 encyclical *Quanta Cura* and the *Syllabus of Errors*, see http://www.papalencyclicals.net/Pius09/p9quanta.htm and http://www.papalencyclicals.net/Pius09/p9syll.htm. Before he issued the *Syllabus*, Pius had consulted with his bishops about the contents. Ninety-six refused to give an opinion, and of the 159 who did reply, a third were opposed.
92 Wills, *Papal Sin*, 244.
93 Chadwick, *A History of the Popes*, 176–78.
94 Ibid., 195–98.
95 It is impossible to obtain an accurate vote since there was no public tally. An early report had the bishops in favor 451 to 88. But some historians believe 62 of those preferred an amended version with a more limited power of infallibility.
96 Hales, *Pio Nono*, 244.
97 Ferguson, *The House of Rothschild*, Kindle edition, location 2792 of 15319.
98 Frank J. Coppa, *The Italian Wars of Independence* (New York: Longman, 1992), 139–41.
99 Chadwick, *A History of the Popes*, 216.
100 Riccards, *Vicars of Christ*, 28.
101 Carlo F. Passaglia (trans. by Ernest Filalete). *De l'obligation pour le Pape Eveque de Rome de rester dans cette ville quoque elle devienne la capitale du Royame Italien* (Paris: Molini, 1861), 77–82.
102 Alvarez, *Spies in the Vatican*, 51; Chadwick, *A History of the Popes*, 226.
103 Coppa, *Cardinal Giacomo Antonelli and Papal Politics in European Affairs*, 165.
104 Pollard, *Money and the Rise of the Modern Papacy*, 30; Cameron, "Papal Finance," 137.
105 Carlo Crocella, *Augusta miseria: aspetti delle finanze pontificie nell'età del capitalismo* (Milan: Nuovo 1st ed. Italia, 1982), 66.
106 Coppa, *Cardinal Giacomo Antonelli*, 169.
107 Corrado Pallenberg, *Inside the Vatican* (New York: Hawthorn Books, 1960).
108 Pollard, *Money and the Rise of the Modern Papacy*, 30.
109 Segreteria di Stato (SdS), Spoglio di Pio X, b. 4, fasc. 16, Pensioni, undated, *Archivio Segreto Vaticano*, Vatican City, cited in Pollard, *Money and the Rise of the Modern Papacy*.
110 *Obolo dil San Pietro* [Peter's Pence]: http://www.vatican.va/roman_curia/secretariat_state/obolo_spietro/documents/index_it.htm; see Chadwick, *A History of the Popes*, 145. Until the eighteenth century, church historians referred to it only by its Latin name, *Denarius Sancti Petri*. See also F. Lieberman, "Peter's Pence and the Population of England about 1164," *The English Historical Review*, Vol. 11, no. 44, October 1896, 744–47.
111 Ralph Della Cava, "Financing the Faith: The Case of Roman Catholicism," *Church and State* 35 (1993): 37–61. Through the 1990s, Peter's Pence was all cash. Many times, Catholics granted an audience with the Pope passed large gifts of cash (which the Pope in turn handed to someone in his entourage). In the twenty-first century, the Vatican has adapted Peter's Pence to the digital age, allowing the faithful to use credit cards or bank wire transfers for their contributions. On the Vatican's website, Peter's Pence is described as "an ancient custom still alive today" and is "the financial support offered by the faithful to the Holy Father as a sign of the sharing in the concern of the Successor of

Peter for the many different needs of the Universal Church and for the relief of those most in need." See http://www.vatican.va/roman_curia/secretariat_state/obolo_spietro/documents/index_en.htm.

112 Thomas J. Reese, SJ, *Inside the Vatican: The Politics and Organization of the Catholic Church* (Cambridge: Harvard University Press, 1996), 225; Benny Lai, *Finanze Vaticane: Da Pio XI a Benedetto XVI* (Rome: Rubbettino Editore, 2012), 9.

113 Chadwick, *A History of the Popes*, 24. There were also sales of coupons that could be cashed in once the buyer arrived in Heaven. It is not clear if that was done with the church's blessing. Nino Lo Bello, *The Vatican Empire* (New York: Trident, 1968), 57–58.

114 Crocella, *Augusta Miseria*, 108.

115 Ambasciata d'Italia agli Stati Uniti, Pacco 33, 1903–07, April 17, 1903, Archivio Storico del Ministero degli Affari Esteri, Archive of the Italian Foreign Ministry (Rome), cited in Pollard, *Money and the Rise of the Modern Papacy.*

116 Sachs, *L'Italie, ses finances*, 456; see also Lo Bello, *The Vatican Empire*, 54–56.

117 Cameron, "Papal Finance," 137.

118 James Gollin, *Worldly Goods: The Wealth and Power of the American Catholic Church, the Vatican, and the Men Who Control the Money* (New York: Random House, 1971), 63–70.

119 On November 1, 1745, Pope Benedict XIV issued *Vix Pervenit: On Usury and Other Dishonest Profits*. It is available in its entirety at http://www.papalencyclicals.net/Ben14/b14vixpe.htm; see also Pollard, *Money and the Rise of the Modern Papacy,* 210, n. 1. Earning interest is still a contentious issue in Muslim countries, because the Koran bans it. But Muslims have largely skirted the prohibition since Islamic banks and investment companies deem the interest paid as "profits" from the money deposited, a financial transaction not prohibited by the Koran.

120 Joseph Clifford Fenton, "Sacrorum Antistitum and the Background of the Oath Against Modernism," CatholicCulture.org. See www.vatican.va/holy_father/pius_x/motu_proprio/documents/hf_p-x_motu-proprio_19100901_sacorum-antistitum_it.html/.

121 Guido Mazzoni, *Papa Pio IX,* 1849, pamphlet collection at Duke University Libraries, E.331.VI.

122 Pollard, *Money and the Rise of the Modern* Papacy, 38.

123 Ibid., 211; see also Kertzer, *The Popes Against the Jews*; and see also Wills, *Papal Sin*, 37–38.

124 David Chidester, *Christianity, A Global History* (New York: HarperCollins, 2000), 479-480.

125 Donald A. Nielsen, "Sects, Churches and Economic Transformations in Russia and Western Europe," *International Journal of Politics, Culture, and Society*, vol. 2, no. 4 (summer 1989), 496–97, 503–04, 517. The symbol of Protestant encouragement that workers get involved in free enterprise is the 1904 book—*The Protestant Ethic and the Spirit of Capitalism*—written by German sociologist Max Weber.

126 Chidester, *Christianity,* 480.

127 Samuel Gregg, "Did the Protestant Work Ethic Create Capitalism," *The Public Discourse*, January 21, 2014. See generally Chidester, *Christianity,* 487.

128 The law passed 185 to 106, with 217 abstentions.

129 Chadwick, *A History of the Popes*, 228–29.

130 Falconi, *Il Cardinale*, 488; see also Coppa, *Cardinal Giacomo Antonelli*, 118. Pius prayed that Jesus might show mercy to the "perverted and adulterous" lawmakers who had passed the legislation.

131 The encyclical, *Ubi Nos*, is available in English at http://www.papalencyclicals.net/Pius09/p9ubinos.htm.

132 Ibid.

133 The only thing to which Pius did not protest was the portion that converted the Church's large debt into an obligation assumed by the government: Cameron, "Papal Finance," 139.

134 Chadwick, *A History of the Popes*, 231–34.

135 Ibid., 271–72; see also John Thavis, *The Vatican Diaries: A Behind-the-Scenes Look at the Power, Personalities and Politics at the Heart of the Catholic Church* (New York: Viking, 2013), 7.

136 Collections in Segreteria di Stato, Archivo Nunziatura Napoli, scatole 125–27, Archivio Segreto Vaticano, Vatican City (ASV), cited in Alvarez, *Spies in the Vatican.*

Chapter 3: Enter the Black Nobles

1 Reese, *Inside the Vatican*, 96.

2 Chivot, *Vatican*, 49.

3 Norwich, *Absolute Monarchs*, Kindle edition, location 7538 of 8891.
4 Carlo Fiorentino, *La questione romana intorno al 1870: studi e documenti* (Rome: Archivo Guido Izzi, 1997), as relates to footnote f, 215.
5 Cameron, "Papal Finance," 13; Pollard, *Money and the Rise of the Modern Papacy*, 35.
6 Phillipe Levillain and François-Charles Uginet, *Il Vaticano e le frontiere della Grazia* (Milan, 1985), 100–101.
7 R. de Cesare, *The Last Days of Papal Rome* (Boston: Houghton Mifflin, 1909), 259. A full digital copy of *The Last Days of Papal Rome* is made available by the Sage Endowment Fund at http://archive.org/stream/lastdaysofpapalr00dece#page/n7/mode/2up. See also Coppa, *Cardinal Giacomo Antonelli*, 3, 80; Michael Walsh, *The Cardinals: Thirteen Centuries of the Men Behind the Papal Throne* (Grand Rapids, MI: Wm. B. Eerdmans Publishing, 2011), 188.
8 The Black Nobles reached their peak of power in the late nineteenth century. Benedict XIV slashed their numbers in the early twentieth century. In 1968, Pope Paul VI eliminated most of the titles still in use.
9 Falconi, *Il Cardinale*, 494–95.
10 Crocella, *Augusta miseria*, 177–78.
11 Coppa, *Cardinal Giacomo Antonelli*, 181.
12 Chadwick, *A History of the Popes*, 93–94; Coppa, *Cardinal Giacomo Antonelli*, 181. The sensational court case brought by Lambertini captivated the public. The judges thought it likely she might be Antonelli's daughter but said the evidence fell short of certainty. As a result, they let his original will stand.
13 Benny Lai, *Finanze e finanzieri vaticani tra l'ottocento e il novecento da Pio IX a Benedetto XV* (Milan: A. Mondadori, 1979), 87, 89 n. 2 (this book was updated in 2012 to *Finanze Vaticane: Da Pio XI a Benedetto XVI*, both are cited separately in these notes).
14 Ron Chernow, *The House of Morgan: An American Banking Dynasty and the Rise of Modern Finance* (New York: Grove, 1990), 285; iBook edition, 513.
15 Freemasonry was founded in England in the sixteenth century and before long it counted as members prominent rationalists and secularists throughout Europe. In Austria and France, in particular, Freemasons worked to destabilize the church and promote atheism. Since 1738 Catholics have been threatened with excommunication if they became Freemasons. See generally Chadwick, *A History of the Popes*, 304–7 and John J. Robinson, *Born in Blood: The Lost Secrets of Freemasonry* (New York: M. Evans, 1989), 307–12, 344–59.
16 Pollard, *Money and the Rise of the Modern Papacy*, 63.
17 Alberto Caracciolo, *Roma capitale. Dal Risorgimento all crisi dello stato liberale* (Rome, 1956), 162–64.
18 Richard A. Webster, *Industrial Imperialism in Italy, 1908–1915* (Berkeley: University of California Press, 1975), 154–55.
19 Malachi Martin, *Rich Church, Poor Church* (New York: G. P. Putnam's Sons, 1984), 175–76; Lo Bello, *The Vatican Empire*, 58.
20 The fascists had a small network of agents inside the city-state, all run by Arturo Bocchini, Rome's police chief. Through World War II, a midlevel cleric, Monsignor Enrico Pucci, directed three others: a Secretary of State employee, Stanislao Caterina; Virgilio Scattolini, a journalist at *L'Osservatore Romano;* and Giovanni Fazio, a Vatican policeman. Eric Frattini, *The Entity: Five Centuries of Secret Vatican Espionage* (New York: St. Martin's Press, 2008), 265, 460. See generally Alvarez, *Spies in the Vatican*, 53–55.
21 Levillain, and Uginet, *Il Vaticano e le frontiere della Grazia*, 104.
22 *The Irish Catholic Directory and Almanac for 1900 with Complete Directory in English* (Dublin: James Duffy and Co., 1900).
23 Mocenni quoted in Lai, *Finanze e finanzieri vaticani*, 178.
24 Pollard, *Money and the Rise of the Modern Papacy*, 67, n. 66.
25 Pius had an antiquated view even of the appropriate music to be played in the church. In addition to ending the practice of using castrati, he also banned women from choirs. Orchestras were abolished, as were pianos. Pius preferred only organs and Gregorian chants.
26 Chadwick, *A History of the Popes*, 280.
27 Michael Phayer, *Pius XII, the Holocaust, and the Cold War* (Bloomington: Indiana University Press, 2008), 138–39; see full encyclical at http://www.vatican.va/holy_father/leo_xiii/encyclicals/documents/hf_l-xiii_enc_15051891_rerum-novarum_en.html; see also Berry, *Render Unto*

Rome, 51. For a fuller discussion of the encyclical and its impact on Catholic trade unions in the political context of that era, see Chadwick, *A History of the Popes*, 312–20.

28 Historians seem perplexed at the apparent contradiction. See generally Pollard, *Money and the Rise of the Modern Papacy*, 76–77.

29 Giovanni Grilli, *La finanza vaticana in Italia* (Rome: Editori Riuniti, 1961), 26.

30 John F. Pollard, "Conservative Catholics and Italian Fascism: The Clerico-Fascists" and "Religion and the Formation of the Italian Working Class," in Martin Blinkhorn, ed., *Fascists and Conservatives: The Radical Right and the Establishment in Twentieth-Century Europe* (London: Routledge, 2003), 45, 171.

31 Chadwick, *A History of the Popes*, 281–84; 32030; 516–17.

32 Riccards, *Vicars of Christ*, 38–39.

33 Leo XIII condemned Americanism in January 1899. He addressed the issue of Christian democracy in Italy in January 1901 (*Graves de Communi*). Leo feared that "an era of liberty" meant that "spiritual direction . . . was less necessary." See also Allen, *All the Pope's Men*, 315; "Religion: America in Rome," *Time*, February 25, 1946.

34 Thomas T. McAvoy, "Leo XIII and America," in *Leo XIII and the Modern World*, ed. Edward T. Gargan (New York: Sheed & Ward, 1961); see also John Tracy Ellis, *The Life of James Cardinal Gibbons*, Vol. 2 (Milwaukee: Bruce Publishing, 1952); John C. Fenton, "The Teachings of the Testem Benevolentiae," *American Ecclesiastical Review* 129 (1953): 124–33.

35 *Diuturnum*, an encyclical on Civil Power, issued June 29, 1881. A digital copy is at http://www.vatican.va/holy_father/leo_xiii/encyclicals/documents/hf_l-xiii_enc_29061881_diuturnum_en.html.

Chapter 4: "Merely a Palace, Not a State"

1 Reese, *Inside the Vatican*, 88; The longest conclave was in the thirteenth century in which eighteen deadlocked cardinals argued for three years before settling on Gregory X.

2 Hoffman, *Anatomy of the Vatican*, 59–60.

3 Francis X. Seppelt and Klemens Löffler, *A Short History of the Popes* (St. Louis: B. Herder, 1932), 498; Chadwick, *A History of the Popes*, 332–41.

4 Kelly, *Dictionary of Popes*, 313.

5 Riccards, *Vicars of Christ*, 58.

6 Katherine Burton, *The Great Mantle: The Life of Giuseppe Melchiore Sarto, Pope Pius X* (New York: Longmans, Green, 1950), 157–58; Chadwick, *A History of the Popes*, 345.

7 For a detailed discussion of the history of the Curia, see Reese, *Inside the Vatican*, 106–39, 158–72; Norwich, *Absolute Monarchs*, Kindle edition, location 1736 of 8891; Allen, *All the Pope's Men*, 28–44, 68.

8 Chadwick, *A History of the Popes*, 367.

9 Norwich, *Absolute Monarchs*, Kindle edition, location 7544 of 8891.

10 Francis Xavier Murphy, "A Look at the Earth's Tiniest State," *Chicago Tribune*, August 31, 1982, 11.

11 In *Sapienti Consilio* (Wise Counsel) Pius wanted to eliminate eighteen dicasteries (departments of the Roman Curia). He managed to close ten and created two new ones. But the number of Curial workers stayed virtually the same. See a digital English translation at http://www.vatican.va/holy_father/pius_x/apost_constitutions/documents/hf_p-x_apc_19080629_ordo-servandus-normae-1_lt.html.

12 Alvarez, *Spies in the Vatican*, 73–74.

13 Anthony Rhodes, *The Power of Rome in the Twentieth Century* (New York: Franklin Watts, 1983), 195.

14 *Lamintabili Sane* (Lamentable Certainly—Syllabus Condemning the Errors of the Modernists), July 3, 1907. A digital copy is at http://www.papalencyclicals.net/Pius10/p10lamen.htm.

15 Cornwell, *Hitler's Pope*, 36–39.

16 Norwich, *Absolute Monarchs*, Kindle edition, location 7544 of 8891.

17 It was the Oath Against Modernism (*Motu Proprio Secrorum Antistium*). Fewer than fifty priests refused to take it, most of them German. See generally Chadwick, *A History of the Popes*, 355–59; see also Cornwell, *Hitler's Pope*, 39–40.

18 Historian John Cornwell theorized that the decree from Pius to lower the confessional age to seven inadvertently "prompted sex complexes" and that pedophile clerics used it to target their victims. John Cornwell, *The Dark Box: A Secret History of Confession* (New York: Basic Books, 2014).

19 M. De Bujanda and Marcella Richter, ed., *Index librorum prohibitorum: 1600–1966,* Vol. XI (Geneva: Librairie Droz, 2002).

20 Chadwick, *A History of the Popes,* 356.

21 In a 1907 decree, Pius branded the burgeoning "modernist movement"—represented in part by the works of Sigmund Freud, Albert Einstein, and Friedrich Nietzsche—as heresy. Intellectuals universally castigated Pius's thinking as a giant backward step for the church.

22 Archivo Segreto Vaticano, SdS, Spoglio di Pio X, fasc. 1, letter of April 2, 1905; fasc. 10, three receipts for a total of 500,000 lire, dated August 14, 1907, and September 28, 1914; see Pollard, *Money and the Rise of the Modern Papacy.*

23 Riccards, *Vicars of Christ,* 67.

24 Pius concentrated on Catholics in Poland, then under Russian control. The tsar considered it to be Papal interference in Russia's westernmost province.

25 Lai, *Finanze e finanzieri vaticani,* 262; see also Burton, *The Great Mantle,* 157, 205–6.

26 Lai, *Finanze e finanzieri vaticani,* 210–13. It is quoted slightly different in Spadolini, ed., *Il Cardinale Gasparri e la questione romana: Con brani delle memorie inedite* (Florence: 1971), 234: "The Vatican is merely a palace with a garden on the edge of Rome."

27 Lai, *Finanze e finanzieri vaticani,* 207.

28 Ibid., 259–60; Author interview with Benny Lai, September 20, 2006.

29 SdS, Spoglio de Pio X, fasc. 1, letter from Pius of September 28, 1912, ASV; see Pollard, *Money and the Rise of the Modern Papacy.*

30 Christopher Seton-Watson, *Italy from Liberalism to Fascism, 1870–1925* (Oxford: Routledge & Kegan Paul, 1979), 323.

31 Seton-Watson, *Italy from Liberalism to Fascism,* 323; Lai, *Finanze e finanzieri vaticani,* 262–63.

32 Daniel A. Binchy, *Church and State in Fascist Italy* (New York: Oxford University Press, 1941), 157–58. Seemingly everyone in the church noted that Karl Marx was Jewish. Although he was a secular Jew, most prelates incorrectly thought that his faith was instrumental to his political treatises that fueled socialism. The 1848 *The Communist Manifesto*—which Marx co-wrote with Friedrich Engels—was the anti-bible to the Vatican. It reinforced the widespread prejudice that Jews were inherently revolutionary, seeking by design the destabilization of established monarchies and the church. Anti-Semites pointed to Marx's celebration of the assassination of Paris's archbishop in 1871 by members of a revolutionary worker's commune. "The Jew is behind it all," wrote the hugely successful Catholic populist Edouard Drumont. See Carroll, *Constantine's Sword,* 426–38.

33 Richard A. Webster, *The Cross and the Fasces: Christian Democracy and Fascism in Italy* (Stanford: Stanford University Press, 1960), 14–15; Chadwick, *A History of the Popes,* 404.

34 Seton-Watson, *Italy from Liberalism to Fascism,* 388–89.

35 John F. Pollard, "Conservative Catholics and Italian Fascism: The Clerico-Fascists," in Martin Blinkhorn, ed., *Fascists and Conservatives: The Radical Right and the Establishment in Twentieth-Century Europe* (London: Routledge, 2003), 32–33.

36 Chadwick, *A History of the Popes,* 232; ibid., Lai, *Finanze e finanzieri vaticani,* 242, 243, n. 3; Italia e Principato di Monaco, 43, 80–84, Archivio degli Affari Ecclesiastici Straordinari, Archive for Extraordinary Ecclesiastical Affairs, Vatican Archives, Secretariat of State, Vatican City.

37 The formal title for the cleric who ran the Holy Office of the Inquisition was Inquisitor General. Some prelates preferred Secretary of the Inquisition. Inquisitor General, which raised connotations of the dark Spanish crusade to convert Jews, was last used in 1929.

38 Luigi De Rosa and Gabriele De Rosa, *Storia del Banco Di Roma,* Vol. 1 of 3 (Rome: Banco di Roma, 1982), 268; Account summaries listed in SdS, Spoglio di Pio X, fasc. 7, Rendiconto per il primo Trimestre del 1912, ASV, Rendiconto del secondo Trimestre del 1913, cited Pollard, *Money and the Rise of the Modern Papacy.*

39 Alberto Theodoli, *A cavallo di due secoli* (Rome: La Navicella, 1950), 49.

40 Richard A. Webster, "The Political and Industrial Strategies of a Mixed Investment Bank: Italian Industrial Financing and the Banca Commerciale, 1894–1915," *VSWG*: Vierteljahrschrift für Sozial-und Wirtschaftsgeschichte, 61. Bd., H. 3 (1974), 354. See note 25, Webster, *Industrial Im-*

perialism in Italy, 367; Anna Caroleo, *Le banche cattoliche dalla prima guerra mondiale al fascismo* (Venice: Studio Bibliografico Malombra, 1976), 30.
41 Lai, *Finanze e finanzieri vaticani*, 259; Pollard, *Money and the Rise of the Modern Papacy*, 100.
42 Webster, *Industrial Imperialism in Italy*, 157.
43 Webster, *The Political and Industrial Strategies of a Mixed Investment Bank*, 357–59, 362, 364.
44 Riccards, *Vicars of Christ*, 69.
45 Annibale Zambarbieri, "La devozione al papa," Part of the collection of Fondazione per le scienze religiose Giovanni XXIII, Catalogo pregresso della Biblioteca Giuseppe Dossetti (1953–2000), Location G-I-a-29bis-(22/II), Bologna, 71.
46 Webster, *Industrial Imperialism in Italy*, 150–55.

Chapter 5: An Unholy Alliance

1 Much is known about the behind-the-scenes politicking at the conclave that led to Benedict's election since Vienna's Cardinal Friedrich Gustav Piffl violated the rules by keeping a daily diary.
2 Alvarez, *Spies in the Vatican*, 86–87.
3 Walter H. Peters, *Life of Benedict XV* (Milwaukee: Bruce, 1959), 32–35.
4 Riccards, *Vicars of Christ*, 74; see also Cornwell, *Hitler's Pope*, 59.
5 John Pollard, "The Vatican and the Wall Street Crash: Bernardino Nogara and Papal Finances in the Early 1930s," *The Historical Journal*, 42, 4 (1999), 1081.
6 George Seldes, *The Vatican—Yesterday, Today and Tomorrow* (New York: Harper & Bros., 1934), 246; John N. Molony, *The Emergence of Political Catholicism in Italy: Partito Popolare, 1919–1926* (London, Croom Helm, 1977), 59.
7 John F. Pollard, *The Unknown Pope: Benedict XV (1914–1922) and the Pursuit of Peace* (London: Bloomsbury Academic, 2000), 115.
8 Molony, *The Emergence of Political Catholicism in Italy*, 59–61; Lo Bello, *The Vatican Empire*, 6263; see also Gollin, *Worldly Goods*, 437. For a counterview of Benedict's financial directorship of the church, see Pollard, *Money and the Rise of the Modern Papacy*, 110–26.
9 Douglas J. Forsyth, *The Crisis of Liberal Italy: Monetary and Financial Policy, 1914–1922* (Cambridge: Cambridge University Press, 1993), 330.
10 Klaus Epstein, *Matthias Erzberger and the Dilemma of German Democracy* (Princeton: Princeton University Press, 1959), 103–5.
11 De Rosa, *Storia del Banco di Roma*, Vol. 1, 82.
12 Ibid., Vol. 3, 101.
13 *Il Massager* (Pisa), *L'Eco di Bergamo* and *Il Corriere d'Italia* (Rome), *Il Momento* (Turin), and *L'Avvenire* (Bologna); Pollard, "The Vatican and the Wall Street Crash," 1081.
14 Records of the Apostolic Delegation in Washington (DAUS), b. 70, Prestito a favore dell'Unione Editoriale Romana (1915–16), letter of Archbishop Farley to Archbishop Bonzano, January 5, 1916, ASV; see also Pollard, *Money and the Rise of the Modern Papacy*,118–19.
15 Archives of the Vatican Secretariat of State, 1914–1918, 335, 833, 930; cited in Pollard, *Money and the Rise of the Modern Papacy.*
16 Franz von Stockhammern was a German diplomat, based in Rome, responsible for intelligence and propaganda programs in Italy. Alvarez, *Spies in the Vatican*, 92–94, 98.
17 Ibid., 91–93, 95–96.
18 Henri Daniel-Rops [Henri Jules Charles Petiot], *A Fight for God*, trans. John Warrington (New York: E. P. Dutton,1966), 234.
19 Dragoljub Zivojinovic, *The United States and the Vatican Policies: 1914–1918* (Boulder, CO: Colorado Associated University Press, 1978), 12–14.
20 Forsyth, *The Crisis of Liberal Italy*, 120.
21 Gaetano Salvemini, *Chiesa e stato in Italia* (Milan: Feltrinelli, 1969), 384.
22 General Directorate of Public Security (DGPA), H4, Vaticano, Notizie, Commissarato del Borgo, 1915, October 22, 1915, Archivio Centrale dello Stato, Italian Central State Archives, Rome (ACS).
23 Alvarez, *Spies in the Vatican*, 92.

24 William Renzi, *In the Shadow of the Sword: Italy's Neutrality and Entrance into the Great War 1914–1915* (New York: Peter Lang, 1987), 156–58; Epstein, *Matthias Erzberger*, 102.
25 Renzi, *In the Shadow of the Sword*, 156–57; Alvarez, *Spies in the Vatican*, 92, 305.
26 Peters, *Life of Benedict*, 127–38; Pollard, *The Unknown Pope*, 103–7.
27 Memo (unsigned), March 24, 1917, Uffico Centrale d'Investigazione, busta 3, f. 39, Direzione Generale della Pubblica Sicurezza, Archivo Centrale dello Stato, cited in Alvarez, *Spies in the Vatican*.
28 Letter, Monsignor Giuseppe Aversa to Cardinal Secretary of State, Pietro Gasparri, January 1917, Guerra Europe, 1914–1918: Iniziative Pace Santa Sede, January 1916–April 1917, Archivio degli Affari Ecclesiastici Straordinari, ACS.
29 Alvarez, *Spies in the Vatican*.
30 Frank J. Coppa, ed., *Controversial Concordats: The Vatican's Relations with Napoleon, Mussolini, and Hitler* (Washington, DC: Catholic University of America Press, 1999), 84.
31 Italian intelligence received reports that three ranking clerics in Switzerland, with covert connections to Vienna and Berlin, had drafted the Pope's peace plan. That was never confirmed. When John Francis Charles, the British Envoy Extraordinary to the Holy See, later heard that, he dismissed it as ludicrous. See generally Alvarez, *Spies in the Vatican*, 107.
32 Ibid., 110–11.
33 Memorandum, Eastern Report No. 37, Foreign Office, October 11, 1917, 24/144/12, 109–11, British Cabinet Papers, National Archives, Kew, UK; see also Alvarez, *Spies in the Vatican*, 110.
34 Pollard, *The Unknown Pope*, 68.
35 Ibid., 103.
36 Alvarez, *Spies in the Vatican*, 112. Italy's anticlerical Foreign Minister, Baron Sidney Constantino Sonnino, was the force behind Article XV of the Treaty of London, the clause barring any Papal participation.
37 For the widespread fear about the spread of communism in the aftermath of World War I, see Directorate of Intelligence, A Monthly Review of Revolutionary Movements in British Dominions Overseas and Foreign Countries, No. 32, June 1921, (CP 3168), 24/126/70, Cabinet Papers, National Archives, Kew, UK.
38 Giovanni Spadolini, ed., *Il Cardinale Gasparri* (Grassina, Italy: Le Monnier, 1997), 376–77; Pollard, *Money and the Rise of the Modern Papacy*, 121.
39 Molony, *The Emergence of Political Catholicism*, 59–60.
40 Ibid., 59.
41 Zambarbieri, "La devozione al papa," 72; Chadwick, *A History of the Popes*, 398.
42 Pollard, *Money and the Rise of the Modern Papacy*, 121; Scottá, ed., *La Conciliazione Ufficiosa*, Vols. 2, 3, January 3, 1917.
43 James J. Hennesey, *American Catholics: A History of the Roman Catholic Community in the United States* (New York: Oxford University Press, 1981), 234–36.
44 DAUS, letter of Bishop John T. McNicholas to Cardinal Giovanni Bonzano, September 27, 1919, Box 284, ACS, cited in Pollard, *Money and the Rise of the Modern Papacy*.
45 Berry, *Render Unto Rome*, 61; Seldes, *The Vatican*, 249; see also "Una firma per l'Italia pensando al mondo," *L'Osservatore Romano*, http://www.vatican.va/news_services/or/or_quo/cultura/2009/034q04a1.html); see also Indice Dei Fondi e relative mezzi di descrizione e di ricerca dell'Archivio Segreto Vaticano 2011, for additional reference points for Bonaventura Cerretti in the Vatican Archives, http://www.archiviosegretovaticano.va.
46 Pollard, *Money and the Rise of the Modern Papacy*, 114.
47 Lai, *Finanze Vaticane*, 12; Lo Bello, *The Vatican Empire*, 62, 131, 280. Some historians contend that no loan was necessary, and that Gasparri found the money he needed in a locked box in the late Pope's desk. But Gasparri himself said there was only 75,000 lire in the Pope's quarters, and he needed millions for the burial and ensuing conclave. Others suggest the American bishops made up the difference. But a loan from the Chicago Archdiocese did not come until 1928, six years after Benedict's death. Professor John Pollard, a Papal historian, says the report of the loan is "almost certainly an exaggeration," since a Rothschild archivist wrote him a letter in 1998 saying the bank had no record of it. However, if any loan was issued, it likely came from the Vienna branch of the Rothschilds. That cannot be confirmed since the Nazis seized those bank records in 1939 and they were never recovered.

48 Riccards, *Vicars of Christ,* 103.
49 Kertzer, *The Pope and Mussolini: The Secret History of Pius XI and the Rise of Fascism in Europe* (New York: Random House, 2014), Kindle edition, location 1628 of 10577.
50 Ministry of the Interior, Direzione Generale della Pubblica Sicurezza (General Directorate of Public Security), 1926, Box 113, H4, Notizie Vaticane, reports of October 3, 1926, and November 1, 1926, ACS; Luigi Lazzarini, *Pio XI* (Milan: Sesto San Giovanni, 1937), 312.
51 Pollard, *Money and the Rise of the Modern Papacy,* 132.
52 John F. Pollard, *The Vatican and Italian Fascism, 1929–32: A Study in Conflict* (Cambridge: Cambridge University Press, 2005), 22.
53 Peter C. Kent, *The Pope and the Duce: The International Impact of the Lateran Agreements* (New York: St. Martins, 1981), 5.
54 See generally Thomas B. Morgan, *A Reporter at the Papal Court: A Narrative of the Reign of Pope Pius XI* (New York: Longmans, Green, 1937).
55 See generally E. Pacelli, *Erster Apostolischer Nuntius beim deutschen Reich, Gesammelte Reden,* ed. Ludwig Kaas (Berlin, 1930), 58 ("Primate des Reichsgedankens/Triumph über den düsteren Dämon der Gewalt").
56 Kertzer, *The Pope and Mussolini,* Kindle edition, location 1684 of 10577; Edward R. Tannenbaum, *The Fascist Experience: Italian Society and Culture, 1922–1945* (New York: Basic Books, 1972), 186–88.
57 William Teeling, *Pope Pius XI and World Affairs* (New York: Fredrick A. Stokes, 1937), 129.
58 Coppa, *Controversial Concordats,* 20–21.
59 Pollard, *Money and the Rise of the Modern Papacy,* 133.
60 Coppa, *Controversial Concordats,* 22–23.
61 Alexander J. De Grand, *Italian Fascism: Its Origins and Development* (Lincoln: University of Nebraska Press, 2000), 46; Binchy, *Church and State in Fascist Italy,* 139–40.
62 Pollard, "Conservative Catholics and Fascism: The Clerico-Fascists," 39.
63 William Teeling, *Pope Pius XI,* 112–13.
64 Pollard, *Money and the Rise of the Modern Papacy,* 133.
65 Pollard, "Conservative Catholics and Fascism: The Clerico-Fascists," 38–39; John N. Molony, *The Emergence of Political Catholicism in Italy: Partito Popolare 1919-1926* (London: Rowman and Littlefield, 1977), 130-31.
66 Pollard, *Money and the Rise of the Modern Papacy,* 130, n. 9; Lo Bello, *The Vatican Empire,* 59–61.
67 Caroleo, *Le banche cattoliche,* 120.
68 Leone Castelli *Quel tanto di territorio: ricordi di lavori ed opera eseguiti nel Vaticano durante il Pontificato di Pio XI (1922–1939)* (Rome: Edizioni Fuori Comercio, 1948), 46–50.
69 See generally Italo Insolera, *Roma Moderna* (Turin, 1971); see also Pollard, *Money and the Rise of the Modern Papacy,* 134–35.
70 DAUS, b. 70, Prestito a favore dell'Unione Editoriale Romana (1915–16), letter of Bonzano to Gasparri, January 10, 1916, ASV, cited in Pollard, *Money and the Rise of the Modern Papacy.*
71 Edward R. Kantowicz, *Corporation Sole: Cardinal Mundelein and Chicago Catholicism* (North Bend, IN: University of Notre Dame Press, 1983), 47, 562; Berry, *Render Unto Rome,* 64; Lo Bello, *The Vatican Empire,* 59. The Pope even asked a young American monsignor, Francis Spellman, for three cars. See Berry, *Render Unto Rome,* 64.
72 Riccards, *Vicars of Christ,* 117.
73 Ibid., 49; see also Pollard, *Money and the Rise of the Modern Papacy,* 136–37.
74 Thomas E. Hachey, ed., *Anglo-Vatican Relations, 1914–1939: Confidential Annual Reports of the British Ministers to the Holy See* (Boston: G. K. Hall, 1972), 70–71.
75 Seldes, *The Vatican,* 23.
76 Kertzer, *The Pope and Mussolini,* Kindle edition, location 1067 of 10577; Lo Bello, *The Vatican Empire,* 64.
77 Coppa, *Controversial Concordats,* 94. The suggestion that the fascists might reach an accommodation with the church caused an uproar at the party's first national congress in 1919. For a fuller history of the fascist opposition to any accord with the church: Arnaldo Suriani Cicchetti, "L'Opposizione italiana (1929–1931) ai Patti Lateranensi," *Nuova Antologia,* July 1952; see also Berry, *Render Unto Rome,* 63.
78 The OSS concluded later that Tacchi Venturi was one of two ranking Jesuits who was a "tireless supporter of Fascist political movements in every country including Italy" and that he "initiated

the negotiations for a concordat between the Vatican and the Fascist State." J.C.H. to A.W.D. (Allen Dulles), OSS, September 10, 1942, RG 226, E217, Box 20, Location 00687RWN26535, National Archives and Records Administration (NARA), Washington, DC/College Park, Maryland. See also Riccards, *Vicars of Christ*, 107; "Why the Pope Chose to Sign the Concordat," *The New York Times*, March 31, 1929; citations to the Lateran Treaty: a digital copy is available at http://www.vaticandiplomacy.org/laterantreaty1929.htm. It is an accurate English translation of the original maintained in the Vatican Archives.

79 F. Pacelli, Journal de la réconciliation—With an appendix of records and documents, Libreria Editrice Vaticana, Vatican City 1959: these are notes of the negotiations by Francesco Pacelli, inherited from Eugenio Pacelli, under direction not to be made public until 1959, at which point they were published by Monsignor Michele Maccarrone, Director of the "Journal of the History of the Church in Italy." See the discussion in Lai, *Finanze Vaticane*, 103.

80 Francesco was a cousin to Ernesto Pacelli, who had been the financial advisor to Pius X. Salvatore Cortesi, "Italy to Indemnify Church, Rome Hears," *The New York Times*, February 11, 1928, 4. The *Times* referred to Tacchi Venturi as "a scholar in history and literature" who was the Vatican's "chief negotiator" but was also someone who "remains in the dark and is almost unknown." It was not possible for the Pope to send his Secretary of State to the talks since the church did not yet recognize Italy's sovereignty and it was considered more likely for there to be a leak if a high ranking official represented the Vatican. See Kertzer, *The Pope and Mussolini*, Kindle edition, location 1872 of 10577.

81 The retiring Secretary of State, Pietro Gasparri, was Pacelli's mentor and had strongly backed his appointment.

82 Arnaldo Cortesi, "Vatican and Italy Sign Pact Recreating a Papal State: 60 Years of Enmity Ended," *The New York Times*, February 12, 1929, 1. An original of the Lateran Pacts is maintained by the Vatican.

83 Chivot, *Vatican*, 70; P. C. Kent, *The Pope and the Duce: The International Impact of the Lateran Agreements* (London: Macmillan, 1981), Ch. 9, 10.

84 Coppa, *Controversial Concordats*, 95–99.

85 Thomas J. Reese, SJ, *Inside the Vatican: The Politics and Organization of the Catholic Church* (Cambridge: Harvard University Press, 1996).

86 Susan Zuccotti, *Under His Very Windows: The Vatican and the Holocaust in Italy* (New Haven: Yale University Press, 2002), 19.

87 Gerhard Besier, with the collaboration of Francesca Piombo, translated by W. R. Ward, *The Holy See and Hitler's Germany* (New York: Palgrave Macmillan, 2007), 67–71.

88 Pollard, "The Vatican and the Wall Street Crash," 1079. Pollard estimates the conversion was 19 lire to the dollar.

89 Mussolini later tried discounting how much Italy gave the Vatican by claiming in a speech to Parliament that the billion lire in bonds was really worth "only" 800 million lire. Others tried minimizing the impact of such an enormous payout to the church by arguing that the Vatican would end up spending much of it back into Italy between employment, construction, and property purchases. Ibid., 1080; See also M. McGoldrick, "New Perspectives on Pius XII and Vatican Financial Transactions During the Second World War," *The Historical Journal* 55, no. 4 (December 2012): 1030; Gollin, *Worldly Goods*, 438. See the text of the Lateran Financial Convention at http://www.concordatwatch.eu/showtopic.php?org_id=878&kb_header_id=39241.

As a concession, the Vatican agreed not to sell the bonds it received as part of the settlement for at least ten years. That meant that the church had a direct stake in Mussolini's success; see "Pope and Politics," *The Nation*, December 11, 1937, 662.

90 Francesco Pacelli, *Diario della conciliazione* (Libreria Editrice Vaticana, 1959), 19, 26, 39. See generally Pollard, *Money and the Rise of the Modern Papacy*, 138–43, and Lai, *Finanze Vaticane*, 8; see also Salvatore Cortesi, "Italy to Indemnify Church, Rome Hears," *The New York Times*, February 11, 1928, 4.

91 Lo Bello, *The Vatican Empire*, 67.

92 *L'Osservatore Romano*, February 12, 1929; "Pope Praises Agreement," *The New York Times*, February 14, 1929; *Il Monitore Ecclesiastico*, March 1929; see also Berry, *Render Unto Rome*, 65.

93 Godman, *Hitler and the Vatican*, 15.

94 Ronald J. Rychlak, *Hitler, the War, and the Pope* (Columbus, MS: Genesis, 2000), 36–37.

95 Ludwig Kaas, "Der Konkordatstyp der faschischten Italien," in the *Zeitschrift fur auslandische offentliches Recht und Volkerrecht* (Berlin: 1933), 510–11.

96 Lo Bello, *The Vatican Empire*, 66.
97 Cornwell, *Hitler's Pope*, 115; see generally Kertzer, *The Pope and Mussolini*, Kindle edition, location 2065 of 10577.
98 Riccards, *Vicars of Christ*, 109.
99 Binchy, *Church and State in Fascist Italy*, 186.
100 Quoted in Godman, *Hitler and the Vatican*, 11; see also Paul Blanshard, "The Roman Catholic Church and Fascism," *The Nation*, March 1948, 392.
101 Robert Dell, in *The Nation*, made an assumption that was widespread at the time about the concordat: "It seems hardly doubtful that this agreement ties the church up with Fascism and that henceforth they stand or fall together in Italy. It becomes the interest of the Papacy to support Fascist policy at home and abroad, for, although any regime that might succeed to Fascism might well accept the 'Vatican City,' no other regime would accept the Concordat." Dell and others were right that the concordat inextricably bound the church and the fascist state. The mistake was in believing that no future secular government would embrace the deal Mussolini brokered. In fact, although Italians abandoned fascism in 1943, no subsequent Italian government has challenged the substance of the Lateran Pacts. See generally Robert Dell, "The Papal-Fascist Alliance," *The Nation*, March 27, 1929, vol. 128, no. 3325, 368–69.

Chapter 6: "The Pope Banker"

1 Lai, *Finanze Vaticane*, 105–6.
2 While an undergraduate student, he also had a brief mining job at Brescia.
3 At that time, BCI was far more than simply a bank. It was the financial element in an international syndicate, giving BCI interlocking ownership and management stakes in many industries.
4 Nogara worked for Volpi in several ventures. In Bulgaria it was a mining operation (Société Minière de Bulgarie), and in Istanbul the BCI-funded conglomerate Società Commerciale d'Oriente. In Montenegro, Nogara had small equity with Volpi in a government tobacco monopoly. Volpi also used Nogara as a consultant at Thessaloniki Limited Partnership G. Volpi, A. & C. and Corinaldi at Geneva.
5 BCI was the primary financier for Volpi's business ventures since the start of his career. Sometimes the bank even took small ownership interests in the projects. In Istanbul, BCI had enormous sums at stake. Professor Richard Webster, in his definitive history of industrial development in Italy at the start of the twentieth century, called Volpi and Nogara "the great international agents of the Banca Commerciale." Webster, *Industrial Imperialism in Italy*, 158. Volpi's surviving papers and correspondence are split between the archives of the Ministry of Foreign Affairs, Rome, and the private archives of Banca Commerciale and the Banca d'Italia (Bank of Italy), most of which are in Rome. See also Lai, *Finanze Vaticane*, 105–6.
6 The Rome Chamber of Commerce was the representative of the Italian creditors to the Ottoman Empire. Donald Quataert, *The Ottoman Empire, 1700–1922* (Cambridge: Cambridge University Press, 2000); see also Memorandum, Treaty of Peace with Turkey from the Supreme Council of the Allied Powers, February 17, 1920, 24/98/65, 253, Cabinet Papers, National Archives, Kew, UK; see also Webster, *Industrial Imperialism in Italy*, 195, 255.
7 Pollard, *Money and the Rise of the Modern Papacy*, 145; and "The Vatican and the Wall Street Crash," 1078.
8 Pollard, "The Vatican and the Wall Street Crash," 1079. Nogara also had briefly bought some bonds for the Vatican in 1914, while he was working in Istanbul. It is not clear whether Pius knew about that work or if it played a factor in his hiring of Nogara.
9 Alessandra Kersevan and Pierluigi Visintin, *Giuseppe Nogara: luci e ombre di un arcivescovo, 1928–1945* (Udine: Kappa Vu, 1992), 10–11.
10 Gollin, *Worldly Goods*, 439–40.
11 Chernow, *The House of Morgan*, iBook edition, 513.
12 Lai, *Finanze Vaticane*, 108, citing an interview by Lai of Massimo Spada, March 7, 1979.
13 See generally Pollard, *Money and the Rise of the Modern Papacy*, 143–49; see also Giovanni Belardelli, "Un viaggio di Bernardino Nogara negli Stati Uniti" (November 1937), in *Storia Contemporanea*, XXIII, (1992), 321–38.
14 Pollard, "The Vatican and the Wall Street Crash," 1080.

15 Lai, *Finanze Vaticane*, 13.
16 Chernow, *The House of Morgan*, iBook edition, 514.
17 Lai, *Finanze Vaticane*, 10–11.
18 Nogara took notes of his meetings with Pius XI, stopping when Pius XII became Pope in 1939. The journals are in the custody of the Nogara family, which has selectively made them available to historians, most extensively for John F. Pollard in his 2005 book, *Money and the Rise of the Modern Papacy: Financing the Vatican, 1850–1950* (Cambridge: Cambridge University Press); Renzo De Felice also cited information from Nogara's journals in "La Santa Sede e il conflitto italo-etiopico nel diario di Bernardino Nogara," *Storia Contemporanea*, 4 (1977): 823–34; as did Belardelli in "Un viaggio di Bernardino Nogara," 321–8. My inquiries to the Nogara family went unanswered. I asked Professor Pollard for assistance. In February 2013, he informed me by email that he had "tried to persuade" the family to publish the papers, but they had declined. Since I was unable to personally review the journals, the citations to the Archivo Famiglia Nogara (AFN) are from Pollard's book, unless otherwise indicated.
19 Tardini quoted in Lai, *Finanze Vaticane*, 110.
20 Corrado Pallenberg, *Inside the Vatican* (New York: Hawthorn, 1960), 188.
21 Archivo Famiglia Nogara, Personal Papers of Bernardino Nogara, Rome, diary entry for January 18, 1933, cited in Pollard, *Money and the Rise of the Modern Papacy*, 156.
22 Nogara did not then expect that the different Curia departments would still run a deficit and expect a subsidy from his well-funded ASSS. His diary reveals his frustration at the lack of adequate oversight inside the Vatican. See generally Pollard, "The Vatican and the Wall Street Crash," 1084.
23 Massimo Spada, a layman who started working in 1929 in the Special Administration, said at that time "there were only bonds." Lai, *Finanze Vaticane*, 107; Benny Lai interview with Spada, March 7, 1979.
24 Lai, *Finanze Vaticane*, 14, 17; Hachey, *Anglo-Vatican Relations*, 202, 226; Chernow, *The House of Morgan*, 286.
25 Seldes, *The Vatican*, 307–8.
26 See generally Mark Aarons and John Loftus, *Unholy Trinity: The Vatican, the Nazis, and the Swiss Banks* (New York: St. Martin's/Griffin, 1998), 294–95.
27 Ibid., 294–95.
28 Giuseppe Guarino and Gianni Toniolo, eds., *La Banca d'Italia e il sistema bancario, 1919–1936* (Bari and Rome: 1993), 582–83. See digital copy at http://www.bancaditalia.it/pubblicazioni/pubsto/collsto/docu/coll_sto_docum.pdf. Also Pollard, "The Vatican and the Wall Street Crash," 1083.
29 Pollard, *Money and the Rise of the Modern Papacy*, 150.
30 See generally ibid., 150–53; Pollard, "The Vatican and the Wall Street Crash," 1082–83.
31 Lai, *Finanze Vaticane*, 13.
32 Not all the expansion worked as planned. The telegraph office, for instance, sat mostly dormant, used only for sending out devotional prayers. The post office workers who sold the Vatican commemorative stamps kept the money instead of putting it into the church's coffers. And the railway never turned a profit. See generally Cameron, "Papal Finance." The Vatican prison, seldom used, was closed in the 1960s (in 2012, the prison was briefly reopened). Lo Bello, *The Vatican Empire*, 42–48. But the expansion of Vatican City was impressive, eventually counting between eleven and twelve thousand rooms in the connecting buildings.
33 Castelli, *Quel tanto di territorio*, 47–49.
34 Pollard, *Money and the Rise of the Modern Papacy*, 151, n. 5; The building frenzy was not limited to the property inside the mini-state's walls. On church land in Trastevere, the Palazzo San Calisto was built for the expanding Vatican bureaucracy. The Papal villa, Castel Gandolfo, was restored, and near it a modern observatory erected. Eventually, the Via della Conciliazione was built, creating a triumphal avenue from the Tiber River to the Vatican.
35 Pollard, "The Vatican and the Wall Street Crash," 1082.
36 Hachey, *Anglo-Vatican Relations*, 228.
37 Arnaldo Cipolla, "Due Giorni in Vaticano," *La Stampa*, November 16, 1931.
38 Binchy, *Church and State*, 514, 517–22.
39 See a digital copy of the encyclical at http://www.papalencyclicals.net/Pius11/P11FAC.HTM.
40 Alvarez, *Spies in the Vatican*. 159–65.

41 The previous month, Pius had issued another encyclical, *Quadragesimo Anno* (The 40th Year), that included an oblique criticism about Jewish control of international finances: "[I]t is obvious that not only is wealth concentrated in our times but an immense power and despotic economic dictatorship is consolidated in the hands of a few, who often are not owners but only the trustees and managing directors of invested funds which they administer according to their own arbitrary will and pleasure. This dictatorship is being most forcibly exercised by those who, since they hold the money and completely control it, control credit also and rule the lending of money. Hence they regulate the flow, so to speak, of the life-blood whereby the entire economic system lives, and have so firmly in their grasp the soul, as it were, of economic life that no one can breathe against their will." See *Quadragesimo Anno* at http://www.vatican.va/holy_father/pius_xi/encyclicals/documents/hf_p-xi_enc_19310515_quadragesimo-anno_en.html.

42 Kent, *The Pope and the Duce*, 119–24; see Kertzer, *The Pope and Mussolini*, Kindle edition, location 1173, 1912 of 10577.

43 Pollard, *Money and the Rise of the Modern Papacy*, 157.

44 Hachey, *Anglo-Vatican Relations*, 229.

45 Ibid., 259.

46 R. J. B. Bosworth, "Tourist Planning in Fascist Italy and the Limits of Totalitarian Culture," *Contemporary European History* 6, no. 1 (March 1997): 17. Holy Years are always profitable for the church, and normally held every twenty-five years. Sometimes, new saints were rushed through the canonization process in order to attract pilgrims and tourists. For instance, to meet the 1950 deadline for a Holy Year celebration, Pius XII crammed through in near record time the sainthood of Maria Goretti, an eleven-year-old Italian girl who had been killed while resisting a rape. Many church elders were skeptical of her qualifications for sainthood. However, her case drew front-page newspaper coverage and her elevation to a saint resulted in record numbers of Italian worshippers at that year's event. See Hoffman, *Anatomy of the Vatican*, 118. See also Kertzer, *The Pope and Mussolini*, Kindle edition, location 1567 of 10577.

47 Archives of the Archdiocese of Chicago, Mundelein Papers, 1872–1939, 3/36, letter of Pius to Cardinal Mundelein, December 12, 1933; Pius reveals in that letter that he had seriously underestimated the impact of the Great Depression, especially as it had affected America, a country whose Catholics he considered a reliable source of money.

48 Archivo Famiglia Nogara, Personal Papers of Bernardino Nogara, Rome, diary entry for February 25, 1931, cited in Pollard, *Money and the Rise of the Modern Papacy*.

49 Ibid., March 23, 1932; see also Pollard, "The Vatican and the Wall Street Crash," 1086.

50 Pollard, "The Vatican and the Wall Street Crash," 1086.

51 Ibid., April 6, 1933.

52 Ibid., August 19, 1932, and July 30, 1933.

53 Pollard, "Conservative Catholics and Fascism: The Clerico-Fascists," 39.

54 Lai, *Finanze Vaticane*, 13.

55 Pius might have considered it a relief not to be bothered with too many details of what Nogara was doing. A trait that one author noted in his book about the modern-day Vatican was also true about church officials then: "Vatican officials would sooner talk about sex than money." Kenneth L. Woodward, *Making Saints: How the Catholic Church Determines Who Becomes a Saint, Who Doesn't, and Why* (New York: Touchstone, 1996), 110.

56 Archivo Famiglia Nogara, Personal Papers of Bernardino Nogara, Rome, diary entry for September 21, 1933, cited in Pollard, *Money and the Rise of the Modern Papacy*.

57 Lai, *Finanze Vaticane*, 108. This was a long-term strategy, picking up steam with even larger purchases in 1933.

58 The church still owns some of the property Nogara bought. David Leigh, "How the Vatican Built a Secret Property Empire Using Mussolini's Millions," *The Guardian*, January 21, 2013, 1; Regarding the actions undertaken by Nogara at the time, see Nogara's diary, entry of Archivo Famiglia Nogara, Personal Papers of Bernardino Nogara, Rome, diary entry for July 24, 1933, as cited in Pollard, *Money and the Rise of the Modern Papacy*, AFN; McGoldrick, "New Perspectives on Pius XII and Vatican Financial Transactions During the Second World War," 1033.

59 Archivo Famiglia Nogara, Personal Papers of Bernardino Nogara, Rome, diary entry for February 15, 1932, cited in Pollard, *Money and the Rise of the Modern Papacy*; Gollin, *Worldly Goods*, 442–44.

60 Nogara's eight years of diary entries do not provide details about how, where, or why he invested the Vatican's money. It is instead a generic listing of his audiences with Pius XI, one about every ten days. It resembles more an expanded day journal than a comprehensive personal diary.

61 John F. Pollard, "The Vatican and the Wall Street Crash: Bernardino Nogara and Papal Finances in the Early 1930s," *The Historical Journal* 42, no. 4 (December 1999): 1087–88.

62 Nogara first used a shell corporation in 1913 when he was in Constantinople and bid on government contracts that could be issued only to Ottoman subjects. By the time he was utilizing shell and holding companies at the Vatican almost twenty years later, he was as knowledgeable as any banker of his day.

63 In March 1939, not long before Henri de Maillardoz moved from Credit Suisse to the Vatican, he presided over a special board meeting of Grolux, Nogara's Luxembourg holding company. Maillardoz ensured that the company's bylaws were amended so it could operate in secrecy from Switzerland for the remainder of the war. The Luxembourg holding company's full name was Groupement Financier Luxembourgeois (Grolux S.A.). Grolux also worked in tandem with another of Nogara's Swiss-based holding companies, Profima. *Memorial du Grand Duché de Luxembourg, Recueil Special, 1931.* 1037–44, 1177–78; see also Ernest Muhlen, *Monnaie et circuits financiers au Grand Duché de Luxembourg* (Luxembourg, 1968), 105; Pollard, *Money and the Rise of the Modern Papacy*, 161; and McGoldrick, "New Perspectives on Pius XII and Vatican Financial Transactions During the Second World War," 1032–35.

64 Companies House, London, File 270820, British Grolux Ltd., Annual Returns, 1932–33; 1936–37; 1945–46; Pollard, *Money and the Rise of the Modern Papacy*, 160–61; see also Archivo Famiglia Nogara, Personal Papers of Bernardino Nogara, Rome, diary entry for April 20, 1932, cited in Pollard, *Money and the Rise of the Modern Papacy.*

65 Pollard, "The Vatican and the Wall Street Crash," 1088.

66 OSS files, Box 168, XL 1257, report from Berne, July 7, 1945, NARA.

67 Chernow, *The House of Morgan*, 96, iBook edition, 514.

68 Ibid., hardcover edition, 495–97.

69 Chernow, *The House of Morgan,* iBook edition, 514.

70 ScdA, "CV di Bernardino Nogara," November 14, 1958, Archivo Storico della Banca Commerciale Italiana, Historical Archive of the Banca Commerciale Italiana, Milan, ASBCI. Nogara became a director on the board of Montecatini Company, later Montecatini Edison. His experience there encouraged him to subsequently invest in synthetic resins, textiles, and electric power.

71 Nogara was a director, among others, of a leading bank, Istituto Italiano di Credito Fondiario; Italy's biggest insurance firm, the Assicurazioni Generali; one of the country's largest railway companies, the Società Italiana per le Strade Ferrate Meridionali; the property behemoth Istituto Romano per di Beni Stabili; chemical conglomerate Società Elettrica ed Elettrochimica del Caffaro; petrochemical society per l'Industria Petrolifera e Chimica; the mining company Società Mineraria e Metallurgica de Pertusola; the papermaker Cartiere Burgo; and the electrical supply utility Società Adriatica di Elettricità.

72 Pollard, *Money and the Rise of the Modern Papacy*, 173.

73 Vera Zamagni, *The Economic History of Italy, 1860–1990: Recovery After Decline* (Oxford: Clarendon Press, 1997), 300–3.

74 Gollin, *Worldly Goods*, 445–46.

75 See generally De Rosa and De Rosa, *Storia del Banco di Roma*, Vols. 1–3, an authorized history of the bank.

76 Lo Bello, *The Vatican Empire*, 70–71.

77 Pollard, *Money and the Rise of the Modern Papacy*, 172–73.

78 Ibid., 173; Christopher Kobrak and Per H. Hansen, eds., *European Business, Dictatorship, and Political Risk 1920–1945* (New York: Berghahn Books, 2004), 225–26.

79 Raghuram Rajan and Luigi Zingales, *Saving Capitalism from the Capitalists: How Open Financial Markets Challenge the Establishment and Spread Prosperity to Rich and Poor Alike* (New York: Random House, 2003), 213.

80 Lo Bello, *The Vatican Empire*, 69–70.

81 Archivo Famiglia Nogara, Personal Papers of Bernardino Nogara, Rome, diary entry for September 21, 1933, cited in Pollard, *Money and the Rise of the Modern Papacy*; Grilli, *La finanza vaticana,* 71; Some of the key directors Nogara selected included Felippo Cremonesi, the Marquis

Giuseppe Della Chiesa (Benedict XV's nephew), Giuseppe Gualdi, Francesco Mario Odasso, Giovanni Rosmini, Prince Francesco Boncompagni Ludovisi, and Count Franco Ratti (Pius XI's nephew).

82 Gianni Toniolo, *L'economia dell'Italia fascista* (Bari, Italy, 1980), 135; Gollin, *Worldly Goods*, 446–47.

83 Archivo Famiglia Nogara, Personal Papers of Bernardino Nogara, Rome, diary entry for November 4, 1931, cited in Pollard, *Money and the Rise of the Modern Papacy*: The church was the most powerful financial force in Rome. In Milan, Nogara installed his son-in-law as head of a holding company that became the city's largest purchaser of real estate.

84 Pollard, *The Vatican and Italian Fascism*, 154, 187–89; Pallenberg, *Inside the Vatican*, 31. Pacelli helped Pius XI draft a series of anticommunist decrees. See generally Godman, *Hitler and the Vatican*, 99.

85 See generally, Pollard, *Money and the Rise of the Modern Papacy*, 176–77.

86 Owen Chadwick, *Britain and the Vatican During the Second World War* (Cambridge: Cambridge University Press, 1986), 28.

87 Frederic Sondern Jr., "The Pope: A Great Man and a Great Statesman Works for the Peace of the World," *Life*, December 4, 1939, 86–87. For Pacelli's attitude toward communism, and how it affected his tenure later as Pope, see Ludwig Volk, *Das Reichskonkordat von 20 Julie 1933* (Ostfildern: Matthias Grünewald Verlag, 1976), 64–65. See also the concerns of the Vatican about unrelenting oppression of religion in Russia: Memorandum, Alleged Religious Persecution in Russia, Arthur Henderson, Foreign Office, March 3, 1930, 24/210/24, 171–74, Cabinet Papers, National Archives, Kew, UK.

88 Alvarez, *Spies in the Vatican*, 130–31, 133, 141–43; Coppa, *Controversial Concordats*, 27.

89 *Quadragesimo Anno*, May 1931; *Nova Impendet*, October 1931; and *Caritate Christi Compulsit*, May 1932.

90 Claudia Carlen, IHM, ed., *The Papal Encyclicals*, 5 vols. (Ypsilanti, MI: Pierian Press, 1990), vol. 3, 431–32, 475.

91 Ibid., Vol. 3, 481.

92 Gollin, *Worldly Goods*, 440; Lo Bello, *The Vatican Empire*, 26.

93 Gollin, *Worldly Goods*, 131, 451–52; Pollard, *Money and the Rise of the Modern Papacy*, 165–66.

94 Archivo Famiglia Nogara, Personal Papers of Bernardino Nogara, Rome, diary entry for February 15, 1932, cited in Pollard, *Money and the Rise of the Modern Papacy*.

Chapter 7: Prelude to War

1 Quoted in Cornwell, *Hitler's Pope*, 106.

2 Ibid.

3 Carroll, *Constantine's Sword*, 495–97; Phayer, *Pius XII, the Holocaust, and the Cold War*, 139.

4 Anthony Rhodes, *The Vatican in the Age of the Dictators, 1922–1945* (London: Hodder & Stoughton, 1973), 167; Cornwell, *Hitler's Pope*, 133.

5 Coppa, *Controversial Concordats*, 22–23; see generally Klaus Scholder, *The Churches and the Third Reich*, trans. John Bowden (Philadelphia: Fortress Press, 1988), 52–73; 146–67.

6 There is some dispute among historians as to whether the Nazis or the Vatican made the first overture to negotiate a concordat. The credible evidence is that the Third Reich put out a feeler to which the Vatican was receptive. The talks with Germany were important for Secretary of State Pacelli, since he feared that his career would be finished if the agreement turned sour and he was also blamed for having chased the Third Reich for the deal. For a summary of the conflicting sources, see generally Coppa, *Controversial Concordats*, 129–30; and Besier, *The Holy See and Hitler's Germany*, 165–67.

7 *Germania* 1937–38, Pos. 720, fasc. 329, 23–24, ASV, AES. Pacelli negotiated on his own, much to the consternation of the German bishops, who were largely shut out of the agreement by which they would be most affected: Cornwell, *Hitler's Pope*, 145–46. See also Reinhold Niebuhr, "Pius XI and His Successor," *The Nation*, January 30, 1937, 120–22.

8 Carroll, *Constantine's Sword*, 508.

9 The storm troopers included SS, Schutzstaffel, and SA (Sturm Abteilung).

10 Clifford J. Hynning, *Germany: Preliminary Report on Selected Financial Laws, Decrees and Regula-*

tions, Vol. 2, Appendices (Washington, DC: Treasury Department, Office of the General Counsel, 1944), E48.

11 Gregg J. Rickman, *Conquest and Redemption: A History of Jewish Assets from the Holocaust* (Piscataway, NJ: Transaction Publishers, 2006), 10.

12 Hynning, *Germany: Preliminary Report*, E48-50. See also Gerald D. Feldman, *Allianz and the German Insurance Business, 1933–1945* (Cambridge: Cambridge University Press, 2001), 67.

13 The Nazis created different categories. A person with two Jewish grandparents was considered fully Jewish. Those Germans were classified as Geltungsjude (legally Jewish). One Jewish grandparent meant the descendant was not Aryan and those were called Mischlinge (mixed breeds). The Nazis did not apply their racial laws to the groups uniformly. An estimated 150,000 German soldiers who fought for the Reich were either Mischlinge or Geltungsjude who had earlier converted. See Bryan Mark Rigg, *Hitler's Jewish Soldiers: The Untold Story of Nazi Racial Laws and Men of Jewish Descent in the German Military* (Lawrence: University Press of Kansas, 2004), 7. Document Archives, Laws and Legislation, NSDAP, 1933–1936, Archives, National Holocaust Museum, Washington, DC. See also Klaus Hentschel, editor, and Ann Hentschel, editorial assistant and translator, *Physics and National Socialism: An Anthology of Primary Sources* (Berlin: Birkhäuser, 1996). The church had considered a blood definition for Jews during the Inquisition, but decided against it since it diminished the lure of converting to Catholicism. However, as late as World War II, the Jesuits applied "purity of blood" restrictions to aspiring priests. See generally Robert A. Maryks, *The Jesuit Order as a Synagogue of Jews: Jesuits of Jewish Ancestry and Purity-of-Blood Laws in the Early Society of Jesus* (Boston: Brill Academic Publishers, 2009).

14 Appeals for condemnation of the Nazi persecution were made to Pius XI that April from prominent rabbis in New York and Vienna. An Austrian rabbi, Dr. Arthur Zacharias Schwarz, knew Pius from when he was Milan's cardinal. Pacelli's office intercepted the letters and decided that such matters were better left to the German bishops. However, neither were the appeals ever passed to the German clerics. Besier, *The Holy See and Hitler's Germany*, 126–27.

15 The Nazis banned not only Jewish authors; many non-Jews were also put on the prohibited list. Thomas Mann was taboo because he had a Jewish wife. Helen Keller was deaf blind and her handicap got her listed. Ernest Hemingway was banned because *A Farewell to Arms* was judged as antiwar. Jack London's socialist politics got him blacklisted. "Book Burnings in Germany, 1933," PBS: *American Experience*, April 25, 2006.

16 Carroll, *Constantine's Sword*, 508, n30, 684.

17 Bertram quoted in Ibid; see also Godman, *Hitler and the Vatican*, 32–34.

18 Faulhaber quoted in Guenter Lewy, *The Catholic Church and Nazi Germany* (New York: McGraw-Hill, 1964), 41. Cardinal von Faulhaber emphasized during his 1933 Advent sermons that he was interested only in defending the Old Testament, not commenting on any contemporary matters affecting German Jews. And the cardinal—who believed Hitler was a gifted leader—began inserting anti-Semitic clichés into his weekly sermons. Godman, *Hitler and the Vatican*, 124.

19 Ernest Christian Helmreich, *The German Churches Under Hitler: Background, Struggle and Epilogue* (Detroit: Wayne State University Press, 1979), 276–77.

20 One of the many things that Pius could have done to slow the Nazis was to instruct parish priests across Europe to destroy or hide their baptismal records once it became apparent they were being used to uncover Jewish ancestry. A few priests did try to keep their records from the Nazis, but they were the exception. See generally Cornwell, *Hitler's Pope*, 154.

21 AES, *Germania* 1932–36, Pos. 632, fasc. 150, 3–5; see also Godman, *Hitler and the Vatican*, 36–37.

22 AES, 51; see also Friedländer, *Nazi Germany and the Jews*.

23 Gitta Sereny, *Into That Darkness: An Examination of Conscience* (New York: Vintage, 1983), 75, 282.

24 Godman, *Hitler and the Vatican*, 40–42, 47; See also Chad Ross, *Naked Germany: Health, Race and the Nation* (New York: Berg Publishers, 2005).

25 As for Pacelli and his view of the Reichskonkordat, see Hubert Wolf, *Pope and Devil: The Vatican's Archives and the Third Reich*, trans. Kenneth Kronenberg (Cambridge, MA: Belknap Press of Harvard University Press, 2010), 170–78. For an English language translation of the *Concordat Between the Holy See and the German Reich, July 20, 1933*, see http://www.newadvent.org/library/docs_ss33co.htm.

26 Although the Nazis affirmed the right to a Catholic education, they did their best to undermine

it. They often demanded that parents explain why they had chosen a Catholic over a state school. The pressure worked. In the Catholic stronghold of Munich, for instance, in the four years following the Reichskonkordat, the number of families who sent their children to Catholic schools dropped from 655 to 20. See Coppa, *Controversial Concordats*, 148.

27 Besier, *The Holy See and Hitler's Germany*, 102–23; Coppa, *Controversial Concordats*, 139–42.

28 Even Hitler paid his church tax. In a supplementary protocol to Article 13 of the Reichskonkordat, the parties "agreed that the right of the Church to levy taxes remains guaranteed." David Cymet, *History vs. Apologetics: The Holocaust, the Third Reich, and the Catholic Church* (Lanham, MD: Lexington, 2010), 60. It took the Third Reich until 1935 to fully implement the state collection of church taxes. See generally Stephanie Hoffer, "Caesar as God's Banker: Using Germany's Church Tax as an Example of Non-Geographically Bounded Taxing Jurisdiction," *Washington University Global Studies Law Review*, Vol. 9, no. 4, January 2010.

29 Robert P. Ericksen, *Complicity in the Holocaust: Churches and Universities in Nazi Germany* (Cambridge: Cambridge University Press, 2012), 54–57; see also Ira Katznelson and Gareth Stedman Jones, *Religion and the Political Imagination* (Cambridge: Cambridge University Press, 2010), 322.

30 Margherita Marchione, *Man of Peace: Pope Pius XII* (Mahwah, NJ: Paulist Press, 2004), 15; Cornwell, *Hitler's Pope*, 164.

31 Lewy, *The Catholic Church and Nazi Germany*, 3; Coppa, *Controversial Concordats*, 126–27; Cornwell, *Hitler's Pope*, 10. The German bishops had lifted their excommunication ban on Nazi Party membership in March, paving the way for the Reichskonkordat. German historian Michael Hesemann concluded: "History tells us that this ultimately was a mistake but one that could not be predicted." Gary L. Krupp, ed., *Pope Pius XII and World War II—The Documented Truth: A Compilation of International Evidence Revealing the Wartime Acts of the Vatican* (Wantagh, NY: Pave the Way Foundation, 2012), Kindle edition, location 446 of 5877. That the Reichskonkordat led to the demise of the Catholic Center Party does not mean that the church embraced with any enthusiasm that trade-off with the Third Reich. British diplomat Ivone Kirkpatrick sent a report to London in 1933 in which he said Pacelli told him "that he had to choose between an agreement on their [Third Reich] lines and the virtual elimination of the Catholic Church in the Reich." Pacelli quoted in Wolf, *Pope and Devil*, 177.

32 Lewy, *The Catholic Church and Nazi Germany*, 71–72. See also Robert A. Krieg, "The Vatican Concordat With Hitler's Reich," *America*, September 1, 2003.

33 John Jay Hughes, "The Reich Concordat 1933: Capitulation or Compromise?," *Australian Journal of Politics and History* 20 (1974): 165.

34 The Reichskonkordat did not address the relationship between the Catholic press and the Third Reich. Evidently, the church intended that papers concentrate only on religious matters, and as such, did not expect any problems. The Nazi control of the Catholic press began with state qualifications for journalists. On April 24, 1934, nine months after the Reichskonkordat was signed, the Third Reich shuttered all Catholic dailies.

35 Pierre Blet, SJ, *Pius XII and the Second World War: According to the Archives of the Vatican* (New York: Paulist Press, 1997), 153. Blet, who passed away in 2009, was a French Jesuit and leading church historian. He assisted in the compilation of the Vatican's first multivolume release of documents from the Secret Archives about World War II and Pius, *Actes et Documents du Saint Siège relatifs à la Seconde Guerre Mondiale*. Blet's 1997 book was essentially a 392-page condensed version of the eleven-volume *Actes*.

36 Carroll, *Constantine's Sword*, 509–10.

37 The church tried to stake a claim to baptized Jews. Whenever bishops and other church officials criticized the Third Reich it was always in language about "racism" (since the definition of race included converts), as opposed to "anti-Semitism" (which would have condemned only anti-Jewish actions). Walther Hofer, *Der Nationalsozialismus Dokumente, 1933–1945* (Frankfurt: Fischer Taschenbuch Verlag GmbH, 1957), 130; see also Klaus Scholder, *The Churches and the Third Reich: Preliminary History and the Time of Illusions* (Philadelphia: Fortress Press, 1988), 228, 240. As for the Nazi view on the threat posed by converted Jews, see Phayer, *The Catholic Church and the Holocaust*, 10. Catholic converts who were forced to later wear yellow Stars of David identifying their Jewish ancestry were frequently shunned by other Catholics (some refused to kneel next to them when attending a Mass or waiting to receive the Eucharist).

38 German historian Michael Hesemann was granted special access to the Vatican's Pius XII archives

and in 2008 made headlines with his discovery of four letters from the Pope seeking exit visas. Defenders of the Pontiff seized on those letters to contend that "non-Aryan Catholics" was a code word for persecuted Jews. But there is no evidence that the Pope used the terms interchangeably. Only to the Nazis, with their strict race interpretation of Jewishness, were non-Aryan Catholics the same as Jews. Pacelli's effort saved the lives of baptized converted Jews, or in the eyes of the church, Catholics. For more on the letters, see generally Michael Hesemann, *Der Papst, der Hitler trotzte. Die Wahrheit über Pius XII* (Augsburg: Sankt Ulrich Verlag GmbH, 2008); David G. Dalin, *The Myth of Hitler's Pope: How Pope Pius XII Rescued Jews from the Nazis* (Washington, DC: Regenery; annotated edition, 2005).

39 Cornwell, *Hitler's Pope*, 130.

40 Ibid., 507.

41 Carroll, *Constantine's Sword*, 499–506.

42 The British were disappointed that the Reichskonkordat eliminated the possibility the Vatican would marshal their rank-and-file followers to oppose Hitler: Memorandum, The German Danger; A collection of Reports from His Majesty's Embassy at Berlin between the accession of Herr Hitler to Power in the Spring of 1933 and the end of 1935, January 17, 1936, 24/259/13, 60–61, Cabinet Papers, National Archives, Kew, UK.

43 See generally Michael Berenbaum, *The World Must Know: The History of the Holocaust as Told in United States Holocaust Memorial Museum* (New York: Back Bay, 1993), 40; see also, Ludwig Volk, *Das Reichskonkordat*; Klaus Scholder, "The Churches and the Third Reich," Vol. 1, Ch. 10, "Concordat Policy and the Lateran Treaties" (1930–33); and Vol. 2, "The Capitulation of Catholicism" (February–March 1933); see also Krieg, "The Vatican Concordat With Hitler's Reich," *America*.

44 Lewy, *The Catholic Church and Nazi Germany*, 104; see also Coppa, *Controversial Concordats*, 142.

45 Walther Hofer, ed., with commentary. *Der Nationalsozialismus Dokumente, 1933–1945* (Frankfurt: Fisher Bucherei, 1959), 129–30; Cornwell, *Hitler's Pope*, 130, 152.

46 Cymet, *History vs. Apologetics*, 94.

47 Ludwig Volk, *Das Reichskonkordat vom 20, Juli, 1933. Von den Ansätzen in der Weimarer Republik bis zur Ratifizierung am 10, September 1933*, Veröffentlichung der Kommission für Zeitgeschichte (VKZ), B, 5 (Mainz, 1972).

48 Cymet, *History vs. Apologetics*, 95. The Jesuit periodical *La Civiltà Cattolica* had gone so far as to criticize Nazi anti-Semitism as not being ecclesiastically pure since it did "not stem from the religious convictions or the Christian conscience." *La Civiltà Cattolica* had published stories about supposed Jewish ritual murders of Christian children. Benedict XV had banned in 1914 any Vatican newspaper from printing anything about blood libel, but in the decades after his death the prohibition was not strictly enforced.

49 Archivo della Congregazione per la dottrina della fede, S.O., 125/28 [R.V. 1928 n. 2], vol. 1.

50 Kevin J. Madigan, "Two Popes, One Holocaust," *Commentary*, December 1, 2010; see also Godman, *Hitler and the Vatican*, 25.

51 Theodor Herzl, Account of Audience with Pope Pius X (1904), *Dialogika*, Council of Centers on Jewish-Christian Relations, online at http://www.ccjr.us/dialogika-resources/primary-texts-from-the-history-of-the-relationship/1253-herzl1904.

52 Godman, *Hitler and the Vatican*, 24–26; see Wolf, *Pope and Devil*, 108–17.

53 "Obelisk arrives back in Ethiopia," BBC, April 19, 2005.

54 The Vatican often encouraged Mussolini's grander ambitions, supporting him in one of his first disputes with the British, over Malta in 1933. Cabinet 50 (33), September 5, 1933, 23/77/1, 29–30, Cabinet Papers, National Archives, Kew, UK.

55 Bernard Bridel, "Le Temps Les ambulances à Croix-Rouge du CICR sous les gaz en Ethiopie," International Committee of the Red Cross archives, August 13, 2003.

56 Six years later, in 1941, Nogara applied for an exemption to U.S. wartime Treasury restrictions. The Vatican wanted to import for safekeeping to New York's J. P. Morgan some of the stocks that had been transferred to it during the early stages of the Ethiopian invasion. In a written statement to U.S. officials, Nogara said the securities were a gift from an unidentified donor. Since receiving them, the Vatican had supposedly kept the stocks on deposit at the Banque de l'Etate de Fribourg in Switzerland. McGoldrick, "New Perspectives on Pius XII and Vatican Financial Transactions During the Second World War," 1031–32.

57 For instance, when the League tried issuing sanctions on oil, the British and French successfully

argued that if they were not allowed to sell oil to the Italians, then America—which was not a League member—would simply fill the void and make all the profit.

58 Gollin, *Worldly Goods*, 447.

59 Coppa, *Controversial Concordats*, 115; see also Anthony Rhodes, *The Vatican in the Age of the Dictators*, 69.

60 Chadwick, *Britain and the Vatican During the Second World War*, 8.

61 Rhodes, *The Vatican in the Age of the Dictators*, 77.

62 Paul I. Murphy, *La Popessa: The Controversial Biography of Sister Pascalina, the Most Powerful Woman in Vatican History* (New York: Warner, 1983), 138; Lo Bello, *The Vatican Empire*, 72.

63 Murphy, *La Popessa*, 140. British professor John F. Pollard, in his study of modern Vatican finances (*Money and the Rise of the Modern Papacy*), believes the loan "is highly unlikely" and that references to it in other accounts refer to the fact that the church was "*indirectly* propping up the war effort through its massive holding of Italian government stock and IRI bonds." However, Paul Murphy, in his biography of Sister Pascalina, Pius XII's confidant (*La Popessa*) describes the loans as having been initiated by the fascist government, and that the church agreed only to protect its other investments that were intertwined with Italy.

Massimo Spada, Nogara's deputy, told Benny Lai in 1979 that he had opposed making the wartime loan to Italy. He thought it too risky for the Vatican. Lai, *Finanze Vaticane*, 109, citing Lai interview with Spada, March 7, 1979.

64 Lo Bello, *The Vatican Empire*, 132.

65 See generally Renzo De Felice, "La Santa e il confitto Italio-Etiopico del diario di Bernardino Nogara," *Storia Contemporanea* 9 (1977): 821–34.

66 Archivo Famiglia Nogara, Personal Papers of Bernardino Nogara, Rome, diary entry for November 23, 1935, cited in Pollard, *Money and the Rise of the Modern Papacy*.

67 Lo Bello, *The Vatican Empire*, 170.

68 Cooney, *The American Pope*, 66–71; Cornwell, *Hitler's Pope*, 176–77.

69 Western governments also noted that the Vatican tacitly supported Generalissimo Francisco Franco's fascists in the Spanish Civil War. Chadwick, *Britain and the Vatican During the Second World War*, 8–9.

70 Belardelli, "Un viaggio di Bernardino Nogara," 321–38.

71 Ibid., 327; see also Pollard, *Money and the Rise of the Modern Papacy*, 180–81.

72 Pollard, "The Vatican and the Wall Street Crash," 117.

73 Coppa, *Controversial Concordats*, 159; Cornwell, *Hitler's Pope*, 180–81; see also Rychlak, *Hitler, the War, and the Pope*, 63–64.

74 Alvarez, *Spies in the Vatican*, 163–65.

75 Riccards, *Vicars of Christ*, 122. Leading Vaticanologist Andrea Tornielli tried bolstering Pacelli's anti-Hitler credentials in a well-received biography. He dedicated an entire chapter to "seventy useless protests" the Secretary of State issued on behalf of the Holy See to Berlin from 1933 to 1937, all complaining about Nazi violations of the Reichskonkordat. (See Andrea Tornielli, *Pio XII: Eugenio Pacelli. Un uomo sul trono di Pietro* [Pio XII: Eugenio Pacelli. A Man on the Throne of Peter] [Milan: Arnoldo Mondadori. 2007], chapter 7). But most of the protests were about relatively minor matters, not material disagreements with the Nazi ideology and nothing about its campaign against Germany's Jews. Professor Roy Domenico, chair of the history department at the University of Scranton—a Jesuit school—notes that, "Many of these complaints, however, dealt with holding Nazi rallies on Sundays or with details on religious education." (Roy Domenico, "*Pio XII: Eugenio Pacelli. Un uomo sul trono di Pietro* [review]," *The Catholic Historical Review* 94, no. 4, October 2008, 752–53.)

76 "The Holy Office's First Proposed Condemnation of National Socialism 1935," ACDF, R.V. 1934, 29; Prot. 3375/34, Vol. 1, fasc. 3b (May 1, 1935), 16–26; "The Holy Office's Revised Condemnation 1936," ACDF, R.V., 1934; Prot. 3375/34, Vol. 4, fasc. 13 (October 1936); "The Holy Office's Comparison Between Its Draft Condemnations and *Mit brennender Sorge 1937*," ACDF, R.V., 1934; Prot. 3375/34, Vol. 4, fasc. 18 (April 1937); see also description of early drafts at Godman, *Hitler and the Vatican*, 141–49.

77 See the English translation of the encyclical at the Vatican's archival online website: http://www.vatican.va/holy_father/pius_xi/encyclicals/documents/hf_p-xi_enc_14031937_mit-brennender-sorge_en.html.

78 Allen, *All the Pope's Men*, 201–2. Paul Beecher Blanshard, an editor of *The Nation*, said about

Mit Brennender: "It is this encyclical that is used in American Catholic propaganda to prove that the Pope was anti-Fascist. Actually, the Pope rebuked Mussolini not as a Fascist but as an anti-clerical." "The Roman Catholic Church and Fascism," *The Nation*, April 10, 1948, 393.

79 Ludwig Volk, "Die Enzyklika *Mit brennender Sorge*," in *Katholische Kirche und Nationalsozialismus*, ed. Dieter Albrecht (Ostfildern: Matthias Grünewald Verlag, 1987), 34–55.

80 Martin Rhonheimer, "The Holocaust: What Was Not Said," *First Things*, November 2003, 18–28.

81 Besier, *The Holy See and Hitler's Germany*, 167.

82 Rychlak, *Hitler, the War, and the Pope*, 93–94; Cornwell, *Hitler's Pope*, 182–83.

83 Coppa, *Controversial Concordats*, 157–58.

84 In July 1941, Hitler publicly expressed what he had told others privately. "Christianity is the hardest blow that ever hit humanity. Bolshevism is the bastard son of Christianity; both are the monstrous issue of the Jews." A few months later he warned, "The war will come to an end, and I shall see my last task as cleaning up the Church problem." Cornwell, *Hitler's Pope*, 261; John S. Conway, *The Nazi Persecution of the Churches, 1933–45* (London: Weidenfeld & Nicolson, 1968), 236–39; 243–44; 254–61; Coppa, *Controversial Concordats*, 178.

85 Bergen to Berlin, July 23, 1937, Documents of German Foreign Policy, 1918–1945, Series D, Vol. 1, 990–92.

86 Rychlak, *Hitler, the War, and the Pope*, 94; Cornwell, *Hitler's Pope*, 183.

87 Wills, *Papal Sin*, 29.

88 Robert G. Weisbord and Wallace P. Sillanpoa, *The Chief Rabbi, the Pope, and the Holocaust: An Era in Vatican–Jewish Relations* (New Brunswick, NJ: Transaction, 1992), 36. Pacelli did not show any sign that he was reconsidering the issue of anti-Semitism and the church. That May, he was the Papal Delegate at the International Eucharistic Conference in Budapest. More than 100,000 of the faithful attended, including 330 bishops and fifteen cardinals. That conference coincided with the Hungarian legislature passing the country's first slew of anti-Semitic laws. Pacelli made a reference that some interpreted as a slight toward Jews when he castigated those people "whose lips curse [Christ] and whose hearts reject him even today." See "Pope Pius XII and the Holocaust." Online at www.general-books.net/sw2.cfm?q=Pope_Pius_XII_and_the_Holocaust.

89 Conway, *The Nazi Persecution of the Churches*, 166; see Weisbord and Sillanpoa, *The Chief Rabbi, the Pope, and the Holocaust*, 35.

90 Alexander Stille, *Benevolence and Betrayal: Five Italian Jewish Families Under Fascism* (New York: Picador 2003), 70.

91 Peter C. Kent, "A Tale of Two Popes: Pius XI, Pius XII and the Rome-Berlin Axis," *Journal of Contemporary History* 23 (1988): 600.

92 Osborne sent a coded cable to London describing Pius's transformation over a couple of years from "a Fascist Pope" to "an old and probably dying man, for whatever reasons he is following a policy in international affairs which on the major issues of principle corresponds very closely indeed with our own." Chadwick, *Britain and the Vatican*, 25–26. Osborne's official title was Envoy Extraordinary and Minister Plenipotentiary to the Holy See.

93 Cornwell, *Hitler's Pope*, 190; see also Godman, *Hitler and the Vatican*, 160; and Berry, *Render Unto Rome*, 66.

94 John LaFarge, *Interracial Justice as a Principle of Order* (Washington, DC: Catholic University of America Press, 1937); see also Wills, *Papal Sin*, 30.

95 One was a German, Gustav Gundlach, who had worked on Pius's 1931 *Quadragesimo Anno*, in which he presented nonsocialist alternatives to equality and workers' rights under capitalism. The other Jesuit, Gustave Desbuqois, was French, and had worked on the same 1931 encyclical, as well as an anticommunist encyclical, the 1937 *Divini Redemptoris*.

96 Alvarez, *Spies in the Vatican*, 167. The source, who provided among other things the confidential minutes of the annual meeting of the German bishops, remains unidentified. It is one of the war's great unsolved espionage mysteries.

97 J.C.H. to A.W.D. (Allen Dulles), OSS, September 10, 1942, RG 226, E217, Box 20, Location 00687RWN26535, NARA; see Weisbord and Sillanpoa, *The Chief Rabbi, the Pope, and the Holocaust*, 36; and Wills, *Papal Sin*, 31. German intelligence managed to place an agent in Ledochowski's inner circle; see Report of Interrogation of Walter Schellenberg, June 27 to July 12, 1945, Top Secret, RG 226, E119A, Folder 2051, NARA.

98 Georges Passelecq and Bernard Suchecky, *The Hidden Encyclical of Pius XI*, translated from the

French by Steven Rendall, with an introduction by Garry Wills (New York: Harcourt Brace, 1997), 124–35; Wolf, *Pope and Devil,* 116–17; see also Wills, *Papal Sin*, 38.

99 Some historians believe Pius was afflicted since childhood with epilepsy. A few anecdotal accounts support this conclusion, but there are no verified reports of seizures associated with the condition. Instead, there are many instances during his tenure marked by a fierce and uncontrollable temper as well as assaultive verbal explosions filled with invective and cruelness. Whatever their cause, those outbursts and fits became his feared trademark as Pope. Godman, *Hitler and the Vatican*, 133, 143; Chadwick, *Britain and the Vatican During the Second World War*, 43, 56.

100 Wills, *Papal Sin*, 39; Lo Bello, *The Vatican Papers*, 23.

101 Maura Hametz, "Zionism, Emigration, and Anti-Semitism in Trieste: Central Europe's 'Gateway to Zion,' 1896–1943," Jewish Social Studies, New Series, Indiana University Press 13, no. 3 (Spring–Summer, 2007): 121–24. Michele Sarfatti, *The Jews in Mussolini's Italy: From Equality to Persecution*, trans. John and Anne C. Tedeschi (Madison: University of Wisconsin Press, 2006), 103–5, 130.

102 "Italy's 'Race Laws Take 15,000 Jobs: Jews to Be Restricted to Labor and Small Trade—Police Warn 'Aryan' Servants," *The New York Times*, November 20, 1938, 33.

103 *Germania* 1938, Pos. 742, fasc. 354, 40ff, ASV, AES; see also Besier, *The Holy See and Hitler's Germany*, 185.

104 Phayer, *The Catholic Church and the Holocaust,* 16, n. 90.

105 Rychlak, *Hitler, the War, and the Pope*, 103.

106 The day before Chamberlain met Pius, the Prime Minister met Mussolini. In that meeting, Il Duce told Chamberlain, "Another European war would mean the destruction of civilization." Chamberlain was joined by his Foreign Secretary, Lord Halifax, and Mussolini by his Secretary of State, Count Galeazzo Ciano. They also talked about "the Jewish refugee problem," and Mussolini pushed the British representatives to consider a "sovereign Jewish state" in some country that had a lot of spare land. Il Duce suggested Brazil, Russia, or the United States. Chamberlain asked Mussolini if he might intercede with Hitler to see if he would not only let German Jews leave Germany, but also take some of their money with them. Mussolini said, "It would not be of much use to ask for a great deal as the Germans had suffered great hardships and had become very poor in consequence of the actions of Jews." The persecution of the Jews, said Mussolini, was "an internal policy in Germany," "The Visit to Rome of the Prime Minister and the Secretary of State for Foreign Affairs from January 11 to January 14, 1939," Foreign Office, War Cabinet, January 11, 1939, 24/282/8, 81–82, Cabinet Papers, National Archives, Kew, UK. Chamberlain returned to London "very favorably" impressed with Mussolini. Cabinet 1 (39), January 18, 1939, 23/97/1, 4, Cabinet papers, National Archives, Kew, UK.

107 "The Visit to Rome of the Prime Minister," 86.

108 On the morning that Pius XI died, Massimo Spada later recounted that Pacelli had found money left behind by the Pope: "Monsignor Angelo Pomato and I took all the money that Camerlengo Pacelli found in the study of the deceased Pope. Wrapped inside a handkerchief were Italian bank notes for 1,650,000 lire and also $1,200. That lire was deposited into the bank account number 1617 made payable to the Secretary of State, and the dollars to the current account 51170, with the same header as the other. It all went to pay homage to the mortal remains of the deceased." Lai, *Finanze Vaticane*, 111, citing an interview by Lai with Massimo Spada, March 7, 1979. As for Pius's desire to personally deliver a speech to the cardinals on February 11, see Kertzer, *The Pope and Mussolini,* Kindle edition, location 274, 295 of 10577.

109 Jean Charles-Roux, "How the Rumors Began that Pius XI was Murdered," *The Catholic Herald,* July 7, 1972; Peter Eisner, "Pope Pius XI's Last Crusade," *Huffington Post*, April 15, 2013.

110 Weisbord and Sillanpoa, *The Chief Rabbi, the Pope, and the Holocaust*, 36; Cornwell, *Hitler's Pope*, 192.

111 Jim Castelli, "Unpublished Encyclical Attacked Anti-Semitism," *National Catholic Reporter*, December 15, 1972, 1.

112 Georges Passelecq and Bernard Suchecky, "The Hidden Encyclical of Pius XI," available at washingtonpost.com/wp-srv/style/longterm/books/chap1/hiddenencyclicalofpiusxi.htm; Wills, *Papal Sin*, 32.

113 Archivo della Congregazione per la dottrina della fede, S.O., 125/28 [R.V. 1928 n. 2], Vol. 1.

114 Georges Passelecq and Bernard Suchecky, *The Hidden Encyclical of Pius XI,* translated by *Ste-*

ven Rendall (New York: Harcourt Brace, 1997), 247–49; "Humanis Generis Unitas," paragraphs 133–36; Wills, *Papal Sin*, 36.

115 Cornwell, *Hitler's Pope*, 191.

116 Passelecq and Suchecky, *The Hidden Encyclical*, 251–53; "Humanis Generis Unitas," paragraphs 141–42; Lo Bello, *The Vatican Papers*, 22–23.

117 "Humanis Generis Unitas," 88. A copy of the encyclical is available at the Father Edward Stanton papers at Boston College (Burns Library).

118 The writer and editor Conor Cruise O'Brien thinks the failure to release the encyclical was "one of the most tragic missed opportunities in history." He argues that millions of Jewish lives would have been saved. Father Walter Abbot, an editorial writer at the Jesuits' *America*, believes that Hitler would have cracked down even harder in the wake of the release of such an encyclical. This time the victims would not only be Jewish but also bishops and lay Catholic. Conor Cruise O'Brien, "A Lost Chance to Save the Jews?," *The New York Review of Books*, April 27, 1989, 35. And see generally Weisbord and Sillanpoa, *The Chief Rabbi, the Pope, and the Holcaust*, 38.

Chapter 8: A Policy of Silence

1 Cornwell, *Hitler's Pope*, 205–8.

2 Alvarez, *Spies in the Vatican*, 170–71.

3 Chadwick, *Britain and the Vatican*, 40–42.

4 Pius was a master linguist. He was fluent in German, Italian, English, Spanish, and Portuguese. He also had given short speeches in Swedish, Dutch, and Danish. Before his death he studied Russian, hoping to address the Russian people.

5 Rychlak, *Hitler, the War, and the Pope*, 184.

6 Alvarez, *Spies in the Vatican*, 168–70.

7 See generally, Godman, *Hitler and the Vatican*, 32–38. Pacelli sometimes expressed personal disdain for Hitler but only in private. His statement about Hitler's incapability to be a moderate was in 1937 to Alfred Klieforth, the American consul general to Berlin. Klieforth summarized his talk with Pacelli in a cable to the State Department. The Cardinal Secretary of State also said that he supported the German bishops in their anti-Nazi stand. (Frances D'Emilio, "Jesuit Researcher Says Wartime Pope's Anti-Nazi Stand Was Strong in 'Private' Contacts," Associated Press, International News, Vatican City, August 21, 2003). As for the comments to Ambassador Joseph Kennedy, they were made during a series of meetings the two had in Rome in 1938, only six months before the start of World War II. Pacelli gave Kennedy a document he said were his "personal views, delivered for your confidential use." In it he chastised Nazism as "pro-paganism" and complained about a new Kulturkampf (referring to the anti-Catholic policies enacted by German Chancellor Otto von Bismarck in the 1870s). Pacelli told Kennedy it was all right to pass his "personal private views of mine on to your Friend," meaning Franklin Roosevelt. The document was made public in 2003 by the John F. Kennedy Library (Charles R. Gallagher, "Personal, Private Views," *America*, September 1, 2003).

8 John P. McKnight, *The Papacy: A New Appraisal* (New York: Rinehart, 1952), 218.

9 Frederic Sondern Jr., "The Pope: A Great Man and Great Statesman Works for the Peace of the World," *Life*, December 4, 1939, 88.

10 Besier, *The Holy See and Hitler's Germany*, 2–3.

11 *La Conciliazione Ufficiosa: Diario del barone Carlo Monti "incaricato d'affari" del governo italiano presso la Santa Sede (1914-1922)*, (Vatican City: Antonio Scotta, 1997), 51; see also Cornwell, *Hitler's Pope*, 62. Defenders of Pius try to discredit Monti since he bore Pacelli a personal grudge. Moreover, they claim the Pope could not have been that upset since he did not rebuke Pacelli. See Rychlak, *Hitler, the War, and the Pope*, 293.

12 Sondern "The Pope," 86–95.

13 Ibid., 91; Hoffman, *Anatomy of the Vatican*, 20.

14 Rychlak, *Hitler, the War, and the Pope*, 107–8.

15 Pius XII had telephones installed in his study by International Telephone & Telegraph. His private phone had a solid gold receiver on which was engraved the Papal coat of arms. He used it over the Vatican's internal switchboard to call Curia officials, usually for short, all-business

monologues. See Paul L. Williams, *The Vatican Exposed: Money, Murder, and the Mafia* (New York: Prometheus, 2003), 59; see also Sondern, "The Pope," 91; and Hoffman, *Anatomy of the Vatican*, 19.

16 Murphy, *La Popessa*, 60, 88.

17 Ibid., 66. Some Italian priests working in the Curia did live at home with their parents for years while tending to duties inside Vatican City, but Pacelli bypassed living quarters offered to him by the Vatican in order to stay at home.

18 Carl Steinhouse, *Improbable Heroes: The True Story of How Clergy and Ordinary Citizens Risked Their Lives to Save Jews in Italy* (Bloomington, IN: AuthorHouse, 2005), 30.

19 Murphy, *La Popessa*, 54. She was born Josefine Lehnert and took the name Pascalina when she took her vows as a nun. And although she was never a mother superior of a convent, it became part of her widely accepted title. Canon code 133, set forth by Pope Benedict XV, ordered that the women who took care of the households of ranking clerics be beyond "canonical age," lest it might give rise to suspicion of "something evil." Canon Law encouraged that priests use their mothers, aunts, or elderly women for overseeing their households. *Canonical age* was the church's oblique way of referring to menopause. See generally Hoffman, *Anatomy of the Vatican*, 134.

20 After Pius had become Pope, the U.S. Secretary of State John Foster Dulles met with him at the Vatican. During that meeting, Mother Pascalina entered unannounced and leaned over to Pius and spoke to him sternly in German. His soup was on the table. The Pope excused himself. Hoffman, *Anatomy of the Vatican*, 22; "Pope Takes Orders from Housekeeper," *Sarasota Herald-Tribune*, UPI, April 25, 1954, 32.

21 Pius appointed Pascalina as the head of Vatican housekeeping. But she was much more than that, serving as a trusted confidante. Paul Hoffman covered the Vatican for *The New York Times* during the 1970s and later penned a book about the church (*Anatomy of the Vatican*). Hoffman wrote that while only a few women ever wielded "influence in the papal entourage"—such as the fourteenth-century mystic Catherine of Siena, and the seventeenth-century Swedish Queen Christina—that Pascalina was the "one woman alone in modern times [who] has exercised considerable, if unofficial, power in the Vatican." See generally "Pope Takes Orders from Housekeeper," 32. Also, Pascalina wrote a hagiographic account of her service for Pius after his death. An English language edition was not published until 2014. Pascalina Lehnert and Susan Johnson, *His Humble Servant: Sister M. Pascalina Lehnert's Memoirs of Her Years of Service to Eugenio Pacelli, Pope Pius XII* (South Bend, IN: St. Augustine Press, 2014).

22 Peter C. Kent, *The Lonely Cold War of Pope Pius XII: The Roman Catholic Church and the Division of Europe, 1943–1950* (Montreal: McGill Queens University Press, 2002), 64.

23 "Religion: America in Rome," *Time*, February 25, 1946.

24 Murphy, *La Popessa*, 54–55, 57, 59. Two dozen reporters had camped out at Rome's main rail station to capture Pacelli's and Spellman's return. They got past the reporters unnoticed, with Pacelli dressed as an ordinary priest and hiding behind large sunglasses, and Spellman disguised as a layman. A visiting New York priest remarked to friends back home that Spellman was utterly entranced by Pacelli, and jokingly said that Spellman seemed to be like a poodle being shown off and walked on Fifth Avenue by his owner. As for Spellman, he wrote to his mother about Pacelli: "He is very kind and pleasant and confidential with me." And Spellman wrote home somewhat facetiously that the Pope (Pius XI) called him "Monsignor Precious." One of Pacelli's first acts as Pope was to appoint Spellman the Archbishop of New York in 1939—that caused a ruckus among senior clerics who knew that Pius XI had intended to appoint Cincinnati's Archbishop John McNicholas, but the Pope had died before he signed the papers. Seven years later, when the war ended, Pacelli made Spellman a cardinal (see generally, Francis Beauchesne Thornton, *Our American Princes: The Story of the Seventeen American Cardinals* [New York: Putnam, 1963], 200–202). John Cooney, Spellman's biographer, recounted several secondhand stories that Spellman—an exacting public moralist—was in fact gay: John Cooney, *The American Pope: The Life and Times of Francis Cardinal Spellman* (New York: Crown, 1984). The allegation caused an uproar when it was published. Spellman's longtime clerical personal assistant dismissed it as "utterly ridiculous." New York journalist Michelangelo Signorile followed up the leads in Cooney's book and concluded in 2002 that Spellman was "one of the most notorious, powerful and sexually voracious homosexuals in the American Catholic Church's history," a closeted gay man who was "known as 'Franny' to assorted chorus boys and others." Michelangelo Signorile, "Cardinal Spellman's Dark Legacy," *New York Press*, May 7, 2002. The information provided about Spellman by author Paul Murphy

in *La Popessa* is based in part on Murphy's exclusive access to personal papers, diaries, and letters of Cardinal Spellman, provided by the cardinal's brother, Dr. Martin Spellman.

25 Phayer, *Pius XII, the Holocaust, and the Cold War*, 9; see also Besier, *The Holy See and Hitler's Germany*, 2–3.

26 Domenico Cardinal Tardini, *Memories of Pius XII,* trans. Rosemary Goldie (Westminster, MD: Newman Press, 1961), 73. Many thought Pacelli was too influenced by his cautious and accommodating predecessor, Cardinal Pietro Gasparri. Gasparri was also an energetic Secretary of State, but few of his colleagues thought him capable of administering the church. See Frank J. Coppa, *The Policies and Politics of Pope Pius XII: Between Diplomacy and Morality* (New York: Peter Lang, 2011), 57.

27 Godman, *Hitler and the Vatican*, 82–83.

28 Osborne quoted in Rhodes, *The Vatican in the Age of the Dictators*, 222–23; McKnight, *The Papacy*, 257, 291; Tardini, *Memories of Pius XII*, 73.

29 Chadwick, *Britain and the Vatican*, 50–52.

30 A two-thirds majority of the eligible sixty-two cardinals was necessary for selection as Pope. Pacelli polled the most votes from the first ballot, but it took two additional ballots before he garnered the necessary forty-eight votes. See Cornwell, *Hitler's Pope*, 207. Pacelli's coronation was the first time the U.S. government sent an emissary. FDR dispatched the Catholic Joseph Kennedy, then ambassador to the U.K. The British, recognizing that having a friendly relationship with the new Pope was critical given the tensions in Europe, appointed the Duke of Norfolk to the new post of Special Ambassador to the Vatican for the Papal Coronation. Cabinet 1 (39), January 18, 1939, 23/97/1, 380, Cabinet Papers, National Archives, Kew, UK.

31 J. N. D. Kelly, *Dictionary of Popes*, 318. Pacelli's coronation was the grandest in modern times, principally because it was the first since the Lateran Pacts and as a result was the only one in a century to be held outdoors. See also G. A. Borgese, "Pius XII and the Axis," *The Nation*, March 11, 1939, 285–88.

32 Chadwick, *Britain and the Vatican*, 57; see also *The Pope Speaks*, with a preface by Cardinal Arthur Hinsley (London: Faber & Faber, 1940), 60–63.

33 Blet, *Pius XII and the Second World War*, 53–54.

34 Cornwell, *Hitler's Pope*, 208–9.

35 Pie XII à Hitler (minute de letter), Records and Documents of the Holy See Relating to the Second World War (Vatican City: Liberia Editrice Vaticana, 1965–1981), Vol. 2, Appendix No. 6, 420.

36 Coppa, *Controversial Concordats*, 165; Phayer, *The Catholic Church and the Holocaust*, 45; Pius XII and Franklin Roosevelt had maintained a cordial correspondence since their meeting during the Pope's 1936 trip to the U.S. A month after Pacelli became Pope, FDR wrote asking for his support for Roosevelt's request to Hitler and Mussolini that they agree to no further aggression for at least a decade. Pius declined, telling him that the Vatican would address both Hitler and Mussolini in good time, and on its own terms. See generally Blet, *Pius XII and the Second World War*, 9–10.

37 Sondern, "The Pope," 91, 93–94. Pius did not trust the telephones for calls outside the Vatican, convinced that Italy's security services monitored them. During the war he learned that the Soviets regularly intercepted phone calls between the Vatican and Castel Gandolfo. See Hoffman, *Anatomy of the Vatican*, 253.

38 Sondern, "The Pope," 91, 93–94.

39 Mother Pascalina later recounted that during Pius's nineteen-year tenure, he only broke his silent meal tradition once, inviting Munich's Cardinal von Faulhaber to stay for dinner after a meeting had run late. Even those who knew him best, like his secretary Father Robert Leiber, a German Jesuit who met with him daily, observed that it was tough to break through his great reserve: "One of his classmates said that as a boy he had been difficult to approach. He stayed that way. . . . He remained solitary. It was hard to penetrate the depths of his soul." Hoffman, *Anatomy of the Vatican*, 21–22, 140.

40 Chernow, *The House of Morgan*, iBook edition, location 789.

41 Murphy, *La Popessa*, 85.

42 Webster, *Industrial Imperialism in Italy*, 153, 58.

43 Giovanni Preziosi, *Germania alla Conquista dell'Italia: Con prefazione di G.A. Colonna di Cesaro' e con nota del prof. Maffeo Pantaleoni* (Florence: 1915).

44 Lo Bello, *The Vatican Empire*, 28; Martin, *Rich Church, Poor Church*, 41–42; Gollin, *Worldly Goods*, 453–54.

45 Giovanni Preziosi, *Germania alla Conquista dell'Italia: Con pefazione di G.A. Colonna di Cesaro' e con nota del prof. Maffeo Pantaleoni* (Florence: 1915). Preziosi, a former priest who left the order to become the chief anti-Semitic spokesman for Mussolini's Fascist Party, set forth the nationalist suspicions about foreign, Jewish, and Freemason influence at Banca Commerciale Italiana (BCI). Mussolini rewarded Preziosi with a 1942 appointment as Minister of State. He committed suicide after the war when his arrest by the Allies was imminent.

46 Lo Bello, *The Vatican Empire*, 28; Martin, *Rich Church, Poor Church*, 41–42; see also Murphy, *La Popessa*, 76.

47 Lai, *Finanze Vaticane*, 21–22; see also Martin, *Rich Church, Poor Church*, 42.

48 The most likely replacement was Monsignor Alberto di Jorio, the Curia bureaucrat who was Nogara's most trusted colleague. He kept the finances balanced while Nogara was under scrutiny.

49 Martin, *Rich Church, Poor Church*, 42. Gollin, *Worldly Goods*, puts the sum as low as $150 million, while Lo Bello, *The Vatican Papers*, puts it as high as $2 billion.

50 Martin, *Rich Church, Poor Church*, 42.

51 McGoldrick, "New Perspectives on Pius XII and Vatican Financial Transactions During the Second World War," 1031. Nogara kept notes of his meetings with Pius XI for a decade. It is not clear whether the decision to leave no written record was made by Pius or Nogara. The answer is possibly sealed inside the Vatican's Secret Archives. The Vatican has not even released a log of the days and times during Pius's Papacy during which the two met.

52 Pius had floated a diplomatic proposal several months before Hitler invaded Poland. He wanted the Vatican to mediate negotiations with Germany over contested lands in Czechoslovakia and Austria. France and Britain rejected the idea. Cabinet 27 (39), May 10, 1939, 23/99/6, 161, Cabinet Papers, National Archives, Kew, UK. Pius also suggested a truce that December, after the Nazis had taken Poland and were marching on Finland. The Allies thought it a terrible idea, as a lull would provide the Germans a short rest, after which they could renew the fighting with vigor; Notebook, Foreign Policy in Europe, December 11, 1939, (WP-39-155), 66/4/5/1, Cabinet Papers, National Archives, Kew, UK.

53 *Veröffentlichungen der Kommission für Zeitgeschichte*, Series A, Vol. 34, 550–51.

54 The following month the Third Reich instituted its euthanasia program (*Gnadentod*, "mercy death"), with a goal of eliminating those with physical abnormalities or mental illnesses. It was supposed to be a closely held secret within the Reich, but that was impossible since the program employed more than a thousand people in its administration and execution. Rumors of what was happening were soon widespread throughout Germany. German bishop August von Galen ignored entreaties from the Vatican to stay silent and condemned the program in his sermons. Some top Nazis, including Martin Bormann, wanted Galen arrested and executed, but the Nazis did not move against him because they feared they would lose popular support if they harmed him. Over time, the public denunciations of the "secret" murders grew. Hitler's response was to end the German program after two years, with a tally of 70,273 dead. The Nazis moved the killings to Poland and Russia, where they were lost under the chaos of the fighting there. Another 130,000 were killed before the war's end. But that the Nazis had to backpedal in Germany has been cited by some scholars as evidence that wider Catholic protests might have slowed or even stopped the Holocaust; see Cornwell, *Hitler's Pope*, 195–99.

55 See *Documents on German Foreign Policy*, Series C, Vol. 1, No. 501; Series D, Vol. 13, No. 309, cited in George Kent, "Pope Pius XII and Germany: Some Aspects of German-Vatican Relations, 1933–1943, *American Historical Review* 70 (October 1964). Pius never used the church's influence with prominent Italians to try and stem Il Duce's embrace of the Führer. Instead, the Pope merely complained sub rosa to the British. The U.K. government took notice, but of course had no sway when it came to Mussolini. Summary of the War Cabinet, March 6, 1940 (WM-40-61), 65/6/6, 39–40, Cabinet Papers, National Archives, Kew, UK.

56 Friedländer, *Nazi Germany and the Jews*, 223.

57 Moshe Y. Herczl, *Christianity and the Holocaust of Hungarian Jewry*, trans. Joel Lerner (New York: Harper & Row, 1971), 118.

58 American diplomat George Kennan was assigned to Prague until the Nazis took control. In his memoirs, he recounted that Rudolph Mikuš, the influential chief of the Jesuits in Slovakia, gave a "carefully prepared interview" in 1939 to the country's semi-official newspaper. Mikuš "favors the segregation of the Jew and the elimination of their influence in political and economic life in

Slovakia." He only allowed an exemption for baptized Jews. George F. Kennan, *From Prague After Munich: Diplomatic Papers, 1938–1940* (Princeton: Princeton University Press, 1968), 51–52.

59 Phayer, *The Catholic Church and the Holocaust*, 87; Gabriel Wilensky, *Six Million Crucifixions: How Christian Teachings About Jews Paved the Road to the Holocaust* (San Diego, CA: Qwerty Publishers, 2010), Kindle edition, 3906 of 8032.

60 Quoted in Ladislav Lipscher, "The Jews of Slovakia: 1939–1945," *The Jews of Czechoslovakia*, ed. Avigdor Dagan, Vol. 3 of Historical Studies and Surveys (New York: Society for the History of Czechoslovak Jews, 1984), 166.

61 Michael Robert Marrus, *The Nazi Holocaust, Part 8: Bystanders to the Holocaust*, Vol. 3 (Berlin: De Gruyter, 1989), 1313.

62 Phayer, *The Catholic Church and the Holocaust*, 46.

63 See generally Le nonce à Berlin Orsenigo au cardinal Maglione (Report of Apostolic Nuncio Cesare Orsenigo regarding his meeting with Hitler), Vol. 1, No. 28–29, 128ff, Records and Documents of the Holy See Relating to the Second World War, *Actes et Documents du Saint Siège relatifs à la Seconde Guerre Mondiale, Le Saint Siège et la guerre en Europe* (Vatican City: Liberia Editrice Vatican), (ADSS); Notes du cardinal Maglione (Note of the Italian Ambassador [Ciano] the Vatican Secretary of State [Maglione]), May 9, 1938, No 36, 138, Records and Documents of the Holy See Relating to the Second World War, ADSS; Sir Neville Henderson to the British Foreign Office, Series 371/23790/190, file of the Foreign Office, National Archives, Kew, UK. French suspicions about Pius and Maglione working with Italian intelligence were largely based on the extent to which the Vatican was intertwined with Mussolini's government during the summer of 1939, just before the breakout of hostilities. See generally the archival documents relating to British Foreign policy, 3rd Series, 1919–1939, Vol. 7, National Archives, Kew, UK; see also Chadwick, *Britain and the Vatican*, 65, 68.

64 Ronald Modras, *The Catholic Church in Poland and Anti-Semitism, 1933–1939* (Abingdon-on-Thames: Routledge, 2000), 186.

65 Chadwick, *Britain and the Vatican*, 82.

66 Phayer, *The Catholic Church and the Holocaust*, 25.

67 Memo, Harold H. Tittmann, U.S. Department of State, *Foreign Relations of the United States, Diplomatic Papers, Europe, 1942*, University of Wisconsin, Digital Collection, http://digicoll.library.wisc.edu/cgi-bin/FRUS/FRUS-idx?type=turn&entity=FRUS.FRUS1942v03.p0783&id=FRUS.FRUS1942v03&isize=text.

68 Walter Hannot, *Die Judenfrage in der katholishen Tagespresse Deutschlands and Osterreichs, 1923–1933* (Mains: Grünewald, 1990), Series B of *Veröffentlichungen der Kommission für Zeitgeschichte*, Vol. 51, 286ff.

69 Modras, *The Catholic Church and Anti-Semitism*, 195. In 1995, on the fiftieth anniversary of the end of World War II, the Polish clergy issued a formal apology for not having condemned the Nazi slaughter of Polish Jews.

70 The Polish cardinals who promoted blood libel included Józef Sapieha and Karol Radonski. Paper presented by Andrzej Bryk, "Polish-Jewish Relations During the Holocaust: The Hidden Complex of the Polish Mind," at the History and Culture of the Polish Jews, 1988, Jerusalem; see also Friedländer, *Nazi Germany and the Jews*, 47–48; Phayer, *The Catholic Church and the Holocaust*, 14–15. Hlond later tempered his anti-Jewish remarks and became a critic of Nazi crimes. Hlond's rant about Jews was part of a 1936 pastoral letter that was read during Sunday mass at churches across Poland. Cymet, *History vs. Apologetics*, 152. See generally Besier, *The Holy See and Hitler's Germany*, 134–35; Natalia Aleksiun, "The Polish Catholic Church and the Jewish Question in Poland, 1944–1948," Holocaust Studies, Yad Vashem, vol. 33, 2005.

71 The Nazis had begun targeting clerics they thought were not enthusiastic about the new German General Government. Richard C. Lukas, *The Forgotten Holocaust: The Poles Under German Occupation, 1939–1944* (Lexington: University Press of Kentucky, 1986), 13–14; August Hlond, *The Persecution of the Catholic Church in German-Occupied Poland. Reports presented by H. E. Cardinal Hlond, Primate of Poland, to Pope Pius XII, Vatican Broadcasts and Other Reliable Evidence*—preface by Cardinal Hinsley (New York: Longmans, Green, 1941), 110–17; see also Phayer, *The Catholic Church and the Holocaust*, 22–23; and Phayer, *Pius XII, the Holocaust, and the Cold War*, 21–24, 28.

72 George La Piana, "Vatican-Axis Diplomacy," *The Nation*, November 30, 1940, 530–32.

73 Phayer, *The Catholic Church and the Holocaust*, 25.

74 Lukas, *The Forgotten Holocaust*, 16.
75 Phayer, *The Catholic Church and the Holocaust*, 29.
76 Burzio's most detailed warning was an early March 1942 letter in which he reported the imminent deportation of 80,000 Slovakian Jews, Burzio to Maglione, March 9, 1942, Vol. 8, 153, ADSS; see Livia Rothkirchen, "The Churches and the Deportation and Persecution of Jews in Slovakia," Shoah Resource Center, The International School for Holocaust Studies, 2000; Morley, *Vatican Diplomacy and the Jews During the Holocaust*, 78–81; Chadwick, *Britain and the Vatican*, 205, citing the diary of British envoy D'Arcy Osborne.
77 Phayer, *The Catholic Church and the Holocaust*, 87.
78 Ibid., 88. See also Livia Rothkirchen, "Vatican Policy and the 'Jewish Problem' in 'Independent' Slovakia 1939-1945, *Yad Vashem Studies*, 6 (1967), 36. Secretary of State Maglione made a more direct appeal in May 1943.
79 "Notes de Mgr Tardini," Vol. 8, Doc. 426, 597–98, Records and Documents of the Holy See Relating to the Second World War, ADSS; see also John S. Conway, "The Vatican, Germany and the Holocaust," in *Papal Diplomacy in the Modern Age*, ed. Peter C. Kent and John F. Pollard (Westport, CT: Praeger, 1994), 113.
80 Phayer, *Pius XII, The Holocaust, and the Cold War*, 10.
81 Marco Aurelio Rivelli, *L'arcivescovo del genocidio: Monsignor Stepinac, il Vaticano e la dittatura ustascia in Croazia, 1941–1945* (Milan: Kaos, 1999), 12–13. It appears that Pavelić made two appointments as military vicar. One was Monsignor Stipe Vučetić, and subsequently Stepinac. When Stepinac was charged after the war with war crimes, his position as military vicar was cited in the indictment. See generally Stella Alexander, *The Triple Myth: A Life of Archbishop Alojzije Stepinac* (Boulder, CO: East European Monographs, 1987), 86-87.
82 Mussolini also was an early Ustaša supporter, providing them with logistical and military support.
83 Alexander, *The Triple Myth*, 57-58, citing *Katolički List*, the semi-official journal of the Zagreb diocese, as KL 8 (92) 20.2.41, 93.
84 Blet, *Pius XII and the Second World War*, 108; see also Harold H. Tittmann Jr., *Inside the Vatican of Pius XII: The Memoir of an American Diplomat During World War II* (New York: Image Books/Doubleday, 2010), Kindle edition, location 746 of 3089.
85 Blet, *Pius XII and the Second World War*, 108–9.
86 Quoted in Aarons and Loftus, *Unholy Trinity*, 71.
87 Miha Krek passed the request to Pius XII through Ljubljana's Bishop Gregory Rozman; see Mark Aarons, *Sanctuary: Nazi Fugitives in Australia* (Melbourne: William Heinemann, 1989), 19.
88 Alexander, *The Triple Myth*, 59–60.
89 Menachem Shelah, "The Catholic Church in Croatia, the Vatican and the Murder of the Croatian Jews." Included in *Remembering for the Future: The Holocaust in an Age of Genocides*, Vol. 1 (Oxford: Pergamon, 1988), 266, 274.
90 Aarons and Loftus, *Unholy Trinity*, 71–72; On the same day as Pavelić saw Pius, Secretary of State Maglione issued a letter declaring the visit did not constitute an official recognition of the new Croatian government. Blet, *Pius XII and the Second World War*, 109.
91 Alexander, *The Triple Myth*, 63-65. See also Raul Hilberg, *Destruction of European Jews*, Vol. 1 (New Haven: Yale University Press, 2003), 710–11; see also Phayer, *The Catholic Church and the Holocaust*, 32–33. Besides meeting Pavelić that day, Pius blessed a delegation of the Great Crusader's Brotherhood, a Croatian nationalist group whose goal was to convert Serbs to Catholicism.
92 Chadwick, *Britain and the Vatican*, 193–95; see also Phayer, *Pius XII, the Holocaust, and the Cold War*, 39–40.
93 According to statistics compiled by the German High Command, from the time of the invasion, June 1941, through the end of the war, more than 90 percent of all Nazi casualties were on the Eastern Front.
94 Fritz Menshausen to State Secretary Weizsäcker, September 12, 1941, *Documents on German Foreign Policy 1918-1945*, Series D, Vol. 13 (Washington, DC: United States Government Printing Office, 1964), 489.
95 *Encyclopedia of the Holocaust*, ed. Israel Gutman (New York: Macmillan, 1990), 39.
96 Jonathan Steinberg, *All or Nothing: The Axis and the Holocaust, 1941–43* (London: Routledge, 2002), 36; Phayer, *The Catholic Church and the Holocaust*, 33, n. 11
97 Aarons, *Sanctuary*, 61–62: During the first months of Pavelić's regime, there was no doubt that an anti-Jewish and intra-Slavic race war was under way. Serbs were ordered to wear blue armbands

and Jews yellow Stars of David. All public transport and retail stores had to post signs that announced, "No Serbs, Jews, Gypsies and dogs allowed."

98 Cornwell, *Hitler's Pope*, 250–51. The Vatican did not even officially express its disapproval of forced conversion until 1942. See Rychlak, *Hitler, the War, and the Pope*, 303, citing a memorandum from the Vatican Secretary of State to the Legation to Yugoslavia, January 25, 1942.

99 Quoted in Shelah, "The Catholic Church in Croatia, the Vatican and the Murder of the Croatian Jews," 266–80; see also Aarons, *Sanctuary*, 59–60. Sarić appropriated real estate and bank accounts from Jews. After the war he found safe haven at Rome's Pontificium Institutum Orientalium, a Pontifical school that studies Eastern Christianity. Wilensky, *Six Million Crucifixions*, Kindle edition, 3207 of 8032.

100 Carlo Falconi, *The Silence of Pius XII*, English translation (Boston: Little, Brown, 1970), 273–75, 307–8.

101 Cornwell, *Hitler's Pope*, 254; Phayer, *The Catholic Church and the Holocaust*, 34–35, 38.

102 Williams, *The Vatican Exposed*, 67; the three priests were Josef Culina, Zvonko Brekalo, and Zvonko Lipovac.

103 Phayer, *The Catholic Church and the Holocaust*, 34, n. 14.

104 Falconi, *The Silence of Pius XII*, 308.

105 Branko Bokun, *Spy in the Vatican, 1941–45* (London: Vita, 1973), 11.

106 Through 1941, Bokun tried repeatedly to get the file to Pius, even once trying to hand it to him during a public blessing. The Pope's advisors blocked Bokun's efforts to pass the documents. See generally Bokun, *Spy in the Vatican*; Cornwell, *Hitler's Pope*, 255–57.

107 Phayer, *The Catholic Church and the Holocaust*, 37.

108 Aarons, *Sanctuary*, 62; see also Stevan K. Pavlowitch, *Hitler's New Disorder: The Second World War in Yugoslavia* (New York: Columbia University Press, 2008), in which he cites Pavelić bragging to the Italian Foreign Minister that only twelve thousand Jews are still in the territory controlled by the Ustaša; see also Sergio Romano, *Giuseppe Volpi: industria e finanza tra Giolitti e Mussolini* (Milan: Bompiani, 1979) and Sergio Romano, *Giuseppe Volpi et l'Italie moderne: Finance, industrie et état de l'ère Giolittienne à la Deuxième Guerre Mondiale* (Rome: Ecole Française de Rome, 1982). Author Ronald Rychlak cites an August 4,1942 letter from Miroslav Freiberger, the chief rabbi of Zagreb, to Pius, in which he thanked the Pope for the "limitless goodness that the representatives of the Holy See and the leaders of the Church showed to our poor brothers." Rychlak omits, however, the rabbi's urgent appeal to the Pontiff: "Now, at the moment when the last remnants of our community find themselves in a most crucial situation—at a moment when decisions are being made about their lives—our eyes are fixed upon Your Holiness. We beseech Your Holiness in the name of several thousand women and abandoned children, whose supports are in concentration camps, in the name of widows and orphans, in the name of elderly and the feeble, to help them so that they may remain in their homes and spend their days there, even, if necessary, in the most humble circumstances." The Vatican responded through a Benedictine Abbot, Giuseppe Ramiro Marcone, who acted as the de facto nuncio to Croatia. The church always did what it could to help the suffering, he told Freiberger, and would continue to do so. Freiberger and his wife died at Auschwitz the following year. See Mordecai Paldiel, *Churches and the Holocaust: Unholy Teaching, Good Samaritans, and Reconciliation* (Brooklyn, NY: Ktav Publishing House, 2006), 302.

109 Cornwell, *Hitler's Pope*, 283. From 1944 on the Germans were furious at Pius for his failure to explicitly condemn the Allied carpet-bombing of German cities, in which hundreds of thousands of civilians died. It is not clear if Pius's silence late in the war was due to a shift in his view of who would prevail on the battlefield. See generally Chadwick, *Britain and the Vatican*, 198–99, 207.

110 Chadwick, *Britain and the Vatican*, 193–95; see also Phayer, *Pius XII, the Holocaust, and the Cold War*, 39–40.

111 The Minister in Switzerland (Harrison) to the Secretary of State, March 19, 1942, *Foreign Relations of the United States, Diplomatic Papers, Europe, 1942* (Washington, DC: U.S. Government Printing Office, 1964), 785–86.

112 Report by Oliver Lyttelton, MP, on his Period of Office as Minister of State, Oliver Lyttelton, (WP-42-139), 66/23/19, 79–80, Cabinet Papers, National Archives, Kew, UK.

113 Phayer, *The Catholic Church and the Holocaust*, 45.

114 Letter, Robert Leiber to Cardinal Konrad Graf von Preysing, October 28, 1945, Diözesanarchiv Berlin, V/16-4, Collection of Preysing, Berlin.

115 Phayer, *The Catholic Church and the Holocaust*, 45–46.

116 Coppa, *Controversial Concordats*, 163–65, 177; see also Phayer, *The Catholic Church and the Holocaust*, 67–81. Some German bishops cited what happened in Holland in 1942 as a reason not to act. There, bishops issued a condemnation of Nazi racial policies and deportations. The Germans responded by accelerating the roundup of Jews, sending some twenty thousand to their death in Auschwitz. Among them was Edith Stein, a Carmelite nun who had converted from Judaism before the war (she was canonized in 1998). After the war, Pius's personal aide and housekeeper, Pascalina Lehnert, claimed that Pius had intended to publicly condemn Nazi atrocities but had destroyed his handwritten statement in the Vatican kitchen after the Nazi response in the Netherlands made him fear the consequences of such a denunciation. According to Pascalina, the Pope said, "I now think that if the letter of the bishops has cost the lives of 40,000 persons, my own protest, that carries an even stronger tone, could cost the lives of perhaps 200,000 Jews." She told that story for the first time in 1968, twenty-six years after it allegedly happened. She disclosed it during her testimony before the beatification tribunal completing Pius's first stage toward sainthood. Pascalina never explained how Pius supposedly knew that the Dutch Jews had been gassed. Their ultimate fate was only confirmed from Nazi records after the war. In any case Maria Conrada Grabmair, a domestic worker who was there that evening, testified that she had seen Pius burn some papers but did not know what was in them, nor did she hear him say anything. Pius's nephew also testified before the beatification tribunal. While he also could not confirm Pascalina's account, he said his uncle should be credited for doing more than merely staying silent during the war. He claimed that in the middle of the night, in the Papal chapel, Pius often performed a customized type of exorcism to cast the devil out of Hitler. See also Pascalina Lehnert, *Pio XII il privilegio di servirlo*, trans. Marola Guarducci (Milan: Rusconi, 1984), 148-49.

117 Alexander, *The Triple Myth*, 102. Accompanying Stepinac on his trip to Pius was Father Krunoslav Draganović, one of Bishop Ivan Saric's personal secretaries. Draganović would play an important postwar role in helping Ustašans charged with war crimes evade justice. See Chapter 12, The Ratline. Also Phayer, *The Catholic Church and the Holocaust*, 169.

118 See "Fate of the Wartime Ustaša Treasury," Report of U.S. State Department, June 2, 1998, 2–4; see also, Alexander, *The Triple Myth*, chapter 8, "The Disenchantment," 88–106; Rychlak, *Hitler, the War, and the Pope*, 304; Phayer, *The Catholic Church and the Holocaust*, 31–40 and *Pius XII, the Holocaust, and the Cold War*, 11–12. Although Stepinac was convicted of war crimes in 1946 by the communist government that came to power in the reassembled Yugoslavia, the Vatican maintained he was the victim of a Soviet-inspired witch-hunt against church officials. He died in 1960 while still under house arrest.

119 Carroll, *Constantine's Sword*, 230–31; Robert S. Wistrich, "Reassessing Pope Pius XII's Attitudes Toward the Holocaust," Jerusalem Center for Public Affairs, October 19, 2009.

120 Carroll, *Constantine's Sword*, 231.

121 Carlo Falconi, *The Popes in the Twentieth Century: From Pius X to John XXIII* (Boston: Little, Brown, 1968), 260.

122 Although Pius did not authorize any condemnation of the civilian murders, he was so pleased with the Nazi invasion of the Soviet Union that he allowed Archbishop (later Cardinal) Celso Constantini, the Secretary of the Congregation of the Propagation of the Faith, to give a speech in which the cleric praised German troops as "brave soldiers" locked in a war with "Satan's deputies." The Allies pleaded with the Pope to tone down any language that might convert the German aggression into an anticommunist crusade that generated support among the Catholic faithful: Memorandum, Reports for the Month of June 1941 for the Dominions, July 21, 1941 (WP-R-41-48), 68/8/48, 50–51, Cabinet Papers, National Archives, Kew, UK.

123 Conclusion, Confidential Annex (WM-43-114), 65/39/10, 47, Cabinet Papers, National Archives, Kew, UK. U.S. Intelligence intercepted a 1941 church cable expressing concerns that a priest known only as Father Hoffman, who supposedly worked for the Gestapo and was also a prior of a large Benedictine monastery, had penetrated the Vatican. See NNO32947, September 29, 1941, RG 59, IWG (Nazi war crimes working group), FBI Secret Intercepts, NARA.

124 See generally "Le president de la Unione delle comunità israelitiche Alatri au cardinal Maglione,"(interpretation over the failure of the church to reply to a plea for help in August 1941 from the Union for the Israelite Community of Altari), Vol. 8, 250, Records and Documents of the Holy See Relating to the Second World War, ADSS.

125 Le métropolite de Léopol des Ruthènes Szeptyckyj au pape Pie XII (Szeptycyki to Pius XII),

August 29–31, 1942, (Vatican City: Liberia Editrice Vaticana, 1965–1981), Vol. 3B, Doc. 406, 625, ADSS. Three years earlier Szeptycyki had asked Pius in vain for permission to kill himself as a sign of protest against the Nazi crimes. Pius ignored that entreaty. In his August 1942 letter, he also informed the Pope that the Nazis had killed or rounded up "hundreds of thousands of Christians." The Pope's response two weeks later congratulated Szeptycyki on the fiftieth anniversary of his ordination as a priest and empathized over the hard time that "pastors" were undergoing in Russia. There was no mention of the Jews or the Nazi murders.

126 See generally "La Nonciature en Italie au Ministère des affaires étrangères," 8, Doc. 276, 431, Records and Documents of the Holy See Relating to the Second World War, ADSS; John F. Morley, *Vatican Diplomacy and the Jews During the Holocaust* (New York: Ktav, 1980), 136–37; Phayer, *The Catholic Church and the Holocaust*, 47–48.

127 Sereny, *Into That Darkness*, 139.

128 Memorandum of Sir R. Geoffrey A. Meade, British Foreign Office, August 12, 1942, Foreign Office collection, National Archives, Kew, UK, cited in Chadwick, *Britain and the Vatican*, 209.

129 Harold Tittmann, Taylor's assistant, had remained in Rome when hostilities broke out and found sanctuary inside Vatican City. He was joined by D'Arcy Osborne and other diplomats who had stayed behind. Some envoys, like Taylor, had returned to their native countries and conducted diplomacy from a distance, only occasionally visiting Rome. Since the Vatican did not have an airport, Mussolini's government—as a courtesy to the church—had to approve each of Taylor's landings and departures.

130 Harold Tittmann to the U.S. State Department, Memo No. 114, September 15, 1942, Myron C. Taylor Papers (also available at the Harry S. Truman Library, Independence, MO); also listed as The Minister in Switzerland (Harrison) to the Secretary of State, August 3, 1942, *Foreign Relations of the United States*, Vol. 3, 1943, 926–28, NARA; Chadwick, *Britain and the Vatican*, citing diary of D'Arcy Osborne, 204–5.

131 See Memorandum, Mr. Myron Taylor's visit to Rome, Anthony Eden, October 13, 1942 (WP-42-466), 66/29/46, 228–32, Cabinet Papers, National Archives, Kew, UK; Blet, *Pius XII and the Second World War*, 159.

132 Riccards, *Vicars of Christ*, 135. Although Pius did not excommunicate either Hitler or Mussolini, when the Western powers asked him after the war to do so to communist leaders, he obliged with a 1949 decree that excommunicated all of them from the church. And in 1955 he did the same to Juan Perón, not because the Argentine dictator was pro-Nazi and provided safe haven to war criminals, but because Perón had introduced a divorce law, banned religious education in schools, and issued an edict that the Catholic Feast of Corpus Christi was no longer a national holiday. See generally Records of the German External Assets Branch of the U.S. Allied Commission for Austria (USACA), Section 1945–1950 in USACA Semi-Monthly Flash Reports 15 January–31 July 1949, No. 21–34, File 28, Roll 113, 3–4, NARA.

133 Coppa, *Controversial Concordats*, 175; Cornwell, *Hitler's Pope*, 288–90; Phayer, *The Catholic Church and the Holocaust*, 49, 39.

134 "A Summary of the Conversations Between His Holiness Pope Pius XII and Myron Taylor, Personal Representative of the President of the United States of America to His Holiness Pope Pius XII at Vatican City, September 19, 22, 26, 1942," 25, Vatican: Taylor, Myron C.: Report on 1942 trip (i467) Index, Box 52, Franklin Roosevelt Presidential Library, Hyde Park, NY.

135 "Memorandum of His Holiness Pope Pius XII re Prisoners of War," September 26, 1942, 25, Vatican: Taylor, Myron C.: Report on 1942 trip (i467) Index, Box 52, Franklin Roosevelt Presidential Library, Hyde Park, NY; see also Pope Pius to Myron Taylor, 7001/42, 723, ADSS, cited and reprinted in Margherita Marchione, *Pope Pius XII: Architect for Peace* (Mahwah, NJ: Paulist Press, 2000), 240.

136 See generally "Informal Notes of Myron Taylor," September 27, 1942, 49, Vatican: Taylor, Myron C.: Report on 1942 trip (i467) Index, Box 52, Franklin Roosevelt Presidential Library, Hyde Park, NY.

137 "Strictly Personal Memorandum, Giving Summary of Considerations Expressed by H. E. Monsignor Tardini, in Conversation with H.E. Mr. Myron C. Taylor," September 26, 1942, 73, Vatican: Taylor, Myron C.: Report on 1942 trip (i467) Index, Box 52, Franklin Roosevelt Presidential Library, Hyde Park, NY.

138 The translator for the Taylor-Maglione talks was an American priest, Walther Carroll, who was

stationed at the Vatican. Several days after the meetings, Carroll used his hurriedly scribbled notes to write a detailed account.

139 Cornwell, *Hitler's Pope*, 290; see generally Friedländer, *Nazi Germany and the Jews*.

140 Chadwick, *Britain and the Vatican During the Second World War*, 214, citing Maglione to Taylor, Vol. 5, September 1942, ADSS, 705, 721.

141 Notes of Montini, memo from Myron Taylor, 7247/42, Vatican City, September 27, 1942, ADSS; see also Blet, *Pius XII and the Second World War*, 159–60.

142 Telegram from the Minister in Switzerland (Harrison) to the Secretary of State, October 16, 1942, United States Department of State, *Foreign Relations of the United States*, "Diplomatic Papers," *Europe, 1942* (Washington, DC: U.S. Government Printing Office, 1964), 777.

143 Typical of the type of on-the-ground information available to the Vatican were the accounts of the Ustašan atrocities sent by Croatia's Monsignor Vlatko Maček to both the Catholic Episcopate in Croatia and to an OSS source in Switzerland. "L'Episcopat Catholique en Croatie: Son point de vue à l'égard du raceme-Son attitude à l'égard e la persecution des Orthodoxes-Son activité charitable," RG 226, Entry 210, Box 94, Proj. 974345, NARA. Phayer, *The Catholic Church and the Holocaust*, 43; Pius did issue some public statements about the ravages of war during 1942. For instance, in May, he bemoaned the deaths of innocent civilians. He was not talking about the Jews, but rather the Allied air raids over Japan and Germany that resulted in thousands of civilian deaths. See Rychlak, *Hitler, the War, and the Pope*, 170.

144 Between 1965 and 1981, the Vatican published an eleven-volume set of documents about World War II and Pius XII. Four Jesuit historians compiled the documentation (*Actes et Documents du Saint Siège relatifs à la Seconde Guerre Mondiale, Le Saint Siège et la guerre en Europe*–ADSS). Although most historians acknowledge ADSS as an important historical contribution, some shortcomings are also notable. Michael Phayer, an American professor who has written two acclaimed books about Pius XII and World War II, has criticized the ADSS document release as "critically flawed because of its many omissions." For instance, no documents of the German bishops were published; the private papers of the Nazi sympathizer Bishop Alois Hudal were not unsealed; few papers from Eastern Europe, the center of the death camps, were included. Berlin's Bishop Konrad von Preysing's letters to Pius in 1943 and 1944 were missing. It is not clear whether those are still in the Vatican's archives or were destroyed after the war. Some critical documents given to the Vatican during the war from the Polish representative in exile to the Holy See were added only after historian Gitta Sereny noted their absence. See generally Phayer, *The Catholic Church and the Holocaust*, xvii; see also Sereny, *Into That Darkness*, 329, 334. As for the frequency of the meetings between Pius and Leiber, see Chadwick, *Britain and the Vatican*, 187.

145 For more information see http://www.imdb.com/title/tt0035177/.

146 Cornwell, *Hitler's Pope*, 271; John O'Hanlon, *The Life of St. Malachy O'Morgair, Bishop of Down and Connor, Archbishop of Armagh* (Memphis, TN: General Books LLC, 2013), 111–12.

147 Cornwell, *Hitler's Pope*, 270–71.

148 "A film is being made here," D'Arcy Osborne wrote in his diary on July 31,1942, "for world distribution . . . I cannot say how I deplore this. It is like Hollywood publicity." Separately Osborne wrote that the "Pope's silence is deafening" about "the German crimes." Osborne's diary was the only personal memoir of any of the diplomats stationed at the Vatican that survived the war intact. He took it with him when he returned to England. The other diplomats had burned their files at the request of the Vatican Secretary of State when the Nazis occupied Rome in 1943: Cornwell, *Hitler's Pope*, 285; see also Chadwick, *Britain and the Vatican*, 210–11.

149 John Evangelist Walsh, *Bones of St. Peter: The First Full Account of the Apostle's Tomb* (New York: Doubleday, 1982), 17; Pallenberg, *Inside the Vatican*, 231–33; Kaas and Pius had become friends when the Pope—then Pacelli—served as the Nuncio to Germany during the 1920s. Pacelli had lobbied for Kaas's appointment as a monsignor. Mother Pascalina said the duo were "extremely close." Kaas selected for his team two Jesuits, Engelbert Kirschbaum and Antonio Ferrua; the Vatican's then current architect, Bruno Appolonj-Ghetti; and an anthropology professor, Enrico Josi, who held the title Inspector of the Catacombs. See also Paul Hoffman, *The Vatican's Women: Female Influence at the Holy See* (New York: St. Martin's Griffin, 2003), Kindle edition, location 822 of 2992.

150 Pallenberg, *Inside the Vatican*, 232–33; see also Walsh, *Bones of St. Peter*.

151 Walsh, *Bones of St. Peter*, 27.

152 Pallenberg, *Inside the Vatican*, 235–36. When Kaas died in 1952, he was initially buried at the

Vatican's Campo Santo cemetery. But Pius had him reinterred in the crypt of St. Peter's Basilica, making Kaas the only monsignor buried near virtually all of the twentieth-century Popes; see also Walsh, *Bones of St. Peter*, 57–58.

153 Robert Katz, *The Battle for Rome: The Germans, the Allies, the Partisans, and the Pope, September 1943–June 1944* (New York: Simon & Schuster, 2003), 54. Katz relied on new testimony and freshly released documentation for his book, which was received to widespread critical acclaim on its publication. Katz charged that Pius XII had advance warning—nineteen hours—of the Nazi massacre of civilians at the Ardeatine Caves. Katz's evidence that Pius had known and failed to act was circumstantial. The Vatican condemned the book. The late Pope's sister and niece sued Katz in Rome. Italian law allows surviving relatives to sue for defamation and libel. A Roman judge ruled in the family's favor, concluding that, "Robert Katz wished to defame Pius XII, attributing to him actions, decisions and sentiments which no objective face and no witness authorized him to do." The court fined Katz and gave him a thirteen-month suspended jail sentence. Some pro-Vatican historians, such as Professor Ronald Rychlak, contend that the court ruling means "Someone truly interested in the truth about Pius XII would [be] dissuaded from relying on any of Katz's work." This author believes that while the evidence presented by Katz about Pius's foreknowledge of the massacre is circumstantially persuasive, it is not conclusive. However, the remainder of his book is thoroughly researched and reported. Any citations to Katz's work are separate to those portions from any issue about whether Pius may have known beforehand that the Nazis were about to kill Romans.

154 Walsh, *Bones of St. Peter*, 59.

155 McDowell, *Inside the Vatican*, 30–31.

156 Walsh, *The Bones of St. Peter*, 122–26, 128–31; Hoffman, *The Vatican's Women*, Kindle edition, location 822 of 2992; "Vatican displays Saint Peter's bones for the first time," *The Guardian*, November 24, 2013.

157 Sereny, *Into That Darkness*, 142.

158 Polish Ambassador to Secretary of State, December 19, 1942, Vol. 8, ADSS, 755.

159 Papée met with Pius about ten times while he was in Rome during the war. He also met frequently with Cardinals Maglione and Montini. In one of his last meetings with Pius, in 1944, the Pope greeted him by raising both his arms as if exasperated: "I have listened again and again to your representations about our unhappy children in Poland. Must I be given the same story yet again?" Sereny, *Into That Darkness*, 330, 332.

160 Summary from a War Cabinet Meeting, December 12, 1939 (WM-39-112), 65/2/46, 264–65, Cabinet Papers, National Archives, Kew, UK.

161 Rafael Medoff, "Sidestepping Genocide, Then and Now," *Commentary*, December 13, 2007; see the declaration at http://www.jewishvirtuallibrary.org/jsource/UN/un1942a.html.

162 A digital copy of Pius's 1942 Christmas address is at http://www.papalencyclicals.net/Pius12/P12CH42.HTM; Cornwell, *Hitler's Pope*, 268, n. 1.

163 Defenders of Pius, such as author Ronald Rychlak, argue that since Pius "used the Latin word *stirps*, which means race," he was therefore referring to Jews since it "had been used throughout Europe for centuries as an explicit reference to Jews." Rychlak, *Hitler, the War, and the Pope*, 177. The problem with that contention is that Pius did not use *stirps* when talking about Jews in any other instance. Why would the Pope decide that on the most important address of his Papacy about the Holocaust to be indirect about calling a Jew a Jew?

164 Cornwell, *Hitler's Pope*, 291; see also, Chadwick, *Britain and the Vatican*, 216–17.

165 Chadwick, *Britain and the Vatican*, 219.

166 Palazzo Ciano, *Diary 1937–1947*, English reprint of 1947 book (New York: Enigma, 2002), 536–38. Pius's defenders interpret the broad language of the 1942 Christmas message to be a resounding condemnation of Nazi crimes. They emphasize in particular the sentence about those who "because of their nationality or race, have been consigned to death or to a slow decline." Other historians contend that that single sentence was unfortunately lost in the forty-four-minute talk. What is undeniable is that it unquestionably had no impact. See generally Rychlak, *Hitler, the War, and the Pope*, 177–78; Justus George Lawler, *Popes and Politics: Reform, Resentment, and the Holocaust* (New York: Continuum, 2002), 109–17.

167 M. James Hennesey, "American Jesuit in Wartime Rome: The Diary of Vincent A. McCormick, SJ. (1942–1945)," *Mid America: An Historical Review* 56, No. 1 (1974): 36.

168 Phayer, *Pius XII, the Holocaust, and the Cold War*, 58.

169 Myra Noveck, "Israel's Holocaust Museum Softens Its Criticism of Pope Pius XII," *The New York Times*, July 1, 2012.
170 The Minister in Switzerland (Harrison) to the Secretary of State, recounting Tittmann meeting with Pius XII, January 5, 1943, *Foreign Relations of the United States, 1943, Volume II, Europe* (Washington, DC: U.S. Government Printing Office, 1964), 911–12; see Lawler, *Popes and Politics*, 110–11. Defenders of Pope Pius cite Vatican Radio broadcasts in 1942 about the atrocities in Poland as evidence the church spoke out about the crimes. The few broadcasts addressed the abuses against the church, however, not the Nazi war against the Jews. The American bishops did release a November 1942 statement expressing "a deep sense of revulsion against the cruel indignities heaped upon the Jews in conquered countries." It was the very type of declaration most diplomats hoped in vain the Vatican might issue. See generally Rychlak, *Hitler, the War, and the Pope*, 175.
171 Tittmann to Secretary of State, October 6, 1942, *Foreign Relations of the United States*, Vol. III (Europe), (Washington, DC: U.S. Government Printing Office, 1964), 777.
172 Lawler, *Popes and Politics*, 116.
173 Phayer, *The Catholic Church and the Holocaust*, 86–87, 89–90. Slachta had also implored Hungarian church leaders to influence their Slovakian counterparts. She feared that the "hellish and Satanic" treatment of Jews she had witnessed in Slovakia might spill over to Hungary. She inquired about possibly excommunicating Monsignor Tiso, or the country's prime minister, Bella Tuka, a daily communicant. Her pleas went unanswered.
174 Maria Schmidt, "Margit Slachta's Activities in Support of Slovakian Jewry, 1942–43." Included in *Remembering for the Future: The Holocaust in an Age of Genocides*, Vol. 1 (New York: Pergamon, 1989), 207–11.
175 Morley, *Vatican Diplomacy and the Jews During the Holocaust*, 82.
176 Rychlak, *Hitler, the War, and the Pope*, 304–6. See also Livia Rothkirchen, "Vatican Policy and the 'Jewish Problem' in 'Independent' Slovakia 1939–1945," *Yad Vashem Studies*, 6 (1967), 36.
177 ADSS 9.147, Pressburg (Bratislava), Chargé d'affaires Bratislava, Giuseppe Burzio to Cardinal Maglione, April 10, 1943, ADSS. Reference: Report number 1517 (AES 2754/43), location and date: Presburg (Bratislava). On March 7, 1943, Burzio sent an Italian translation of the letter dated February 17, 1943 (No. 403/I/1943, AES 2754/43).
178 Phayer, *Pius XII, the Holocaust, and the Cold War*, Kindle edition, location 632 of 4256. According to Phayer, Stepinac presented the report to Pius a year later during his April 1942 visit. The precise visit during which he passed the grim report is not clear because the Vatican has not released details about the document. However, Secretary of State Maglione wrote to Stepinac a month after his 1943 visit, thanking him for the documentation about what was happening to Jews and Serbs inside Croatia. Maglione was likely commenting on the nine-page report. See Alexander, *The Triple Myth*, 102–3.
179 George Weigel, "The Vatican Secret Archives Unveiled," *National Review Online*, June 27, 2012; Aarons and Loftus, *Unholy Trinity*, 73; Cromwell, *Hitler's Pope*, 260.
180 Phayer, *The Catholic Church and the Holocaust*, 96–97. The document given by Marie-Benoît to Pius was also omitted from the Vatican's eleven volumes of Acts and Documents of the Holy See related to the Second World War, *Actes et Documents du Saint Siège Relatifs á la Seconde Guerre Mondiale*, ADSS. See also Susan Zuccotti, *Père Marie-Benoit and Jewish Rescue* (Bloomington: Indiana University Press), 2013.
181 Phayer, *The Catholic Church and the Holocaust*, 96.
182 Confidential Annex, Conclusions, Minute 3, Air Policy—Bombing Policy, 65/39/3, 16, Cabinet Papers, National Archives, Kew, UK; "Roman Catholics would be gravely distressed by an air bombardment of Rome," concluded the secret memo distributed to the British civilian and military leadership; Report of 1940 Vatican notice to the Allies, see The Minister in Switzerland (Harrison) to the Secretary of State, January 5, 1943, *Foreign Relations of the United States, 1943*, Europe, 1943, 913–14; see also Blet, *Pius XII and the Second World War*, 106.
183 Myron Taylor to FDR, January 1, 1943, *Foreign Relations of the United States, Diplomatic Papers, 1943, Volume II, Europe* (Washington, DC: U.S. Government Printing Office, 1964), 910–11; see also Minister in Switzerland (Harrison) to the Secretary of State, summarizing Tittmann's audience with Pius XII, January 5, 1943, *Foreign Relations of the United States*, Europe, 1943, 911–12, 910-53; Blet, *Pius XII and the Second World War*, 201–2; Phayer, *The Catholic Church and the Holocaust* 62, n. 97.

184 Although Rome was the focus of the Pope's entreaties, Secretary of State Maglione lobbied that the bombers should also avoid hitting his own ancestral house near Naples. The Allies, meanwhile, had pleaded in vain with the Pope to condemn the massive civilian casualties from the Nazi aerial attacks on Birmingham and Coventry in November 1942. Monsignor Tardini, one of the Pope's aides, told the British envoy that while Pius was "very distressed" about those bombings, he would not comment publicly. As for FDR's assurance about the bombing, see President Roosevelt to Pius XII, June 16, 1943, reprinted in *Foreign Relations of the United States, Diplomatic Papers, 1943, Volume II, Europe* (Washington, DC: U.S. Government Printing Office, 1964), 919–20. As for Eden's threats, see in the same volume "Memorandum by the Acting Chief of the Division of European Affairs (Atherton) to the Under Secretary of State (Welles), March 8, 1943, 915–16.

Behind the scenes, the British aggressively kept open their options about whether to bomb Rome. Churchill himself pressed the issue at a dinner party with Myron Taylor: The Ambassador in the United Kingdom (Winant) to the Secretary of State, London, December 8, 1942, *Foreign Relations of the United States*, Europe, 794.

185 Osborne quoted in Chadwick, *Britain and the Vatican*, 216.

186 Blet, *Pius XII and the Second World War*, 208; Memorandum, Report for the month of July 1943 for the Dominions, India, Burma and the Colonies and Mandated Territories, August 27, 1943 (WP-43-381), 66/40/31, 125, Cabinet Papers, National Archives, Kew, UK.

187 Blet, *Pius XII and the Second World War*, 207-08; Phayer, *The Catholic Church and the Holocaust*, 63.

188 Pius XII to President Roosevelt, July 20, 1943, *Foreign Relations of the United States, Diplomatic Papers, 1943, Volume II, Europe* (Washington, DC: U.S. Government Printing Office, 1964), 931–32; Phayer, *The Catholic Church and the Holocaust*, 63, n. 103.

189 Although prime ministers such as Mussolini ruled effectively with full power, Italy remained technically a monarchy. The royal rule was dissolved finally by a popular referendum on June 2, 1946.

190 Daniel Jonah Goldenhagen, *Hitler's Willing Executioners: Ordinary Germans and the Holocaust* (New York: Alfred A. Knopf, 1996), 159–60.

191 Cornwell, *Hitler's Pope*, 273.

192 Mussolini established his new government—the Italian Social Republic (Repubblica Sociale Italiana)—at Salò on Lake Garda, a Nazi stronghold in northern Italy. See generally Katz, *The Battle for Rome*, 49.

193 For details about the Nazi plans to possibly kidnap Pius, see Dan Kurzman, *A Special Mission: Hitler's Secret Plot to Seize the Vatican and Kidnap Pope Pius XII* (New York: Da Capo, 2008).

194 Katz, *The Battle for Rome*, 39.

195 David Alvarez and Robert Graham, *Nothing Sacred: Nazi Espionage Against the Vatican, 1939–1945* (Studies in Intelligence) (London: Routledge, 1998), 83–85.

196 It is not clear if Nogara was in Rome when the German occupation began. There are no reports of what, if anything, was done inside the IOR to protect its financial records in case the Nazis entered the city-state.

197 Saul Friedländer, *Pius XII and the Third Reich: A Documentation* (New York: Alfred A. Knopf, 1966), 182.

198 Weisbord and Sillanpoa, *The Chief Rabbi, the Pope, and the Holocaust*, 118.

199 Eugenio Zolli, *Before the Dawn: Autobiographical Reflections* (San Francisco: Ignatius Press, 2008), 169-70.

200 Rychlak, *Hitler, the War and the Pope*, 204-05; Zolli, *Before the Dawn*, 170; Weisbord and Sillanpoa, *The Chief Rabbi, the Pope, and the Holocaust*, 120-21.

201 Letter from Nogara to Cardinal Maglione, Vol. 9, ADSS, 494. See also Weisbord and Sillanpoa, *The Chief Rabbi, the Pope, and the Holocaust*, 118–22, 135; Rychlak, *Hitler, the War and the Pope*, 204–05.

202 Weisbord and Sillanpoa, *The Chief Rabbi, the Pope, and the Holocaust*, 121.

203 Robert Katz, *Black Sabbath: A Journey Through a Crime Against Humanity* (West Sussex, UK: Littlehampton Book Services, 1969), 85–87.

204 Katz, *The Battle for Rome*, 103.

205 Zuccotti, *The Italians and the Holocaust*, 101, 104.

206 Eitel Friedrich Molhausen, the German Consul in Rome, inadvertently saw the secret message from SS chief Heinrich Himmler to Obersturmbannführer Kappler, ordering the implementation of the Final Solution against Rome's Jews. Molhausen warned Weizsäcker who in turn passed

along the word to the Vatican. Leonidas G. Hill, "The Vatican Embassy of Ernst Von Weizsäcker," 1943–1945, *The Journal of Modern History*, 39, no. 2, June 1967, 144–47; Weisbord and Sillanpoa, *The Chief Rabbi, the Pope, and the Holocaust*, 65–66; Robert Katz, *Death in Rome* (New York: Macmillan, 1967), 25.

207 Weisbord and Sillanpoa, *The Chief Rabbi, the Pope, and the Holocaust*, 65–66.

208 Morley, *Vatican Diplomacy and the Jews*, 151; Cornwell, *Hitler's Pope*, 301, 304.

209 Maglione quote in Morley, *Vatican Diplomacy and the Jews*, 152,181.

210 Phayer, *The Catholic Church and the Holocaust*, 100.

211 Katz, *The Battle for Rome*, 106.

212 Hitler was not the only dictator Hudal admired. He called Mussolini the "brilliant Duce." Archivo della Congregazione per la dottrina della fede, S.O., R.V. 1934, 29; Prot. 3373/34, Vol. 1, 3–4; see also, Godman, *Hitler and the Vatican*, 76–81; 116–24.

213 Godman, *Hitler and the Vatican*, 169–70. It was the Pope's nephew, Count Carlo Pacelli, the General Counsel of the State of the Vatican, who asked Hudal to intervene. The bishop's German connections were impeccable, so the Vatican considered him the ideal go-between.

214 Phayer, *Pius XII, the Holocaust, and the Cold War*, 77; Steinacher, *Nazis on the Run*.

215 Blet, *Pius XII and the Second World War*, 216–17. As for the Hudal-Pius friendship, see Alfred Persche, unpublished manuscript titled "Die Aktion Hudal: Das letzte Aufgebot des Abendlandes," 72–73, archives of Dokumentationsarchiv des Österreichischen Widerstandes (Documentation Center of Austrian Resistance), Vienna. See generally Aarons and Loftus, *Unholy Trinity*, 31–33.

216 Telegram from Weizsäcker to Foreign Office, Berlin, October 17, 1943, *Inland Il Geheim*, quoted in full in Katz, *Black Sabbath*, 215. Defenders of Pius make an energetic case that the Pope personally intervened to stop the roundup of Rome's Jews, and none more so than Gary L. Krupp and his New York–based Pave the Way Foundation. *La Stampa*'s "Vatican Insider" column described Pave the Way as "the American foundation established and led by the Jew Gary Krupp has been fighting for years to uncover the balanced historical truth on the figure and work of Pope Pacelli, the victim of a 'black legend' born in the 60s and now still very much alive, despite the efforts of many historians on both sides, Jews and Christian, to dispel it." Krupp contends that Pius dispatched his nephew, Carlo Pacelli, and Father Pankratius Pfeiffer, the superior general of the Salvatorian Order, to plead with the German military commander of Rome, Generalleutnant Reiner Stahel, "to interfere personally in this affair." Krupp claims as a result, Stahel intervened with SS Chief Heinrich Himmler and "persuaded him to cease the persecution of Jews in Rome." But that account is predicated on double hearsay given decades after the war from the Jesuit priest who had been appointed by the church to present the case for Pius XII's beatification. The story of what happened with Stahel relies on an account told by Father Peter Gumpel. He related a conversation he had with another German general, Dietrich Beelitz, who purportedly claimed to have overheard the telephone conversation between Stahel and Himmler. The problem is that Father Gumpel did not disclose any of it until a 2004 publication setting forth the case in favor of making Pius XII a saint. By that time, both Stahel and Beelitz were dead and the account could not be independently confirmed. Further clouding the account is that Gumpel's objectivity about Pius XII has been called into question. In 2009, for instance, he blamed the World Jewish Congress and Anti-Defamation League for blocking Pius's ascent to sainthood. In 2014, the ninety-one-year-old Gumpel affirmed his belief that "sooner or later Pius XII's beatification will happen." (Gumpel quoted in Sarah Delaney, "Pope Pius XII Promoter Says Jewish Pressure an Obstacle to Sainthood," Catholic News Service, June 23, 2009; Gumpel quoted in Federico Cenci, "Sooner or Later, Pius XII Will Be Beatified," Zenit, Vatican City, June 30, 2014; description of Pave the Way in Marco Tosatti, "Pius XII and October 17, 1943: new documents," "Vatican Insider," *La Stampa*, July 31, 2011); Gary L. Krupp, *Pope Pius XII and World War II*, Kindle edition, location 1528–53).

217 Some historians have suggested that Pius feared that if he protested, the Germans might detain him or take him as prisoner to Germany.

218 See Zuccotti, *Under His Very Windows*, 155; see also Weisbord and Sillanpoa, *The Chief Rabbi, the Pope, and the Holocaust*, 63; Katz, *The Battle for Rome*, 109.

219 Susan Zuccotti, "Pius XII and the Holocaust: The Case in Italy," in *The Italian Refugee: Rescue of Jews during the Holocaust*, eds. I. Herzer, Kathleen Voight, and J. Burgwin (Washington, DC: Catholic University of America Press, 1989), 133.

220 Carroll, *Constantine's Sword*, 524.

221 Phayer, *The Catholic Church and the Holocaust*, 98. Some Catholic writers, such as Britain's Joanna Bogle, have argued that the nuns and priests who sheltered Jews did so only as part of an authorized directive from Pius XII. But the work, while highlighting the bravery of many individual clerics and nuns when it came to saving Jews, falls short of conclusively establishing that it was official church policy. See Joanna Bogle, *Courage and Conviction: Pius XII, the Bridgettine Nuns and the Rescue of the Jews* (Herefordshire, UK: Gracewing, 2013). See also Dalin, *The Myth of Hitler's Pope*, Kindle edition, location 1465–1563 of 4813.

222 Weisbord and Sillanpoa, *The Chief Rabbi, the Pope, and the Holocaust*, 65, 69–82; 121; Blet, *Pius XII and the Second World War*, 165, 200, 218; Krupp, *Pope Pius XII and World War II*, Kindle edition, location 2449 of 5877.

223 *L'Osservatore Romano*, June 21, 1948; This was the time during which Pius worked on the two most important encyclicals of his Papacy. But neither was focused on the war or the moral duty of Catholics at times of such unprecedented civilian carnage. *Mystic Corporis Christi* (On the Mystical Body of Christ) was released in June. It was an ecclesiastical insider's discourse on why the Pope believed the Church was the living mystical body of Christ: http://www.papalencyclicals.net/Pius12/P12MYSTI.HTM. The second—*Divino Afflante Spiritu* (On the Promotion of Biblical Studies)—was released a few months later on September 30. *Divino* strongly condemned the spiritual exegesis of modernists: http://www.papalencyclicals.net/Pius12/P12DIVIN.HTM.

224 Chadwick, *Britain and the Vatican*, 289.

225 Ibid., 289.

226 Osborne's memo describing the meeting was not declassified by the British government until December 1998; Richard Z. Chesnoff, *Pack of Thieves: How Hitler and Europe Plundered the Jews and Committed the Greatest Theft in History* (New York: Doubleday, 1999), 249–50.

227 Hoffman, *Anatomy of the Vatican*, 281–82.

228 Martin Gilbert, *The Holocaust: A History of the Jews of Europe During the Second World War* (New York: Holt, Rinehart & Winston, 1985), 623. In 1944, the Pope covertly asked the American government to do its best to stop the resettlement of Jews in northern Italy. By that time, however, the German army had fled Rome and Pius might have felt a bit braver, although still subdued in his opposition to the plight of the Jews.

229 Vol. 9, ADSS, 426, 274, as cited in Marrus, *The Nazi Holocaust, Part 8: Bystanders to the Holocaust*, Vol. 3, 1264.

230 Wistrich, "Reassessing Pope Pius XII's Attitudes Toward the Holocaust."

231 Herczl, *Christianity and the Holocaust of Hungarian Jewry*, 206.

232 Pius had set a poor precedent in Hungary with his 1943 appointment of Josef Grosz as the country's second-ranking bishop. Grosz was an avid supporter of Hungary's fascist party, the Arrow Cross. Many Hungarian Catholics, and even other prelates, interpreted Grosz's appointment as a tacit approval by Pius of the new bishop's political views.

233 Blet, *Pius XII and the Second World War*, 166.

234 Amiram Barkat, "New Research Bares Vatican Criticism of Nazi-Era Pope," *Haaretz*, December 1, 2006, 1. The accounts of both Bishops Burzio and Roncalli indicate that the Vatican had the Auschwitz Protocols by May 1944, although the church's official position is that Pius did not see the document until October.

235 Blet, *Pius XII and the Second World War*, 166–67; see also David B. Woolnera and Richard G. Kuria, eds., *FDR, the Vatican, and the Roman Catholic Church in America, 1933–1945* (New York: Palgrave Macmillan, 2003), chapter 13.

236 Katz, *The Battle for Rome*, 188.

237 Blet, *Pius XII and the Second World War*, 223–24.

238 Katz, *The Battle for Rome*, 189.

239 Foreign Office files, 371/43869/21, National Archives, Kew, UK, cited in Chadwick, *Britain and the Vatican*, 290; see also Robert G. Weisborg and Michael W. Honhart, "A Question of Race: Pope Pius XII and the 'Colored Troops' in Italy," *The Historian*, vol. 65, issue 2, winter 2002, 415).

240 As early as 1920, when he was Secretary of State, Pacelli had requested Pius XI's intervention to stop France's deployment of black troops, mostly of African heritage, in fighting in the Rhineland. That was because he said they were routinely raping German women and children. It was a charge the French adamantly rejected and called "odious." Credible proof of such widespread behavior was never forthcoming. Foreign Office Papers, in Public Records Office, Kew, UK,

371/43869/21. For more information on the British national archives depository, see http://www.nationalarchives.gov.uk/default.htm See also Cornwell, *Hitler's Pope*, quoting an interview with P. Gumple, S.J., 319, 320.

241 Katz, *The Battle for Rome*, 157.

242 Blet, *Pius XII and the Second World War*, 287.

243 Katz, *The Battle for Rome*, 324–25.

244 Hoffman, *Anatomy of the Vatican*, 21–22.

245 Squires, "Wartime Pope Pius XII 'More Concerned About Communism than Holocaust,'" 1, referring to the discovery of previously classified wartime correspondence from D'Arcy Osborne to the British Foreign Office recounting details of one of his meetings with Pius XII.

246 David Kranzler, "The Swiss Press Campaign That Halted Deportations to Auschwitz and the Role of the Vatican, the Swiss and Hungarian Churches," in *Remembering for the Future: The Holocaust in an Age of Genocide*, Vol. 1, 162. Since the Nazi invasion a few months earlier, Horthy was mostly sidelined and the nation's power was held by its Nazi Governor General, SS Brigadeführer Edmund Veesenmayer.

247 Phayer, *The Catholic Church and the Holocaust*, 107.

248 Ibid., 108–9.

249 Cooney, *The American Pope*, 141.

250 In May 2014, to the consternation of church traditionalists, Pope Francis announced he was not ready to allow Pius's beatification. "There's still no miracle," Francis told reporters as he returned to Rome after a two-day visit to Israel. "If there are no miracles, it can't go forward. It's blocked there." Before 1983, two miracles were necessary for beatification. Only one is now required. Nicole Winfield, "Pope Francis Says Pius XII's Beatification Won't Go Ahead," *The Times of Israel*, May 27, 2014.

251 See generally Lawler, *Popes and Politics*, 133.

252 Phayer, *The Catholic Church and the Holocaust*, 25–26; see also Chadwick, *Britain and the Vatican*, 259–60, 275; Cornwell, *Hitler's Pope*.

253 Lawler, *Popes and Politics*, 125. See generally Christina Susanna House, "Eugenio Pacelli: His Diplomacy Prior to His Pontificate and Its Lingering Results," (thesis, Bowling Green State University, August 2011). According to Charles R. Gallagher, a Jesuit and a history professor, "[I]t is clear that at least diplomatically, during World War II Pope Pius XII engaged in an excruciating tussle between employing the secrecy of 19th-century practice with the principles of open dialogue and public discussion of the 20th." It was Gallagher who first found a 1938 document criticizing Nazis that the then Cardinal Pacelli had given to Joseph Kennedy. "[I]t also shows that Pacelli preferred to make such remarks in private, only to high-ranking diplomats and within the context of formal discussion. Like many other diplomats of his time, he was not yet able to break completely from the old rules of diplomatic conduct." Gallagher, "Personal, Private Views."

254 Foreign Office files, Osborne to Halifax, December 7, 1940, 380/106, National Archives, Kew, UK.

255 Kertzer, *The Pope and Mussolini*, Kindle edition, location 468 of 10577.

256 When Pacelli was in Germany after World War I, there were violent pro-communist demonstrations. Pacelli wrote to the Vatican Secretary of State about how the three red leaders were all Jews. That experience helped form his later view that socialism, communism, and Jews were all intertwined. He described a trip by a colleague to meet representatives of the new Bolshevik government that controlled Munich. "An army of employees were dashing about to and fro, giving out orders, waving bits of paper, and in the middle of this, a gang of young women, of dubious appearance, Jews like all the rest of them, hanging around in all the offices with lecherous demeanor and suggestive smiles. The boss of this female rabble was Levien's mistress, a young Russian woman, a Jew and divorcée, who was in charge. . . . This Levien is a young man, of about thirty to thirty-five, also Russian and a Jew. Pale, dirty, with vacant eyes, hoarse voice, vulgar, repulsive, with a face that is both intelligent and sly." (Max Levien was head of the Munich Soviet movement.) See also Cornwell, *Hitler's Pope*, pp. 295–96. Defenders of Pius, like Jesuit historian Pierre Blet, counter that the letter to the Vatican Secretary of State was probably only signed by Pacelli, as such matters were often prepared by one of the Nuncio's aides. Of course, that overlooks Pacelli's micromanagement. It would have been out of character for Pacelli to send such a letter to his superiors without signing off on every word.

257 David L. Kertzer, "The Popes Against the Jews: The Vatican's Role in the Rise of Modern Anti-Semitism," *The New York Times*, September 23, 2001.

258 The International Catholic-Jewish Historical Commission—consisting of three Catholic scholars appointed by the Vatican and three Jewish scholars selected by a group of Jewish organizations—concluded a ten-year study into the question of Pius XII and his role during World War II in 2009. The reassessment of Pius was that "Pius XII was neither 'Hitler's pope' nor a 'righteous Gentile.' The polished diplomat ultimately won out over the voice of conscience in facing the formidable trial of the Holocaust." In July 2012, Yad Vashem, Israel's Holocaust Memorial and Museum, modified text in an exhibit so it was less critical of Pius. The title of that portion of the exhibit was changed from "Pius XII" to "The Vatican." The previous text noted that Pius had signed the Reichskonkordat with Germany "even if this meant recognizing the Nazi racist regime." The revision noted that Pius was only the Papal Nuncio when the Concordat was negotiated and it removed the last sentence. In another instance, the previous text addressed the deportation of Rome's Jews by concluding that Pius "did not intervene." The revision states that Pius merely "did not publicly protest." In September 2013, Yad Vashem further moderated its position, adding that the Vatican was sometimes aware that convents sheltered Jews hiding from the Nazis.

Although the changes seem minor, considering they were made at Israel's most important tribute to the Holocaust, they were significant. It was a confirmation that judging Pius's wartime actions had become more complex and nuanced over time with the release of more documents. It was also a victory for the Vatican, which had for years bitterly protested the Yad Vashem text. In 2007, Archbishop Antonio Franco, the Papal Nuncio to Israel and the Palestinian territories, had threatened to not take part in Israel's Holocaust Remembrance Day ceremony because of it. After the changes, Franco told the Catholic News Service that the revision was "a step forward"; see Wistrich, "Reassessing Pope Pius XII's Attitudes Toward the Holocaust."

Chapter 9: The Blacklist

1 The Nazis also collected a similar tax on behalf of Protestants. Ninety-five percent of all Germans paid the church tax during the years Hitler was in power. The concept of the tax has since spread to other countries, presently covering Catholics in Germany, Sweden, Austria, Denmark, Finland, and Iceland, as well as parts of Switzerland and Italy. The average tax is 9 percent of the person's income tax. So someone paying a $5,000 income tax would pay another $450 as a church tax. In 2010, the last year for which the church released information, the tax brought in about $14 billion, paying 70 percent of the Vatican's expenses. That year, a retired German professor of church law filed a lawsuit demanding that he be allowed to receive Communion and have a Catholic burial, but not be forced to pay the tax. A German court ruled against him, in a decision the national press dubbed "pay to pray." An extension of the tax to cover capital gains as of 2015 has caused thousands of Germans to quit their parishes. See Tom Hehegan, "Capital Gains Mean Church Losses in New German Tax Twist," Reuters, August 29, 2014. See also Doris L. Bergen, "Nazism and Christianity: Partners and Rivals? A Response to Richard Steigmann-Gall, *The Holy Reich: Nazi Conceptions of Christianity, 1919–1945*," *Journal of Contemporary History* 42, no. 1 (January 2007): 29–30.

2 Clemens Vollnhals, "Das Reichskonkordat von 1933 als Konfliktfall im Alliierten Kontrollrat," *Vierteljahrshefte für Zeitgeschichte*, 35, Jahrg., October 4, 1987), 677, 695–97. See also Paul L. Williams, *The Vatican Exposed* (Amherst, NY: Prometheus Books, 2003), Kindle edition, 428 of 2622.

3 Because of Luxembourg's restrictions on access to company files, it is not possible to determine how Grolux was ultimately dissolved or what happened to its 36 million Luxembourg francs (then worth approximately $2.25 million). McGoldrick, "New Perspectives on Pius XII and Vatican Financial Transactions During the Second World War," 1033.

4 RG 226, Office of Strategic Services (OSS), Box 168, XL12579, NARA.

5 Pollard, *Money and the Rise of the Modern Papacy*, 190.

6 William Harvey Reeves, "The Control of Foreign Funds by the United States Treasury," *Law and Contemporary Problems*, Duke University Law School, 1945, 22.

7 Pollard, *The Vatican and the Wall Street Crash*, 1085, 1091. Some reports claim that the amount

of gold transferred was substantially higher, approximately $22 million; see Lo Bello, *The Vatican Empire*, 27; see also McGoldrick, "New Perspectives on Pius XII and Vatican Financial Transactions During the Second World War."

8 Gollin, *Worldly Goods*, 457–58; see Pollard, *Money and the Rise of the Modern Papacy*, 190. Nogara added to the church's American gold reserves during the war. As late as February 1942, the Vatican Bank bought $1.5 million of additional bullion. See Memo, National City Bank to Amministrazione Pontificia per le Opere di Religione, "Purchase of Gold Value $1,499,935.35 by Vatican," FBI Intercepts, RG 59, IWG (Nazi war crimes working group), Section 2, NNU32771, NARA.

9 In 2012, documents released from the National Archives of the United Kingdom revealed that from 1941 through mid-1943 the British government had intercepted many Vatican cables and communications about the church's investments to the U.S. and U.K. They provide a limited view of Nogara's overall strategy. Other documents that provide a fuller portrait of Nogara's financial management are sealed in the British National Archives; a year of ABSS statements at J. P. Morgan are missing; and the diary of the British envoy to the Vatican, Sir D'Arcy Osborne, is in the British library but heavily redacted. U.S. Treasury Department, Treasury Financial Agent, Form 1, November 10, 1941, part of the collection of T series, 231/140, National Archives, Kew, UK; also McGoldrick, "New Perspectives on Pius XII and Vatican Financial Transactions During the Second World War," 1032.

10 Executive Order No. 8839, April 10, 1940, Documents Pertaining to Foreign Funds Control, U.S. Treasury Department, Washington: March 30, 1943, 6, Papers of Bernard Bernstein, Subject File, Box 23, Harry S. Truman Library, Independence, MO.

11 American isolationists objected to the freezing order, criticizing it as a provocative act that could encourage an Axis retaliation against the U.S. FDR claimed authority for his executive order from a broad World War I–era statute, the Trading with the Enemy Act.

12 U.S. Treasury Department, "Documents Pertaining to Foreign Funds Control," Washington, March 30, 1943, 6, Papers of Bernard Bernstein Subject File, Box 23, Harry S. Truman Library, Independence, MO; see also Mira Wilkins, *The History of Foreign Investment in the United States, 1914–1945* (Cambridge: Harvard University Press, 2004), 451–52, 829, citing U.S. Department of the Treasury, Documents Pertaining to Foreign Funds Control (Washington, DC, 1945).

13 Executive Order 8785, 6 Federal Register, 2897, 1941. And in Documents Pertaining to Foreign Funds Control, U.S. Treasury Department, Washington: March 30, 1943, 6, 11, Papers of Bernard Bernstein, Subject File, Box 23, Harry S. Truman Library, Independence, MO.

14 Shortly after that amendment, the Nazis attacked the Soviet Union. Russia was then removed from the blacklist.

15 "Italians Take $480,000,000 from the U.S.," *New York Post*, May 3, 1941.

16 General License No. 44, Roman Curia—Generally Licensed National, Documents Pertaining to Foreign Funds Control, U.S. Treasury Department, Washington, March 30, 1943, 44, Papers of Bernard Bernstein, Subject File, Box 23, Harry S. Truman Library, Independence, MO.

17 "Nephew of Pius XI Dies," *The New York Times*, January 29, 1953, 28.

18 Cardinal Carlo Salotti, Prefect of the Sacred Congregation of Rites, and one of Pius's closest advisors, "is pro-Fascist and a close friend of Pius XII." Cardinal Adolf Bertram, Director of the Confraternity of German Bishops, "is a weak man who has collaborated with the Nazis." Genoa's cardinal, Pietro Boetto, "is unquestionably the ringleader of the Fascist clique within the College of Cardinals." Cardinal Raffaele Carlo Rossi, Secretary of the Consistorial Congregation, "is decidedly pro-Fascist." Cardinal Celso Benigno Luigi Constantini is "a Fascist." Argentina's Cardinal Santiago Luis Copello is "a Fascist, [and] anti-United States." Paris's Cardinal Emmanuel Célestin Suhard is "a collaborationist." And Cardinal Nicola Canali, President of Vatican City, is "a Fascist." J.C.H. to A.W.D. (Allen Dulles), OSS, September 10, 1942, RG 226, E217, Box 20, Location 00687RWN26535, NARA.

19 Foreign Office files, 37150078, Financial Activities of the Vatican, John Crump, Ministry of Economic Warfare, to Peter Hebblethwaite, Foreign Office, March 29, 1945, National Archives, Kew, UK; U.S. Treasury Department, "Documents Pertaining to Foreign Funds Control," Washington, March 30, 1943, 24, Papers of Bernard Bernstein, Subject File, Box 23, Harry S. Truman Library, Independence, MO.

20 Besier, *The Holy See and Hitler's Germany*, 163.

21 RG 131, Department of Justice, Foreign Funds and Control Records, Box 487, Letter of John

Pehle to Henry Morgenthau, April 21, 1942, NARA; see also Charles Higham, *Trading with the Enemy: An Exposé of the Nazi-American Money Plot, 1933–1949* (New York: Delacorte, 1983), 191. The U.S. did more than simply fail to list the Vatican as a blocked country under the president's executive order. At times, the U.S. gave the church, under the direction of Pius XII's nephew Carlo Pacelli, permission to import supplies through an Allied naval blockade.

22 Harold H. Tittmann Jr., *Inside the Vatican of Pius XII*, Kindle edition, locations 665–77.

23 Ibid.

24 McGoldrick, "New Perspectives on Pius XII and Vatican Financial Transactions During the Second World War," 1045; Phayer, *Pius XII, the Holocaust, and the Cold War*, 96, citing J. Edgar Hoover, FBI Director, to Adolf Berle Jr., Assistant Secretary of State, September 22, 1941, Decimal File 1940–44, Box 5689, File 866A.001/103, RG 59, NARA. For details on the Pope's personal account, see Memo from Chase National Bank to Ferdinando Federici, September 30, 1941, and to Nelson A. Rockefeller, December 6, 1941, "Pope's Account with Chase National Bank, New York," RG 59, IWG (Nazi war crimes working group), FBI Secret Intercepts, NARA.

25 "Authorizing a Proclaimed List of Certain Blocked Nationals and Controlling Certain Exports," July 22, 1941, Documents Pertaining to Foreign Funds Control, U.S. Treasury Department, Washington: March 30, 1943, 14–15, Papers of Bernard Bernstein Subject File, Box 23, Harry S. Truman Library, Independence, MO. See also Reeves, "The Control of Foreign Funds by the United States Treasury," 57.

26 A historical review of the Proclaimed List for just Latin America—in which most of the countries were neutral during the war—reveals that in the first year it was issued some six thousand businesses were listed. Those marked as pro-Axis by the State Department, relying invariably on undisclosed evidence assembled by the FBI, included a diverse group, ranging from accountants, lawyers, even landlords who had done business with a German, Italian, or Japanese national: Max Paul Friedman, *Economic Warfare, Enemy Civilians, and the Lessons of World War II Nazis and Good Neighbors: The United States Campaign Against the Germans of Latin American World War II* (Cambridge: Cambridge University Press, 2005), 418.

27 F. W. W. McCombe's Report on Vatican Funds, May 16, 1941, T 231, 1131, National Archives, Kew, UK. The TWE (Trading with the Enemy) files were released by the British government mostly between 1999 and 2008 and are maintained at the Department of Trade and Industry: Enemy Property Claims Assessment Panel (EPCAP) Secretariat; Database of Seized Property, Reference Section NK 1, National Archives, Kew, UK. The British published a "Statutory List," which was their blacklist.

28 McGoldrick, "New Perspectives on Pius XII and Vatican Financial Transactions During the Second World War," 1043.

29 On January 21, 2013, *The Guardian* published a "special investigation" under the banner headline, "How the Vatican Built a Secret Property Empire Using Mussolini's Millions." The newspaper followed the Lateran Pacts money that was deposited into British Grolux to list the properties the church had acquired over the years. "Behind a disguised offshore company structure, the church's international portfolio has been built up over the years, using cash originally handed over by Mussolini in return for papal recognition of the Italian fascist regime in 1929. Since then the international value of Mussolini's nest-egg has mounted until it now exceeds £500m." A Vatican spokesman dismissed it the following day: "I am amazed by this article in the *Guardian*, which seems to come from someone who is among the asteroids. . . . These things have been public knowledge for 80 years." David Leigh, Jean François Tanda, and Jessica Benhamou, "Mussolini, a Vatican Vow of Silence and the Secret £500m Property Portfolio: Offshore Structure Veils List of London Properties Fascist Origins of Papacy's Wealth Hidden from 1931," *The Guardian*, January 22, 2013, 1.

As for Nogara's transfer of the Vatican's share of British Grolux to the Morgan Bank, see Foreign Commonwealth Office files, 371/30197, letter of P. W. Dixon to F. W. Combe, Trading with the Enemy Branch, August 27, 1941, National Archives, Kew, UK; see also Pollard, *Money and the Rise of the Modern Papacy*, 189, and "The Vatican and the Wall Street Crash," 1088.

30 Conclusion Former Reference regarding the Foreign Secretary: WM (40) 99, 65/6/44, 388, Cabinet Papers, National Archives, Kew, UK.

31 Foreign Office files, 37150078, Financial Activities of the Vatican, John Crump, Ministry of Economic Warfare, to Peter Hebblethwaite, Foreign Office, March 29, 1945, National Archives, Kew, UK; see also Nechama Janet Cohen Cox, "The Ministry of Economic Warfare and Britain's

Conduct of Economic Warfare, 1939–1945," King's College London, 2001, online at https://kclpure.kcl.ac.uk/portal/files/2935689/246631.pdf; see Pollard, *Money and the Rise of the Modern Papacy*, 190.

32 Maurizio Pegrari, *Dizionario Biografico degli Italiani*, Vol. 78, (Rome: Istituto della Enciclopedia Italiana, 2013).

33 "Italy's Money Mart Here Shut by U.S. Order," *New York Herald Tribune*, June 22, 1941.

34 RG 84, Safehaven Files, Banca della Svizzera Italiana, memo from managing director to United States consul in Berne, March 30, 1943, Entry 323, Box 6, NARA. In 1947, Banca della Svizzera Italiana formed a partnership with the Bank of Rome and opened the Banco di Roma per la Svizzera. One of Pius XII's nephews, Prince Marcantonio Pacelli, was appointed as President. See Hoffman, *Anatomy of the Vatican*, 181.

35 Sudameris was actually a collection of eight banks operating in five countries. Phayer, *Pius XII, the Holocaust, and the Cold War*, 108; see generally Chernow, *The House of Morgan*, iBook edition, 795–96. The Sudameris banks had shares in Nogara's interlocking network, the same one he used to help German firms move assets to South America.

36 RG 226, Research and Analysis Branch, Letter from R. Fenton, UK, Entry 19, Box 90, XL6425, NARA; see also Pollard, *Money and the Rise of the Modern Papacy*, 191; and Leigh et al., "Mussolini, a Vatican Vow of Silence and the Secret £500m Property Portfolio."

37 After the war Malagodi served as secretary to Italy's Liberal Party and in the 1980s was the President of the Italian Senate. Pegrari, *Dizionario Biografico degli Italiani*.

38 Fondo AD2 (Nogara), Cart. 15, fasc. 40–45, telegram of Giovanni Malagodi to Bernardino Nogara, May 15, 1943, ASBCI, cited in Pollard, *Money and the Rise of the Modern Papacy*.

39 Phayer, *Pius XII, the Holocaust, and the Cold War*, 110–11; Confidential cable dated December 21, 1945, RG 59, Department of State, Rome Embassy, File 851, Box 161, NARA.

40 The State Department Report that covers Sudameris, Nogara, and the Vatican is the "Report of Recent Activities of the Banque Francaise et Italienne pour L'Amerique du Sud (Sudameris)," by Virginia Marino of the Economic Warfare Section of the War Division of the U.S. Department of Justice, May 9, 1944, Entry 16, Box 850, File 70712, RG 226, Location 190/2/28/6, NARA.

41 Ministry of Economic Warfare, letter to Berne Embassy, April 10, 1945, National Archives, Kew, UK; see also Pollard, *Money and the Rise of the Modern Papacy*, 192; see also Phayer, *Pius XII, the Holocaust, and the Cold War*, 110.

42 See generally Pollard, *Money and the Rise of the Modern Papacy*, 192.

43 Nogara to J. P. Morgan & Co., New York, November 10, 1941, T 231, 140, National Archives, Kew, UK; see also McGoldrick, "New Perspectives on Pius XII and Vatican Financial Transactions During the Second World War," 1039.

44 General Ruling No. 17, 8 Federal Register, 14, 351, 1943; Reeves, *The Control of Foreign Funds by the United States Treasury*, 42–43; US Treasury Department, "Documents Pertaining to Foreign Funds Control," Washington, March 30, 1943, 6–17, 19–20; Treasury Department, Office of the Secretary, April 13, 1943, General License No. 68A, As Amended, 67, 106, Papers of Bernard Bernstein, Subject File, Box 23, Harry S. Truman Library, Independence, MO.

45 Journal entries for January 2, 1942, and March 19, 1942, Series T 231, 141–42, National Archives, Kew, UK.

46 Reeves, *The Control of Foreign Funds by the United States Treasury*, 31. It is also possible that the Vatican investigation merely got lost in the volume of cases into possible evasions of the economic warfare laws that flooded into the Treasury Department. Treasury received nearly 600,000 reports of violations over four years.

47 U.S. Treasury Department, "Documents Pertaining to Foreign Funds Control," Roman Curia—Generally Licensed National—General License No. 44, Washington, March 30, 1943, 44–45, Papers of Bernard Bernstein, Subject File, Box 23, Harry S. Truman Library, Independence, MO.

48 Germany and Japan were excluded from the list of countries from which it could operate. In the spring of 1943, U.S. officials were furious to intercept an SS cable that reported the Vatican had sent $45,000 to Japan to care for wounded soldiers. Treasury threatened to terminate the church's special status, but the Vatican was spared any punishment after claiming the money was sent to the church's Apostolic Delegate there for "relief of prisoners of war in Japanese hands." Phayer, *Pius XII, The Holocaust, and the Cold War*, 103–5; see also Memorandum, U.S. Treasury Department, regarding the transfer of sums in U.S. currency to the currency of European countries, Box

5690, RG 59, Location 250/34/11/1, and letter to Secretary Morgenthau, "Treasury Provision of Swiss Francs for the Holy See," March 8, 1943, RG 131, APC-FFC General Correspondence 1942–60, Box 482, Transfer of Funds, Vatican City, NND 968103, NARA. Records at the National Archives, RG 59, IWG (Nazi war crimes working group), FBI Secret Intercepts, has hundreds of pages of government tracking of transfers between Vatican-owned bank accounts in the U.S. and banks abroad, as well as details about the dividends earned on shares and bonds, from the company stocks held by the church in its U.S. accounts.

The presence of church missions in otherwise blacklisted or sanctioned countries continued as a problem between the U.S. and the Vatican long past World War II. Information contained in a WikiLeaks cable shows that as late as 2002, the Treasury Department had blocked Vatican funds sent to Cuba, prompting a furious response from the church's Secretary of State. Treasury, as it did in World War II, backed off and released the money: https://www.wikileaks.org/plusd/cables/02VATICAN83_a.html.

49 The IOR's roots go back to an 1887 commission of cardinals appointed by Pope Leo XIII. Their role was to use some cash donations from the faithful to buy property. That commission morphed in 1904 under Pius X into the Commission of Religious Works. And in 1908, the Pope removed its "cardinal only" status, and renamed the small group the Prelate's Administrative Commission for the Works of Religion. His successor, Pius XI, approved in 1934 some expanded powers that allowed the commission to act as a financial clearinghouse for other Vatican branches. In 1941, a year before he created the IOR, Pius XII had placed the commission under the oversight of a panel of cardinals, and gave it limited rights to accept deposits from some clerics, only for the "works of religion and Christian piety." The commission was subsumed by the IOR. See generally Raw, *The Moneychangers*, 53.

50 See Reese, *Inside the Vatican*, 205–6.

51 See J. Paul Horne, "How the Vatican Manages Its Money," *Institutional Investor*, January 1971, 78. Canon lawyers made a point that the IOR was "in Vatican City" not "of the Vatican." That seemed to create some distance between the IOR and the Pope in case the bank ended up in any difficulty. See Hoffman, *Anatomy of the Vatican*, 185.

52 "Marcinkus Comments," *Il Sabato*, October 22, 1982.

53 Martin, *Rich Church, Poor Church*, 45.

54 Pollard, *Money and the Rise of the Modern Papacy*, 200; see also Martin, *Rich Church, Poor Church*, 45.

55 Raw, *The Moneychangers*, 53.

56 The countries that share a border with Italy are France, Switzerland, Slovenia, Austria, San Marino, and the Vatican.

57 "Declaration of attorney, Franzo Grande Stevens, in support of the IOR's motion to dismiss plaintiffs third amended complaint," October 30, 2000, Turin, Case No. C-99-4941 MMC, United States District Court, Northern District of California, § 21: "It is the custom and practice of the IOR not to retain records after ten years."

58 Raw, *The Moneychangers*, 54.

59 For examples of U.S. intelligence efforts to keep track of Vatican financial transactions, see in general Federal Bureau Investigation, Secret, Interagency Working Group (IWG), Nazi War Crimes, FBI Secret Intercepts—Vatican, RG 59, NARA.

60 Executive Order 8785, 6 Federal Register, 2897, 1941.

61 The Allies also had learned that a fascist finance official had thanked one of the IOR's lay officers, Massimo Spada, for the IOR's purchase of fascist-issued bonds that helped support Mussolini's government. Lai, *Finanze Vaticane*, 24–25.

62 Susan Headden, Dana Hawkins, and Jason Vest, "A Vow of Silence: Did Gold Stolen by Croatian Fascists Reach the Vatican," *U.S. News & World Report*, March 22, 1998.

63 The British were the first to put the Bank Suisse Italienne of Lugano on the blacklist in 1940 and the Americans followed late the following year.

64 "Papers Link Vatican to Illegal Deals with Nazis Swiss Bankers Used as Conduit, U.S. Intelligence Documents Say," *The Toronto Star*, Reuters, August 4, 1997, A3; see also Arthur Spiegelman, "Vatican Bank Dealt With Reichsbank in War-Document," Reuters, International, August 3, 1997.

65 The accounts in Germany were not significant investments, but that the church could maintain them without discovery is evidence that the Allies were not fully capable of following the money

trail. Files maintained at Entry 1069, Box 287, RG 59, Location 250/48/29/05, NARA; see also Phayer, *Pius XII, the Holocaust, and the Cold War,* 103–6.

Chapter 10: Blood Money

1 When I was far enough along on my research—which had started in 2005—to know precisely what IOR-related information might be in the Secret Archives, I sought access from the Vatican. The Archbishop of Miami, Thomas Wenski, formally passed my request for access to Archbishop Carlo Maria Viganò, the Apostolic Nuncio to the United States. Viganò in turn forwarded my request to Archbishop Jean-Louis Bruguès, the Archivist of the Secret Archives. After several weeks, my request for access was formally denied in 2013.

2 Feldman, *Allianz and the German Insurance Business*, viii–ix.

3 Ibid., xii.

4 Joseph Belth, ed., "Life Insurance and the Holocaust," *The Insurance Forum*, Special Holocaust Issue 25, no. 9 (September 1998): 81, 92–93.

5 After the war, Italian and German businessmen feverishly tried convincing the Allies that their collaboration with the fascists had only been for business expediency, not because of ideology. See, for instance, interrogation of Kurt Schmitt, Allianz's General Director, July 8, 1947, Office of Military Government, RG 260, Folder 2/58/2-7, NARA. The same was true in Germany, see generally Feldman *Allianz and the German Insurance Business*, 51. During the war, the business relationships were incestuous between a handful of the largest companies. For instance, U.S. intelligence uncovered that Schmitt secretly owned shares in Generali's American subsidiary. See "The Pilot Reinsurance Company of New York Shareholders of Record," February 4, 1942, RG 131, Box 26, Folder 230/38/110/5, NARA.

6 Ranking Officials, Assicurazioni Generali, also Washington Reports 1943, RG 59, Department of State, Rome Embassy, File 851, Box 161, NARA.

7 Webster, "The Political and Industrial Strategies of a Mixed Investment Bank," 329.

8 The company was Galata, a mining and mineral exploration firm. See *Transactions of the Institution of Mining Engineers*, ed. Percy Strzelecki, Vol. 34, (Newcastle-upon-Tyne, UK: The Institution, 1908), 234.

9 Webster, "The Political and Industrial Strategies of a Mixed Investment Bank," 329.

10 Webster, *Industrial Imperialism in Italy 1908–1915*, 111; Romano, *Giuseppe Volpi*, 18. At that time, BCI was more than simply a bank. It had equity and management stakes in many companies, with its largest interests in armaments, shipping, and steel. Italy sometimes committed public money or gave special tax breaks to BCI-led industries that were considered critical to the nation (such as the chemical industry in central Italy in 1912). The Bank of England, the Morgans, and the Mellons had minority shares in some BCI industrial syndicates.

11 Romano, *Giuseppe Volpi*, 52, citing *Carte Nogara*, correspondence between Nogara and Volpi between 1912 and 1914. The BCI archives have two files dealing with the Merkur Gewerkschaft (German) and Monte Amiata (Italian) mines: that correspondence covers from 1919 to 1926 and includes an attempt by Nogara, then a BCI executive and mining engineer, to get the Amiata corporation to take an interest in Anatolian mining (Turkish) from 1920 through 1922. When Volpi became the chief Italian representative in peace talks with the Turks, he tapped Nogara to fill his vacant spot on the Ottoman Public Debt Administration. "Italy: Volpi's Commission," *Time*, November 2, 1925; Donald Quataert, *The Ottoman Empire, 1700–1922* (Cambridge: Cambridge University Press, 2000); see also Memorandum, Treaty of Peace with Turkey from the Supreme Council of the Allied Powers, February 17, 1920, 24/98/65, 253, Cabinet Papers, National Archives, Kew, UK.

12 Webster, "The Political and Industrial Strategies of a Mixed Investment Bank," 359.

13 Franco Amatori, "Entrepreneurial Typologies in the History of Industrial Italy (1880–1960)," *The Business History Review* 54, no. 3 (Autumn, 1980): 371.

14 Bosworth, "Tourist Planning in Fascist Italy and the Limits of Totalitarian Culture," 13, n. 62.

15 Volpi was not only a power with which to be reckoned in Italy, but he was a respected businessman in other Western countries. In 1928, *Time*, in covering Volpi's decision to peg the weak lira to the gold standard and undertake a comprehensive renegotiation of Italy's debt, said he "epitomizes the best type of self-made Italian business man" and described his work for Mussolini as

"brilliant." He was also famous for a glittering social life. His fifteen-thousand-square-foot palace surrounded by formal gardens, at the foot of the Spanish Steps at Via del Quirinale, was widely acknowledged as one of the most sumptuous homes outside Vatican City. There, at dazzling parties, his regular guests included everyone from the Duke and Duchess of Windsor, Cole Porter, Jean Cocteau, Cecil Beaton, Maria Callas, and Orson Welles. His 1933 launch of the Venice Film Festival was in keeping with his outsized personality.

16 It was not easy to be successful in private industry in Italy under fascism. By the mid-1930s only the Soviet Union owned a larger share of private industry than the Italian government. The capitalism that was the backdrop for businessmen like Nogara and Volpi thrived on a steady stream of preferential state policies and government subsidies that would have defied the words "free market" in many countries. See Franco Amatori, "Entrepreneurial Typologies in the History of Industrial Italy (1880–1960)," *The Business History Review* 54, no. 3 (Autumn 1980): 361; and *L'Italia di Fronted alla Prima Guerra Mondiale* by Brunello Vigezzi, review by Richard Webster, *The Journal of Modern History* 41, no. 4 (December, 1969): 626.

17 Webster, "The Political and Industrial Strategies of a Mixed Investment Bank," 329.

18 "The Regeneration of Tripolitania," La Rinascita Della Tripolitania: Memorie e studi sui quattro anni di governo del Conte Giuseppe Volpi di Misurata, *The Geographical Journal* 71, no. 3 (March 1928): 280–82; "Italy: Volpi Out," *Time*, July 16, 1928.

19 The company's full name was Compagnie Internationale des Wagons-Lits. Bosworth, "Tourist Planning in Fascist Italy and the Limits of a Totalitarian Culture," 17–18; see Pollard, "The Vatican and the Wall Street Crash," 1087.

20 Romano, *Giuseppe Volpi*, 218. Volpi had an edge in Croatia over his Italian counterparts. Mussolini had chosen him to be the lead negotiator in a 1941 economic pact the fascist government signed with Pavelić. It meant that Volpi had a status in Catholic Croatia that competitors could not match. Srdjan Trifković, "Rivalry Between Germany and Italy in Croatia, 1942–1943," *The Historical Journal* 36, no. 4 (December 1993), 886.

21 Everyone in Italy refers to the holding company as Bastogi, named after Pietro Bastogi, the first Finance Minister of the Italian Republic, who founded the company in 1862. Its official name is Italiane Strade Ferrate. Luciano Segreto, "Models of Control in Italian Capitalism from the Mixed Bank to Mediobanca, 1894–1993," *Business and Economic History* 26, no. 2 (Winter 1997): 652. See also Parliamentary Commission Report of Inquiry on the Case of Sindona, Chamber of Deputies Senate, VIII Legislature, Doc. XXIII, Read 22 May 1980, n. 204, June 23, 1981, 27–28.

22 Marco Parenti was a cofounder and had business links to the Rothschilds. Other Jewish founding members of Generali included: Vidal Benjamin Cusin, the grandfather of two future directors of the company; a lawyer, Giambattista Rosmini; a competing insurance executive, Alessio Paris; shipbuilder Michele Vucetich; and a Frankfurt native, Giovanni Cristoforo Ritter de Zahony. Morpurgo's father was a banker who was all too familiar with institutionalized Italian anti-Semitism. On a few occasions under the Papacy of Benedict XIV, when he entered the Vatican for business, he was required to pin a small piece of colored fabric on his suit so that those who dealt with him knew he was Jewish. John Authers and Richard Wolffe, *The Victim's Fortune: Inside the Epic Battle over the Debts of the Holocaust* (New York: HarperCollins, 2002), 108–9.

23 Pollard, *Money and the Rise of the Modern Papacy*, 171; Segreto, "Models of Control in Italian Capitalism," 652; Tom Weiss, interviewed by Brendan Howley, November 13, 2005.

24 Maura Hametz, "Zionism, Emigration, and Anti-Semitism in Trieste," 126–32.

25 The resignation of Edgardo Morpurgo caused an international outcry, but the Italians ignored the criticism.

26 The new chairman of RAS was a strident fascist, Fulvio Suvich, the ex-ambassador to the United States, and a Trieste native who was good friends with Volpi. Italian Jewish insurance executives were not the only ones being shoved aside by race laws. The Nazis set the example by excluding Jews from all German business life, including their removal as shareholders and directors of insurance companies. They were excluded from the industry by the time the violence against Jews had created financial problems for insurance companies. State-organized hooliganism, for instance, in Germany culminated in Kristallnacht—the Night of Broken Glass in November 1938—in which Jewish businesses and synagogues were torched and vandalized nationwide. German insurers were on the line for tens of millions of dollars in insurable losses. But those executives worked with the Third Reich to devise ways to avoid paying most of the claims. They used several pretexts to cheat their customers, with the most common excuse being that the

riots and vandalism were a public disturbance and therefore not subject to compensation. Some insurers fretted that their failure to pay the claims were a "black spot on the coat of honor of the German insurance industry," so they conspired with the Nazis to levy a one-billion-mark fine on the Jews, from which some funds would be recycled back to the victims as payments for broken glass and stolen goods. Ultimately, German insurance companies started a massive repurchase of life insurance policies from Jewish clients as it became clear that Jews were not insurable under the race laws.

27 Quoted in Romano, *Giuseppe Volpi, industria e finanza tra Giolitti e Mussolini*, 221.

28 Pollard, *Money and the Rise of the Modern Papacy*, 105, 171.

29 See Report on Internationale Unfall & Schadensversicherungs Ges A.G. from GEA Branch, NARA, Exhibits 6–12, 18, 26A, 30–31; Confidential Memo from the American Embassy in Rome to the Secretary of State, March 19, 1945, RG 59, Department of State, Rome Embassy, File 851, Box 161, NARA; Tom Weiss, interviewed by Brendan Howley, November 13, 2005.

30 Joseph B. Treaster, "Holocaust Survivors' Insurance Ordeal," *The New York Times*, April 8, 2003, 8.

31 Authers and Wolffe, *The Victim's Fortune*, 109. Morpurgo sent his agents throughout Eastern Europe, the Balkans, and the Pale of Settlement, an enormous region Russia set aside in the eighteenth century in which Jews were allowed to live and work. The Pale of Settlement comprised about 20 percent of western Russia and what is today most of Poland, Lithuania, Ukraine, Belarus, and Moldova.

32 Franz Kafka worked in Generali's Prague office for nine months. According to company records, he left because of a "nervous ailment."

33 Belth, "Life Insurance and the Holocaust," 90.

34 Christopher Kobrak and Per H. Hansen, eds., *European Business, Dictatorship, and Political Risk, 1920–1945* (New York: Berghahn, 2004), 43.

35 Ibid., 42. Generali accounted for 8 percent of Italy's GDP. In comparison, in 2013, ExxonMobil had revenues of $500 billion, but accounted only for .03 percent of U.S. GDP.

36 German insurance companies instituted a "risk supplement" that increased life insurance premiums between 20 percent and 30 percent. Still, the longer the war continued it took a heavy toll on insurers. For instance, during 1942, Allianz, the largest German insurer, had 17,537 policyholders killed in combat, resulting in payouts of 40.3 million reichsmarks. The battle of Stalingrad meant that in the first three months of 1943, another twenty thousand policyholders were dead, costing the insurer another 50 million reichsmarks.

37 Feldman, *Allianz and the German Insurance Business*, 347.

38 Kobrak and Hansen, *European Business, Dictatorship, and Political Risk*, 51–52.

39 Kurt Schmitt to Giuseppe Volpi, Action Note (Aktennote), September 24, 1938; and Volpi to Schmitt, September 27, 1938, FHA, MR A 1/2; Kobrak and Hansen, *European Business, Dictatorship, and Political Risk*, 51; see also Stefan Karlen, Lucas Chocomeli, Kristin D'haemer, Stefan Laube, and Daniel C. Schmid, "Schweizerische Versicherungsgesellschaften im Machtbereich des Dritten Reich" (Swiss insurance companies in the area governed by the Third Reich), Independent Commission of Experts, ICE, Vol. 12 (Zürich: Pendo Verlag GmbH, 2002).

40 *Elimination of German Resources for War*, Vols. 1–9, U.S. Congress, Hearings Before the Subcommittee of the Senate Committee on Military Affairs, 79th Congress, 2nd Session, (Washington, DC: U.S. Government Printing Office, 1945), 381. There are additional volumes of documents and testimony printed from these hearings under the same general title, but it is in the book published as Volumes 1–9 covering German and Italian insurance companies.

41 Memorandum re Assicurazioni Generali, Rome, August 17, 1945, RG 59, Department of State, Rome Embassy, File 851, Box 161, NARA; *Elimination of German Resources for War*, Senate Military Affairs Subcommittee on War Mobilization,1945, RG 226, Files 184–212, 222–230. The template Volpi used to gain a share of the business was the 1936 collapse of Europe's third largest insurer, Austria's Jewish-owned Phönix Life. There a consortium of Germany's Munich Re, Austria's Städtische, and Italy's Generali divided the spoils. Records of the German External Assets Branch of the U.S. Allied Commission for Austria (USACA) Section, 1945–1950, Società Anonima Di Assicurazioni "Acciai Alpine," Milan, Italy, General Records series, publication Microfilm Series M1928, File 2-203, Roll 0095, catalogue identification 1561456, NARA; see also Aktennote Kissakalt, September 17, 1935, Archives of Munich Reinsurance Company, A 2.13/46, Munich.

42 Nogara was familiar with shell companies from his work in Constantinople. There he had formed his first in 1913 in order to bypass a Turkish ban on foreigners bidding for development rights in an ambitious coastal development. See Webster, *Industrial Imperialism in Italy*, 262.

43 See generally Kobrak and Hansen, *European Business, Dictatorship, and Political Risk*, 55.

44 Munich Re (Münchener Rück) is used in the insurance industry to refer to Munich Reinsurance Company (Münchener Rückversicherungs-Gesellschaft AG). Munich Re and RWM, September 28, 1939, A. 2.14/55, Center for Corporate History of Allianz, historical archives of the Munich Reinsurance Company, Munich; Economic Advisory Branch report, undated, Property Control, German Intelligence and Investments 1945–50, Appendix II, "German and Italian Insurance Companies known to have been operating in German Occupied and Allied Countries," RG 260, Records Property Division, Box 651, 3, NARA.

45 See Feldman, *Allianz and the German Insurance Business*, 321, 321n, Aktennote Kurt Schmitt, May 12, 1941; see Stefan Karlen et al., "Schweizerische Vericherungsgesellschaften im Machtbereich des 'Dritten Reichs'" (2002).

46 See Italian Foreign Ministry files generally for Volpi's efforts to keep the Germans from getting any business in Croatia; Trifković, "Rivalry Between Germany and Italy in Croatia, 1942–1943," 879–904; R. A. H. Robinson, *The English Historical Review* 101, no. 398 (January 1986): 303.

47 Richard J. Overy, "The Economy of the German 'New Order,'" ed., Richard J. Overy, Gerhard Otto, and Johannes Houwink ten Cate, *Die "Neuordnung" Europas. NS-Wirtschaftspolitik in den besetzten Gebieten* (Berlin: Metropol, 1997), 11–26; Harm G. Schröter, *Außenpolitik und Wirtschaftsinteresse: Skandinavien im außenwirtschaftlichen Kalkül Deutschlands und Großbritanniens*, 1918–1939 (Frankfurt/Main: Peter Lang, 1983), 15–19, available at Columbia University Collection, New York; see generally Alice Teichova, "Instruments of Economic Control and Exploitation: The German Occupation of Bohemia and Moravia," in Richard J. Overy, G. Otto and Johannes Houwink ten Cate, *Die 'Neuordnung' Europas: NS-Wirtschaftspolitik in den besetzten Gebieten* (Berlin: Metropol, 1997), 83–107.

48 Report to Arnoldo Frigessi, January 21, 1941, papers of Arnoldo Frigessi di Rattalma, Banca Commerciale Archives, Milan, Cart. 108, fasc. 3; see also Kobrak and Hansen, *European Business, Dictatorship, and Political Risk*, 56.

49 Protocol of Meetings, September 20–21, 1942, and appended documents, FHA, MR, C/210; see also Kobrak and Hansen, *European Business, Dictatorship, and Political Risk*, 58–59. Volpi was also active in Croatia extending his electrical utility conglomerate, SADE, eventually providing half the country's power during the war.

50 Report on Internationale Unfall & Schadensversicherungs Ges A.G. from GEA Branch, Records of the German External Assets Branch of the U.S. Allied Commission for Austria (USACA) Section, 1945–1950, Reports on Businesses, compiled 1945–1950, see particularly report "Preliminary Report on Internationale Unfall & Schadensversicherungs-Gesellschaft A.G., September 5, 1947," RG 260, M1928, 49B, Roll 0017, NARA.

51 Economic Advisory Branch report, undated, Property Control, German Intelligence and Investments 1945–50, RG 260, Records Property Division, Box 651,13–14, NARA.

52 Volpi tried to evade the U.S. ban by trading real estate in Italy for blocked funds in the U.S. See RG 131, Box 26, Folder 230/38/10/5; and Louis Pink, Superintendent of Insurance, New York State, to John Pehle, Assistant to the Secretary, Treasury Department, July 22, 1941, RG 131, NN3-131-94-002, Box 15, Folder 48B, 230/8/3414, NARA; see telex from J. W. Pehle to Herbert Kimball, October 28, 1942, RG 131, NN3-131-94-002, Box 15, Docket Files of 1940/60, Bis Enterprises, Folder 48/A, 230/38/34/4, NARA.

53 See for instance the shares owned in Riunione Adriatica di Sicurtà, an investment that Nogara duplicated across all top-shelf Italian insurance companies. Report on Internationale Unfall & Schadensversicherungs Ges A.G. from GEA Branch, Records of the German External Assets Branch of the U.S. Allied Commission for Austria (USACA) Section, 1945–1950, Reports on Businesses, compiled 1945–1950, RG 260, M1928, 49B, Roll 0017, Exhibit 4, NARA.

54 Phayer, *Pius XII, the Holocaust, and the Cold War*, 115, citing a file summarizing foreign insurance company operations in Italy, Entry 196, Box 16, File 30, RG 226, location 190/10/9/5, NARA.

55 Nogara purchased controlling shares in both Fondiaria Vita (the life insurance branch) and Fondiaria Infortuni (accident insurance). This information is contained as part of the so-called Safehaven Report, at the National Archives. During World War II, the U.S. tried to persuade neutral

countries to seize German assets deposited in their countries. See Donald P. Steury, "The OSS and Project Safehaven," CIA, at https://www.cia.gov/library/center-for-the-study-of-intelligence/csi-publications/csi-studies/studies/summer00/art04.html. The effort was code-named Operation Safehaven. This information about Fondiaria and the Vatican is from the Safehaven Report, April 1, 1945, Entry 210, Box 337, RG 226, Location 250/64/28/1, NARA. The Safehaven probe of all Italian insurance firms is April 1945, COI/OSS Central Files, Entry 92, Box 502, File 8, RG 226, Location 190/6/1/4, NARA.

56 Nogara was a director of the Istituto di Credito Fondiario, so even without help from Volpi, he may have been able to get the advance scoop.

57 Webster, "The Political and Industrial Strategies of a Mixed Investment Bank," 356.

58 Phayer, *Pius XII, the Holocaust, and the Cold War,* 115.

59 U.S. Treasury Department, "Documents Pertaining to Foreign Funds Control," Washington, March 30, 1943, 23–24, Papers of Bernard Bernstein, Subject File, Box 23, Harry S. Truman Library, Independence, MO; see Phayer, *Pius XII, the Holocaust, and the Cold War,* 111–20.

60 Phayer, *Pius XII, the Holocaust, and the Cold War,* 126ff, 132.

61 Economic Advisory Branch report, undated, Property Control, German Intelligence and Investments 1945–50, RG 260, Records Property Division, Box 651,10–13, NARA. One of the most comprehensive intelligence overviews of German and Italian insurers and their interrelationships is Memo, Saint JJI to Saint BB, Response to Questionnaire by Reinhard Karl Wilhelm Reme, October 25, 1945, Washington Registry SI Intel Field Files, records of the Office of Strategic Services, RG 226, Box 214, NND 897108, Entry 108A; see also "Memorandum for Listing: Insurance," RG13, NN3-131-94-002, Box 15, Folder 48B, 230/8/3414, NARA.

62 Confidential Memo, No. 2236, Subject: Status of Assicurazioni Generali, September 11, 1945, RG 59, Department of State, Rome Embassy, File 851, Box 161, NARA.

63 Economic Advisory Branch report, undated, Property Control, German Intelligence and Investments 1945–50, Appendix II, "German and Italian Insurance Companies known to have been operating in German Occupied and Allied Countries," RG 260, Records Property Division, Box 651, 3, NARA.

64 Memo, Saint JJI to Saint BB, Response to Questionnaire by Reinhard Karl Wilhelm Reme, October 25, 1945, Washington Registry SI Intel Field Files, records of the Office of Strategic Services, RG 226, Box 214, NND 897108, Entry 108A, NARA, 16. Also, Economic Advisory Branch report, undated, Property Control, German Intelligence and Investments 1945–50, Appendix II, "German and Italian Insurance Companies known to have been operating in German Occupied and Allied Countries," RG 260, Records Property Division, Box 651, 5–6, NARA; see also in the same document and file, Appendix 3, one page, "The distribution of foreign business of German Insurance Companies."

65 Without Albula, the Germans could not have obtained Swiss francs, the currency demanded by the selling company, Dorna Vatra. See Ibid., Memo, Saint JJI to Saint BB, NARA, 8–10.

66 From Vincent La Vista to Herbert J. Cummings, Subject: SAFEHAVEN Italian Insurance Companies, October 24, 1945, Record Group 84, PRFSP State Department, Rome Embassy and Consulate, Confidential Files, 1946, 851 A.C. Finance, Section 851.5, Box 11; also Economic Advisory Branch report, undated, Property Control, German Intelligence and Investments 1945–50, RG 260, Records Property Division, Box 651; and Memorandum, untitled, August 17, 1945, Rome, State Department, NARA.

67 See memorandum regarding reinsurance in Chile, to the Foreign Funds Control, U.S. Treasury, February 23, 1942, RG 131, NN3-131-94-002, Box 15, Folder 48B, 230/8/3414, NARA; see generally list of companies involved, in part, M1928, "Records of the German External Assets Branch of the U.S. Allied Commission for Austria (USACA) Section, 1945–1950, part of RG 260, 2003, NARA.

68 "Copy for US Embassy," Board of Trade, Secret, January 24, 1945, RG 84, File 850.6, 851, Box 272, NARA.

69 Memo, for the Ambassador, August 29, 1945, RG 59, Department of State, Rome Embassy, File 851, Box 161, NARA; see also "The Export of Insurance, Business and Finance Section," *The Economist,* August 25, 1945, 24.

70 Confidential Memo, No. 2236, Subject: Status of Assicurazioni Generali, September 11, 1945, RG 59, Department of State, Rome Embassy, File 851, Box 161, NARA.

71 Report of Finance Sub-Commission, HQ AC for February, 1945, from Headquarters of the

Allied Commission, APC 394, March 10, 1945, RG 59, Foreign Service Post, Rome Embassy and Consulate, General Records, 1945, Box 861, 850.9.851, NARA; see also "Italians Take $480,000,000 from the U.S.," *New York Post*, May 3, 1941.

72 See generally Annual Statement of The Generali Insurance Company, United States Branch, 1940, RG 131, Box 15, folder 48B, setting forth reinsurance dealings between Generali and some blacklisted firms; see also Phayer, *Pius XII, the Holocaust, and the Cold War*, 116–17.

73 For a straight listing of their status in fascist Italy, see "Who's Who in Fascist Italy," Confidential memorandum, December 26, 1942, RG 226, E179, Box 4, NARA.

74 McGoldrick, "New Perspectives on Pius XII and Vatican Financial Transactions During the Second World War," 1044.

75 Ibid. The Vatican also received income from bonds of at least several other countries in the Allied alliance, Canada, Costa Rica, and the Dominican Republic, as well as nations technically neutral but Axis-leaning, such as Argentina, Brazil, Spain, and Chile. Nogara still had government bonds in Nazi-occupied Greece and Italy, and in a list of blocked Italian companies such as Pirelli Tire. See Memo from National City Bank to Amministrazione Pontificia per le Opere di Religione, March 3, 1942; and J. P. Morgan to Amministrazione Speciale della Santa Sede, March 6 and March 10, 1942; National City Bank to Amministrazione Pontificia per le Opere di Religione, February 16, 1942; and National City Bank to Amministrazione Pontificia per le Opere di Religione, titled "Vatican City Holdings in U.S.A.," January 17, 1942; J. P. Morgan & Co. to Amministrazione Speciale Della Santa Sede, titled "Vatican City Holdings in U.S.A.," January 30, 1942; Amministrazione Special della Santa Sede to J. P. Morgan & Co., titled "Vatican Holdings of Italian Bonds in U.S. Dollars," January 24, 1942, RG 59, IWG (Nazi war crimes working group), FBI Secret Intercepts, NARA.

76 McGoldrick, 1044. McGoldrick cites the Vatican's American portfolio as evidence that the church and Nogara favored the Allies since she says the large industrial companies in which it invested were "war-related industries" and that "they all . . . fed directly into the military production of the US war economy." In comparison to the investments that Nogara directed into Italian and German insurers, McGoldrick contends that, "If the weight of investment counts, Vatican money was clearly behind the Allies." Ibid., 1045. However, there is no evidence that Nogara used any metrics beyond profitability and safety in investing the church's money. Publicly traded, large American industrial companies were not only conservative investments but provided steady dividend income. Whether or not those firms were involved in the Allied war effort was almost certainly not an inducement nor cause of concern for Nogara. Nogara's primary focus—as with all his investments on both sides of the war—was to safely maximize profits and preserve capital. Even McGoldrick acknowledges that, "It might be argued that these investments represented the shrewd judgment of the Vatican's delegate, Nogara, who recognized that war is profitable and who, acting on his own initiative, made these investments with an eye only to maximizing gain." Ibid., 1045.

77 Insurance, Confidential, Series 24932, RG 131, NN3-131-94-002, Box 15, Folder 48B, 230/8/3414, NARA.

78 See generally Ranking Officials, Assicurazioni Generali, Record Group 59, Department of State, Rome Embassy, File 851, Box 161, NARA.

79 Phayer, *Pius XII, the Holocaust, and the Cold War*, 108.

80 Memo to S. S. Gilbert and S. Klotz, June 22, 1942, RG 131, NN3-131-94-002, Box 15, Folder 48B, 230/38/34/4, NARA. In the memo, the Mexican bank was identified as Banco Nacional de Mexico. But it had long ago merged with Banco Mercantil Mexicano to form Banamex.

81 Memorandum for the Files, 1942, recounting a July 25, 1942, meeting, NND 968123, NARA.

82 Gold was a favorite way Germans and Italians circumvented currency restrictions: Switzerland and Gold Transactions in the Second World War (*Die Schweiz und die Goldtransaktionen im Zweiten Weltkrieg*), The Independent Commission of Experts, Switzerland: World War II, Vol. 16.

83 RG 84, Safehaven Files, Banca della Svizzera Italiana, memo from managing director to United States consul in Berne, March 30, 1943, Entry 323, Box 6, NARA.

84 See generally Authers and Wolffe, *The Victim's Fortune*.

85 "Life Insurance and the Holocaust," 81–100; Becker to Bernstein, November 27, 1946, RG 260, OMGUS, Finance, Box 60, 17/60/10, NARA. In Germany, the insurance companies became partners with the Third Reich. The Reichsbank took 75 percent of the profits from policies in return for cloaking the source of the money.

86 Author interview with Elan Steinberg, April 2, 2006; Interagency Task Force on Nazi Assets Di-

rected by Under Secretary of State Stuart Eizenstat: U.S. Department of State, "U.S. and Allied Efforts to Recover and Restore Gold and Other Assets Stolen or Hidden by Germany During World War II: Preliminary Study" (1997); see also Authers and Wolffe, *The Victim's Fortune*. As for the figure of $200 billion, that is from Professor Joseph Belth, *Insurance Forum* 25, no. 9 (September 1998), who calculated that half of those who died in the Holocaust owned life insurance and that the average policy was for several thousand dollars. In 2004, the Holocaust Insurance Claims Research Project reached the same conclusion that previous estimates of restitution had not included property insurance claims and unclaimed bank accounts. See Sidney Zabludoff, "Restitution of Holocaust-Era Assets: Promises and Reality," *Jewish Political Studies Review*, March 1, 2007; see also Reports on Archival Research, The International Commission on Holocaust Era Insurance Claims, April, August and October 2004.

87 Becker to Bernstein, November 27, 1946, RG 260, OMGUS, Finance, Box 60, 17/60/10, NARA.

88 Author interview with Elan Steinberg, April 2, 2006; see generally "Subject to Questionnaire by Reinhard Karl Wilhelm Reme," October 25, 1945, Washington, records of the Office of Strategic Services, RG 226, Box 214, NND 897108, Entry 108A, 16-17, 24, NARA. See also Belth, "The Insurance Forum," 82.

89 Letter from Archbishop Carlo Maria Viganò, Apostolic Nuncio to the United States, to Archbishop Thomas G. Wenski, March 20, 2013, in the Gerald Posner collection, Howard Gotlieb Archival Research Center, Boston University. Professor Gerald Steinacher notes that "[t]he Vatican remains the only European state that withholds free access to its archives to contemporary historians." Gerald Steinacher, *Nazis on the Run: How Hitler's Henchmen Fled Justice* (Oxford: Oxford University Press, 2012), Kindle edition, 2342 of 9472; see also Wolf, *Pope and Devil*, 15.

90 From Vincent La Vista to Herbert J. Cummings, Subject: SAFEHAVEN Italian Insurance Companies, October 24, 1945, Record Group 84, PRFSP State Department, Rome Embassy and Consulate, Confidential Files, 1946, 851 A.C. Finance, Section 851.5, Box 11, NARA.

91 Economic Advisory Branch report, undated, Property Control, German Intelligence and Investments 1945–50, RG 260, Records Property Division, Box 651,13–14, NARA. In Croatia, for instance, Mussolini was not long out of office when a new law created the Croatian Reinsurance Company of Zagreb, which redirected almost all the insurance work that had been the province of the Italian and German Croat companies.

92 Ranking Officials, Assicurazioni Generali, RG 59, Department of State, Rome Embassy, File 851, Box 161, NARA.

93 Romano, *Giuseppe Volpi*, 235–36.

94 Ibid., 236.

95 See generally Headquarters Allied Commission, Finance Sub-Commission, APO 394, Confidential, RG 59, Department of State, Rome Embassy, File 851, Box 161, NARA.

96 Headquarters Allied Commission, Finance Sub-Commission, APO 394, Confidential, RG 59, Department of State, Rome Embassy, File 851, Box 161, NARA; also Memo, Saint JJI to Saint BB, Response to Questionnaire by Reinhard Karl Wilhelm Reme, October 25, 1945, Washington Registry SI Intel Field Files, records of the Office of Strategic Services, RG 226, Box 214, NND 897108, Entry 108A, NARA, 24–26. See also Claudio Lindner and Giancarlo Mazzuca, *Il leone di Trieste: il romanzo delle Assicurazioni Generali dalle origini austroungariche all'era Cuccia* (Milan: Sperling & Kupfer), 1990.

97 See Giorgio Bocca, *La Repubblica di Mussolini* (Bari, Italy: Laterza, 1977); Romano, *Giuseppe Volpi*, 236.

98 Romano, *Giuseppe Volpi*, 237. The Allied High Commission for Sanctions Against Fascism later seized whatever Volpi assets the Germans had missed, and charged him with crimes for aiding the fascists. He stayed in Switzerland during the trial that resulted in a guilty verdict in January 1947. The court, however, extended amnesty to him. By then it was clear that few German or Italian businessmen would pay any price for having helped the Axis war effort. The American embassy had complained at the end of the war to the Secretary of State, "there are some forty-five high ranking insurance executives in Rome whom the Allied Commission consider 'undesirable elements.'" The Italians were resistant to putting any on trial. In Germany, General Lucius Clay, the U.S. Military Governor, aborted all the war crimes trials of the German insurance industry executives. Volpi's German counterparts walked free, many returning to the only business they knew, insurance.

Chapter 11: A Nazi Spy in the Vatican?

1 Declaration on Gold Purchases, February 22, 1944, Documents Pertaining to Foreign Funds Control, U.S. Treasury Department, Washington: March 30, 1944, 15–16, Papers of Bernard Bernstein, Subject File, Box 23, Harry S. Truman Library, Independence, MO.

2 BIS was the subject of furious wartime debates inside the U.S. and other countries. U.S. Treasury Secretary Henry Morgenthau pressed the case that since BIS was effectively controlled by the Nazis, there should be no U.S. delegates. Higham, *Trading with the Enemy*, 26–33.

3 BIS attracted prominent names from its inception. Its first president was Gates McGarrah, who had previously been the president of Chase National Bank before becoming chairman of the New York Federal Reserve Bank. U.S. Treasury Secretary Henry Morgenthau worried that at the very start of the war that BIS was Axis-controlled. William C. Bullitt to Henry Morgenthau, May 9, 1939, Telegram 907, Charles Higham "Trading with the Enemy" Collection, Box 1, Folder 1, University of Southern California Cinematic Arts Library.

4 Schröder managed J. H. Stein Bank, the German side of an international banking family that included one of London's oldest merchant banks, Schrobanco. John Foster Dulles, as a Sullivan and Cromwell partner, represented Schrobanco's American subsidiary. There were concerns in both the British and American governments about whether Schrobanco did business with some blacklisted companies. Published reports in 1944 in Britain suggested the company was loyal to Germany. Still, one senior Schrobanco executive worked for the OSS in Cairo and Zurich. After the war, when U.S. forces detained Kurt von Schröder, he provided information that helped prosecutors prepare some of their war crimes trials. In return, he was not personally charged with any crimes although the Allies knew the SS had freely used his bank, J. H. Stein, as a repository of plundered assets throughout the war. See Richard Roberts, *Schroders: Merchants and Bankers* (London: Macmillan, 1992), 292–97; U.S. Counsel for the Prosecution of Axis Criminality 1945–46, Miscellaneous Reference Materials, Transcripts of Interrogations, Baron Kurt von Schröder, RG 238, World War II War Crimes, Box 2, NARA.

5 See generally Murphy to Mowinckel, Records of the OSS, Office of the Director, RG 226, Entry 116, June 4, 1945, NARA.

6 The Independent Commission of Experts was a group of financial, political, and historical researchers who for six years, starting in 1996, reviewed and prepared a report on the armaments industry/trade; Swiss insurance companies in the Third Reich; use of Switzerland as a financial center; gold transactions and Aryanization in Austria; and Franco-Swiss financial relations. Their final report was issued in 2002. *Switzerland, National Socialism and the Second World War* (Zürich: Pendo Verlag GmbH, 2002); see also Jean Ziegler, *Die Schweiz, das Gold und die Toten* (Munich: Bertelsmann, 1997); and Werner Rings, *Raubgold aus Deutschland. Die 'Golddrehscheibe' Schweiz im Zweiten Weltkrieg* (Munich: Piper, 1996).

7 Die Schweiz und die Goldtransaktionen im Zweiten Weltkrieg Überarbeitete und ergänzte Fassung des Zwischenberichts von 1998: http://www.uek.ch/de/publikationen1997-2000/gold.pdf. Unabhängige Expertenkommission Schweiz—Zweiter Weltkrieg—Switzerland, National Socialism and the Second World War, Final Report, the Independent Commission of Experts, Switzerland, March 22, 2002.

8 Interrogation of Walter Funk, July 6, 1945, Collection of World War II War Crimes Records, RG 238, 1933–50 and 1943–50, Box 73, NARA.

9 Elizabeth White, "The Disposition of SS-Looted Victim Gold During and After World War II," *American University International Law Review*, 14, no. 1, Article 15 (January 1998): 212–13; see also Higham, *Trading with the Enemy*, 39–40.

10 Interrogation of Walter Funk, October 22, 1945, Box 186, PS 3544, Collection of World War II War Crimes Records, NARA. For an in-depth investigation of the disposition of looted Nazi gold during and immediately after the war, as well as the question of the missing files about gold and the Reichsbank, see the two reports issued by the Interagency Task Force on Nazi Assets Directed by Under Secretary of State Stuart Eizenstat: U.S. Department of State, "U.S. and Allied Efforts to Recover and Restore Gold and Other Assets Stolen or Hidden by Germany During World War II: Preliminary Study (1997)," and U.S. Department of State, "U.S. and Allied Wartime and Postwar Relations and Negotiations with Argentina, Portugal, Spain, Sweden, and Turkey on Looted Gold and German External Assets and U.S. Concerns About the Fate of the Wartime Ustaša Treasury (1998)."

11 "Jewish Group Rejects Report On Nazi Gold," *Chicago Tribune*, March 10, 1997; author interview with Elan Steinberg, April 2, 2006.
12 "BIS Archive Guide," Bank of International Settlements (Basel: 2007), 2, https://docs.google.com/viewer?url=http%3A%2F%2Fwww.bis.org%2Fabout%2Farch_guide.pdf; see also Aarons and Loftus, *Unholy Trinity*, 296.
13 Aarons and Loftus, *Unholy Trinity*, 276.
14 Higham, *Trading with the Enemy*, 32–33, citing Interrogation Statement of Heinrich Otto Abetz to U.S. military, June 21, 1946. See generally Robert O. Paxton, *Vichy France: Old Guard and New Order, 1940–1944* (New York: Columbia University Press, 2001), 100, 108, 124; Roland Ray, *Annäherung an Frankreich im Dienste Hitlers? Otto Abetz und die deutsche Frankreichpolitik, 1930–1942* (Munich: Oldenbourg Wissenschaftsverlag, 2000); Aarons and Loftus, *Unholy Trinity*, 276–77. Statement of Heinrich Otto Abetz to U.S. military, June 21, 1946. Abetz, the German ambassador to Vichy France, was tried and convicted of war crimes for his role in sending French Jews to death camps. He served five years of a twenty-year sentence.
15 Heinrich Otto Abetz told American interrogators that in return for a share of the profits, the Vatican's espionage unit had divulged the secret to Pierre Pucheu, a Vichy cabinet minister and director of a private bank in Paris. Pucheu in turn passed the secret to Yves Bréart de Boisanger, the governor of the Bank of France and a BIS director. Higham, *Trading with the Enemy*, 32–33, citing Interrogation Statement of Heinrich Otto Abetz to U.S. military, June 21, 1946. See generally Paxton, *Vichy France*, 100, 108, 124; Ray, *Annäherung an Frankreich*; Aarons and Loftus, *Unholy Trinity*, 276–77. Statement of Heinrich Otto Abetz to U.S. military, June 21, 1946.
16 The United Nations Monetary and Financial Conference, known as the Bretton Woods Conference, recommended in 1944 that BIS be dissolved since it had operated as an Axis-dominated entity in outright violation of its neutral charter. But its solid business and government connections, chiefly through Allen Dulles, helped it successfully resist the dissolution order. Today, BIS thrives in a role that mirrors the International Monetary Fund. See generally "BIS Archive Guide," 2.
17 U.S. State Department Post Files, Switzerland, 1945, Interrogation of Allen Dulles, NARA; see also Aarons and Loftus, *Unholy Trinity*, 277.
18 Aarons and Loftus, *Unholy Trinity*, 277–78.
19 Ibid., 295.
20 SCI Unit Memo, May 27, 1945, supplementary Interrogation Report of Reinhard Karl Wilhelm Reme, Abwehr II Recruiter, Washington Registry SI Intel Field Files, records of the Office of Strategic Services, RG 226, Box 214, NND 897108, Entry 108A; the document is an attachment to a longer memo dated October 25, 1945, "Subject to Questionnaire by Reinhard Karl Wilhelm Reme," NARA.
21 Aarons and Loftus, *Unholy Trinity*, 38.
22 There is a May 27, 1945, two-page summary of an interrogation with Reme. Another one-page summary dated June 6, 1945. That document notes "attached herewith Supplementary Interrogation Report of Reinhard Karl Wilhelm REME," but all that is attached to that sheet is "Appendix C." And there is also a twenty-six-page questionnaire answered by Reme dated October 25, 1945. The National Archives declassified all three documents on April 28, 2006. On June 22, 2006, the National Archives released supplementary documents related to Reme, including an intelligence twelve-page "Top Secret" summary about Reme and his intelligence service, complete with drawings of his Milan office. On June 27, 2006, the National Archives declassified a fifteen-page OSS file on Reme, including notes again about his supplementary interrogation. American intelligence determined that SD agents—Sicherheitsdienst, the SS spy agency—had penetrated Jauch and Hübener: "Eilers, Edith, PF 608.624," OSS Archives, London, RG 226, DSS E119A, subdocument "Eilers, Edith Ida Johanna," June 6, 1945, Folder 309, 2, NARA. The SD had in fact inserted into the firm in 1941 one of its own operatives, Dr. Herbert Worch. See also Memo, Saint JJI to Saint BB, Response to Questionnaire by Reinhard Karl Wilhelm Reme, October 25, 1945, Washington Registry SI Intel Field Files, records of the Office of Strategic Services, RG 226, Box 214, NND 897108, Entry 108A, NARA, 12.
23 Report on "FIDE Group, Abwehr II, Background Notes, Top Secret, RG 226, Box 13, File 79, 2.
24 Appendix C of SCI Unit Memo, May 27, 1945, supplementary Interrogation Report of Reinhard Karl Wilhelm Reme, Abwehr II Recruiter, Washington Registry SI Intel Field Files, records of the Office of Strategic Services, RG 226, Box 214, NND 897108, Entry 108A, NARA.

25 Preliminary Interrogation Report of Reinhard Karl Wilhelm Reme, SCI Unit Rome, Top Secret, May 18, 1945, OSS Archives, RG 226, OSS E119A/File 1359, NARA.
26 Supplementary Interrogation Report of Reinhard Karl Wilhelm Reme, May 27, 1945, Washington Registry SI Intel Field Files, records of the Office of Strategic Services, RG 226, Box 214, NND 897108, Entry 108A, NARA, 2.
27 Preliminary Interrogation Report of Reinhard Karl Wilhelm Reme, SCI Unit Rome, Top Secret, May 18, 1945, OSS Archives, RG 226, OSS E119A/File 1359, NARA. Elsewhere, in the typed notes in the same file, unattributed comments say Reme "recruited agents for Italian Sabotage Agency in Milan" based on information from "Antonio Calrari [a] captured saboteur."
28 An Argentine insurance company, Mackenzie Limitada, was blacklisted by the United States Treasury for its business dealings with the Axis powers. The firm was reported to have operations in Genoa and Milan. During his interrogation and investigation of Reme, Angleton discovered that Reme's operating alias was Carlo Mackenzie. Angleton did not know about the eponymously named blacklisted firm in Argentina, operating in the same industry–insurance–in which Reme was a senior executive before his transfer to Milan. Declassified files reviewed by the author do not answer whether the Mackenzie/ insurance overlap between a blacklisted firm and Reme are simply a coincidence or are somehow linked. See generally "Memorandum for Listing, Insurance," British Embassy, Washington, DC, February 6, 1942, RG 131, Box 15, Folder 48B, 230/8/34/4, NARA.
29 Some Abwehr files about its battle with the SS are available in the so-called Himmler Collection, about nine thousand pages of Gestapo intelligence and counterintelligence files released by the National Archives in 2002; Interagency Working Group, the Nazi War Crimes and Japanese Imperial Government Records Interagency Working Group.
30 Reme told his interrogators that "some agents" of SD's Ämter VI had approached his senior partners in Jauch and Hübener in 1941. The work they requested got the firm "into serious difficulties."
31 "Zeidler, PF. 602.690," OSS Archives, London, RG 226, DSS E119A, subdocument "Obtaining of Technical Intelligence," Folder 1617, NARA.
32 Interim Report of Dr. Hans Martin Zeidler, AMT VI Wi, Secret, "Incorporation of OK/AMT AUSLAND u ABWEHR I Wi IN AMT VI Wi (Feb 44), No. 15, RG 319, Entry Oskar Turina XE1G186, Box 469, NARA. Angleton says that Reme did not leave Italy because he thought it "would have been suicide." Supplementary Interrogation Report of Reinhard Karl Wilhelm Reme, May 27, 1945, Washington Registry SI Intel Field Files, records of the Office of Strategic Services, RG 226, Box 214, NND 897108, Entry 108A, NARA, 2
33 Schellenberg also said that the Abwehr agents in the Vatican had been "broken when the Allies took Rome." But that was only an assumption by Schellenberg, since his group had no way of knowing what the embedded Abwehr units did after the occupation of Rome. Report of Interrogation of Walter Schellenberg, June 27 to July 12, 1945, Top Secret, RG 226, E119A, Folder 2051, NARA. See also Reinhard R. Doerries, ed., *Hitler's Last Chief of Foreign Intelligence: Allied Interrogations of Walter Schellenberg* (London: Cass, 2003).
34 See generally Report of Interrogation of Walter Schellenberg, June 27 to July 12, 1945, Top Secret, RG 226, E119A, Folder 2051, NARA.
35 Frattini, *The Entity*, 277–79.
36 One of Angleton's informants was Virgilio Scattolini, who was also providing intelligence to the Germans. Although he was an opportunist and a writer of pornography, he had excellent connections inside St. Peter's. Another Angleton source was Monsignor Enrico Pucci, the Vatican aide who gave daily press briefings. Pucci secretly sold to the fascists the same reports he peddled to the Allies. Cooney, *The American Pope*, 144. See also Frattini, *The Entity*, 278.
37 Aarons and Loftus, *Unholy Trinity*, 301–2.
38 London, OSS Archives, Appendix F, RG 226, OSS E119A, Folder 1359, NARA.
39 Webster, *Industrial Imperialism in Italy*, 252, discussing how during the time Nogara was there "Constantinople became a center of international agents, influence peddlers, and journalists selling their pens, in addition to the customary concession-seekers and promoters who claimed foreign backing."
40 Ibid., 252–53; Roman, *Giuseppe Volpi*, 37–38. Nogara had worked closely in 1912-13 in Constantinople with German businessmen on a plan for a rail link from Turkey to the new state of Albania.

41 "Subject: Nogara Bruno, BIETOLETTI Nino, FABRI William, MENEGAZZI Angelo," from HQ Fifteenth Army Group, 1456/523/GSI(b), to the GSI Eighth Army, copy to 2 SCI Unit, April 23, 1945, War Office/Headquarters Papers, Allied Forces in North Africa, Italy and France 1942–1945, W0 204/12143, UK National Archives, retrieved by Tina Hampson.

42 Giuseppe Casarrubea, *Storia segreta della Sicilia: Dallo sbarco alleato a Portella della Ginestra (Tascabili Saggi)* (Secret History of Sicily by the Allied Landing at Portella della Ginestra) (Turin, Italy: Bompiani, 2012), Kindle edition, location 5955 of 6114. On the chart that Angleton constructed from his debrief of Reme, Pfannenstiel's unit is correctly listed as one of four independent branches operating in northern Italy under Abwehr II command, under außenstelle-lager FAI.

43 Schmidt-Bruck had moved to take charge of Abwehr unit 254 sometime around May 1944, previously having directed unit 253, responsible for carrying out sabotage in central and southern Italy. Schmidt-Bruck's assistant, Dr. Viktor Fadrus, took charge of that unit 253. Op. Cit. "Key: FIDE Group (ABWEHR II), I. Background Notes," 19, NARA.

44 Until approximately May 1944, Reme was in Abwehr unit 253 in Bozzolo, about seventy miles southeast of Milan. After that he was in unit 254 as the chief recruiter in the northern city of Reggio Emilia. Op. Cit. "Key: FIDE Group (ABWEHR II), I. Background Notes," NARA (in that document Bozzolo is misspelled as *Boxxolo*).

45 "Subject: Nogara Bruno, BIETOLETTI Nino, FABRI William, MENEGAZZI Angelo," from HQ Fifteenth Army Group, 1456/523/GSI(b), to the GSI Eighth Army, 6, U.K. National Archives.

46 Two-page letter within the SCI Unit Memo, May 27, 1945, supplementary Interrogation Report of Reinhard Karl Wilhelm Reme, Abwehr II Recruiter, Washington Registry SI Intel Field Files, records of the Office of Strategic Services, RG 226, Box 214, NND 897108, Entry 108A, NARA.

47 Ibid.

48 A 1958 Italian obituary of Nogara, listed him as the Vatican's representative to the Committee of National Liberation, Rome's underground resistance movement. The author could not substantiate any such affiliation from government archives about Nogara nor from available files concerning the history of the Committee of National Liberation. The listing could have been inserted by the Vatican or by Nogara's family as a way to posthumously create antifascist credentials. Or it could have been added to his biography by a Western intelligence agency as a way of further burying any link to the Abwehr. Finally, it is also possible that Nogara belonged to the Abwehr as well as the Committee of National Liberation, serving both in order to best protect his Vatican investments.

Chapter 12: The Ratline

1 Generally Briefing by Stuart Eizenstat, Undersecretary for Economic, Business, and Agricultural Affairs, regarding release of the report, U.S. and Allied Wartime and Postwar Relations and Negotiations with Argentina, Portugal, Spain, Sweden, and Turkey on Looted Gold and German External Assets and U.S. Concerns About the Fate of the Wartime Ustaša Treasury, June 2, 1998.

2 Report of Interrogation of Walter Schellenberg, June 27 to July 12, 1945, Top Secret, RG 226, E119A, Folder 2051, Section 107, "Faked Pound Notes," NARA. Schwend's name is also spelled as Schwendt in some U.S. military files as well as in some books by historians. The first spelling is used here because on documents in which Schwend signed his name, he did so without the *t*. For more on Schwend and his counterfeiting plot—Operation Bernhard—see Auszug aus den Akten Friedrich Schwendt, RG 242, T-120, Roll 5781, Frame FH297319-55, NARA. See Dr. Kevin C. Ruffner, "On the Trail of the Nazi Counterfeiters," *The Daily Beast*, September 20, 2014.

3 The OSS used Schwend on so-called bird-dog operations, designed to find wanted Nazis. His code name was Flush. Schwend wrote a long report about his counterfeiting operation for the OSS, but according to the intelligence agency, and its successor the CIA, that report was inadvertently destroyed. The Americans cut Schwend loose in 1946 when they discovered he was running yet another counterfeiting operation in Italy. He ended up in Peru where he produced fake dollars and trafficked in small arms. Cables of December 12, 1966, and August 19, 1969, Memorandum for CIA Deputy Director for Plans, RG 263, Freidrich Schwend Name File, Vol. 2, NARA. See generally Kevin C. Ruffner, "On the Trail of the Nazi Counterfeiters," *Studies in Intelligence* (2002), 44, https://www.cia.gov/library/center-for-the-study-of-intelligence/kent-csi

/vol40no5/html/v40i5a12p.htm. See also release of "Studies in Intelligence" document by the CIA, September 18, 2014.

4 Aarons and Loftus, *Unholy Trinity,* 297; see also Auszug aus den Akten Friedrich Schwendt, RG 242, T-120, Roll 5781, Frame FH297319-55, NARA; Richard Breitman, Norman J. W. Goda, Timothy Naftali, and Robert Wolfe, *U.S. Intelligence and the Nazis* (Cambridge: Cambridge University Press, 2005). As for the exchange of British sterling in 1945, see John Hooper and Richard Norton-Taylor, "The Pope Has a Problem; The Vatican Is Still Trying to Hide What May Be Ugly Secrets About Nazi Loot," *The Guardian*, February 12, 1998, 19. Besides his cash, Schwend had buried about 7,000 pieces of gold in a remote stretch of Austrian countryside. But before he could retrieve it and send it to the Vatican or other safe haven, the OSS took it as part of their convoluted bargain with Schwend. See Ruffner, "On the Trail of the Nazi Counterfeiters."

5 The Yugoslavian government later claimed that 258 pounds of gold were stolen. An early detailed accounting about the Ustaša looting of gold reserves is a January 1946 intelligence report from James Jesus Angleton. He reported that Ustašan fugitives had fled into Austria with two crates of gold. U.S. Strategic Services Unit report of James Angleton, January 22, 1946, Entry 210, Box 6, RG 226, Location 250/64/28/02, NARA; see also Phayer, *Pius XII, the Holocaust, and the Cold War*, 211, Aarons and Loftus, *Unholy Trinity*, 301–2. As for the U.S. intelligence assessment that the Croatian gold included some plundered from victims, see "Subject: Pending Release of Amb. Eizenstat's Vol. II Report on WWII Victim Gold," CIA, Secret, May 29, 1998, declassified pursuant to the Nazi War Crimes Disclosure Act, available online at http://www.foia.cia.gov/sites/default/files/document_conversions/1705143/DRAGANOVIC,%20KRUNOSLAV_0094.pdf.

In the CIA summary as well: "Available information indicates that there was some quantity of gold at the disposal of the Ustashi in Rome, Austria, and Switzerland. From the character of the Ustasha regime and the nature of its wartime activities, this sum almost certainly included some quantity of victim gold."

6 Deposition of William E. W. Gowen, *Emil Alperin v. Vatican Bank*, Case No. C99–04041 MMC, USDC Northern District of California, March 9, 2006, Vol. 4, 759–61, 775.

7 "The largest estimate of Croatian state treasury reaching the Vatican was made in an October 1946 report to the treasury department, which estimated that 200 million Swiss francs (about $47 million) was originally held in the Vatican before being moved to Spain and Argentina," ibid., "Subject: Pending Release of Amb. Eizenstat's Vol. II Report on WWII Victim Gold," CIA, Secret, May 29, 1998; Historian John Pollard thinks the sum is "inconceivable" unless the Ustaša had also emptied Belgrade's Yugoslav National Bank, and "we have no evidence they did so." Pollard, *Money and the Rise of the Modern Papacy*, 198–99. See also Bigelow to Glaser, July 19, 1946, Entry 183, Box 27, RG 226, Llocation 190/9/22/05, NARA.

8 Argentina: Economic/Safehaven: German Capital Invested in Argentina, Report F-3627-A, RG 260, Office of the Military Government, United States (OMGUS), Property Division, Box 645, Argentina, NARA.

9 Emerson Bigelow worked for the Strategic Services Unit, an intelligence organization that existed briefly between the winding down of the OSS and the start-up of the CIA. He was not an intelligence officer but rather a financial analyst who sent his report to Harold Glasser, the Treasury Department's Director of Monetary Research. Bigelow's memo was declassified on December 31, 1996, as part of the State Department's normal review of historical documents. In July 1997, the document was released pursuant to a Freedom of Information and Privacy Act request to two television producers, Gaylen Ross and Stephen Crisman, who were filming a two-hour documentary for the Arts and Entertainment Network about how Switzerland handled Nazi gold during and after the war. The State Department released the document too late to be included in the July 26 show, so instead the producers released it to several newspaper reporters and wire services. Bigelow to Glasser, July 19, 1946, Entry 183, Box 27, RG 226, Location 190/9/22/05; Memo from Emerson Bigelow to Harold Glasser, Director of Monetary Research, U.S. Treasury Department, October 21, 1946, RG 226, Entry 183, Box 29, File 6495; also Entry 183, Box 27, RG 226, Location 190/9/22/05, NARA.

10 Gowen's father, Franklin, was assigned at the same time to the State Department's Vatican mission. During the war, he had served as Myron Taylor's assistant.

11 There was some debate among CIC investigators about whether the British troops and priests were authentic or merely Ustašan officers in stolen uniforms and clerical robes. CIC agent Gowen believed that the uniforms were stolen and had been taken from the headquarters of the British

8th Army. Letter from Dr. Jonathan Levy to Rene Brülhart, Autorita di Informazione Finanziaria, March 25, 2013, Re: Offer to Compromise Without Prejudice on the Matter of the Ustaša Treasury; Deposition of William W. Gowen, *Emil Alperin v. Vatican Bank,* Case No. C99-04041 MMC, USDC Northern District of California, December 12, 2005, 56.

12 The lieutenant colonel was Ivan Babic, a decorated Ustašan veteran who had fought against Russian troops. Deposition of William W. Gowen, *Emil Alperin v. Vatican Bank,* Case No. C99-04041 MMC, USDC Northern District of California, December 12, 2005, 45.

13 Headden, Hawkins, and Vest, "A Vow of Silence," 34.

14 Ibid., 34; Declaration of William W. Gowen, *Emil Alperin v. Vatican Bank,* Case No. C99-4941 MMC, USDC Northern District of California, January 16, 2003, 6.

15 Aarons and Loftus, *Unholy Trinity,* 113.

16 Declaration of William W. Gowen, *Emil Alperin v. Vatican Bank,* Case No. C99-4941 MMC, USDC Northern District of California, January 16, 2003, 5–6; see also Deposition of William W. Gowen, *Emil Alperin v. Vatican Bank,* Case No. C99-04041 MMC, USDC Northern District of California, December 12, 2005, 45–47. See also Steinacher, *Nazis on the Run,* xx, 13.

17 Wilensky, *Six Million Crucifixions,* Kindle edition, 3207 of 8032.

18 Deposition of William W. Gowen, *Emil Alperin v. Vatican Bank,* Case No. C99-04041 MMC, USDC Northern District of California, March 9, 2006, 796; see also Exhibit, Declaration of William W. Gowen, January 16, 2003.

19 Declaration of William W. Gowen, January 16, 2003, 15–18. The Foreign Service officer was J. Graham Parsons. He had replaced Gowen's father, Franklin, as Myron Taylor's assistant. The elder Gowen left his post in 1945, shortly after his son had arrived in Italy on behalf of the CIC.

20 Declaration of William W. Gowen, 18. Decades later, Gowen said that he believed there had been an official cover-up of his investigation. "Many other documents, including some of my Rome CIC Reports and those of Major Leo Pagnotta, had not surfaced, and thus there were many remaining gaps in the story of our Rome CIC hunt for Ante Pavelic. As I testified, I believe that many documents, including the Registration Files of San Girolamo, and our 1946–47 'Operation Circle' reports on the hunt for 23 'escaped' SS officers, have mysteriously disappeared, and may have been deliberately destroyed." Letter from William E. Gowen to Jonathan Levy, Esq., September 29, 2008, made available by Jonathan Levy.

21 Letter from Dr. Jonathan Levy to Rene Bruelhart, Autorita di Informazione Finanziaria, March 25, 2013, Re: Offer to Compromise Without Prejudice on the Matter of the Ustašan Treasury. Secret Staff Summary for the Director, CIA, "Subject: Pending Release of Amb. Eizenstat's Vol. II Report on WWII Victim Gold," pages 1–3CIA, Secret, May 29, 1998, declassified and released by the CIA under the Nazi War Crimes Disclosure Act. Secret Staff Summary for the Director, CIA, Subject: Pending Release of Amb. Eizenstat's Vol. II Report on WWII Victim Gold, May 29, 1998, pages 1–3, declassified and released by the CIA under the Nazi War Crimes Disclosure Act.

22 Deposition of William W. Gowen, *Emil Alperin v. Vatican Bank,* Case No. C99-04041 MMC, USDC Northern District of California, December 12, 2005, 82–84.

23 From Vincent La Vista to Herbert J. Cummings, Subject: SAFEHAVEN: FLIGHT OF CAPITAL BY PETACCI FAMILY, Secret, Report No. 11, Rome, June 19, 1946, RG 84, PRFSP, State Department, Rome, Embassy and Consulate, Confidential Files, 1946, 851 AC, Finance Section, 851.5, Box 11, NARA.

24 Ibid.

25 Ibid.

26 Rick Hampson, "Pope Changed the World," *USA Today,* April 3, 2005.

27 Myron C. Taylor to Secretary of State (Edward Stettinius), April 20, 1945, RG 59, Box 28, Entry 1069, Location 250/48/29/05, NARA.

28 The Italian communist chief was Palmiro Togliatti. Phayer, *Pius XII, the Holocaust, and the Cold War,* 135. Pius in part blamed the Allies for the strong postwar power of the Soviets. He was convinced that if America and Britain had not so thoroughly destroyed the Germans, the Russians would not have been able to grab half of Europe.

29 Cooney, *The American Pope,* 145, citing undated OSS documents in note 54.

30 Phayer, *Pius XII, the Holocaust, and the Cold War,* 141.

31 Ibid., 238.

32 Aarons and Loftus, *Unholy Trinity,* 25.

33 Pascalina was put in charge of Church Asylum, which focused in large part on German POWs in gigantic Allied makeshift detention camps. See Steinacher, *Nazis on the Run*, 102. Montini had worked with Draganović during the war as the de facto representative for Croatian refugees. Subject Dr. Krunoslav DRAGANOVIC, Secret: U.S. Officials Only, Date of Info: 1945–1952, Date Acquired: July 1952, Date of Report, July 24, 1952, Approved for release Feb 1998, (262), NARA; see also Phayer, *Pius XII, the Holocaust, and the Cold War*, 233. The postwar Confraternity of San Girolamo was a charity founded in July 1945 for Croatian refugees. It provided a cover for Draganović to continue his work with the Vatican and Monsignor Montini.

34 The Allies had compiled a Central Registry of War Crimes and Security Suspects (CROWCASS). By the time it was phased out in 1948, it had 85,000 wanted reports and forty book-length reports of wanted criminals. As the largest database of its kind, investigators in a dozen countries used CROWCASS, as well as military and army police files, cross-referencing names against the millions detained in POW or displaced persons' camps. Christopher Simpson, *Blowback: America's Recruitment of Nazis and Its Effects on the Cold War* (New York: Weidenfeld & Nicolson, 1988), 67.

35 Vatican passports were only for clerics, although a few were issued to Black Nobles. The church's alliance with the International Red Cross, which was itself under tremendous pressure and operating at full capacity because of the flood of refugees, was natural. Some Red Cross passports used by Nazi fugitives were fake.

36 See generally Sereny, *Into That Darkness*, 275–91.

37 Stephanie Stern, "Papal Responses to the Holocaust: Contrast Between Pope Pius XII and Pope John Paul II," *Colgate Academic Review* 8, Article 5 (Fall 2010). Even when Pius was offered opportunities to make up for some of the church's inaction during the war, he failed to do so. Five months after hostilities ended, the World Jewish Congress's Gerhart Riegner met with Monsignor Montini and Pius. Riegner pleaded for assistance in finding any Jewish children who might have survived the death camps. He informed the two church leaders that the Nazis had murdered 1.5 million Jewish children. Montini dismissed that as exaggerated. Pius promised the church would help. It did nothing. It was not until 2004 that historians uncovered in France an unsigned letter approved by Pius XII instructing that Jewish children who had been baptized to save them from the gas chambers should be entrusted only to families who agreed to raise them as Catholic. Jewish groups raised an uproar. Vatican spokesman Father Sergio Pagano contended the letter was only meant to apply to "abandoned" children. "It would be another thing if the children were requested back by their parents," he said. John Thavis, "Vatican Not Impressed with Threat to Sue over Access to Archives," Catholic News Service, January 28, 2005.

38 Headden, Hawkins, and Vest, "A Vow of Silence," 34. Schellenberg was sent later to Great Britain. During extensive interrogations there he gave the most complete accounts of Nazi wartime intelligence. See Ruffner, "On the Trail of Nazi Counterfeiters."

39 In a World Peace Rally in New York, Cardinal Spellman told a large crowd that Stepinac's only crime was "fidelity to God and country."

40 Uki Goñi, *The Real Odessa: How Perón Brought the Nazi War Criminals to Argentina* (London: Granta, 2002), 346; Michael Phayer, "Canonizing Pius XII: Why Did the Pope Help Nazis Escape?," Ohlendorf testimony in Case 9 Transcripts, RG 238, Entry 92, Box 1, Vol. 2, 510, NARA.

41 Catherine Epstein, *Model Nazi: Arthur Greiser and the Occupation of Poland* (Cary, NC: Oxford University Press USA, 2012), 330–31. Greiser's case is typical of others in which Pius intervened for clemency. Greiser wrote to Pius and two British politicians—Anthony Eden and Alfred Duff Cooper—he thought might be sympathetic to his appeal to avoid a death sentence. The politicians were smart enough to ignore him. Only Pius responded, asking the Poles to spare Greiser, in part "following the divine example of our Lord, who, on the cross, praying for his executioners." Greiser had met the Pope (then Secretary of State Pacelli) during a visit to Rome in 1938.

42 Epstein, *Model Nazi*, 330; see also Goñi, *The Real Odessa*, 346.

43 Glenn Yeadon, *The Nazi Hydra in America: Suppressed History of a Century* (Palm Desert, CA: Progressive Press, 2008), 276.

44 Phayer, *The Catholic Church and the Holocaust*, 154, 201; see also Suzanne Brown-Fleming, *The Holocaust and Catholic Conscience: Cardinal Aloisius Muench and the Guilt Question in Germany* (Notre Dame, IN: Notre Dame University Press, 2006).

45 Brown-Fleming, *The Holocaust and Catholic Conscience*, 88, 188–89; Phayer, *Pius XII, the Holocaust, and the Cold War*, 136.

46 Aarons and Loftus, *Unholy Trinity*, 148–49.

47 Jakob Weinbacker interview with Gitta Sereny, in Sereny, *Into That Darkness,* 305–6.
48 William Gowen and Louis Caniglia, Counter Intelligence Corps, Rome, August 29, 1947, RG 319, Box 173, File IRR XE001109 Pavelić, Location 270/84/1/4, NARA; Antonio Vucetich, El Socorro, Argentina, to Olga Vucetich-Radic, May 6, 1947, RG 59, Box 17, Entry 1068, Location 250/48/29/01-05, NARA. See also for a general discussion Phayer, *Pius XII, the Holocaust, and the Cold War*, 234–45.
49 Aarons, *Sanctuary*, 216–17; Phayer, *Pius XII, the Holocaust, and the Cold War*, 245–46, 263.
50 Pavelić was no newcomer to Italy as a fugitive. In 1934 he had found safe haven there after assassinating Serbian King Alexander and the French Foreign Minister. Mussolini refused to extradite him. In 1941 he returned to Croatia to lead the new fascist state.
51 Phayer, *Pius XII, the Holocaust, and the Cold War*, 222–23, 225.
52 Goñi, *The Real Odessa*, 343, citing CIC memorandum, Life and Work of Dr. Dominik Mandic, October 10, 1946, CIA Operational Files M; Blazekovic, *Studia Croatica*, 1973, Issues 50–51; Headden, Hawkins, and Vest, "A Vow of Silence," 34.
53 Headquarters of Counter Intelligence Corps, Allied Forces Headquarters, APO 512, Subject: Father Krunoslav DRAGANOVIC, Re: PAST Background and PRESENT Activity, February 12, 1947, NARA. San Girolamo was the busiest of the ratline seminaries, but it was not the only one. It catered to Croatian fugitives. Lithuanians went to a Father Jatulevicius on the Via Lucullo, while Hungarians were directed to a small house on Via dei Parione run by Father Gallov. See generally Simpson, *Blowback*, 179.
54 Headden, Hawkins, and Vest, "A Vow of Silence," 34 .
55 Lt. Col. G. F. Blunder, Headquarters, Mediterranean Theater of Operations, to Col. Carl Fritzsche, Assistant Deputy Director of Intelligence, November 8, 1947, RG 319, Box 173, File IRR XE001109 Pavelić, Location 270/84/14, NARA.
56 Headden, Hawkins, and Vest, "A Vow of Silence," 34. The British Foreign Office in 1998 denied any involvement in the escape of the Ustašan fugitives, but refused to release any military intelligence records about Pavelić.
57 It took the Vatican fifty years to respond to the charges that it had helped Pavelić escape, and it did so only after Vienna-based Nazi hunter Simon Wiesenthal had released a damning report about the church's role as Pavelić's postwar protector. The Vatican's response? It claimed only that it could not find any evidence of payments to anyone named Pavelić in the records of the IOR. "Vatican Will Attend Nazi Gold Conference in London," Agence France-Presse, December 1, 1997 See also Yossi Melman, "Pope Paul VI Allegedly Helped Croatian Fascists," *Ha'aretz*, January 16, 2006.

General funding for Croatian refugees also came from the American National Catholic Welfare Council, a charitable organization directed by the U.S. cardinals. Chicago's Cardinal Samuel Stritch was the best fundraiser, but he had good reason to do so since he oversaw the largest Croatian congregation in the U.S. See generally Phayer, *Pius XII, the Holocaust, and the Cold War*, 247–48. The CIA declassified what it claimed were the last two pages in its possession about Draganović, but both are completely redacted.
58 "Ante Pavelic Dies in Madrid at 70," Reuters, Madrid, December 29, 1959; Aarons and Loftus, *Unholy Trinity*, 143–50.
59 Telegram from Weizsäcker to the Foreign Office, Berlin, October 17, 1943, *Inland Il Geheim*, quoted in full in Katz, *Black Sabbath*, 215.
60 Steinacher, *Nazis on the Run*, 119–20. Disguised as an Austrian refugee organization, the Austrian Liberation Committee and Hudal received financial aid from the American Catholic Bishops Conference among other church groups.
61 Stangl interview with Gitta Sereny in Sereny, *Into That Darkness*, 274
62 Ibid., 289.
63 Tony Paterson, "How the Nazis Escaped Justice," *Independent Press*, January 28, 21=013, 26.
64 Yitzhak Arad, *Belzec, Sobibor, Treblinka: The Operation Reinhard Death Camps* (Bloomington, IN: 1987), Kindle edition, location 4025 of 9931. In 1979, BBC investigative journalist Tom Bower tracked Wagner to Sao Paulo. In an interview, when asked about his savage role at the death camp, said: "I had no feelings, although at the beginning I did. It just became another job. In the evenings we never discussed our work, but just drank and played cards. . . . I feel like an ordinary man, no different from others." Tom Bower, "The Tracking and Freeing of a Nazi Killer: The Life and Deaths of Gustav Wagner," *The Washington Post*, August 19, 1975, E1.

65 See Holger M. Meding, *Flucht vor Nurnberg?: Deutsche und osterreichische Einwanderung in Argentinien, 1945–1955* (Vienna: Köln, Weimar, Wien, Böhlau Verlag, 1992).
66 Sereny, *Into That Darkness*, 290.
67 Interrogation Report on SS-Standartenführer Rauff Walther. CSDIC.SC/15AG/SD 11, May 29, 1945, RG 263, Walter Rauff Name File (note: different spellings of Walther/Walter are as reflected in the files), NARA.
68 Sworn statement (translated) of Hermann Julis Walter Rauff Bauermeister, Santiago, Chile, December 5, 1962, Simon Wiesenthal Center, Los Angeles; see Aarons and Loftus, *Unholy Trinity*, 38; see also Simpson, *Blowback*, 92–94.
69 Aarons and Loftus, *Unholy Trinity*, 38.
70 Kevin Freeman, "Wiesenthal Center Releases Documents Which Link Rauff to Important Figures in the Catholic Church," Jewish Telegraph Agency, May 9, 1984; see also Simpson, *Blowback*, 93–94.
71 Simon Wiesenthal interview with Mark Aarons and John Loftus, *Unholy Trinity*, 28; Steinacher, *Nazis on the Run*, 134.
72 Sereny, *Into That Darkness*, 319.
73 Summary Report, by Special Agent Robert Mudd, RG 262, Box 12, Entry A1-86, NARA; see also Phayer, *Pius XII, the Holocaust, and the Cold War*, 235.
74 Anton Weber interview with Gitta Sereny in Sereny, *Into That Darkness*, 318. Some countries that were willing to accept baptized Jews still wanted to ensure they were getting real converts and not merely Jews who claimed to be Catholic to avoid being killed. Brazil, for instance, offered the Vatican three thousand visas but insisted they only be issued to Jews who had been Catholics for at least two years.
75 Anton Weber interview with Gitta Sereny in Sereny, *Into That Darkness*, 319.
76 Adolf Eichmann, "Meine Flucht: Bericht aus der Zelle in Jerusalem," CIA, War Crimes, CIA name files, IWG, RG 263, Box 14, Eichmann, Adolf, Vol. 1, NARA.
77 Sereny, *Into that Darkness*, 321–22.
78 Monsignor Karl Bayer interview with Gitta Sereny, *Into That Darkness*, 309; Goñi, *The Real Odessa*, 342. As for the misplaced hope in the Vatican leadership that the Ustaša might be able to return to power, see Phayer, *Pius XII, the Holocaust, and the Cold War*, 234.
79 Most of the files about Pius's overt support of the efforts to free Ustašan and other war criminals were released by the U.K. National Archives in 2001 and 2002. One of the first journalists to put those files into their historical context was Uki Goñi, *The Real Odessa*, 328–34. Osborne to Foreign Office, August 27, 1945, Foreign Office, 371/48920 R14525; Appeal of the Vatican, March 27, 1946, War Office 204/1113; Osborne to Foreign Office, January 16, 1947, Foreign Office, 371/67370 R 1166, all files at the National Archives, Kew, UK.
80 Appeal of the Vatican, March 27, 1946, War Office 204/1113, National Archives, Kew, UK.
81 In fact, the Italians and Allies never searched monasteries. Church officials even successfully extended their Lateran Pact sovereignty to many schools, churches, and convents. See Steinacher, *Nazis on the Run*,143–46.
82 Quoted in Goñi, *The Real Odessa*, 330
83 Osborne, instructions provided by the Foreign Office, 1947, Foreign Office files, 371/59423 R17521 and R17586, cited in Goñi, *The Real Odessa*, 330–31.
84 Quoted in Goñi, *The Real Odessa*, 331.
85 D'Arcy Osborne to Foreign Office, January 16, 1947, Foreign Office files, 371/67370, R1166, National Archives, Kew, UK.
86 Deposition of William E. W. Gowen, *Emil Alperin v. Vatican Bank*, Case No. C99-04041 MMC, USDC Northern District of California, December 12, 2005, 40–41.
87 Aarons and Loftus, *Unholy Trinity*, 59, citing Draganović's statement to the Yugoslav authorities, September 1967, 26; Ibid., 108, citing the report of a British diplomat in Italy in 1947. Major Stephen Clissold was sent to Genoa to detain some Ustašan criminals, but they managed to escape by sea. According to Clissold, the fugitives were "sponsored by the Pontifical Commissione de Assistenza," and a "trusted collaborator" of Draganović had given them safe shelter while in Genoa; citing telegram from Rome to Foreign Office, February 22, 1947, Public Records Office, Foreign Office, 371 673372, and an unpublished manuscript of Stephen Clissold. See also Goñi, *The Real Odessa*, 332. Further evidence that Pius personally protected Draganović is that the Croatian remained in his position as the head of San Girolamo until Pius's death in 1958, at which point the next Pope, John XXIII, promptly evicted him.

88 Aarons and Loftus, *Unholy Trinity*, 32.
89 Father Ciro Benedettini quoted by Diana Jean Schemo, "A Nazi's Trail Leads to a Gold Cache in Brazil," *The New York Times*, September 23, 1997, 1.
90 Since the 1944 death of Cardinal Secretary of State Maglione, Pius had relied on two undersecretaries, Monsignors Domenico Tardini and Giovanni Montini, for all foreign policy and refugee issues. Goñi, *The Real Odessa*, 331; see also Aarons and Loftus, *Unholy Trinity*, 34–35.
91 CIA memorandum, "A Dangerous and Uncompromising Extremist," Subject: Dr. Krunoslav DRAGANOVIC, Report No (redacted), Date of Intelligence Information 1945–1952, Date of report, July 24, 1952, CIA Operational Files, Declassified, NARA.
92 Deposition of William W. Gowen, *Emil Alperin v. Vatican Bank*, Case No. C99-04041 MMC, USDC Northern District of California, March 9, 2006, 760–61; John Triggs, "The True Story of the Looted 'Nazi Gold,'" *The Express*, November 20, 2004, 53.
93 Triggs, "The True Story of the Looted 'Nazi Gold,'" 53.
94 "Illegal Emigration Movements in and Through Italy," Vincent La Vista to Herbert J. Cummings, May 15, 1947, Holocaust-Era Assets, Civilian Agency Records, RG 19, File 10, NARA.
95 Memo to J. Graham Parsons, State Department, July 28, 1947, "Political General 1947," RG 59, Box 17, Entry 1068, Location 250/488/29/01-05, NARA; see Aarons and Loftus, *Unholy Trinity*, 44.
96 CIC documents set forth "the provisional agreement" to work with Draganović, describing him as "head of the Vatican resettlement project for refugees." Steinacher, *Nazis on the Run*, 200. When John Moors Cabot, the U.S. ambassador to Belgrade, learned about the Allied intelligence–Vatican ratline, he complained to Washington, "We are conniving with [the] Vatican and Argentina to get people to haven in latter country." The OSS was under no illusion about Draganović, calling him a "Fascist, war criminal." "Klaus Barbie and the United States Government," A Report to the Attorney General of the United States, August 1983, Office of Special Investigations, U.S. Department of Justice, 136; see also Mark Fritz, "The Secret History of World War II: From Hot Conflict to Cold War; US Made Moral Compromises in Using Former Nazi Spy Network Against Soviet Threat," *The Boston Globe*, Part 9 of 9, December 26, 2001, 1.
97 Operations Paperclip and Overcast were OSS programs that recruited 765 Nazi rocket scientists and engineers in the decade following the war. The recruits ranged from Wernher von Braun, the "father of rocket science," to Hubertus Strughold, who was involved in medical experiments at the Dachau concentration camp. Reinhard Gehlen, a Catholic and Wehrmacht officer, was put in charge of an eponymously named counterintelligence group that spied on the East Germans and the Soviets. The Gehlen Group consisted of ex-Nazis, quite a few of whom were involved in wartime atrocities. (The Gehlen Group was eventually absorbed into West Germany's Federal Intelligence Service or Bundesnachrichtendienst, the BND.)

The same was true of Allied intelligence recruitment in other fields such as chemical warfare, electronics, and to a smaller extent medicine and cryptography. In some instances, after supplying information, fugitives were simply given a free pass to a safe country. SS Officer Klaus Barbie is the most prominent example. See generally Linda Hunt, *Secret Agenda: The United States Government, Nazi Scientists, and Project Paperclip, 1945 to 1990* (New York: St. Martin's/Thomas Dunne, 1991); Heinz Hone and Hermann Zolling, *The General Was a Spy: The Truth About General Gehlen and His Spy Ring* (New York: Putnam, 1972); Magnus Linklater, Isabel Hilton, and Neal Ascherson, *The Nazi Legacy: Klaus Barbie and the International Fascist Connection* (New York: Henry Holt, 1985); Simpson, *Blowback*.
98 Paul S. Lyon, "Rat Line from Austria to South America," appendix to "Klaus Barbie and the United States Government," A Report to the Attorney General of the United States, August 1983, Office of Special Investigations, U.S. Department of Justice, http://www.justice.gov/criminal/hrsp/archives/1983/08-02-83barbie-rpt.pdf.
99 Bishop Hudal to Juan Perón, August 31, 1948, Collegio Santa Maria dell'Anima, Nachlass Hudal, Box 27, August 1948.
100 John Hobbins, "Memorandum for the Record, Subject: Informant Disposal, Emigration Methods of the 430th CIC Detachment," Top Secret, reproduced in "Klaus Barbie and the United States Government," A Report to the Attorney General of the United States, August 1983, Tab 96 and 145n.
101 Dianne Kirby, "Divinely Sanctioned: The Anglo-American Cold War Alliance and the Defence of Western Civilization and Christianity, 1945–48," *Journal of Contemporary History* 35, no. 3 (July 2000): 385–412.

102 Kent, *The Lonely Cold War*, 239.
103 Adriano Ercole Ciani, "The Vatican, American Catholics and the Struggle for Palestine, 1917–1958: A Study of Cold War Catholic Transnationalism" (PhD thesis, University of Western Ontario, Canada, 2011).
104 Cooney, *The American Pope*, 161, citing undated Spellman memo to Marshall; Simpson, *Blowback*, 91.
105 Telegram to the State Department from J. Graham Parsons, January 16, 1948, J. Graham Parsons Papers, Series 4, Special Collections, Georgetown University. Myron Taylor also reported to the State Department that Pius's main worries were that the election could easily result in a "leftist dictatorship" and that the communists "remain the best organized and most active party with indefatigable will to [gain] power and seemingly limitless funds."
106 Griffiths memo to Cardinal Spellman, March 4, 1948, cited in Cooney, *The American Pope*, 159.
107 "Pope Sees Senators; Says Hate and Greed Bar Peace," *The New York Times*, November 11, 1947, 29; Pope Receives Congressman," *The New York Times*, 42; Cooney, *The American Pope*, 157; see also Pollard, *Money and the Rise of the Modern Papacy*, 224.
108 Phayer, *Pius XII, the Holocaust, and the Cold War*, 145–46.
109 Martin, *Rich Church, Poor Church*, 48.
110 Aarons and Loftus, *Unholy Trinity*, 56, 237–38.
111 The extent of fear in the Truman administration about a communist electoral victory in Italy was revealed by George Kennan, then chief of the State Department's Policy Planning Staff, when he cabled U.S. diplomats in Europe: "As far as Europe is concerned, Italy is obviously key point. If Communists were to win the election there our whole position in Mediterranean, and possibly in Europe as well, would probably be undermined." Kennan recommended American military intervention and occupation of Italy if the communists won. Thomas Powers, *The Man Who Kept the Secrets: Richard Helms and the CIA* (New York: Alfred A. Knopf, 1979), 31–32; Simpson, *Blowback*, 89–92; Steinacher, *Nazis on the Run*.
112 Author interview with Elan Steinberg, April 12, 2006. See also Chalmers Johnson, *Dismantling the Empire: America's Last Best Hope* (New York: Metropolitan Books/Henry Holt), 79; James E. Miller, "Taking Off the Gloves: The United States and the Italian Elections," *Diplomatic History* 7, 1983. See generally George J. Gill, "The Truman Administration and Vatican Relations," *The Catholic Historical Review* 73, no. 5, July 1987; Martin A. Lee, "Their Will Be Done," *Mother Jones*, July/August 1983.
113 Quoted in Gollin, *Worldly Goods*, 464.
114 John F. Pollard, "The Vatican, Italy and the Cold War," in Diane Kirby, *Religion and the Cold War* (London: Palgrave Macmillan, 2002), 110.
115 Pollard, *Money and the Rise of the Modern Papacy*, 202; Cooney, *The American Pope*, 155–58; Phayer, *Pius XII, the Holocaust, and the Cold War*, 146-47.
116 The Popular Democratic Front consisted of the Italian Communist Party and the Italian Socialist Party. The disclosure of some of the money spent ($1 million to the center-right political parties) was made in a CIA memorandum to the Forty Committee (National Security Council), presented to the Select Committee on Intelligence, United States House of Representatives in 1975. The U.S. government provided overt aid in excess of $350 million ($3.6 billion in 2014 dollars) to Italy just in the year leading up to the election. The communists tried countering the Vatican's influence among voters by publicizing the case of a priest in the Secretary of State's office, Edward Prettner Cippico, who was arrested before the vote for stealing money from wealthy Italians who had used the IOR to evade currency restrictions. The church defrocked Cippico. The Cippico revelations titillated Italians but had no discernible impact on the election. (Sentenced to nine years in prison, an appellate court overturned his conviction and after the election the church reinstated him into the priesthood.) See Hoffman, *Anatomy of the Vatican*, 182–83. The church and CIA were not stymied simply if a country did not have free elections. In Guatemala, the CIA and Cardinal Spellman joined forces in backing a 1954 coup that put into power their handpicked anticommunist, Colonel Castillo Armas. See generally Dermot Keogh, "Ireland, The Vatican and the Cold War: The Case of Italy, 1948," *The Historical Journal* 34, no. 4 (December 1991): 931–52.
117 John Tagliabue, "Giulio Andreotti, Premier of Italy 7 Times, Dies at 94," *The New York Times*, May 6, 2013, 1. Mussolini had imprisoned De Gasperi in 1927, but released him two years later to the "custody" of Pope Pius XI. See Berry, *Render Unto Rome*, 25.
118 Cardinal Francis Spellman, "The Pope's War on Communism," *Look*, May 24, 1949.

119 "Vatican Decree in Scots Churches: Anti-Communist Move," *The Glasgow Herald*, August 9, 1949, 5; "Catholic Communists to Be Excommunicated," *The Advocate*, July 15, 1949, 3.

Chapter 13: "He's No Pope"

1 Simpson, *Blowback*, 67.
2 Martha Hopkins, "For European Recovery," Library of Congress, Information Bulletin, Vol. 56, No. 11, June 23, 1997.
3 Article 37 in the armistice with Italy, on September 29, 1943, established the Allied Control Commission for Italy. The Allied Military Government for Occupied Territories ran the country until the Italian peace treaty was signed at the Paris Peace Conference in 1947. While under Allied military command, Italian public companies were held in the equivalent of nontrading escrow accounts, and shareholders like the Vatican had to wait until 1947 before their ownership rights in those firms were fully restored.
4 Hoffman, *Anatomy of the Vatican*, 181.
5 Pollard, *Money and the Rise of the Modern Papacy*, citing H. J. A. Sire, *The Knights of Malta* (New Haven: Yale University Press, 1994), 258–59; see also Paul Hoffman, "Curia Cardinals Rule Informally," *The New York Times*, October 8, 1958, 3.
6 Pollard, *Money and the Rise of the Modern Papacy*, 208.
7 Cornwell, *Hitler's Pope*, 200; see also Gollin, *Worldly Goods*, 465. Carlo Pacelli was the Vatican official who asked Bishop Hudal to represent the church in the October 1943 talks with the German ambassador about the Nazi roundup of Rome's Jews. Pacelli was also at the center of a family scandal, taking a picture of Sister Pascalina and Pius's doctor, Ricardo Galeazzi-Lisi, in what Vatican insiders said was a "compromising situation." The picture evidently made its way back to Pius, but whatever the private fallout, it did not affect Pius's close attachment to his doctor, nephew, or Sister Pascalina. Cornwell, *Hitler's Pope*, 201.
8 Cornwell, *Hitler's Pope*, 350–51.
9 Lai, *Finanze vaticane*, 107, citing Lai interview with Spada, March 7, 1979. That department was one of the few paying a competitive salary compared to private industry.
10 Pollard, *Money and the Rise of the Modern Papacy*, 207.
11 Lai, *Finanze vaticane*, 12; Grilli, *La finanza vaticana in Italia*, 76–77; see also Raw, *The Moneychangers*, 53.
12 Most sources list fourteen children for Mennini, although one writer says it was ten. Hebblethwaite, *Pope John Paul II and the Church*, 108.
13 Martin, *Rich Church, Poor Church*, 39; Gollin, *Worldly Goods*, 465. One of Mennini's sons was a Jesuit priest and a daughter was a nun. See generally Raw, *The Moneychangers*, 64.
14 Lai, *Finanze vaticane*, 107, n. 24.
15 See Pollard, *Money and the Rise of the Modern Papacy*, 189; Chernow, *The House of Morgan*, hardcover, 286.
16 Grilli, *La finanza vaticana in Italia*, 61.
17 See John Lukacs, "The Diplomacy of the Holy See During World War II: Review Article," *The Catholic Historical Review* 60, no. 2 (July 1974): 273; and Pollard, *Money and the Rise of the Modern Papacy*, 192, citing APSS (Ambasciata presso la Santa Sede), pacco 71, memorandum to the minister, 4 and 24, November 1942.
18 In addition to the handful of men who comprised Nogara's close circle, there was a second tier that also wielded reduced but still considerable influence. Some worked inside the Vatican, and a few represented Nogara outside the church but without any formal arrangement. They included two of Carlo Pacelli's cousins, Marcantonio and Giulio Pacelli; and Baron Francesco Maria Oddasso, a director at Nogara's SNIA Viscosa, the country's largest textile company. Luigi Gedda, an ex-president of Catholic Action, was a Nogara insider, as was Antonio Rinaldi, vice president of the Apostolic Chamber and a private finance company that did business with the IOR. There were also Nogara's longtime friends Vittorio Cerruti, Giovanni Battista Sacchetti, Count Enrico Galeazzi, and Count Paolo Blumensthil (whose father, Colonel Bernardino Blumensthil, had led the Vatican's last Pontifical Army, which was disbanded in 1906). See Romano, *Giuseppe Volpi*, 46-47; Grilli, *La finanza vaticana in Italia*, 27, 97, 135; Martin, *Rich Church, Poor Church*, 39; "Who's Who in Fascist Italy," December 26, 1942, RG 226, Box 4, File 174, NARA.

19 Pallenberg, *Inside the Vatican*, 188; Lai, *Finanze vaticane*, 14, 17; see Hachey, *Anglo-Vatican Relations*, 202, 226; and Chernow, *The House of Morgan*, hardcover, 286.
20 Gollin, *Worldly Goods*, 466–67.
21 Ibid., 467.
22 Pollard, *Money and the Rise of the Modern Papacy*, 207.
23 Grilli, *La finanza vaticana in Italia*, 131–32, 159–60.
24 Martin, *Rich Church, Poor Church*, 53.
25 Lai, *Finanze vaticane*, 18.
26 Ibid., 20; see also Martin, *Rich Church, Poor Church*, 52–53.
27 Grilli, *La finanza vaticana in Italia*, 91–92, 102; Pollard, *Money and the Rise of the Modern Papacy*, 207.
28 In addition to buying ownership stakes in companies, the Vatican also bought bonds, some offered by the government, and others of state-owned companies such as Italy's oil and gas enterprise, Ente Nazaionale Idrocarburi. By 1950, the church earned approximately $3 million annually in interest from its Italian bond investments. See generally Martin, *Rich Church, Poor Church*, 52–54.
29 Lai, *Finanze vaticane*, 20, citing Lai interview with Massimo Spada, March 7, 1979; Lo Bello, *The Vatican Empire*, 100.
30 Ernst A. Lewin, "The Finances of the Vatican," *Journal of Contemporary History* 18, no. 2 (April 1983): 195; Grilli, *La finanza vaticana in Italia*, 116, 119–20, 122–23; see also Horne, "How the Vatican Manages Its Money," 80.
31 "Italy: Hens Nesting on Rocks," *Time*, September 19, 1969.
32 Romano, *Giuseppe Volpi*, 238. See also "German Penetration into European Insurance," Economic Advisory Branch, Financial Investigative Branch, RG 260, Box 651, file 390/46/1, 6–7; Supplementary Reports, June to October 1946, RG 260, OMGUS Records, Property Division, Box 647, file 742, 1–5.
33 While Nogara and his financial administration prepared for the postwar era, Pius also set about to make his permanent mark on Catholicism. In 1950, he announced *Munificentissimus Deus*, the dogma of the Assumption of Mary. It decreed that God had taken to heaven the physical body of the mother of Jesus. The doctrine had been debated in earlier centuries and rejected by other Popes since scripture did not support it. Pius definitively settled the issue by invoking the Papal doctrine of infallibility (no other Pope has *ever* claimed infallibility on a matter of faith). Four years later, in his encyclical *Sacra Virginitas*, Pius cited Mary for the concept that virginity was more perfect than marriage. See *Sacra Virginitas*, March 25, 1954, http://www.vatican.va/holy_father/pius_xii/encyclicals/documents/hf_p-xii_enc_25031954_sacra-virginitas_en.html. See generally Hoffman, *Anatomy of the Vatican*, 21.
34 Martin, *Rich Church, Poor Church*, 57.
35 Grilli, *La finanza vaticana in Italia*, 131, 139–41.
36 Montini and Monsignor Domenico Tardini had jointly filled the office—subject to Pius's tight supervision—that had been vacant since Cardinal Maglione's 1944 death.
37 Steinacher, *Nazis on the Run*, 106.
38 Martin, *Rich Church, Poor Church*, 57–58.
39 Hoffman, *Anatomy of the Vatican*, 136.
40 "New Cardinals Receive Symbolic Hats from Pope," *The Boston Globe*, January 14, 1953, 8.
41 Pius also passed over his other Undersecretary of State, Monsignor Tardini. In a January 12, 1953, meeting of some cardinals, Pius said he had wanted to appoint both Montini and Tardini, but that they had declined. Their decision, said Pius, was "palpable evidence of their virtue." Few in the Curia believed that the duo had voluntarily passed the chance to become to cardinals. Hoffman, *Anatomy of the Vatican*, 112.
42 Francis Xavier Murphy, "City of God," *The Wilson Quarterly* 6, no. 4 (Autumn 1982): 105.
43 See Roland Flamini, *Pope, Premier, President* (New York, Macmillan, 1980), 166–67; Michael Novak, *The Open Church* (New Brunswick, NJ: Transaction, 2002), 31–32. Theoretically any Catholic man can be selected at a conclave to serve as Pope. But the last noncardinal, Urban VI, was picked in 1378, and his choice led to the Western Schism in which Urban had to fight for legitimacy against Clement VII.
44 Lo Bello, *The Vatican Empire*, 22.
45 Pollard, *Money and the Rise of the Modern Papacy*, 146; Lo Bello, *The Vatican Empire*, 29.

46 Martin, *Rich Church, Poor Church*, 52–56.
47 See generally Raw, *The Moneychangers*, 52;. At the Ceramica Pozzi (earlier Pozzi-Ginori), Paolo Nogara served with Prince Marcantonio Pacelli, who represented the church's investment in the firm. Paolo also served on a series of boards in the chemical industry, all of which had Vatican investments.
48 Grilli, *La finanza vaticana in Italia*, 114–15, 156–57.
49 Ibid., 114–15.
50 Arnaldo Cortesi, "Pope over Crisis, His Doctors Feel; New Therapy Set," *The New York Times*, December 5, 1954, 1; Lehnert, *His Humble Servant*, 155.
51 Pascalina later wrote admiringly of Niehans, see generally Lehnert, *His Humble Servant*, 154–58, 179.
52 Sister Pascalina wrote in her memoirs about Pius's "serious illness" and that "his stomach rejected all food." He was beset daily with nausea and "the continued, cruelly debilitating hiccupping. The only periods of respite were the brief half hours of sleep." Lehnert, *His Humble Servant*, 155.
53 Hoffman, *Anatomy of the Vatican*, 22–23.
54 Niehans convinced the Pope not to undergo exploratory surgery to check further on what was causing his stomach problems. Instead, Niehans continued administering a combination of his specially formulated injections and as well as blood transfusions. Lehnert, *His Humble Servant*, 158.
55 Lehnert, *His Humble Servant*, 156–57.
56 By that time, Niehans had formed his own Swiss clinic that was shipping its products worldwide. Although he died in 1981, the eponymously named clinic flourished. On its website—http://www.paulniehans.ch/clinic.htm—the Clinic Paul Niehans claims it can "rejuvenate and revitalize your body" and cites famous patients including Pope Pius XII, Charlie Chaplin, Saudi King Ibn Saud, and German Chancellor Konrad Adenauer.
57 Niehans returned to treat Pius in October 1958. He was there during the Pope's final days; Pascalina "Niehans never left the bedside." Lehnert, *His Humble Servant*, 187, 190, 192.
58 Robert A. Ventresca, *Soldier of Christ: The Life of Pope Pius XII* (Cambridge: Harvard University Press/Belknap Press, 2013), 294. "I shall die quite suddenly one day and I'm glad I've written my testament. . . . I asked God for a day." Lehnert, *His Humble Servant*, 164.
59 Sister Pascalina later recounted how she and a few other Papal confidants had tried but failed to see what Pius described. "The following day was a Sunday. Full of expectation we went into the garden, hoping to see the spectacle as well, but we came home again disappointed." Lehnert, *His Humble Servant*, 136. See also Hoffman, *Anatomy of the Vatican*, 20–21.
60 Ventresca, *Soldier of Christ*, 292–93.
61 See for example Cortesi, "Pope over Crisis, His Doctors Feel; New Therapy Set," 1.
62 Although embalming was against Vatican tradition, Dr. Galeazzi-Lisi persuaded Cardinal Tisserant that Pius had secretly authorized him to do it utilizing a method the doctor swore was the same ancient formula used for Jesus. But he botched the herbal and chemical preparation. While Pius's body was still at Castel Gandolfo, where he died, Galeazzi-Lisi wrapped it in plastic in a failed attempt to minimize the horrific odor. During the public procession from the summer palace to Rome, Pius's chest exploded and some of the body began disintegrating before the horrified crowd. After spending a full night repairing the corpse, the following day Pius was laid in a transparent sheath on a colossal catafalque in St. Peter's. As thousands slowly passed to pay their respect, yellowish gray splotches began appearing on Pius's face. The decaying odor was soon so strong that one of the Swiss Guards fainted. At night, with the crowds gone, Galeazzi-Lisi climbed a ladder to pour more of his herbal concoction into the Pope. It was for naught. The casket had to be sealed and placed into a larger lead coffin before it could be buried without further incident. Galeazzi-Lisi compounded his bungled embalming by selling to *Paris Match* photos of the dead Pontiff as well as what he claimed was his diary of the last four days of Pius's life. Italy's medical association expelled him for "infamous conduct," and the Catholic church censured him. But he incredibly reclaimed his medical license because of a technical flaw in the administrative proceedings against him. "Funeral of Pope Pius XII and Coronation of John XXIII," 1958, DO 35/8036 (reference prior department CON 221/1), National Archives, Kew, UK; see generally Hoffman, *Anatomy of the Vatican*, 23–26; Cornwell, *Hitler's Pope*, 356; and Murphy, *La Popessa*, 15–16.

63 Flamini, *Pope, Premier, President*, 31; Cooney, *The American Pope*, 258; see also Arnaldo Corteri, "Cardinal Roncalli Elected Pope; Venetian, 76, Reigns as John XXIII," *The New York Times*, October 29, 1958, 1.
64 Peter Hebblethwaite, *The Year of Three Popes* (Cleveland, OH: William Collins, 1978), 73–74.
65 When Venice was a republic, its top cleric was titled a Patriarch. That title from the days of the empire of the Papal States carried over to modern times. "Elections of Popes John XXIII and Paul VI; visit of Archbishop of Canterbury to Rome, 2 December 1960," 1958–1963, PREM 11/4594, National Archives, Kew, UK.
66 Reese, *Inside the Vatican*, 95.
67 Cooney, *The American Pope*, 260; see also Flamini, *Pope, Premier, President*, 41. A continuing conspiracy theory emerged from the conclave that Cardinal Siri was in fact elected, and then either not allowed to become Pope or for reasons not clear was afraid to accept the post. The so-called Siri Thesis is promoted by a small clique of Catholic traditionalists—called Sirianists—who believe that Roncalli was selected to liberalize the church by calling for the reform-minded Second Vatican Council. The "Siri-was-elected thesis" is based on several minutes of white smoke after a vote on the second day, as well as some incorrect Italian newspaper accounts. It has been repeated everywhere from self-published books to YouTube videos. Some proponents have cited still classified FBI reports (conveniently not available for independent review) to support the theory. At the next three conclaves, in 1963 and 1978 (two that year), Siri was the top vote getter on the first ballots. See Reese, *Inside the Vatican*, 78, 85, 91, 93, 95.
68 Flamini, *Pope, Premier, President*, 41; "Religion: I Choose John . . . ," *Time*, November 10, 1958.
69 "Religion: I Choose John . . . ," *Time*.
70 Hoffman, *Anatomy of the Vatican*, 111–12.
71 Flamini, *Pope, Premier, President*, 48.
72 Wynn, *Keepers of the Keys*, 17–18; Flamini, *Pope, Premier, President*, 48–49.
73 Cornwell, *Hitler's Pope*, 325.
74 Sereny, *Into That Darkness*, 323, note.
75 Wilton Wynn, *Keepers of the Keys: John XXIII, Paul VI, and John Paul II—Three Who Changed the Church* (New York: Random House, 1988), 17–18.
76 Flamini, *Pope, Premier, President*, 19.
77 Lehnert, *His Humble Servant*, 189.
78 One version (Murphy, *La Popessa*, 301) has Pascalina slapping Tisserant. See also Hoffman, *Anatomy of the Vatican*, 137—38; and Cooney, *The American Pope*, 262.
79 Spellman quoted in Cooney, *The American Pope*, 261.
80 John XXIII ordered the Vatican daily, *L'Osservatore Romano*, to stop referring to him as "The Illuminated Holy Father," or "The Highest Pontiff," and instead use the simpler "Pope." "Religion: I Choose John . . . ," *Time*.
81 Hoffman, *Anatomy of the Vatican*, 27.
82 Wynn, *Keepers of the Keys*, 236.
83 Patrick Allitt, "Catholics and the New Conservatism of the 1950s," *U.S. Catholic Historian* 7, no. 1, "Transitions in Catholic Culture: The Fifties" (Winter 1988): 15–37. The U.S. intelligence report is from Cooney, *The American Pope*, 278–79, citing memorandum, CIA staff report, "Change in the Church," No. 27-63, May 13, 1963.
84 Flamini, *Pope, Premier, President*, 14–17.
85 Pope John refused repeated entreaties from the conservatives to mobilize the church in Italian elections on behalf of the Christian Democrats. In Latin America, John allowed bishops to criticize some totalitarian regimes backed by the U.S. When Spellman visited Nicaragua, the Pope personally requested that the New York cardinal not pose for any pictures with the right-wing strongman, Anastasio Somoza. Spellman ignored the directive and not only was photographed with Somoza but even gave his permission for his image to be put on a stamp with the dictator. "Visit by Cardinal Spellman, Archbishop of New York to Nicaragua," Code AN File 1781, FO 371/139625, National Archives, Kew, UK.
86 "Nogara, 88, Directed Vatican's Finances," *The New York Times*, November 16, 1958, 88.
87 See for instance "Bernardino Nogara," *The Boston Globe*, November 16, 1958. The *Globe*, as did many other newspapers, had trouble describing what Nogara had done during his twenty-five years in the city-state. Some obituaries mistakenly referred to him as *monsignor*. Also, a few

books and articles cite a statement attributed to Cardinal Spellman at the time of Nogara's death: "Next to Jesus Christ the greatest thing that has happened to the Catholic Church is Bernardino Nogara." However, no citation is provided. In his comprehensive biography of Cardinal Spellman (*The American Pope*), John Cooney does not repeat it, nor does John Pollard in his book, in which Nogara figures prominently, *Money and the Rise of the Modern Papacy*.

88 R. García Mateo, Rafael Wirth, and J. M. Puig de la Bellacasa, "Las finanza del Vaticano," *El Ciervo* 19, no. 198 (August 1970): 10–11.

89 Francis Xavier Murphy, "A Look at the Earth's Tiniest State," *Chicago Tribune*, August 31, 1982, 11; Murphy, "City of God," 104.

90 The First Vatican Council, called in 1864 by Pius IX, debated the role of the church in the modernist movement, and addressed whether the Pope was infallible when it came to matters of faith. Earlier Ecumenical Councils summoned in the church's history—one in 325 to set the date for Easter or one in 431 to declare Mary the mother of God—did not require that all bishops assemble in Rome.

91 Cornwell, *Hitler's Pope*, 361. The Second Vatican Council led to the removal of some of the most incendiary anti-Jewish language that had been a hallmark of the Catholic liturgy for centuries. Many traditionalists resented the changes, charging that the removal diluted the faith. A few conservative congregations refused to abide by the new rules. French Archbishop Marcel Lefebvre in 1970 led a breakaway group of uncompromising conservatives he called the Society of Saint Pius X (SSPX). Lefebvre was excommunicated, although in 2009, Pope Benedict XVI reversed the excommunication posthumously.

92 "Pope Acts to Unite All Christians: Summons First Ecumenical (World-Wide) Council in Nearly a Century," *The Boston Globe*, January 26, 1959, 1.

93 Wynn, *Keepers of the Keys*, 153.

94 Lai, *Finanze vaticane*, 35.

95 Lewin, "The Finances of the Vatican," 187; Lo Bello, *The Vatican Empire*, 96–97. One of the best estimates of the value of the Vatican's real estate holdings was a 1978 survey mostly from public records, and excluding real estate held by foreign dioceses, by the *International Herald Tribune*. It put the value at $36 billion ($176 billion in 2014 dollars). In 1985, *New York Times* reporter Paul Hoffman reported that the church owned between 20 percent of all land and 25 percent of all buildings in Rome's city limits: Hoffman, *Anatomy of the Vatican*, 171.

96 Raw, *The Moneychangers*, 51; Lo Bello, *The Vatican Empire*, 97

Chapter 14: The Men of Confidence

1 Anonymous business colleague of Sindona quoted in Gordon Thomas and Max Morgan-Witts, *Pontiff* (Garden City, NY: Doubleday, 1983), 145.

2 Sindona's father had trouble holding a regular job and his mother was an invalid. Sindona's maternal grandmother raised him and his brothers. Raw, *The Moneychangers*, 56.

3 Galli, *Finanza bianca*, 65. Author John Cornwell charged that immediately after the war, Sindona was "illegally trafficking in grains, with the benign acquiescence of the Allied Military Government on the island [Sicily]." Cornwell, *God's Banker*, 36. Cornwell does not provide a citation for the allegation, and this author did not find documentary evidence to support it.

4 Luigi DiFonzo, *St. Peter's Banker: Michele Sindona* (New York: Franklin Watts, 1983), 13–14, 22.

5 Jennifer Parmelee, Untitled, Associated Press, International News, Rome, BC cycle, May 18, 1986.

6 Gianni Simoni and Giuliano Turone, *Il caffè di Sindona: Un finanzieri d'avventura tra politica, Vaticano e mafia* (Milan: Garzanti Libri, 2009), 33–34; see also Galli, *Finanza bianca*, 72.

7 Hoffman, *Anatomy of the Vatican*, 189.

8 Ibid., 190.

9 DiFonzo, *St. Peter's Banker*, 31; Thomas and Morgan-Witts, *Pontiff*, 146. Some writers, such as Charles Raw (*The Moneychangers*) believe that Sindona did not meet Spada until 1958. But their correspondence predates that.

10 Giorgio Montini was a member of the Partito Popolare.

11 Nick Tosches, *Power on Earth* (New York: Arbor House, 1986), 22; see also Galli, *Finanza bianca*, 65.

12 Murphy, "City of God," 111; historian Carlo Pellegrini Bellavite, in a 2002 history of the Banco Ambrosiano (*Il caso del controllo del Banco Ambrosiano*), noted that "Montini had a good impression of Sindona. It was unlikely to find two people more different, Montini on the one hand a slender figure and ascetic, the disciple of Maritain, and the other figure a cold and ruthless Sicilian financier." Cited in Galli, *Finanza bianca*, 69.

13 Michael Arthur Ledeen, *West European Communism and American Foreign Policy* (New Brunswick, NJ: Transaction, 1987); "Chief Italian Red Sees Rightist Plot," *The New York Times*, August 2, 1948, 3.

14 DiFonzo, *St. Peter's Banker*, 35.

15 Although Montini and Sindona were energized over the battle for control of the trade union because Secchia was a communist, neither man liked labor unions. Sindona thought they crippled fast-growing Italian companies from competing internationally, and Montini feared that if they grew too powerful, it would only be a matter of time before the Vatican's menial lay workers would want to organize. In fact, in 1979, many Vatican employees did join the Association of Lay Vatican Workers. Although unions were still banned inside the city-state, the association operated loosely as a central bargaining authority when it came to salary increases, adjustments in work hours, and changes to pension rights. DiFonzo, *St. Peter's Banker*, 34–35; Tosches, *Power on Earth*, 37.

16 "Italy: Beating the Cycle," *Time*, September 25, 1964; see also Malachi Martin, *The Final Conclave* (Briarcliff, NY: Stein & Day, 1978), 28; Galli, *Finanza bianca*, 72.

17 Within three weeks of assuming the Papacy, Pope John broke a 372-year history by expanding the College of Cardinals to seventy, the largest ever. During his Pontificate, he added another fifteen, including five Americans. Senior cardinals were not pleased with the expansion since it diluted their exclusive club. Although John is often deemed a reformer since he appointed the first cardinals from the Philippines and Japan, the college became more Italian under him than it had been since the turn of the century. He also increased, to one third, the number of cardinals who were Curia officials.

18 Account of unnamed priest recounted in DiFonzo, *St. Peter's Banker*, 35.

19 Martin, *Rich Church, Poor Church*, 59.

20 David Yallop, *In God's Name: An Investigation into the Murder of Pope John Paul* (New York: Carroll & Graf, 2007), 97–98; Paul L. Williams, *The Vatican Exposed: Money, Murder, and the Mafia* (Amherst, NY: Prometheus Books, 2003), 100–1.

21 Between 1958 and 1965, the percentage of Italian families that owned televisions rose from 12 percent to 49 percent, refrigerators from 13 percent to 55 percent, and washing machines from 3 percent to 23 percent. Paul Ginsborg, *A History of Contemporary Italy: Society and Politics, 1943–1988* (Basingstoke, UK: Palgrave Macmillan, 2003), 239; see also William Easterly, "Reliving the 1950s: The Big Push, Poverty Traps, and Takeoffs in Economic Development," *Journal of Economic Growth* 11, no. 4 (December 2006): 289–318; see also Cornwell, *God's Banker*, 33.

22 Galli, *Finanza bianca*, 72–73; see also Thomas and Morgan-Witts, *Pontiff*, 146.

23 Simoni and Turone, *Il caffè di Sindona*, 34–35.

24 The Nogara-created SNIA Viscosa textile conglomerate—for which Sindona did some legal work—bought 10 percent of BPF. And another 10 percent stake went to a Sindona friend, Tito Carnelutti, who owned the Banque de Financement of Geneva. See generally Martin, *Rich Church, Poor Church*, 59; and Tosches, *Power on Earth*, 44–45.

25 Cornwell, *God's Banker*, 38; DiFonzo, *St. Peter's Banker*, 37–38. Sindona also aggressively utilized the confidentiality shield of the attorney-client privilege to protect his clients' identity in deals.

26 Simoni and Turone, *Il caffè di Sindona*, 34–35; DiFonzo, *St. Peter's Banker*, 38–42; as for Di Jorio's role, see Lai, *Finanze vaticane*, 38–39.

27 Tosches, *Power on Earth*, 47.

28 The two Liechtenstein firms were Ravoxr A.G. and Tuxanr A.G. See generally DiFonzo, *St. Peter's Banker*, 56–57; Martin, *Rich Church, Poor Church*, 59.

29 "Italy: Beating the Cycle," *Time*.

30 Simoni and Turone, *Il caffè di Sindona*, 33.

31 Tosches, *Power on Earth*, 60–61.

32 Ibid., 53.

33 Ibid., 118; Simoni and Turone, *Il caffè di Sindona*, 3536.

34 The tales of Sindona's sponsorship by a Mafia cartel are oft repeated if unproven. In Larry Gurwin's *The Calvi Affair*, Vito Genovese, representing all Sicilian mob families, picked Sindona to

run a black-market produce business during the last few years of World War II, giving him the seed money to establish his career as an attorney while simultaneously indebting Sindona forever to the Mafia (page 10). Paul Williams, in *The Vatican Exposed*, even tied in the church, asserting that Sindona was introduced to Genovese by the archbishop of Messina (page 104). While clerics have been involved with the mob—four Franciscan monks were convicted in 1962 as made members of the Sicilian Mafia, and the prior of Rome's St. Angelo's Cathedral was convicted in 1978 of laundering ransom money for his Mafia family—there is no credible evidence linking any of the criminal clerics to Sindona. In 1972, Jack Begon, an ABC stringer in Rome, filed a story that in 1957 Sindona attended a summit meeting with leading Mafiosi in the penthouse of Palermo's Hotel et des Palmes. Supposedly joining him were mob luminaries including Lucky Luciano, Joseph Bonanno, Carmine Galante, and representatives of the Genovese, Lucchese, and Gambino families. At that meeting, according to Begon, the mob bosses gave the young attorney "total control over the profits of the heroin trade for investment in Europe and the Americas." Begon claimed that the following year some unidentified Mafiosi kidnapped and interrogated him to discover his sources. After an investigation, Italian authorities ultimately charged Begon with faking his own kidnapping and also embezzling $5,000 from ABC. A Rome court cleared him of any criminal liability but most journalists who have studied Begon's story dismiss it as unsubstantiated. Nick Tosches, *Power on Earth*, is typical in dubbing it "fanciful" and an "apocryphal history." Still, other authors—including Luigi DiFonzo in *St. Peter's Banker* and Malachi Martin in *Rich Church, Poor Church*—have repeated the story without any caveat. In Williams's *The Vatican Exposed*, the author goes so far as to list what food and wine the group ordered and says that it was the night in which "La Costra Nostra . . . came into being."

While both the postwar produce story and the Hotel et des Palmes tale seem false, they were circulated so widely that many people simply accepted Sindona's link to the Mafia as an uncontested fact.

There is an unresolved matter about Sindona and a possible underworld criminal connection. On November 1, 1967, Fred J. Douglas, a director in Interpol's Washington, D.C., office, sent a letter to the police in Milan. It was an inquiry about four men, including Sindona and one of his trusted American executives, an accountant, Daniel Porco. The inquiry said that the men "are involved in the illegal trafficking of sedatives, stimulants and hallucinogens between Italy and the United States and other regions of Europe." According to the Final Report of Italy's Parliamentary Committee that ultimately investigated all civil and criminal matters that had arisen concerning Sindona, "The superintendent of Milan responded with a letter of bureaucratic style, which acknowledged a business relationship between Porco and Sindona, but concluded categorically that 'based on the status of the investigation carried out by us, there is no evidence to say that the persons referred to, especially Porco and Sindona, are involved in drug trafficking between Italy and the USA.'" There is no indication the Milanese police opened a formal investigation, nor did anything more than make a few casual inquiries and rely on the truthfulness of the denials they received. (Relazioni di Commissioni Parlamentari di Inchiesti, Relazione conclusiva della Commissione parlamentare d'inchiesta sul caso Sindona e sulle responsabilità politiche ed amministrative ad esso eventualmente connesse, VIII legislatura—Doc. XXIII n. 2-sexies, Relazione conclusiva di maggioranza, relatore on. Giuseppe Azzaro, Rome, March 24, 1982, 163.)

In the late 1970s, after Sindona's empire had collapsed and he was jailed for financial crimes, some mobsters—like Francesco Marino Mannoia and Antonino Giuffrè—tried implicating him in drug trafficking. Those proffers were inevitably in exchange for leniency on pending charges or to deflect the investigation from the suspects that prosecutors thought were the real masterminds. In January 1982, Sindona was one of 470 men indicted in Italy in the then largest heroin smuggling case in history. But the charges against him were dismissed before the trial began, and the evidence was based solely on the account of a top mobster trying in part to buy his freedom by fingering the financier. In 1985, Sindona, from prison, bragged to author Nick Tosches, "Never did I lie down with the Mafia. . . . And never, despite their greatest efforts, blackmails, and dreams, have the prosecutors here or in America been able to produce one Mafioso to say otherwise. In all their wiretaps, not once have they heard the name of Michele Sindona mentioned." Tosches, *Power on Earth*, 98, 240–42.

Ivan Fisher, a prominent New York criminal defense lawyer, represented Sindona on an appeal in 1979–80. Fisher had by then carved out a specialty in the high-profile defense bar by representing some top drug traffickers and Italian mobsters. He had been the lead counsel in the 1973 defense of the Pizza Connection, at the time the largest heroin conspiracy. "To the extent I know a negative," Fisher told me, "I know Sindona was not into drugs or a member of the Mafia. My information goes well beyond whatever he and I discussed. The government tried hard to connect him to the Mafia, but it wasn't possible. He did know some of the big New York mobsters, but that is because he was like a rock star among the Italians in America. Everybody wanted to hang out with Michele. But he wasn't one of them." Author interview with Ivan Fisher, June 19, 2013.

35 DiFonzo, *St. Peter's Banker*, 44; Simoni and Turone, *Il caffè di Sindona*, 34.

36 "Cardinal Canali Is Dead at 87; Administrative Head of Vatican," *The New York Times*, August 4, 1961, 21; Grilli, *La finanza vaticana in Italia*, 76.

37 Wynn, *Keepers of the Keys*, 47–48.

38 Hebblethwaite, *The Year of Three Popes*, 15.

39 Flamini, *Pope, Premier, President*, 96–98.

40 Ibid., 97–98.

41 Cooney, *The American Pope*, 278–79.

42 Flamini, *Pope, Premier, President*, 168–69; Cooney, *The American Pope*, 278.

43 Cardinal Siri quoted in Hebblethwaite, *The Year of Three Popes*, 142; see also Hoffman, *Anatomy of the Vatican*, 29.

44 Flamini, *Pope, Premier, President*, 162–63.

45 Victor L. Simpson, "Today's Topic: Inside the Conclave," Associated Press, Vatican City, P.M. cycle August 8, 1978.

46 Hoffman, *Anatomy of the Vatican*, 151–52; See also *Persona Humana*, Sacred Congregation for the Doctrine of the Faith, Declaration on Certain Questions Concerning Sexual Ethics, December 29, 1975; Franco Bellegrandi, *Nichitaroncalli: Controvita di un papa* (Rome: Edizione Internazionali di Letteratura e Scienze, 1994; Hoffman, *Anatomy of the Vatican*, 151; Author interviews with a U.S. diplomat stationed in Rome during 1975 to 1979, October 13, 2012; Author interview with an Italian priest who had worked for the Secretariat of State during Pope Paul VI's Papacy, June 5, 2006.

47 Hoffman, *Anatomy of the Vatican*,145–51. Sindona knew Macchi well and thought he was an ambitious and mean-spirited gatekeeper. "He talks like Mao Tse-Tung but lives like Louis XIV," Sindona said about him. Tosches, *Power on Earth*, 51.

48 Thomas and Morgan-Witts, *Pontiff*, 31.

49 The other cardinals were Chicago's Albert Meyer, St. Louis's Joseph Ritter, Pittsburgh's John Wright, and Boston's Richard Cushing; Cooney, *The American Pope*, 280.

50 Reese, *Inside the Vatican*, 84; see also Giancarlo Zizola, *Quale papa?* (Rome: Borla, 1977).

51 Some controversy developed when Italian newspapers reported that the CIA had the news about the new Pope before it was announced outside the sealed conclave. That led to speculation that the CIA had bugged the Apostolic Palace. Flamini, *Pope, Premier, President*, 173–74.

52 "Reign of 'Pope of Unity' Studded with Landmarks," *Chicago Tribune*, June 4, 1963, 8; Hoffman, *Anatomy of the Vatican*, 28.

53 Wynn, *Keepers of the Keys*, 126–27.

54 "Reign of 'Pope of Unity' Studded with Landmarks," *Chicago Tribune*, 8.

55 Hoffman, *Anatomy of the Vatican*, 30.

56 In 1966, Paul built a roof garden on top of the Apostolic Palace, with direct access from his apartment. That meant he no longer had to walk through the more public Vatican gardens when he wanted to get fresh air. "Faceliftng Due on Papal Palace," AP, Vatican City, July 10, 1966.

57 Lewin, "The Finances of the Vatican," 193; Peter Hebblethwaite, *Paul VI: The First Modern Pope* (London: HarperCollins, 1993). See also Hoffman, *Anatomy of the Vatican*, 169.

58 Hoffman, *Anatomy of the Vatican*, 52.

59 Ibid., 164–65.

60 "Vatican's Budget Is Vetoed by Pope," *The New York Times*, January 23, 1975. *The New York Times* reported about Paul VI, "He is known to take a personal interest in budgetary matters. He made a reputation as a top administrator while Archbishop of Milan."

61 David S. McLellan and Robert McLellan, "The 1963 Italian Elections," *The Western Political Quarterly* 17, no. 4 (December 1964): 671–89.

62 Martin, *Rich Church, Poor Church*, 53; Lo Bello, *The Vatican Empire*, 112.

63 "Italy: Hens Nesting on Rocks," *Time*, September 19, 1969; DiFonzo, *St. Peter's Banker*, 59–64.

64 See generally Tosches, *Power on Earth*, 53–55.

65 Robert C. Doty, "Italian Collector's Treasures Include 2 American Companies," *The New York Times,* August 16, 1964, F1; see DiFonzo, *St. Peter's Banker*, 74, and Martin, *Rich Church, Poor Church*, 59.
66 Moneyrex's legal name was Euro-Market Money Brokers, S.p.A. It was incorporated in Liechtenstein by Sindona's Luxembourg-based holding company, Fasco. See generally Raw, *The Moneychangers*, 58, and Tosches, *Power on Earth*, 139, 145; Parliamentary Commission of Inquiry into the Case of Sindona and Responsibilities and the Political and Administrative Connected To It, 41.
67 Gianni Simoni and Giuliano Turone, *Il caffè di Sindona: Un finanzieri d'avventura tra politica, Vaticano e mafia* (Milan: Garzanti Libri, 2009), 35, 162; Raw, *The Moneychangers*, 66–67, 331.
68 Parliamentary Commission of Inquiry into the Case of Sindona and Responsibilities and the Political and Administrative Connected To It, n. 204, and June 23, 1981, n. 315, 26; DiFonzo, *St. Peter's Banker*, 75–84.
69 Two of his most profitable banks turned out to be Milan's Banca Unione and Sicily's Messina Banca. Tosches, *Power on Earth*, 118; Simoni and Turone, *Il caffè di Sindona*, 35–36.
70 Banca Unione is typical of how enmeshed Sindona was with the Vatican. The church had been an equal partner with a publishing company, Giangiacomo Feltrinelli. The IOR provided the financing for Sindona to buy the bank. The church retained a 20 percent stake. Luigi Mennini was the bank's executive director and also a member of the board. Mennini was also on the board of Sindona's Finabank and Banca Privata Finanziaria. Tosches, *Power on Earth*, 118; Raw, *The Moneychangers*, 56–57.
71 Spada quoted in Raw, *The Moneychangers*, 57.
72 Hoffman, *Anatomy of the Vatican*, 189; Gurwin, *The Calvi Affair*, 12.
73 Ginder in *Our Sunday Visitor*, quoted in Gollin, *Worldly Goods*, 6. In 1969, Ginder was arrested for possession of child porn and sentenced to ten years of probation. After he published a book in 1976 in which he excoriated the church's doctrines on sexuality, he was evicted from the priesthood. Two years later, 1978, he was arrested, tried, and convicted of sodomizing two underage boys. He was sentenced to four years in prison. "5 Pittsburgh Priests Went to Prison," *Pittsburgh Post-Gazette*, February 28, 2004.
74 "Italy: Beating the Cycle," *Time*.
75 *Business Week, Part 2*, referring to an article "Italy: A Sicilian Financier" (New York: McGraw-Hill, 1972), 928; *Fortune, Volume 88* (New York: Time Inc., 1973), 174; Doty, "Italian Collector's Treasures Include 2 American Companies," F1; Nick Tosches, *The Nick Tosches Reader* (Boston: Da Capo, 2000), 257. A few years later, in 1969, *Time* said about Sindona that "no one has done more to shake the country's old financial structure," and that his "financial empire [that] spans three continents" helped him "leap from obscurity to international prominence." "Italy: Hens Nesting on Rocks."
76 "Watergate's Landlord," *The Economist*, June 16, 1973, 105–6.
77 DiFonzi, *St. Peter's Banker*, 68–69. For the fullest biography of Gelli, see Gianfranco Piazzesi, *Gelli: La carriera di un eroe di questa Italia* (Milan: Garzanti Libri, 1983).
78 Even fewer knew that after Mussolini's fall in July 1943, the fascist Gelli had become a liaison officer with the SS. He later told author Charles Raw that his only choice was either to work with the SS or be sent to a German prison camp. He was detained and released four times by Allied forces, suspected on each occasion of having collaborated with the Nazis. Somehow, he ended up working with American counterintelligence, and later went on to assist Italy's postwar intelligence services. Willan, *The Last Supper*, 118–19; Raw, *The Moneychangers*, 140; Gurwin, *The Calvi Affair*, 50–51.
79 Some accounts list 962 names and others 953. Henry Tanner, "Italian Elite Embroiled in Scandal," *The New York Times*, May 24, 1981, 1, and Willan, *The Last Supper*, 15. Gelli chose "Propaganda" as the name for his lodge since it had been the same name used for a lodge by Giuseppe Mazzini, one of the heroes of the 1848 Italian revolution that led to a unified national government.
80 Memo, "Cossiga Orders Study of CIA-Terrorism Links," Ref: AU2307110890 Paris, Source ROME ANSA in English, Approved for Release May 1998, pages 0089-0091, released pursuant to a Freedom of Information and Privacy request to the CIA.
81 Victor L. Simpson, "Scandal in Italian Masonic Lodge Clouds Movement Long Criticized by the Church," Associated Press, A.M. cycle, May 27, 1981.
82 In introducing the Anti-Masonic Law of 1925, Mussolini said that Freemasonry was "a danger to

the peace and quietude of the State." 1948 Official Proceedings, Grand Lodge of Missouri, The Grand Lodge of Ancient Free and Accepted Masons of the State of Missouri, The One Hundred Twenty-Seventh Annual Communication, St. Louis, September 28–30, 12c–13c, available at http://issuu.com/momason/docs/gl_proceedings_1948.

83 Simpson, "Scandal in Italian Masonic Lodge Clouds Movement Long Criticized by the Church"; Willan, *The Last Supper*, 118.

84 Ibid., 120.

85 Hearings Before the Committee on Standards of Official Conduct, House of Representatives, 1976.

86 Tosches, *Power on Earth*, 167. In an interview with author Nick Tosches, Sindona recounted meeting Gelli in 1974. But it was almost certainly a decade earlier according to P2 documentation seized by Italian authorities.

87 Although Sindona said he turned down the offer of a P2 membership card, and that he and Gelli were only political allies, when Italian authorities seized P2's records, they found Sindona's entry, #1612, in the ledger. Some others listed in the P2 files claimed they were not in fact members, but investigators determined the documents to be accurate. Tosches, *Power on Earth*, 169; Willan, *The Last Supper*, Notes on Text.

According to DiFonzo in *St. Peter's Banker* (65–71), "There is no way to be sure how the oath [was] read or how it was taken because Gelli quite often would change the ceremony and the oath to fit his own moods." Still, DiFonzo spends four pages setting forth a version of what the ceremony might have looked like, complete with KKK-like black hoods, pictures of Hitler, Mussolini, and Perón, live serpents, a blood oath, and a pagan rite during which Sindona swore loyalty to Gelli and P2 under threat of death. While it seems certain that Sindona was in fact a P2 member, and some inductees did go through a jazzed-up Masonic ceremony, there is no evidence that Sindona ever underwent one.

88 Clyde H. Farnsworth, "Sindona's Empire: Sharp Trading, Big Losses," *The New York Times*, September 30, 1974, 57.

89 Tosches, *Power on Earth*, 168–69.

90 Lo Bello, *The Vatican Empire*, 90–97; see also Martin, *The Final Conclave*, 26–27.

91 Martin, *The Final Conclave*, 27.

92 Lo Bello, *The Vatican Empire*, 94–96.

93 See generally ibid., 100–104. Montecatini had merged with the Edison Company in 1966 to become Montedison.

94 "Finance: Diversification at the Vatican," *Time*, January 25, 1971; Lewin, "The Finances of the Vatican," 194; see also Horne, "How the Vatican Manages Its Money," 34; Martin, *Rich Church, Poor Church*, 65.

95 This was a title often given to the Black Nobles, and before the Second Vatican Council it was the Papal Chamberlains of the Sword and Cape (Cameriere di spada e cappa); John Hooper, "Luigi Mennini: Shadow over the Vatican," *The Guardian*, August 14, 1997, 14.

96 See *Nostra Aetate*, Declaration on the Relation of the Church to Non-Christian Religions Proclaimed by His Holiness Pope Paul VI on October 28, 1965.

97 Cardinal Siri quoted in Hebblethwaite, *The Year of Three Popes*, 142.

98 James Franklin, "John Paul and Changes in Vatican," *The Boston Globe*, August 27, 1978, 11.

99 "Catholics Plan Aid to Hanoi," *The Boston Globe*, April 1, 1967, 1; "Pope Eyed Trip to Hanoi," *The Boston Globe*, November 22, 1968, 3. The two monsignors sent were Pope Paul's personal secretary, Don Pasquale Macchi, and Paul Marcinkus, then an up-and-coming American cleric in the Secretary of State's office. "2 Papal Aides Visited Viet, Vatican Says," *Chicago Tribune*, October 29, 1966, 5. When reporters found out about the trip and asked Marcinkus why he had gone, he replied simply, "Vacation."

100 Flamini, *Pope, Premier, President*, 6. In 1973, Paul VI dispatched one of his diplomats, Monsignor Agostino Casaroli, to visit Moscow. Two years later Casaroli (later Secretary of State) made a state visit to Cuba and Fidel Castro. Conservative Curialists had reservations about each journey.

101 See http://www.vatican.va/holy_father/paul_vi/encyclicals/documents/hf_p-vi_enc_26031967_populorum_en.html; see also Horne, "How the Vatican Manages Its Money," January 1971, 30.

102 The Pope kept moving further to the left. He caused an uproar when he said that Mao Tse-tung's atheistic philosophy shared "Christian values" with Catholicism. Paul Hoffman, "Vatican Sees

Christian Ideas in Maoism," *The New York Times*, April 19, 1973, 3; Flamini, *Pope, Premier, President*, 5. See also for the full encyclical: http://www.vatican.va/holy_father/paul_vi/encyclicals/documents/hf_p-vi_enc_26031967_populorum_en.html.

During his tenure, Paul VI expanded the College of Cardinals from the record number of eighty that he had inherited from John XXIII, to 136. He "internationalized" the Curia with many non-Italian appointees and ensured they had no connection to the traditional Roman bureaucracy. In some cases, as in Benin's Bernardin Gantin, Brazil's Alosio Lorscheider and Paulo Evaristo Arns, Argentina's Eduardo Pironio, the Philippines' Jaime Sin, and Senegal's Hyacinthe Thiandoum, he picked avowed progressives, not only rankling traditionalists, but most of the Curia, who did not like to see their Italian-centric power diluted. And he tried to tilt any future conclave toward choosing a younger Pope by his ruling that all cardinals had to submit their resignations by seventy-five. Even in instances in which the Pope asked them to continue to serve, they had to step aside on their eightieth birthday. After eighty they no longer could cast a vote in the conclave. When Pope Paul issued the decree in 1970, it meant that twenty-five of the 127 cardinals were automatically excluded from electing the next Pontiff. The edict caused considerable griping from those affected. See generally Hoffman, *Anatomy of the Vatican*, 72–73; and "Roman Catholics: Princely Promotions," *Time*, April 4, 1969.

103 See "The Deception of the Century," http://www.tldm.org/News3/impostor.htm.

104 Lo Bello, *The Vatican Empire*, 108–22. Although the investments sound straightforward, they were usually done through holding companies and proxy subsidiaries. For instance, the Vatican had, among other banks, an interest in a small regional bank near Genoa, Banca Naef Ferrazzi Longhi of Spezia. Its ownership there was hidden under the Istituto Bancario Italiano, a financial holding company established in 1967 by the cement company Italcementi. The only tangential evidence of the church's role in newly acquired banks such as Naef Ferrazzi Longhi was when Italcementi's president appointed Massimo Spada as vice president and a director of the new financial consortium.

105 Lo Bello, *The Vatican Empire*, 168–69.

106 Lewin, "The Finances of the Vatican," 194–95.

107 The wealthiest Italians continued to avoid any tariff by holding their stocks in foreign shell companies through proxies. The foreign agent who held the stock would be listed as the owner for Italian tax purposes and pay only the 15 percent rate. The foreign agent would then deduct a service commission, but still the Italian taxpayer would pay far less than Italy's punitive 30 percent tax. A flourishing part of Sindona's law practice was the use of Swiss fiduciary contracts to evade taxes for wealthy clients. See Commissione Parlamentare D'inchiesta Sul Caso Sindona E Sulle Responsabilita Politiche Ed Amministrative Ad Esso Eventualmente Connesse, hereinafter Parliamentary Commission of Inquiry into the Case of Sindona and Responsibilities and the Political and Administrative Connected to It), Chamber of Deputies of the Senate, VIII Legislature, Doc. XXIII, May 22, 1980, n. 204, and June 23, 1981, n. 315, 44–45, 49–50.

108 Lai, *Finanze vaticane*, 139; Lo Bello, *The Vatican Empire*, 132.

109 Lo Bello, *The Vatican Empire*, 126.

110 Sindona interview in Tosches, *Power on Earth*, 87.

111 Lewin, "The Finances of the Vatican," 195.

112 Horne, "How the Vatican Manages Its Money," 31–32; Lo Bello, *The Vatican Empire*, 127–28.

113 Robert C. Doty, "Vatican Is Stunned by Plan to Tax It," *The New York Times*, July 13, 1968, 1.

114 Before there was a press office, the Vatican unofficially allowed some prelates to sell to reporters a daily typewritten list of Papal audiences and other tidbits of Vatican news. Monsignor Emilio Pucci's onionskin paper bulletins—although not always reliable—were required reading by news organizations for more than a decade. Pucci was forced to resign from his Secretariat of State position after World War II when he was exposed as a paid informant for Mussolini's secret police. A successor to the business, a layman, Virgilio Scattolini, ended up in jail after he was unmasked for fabricating stories and passing them along as news (his fake stories ended up in U.S. and British newspapers). See Hoffman, *Anatomy of the Vatican*, 255–61.

115 "An Official Press Office Is Established by Vatican," *The New York Times*, October 19, 1966, 27. Another early issue Vallainc addressed was publicity over the publication of Robert Katz's critically acclaimed *Death in Rome*, in which Katz contended that although Pius XII knew some nineteen hours in advance about the Nazi plan to massacre civilians at the Ardeatine Caves, he did nothing. "This is not a book of history but a polemic in which the special interests of the author

are dominant and in conflict with the interests of research presentation for the facts," said Vallainc. This type of generic dismissal, without contesting facts or providing additional information, became the template for how the press office handled subsequent questions raised by historians over the wider issue of Pius's silence during the Holocaust.

116 Doty, "Vatican Is Stunned by Plan to Tax It," 3.

117 Reese, *Inside the Vatican*, 204–5. The subsidy amounted to $280 million annually when it was finally terminated ($506 million in 2014 dollars). See also Lai, *Finanze vaticane*, 46.

118 "Finance: Diversification at the Vatican," *Time*, January 25, 1971; Horne, "How the Vatican Manages Its Money," 31.

119 Lewin, "The Finances of the Vatican," 187.

120 Maillardoz had helped run the Special Administration, under Nogara. Some of its liquid assets had been moved to the Vatican Bank over the years, leaving mostly the real estate that was at the core of the newly formed APSA.

121 Horne, "How the Vatican Manages Its Money," 31; Lai, *Finanze vaticane*, 43–44; Raw, *The Moneychangers*, 52.

122 Lai, *Finanze vaticane*, 44.

123 Ibid., 122, Lai interview with Massimo, April 3, 1972.

124 James Franklin, "John Paul and Changes in Vatican," *The Boston Globe*, August 27, 1978, 11.

125 Lewin, "The Finances of the Vatican," 189.

126 Hoffman, *Anatomy of the Vatican*, 176.

127 Cardinal Egidio Vagnozzi, the new chief of the Prefecture, at least claimed he could read a balance sheet. And one of his early goals was to initiate a single balance sheet that would cover all Vatican departments that had anything to do with money. The staunchly independent IOR put a quick stop to such talk. See Horne, "How the Vatican Manages Its Money," 32.

128 Lo Bello, *The Vatican Empire*, 32.

129 Francis Xavier Murphy, "City of God," *The Wilson Quarterly* (1976), 6. no. 4 (autumn 1982): 110–11.

130 Lo Bello, *The Vatican Empire*, 31–32.

131 Lai, *Finanze vaticane*, 46–47, 57.

132 Francis Xavier Murphy, "A Look at the Earth's Tiniest State," *Chicago Tribune*, August 31, 1982, 11; Murphy, "City of God," 111. Vagnozzi soon added an additional two more cardinals as aides, Chicago's John Cody and Cologne's Joseph Höffner. Although they were in theory more adept at financial administration since they ran their own dioceses, both were so far removed from day-to-day events at the Vatican that they afforded little guidance.

133 Reese, *Inside the Vatican*, 203–4.

134 Walter Scott, "Personality Parade," *The Boston Globe*, October 12, 1969, C2; Thomas and Morgan-Witts, *Pontiff*, 140; Lewin, "The Finances of the Vatican," 199; see also Hoffman, *Anatomy of the Vatican*, 177.

135 Horne, "How the Vatican Manages its Money," 80.

136 Grilli, *La finanza vaticana in Italia*, 149.

137 Pope John XXIII had established a commission to study what policy was best for the church to adopt about birth control. The advent of a daily pharmaceutical pill in the early 1960s had made birth control both affordable and widely available. The church's only previous pronouncement had been Pius XII's 1951 declaration that the church would sanction the use of the rhythm method as a "natural" means of birth control. Before that, the only approved option was abstinence. Pope John's committee finished its work after his death. Its recommendation to Paul VI was that the church should consider liberalizing its ban on all forms of artificial birth control. The conservatives on the committee leaked word of the panel's suggestion. Traditionalists raised a fury, so much so that Paul felt compelled to issue a blanket ban in *Humanae Vitae*. See http://www.vatican.va/holy_father/paul_vi/encyclicals/documents/hf_p-vi_enc_25071968_humanae-vitae_en.html.

The bishop who later run the IOR, Paul Marcinkus, claimed—without proof—that the church's stake in the manufacturer of birth control was only "one share, that somebody had left in a will." See Marcinkus interviewed in John Cornwell, *A Thief in the Night: Life and Death in the Vatican* (New York: Penguin, 2001), 134. Marcinkus also asserted that after he took control of the IOR in 1969, "I gave orders: no pharmaceuticals, no armaments, no luxury buildings of any sort." Marcinkus also claimed that under his direction, the IOR had "no exposure in South

Africa," which was then off limits because of international sanctions over the white-controlled apartheid government. "But some of our clients do." Handwritten notes by Philip Willan of audiotaped interviews between John Cornwell and Marcinkus, February 8, 1988, 6b, 7a, provided to author courtesy of Willan.

138 "Investment: Low Profile for the Vatican," *Time*, November 28, 1969; Andrew Blake, "Financier's Fall Costly to Vatican," *The Boston Globe*, February 2, 1975, 21; see also Martin, *The Final Conclave*, 24.

139 Thomas and Morgan-Witts, *Pontiff*, 146–47. After Paul VI's death in 1978, Macchi worked to move along the church bureaucracy responsible for putting Paul on track for sainthood. During those years, Macchi claimed to reporters that Paul had never met Sindona. To others he said they met only once, "at a formal dinner in New York." As author Giancarlo Galli wrote, Macchi considered a Sindona friendship with Pope Paul VI to be "shadows best deleted." *Finanza bianca*, 71.

140 Neal Ascherson, "Revolution on World's Campuses: Students' Target: The Bureaucratic State," *The New York Times*, May 27, 1968, 13; "Students in Rome Gain Supporters," *The New York Times*, March 4, 1968, 8.

141 Wynn, *Keepers of the Keys*, 155.

142 "Investment: Low Profile for the Vatican," *Time*; Wynn, *Keepers of the Keys*, 156; see Raw, *The Moneychangers*, 52; Hoffman, *Anatomy of the Vatican*, 190; and Lai, *Finanze vaticane*, 47.

143 DiFonzo, *St. Peter's Banker*, 11–12.

144 Cardinal Vagnozzi interview, in Horne, "How the Vatican Manages Its Money," 32.

145 Ibid., 30

146 "Paul VI considered Sindona a great genius of finance," noted Giuseppe D'Alema, a member of parliament who was later a member of inquiry in Sindona's affairs. See Gurwin, *The Calvi Affair*, 13.

147 Clyde H. Farnsworth, "Michele Sindona, the Outsider as Insider in Worldwide Finance," *The New York Times*, May 20, 1974, 47. Malachi Martin in *Rich Church, Poor Church* claimed that Pope Paul had signed a document "giving Sindona total control over all Vatican investments." There is no source for the charge, and the author has not found any independent proof that such a document was executed.

148 "Investment: Low Profile for the Vatican," *Time*.

149 Thomas and Morgan-Witts, *Pontiff*, 147; Andrew Blake, "Financier's Fall Costly to Vatican," *The Boston Globe*, February 2, 1975, 21.

150 Years later, when the wisdom of that sale was under attack, the IOR's chief cleric, Archbishop Paul Marcinkus, disingenuously said, "APSA sold him [Sindona] the shares for Immobiliare. . . . I had nothing to do with it." Cornwell, *A Thief in the Night*, 131–32. For details of the sale, see Horne, "How the Vatican Manages Its Money," 80. As for Spada's role, see Lai, *Finanze vaticane*, 48.

151 "Investment Shift by Vatican Seen," *The New York* Times, June 19, 1969, 19. The sale technically came from APSA. When Nogara ran both the IOR and APSA's predecessor department, the Special Administration, he had blurred the separation of responsibilities and duties between the two. In the restructured Vatican the company investments and stocks were sold by APSA, but the reinvested monies were directed by the IOR. See also "Hear Vatican Disposing of Italy Stocks," *Chicago Tribune*, June 19, 1969, A6.

152 "Vatican Stock Sale Hinted," *The Boston Globe*, June 19, 1969, 3; see also "Vatican Confirms Sale of Holdings," *The New York Times*, June 21, 1969, 9. As for the Sindona purchase of the church's shares, see Cornwell, *God's Banker*, 40–41.

153 No reporter knew that Sindona himself had bought the church's SGI shares. He did so in typically convoluted Sindona-style. He first arranged for the Vatican Bank's shares to be sent to Paribas Transcontinental of Luxembourg, a wholly owned subsidiary of Banque de Paris et des Pays-Bas (Paribas). Paribas then transferred the shares to Sindona's Luxembourg holding company, Fasco. Two different Swiss holding companies acted as the owner at different stages of the transfer. As for the money, Fasco joined British merchant bank Hambros in forming Distributor, a Luxembourg holding company. Most of the funding passed through that new entity, coupled with some fiduciary deposits from Sindona's Banca Privata. See generally "Sindona, Self-Made Man of 53, Rules a Vast Industrial Empire," *The New York Times*, May 13, 1974, 48; Farnsworth, "Michele Sindona, the Outsider as Insider," 47; see also Raw, *The Moneychangers*, 59; and Lai, *Finanze vaticane*, 48; see also Parliamentary Commission of Inquiry into the Case of Sindona and Responsibilities and the Political and Administrative Connected To It. SGI soared 300 percent in the year after

Sindona bought the church's stake, and it doubled in just six weeks in 1972: "Italian Bourse: Is Now the Time?," *The Economist,* July 6, 2002, 104.

154 Farnsworth, "Michele Sindona, the Outsider as Insider."

155 Horne, "How the Vatican Manages Its Money"; "Finance: Diversification at the Vatican," *Time,* January 25, 1971, 32, 35. The Prefecture for the Economic Affairs of the Holy See had some assets, but far smaller than that what the IOR or APSA controlled. The interview by Horne was trumpeted by *Institutional Investor* as "the first time key Vatican financial officials have talked so freely with a reporter." The then IOR chief Bishop Marcinkus refused to meet Horne, but did talk to him by phone. The journalist described him as "reticent." Marcinkus said it would take time for the IOR to implement any changes and he downplayed the size of the IOR's holdings.

156 The *Institutional Investor* article erred on the low side of the Vatican's net worth because Horne had been blocked from getting any accurate information about the IOR. But other reports wildly inflated the church's wealth. An Episcopalian bishop, James Pike, who had formerly worked with the SEC, wrote an article in *Playboy* in which he asserted—without any evidence—that the Jesuits alone owned 51 percent of Bank of America. They also had a majority stake, claimed Pike, in Phillips Petroleum and owned large portions of Boeing and Lockheed. Pike declared that the Jesuits' investments returned $250 million annually. Gollin, *Worldly Goods,* 12–13.

157 The estimates of the size of the Vatican's investment assets ranged in the Italian press from $5 billion to $13 billion. The Vatican newspaper, *L'Osservatore Romano,* went even further than Vagnozzi, estimating the church's total investment capital only as $128 million. The newspaper provided no details or sources for how it reached its low conclusion. See Horne, "How the Vatican Manages Its Money," 35.

158 As of 1971, when Vagnozzi spoke to *Institutional Investor,* the Vatican still had small stock positions in fifty-eight public Italian companies. It was a fraction of its ownership just a year earlier. Horne, "How the Vatican Manages Its Money," 35.

159 Even inside the IOR, laymen dominated. Of the sixty employees at the time of this sea change in investment policy, only four were clerics. Horne, "How the Vatican Manages Its Money," 78; see also Gurwin, *The Calvi Affair,* 13.

Chapter 15: "You Can't Run the Church on Hail Marys"

1 The name on his birth certificate is Paulius Casimir Marcinkus, but it appears that family and friends always called him Paul, the Anglicized version of his first name.

2 Hoffman, "Bishop with Chicago Roots Is Managing Pope's Travels." *The New York Times,* October 1, 1979.

Marcinkus later said, "You read these books about me and you get the impression I was raised by Al Capone in the streets. That's because of Cicero, see?" Marcinkus interviewed in Cornwell, *A Thief in the Night,* 81. The Al Capone/Cicero connection even found its way into a *Chicago Tribune* profile about an eighty-five-year-old barber who ran a Cicero barbershop for almost seventy years. He boasted to the *Tribune* that his two most famous customers were Marcinkus and mobster Ralph "Bottles" Capone, Al's brother. Kristen Scharnberg, "A Traditional Cut Above the Rest," Chicagoland, *Chicago Tribune,* March 18, 2001, 1.

Francesco Pazienza, an Italian intelligence agent who was a friend of Marcinkus, told the author: "One day, Marcinkus confided to me that his father had been the preferred driver for Al Capone. He told me that very straight, no bullshit." There is no evidence to support that, and Marcinkus was likely saying it to impress Pazienza, who had a reputation as a self-described "tough guy." Author interview with Francesco Pazienza, September 18, 2013.

Besides being famous as Capone's hometown, Marcinkus said that Cicero "became famous . . . for the race riots which they had" (1951 riots by thousands of white residents violently protesting the arrival of the first blacks). Handwritten notes by Philip Willan of audiotaped interviews between John Cornwell and Marcinkus, January 15, 1988, 1a, provided to author courtesy of Willan.

3 Marcinkus interviewed in Cornwell, *A Thief in the Night,* 81; Jim Gallagher, "The Pope's Banker," *Chicago Tribune,* March 13, 1983, G15–16.

4 Handwritten notes by Philip Willan of audiotaped interviews between John Cornwell and Marcinkus, January 15, 1988, 1b, provided to author courtesy of Willan.

5 He had been in a junior day seminary—Quigley Preparatory Seminary—since he was thirteen. It offered a classical Catholic education and was designed for youngsters who were considering the priesthood. His Lithuanian neighborhood where he grew up was overwhelmingly Catholic, with three churches in a four-block radius. Years later, when asked if he had ever dated a girl before he joined a full time seminary at eighteen, he said, "Maybe once in a while I would go out on a date . . . I wasn't scared of them or anything." Marcinkus interviewed in Cornwell, *A Thief in the Night*, 82. He also later described himself while a student as a "sports nut; I enjoyed sports more than anything else I did as a kid." Marcinkus interviewed in Gallagher, "The Pope's Banker," G16.

6 Handwritten notes by Philip Willan of audiotaped interviews between John Cornwell and Marcinkus, February 8, 1988, 2a, provided to author courtesy of Willan.

7 Galli, *Finanza bianca*, 62.

8 While working at the marriage bureau, he lived in a parish that was 90 percent black. Handwritten notes by Philip Willan of audiotaped interviews between John Cornwell and Marcinkus, February 8, 1988, no. 3, 2b, provided to author courtesy of Willan.

9 "Cicero Priest Makes Good in Vatican Post," *Chicago Tribune*, January 4, 1969, A12. In a *Chicago Tribune* article seven years earlier, Marcinkus's first and only Chicago parish was listed as Holy Cross. The Chicago Diocese informed the author that St. Christina's is the correct parish. Gwen Morgan, "Mrs. Kennedy in New Delhi," *Chicago Tribune*, May 12, 1962, 1–2; Cornwell, *A Thief in the Night*, 63–64.

10 Jim Gallagher, "The Pope's Banker," *Chicago Tribune*, March 13, 1983, G12.

11 Marcinkus said his "thesis [was] on baptism in relation to marriage." Handwritten notes by Philip Willan of audiotaped interviews between John Cornwell and Marcinkus, February 8, 1988, 2a, provided to author courtesy of Willan. See also Henry Gaggiottini, "Marcinkus Consecrated Bishop," *Chicago Tribune*, January 7, 1969, A9; Gallagher, "The Pope's Banker," G18.

12 Marcinkus served as the secretary to the Papal Nuncio in Bolivia from January 1955 to September 1956. While there he was given the rank of a Papal Chamberlain, with the title of "Very Reverend Monsignor." He then served at the Nuncio's office in Ottawa, returning to Rome in 1960.

13 Handwritten notes by Philip Willan of audiotaped interviews between John Cornwell and Marcinkus, February 8, 1988, 2a, provided to author courtesy of Willan.

14 Nino Lo Bello, "Bodyguard to Pope," *The Boston Globe*, January 5, 1969, A19.

15 "Cicero Priest Makes Good in Vatican Post," *Chicago Tribune*, 124.

16 Marcinkus interviewed in Cornwell, *A Thief in the Night*, 77.

17 Cornwell, *A Thief in the Night*, 64–65.

18 Gallagher, "The Pope's Banker," G18.

19 "Cicero Priest Makes Good in Vatican Post," *Chicago Tribune*; see Gallagher, "The Pope's Banker," 22.

20 Hoffman, "Bishop with Chicago Roots Is Managing Pope's Travels."

21 Marcinkus interviewed in Cornwell, *A Thief in the Night*, 86.

22 Ibid., 142–43.

23 Ibid., 142. "One has many colleagues but few friends in the halls of the Vatican," wrote Hoffman in *Anatomy of the Vatican*, 11.

24 Marcinkus interviewed in Gallagher, "The Pope's Banker," G18.

25 Author interview with Peter K. Murphy, Deputy Chief of Mission at the embassy, 1984–89, January 31, 2014.

26 "In Italy, Presidentessa: In India, Amriki Rani," *The Boston Globe*, May 27, 1962, E11.

27 Marcinkus interviewed in Gallagher, "The Pope's Banker," G18.

28 Marcinkus worked with a Yugoslavian emigrant, Stefano Falez, whom he had met in Rome. Falez went on to found Catintour, one of the most successful Vatican-approved travel agencies. See Willey, *God's Politician*, 209.

29 Cornwell, *A Thief in the Night*, 65.

30 Marcinkus interviewed in ibid., 140.

31 Marcinkus later said, "I never ran a tourist agency. I've never been involved in a tourist agency. I used people that were involved. I needed a guy who knew how to handle the logistics, tickets, the baggage; we never lost a bag. Same with the Pope's trips." Cornwell, *A Thief in the Night*, 140. When John XXIII died, Marcinkus learned that the Pontiff had selected him to be one of only four clerics to serve as the honor guard at his funeral.

32 Gwen Morgan, "Pope in Death, Tranquil and Benign Figure," *Chicago Tribune*, June 5, 1963, 1; "Chicagoan in Guard," *Chicago Tribune*, June 5, 1963, 3.

33 Marcinkus interviewed in Gallagher, "The Pope's Banker," G18. Also handwritten notes by Philip Willan of audiotaped interviews between John Cornwell and Marcinkus, February 8, 1988, 3b, provided to author courtesy of Willan.
34 Robert C. Doty, "Pope Paul, Class of '23, Visits Vatican's School for Diplomats," *The New York Times*, January 18, 1965, 6; see also Cornwell, *A Thief in the Night*, 65.
35 Marcinkus interviewed in Gallagher, "The Pope's Banker," G18.
36 Barry Bishop, "Bogota Meet Is Aided by Cicero Priest," *Chicago Tribune*, August 20, 1968, A5.
37 Galli, *Finanza bianca*, 74; Wynn, *Keepers of the Keys*, 159–60; Paul Hoffman, "Bishop with Chicago Roots Is Managing Pope's Travels," A9. Marcinkus was the advance man on seven international trips: India, New York, Portugal, Chile, Turkey, the Philippines, and Uganda. He also handled all the Pontiff's personal travel. Those trips marked the first time a Pope had ever traveled in a jet. See Gallagher, "The Pope's Banker," G18.
38 Marcinkus interviewed in Cornwell, *A Thief in the Night*, 85–86.
39 Handwritten notes by Philip Willan of audiotaped interviews between John Cornwell and Marcinkus, January 15, 1988, 2b, provided to author courtesy of Willan.
40 Wynn, *Keepers of the Keys*, 160; Gallagher, "The Pope's Banker," G18.
41 Marcinkus interviewed in Cornwell, *A Thief in the Night*, 84–85.
42 Bishop, "Bogota Meet Is Aided by Cicero Priest," A6. Marcinkus thought he "was a good man" for the job because he was "very methodical [and] I had a good memory." Handwritten notes by Philip Willan of audiotaped interviews between John Cornwell and Marcinkus, January 15, 1988, 2a, provided to author courtesy of Willan.
43 Handwritten notes by Philip Willan of audiotaped interviews between John Cornwell and Marcinkus, January 15, 1988, 2a, provided to author courtesy of Willan.
44 The *Chicago Tribune* ran "local boy makes good" stories and photos of Marcinkus and Paul VI with the city's mayor, Richard Daley (1964); Martin Luther King Jr. (1964); British Prime Minister Harold Wilson (1965); and Robert Kennedy (1967): see "Pope Greets Daleys," *Chicago Tribune*, May 10, 1964, 1; Richard Philbrick, "Professor Recalls His Doggedness and Integrity," *Chicago Tribune*, April 7, 1968, A4; "Prime Minister, Wife Visit Pope," *Chicago Tribune*, April 30, 1965, A13; "Kennedy Sees Loss of U.S. Prestige over War in Viet," *Chicago Tribune*, February 5, 1967, 4.
45 Marcinkus interviewed in Gallagher, "The Pope's Banker," G18.
46 Robert C. Doty, "Pope Will Visit New York Oct. 4," *The New York Times*, September 9, 1965, 16; "Two Papal Aides Arrive," *The New York Times*, September 9, 1965, 16. President Johnson informed the Pope that America was "quite heartened" at Paul VI's "appointment of a Negro as the auxiliary bishop of New Orleans." See Douglas Kiker, "Pontiff's Visit 'May Be Just What World Needs'—LBJ," *The Boston Globe*, October 5, 1965, 11.
47 In 1968, Paul VI appointed Marcinkus as the rector of St. Mary of the Lake villa. It was informally called Villa Stritch, after the Chicago cardinal who had founded the American chapter of Opus Dei. Another Chicago cardinal, George Mundelein, had bought the walled-in villa, adjacent to Rome's large Borghese Park, in 1935. Mundelein set it aside as a center for American clerics studying in Rome. Many in the Curia referred to the center simply as the Chicago House. There were only ten Americans at the Vatican at the time Marcinkus was appointed the rector. He had overseen the building's multimillion-dollar renovation in 1963, and to the amazement of his Italian colleagues managed to accomplish it on time and within the original budget. See Gwen Morgan, "Meyer in Villa," *Chicago Tribune*, June 16, 1963, 5; and Gallagher, "The Pope's Banker," G18.
48 Timothy M. Dolan, "'Hence We Cheerfully Sent One Who Should Represent Our Person': A Century of Papal Representation in the United States," *U.S. Catholic Historian* 12, no. 2, The Apostolic Delegation/Nunciature 1893–1993 (Spring 1994): 21.
49 It is not clear if Marcinkus had such contacts or merely boasted about it in the hope that Spellman's death presented an opportunity for advancement. He lobbied in particular Father Pasquale Macchi, Pope Paul's close personal assistant, Tosches, *Power on Earth*, 122; see also Gurwin, *The Calvi Affair*, 13. See also Lehnert, *His Humble Servant*, 105. As for Spellman's replacement, Terence Cooke, he was not elevated cardinal until March 1969.
50 Sylvana Foa, "Vatican's American Priests Are Bitter," *Chicago Tribune*, July 31, 1977, 12.
51 "U.S. Priest in Vatican Post," *The New York Times*, 45.
52 Marcinkus interviewed in Cornwell, *A Thief in the Night*, 83. Marcinkus said that his "real finan-

cial experience [was] I'd count Sunday collection and it was never wrong." He also thought the focus on his lack of training was misplaced. "Actually, you see, these people don't understand. I am not making the transactions, I just set policy. We have people here who are technicians who've been doing it for thirty to forty years." Handwritten notes by Philip Willan of audiotaped interviews between John Cornwell and Marcinkus, January 15, 1988, 1b, 2a, provided to author courtesy of Willan.

53 Hoffman, *Anatomy of the Vatican*, 188.

54 *New York Times* reporter Paul Hoffman wrote that Marcinkus took business administration courses at Harvard. The author was unable to confirm that Marcinkus had taken any classes there. Forty-five years after Marcinkus's appointment at the IOR, former Vatican correspondent for the BBC David Willey wrote that the Pope had dispatched the bishop to Harvard for a six-week crash course about finances. According to the school, that never happened. David Willey, "The Vatican Bank Is Rocked by Scandal Again," BBC News, July 17, 2013, http://www.bbc.co.uk/news/business-23289297.

55 Handwritten notes by Philip Willan of audiotaped interviews between John Cornwell and Marcinkus, January 15, 1988, 1b, provided to author courtesy of Willan.

56 Ibid., 4a.

57 In any case, as far as Marcinkus was concerned, "Money is a tool. It's a means, not a goal in itself." Handwritten notes by Philip Willan of audiotaped interviews between John Cornwell and Marcinkus, February 8, 1988, 41, provided to author courtesy of Willan. See also Thomas and Morgan-Witts, *Pontiff*, 142.

58 Colleague of Marcinkus quoted anonymously in Willey, *God's Politician*,, 210.

59 Sindona interviewed in Raw, *The Moneychangers*, 64.

60 Tosches, *Power on Earth*, 123.

61 Sindona quoted in Lernoux, *In Banks We Trust*, 209.

62 Reporter Jim Gallagher interviewed Sindona in 1983 while he was in a federal prison serving a sentence for a fraud conviction. Gallagher, "The Pope's Banker," G15.

63 Sindona also thought that Marcinkus was upset with him. When the IOR sold Immobiliare to Sindona, Marcinkus lost his status at the company's Roman golf course. Sindona believed Marcinkus blamed him for the fall-off in his VIP status. Tosches, *Power on Earth*, 123–24.

64 Galli, *Finanza bianca*, 79; Raw, *The Moneychangers*, 62.

65 Leo Sisti and Gianfranco Modolo, *Il banco paga: Roberto Calvi e l'avventura dell'Ambrosiano* (Milan: Mondadori Milano, 1982). There are some incorrect published reports that the BCI branch was in Lecce.

66 Galli, *Finanza bianca*, 80.

67 Cornwell, *God's Banker*, 27.

68 Raw, *The Moneychangers*,17; Hoffman, *Anatomy of the Vatican*, 195–96.

69 Grilli, *La finanza vaticana in Italia*, 32, 34.

70 "Marcinkus—Sindona con l'oro a Milano Fini la Capitale Morale," *La Repubblica*, April 19, 1992; Gurwin, *The Calvi Affair*, 5–6; see also Giovanni Bazoli, "The Ambrosiano Failure," *The American Banker*, July 12, 1983, 16.

71 Calvi's business wardrobe consisted of identical dark gray suits, white shirts, dark blue ties, and black shoes. In the summer, he changed to a lighter shade of gray. See Francesco Pazienza interviewed in Willan, *The Last Supper*, 39; see also Gurwin, *The Calvi Affair*, 6; Cornwell, *God's Banker*, 31.

72 "Marcinkus—Sindona con l'oro a Milano Fini la Capitale Morale," *La Repubblica*; Willan, *The Last Supper*, 35.

73 Calvi crammed in his self-taught language study at nights. Galli, *Finanza bianca*, 81–82.

74 "Marcinkus—Sindona con l'oro a Milano Fini la Capitale Morale," *La Repubblica*; Cornwell, *God's Banker*, 31.

75 Cornwell, *God's Banker*, 32; Willan, *The Last Supper*, 35; Lo Bello, *The Vatican Empire*, 115.

76 Gurwin, *The Calvi Affair*, 7, citing Andrea Barberi et al., "*L'Italia della P2* (Milan: Mondadori, 1981). The Vatican institutions that offered stakes in foreign mutual funds were the Banca Provinciale Lombarda and the La Centrale financial holding company.

77 Galli, *Finanza bianca*, 82.

78 Raw, *The Moneychangers*, 62–63.

79 Rosone interviewed in Willan, *The Last Supper*, 34–35.

80 The son-in-law, Piersandro Magnoni, had married Sindona's daughter, Maria Elisa, in 1967. Sindona brought him into his business. Piersandro's father, Giuliano Magnoni, knew Sindona since college, and it was the senior Magnoni who knew Calvi and wanted Sindona to meet him. The younger Magnoni simply passed along the message. See Simoni and Turone, *Il caffè di Sindona*, 121.
81 Tosches, *Power on Earth*, 118–19.
82 Sindona describing conversation with Calvi in ibid., 120.
83 Marcinkus later claimed that he met Calvi through "the Milanese Curia," but Sindona's version was that he introduced Calvi to the top tier of IOR officials and Luigi Mennini later confirmed that. See generally Cornwell, *God's Banker*, 54. See also Simoni and Turone, *Il caffè di Sindona*, 122; and Raw, *The Moneychangers*, 62.
84 Gurwin, *The Calvi Affair*, 26; Raw, *The Moneychangers*, 64–65.
85 All bishops are assigned titular titles. Marcinkus was the Bishop of Horta in Carthage (Italianized as Orta), after a Cypriot son of pagan parents who converted to Catholicism and became the bishop of Carthage in 248. Marcinkus's mother, Helen, traveled to Rome for the consecration, as did Chicago's cardinal, John Cody. "Cicero Priest Named Bishop by Pope Paul," *Chicago Tribune*, December 25, 1968, C19; "Mother to See Son Become Bishop," *Chicago Tribune*, December 27, 1968, 3; "Cody to See Marcinkus Elevated, *Chicago Tribune*, December 26, 1968, B3.
86 "Cicero Native Named Vatican Financial Aide," *Chicago Tribune*, December 21, 1968, 11. "Finance: Diversification at the Vatican," *Time*, January 25, 1971. See generally "Names and Faces," *The Boston Globe*, February 25, 1969, 40.
87 *The New York Times*, "Investment Shift by Vatican Seen," referred to Sindona as "Milan lawyer" and "secretary" of Generali. He had no public comment, according to the paper. *The Boston Globe*, "Vatican Stock Sale Hinted," June 19, 1969, 3, referred to Marcinkus as "the Vatican's American-born 'finance minister.'" The *Chicago Tribune* noted, "The bishop's robes also go with Marcinkus' new post as second-in-command—but effective head—of the Vatican Bank," "Cicero Priest Makes Good in Vatican Post," January 4, 1969, A12. See also Hoffman, "Bishop with Chicago Roots Is Managing Pope's Travels." See also Lai, *Finanze vaticane*, 51.
88 In obtaining direct access to Pope Paul, Marcinkus had outmaneuvered Archbishop Giovanni Benelli, the Sostituto (substitute) Secretary of State, to whom he would have normally reported. The two clashed repeatedly inside the Curia, and Marcinkus made it clear to the Pope that reporting to Benelli would only hinder his work at the IOR. Benelli was nicknamed "the Master Sergeant" inside the Curia for his authoritarian "stickler for detail" attitude. Benelli, meanwhile, thought it demeaning that Marcinkus could bypass the traditional chain of authority. Bishop Marcinkus, and Director of FBI field office in Rome, Tom Biamonte, both interviewed in Cornwell, *A Thief in the Night*, 17–18, 85–86, 170–71. For Benelli's reputation, see Hoffman, *Anatomy of the Vatican*, 116.
89 Marcinkus interviewed in "Finance: Diversification at the Vatican," *Time*. "From the organizational viewpoint," Marcinkus later said, "I think maybe I've always been very methodical." Handwritten notes by Philip Willan of audiotaped interviews between John Cornwell and Marcinkus, January 15, 1988, 1b, provided to author courtesy of Willan.
90 "Finance: Diversification at the Vatican," *Time*, January 25, 1971.
91 Lai, *Finanze vaticane*, 52–53. Macchi had been elected to a Monsignor soon after Paul VI assumed the Papacy.
92 Henry Gaggiottini, "Marcinkus Consecrated Bishop," *Chicago Tribune*, January 7, 1969, A9.
93 Francesco Pazienza, an Italian intelligence agent, told the author, "The Pope knew the IOR needed a son of a bitch." Author interview, September 18, 2013.
94 Cody interviewed in "Cody to See Marcinkus Elevated," *Chicago Tribune*, December 26, 1968, B3.
95 Hooper, "Luigi Mennini: Shadow over the Vatican," 14. There was little doubt Marcinkus took charge at an important time. A thinly sourced but widely covered book about Vatican finances was coincidentally published just before his appointment. In *The Vatican Empire*, former *Boston Globe* reporter Nino Lo Bello asserted the IOR had close to $13 billion in cash ($85 billion in 2014 dollars) and exposed some of the bank's secret business deals. After Germany's *Der Spiegel* and Italy's *Il Mondo* widely covered the book's revelations, the Vatican issued its answer in an unsigned article in the church's *L'Osservatore Romano*, in which it claimed that its cash wealth was "in reality . . . a hundredth" of what Lo Bello asserted. The church did not comment on Lo Bello's claim that Marcinkus was a good manager in part because he had "established close links with

[the] Rothschild banking interests." Alfred Friendly Jr., "Vatican Denies It Has Billions: Book on Wealth Is Termed Greatly Exaggerated," *The New York Times*, July 22, 1970, 8.

96 The fifteenth-century tower, sometimes called the bastion of Nicholas V, has walls nearly thirty feet thick near its base. They were built to withstand an armed assault.

97 Cornwell, *A Thief in the Night*, 159. Marigonda was also a former USIA officer assigned to the U.S. embassy at Rome before leaving to take a position with Marcinkus; email from Peter K. Murphy to Gerald Posner, January 30, 2014.

98 Sindona interviewed in Tosches, *Power on Earth*, 124.

99 Hoffman, *Anatomy of the Vatican*, 187.

100 Eight-page attachment to Letter from William Wilson to William French Smith, July 15, 1982, William A. Wilson Papers, Box 2, Folder 66, Georgetown University Library, Special Collections Research Center, Washington, D.C.

101 Marcinkus and Marigonda interviewed in Cornwell, *A Thief in the Night*, 87–88, 141.

102 Sindona interviewed in Tosches, *Power on Earth*, 124–25.

103 Author interview with Philip Willan, Rome, September 19, 2013; Philip Willan, "Three Jailed for 1969 Milan Bomb," *The Guardian*, July 1, 2001, 14; "U.S. supported anti-left terror in Italy," June 24, 2000, 19; Giovanni Mario Ceci, "The Explosion of Italian Terrorism and the Piazza Fontana Massacre Seen by the United States," *Historia*, vol. 31, February 9, 2013, 29–40. See also Hutchinson, *Their Kingdom Come*, 269–75. Author interview with Francesco Pazienza, Rome, September 21, 2013.

104 Robert C. Doty, "Pontiff Sees a Difficult Road to Unity," *The New York Times*, June 11, 1969, 14.

105 "Pope to Meet African Heads on Next Trip," *Chicago Tribune*, July 23, 1969, A5; "Pope Paul, Nigerian Peace Official Meet," *Chicago Tribune*, August 2, 1969, W13.

106 Hoffman, "Bishop with Chicago Roots Is Managing Pope's Travels."

107 Nino Lo Bello, "Bodyguard to Pope," *Boston Globe*, January 5, 1969, A19.

108 "They use the word here [Italy] and everyone knows it is *bodyguard*." Handwritten notes by Philip Willan of audiotaped interviews between John Cornwell and Marcinkus, January 15, 1988, 2a, provided to author courtesy of Willan. See also Thomas and Max Morgan-Witts, *Pontiff*, 139; and see also Marcinkus interviewed in Cornwell, *A Thief in the Night*, 84.

109 "Archbishop Paul Marcinkus: Vatican Bank Head Hit by Scandal," *The Independent* (London), February 23, 2006.

110 Published reports agree that Compendium was a Luxembourg holding company, that Calvi renamed it Banco Ambrosiano Holding, and that Calvi used Compendium to start Cisalpine (which means South of the Alps). Three authors write that Compendium was founded in 1963 by Ambrosiano, in connection with Lovelok, a Liechtenstein holding company: Robert Hutchinson, *The Kingdom Come: Inside the Secret World of Opus Dei* (New York: St. Martin's, 1999), 241; Raw, *The Moneychangers*, 63; Rupert Cornwell, *God's Banker*, 33. Two other authors write instead that Sindona owned Compendium and that Calvi bought it from him in 1970: Gurwin, *The Calvi Affair*, 17; Tosches, *Power on Earth*, 120. Tosches was the only author who had unrestricted access to Sindona. But Sindona's recollection, years after the event, does not guarantee it is accurate. His recall is often incorrect when compared to the documentary record. The problem with settling the issue of precisely when and by whom Compendium was founded is that its records are no longer available for public review in Luxembourg, nor are any records available in the Bahamas for the Cisalpine Bank.

All the authors agree that by 1980, Calvi built Cisalpine into the second largest bank in the Bahamas, with about $500 million under its control. "Banks Ranked," *The American Banker*, July 25, 1980. *Time*, in a 1982 special investigation, sided with the 1963 incorporation of Compendium by the Ambrosiano, without any Sindona involvement. Peter Stoler, with Jonathan Beaty and Barry Kalb, "The Great Vatican Bank Mystery," *Time*, September 13, 1982, 24.

111 The IOR started by buying five thousand of the initially offered fifteen thousand Class A shares. Over several years, the church's stake grew to 16,667 shares, 8.3 percent of the bank. Sindona, through his Finabank, owned 2.5 percent. Tosches, *Power on Earth*, 120; Rupert Cornwell, *God's Banker*, 50; memorandum of Paul Marcinkus to the Joint Investigating Committee, Vatican and Italy, into the Affairs of the IOR, quoted in Raw, *The Moneychangers*, 67; see also pages 66–71.

112 Unnamed Bank of Italy official quoted in Gurwin, *The Calvi Affair*, 17. When Cisalpine's links to Calvi, Sindona, and the church later became public, the Nassau bank became a fulcrum of

conspiracy theorists. One of the most often repeated is a tale in which Cisalpine laundered Mafia heroin profits through an Asian bank run by a CIA-linked Cuban expatriate. All that is missing is credible evidence.

113 Ann Crittenden, "Growing Bahamian Loan Activity by U.S. Banks Causes Concern," *The New York Times*, March 3, 1977, 1. Penny Lernoux, in her 1984 book, *In Banks We Trust*, wrote: "Then, as now [1984], the Eurocurrency market was a giant floating crap game in which exchange dealers (mostly banks) bet on the rise or fall of national currencies."

114 Sindona quoted in Stoler, Beaty, and Kalb, "The Great Vatican Bank Mystery."

115 Handwritten notes by Philip Willan of audiotaped interviews between John Cornwell and Marcinkus, February 8, 1988, 7a, provided to author courtesy of Willan.

116 Marcinkus quoted in Raw, *The Moneychangers*, 71.

117 Raw, *The Moneychangers*, 8, 219; Cornwell, *God's Banker*, 50.

118 Cornwell, *God's Banker*, 50.

119 Willey, *God's Politician*, 211.

120 Clara Calvi quoted in Gurwin, *The Calvi Affair*, 26.

121 Marcinkus also visited the following year. Raw, *The Moneychangers*, 94; Cornwell, *God's Banker*, 50, 54; DiFonzo, *St. Peter's Banker*, 65; Tosches, *Power on Earth*, 170.

122 Stoler, Beaty, and Kalb, "The Great Vatican Bank Mystery."

123 Raw, *The Moneychangers*, 81–83. The back-to-back operations picked up steam after an April 25, 1972, Cisalpine board meeting in New York. Marcinkus and Calvi agreed to expand the scope of the deposits, although they kept their agreement secret from the other directors, as well as from Cisalpine's titular president, Peter Siegenthaler. Radowal, a Liechtenstein holding company owned by Calvi, became a key way station between the Vatican Bank and other elements of the Calvi empire.

124 The back-to-back arrangements, which also involved joint IOR and Ambrosiano accounts at Banca del Gottardo in Lugano, were initially oral agreements, but were committed to writing in two November 1976 letters from Calvi to Marcinkus. Stoler, Beaty, and Kalb, "The Great Vatican Bank Mystery"; Raw, *The Moneychangers*, 74, 131–37.

125 Marcinkus made that statement to Paul Horne during a telephone interview for the in-depth 1971 *Institutional Investor* article about the finances of the church. Horne attributed it in the published piece only to "one Vatican insider," but it was widely known in the Vatican that it was Marcinkus. (Horne, "How the Vatican Manages Its Money," 83.) Marcinkus later tried to step back from that quote: "The bank we have here is a service organization for the Church; it's involved particularly in apostolic works. Somebody asked me one time, 'Why this?' I said, 'When my workers here come to retire they expect a pension; it's no use my saying to them, 'I'll pay you 400 Hail Marys.' Now that's been misquoted all over the place. They use that all the time, see? I'm quoted as saying, 'You can't run the Church on Hail Marys.' It would be very nice if the Church could live without depending on these things, but you find a church you have to buy bricks, have a bricklayer." Marcinkus interviewed in Cornwell, *A Thief in the Night*, 76. See also reference to a November 1982 interview by Marcinkus with *Il Sabato*, the weekly publication of the influential lay organization Comunione e Liberazione (Communion and Liberation); Cornwell, *God's Banker*, 58. See also Hooper, "Luigi Mennini: Shadow over the Vatican," 14; and see also Gurwin, *The Calvi Affair*, 14.

Chapter 16: Operation Fraulein

1 Infighting between the two principals gave him an opportunity to seize the company. Raw, *The Moneychangers*, 69; Tosches, *Power on Earth*, 127–28; see also Henry Tanner, "Italy Suspends All Stock Trading: Moves to Halt Price Collapse," *The New York Times*, July 9, 1981, D4.

2 Carl Bernstein, "The CIA and the Media," *Rolling Stone*, October 20, 1977. Sindona interviewed in Tosches, *Power on Earth*, 131–32. *The Daily American*, started by three American soldiers after World War II, was the only competitor in Italy to the *International Herald Tribune*. It went out of business in 1986.

3 Hoffman, *Anatomy of the Vatican*, 191.

4 Felix Kessler, "Italy's 'Howard Hughes' Said to Prepare for Sizable Increase in His U.S. Investments," *The Wall Street Journal*, February 17, 1972, 12.

5 Ibid.

6 H. Erich Heinemann, "Loews Sells Million Franklin Shares," *The New York Times*, July 13, 1972, 47.

7 H. Erich Heinemann, "A Question of Control: European Encounters American Bank Rules," *The New York Times*, F5. Through Fasco, Sindona bought 18.4 percent of Franklin, less than the 25 percent that would have required Fasco to register with the Federal Reserve as a bank holding company. That would have immediately subjected Fasco to far greater scrutiny. New York State law presumed that control of a bank existed with as little as 10 percent ownership.

8 H. Heinemann, "Loews Sells Million Franklin Shares, 47; see also DiFonzo, *St. Peter's Banker*, 138–39; "Sindona: He's Popped Up Again," *The Economist*, July 23, 1972.

9 In June 1972, one of Calvi's companies, Cimafin Finanza Anstalt, agreed to buy Sindona's Zitropo Holding S.A. and Pacchetti S.p.A. for $44,317,876 (the IOR made $860,000 on currency conversion commissions on that sale, on its way to earning $5.6 million that year just on exchanging lire for Calvi). Full transfer of ownership and payment for Franklin was not until February 1973. All money passed through Sindona's Fasco. "Sindona Speaks," *The Economist*, September 16, 1972, 100. See also Turone, *Il caffè di Sindona*, 123–24, 126; DiFonzo, *St. Peter's Banker*, 145–47; Raw, *The Moneychangers*, 84–86, 94–95.

10 Sindona interviewed in Manny Topol and Adrian Peracchi, *Newsday*, October 17, 1982, 1

11 H. Erich Heinemann, "Roth Asks Inquiry on Bank-Stock Sale," *The New York Times*, July 18, 1972, 41.

12 Ibid.; DiFonzo, *St. Peter's Banker*, 148–49. Tisch ignored Roth's campaign to further question Sindona. Six years later (1978), the FDIC, in its role then as a receiver of a bankrupt Franklin, filed a federal lawsuit against Tisch, charging that he failed to thoroughly investigate Sindona's bona fides. The FDIC asked in its complaint for Tisch to return the profit he had made by selling his Franklin shares to Sindona. The lawsuit was settled out of court. See Max H. Seigel, "F.D.I.C. Suit Against Franklin National Head," *The New York Times*, July 13, 1978, D6.

13 John V. Conti, "Oxford Electric, Interphoto Data Show Tangled Debts and Conflict of Interest," *The Wall Street Journal*, January 17, 1972, 10; see also Farnsworth, "Sindona's Empire: Sharp Trading, Big Losses," 57.

14 Kessler, "Italy's 'Howard Hughes' Said to Prepare for Sizable Increase in His U.S. Investments," 12.

15 Federal regulatory authorities deferred usually to the classifications given the buyers by state regulators. When Sindona used Fasco to buy Franklin, since he was Fasco's sole owner, for New York State banking rules he was considered an "individual purchaser." That meant he was not subject to the scrutiny to which a company would have undergone. "Sindona Speaks," *The Economist*, 100.

New York's Superintendent of Banks proposed a change to state law so that after Franklin, all individuals were subject to the same rigorous examination as companies. See also Heinemann, "A Question of Control," F5.

16 Bordoni had been dismissed from Citibank in 1965, allegedly for having exceeded the trading limits set by the bank. Against the advice of David Kennedy, the respected chairman of Continental Illinois, Sindona had picked Bordoni to run Moneyrex. Bordoni was later a director of Sindona's Banca Unione. See Raw, *The Moneychangers*, 58.

Sindona was appointed to a specially created executive board, a technical distinction that allowed him, despite being an Italian citizen, to perform all the duties of any normal director at a U.S. financial institution. At the time, foreigners were not allowed to serve directly on U.S. bank boards: "Sindona Is Named to Bank's Board," *The New York Times*, August 18, 1972, 45.

17 That money came from part of a $24 million loan from the IOR; Gurwin, *The Calvi Affair*, 22; Raw, *The Moneychangers*, 98.

18 Author interview with Carlo Calvi, September 10, 2006.

19 David Burnham, "Sindona Discusses Issuing Role with U.S. Controller," *The New York Times*, May 15, 1974, 61; Robert E. Bedingfield, "Franklin Bank Solvency Reiterated by Controller," *The New York Times*, May 23, 1974, 59. Kennedy and Sindona had met when Continental Illinois Bank bought a minority interest in Banca Privata, the Sindona-IOR-owned institution; see Farnsworth, "Michele Sindona, the Outsider as Insider."

20 Tosches, *Power on Earth*, 77. Kennedy and Sindona are at the center of a long-standing conspiracy theory that has Continental Bank transferring $4 million in 1967 to Sindona's PBF, which he in turn loaned to a right-wing Greek army colonel, Georgios Papadopoulos. In April of that year Papadopoulos led a coup d'état in his native country. Conspiracy theorists believe it was all part

of a P2 subplot to topple Greece with the hope it would encourage the Italian military to do the same in Italy. Although the plot was reprinted in one book as fact (DiFonzo, *St. Peter's Banker*), the author is unable to find any credible evidence of it.

21 Lucinda Franks, "Sindona's $1-Million Offer to Nixon Group Examined," *The New York Times*, July 15, 1974, 1. Foreigners are not allowed to contribute to U.S. elections unless they have a so-called green card, a permanent resident's permit. Stans later said he was not certain if the banker had a green card or merely a work visa that allowed him to temporarily conduct business in the country.

22 Tosches, *Power on Earth*, 134; "Hambros in Italy," *The Economist*, October 16, 1971, 100, 103; Raw, *The Moneychangers*, 79–80, 91–93. Calvi bought Hambros Bank's share in Le Centrale (the IOR had historically owned a substantial minority share in Hambros). Calvi took a share in the Le Centrale interests held by Credito Varesino and the Pacchetti Group, both of which were consolidated under a Sindona holding company, Zitropo. And as a final element in the deal, Sindona gave Calvi the first option he owned to purchase Invest, a trading company. Marcinkus stayed involved by authorizing a short-term $43.5 million loan to Cisalpine on November 30, 1972. That money was used by Calvi to pay Sindona what he still owed on Varesino, Pacchetti, and Zitropo. Marcinkus also helped the sellers of the Varesino shares transfer part of their profits to a Lugano holding company, and earned for the IOR an additional $930,000 in the conversion of those funds from lire to Swiss francs. See also Cornwell, *God's Banker*, 62–63.

23 Raw, *The Moneychangers*, 134.

24 In 1978, Italy's banking regulators discovered that the IOR's accountant, Pellegrino de Strobel, had written a 1975 letter to the Ambrosiano in a clumsy effort to mask Calvi's ownership share in Suprafin S.p.A. The plan to secretly accumulate the Ambrosiano shares also involved two Swiss banks, Zurich's Credit Suisse and Chiasso's Union de Banques Suisses, as well as an Ambrosiano holding company in Lausanne, Banca del Gottardo. Two offshore accounts were also used, Ehrenkreuz Anstalt and Radowal Financial Etablissement. Calvi's wife, Clara, held an undisclosed power of attorney in each offshore company. Benton E. Gup, *Bank Failures in the Major Trading Countries of the World: Causes and Remedies* (Westport, CT: Greenwood/Quorum, 1998), 31–32; Tosches, *Power on Earth*, 135.

25 Tosches, *Power on Earth*, 131.

26 During World War II, the Banca Cattolica had come under Mussolini's state ownership, but in 1946 the Vatican reclaimed private control. See Raw, *The Moneychangers*, 56.

27 Gallagher, "The Pope's Banker," G15–16.

28 Raw, *The Moneychangers*, 70.

29 Gurwin, *The Calvi Affair*, 19.

30 Calvi quoted in ibid.

31 According to Pollard, "It was Spada who masterminded the passage of the majority share-holding of the Banca Cattolica to the IOR." Pollard, *Money and the Rise of the Modern Papacy*, 207; Tosches, *Power on Earth*, 135. Calvi used his Le Centrale holding company for the Cattolica purchase. Raw, *The Moneychangers*, 77–78.

32 Raw, *The Moneychangers*, 77–78.

33 Ibid., 70.

34 The initial $12 million was paid by the Swiss holding company Lovelok to the IOR, and then deposited by Marcinkus that same day into Cisalpine. Each subsequent installment involved an extra step of obfuscation. Calvi formed Vertlac, another Liechtenstein holding company. Cisalpine made loans to Vertlac in the exact amount of each installment due to the IOR. Vertlac then wired the money to the Vatican Bank, which in turn deposited it into six-month certificates of deposit at Cisalpine. The IOR even managed to squeeze $2.5 million in profit by getting an artificially high exchange rate at Cisalpine when converting the U.S. dollars used in the installment payments into lire. Raw, *The Moneychangers*, 70, 74, 78; see also Gurwin, *The Calvi Affair*, 19.

35 Raw, *The Moneychangers*, 110.

36 Marcinkus's reported dismissal of Luciani is cited. in Gurwin, *The Calvi Affair*, 20–21.

37 See generally Gallagher, "The Pope's Banker," 20.

38 "A Pontiff from Cicero?," *Chicago Tribune*, June 25, 1972, A6.

39 As for the directors' meeting, see generally Raw, *The Moneychangers*, 89.

40 Securities and Exchange Commission, 39th Annual Report, for the fiscal year ending June 30, 1973, U.S. Government Printing Office, 73–74.

41 SEC News Digest, A Daily Summary from the Securities and Exchange Commission, "Irving Eisenberger, Able Associates Enjoined; Trading Suspended in Vetco Offshore Industries Stock," Issue No. 73-42, March 2, 1973, Court Enforcement Actions, 1; see also Felix Belair Jr., "Court Bars Sale of Vetco Stock," *The New York Times*, March 2, 1973, 47.
42 Everett Hollis, "Vatican Refund Sought by Vetco," *The New York Times*, March 5, 1973, 43; see also Belair Jr., "Court Bars Sale of Vetco Stock," 47. See "Statement on Behalf of Ragnar Option Co. and Victor Sperandeo," included as an attachment in an unsigned letter from Willkie Farr & Gallagher to Richard Kraut, Harold Halperin, and Charles Lerner, all of the Securities and Exchange Commission, Re: Vetco Offshore Industries—Ragnar Option Co., October 31, 1973, copy in possession of author.
43 Fiduciary Investment Services was owned by Sindona. It is not clear who introduced Marcinkus and Eisenberger. Much later, Sindona told author Charles Raw that he was not responsible for the link between the IOR and Eisenberger, and moreover said that he repeatedly warned Marcinkus against doing business with small advisors. Raw, *The Moneychangers*, 101; Hollis, "Vatican Refund Sought by Vetco," 43.
44 Hollis, "Vatican Refund Sought by Vetco," 43.
45 Raw, *The Moneychangers*, 101; see also Thomas and Morgan-Witts, *Pontiff*, 149; and Martin, *The Final Conclave*, 30.
46 Belair Jr., "Court Bars Sale of Vetco Stock," 47. For later Vetco legal problems with a Swiss subsidiary and U.S. tax laws, see *United States v. Vetco, Inc.*, 691 *Federal Reporter*, 2d Series, 1981, 1282–91.
47 Paul VI elevated Luciani to a cardinal on March 5, 1973.
48 Robert J. Cole, "U.S. Inquiry in 1973 at Vatican Bank Is Disclosed," *The New York Times*, August 7, 1982, 34.
49 Author interview with William Aronwald, February 16, 2007; Richard Hammer, *The Vatican Connection* (New York: Charter, 1983), 150–53. Hammer's book is about Operation Fraulein. It won a 1982 Edgar Award for the year's best true crime book. Aronwald and Tamarro told me that the book's factual errors are because it relied too much on Coffey's version of events. "That book is a story as told to the author by Joe Coffey," says Aronwald. "Neither Dick Tamarro or I were interviewed for the book."

"Coffey and I never spoke after that pulp fiction book was published," Tamarro told me. *Newsweek*, in a September 13, 1982, review of *The Vatican Connection*, noted that while Coffey was a "key source for the book," Hammer "bases his case chiefly on a far-from impeccable source: the unsworn testimony of two convicted con men and an accomplice."
50 Hammer, *The Vatican Connection*, 51–52.
51 Ibid., 64–70.
52 Jane Mayer, "Vatican Bank's Marcinkus Was Queried in U.S. Counterfeiting Case 9 Years Ago," *The Wall Street Journal*, August 6, 1982, 2.
53 Hammer, *The Vatican Connection*, 100.
54 Author interview with William Aronwald, February 16, 2007; see also Hammer, *The Vatican Connection*, 76–98.
55 Hammer, *The Vatican Connection*, 77–78.
56 Ibid., 210–11.
57 Alfred Scotti, Deputy District Attorney, New York, quoted in Arnold H. Lubasch, "Disposal of Illicit Paper Is Charged Here," *The New York Times*, July 12, 1973, 1.
58 Author interview with William Aronwald, February 16, 2007. Aronwald's Strike Force was a specially formed group inside the Organized Crime and Racketeering Division, assigned to the Southern District of New York.
59 Author interview with William Aronwald, February 16, 2007; see also Mayer, "Vatican Bank's Marcinkus Was Queried in U.S. Counterfeiting Case 9 Years Ago," 2.
60 Hammer, *The Vatican Connection*, 154–55.
61 Ibid., 144, 158–59.
62 Ibid., 210–12.
63 Author interview with William Aronwald, February 16, 2007. Before Tamarro's trip to Germany, the FBI had relied exclusively on its legal attachés in U.S. embassies when it came to any foreign case.
64 Author interview with Richard Tamarro, February 28, 2007.

65 Ibid.
66 Author interview with William Aronwald, February 16, 2007; Hammer, *The Vatican Connection*, 219.
67 Cole, "U.S. Inquiry in 1973 at Vatican Bank Is Disclosed," 34.
68 Author interview with William Aronwald, February 16, 2007; see also DiFonzo, *St. Peter's Banker*, 108–14; "Hambros in Italy," *The Economist*, October 16, 1971, 100, 103; "The End: Bastogi," *The Economist*, October 23, 1971, 103, 104; "End of the Italian Affair," *The Economist*, January 8, 1972, 72–73; see also Simoni and Turone, *Il caffè di Sindona*, 122.
69 Author interview with William Aronwald, February 16, 2007.
70 Ibid.
71 In 1946, Cardinal Tisserant—a French intelligence agent during World War I—met with Argentine Cardinal Antonio Caggiano at the Vatican. The two prelates facilitated the flight of French war criminals to Argentina. Since that information was made public in 2003, the Vatican has refused to release any files about the matter. The Argentine Catholic Church claimed to the author that the relevant records were destroyed in a 1955 fire. Kevin G. Hall, "Argentina's New President Pressured to Open Perón Files on Nazis," Knight Ridder Washington Bureau, International News, June 1, 2003.
72 Author interview with Richard Tamarro, February 28, 2007; author interview with William Aronwald, February 16, 2007; Hammer, *The Vatican Connection*, 235–38.
73 Author interview with William Aronwald, February 16, 2007; see also Mayer, "Vatican Bank's Marcinkus Was Queried in U.S. Counterfeiting Case 9 Years Ago," 2.
74 Hammer, *The Vatican Connection*, 216.
75 Author interview with Richard Tamarro, February 28, 2007.
76 Lubasch, "Disposal of Illicit Paper Is Charged Here."
77 Author interview with Richard Tamarro, February 28, 2007.
78 Hammer, *The Vatican Connection*, 249–50.
79 Mayer, "Vatican Bank's Marcinkus Was Queried in U.S. Counterfeiting Case 9 Years Ago," 2; also author interview with William Aronwald, February 16, 2007.
80 James Bacque, "How a Manhattan Detective Trailed a Small-Time Hood and Ended Up Investigating Some Strange and Possibly Illegal Dealings of the Vatican Bank," *The Globe and Mail* (Canada), January 15, 1983.
81 Hammer, *The Vatican Connection*, 215–16.
82 Author interview with William Aronwald, February 16, 2007; author interview with Richard Tamarro, February 28, 2007; see also Hammer, *The Vatican Connection*, 241–45.
83 Author interview with Richard Tamarro, February 28, 2007.
84 Author interview with William Aronwald, February 16, 2007; author interview with Richard Tamarro, February 28, 2007.
85 Author interview with William Aronwald, February 16, 2007.
86 Ibid.
87 Ibid.
88 Seymour had recently announced his resignation for personal reasons. Nixon had announced his replacement, Paul Curran, the Chairman of the New York State Commission of Investigation, but the Senate had not yet approved him. Aronwald fully briefed Curran on the meeting and the investigation once he took charge later that month (April 1973).
89 Author interview with William Aronwald, February 16, 2007.
90 Hammer, *The Vatican Connection*, 301–2. Aronwald told the author: "Sure he [Coffey] was upset, but it was simply our jurisdiction at that stage. The meeting at the Vatican was super sensitive, and we didn't want to mess it up by taking a large group there. There were plenty of people besides Coffey who wanted to go. My biggest concern was that if we started to get too large on our side, the Vatican might change its mind and cancel." Years later, Coffey speculated to author Richard Hammer that the Nixon administration had sidetracked a harder investigation because the President feared upsetting Catholic voters before the reelection. Aronwald insists, however, "No one ever pressured me and I was running the case."
91 Author interview with William Aronwald, February 16, 2007.
92 Author interview with Richard Tamarro, February 28, 2007.
93 Ibid.
94 Ibid.

95 Ibid.
96 Author interview with William Aronwald, February 16, 2007. Tom Biamonte, the FBI liaison officer at the American embassy in Rome, had lobbied Marcinkus to speak to the Justice Department trio. "We had no right to enter the Vatican unless specifically invited," Biamonte later said. "But out of courtesy to us at the embassy, he [Marcinkus] agreed to answer any questions they wanted to throw at him." Biamonte interviewed in Cornwell, *A Thief in the Night*, 172.
97 Author interview with Richard Tamarro, February 28, 2007.
98 Author interview with William Aronwald, February 16, 2007; author interview with Richard Tamarro, February 28, 2007.
99 Biamonte interviewed in Cornwell, *A Thief in the Night*, 172.
100 Monsignor Fornasari was a well-known Vatican attorney who practiced before the Apostolic Tribunal of the Roman Rota, the church's equivalent of the Supreme Court. He also had a side business in manufacturing rosaries and crucifixes.
101 Hammer, *The Vatican Connection*, 305–6.
102 FBI File summary of the interview with Marcinkus, quoted and cited in Raw, *The Moneychangers*, 102.
103 Mayer, "Vatican Bank's Marcinkus Was Queried in U.S. Counterfeiting Case 9 Years Ago," 2.
104 Cornwell, *A Thief in the Night*, 172.
105 Author interview with William Aronwald, February 16, 2007; author interview with Richard Tamarro, February 28, 2007.
106 Jane Mayer, "Vatican Bank's Marcinkus Was Queried in U.S. Counterfeiting Case 9 Years Ago," *The Wall Street Journal*, August 6, 1982, 2.
107 Author interview with William Aronwald, February 16, 2007.
108 Author interview with Richard Tamarro, February 28, 2007.
109 Interview with William Aronwald, February 16, 2007.
110 Lubasch, "Disposal of Illicit Paper Is Charged Here," 1; Mayer, "Vatican Bank's Marcinkus Was Queried in U.S. Counterfeiting Case 9 Years Ago," 2.
111 Lubasch, "Disposal of Illicit Paper Is Charged Here," 1; the case, *U.S. v. Amato, et al.*, is on Pacer, the legal database, at 1:73-cr00672-MGC, filing date of July 10, 1973.
112 Rizzo pled guilty and was given a five-year sentence to serve concurrently with his drug trafficking conviction. The government never pursued extradition requests against either Ledl or Foligni, both of whom were never tried.
113 Mayer, "Vatican Bank's Marcinkus Was Queried in U.S. Counterfeiting Case 9 Years Ago," 2; author interview with William Aronwald, February 16, 2007.
114 Author interview with William Aronwald, February 16, 2007.

Chapter 17: *Il Crack Sindona*

1 Paul Hofmann, "War Raids Incite Anti-U.S. Feelings in Italy," *The New York Times*, January 3, 1973, 8. In the State Department that year, 1973, there was a flurry of diplomatic cable traffic over the "Vatican's 'contacts' with Communists" in Vietnam. It was about fears the Pope might reach out to the Vietcong. See generally 09-25-73 WikiLeaks Vatican "Contacts" with Communists Cable: 1973ROME10199_b; https://www.wikileaks.org/plusd/cables/1973ROME10199_b.html; also 09-28-73 WikiLeaks Audience with Pope Paul VI (Held at Vatican Suggestion) Cable: 1973ROME10410_b; https://www.wikileaks.org/plusd/cables/1973ROME10410_b.html.
2 "Two Bombings in Milan," *The New York Times*, January 16, 1973, 14.
3 Paul Hofmann, "El Al Employe [*sic*] in Rome Is Shot to Death by an Arab: 3 Seized at Beirut Airport," *The New York Times*, April 28, 1973, 6.
4 Paul Hofmann, "Italian Neo-Fascists Are Linked to a Synagogue Fire in Padua," *The New York Times*, April 30, 1973, 3.
5 "Anarchist Seized in Blast in Milan," *The New York Times*, May 18, 1972, 7.
6 Paul Hofmann, "If Surge of Gunfire Is a Sign, Sicilian Mafia Is in Trouble," *The New York Times*, May 15, 1973, 41.
7 Paul Hofmann, "Italians Suspect Violence Is Plot: International Police Aid Is Asked After Milan Blast," *The New York Times*, May 21, 1973, 9.
8 "Again Italy's Premier: Mariano Rumor," *The New York Times*, July 9, 1973, 3.

9 Ibid.
10 "Milan Offices Bombed," *The New York Times*, July 29, 1973, 3.
11 "Libyan Jets Attack an Italian Warship off African Coast," *The New York Times*, September 22, 1973, 2.
12 William D. Smith, "The Arab Oil Weapon Comes into Play," *The New York Times*, October 21, 1973, 185; DiFonzo, *St. Peter's Banker*, 194–95.
13 Robert D. Hershey Jr., "10 Years After Oil Crisis: Lessons Still Uncertain," *The New York Times*, September 25, 1983, 1.
14 "Europeans Move to Conserve Oil," *The New York Times*, November 8, 1973, 71.
15 Clyde H. Farnsworth, "Oil: Alarms Growing in Europe and U.S.: Continent Worries About a Possible '74 Recession," *The New York Times*, November 21, 1973, 51; "Deep Recession Seen for Europe," *The New York Times*, December 1, 1973, 47; "Oil Shortage Abroad Puts Stocks in Different Light," *The New York Times*, December 3, 1973, 63.
16 Terry Robards, "Oil-Short Europe Is Facing Hardest Winter Since War," *The New York Times*, December 11, 1973, 1.
17 "Kuwait Considers Giving Hijackers to Guerrilla Group for Trial," *The New York Times*, December 21, 1973, 14.
18 "Pope Urges Italians to Shun A 'Mafia-Style Mentality,'" *The New York Times*, January 2, 1974, 13.
19 Martin Andersen, "Argentina Can't Exorcise Fascination with Perón," *The Miami Herald*, July 3, 1987, Q17; Martin Andersen, "$10 Million Demanded for Return of the Hands Cut from Perón's Body," *The Globe and Mail* (Canada), July 3, 1987; Susana Viau and Eduardo Tagliaferro, "Carlos Bartffeld, Mason y Amigo de Massera," December 14, 1998, 12.
20 Tosches, *Power on Earth*, 169–71.
21 There are conflicting accounts of precisely when Calvi and Gelli met, but the best evidence is that it was sometime in 1974, although they did not do regular business together until the following year. Calvi's wife, Clara, thought it could have been as early as 1973, but she was not present. Willan, *The Last Supper*, 112–13. See also Raw, *The Moneychangers*, 139.
22 Sindona interviewed in Tosches, *Power on Earth*, 171
23 Calvi quoted in Willan, *The Last Supper*, 112.
24 Gelli interviewed in ibid., 126–27.
25 When the police eventually seized Gelli's P2 records, it showed Calvi was initiated into the Rome branch in 1974, and became a member of a Geneva lodge the following year. See Willan, *The Last Supper*, 111–12. Some publications also link Calvi to a London Masonic lodge, but there is no evidence he was a member there. It appears that P2 had an affiliation to a London lodge, and that was sufficient for Calvi in case he needed to call upon one of its British members.
26 Sindona interviewed in Tosches, *Power on Earth*, 172.
27 Ibid., 172–73.
28 Bastogi had large interests in Italian utility, mining, and cement industries. Count Giuseppe Volpi owned it during World War II. Sindona secretly acquired some shares starting in the late 1960s. In 1971, he enlisted Calvi and the British merchant bank Hambros to quietly accumulate more of Bastogi, using Ultrafin, a Swiss holding company that could not easily be traced to them. When Bastogi's board learned of Sindona and Calvi's takeover interest, they put up a fierce battle—much of which played out publicly—to successfully retain control. Hostile takeovers were unheard of in Italy at the time, and in its aftermath Sindona was the public relations loser, seeming by Italian business standards too hungry a predator. See Galli, *Finanza bianca*, 82.
29 The Pierre was best known as a five-star luxury hotel, but it also had seventy-seven condominium apartments that were maintained under the hotel's general management. Parliamentary Commission of Inquiry into the Case of Sindona and Responsibilities and the Political and Administrative Connected To It, n. 315 (citing Exhibit Carli, January 28, 1981 Mec. I/5), 18.
30 Affidavit of John McCaffrey, February 3, 1981, quoted at length in DiFonzo, *St. Peter's Banker*, 1046; see also Willan, *The Last Supper*, 86–87.
31 Marcinkus interviewed in Cornwell, *A Thief in the Night*, 132.
32 Tosches, *Power on Earth*, 149.
33 Parliamentary Commission of Inquiry into the Case of Sindona and Responsibilities and the Political and Administrative Connected To It, 20–22.
34 Farnsworth, "Sindona's Empire: Sharp Trading, Big Losses," 57. Sindona's merged bank had no assets: see Lai, *Finanze vaticane*, 53.

35 The Bank of Italy conducted four investigations of Sindona's businesses, dating back to his failed attempt to take over Bastogi. Farnsworth, "Sindona's Empire: Sharp Trading, Big Losses," 57. See also Turone, *Il caffè di Sindona,* 122; and "Hambros in Italy," *The Economist,* October 16, 1971, 100. As for the questions over the Bank of Italy's failure to find evidence during its regularly scheduled annual reviews, see Parliamentary Commission of Inquiry into the Case of Sindona and Responsibilities and the Political and Administrative Connected To It, 19–20; Turone, *Il caffè di Sindona,* 40.

36 DiFonzo, *St. Peter's Banker,* 182–83. Some published reports assert that in exchange for his donation, Sindona demanded and got his friend Mario Barone appointed as the chief of the Bank of Rome (Willan, *The Last Supper,* 81). The author was unable to confirm this was a quid pro quo for the Sindona contribution to the anti-divorce battle. See also William Tuohy, "Italy Retains Divorce, 3–2; Rebuff to Vatican, State," *The Boston Globe,* May 14 1974, 1.

37 John O'Neill, "'Coition Death': Are Only the Famous Prone to Final Fun?" *Sydney Morning Herald* (Australia), July 1, 1987, 21; Alexander Chancellor, "Long Life," *The Spectator,* July 27, 2013; author interview with a priest recounting a personal conversation with Sindona, September 21, 2013.

38 Robert E. Bedingfield, "Strains at Bank Multiplied in Big-City Competition," *The New York Times,* May 18, 1974, 39; "Banking, A Shocking Drama," *Time,* May 27, 1974.

39 DiFonzo, *St. Peter's Banker,* 163–65. This trade was a staple of Sindona financial institutions: see Parliamentary Commission of Inquiry into the Case of Sindona and Responsibilities and the Political and Administrative Connected To It, 28–30.

40 Farnsworth, "Sindona's Empire: Sharp Trading, Big Losses," 57.

41 Harold Gleason quoted in DiFonzo, *St. Peter's Banker,* 191.

42 Parliamentary Commission of Inquiry into the Case of Sindona and Responsibilities and the Political and Administrative Connected To It, 14.

43 John A. Allan, "Lag at Franklin Cited," *The New York Times,* May 2, 1974, 75.

44 Richard E. Mooney, "When a Big Bank Stumbles," *The New York Times,* June 9, 1974, 164.

45 Tosches, *Power on Earth,* 152.

46 "Sindona, Self-Made Man of 53, Rules Vast Industrial Empire," *The New York Times,* May 13, 1974, 48.

47 John H. Allan, "Franklin National Bank Dismisses Its President," *The New York Times,* May 14, 1974, 1; see also Robert E. Bedingfield, "Franklin Urged to Omit Payment," *The New York Times,* May 11, 1974, 39; "Banking: A Shocking Drama," *Time*; "Poor Sindona," *The Economist,* May 18, 1974, 126.

48 DiFonzo, *St. Peter's Banker,* 198.

49 John H. Allan, "10-Day Ban Intended to Allow Bank to Arrange Affairs," *The New York Times,* May 15, 1974, 61.

50 Farnsworth, "Sindona's Empire: Sharp Trading, Big Losses," 57.

51 Robert D. Hershey Jr., "Tremors in the Banking System," *The New York Times,* May 19, 1974, 159.

52 "Poor Sindona," *The Economist,* 126.

53 Sindona interviewed in Tosches, *Power on Earth,* 170–71.

54 Ibid.,171.

55 Ibid.

56 Ibid., 172.

57 DiFonzo, *St. Peter's Banker,* 158.

58 Raw, *The Moneychangers,* 111.

59 Farnsworth, "Sindona's Empire: Sharp Trading, Big Losses," 57; Turone, *Il caffè di Sindona,* 42–43.

60 Parliamentary Commission of Inquiry into the Case of Sindona and Responsibilities and the Political and Administrative Connected To It, 33–35; see also "Loan to Sindona by Rome Bank Is Not Expected to Aid Franklin," *The New York Times,* July 12, 1974, 55.

61 Paul Hofmann, "Italian Financier Said to Make Concessions for $100-Million Loan," *The New York Times,* July 10, 1974, 51; Farnsworth, "Sindona's Empire: Sharp Trading, Big Losses," 57.

62 Farnsworth, "Sindona's Empire: Sharp Trading, Big Losses," 57.

63 "Sindona: A £100m Loss?," *The Economist,* September 21, 1974, 119.

64 "Franklin Fizzles Out," *Time,* October 21, 1974; see generally Parliamentary Commission of Inquiry into the Case of Sindona and Responsibilities and the Political and Administrative Connected To It, 120–22.

65 DiFonzo, *St. Peter's Banker*, 206.
66 Farnsworth, "Sindona's Empire: Sharp Trading, Big Losses," 57; "More Collateral Put Up by Sindona," *The New York Times*, July 16, 1974, 51. As for how Sindona tried to insulate SGI from being infected by losses in his other financial companies, see generally Parliamentary Commission of Inquiry into the Case of Sindona and Responsibilities and the Political and Administrative Connected To It, n. 315, 35–36.
67 Farnsworth, "Sindona's Empire: Sharp Trading, Big Losses," 57. See also advertisement, "A Great Bank Is Born, Banca Privata Italiana," *The Economist*, July 6, 1974, 121. Sindona's streak of bad luck continued in Italian courts that month, when shareholders of his financing company, Finambro, prevailed in their lawsuit to stop him from raising more capital.
68 John H. Allan, "63-Million Lost by Franklin Bank in 5 Months of '74," *The New York Times*, June 21, 1974, 1.
69 John H. Allan, "Sindona Associate Leaving Franklin," *The New York Times*, June 24, 1974, 43.
70 Tosches, *Power on Earth*, 153; DiFonzo, *St. Peter's Banker*, 206.
71 "Franklin Fizzles Out," *Time*.
72 Michael C. Jensen, "S.E.C. Said to Be Investigating Franklin Bank's Sindona Deals," *The New York Times*, July 18, 1974, 49; Robert J. Cole, "S.E.C. Files Fraud Charges Against Nine Once at Franklin," *The New York Times*, October 18, 1974, 57. Sindona was in fact involved in shuffling money between Franklin and his other businesses in an effort to minimize the bank's trading losses and artificially increase paper profits. See generally DiFonzo, *St. Peter's Banker*, 192–94.
73 "Sindona Said to Vow to Save Franklin," *The New York Times*, July 2, 1974, 54. "After so many Italians who have come here to trade in vegetables or enroll with the gangsters, here's now someone who has Wall Street listening to him, but instead of assisting me, they [his Italian critics] attack me," Sindona told *Corriere della Sera*. He was angry at the widespread commercial success of Francis Ford Coppola's 1972 *The Godfather*. Sindona told friends and business colleagues that the film reinforced the worst stereotypes of Italians in America and made it more difficult for businessmen to work with him. Meanwhile, Sindona's former partner, Calvi, did not worry about how Americans judged him since he did so little business in the U.S. Calvi loved the film; he told a fellow financier, "Do you know *The Godfather*? It's a masterpiece, because everything is in it." Calvi quoted in Gurwin, *The Calvi Affair*, 36.
74 "Sindona, Big Franklin Holder, Reported Selling a Bank in Italy," *The New York Times*, September 5, 1974, 62; Raw, *The Moneychangers*, 119.
75 DiFonzo, *St. Peter's Banker*, 175–77.
76 Clyde H. Farnsworth, "Bank Closes in Germany; Sindona Owned Half of It," *The New York Times*, August 24, 1974, 31.
77 "Vatican Denies Report of Big Banking Losses," *The New York Times*, August 28, 1974, 39.
78 Herbert Koshetz, "Sindona Unit Selling 53% of Talcott for 5.6-Million," *The New York Times*, September 28, 1974, 35; "The American Connection," *The Economist*, October 5, 1974, 106.
79 Parliamentary Commission of Inquiry into the Case of Sindona and Responsibilities and the Political and Administrative Connected To It, 22, 37–42.
80 See Raw, *The Moneychangers*, 119–20.
81 Although Italian authorities closed Finabank's Italian branch that September, Switzerland did not shutter its headquarters until the following January; see Turone, *Il caffè di Sindona*, 41–42.
82 DiFonzo, *St. Peter's Banker*, 89.
83 Tosches, *Power on Earth*, 171–72.
84 Farnsworth, "Sindona's Empire: Sharp Trading, Big Losses," 57.
85 Ibid.; Clyde H. Farnsworth, "Italy Is Making Good on the Failure of Sindona's Bank: $500-Million in Losses Books Examined," *The New York Times*, September 20, 1974, 51.
86 "Sindona Reported in a Court Inquiry," *The New York Times*, September 16, 1974, 54.
87 In just one instance, Sindona arranged for some customer deposits at the Banca Privata Finanziaria to serve as collateral for debt issues at one of his holding companies, Moizzi & Co. Those funds were sometimes transferred to the IOR, which in turn made them available to a Finabank account in Geneva. That account, nicknamed MANI, after the first two letters of Sindona's sons' names (Marco and Nino), served as collateral for foreign currency speculation. See generally DiFonzo, *St. Peter's Banker*, 91.
88 Farnsworth, "Sindona's Empire: Sharp Trading, Big Losses," 57.
89 Ibid.

90 John A. Allan, "Sindona Resigns His Post as Franklin Bank Director," *The New York Times*, September 22, 1974, 1.
91 John A. Allan, "F.D.I.C. Rejects Franklin's Plan," *The New York Times*, October 4, 1974, 1.
92 For a full background of the criminal charges filed against Sindona, see M. De Luca, ed., *Sindona. The Indictments of the Courts of Milan* (Rome: Riuniti, 1986); and Israel Shenker, "Warrant Seeks Sindona Arrest," *The New York Times*, October 10, 1974, 81.
93 Martin, *The Final Conclave*, 30.
94 European-American Bank bought what was left of Franklin for $125 million, outbidding Manufacturers Hanover by $2 million. DiFonzo, *St. Peter's Banker*, 213-14.
95 Patrick J. Sloyan, "Franklin Failure Almost Caused World Panic, Burns Says," *The New York Times*, December 22, 1974, 58; "Franklin Fizzles Out," *Time*.
96 "Italy Is Liquidating Bank in the Group Headed by Sindona," *The New York Times*, September 29, 1974, 4. "Sindona: Worse and Worse," *The Economist*, October 5, 1974, 106.
97 Generale Immobiliare, Revealing All," *The Economist*, April 5, 1975, 84.
98 See generally Untitled, Associated Press, Rome, A.M. cycle, August 8, 1979.
99 Sindona quoted in "Sindona Declares He Can Incriminate Leading Italians," *The New York Times*, April 7, 1975, 33.
100 Cole, "S.E.C. Files Fraud Charges On Nine Formerly at Franklin," 57. Although the SEC described the action as "one of the biggest actions ever brought against a bank and its officers," it admitted that its investigation had not found any "evidence of looting."
101 Ibid., 57, 68.
102 Israel Shenker, "Warrant Seeks Sindona Arrest," *The New York Times*, October 10, 1974, 81; "Sindona Picks Defense Lawyers," *The New York Times*, October 16, 1974, 67.
103 DiFonzo, *St. Peter's Banker*, 214.
104 Gelli quoted in Ibid., 215.
105 Ibid., 218–19; Sindona's mistress had been married to an American, but was divorced by the time she met Sindona at a Lehman Brothers reception in New York in 1960. Although he was married, he had had several mistresses over the years. He had a longer relationship with her than with any other woman.
106 DiFonzo, *St. Peter's Banker*, 219.
107 Leonard Sloane, "Sindona Appears in Public to Address College Group," *The New York Times*, April 16, 1997, 51; Terry Robards, "Sindona Says He Lives on Help," *The New York Times*, November 27, 1975, 55. Sindona told friends and colleagues that although he was still living in his condominium at the Pierre, he had sold it to raise money and was now renting it by the day from an undisclosed buyer. In fact, Sindona still owned it. That woud be disclosed when the following year he posted its deed to help make bail.
108 Sindona quoted in DiFonzo, *St. Peter's Banker*, 220.
109 *The New York Times*, January 8, 1975, 51 (no article title or byline).
110 Lloyd Shearer, "Intelligence Report," *The Boston Globe, Parade* supplement, titled "The Vatican Takes a Bath," March 23, 1975, H16, referring to how Pope Paul VI "also brought in his old friend, Michele Sindona [to the IOR]." See also "Allah Be Praised," *Forbes*, February 15, 1975, 8; "Vatican's Budget Is Vetoed by Pope," *The New York Times*, January 23, 1975, 14. No article title for the statement by Vatican spokesman, Federico Alessandrini, about the church's limited losses, *The New York Times*, February 1, 1975, 4. See also *The New York Times*, January 23, 1975, 14 (no title to article and no byline). And see also Raw, *The Moneychangers*, 120.
111 Italian magazine *Panorama*, cited in "Report Chicagoan Out as Vatican Bank Head," *Chicago Tribune*, November 22, 1974, 1.
112 Italian magazine *Panorama*, cited in Andrew Blake, "Financier's Fall Costly to Vatican," *The Boston Globe*, February 2, 1975, 21.
113 Kay Withers, "Vatican Aide Denies Pope May Fire Him," *Chicago Tribune*, November 23, 1974, D11.
114 Kay Withers, "Vatican Wealth: The Bottom Line Isn't Too Blessed," *Chicago Tribune*, April 20, 1975, A1.
115 "Vatican's Finances: Paul's Pence," *The Economist*, February 8, 1975, 71.
116 "Vatican's Budget Is Vetoed by Pope," *The New York Times*, January 23, 1975, 14; "Vatican Finances; Paul's Pence," *The Economist*, 71.

117 Edward Magri, "Vatican Reportedly Lost $56m in Bank Scandal," *The Boston Globe*, January 31, 1975, 40.
118 "Vatican's Finances; Paul's Pence," *The Economist*, 71.
119 Cornwell, *God's Banker*, 131–34.
120 Sindona quoted in Tosches, *Power on Earth*, 173; see also Brendan Jones, no title to article, *The New York Times*, February 21, 1975, 41.
121 DiFonzo, *St. Peter's Banker*, 222.
122 "People and Business: Problems as Banks Flee Saigon," *The New York Times*, April 10, 1975, 62.
123 Sloane, "Sindona Appears in Public to Address College Group," 51. The article is one of the few that mentions that Sindona's English was not good, describing him as "Speaking in a heavily accented English." New York criminal defense attorney Ivan Fisher told me that when he first met Sindona, "One of my biggest problems representing him was how poorly he spoke English. He told me in our first meeting that I should contact *A*, to see if he might be able to help. He said it with such respect that I didn't want to admit I didn't know who *A* was. It took until our third meeting before I realized he was saying *Haig* (then the Supreme Commander of NATO, and someone Sindona knew from Haig's tenure as chief of staff for Nixon). I could not get close to him in the way I am most comfortable because it was so difficult to understand him. I suggested an interpreter. He was really offended because he thought his English was magnificent." Author interview with Ivan Fisher, June 19, 2013.
124 DiFonzo, *St. Peter's Banker*, 222.
125 "An Unlikelääy Lecturer," *Time*, December 8, 1975. Between 1975 and 1977, Sindona spoke at sixteen university business schools.
126 Michael C. Jensen, "Sindona Assails Governmental Bailouts," *The New York Times*, June 13, 1975, 51.
127 Prosecutors were particularly incensed by photos in the *New York Post* of Sindona partying with New York Mayor Abraham Beame.
128 "Carli and Others Are Investigated," *The New York Times*, June 27, 1975, 47.
129 Arnold H. Lubasch, "8 Former Aides of Franklin Bank Indicted by U.S.," *The New York Times*, April 13, 1975, 1.
130 Kay Withers, "Legendary Vatican Wealth May Be Just a Myth," *The Boston Globe*, May 11, 1975, B2.
131 Horne, "How the Vatican Manages Its Money."
132 Withers, "Vatican Wealth: The Bottom Line Isn't Too Blessed," A1; Kay Withers, "Legendary Vatican Wealth May Be Just a Myth," B2.
133 Vagnozzi revealed that salaries consumed 10 percent of the Holy See's budget. Their employment included a generous health plan and pension coverage, and some fifteen hundred retired lay employees received their full salaries for the rest of their life. "A trend to internationalization" meant there were "many [lay] non-Italians now in the Curia." That meant "considerably" increased costs since they brought their families to Rome at church expense.
134 Withers, "Vatican Wealth: The Bottom Line Isn't Too Blessed," A1.
135 "Milan's Prosecutor Visiting U.S. to Ask Sindona Extradition," *The New York Times*, November 25, 1975.
136 "An Unlikely Lecturer," *Time.*
137 Robards, "Sindona Says He Lives on Help," *The New York Times* 55. Sindona claimed he had received anonymous telephone calls and letters urging him to commit suicide.
138 Enrico Cuccia quoted in Tosches, *Power on Earth*, 167.
139 Lubasch, "Ex-Franklin Bank Aide Pleads Guilty," 43.
140 Raw, *The Moneychangers*, 119.
141 Tosches, *Power on Earth*, 120; Raw, *The Moneychangers*, 138–39.
142 Gurwin, *The Calvi Affair*, 28.
143 Willan, *The Last Supper*, 36–37; see Calvi statement to judicial magistrates in July 1981, quoted in Raw, *The Moneychangers*, 146.
144 Willan, *The Last Supper*, 113.
145 Raw, *The Moneychangers*, 145, 149. Marcinkus interviewed in Cornwell, *A Thief in the Night*, 134.
146 Gurwin, *The Calvi Affair*, 31; Willan, *The Last Supper*, 36–37.
147 Handwritten notes by Philip Willan of audiotaped interviews between John Cornwell and Marcinkus, February 8, 1988, 4b, 5a, 9b, provided to author courtesy of Willan.

148 Ibid., 4b.
149 Raw, *The Moneychangers*, 119, 125–26, 129–31.
150 Ibid., 124–25.
151 Laura Colby, "Vatican Bank Played a Central Role in Fall of Banco Ambrosiano," *Wall Street Journal*, April 27, 1987, 1.
152 Raw, *The Moneychangers*, 135–36.
153 Ibid., 137.
154 The dollar and Swiss franc back-to-back schemes were so useful for Calvi and profitable for Marcinkus that by December 1975 the duo also began back-to-back lira transfers. Raw, *The Moneychangers*, 161–72, 176, 184–94, 209–12, 247–49, 365–66.
155 Based on Calvi's new advice, Marcinkus made substantial investments into United Trading Corporation, a Panamanian holding company with nominee subsidiaries (Teclefin and Imparfin) based in Liechtenstein. Cornwell, *God's Banker*, 71; see also Raw, *The Moneychangers*, 49, 95, 108–9. In December 1974, the IOR had made its first installment payment to United Trading, sending the funds through Cisalpine in Nassau. The IOR had also made a $43.5 million loan in May 1972 to Radowal, a Liechtenstein company that later became United Trading. Marcinkus had also approved in late 1973 a Vatican Bank loan of $45 million to Manic, the newly formed Calvi holding company headquartered in Luxembourg. In each case, the IOR got above-market interest rates on its money, as well as lump-sum commission payments of nearly $4 million for the loans. Criminal investigators later examined those commissions, scattered across the books of banks and holding companies in several countries, to determine if they constituted bribes to Marcinkus for the use of the church's money. Although the prosecutors suspected they were, they never developed enough evidence to make a criminal case.

By 1978, the IOR secretly owned United Trading, although Vatican Bank attorneys later contended the IOR "did not control" it. This was in reference to what the lawyers considered administrative control exerted by Calvi, that United Trading "was directly managed by the [Ambrosiano] Group in its own sole interest." See generally Colby, "Vatican Bank Played a Central Role in Fall of Banco Ambrosiano," 1; see also "Memo prepared by IOR's lawyers re Laura Colby's article," reproduced in its entirety in Cornwell, *A Thief in the Night*, 354–58.

Chapter 18: The Battle of Two Scorpions

1 Raw, *The Moneychangers*, 177. Some of the companies that owed the IOR money, such as Zitropo with a $12 million loan, were essentially bankrupt. But Calvi kept shuffling money disguised as "dividends" to Zitropo so it could at least make its interest payments to the Vatican Bank. It is not clear if Marcinkus was aware of the dire state of Zitropo, although he agreed to a reduction of the loan's interest rate from 11 percent to 2 percent at the close of 1975.
2 Bafisud was the acronym for Banco Financiero Sudamericano. Not only did Calvi direct the Ambrosiano and the IOR to invest in Bafisud, but he also persuaded Italy's then largest bank, the Banca Nazionale del Lavoro (BNL), to become an equity partner. The top five BNL executives were all P2 members. See Gurwin, *The Calvi Affair*, 56.
3 Minutes of Cisalpine shareholders meeting of February 4, 1976, in Geneva, cited in Raw, *The Moneychangers*, 177.
4 Ibid., 177–78.
5 Law 159 is still on the books in Italy. See generally Cornwell, *God's Banker*, 81.
6 Raw, *The Moneychangers*, 178–79.
7 Ibid., 183–94.
8 Ibid., 197. Marcinkus and Calvi attended a Cisalpine board meeting at the Bristol Hotel in Paris on October 20, 1977, and in Zurich on March 2, 1978. At neither meeting did Marcinkus mention that Calvi was using Cisalpine's cash—with the IOR's assistance—to buy the nonpublic shares of United Trading, Cisalpine's parent. Instead, Calvi showed the money as being on deposit at the IOR, something that he and Marcinkus knew to be false.
9 Calvi to Marcinkus, letter, July 26, 1977, cited in Raw, *The Moneychangers*, 198.
10 Colby, "Vatican Bank Played a Central Role in Fall of Banco Ambrosiano," 1; Cornwell, *A Thief in the Night*, citing "Marcinkus Replies to the *Wall Street Journal*," 354–58; Raw, *The Moneychangers*, 358–62, 373.

11 Raw, *The Moneychangers*, 62, 126–29. And despite its management contracts with some of the offshore companies, the IOR later contended through its Italian attorneys that none of its "executives were aware of the existence and unethical nature of Calvi's schemes." Anything to the contrary, said the attorneys, was based on "conjectures and hypotheses that are not supported by any evidence." "Memo prepared by IOR's lawyers re Laura Colby's article," reproduced in its entirety in Cornwell, *A Thief in the Night*, 354–58.

12 That November, Calvi put into writing a confirmation of the back-to-back arrangements that had existed for several years between Cisalpine, the Vatican Bank, and United Trading. A separate letter did the same for the Gottardo-IOR back-to-back deposits. It is not clear what prompted the duo to commit this part of their dealings to writing. See generally Raw, *The Moneychangers*, 132.

13 Marcinkus interviewed in Cornwell, *A Thief in the Night*, 131.

14 "Milan's Prosecutor Visiting U.S. to Ask Sindona Extradition," *The New York Times*, November 25, 1975; Parliamentary Commission of Inquiry into the Case of Sindona and Responsibilities and the Political and Administrative Connected To It, 122–32.

15 "Sindona Is Sentenced to Prison in Italy," *The New York Times*, June 26, 1976, 34.

16 Although Sindona was disappointed by Carter's election, that a former peanut farmer could become president reinforced for him the idea that in America anything is possible: Tosches, *Power on Earth*, 181. See generally Parliamentary Commission of Inquiry into the Case of Sindona and Responsibilities and the Political and Administrative Connected To It.

17 "Sindona Bail $3m," *The Boston Globe*, September 9, 1976, 27. In October 1976, the Italian government expanded its charges against Sindona with a detailed filing that compiled some of his efforts to evade the country's currency laws; see Robert J. Cole, "Italians Amplify Looting Charges Against Sindona," *The New York Times*, October 27, 1976, 72.

18 Gelli convinced Spagnuolo that the case against Sindona was a leftist smear plot. Robert J. Cole, "Court Papers Filed by Sindona in Fight to Bar Extradition," *The New York Times*, December 14, 1976, 66.

19 Terry Robards, "Sindona to Face Charges in Italy After Surrender," *The New York Times*, September 9, 1976, 57; "Ex-Franklin Aides File Guilty Pleas," *The New York Times*, January 21, 1976, 76.

20 Lubasch, "Ex-Franklin Bank Aide Pleads Guilty," 43.

21 Robards, "Sindona to Face Charges in Italy After Surrender," 57; Raw, *The Moneychangers*, 205, puts the amount at $334 million, which it did eventually reach.

22 Robert Lenzner, "Mario Barone: Muscle at the Banco," *The Boston Globe*, July 30, 1976, 33. Barone was a power in Italy's banking industry, having run the Bank of Italy for decades. The following year he stepped down from his post after an internal review found that he refused to fully cooperate with prosecutors trying to find the names of up to five hundred Italian businessmen and politicians who had deposited money into Sindona-controlled Swiss bank accounts. Barone had been the chief official responsible for approving the Bank of Rome's $200 million in loans shortly before Sindona's empire collapsed.

23 "Sindona Loses in Court in Banco di Roma Case," *The New York Times*, July 7, 1976, 66.

24 Raw, *The Moneychangers*, 205; Andreotti, who had resigned as Prime Minister—the fifty-ninth since World War I—was back as the country's sixty-second Prime Minister in July 1976.

25 Parliamentary Commission of Inquiry into the Case of Sindona and Responsibilities and the Political and Administrative Connected To It, 18–20.

26 Raw, *The Moneychangers*, 205.

27 Simoni and Turone, *Il caffè di Sindona*, 123–24.

28 Raw, *The Moneychangers*, 207.

29 See generally Parliamentary Commission of Inquiry into the Case of Sindona and Responsibilities and the Political and Administrative Connected To It, 151–59.

30 Simoni and Turone, *Il caffè di Sindona*, 125–26.

31 The names of the accounts were Ehrenkreuz and Rolrov. Gurwin, *The Calvi Affair*, 38–39; see also Simoni and Turone, *Il caffè di Sindona*, 125; and Raw, *The Moneychangers*, 205–6.

32 Robert Hutchison, *Their Kingdom Come: Inside the Secret World of Opus Dei* (New York: Thomas Dunne Books/St. Martin's Griffin, 1997), 246.

33 Cornwell, *God's Banker*, 83–84; see also Gurwin, *The Calvi Affair*, 37–38; Tosches, *Power on Earth*, 184; and DiFonzo, *St. Peter's Banker*, 228.

34 See Tosches, *Power on Earth*, 184, 193–93.

35 Cavallo letter to Calvi, December 1977, quoted in part in Simoni and Turone, *Il caffè di Sindona*,

126–27; and Raw, *The Moneychangers*, 206. Sindona's squeeze was a tremendous distraction for Calvi, who was in the middle of an ambitious expansion into Nicaragua. Bosco Matamoros, the Nicaraguan ambassador to the Vatican, had encouraged Calvi to buy property in the country, obtain Nicaraguan passports for himself and his wife, and open a new subsidiary, Ambrosiano Groupo Banco Comercial, in Managua. Calvi hit it off so well with Anastasio Somoza, the country's right-wing strongman, that Somoza soon used him to suggest changes to the country's offshore banking laws. And in return for the warm reception, Calvi arranged for several million dollars in loans on favorable terms to Somoza-affiliated companies (Calvi's loans into Nicaragua totaled about $8 million, and half of that went to firms linked to Somoza). Marcinkus for once urged caution about the expansion into Nicaragua. He told Calvi that it seemed risky since left-wing guerrillas, the Sandinistas, were giving Somoza's army a tough fight. Mexico, Marcinkus suggested, might be a better investment because of its proximity to America. But Calvi was not dissuaded. He also launched a Peruvian-based firm, Central American Service, which bought large tracts of land for oil and precious metals speculation and also acted as an agent in arranging Italian armaments sales to the Peruvian military.

36 Galli, *Finanza bianca*, 83–84; Willan, *The Last Supper*, 54; Gurwin, *The Calvi Affair*, 38–39.

37 Calvi met with Sindona's attorney, Rodolfo Guzzi, at the popular Caffè Greco in central Rome. Guzzi passed him a scrap of paper with a handwritten notation of the bank and account number to which Calvi should wire the money. Calvi put that paper into his safe, and after his death prosecutors retrieved it and analyzed the handwriting. It belonged to Sindona. As for using United Trading, Calvi did not mention a word to Marcinkus. United Trading was already responsible for $15 million annually to the IOR just in interest payments servicing its loans. See generally *The Sunday Times* (London), February 13, 1983.

38 Raw, *The Moneychangers*, 218–20.

39 Cornwell, *God's Banker*, 114–15; see also, Raw, *The Moneychangers*, 213, 308–9.

40 Raw, *The Moneychangers*, 215.

41 Raw, *The Moneychangers*, 362–66.

42 The Bank of Italy had dispatched a remarkable quarter of all its inspectors for the Ambrosiano probe. See generally Cornwell, *God's Banker*, 90.

43 See generally Tosches, *Power on Earth*, 235.

44 Raw, *The Moneychangers*, 207, 259.

45 Sindona had hired Luigi Cavallo to send Bank of Italy inspectors about 30 pages of copies of some of Calvi's Swiss bank accounts, see Willan, *The Last Supper*, 55; Cornwell, *God's Banker*, 82.

46 Gurwin, *The Calvi Affair*, 53.

47 "Sidona's [*sic*] Extradition Tentatively Approved," *The New York Times*, November 12, 1977, F32; Arnold H. Lubasch, "Sindona's Extradition to Italy Is Granted by Court," *The New York Times*, May 19, 1978, D11.

48 Arnold H. Lubasch, "3 Franklin Indictments," *The New York Times*, July 14, 1978, D3.

Chapter 19: "A Psychopathic Paranoid"

1 Hoffman, *Anatomy of the Vatican*, 148.

2 Paul Hoffman, "Speculation on Pope: Will He Resign at 80?," *The New York Times*, August 29, 1977, 6.

3 Henry Tanner, "Election to Be Held," *The New York Times*, August 7, 978, A1.

4 Hoffman, "Speculation on Pope: Will He Resign at 80?," 6; Paul had told some colleagues that he "saw the end of my life approaching." William Claiborne, "Thousands Mourn Pope's Death; Cardinals Gather for Rites, Election," *The Washington Post*, August 8, 1978, A1.

5 Hoffman, "Speculation on Pope: Will He Resign at 80?," 6.

6 For a few Vaticanologists, the question of whether Paul VI would be the first modern Pope to resign arose first in 1967, only four years into his Papacy. That was when he made an unscripted visit to Fumone Castle, an isolated mountaintop retreat between Rome and Naples. There he spoke about feeling resigned to life. His words were interpreted to be a cloaked allusion to his own desire to step down from the Papacy. Fumone Castle was famous as the place where the so-called hermit Pope, Celestine V, spent the last five months of his life after resigning from the Papacy in 1296. Hoffman, "Speculation on Pope: Will He Resign at 80?," 6; Thomas and Morgan-Witts,

Pontiff, 37; "Rumors Pope May Retire Laid to Vatican Rifts," *The New York Times*, September 1, 1977, 5; "Pontiff Turns 80; He Shows No Sign of Wanting to Quit," *The New York Times*, September 27, 1977, 13.

7 Martin, *The Final Conclave*, 86.

8 Hoffman, *Anatomy of the Vatican*, 32.

9 John Deedy, "The Clergy's Revolution in Sexual Mores," *The New York Times*, February 6, 1977, E16.

10 Martin, *The Final Conclave*, 49. Martin, a former Jesuit, wrote several nonfiction books about the Vatican. *The Final Conclave* is an unusual hybrid because the first 112 pages are nonfiction, and Martin writes that in the account of the conclave that took place upon the death of Paul VI, beginning on page 113, "the participants are fictional." In an "Author's Note" he claims that the fictional portion is based on "accurate knowledge of the issues and factions at work in the choice of Pope Paul's successor." Still, the author has restricted any information and citation of *The Final Conclave* to only the first 112 pages, the nonfiction portion.

11 "Pope Paul Distressed over Defection of Priests," *The Boston Globe*, February 11, 1978, 7.

12 "Murdered Congo Cardinal Is Buried in Brazzaville," *The New York Times*, March 28, 1977, 5.

13 This offer was especially risky since the Pope was on a Red Brigades short list for assassination. Tanner, "Election to Be Held," A1.

14 A coincidental footnote to the Moro assassination is that the priest who had heard Moro's final confession was Father Antonio Mennini, one of the sons of Luigi Mennini, the Vatican Bank director. Peter Hebblethwaite, *Pope John Paul II and the Church* (Kansas City: Sheed & Ward, 1995), 108. In 2015, Pope Francis departed from the Vatican's doctrine that the sanctity of a confessional must never be breached, and allowed Mennini (then an archbishop and the Papal Nuncio to the UK), to testify in closed session before an Italian parliamentary committee still investigating the assassination. "Pope Orders Priest who Confessed Aldo Moro to Testify Before Parliamentary Committee," *Malta Independent*, March 7, 2015.

15 There were unconfirmed reports that the Pope refused to forgive the sin of the killers, something that would have gone against Catholic teaching that every sin, no matter how grievous, can be forgiven through confession and penance. See generally Thomas and Morgan-Witts, *Pontiff,* 25.

16 Tanner, "Election to Be Held," A1.

17 "Bitter Family Buries Moro Privately," *The Boston Globe*, May 11, 1978, 1.

18 "General and Aide Are Killed in Spain," *The New York Times*, July 22, 1978, 3.

19 Michael T. Kaufman, "12 White Teachers and Children Killed by Guerillas in Rhodesia," *The New York Times*, June 25, 1978, 1.

20 Jonathan Kandell, "2 Slain at Terrorist Siege in Paris Embassy," *The New York Times*, August 1, 1978, A1.

21 "Bomb Kills Five on Jerusalem Bus," *The Boston Globe*, June 3, 1978, 24.

22 See generally about fighting in the Curia, Thomas and Morgan-Witts, *Pontiff,* 93.

23 James L. Franklin, "Catholic Scholar Says Vatican Is Tilting to the Left," *The Boston Globe*, March 2, 1978, 1. In a 1975 decree that modified the conclave, Paul VI had expressly rejected expanding the voting for a new Pontiff to patriarchs of the Eastern Rite, or any other non-Catholic clerics. Conservatives, however, did not trust him. They believed he had adopted that position because he did not yet have broad-based enough support to push a more liberal agenda.

24 Robert D. McFadden, "Cardinals to Meet to Elect Successor," *The New York Times*, August 7, 1978, A14; see Martin, *The Final Conclave*, 57, 73.

25 Franklin, "Catholic Scholar Says Vatican Is Tilting to the Left," *Boston Globe*, 1. Martin gave his *Boston Globe* interview to promote his just published book, *The Final Conclave*.

26 Thomas and Morgan-Witts, *Pontiff,* 140. An unidentified Monsignor interviewed in Cornwell, *A Thief in the Night*, 90. The gossip intended to undermine clerics with power such as Marcinkus and Macchi often centered on secret sex lives. Much dismissed stories of a too-close relationship between Macchi and the Pope continued making the rounds. As for Marcinkus, the tales were instead that he was having an affair with a former Miss France, who was married to a Marcinkus friend, Steve Barclay, a former B-grade Hollywood actor who had become a star in Italian cinema. Over a stretch of several years in the mid-1970s, Marcinkus was at the couple's house a few times a week. That set off the Curia rumor mill. Evidence, as was the case with most innuendos and aspersions inside the Vatican, was not necessary. See Biamonte interviewed in Cornwell, *A Thief in the Night*, 173–74.

Ex–Italian intelligence agent Francesco Pazienza, who later investigated Marcinkus in order to turn up dirt at the request of the Secretary of State, did not believe the IOR chief had any sexual weaknesses. "He was in love with power and la dolce vita, not women or men," Pazienza told the author. Marcinkus himself had commented about it once. "You don't play with fire if you don't want to get burned. If you want to take on the priesthood you have to know it's a celibate life." Handwritten notes by Philip Willan of audiotaped interviews between John Cornwell and Marcinkus, February 8, 1988, 2a, provided to author courtesy of Willan.

27 Galli, *Finanza bianca*, 64.

28 Peter Steinfels, "Andrew M. Greeley, Priest, Scholar and Scold, Is Dead at 85," *The New York Times*, May 30, 2013.

29 Greeley had founded the U.S.-based group the Committee for the Responsible Election of the Pope (CREP) in which he urged that all priests worldwide vote for successor Pontiffs.

30 Andrew M. Greeley, *Furthermore! Memories of a Parish Priest* (New York: Tom Doherty Associates, 2000), Google ebook edition 2011: 88–89.

31 Ibid., 88.

32 Kenneth A. Briggs, "Center of Strife Under Cody: All Charges Denied," *The New York Times*, September 20, 1981, 20.

33 Clements, Mustain & Larson, "Federal Grand Jury probes Cardinal Cody's Use of Church Funds," *Chicago Sun-Times*, September 10, 1981, 1; D. Winston, "Chicago Archbishop Under US Inquiry on Funds," *The New York Times*, September 11, 1981, 16. See also Andrew M. Greeley, *Furthermore! Memories of a Parish Priest* (New York: Tom Doherty Associates, 2000), Google ebook edition 2011, 88–89; Hoffman, *Anatomy of the Vatican*, 64; Alexander L. Taylor III, "God and Mammon in Chicago," *Time*, September 21, 1981; Linda Witt and John McGuire, "A Deepening Scandal Over Church Funds Rocks a Cardinal and His Controversial Cousin," *People*, September 28, 1981.

34 Ibid.; Barry W. Taylor, "Diversion of Church Funds to Personal Use: State, Federal and Private Sanctions," *Journal of Criminal Law and Criminology* 73, no. 3, Article 16, 1205–06. See also Thomas and Morgan-Witts, *Pontiff*, 28–29, 71, 109.

35 Greeley, recounting his talk with Cardinal Baggio, May 11, 2007. Marcinkus heard the rumors, but did not give his opinion. He hoped Cody would not have to leave his post since he thought his friend had "been maligned, very much so. . . . The picture they paint of him in Chicago is, I think, unreal, too brutal." Handwritten notes by Philip Willan of audiotaped interviews between John Cornwell and Marcinkus, February 8, 1988, 9b, 10a, provided to author courtesy of Willan.

36 Greeley, *Furthermore! Memories of a Parish Priest*, 88–89. Thomas and Morgan-Witts, *Pontiff*, 71–72; see generally Peter Hebblethwaite, "Obituary: Cardinal Sebastiano Baggio," *The Independent* (London), March 23, 1993.

37 Thomas and Morgan-Witts, *Pontiff*, 71. Greeley, *Furthermore! Memories of a Parish Priest*, 544–45.

38 Thomas and Morgan-Witts, *Pontiff*, 67–68.

39 Moshe Brilliant, "Israeli Jets Strike Lebanon to Avenge Bombing in Tel Aviv," *The New York Times*, August 4, 1978, 1.

40 Thomas and Morgan-Witts, *Pontiff*, 67.

41 Hebblethwaite, *The Year of Three Popes*, 1-2.

42 Ibid., 72–73. Later, when the Pope died, some noted doctors broke with the tradition of not publicly criticizing physicians in other cases. South African heart transplant pioneer Dr. Christiaan Barnard told *Salve*, an Italian health magazine, that Pope Paul VI's life might have been saved. "An acutely sick patient is given intensive therapy. If this was not done for Pope Paul VI, I must say the doctor's behavior was unacceptable." See also Thomas and Morgan-Witts, *Pontiff*, 72–73.

43 Hebblethwaite, *The Year of Three Popes*, 2. The Pope's brother was Ludovico Montini, an Italian senator, and the nephew was Marco Martini.

44 See generally regarding the traditional use of the silver hammer to confirm the death of the Pope, Russell Watson, Loren Jenkins, Paul Martin, and Elaine Sciolino, "A Death in Rome," *Newsweek*, October 9, 1978, 70.

45 Associated Press, Rome, P.M. cycle, August 7, 1978.

46 Hebblethwaite, *The Year of Three Popes*, 2-3.

47 Dennis Redmont, no title, Associated Press, Vatican City, A.M. cycle, August 6, 1978.

48 Villot quoted in Thomas and Morgan-Witts, *Pontiff*, 78.

49 Thomas and Morgan-Witts, *Pontiff*, 78.

50 Claiborne, "Thousands Mourn Pope's Death," *The Washington Post*, August 8, 1978, A1.

51 Telegram cited in full in Thomas and Morgan-Witts, *Pontiff*, 81. See also "Cardinal Villot Takes the Reins," *Boston Globe*, August 7, 1978.

Chapter 20: The Year of Three Popes

1 See generally Stephen Schloesser, "Against Forgetting: Memory, History, Vatican II," *Theological Studies* 67, no. 2 (June 1, 2006).

2 *Romano Pontifici Eligendo* was Pope Paul VI's 1975 reform of the way the church elected Popes. Besides banning voting by cardinals over the age of eighty, it instituted other rules that governed the pre-conclave gathering (cardinals should not do any politicking but were allowed to get together for permissible "consultations"). *Eligendo* also set new features for the conclave itself, such as boarding up all windows in the Sistine Chapel (John Paul II abolished that unpopular change in 1996). And although Paul VI had given away the Pope's triple tiara crown, *Eligendo* left it up to the successor Popes as to whether they wanted a coronation. John Paul II also eliminated that option in 1996, saying that it was "wrong" since it was "a symbol of the temporal power of the Popes." See http://www.vatican.va/holy_father/paul_vi/apost_constitutions/documents/hf_p-vi_apc_19751001_romano-pontifici-eligendo_it.html. See also Hebblethwaite, *The Year of Three Popes*, 4–5.

3 Thomas and Morgan-Witts, *Pontiff*, 97. Kelly, *The Oxford Dictionary of Popes*, 326.

4 Thomas and Morgan-Witts, *Pontiff*, 106. Sometimes it appeared the extra time might be necessary just to educate cardinals who had never before participated in a conclave. Traditionalists grimaced when St. Louis's Cardinal John Carberry told American reporters, "This is my first conclave. I don't have a clue as to how we go about it. I don't even know if we have roundtable discussions or not. I don't know now, and when I come out I'll have taken an oath of secrecy so I won't be able to tell you." Adding to the irritation of some in Rome, Carberry also was widely quoted for speculating it might be time for an American Pope. "The Italians have been at this job for years." "Cardinal Unsure on Rules," *The Boston Globe*, August 10, 1978, 18.

5 Pope Paul VI had modified the conclave election rules in 1975. They had been established by Pope Alexander III in 1179, then amended for modern elections first by Pius XII (December 1945), and then John XXIII (October 1962). See also "115 Cardinals to Vote for Pope," *Boston Globe*, August 7, 1978.

6 Hebblethwaite, *The Year of Three Popes*, 41.

7 Thomas and Morgan-Witts, *Pontiff*, 104; see also Victor L. Simpson, "Today's Topic: Inside the Conclave," Associated Press, Vatican City, P.M. cycle, August 8, 1978. By the time the conclave got under way, Monsignor Macchi had left the Vatican for a small seminary, taking with him "several truckloads" of personal effects accumulated over the years, including "works of art" he had acquired. See generally Hoffman, *Anatomy of the Vatican*, 149.

8 Cibin's official title was Inspector General of the Corpo della Gendarmeria.

9 See generally about security concerns in Thomas and Morgan-Witts, *Pontiff*, 134, 173.

10 Thomas and Morgan-Witts, *Pontiff*, 134, 172–73; see also Aidan Lewis and Jim Krane, "New Challenge for Papal Conclave: Feast of Spy Technology for Prying Eyes and Ears," *International News*, Vatican City, Associated Press, April 11, 2005.

11 Harry F. Waters and Loren Jenkins, "Cardinal Candidates," *Newsweek*, August 21, 1978, 50. See also Hebblethwaite, *The Year of Three Popes*, 45–46.

12 Waters and Jenkins "Cardinal Candidates." The Secretariat for Non-Christians was subsequently renamed the Congregation for the Evangelization of Peoples.

13 Tammy Oaks, "Bookmakers Lay Odds on New Pope," CNN, April 19, 2005, http://www.cnn.com/2005/WORLD/europe/04/18/pope.betting.

14 Henry Tanner, "Election to Be Held," *The New York Times*, August 7, 1978, A1.

15 Associated Press, Vatican City, *The Boston Globe*, October 13, 1978, 2.

16 David Browne, "Ladbrokes Regret but Carry On Taking Bets," *Catholic Herald* (UK), August 11, 1978, 5.

17 When a Labour MP, Simon Mahon, publicly condemned the betting and asked Ladbrokes to stop, a spokesman for the London-based bookmakers refused: "There are a number of precedents for this sort of betting. We opened books on the new Archbishop of Canterbury in 1974 and on the Archbishop of Westminster in 1976 without any trouble. And this week the newspapers are full of speculation about 'frontrunners,' 'contenders,' 'outsiders' and so on. All that we are doing

is putting prices to the prospects in a sporting way. . . . I am sorry if we have given any offense." Ladbrokes has continued the tradition unabated since introducing it in 1978.

18 Thomas and Morgan-Witts, *Pontiff*, 149.

19 For a detailed breakdown of the votes by ballots, based on a number of sources that subsequently spoke to reporters, see Hebblethwaite, *The Year of Three Popes*, 81–82.

20 Among the changes that Paul VI instituted for the eighty-second conclave was a rule that if the cardinals did not come to an agreement in three days, they would be forced to take a day off for prayer and contemplation before voting again.

21 In 2012, on the anniversary of what would have been the one hundredth birthday of Luciani, his former priest secretary, Father Diego Lorenzi, gave an hour radio interview on Sat2000, the network of Italian bishops. Lorenzi tried downplaying that Luciani was such a long shot, claiming instead that the cardinal himself knew there was much talk about him before the vote. But no matter what Luciani thought his odds, it is clear his colleagues did not expect him to be a contender. See generally John L. Allen, Jr., "Debunking Four Myths About John Paul I, the 'Smiling Pope,'" *National Catholic Reporter*, November 2, 2012.

22 Hebblethwaite, *The Year of Three Popes*, 63–64, 79–80.

23 Kelly, *Oxford Dictionary of Popes*, 325. Although he had some minor health issues, including occasional bouts of asthma, and was hobbled by phlebitis, a painful circulatory condition, those were not an obstacle to his election. None of the cardinals, especially the older ones, were free of health problems. Luciani's blood pressure was not made better by the fact that he was a constant worrier. "Pope Had a History of Minor Illnesses," *The Milwaukee Journal*, September 29, 1988, 1. A month into his Papacy, at a public blessing of the infirm, the Pope offered them some solace by talking about his own health: "I wish you to know that your Pope understands and loves you very much. You perhaps do not know that your Pope has been eight times to the hospital and has undergone four operations." The hospital visits had been twice for gallstones, once for an eye infection, and another time to set a broken nose. Watson, Loren, et al., "A Death in Rome," 70.

24 Hebblethwaite, *The Year of Three Popes*, citing the pastoral letter of Cardinal Joseph Höffner, 77.

25 The Roman numerals that are part of any modern Pope's name were used for the first time by Gregory III in 731, and didn't become a firm rule until the eleventh century. Before Gregory, if a Pope took the same name as a predecessor, the appellation *junior* was used. If a name was used a third time, it became *secundus junior*. See Philippe Levillain, *The Papacy: An Encyclopedia* (Oxford: Routledge, 2002), 1065. As for the first original name in one thousand years, see Associated Press, Vatican City, *The Boston Globe*, August 27, 1978, 1; Kelly, *The Oxford Dictionary of Popes*, 121.

26 William Tuohy, "The 263d Pope: John Paul I: The Man A Career Shaped by Simplicity," *The Boston Globe*, August 27, 1978, 1; Thomas and Morgan-Witts, *Pontiff*, 217.

27 His father's first wife had died, leaving him with two young daughters, both deaf mutes. "Whence Albino Luciani," Reuters, *The Boston Globe*, August 28, 1978, 11; Raymond and Lauretta Seabeck, *The Smiling Pope: The Life and Teachings of John Paul I* (Huntington, IN: Our Sunday Visitor Publishing, 1988), 11.

28 "Whence Albino Luciani," Reuters, *The Boston Globe*, 11. See also Hebblethwaite, *The Year of Three Popes*, 89–90.

29 Luciani's first seminary rector was later interviewed by Kay Withers, a *Chicago Tribune* reporter. When she asked if the youngster showed any interest in girls, the rector told her none at all since he was enrolled in the seminary. "Well, did he have any interest in boys?" Withers asked. "Well, the priest almost died," Marcinkus later recalled. Handwritten notes by Philip Willan of audio-taped interviews between John Cornwell and Marcinkus, February 8, 1988, 11a, provided to author courtesy of Willan.

30 Seabeck, *The Smiling Pope*, 20; "Whence Albino Luciani," Reuters, *Boston Globe*, 11; Official Vatican summary, "Highlights of the Life of His Holiness John Paul I," http://www.vatican.va/holy_father/john_paul_i/biography/documents/hf_jp-i_bio_01021997_biography_en.html.

31 His thesis was "The Origin of the Human Soul According to Antonio Rosmini-Serbati" (a nineteenth-century priest and philosopher). Hebblethwaite, *The Year of Three Popes*, 91–92.

32 Seabeck, *The Smiling Pope*, 22; "A Product of Italy's Countryside," Associated Press, Vatican City, A.M. cycle, August 27, 1978.

33 Hebblethwaite, *The Year of Three Popes*, 97–99.

34 "A Product of Italy's Countryside," Associated Press.

35 Tuohy, "The 263d Pope: John Paul I: The Man A Career Shaped by Simplicity," 1; see also Kelly, *Oxford Dictionary of Popes*, 325.
36 Bernard Nossiter, "The Election: Cardinal Luciani, Patriarch of Venice," *The Boston Globe*, August 27, 1978, 1.
37 Hebblethwaite, *The Year of Three Popes*, 112–13.
38 Watson, et al., "A Death in Rome," 70.
39 Hebblethwaite, *The Year of Three Popes*, 42; see also Waters and Jenkins, "Cardinal Candidates."
40 Marcinkus quoted in Gurwin, *The Calvi Affair*, 20, 21.
41 The date is determined as seventy-five years from the death of John Paul I.
42 "Pope's Popularity Helps Improve Financial Situation at Vatican," Vatican City, Associated Press, August 25, 1979, citing a peak of $15 million in Peter's Pence at end of John XXIII's Papacy to only $4 million by the time Paul VI died fifteen years later. In contrast, more than halfway through the Papacy of the popular John Paul II, Peter's Pence was a robust $67 million in 1992. Reese, *Inside the Vatican*, 225.
43 Thomas and Morgan-Witts, *Pontiff*, 231, 233–34.
44 The charter is cited at *Acta Apostolicae Sedis*, 8 (1942), Chirographus, 1.
45 "Russian Prelate Dies During Papal Audience," *The Boston Globe*, September 6, 1978, 66; "Deaths," *Newsweek*, September 18, 1978, 93; Edward Magri, "Today's Focus: The 34 Days," Associated Press, A.M. cycle, September 29, 1978. Thomas and Morgan-Witts, *Pontiff*, 236–37.
46 Hebblethwaite, *The Year of Three Popes*, 126–27.
47 There was nothing sinister about the decision not to perform an autopsy since it was a firm policy in the Russian Orthodox faith. Italian law requires a postmortem in the case of a sudden unexplained death in which the deceased person had not recently seen a physician. But the sovereign Vatican had no such rule, and avoided at all times autopsies of its own prelates who died inside the confines of the city-state. For a general discussion of how autopsies are treated differently by various religions, see Walter E. Finkbeiner, Philip C. Ursell, and Richard L. Davis, *Autopsy Pathology: A Manual and Atlas* (Philadelphia: Saunders, 2009), 21. As for the number of Nikodim's previous heart attacks, it ranges in published accounts from two to five (Hilmi Toros, Associated Press, A.M. cycle, September 5, 1978).
48 Hoffman, *Anatomy of the Vatican*, 35.
49 Michael Dobbs, "Ukraine Prelate Predicts Legalization of Church; Gorbachev, Pope Expected to Find Accord," *The Washington Post*, November 29, 1989, A31. See generally John Koehler, *Spies in the Vatican: The Soviet Union's Cold War Against the Catholic Church* (New York: Pegasus, 2009).
50 Magri, "Today's Focus."
51 Cornwell, *A Thief in the Night*, 334.
52 Marcinkus interviewed in Cornwell, *A Thief in the Night*, 131–32.
53 Ibid., 138–39.
54 Magee interviewed in Cornwell, *A Thief in the Night*, 254.
55 Cornwell, *A Thief in the Night*, 85.
56 Marcinkus interviewed in ibid., 85, 138.
57 Shortly before Pope Paul's death, Canadian archbishop Édouard Gagnon had led a commission that tried to determine which parts of the Curia were redundant or in other cases were bloated and could be trimmed. That report was also waiting for the new Pope. See Hebblethwaite, *The Year of Three Popes*, 24–25, 42.
58 See generally Thomas and Morgan-Witts, *Pontiff*, 251.
59 Watson, et. al., "A Death in Rome," 70.
60 Luciani quoted in Hebblethwaite, *The Year of Three Popes*, 127.
61 Marcinkus interviewed in Cornwell, *A Thief in the Night*, 79.
62 Hebblethwaite, *The Year of Three Popes*, 103–04.
63 Seabeck, *The Smiling* Pope, 70. In a way similar to how Pascalina and Pope Pius XII had been the subject of rumors, so were Luciani and Sister Vincenza. She not only had regular access to the new Pontiff, but he had told his aides that in the case of an emergency, she was the one who had permission to first enter his room. Curialists spent hours dissecting what she said, whether or not she helped write his finely honed speeches, and how he included her in discussions he held over meals. During her first weeks at the Vatican she had set about bringing color into the monotonous beige and gray that was the trademark of Paul's contemporary decor. There was little doubt that

Vincenza had influence with Luciani. The question was how much and how best she could be dealt with.

64 "Pope Had a History of Minor Illnesses," 1; see also Paul Hoffman, *The Vatican's Women: Female Influence at the Holy See* (New York: St. Martin's, 2002), Kindle edition, location 2091 of 2992; see also Cornwell, *A Thief in the Night*, 187.

65 Magee interviewed in Cornwell, *A Thief in the Night*, 234–35. Lorenzi, a member of the Sons of Divine Providence (Orione Fathers), served as Luciani's private secretary for two years in Venice before moving with him to Rome after the conclave.

66 Sister Irma interviewed in Cornwell, *A Thief in the Night*, 215.

67 Lorenzi interviewed in Cornwell, *A Thief in the Night*, 110; recounted in Thomas and Morgan-Witts, *Pontiff*, 258–59.

68 Lorenzi interviewed in Cornwell, *A Thief in the Night*, 247–48; Hutchison, *Their Kingdom Come*, 253–54; Thomas and Morgan-Witts, *Pontiff*, 259.

69 Buzzonetti and Magee interviewed in Cornwell, *A Thief in the Night*, 220, 247; see also Christopher Hudson, "20 years ago this week John Paul I died after 33 days as Pope. Now even one of his own cardinals says he may have been poisoned," *Daily Mail* (London), August 27, 1998, 11. Also Seabeck, *The Smiling Pope*, 70.

70 Recounted in Thomas and Morgan-Witts, *Pontiff*, 258–60. Sister Vincenza only was interviewed twice, once by a fellow nun, Sister Irma, and another time by author David Yallop. She died on June 28, 1983.

71 Magee later recalled two other nuns coming to get him, but it was evidently Vincenza, with the other nuns arriving moments later. See Cornwell, *A Thief in the Night*, 247.

72 Magee interviewed in Cornwell, *A Thief in the Night*, 248.

73 Ibid.; see also Thomas and Morgan-Witts, *Pontiff*, 260. The death of John Paul, on his thirty-fourth day, marked his Papacy as the seventh shortest in church history. Pope Stephen II died only three days after his selection in 752; both Marcellus II, in 1555, and Urban VII, in 1590, died after thirteen days as Pope; Boniface VI's Papacy was fifteen days in 896; Leo XI served seventeen days in 1605; and Theodore II twenty days in 897.

74 "He [Villot] used to take a walk every day with John Paul I," Marcinkus later recalled. "He was destroyed [by the Pope's death]." Handwritten notes by Philip Willan of audiotaped interviews between John Cornwell and Marcinkus, February 8, 1988, 10b, provided to author courtesy of Willan.

75 "Cardinal Villot, Holder of Vatican's Second Highest Post," *The Boston Globe*, March 10, 1979, 15; Buzzonetti interviewed in Cornwell, *A Thief in the Night*, 219.

76 Lorenzi interviewed in Cornwell, *A Thief in the Night*, 104.

77 John Julius Norwich, "Was Pope John Paul I Murdered?," *The Daily Mail*, May 7, 2011. Aside from that, and an interview with the Associated Press a few days later, Dr. da Ros later declined all interviews, citing doctor-patient confidentiality. As a result, it is not clear what type of exam he had conducted with Luciani just a week before his death. The question asked most often by other doctors—and still unanswered—was if da Ros had performed an electrocardiogram, which would have given a good snapshot of the state of the Pontiff's heart. See generally "Doctor Warned John Paul of Stress," Associated Press, Vatican City, P.M. cycle, October 4, 1978. See also "Pope Had a History of Minor Illnesses," *The Milwaukee Journal*, 1.

78 Da Ros quoted in Untitled, Hilmi Toros, dateline Vatican City, A.M. cycle, *Associated Press*, October 16, 1978.

79 Cornwell, *A Thief in the Night*, 249.

80 Norwich, "Was Pope John Paul I Murdered?"; see also John Julius Norwich, *The Popes: A History* (London: Chatto & Windus, 2011).

81 Victor L. Simpson, Associated Press, Vatican City, A.M. cycle, September 29, 1978.

82 Russell Watson, Loren Jenkins, Paul Martin, and Elaine Sciolino, "A Death in Rome," *Newsweek*, October 9, 1978, 70; Cornwell, *A Thief in the Night*, 244; Untitled, dateline Canale D'Agordo, Italy, P.M. cycle, Associated Press, September 29, 1978; Untitled, Dennis Redmont, dateline Vatican City, P.M. cycle, Associated Press, September 29, 1978; "The Original Engelbert," *Irish Daily Mail*, October 19, 2012, 38.

83 Buzzonetti interviewed in Cornwell, *A Thief in the Night*, 218.

84 Lorenzi interviewed in Cornwell, *A Thief in the Night*, 111.

85 Claiborne, "Thousands Mourn Pope's Death," A1.

86 Villot quoted in Thomas and Morgan-Witts, *Pontiff,* 263; see also Hoffman, *The Vatican's Women,* Kindle edition, location 2091 of 2992; and Sister Irma interviewed in Cornwell, *A Thief in the Night,* 215.

87 Magee interviewed in Cornwell, *A Thief in the Night,* 249.

88 Hoffman, *The Vatican's Women,* Kindle edition, location 2077 of 2992; see also Thomas and Morgan-Witts, *Pontiff,* 263.

89 In a two-page "Vatican Memorandum Supplied to Episcopal Conference, dated 1984," the Vatican played down the significance of who first found the Pope. "While it makes no difference whether the Pope was found dead by a sister, or, as the Vatican communiqué said, by the private secretary of the Pontiff, in fact, the secretary instantly ran to the bedside of Pope John Paul I when he was summoned by the sister who suspected that something might be wrong." The 1984 Vatican memo is reprinted in English in Cornwell, *A Thief in the Night,* 347–48.

90 Ibid., 196, 201.

91 Pope Paul VI was an avid fan of British novelist Graham Greene, and even arranged a meeting with him. Marcinkus recalled that Greene "almost dropped dead" when the Pope told him he had read "every one of your books." The Vatican ensured that the news of Paul VI's popular cultural preferences was never publicized. Handwritten notes by Philip Willan of audiotaped interviews between John Cornwell and Marcinkus, January 15, 1988, 1a, provided to author courtesy of Willan. See also Farusi interviewed in Cornwell, *A Thief in the Night,* 202–3; in the "Vatican Memorandum Supplied to Episcopal Conference, dated 1984," it was emphasized that "No *official* document ever mentioned it [the *Imitation of Christ*]." Cornwell, *A Thief in the Night,* 347–48. For an example of how the story ran internationally, see "Book a 15-Century Work," *The Boston Globe,* September 30, 1978, 9.

Twenty-five years after the event, Lorenzi told the *National Catholic Reporter*'s John L. Allen Jr. that the papers in John Paul's hand were some notes from his days as the Patriarch of Venice, which he was reviewing in preparation for the next Sunday sermon. "I'd like to know how anyone can say anything different," Lorenzi told Allen. "Who else was there? Only we [Lorenzi, Magee, and Vincenza] were there." John L. Allen Jr., "Lessons from a 33-Day Pontificate: John Paul I's Secretary Reminisces on the Man and His Life," *National Catholic Reporter,* September 5, 2003.

92 Arnaldo Signoracci interviewed in Cornwell, *A Thief in the Night,* 271. The Signoraccis, who claimed to use their own secret formula based on formaldehyde, considered John XXIII their finest work. His coffin was opened in 2001, thirty-eight years after his death, in order to move his remains from the crowded crypt in St. Peter's to a new tomb in the basilica above. The body was still perfectly preserved. The Signoracci business was closed in 2002 after the death of the last brother, Renato. At the time, *La Repubblica* noted it was ironic that John Paul II, then eighty-one and in the twenty-fourth year of his Papacy, had outlived the Papal embalmers.

93 Cornwell, *A Thief in the Night,* 283–85.

94 Arnaldo and Ernesto Signoracci interviewed in Cornwell, *A Thief in the Night,* 272–73, 275.

95 Thomas and Morgan-Witts, *Pontiff,* 263; unidentified Curial monsignor quoted in Cornwell, *A Thief in the Night,* 52.

96 Although Vatican entry logs show the morticians arrived that morning, the eyewitnesses to the traumatic event do not always recall it correctly. A decade later, Monsignor Lorenzi told John Cornwell that he did not remember the Signoracci brothers arriving until the evening. He then recounted that he, Villot and Dr. Buzzonetti had laid out the body. In fact, the morticians did that. As for the Signoraccis, when Cornwell interviewed them a decade later, they could not remember precisely when they got to the Vatican. Ernesto said, "It could have been at seven in the morning . . . it could have been ten in the morning . . . or at three in the afternoon, I don't know."

97 Arnaldo Signoracci interviewed in Cornwell, *A Thief in the Night,* 278; Thomas and Morgan-Witts, *Pontiff,* 263.

98 Ernesto Signoracci interviewed in Cornwell, *A Thief in the Night,* 275–77.

99 Evan Whitton, "The Road to Rome," *Sydney Morning Herald,* November 22, 1986, 41; Norwich, "Was Pope John Paul I Murdered?" The medication that was later confirmed as having been in the room was Effortil, an analeptic used to stabilize blood pressure, and often prescribed in instances of persistent low blood pressure. See also Watson, et. al., "A Death in Rome," 70. As for the missing pages in the records of the Vatican pharmacy, see Cornwell's interview with Brothers Fabian and Augusto in *A Thief in the Night,* 312–13.

"He [Pope John] had no medical attention throughout his brief pontificate." Peter Hebblethwaite, "Death of a Rumour," *The Spectator*, June 16, 1989, 30.

100 Associated Press, Vatican City, A.M. cycle, September 29, 1978. For the way the press release by the Vatican was placed into full news coverage, see generally "Pope John Paul Dies in Sleep: Succumbs to Heart Attack After Month in Office," Associated Press, *The Boston Globe*, September 29, 1978, 1.

101 Paul Hoffman, "Bungling and Surmises," *The New York Times*, July 8, 1984, BR32. When Villot died of "acute bronchial pneumonia" at age seventy-three the following March, he was in Gemelli Hospital. He had been admitted two days earlier. But that did not stop his own death from being the subject of false speculation inside the Curia. An unnamed monsignor told John Cornwell that the "real" story was that Villot "collapsed outside the Vatican and got taken to the Gemelli. The Vatican people rushed around and snatched the body. . . . They pretended the corpse was still alive, took it back to the Vatican, and said he died holily in bed." Unnamed monsignor interviewed in Cornwell, *A Thief in the Night*, 96.

102 "Catholic Group Calls for Inquest into John Paul's Sudden Death," *The Globe and Mail* (Canada), October 4, 1978.

103 Thomas and Morgan-Witts, *Pontiff*, 269.

104 Magee interviewed in Cornwell, *A Thief in the Night*, 251, 253.

105 Ibid., 253.

106 Thomas and Morgan-Witts, *Pontiff*, 269; see generally Sandra Miesel, "A Quiet Death in Rome: Was Pope John Paul I Murdered," *Crisis Magazine*, April 1, 2009.

107 Obituary: "Archbishop Romeo Panciroli: Ponderous Vatican Press Officer," *The Independent* (London), March 21, 2006, http://www.independent.co.uk/news/obituaries/archbishop-romeo-panciroli-470769.html.

108 Thomas and Morgan-Witts, *Pontiff*, 270.

109 Cardinal Felici spent the next two days combing through the Secret Archives to see if he might find any precedent for a postmortem exam. He discovered that in the diary of Agostino Chigi, heir to a Renaissance banking family, there was an entry that a secret autopsy had been conducted on Pius VIII, a day after his November 30, 1816, death. Pius died at the age of sixty-nine, after eighteen months as Pope. The purpose had been to see if his organs showed any evidence he had been poisoned (he had not). Thomas and Morgan-Witts, *Pontiff*, 271, 277–79.

110 Whitton, "The Road to Rome," 41; see also Thomas and Morgan-Witts, *Pontiff*, 272.

111 Article 17 of Pope Paul VI's Apostolic Constitution implicitly ruled out any autopsy since the only official method approved for certifying the death of a Pontiff is for the Camerlengo to confirm the death in the presence of witnesses and to then draw a death certificate. Some news accounts incorrectly reported that an autopsy was explicitly banned. See for instance, Watson, et al., "A Death in Rome," 70: "[t]he papal constitution forbids autopsies for popes."

112 Sari Gilbert, "Some Wonder Why No Autopsy on Pope," *The Boston Globe*, October 2, 1978, 2. One of Italy's preeminent surgeons, Dr. Pier Luigi Prati, told reporters for *La Stampa* and the Associated Press that it was possible that Pope John Paul died of a heart attack. "But it also could have been a cerebral hemorrhage. . . . In order to ascertain this, an autopsy would be necessary." Dennis Redmont, Associated Press, Vatican City, A.M. cycle, September 30, 1978.

113 Lorenzi interviewed in Cornwell, *A Thief in the Night*, 111–12.

114 Ernesto Signoracci interviewed in Cornwell, *A Thief in the Night*, 277. The Signoraccis were not paid for their services. "Absolutely nothing, only medals," Arnaldo later recalled. "They made us [a] Knight of Gregory, with a diploma and that sort of thing," confirmed Ernesto. Arnaldo and Ernesto Signoracci interviewed in Cornwell, *A Thief in the Night*, 279.

115 Hilmi Toros, Associated Press, Vatican City, A.M. cycle, October 2, 1978.

116 Signoracci interviewed in Cornwell, *A Thief in the Night*, 272.

117 Jose Torres, Associated Press, Rome, P.M. cycle, October 6, 1978. For Pope Paul VI and his comment on Satan entering the Vatican, see Donald R. McCleary, "Pope Paul VI and the Smoke of Satan," *An American Catholic*, December 4, 2011.

118 Gilbert, "Some Wonder Why No Autopsy on Pope," 2.

119 Thomas and Morgan-Witts, *Pontiff*, 283.

120 The Vatican decided at that point not to make records related to John Paul's death available for any independent review. Author John Cornwell was refused in 1988 access to any documentation

about the Pope's passing, from his death certificate to medical records to his will. The author's own requests for such materials twenty-five years later went unanswered.

As for *In God's Name*, by David Yallop, the book that later claimed the Pope was poisoned, the fact that many critics trashed it did not prevent it from becoming a bestseller. Steve Weinberg, the editor of Investigative Reporters and Editors, wrote in the Balitmore *Sun*, "The shame of publishing: truth is of no concern; neither factual accuracy nor overall truthfulness is taken seriously by many book publishers" (Steve Weinberg, "The Shame of Publishing," Baltimore *Sun*, August 2, 1998, p. 11F). In a meticulous deconstruction in the *Columbia Journalism Review*, Weinberg called it "the Kitty Kelley syndrome," and noted that Yallop's book "proved none of its fantastic claims," and had no source notes or bibliography (Steve Weinberg, "The Kitty Kelley Syndrome; Why You Can't Always Trust What You Read in Books," *Columbia Journalism Review* 30, no. 2 [July/August 1991]: 36). The *Chicago Tribune* said *In God's Name* "was so conspiratorial that it bordered on the ludicrous," and that although Yallop "fudged his sources," and that "despite savage reviews, repeated Vatican denunciations and bewilderment and outrage by people Yallop claimed to have interviewed," book sales had soared (Peter Former and John Blades, "Fiction Passing as Fact Fuels a Crisis in Print," *Chicago Tribune*, May 5, 1985, p. C1].

121 David Yallop, *In God's Name: An Investigation Into the Murder of Pope John Paul I*, 240–42, 289–92; Cornwell, *A Thief in the Night*, 313–25. See also George Rush and Joanna Molloy, for church comments regarding *In God's Name*, see generally Untitled, dateline Vatican City, International News, A.M. cycle, Associated Press, June 12, 1984. "Elton John's Movie Plans Provoke Vatican's Wrath," *The Toronto Star*, February 17, 1999.

In 2014, a successful play about foul play in John Paul's death titled *The Last Confession* kicked off an international tour in Toronto. "*The Last Confession* Probes Papal Death, Vatican Intrigue," *CBC News*, April 19, 2014.

122 Martin, *Final Conclave*; Thomas and Morgan-Witts, *Pontiff*, 295.
123 Thomas and Morgan-Witts, *Pontiff*, 309.
124 They included Madrid's Vicente Enrique y Tarancón, Samoa's Pio Taofinu'u, Holland's Johannes Willebrands, England's Basil Hume, and São Paulo's Paulo Evaristo Arns.
125 Malula quoted in "A Foreign Pope," *Time*, October 30, 1978.
126 Günther Simmermacher, "Electing a Pope: The Conclave of October 1978," *The Southern Cross*, March 7, 2013; see also Hebblethwaite, *The Year of Three Popes*, 152.
127 König interviewed in George Weigel, *Witness to Hope: The Biography of Pope John Paul II* (New York: Cliff Street, 1999), 253.
128 Author interview with Andrew Greeley, May 11, 2007.
129 Simmermacher, "Electing a Pope: The Conclave of October 1978"; Thomas and Morgan-Witts, *Pontiff*, 313–14.
130 Hebblethwaite, *The Year of Three Popes*, 153.
131 Whitton, "The Road to Rome," 41; see also Thomas and Morgan-Witts, *Pontiff*, 314–16.
132 Wojtyla quoted in Thomas and Morgan-Witts, *Pontiff*, 319.
133 Simmermacher, "Electing a Pope: The Conclave of October 1978"; Whitton, "The Road to Rome," 41.
134 Cardinal Hume quoted in Hebblethwaite, *The Year of Three Popes*, 156.
135 He was a moderate by the standards of the church's six Eastern European cardinals, but considered somewhat of a conservative by Western standards.
136 Ronald Koven, "Cardinal Wojtyla of Poland Breaks Line of Italian Popes," *The Washington Post*, October 17, 1978, A1.
137 Weigel, *Witness to Hope*, 254.

Chapter 21: The Backdoor Deal

1 Weigel, *Witness to Hope*,16, 23. His mother's family came from Silesia, and his father served in the Austro-Hungarian army. That meant Wojtyla's second language at home was German. Hebblethwaite, *Pope John Paul II and the Church*, 260.
2 Edward Stourton, *John Paul II: Man of History* (London: Hodder & Stoughton, 2006), 25; Weigel, *Witness to Hope*; see also Hebblethwaite, *The Year of Three Popes*, 157–60.

3 Official biography [short] of John Paul II, Holy See Press Office, last updated June 30, 2005.
4 Weigel, *Witness to Hope*, 44.
5 Years later he bemoaned that he had not been present for the death of either of his parents or for a brother who died during the war. "At twenty, I had already lost all the people I loved." See generally Stourton, *John Paul II: Man of History*, 60. As for Kraków's Black Sunday, see generally Norman Davies, *Rising '44: The Battle for Warsaw* (London: Viking, 2004), 253–55.
6 See "When Karol Wojtyla Refused to Baptize an Orphan," *Zenit*, January 18, 2005, online at http://www.zenit.org/en/articles/when-karol-wojtyla-refused-to-baptize-an-orphan.
7 Patricia Rice, "They Call Him 'Wujek,'" *St. Louis Post-Dispatch*, January 24, 1999, 18.
8 Hebblethwaite, *The Year of Three Popes*, 165-66.
9 Whitton, "The Road to Rome," 41.
10 Ibid., citing National Foreign Assessment Center report for the CIA, 59.
11 Koehler, *Spies in the Vatican*, 257.
12 Thomas and Morgan-Witts, *Pontiff*, 347.
13 See Lai, *Finanze vaticane*, 149.
14 Thomas and Morgan-Witts, *Pontiff*, 348.
15 Marcinkus was raised in a household in which Lithuanian was his first language. His parents spoke it exclusively at home. He also studied it at school. Handwritten notes by Philip Willan of audiotaped interviews between John Cornwell and Marcinkus, January 15, 1988, 1b, provided to author courtesy of Willan. "Marcinkus spoke good Polish": Curzio Maltese, in collaboration with Carlo Pontesilli and Maurizio Turco, "Scandal, Intrigue and Mystery; The Secrets of the Vatican Bank," translated by Graeme A. Hunter, *La Repubblica*, January 26, 2008.
16 The shrine was located in Doylestown, Pennsylvania, a suburb about thirty miles from Philadelphia; in the U.S. the monastic order is referred to as the Pauline Fathers, but in Poland the 770-year-old sect is known officially as the Order of St. Paul the First Hermit.
17 Gannett was awarded a 1980 Pulitzer for Public Service for its investigative series. It also resulted in a $110 million libel suit by the former father superior of the Pauline shrine. That lawsuit was dismissed.
18 The first signs of something amiss came up after a routine 1972 audit conducted by the Philadelphia diocese. See generally Ben A. Franklin, "Cover-Up Alleged in Monastic Scandal," *The New York Times*, September 21, 1979, 14; "Pope Reportedly Blocked Investigation of Pauline Father's Financial Dealings," *The Washington Post*, September 10, 1979, A3.
19 Vatican report cited in "Pope Reportedly Blocked Investigation of Pauline Father's Financial Dealings," *The Washington Post*, A3. See also "Vatican Refuses to Comment," *Observer-Reporter* (Pennsylvania), September 11, 1979, A7.
20 "Gannett Sued for $110 Million," Associated Press, Domestic News, New York, P.M. cycle, September 16, 1980; see also "Catholic Order's Squandering of Millions in Contributions, Loan, Investments Alleged," *The Blade* (Ohio), September 10, 1979, 8.
21 "Pope Reportedly Blocked Investigation of Pauline Father's Financial Dealings," *The Washington Post.*
22 Untitled, Associated Press, Washington, A.M. cycle, September 10, 1979.
23 Franklin, "Cover-Up Alleged in Monastic Scandal," 14.
24 Untitled, Associated Press, Washington, A.M. cycle, September 10, 1979; see also Franklin, "Cover-Up Alleged in Monastic Scandal."
25 "Probe of Monks Cites Kickbacks," *Pittsburgh Post-Gazette*, September 11, 1979, 3; Untitled, Associated Press, Washington, A.M. cycle, September 10, 1979.
26 Untitled, Associated Press, Washington, A.M. cycle, September 10, 1979.
27 Untitled, Associated Press, Washington, A.M. cycle, September 9, 1979; see also "Pope Reportedly Blocked Investigation of Pauline Father's Financial Dealings," *The Washington Post.*
28 "Pope Reportedly Blocked Investigation of Pauline Father's Financial Dealings," *The Washington Post.*
29 Franklin, "Cover-Up Alleged in Monastic Scandal"; untitled, Associated Press, Washington, P.M. cycle, September 10, 1979.
30 Untitled, Associated Press, Washington, A.M. cycle, September 11, 1979.
31 Cardinal Krol personally oversaw the distribution of the funds through his own diocese so the source of the money appeared to be from Philadelphia as opposed to Rome. The order of payments was determined with the assistance of attorneys from the Philadelphia law firm of Eastburn &

Gray. A fundraising drive among the faithful—"to honor their Polish ancestors"—to pay some of the Pauline debts raised some $2 million. The author could not determine if that money was returned to Marcinkus and the IOR. Francesco Pazienza recounting contemporaneous conversations with Marcinkus, interview with author, September 18, 2013. See also Untitled, Associated Press, Domestic News, Camden, NJ, A.M. cycle, September 12, 1979. "When Marcinkus made it go away quickly he had earned the immediate loyalty of John Paul," said Francesco Pazienza.

32 Willan, *The Last Supper*, 177-78, citing in part Pazienza's autobiography, *Il Disubbidient* (Milan: Longanesi, 1990).

33 See generally Roy Larson, "In the 1980's, a Chicago Newspaper Investigated Cardinal Cody," *Niemen Reports*, The Niemen Foundation for Journalism at Harvard, spring 2003; John Conroy, "Cardinal Sins," *Chicago Reader*, June 4, 1987.

34 See generally about Vienna's Cardinal König aware of the KGB's Department D; Thomas and Morgan-Witts, *Pontiff*, 265–66.

35 Author interview with Francesco Pazienza, September 22, 2013.

36 Willey, *God's Politicians*, 234.

37 The letter is undated except that on page 1 it has a time stamp "March 23, 1979." It was passed to Marcinkus on March 26, 1979, by P. Peter Sarros, a Deputy Presidential Envoy to the Vatican. See Letter from P. Peter Sarros, Deputy Presidential Envoy, to Bishop Marcinkus, March 26, 1979, with handwritten notation in the upper-right-hand corner of the one-page cover note "Rcd 26-3-79 BM." The Sarros letter included a three-page attached telex. That attachment is the same as the contents of the letter from Benjamin R. Civiletti, Deputy Attorney General, Department of Justice, to Bishop Paul C. Marcinkus, President, Institute of Religious Works, date-stamped March 23, 1979, William A. Wilson Papers, Box 2, Folder 66, Georgetown University Library, Special Collections Research Center, Washington, D.C.

38 The accounts were opened in 1974 by Howard Mitnick, through a power of attorney of Ellis Shore, chairman of ATS. One account with $3.6 million was held in the name of RAE Advertising, a wholly owned ATS subsidiary, while the other, with $4.1 million, was in the name of another ATS subsidiary, Analysis and Research Associates. Letter from Benjamin R. Civiletti, Deputy Attorney General, Department of Justice, to Bishop Paul C. Marcinkus, President, Institute of Religious Works, date-stamped March 23, 1979, William A. Wilson Papers, William A. Wilson Papers: Box 2, Folder 66, Georgetown University Library, Special Collections Research Center, Washington, D.C.

39 Marcinkus incorrectly told Civiletti that the IOR was "an organization established by Pope Leo XIII to husband monies destined for religious works of the Church, all over the world." Leo XIII had began what was a generic predecessor organization, the Administration of Religious Works, but the IOR to which Marcinkus referred was started by Bernardino Nogara and Pope Pius XII in June 1942. See Letter from Paul C. Marcinkus to Benjamin R. Civiletti, April 3, 1979, William A. Wilson Papers, Box 2, Folder 66, Georgetown University Library, Special Collections Research Center, Washington, D.C.

40 Letter from Paul C. Marcinkus to Benjamin R. Civiletti, April 3, 1979, William A. Wilson Papers, Box 2, Folder 66, Georgetown University Library, Special Collections Research Center, Washington, D.C., 2.

41 The Vatican refused to allow the author to have access to any of the records of the IOR.

42 Letter from Paul C. Marcinkus to Benjamin R. Civiletti, April 24, 1979, William A. Wilson Papers, Box 2, Folder 66, Georgetown University Library, Special Collections Research Center, Washington, D.C.

43 Ibid.

44 Author interview with William Aronwald, February 16, 2007.

Chapter 22: "The Vatican Has Abandoned Me"

1 Galli, *Finanza bianca*, 83–84.

2 In discussing how the Bank of Italy uncovered that foreign corporations of unknown ownership, based primarily in Panama and Liechtenstein, had purchased large blocks of the Ambrosiano, the report concluded, "It cannot be excluded that the above mentioned purchasers could be part of the 'Ambrosiano group,' given the wide and uncontrollable possibilities for maneuver by banks and foreign financial affiliates, or of IOR."

3 This report was the culmination of the investigation that began in April 1978 when Bank of Italy inspectors had shown up unannounced at the Ambrosiano's headquarters. It was a probe kicked off by tips provided to the inspectors by Sindona. Neither Padalino, the chief inspector, nor anyone on his team was a P2 member. So when Calvi asked Licio Gelli for help, the P2 chief was of no assistance. See Cornwell, *God's Banker*, 91; Tosches, *Power on Earth*, 191.

4 Since the IOR was the central bank of a sovereign nation, the Bank of Italy had no jurisdiction over it. Instead, its investigation started and stopped with the Ambrosiano. Almost all questions about the Vatican's role were left unanswered. See Gurwin, *The Calvi Affair*, 41–43.

5 Sergio Bocconi, "Quelle missioni da Berlinguer e Craxi per i crediti del vecchio Ambrosiano," *Corriere della Sera*, October 26, 2007, 35.

6 Padalino Report excerpt quoted in Cornwell, *God's Banker*, 91.

7 Gurwin, *The Calvi Affair*, 41.

8 It is part of the Italian armed forces and is a policing authority under the Ministry of Economy and Finance.

9 See Cornwell, *God's Banker*, 96.

10 *L'Espresso* cited in Cornwell, *God's Banker*, 96; Raw, *The Moneychangers*, 272.

11 Henry Tanner, "Italian Prime Minister Defends Government's Record as Terrorism Rises: Communists Withdrew Support," *The New York Times*, January 30, 1979, A2.

12 "Parliament Is Cool to Andreotti Plea," *The Boston Globe*, January 30, 1979, 4; Henry Tanner, "Andreotti Resigns, Bringing Fears of Rise in Italian Terrorist Activity: Murder Is Linked to Politics," *The New York Times*, February 1, 1979, A3; Raw, *The Moneychangers*, 255.

The fact that Calvi was not involved in Alessandrini's death has not stopped some writers from reporting it as if it were somehow connected to a larger conspiracy: "Alessandrini could not be bought," wrote David Yallop in *In God's Name*. The investigating magistrate posed "a very serious threat . . . for Calvi, Marcinkus, Gelli and Sindona. . . . Something had to be done."

13 Tanner, "Andreotti Resigns, Bringing Fears of Rise in Italian Terrorist Activity: Murder Is Linked to Politics."

14 Raw, *The Moneychangers*, 255.

15 Ibid., 138, 272.

16 Gurwin, *The Calvi Affair*, 56.

17 Calvi ultimately completed the transfer of all his Latin American operations to Banco Ambrosiano Andino only four months after the Sandinistas defeated Somoza's army. See Raw, *The Moneychangers*, 265.

18 Gurwin, *The Calvi Affair*, 56, 58.

19 Marcinkus later claimed in a written submission to an Italian government investigating committee about the Ambrosiano that the transfer of the loans from United Trading to Andino had been "ordered and executed without the knowledge of the IOR." But the government investigators doubted that was true. Calvi had sent letters to Marcinkus on December 17, 1979, stating that the obligations of the IOR had been extended to Andino. Marcinkus later contended that letter was not sufficient notice to the Vatican Bank, but never to the complete satisfaction of the government probe. The Joint Investigating Committee submission by Marcinkus, cited in Raw, *The Moneychangers*, 266–67.

20 Raw, *The Moneychangers*, 263.

21 Sindona quoted in Lernoux, *In Banks We Trust*, 209.

22 Raw, *The Moneychangers*, 282, 284, 323.

23 Ibid., 214–16, 227–28, 261–62, 306–9.

24 Arnold H. Lubasch, "A Nixon Treasury Secretary Queried on $200,000 He Got from Sindona," *The New York Times*, January 23, 1979, B7. Kennedy eventually testified before the grand jury without a grant of immunity. There were questions as to whether Kennedy had broken the law by taking and not disclosing the short-term $200,000 loan from Sindona in 1974. Kennedy said he had used the money for a land development in Arizona, to which Sindona had no connection. Prosecutors also asked Kennedy about his service as a director at Sindona's Fasco holding company. No charges were filed against Kennedy. As for the Kennedy-Marcinkus friendship, see Simoni and Turone, *Il caffè di Sindona*, 34, 37. Also, Marcinkus talked to author John Cornwell about some "friends" in Chicago that introduced him to "people at Continental Bank." Kennedy became the chairman of that bank the same year Pope Paul VI appointed Marcinkus as the chief prelate of the IOR. The two men were good friends. See Marcinkus interviewed in Cornwell, *A*

Thief in the Night, 83; also Robert D. Hershey, Jr., "David Kennedy, Ex-Treasury Chief, Dies at 90," *The New York Times*, May 3, 1996.

25 Arnold H. Lubasch, "3 Former Officials of Franklin Bank Convicted of Fraud," *The New York Times*, January 24, 1979, A1. Harold Gleason had been the chairman, Paul Luftig the president, and J. Michael Carter the senior vice president.

26 Paul Serafini, Associated Press, Business News, New York, A.M. cycle, March 19, 1979; DiFonzo, *St. Peter's Banker*, 237.

27 "U.S. Indicts Sindona on Bank Role: U.S. Accuses Sindona of Fund Misappropriation," *The New York Times*, March 20, 1979, D1. The banks cited in the indictment were Banca Unione and Banca Finanziaria, which failed in 1974 but were merged into Sindona's new Banca Privata Italiana. See also "Gunshots and Persons Unknown," *The Economist*, October 6, 1979, 114; Parliamentary Commission of Inquiry into the Case of Sindona and Responsibilities and the Political and Administrative Connected To It, 63–77.

28 Robert Fiske Jr. quoted in "U.S. Indicts Sindona on Bank Role: U.S. Accuses Sindona of Fund Misappropriation," *The New York Times*. Robert Fiske, the U.S. Attorney, told the press within hours of filing the indictment that the case would not stop the extradition proceedings against Sindona. If the government prevailed in its effort to send him back to Italy, that deportation would be stayed pending an outcome on the American criminal charges.

29 Paul Serafini, Associated Press, Business News, New York, A.M. cycle, March 19, 1979. Eight days after the indictment, Thomas C. Platt Jr., the federal judge who had overseen each of the Franklin trials and was familiar with the facts of the different cases, disqualified himself from Sindona's case as the result of an uproar by defense lawyers over a joke he made in open court. The joke had actually been made the previous Halloween, but Sindona's attorneys did not use it as the basis for a recusal until their client was formally indicted. It was not possible to tell precisely what the joke was since Judge Platt sealed the transcript that contained it, but leaks from defense counsel indicated that it referred to the defenses by key Franklin executives as a "fairy tale." One of the most distinguished justices in the New York district courts, Jack B. Weinstein, took over the Sindona trial. See Robert J. Cole, "Judge Out in Sindona Bank Suit," *The New York Times*, March 29, 1979, D1.

30 Marcinkus interviewed in Cromwell, *A Thief in the Night*, 132.

31 Robert Suro, "Sindona Gets Life Term in Murder Case in Italy," *The New York Times*, March 19, 1986, D17.

32 Luigi DiFonzo, "Justifiable Homicide," *New York*, April 11, 1983, 31–32.

33 Parliamentary Commission of Inquiry into the Case of Sindona and Responsibilities and the Political and Administrative Connected To It, 37–40, 44.

34 Raw, *The Moneychangers*, 86. Ambrosoli demonstrated that Sindona did not use any of his own money to buy Franklin, but instead improperly used the proceeds of the Zitropo/Pachetti deal.

35 "Gunshots and Persons Unknown," *The Economist*, 114.

36 Ambrosoli Report cited in Raw, *The Moneychangers*, 87. See also Galli, *Finanza bianca*, 84; and Gurwin, *The Calvi Affair*, 45.

37 Alexander L. Taylor III, "Scandal at the Pope's Bank; Outside Experts Are Called in to Investigate Some Shady Financial Dealings," *Time*, July 26, 1982, 34; "Official Italian sources later confirmed that Ambrosoli was referring to Marcinkus and Calvi." Lernoux, *In Banks We Trust*, 187. Jennifer Parmelee, Untitled, Associated Press, International News, Rome, BC cycle, May 18, 1986. Sindona told *Newsweek* in 1982 that he had paid half that amount to Calvi's wife, but not any money to Marcinkus. It is doubtful Sindona told the truth. He was in prison in the U.S. at the time awaiting extradition to Italy. Sindona also denied to *Newsweek* that he had anything to do with the death of an Italian prosecuting magistrate, a case in which he was eventually convicted of ordering the murder. Harry Anderson with Rich Thomas in London and Rome and Hope Lamfert in New York, "Inside the Vatican Bank," *Newsweek*, September 13, 1982, 62.

38 Giacomo Vitale, the brother-in-law of Mafia don Stefano Bontade, was later identified as the caller; see judicial hearings, Palermo, December 18, 1997, and February 24, 1998, on the basis of the declarations made by collaborators of justice Angelo Tullio Siino and Cinnamon (Palermo Court, judgment of 23 October 1999 Andreotti, ch. VI, § 1, p. 1845ss).

39 Tosches, *Power on Earth*, 192.

40 Andrew Gumbel, "Obscure Magistrate Began Downfall of a Corrupt Generation," *The Independent* (London), March 23, 1995, p. 11; see Raw, *The Moneychangers*, 258; and Gurwin, *The Calvi Affair*, 45.

41 Sindona's U.S. trial was scheduled to start in September 1979 and the U.S. Attorney's Office hoped that Ambrosoli might have uncovered additional information to assist them. Raw, *The Moneychangers*, 258.
42 "Gunshots and Persons Unknown," 114.
43 Henry Tanner, "A Sindona Inquiry by Italian Parliament Gets Support," *The New York Times*, August 10, 1979, B3.
44 Joseph P. Fried, "U.S. Bids to Send Sindona to Italy," *The New York Times*, December 18, 1983, 49.
45 Tosches, *Power on Earth*, 196; DiFonzo, *St. Peter's Banker*, 240.
46 Luigi DiFonzo, "Justifiable Homicide," 30; see Raw, *The Moneychangers*, 87.
47 Ibid., Di Fonzo, *St. Peter's Banker*; Raw, *The Moneychangers*, 259.
48 See generally Claire Sterling, *The Terror Network: The Secret War of International Terrorism* (New York: Henry Holt, 1981).
49 Tanner, "A Sindona Inquiry by Italian Parliament Gets Support," B3.
50 Ibid.; DiFonzo, *St. Peter's Banker*, 241.
51 Gurwin, *The Calvi Affair*, 44, 46.
52 "Execution Deadline for Sindona Passes," *The Boston Globe*, August 12, 1979, 18; "Indicted Italian Financier Reported Kidnapped in US," *The Boston Globe*, August 7, 1979, 11.
53 Arnold H. Lubasch, "Sindona Missing; Suspect in Fraud at Franklin Bank," *The New York Times*, August 7, 1979, A1; "Disappearance of Italian Financier Indicted in Fraud Is Still a Mystery," *The New York Times*, August 8, 1979, B3; "A Letter from Missing Financier Reported by Lawyer," *The New York Times*, August 16, 1979, B3.
54 Arnold H. Lubasch, "Family Awaits News of Fate of Sindona," *The New York Times*, August 12, 1979, 35.
55 "Death Threat for Sindona," *The Boston Globe*, August 11, 1979, 11.
56 Arnold H. Lubasch, "Caller Asserts Missing Sindona Is to Be Shot 'at Dawn,'" *The New York Times*, August 11, 1979, 1; "Family Awaits News of Fate of Sindona," *The New York Times*, August 12, 1979, 35; "Death Threat for Sindona," 11.
57 Lubasch, "A Letter from Missing Financier Reported by Lawyer," B3; Arnold H. Lubasch, "A Letter in Sindona's Handwriting Says Captors Do Not Seek Ransom," *The New York Times*, August 22, 1979, A21.
58 "Message Reported in Sindona Case," *The New York Times*, September 1, 1979, 23.
59 "Key Sindona Witness Gets Protection," *The Boston Globe*, August 10, 1979, 10; "The City: Public Aid Sought in Finding Sindona," *The New York Times*, August 15, 1979, B4.
60 "The City: Search for Financier," *The New York Times*, August 9, 1979, B3. In Italy, Sindona's disappearance dominated the headlines and caused an uproar in Parliament. Italian lawmakers—many of whom were suspicious that Sindona had merely fled to avoid the start of his criminal trial in New York—responded by establishing a new parliamentary committee with greater powers to investigate possible links between Sindona and leading government ministers and Christian Democrats. Tanner, "A Sindona Inquiry by Italian Parliament Gets Support," B3.
61 "Banker Sindona's Family Asks Help," *The Boston Globe*, August 22, 1979, 16.
62 Nicholas Gage, "Sindona Photo Received; Kidnap Report Bolstered," *The New York Times*, September 24, 1979, B1.
63 Ibid.; see also Paul Hoffman, "Sindona Lawyer Receives a Photo," *The New York Times*, September 15, 1979, 22; "Photo of Sindona Reported," *The Boston Globe*, September 15, 1979, 19.
64 DiFonzi, *St. Peter's Banker*, 249.
65 "2 Suspects Arrested in Sicily," *The New York Times*, October 18, 1979, A19; Tosches, *Power on Earth*, 199.
66 DiFonzo, *St. Peter's Banker*, 256–57.
67 Ibid., 215–16, 221–22.
68 Joseph B. Treaster, "Sindona Enters a Hospital Here with a Wound," *The New York Times*, October 17, 1979, A1.
69 "Sindona Account Blames 'Leftists,'" *The Boston Globe*, October 21, 1979, 83; Selwyn Raab, "Sindona Gives Account of 10-Week Disappearance," *The New York Times*, October 21, 1979, 1.
70 Joseph B. Treaster, "Sindona in U.S. Court, Recounts Abduction Ordeal," *The New York Times*, October 25, 1979, A1.

71 DiFonzo, *St. Peter's Banker*, 256–57.
72 Joseph B. Treaster, "Judge Orders Silence on the Sindona Case," *The New York Times*, October 20, 1979, A1.
73 Paul Serafini, "How Federal Agents Discovered Sindona Was Not Kidnapped," Associated Press, New York, A.M. cycle, April 3, 1980.
74 Raab, "Sindona Gives Account of 10-Week Disappearance"; see also Joseph B. Treaster, "Italian Suspect Said to Have Been in City at Time Sindona Vanished," *The New York Times*, October 22, 1978, B3.
75 Serafini, "How Federal Agents Discovered Sindona Was Not Kidnapped"; Gurwin, *The Calvi Affair*, 45, 64–65.
76 Raw, *The Moneychangers*, 261.
77 Marjorie Hyer, "U.S. Catholic Budget Set," *The Washington Post*, November 16, 1979, C1; Theodora Luriealso, "$20 Million in Debt, Says the Vatican in Its First-Ever Public Disclosure," *The Globe and Mail* (Canada), November 10, 1979; correspondent Leslie Childe for *The Telegraph*, cited in Raw, *The Moneychangers*, 274.
78 Luriealso, "$20 Million in Debt, Says the Vatican in Its First-Ever Public Disclosure." There was also speculation that John Paul II was considering streamlining the Curia—seemingly a favorite theme of every newly elected Pope since Pius XII—and that reform of the IOR might be in the offing. John Paul II did not tackle any change at the Vatican Bank. See generally Joseph McLellan, "The Vatican: John Paul II May Make the Bureaucracy That Runs the Church Change," *The Washington Post*, October 7, 1979, 22.
79 Victor Simpson, Associated Press, International News, Vatican City, A.M. cycle, November 9, 1979.
80 Lai, *Finanze vaticane*, 59–60.
81 Marcinkus set the meeting with Garner for the day after a Cisalpine board meeting in Geneva. Raw, *The Moneychangers*, 274–75.
82 Garner made several pages of written notes about the meeting five days later, on December 10. They are the basis for this brief reconstruction of what happened at their discussion. In 1985, Cisalpine's liquidators sued Coopers & Lybrand, alleging it had been grossly negligent in its accounting. Coopers & Lybrand in turn countersued Marcinkus and the IOR, charging that Marcinkus had "by reason of misrepresentations made fraudulently or otherwise wrongfully" caused the accountants to rely on the wrong information. As part of its answer, the IOR did not admit that Garner's version of the December 5 meeting was correct. But it also did not provide an alternative version. See generally Raw, *The Moneychangers*, 276.
83 Ibid., 279.
84 Ibid., 279–80.
85 The IOR had reduced the amount owed by Cisalpine by $90 million during 1978–79. As for the promissory notes bought by the IOR in 1980, they were issued by Andino and BAH. Raw, *The Moneychangers*, 279–80, 310.
86 Hoffman, *Anatomy of the Vatican*, 193.
87 Tosches, *Power on Earth*, 217.
88 Hoffman, *Anatomy of the Vatican*, 193; Tosches, *Power on Earth*, 217.
89 Raw, *The Moneychangers*, 279. Pope John Paul II had promoted Casaroli to the Secretary of State position on April 30, 1979.
90 Tosches, *Power on Earth*, 218.
91 Gurwin, *The Calvi Affair*, 46.
92 A few years later, author Nick Tosches wrote to Cardinal Guerri about Sindona. The cardinal wrote a reply: "I must attest that in all negotiations Avvocato Sindona behaved in an extremely correct manner and with the greatest fairness." Tosches, *Power on Earth*, 218–19.
93 Author interview with Francesco Pazienza, September 20, 22, 2013. Archbishop Celata did not respond to a request for an interview. Over half a dozen interviews with the author, Pazienza reiterated and expanded on much of the information he had provided to journalists in earlier years, especially his 1986 talk, while he was incarcerated in Manhattan's Metropolitan Correctional Center awaiting extradition to Italy, with author Charles Raw. See also Pazienza interviewed in Raw, *The Moneychangers*, 323.

In some published accounts, Santovito and Pazienza are described as relatives (see Gurwin,

The Calvi Affair, 180). "That is completely false," Pazienza told the author. "Our families come from the same town in Italy, that's all." Author interview with Francesco Pazienza, September 20, 2013.

94 Author interview with Francesco Pazienza, September 21, 2013.

95 Ibid.

96 Ibid.

97 Tosches, *Power on Earth*, 219.

98 Sindona actually left the U.S. on August 2, the day he was reported missing, on a TWA flight to Vienna, traveling as Bonamico. He was met by Masonic friends of Gelli, who drove him to Sicily. In 1985, Sindona proved himself a creative fabulist when he gave author Nick Tosches a convoluted explanation for the motive behind his fake kidnapping. According to Sindona, communists in Sicily had plotted to steal nuclear missiles from an American military base. Sindona told Tosches that "my reputation in the region was powerful enough to attract huge numbers of Sicilians." Just by being there, he was certain he could assist Gelli's Masons in thwarting the communist plot. See Simoni and Turone, *Il caffè di Sindona*, 14, n. 2; Tosches, *Power on Earth*, 203–9; DiFonzo, *St. Peter's Banker*, 243–57.

99 Parliamentary Commission of Inquiry into the Case of Sindona and Responsibilities and the Political and Administrative Connected To It, 163–74; see also statement made by Francesco Di Carlo at the hearing on October 30, 1996, of the Andreotti trial (Palermo Court, Judgment of October 23, 1999, cap. VI, § 1, p. 1910).

100 "Financier Indicted in Mafia Drug Investigation," Associated Press, International News, Palermo, A.M. cycle, December 11, 1981.

101 DiFonzo, *St. Peter's Banker*, 254–56.

102 Paul Serafini, "Financier's Bail Revoked Before His Trial Begins," Associated Press, Domestic News, New York, A.M. cycle, February 6, 1980.

103 Arnold H. Lubasch, "Ex-Associate Heard at Sindona's Trial," *The New York Times*, February 8, 1980, D3. In return for his testimony, Bordoni served only five months of a seven-year sentence at Danbury, Connecticut's minimum-security camp. Allowed to remain free on bail while preparing to testify against Massimo Spada and others in Italy, he vanished. He was eventually run to ground and tried and convicted of financial crimes in Italy. See Parliamentary Commission of Inquiry into the Case of Sindona and Responsibilities and the Political and Administrative Connected To It.

104 "Govt. Set to Rest Case on Sindona with Charge of Faked Kidnapping," *The American Banker*, March 6, 1980. Four and a half years after Sindona's trial, the U.S. Attorney in New Jersey charged Rosario Gambino, a foot soldier in the Gambino crime family, with having facilitated Sindona's fake kidnapping. That count was subsumed under heroin trafficking for which he was subsequently indicted and convicted.

105 Ann Crittenden, "Sindona Faces a Lifetime in Jail, Here and Abroad," *The New York Times*, March 30, 1980, E6.

106 The original ninety-nine-count indictment had been replaced with a superseding indictment of sixty-nine counts on January 11, 1980. Sindona was found guilty of sixty-five counts. Arnold H. Lubasch, "Sindona Is Convicted by U.S. Jury of Fraud in Franklin Bank Failure," *The New York Times*, March 28, 1980, A1; "Michele Sindona: Convicted," *The Economist*, April 5, 1980, 78. See also Harry Anderson and Rich Thomas, "Inside the Vatican Bank," *Newsweek*, September 13, 1982, 62.

107 Sindona interviewed in Tosches, *Power on Earth*, 229–30; DiFonzo, *St. Peter's Banker*, 258.

108 "Sindona Back in Jail," *The New York Times*, June 11, 1980, B5.

109 Lee A. Daniels, "Sindona Is Given a 25-Year Term, Fined $207,000," *The New York Times*, June 14, 1980, 25. The U.S. Attorney indicted Sindona again on October 7, five months after his conviction of fraud for misappropriating millions from Franklin National. The new charges were for jumping bail and perjury related to his kidnapping fairy tale. He was convicted in April 1981, and two and a half years were added to his twenty-five-year Franklin sentence. See generally DiFonzo, *St. Peter's Banker*, 258–59.

110 Hill had provided critical information to the FBI regarding the $6 million Lufthansa cargo heist at JFK Airport as well as about a mob ring that fixed college basketball games. Joseph P. Fried, "U.S. Bids to Send Sindona to Italy," *The New York Times*, December 18, 1983, 49.

111 Ibid.; see also Gregg Hill, *On the Run: A Mafia Childhood* (New York: Warner, 2004).

112 DiFonzo, "Justifiable Homicide," 32.

113 Hill independently told the FBI that Sindona, and his son, Nino, had invested in a food import company that was a front for importing heroin. Notwithstanding many suspicions, the FBI never developed enough evidence to prove Ace Pizza was a front for an illegal business.

114 Nino Sindona interviewed in DiFonzo, "Justifiable Homicide," 33. DiFonzo wrote in his 1983 *New York* magazine article, "U.S. government sources say they expect that Nino Sindona will be arrested and charged with obstruction of justice and being an accessory after-the-fact." Federal prosecutors, wrote DiFonzo, were confident that they could leverage Sindona with an indictment against his son. But Nino was never charged.

115 DiFonzo, "Justifiable Homicide," *New York Magazine*.

116 "Italian Police Charge Sindona with Ordering Murder," Associated Press, Milan, International News, A.M. cycle, July 17, 1981.

117 "Alleged Sindona Hit Man Dies in Escape Attempt," Associated Press, New York, Domestic News, A.M. cycle, February 20, 1984.

118 Months before Arcio was to be extradited to Italy in 1984 to stand trial as the Ambrosoli gunman, he fell to his death while trying to escape from Manhattan's Metropolitan Detention Center. Police claimed he fell five floors after cutting through the bars of his ninth-floor cell and then losing his grip on a makeshift rope cobbled together from bedsheets. "Alleged Sindona Hit Man Dies in Escape Attempt," Associated Press.

As for Italian efforts behind the scenes to get Sindona brought back to Italy for trial, see generally Parliamentary Commission of Inquiry on the Case Sindona and Responsibilities both Political and Administrative related to it, VIII legislature, Doc No. XXIII, 2-series, Final Report of the majority, Report of Joseph Azzaro, Rome, March 24, 1982.

119 Cornwell, *God's Banker*, 125–26; Gurwin, *The Calvi Affair*, 63.

120 "Police Arrest Two Suspected Accomplices of Michele Sindona," International News, Rome, A.M cycle, Feburary 5, 1981.

121 "Vatican Banker Linked to Sindona Is Arrested," *The New York Times*, February 6, 1981, A3; Raw, *The Moneychangers*, 316.

122 John Hooper, "Luigi Mennini: Shadow over the Vatican," *The Guardian*, August 14, 1997, 14.

123 Forty days in jail according to Paul Hoffman, *Anatomy of the Vatican*, 195; Raw, *The Moneychangers*, 316; As for Mennini released without any charges, see "Vatican Banker to Stand Trial in Sindona Case," International News, Rome, P.M. cycle, July 22, 1982.

124 Gurwin, *The Calvi Affair*, 64.

125 Gelli maintained an office at the Arezzo office of the textile firm, Giole, in Castiglion Fibocchi, Simoni and Turone, *Il caffè di Sindona*, 130.

126 Gurwin, *The Calvi Affair*, 51.

127 Rupert Cornwell, *God's Banker*, 134.

128 Lernoux, *In Banks We Trust*, 179; Craig Unger, "The War They Wanted, the Lies They Needed," *Vanity Fair*, July 2006; see also Tosches, *Power on Earth*, 238.

129 Simoni and Turone, *Il caffè di Sindona*, 130, citing Massimo Teodori, Commissione parlamentare d'inchiesta sul caso Sindona, Relazione di minoranza (Minority Report of the Parliamentary Commission of Inquiry on the Case and Sindona Report), Rome, April 15, 1982, 550ss.

130 Warrant subsequently executed on Michele Sindona, cited in Gurwin, *The Calvi Affair*, 67; Cornwell, *God's Banker*, 134.

131 A Parliamentary Commission of Inquiry into P2 was established on September 23, 1981, and finished its work on July 12, 1984. Its final report was published as *Dossier P2* in 2008 by Kaos Publishing in Milan.

132 See generally A. Barbieri, E. Scalfari, G.Turani, and N. Pagani, *L'Italia della P2* (Milan: Mondadori Editore, 1981); Gianfranco Piazzesi, *Gelli: La carriere di un eroe di questa Italia* (Milan: Garzanti, 1983).

133 Vanni Nisticò quoted in *L'Espresso*, July 6, 1981, cited in Gurwin, *The Calvi Affair*, 51. Father Lorenzo Zorza, a New York priest with whom the author spoke, was a close friend of Francesco Pazienza, an Italian intelligence agent and Calvi confidant. Zorza had seen and was familiar with the photo of the naked Pontiff. "It was obtained by Gelli," Zorza told the author. "In part to show his power." Interview with Father Lorenzo Zorza, September 6, 2013.

134 Raw, *The Moneychangers*, 299, 320–21.

135 Ortolani was also a Catholic nobleman who once served as the Knights of Malta ambassador to Uruguay. The Grand Military Order of the Knights of Malta is a Catholic order and recognizes

the Pope's authority over all its members. It also has sovereign diplomatic relations with over one hundred countries, including, among others, Spain, Italy, Russia, Austria, Egypt, Brazil. The Knights of Malta has a fully accredited ambassador to the European Union. Since 1994 it is a permanent observer at the United Nations. Parliamentary Commission of Inquiry into the Case of Sindona and Responsibilities and the Political and Administrative Connected To It, 16. See also ww.orderofmalta.int.

136 Philip Pullella, "Italian Government Collapses over Masonic Scandal," UPI, International News, Rome, A.M. cycle, May 26, 1981; see also Cornwell, *God's Banker*, 46–47.

137 Louise Branson, "Italian Masonic Leader Arrested at Swiss Bank," UPI, International News, Geneva, P.M. cycle, September 14, 1982; Tanner, "Italian Elite Embroiled in a Scandal."

138 Also included on the list besides Marcinkus was an IOR monsignor, Donato de Bonis, and also Secretary of State Villot and Foreign Minister Casaroli. See Nuzzi, *Vaticano S.p.A.*, 17; Willan, *The Last Supper*, 121; Raw, *The Moneychangers*, 145. As for Freemasonry inside the Vatican, Marcinkus said, "there is no such thing. Promise. I swear it." Handwritten notes by Philip Willan of audiotaped interviews between John Cornwell and Marcinkus, February 8, 1988, 8b, 9a, provided to author courtesy of Willan. Pope John Paul II later eliminated excommunication as a punishment for being a Freemason, although technically membership remained incompatible with church dogma. See Nuzzi, *Vaticano S.p.A.*, 26 and 29, n. 14.

139 Paddy Agnew, "Andreotti Verdict Welcomed by Right and the Vatican," *The Irish Times*, October 25, 1999, 9.

Chapter 23: "You Have to Kill the Pope"

1 Henry Tanner, "2 Bullets Hit Pontiff," *The New York Times*, May 14, 1981, A1.

2 The Pope believed that the Virgin Mary had interceded to save him, part of what he later called a "divine call." Hebblethwaite, *Pope John Paul II and the Church*, 94.

3 "Bulgaria and the Pope," *The MacNeil/Lehrer Report*, transcript, January 5, 1983. The day after Ağca had killed the Turkish editor, he mailed letters to the dead man's newspaper warning that if the Pope visited Turkey, he would kill the "Crusader Commander." Koehler, *Spies in the Vatican*, 115. See generally Paul Henze, *The Plot to Kill the Pope* (New York: Charles Scribner's Sons, 1983).

4 Wendy Owen, "Agca Wasn't the Only One Who Said There Was a Plot," Associated Press, International News, Rome, A.M. cycle, March 29, 1986.

5 "Bulgaria and the Pope," *The MacNeil/Lehrer Report*.

6 Owen, "Agca Wasn't the Only One Who Said There Was a Plot." Two years later the Bulgarian government, still stinging from the charges it was behind the plot to kill the Pope, published a report that concluded it was highly likely that John Paul I had been poisoned in 1978. The Bulgarians said John Paul had been murdered by Vatican insiders intent on preventing him from overhauling the Curia. "Bulgaria Suggests John Paul I was Poisoned," UPI, International News, A.M. cycle, Vienna, February 4, 1983.

7 "Bulgaria and the Pope," *The MacNeil/Lehrer Report*.

8 Koehler, *Spies in the Vatican*, 117–19, 127.

9 See Willan, *The Last Supper*, 279–81; Thomas and Morgan-Witts, *Pontiff*, 331; Abdul Alim, "Khomeni himself asked me to kill the Pope," *The Muslim Times*, February 2, 2013.

10 Vladimir Zhirinovsky quoted in "Russia's Zhirinovskiy Tries to Justify Attempt on Polish Pope's Life," BBC Monitoring Former Soviet Union—Political, Supplied by BBC Worldwide Monitoring, January 12, 2006; see also Matthew Day, "CIA 'Framed Bulgaria' for Shooting Pope John Paul II," *The Daily Telegraph*, April 22, 2011, Edition 3, 20.

11 Victor L. Simpson, "Close Encounters with St. Peter's Successors on Papal Plane and Behind Vatican's Bronze Doors," Postmedia Breaking News, Associated Press, February 27, 2013.

12 George Brodzki, "Strikers Reportedly Form Unified Committee," International News, A.M. cycle, Gdańsk, Poland, Associated Press, August 17, 1980.

13 Carl Bernstein and Marco Politi, *His Holiness: John Paul II and the History of Our Time* (New York: Penguin, 1996), 231, 244–47. See generally Jack M. Bloom, "The Solidarity Revolution in Poland, 1980–1981," *The Oral History Review* 33, no. 1 (Winter/Spring, 2006), published by Oxford University Press on behalf of the Oral History Association, 33–64; Gregory F. Domber,

"The AFL-CIO, the Reagan Administration and Solidarność," *The Polish Review* 52, no. 3 (2007), published by the University of Illinois Press on behalf of the Polish Institute of Arts & Sciences of America, 277–304.

14 Thomas and Morgan-Witts, *Pontiff*, 406–7.

15 Owen, "Agca Wasn't the Only One Who Said There Was a Plot"; "Bulgaria and the Pope," *The MacNeil/Lehrer Report*.

16 Wojciech Adamiecki, the editor of the underground Solidarity newspapers, interviewed by Carl Bernstein, "The Holy Alliance," *Time*, February 24, 1992. "We were told the Pope had warned the Soviets that if they entered Poland he would fly to Poland and stay with the Polish people. The church was of primary assistance."

17 Agostino Bono, "Officials Say Pope, Reagan Shared Cold War Data, but Lacked Alliance," Catholic News Service, November 17, 2004, 31.

18 Bernstein and Politi, *His Holiness*, 267. The KGB was aware of the White House relationship with Krol. See generally Koehler, *Spies in the Vatican*, 97–98.

19 Laghi always used a southwest gate so he could avoid reporters. "By keeping in such close touch, we did not cross lines. My role was primarily to facilitate meetings between Walters and the Holy Father. The Holy Father knew his people. It was a very complex situation." Bernstein, "The Holy Alliance."

20 Bernstein and Politi, *His Holiness*, 269; see also Koehler, *Spies in the Vatican*, 188, n. 6.

21 Author interview with Michael Hornblow, January 28, 2014.

22 Ibid.

23 Koehler, *Spies in the Vatican*, 187.

24 Ronald Reagan interviewed in Bernstein, "The Holy Alliance."

25 Author interview with William P. Clark, September 15, 2005. That same year, 1984, the Reagan administration announced at the World Conference on Population in Mexico City that it was reversing America's many years of commitment to international family planning and withdrew funding from the United Nations Fund for Population Activities as well as the International Planned Parenthood Federation. The quid pro quo between the U.S. and the Vatican seemed to continue when Reagan introduced a new generation of more powerful cruise missiles into Europe, and the normally pacifist Papacy did not object. Domestically, the president had proposed tuition tax credits for private schools, introducing the idea in a speech before the National Catholic Educational Association. That led to decades of mostly unsuccessful court challenges by opponents who argued it violated the Constitution's separation of church and state.

26 Richard Allen interviewed in Bernstein, "The Holy Alliance."

27 Robert M. Gates, *From the Shadows: The Ultimate Insider's Story of Five Presidents and How They Won the Cold War* (New York: Simon & Schuster, 1996), 237.

28 Bernstein, "The Holy Alliance." According to Bernstein, "Lech Walesa and other leaders of Solidarity received strategic advice—often conveyed by priests or American and European labor experts working undercover in Poland—that reflected the thinking of the Vatican and the Reagan Administration."

29 Koehler, *Spies in the Vatican*, 177–79, citing a document in the Archive of the former East Germany Ministry for State Security [Stasi], 1083/81 BSTU Nr. 00008, translated from the Russian.

30 Ibid., citing a document in the Archive of the former East Germany Ministry for State Security [Stasi], HA XX/4-233 BSTU Nr. 000058.

31 Ibid., citing a document in the Archive of the former East Germany Ministry for State Security [Stasi], HA XX/4-8751 BSTU Nr. 000197.

32 "The information from the Vatican was sometimes better than we obtained," recalls the State Department's Hornblow: author interview with Michael Hornblow, January 28, 2014.

33 A month after martial law was imposed, General Jaruzelski said that the "counterrevolution was crushed." But Brezhnev felt the imposition of martial law would ultimately "only ruin things." Koehler, *Spies in the Vatican*, 203.

34 See generally Bernstein, "The Holy Alliance;" William A. Wilson Papers, Georgetown University Library, Special Collections Research Center, Washington, D.C. Also Hutchison, *Their Kingdom Come*, 359.

35 Laura Colby, "Vatican Bank Played a Central Role in Fall of Banco Ambrosiano," *The Wall Street Journal*, April 27, 1987, 1.

36 Galli, *Finanza bianca*, 84–85; see also Lernoux, *In Banks We Trust*, 212. Marcinkus denied any higher ambitions. "None, whatsoever. . . . I don't see any reason why they should make me a

cardinal. Nobody has a right to be made a cardinal." Handwritten notes by Philip Willan of audiotaped interviews between John Cornwell and Marcinkus, February 8, 1988, 11a, provided to author courtesy of Willan.

37 Raw, *The Moneychangers*, 277–78.

38 Calvi quoted in Gurwin, *The Calvi Affair*, 103; handwritten notes by Philip Willan of audiotaped interviews between John Cornwell and Marcinkus, February 8, 1988, 8a, provided to author courtesy of Willan.

39 Author interview with Francesco Pazienza, September 18, 2013. According to Pazienza, $3.5 million of the money came from the Vatican while $500,000 came from the Ambrosiano.

40 See generally Hebblethwaite, *Pope John Paul II and the Church*, "Pope Repudiates Liberation Theology," 113-19, 264-65; Willey, *God's Politician*, "Salvation Politics," 113–37.

41 In Guatemala in May 1981, General Vernon Walters visited the country as goodwill ambassador-at-large for the Reagan administration. Walters was also representing a Luxembourg-based company, Basic Resources International SA (BRISA). British tycoon Sir James Goldsmith owned BRISA, and Antonio Tonello was a director. In addition to having executive positions in Calvi's La Centrale and Toro Assicuranzioni, Tonello was a close associate of P2's Licio Gelli. And Tonello was also a director of Cisalpine, serving with Marcinkus on the board. During Walters's visit, the Guatemalan military government signed a multiyear oil export deal with BRISA. Some of that revenue passed through the Ambrosiano subsidiaries in which the IOR owned stakes. See generally Gurwin, *The Calvi Affair*, 194; Lawrence Minard, "I Don't Give a Damn What Anybody Says!," *Forbes*, September 18, 1979, 41.

The money flow from the Vatican continued in 1980 despite the conviction of members of the right-wing Salvadoran army for murdering four Maryknoll sisters.

42 Francis Rooney, *The Global Vatican: An Inside Look at the Catholic Church, World Politics, and the Extraordinary Relationship between the United States and the Holy See* (New York: Rowman & Littlefield, 2013), 268–70; Willey, *God's Politician*, 191; "Vatican Blasts U.S.: Calls It 'Occupying Power' and Urges Noriega to Leave," *Los Angeles Times*, December 29, 1989, 1.

43 "Marcinkus—Pope Is Not Commission's Formal President," UPI, International News, Vatican City, P.M. cycle, September 29, 1981; "American in Key Vatican Job," *The New York Times*, September 30, 1981, A12.

44 "Marcinkus—Pope Is Not Commission's Formal President," UPI, International News, Vatican City, P.M. cycle, September 29, 1981; "Pope Names American Bishop as Top Vatican Manager," Associated Press, International News, Vatican City, P.M. cycle, September 29, 1981; "American in Key Vatican Job," *The New York Times*.

Chapter 24: "Tell Your Father to Be Quiet"

1 Gurwin, *The Calvi Affair*, 67. In April, while prosecutors assembled their case against Calvi, he tried rehabilitating his damaged reputation by making a successful bid to buy Rizzoli, one of Italy's most prestigious publishing houses. Calvi managed to raise $200 million from investors because of Rizzoli's sterling name, but he paid a significant premium for the shares, and an enormous commission. Investigators later concluded that the premium was in part a theft of funds from some of Calvi's offshore banks. See generally Raw, *The Moneychangers*, 286–87, 290–91.

2 Cornwell, *God's Banker*, 138; Gurwin, *The Calvi Affair*, 71.

3 "7 Arrested in Italy on Lire Outflow," *The New York Times*, May 21, 1981, D14; "Italian Financiers Arrested over Alleged Illegal Funds Transfers," Associated Press, Business News, Milan, A.M. cycle, May 20, 1981. As for currency regulation discussion, see generally Parliamentary Commission of Inquiry into the Case of Sindona and Responsibilities and the Political and Administrative Connected to It, 110–11.

4 United Press International, Milan, Financial, BC cycle, May 29, 1981; the sell-off culminated in a 20 percent dip in the indexes on July 8, when the Treasury Ministry suspended stock trading to restore order. "Financier Attempts Suicide," Associated Press, International News, Milan, P.M. cycle, July 8, 1981.

5 Paul Lewis, "Italy's Mysterious, Deepening Bank Scandal," *The New York Times*, July 28, 1982, A1; "3 Named by Vatican to Study Bank Ties," *The New York Times*, July 14, 1982, D1.

6 Author interviews with Carlo Calvi, September 27, 2005, and September 10, 2006.

7 Cornwell, *God's Banker*, 123–24; see generally Benten E. Gup, *Bank Failures in the Major Trading Countries of the World: Causes and Remedies* (Westport, CT: Quorum, 1998), 31–33. In 1973, when Manic was founded in Luxembourg, the IOR subscribed to a $40 million bond issue from the new company (the money made available from a loan from the Ambrosiano to Manic). And the Vatican Bank bought control of Manic at the same time for a price listed in documents as only $5 million. In 1979, the IOR was repaid its $45 million, plus an agreed upon 10 percent interest. But it retained the physical shares of Manic, representing controlling ownership. After the entire web of companies collapsed, Marcinkus tried putting some distance between the IOR and the offshore subsidiaries. In a 1982 statement to an Italian parliamentary investigating committee, Marcinkus said that he only learned about the extent of the IOR's ownership in Manic earlier that year, and proof of that was the failure of the IOR to receive a balance sheet after 1997. Few believed that to be true, since Manic had seven subsidiaries managed by the Nassau-based Cisalpine, of which Marcinkus was a director. One typewritten letter dated March 6, 1980, to Cisalpine, and signed simply "Manic S.A.," is about "our various Panamanian subsidiaries which you are managing on our behalf." That would not stop Marcinkus from later claiming, "These companies and stuff, I never even heard of them. . . . I say that with all honesty." See generally Laura Colby, "Vatican Bank Played a Central Role in Fall of Banco Ambrosiano," *The Wall Street Journal*, April 27, 1987, 1; "Memo prepared by IOR's lawyers re Laura Colby's article," reproduced in its entirety in Cornwell, *A Thief in the Night*, 354–58; Raw, *The Moneychangers*, 347–49; see also Marcinkus interviewed in Cornwell, *A Thief in the Night*, 132.

8 Raw, *The Moneychangers*, 352.

9 Gurwin, *The Calvi Affair*, 72–73.

10 Simoni and Turone, *Il caffè di Sindona*, 135–36.

11 Clara Calvi account recounted in Lernoux, *In Banks We Trust*, 199; see also Cornwell, *God's Banker*, 143; and Raw, *The Moneychangers*, 338.

12 Gurwin, *The Calvi Affair*, 69–70; see also Willan, *The Last Supper*, 147.

13 Cornwell, *God's Banker*, 140; Tosches, *Powers on Earth*, 242–43; Raw, *The Moneychangers*, 322–23.

14 See generally, Lernoux, *In Banks We Trust*, 216–17.

15 Author interview with Francesco Pazienza, September 18, 2013.

16 Tosches, *Power on Earth*, 236.

17 Ralph Blumenthal, "Italian Ex-Agent Ordered Extradited from U.S.," *The New York Times*, September 12, 1985, A12.

18 Author interviews with Francesco Pazienza, September 18, 20, and 21, 2013. See also Loren Jenkins, "Italian Judge Said to Drop Probe of Agca Being Coached," *The Washington Post*, December 19, 1985, A31; "Rome Inquiry: Was Agca Coached?," *The New York Times*, October 8, 1985, A3; Blumenthal, "Italian Ex-Agent Ordered Extradited from U.S."

19 Author interviews with Francesco Pazienza, September 18, 20, 21, 2013; Ralph Blumenthal, "Italian Ex-Agent Ordered Extradited From U.S.," *The New York Times*, September 12, 1985, A12; Lernoux, *In Banks We Trust*, 216–17; Tosches; *Power on Earth*, 242–43, 260–61.

20 Author interview with Carlo Calvi, September 10, 2006. Even the State Department, in some 350 pages of documents released pursuant to a Freedom of Information request, referred in contemporaneous documents to Pazienza as a "fixer." Author interview with Francesco Pazienza, September 18, 2013.

21 Author interview with Francesco Pazienza, September 18, 2013.

22 One of those Pazienza puts at the center of his efforts to sell the Ambrosiano was Roberto Armao, the president of a private Vatican lay foundation that raised donations from the faithful. Armao had worked for the Shah of Iran, and was close to David Rockefeller and senior executives at Chase Manhattan. Armao's connections later fueled conspiracy theories tying the Ambrosiano to a much broader and more complicated global intelligence and business scheme. Author interviews with Francesco Pazienza, September 18 and 19, 2013. See generally Lernoux, *In Banks We Trust*, 216. Also see Cornwell, *God's Banker*, 170–73; and Raw, *The Moneychangers*, 323–25, 377–78, 382–84, 413.

23 Carlo Calvi recalled the bank as a branch of the elite private British bank Coutts. But documents in subsequent government investigations reveal that the senior Calvi kept about 1,500 pages of documents and journal entries at Roywest.

24 Author interview with Carlo Calvi, September 10, 2006.

25 Ibid.
26 Author interview with Francesco Pazienza, September 18, 2013.
27 Author interview with Francesco Pazienza, September 20, 2013; Raw, *The Moneychangers*, 339.
28 Raw, *The Moneychangers*, 352.
29 Gurwin, *The Calvi Affair*, 70. Cheli was himself somewhat controversial, having sent more than $100,000 of church money in donations to Palestine. It was Cheli who made the Pontifical Mission for Palestine a diplomatic priority for the Vatican, and behind the scenes at the United Nations he was known for his often biting criticism of Israel. See generally "Vatican Gives $10,000 to Refugees," Associated Press, International News, Vatican City, A.M. cycle, November 27, 1981.
30 "Report Archbishop Marcinkus Has Resigned," United Press International, International News, Vatican City, A.M. cycle, July 7, 1982.
31 Raw, *The Moneychangers*, 58.
32 Author interview with Father Lorenzo Zorza, September 6, 2013. See "Association Between the Families of Victims, the Massacre at the Station of Bologna," August 2, 1980, 5th Assize Court, Rome, http://www.uonna.it/bologna-strage-1980-sentenza.htm; author interview with Francesco Pazienza, September 19, 2013.
33 Zorza was "in residence" at St. Agnes, a situation in which a priest is on special assignment—as Zorza was with UN staff—and allowed to reside in a local parish without any pastoral duties. Author interview with Father Lorenzo Zorza, September 6, 2013; William G. Blair, "Priest Arrested in Smuggling of Art Is Suspended from his U.N. Duties," *The New York Times*, March 3, 1982, B3.
34 Author interviews with Carlo Calvi, September 27, 2005, and September 10, 2006.
35 Prior published accounts have reported that Zorza, Pazienza, and another Italian businessman had offered $4.5 million for a small island near Antigua, in the hope of creating their own state with an independent currency, a central bank, and liberal tax laws. But according to those reports, the deal fell through when Antigua refused to cede sovereignty over the island. See generally Rick Hampson and Larry McShane, "Accusations of Drug, Art Smuggling; Odyssey Takes Priest Outside Law, the Church," *Los Angeles Times*, August 13, 1988, Part 2, 7. However, Father Zorza told this author that he was not involved with Pazienza's deal for a sovereign state. Zorza claims that the Knights of Malta were behind Pazienza's attempt to create a tiny nation from an island belonging to Belize, not Antigua. The price, several million dollars' worth of construction equipment required by Belize to build roads, was never delivered and the deal was not completed. Author interview with Father Zorza, September 6, 2013. As for Zorza's claim about his Ambrosiano application for a $5 million loan, and the required 50 percent kickback of the principal, it is from a ten-page undated document titled, "Subject: My Life: Some explanations . . ." written by Father Zorza, and provided to the author on September 6, 2013.
36 William G. Blair, "Priest Arrested in Smuggling of Art Is Suspended from his U.N. Duties," *The New York Times*, March 3, 1982, B3; "Priest Held in Theft," *The New York Times*, August 21, 1987, A8; Ralph Blumenthal, "U.S. and Italy Join in Breaking a Vast Drug Ring," *The New York Times*, April 1, 1988, A1; "Priest Arrested in Italy On U.S. Drug Charges," *The New York Times*, April 7, 1998; Hutchison, *Their Kingdom Come*, 324; Assorted author email and interviews with Father Zorza, 2013 and 2014.
37 Author interviews with Carlo Calvi, September 10, 2006; and Lorenzo Zorza, September 6, 2013.
38 Author interviews with Carlo Calvi, September 27, 2005, and September 10, 2006.
39 Author interview with Carlo Calvi, September 10, 2006.
40 "Financier on Trial Dies," Associated Press, International News, Milan, A.M. cycle, June 15, 1981; Cornwell, *God's Banker*, 143–44.
41 Raw, *The Moneychangers*, 345–46.
42 "Financier Attempts Suicide," Associated Press, International News, Milan, P.M. cycle, July 8, 1981; Cornwell, *God's Banker*, 145.
43 "Financier Attempts Suicide," Associated Press; as for the warden, see Gurwin, *The Calvi Affair*, 75.
44 Author interview with Carlo Calvi, September 10, 2006.
45 Raw, *The Moneychangers*, 349–50.
46 Ibid., 355.
47 Cornwell, *God's Banker*, 145.
48 Gurwin, *The Calvi Affair*, 76.

49 Willan, *The Last Supper*, 58–59.
50 Cornwell, *God's Banker*, 148–49; Raw, *The Moneychangers*, 353.
51 Marcinkus interviewed in Cornwell, *A Thief in the Night*, 134.
52 Gurwin, *The Calvi Affair*, 79.
53 Raw, *The Moneychangers*, 353.
54 Viviane Hewitt, "Lawmen: Mobster May Help Destroy Mafia for First Time Since Middle Ages, Italians Speak of Ending Mob Rule," *The Miami Herald*, October 7, 1984, 1. Gurwin, *The Calvi Affair*, 80.
55 Raw, *The Moneychangers*, 264, 266.
56 Ibid., 197–98. The IOR at this point had $205 million at stake, all with no collateral other than Calvi's promise to make good on the debt.
57 Simoni and Turone, *Il caffè di Sindona*, 133.
58 Calvi was with Pazienza, meeting and entertaining potential investors for the Ambrosiano. Raw, *The Moneychangers*, 355, 358.
59 The companies were those at the heart of the Ambrosiano-Vatican business relationship. They were from Panama (Astolfine, Bellatrix, Belrosa, Erin, Laramie, Starfield, United Trading, and Worldwide Trading), Liechtenstein (Nordeurop), and Luxembourg (Manic). Money was shuffled between them at sometimes dizzying speeds. In the spring of 1980, for instance, Nordeurop owed nothing to the Ambrosiano. By September Nordeurop's debts to the Ambrosiano were $400 million. Colby, "Vatican Bank Played a Central Role in Fall of Banco Ambrosiano," 1.

The companies later proved a mystery to most reporters, who were unfamiliar with them. *The New York Times* said of the companies: "Most of this money was then lent to a series of Panamanian companies with names such as Bellatrix Inc., Manic Inc., and Astrolfine Inc., most of which are thought to have no more than mail addresses." Paul Lewis, "Italy's Mysterious, Deepening Bank Scandal," *The New York Times*, July 28, 1982, A1. The stationery on which the letters of patronage were written was headed *Istituto per le Opere di Religione, Città del Vaticano*. See also Gurwin, *The Calvi Affair*, 83.
60 Cornwell, *God's Banker*, 151; Raw, *The Moneychangers*, 358.
61 As for Alessandro Mennini's influence at the Ambrosiano, see generally Gurwin, *The Calvi Affair*, 69; see also author interview with Father Lorenzo Zorza, September 6, 2013.
62 Colby, "Vatican Bank Played a Central Role in Fall of Banco Ambrosiano," 1; Raw, *The Moneychangers*, 358.
63 De Strobel had also reviewed the Gottardo numbers on July 3 in Lugano, so he knew the numbers on the attachment to the patronage letters were wrong. When de Strobel and Mennini signed the patronage letters, they also initialed each of the eight pages of the balance sheet attachments. Raw, *The Moneychangers*, 358, 361, 367; also Willan, *The Last Supper*, 191.
64 Gurwin, *The Calvi Affair*, 83.
65 The IOR had the contractual right to call its loans due at any time on fifteen days' notice. But Marcinkus knew Calvi did not have the money to repay the church, so it would only cause a creditors' crisis. Raw, *The Moneychangers*, 363–65.
66 Raw, *The Moneychangers*, 359; Simoni and Turone, *Il caffè di Sindona*, 136. The indemnity letter also extended the Vatican's exit to four companies not listed in the patronage letters; these were Inparfin, Intermax, Suprafin, and Intermax. See also Assize Court of Rome, 6 June 2007, Calō + 4, cit., 22; referring to April 22, 1998, interview with Orazio Bagnasco by the magistrate.
67 Calvi gave the patronage letters to the Banca del Gottardo and the Ambrosiano Services holding company, among others. Harry Anderson, Rich Thomas, and Hope Lamfert, "Inside the Vatican Bank," *Newsweek*, September 13, 1982, 62; Raw, *The Moneychangers*, 372–73.
68 Marcinkus interviewed in Cornwell, *A Thief in the Night*, 133. Even when Marcinkus's staunchest defenders acknowledge those facts they still invariably excuse him. Typical is Pope John Paul II's biographer, George Weigel: "It looked to some like fraud, but to those who knew Marcinkus, it was indicative of his naïveté." Weigel, *Witness to Hope*, 747.
69 Sindona interviewed in Tosches, *Power on Earth*, 247–48.
70 Calvi eventually sent more than $8.8 million to Pazienza-controlled accounts at two of the ghost companies, Realfin and Finanzco. Some of that was traced later to Carboni, who evidently used it mostly to buy cars and jewelry. Pazienza spent $2.5 million on two yachts.
71 Galli, *Finanza bianca*, 85–86.
72 Italian investigators concluded that the patronage letters were prima facie evidence of high-level collusion between Calvi and Marcinkus. See Colby, "Vatican Bank Played a Central Role in Fall

of Banco Ambrosiano," 1. As for the October 26, 1981, letters, signed by de Strobel and Mennini, they are cited in Raw, *The Moneychangers*, 373–74. (*The Wall Street Journal* reported the power of attorney letter as being dated October 16.)

73 "Memo prepared by IOR's lawyers re Laura Colby's article," reproduced in its entirety in Cornwell, *A Thief in the Night*, 354–58.

74 It was Marcinkus's nineteenth board meeting for Cisalpine since becoming a director in 1971.

75 Henry Kamm, "Pope Vows to Assist Bank Study," *The New York Times*, November 27, 1982, 35.

76 George Cornell, "Church Plans to Open Books on Troubled Vatican Finances," *The Globe and Mail* (Canada), September 19, 1981.

77 Benny Lai interview of Cardinal Palazzini, in Lai, *Finanze vaticane*, 141.

78 Lai, *Finanze vaticane*, 58–59.

79 Paul Lewis, "Sharing Ambrosiano's Losses," *The New York Times*, December 18, 1982, 35.

80 Assize Court of Rome, 6 June 2007, cit., 4; Simoni and Turone, *Il caffè di Sindona*, 137. Carboni was also partners with Italy's future three-time Prime Minister, Silvio Berlusconi, who then owned a television station and had wide-ranging real estate interests. They shared the same grand villa, Villa Certosa, on Sardinia's northern coast. See generally Philip Willan, *The Vatican at War: From Blackfriars Bridge to Buenos Aires* (iUniverse LLC: Bloomington, IN, 2013), Kindle edition, locations 5132, 5080 of 6371.

81 Raw, *The Moneychangers*, 356–57; Willan, *The Last Supper*, 184.

82 Calvi knew, for instance, that Carboni was close to Giovanni Spadolini, head of the Republican Party and the current Prime Minister. Calvi overlooked, as did Carboni's other political acquaintances, that the Sardinian was also friends with the mobster Domenico Balducci.

83 Cornwell, *God's Banker*, 174–75.

84 Gurwin, *The Calvi Affair*, 85–86.

85 "Carlo de Benedetti; Yesterday Italy, Today Europe, Tomorrow the World?," *The Economist*, February 22, 1986, 70 (U.S. edition, p. 68).

86 Cornwell, *God's Banker*, 153–54; Gurwin, *The Calvi Affair*, 87–91.

87 Galli, *Finanza bianca*, 85.

88 Author interview with Carlo Calvi, September 10, 2006.

89 Lewis, "Italy's Mysterious, Deepening Bank Scandal," A1. See also Cornwell, *God's Banker*, 155–62.

90 "Banco Ambrosiano: Exit de Benedetti," *The Economist*, January 30, 1982, 83 (U.S. edition, p. 77); Gurwin, *The Calvi Affair*, 91. Eleven years later, in 1992, De Benedetti was convicted of a fraud in the Ambrosiano's collapse. He had been the bank's deputy chairman for only sixty-five days. An appeals court upheld the conviction in 1996, but in 1998 the equivalent of the Italian Supreme Court reversed it. Alan Riding, "Olivetti's Chief Convicted in Collapse of Bank in 1982," *The New York Times*, April 17, 1982; "High Court Overturns Conviction of Olivetti Chairman in Bank Collapse," Associated Press, Business News, Rome, April 22, 1998; Raw, *The Moneychangers*, 380–82, 388–91.

91 Colby, "Vatican Bank Played a Central Role in Fall of Banco Ambrosiano," 1. The unidentified official in Colby's article was later identified by Benedetti as Cardinal Casaroli. Calvi and De Benedetti turned to the media to spin their own versions of who was to blame for the fast divorce. "Why I Married De Benedetti" was Calvi's take in *L'Espresso* in December 1981. De Benedetti followed three months later with "My 65 Days with Calvi" in Italy's *Panorama*.

92 Raw, *The Moneychangers*, 385.

93 "Banco Ambrosiano; Calvinism," *The Economist*, June 19, 1982, 103 (U.S. edition, p. 93); Raw, *The Moneychangers*, 392–93; see also Galli, *Finanza bianca*, 85.

94 Cornwell, *God's Banker*, 163.

95 Typical was the *Financial Times*: "Banco Ambrosiano Is Doing Fine." Raw, *The Moneychangers*, 402. See also Gurwin. *The Calvi Affair*, 93.

96 Cornwell, *God's Banker*, 168–69.

97 Gurwin. *The Calvi Affair*, 93.

98 Ibid., 79.

99 Calvi quoted in Raw, *The Moneychangers*, 408.

100 Anna Calvi gave this statement in a sworn deposition before the Court of Assizes of Rome, Assize Court of Rome, 6 June 2007, cit. 86.

101 Raw, *The Moneychangers*, 403.

102 "Banco Ambrosiano; Liquidated," *The Economist*, August 28, 1982, 59 (U.S. edition, p. 61); see also Cornwell, *God's Banker*, 175; and Raw, *The Moneychangers*, 403–4.
103 Author's written inquiries to Vatican Press Office, 2006.
104 Calvi quoted in Raw, *The Moneychangers*, 403.
105 "Banco Ambrosiano; Liquidated," *The Economist*, 59 (U.S. edition, p. 61).
106 Cornwell, *God's Banker*, 170.
107 Gurwin, *The Calvi Affair*, 102.
108 Letter, Calvi to Palazzini, quoted in Simoni and Turone, *Il caffè di Sindona*, 139–40.
109 Carboni interviewed in Raw, *The Moneychangers*, 400.
110 Raw, *The Moneychangers*, 389.
111 Gurwin, *The Calvi Affair*, 103.
112 Raw, *The Moneychangers*, 406.
113 Hoffman, *Anatomy of the Vatican*, 214, 230–31, 270; see also Simoni and Turone, *Il caffè di Sindona*, 139.
114 Willan, *The Last Supper*, 46–48; Cornwell, *God's Banker*, 177. For his long-shot deal with Opus Dei, Calvi likely relied on his business and personal connections at Madrid's Banco Occidental. Gregorio de Diego, that bank's owner, and most of its top executives, were Opus Dei members. Calvi had done business with the bank since the mid-1970s. Hutchison, *Their Kingdom Come*, 264-66, 282-84.
115 Letters, possibly forged, found after Calvi's death are cited sometimes to show that the troubled financier was in touch with Opus Dei through Carboni and Monsignor Hilary Franco, who held the honorary title of Prelate of the Pope. Franco's name was on a scrap of paper, along with several others, found in one of Calvi's suit pockets when his corpse was recovered under Blackfriars Bridge. Monsignor Franco was charged in 1986 over the illegal currency export of $13.2 million. In his defense, he said that his three co-conspirators were generous contributors to church charities and that he believed in their "good and pious intentions." Franco was acquitted. Lernoux, *In Banks We Trust*, 215–16; Gurwin, *The Calvi Affair*, 102–3; Raw, *The Moneychangers*, 406, 421; Cornwell, *God's Banker*, 198.
116 Cornwell, *God's Banker*, 127–29, 166; Gurwin, *The Calvi Affair*, 100–101; Raw, *The Moneychangers*, 386–87.
117 Raw, *The Moneychangers*, 410.
118 Gurwin, *The Calvi Affair*, 105; Lernoux, *In Banks We Trust*, 197–98, 218.
119 Lewis, "Italy's Mysterious, Deepening Bank Scandal," A1; Cornwell, *God's Banker*, 180.
120 Lewis, "Italy's Mysterious, Deepening Bank Scandal," A1; Cornwell, *God's Banker*, 179; Raw, *The Moneychangers*, 408.
121 Richard Owen, "Plea to Pope from 'God's Banker' Revealed as Murder Trial Begins," *The Times* (London), October 6, 2005.
122 Andrea Perry, Mark Watts, and Elena Cosentino, "Help Me. Murdered Banker Calvi's Last Desperate Plea to the Pope," *Sunday Express* (London), April 16, 2006, 39.
123 Owen, "Plea to Pope from 'God's Banker' Revealed as Murder Trial Begins."
124 For a full copy of the June 5, 1982, letter, see Simoni and Turone, *Il caffè di Sindona*, 141–43.
125 Raw, *The Moneychangers*, 410–11.
126 Ibid., 419, 440; Cornwell, in *God's Banker*, 185–86, has Calvi calling Luigi Mennini within forty-eight hours, but in fact it was two of Calvi's Rome attorneys who got the call.
127 Gurwin, *The Calvi Affair*, 108. Calvi was anything but calm. On June 5, Luciano Rossi, a lieutenant colonel in a special criminal financial investigative unit was found shot to death in his Rome office. Rossi had been at the center of a probe into law enforcement corruption relating to P2 and some offshore Licio Gelli accounts. The death was listed as suicide, even though there was no note and some conflicting forensics evidence. Calvi was convinced that Rossi had been murdered, the same as he believed another financial inspector, Lieutenant Colonel Salvatore Florio, had been killed in a single car accident a couple of years earlier. See generally Charles Ridley, "Colonel Linked to Scandal Commits Suicide," United Press International, International News, Rome, A.M. cycle, June 5, 1981.
128 According to Father Lorenzo Zorza, Pazienza helped obtain the passport through the Knights of Malta. "Back then," Zorza told me, "a Knights of Malta passport was good for entry into England." Author interview with Father Lorenzo Zorza, September 6, 2013.
129 Raw, *The Moneychangers*, 424.

130 The loans totaled 123,965,000 Swiss francs, then trading at 2.03 to the dollar.
131 Raw, *The Moneychangers*, 424.
132 Handwritten notes by Philip Willan of audiotaped interviews between John Cornwell and Marcinkus, February 8, 1988, 7a, provided to author courtesy of Willan.
133 See generally Hoffman, *Anatomy of the Vatican*, 201–2.
134 Lai, *Finanze vaticane*, 61.
135 Ibid., 64.
136 Handwritten notes by Philip Willan of audiotaped interviews between John Cornwell and Marcinkus, February 8, 1988, 9a, provided to author courtesy of Willan.
137 Willan, *The Last Supper*, 247-48; Cornwell, *God's Banker*, 188.
138 Gurwin, *The Calvi Affair*, 109–10, 171; Cornwell, *God's Banker*, 188.
139 Raw, *The Moneychangers*, 430–31.
140 Rosone quoted in Gurwin, *The Calvi Affair*, 110.
141 Cornwell, *God's Banker*, 188.
142 Leemans and Marcinkus quoted in Raw, *The Moneychangers*, 436–37; see also Cornwell, *God's Banker*, 189; and Gurwin, *The Calvi Affair*, 119–20.
143 Some journalists report it as fifth floor window. Hoffman, *Anatomy of the Vatican*, 199.
144 Cornwell, *God's Banker*, 191; "Italy Banker Linked to Scandal Found Hanged," *Miami Herald*, June 20, 1982, A6. In some published accounts, the note is quoted as saying, "Curse him for all the wrong he is doing to all of us from the bank and the group of whose image we were once so proud." See generally Mark S. Smith, untitled, Associated Press, International News, London, A.M. cycle, June 19, 1982.
145 Cornwell, *God's Banker*, 186.
146 Author interview with Father Lorenzo Zorza, September 6, 2013.
147 Sindona was certain Calvi had been murdered: "Calvi's death was certainly not suicide . . . he was terrified of heights. He would never have climbed over a bridge on the high scaffolding. . . . Calvi was murdered, and those who killed him made it appear to be some sort of ritual Masonic execution." Sindona interviewed in Tosches, *Power on Earth*, 245.

Chapter 25: "Protect the Source"

1 Michael Sheridan, "Loss of Face—and Funds—Worries Church," *Chicago Tribune*, July 7, 1982, A5.
2 "Archbishop Quit Bank, Paper Says," *The Miami Herald*, July 8, 1982, A2, cited in Cornwell, *God's Banker*, 207.
3 Clara Calvi, the banker's wife, was outspoken, offering her testimony to the parliamentary investigating committee as well as the prosecutors looking into the Ambrosiano's collapse. "I could be very upset about what she has said," Marcinkus later told author John Cornwell. "She called me all kinds of names and accused me of a lot of things. That's something she'll have to answer for, not me." Marcinkus interviewed in Cornwell, *A Thief in the Night*, 132.
4 Beniamino Andreatta quoted in "Italian Bank Probe Faces Wall of Silence," *The Globe and Mail* (Canada), July 24, 1982; Daniela Iacono, "Official Links Vatican to Scandal-Ridden Bank," United Press International, International News, Rome, A.M. cycle, July 3, 1982; Kay Withers, "Marcinkus Says He'll Stay, Denies Tie to Bank Scandal," *Chicago Tribune*, July 8, 1982, 1.
5 Cornwell, *God's Banker*, 210.
6 Beniamino Andreatta quoted in John Winn Miller, "Says Pope Should Order Bank Liable for $1.2 Billion," Associated Press, International News, Rome, A.M. cycle, October 8, 1982. The Treasury Ministry was also furiously trying to determine how much the IOR owned of the Ambrosiano. The Vatican said it was 1.58 percent, but some press reports put the share much higher, at 16 percent. See "Special Commission to Probe Dealings of Vatican Bank," United Press International, International News, Vatican City, A.M. cycle, December 24, 1982. Calvi's son, Carlo, claimed that with a 16 percent share, the Vatican was the effective owner of the Ambrosiano. See Gurwin, *The Calvi Affair*, 172. Investigators had difficulty determining an accurate number because the Vatican Bank likely held some of its shares through Calvi's offshore proxies, accounts to which Italian investigators could not get access. There was evidence suggesting that the IOR controlled an additional 7.5 percent of the Ambrosiano through its Luxembourg holding company, Manic.

Marcinkus had no incentive to reveal that the church had a larger stake in the parent company under attack for improper and illegal behavior. He knew that any equity stake, whether 2 percent or16 percent, would be worthless once Italian regulators dissolved the bank. Vatican attorneys later admitted that the shell companies "had de facto control" of the Ambrosiano, but emphasized that the shells "were never owned by the IOR." See generally Colby, "Vatican Bank Played a Central Role in Fall of Banco Ambrosiano," 1; and "Memo prepared by IOR's lawyers re Laura Colby's article," reproduced in its entirety in Cornwell, *A Thief in the Night*, 354–58.

7 They were Giovanni Arduino and Antonio Occhiuto, two veteran bankers.

8 "Italian Bank Probe Faces Wall of Silence," *The Globe and Mail* (Canada); Cornwell, *God's Banker*, 208–9.

9 Cornwell, *God's Banker*, 208–9.

10 Sheridan, "Loss of Face—and Funds—Worries Church," A5.

11 Franco Calamandrei quoted in "Financier Linked to Arms Deal," *The Globe and Mail* (Canada), July 8, 1982. This story developed into one in which MI6, British secret service, had targeted the Ambrosiano because Calvi's bank financed Argentine purchases of $200 million to buy Exocet missiles during the Falklands War between the two countries. Although a handful of ex-intelligence agents made some sensational claims, there was ultimately no hard proof that the Ambrosiano played such a role. When Marcinkus was asked about whether some of the money from the IOR-Ambrosiano ventures ended up in Argentine deals, he said, "I never saw it." See generally Lewis, "Italy's Mysterious, Deepening Bank Scandal," A1; Lernoux, *In Banks We Trust*, 207; Marcinkus interviewed in Cornwell, *A Thief in the Night*, 134.

12 "Vatican Bank's Head Is Reported Resigning," *The New York Times*, July 8, 1982, A4; "Report Archbishop Marcinkus Has Resigned," United Press International, International News, Vatican City, A.M. cycle, July 7, 1982.

13 Withers, "Marcinkus Says He'll Stay, Denies Tie to Bank Scandal," 1; "Vatican City Bank Chief's Job on Line," *Chicago Tribune*, July 7, 1982, 1; "Report Archbishop Marcinkus Has Resigned," United Press International. When reporters called Father Romeo Panciroli, the Vatican's press spokesman, and asked if Marcinkus was about to become a cardinal, he offered no comment. John Winn Miller, Untitled, Associated Press, International News, Rome, A.M. cycle, July 7, 1982.

14 "Archbishop Quit Bank, Paper Says," *The Miami Herald*, A2; Kay Withers, "Marcinkus Says He'll Stay, Denies Tie to Bank Scandal," *Chicago Tribune*, July 8, 1982, 1.

15 Hornblow returned to the Vatican for six months of additional service in 1989.

16 Author interview with Michael Hornblow, January 28, 2014.

17 "Pope Reportedly Asked to Remove Marcinkus," *Chicago Tribune*, July 9, 1982, 8, citing *The Daily American*, reporting from Rome.

18 Marcinkus interviewed in Withers, "Marcinkus Says He'll Stay, Denies Tie to Bank Scandal."

19 "Marcinkus Link Seen in Choice of Bernardin," *Chicago Tribune*, July 12, 1982, A5.

20 Marcinkus quoted in "Marcinkus Vows to See Scandal 'Through to End,'" United Press International, International News, Vatican City, A.M. cycle, November 27, 1982.

21 "Banco Ambrosiano; Enter God's Sleuths," *The Economist*, July 17, 1982, 76 (U.S. edition, p. 80); Paul Lewis, "Italy's Mysterious, Deepening Bank Scandal," *The New York Times*, July 28, 1982, A1.

22 John Winn Miller, "Under Pressure, Vatican Calls in Bank Consultants," Associated Press, International News, Vatican City, A.M. cycle, July 13, 1982.

23 "3 Named by Vatican to Study Bank Ties," *The New York Times*, July 14, 1982, D1. Cerutti had been a financial advisor to every Pope since Pius XII: Cornwell, *God's Banker*, 209.

24 "Some Italian bankers and officials feel that, with the exception of Mr. de Wech [*sic*], the commission is an ineffective group that may not make much of an impact on the Vatican's ponderous administrative machinery": Lewis, "Italy's Mysterious, Deepening Bank Scandal," A1.

25 Miller, "Under Pressure, Vatican Calls in Bank Consultants."

26 Untitled from LexisNexis, *The Wall Street Journal*, July 16, 1982, 20.

27 Paul Lewis, "Italy Bank's Subsidiary Defaults," *The New York Times*, July 17, 1982, 25.

28 Cornwell, *God's Banker*, 210.

29 Robert Trigaux, "The Ambrosiano Affair: 'Gang of 88' Wants Its Money Back," *The American Banker*, July 12, 1983.

30 "Italy liquidates Ailing Banco Ambrosiano," *The Globe and Mail* (Canada), August 10, 1982.

31 "Rome Suicide Widens Freemason Scandal," *The Globe and Mail* (Canada), June 6, 1981.
32 Marcinkus interviewed in Cornwell, *A Thief in the Night*, 136.
33 "Vatican Banker to Stand Trial in Sindona Case," United Press International, International News, Milan, July 22, 1982; Tosches, *Power on Earth*, 246.
34 Since Mennini had refused to return for the trial, he was convicted in absentia. Mennini's attorneys appealed, which forestalled any immediate crisis between the church and Italy.
35 Hebblethwaite, *Pope John Paul II and the Church*, 108–9.
36 The notice was not a subpoena. Still it caused concern inside the IOR. "Says Italy Investigating American Archbishop," Associated Press, International News, Rome, A.M. cycle, July 29, 1982; Cornwell, *God's Banker*, 225.
37 As for Wilson's devout faith, author interview with Michael Hornblow, January 28, 2014.
38 See Substitution of Co-Trustees, June 11, 1985, William A. Wilson Papers, Georgetown University Library, Special Collections Research Center, Washington, D.C.
39 Wilson had been the president's personal envoy at the Vatican since February 1981, before the mission was upgraded to an ambassador's post with full diplomatic recognition of the Holy See. Author interview with Peter K. Murphy, Deputy Chief of Mission (DCM) at the embassy, 1984–89, January 31, 2014. The Vatican embassy consisted of only three consular officers: the ambassador, the DCM, and a political officer. It also employed three full-time secretaries, and relied on support from the much larger American embassy in Rome. See also the Association for Diplomatic Studies and Training, Foreign Affairs Oral History Project, Peter K. Murphy, interviewed by William D. Morgan, Initial Interview Date, April 4, 1998, Copyright 1998 ADST, 84–85.
40 Letter, William Wilson to Robert H. McBride, July 30, 1982, Box 1, Series 2, Correspondence 1982, William A. Wilson Papers, Georgetown University Library, Special Collections Research Center, Washington, D.C.
41 Author interview with Michael Hornblow, January 28, 2014.
42 Cable from Michael Hornblow, U.S. Embassy, Rome, to Secretary of State, Washington, DC, Secret, Section 01, October 1, 1980, part of the Department of State Freedom of Information request by the author. Also see the collected 1982–84 correspondence of William A. Wilson, William A. Wilson Papers, Georgetown University Library, Special Collections Research Center, Washington, D.C.
43 Cable from Michael Hornblow, U.S. Embassy, Rome, to Secretary of State, Washington, DC, Secret, Section 01, October 1, 1980, part of the Department of State Freedom of Information request by the author.
44 Ibid.
45 Ibid., point 8.
46 Author interview with Peter K. Murphy, Deputy Chief of Mission at the embassy, 1984–89, January 31, 2014.
47 See generally letter, William Wilson to Robert H. McBride, July 30, 1982, Box 1, Series 2, Correspondence 1982, William A. Wilson Papers, Georgetown University Library, Special Collections Research Center, Washington, DC.
48 Richard Hammer, *The Vatican Connection: The Astonishing Account of a Billion-Dollar Counterfeit Stock Deal Between the Mafia and the Church* (New York: Holt, Rinehart & Winston, 1982).
49 Letter from William Wilson to William French Smith, July 15, 1982, William A. Wilson Papers, Box 2, Folder 66, Georgetown University Library, Special Collections Research Center, Washington, DC.
50 Ibid.
51 Ibid.
52 Letter from John G. Roberts Jr. to William A. Wilson, August 9, 1982, William A. Wilson Papers, Box 2, Folder 66, Georgetown University Library, Special Collections Research Center, Washington, DC.
53 Robert Wagner to Stanley Frank, August 20, 1982, Correspondence Files, William A. Wilson Papers, Box 2, Folder 66, Georgetown University Library, Special Collections Research Center, Washington, DC.
54 Letter from William A. Wilson to His Excellency, Archbishop Paul Marcinkus, August 12, 1982, William A. Wilson Papers, Box 2, Folder 66, Georgetown University Library, Special Collections

Research Center, Washington, DC. The letter from Roberts was time-stamped as received by Wilson on August 11; hence Wilson was writing to Marcinkus only a day later.

55 Ibid.

56 In an August 30 letter from Marcinkus to Wilson, the archbishop indicated he had spoken to Wagner and his aides and "it seems that there is very little we really can do without getting involved in a long process of litigation." William A. Wilson Papers, Box 2, Folder 66, Georgetown University Library, Special Collections Research Center, Washington, DC.

57 Susan Dentzer and Hope Lambert, "A Book of Revelations," *Newsweek*, September 13, 1982, 69.

58 Letter, William Wilson to Robert H. McBride, July 30, 1982, Box 1, Series 2, Correspondence 1982, William A. Wilson Papers, Georgetown University Library, Special Collections Research Center, Washington, DC.

Chapter 26: "A Heck of a Lot of Money"

1 Gurwin, *The Calvi Affair*, 162.

2 Louise Branson, "Italian Masonic Leader Arrested at Swiss Bank," United Press International, International News, Geneva, P.M. cycle, September 14, 1982; "Gelli Deported Back to Italy," *BBC News*, October 16, 1998.

3 Lernoux, *In Banks We Trust*, 209; Gurwin, *The Calvi Affair*, 165–66; Cornwell, *God's Banker*, 239–40; DiFonzo, *St. Peter's Banker*, 259.

4 Henry Kamm, "Pope Vows to Assist Bank Study," *The New York Times*, November 27, 1982, 35.

5 Henry Kamm, "Cardinals Discuss Tie to Bank," *The New York Times*, November 26, 1982, 25; Gurwin, *The Calvi Affair*, 170.

6 Gurwin, ibid., 170–71; Cornwell, *God's Banker*, 213–14.

7 Marcinkus quoted in Cornwell, *God's Banker*, 233.

8 Lai, *Finanze vaticane*, 66, in particular Lai interview with Cardinal Giuseppe Caprio, December 4, 1982, 135.

9 Hoffman, *Anatomy of the Vatican*, 204.

10 See Laura Colby, "Vatican Bank Played a Central Role in Fall of Banco Ambrosiano," *Wall Street Journal*, April 27, 1987, 1.

11 Untitled, Associated Press, International News, Rome, A.M. cycle, December 5, 1982; Raw, *The Moneychangers*, 34–49.

12 Clara Calvi quoted in Willey, *God's Politician*, 213–14; "Bank President's Wife Says Husband Killed, Not Suicide," International News, A.M. cycle, Turin, United Press International, October 7, 1982; Untitled, dateline Rome, International News, A.M. cycle, Associated Press, December 5, 1982 (referring to Clara mistakenly as Carla).

13 "Special Commission to Probe Dealings of Vatican Bank," United Press International, International News, Vatican City, A.M. cycle, December 24, 1982.

14 Joan Goulding, "Jewish Groups Protest Sparks Vatican Probe," United Press International, Domestic News, Los Angeles, BC cycle, January 5, 1983.

15 "Vatican Said Investigating Banker's Alleged Ties to Nazis," Associated Press, Domestic News, Los Angeles, P.M. cycle, January 6, 1983.

16 Jay Arnold, "Jews Ask Pope to Rescind Appointment of Alleged Nazi Collaborator," Associated Press, Domestic News, Los Angeles, A.M. cycle, December 29, 1982.

17 "Vatican Said Investigating Banker's Alleged Ties to Nazis," Associated Press.

18 Pawlikowski quoted in Joan Goulding, "Catholic Theologian Calls for Probe of Papal Appointee," United Press International, Domestic News, Los Angeles, A.M. cycle, January 7, 1983.

19 The company was Deutsche Solvay-Werke A.G., a Belgian conglomerate controlled by the Nazis after Belgium fell to German troops in 1940. "Records Show Papal Appointee Helped Run Nazi Camp Where Pope Worked," United Press International, Domestic News, Los Angeles, P.M. cycle, January 11, 1983. Author Charles Higham added to the pressure by calling Abs "Hitler's Banker." In his 1983 book (*Trading with the Enemy*), about how Allied and German companies clandestinely did business throughout the war, he contended that Abs was part of "Hitler's immediate circle" (p. 240).

20 John Paul quoted in "Pope Cautions Faithful Against News Reports," Associated Press, International News, Rome, A.M. cycle, February 27, 1983.
21 Author interview with Rabbi Marvin Heir, June 24, 2006.
22 Sergio Itzhak Minerbi, "Pope John Paul II and the Jews: An Evaluation," *Jewish Political Studies Review* 18: 1, 2 (Spring 2006).
23 Heir quoted in Untitled, United Press International, International News, Rome, A.M. cycle, April 25, 1983.
24 Michael Day, "Vatican Turns to Fox News Man Greg Burke for Image Makeover," *The Independent* (London), June 25, 2012.

Chapter 27: "I've Been Poisoned"

1 "Red Hats for Six Continents," *Time*, January 17, 1983.
2 In keeping with the shift since Pope Paul VI to reduce the influence of Italians in the College of Cardinal, only three of the eighteen new appointees were Italian. "Pontiff Names Bernardin and Glemp Cardinals," *Chicago Tribune*, January 6, 1983, 1; "Josef Glemp Is Among 18 New Cardinals," *The Boston Globe*, January 5, 1983, 1; see also Hoffman, *Anatomy of the Vatican*, 206.
3 "Pontiff Names Bernardin and Glemp Cardinals," *Chicago Tribune*, 1.
4 "Answers to Quiz," *The New York Times*, January 8, 1983, 12; see Henry Kamm, "Inside the College of Cardinals," *The New York Times*, January 9, 1983: "Archbishop Paul C. Marcinkus, the head of the Vatican Bank, did not receive the accolade that before the bank scandal was assumed to be a certainty." And "18 Become Cardinals Today: Family and Friends Gather in Vatican City for Ceremonies," *The Boston Globe*, February 2, 1983, 1: "Archbishop Marcinkus had been expected to be named a cardinal but was not."
5 Henry Kamm, "Vatican-Italy Study Set on Ambrosiano Links," *The New York Times*, December 25, 1982, 29; see also Nancy Frazier, "Vatican, Italy Form Ambrosiano Commission," *Catholic Courier Journal* (New York), January 5, 1983, 18. Charles Raw says that all three Vatican appointees were lawyers. *The Moneychangers*, 47.
6 Raw, *The Moneychangers*, 43, 47. See formation order of the commission in Nuzzi, *Vaticano S.p.A.*, 19.
7 "Vatican Pact Reported on Banco Ambrosiano," *The New York Times*, May 11, 1984, D1.
8 The long-standing rule for a full Papal indulgence for Jubilees was a requirement that a Catholic visit Rome's four basilicas fifteen times during a single year. Romans had to make thirty visits. John Paul lowered the bar, requiring only that each of the basilicas be visited once. That ensured that millions would travel to Rome for the easier-to-target indulgence.
9 Nuzzi, *Vaticano S.p.A.*, 19.
10 Boniface VIII called the first Holy Year in 1300, and subsequent ones were held every fifty years. But by 1425, they were so popular and lucrative that they were scheduled every twenty-five years. John Paul cited the crucifixion of Jesus as the reason to mark the 1950th anniversary of his death and resurrection. James L. Franklin, "Unusual Holy Years Starts This Weekend," *The Boston Globe*, March 27, 1983, 1; see also Sari Gilbert, "Rome Expects Millions for the Holy Year," *The Boston Globe*, February 27, 1983, 1; Gurwin, *The Calvi Affair*, 176–77.
11 It was a seven-year (1973–80) gasoline-tax-evasion scheme, involving Italian customs agents conspiring with oil company employees who shuffled customs documents that passed off premium fuel as lower-taxed heating oil. "Petroleum Scandal Touches Vatican Bank Official," Associated Press, International News, Rome, A.M. cycle, February 10, 1983; see also "3 Priests Implicated in Rome Tax Scandal," *The New York Times*, February 11, 1983; and "Vatican Bank Officials Linked to a Major Financial Scandal," *The New York Times*, February 3, 1983, A17. See generally John Winn Miller, "Career of Once Powerful American Prelate in Decline," Associated Press, International News, Vatican City, BC cycle, August 26, 1984. Prosecutors notified two other priests, Monsignor Mario Pimpo, secretary for the confidential affairs of the Vicariate of Rome, and a Roman parish priest, Giacomo Ceretto, they were also under investigation.
12 See generally Untitled, *The Wall Street Journal*, February 14, 1983, 21.
13 See generally Hutchison, *Their Kingdom Come*, 290.
14 Lai, *Finanze vaticane*, 87.

15 Massimo Spada, who had spent decades at the bank, said De Bonis had avoided being a target in the Ambrosiano case because he "had only been a clerk then." Benny Lai interview of Massimo Spada, January 14, 1998, and June 7, 1989, in Lai, *Finanze vaticane*, 145; and see also Nuzzi, *Vaticano S.p.A.*, 62, citing Giancarlo Zizola,"Banchiere di san Francescon," *Panorama.*
16 Raw, *The Moneychangers*, 62, 126, 134.
17 John Corry, "TV Reviews Based on Early Tapes," *The New York Times*, February 16, 1983, C31.
18 Raw, *The Moneychangers*, 42.
19 "New Inquest Set in Calvi's Death," *The New York Times*, March 30, 1983, D5.
20 Raw, *The Moneychangers*, 9.
21 Ibid., 42–43.
22 In its published final report, the joint commission stated simply that the three men had been "unavailable for interview." An independent magistrate, Antonio Pizzi, who investigated the IOR's role in the Ambrosiano collapse, later complained to the press, "They have always refused to be questioned in the case." The Italian Court of Cassation, which handles issues of legal procedure, upheld the right of Pizzi to investigate the Vatican officials, but no one could force them to make themselves available for questioning. "Arrest Warrant Issued for Marcinkus in Bank Collapse," Associated Press, International News, Milan, A.M. cycle, February 25, 1987.
23 Some resorted to arguing their case in the press, such as when Cologne's Cardinal Joseph Höffner took a not so subtle swipe at Marcinkus by telling reporters that he favored only "competent" financial laymen to run the Vatican Bank. "Shift Is Urged at Vatican Bank," *The New York Times*, March 8, 1983, D4. In 1986 Höffner asked John Paul to replace Marcinkus with a noncleric as the IOR's chief.
24 IOR/Marcinkus memorandum, July 1, 1983, quoted in Raw, *The Moneychangers*, 45.
25 Andrew Malone and Nick Pisa, "Was This Girl Murdered After Being Snatched for Vatican Sex Parties? Police Try and Solve the Mystery of the 15-Year-Old Who Vanished in 1983," *Mail Online*, May 30, 2012; See Willan, *The Last Supper*, 283–84.
26 Uli Schmetzer, "Extradition Cloaked in Intrigue," *Chicago Tribune*, February 18, 1988, 18; Cornwell, *God's Banker*, 246–47. The Joint Commission also wanted to get the assistance of Gelli's right-hand man, Umberto Ortolani, but he was in Brazil fighting extradition.
27 "Gelli, Fugitive Italian Financier, Gives Himself Up in Switzerland," *The Philadelphia Inquirer*, September 22, 1987; "Top Italian Fugitive Licio Gelli Arrested in France," International News, Rome, Associated Press, September 10, 1998; "Gelli Deported Back to Italy," *BBC*, October 16, 1998; Raw, *The Moneychangers*, 9, 158, 484.
28 Final Report of the Joint Commission, October 1983, in Raw, *The Moneychangers*, 45.
29 Memo to Cardinal Secretary of State, from Agostino Gamboni, Pellegrino Capaldo, and Renato Dardozzi, Vatican City, August 17, 1983, reproduced in Nuzzi, *Vaticano S.p.A.*, 23–24.
30 Statements of Santa Maria and Cattaneo in Final Report of the Joint Commission, October 1983, quoted in Raw, *The Moneychangers*, 47.
31 Statement of Chiomenti in Final Report of the Joint Commission, October 1983, quoted in Raw, *The Moneychangers*, 31–32.
32 "Vatican Bank Is Target," *The New York Times*, March 28, 1983, D2.
33 Raw, *The Moneychangers*, 32–34.
34 Draft document, "The Spirit of Luca," dated August 10, 1983, quoted in Raw, *The Moneychangers*, 33.
35 All Marcinkus statements about his views and what he said regarding whether the Vatican should settle with the Ambrosiano's creditors are from interviews by John Cornwell, *A Thief in the Night*, 136–37. That interview with Cornwell was the first public evidence of the heated debate that had taken place inside the Vatican.
36 Raw, *The Moneychangers*, 35.
37 John Winn Miller, Untitled, Associated Press, International News, Rome, A.M. cycle, April 1, 1984. Italmobiliare had controlling interests in the insurance conglomerate RAS, as well as the country's largest cement maker, Italcementi.
38 Miller, "Career of Once Powerful American Prelate in Decline."
39 "Vatican Bank Inquiry in Italy," *The New York Times*, April 2, 1984, D5.
40 "U.S. Archbishop Says He Has Nothing to Hide in Vatican Loan Probe," Associated Press, Business News, Rome, P.M. cycle, April 3, 1984. "His foes in the Curia were delighted when he got indicted," says Peter Murphy, later the Deputy Chief of Mission for U.S. embassy at the Vatican.

"They barely hid their glee." Author interview with Peter K. Murphy, Deputy Chief of Mission at the embassy, 1984–89, January 31, 2014.

41 "John Paul Completes His Team," *Time*, April 23, 1984.

42 The appointment that got the most attention was of Benin's Cardinal Bernardin Gantin to become the prefect of the Congregation for Bishops. It made Gantin the first non-Italian with the power of appointing—with the Pope's approval—the church's bishops. Gantin also later served on a committee of five cardinals that had some general oversight over financial matters in the wake of Marcinkus's departure.

43 "John Paul Completes His Team," *Time*. Although Marcinkus kept the same title, the changes by John Paul meant that his authority was no longer unchecked when it came to the Vatican City administration.

44 Marcinkus interviewed by John Cornwell, *A Thief in the Night*, 136–37.

45 Marcinkus statements from interviews in ibid.

46 Raw, *The Moneychangers*, 36–37.

47 The first reports were that the accord included 109 creditor banks, but the final agreement covered 120. Paul Lewis, "Vatican Pact Reported on Banco Ambrosiano," *The New York Times*, May 11, 1984, D1; "A Moral Duty," *Time*, May 21, 1984. Also, initially, the Vatican planned to pay $250 million in three installments over twelve months, but the banks gave the church a $6 million discount if it made a single payment by June 30, 1984. "Vatican to Pay in Bank Failure," *Chicago Tribune*, May 22, 1984, B3. In fact, based on fluctuations in currency exchange, the Vatican paid $240.9 million on Monday, July 2, since June 30 was a Saturday. Lewis, "Vatican Pact Reported on Banco Ambrosiano," D1. See also "Tentative Agreement Reportedly Reached on Banco Ambrosiano," Associated Press, Business News, Rome, P.M. cycle, May 21, 1984; "Payment by Vatican," *The New York Times*, July 4, 1984, D14. See also Galli, *Finanza bianca*, 88.

48 Lai, *Finanze vaticane*, 69.

49 The Vatican payment was 60 percent of a $406 million settlement agreed to by the creditors, about two thirds of their claims against the Ambrosiano group. Italy arranged other payments from cash recovered after the Ambrosiano's collapse as well as from the fire sale of some of its assets, including Banca del Gottardo, which Japan's Sumitomo Bank bought for $144 million. Also, $53 million was seized from Licio Gelli's Swiss bank account. "Vatican Pact Reported on Banco Ambrosiano," D1. See also "Payment by Vatican," *The New York Times*, July 4, 1984, D14; "Vatican Payment Reported," *The New York Times*, May 26, 1984, 42.

The execution of the agreement was cloaked in secrecy. Bankers and Vatican representatives gathered at Geneva's grand luxe Hotel des Bergues, but when reporters arrived the group moved to the nondescript European Free Trade Association building.

50 "Vatican Pact Reported on Banco Ambrosiano," *The New York Times*, D1.

51 Charles Raw, a *London Sunday Times* reporter who investigated the matter for nine years, and wrote what many consider the definitive book on the financial details of the crisis—*The Moneychangers*—believes the Vatican lost about $250 million in its dealings with the Ambrosiano and Calvi. See *The Moneychangers*, 39.

52 "A Moral Duty," *Time*; see also "Vatican Pact Reported on Banco Ambrosiano," *The New York Times*, D1.

53 Stella Shamoon, "Untangling the Banco Ambrosiano Scandal; Shadowy Web of Financial Dealings Spreads," United Press International, Financial, London, BC cycle, May 6, 1984. For a full copy of the 1984 changes, see the articles reproduced as Accordo tra la Repubblica italiana e la Santa Sede che apporta modificazioni al Concordato lateranense, Massimo Teodori, *Vaticano rapace: Lo scandaloso finanziamento dell'Italia alla Chiesa* (Venice: Marsilio Editiori, 2013), 145–71. See also "New Concordat with Vatican Is Approved by Italian Senate," *The New York Times*, August 4, 1984.

54 Henry Kamm, "Italy Abolishes State Religion in Vatican Pact," *The New York Times*, February 19, 1984.

55 In 2010, the tax yielded about $900 million to the church.

56 How to break the news of the "murder plot" was coordinated by Jonathan Cape, the U.K. publisher, and Bantam, the U.S. distributor. It was considered a coup to have kept the book's explosive charge secret during months of presales of rights to book clubs and the scheduling of the author on television shows for the day after publication. Curt Suplee, "How the Book Industry Kept Its Pope Story Secret," *The Washington Post*, June 14, 1984, B1.

57 "Envoy's Plea Was Opposed," *The New York Times*, July 10, 1984, A10.

58 Adding to the pressure on Wilson were disclosures that he had received a special exemption from the State Department to continue to serve on the board of two companies, Earle M. Jorgensen, a California-based steel firm, and Pennzoil. Ambassadors usually resign their corporate director's positions to avoid any potential conflict of interest. Mary Thornton, "U.S. Envoy to Vatican Got Special Exemption," *The Washington Post*, July 13, 1984, A2; "Ambassador from Pennzoil?," *Chicago Tribune*, July 20, 1984, 22.

59 Loren Jenkins, "Envoy to Vatican Denies Wrongdoing; Wilson Refuses to Discuss Controversial Ties, Travel to Libya," *The Washington Post*, May 22, 1986.

60 Miller, "Career of Once Powerful American Prelate in Decline."

61 When the AP reporter caught up with Marcinkus, the IOR chief said, "I'd say that 99.9 percent of my life has been an open book. Perhaps that's my problem. Maybe I'm too frank." Ibid.

62 "Italian Financier Suspected in Vatican Bank Collapse Was 77," United Press International, International News, Milan, A.M. cycle, September 21, 1984.

63 It had been made possible by a new treaty between Rome and Washington that was aimed at fighting Mafia drug syndicates. "Financier Sent to Italy to Face Charges," *The Globe and Mail* (Canada), September 26, 1984.

64 "No one [at the Vatican] wanted anything at all to do with the subject [of Sindona]," recalls Peter Murphy, the Deputy Chief of the U.S. embassy at the time, "and [they] pushed everything off on Marcinkus." Email from Peter K. Murphy to author, January 30, 2014.

65 "Italian Financier Jailed for Fraud," *The Globe and Mail* (Canada), March 16, 1985.

66 "Ex-Adviser to Vatican Gets Life for Murder," United Press International, Milan, A.M. cycle, March 18, 1987.

67 Uli Schmetzer, "'I've Been Poisoned,' Stricken Financier Sindona Told Jailers," *Chicago Tribune*, March 22, 1986, 6.

68 "Italian Bank Swindler Rushed to Hospital in Coma," United Press International, International News, Voghera, Italy, P.M. cycle, March 20, 1986; "Jailed Italian Financier Dies of Cyanide Poisoning," *The Washington Post*, March 23, 1986, A18.

69 E. J. Dionne Jr., "Italy Says It Found Cyanide in Sindona," *The New York Times*, March 22, 1986, 3; "Cyanide Was in Sindona's Coffee, Investigators Say," Associated Press, International News, Milan, A.M. cycle, April 1, 1986.

70 Uli Schmetzer, "Jailed Italian Financier in Coma After Poisoning," *Chicago Tribune*, March 21, 1986, 6; "Poisoning Baffles Jail Officials," *The Globe and Mail* (Canada), March 22, 1986, A15.

71 "Magistrate Rules Financier Killed Himself," United Press International, International News, Milan, A.M. cycle, November 3, 1986.

72 Author interview with Ivan Fisher, June 19, 2013.

73 Piero Valsecchi, "Arrest Warrant Reportedly Issued for American Archbishop," Associated Press International News, Milan, BC cycle, February 25, 1987; "Arrest Warrant Issued for Marcinkus in Bank Collapse," Associated Press, International News, Milan, A.M. cycle, February 25, 1987.

74 Uli Schmetzer, "Vatican Bank Official Can Be Arrested, Italy Says," *Chicago Tribune*, March 1, 1987, 27.

75 Valsecchi, "Arrest Warrant for American Prelate in Bank Scandal."

76 See for example Uli Schmetzer, "Italy Trying to Arrest Bishop," *Chicago Tribune*, February 26, 1987, 5. U.S. government officials, in classified cables, had long referred to Marcinkus as "the Pope's Banker." See generally cable from U.S. Embassy, Rome, to Secretary of State, Washington, DC, Secret, Section 01, October 1, 1980, part of the Department of State Freedom of Information request by the Author, August 15, 2007, 15 of 162.

77 Uli Schmetzer, "Marcinkus Among 23 Sought by Italy," *Chicago Tribune*, February 27, 1987, 14.

78 St. Martha Hospice was built in 1891 because of fear that a deadly cholera epidemic might reach Rome. It served mostly as a hospital for pilgrims before it was converted into residential housing for clerics inside the city-state. In 1996, a new structure was built at the site, Casa Santa Marta. It is not only a guesthouse for clergy, but it is where Pope Francis moved his residence in 2013, a much simpler affair than the grander Papal apartment in the Apostolic Palace.

79 Frances D'Emilio, "Independence of Holy See Complicates Scandal Probe," Associated Press, International News, Vatican City, A.M. cycle, February 28, 1987.

80 John Tagliabue, "Vatican Prelate Said to Face Arrest in Milan Bank Collapse," *The New York Times*, February 26, 1987, A1; John Tagliabue, "Warrants for Vatican Bankers Raise Legal Problem for Italy," *The New York Times*, February 27, 1987, A6.

81 Schmetzer, "Marcinkus Among 23 Sought by Italy."
82 Cornwell, *God's Banker*, 226; Hoffman, *Anatomy of the Vatican*, 203.
83 "'Astonished' by Warrants for 3 Bank Officials: Vatican," *Los Angeles Times*, February 27, 1987, 2.
84 D'Emilio, "Independence of Holy See Complicates Scandal Probe," Associated Press.
85 John Tagliabue, "Vatican Denounces Attempt by Italy to Arrest Bank Chief," *The New York Times*, February 28, 1987, 2.
86 Loren Jenkins, "Vatican Issues Defense of Top Bank Officials; American, 2 Aides Charged in Fraud Case," *The Washington Post*, February 28, 1987, A17; see also Lai, *Finanze vaticane*, 72–73, 139.
87 Author interview with Peter K. Murphy, Deputy Chief of Mission at the U.S. Embassy, 1984–89, January 31, 2014.
88 Uli Schmetzer, "Vatican Bank Official Can Be Arrested, Italy Says," *Chicago Tribune*, March 1, 1987, 27.
89 The original estimate for 1987 was a $63 million deficit, but it came in at $80 million. Ruth Gruber, "Vatican Faces 'Radical Insufficiency' of Funds; Appeal for Money Goes to Catholics Worldwide," *The Toronto Star*, March 29, 1987, H5; William Scobie, "Secrets of the Holy See," *Sydney Morning Herald*, May 20, 1987, 17; see also "Vatican Expects Record Deficit, Appeals to Local Churches," *Chicago Tribune*, March 27, 1987, 1.
90 Benny Lai interview with Cardinal Giuseppe Caprio, December 11, 1988, reflecting that donations had dropped from a high of 30 billion lire to "around 6 billion," in Lai, *Finanze vaticane*, 143.
91 Shawn Tully and Marta F. Dorion, "The Vatican's Finances," *Fortune*, December 21, 1987, 28–40.
92 Ibid.
93 Ibid.
94 As of 2014, funding pensions was still one of the biggest problems confronting the church. Longtime workers, with forty years or more of service, retire with 80 percent of their salaries for life. And many employees start young in the city-state and stay through full retirement. Although the Vatican has moved to a smaller "fixed benefit" plan going forward, it is obligated to fund about 1,800 retirees for decades to come. An unnamed "Vatican insider" told *Fortune* that the church's pension fund is short by a "few hundred million dollars." Quoted in Shawn Tully, "This Pope Means Business," *Fortune*, September 1, 2014.
95 "The global image of the Church has suffered," Cardinal Giuseppe Caprio, head of the budget office, told *Fortune*: ibid.; Lai, *Finanze vaticane*, 70.
96 "Cardinals Tackle Vatican's $56M Budget Shortfall," *The Telegraph*, March 25, 1987.
97 Unidentified cleric quoted in Alan Riding, "U.S. Prelate Not Indicted in Italy Bank Scandal," *The New York Times*, April 30, 1989, 22. Toronto's Cardinal Gerald Emmett Carter told *Fortune* that "We [the cardinals] fought for five years for more open accounting": Tully and Dorion, "The Vatican's Finances."
98 Rocco Palmo, "God's Bankers: Not Afraid," *Whispers in the Loggia*, October 14, 2008, online at http://whispersintheloggia.blogspot.com/2008/10/gods-bankers-not-afraid.html; see also Tully and Dorion, "The Vatican's Finances."
99 "Italy Asks Vatican Extradition," *The New York Times*, March 29, 1987, 13; Bill Scott, "Law Closes In on Wanted Vatican Bank Boss," *The Advertiser*, March 27, 1987.
100 "Marcinkus Treated Brutally, Pope Says," *Chicago Tribune*, April 2, 1987, 5; Tana De Zuleta, "Vatican Stands Firm over Calls to Extradite Marcinkus: Pope Fights to Defend His Banker in Scandal," *The Sunday Times* (London), April 5, 1987.
101 Gianluigi Nuzzi, *Ratzinger Was Afraid: The Secret Documents, the Money and the Scandals that Overwhelmed the Pope* (Rome: Adagio, 2013), Google edition, 27.
102 Recounted by Bishop Lynch at Marcinkus's funeral, reported by Margaret Ramirez, "A Final Farewell for 'God's Banker'; Family, Friends Share Their Memories of Cicero Native Who Became Archbishop," *Chicago Tribune*, March 3, 2006, 1. In 1981, Italy's public prosecutors notified Mother Teresa and seventy-four clerics and lay bankers that they were under investigation for violating the country's tough currency exchange statutes. The suspicion was that wealthy Italians had used the IOR and some foreign Catholic charities to smuggle cash out of Italy. No formal charges were ultimately filed. Robert McCartney, "Vatican Bank, Charity Groups Face Currency Probe," Associated Press, International, Rome, A.M. cycle, November 17, 1981.
103 Author interview with Peter K. Murphy, Deputy Chief of Mission at the U.S. Embassy, 1984–89, January 31, 2014. By "sharks" Murphy is referring not to other prelates but to Sindona, Calvi, P2, and Gelli, and some of the lay businesspeople with whom Marcinkus dealt with at the IOR.

104 Ibid.

105 Piero Valsecchi, "Court Upholds Arrest Warrant for Marcinkus," Associated Press, International, Milan, P.M. cycle, April 14, 1987. Some clerics were disappointed since they wanted the legal standoff over before the June feasts of St. Peter and St. Paul, traditionally a time when the faithful gave large donations. They feared that otherwise generous Catholics would be put off by the daily headlines speculating about whether Italian prosecutors or the Pope would first capitulate. Clare Pedrick, "Storm Clouds at Vatican Bank: Officials Urge Sacking of Notorious President as Donation Day Looms," *The Financial Post* (Toronto), May 4, 1987, 11. For general effect of how the scandals caused a drop-off in contributions, see "Poor Image Depletes Vatican Coffers," *Chicago Tribune*, March 18, 1986, 5.

106 Piero Valsecchi, "More Warrants Issued in Collapse of Banco Ambrosiano," Associated Press, International, Milan, A.M. cycle, May 6, 1987.

107 Lai, *Finanze vaticane*, 73.

108 "Vatican Court Reportedly Rejects Extradition of Marcinkus," Associated Press, International, Turin, P.M. cycle, June 19, 1987.

109 George Armstrong, "The Vatican Gives Haven to a Fugitive," *Los Angeles Times*, July 19, 1987, Part 5, 2.

110 Nuzzi, *Vaticano S.p.A.*, 22.

111 Ibid., 37.

112 "Vatican Backs 3 in Bank Case," *The New York Times*, July 14, 1987, D21.

113 "Vatican Official: Marcinkus 'Victim' of Bank Scandal," Associated Press, International, Vatican City, P.M. cycle, July 13, 1987.

114 Ibid.

115 Prosecutors had argued in vain that the IOR was not a "central entity" since it was so heavily involved with secular investments and businesses. See "3 Won't Face Charges in Vatican Bank Case," *Chicago Tribune*, June 9, 1988, 23.

116 "Italy Can't Charge Vatican Bank Archbishop—Court," *Los Angeles Times*, July 17, 1987, 2.

117 Benny Lai interview with De Bonis, July 28, 1987, in Lai, *Vaticane finanze*, 140.

118 Marcinkus quoted in Samuel Koo, "Top Court Upholds Vatican, Rejects Arrest Warrants for Marcinkus," Associated Press, International News, Rome, P.M. cycle, July 17, 1987; Roberto Suro, "Top Italy Court Annuls Warrants Against 3 Vatican Bank Officials," *The New York Times*, July 18, 1987, 2. When author Benny Lai, *Finanze vaticane*, reached Marcinkus, the IOR chief told him, "I am happy with this judgment, because it gave me the proof that justice exists. I've always had faith in justice and I was right" (interview by Lai of Marcinkus, July 28, 1987).

119 Uli Schmetzer, "Court Bars Arrest of Marcinkus," *Chicago Tribune*, July 18, 1987, C1.

120 See generally George Armstrong, "Bank Officials Free to Leave Vatican," *The Guardian*, July 18, 1987.

121 Paul Marcinkus v. Nal Publishing Inc., 138 Misc.2d 256 (1987), Supreme Court, New York County, December 3, 1987, available online at http://scholar.google.com/scholar_case?case=8865799868810149066&q=138+Misc.+2d+256&hl=en&as_sdt=4,33.

122 Roberto Suro, "Italy Presses Case Against Vatican Bank Officials," *The New York Times*, December 11, 1987, A8.

123 "Laywer Asking Court to Rule on Marcinkus Prosecution," Associated Press, International, Milan, December 11, 1987. In 2008, Minister of Justice Angelino Alfano in essence copied the language of the high court in issuing a decree, the Lodo Alfano (Alfano Law). It granted immunity from prosecution to the four highest government offices, the President, two Speakers of the Houses of Parliament, and the Prime Minister. The Lodo Alfano, which was intended to end any investigations of Italy's Prime Minister, Silvio Berlusconi, was voided by the country's Constitutional Court in October 2009.

124 Uli Schmetzer, "Bishop Gets Immunity in Bank Case," *Chicago Tribune*, May 18, 1988, C6; "High Court Rules Italian Courts Can't Prosecute American Archbishop," Associated Press, International, Rome, June 8, 1988.

125 Tully and Dorion, "The Vatican's Finances."

126 The IOR had for decades never exceeded a dozen employees. Not a single employee had an MBA. By 2012, the IOR counted 100 employees, the result of a major growth spurt after the millennium. Ibid.

127 Victor L. Simpson, "Vatican Forecasts Record Deficit; Announces Bank Overhaul," Associated

Press, International, Vatican City, P.M. cycle, March 9, 1989. John Cornwell, "The Dues of the Fisherman; Burdened by Scandal and Bureaucracy, the Vatican Is Living Beyond Its Means, and the Crisis Is Undermining Its Mission. A Miracle is Needed to End the Shortage of Peter's Pence," *The Independent* (London), April 15, 1990, 10; see also Raw, *The Moneychangers,* 38.

128 Roberto Suro, "Vatican Expects Record '88 Deficit," *The New York Times*, March 6, 1988; "Nippon TV and the Vatican," *The New York Times*, May 29, 1990. As for more specifics about the 1985 budget figures, Jason Berry obtained a *General Final Balance Sheet and Profit and Loss Account* from someone he described as a "background source." See Berry, *Render Unto Rome*, 37, 367 n. 5.

129 Tully and Dorion, "The Vatican's Finances."

130 For years, the Vatican had subsidized the Roman diocese—for which it felt responsible—because that diocese had trouble covering its expenses. See Berry, *Render Unto Rome*, 39–40.

131 In the case of the German tax, for instance, large dioceses such as Cologne had 75 percent of their expenses covered by the tax. See Tully and Dorion, "The Vatican's Finances." Desmond O'Grady, "Vatican Plan for Tax on Catholics," *Sydney Morning Herald*, August 28, 1987, 10. One cardinal, Joseph Höffner, sent chills through most Catholics when he suggested a worldwide tax on the faithful.

132 Tully and Dorion, "The Vatican's Finances."

133 Lai, *Finanze vaticane*, 84–85.

134 "We're probably the only organization in Italy that takes rent control seriously," one unnamed prelate moaned to *Fortune*. Tully and Dorion, "The Vatican's Finances."

135 Besides Krol, the commission included New York Cardinal John O'Connor. "The Pope Creates Vatican Bank Panel," Lexis Nexis, *Herald*, Business Section, June 29, 1988, 21. See also Tully and Dorion, "The Vatican's Finances."

136 Shawn Tully and Marta F. Dorion, "The Vatican's Finances," *Fortune*, December 21, 1987.

137 Benny Lai interview with de Caprio, July 28, 1987, in Lai, *Finanze vaticane*, 140.

138 APSA, the Vatican's other chief financial department besides the IOR, was firmly under lay control by this time. Benedetto Argentieri, an ex–market analyst at Brussels' Banque Européenne d'Investissement, directed its twenty-six lay professionals. Compared to Marcinkus and the IOR, APSA had evolved into a more accountable division. Tully and Dorion, "The Vatican's Finances." See also Religious News Service, "American Head of Vatican Bank May Be Ousted," *Los Angeles Times*, July 16, 1988, Part 2, 7.

139 Nuzzi, *Vaticano S.p.A.*, 35.

140 Lai, *Finanze vaticane*, 148, citing G. Zizola, "banker of St. Francis," *Panorama*, March 26, 1989.

141 Benny Lai interviews of Massimo Spada, January 14, 1998, and June 7, 1989, in Lai, *Finanze vaticane*, 142, cited in Nuzzi, *Vaticano S.p.A.*, 62, as "1 2 de julio de 1987." Giancarlo Zizola, "Banchiere di san Francescon," *Panorama*. Author interview with Lai, September 20, 2006.

Chapter 28: White Finance

1 Caloia was the group's secretary, and other founding members included top bankers such as Giovanni Bazoli of Banca Intesa, Cesar Geronzi of Capitalia, and Banca d'Italia's Antonio Fazio. The group also counted Bishop Attilio Nicora, the auxiliary of Milan's Cardinal Martini; Lorenzo Ornaghi, the future rector of the Catholic University of the Sacred Heart; and Father Giampiero Salvini, a Jesuit intellectual and future editor of *La Civiltà Cattolica*. Sandro Magister, "The Pope's Banker Speaks: 'Here's How I Saved the IOR,'" *L'Espresso*, No. 25, June 18–24, 2004.

2 Account provided by Caloia in Galli, *Finanza bianca*, 129. Caloia at times seemed interested in interviewing with this author, but ultimately declined.

3 Ibid., 129–30.

4 Caloia interviewed in Galli, *Finanza bianca*, 130.

5 Galli, *Finanza bianca*, 130.

6 Lai, *Finanze vaticane*, 79.

7 Caloia interviewed in Galli, *Finanza bianca*, 131.

8 Ibid.

9 Lai, *Finanze vaticane*, 77.

10 Michael Sheridan, "Vatican Ends Archbishop's Scandalous Reign," *The Independent* (London), March 10, 1989, 10.

11 Alan Riding, "U.S. Prelate Not Indicted in Italy Bank Scandal," *The New York Times*, April 30, 1989, 22.
12 Marcinkus quoted in Tully and Dorion, "The Vatican's Finances," *Fortune*.
13 "Vatican Bank Gets New Supervising Council," United Press International, Vatican City, BC cycle, June 20, 1989.
14 Caloia interviewed in Galli Financial News, *Finanza bianca*, 132.
15 Angelo Pergolini, "Dimenticare Marcinkus," *Espansione*, November 1, 1988, n. 222. Philippe de Weck, the UBS president, convinced Casaroli that Caloia should chair the IOR's lay supervisory council. See also Lai, *Finanze vaticane*, 79–80.
16 Most press accounts of Bodio's appointment incorrectly reported that he was the first layman to head the IOR. That overlooked both Nogara and Maillardoz. Typical was the coverage in "First Layman Named to Lead Vatican Bank," *Chicago Tribune*, March 18, 1990, 20; and "Vatican Names New Director of Bank," Associated Press, International News, Vatican City, A.M. cycle, March 17, 1990
17 See generally "Ambrosiano Crash: 35 on Trial in Milan," *Australian Financial Review*, May 30, 1990, 57.
18 See Lai, *Finanze vaticane*, 81, n. 45; see also Charles Ridley, "Archbishop Marcinkus Resigns from Vatican Service," United Press International, International News, Vatican City, BC cycle, October 30, 1990.
19 Marcinkus quoted in Victor L. Simpson, "Former Vatican Bank Head Returning to United States," Associated Press, International News, Vatican City, P.M. cycle, October 30, 1990.
20 Memo from Interpol Washington to Justice, Memo of Conversation, 2003/04/05755, 23 April 2003, 450PM, FOIA release to author.
21 Author interview with Peter K. Murphy, January 31, 2014.
22 Marcinkus quoted in Clyde Haberman, "Former Head of Vatican Bank Retires," *The New York Times*, October 31, 1990, A3.
23 Margalit Fox, "Archbishop Marcinkus, 84, Banker at the Vatican, Dies," *The New York Times*, February 22, 2006; John Hooper, "Luigi Mennini: Shadow Over the Vatican," *The Guardian*, August 14, 1997, 14. Author request for information to the Archdiocese of Chicago, December 18, 2013.

Chapter 29: Suitcases of Cash

1 Hebblethwaite, *Pope John Paul II and the Church*, 104-7; Willey, *God's Politician*, 196-97; Hoffman, *Anatomy of the Vatican*, 237–41.
2 Ibid., Galli, 93.
3 Caloia interviewed in Ibid., 89.
4 During his tenure at the Vatican, Dardozzi had acted as registrar of the Pontifical Academy of Sciences, a member of the board of directors of the Libreria Editrice Vaticana, and an auditor of the Pontifical Council for Culture. Lai, *Finanze vaticane*, 78. See Sandro Magister, "All the Denarii of Peter. Vices and Virtues of the Vatican Bank," *L'Espresso*, June 15, 2009.
5 Statement of an anonymous witness to television journalist Paolo Mondani, reported in Willan, *The Vatican at War*, location 5338-5392 of 6371.
6 There is some evidence that the Spellman Foundation account dated back to the 1960s and this was merely the opening of a new account (IOR number 001-3-14774-C). Nuzzi, *Vaticano S.p.A.*, 39; Willan, *The Vatican at War*, location 5301 of 6371.
7 Photocopy of the account application, Istituto per le Opere di Religione, Ufficio Amministrativo, June 15, 1987, stating that the De Bonis was managing the account on behalf of Andreotti. Reproduced in Nuzzi, *Vaticano S.p.A.*, 41.
8 Giacomo Galeazzi, "Karol Wojtyla and the Secrets of Vatican Finances," "Vatican Insider," *La Stampa*, June 6, 2011. De Bonis later changed it so that any proceeds went only to charity, but by then the account was depleted. Last Will and Testament of Donato De Bonis, in Nuzzi, *Vaticano S.p.A.*, 39, 42, 143.
9 €26.4 million, see Nuzzi, *Vaticano S.p.A.*, 43. Fifty billion lire transferred in, and 43 billion out, in Philip Willan, "The Vatican's Dirty Secrets: Bribery, Money Laundering and Mafia Connections," AlterNet, June 4, 2009.
10 Willan, *The Vatican at War*, location 5320 of 6371; Nuzzi, *Vaticano S.p.A.*, 42.

11 Nuzzi describes the charitable contributions from the Spellman account as "marginal." Nuzzi, *Vaticano S.p.A.*, 45; see also Willan, *The Vatican at War*, location 5320–25 of 6371.

12 Nuzzi, *Vaticano S.p.A.*, 44, 47. When de Bonis escorted account holders up the staircase in the Nicholas V Tower, he told them they were "closer to heaven." Curzio Maltese, in collaboration with Carlo Pontesilli and Maurizio Turco, "Scandal, Intrigue and Mystery: The Secrets of the Vatican Bank," translated by Graeme A. Hunter, *La Repubblica*, January 26, 2008.

13 A new word, *tangentopoli*, roughly translated as *bribsesville*, was coined to describe the entire episode. Alan Cowell, "Web of Scandal: Broad Bribery Investigation Is Ensnaring the Elite of Italy," Special Report, *The New York Times*, March 3, 1993, A1; see also Jean-Louis de la Vaissiere, "Clean Hands Probe Enters Its Third Year," Agence France-Presse, International News, Rome, February 15, 1994.

14 The 1992 directive is quoted in Nuzzi, *Vatican S.p.A.*, 47, 165, citing from the "reminder to the Board of Superintendence" of February 1994, signed "*VP*." Those initials belong to Vincenzo Perrone, an IOR consultant and self-described confidant of Angelo Caloia.

15 Caloia interviewed in Galli, *Finanza bianca*, 149.

16 Maltese, "Scandal, Intrigue and Mystery."

17 Ibid.

18 Magister, "All the Denarii of Peter. Vices and Virtues of the Vatican Bank." See also Nuzzi, *Vaticano S.p.A.*, 45, 53–58.

19 Ibid., Nuzzi, 48.

20 Angelo Caloia quoted in ibid., 146.

21 Ibid., 62.

22 Among them was the Cardinal Francis Spellman Foundation, Account No. 001-3-14774-C; the Augustus Louis Jonas Foundation, Account No. 001-3-16764-G; St. Seraphim Fund, Account 001-3-17178; the Mama Roma Fund for the Fight Against Leukemia, Account 001-3-15924; the Rome Charity Fund, Account No. 051-3-10054; Our Lady of Lourdes Fund, Account No. 051-3-02370; Holy House of Loreto, Account No. 001-3-16899; Sanctuary of Loreto and Sacro Monte di Varese, Account No. 051-3-10840; St. Martin Fund, Account No. 001-3-14577; Tumedei and Alina Casalis, Accounts No. 051-1-03972, 051-6-04425, and 051-3-05620; and one account listed without a number, Sisters of Divine Providence-Bisceglie.

23 Nuzzi, *Vaticano S.p.A.*, 145.

24 Ibid., 57–58.

25 Ibid., 68. Those nuns were moved to the Santa Chiara nunnery, at Bisceglie. Years later (2007), the Sisters were embroiled in news reports of fierce, sometimes even violent fights over whether the convent's monastic lifestyle should change. The mother superior, Sister Liliana, dispatched a letter to Pope Benedict, pleading with him in vain to intervene and to restore some order among her fellow nuns. John Hooper, "Nun Sends Plea to Pope over Unholy Row in Convent," *The Guardian*, October 3, 2007, 19.

26 Handwritten letter, Angelo Caloia to Stanislaw Dziwisz, August 5, 1992, reproduced in *Vaticano S.p.A.*, 50.

27 Nuzzi, *Vaticano S.p.A.*, 68–70, also citing the independent investigative work of freelance journalist Gianni Lannes.

28 Enzo D'Errico, "Uno sponsor politico per ogni farmaco," *Corriere della Sera*, October 27, 1993, 11.

29 Galli, *Finanza bianca*, 133, 149; Nuzzi, *Vaticano S.p.A.*, 67.

30 Caloia interviewed in Galli, *Finanza bianca*, 133.

31 Alessandro Speciale, "Unmasking the Vatican's Bank," *Global Post*, January 25, 2011.

32 Nuzzi, *Vaticano S.p.A.*, 63; see the typed one-page document attached to the letter from Caloia to Pope John Paul II, reproduced in *Vaticano S.p.A.*, 66; Galeazzi, "Karol Wojtyla and the Secrets of Vatican Finances."

33 Michael Hornblow, the American diplomat stationed at the Vatican for several years, explained that everything in the city-state played out in slow motion: "A word I heard constantly was *pazienza* [patience]." Author interview with Michael Hornblow, January 28, 2014.

34 "Bishop Indicted in Ambrosiano Case," Associated Press, Business News, Rome, A.M. cycle, April 21, 1992.

35 Bruce Johnston, "Quietly among the sound and fury of falling politicians, a court case has opened that could finally explode the Italian timebomb," *South China Morning Post* (Hong Kong), March 8, 1993, 17.

36 Raw, *The Moneychangers*, citing the March 24, 1992 report of Rome Investigating Magistrate, Mario Almerighi, 478; see also James Moore and Bruce Johnston, "Murder Squad Revisit Roberto Calvi Following the Testimony of Mafia Supergrasses in Rome, Police in London Have Opened a Murder Inquiry into the 1982 Death of the Banker," *The Daily Telegraph* (London), October 4, 2003, 36.

37 "Rome: Slovak Bishop Given Three-Year Sentence," *The Tablet*, April 10, 1993, 10; see also "$4M Vatican Payout," *Sunday Mail* (QLD), May 10, 1992. Some estimates are that Hnilica paid between $3 and $6 million for Calvi's briefcase. See Philip Willan, *The Vatican at War: From Blackfriars Bridge to Buenos Aires* (Bloomington, IN: iUniverse Books, 2013), Kindle edition, 154 of 6371.

38 Raw, *The Moneychangers*, citing De Leo, 478; see also Johnston, "Quietly among the sound and fury of falling politicians, a court case has opened that could finally explode the Italian timebomb," and A. G. D. Maran, *Mafia: Inside the Dark Heart* (New York: Random House, 2011), 25–26.

39 Viyiane Hewitt, "Rome Court Opens Vatican Row," *The Catholic Herald* (UK), October 27, 1989, 1; see also "Rome: Slovak Bishop Given Three-Year Sentence," *The Tablet*. Additional evidence cast doubt on Hnilica's initial defense that the signatures had been faked. After the first two checks totaling 600 million lire ($500,000), Hnilica had signed and delivered an additional twelve checks totaling $700,000 to Lena. See Hutchison, *Their Kingdom Come*, 331–32.

40 "Czech Cigarettes," *USA Today*, April 23, 1992, 10B; see also Hutchison, *Their Kingdom Come*, 330–338.

41 The prosecutors had hoped to prove that the trio had conspired to shake down the Vatican. But the finger pointing made for a confusing trial that worked to the benefit of the defendants. At its conclusion, all three were convicted of Article 648 of the Criminal Code, the knowing receipt of stolen goods. Carboni got the maximum of five years, Hnilica received three years, and Lena got two and a half. According to author Robert Hutchison, all three verdicts were "later overturned because of 'faulty legal procedure.'" Author Philip Willan writes that "The verdict would later be overturned on appeal, Italy's highest court ruling that there was no evidence that the briefcase had not originally been entrusted to Carboni by Calvi of his own free will." Willan, *The Vatican at War*, 3169-3171 of 6371; Hutchison, *Their Kingdom Come*, 338. As for the sentences, see "Rome: Slovak Bishop Given Three-Year Sentence," *The Tablet*. See also Richard Owen, "'God's Banker' to be exhumed: Murder or Suicide? Mafia-linked financier's death still a mystery," *Calgary Herald* (Alberta, Canada), December 16, 1998, A11.

42 The church was strangely silent during this time about some matters that would have seemed natural for the type of activism for which John Paul had earned an early reputation. On September 15, on his fifty-sixth birthday, Father Guiseppe Puglisi was murdered at point-blank range in front of his Palermo parish. Puglisi had for three years spearheaded a campaign against the Mafia. His public execution prompted calls by Sicilian clergy for the Pope to attend the funeral. But to their disappointment, he did not go to the memorial mass for the slain priest. The Vatican did not even send a representative. And the Pope issued no statement condemning the Mafia and its corrosive influence in Italian society.

43 Galli, *Finanza bianca*, 76; Magister, "The Pope's Banker Speaks"; see also Lai, *Finanze vaticane*, 86.

44 Magister, "All the Denarii of Peter. Vices and Virtues of the Vatican Bank."

45 Reese, *Inside the Vatican*, 206–8.

46 Magister, "All the Denarii of Peter. Vices and Virtues of the Vatican Bank." See also Nuzzi, *Vaticano S.p.A.*, 150. In their first meeting, Castillo Lara did not think Caloia was paying enough attention to him and interrupted the banker in front of a packed room: "Look, I'm not here just to shine shoes." The most Caloia later admitted publicly was that he was "not close" to Castillo Lara because "he was surrounded by members of the old system." Angelo Caloia interviewed in Galli, *Finanza bianca*, 152.

47 Berry, *Render Unto Rome*, 103, 162, 175, 278, 336–39; Author faxes to Father Federico Lombardi, September 2013.

48 Berry, *Render Unto Rome*, 100–104, 181, 184, 186.

49 Ibid., 184-85. That arrest had prompted media speculation about whether the church was on the verge of getting sucked further into the ever-expanding criminal web unraveling in Italy. Even the *National Catholic Reporter* noted, "The level of church involvement depends on how rigorously

one can draw the distinction between 'Catholics' and 'the church.'" Peter Hebblethwaite, "Scandal in Rome Has Buffeted the Church; Italian Political Corruption Purges," *National Catholic Reporter* March 26, 1993, 16.

50 Caloia to Sodano, Memo, July 27, 1993, quoted in Magister, "All the Denarii of Peter. Vices and Virtues of the Vatican Bank." And in Nuzzi, *Vatican S.p.A.*, 101n12. Also Caloia, who thought Sodano was "a person of exceptional trust and humanity," realized from their conversation that they "would never agree on the mission of the IOR." Angelo Caloia interviewed in Galli, *Finanza bianca*, 152.

51 Author interview with a former Papal advisor/assistant, identity withheld at their request, in Rome, September 2013.

52 Alessandro Bonanno and Douglas H. Constance, *Stories of Globalization: Transnational Corporations, Resistance, and the State* (University Park, PA: Penn State Press, 2010), 88–89; See also John Tagliabue, "In a Courtroom in Milan, Italian Society Is on Trial," *The New York Times*, February 6, 1994.

53 Recounted by Caloia in Galli, *Finanza bianca*, 159–60; Paddy Agnew, "Vatican Pledges to Help Bribes Inquiry," *The Irish Times*, October 18, 1993, 10; see also John Glover, "New Suicide Stuns Italy," *The Guardian*, July 24, 1993, 1; Nuzzi, *Vaticano S.p.A.*, 84–85.

54 Galli, *Finanza bianca*, 159–60; Willan, *The Vatican at War*, location 5320 of 6371; see also Nuzzi, *Vaticano S.p.A.*, 43. Before he met the prosecutors, Caloia talked to one of his trusted IOR lieutenants, Monsignor Dardozzi. The bank was once again, he told the cleric, "in the shit." Maltese, "Scandal, Intrigue and Mystery."

55 Paddy Agnew, "Illegal Funds Hint Soils the Image of the 'Clean' League," *The Irish Times*, November 25, 1993, 10; Maltese, Pontesilli, and Turco, "Scandal, Intrigue and Mystery; The Secrets of the Vatican Bank"; Launch Ansa, "P2 Lodge: List Names," May 21, 1981, Fasc. 020203, Group 6, cited in Nuzzi, *Vaticano S.p.A.*, 100n4, Dr. Luigi Bisignani, Rome, Code E. 1977, Card 1689 date Init. 1.1.1977, date scad. 31.12.1980.

56 Nuzzi, *Vaticano S.p.A.*, 76, 84. That account, 001-3-16764-G, was opened on October 11, 1990.

57 Obituary, George E. Jonas, *Poughkeepsie Journal* (New York), August 27, 1978, D6; see Gianni Barbacetto, "Luigi Bisignani, l'uomo che college," *Il Fatto Quotidiano*, March 8, 2011.

58 Andrea Gagliarducci, "I.O.R., Is Something Going to Change?" *MondayVatican: Vatican at a Glance*, June 6, 2011; Galli, *Finanza bianca*, 163.

59 Gagliarducci, "I.O.R., is Something Going to Change?" Galli, *Finanza bianca*, 163.

60 Letters from Caloia to Sodano, October 5 and October 20, 1993, in Nuzzi, *Vaticano S.p.A.*, 99, 101.

61 Angelo Caloia interviewed in Galli, *Finanza bianca*, 151; see also Nuzzi, *Vaticano S.p.A.*, 80; and see also "Vatican Bank Director," *Newsday*, March 18, 1990, 12. Antonio Chiminello is still at the Vatican. On April 30, 2012, Pope Francis, only six weeks into his Papacy, promoted Chiminello from the consultor of the prefecture for the Economic Affairs of the Holy See to become the vice director of the Auditors Office of Vatican City State.

62 Bonifaci opened three accounts: No. 91003 on July 11, 1991, immediately after that No. 001-3-17624, and on August 12, 1992, No. 001-6-02660 –Y. All were to "to allow the application of special rates" so they could earn the IOR's highest interest rate, and Bodio approved all.

63 Nuzzi, *Vaticano S.p.A.*, 153.

64 David Agazzi, "Gibellini: Sorry for the IOR in the dirt and no more secrets," L4B Local ANSO, May 30, 2012. Nuzzi, *Vaticano S.p.A.*, 164–66, showing for example the memo to the IOR board of supervisory oversight, February 18, 1994, from "VP."

65 Agnew, "Vatican Pledges to Help Bribes Inquiry,"10; Nuzzi, *Vaticano S.p.A.*, 84–85, 121.

66 Nuzzi, *Vaticano S.p.A.*, 97–98.

67 Ibid., 99. As suspicious as Caloia was of Cardinal Castillo-Lara, he also did not trust Castillo's chief financial aide inside APSA, Monsignor Robert Devine. Devine was a successful Canadian private businessman who turned from earning outsized profits to tending for the sick and giving away most of his personal fortune. He became a priest at fifty-two and landed in Rome as Castillo Lara's investment advisor inside APSA in 1991. As far as Caloia was concerned, Devine might be a talented investor but he was all too willing to second the cardinal's position that "no disclosure was the best policy." See generally Alfred LeBlanc and Mark Anderson, "Devine Intervention," *The Financial Post* (Toronto), *The Magazine*, February 1, 1996, 18.

68 Emilio Colombo quoted as part of a "recent unpublished evidence" in Nuzzi, *Vaticano S.p.A.*, 95;

Colombo had been Foreign Minister when the tug-of-war played out in the early 1980s over the Marcinkus arrest warrants.

69 Peter Semler, "Berlusconi Decree Shackles Top-Level Corruption Probe," *The Sunday Times* (London), July 17, 1994.

70 Author interview with former official in the Secretary of State's office, November 2013.

71 Ibid. Monsignor Dardozzi felt as if they were all on the deck of the *Titanic*, talking about how terrible an accident the ship had just had with an iceberg, but nobody was doing anything to save the sinking vessel, Nuzzi, *Vaticano S.p.A.*, 87. The good news for Caloia by the fall of 1993 was that Pietro Ciocci, who had cosigned some of the questionable De Bonis accounts, as well as Monsignor Carmine Recchia, the chief of the IOR archive, and a close De Bonis ally, were also transferred from the bank. One of the IOR's supervisory lay commission members, former UBS chairman Philippe de Weck, suggested that a fix to all the IOR's battered image was to simply change its name in order to "clearly break with the past." That got no backing.

72 Peter Hebblethwaite, "Vatican Bank Scandal Reappears in Venezuela," *National Catholic Reporter*, December 24, 1993.

73 Ibid.

74 Galli, *Finanza bianca*, 163–64.

75 Author interview with a former official in the Secretary of State's office, November 2013.

76 "Trial Testimony: Scandal Figures Turned to Vatican Bank," Associated Press, International News, Milan, December 13, 1993; Piero Valsecchi, "Financier Sentenced to 8 Years for Kickback Scandal," Associated Press Worldstream, International News, Milan, April 28, 1994.

77 See John Tagliabue, "In a Courtroom in Milan, Italian Society is on Trial," *The New York Times*, February 6, 1994.

78 "Alleged Money Courier: Funds Carried to Vatican Bank," Associated Press, International News, Milan, A.M. cycle, January 12, 1994.

79 Bonanno and Constance, *Stories of Globalization*, 98.

80 Caloia to Sodano, March 1 1994, citied in Willan, *The Vatican at War*, 324–25. See also John Tagliabue, "In a Courtroom in Milan, Italian Society Is on Trial," *The New York Times*, February 6, 1994, A3.

81 Gagliarducci, "I.O.R., is Something Going to Change?"

82 Bonanno and Constance, *Stories of Globalization*, 97.

83 Willan, *The Vatican at War*, location 5356 of 6371.

84 Author interview with a former consultant to the IOR, identity withheld at his request, in Rome, September 30, 2013.

85 Maltese, "Scandal, Intrigue and Mystery; The Secrets of the Vatican Bank."

86 Ibid. See also "Mobster Laundered Cash at Vatican Bank," *Daily Telegraph*, July 9, 1998, 6.

87 "Vatican Rejects Claim of Bank Links to Mafia," *The Herald* (Glasgow), November 18, 1994, 9.

88 Rosario Spatola quoted in "Witness Accuses Marcinkus of Laundering $6.5m of Mafia Money," *The Irish Times*, November 18, 1994, 14.

89 Castillo Lara quoted in "The Vatican Denies That Cardinal Rosalio Castillo Lara was Involved in Money Laundering for the Mafia," *Daily Record*, November 18, 1994, 19; "Cardinal Denies Turncoat's Account of Money Laundering," Associated Press Worldstream, International News, Rome, November 17, 1994.

90 Maltese, Pontesilli, and Turco, "Scandal, Intrigue and Mystery; The Secrets of the Vatican Bank."

91 Magister, "All the Denarii of Peter. Vices and Virtues of the Vatican Bank."

92 Galli, *Finanza bianca*, 151.

93 "Vatican in Black for Third Successive Year," Agence France-Presse, International News, Vatican City, June 19, 1996.

94 Nuzzi, *Vaticano S.p.A.*, 194–95.

95 March 16, 1994, letter from Caloia to Pope John Paul II, reprinted in its entirety in Nuzzi, *Vaticano S.p.A.*, 195–97.

96 Caloia quoted in Antonio Macaluso, "Il risanamento raccontato dal president Angelo Caloia 'Con questa cura ho guarito lo IOR,'" *Corriere della Sera*, March 27, 1995.

97 Philip Willan, "Papal Aide Tried to Swindle €99m From Inheritance Left by Vatican land baron," *The Times* (London), July 22, 2014.

98 The Foundation Gerini was IOR account 90970; see Nuzzi, *Vaticano S.p.A.*, 173–74,188, n. 12. A memo prepared contemporaneously by Dardozzi says: "A lawyer is trying to induce the IOR

to use its good offices to get his fee paid by the foundation and is being wound together with a sum for 'things to accommodate' with the other heirs (grandchildren) of Gerini. He (the lawyer) insinuates that in Montevideo (in a bank) would be lying a large (but impregnable) amount that would have connection with the characters of the former Banco Ambrosiano and Gerini."

99 Ibid., 174–75.

100 "'Così mi truffarono' Salesiani, Bertone sentito in Vaticano «Così mi truffarono»," *Corriere della Sera*, April 19, 2013; "Salesian Congregation Faces Bankruptcy After Losing Case," Rome, Agence France-Press, November 28, 2012; Philip Willan, "Papal Aide Tried to Swindle €99m from Inheritance Left by Vatican Land Baron," *The Times* (London), July 22, 2014.

101 Ibid., 175–78, 189.

102 Letter addressed from Caloia to Sodano, February 1, 1996: "Everything is silent on the front of Father Izzi. The ill-will of the religious order, however, confirmed by small episodes, such as the one that led me to try to collect a check for ten million on a BNL account that we knew had been closed for some time."

103 Caloia to Sodano, February 1, 1996, cited in Nuzzi, *Vaticano S.p.A.*, 176.

104 See generally "Money Laundering: Unequal Fight," Spotlight Section, No. 243, *Intelligence Newsletter*, June 23, 1994.

105 See "History of the FATF" at http://www.fatf-gafi.org/pages/aboutus/historyofthefatf/; and "Who Are We" at http://www.fatf-gafi.org.

106 Nuzzi, *Vaticano S.p.A.*, 33.

Chapter 30: Burying the Trail on Nazi Gold

1 Paddy Agnew, "Trial of Sicilian Archbishop on Fraud and Corruption Charges Adjourned," *The Irish Times*, February 27, 1997, 10.

2 "The central and key point in the IOR is the conservation and management of money and resources entrusted to the institution, in order to enhance and fund religious entities, according to the need of ecclesiastical bodies, religious orders, dioceses and missions, all the while excluding speculation and unethical financial transactions." Angelo Caloia interviewed in Galli, *Finanza bianca*, 150.

3 Celestine Bohlen, "Rome Journal; For Vatican's Lay Staff, Tighter Rules to Live By," *The New York Times*, July 25, 1995, A4.

4 "Italians Hold Ex-CIA Agent in Global Crime Probe: Mafia, Yugoslav Factions Linked to Network Trading in Illegal Arms and Drugs," *The Vancouver Sun*, December 4, 1995.

5 Andrew Gumbel, "Death, Drugs and Diamonds in Tale of Global Conspiracy; A Web of Intrigue Unearthed in Italy," *The Independent* (London), June 3, 1996, 10.

6 "American Arrested in Italian Money-Laundering Investigation," Associated Press, International News, Naples, Italy, A.M. cycle, December 2, 1995; John Hooper, "Odd Deals in High Places," *The Observer*, June 2, 1996, 7.

7 Hooper, "Odd Deals in High Places," 7.

8 "Italian Police Crack Down on International Mafia," Agence France-Presse, International News, Rome, June 2, 1996.

9 "Italians Hold Ex-CIA Agent in Global Crime Probe," *The Vancouver Sun*, A7.

10 "Cardinal Michele Giordano of Italy Dies at 80," *The New York Times*, December 4, 2010.

11 John L. Allen, Jr., "A Hint of Accountability in a New Vatican Financial Scandal," *National Catholic Reporter*, June 21, 2010; see also "Prosecutors Pursue Inquiry into Cardinal Despite Church-State Fears," *Birmingham Post*, August 25, 1998, 9; Philip Willan, "Loan-Sharking Case Fails Against Naples Cardinal," *The Guardian*, December 23, 2000, 12. Giordano retired in 2006. "Retired Naples cardinal Giordano dies at 80," *The Seattle Times*, December 3, 2010.

12 "Investigations: A Status Report on the Volcker Commission," PBS *Frontline*, June 1997; See also John Authers and Richard Wolffe, *The Victim's Fortune*, 27–29.

13 See Greg Bradsher, "Searching for Records Relating to Nazi Gold Part II," *The Record*, May 1998; Rickman, *Conquest and Redemption*, 210-11.

14 "Echoes Of The Nazis' Crimes Still Resound / Swiss Banks List Old Accounts, Invite Heirs To Come Forward," *The Philadelphia Inquirer*, July 23, 1997, A01.

15 Switzerland's Economic Minister, Jean-Pascal Delamuraz, had to formally apologize after he

called the disclosures "blackmail." Carlo Jagmetti, the Swiss ambassador to the U.S., resigned after a document leaked to the press in which he called the charges a "war" by Holocaust groups.

16 David E. Sanger, "McCall and State Dept. Clash on Sanctions Against Swiss Over Gold," *The New York Times*, July 23, 1998; Authers and Wolffe, *The Victim's Fortune*, 63-69; 89-92.

17 Elan Steinberg of the World Jewish Congress considered the Holocaust asset litigation as "plaintiff's diplomacy." Author interview with Elan Steinberg, April 2, 2006. Friedman v. Union Bank of Switzerland, Eastern District of New York, 1996 and Weisshaus v. Union Bank of Switzerland, Eastern District of New York, 1997, together are the core cases for the so-called Swiss Bankers litigation. Michael Bazyler, *Holocaust Justice: The Battle for Restitution in America's Courts* (New York: New York University Press, 2003), Kindle Edition, 325 of 9290; see also Itmar Levin, "Holocaust Survivor Files $20 Bln Class Action Against 100 Swiss Banks," *Globes* (Israel), October 7, 1996.

18 Michael Bazyler, *Holocaust Justice*, 75 of 9290; see in particular Adolf Stern, et al., v. Assicurazioni Generali, California, District Court, SF, 1996.

19 David Briscoe, "U.S. Memo Says Vatican Held Nazi Loot," Associated Press, Washington, A.M. cycle, July 21, 1997; see also "Papers Link Vatican to Illegal Deals with Nazis Swiss Bankers Used as Conduit, U.S. Intelligence Documents Say," *The Toronto Star*, August 4, 1997, A3.

20 Memo from Emerson Bigelow to Harold Glasser, Director of Monetary Research, U.S. Treasury Department, October 21, 1946, RG 226, Entry 183, Box 29, File #6495, NARA.

21 "The Eizenstat Report and Related Issues Concerning United States and Allied Efforts to Restore Gold and Other Assets Looted by Nazis During World War II," Hearing Before the Committee on Banking and Financial Services, House of Representatives, One Hundred Fifth Congress, First Session, June 25, 1997, Volume 4 (Washington, DC: U.S. Government Printing Office), 1997.

22 Slobodan Lekic, "Clinton: U.S. Pursuing Facts on Nazi Gold," Associated Press, International News, Washington, July 22, 1997.

23 Transcript, "Rabbi Marvin Heir Discusses the Latest Developments in the Nazi Gold/Holocaust Victims/Swiss Banks Investigation," CNN Early Edition with Martin Savidge, July 23, 1997; Bruce Johnston, "Vatican Tainted by Holocaust Gold Memo," *Calgary Herald*, July 27, 1997, D1.

24 See, for example, "U.S. Memo Says Vatican Held Nazi Puppet's Cash," *San Francisco Examiner*, July 22, 1997.

25 Lekic, "Clinton: U.S. Pursuing Facts on Nazi Gold."

26 "Vatican Denies Report It Stored Fascists' Gold," *San Jose Mercury News*, July 23, 1997, 16A; Bruce Johnston and Tim Butcher, "Vatican Denies Receiving $184 Million Stolen from Jews During War," reprinted from *The Telegraph* in *The Vancouver Sun*, July 23, 1997, A7; see also Lekic, "Clinton: U.S. Pursuing Facts on Nazi Gold"; and "U.S. Memo Says Vatican Held Nazi Puppet's Cash," *San Francisco Examiner*.

27 Bronfman quoted in Brian Milner, "Settling Holocaust Accounts: Bronfman Turns Sights from Swiss to Vatican in Bid to Open Last Locked Doors of Nazi Era," *The Globe and Mail* (Canada), July 26, 1997, A1.

28 "Survivors Sue Insurance Firms for Failing to Honor Policies," *Jewish Telegraph Agency*, June 5, 1997. Bazyler, *Holocaust Justice*, location 2489 of 9290; Authers and Wolffe, *The Victim's Fortune*, 119–34; see generally "Life Insurance and the Holocaust," *The Insurance Forum*, Special Holocaust Issue, 25, no. 9 (September 1998): 81100; Becker to Bernstein, November 27, 1946, RG 260, OMGUS, Finance, Box 60, 17/60/10, NARA.

29 The documents were Allied intercepts of Swiss bank wire transfers in 1944 and 1945 and they classify the Vatican transactions as "objectionable." One confidential document, dated January 27, 1945, lists a November 12, 1944, transaction in which Credit Suisse sent this message to the IOR: "We credit you 6,407.50 francs on order of the Reichsbank Berlin." That transaction was listed among violations by the Swiss of the Allied war code. According to a second document, labeled "Secret Intelligence Material Confidential," in April 1945 the IOR instructed the Union Bank of Switzerland to pay 100,000 Swiss francs and asked the Swiss central bank to pay 200,000 francs to the Bank Suisse Italienne of Lugano, which the Allies had blacklisted in June 1940. A third document, also in 1945, reported that the IOR asked a Portuguese bank to "forward 2,500 large dollar notes in a sealed packet to the Vatican through the medium of the papal nuncio in Lisbon." See generally "Papers Link Vatican to Illegal Deals with Nazis Swiss Bankers Used as Conduit, U.S. Intelligence Documents Say," *The Toronto Star* A3; "News in Brief: Vatican Bank 'Dealt with Nazis,'" *The Guardian*, August 4, 1997.

30 Edith M. Lederer, "Nazi Victims Should Be Given dlrs 63 Million in Looted Gold," Associated Press, International News, London, March 21, 1997.
31 Hoeckman quoted in "Vatican Won't Open Archives: Pope Remains Silent on Accusations of Wartime Crimes," *The Daily Telegraph*, September 12, 1997, A8.
32 Gordon Legge, "Auschwitz Survivor to Protest at Vatican," *Calgary Herald*, September 18, 1997, B7.
33 Letter from Shimon Samuels, quoted in Bruce Johnston, "Pope's Holocaust Speech Falls Short, Jewish Leaders Say," *Daily Telegraph*, November 2, 1997, C10.
34 Bruno Bartoloni, "Vatican Resists Pressure to Open Archives on Relations with Nazis," Agence France-Presse, International News, Vatican City, November 30, 1997.
35 "Vatican Will Attend Nazi Gold Conference in London," Agence France-Presse, International News, December 1, 1997.
36 Maureen Johnson, "Vatican Has Gold Wrested from Gypsy Victims, Delegate Claims with BC-Nazi Gold Conference," Associated Press, International News, London, December 3, 1997.
37 The other attention-grabbing moment was when Swiss investigators announced they had determined that the amount of gold transferred through the Reichsbank during World War II was $120.05 billion, far more than previously estimated. And at least $1.3 billion came from victims of the Nazis.
38 Henry Meyer, "Nazi Gold Conference Fails to Generate International Solidarity," Agence France-Presse, International News, London, December 4, 1997.
39 Christopher Lockwood, "Vatican Comes Under Heavy Flak, World: 'Archives Hold Key to Nazi Gold,'" *Hamilton Spectator* (Ontario), December 5, 1997, C4.
40 Ray Moseley, "41 States Unite on Probes of Nazi Era Their Aim: Justice for Surviving Victims by Turn of Century," *The Toronto Star*, December 5, 1997, A20.
41 Christopher Henning, "Vatican Remains Mute on Looting—US Calls for Disclosure of Documents," *The Age* (Melbourne), December 6, 1997, 20.
42 Ibid.
43 Lockwood, "Vatican Comes Under Heavy Flak, World: 'Archives Hold Key to Nazi Gold.'"
44 Author interview with Elan Steinberg, April 2, 2006.
45 Navarro-Valls quoted in "Vatican Denies Handling Nazi Gold from Croatia," Agence France-Presse, International News, Vatican City, December 9, 1997; Frances D'Emilio, "Vatican Insists Its Archives Don't Back Up Croatia Link," Vatican City, Associated Press, December 9, 1997.
46 D'Emilio, "Vatican Insists Its Archives Don't Back Up Croatia Link," Associated Press.
47 "Looted Gold Kept at Bank in New York Canada, IMF Owned Bars Marked with Swastikas," *The Toronto Star*, December 18, 1997, A17; John Sweeney, "Steal of the Century: Wall of Silence Guards Gold," *The Observer*, December 7, 1997, 12.
48 "British Legislators to Study Vatican WWII Archives," Associated Press, International News, London, February 9, 1998. "We Remember: A Reflection on the Shoah," Commission for Religious Relations with the Jews, Presentation by Cardinal Edward Idris Cassidy, Vatican City, March 12, 1998, online at http://www.vatican.va/roman_curia/pontifical_councils/chrstuni/documents/rc_pc_chrstuni_doc_16031998_shoah_en.html.
49 Dimitri Cavalli, "The Commission That Couldn't Shoot Straight," *New Oxford Review*, July/August, 2002. The Vatican's response was that it had already released plenty of documents from its archives in the collection *Actes et documents du Saint Siège relatifs a la Seconde Guerre Mondiale*, published between 1965 and 1981.
50 U.S. Government Supplementary Report on Nazi Assets, U.S. Government Printing Office, June 1998; see generally Sid Balman Jr., "Vatican WWII Role Questioned," United Press International, Washington, DC, BC cycle, June 2, 1998. As for the controversy over the change of language between a late draft and the final report, see David E. Sanger, "U.S. Says Nazis Used Gold Loot to Pay for War," *The New York Times*, June 1, 1998, A1.
51 John M. Goshko, "Trade with Neutral Countries Propelled Nazi Army, U.S. Says," *The Washington Post*, June 3, 1998, A3.
52 Transcript of Stuart Eizenstat, Undersecretary of State, briefing, Federal News Service, June 2, 1998. See also "US Study Links Neutral Countries, Switzerland to Nazi War Machine," Agence France-Presse, June 2, 1998.
53 "Neutrals Give Mixed Reaction to U.S. Call to Contribute to Holocaust Victims," Section VIII, Law of War, *International Enforcement Law Reporter* 14, no. 7 (July 1998).

54 Navarro-Valls quoted in David Briscoe, "Nazi Puppets Used Vatican Ties to Protect Gold, Report Says," Associated Press, Business News, Washington, P.M. cycle, June 3, 1998.
55 It began as thirty-nine nations but expanded quickly to forty-one. Barry Schweid, "39 Nations to Search for Loot Taken from Holocaust Victims," Associated Press, Washington, A.M. cycle, June 30, 1998.
56 "Report on Nazi Gold Conference Notes Vatican Failure to Open Archives," Associated Press, Business News, London, A.M. cycle, August 24, 1998.
57 See generally "Vatican Under Fire over Nazi Gold Riddle," *Birmingham Post*, August 25, 1998, 16.
58 See Stephanie A. Bilenker, "In Re Holocaust Victms' Assets Litigation: Do the U.S. Courts Have Jurisdiction over the Lawsuits Filed by Holocaust Survivors Against the Swiss Banks?," *Maryland Journal of International Law* 21, no. 2, Article 5 (1997). See also Authers and Wolffe, *The Victim's Fortune*, 96–100.
59 Author interview with Elan Steinberg, April 2, 2006.
60 "US Asks Russia, Vatican to Release Information on Nazi Gold," *The White House Bulletin*, September 9, 1998.
61 Bruce Johnson, "Pope Prepares to Beatify Controversial Cardinal," *The Daily Telegraph*, October 1, 1998, C5.
62 Ibid.
63 The Vatican was the first nation to recognize the newly independent Croatia in 1991. Journalist Stanko Vuleta wrote: "Croatia of 1991 adopted the ideology, name, flag, coat of arms, currency and linguistics of the Croatia of the Second World War," in "Mere Words No Consolation," *The Ottawa Citizen*, March 19, 2000, A17.
64 Uki Goni, "Argentina Confronts Role as Safe Place for Nazis; Auschwitz Doctor Josef Mengele Spent Decades in Argentina," *The Guardian*, November 18, 1998, 19.
65 Gerald Posner, "The Bormann File," *The New York Times*, November 13, 1991; see also Viviana Alonso, Argentina: Commission Admits Gov't Helped Nazi War Criminals, Buenos Aires, Inter Press Service, November 19, 1998.
66 Desson Howe, "A Wealth of New Information on Holocaust; Declassified Wartime Documents at Archives Are Generating Lots of Interest," *The Washington Post*, November 18, 1998, B1.
67 "Every now and then, you find something that truly surprises, that blows you out of the water." Late Holocaust scholar Sybil Milton quoted in ibid.
68 The list was in a letter released by Bobby Brown, Prime Minister Benjamin Netanyahu's advisor on Diaspora affairs. Nicolas B. Tatro, "Israel Calls for Opening of International Holocaust Archives," Associated Press, International News, Jerusalem, P.M. cycle, November 26, 1998.
69 Ibid.
70 Madeleine Albright quoted in Laura Myers, "Albright Asks Holocaust Conference Delegates to Return Nazi-Looted Art," Associated Press, Washington, A.M. cycle, December 1, 1998.
71 "Vatican Denies Secret Records on Holocaust," Agence France-Presse, International News, Vatican City, December 3, 1998.
72 *Emil Alperin v. Istituto per le Opere di Religione*, U.S. District Court, San Francisco, November 1999. The suit also listed an unspecified number of unidentified international banks as defendants. The use of so-called John Doe defendants is normal in a case in which the plaintiffs believe that others than the named parties were involved but that they do not yet have the evidence to name them. The court allows the pleading so long as the allegation is made on a good faith belief and the plaintiff thinks it will uncover the identity of the unnamed parties through the discovery process.
73 Author interview with Jonathan Levy, February 21, 2012.
74 Ibid.
75 By the time Levy amended the complaint, he had developed a novel argument in an effort to bring the Swiss banks—who were free from liability because they had already settled their original class action—back into the courtroom. He contended that the postwar transfers of the illicit gold and cash made the Swiss co-conspirators with the IOR and therefore their actions with the Ustašan gold fell outside the scope of their settlement. Levy's argument was not successful.
76 The German companies and the plaintiffs were far apart when they began settlement negotiations. The German firms thought that they could settle all the lawsuits for about $1.25 billion, the same as the Swiss banks had paid. The plaintiffs in the forced labor litigation alone were demanding $30 billion for all their claims. Authers and Wolffe, *The Victim's Fortune*, 213, 218–21, 235–40;

Bazyler, *Holocaust Justice*, location 75 of 9290; see also Authers and Wolffe, *The Victim's Fortune*, 188–91.

77 Independent Commission of Experts, *Switzerland and Gold Transactions in WW2*, May 25, 1998. It is often referred to as the Bergier Report, after the commission's director, Jean-François Bergier.

78 "Prepared testimony of Stuart E. Eizenstat, Treasury Deputy Secretary, Before the House Banking and Financial Services Committee," Federal News Service, February 9, 2000. See also Authers and Wolffe, *The Victim's Fortune*, 254–65.

79 Vignolo Mino, "Fatima, ultimo segreto Nel conto del santuario oro rubato dai nazisti," *Corriere della Sera*, April 5, 2000; see also Giles Tremlett, "Nazi Gold Taints Fatima," *Scotland on Sunday*, April 16, 2000, 23.

80 Januario Torgal Ferreira quoted in ibid., Tremlett, "Nazi Gold Taints Fatima."

81 Pope John Paul quoted in Jocelyn Noveck, "In Historic Speech at Holocaust Memorial, Pope Says Church Deeply Saddened," Associated Press, International News, Jerusalem, March 23, 2000.

82 Author interview with Elan Steinberg, April 2, 2006.

83 See 10-31-02 WikiLeaks Vatican Archives: Archivist Confirms Partial Opening for Nazi Germany and WWII Documents Cable: 02Vatican5356_a, https://www.wikileaks.org/plusd/cables/02VATICAN5356_a.html; and 03-13-03 WikiLeaks Holocaust Museum Delegation Works in Secret Archives, Offers Collaboration to Catalogue Closed Records Cable: 03vatican1046_a, https://www.wikileaks.org/plusd/cables/03Vatican1046_a.html.

84 Authers and Wolffe, *The Victim's Fortune*, 321–23.

85 Joseph B. Treaster, "Settlement Approved in Holocaust Victims' Suit Against Italian Insurer," *The New York* Times, February 28, 2007, reporting on a federal judge's approval of the settlement reached in 2006. Authers and Wolffe, *The Victim's Fortune*, 269–73; Author interview with Elan Steinberg, April 2, 2006.

86 "Vatican Claims Immunity in Lawsuit," Reuters, San Francisco, November 24, 2000.

87 Author interview with Jonathan Levy, February 21, 2012.

Chapter 31: "A Criminal Underground in the Priesthood"

1 Colagiovanni's foundation was the Monitor Ecclesiasticus Foundation. See generally Alessandra Stanley, "How 2 Priests Got Mixed Up in a Huge Insurance Scandal," *The New York Times*, June 26, 1999, C1; see also Tom Lowry, "Scandal's Cost: Consumers Probably Will Pay," *USA Today*, July 26, 1999, 3B.

2 See generally Stanley, "How 2 Priests Got Mixed Up in a Huge Insurance Scandal."

3 Simon Fluendy, "Vatican Bank Is Sued in US over Charity Scandal," *Mail on Sunday* (UK), August 11, 2002, 6.

4 Ibid.

5 Lowry, "Scandal's Cost: Consumers Probably Will Pay," 3B.

6 Fluendy, "Vatican Bank Is Sued in US over Charity Scandal," *Mail on Sunday*.

7 See generally Stanley, "How 2 Priests Got Mixed Up in a Huge Insurance Scandal."

8 Author interview with a former consultant to the IOR, identity withheld at his request, in Rome, September 30, 2013.

9 Lai, *Finanze vaticane*, 82. See also "A Life of Faith: Father Edmond C. Szoka, Former Detroit Archbishop, Dies at 86," *The Michigan Catholic*, August 21, 2014.

10 Other cardinals resented that Szoka carried influence with John Paul merely because he had Polish heritage. "If you want to see the real Szoka," Cardinal Giuseppe Caprio told author Benny Lai, "get up early one morning when it does not rain, say 5:00 A.M. Go behind Castel Sant'Angelo. And you will find him jogging. Other than his Polish mother he is a real American." Lai interview with Caprio, February 10, 1997, in Lai, *Finanze vaticane*, 150.

11 Galli, *Finanza bianca*, 157.

12 "Vatican Bank Sounds Out Tietmeyer," *The Australian*, June 1, 1999, 25; Richard Owen, "German Favoured as 'God's Banker,'" *Independent* (Ireland), May 31, 1999.

13 Richard Owen, "Benedict Eager to Modernise Arcane World of Vatican Bank: Averse to Inefficiency, the Pope Is Forming His Own Team to Control Church Finances," *The Times* (London), September 18, 2006.

14 "Vatican Bank Sounds Out Tietmeyer," *The Australian*; Pope John Paul quoted in Sandro Magister, "The Pope's Banker Speaks: 'How I Saved the IOR.'" *L'Espresso*.
15 All the quotes relating to Caloia's reappointment to a third term are from an interview with Caloia set forth in Galli, *Finanza bianca*, 164–66.
16 Caloia interviewed in ibid., 173.
17 Galli, *Finanza bianca*, 169–70.
18 Caloia interviewed in ibid., 179.
19 Thomas P. Doyle and Stephen C. Rubino, "Catholic Clergy Sexual Abuse Meets the Civil Law," *Fordham Urban Law Journal* 31, no. 2, Article 6, (2003): 549. What the Louisiana parents had found—the shuffling of a predator between parishes—was an occurrence far more common than anyone imagined. Another early example was that of Father Joseph Lang, who had been accused of sex abuse by several minors in his Cleveland, Ohio, parish as early as the 1980s. In 1988, Bishop Anthony Pilla loaned Lang to a parish in northern British Columbia. The Canadians were not informed about Lang's predatory history since he was still technically under the control of the Cleveland diocese. It was not until 2012 that Lang was eventually suspended from his clerical duties after it was disclosed he was under a criminal investigation for abuse after the transfer to Canada. David Briggs and James F. Carty, "Prosecutors Didn't Get Names of Four Who Faced Allegations," *The Plain Dealer* (Cleveland), April 11, 2012. These types of stories would, unfortunately, become routine.
20 It was the civil deposition of Bishop Gerard Frey. See Carl M. Cannon, "The Priest Scandal: How Old News at Last Became a Dominant National Story . . . And Why It Took So Long," *American Journalism Review*, May 2002. Chalice proved an important source of information. In his 1992 book about the church's pedophilia scandal, *Lead Us Not into Temptation*, Berry disclosed that Chalice had died. Although he did not name him, Berry revealed that he had been a layman who "through a church-related job, had been molesting teenagers in a diocesan parish. He was eventually . . . imprisoned, and died of AIDS." See also Jason Berry, *Lead Us Not into Temptation: Catholic Priests and the Sexual Abuse of Children* (New York: Doubleday, 1992), 79–82, 167.
21 Jason Berry, "The Tragedy of Gilbert Gauthe," pt. 1, May 23, 1985, *Times of Acadiana*, May 23, 1985, pt. 2 May 30, 1985; "Fallen Priests," *Times of Acadiana*, June 13, 1985; and "Anatomy of a Cover-up," *Times of Acadiana*, January 30, 1986. As for the rejections of his proposal from national publications and some of the reasons given, see Michael D'Antonio, *Mortal Sins: Sex, Crime, and the Era of Catholic Scandal* (New York: Thomas Dunne Books, St. Martin's Press, 2013), 33–35.
22 Ibid.
23 Thomas Fox and Jason Berry in Murray Dubin, ibid. "Church Secrecy on Sex Abuse Has Long History," *The Philadelphia Inquirer*, March 10, 2002.
24 For a thorough review of why the sexual abuse story failed to become a more significant story earlier, see Carl M. Cannon, "The Priest Scandal: How Old News at Last Became a Dominant National Story . . . And Why It Took So Long," 18.
25 See SNAP's self-described history at http://www.snapnetwork.org/about.
26 Berry interviewed in Rorie Sherman, "Legal Spotlight on Priests Who are Pedophiles," *National Law Journal*, April 4, 1998.
27 Robert Matas, "B.C. Priest Goes on Leave as Past in U.S. Revealed; U.S. Investigation into Sexual Abuse by Catholic Clerics Reverberate from Florida to Terrace, B.C."; *The Globe and Mail* (Canada), April 11, 2002, A3.
28 D'Antonio, *Mortal Sins*, 152; Cannon, "The Priest Scandal"; see also Jason Berry, "What Explains Andy Greeley?," America, *The National Catholic Review*, July 2013, online at http://www.americamagazine.org/issue/what-explains-andy-greeley.
29 See generally D'Antonio, *Mortal Sins*.
30 Frank Bruni, "Sins of the Church," *The New York Times*, April 8, 2002, A1.
31 John L. Allen Jr., senior reporter for the *National Catholic Reporter*, later criticized the mainstream American press from going from little to saturation coverage. "To provide just a bit of context, in the same year that the sex abuse scandals finished on the front page of *The New York Times* forty-one days in a row, 2.7 million children were educated in Catholic schools in United States, nearly 10 million persons were given assistance by Catholic Charities USA, and Catholic hospitals spent $2.8 billion in providing uncompensated healthcare to millions of poor and low income Americans." John L. Allen Jr., *All the Pope's Men: The Inside Story of How the Vatican Really Thinks* (New York: Doubleday, 2004), 226.

32 Dubin, "Church Secrecy on Sex Abuse Has Long History."

33 Steven Edwards, "Secrets Shatter Church's Peace: The Archdiocese of Boston Struggles to Deal with Allegations of Sexual Abuse and a Cover-up in Its Highest Office," *National Post* (Canada), March 4, 2002, A12. The scandal in Boston was covered first in a seven-thousand-word investigative article by Kristen Lombardi, a reporter with the alternative *Boston Phoenix*, in 2001. She did a follow-up investigation that same year. *The Boston Globe* won the Pulitzer for its 2002 series on sexual abuse in the Boston archdiocese, and also prompted Cardinal Law's resignation that December, http://www.boston.com/globe/spotlight/abuse/extras/pulitzers.htm. Less than two years after his resignation, Pope John Paul transferred Law to Rome and installed him—over considerable public outcry—as a $12,000-a-month director of the basilica of Santa Maria Maggiore. Law is a member of the Congregation for Bishops, which helps select new bishops. As for the controversy over Law's appointment, see John Phillips, "Reaction Mixed over Cardinal Law's Duties," *The Washington Times*, August 16, 2004, A15.

34 Miro Cernetig, "Pope Speaks Out on Abuse; Says Priests Who Molest Children Cast 'a Dark Shadow of Suspicion' over Innocent Clergymen," *The Globe and Mail* (Canada), March 22, 2002, A14.

35 Pope John Paul quoted in Michael Paulson, "Pope Decries 'Sins' of Priests," *The Boston Globe*, March 22, 2002.

36 John L. Allen Jr. interview in Michael Paulson, "World Doesn't Share US View of Scandal," *The Boston Globe*, April 8, 2002. See also Allen, *All the Pope's Men*, 229-30.

37 Sodano quoted in "Top Cardinal Says Media Overplay Sex Scandal," *The New York Times*, October 11, 2003, A7.

38 Alan Cooperman, "Hundreds of Priests Removed Since '60s; Survey Shows Scope Wider than Disclosed," *The Washington Post*, June 9, 2002, A1; Laurie Goodstein, "Scandals in the Church; the Sexuality Issue; Homosexuality in Priesthood Is Under Increasing Scrutiny," *The New York Times*, April 19, 2002, A1; Frank Walker, "One in 10 Clergy Accused; Church Sex Abuse Total Revealed," *The Sun Herald* (Sydney), July 7, 2002, 24. As for the latest estimate on the possible number of victims—more than 100,000—see "Data on the Crisis: The Human Toll," http://www.bishop-accountability.org/AtAGlance/data.htm.

39 Transcript, "Pope Meeting with American Cardinals at Vatican," reporters Daryn Kagan and Miles O'Brien, *CNN Live Today*, April 23, 2002.

40 "Address of John Paul II to the Cardinals of the United States," April 23, 2002, online at http://www.vatican.va/holy_father/john_paul_ii/speeches/2002/april/documents/hf_jp-ii_spe_20020423_usa-cardinals_en.html; see also Berry, "The Shame of John Paul II."

41 "Cardinals Stop Short of Policy of 'Zero Tolerance' for Priests, *Boston Globe*, April 25, 2002. See also "Bishops Reject Zero Tolerance: U.S. Clerics Demur on One-Time Abuse Cases; Mahony Sees Blanket Policy Emerging in Church's Future," *San Bernardino Sun*, April 29, 2002.

42 Julia Duin, "Bishops Lenient for Past Sex Abuse; Propose Mercy in Isolated Cases," *The Washington Times*, June 5, 2002, A1.

43 "Cardinal's Compromise Comes Up Short," *The Globe and Mail* (Canada), April 27, 2002, A18.

44 "Bishops Reject Zero Tolerance" *San Bernardino Sun*.

45 Herranz Lasado quoted in "Spanish Archbishop Casado: Civil Penalties for Sexual Abuse are Unwarranted," April 29, 2002, online at http://skepticism.org/timeline/april-history/5453-spanish-archbishop-casado-civil-penalties-for-sexual-abuse-are-unwarranted.html

46 Laurie Goodstein, "A Vatican Lawyer Says Bishops Should Not Reveal Abuse Claims," *The New York Times*, May 18, 2002; "Letter to the Bishops of the Catholic Church on the Pastoral Care of Homosexual Persons," Congregation of the Doctrine of the Faith, October 1, 1986; Judy L. Thomas, "Catholic Priests Are Dying of AIDS, Often in Silence," *The Kansas City Star*, January 29, 2000; "Politics Color John Jay Study," *Catholic League/Catalyst*, July/August Issue, 2011; Bill Donohue, "John Jay Study Undermined by Its Own Data," *National Catholic Register*, June 6, 2011.

47 Ghirlanda quoted in Goodstein, "A Vatican Lawyer Says Bishops Should Not Reveal Abuse Claims."

48 Bishop Gregory quoted in Edward Walsh, "Bishops Pass Compromise on Sexual Abuse Policy," *The Washington Post*, June 15, 2002, A1. Walsh, "Bishops Pass Compromise on Sexual Abuse Policy."

49 Bishop Gregory quoted in Edward Walsh, "Bishops Pass Compromise on Sexual Abuse Policy."

50 Alan Cooperman, "Catholics Question Gray Areas of Abuse; Critics Say Some Priests' Misconduct Goes Unpunished Under New Guidelines," *The Washington Post,* November 30, 2002, A2.

51 Peter Isely quoted in Edward Walsh, "Bishops Pass Compromise on Sexual Abuse Policy."

52 Mark Vincent Serrano, "Church unlikely to get tough with all abusive priests," *USA Today*, June 3, 2002; Sam Dillon, "Catholic Religious Orders Let Abusive Priests Stay," *The New York Times*, August 10, 2002, A8. See also Jason Berry, "The Shame of John Paul II: How the Sex Abuse Scandal Stained His Papacy," *The Nation*, May 16, 2011.

53 Matas, "B.C. Priest Goes on Leave as Past in U.S. Revealed," A3.

54 Egan quoted in Cernetig, "Pope Speaks Out on Abuse."

55 Father Thomas P. Doyle and F. Ray Mouton, J.D., "The Problem of Sexual Molestation by Roman Catholic Clergy: Meeting the Problem in a Comprehensive and Responsible Manner," June 1985.

56 When the Vatican's embassy in Washington, DC, became concerned about the fallout from the notorious abuse of Father Gilbert Gauthe—the Louisiana prelate who ultimately pled guilty to molesting eleven boys—the Nuncio assigned Father Doyle to study that case. Doyle later told CBS's *60 Minutes* that the facts left him "bewildered" and "upset" and convinced him "something's got to be done." David Kohn,"The Church on Trial: Part 1, Rage in Louisiana," *60 Minutes,* June 11, 2002. For further details about Doyle, see Colleen Barry, "Former Church Insider, Now Military Chaplain, Helps Victims of Clerical Sexual Abuse," Associated Press, International News, Ramstein, Germany, BC cycle, April 18, 2002.

57 Caroline Overington, "Hundreds Sue Vatican over Child Sex Abuse," *Sydney Morning Herald*, April 6, 2002, 21. Peterson's clinic was The St. Luke Institute, based in Silver Spring, Maryland; see http://www.sli.org.

58 Thomas P. Doyle, A. W. Richard Sipe, and Patrick J. Wall, *Sex, Priests, and Secret Codes: The Catholic Church's 2,000 Year Paper Trail of Sexual Abuse* (Boulder, CO: Taylor Trade Publishing, 2006). See also Michael D'Antonio, *Mortal Sins: Sex, Crime, and the Era of Catholic Scandal* (New York: MacMillan/Thomas Dunne Books, 2013), Kindle edition, 233, 331, 452, 651 of 7845.

59 Berry, "The Shame of John Paul II." For conclusions of the Doyle-Peterson Report, see Michael Powell and Lois Romano, "Roman Catholic Church Shifts Legal Strategy; Aggressive Litigation Replaces Quiet Settlements," *The Washington Post*, May 13, 2002, A1.

For citations to the text quoted from the report, see Martin Edwin Andersen, "Bearing Witness on Sex Scandal Ends Whistleblowing Priest's Career," *The Washington Times*, May 21, 2002, A21; and Fintan O'Toole, "Ruination of Lives, Ruination of Church—The Catholic Church Has Not Learned from the Brendan Smyth Scandal," *The Irish Times,* October 19, 2002, 50. For online citations of text from the report, see http://www.eurekaencyclopedia.com/index.php/Category:Tom_Doyle.

60 Andersen, "Bearing Witness on Sex Scandal Ends Whistleblowing Priest's Career," A21. For more on Doyle, see also Berry, *Lead Us Not into Temptation*, 92–101, 341–44.

61 Cannon, "The Priest Scandal"; see also Steve Twomey, "For 3 Who Warned Church, Fears Borne Out; Priest, Journalist and Professor Who Foresaw Sex Abuse Scandal Frustrated by Bishops' Response," *The Washington Post*, June 13, 2002, A1. See also D'Antonio, *Mortal Sins*, 1959 of 7845.

62 Lindsey Tanner, "Panel Studying Pedophile Priests Brings Praise, Skepticism," Associated Press, Domestic News, Chicago, March 20, 1992; Vickie Chachere, "Lawsuit Accuses Vatican, Three Dioceses of Conspiring to Protect Priests Who Molested Children," Associated Press, International News, St. Petersburg, Florida, April 4, 2002.

63 Michael Paulson and Thomas Farragher, "Bishops Move to Bar Abusers," *The Boston Globe*, June 15, 2002. See also Harold H. Martin, Untitled, United Press International, Domestic News, Philadelphia, BC cycle, November 28, 1992; Overington, "Hundreds Sue Vatican over Child Sex Abuse," 21.

64 Alan Cooperman, "Bishops Urged to Halt Lawsuits; Abuse Victims Group Complains About Defamation Cases," *The Washington Post*, August 31, 2002, A13.

65 Powell and Romano, "Roman Catholic Church Shifts Legal Strategy; Aggressive Litigation Replaces Quiet Settlements," A1.

66 Sarah Schmidt, "Priests Launch Appeal to Vatican over Expulsions: Sexual Abuse Cases: Canadian Expert Says New U.S. Church Policy Contravenes Canon Law," *National Post* (Canada), August 27, 2002, A8; Sheila H. Pierce, "Vatican Approves Policy Revisions For U.S. Church; Those Accused of Abuse to Get Hearing," *The Washington Post*, December 17, 2002, A3.

67 D'Antonio, *Mortal Sins*, 779 of 7845.
68 Transcript, "Palm Beach Bishop Resigns over Sexual Misconduct," *American Morning with Paula Zahn*, CNN, March 12, 2002.
69 "Cardinal's Compromise Comes Up Short," *The Globe and Mail* (Canada).
70 Author interview with a former consultant to the IOR, identity withheld at his request, in Rome, September 30, 2013.
71 Overington, "Hundreds Sue Vatican over Child Sex Abuse."
72 Paulson, "World Doesn't Share US View of Scandal."
73 Berry, *Render Unto Rome*, 59.
74 Ibid., 80–81; 97. See also Nicholas P. Cafardi, "The Availability of Parish Assets for Diocesan Debts: A Canonical Analysis," *Seton Hall Legislative Journal* 29, no. 2 (2005): 361, available online at: http://works.bepress.com/nicholas_cafardi/2.
75 Gregory Viscusi, "Balancing the Vatican Budget: 'The Market Giveth and the Market Taketh Away,'" *The Calgary Herald*, April 10, 2005, E7.
76 "The Catholic Sex Crisis: Money," http://members.shaw.ca/eye-openers/Catholicsexcrisis.htm. (See also "Coverage and Liability Issues in Sexual Misconduct Claims," American Re Insurance Company, Edition 4, 2005; Jerold Oshinksy, Gheiza M. Dias, "Liability of Not-for-Profit Organizations and Insurance Coverage for Related Liability," *The International Journal of Not-For-Profit Law* 4, nos. 2, 3, March 2002. As reported in the John Jay College Report on Sexual Abuse from 1950–2002, during fifty-two years of settlements, $205 million of $475 million paid by dioceses was covered by insurance. The amount covered dropped sharply over time.
77 Dan Gilgoff, "The Archdiocese Agrees to a Record $85 Million. Will Others Follow?," *U.S. News & World Report*, September 22, 2003.
78 Jack Sullivan and Eric Convey, "Land Rich: Archdiocese Owns Millions in Unused Property," *The Boston Herald*, August 27, 2002, A1.
79 See Berry, *Render Unto Rome*, 80–86.
80 Portland filed on 7/6/04; Tucson on 9/20/04; Spokane on 12/6/04; Davenport, Iowa, on 10/10/06; San Diego on 2/27/07; Fairbanks, Arkansas, on 3/1/08; the Oregon province of the Jesuits on 2/17/09; Wilmington, Delaware, and Maryland on 10/18/09; Milwaukee on 1/4/11; the Congregation of the Christian Brothers on 4/28/11; Gallup, New Mexico, on 11/12/13; Stockton, California, on 1/15/14; Helena, Montana, on 1/31/14; and St. Paul-Minneapolis, on 1/16/15. See generally "Bankruptcy Protection in the Abuse Crisis," at http://www.bishop-accountability.org/bankruptcy.htm. Also see Berry, *Render Unto Rome*, 40–41.
81 See "Sexual Abuse by U.S. Catholic Clergy; Settlements and Monetary Awards in 97–98, Civil Suits," http://www.bishop-accountability.org/settlements/. In 2012, John Allen Jr. in "Vatican Abuse Summit: $2.2 Billion and 100,000 Victims in U.S. Alone," *National Catholic Reporter*, February 8, 2012, estimated the payout total at least at $2.2 billion.

The major civil court settlements in the U.S. are: The Dallas diocese in 1998 paid $30.9 million to twelve victims abused by a single priest. In 2003, the Louisville, Kentucky, diocese settled 240 pending lawsuits for $25.7 million. That same year, the archdiocese of Boston paid $85 million to reach an out-of-court settlement with 552 victims. The following year, 2004, the diocese in Orange County, California, settled nearly 90 cases for $100 million. In 2007, the Portland, Oregon, diocese paid $75 million to 177 victims, while the Seattle diocese reached a $48 million settlement with 160 victims. That same year, the Los Angeles diocese paid a stunning $660 million to more than 500 abuse victims (the previous December it settled another 45 lawsuits for $60 million). And also in 2007, the San Diego diocese paid $198.1 million to 144 victims.

In 2008 it was Denver's turn, a relatively small $5.5 million to 18 victims.

For the full effect of parish closures, special assessments, and the impact of clergy pension and retirement funds, see Berry, *Render Unto Rome*.

82 Berry, *Render Unto Rome*, 105–8.
83 Jason Berry, "Cardinal's Profit Mission and an FBI Investigation into Sale of Church Property," *Irish Times*, January 17, 2012; Jose Martinez, "Star's Ex in Vatican Con Plot: High-Living Longtime Hathaway Beau Gets 21M Bail in Money-Launder Rap," *New York Daily News*, June 25, 2008, 4; Thomas Zambito and Corky Siemaszko, "Off to Jail for Hathaway's Ex in Vatican Scam," *New York Daily News*, September 11, 2008, 3; Corinne Lestch, "Arrivederci to Anne's Ex!," *New York Daily News*, May 26, 2012, 15. As for Sodano, see also Berry, *Render Unto Rome*, 120–24, 126–32.

84 Joseph A. Rohner IV, "Catholic Diocese Sexual Abuse Suits, Bankruptcy, and Property of the Bankruptcy Estate: Is the 'Pot of Gold' Really Empty?" *Oregon Law Review*, Vol. 84, 2005, 1203-4; see also Berry, *Render Unto Rome*, 112.

85 Affidavit of Nicolas P. Cafardi, U.S. Bankruptcy Court, Eastern District of Washington, case no. 04–08822, *The Catholic Bishop of Spokane Debtor, Committee of Tort Litigants v. Catholic Bishop of Spokane et al.*, May 27, 2005, 16, cited in Berry, *Render Unto Rome*, 112, n. 48.

86 The document had surfaced in 2003. It addressed only internal church trials and did not tackle the broader question of whether civil authorities should be notified. See generally transcript of "Abuse Victims Seek Court Date with Vatican," National Public Radio, with hosts Linda Wertheimer and Renee Montagne, December 22, 2008. Riazat Butt, "Vatican to Be Sued over Sex Abuse Claims," *The Guardian*, December 15, 2008, 23.

87 As for the Sodano-Rice meeting, see 11-25-05 WikiLeaks Vatican Unhappy with Lawsuits Cable, 05VATICAN538_a; https://www.wikileaks.org/plusd/cables/05VATICAN538_a.html.

88 Ibid., WikiLeaks. Also, "Vatican's Global Importance Evident In Leaked Cables," EWTN, Catholic News Agency, December 14, 2010. "Pope Wants Exemption from U.S. Law," *Vermont Guardian* (Texas), May 31, 2005.

89 Ibid., "Vatican's Global Importance Evident In Leaked Cables," *EWTN*; See 01-08-02 WikiLeaks, "Vatican PM Wants His Money Cable, See also Berry, *Render Unto Rome*, 119-20. 02VATICAN83_a; https://www.wikileaks.org/plusd/cables/02VATICAN83_a.html.

90 John L. Allen Jr., "Vatican Ask Condoleezza Rice to Help Stop a Sex Abuse Lawsuit," *National Catholic Reporter*, March 2, 2005.

91 Karen Terry et al., *The Nature and Scope of Sexual Abuse of Minors by Catholic Priests and Deacons in the United States, 1950–2002*, prepared by the John Jay College of Criminal Justice for the U.S. Conference of Catholic Bishops (Washington, DC: U.S. Conference of Catholic Bishops, 2004) (hereinafter *The John Jay College Report on Sexual Abuse*). Two years later a Supplementary Report was published. Karen Terry, et al., *The Nature and Scope of Sexual Abuse of Minors by Catholic Priests and Deacons in the United States: Supplementary Data Analysis* (March 2006). And again Karen Terry et al., *The Causes and Context of Sexual Abuse of Minors by Catholic Priests in the United States, 1950–2010*, May 18, 2011. The 2011 report focused on the "causes and context of abuse."

92 *The John Jay College Report on Sexual Abuse*, 2, 5. One hundred and ninety-five dioceses and eparchies participated in the study and 140 religious communities submitted answers to confidential surveys sent by John Jay College. The study's authors used a statistical analysis to extrapolate the findings to all dioceses in the U.S. As for the authors' methodology, see *The John Jay College Report on Sexual Abuse*, 13-25.

93 *The John Jay College Report on Sexual Abuse*, 26.

94 "The percentages of accused priests range from a maximum of almost 10% in 1970, decreasing to 8% in 1980 and to fewer than 4% in 1990." Ibid., 26.

95 The serial molesters accounted for nearly a quarter of the assaults. Ibid., 35, 40, 52.

96 Ibid., 47–50, 62.

97 Emphasis added. Ibid., 39, 57.

98 Ibid., 40–43, 45, 47.

99 Ibid., 48, 100.

100 Ibid., 105–20.

101 Tony Kennedy, "Archdiocese Led Lobby to Stop Abuse Law Change," *Star-Tribune* (Minneapolis), November 5, 2013.

102 Berry, "The Shame of John Paul II."

103 Richard McBrien, "The Beatification of John Paul II," *National Catholic Reporter*, February 7, 2011.

104 Ibid. The definitive account of Maciel, his excesses and abuses, and the church's failure to take any action against him for years, is in Jason Berry's *Render Unto Rome*. Berry, and *The Washington Post*'s religion editor, Gerald Renner, exposed charges of sex abuse against Maciel in a February 23, 1997, *Hartford Courant* article. They cited nine seminarians who described multiple instances of abuse. As related by Berry and Renner, Maciel was a morphine addict because of chronic pain. When he kicked his addiction, he told the seminarians that Pius XII had personally given him permission to engage in sex to offset his pain. Maciel's defenders were merciless in attacking Berry and Renner and in defending the bishop. The Pope showed his support by appointing Maciel to a key theological panel in Rome.

105 Berry, "The Shame of John Paul II."
106 When he directed the Congregation for the Doctrine of the Faith, Ratzinger had stopped the probe at the urging of Sodano. "But Ratzinger could not have tabled a case as grave as Maciel's without the approval of John Paul," wrote Jason Berry in *Render Unto Rome*, 186. See also Obituary, The Rev. Marcial Maciel, *The Guardian*, April 28, 2008.
107 Gianluigi Nuzzi, *Sua santità, le carte segrete di Benedetto XVI* (Milan: Chiarelettere, 2012), 196–99, 295; Nuzzi reproduced some confidential Vatican documents in his book. One of them, an October 19, 2011, handwritten note from Benedict's private secretary, Monsignor Gänswein, summarized his meeting with Moreno in which Maciel's abuse was addressed. See also Jason Berry, "The Legion of Christ and the Vatican Meltdown," *National Catholic Reporter*, June 21, 2012.
108 Hugh O'Shaughnessy, "Pope Throws the Book at Wealthy Catholic Legion," *Sunday Tribune* (Ireland), August 8, 2010, N16.
109 See generally Doyle and Rubino, "Catholic Clergy Sexual Abuse Meets the Civil Law."

Chapter 32: "His Inbox Was a Disaster"

1 "Jean Pull II souffrait de la maladie de Parkinson," *Le Monde*, September 10, 1996, 3.
2 "Recovering Pope Keeps Trembling Hand Hidden," *Hobart Mercury* (Australia), October 15, 1996.
3 Freddy Gray, "Pope's Health Prompts Betting Frenzy: Channel 4," *Catholic Herald*, January 16, 2004, 3; the bookmakers were Betfair and Paddy Power.
4 Weigel, *Witness to Hope*, 782–83.
5 Murray was an Australian religious affairs editor. "A Retiring John Paul Is Hard to Imagine," *The Australian*, January 12, 2000, 11.
6 David J. Lynch, "Rumor of Papal Retirement Drifts About Rome," *USA Today*, January 25, 2000, 10A.
7 Author interview with Michael Hornblow, January 28, 2014. "'John Paul was just a terrible administrator,'" a friend of the Pope told author Paul Elie. "Even at his physical peak he had always been indifferent to the operations of the Vatican bureaucracy; now he was barely capable of keeping track of them," concluded Elie. See also Paul Elie, "The Year of Two Popes," *The Atlantic*, January 1, 2006.
8 Philip Willan, "Mafia Caught Attempting Online Bank Fraud," *Network World*, October 9, 2000; "Vatican Bank Involved in Mafia's On-Line Washing Money," Xinhua General News Service, Rome, October 3, 2000.
9 John Walker, "Money Laundering: Quantifying International Patterns," *Australian Social Monitor* 2, no. 6 (February 2000).
10 Ibid., 142. Because of the amount of money laundered through their banks, both the U.S. and the U.K. also made the list.
11 "Legislative and Economic Factors Determining International Flow of Laundered Money," John Walker Crime Trends Analysis, attached paper to the United Nations 10th Congress on Economic and Social Issues, Vienna, Summer 2000, table 1.
12 Michael Becket, "Gangster's Paradise Across the Atlantic," *The Daily Telegraph*, November 19, 2001, 31; *Emil Alperin v. Istituto per le Opere di Religione*, U.S. District Court, San Francisco, November 1999. See also online summary at http://www.vaticanbankclaims.com/vatpr.html.
13 Email from John Walker to author, January 15, 2014. Walker drew this conclusion while admitting that much of the data needed for a more precise calculation is simply "not available for the Vatican."
14 Phillip Smith, "Latin America: Mexican Catholic Church in Narco-Dollar Embarrassment," *Drug War Chronicles* 531, April 11, 2008; Jo Tuckman, "Pope's Visit to Mexico Refocuses Attention on Narco-Church Relations," *The Guardian*, March 22, 2012; Leonor Flores, "Narcolimosnas: "Que partidos e Iglesia reporten operaciones," *El Economista*, February 24, 2011; "Iglesia reconoce recibir limosnas de narcos," *El Economista*, October 31, 2010.
15 See George Dale, *Commissioner of Insurance for the State of Mississippi et al. v. Emilio Colagiovanni and The Holy See et al.*, United States District Court for the Southern District of Mississippi, Jackson Division (Case No. 3:01CV663BN).

16 Simon Fluendy, "Vatican Bank Is Sued in US over Charity Scandal," *Mail on Sunday* (UK), August 11, 2002, 6.
17 Ibid.; see also Lynne Touhy, "Frankel Associate Gets Probation, $10,000 fine," *Hartford Courant*, May 25, 2005, A18.
18 Alexander Walker, "Banned: The Film God's Bankers Don't Want You to See," *The Evening Standard* (London), April 4, 2002, 35.
19 Jim McBeth, "Who Killed God's Banker?," *The Scotsman*, October 2, 2002, 2; "Top Banker 'Murder by the Mafia,'" *The Mirror* (UK), July 24, 2003, 14.
20 Simon Edge, "Leader Italian Police Have Concluded After 21 Years That 'God's Banker' Was Murdered; Who Killed Roberto Calvi . . . The Masons, Mafia or Vatican?," *The Express* (UK), July 25, 2003, 13. For a straightforward review of the developing police and forensics examinations, see James Moore and Bruce Johnston, "Murder Squad Revisit Roberto Calvi," *The Daily Telegraph* (London), October 4, 2003, 36.
21 Author review of LexisNexis search results for "Vatican Bank" in all English language news sources from January 1, 2000, to December 31, 2005; 59 of 111 stories were primarily about Calvi.
22 In 1996, for instance, following an emergency appendectomy, there were widespread reports that his health was so poor he might have to resign. Parkinson's in particular had "implications for the future of his pontificate," since those with the disease frequently have "some mental changes, including depression and features of dementia." Ray Moseley, "Health of Pope Has Vatican Guessing," *Hamilton Spectator* (Ontario), October 19, 1996, B8.

Chapter 33: The Kingmaker Becomes King

1 "Several years ago, the *Financial Times* put the value of the Vatican's real estate holdings at $37.2 billion and its stock portfolio at $23.9 billion," according to Charles W. Bell, "Church Rich in Art, Cash," *New York Daily News*, April 3, 2005, 21.
2 Cardinal Sergio Sebastiani quoted in Victor L. Simpson, "Next Pope Can Add Vatican's Financial Woes to Long List of Responsibilities," Associated Press, International News, Vatican City, BC cycle, April 12, 2005. Father Thomas Reese, a noted writer about the church, was also quoted by Simpson: "The dollar has really hurt them. We're not only talking about money coming from United States. All the rich guys in the Third World also give in dollars."
3 Szoka quoted in "Trouble at God's Bank," *The Toronto Star*, April 17, 2005, A20.
4 Simpson, "Next Pope Can Add Vatican's Financial Woes to Long List of Responsibilities."
5 John Pollard quoted in "Trouble at God's Bank," *The Toronto Star*, A20.
6 Simpson, "Next Pope Can Add Vatican's Financial Woes to Long List of Responsibilities."
7 Ibid.
8 Deirdre Macken, "Next Pope's ID Is in Da Vinci Code; Relativities," *Australian Financial Review*, April 9, 2005, 31.
9 Calum MacDonald, "Politicking Begins as the Cardinals Go into Conclave; Secret Body That Will Choose New Leader," *The Herald* (Glasgow), April 5, 2005, 6; see also Paddy Agnew, "How the Kingmaker Became King," *The Irish Times*, April 23, 2005, 1.
10 Agnew, "How the Kingmaker Became King," 1.
11 Those stories were by *La Repubblica*'s Marco Politi and *L'Espresso*'s Sandro Magister, men who had excellent Curial sources.
12 Peter Stanford, "Pope John Paul II: Who Will Lead One Billion Souls?: The College of Cardinals Must Now Elect a New Pope," *The Observer* (London), April 3, 2005, 16.
13 Grocholewski quoted in Stephen McGinty, "Campaigning Candidates Are Reined In as Agreement Made to Stop All Media Interviews," *The Scotsman*, April 7, 2005, 4.
14 Ibid; see also "Political Wrangle for Potential Popes," *St. Petersburg Times*, April 6, 2005.
15 See generally Lydia Polgreen and Larry Rohter, "Third World Is New Factor in Succession," *The New York Times*, April 5, 2005, 1.
16 Sandro Contenta, Cardinals Divided in Choice for Pope," *Toronto Star*, April 5, 2005, A1; Julia Duin, "Latin America Eyed for Next Pope," *The Washington Times*, April 7, 2005, A14.
17 Charles W. Bell, "The Games Cardinals Play. Mud's Flying as They Angle for Big Job," *New York Daily News*, April 15, 2005, 16.
18 Ibid.

19 Stanford, "Pope John Paul II: Who Will Lead One Billion Souls?"
20 "Will the Cardinals Look Beyond Italy Again?," *Daily Mail*, April 2, 2005, 4.
21 See *Dominus Iesus: On the Unicity and Salvific Universality of Jesus Christ and the Church*, http://www.vatican.va/roman_curia/congregations/cfaith/documents/rc_con_cfaith_doc_20000806_dominus-iesus_en.html. Ratzinger was the principal author and it was issued in 2000.
22 John Follain and Christopher Morgan, "Lobbying Begins for Papal Rivals," *Sunday Times* (London), April 10, 2005, 23.
23 Both quotes repeated widely, see for instance Stephen McGinty and Richard Gray, "Meet the Cardinal Who Will Play Kingmaker in Rome," *Scotland on Sunday*, April 10, 2005, 8.
24 Bruce Johnston, Swing to Ratzinger Boosts Chance of Becoming Pope," *The Daily Telegraph*, April 13, 2005, A12.
25 Bell, "The Games Cardinals Play," 16.
26 Justin Sparks in Munich and John Follain and Christopher Morgan in Rome, "Papal Hopeful Is a Former Hitler Youth," *The Sunday Times* (London), April 17, 2005, 23.
27 Ruini quoted in Charles W. Bell, "A People's Pope Favored. Hints That New Pontiff Will Be Like John Paul," *New York Daily News*, April 22, 2005, 7. Quote is the reporter's summary of the Ruini comments.
28 "Briefly," *The Toronto Star*, September 28, 1997, A11; Thavis, *The Vatican Diaries*, 278–79.
29 Philip Pullella, "Pope Opposed Bob Dylan Singing to John Paul in 1997," Vatican City, Reuters, March 8, 2007.
30 Joseph Ratzinger, while Pope Benedict, *John Paul II, My Beloved Predecessor* (Miami: Pauline Books, 2007): "There was reason to be skeptical—I was, and in a certain sense I still am—to doubt if it was really right to let these types of prophets intervene."
31 Thavis, *The Vatican Diaries*, 279–80; Alessandra Stanley, "Pope's Labor Rally Joins Mass and Rock Concert," *The New York Times*, May 2, 2000, A6. See Eric J. Lyman, "Vatican Pop Culture Guru Backpedals on Lou Reed Tribute," *The Salt Lake Tribune*, October 29, 2013.
32 John L. Allen Jr., *Cardinal Ratzinger: The Vatican's Enforcer of Faith* (New York: Continuum, 2000); John L. Allen Jr., *Pope Benedict XVI: A Biography of Joseph Ratzinger* (London: Bloomsbury Academic, 2005).
33 Joan Vennochi, "A Vote for Pope, an Insult to Abuse Victims," *The Boston Globe*, February 17, 2013.
34 Charles W. Bell, "Vatican Gets Tough to Thwart Leaks," *New York Daily News*, April 15, 1005, 16.
35 Joseph Cardinal Ratzinger, *Milestones: Memoirs, 1927–1977* (San Francisco: Ignatius, 1998).
36 Allen, *Cardinal Ratzinger*, 8, citing Uriel Tal, *Christians and Jews in Germany.*
37 Allen, *Pope Benedict XVI*, 49.
38 See generally "Profile: Emeritus Pope Benedict XVI," BBC News, Europe, May 2, 2013; Greg Sheridan, "Administration Was Not Benedict's Forte," *Real Clear World*, February 11, 2013.
39 Allen, *Cardinal Ratzinger*, 15; see generally David Gibson, *The Rule of Benedict* (NY: Harper, 2006).
40 Sparks, Follain, and Morgan, "Papal Hopeful Is a former Hitler Youth," 23.
41 Ibid.
42 Ratzinger quoted in Charles W. Bell, "New Pope? Nope. 'Relativist' Catholics Ripped by Hard-liner," *New York Daily News*, April 19, 1005, 4.
43 The long shots were Canada's Cardinal Marc Ouellet at 80 to1 and Cardinal Jean-Claude Turcotte at 100 to 1. Scott Stinson, "Italian Favoured in Online Pope Betting," *National Post* (Canada), April 6, 2005, A16.
44 The exact voting tallies for this conclave are known because five months later an Italian political magazine, *Limes*, published the conclave diary believed to have been kept by Cardinal Carlo Maria Martini. It included vote totals on each ballot. In the past, unconfirmed reports had later filtered out about the votes, but never were as credible as the contemporaneous diary. See generally "TV Report: Cardinal's Unauthorized, Anonymous Diary Says Pope Was Elected with 84 Votes," Associated Press Worldstream, International News, Vatican City, September 22, 2005; Nicole Winfield, "Cardinal Diary Details Papal Conclave," Associated Press, International News, Vatican City, September 24, 2005.
45 Bruce Wilson, "Cardinals Set a Ratzinger Trap—Liberals Against Papal Frontrunner—Electing a Pope," *Daily Telegraph* (Sydney), April 19, 2005, 13.

46 John L. Allen Jr., "Profile: New Pope, Jesuit Bergoglio, Was Runner-up in 2005 Conclave," *National Catholic Reporter,* March 3, 2013.

47 See generally Wilson, "Cardinals Set a Ratzinger Trap," 13.

48 On the last ballot, one vote went to the disgraced Boston cardinal, Bernard Law. He was one of the electors, and it is not clear if someone cast a protest vote against Ratzinger, since it was then clear that Ratzinger was about to become Pope, or if he did it himself so he would always remain an odd footnote to the final tally.

The information about what motivated the cardinals was also part of discussions later over the publication of Cardinal Martini's diary. See Daniel J. Wakin, "Ritual and Secrecy Surround Conclave," *The New York Times*, March 11, 2013.

49 Agnew, "How the Kingmaker Became King,"

50 John Hooper, "A Moment Of Doubt, Then A Cry Went Up," *The Guardian*, April 20, 2005.

51 Benedict XXI quoted in "New Pope Admits To 'Inadequacy And Turmoil'" *The Telegraph* (London), April 20, 2005.

Chapter 34: "As Flat as Stale Beer"

1 U.S. Court of Appeals, Ninth Circuit, Opinion No. 03-15208, D.C. No. CV-99-04941-MMC, *Alperin v. Vatican Bank*, Argued and Submitted October 7, 2004—San Francisco, California, filed April 18, 2005, online at "Court Clears Way for Suit Against the Vatican Bank for Nazi Gold," *Silicon Valley Business Journal*, April 18, 2005, reporting on the judgment of the Ninth U.S. Circuit Court, April 12, 2005; see "Nazi Gold–Vatican Bank Ruling, U.S. Ninth Circuit Court of Appeals," *Jurist*, University of Pittsburgh School of Law, April 18, 2005.

2 "Court Clears Way for Suit Against the Vatican Bank for Nazi Gold," *Silicon Valley Business Journal.* The IOR's American lawyers filed an appeal to the U.S. Supreme Court later that fall. On a Petition for a Writ of Certiorari to the United States Court of Appeals for the Ninth Circuit, in the Supreme Court of the United States, in *Istituto per le Opere di Religione v. Emil Alperin et al.*, October 2005, courtesy of Jonathan Levy.

3 Benedict seemed as laid-back that fall when Italy's newspapers were filled with the old IOR-Calvi scandal as five men finally went on trial in Rome charged with murdering the Ambrosiano chairman. Everyone but the Pope seemed to be talking about the prosecutor's opening statement in which he said, "There were many different kinds of interests represented in the Ambrosiano. There was the Vatican, the Mafia, Freemasons and politicians. This trial is going to tell just a part of all of these stories." A Vatican spokesman issued a standing "no comment" to press queries. And the new Pope did not miss a beat that December when headlines were filled with the news of yet another book contending that Pope John Paul I was murdered; this time the motive was supposedly because he knew about money laundering inside the Vatican Bank.

4 Ulrich Schwartz, "'Coded Language' and Yes Men: Cables of Confusion from the Heart of the Vatican," *Der Spiegel*, December 13, 2010; See 02-20-09 WikiLeaks The Holy See: A Failure to Communicate Cable, 09VATICAN28_a; https://www.wikileaks.org/plusd/cables/09VATICAN28_a.html.

5 Ibid.

6 Carla Del Ponte and Chuck Sudetic, *Madame Prosecutor: Confrontations with Humanity's Worst Criminals and the Culture of Impunity* (New York: Other Press, 2011), Kindle edition, location 365 of 7695.

7 Del Ponte and Chuck Sudetic, *Madame Prosecutor*, Kindle Edition, 3586 of 7695.

8 See copy of August 26, 2005 U.S. cable, subject "Del Ponte Makes 'Ugly Impression' at the Vatican," at http://racconta.espresso.repubblica.it/espresso-wikileaks-database-italia/dettaglio_eng.php?id=55. Del Ponte even provided a list of the monasteries to assist the search; see Del Ponte and Sudetic, *Madame Prosecutor*, location 5040, 5057 of 7695.

9 Lajolo quoted in Del Ponte and Sudetic, *Madame Prosecutor*, location 5067 of 7695.

10 See generally Ulrich Schwarz, "'Coded Language' and Yes Men: Cables of Confusion from the Heart of the Vatican," *Der Spiegel*, December 13, 2010. See also August 26, 2005, Del Ponte Makes "Ugly Impression" at the Vatican, https://www.wikileaks.org/plusd/cables/05VATICAN516_a.html.

11 Del Ponte and Sudetic, *Madame Prosecutor*, location 5077 of 7695.

12 See also David Rennie, "Vatican Accused of Shielding 'War Criminal,'" *The Daily Telegraph*, September 20, 2005.
13 "Vatican Denies Knowledge of Indicted War Criminal's Whereabouts," Agence France-Presse, Vatican City, September 20, 2005; "Vatican Hits Back at UN Prosecutor over Wanted Croatian," Deutsche Presse-Agentur, Vatican City/Zagreb/London, September 20, 2005.
14 The Israeli ambassador, for example, received a Vatican statement that was supposed to contain a positive message for Israel, but it was so veiled he missed it, even when he was told it was there: 02-20-09 WikiLeaks The Holy See: A Failure to Communicate cable.
15 Rachel Donadio and Jim Yardley, "Vatican Bureaucracy Tests Even the Infallible," *The New York Times*, March 19, 2013, 1.
16 Tony Blankey, "Pope Benedict in the Lion's Den; A Teacher to Unwilling Students Across the World," *The Washington Times*, November 29, 2006, A19, citing *Time* from the previous week.
17 Thavis, *The Vatican Diaries*. Thavis, a recently retired Rome Bureau chief of the Catholic News Service, provides one of the most astute portraits of Benedict and his personal shortcomings upon assuming the Papacy. See Chapter 10, "The Real Benedict," 278–306.
18 It is customary for Curia officials to resign when reaching seventy-five, but it is subject to the desires of the Pope. Only two days after he was elected, Benedict reappointed Sodano as Secretary of State.
19 According to Edward Pentin, a reporter with the *National Catholic Register*, "A source close to the Vatican said the announcement was made now to halt widespread speculation about new Vatican appointments in the Italian press." Edward Pentin, "Benedict Names Cardinal Bertone Secretary of State," *National Catholic Register*, July 3, 3006, referring to a statement of Pope Benedict dated June 22, 2006
20 Pentin, "Benedict Names Cardinal Bertone Secretary of State," *National Catholic Register*, July 3, 3006, referring to a statement of Pope Benedict dated June 22, 2006.
21 Emiliano Fittipaldi, "Vaticano, le due cordate," *L'Espresso*, May 28, 2012.
22 Rocco Palmo, a veteran Vatican-based journalist, called the process the 'Widows of Sodano," as the Secretary of State put "his dearest aides in high posts as a reward for their loyalty. "Rome Notes," *Whispers in the Loggia*, July 12, 2006.

Sodano also refused to move out of his grand apartment so long as he retained the title as Secretary of State. It forced Bertone to squeeze into an uncomfortable flat, something most Curialists interpreted as a personal slight. Fittipaldi, "Vaticano, le due cordate." *L'Espresso*. Sodano did not leave his office for a year until the renovation was complete on his new one as the Dean of the College of Cardinals. That meant Bertone was stuck in a smaller adjacent room. See Nuzzi, *Ratzinger Was Afraid*, 133.
23 Rocco Palmo, "Rome Notes," *Whispers in the Loggia*, July 12, 1996, online at http://whispersintheloggia.blogspot.com/2006/07/rome-notes.html. Time and again, Benedict was passive when it came to filling top Curial posts. For instance, when it came to the Secretary of the Congregation for Religious Life and Societies of Apostolic Life, Benedict favored Cardinal Crescenzio Sepe. But there was stiff resistance to him from the influential mother superior of the Brigittine Sisters, Tekla Famiglietti. So Benedict sent Sepe to run the diocese in Naples and a Franciscan priest, Franciscan Father Gianfranco Gardin, was the compromise. In 2007, Sepe was embroiled in a broad scandal in which—among other charges—he was accused of giving free Propaganda Fide apartments to Italian politicians in exchange for them directing millions of dollars in public money to his office for never performed restoration work.

In June 2010, Italian magistrates opened a formal investigation. Sepe has denied any wrongdoing and no charges have been filed. John Allen Jr., "Facing Financial Scandals, Pope Creates New Vatican Watchdog," *National Catholic Reporter*, December 30, 2010; see also Philip Pullela, "Vatican Enacts Laws on Financial Transparency; New Laws Adopted in the Wake of Money Laundering Allegations," Reuters, January 1, 2011.
24 Rocco Palmo, "Rome Notes," *Whispers in the Loggia*, July 12, 1996.
25 Lai, *Finanze vaticane*, 93–94; see also Rocco Palmo, *Whispers in the Loggia*, July 12, 1996, online at http://whispersintheloggia.blogspot.com/2006/07/rome-notes.html.
26 Benny Lai interview with Angelo Caloia, June 1, 2007, in Lai, *Finanze vaticane*, 152.
27 02-20-09 WikiLeaks The Holy See: A Failure to Communicate cable.
28 Ibid.
29 Richard Owen, "Benedict Eager to Modernise Arcane World of Vatican Bank: Averse to Ineffi-

ciency, the Pope Is Forming His Own Team to Control Church Finances," *The Times* (London), September 18, 2006.

30 Richard Owen, "Pope to Put His House in Order," *The Australian*, September 20, 2006, 10.

31 Owen, "Benedict Eager to Modernise Arcane World of Vatican Bank."

32 Ibid.; see also Owen, "Pope to Put His House in Order," 10.

33 Lai, *Finanze vaticane*, 95.

34 Rosemary Church and Alessio Vinci, guest Father Thomas Reese, "Pope Benedict XVI," Transcript, CNN International, April 3, 2006.

35 Michael Valpy, "A Look at the Pope Nobody Knows," *The Globe and Mail* (Canada), April 15, 2006.

36 "The AFP Europe news agenda for Sept 10," Agence France Presse, Paris, September 10, 2006.

37 Victor Simpson quoted in Thavis, *The Vatican Diaries*, 280.

38 Thavis, *The Vatican Diaries*, 281.

39 Ibid., 280.

40 Ibid., 281.

41 Benedict quoted in "Pope Benedict vs. The Jihadists," New York *Daily News*, September 14, 2006, 34.

42 Catholic News Service bureau chief John Thavis recalled that by asking Lombardi about the language beforehand the journalists were "offering the Vatican a preemptive defense." In fact, no one around Benedict warned him that repeating such words without also clearly repudiating them might cast him in the popular press as a modern-day crusader against Islam. Thavis, *The Vatican Diaries*, 285–86.

43 Jon Meacham, with Edward Pentin in Rome, "The Pope's 'Holy War'; By Quoting a 14th-Century Christian Emperor on an 'Evil and Inhuman' Islam, Benedict XVI Ignites a Global Storm. What Was He Thinking?," *Newsweek*, September 25, 2006, 36.

44 See, for example, James Mills, "Pope's Criticism of the Prophet Inflames Muslims Worldwide," *The Evening Standard*, September 15, 2006, 7, "Muslims in Pope Rage," *Evening Gazette*, September 15, 2006, 6; Michael Valpy, "Pope's Quote Kindles Islamic Rage; Fury Compared to That over Danish Cartoons," *The Globe and Mail* (Canada), September 16, A1; Geraint Jones, Gordon Thomas, and Julia Hartley-Brewer, "Pope 'Sorry' as Churches Are Bombed by Muslims," *Sunday Express*, September 17, 2006, 7.

45 Alex Jolly and Jack Lefley, " 'Execute the Pope' call at Westminster Protest," *The Evening Standard*, September 18, 2006, 6.

46 Malcolm Moore, "Security Around the Pope Is Stepped up; Six Churches Burned in Weekend of Protests as Muslims Condemn Pontiff's Unflattering Reference to Mohammed," *The Daily Telegraph*, September 18, 2006, 4; James Wickham, "Nun Is Shot Dead in Pope Backlash," *Daily Star* (UK), September 18, 2006. See also Simon Caldwell, "24 Catholic Missionaries Killed in 2006," *Daily Mail*, January 2, 2007, 19. Iran's supreme leader, Ayatollah Ali Khamenei, said the Pope was trying to kick off a "chain of conspiracy to set off a crusade." Ian Fisher and Sebnem Arsu with reporting from Istanbul, Raymond Bonner from Jakarta, Indonesia, and Mona el-Naggar from Cairo, "Pope's Regrets over Statement Fail to Quiet a Storm of Protests," *The New York Times*, September 19, 2006, 15

47 Ağca quoted in Patsy McGarry, "Man Who Tried to Kill Pope Warns Against Trip," *The Irish Times*, September 21, 2006, 12.

48 Nick Pisa, "Pope in Flak Jacket Visit Plea," *The Mirror*, November 27, 2006. Benedict had opposed Muslim Turkey becoming part of the European Union. After the angry response to his remarks about Islam, Benedict was anxious to make amends. So he reversed years of Vatican opposition to Turkey joining the EU and endorsed it. It was to the dismay of the U.S., which had urged him not to do so.

49 For more on the Vatican's excuses about Benedict's 2006 speech addressing Islam, see generally Thavis, *The Vatican Diaries*, 287–88.

50 Author interview with former Papal advisor/assistant, identity withheld at their request, in Rome, September 2013.

51 Benedict quoted in John Hooper, "Pope 'Deeply Sorry' but Muslim Protests Spread: Nun Shot Dead in Somalia; Italy on Security Alert Apology Offends Jews," *The Guardian*, September 18, 2006, 1.

52 Benedict quoted in Ian Fisher, "Pope Tries to Quell Ire over Speech in Brazil," *International Herald Tribune*, May 24, 2007, 3.

53 Pew Research Poll, Religion and Public Life Project, April 7, 2010, online at http://www.pewforum.org/2010/04/07/broad-criticism-of-pope-benedicts-handling-of-sex-abuse-scandal/.
54 Berry, *Render Unto Rome*, 186. See also Berry, "The Shame of John Paul II."
55 Laurie Goodstein, "384 Priests Defrocked over Abuse in 2 Years," *The New York Times*, January 18, 2014, A8.
56 Author interview with former Papal advisor/assistant, identity withheld at their request, in Rome, September 2013.
57 Thomas P. Doyle and Stephen C. Rubino, "Catholic Clergy Sexual Abuse Meets the Civil Law," *Fordham Urban Law Journal*, Volume 31, Issue 2, Article 6, 2003; see also Thavis, *The Vatican Diaries*, 296.
58 Ibid. Thavis, 299.
59 Ibid., 299–300.
60 Ryan Lucas, "New Warsaw Archbishop Quits in Wake of Disclosures," *The Washington Post*, January 8, 2007, A11.
61 Oliver Balch, "British bishop who denied scale of Holocaust loses job," *The Guardian*, February 9, 2009. Bishop Richard Williamson was one of four bishops who adhered to the Society of Saint Pius X (SSPX). SSPX had been founded to oppose the reforms of Vatican II. The four had been excommunicated in 1988.
62 A month after the uproar, Williamson was removed from his position as the chief prelate in his Argentine seminary. Three years later his traditionalist order, SSPX, expelled him. In 2015 Williamson was automatically excommunicated after he ordained another ex-SSPX priest as a "bishop" without the Pope's approval. Oliver Balch, John Hooper, and Riazat Butt, "Vatican Crisis over Bishop Who Denies the Holocaust," *The Guardian*, February 6, 2009; see also Nick Squires, "Holocaust Denying British Bishop Expelled From Religious Order," *The Telegraph* (United Kingdom), October 24, 2012. Andrea Tornielli, "The Fraternity of St. Pius X 'Excommunicates' Williamson," "Vatican Insider," *La Stampa*, March 20, 2015.
63 02-20-09 WikiLeaks The Holy See: A Failure to Communicate Cable, 09VATICAN28_a; https://www.wikileaks.org/plusd/cables/09VATICAN28_a.html.
64 Thavis, *The Vatican Diaries*, 292.
65 Author interview with former Papal advisor/assistant, identity withheld at their request, in Rome, September 2013. Stampa was "one of the Pope's few trusted confidants" according to author Gianluigi Nuzzi. Nuzzi, *Ratzinger Was Afraid*, 23.
66 Nuzzi, ibid.

Chapter 35: Chasing the White List

1 Wang Yunjia, "Old Obstacles, New Crisis Hits Italy's Lagging eEconomy," Xinhua, March 11, 2009.
2 Diego Coletto, "Effects of Economic Crisis on Italian Economy," European Industrial Relations Observatory, University of Milan, January 6, 2010; see also Roberto Di Quirico, "Italy and the Global Economic Crisis," *Bulletin of Italian Politics* 2, no. 2 (2010): 3–19.
3 "Vatican Runs Deficit Amid Global Economic Crisis," Business, *Huffington Post*, July 4, 2009; Kevin Roose, "The Vatican's Financial Empire, in Charts," News & Politics, *New York*, March 12, 2013. The money raised through Peter's Pence dropped every year through 2010. See Nuzzi, *Ratzinger Was Afraid*, 81.
4 Ibid.
5 Benedict quoted in Lorenzo Totaro, "Vatican Says Islamic Finance May Help Western Banks in Crisis," Bloomberg, March 4, 2009.
6 Ibid.
7 "Vatican Bank Safe from Crisis, Bank President Says," EWTN Global Catholic Network, October 15, 2008. Caloia told author Giancarlo Galli that the Holy See maintained gold bullion in Basel, Switzerland, and the United States, the latter in conjunction with the Federal Reserve. The Basel gold was accumulated by Nogara, and according to Caloia had "never been touched." See Galli, *Finanza bianca*, 149. See also Victor L. Simpson, "Official Says Deposits in Vatican Bank Are Safe," Associated Press, Business News, Rome, October 13, 2008.
8 Caloia interview in Galli, *Finanza Bianca*, 168.

9 Caloia quoted in John Thavis, "Vatican Bank Official Says Assets Not Threatened by Global Crisis," Catholic News Service, October 14, 2008; see also Rocco Palmo, "God's Bankers: Not Afraid," *Whispers in the Loggia*, October 14, 2008, online at http://whispersintheloggia.blogspot.com/2008/10/gods-bankers-not-afraid.html; see also Simpson, "Official Says Deposits in Vatican Bank Are Safe."

A comprehensive synopsis of the IOR's strength during the economic crisis, as well as that of other financial departments such as APSA and the Governorate, is by Sandro Magister, "For Peter's Cash, a Calm Amid the Storm," *L'Espresso*, January 30, 2009, including five years of balance sheets for APSA, the Governorate, Peter's Pence, as well as the published consolidated financial statements of the Holy See. See online at http://chiesa.espresso.repubblica.it/articolo/1337147?eng=y.

10 Galli, *Finanza bianca*, 172.

11 Nick Mathiason, "Pope Attacks Tax Havens for Robbing Poor: Vatican Condemns Roots of Credit Crunch, but Critics Say Its Own Bank Hoards Gold, Art and Cash," *The Observer*, December 7, 2008, 7.

12 Benedict quoted in Ibid.

13 Nicole Winfield, "Pope Proposes New Financial Order Guided by Ethics," Associated Press Online, Business News, Vatican City, July 7, 2009; see *Caritas in Veritate* online at http://www.vatican.va/holy_father/benedict_xvi/encyclicals/documents/hf_ben-xvi_enc_20090629_caritas-in-veritate_en.html.

14 Adding to Dardozzi's unhappiness at the IOR, he was convinced the bank had cheated him out of a large commission he was due for arranging the sale of a prime Florentine church property. He wanted that money to ensure that a handicapped daughter he had adopted before he became a priest had enough money to care for herself after his death. When he made no headway in convincing anyone that he had been shortchanged, it only added to his general dissatisfaction.

15 Nuzzi, *Vatican SpA*, 5–7.

16 Gianluigi Nuzzi, "IOR parallelo. Conti segreti in Vaticano," *Panorama*, May 17, 2005.

17 Philip Willan, "How the Vatican Sold," *The Guardian*, June 15, 2009; see also Nuzzi, "IOR parallelo. Conti segreti in Vaticano."

18 Nuzzi quoted in Willan, "The Vatican's Dirty Secrets: Bribery, Money Laundering and Mafia Connections," June 4, 2009.

19 Author interview with former Papal advisor/assistant, identity withheld at their request, in Rome, September 2013.

20 Andreotti quoted in Nuzzi, "IOR parallelo. Conti segreti in Vaticano." Galeazzi, "Karol Wojtyla and the Secrets of Vatican Finances," "Vatican Insider."

21 Ibid.

22 Author interview with former Papal advisor/assistant, identity withheld at their request, in Rome, September 2013.

23 Ibid.

24 Lai, *Finanze vaticane*, 97.

25 Caloia statement as part of a submission of a 2008 financial report to the Secretariat of State; see Magister, "All the Denarii of Peter. Vices and Virtues of the Vatican Bank."

26 Guy Dinmore, "Upheaval Lifts Vatican Bank's Veil of Secrecy," *Financial Times*, October 16, 2009.

27 Ibid. See also an extensive interview with Gotti Tedeschi by Angela Ambrogetti, "Economics from a Catholic Perspective," *Inside the Vatican*, March 7, 2012. See also Stacy Meichtry, "Vatican Revamps Its Bank's Ranks," *The Wall Street Journal*, September 25, 2001, 1.

28 Meichtry, Ibid.

29 John L. Allen Jr., "New Vatican Bank Scandal Threatens to Erupt," *National Catholic Reporter*, September 21, 2010; John Thavis, "Vatican Bank Head Named in Money-Laundering Probe," Catholic News Service, September 21, 2010.

30 "Renewal of the Board of Superintendence of the IOR," Vatican City, Vatican Information Service, September 23, 2009; see also "Supreme Knight Appointed to Board of Vatican Bank," Catholic News Agency, September 23, 2009; Stacy Meichtry, "Vatican Revamps Its Bank's Ranks," *The Wall Street Journal*, September 25, 2001, 1. Anderson carried particular influence at the Vatican because the Knights of Columbus that he ran counted 1.8 million members. That made it the world's largest Catholic service organization.

31 Andreas Wassermann and Peter Wensierski, "Transparency vs. Money Laundering: Catholic Church Fears Growing Vatican Bank Scandal," *Der Spiegel*, July 2, 2012; Jonathan Manthorpe, "Pope Benedict Tries to Purify Scandal-ridden Vatican Bank," *The Vancouver Sun*, July 3, 2012.
32 The best synopsis of Gotti Tedeschi's background is by Sandro Magister, "The Vatican Bank Has a New Laissez-Faire President: Ettore Gotti Tedeschi," *L'Espresso*, October 1, 2009.
33 Gotti Tedeschi interviewed in Ambrogetti, "Economics from a Catholic Perspective." He emphasized his practical business experience. "Don't forget that for twenty years I've been the president of the Italian unit of one of the largest banks in the world. For ten years I have been an independent board member of the Italian government's bank, the Deposits and Loans Fund. I am chairman of the Infrastructure Fund."
34 Magister, "The Vatican Bank Has a New Laissez-Faire President."
35 Rino Cammilleri and Ettore Gotti Tedeschi, *Denaro e Paradiso. L'economia globale e il mondo cattolico* (Money and Paradise: The Global Economy and the Catholic World) (Milan: Piemme, Casale Monferrato, 2004); Gotti Tedeschi's solid connections to the Vatican were evident in the publication of that book: the preface was written by Cardinal Giovanni Battista Re, the Prefect of the Vatican Congregation for Bishops. See Sandro Magister, "A Catholic Banker Tells How to Produce Wealth for the Kingdom of God," *L'Espresso*, October 11, 2004.
36 Sandro Magister, "Financial Crisis. The Good News Is Coming from the Vatican," *L'Espresso*, February 27, 2009.
37 His morality was intertwined with his economic theories. For instance, in an October 24 note to Benedict's private secretary, Monsignor Gänswein, Gotti Tedeschi commented on a credit crunch facing European and American banks: "The excessive lending from banks is an effect, not a cause. The cause is declining birth rates in the Western world, with repercussions on economic growth and increased costs due to an aging population." Letter from Gotti Tedeschi to Gänswein reproduced in Nuzzi, *Ratzinger Was Afraid*, 194, 205.
38 Gotti Tedeschi quoted in David Gibson, "Vatican Bank Probe Threatens New Scandal for Beleaguered Pope," *Politics Daily/Huffington Post*, 2011.
39 Only church historians and coin collectors knew that in a 1930 charter that Pius XI had established the gold lira as the city-state's official currency. But those coins were issued only for commemorative purposes. See Philip W. Willan, "Vatican to Adopt the Euro," *The Guardian*, December 22, 1998.
40 "Vatican, EU Update Financial Accord," Zenit, December 18, 2009.
41 Guy Dinmore, "The Vatican: A Murky See," *Financial Times*, September 24, 2010.
42 Unnamed "Vatican representative" quoted in Rachel Donadio and Andrew Higgins, "Power Struggle on Reforming Vatican Banks," *The New York Times*, March 10, 2013, 1.
43 Andrea Tornielli, "The Vatican's Temptation to Exit the Euro," "Vatican Insider," *La Stampa*, July 24, 2012; Lai, *Finanze vaticane*, 99.
44 The language in the agreement said in part: "The Vatican City State shall undertake to adopt all appropriate measures, through direct transpositions or possibly equivalent actions, for the application of all relevant Community legislation on the prevention of money laundering, on the prevention of fraud and counterfeiting of cash and non-cash means of payment." See online at http://eur-lex.europa.eu/LexUriServ/LexUriServ.do?uri=CELEX:52009PC0570:EN:NOT. "EU and Vatican Sign a New Monetary Accord," Vatican City, *ANSAmed—English*, December 17, 2009; "Vatican, EU Update Financial Accord," Zenit, December 18, 2009.
45 "And only in recent months has the Holy See decided to prosecute money laundering: until April 2010, it did not even consider it a crime." Nuzzi, *Ratzinger Was Afraid*, 28.
46 Dinmore, "The Vatican: A Murky See:" That following January ASPA chief, Cardinal Attilio Nicora, was selected as the chief of a new IOR section whose goal was to facilitate the bank's progress for eventually qualifying for the white list.
47 Nicole Winfield, "US Appeals Court Nixes Vatican Bank Holocaust Suit," Associated Press, International News, Vatican City, December 30, 2009.

Chapter 36: The World Has Changed

1 Jeffrey Owens quoted in Nicole Winfield, "Prosecutors Doubt Vatican Money-Laundering Pledges," *Bloomberg BusinessWeek*, October 30, 2010.

2 Andrea Gagliarducci, "Vatican Finance Group Signs Agreement with German Counterpart," Catholic News Agency, December 4, 2013.
3 Gagliarducci, "Vatican Finance Group Signs Agreement with German Counterpart."
4 Nuzzi, *Ratzinger Was Afraid*, 89.
5 John Thavis, "Vatican Bank Head Named in Money-Laundering Probe," *Catholic News Service*, September 21, 2010; see also "Vatican Bank Board Fires President, Citing Neglect of Duties," *The Catholic Register*, May 28, 2012; Stacy Meichtry and Margherita Stancati, "Vatican Bank's Officials Probed: Italian Prosecutors Look at Allegations Identities of Clients Weren't Disclosed," *The Wall Street Journal*, September 22, 2010.
6 "Vatican Bank 'Investigated over Money-Laundering,'" BBC, News Europe; "Vatican 'Perplexed' by Vatican Bank Probe," *The Catholic Universe*.
7 Giovanni De Censi, the director of Credito Artigiano's parent company, Credito Valtellinese, was a member of the IOR's board of advisors. Meichtry and Stancati, "Vatican Bank's Officials Probed: Italian Prosecutors Look at Allegations Identities of Clients Weren't Disclosed"; Dinmore, "The Vatican: A Murky See."
8 Unnamed Bank of Italy official interviewed in Guy Dinmore, "The Vatican: A Murky See," *Financial Times*, September 24, 2010.
9 The entire statement: "The clear desire for full transparency regarding the financial operations of the Institute for the Works of Religion (IOR), demonstrated many times by the authorities of the Holy See, is well known. That requires that procedures designed to prevent terrorism and money-laundering be put into effect. For this reason, the authorities of IOR for some time have been pursuing the necessary contacts and meetings, both with the Bank of Italy and the relevant international bodies—the Organization for Economic Cooperation and Development, and the Financial Action Task Force—in order to insert the Holy See into the so-called "White List."

"The Holy See, therefore, is perplexed and astonished by the initiative of the Prosecutor of Rome, especially since the information necessary is already available from the relevant offices of the Bank of Italy, and analogous operations are going on concurrently with other Italian institutions of credit.

"Regarding the cited transactions, it should be noted that these are operations of a transfer of credit for non-Italian institutions, the consignee of which is the IOR.

"The Holy See expresses its maximum confidence in the president and director general of the IOR."

As translated in John L. Allen Jr., "New Vatican Bank Scandal Threatens to Erupt," *National Catholic Reporter*, September 21, 2010.
10 Lombardi quoted in John Thavis, "Vatican Bank Head Named in Money-Laundering Probe," Catholic News Service, September 21, 2010. Lombardi letter quoted in Speciale, "Unmasking the Vatican's Bank"; see also "Vatican Finances Aboveboard, Affirms Aide," Zenit, September 23, 2010.
11 Dinmore, "The Vatican: A Murky See."
12 Guy Dinmore, "Sicily Probe Adds to Vatican Bank Pressure," *Financial Times*, November 3, 2010.
13 Ibid.
14 Unnamed Italian official quoted in ibid.
15 Jeffrey Donovan and Lorenzo Totaro, "Nazi Victims Ask EU to Probe Vatican on Looted Assets," Bloomberg, October 26, 2010; author interview with Jonathan Levy, February 21, 2012.
16 Guy Dinmore, "Vatican Bank Goes to Court over Frozen Funds," *Financial Times*, October 7, 2010; "Italian Judge Upholds Seizure of Vatican Assets," Associated Press, Rome, December 20, 2010.
17 Victor Simpson and Nicole Winfield, "Vatican Bank Hit by Financial Scandal . . . Again," *The Independent* (UK), December 19, 2010.
18 Barbie Latza Nadeau, "Vatican Banker Running Scared: Gotti Tedeschi Could Turn Whistle-Blower," *The Daily Beast*, June 10, 2102.
19 According to "a senior FATF official familiar with the negotiations [with the Vatican}" quoted in Winfield, "Prosecutors Doubt Vatican Money-Laundering Pledges."
20 MONEYVAL conducts extensive compliance checks in the central banks of EU member countries, and then monitors them regularly, particularly focusing on whether the banks meet a number of EU conventions: the 1980 Co-operation Group to Combat Drug Abuse and Illicit

Trafficking in Drugs; the 1990 Council of Europe Convention on Laundering, Search, Seizure and Confiscation of the Proceeds of Crime (ETS 141); the subsequent anti-money-laundering "Strasbourg Convention; the 2003 update to the Strasbourg Convention; the 2005 adoption of the Convention on Laundering, Search, Seizure and Confiscation of the Proceeds from Crime and on the Financing of Terrorism (CETS 198); and the 2009 Conference of the Parties to the Convention on Laundering, Search, Seizure and Confiscation of the Proceeds from Crime and on the Financing of Terrorism (CETS 198).

21 In reference to the IOR attempt to move forward on FATF compliance, journalist Nicole Winfield wrote, "Prosecutors, though, aren't buying any of it." Winfield, "Prosecutors Doubt Vatican Money-Laundering Pledges."

22 Amadeu Altafaj, the spokesman for the European Commissioner for Economic and Monetary Affairs, told reporters that the draft discussions set the groundwork for a substantive, new Vatican law. Amadeu Attafaj quoted in Sarah Paulsworth, "Vatican to implement EU financial crimes legislation by end of year," *Jurist,* October 30, 2010. For a detailed overview of the European Union's Financial Crimes statutes, see online at http://ec.europa.eu/internal_market/company/financial-crime/index_en.htm.

23 Unnamed FATF official interviewed in Winfield, "Prosecutors Doubt Vatican Money-Laundering Pledges." Author interview with former Papal advisor/assistant, identity withheld at their request, in Rome, September 2013; Dinmore, "Sicily Probe Adds to Vatican Bank Pressure."

24 Lai, *Finanze vaticane,* 100, 160; see also Andrea Tornielli, "The Vatican's Temptation to Exit the Euro," "Vatican Insider," *La Stampa,* July 24, 2012; and "Influential Prelate Said Vatican Should Drop Euro, Author Reports," *Catholic World News,* July 25, 2012. The author requested to interview Archbishop Viganò through the Vatican press office where it went unanswered.

25 Tornielli, "The Vatican's Temptation to Exit the Euro."

26 Author interview with former Papal advisor/assistant, identity withheld at their request, in Rome, September 2013.

27 Reprinted in full in Mutual Evaluation Report, Anti-Money Laundering and Combating the Financing of Terrorism, Committee of Experts on the Evaluation of Anti-Money Laundering Measures and the Financing of Terrorism, The Holy See (Including Vatican City State) (MONEYVAL), July 4, 2012, 12; see also Rachel Donadio, "The Vatican Creates a Financial Watchdog," *The New York Times,* December 30, 2010.

28 Press accounts sometimes confuse the names, using them interchangeably, or as if they are two separate entities. Reuters' Philip Pullella and Andrea Tornielli, respected Vaticanisti, use FIA as the abbreviation to refer to this financial watchdog unit set up in the Pope's motu propio (so does *The New York Times*). The Vatican, however, cites it on its own website as AIF, the initials used in this book. Also, the Autorità di Informazione Finanziaria has its own webpage. In the English translation provided by the Vatican, the unit is called the Financial Intelligence Authority. This book follows the names and initials as used by the Vatican.

See Tornielli at http://vaticaninsider.lastampa.it/en/the-vatican/detail/articolo/vaticano-vatican-finanza-finance-financia-19443/; Pullella at http://www.reuters.com/article/2011/01/19/us-vatican-bank-watchdog-idUSTRE70I39020110119; the AIF website at http://www.vatican.va/roman_curia/institutions_connected/aif/index.htm; and the Vatican's English translation of the name at http://w2.vatican.va/content/francesco/en/motu_proprio/documents/papa-francesco-motu-proprio_20131115_statuto-aif.html. See also the AIF's website in English at http://www.aif.va/ENG/Statuto.aspx.

29 Tully, "This Pope Means Business," *Fortune.*

30 It is online at http://www.vatican.va/holy_father/benedict_xvi/motu_proprio/documents/hf_ben-xvi_motu-proprio_20101230_attivita-illegali_en.html.

31 Dinmore, "The Vatican: A Murky See."

Bertone lobbied that the AIF chief be a friend of his, Professor Giovanni Maria Flick. But Benedict wanted to have a cleric, not a layman, at the helm. So Nicora was the compromise.

32 Nicora's fellow directors were Marcello Condemi, an economics law professor at Rome's Marconi University; Claudio Bianchi, an accounting professor at Rome's La Sapienza University; Professor Giuseppe Dalla Torre del Tempio di Sanguinetto, the rector of Rome's LUMSA university; and Cesare Testa, head of the department that manages the funds responsible for the salaries of priests in Italy. Philip Pullella, "Vatican Names Board of New Financial Authority," Reuters, Vatican City, January 19, 2011.

33 "Fr. Lombardi's Note Concerning the Motu Proprio," Vatican City, Vatican Information Service, December 30, 2010.
34 Ibid.
35 Email message from Jeffrey Owens, cited in Donadio, "The Vatican Creates a Financial Watchdog."
36 Gianluigi Nuzzi quoted in ibid.
37 Donadio, "The Vatican Creates a Financial Watchdog."

Chapter 37: The Powerbroker

1 Tom Kington, "Vatican Leaks: No Respite for Pope Benedict as More Documents Published," *The Guardian*, June 3, 2012; "Secrets of the Vatican," *Frontline*, PBS, February 2014.
2 "Vatican Diary / The strange case of the new prelate of the IOR," *La Repubblica*, July 30, 2012.
3 Author interview with Joan Lewis, February 10, 2014. "When the dust settles, the most obvious beneficiary of these moves would seem to be Italian Cardinal Tarcisio Bertone, the Secretary of State," wrote the *National Catholic Reporter*'s John Allen. John L. Allen Jr., "A Triptych on Benedict's Papacy, and Hints of What Lies Beyond," *National Catholic Reporter*, May 23, 2011.
4 Rocco Palmo, "Vatiwar: For the Italians, Retreat Week Becomes 'Fight Club'" *Whispers in the Loggia*, February 23, 2013; Palmo, "'Super-Nuncio,' Rome-Bound?," *Whispers in the Loggia*, July 13, 2011; Marco Tosatti, "A Tsunami of Italian Prelates in the Roman Curia," "Vatican Insider," *La Stampa*, July 18, 2011.
5 Andrea Tornielli, "Clash Between Cardinals Over the Cattolica University," "Vatican Insider," *La Stampa*, May 26, 2011; see also Nuzzi, *Ratzinger Was Afraid*, 140–44; "God's Bankers," *The Economist*, July 7, 2012.
6 "Mario Cal: The Mysterious Suicide That Has Rocked the Vatican," *The Independent* (UK), October 3, 2011.
7 Gotti Tedeschi quoted in Nuzzi, *Ratzinger Was Afraid*, 145, see also 144–49; Sandro Magister, "No Glorious Sunset for Cardinal Bertone," *L'Espresso*, February 2, 2012; Kington, "Vatican Leaks." See also "God's Bankers," *The Economist*. Giuseppe Rotelli, a prominent lawyer and government official, led a group of investors who subsequently bought the hospital for nearly $500 million.
8 Kington, "Vatican Leaks."
9 Edward Pentin, "Naming of New Cardinals Prompts Speculation About New Pope," Newsmax, January 10, 2012, http://www.newsmax.com/EdwardPentin/Cardinals-Pope-Benedict-Successor/2012/01/10/id/423629.
10 Nicole Winfield, "22 Cardinals Join Club to Elect Pope's Successor," Associated Press, February 18, 2012.
11 "Pope Butler Arrested, Vatileaks Tip of Iceberg: Dirt-Digging Cardinals Positioning Selves to Become Pope," http://specialguests.com/guests/viewnews.cgi?id=EFFlkuZVuZvDkOhDaO&style=Full%20Article.
12 Kington, "Vatican Leaks."
13 Unnamed Vatican analyst interviewed in ibid.
14 Author interview with Joan Lewis, February 10, 2014.
15 Mutual Evaluation Report, Anti-Money Laundering and Combating the Financing of Terrorism, Committee of Experts on the Evaluation of Anti-Money Laundering Measures and the Financing of Terrorism, The Holy See (Including Vatican City State) (MONEYVAL), July 4, 2012, 5.
16 Resolution CM/Res (2011) 5, on the participation of the Holy See (including the Vatican City State) in the mutual evaluation processes and procedures of the Committee of Experts on the Evaluation of Anti-Money Laundering Measures and the Financing of Terrorism (MONEYVAL) (Adopted by the Committee of Ministers on 6 April 2011 at the 1111th meeting of the Ministers' Deputies).
17 Gaia Pianigiani, "Vatican: Visitors Must Declare Cash," *The New York Times*, April 1, 2011.
18 Avi Jorisch, "The Vatican Bank: The Most Secret Bank in the World," *Forbes*, June 26, 2012.
19 Mutual Evaluation Report, Anti-Money Laundering and Combating the Financing of Terrorism, (MONEYVAL), 5.
20 The Moneyval team included: legal evaluator William Gilmore, a professor of International Criminal Law at the University of Edinburgh and a Moneyval Legal Scientific Expert; two financial examiners, Philipp Roeser, head of Liechtenstein's regulatory Financial Market Au-

thority, and Andrew Strijker, a Moneyval Financial Scientific Expert; two law enforcement evaluators, Boudewijn Verhelst, the Deputy Director of Belgium's Financial Intelligence Unit and a Moneyval Law Enforcement Scientific Expert, as well as Vladimir Nechaev, a senior member of Moneyval Russian Federation. General team members included John Ringguth, Moneyval Executive Secretary, and John Baker, a Moneyval Secretariat director.

21 Fr. Alexander Lucie-Smith, "Italy Is Now 'in the Abyss'—and the Vatican Will Not Escape This Disaster," *Catholic Herald*, November 11, 2011.

22 Besides the IOR, the Moneyval team met with representatives from the Prefecture for Economic Affairs, Secretariat of State, the Juridical Offices, the Governorate, the Administration of the Patrimony of the Apostolic See (APSA), the Gendarmerie, and the recently formed Financial Intelligence Authority (AIF). For a complete list of all the people the Moneyval team met with during their visits to the Vatican, see Annex 1 to Mutual Evaluation Report, Anti-Money Laundering and Combating the Financing of Terrorism, (MONEYVAL).

23 John Ringguth quoted in Elisabetta Povoledo, "Report Sees Flaws in Workings of the Vatican Bank," *The New York Times*, July 19, 2012, B9.

24 Avi Jorisch, "The Vatican Bank: The Most Secret Bank in the World."

25 Sanya Khetani, "A Vatican Whistleblower Was Transferred After Exposing Catholic Corruption," *Business Insider*, January 26, 2012; Philip Pullella, "Corruption Scandal Shakes Vatican as Internal Letters Leaked," Reuters, January 26, 2012.

See also: http://www.businessinsider.com/carlo-maria-vigano-vatican-corruption-2012-1#ixzz2sx6CZwyO.

26 An article in *Il Giornale* in March 2011 accused Viganò of being a reactionary who was upset with the reforms in the church. The opposite was in fact true.

27 Nuzzi, *Ratzinger Was Afraid*, 54–55, 67–69.

28 Viganò letter to Bertone, quoted in Nuzzi, *Ratzinger Was Afraid*, 57.

29 Viganò letter to Pope Benedict, March 27, 2011, quoted in Nuzzi, *Ratzinger Was Afraid*, 58, and reproduced in the original Italian at 244. See also Pullella, "Corruption Scandal Shakes Vatican."

30 Nuzzi, "Ratzinger Was Afraid," 58.

31 Viganò letter to Pope Benedict, quoted in Nuzzi, *Ratzinger Was Afraid*, 58-62.

32 Ibid., 61. Pullella, "Corruption Scandal Shakes Vatican." See also Sandro Magister, "Vatican Diary/Viganò, the Untouchable," *L'Espresso,* January 26, 2012.

33 Giacomo Galeazzi, "Vatican, the New Appointments," "Vatican Insider," *La Stampa*, February 11, 2011.

34 They were ex-Secretary of State, Angelo Sodano; the former chair of the Congregation of Bishops, Giovanni Battista Re; Raffaele Farina, head of the Vatican Library;, and Agostino Cacciavillan, who had been the ambassador to the U.S. for eight years. See Nuzzi, *Ratzinger Was Afraid*, 70.

35 Nuzzi, *Ratzinger Was Afraid*, 71–72. Also Author interview with former Papal advisor/assistant, identity withheld at their request, in Rome, September 2013.

Chapter 38: The Butler

1 Sandro Magister, "No Glorious Sunset for Cardinal Bertone," *L'Espresso*, February 2, 2012.

2 Author interviews, Rome, September 2013.

3 John Hooper, "Gentleman of his Holiness and his Prostitutes Stun Vatican: Papal Usher Linked to Gay Prostitution," *The Guardian* (London), March 5, 2010.

4 Kertzer, *The Pope and Mussolini*, Kindle edition, locations1712–1832 of 10577.

5 Author interview with Peter K. Murphy, January 31, 2014.

6 Marinelli used the pseudonym "The Millenaria"; taken from the Latin *millenarius*, it refers literally to a society or religious movement "containing a thousand." Because of that name, critics initially thought a group wrote the book. It was published the following year, 2000, in the U.S. under the title *Shroud of Secrecy: The Story of Corruption Within the Vatican* (Toronto: Key Porter, 2000).

7 Millenari, *Shroud of Secrecy*, 110–11.

8 Alessandra Stanley, "Tell-All Book Creates Furor at Vatican," *The New York Times*, July 17, 1998.

9 Francis quoted in Daniel Burke, "Pope Francis: 'Gay Lobby' Exists Inside Vatican," CNN, June 11, 2013.

10 Francis quoted in Rachel Donadio, "On Gay Priests, Pope Francis Asks, 'Who Am I to Judge?,'" *The New York Times*, July 29, 2013.
11 Lizzy Davies, "Swiss Guard Veteran Claims Existence of 'Gay Network' at the Vatican," *The Guardian*, January 20, 2014.
12 John Follian and Gretchen Achilles, *City of Secrets: The Truth Behind the Murders at the Vatican* (New York: William Morrow, 2003); John L. Allen Jr., "Power and Secrecy Feed Conspiracy Theories in Vatican City," *National Catholic Reporter*, July 31, 1998; Barbie Latza Nadeau, "Vatican Murder Mystery: Was it a Gay Love Triangle," *The Daily Beast*, November 14, 2011. See also Nuzzi, *Ratzinger Was Afraid*, 116.
13 Christina Boyle and Stephen Rex Brown, "Report: Vatican Owns Building That Houses Cardinals and Europe's Biggest Gay Bathhouse," *New York Daily News*, March 11, 2013.
14 David Badash, "Catholic Church Threatens Lawsuits: We Sell 'Erotica,' Not Pornography!," *The New Civil Rights Movement*, November 3, 2011, online at http://thenewcivilrightsmovement.com/catholic-church-threatens-lawsuits-we-sell-erotica-not-pornography/news/2011/11/03/29594.
15 Author interview, Rome, September 2013; Katie McDonough, "The Vatican Plays Landlord to Europe's Biggest Gay Bathhouse," *Salon*, March 12, 2013, online at http://www.salon.com/2013/03/12/the_vatican_plays_landlord_to_europes_biggest_gay_bathhouse/.
16 Nuzzi, *Ratzinger Was Afraid*, 8.
17 Author interview with retired Vatican colleague of Gabriele, September 19, 2013.
18 Giacomo Galeazzi, "The 'Family' That Lives With Benedict XVI," "Vatican Insider," *La Stampa*, May 26, 2012.
19 Magister, "Vatican Diary/Viganò, the Untouchable." The Finance and Management Committee that was the focus of particular criticism consisted of Massimo Ponzellini, Pellegrino Capaldo, Carlo Fratta Pasini, and before he became the president of the IOR, Ettore Gotti Tedeschi. See also Nuzzi, *Ratzinger Was Afraid*, 28-30.
20 Nicole Winfield, "Exclusive: Vatican Rewrites Money Launder Law," Associated Press, January 27, 2012; see also Andrea Tornielli, "The Vatican Anti-Money Laundering Law Has Responded to Moneyval," "Vatican Insider," *La Stampa*, June 21, 2012.
21 Andrea Gagliarducci, "Holy See and Financial Transparency. The Path to the White List," *Monday Vatican*, June 25, 2012.
22 "Fr. Lombardi: Statement Regarding Italian TV Program," Vatican Radio, January 26, 2012.
23 Ibid.
24 Marco Tosatti, "The Secretariat of Mysteries and the Shadows of Accomplices," "Vatican Insider," *La Stampa*, May 29, 2012.
25 Ibid; also Nuzzi, *Ratzinger Was Afraid*, 122.
26 Andrea Tornielli, "IOR: A Subtle Transparency," "Vatican Insider," *La Stampa*, February 1, 2012; see also John L. Allen Jr., "Yet More Vatican Leaks," *National Catholic Reporter*, February 15, 2012.
27 Nuzzi, *Ratzinger Was Afraid*, 21, 34.
28 Ibid., 18, 21, 29, 33. Tom Kington, "Pope's Butler Arrested After Inquiry into 'Vatileaks': Documents Found in Search of Vatican Flat: Journalist Says Source Wanted to Fight 'Hypocrisy,'" *The Guardian*, May 26, 2012, 34; Barbie Latza Nadeau, "VatiLeaks Exposes Internal Memos of the Catholic Church," *The Daily Beast*, May 24, 2012.
29 Magister, "No Glorious Sunset for Cardinal Bertone."
30 See generally http://www.vatileaks.com/_blog/Vati_Leaks/post/The_leaked_Vatican_documents/.
31 John L. Allen Jr., "Roman Notebook: Yet Another Vatican Financial Scandal," *National Catholic Reporter*, February 8, 2012.
32 Francesco Antonio Grana, "Dalla finanza alla sanità: le manovre di Bertone, vero potere nel papato Ratzinger," *Il Fatto Quotidiano*, February 23, 2013.
33 "Holy See Press Office Rejects Unfounded Claims About the IOR and the AIF," Vatican Information Service, Vatican City, February 9, 2012.
34 "Vatican Rejects Prelate's Corruption Allegations," Associated Press, Vatican City, February 4, 2012.
35 Stacy Meichtry, "After Centuries of Secrecy, Vatican Vexed by Leaks," *The Wall Street Journal*, February 18, 2012.
36 John L. Allen Jr., "Vatican Abuse Summit: $2.2 Billion and 100,000 Victims in U.S. Alone," *National Catholic Reporter*, February 8, 2012; Nuzzi, *Ratzinger Was Afraid*, 80, citing "Vatican

Insider." The estimate of the total amount paid to victims does not include the amounts in sealed settlements. In those cases, a condition of the victim dropping the case is agreeing not to disclose what the church paid.

37 "The Catholic Church's Vatileaks Scandal: A Guide," *The Week*, July 27, 2012.

38 Nick Squires, "Vatileaks: '20 People Involved in Stealing Documents,' Says Pope's Butler," *The Telegraph*, September 6, 2012.

39 Nick Squires, "Vatican Ruled by 'Omerta' Code of Silence, Whistle-blower Claims," *The Telegraph*, February 23, 2014.

40 Magister, "No Glorious Sunset for Cardinal Bertone."

41 The other cardinals were Salvatore De Giorgi, Julián Herranz, and Jozef Tomko.

42 Rachel Donadio, "After Pledging Loyalty to Successor, Pope Leaves Vatican," *The New York Times*, February 28, 2013; "The Vatican Gendarmerie for a year has intercepted all the curia—Clarification of *Panorama*; "Lombardi: 'Checks may have been carried out on two or three individuals'," "Vatican Insider" and Panorama.it, February 28, 2103.

43 Winfield, "22 Cardinals Join Club to Elect Pope's Succcessor."

44 Pope Benedict quoted in Ingrid D. Rowland, "The Fall of the Vice-Pope," *The New York Review of Books*, June 16, 2014.

45 Winfield, "22 Cardinals Join Club to Elect Pope's Succcessor."

Chapter 39: A Vote of No Confidence

1 Philip Pullella, "U.S. Adds Vatican to Money-Laundering 'Concern' List," Reuters, March 8, 2012; Nick Squires, "Vatican Bank Faces Fresh Controversy," *London Telegraph*, March 19, 2012.

2 Phillip Pullella and Lisa Jucca, "Vatican Bank Image Hurt as JP Morgan Closes Account," Reuters, March 19, 2012; "Vaticano, dai dossier di Gotti Tedeschi spunta il giallo di JP Morgan Vaticano, dai dossier di Gotti Tedeschi spunta il giallo di JP Morgan," *Il Messaggero*, June 10, 2012.

3 Rachel Sanderson, "The Scandal at the Vatican Bank," *The Financial Times Magazine*, December 6, 2013.

4 Andrea Tornielli, "The Vatican and Transparency: Moneyval's Objections," "Vatican Insider," *La Stampa*, May 8, 2012. See Committee of Experts on the Evaluation of Anti-Money Laundering Measures and the Financing of Terrorism (MONEYVAL), June 2, 2014.

5 Author interview with former associate at the IOR, identity withheld at their request, Rome, September 2013.

6 Tornielli, "The Vatican and Transparency"; Andreas Wassermann and Peter Wensierski, "Transparency vs. Money Laundering: Catholic Church Fears Growing Vatican Bank Scandal," *Der Spiegel*, July 2, 2012.

7 Author interview with former associate at the IOR, identity withheld at their request, Rome, September 2013.

8 Nick Pisa, "Prosecutors Investigate Vatican Bank Mafia Link," *The Telegraph*, June 10, 2012.

9 Ibid.

10 The bishop, Francesco Micciché, was removed for "alienation of property," a violation of canon law in which a prelate's conduct puts the financial health of a diocese at risk. See John L. Allen Jr., "Hard Lesson for the Vatican: Firing a Bishop Doesn't End the Story," *National Catholic Reporter*, June 15, 2012; see also "Mafia Vatican Funds 'Explosive,'" *The Australian*, June 18, 2012.

11 Gianluigi Nuzzi, *Sua Santità: Le carte segrete di Benedetto XVI* (Milan: Chairelettere Editorie, 2012); see also Nuzzi, *Ratzinger Was Afraid*, 27.

12 A few journalists were hesitant to accept as true everything leaked to Nuzzi. "First, this caution: The mere fact that a document exists does not automatically make its content credible. Some official documents, even if they're stamped 'top secret,' do little more than record gossip, spin or self-serving opinion," in John L. Allen, Jr., "Pondering the 'What,' Not the 'Who,' of Vatileaks," *National Catholic Reporter*, June 1, 2012.

13 Nuzzi, *Ratzinger Was Afraid*, 85–86.

14 Ibid., 116–120.

15 Although Boffo had been accused in 2002 of sexual harassment, the part of the accusation that was false was that he was gay and it was known to the police. The document with that conclusion,

that purported to be from the prosecutor's office, was a forgery. Ibid., 33–35. See also Barbie Latza Nadeau, "VatiLeaks Exposes Internal Memos of the Catholic Church," *The Daily Beast*, May 24, 2012; Nadeau writes that the false "allegations [were] that Boffo had harassed the wife of his gay lover." In under a year, Boffo got a new job as an editor at Tv2000, the official bishop's television channel.

16 Some generic published reports after Gotti Tedeschi was subsequently fired from the IOR said he had compiled a folder he was anxious to show the Pope, but no specifics were provided. See Nick Squires, "Ex-Head of Vatican Bank 'Planned to Give Dossier to Pope,'" *The Telegraph*, June 8, 2012.

17 John L. Allen, Jr., "Hard Lesson for the Vatican: Firing a Bishop Doesn't End the Story," *National Catholic Reporter*. Also, author interview with former associate at the IOR and with former Papal advisor/assistant, identity withheld at their request, Rome, September 2013.

18 Pisa, "Prosecutors Investigate Vatican Bank Mafia Link."

19 John L. Allen, Jr., "Hard Lesson for the Vatican: Firing a Bishop Doesn't End the Story," *National Catholic Reporter*. Also, author interview with former associate at the IOR and with former Papal advisor/assistant, identity withheld at their request, Rome, September 2013.

20 Author interview with former associate at the IOR, September 2013.

21 Ibid., and with former Papal advisor/assistant, identity withheld at their request, Rome, September 2013.

22 "IOR, il memoriale di Gotti Tedeschi. Ecco chi non voleva la norma antiriciclaggio," *Il Fatto Quotidiano*, June 12, 2012, 1.

23 Author interview with former associate at the IOR and with former Papal advisor/assistant, identity withheld at their request, Rome, September 2013. Requests to interview Monsignor Gänswein were submitted through press secretary, Father Federico Lombardi, and went unanswered.

24 Nicole Winfield, "Intrigue Mounts over Ouster of Vatican Bank Chief," Associated Press, Vatican City, June 9, 2012.

25 John Hooper, "Vatican Bank's Former President Accused of Negligence," *The Guardian*, June 10, 2012.

26 Andrea Gagliarducci, "I.O.R., Is Something Going to Change?," *Monday Vatican*, June 6, 2011.

27 Philip Pullella and Silvia Aloisi, "Insight: Vatican Bank—Money, Mystery and Monsignors."

28 Author interview with former associate at the IOR, identity withheld at their request, Rome, September 2013 see also Pullella and Silvia Aloisi, "Insight: Vatican Bank—Money, Mystery and Monsignors."

29 Marco Bardazzi, "No Transparency. That's Why We Fired Gotti Tedeschi," "Vatican Insider," *La Stampa*, May 27, 2012; "Vatican Bank Board Fires President, Citing Neglect of Duties," *The Catholic Register*, May 25, 2012.

30 Pullella and Silvia Aloisi, "Insight: Vatican Bank—Money, Mystery and Monsignors."

31 Bardazzi, "No Transparency. That's Why We Fired Gotti Tedeschi."

32 Philip Pullella, "Vatican Faces Widening of Leaks Scandal," Vatican City, Reuters, May 27, 2012.

33 Andrea Tornielli, "Tobin and His Coming and Going from the Roman Curia," "Vatican Insider," *La Stampa*, October 20, 2012, online at http://vaticaninsider.lastampa.it/en/world-news/detail/articolo/tobin-stati-uniti-united-states-estados-unidos-vescovi-bishops-obispos-19061/.

34 "Vatican Bank Board Fires President, Citing Neglect of Duties," *The Catholic Register*.

35 Ibid.

36 Andrea Gagliarducci, "Holy See and Financial Transparency. The Path to the White List," *Vatican-Monday*, June 25, 2012; see also Francesca Biagiotti, "Ior, Gotti Tedeschi ai pm: 'Tarantola mi fa sempre vedere le lettere che manda,'" *Il Fatto Quotidiano*, June 15, 2012.

37 Gotti Tedeschi quoted in "Vatican Bank Board Fires President, Citing Neglect of Duties," *The Catholic Register*.

38 Gotti Tedeschi quoted in Pullella and Silvia Aloisi, "Insight: Vatican Bank—Money, Mystery and Monsignors."

39 "Benedict XVI Surprised by IOR Chief Sacking, Says Secretary; Prelate Describes Relationship of Mutual Esteem Between Popes," ANSA English Media Service, Vatican City, October 22, 2013.

Chapter 40: "A Time Bomb"

1 Nick Pisa, "The Pope's Butler Arrested Following Vatileaks Investigation," *The Telegraph*, May 25, 2012, 1.
2 Tom Kington, "Vatican Leaks." See generally Jeffrey Kofman and Phoebe Natanson, "Vatican Documents Leaked: Did Butler Paolo Gabriele Do It?" ABC News, May 28, 2012.
3 Anderson interviewed in Bardazzi, "No Transparency. That's Why We Fired Gotti Tedeschi."
4 Marco Lillo, "IOR, Gotti Tedeschi 'spiato' da un medico. 'Disfunzioni psicopatologiche, va cacciato,'" *Il Fatto Quotidiano*, June 9, 2012, 1; see also John Hooper, "Vatican Bank's Former President Accused of Negligence," *The Guardian*, June 10, 2012.
5 Andrea Gagliarducci, "Holy See and Financial Transparency. The Path to the White List."
6 Avi Jorisch, "The Vatican Bank: The Most Secret Bank in the World."
7 Anderson interviewed in Bardazzi, "No Transparency. That's Why We Fired Gotti Tedeschi."
8 Ibid. See also Maria Antonietta Calabrò, "Così lo Ior ha sfiduciato Gotti Tedeschi," *Corriere della Sera*, May 26, 2012.
9 Letters quoted in Winfield, "Intrigue Mounts over Ouster of Vatican Bank Chief."
10 Kington, "Vatican Leaks: No Respite for Pope Benedict."
11 Andrea Gagliarducci, "Vatican Communications, Changes in the Making?" *Monday Vatican*, July 2, 2012.
12 "Mafia Vatican Funds 'Explosive,'" *The Australian*, June 18, 2012.
13 Unnamed priest quoted in ibid.
14 Author interview with former consultant to the IOR, identity withheld at their request, Rome, September 2013.
15 See Andrea Tornielli, "Vatican Bank's Former Head Under Shock After House Search," "Vatican Insider," *La Stampa*, June 6, 2012.
16 Ibid. Also author interview with attorney, name withheld at their request, Rome, September 2013; see also Wassermann and Wensierski, "Transparency vs. Money Laundering: Catholic Church Fears Growing Vatican Bank Scandal."
17 See generally for Vatican resistance to EU oversight Pullella and Silvia Aloisi, "Insight: Vatican Bank—Money, Mystery and Monsignors."
18 Author interview with attorney, name withheld at their request, Rome, September 2013.
19 There were four prosecutors waiting for Gotti Tedeschi: Vincenzo Piscitelli and Henry J. Woodcock from Naples, and Giuseppe Pignatone and Nello Rossi of Rome.
20 Author interview with attorney, name withheld at their request, Rome, September 2013.
21 See also John Hooper, "Vatican Bank's Former President Accused of Negligence," *The Guardian*, June 10, 2012.
22 Stacy Meichtry, "Vatican Peels Back Veil on Its Secretive Bank," *The Wall Street Journal*, June 29, 2012, C3.
23 Memo entry quoted in Wassermann and Wensierski, "Transparency vs. Money Laundering: Catholic Church Fears Growing Vatican Bank Scandal."
24 "If we continue with Bertone's line, we'll never get off the blacklist," Gotti Tedeschi reportedly told the prosecutor. Ibid.
25 Ibid.
26 Marco Lillo, "IOR, Gotti Tedeschi 'spiato' da un medico. 'Disfunzioni psicopatologiche, va cacciato,'" *Il Fatto Quotidiano*, June 9, 2012, 1.
27 Ibid. See also Andrea Gagliarducci, "Too much talking about Gotti Tedeschi. While the Holy See is working to gain financial transparency," *Monday Vatican*, June 11, 2012.
28 Vatican statement quoted in Winfield, "Intrigue Mounts over Ouster of Vatican Bank Chief."
29 Philip Pullella and Silvia Aloisi, "Insight: Vatican Bank—Money, Mystery and Monsignors," Vatican City, June 8, 2012; see also Bardazzi, "No Transparency. That's Why We Fired Gotti Tedeschi"; Winfield, "Intrigue Mounts over Ouster of Vatican Bank Chief."
30 Bertone quoted in "Vatican Blames Media for Scandals," *The Independent* (London), June 18, 2012.
31 Meichtry, "Vatican Peels Back Veil on Its Secretive Bank."
32 As for how the brief visit to the IOR was reported, see Wassermann and Wensierski, "Transparency vs. Money Laundering: Catholic Church Fears Growing Vatican Bank Scandal."

Chapter 41: The Swiss James Bond

1 The report is dated July 4, which is the date on which Moneyval provided a copy to the Vatican. It then provided the city-state time to respond, causing some final edits to the draft. After that response period, the report was released publicly on the 18th. For a digital copy see http://www.coe.int/t/dghl/monitoring/moneyval/Evaluations/round4/MONEYVAL(2012)17_MER_HS_en.pdf.

2 Half the bank's clients are from religious orders; 15 percent are Holy See institutions, 13 percent are cardinals, bishops, and clergy, 9 percent are from Catholic dioceses. The remainder should have some "affiliation to the Catholic Church." See Sanderson, "The Scandal at the Vatican Bank."

3 Povoledo, "Report Sees Flaws."

4 Mutual Evaluation Report, Anti-Money Laundering and Combating the Financing of Terrorism (MONEYVAL).

5 Ibid., par. 797, 147.

6 "Moneyval Report: Giving Concrete Form To The Moral Commitment Of The Vatican And The Holy See," Holy See Press Office, Vatican Information Services (VIS), Wednesday, July 18, 2012.

7 Nicole Winfield, "Pope's Butler Pleads Innocent to the Theft Charge," Vatican City, Associated Press, October 2, 2012; Elisabetta Povoledo, "Pope's Former Butler Admits He Leaked Documents," *The New York Times*, October 2, 2012.

8 See "Vatileaks, Sentenced to Two Months the Computer Sciarpelletti," *Il Fatto Quotidano*, November 10, 2012; Giacomo Galeazzi, "The Poison-Pen Writer Has an Accomplice," "Vatican Insider," *La Stampa*, August 13, 2012.

9 Gabriele trial testimony quoted in Nicole Winfield, "Pope's Butler Pleads Innocent to the Theft Charge."

10 Gabriele trial testimony quoted in Elisabetta Povoledo, "Pope's Former Butler Admits He Leaked Documents."

11 Author interview with René Brülhart, Rome, September 23, 2013.

12 "On His Holiness's Public Service: Can the Man Who Cleaned Up One Tiny State Do the Same for Another?," *The Economist*, October 20, 2012.

13 Rachel Donadio and Andrew Higgins, "Power Struggle on Reforming Vatican Banks."

14 Author interview with René Brülhart, Rome, September 23, 2013.

15 Ibid.

16 Ibid.

17 "On His Holiness's Public Service," *The Economist*.

18 Author interview with René Brülhart, Rome, September 23, 2013.

19 Ibid. Much of what he instituted was a rigorous KYC "know your customer" protocol. KYC had been in place since 2002 but poorly executed. Now, under Brülhart, client profiles are extensive. Background information is obtained about the account holder, the source of the money, and what it is used for. All of that is rudimentary to virtually every modern bank, but at the IOR, where secret proxies had controlled accounts for decades, it seemed revolutionary.

20 Elisabetta Povoledo and Harvey Morris. "Debit and Credit Card Purchases Shut Down at Vatican," *The New York Times*, January 4, 2013.

21 Ibid.

22 Sanderson, "The Scandal at the Vatican Bank."

23 "Vatican Radio—Vatican Finance Expert Responds to Moves by Bank of Italy," January 13, 2013, as reported in M. Antonietta Calabro, "The Vatican Surprised to Block Bank of Italy," *Corriere della Sera*, January 13, 2013.

24 Author interview with René Brülhart, Rome, September 23, 2013.

25 Ibid.

26 Ibid.

27 Declaratio (declaration) of Pope Benedict, February 10, 2013, online at http://www.vatican.va/holy_father/benedict_xvi/speeches/2013/february/documents/hf_ben-xvi_spe_20130211_declaratio_en.html.

28 Author interview with René Brülhart, Rome, September 23, 2013. As for general speculation about why Benedict might have resigned, see generally Mark Dowd, "Why Did Pope Benedict XVI Resign," BBC Radio 4, November 28, 2013.

29 The three cardinals were Spain's Julián Herranz, Slovakia's Jozef Tomko, and Palermo's Salvatore De Giorgi. See generally John Hooper, "Papal Resignation Linked to Inquiry into 'Vatican Gay Officials', Says Paper," *The Guardian*, February 21, 2013; Bill Hutchinson, "Vatican Clergy Gay-Sex Shock Priest Pics Real Drag for Benedict," New York *Daily News*, February 23, 2013, 4.
30 Dowd, "Why Did Pope Benedict XVI Resign."
31 Tom Kington, "Ex-Pope Benedict Says God Told Him to Resign During 'Mystical Experience,'" *The Guardian*, August 21, 2013; Cindy Wooden, "Retired Pope's Secretary Says 'Mystical Experience' Story Is Untrue," *Catholic News Service*, August 26, 2013.
32 Assorted author interviews, names withheld on request, Rome, September 19, 21, 23, 2013; as for general speculation about why Benedict might have resigned, see generally Dowd, "Why Did Pope Benedict XVI Resign."
33 Paolo Rodari, quoted in Rachel Donadio, "'Constant Drumbeat' Hastened the Pope's Exit," *The New York Times*, February 13, 2013, A11.
34 Nuzzi, *Ratzinger Was Afraid*, 9–10.
35 Lombardi statement quoted in Mark Dowd, "Why Did Pope Benedict XVI Resign?" *BBC News Magazine*, BBC Radio 4, November 27, 2013.
36 Rachel Donadio, "Pope Names German Industrialist to Head Vatican Bank," *The New York Times*, February 16, 2013, A6.
37 "Pope Approves German Lawyer to Head Embattled Bank," *USA Today*, February 15, 2013.
38 Alessandro Speciale, "Ernst von Freyberg: Controversial New Vatican Bank President Appointed By Pope Benedict," *The Huffington Post*, February 15, 2013.

Chapter 42: "The People's Pope"

1 Tracy Wilkinson, "As a New Pope Is Chosen, Latin America Hopes for More Sway—Although a Latin American Pope Appears Unlikely, the 19 Cardinals from the Region Who Have a Vote at Next Month's Conclave Are Hoping to Have More Influence This Time," *Los Angeles Times*, February 23, 2013.
2 John L. Allen Jr., "Profile: New Pope, Jesuit Bergoglio, Was Runner-up in 2005 Conclave," *National Catholic Reporter*, March 3, 2013.
3 Howard Chua-Eoan and Elizabeth Dias, "Pope Francis, the People's Pope," *Time*, December 11, 2013.
4 Paul Byrne, "Will the Next Pope Be Black?; Benedict XVI Quits—Who'll Succeed Him? Ghanaian Cardinal Is Front-runner to Take Over," *Daily Mirror*, February 12, 2013, 6–7.
5 Matthew Fisher, "Ouellet Was 'Very Close' to Papacy; Canadian Cardinal Was in a Two-Man Race with Argentina's Bergoglio, Media Reports Claim," *The Gazette* (Montreal), March 16, 2013, A3.
6 Nick Squires, "Division Among Cardinals Paved Way for Selection of Pope Francis," *The Christian Science Monitor*, March 15, 2013.
7 Fisher, "Ouellet Was 'Very Close' to Papacy," A3.
8 Brady and Dolan quoted in Squires, "Division Among Cardinals Paved Way for Selection of Pope Francis."
9 "Pope Francis Reveals Why He Chose His Name," *Catholic Herald*, March 16, 2013.
10 Squires, "Division Among Cardinals Paved Way for Selection of Pope Francis."
11 Sharon Churcher and Tom Worden, "Special report: The damning documents that show new Pope DID betray tortured priests to the junta," *The Daily Mail*, March 16, 2013; "Pope Francis: What Did He Really Do in Argentina in the 1970s?" *The Guardian*, March 20, 2013; Jeevan Vasagar, "Pope Francis Pledged to Fight for Priest Kidnapped by Junta, 1976 Letter Reveals," *The Telegraph*, March 18, 2013.
12 *Pope Francis: From the End of the Earth to Rome*, compiled by reporters from *The Wall Street Journal* (New York: ePub, 2013), Kindle edition, 406-466 of 1782.
13 Ibid., 558, 560, and 615 of 1782.
14 See "Jorge Mario Bergoglio is the new Pope of the Catholic Church: Francis I," "Vatican Insider," *La Stampa*, March 13, 2013.
15 See Sandro Magister, "The 'Segretariola' of Francis, the Pope Who Wants To Do It All Himself," *L'Espresso*, August 9, 2013. Benedict, meanwhile, moved into a 600-year-old unused convent in

the Vatican. The internet carried the unsourced story that he wanted to retire and end his days in his native Germany but he feared that without the protection of Vatican sovereignty, he could be arrested by the International Criminal Court in the Hague for crimes against humanity for protecting pedophile clerics. In fact, some U.S. sex abuse victims had made such a request in 2011, but the Hague never acted on it. The Vatican dismissed it at the time as a "ludicrous publicity stunt." Manuel Roig-Franzia, "Despite Investigating Catholic Scandals, Author Jason Berry Keeps the Faith," *The Washington Post*, September 20, 2011.

16 See generally "Cardinal Pell: Pope Francis's Good Press Won't Last Forever," *Catholic Herald*, August 8, 2013.

17 Pope Francis quoted in Jon Favreau, "The Social-Minded Pope Francis is a Very Different Kind of Pontiff," *The Daily Beast*, January 14, 2014.

18 Pope Francis quoted in Laurie Goodstein and Elisabetta Povoledo, "Pope Sets Down Goals for an Inclusive Church, Reaching Out 'on the Streets,'" *The New York Times*, November 26, 2013. In September 2014, Pope Francis witnessed the marriages of twenty Roman couples, some of whom had lived together or had previous annulments. Some press reports cited it as further evidence that Francis was breaking with tradition. But Catholic periodicals pointed out that the Pope had not in fact formally veered from church dogma. See "No Scandal Here: The 20 Couples Married by Pope Francis Were Legit," *National Catholic Register*, September 16, 2014.

19 Pope Francis quoted in Antonio Spadaro, S.J., "A Big Heart Open to God," *America—National Catholic Review*, September 19, 2013.

20 Pope Francis quoted in Laurie Goodstein and Elisabetta Povoledo, "Pope Sets Down Goals for an Inclusive Church, Reaching Out 'on the Streets;'" and Chua-Eoan and Dias, "Pope Francis, the People's Pope."

21 "Pope Francis, The People's Pope," *TIME*, December 11, 2013; "Person of the Year," *The Advocate*, December 16, 2013.

22 Mark Binelli, "Pope Francis: The Times They Are A-Changin'," *Rolling Stone*, January 28, 2014.

23 William Saletan, "Pope Francis Is a Liberal," *Slate*, September 19, 2013.

24 See Marshall Connolly, "The Secret to Pope Francis' Fame REVEALED," *Catholic Online*, December 26, 2013, online at https://www.catholic.org/hf/faith/story.php?id=53689.

In 2014, *Fortune* ranked Francis number one on its list of "World's Greatest Leaders." And a magazine focused just on Francis was launched. *Il Mio Papa* promised to run pictures and news weekly to update Pope Francis's followers and fans. See Elisabetta Povoledo, "A New Magazine for Fans of the Vatican's Biggest Star," *The New York Times*, March 4, 2014; "Fortune Ranks the World's 50 Greatest Leaders," *Fortune*, March 20, 2014.

25 Eric Marrapodi, CNN Belief Blog editor.

26 Simon Edge, "Top of the Popes: Could Pope Francis Be the Most Popular One Yet?," *Express*, January 10, 2014.

27 Antonio Spadaro, S.J., "A Big Heart Open to God."

28 Pope Francis quoted in Francis X. Rocca, "Pope Condemns Abortion as Product of 'Throwaway Culture,'" Catholic News Service, September 20, 2013.

29 Pope Francis quoted in Steven Ertelt, "Pope Francis: Catholic Church Must Minister More to Women After Abortion," *LifeNews*, September 19, 2013, online at http://www.lifenews.com/2013/09/19/pope-francis-catholic-church-must-minister-more-to-women-after-abortion/. See generally Cheryl K. Chumley, "Pope Francis Takes Veiled Swipe at 'Progressive' Democrats," *The Washington Times*, November 26, 2013.

30 Pope Francis quoted in Matthew Schmitz, "Pope Francis on How to Talk About Abortion, Gay Marriage, and Contraception," *First Things*, online at http://www.firstthings.com/blogs/firstthoughts/2013/09/pope-francis-advice-on-how-to-talk-about-abortion-gay-marriage-and-contraception/.

31 "UN Panel Confronts Vatican on Child Sex Abuse by Clergy," *BBC News Europe*, January 16, 2014.

32 Kharunya Paramaguru, "Vatican Snubs U.N. Probe on Sex Abuse Cases," *Time*, December 4, 2013.

33 "U.N. Expresses "Deepest Concern" over Widespread Sexual Abuse by Clergy, Finding Vatican Failed to Protect Children," Center for Constitutional Rights, February 5, 2014; "The Vatican: Criticism From the U.N. Panel, *The New York Times*, May 24, 2014, A7. To its credit, in September 2014, the church put Archbishop Jozef Wesolowski under house arrest inside the Vatican

and announced it would hold its first ever criminal trial of a cleric on charges of sex abuse. The Polish-born Wesolowski had been recalled to Rome in 2012 after numerous allegations of sex with young boys in the Dominican Republic, where he was stationed as Nuncio. Laurie Goodstein, "Former Vatican Ambassador Is Facing Sexual Abuse Trial," *The New York Times*, September 23, 2014. In November, Francis excommunicated an Argentine priest who had been criminally convicted in 2011 of molesting four boys. Victims had been outraged that he had been allowed to spend all but 15 days of his sentence in a Buenos Aires monastery.

34 O'Malley quoted in John L. Allen Jr. and Lisa Wangsness, "Pope Softening Tone, Not Stance, O'Malley Says," *The Boston Globe*, February 9, 2014.

35 Ross Douthat, "The Pope and the Precipice," *The New York Times*, October 25, 2014.

36 Francis echoed many of his predecessors in condemning the greed and excesses of capitalism. But what set him apart was the vigor with which he tried to redirect the church toward serving the poor. When President Barack Obama met with Francis in 2014, they focused on a subject about which both agreed: the need to fight the growing disparity between rich and poor. See "A Pope for the Poor," *TIME*, July 29, 2013; "Obama Meets Pope Francis; Stressing Fight Against Inequality," *Boston Globe*, March 27, 2014.

37 "CNN Poll: Pope's Approval Rating Sky-High," CNN, December 24, 2013, online at http://religion.blogs.cnn.com/2013/12/24/cnn-poll-popes-approval-rating-sky-high/.

38 Simon Edge, "Top of the Popes: Could Pope Francis be the most popular one yet?" *The Express*, January 10, 2014.

39 "U.S. Catholics Admire the Pope Yet Differ With Many of His Views," ABC/Washington Post poll: The Pope and the Church," October 13, 2003, released October 15, 2003.

40 Kay Campbell, "Rock Star Pope Francis Makes Cover of 'Rolling Stone'—What's up with That?," *AL.com*, February 12, 2014, online at http://www.al.com/opinion/index.ssf/2014/02/rock_star_pope.html.

Chapter 43: "Back from the Dead"

1 Carol Glatz, "Vatican says number of Catholics, priests, bishops worldwide increased," *Catholic News Service*, March 12, 2012; Nuzzi, *Ratzinger Was Afraid*, 81.

2 Sanderson, "The Scandal at the Vatican Bank."

3 Phillip Pullella, "Insight: Pope to Review Vatican Bureaucracy, Scandal-Ridden Bank," Reuters, Vatican City, April 2, 2013.

4 For a full online copy of the 64-page AIF annual report for 2012, see http://goo.gl/715NOC. Andrea Tornielli, "Vatican Insider First Report by Vatican Financial Watchdog Reveals Suspicious Transactions," *La Stampa*, May 22, 2013.

5 Vatican Radio interview with IOR President Ernst von Freyberg, May 31, 2013.

6 Freyberg interviewed in ibid.

7 Cipriani quoted in Andrea Tornielli, "The Vatican Bank's Media 'War,'" "Vatican Insider," *La Stampa*, June 14, 2013.

8 The members were Cardinal Raffaele Farina, president; Cardinal Jean-Louis Tauran; Bishop Juan Ignacio Arrieta Ochoa de Chinchetru; Monsignor Peter Bryan Wells, secretary; and Dr. Mary Ann Glendon, a Harvard law professor and former U.S. ambassador to the Holy See. Letter of the Holy Father Francis for the Establishment of a Representative School Papal Commission for the Works of Religion, Vatican.va, June 26, 2013.

9 Rachel Donadio, "Pope Fills Key Job at Troubled Vatican Bank," *The New York Times*, June 16, 2013, 11.

10 Sandro Magister, "The Prelate of the Gay Lobby," *L'Espresso*, July 18, 2013.

11 Michael Day, "Pope's Bank Clean-Up Man Found Stuck in Elevator with Rent Boy," *Belfast Telegraph*, July 20, 2013; see also "Catholic Bishop in Charge of Cleaning Up Vatican Finances Got Stuck in a Lift with a Rent Boy and Lived with his Gay Lover in Uruguay," *Daily Mail Online*, July 20, 2013.

12 John Hooper, "Francis in Brazil: Vatican Politics: Sex Claims Raise Questions Over Key Papal Decision," *The Guardian*, July 22, 2013; see Barbie Latza Nedeau, "A Reformer in Rome: Pope Francis Appears Serious About Changing the Vatican, but a Scandal Looms," *Newsweek*, July 24, 2013.

13 "New Vatican Bank Official Reportedly Part of 'Gay Lobby,'" Catholic News Agency, July 18, 2013; John L. Allen, Jr., "Vatican Denies Scandal Report on Vatican Prelate," *National Catholic Reporter*, July 19, 2013.
14 The six were Jochen Messemer, a director of the German insurer, ERGO; Jean-Baptiste de Franssu, ex-chief of Invesco Europe's asset-management; George Yeo, Singapore's ex-Foreign Minister; Joseph Zahra, the former chairman of Malta's largest bank; Professor Enrique Llano, an economist from the University of Madrid; and Jean Videlain-Sevestre, a former senior executive at Citroën. Tully, "This Pope Means Business," *Fortune*.
15 Pope Francis quoted in Tully, "This Pope Means Business," *Fortune*.
16 The six laymen—together with a PR specialist, Francesca Immacolata Chaouqui, and a Spanish Bishop, Lucio Angel Vallejo Balda—became directors of the Pontifical Commission for Reference on the Organization of the Economic-Administrative Structure of the Holy See (COSEA). See "Chirograph of the Holy Father Francis for the Institution of a Pontifical Commission for Reference on the Organization of the Economic-Administrative Structure of the Holy See," Communique from the Secretary of State, July 18, 2013; Anita Bourdin, "Le pape veut simplifier et rationaliser les organismes du Vatican," Zenit, July 19, 2013.
17 Nick Schifrin, "Vatican Accountant Accused of Smuggling $26 Million in Private Jet with Ex-Italian Spy," ABC News, June 28, 2013.
18 Brülhart told the author that it was an STR—a suspicious transaction report—generated by the IOR that tripped up Scarano. It was a system about which he took great pride since he had introduced it after he became AIF's director. See also Michael Day, "The Bank of Keeping Mum or Being Dead: The Financial Scandals Just Keep Piling Up for the Vatican's Money-Men," *The Independent*, July 14, 2013, citing a report by Italian magistrates concluding a thirty month investigation into the Vatican Bank.
19 Philip Pullella, "A Look at the Arrested Vatican Monsignor's Lush Life, "ABS.CBN News, July 5, 2013.
20 Nick Squires, "Spy, Monsignor and Banker Arrested in Vatican Bank Fraud 'Plot,'" *The Telegraph*, June 28, 2013, 1. The tales about Scarano have grown more outlandish since his arrest. One acquaintance has told police he spotted the wayward monsignor in front of St. Peter's Square loading two suitcases of gold bullion into a van. But, as with many other stories that are often recounted in press reports or on the internet as if a proven fact, it is impossible to determine whether or not it is true.
21 Alessandro Speciale, "Pope Francis Cleans House at the Vatican Bank," Religion News Service, July 1, 2013. It took nearly two years before Tulli's replacement was picked: Gianfranco Mammì, a longtime IOR administrator with a reputation for independence.
22 Barbie Latza Nadeau, "Heads Roll at Vatican Bank," *The Daily Beast*, July 2, 2013.
23 Rolando Marranci, the ex-CFO of BNP Paribas's Italian subsidiary, became the deputy director and Antonio Montaresi, chief risk and regulatory officer for the New York branches of Italy's Banca Nazionale del Lavoro and Banca di Roma, was selected as the chief risk officer. Speciale, "Pope Francis Cleans House at the Vatican Bank."
24 Nicole Winfield, "Vatican Bank Director, Deputy Resign Amid Scandal," Associated Press, Business News, July 1, 2013. One of the Vatican names that kept coming up with Scarano was Paolo Mennini, APSA's Director General. He also happened to be one of the sons of Luigi Mennini, Marcinkus's former right-hand man at the Vatican Bank. Mennini, however, has never been charged with any wrongdoing. See Day, "The Bank of Keeping Mum or Being Dead: The Financial Scandals Just Keep Piling Up for the Vatican's Money-Men."
25 Author interview, IOR official, Rome, September 2013.
26 Carlo Bonini, "The Sins of the Bank of God: Money Laundering Prevention Circumvented for Years," *La Repubblica*, July 6, 2013.
27 "Ex-Vatican Bank Officials Broke Anti-Money Laundering Laws, Prosecutors Say," Reuters, July 15, 2013.
28 Gotti Tedeschi quoted in Philip Pullella, "Former Vatican Bank Head's Lawyers Threaten to Sue to Clear Name," Reuters, March 28, 2014.
29 Rachel Sanderson, "The Scandal at the Vatican Bank," *The Financial Times Magazine*, December 6, 2013.
30 John L. Allen Jr. "For Once, an Exposé That Helps the Vatican Bank," *National Catholic Reporter*, September 28, 2013. See also Speciale, "Pope Francis Cleans House at the Vatican Bank"; and

Sanderson, "The Scandal at the Vatican Bank." Freyburg quoted Stephanie Kirchgaessner, "Vatican Bank Agrees Landmark Tax Treaty with Italian Regulators," *The Guardian*, April 1, 2015.

31 See for example "Secretive Vatican Bank Takes Step to Transparency," *The New Zealand Herald*, October 1, 2013.

32 Andrea Tornielli, "Exit Bertone, Enter Parolin," "Vatican Insider,", *La Stampa*, August 31, 2013.

33 Sutherland quoted in Sanderson, "The Scandal at the Vatican Bank"; "Vatican Spurns UN Child Law Committee's Call for Changes to Canon Law," Catholic News Agency, September 30, 2014.

34 Pope Francis quoted in Laurie Goodstein, "Pope Assails Bureaucracy of Church as Insular," *The New York Times*, October 2, 2013, A6; "Pope Francis Sets Up a Group of Eight Cardinals to Advise Him," "Vatican Insider," *La Stampa*, April 13, 2013; "Secrets of the Vatican," *Frontline*, PBS, February 2014.

35 *Motu Proprio for the prevention and countering of money laundering, the financing of terrorism and the proliferation of weapons of mass destruction*, October 8, 2013.

36 Statuto Dell'autorità Di Informazione Finanziaria, Vatican News.va, November 18, 2013.

37 "Pope Names Private Secretary to Supervise Vatican Bank," Reuters, Rome, November 28, 2013.

38 Cheryl K. Chumley, "Pope Francis Sends Right-Hand Man to Oversee Vatican Inquiry," *The Washington Times*, November 28, 2013.

39 Freyberg had been under pressure to fill the post left empty since Cipriani's resignation in the spring, especially since it was only days before Moneyval was due back at the Vatican for yet another on-site evaluation. Kevin McCoy, "Rolando Marranci Named Vatican Bank General Director," *USA Today*, November 30, 2013.

40 "Vatican Finance Group Signs Agreement with German Counterpart," *Patheos*, December 4, 2013.

41 Author interview with René Brülhart, Rome, September 23, 2013; see also Sanderson, "The Scandal at the Vatican Bank."

42 Nigel Baker interviewed in Laura Powell, "Inside the World's Most Secretive Bank," *Economia*, December 12, 2013.

43 They were Vienna's Christoph von Schönborn, Toronto's Thomas Christopher Collins, and Cardinal Santos Abril y Castelló, archpriest of the Papal Basilica of St. Mary Major. Arjun Kharpal, "Pope Sacks 4 Cardinals in Vatican Bank in Cleanup," CNBC, January 16, 2014.

44 Di Taranto quoted in Arjun Kharpal, "Pope Sacks 4 Cardinals in Vatican Bank in Cleanup."

45 John L. Allen Jr., "Francis Taps Reformer for Financial Cleanup," *National Catholic Reporter*, January 30, 2014. When Moneyval made its first on-site evaluation in November 2001, Corbellini was undersecretary of the Vatican City administration, and in that role dealt with the European inspectors.

46 Andrea Gagliarducci, "Vatican's Financial Intelligence Authority Receives new President," Catholic News Agency, January 31, 2014.

47 Kharpal, "Pope Sacks 4 Cardinals in Vatican Bank in Cleanup."

48 Guy Dinmore, "Pope Decrees Sweeping Overhaul of Vatican's Financial System," *Financial Times*, February 24, 2014; see also Andrea Gagliarducci, "Pope Francis Shapes Vatican Finances Under Advice from His Cardinals," Catholic News Agency, April 1, 2013.

49 "Australian Cardinal to Head New Vatican Secretariat for Economy," News.Va (The Official Vatican Network), February 24, 2014. British Monsignor Brian Ferme, the ex-dean of the Faculty of Canon Law at Washington's Catholic University, was appointed as Pell's deputy. Francis's fifteen-member Council for the Economy was tasked with setting broad economic polices that the new Secretariat would then implement. Guy Dinmore, "Pope Decrees Sweeping Overhaul of Vatican's Financial System," *Financial Times*, February 24, 2014. The Pope also promised to name an auditor-general, who the Vatican said "will be empowered to conduct audits of any agency of the Holy See and Vatican city-state at any time."

50 Tom Kington, "Pope Francis Opts to Keep Scandal-Plagued Vatican Bank Alive," *Los Angeles Times*, April 7, 2014.

51 Barbie Latza Nadeau, "The Vatican Bank Is Back from the Dead," *The Daily Beast*, April 9, 2014.

52 Josephine McKenna, "Vatican's Financial Watchdog Reports 'Notable' Spike in Shady Transactions," Religion News Service, May 19, 2014.

53 Massimo Faggioli quoted in Sanderson, "The Scandal at the Vatican Bank."

54 Rachel Sanderson and Giulia Segreti, "Pope Cuts Scandal-Prone Vatican Bank Down to Size," *Financial Times*, July 7, 2014. Another public ruckus over Bertone at the same time was press re-

ports that Pope Francis was reportedly furious about Bertone's lavish spending on a 3,700-square-foot penthouse. Not only was the renovation expensive but it was a retirement home nearly five times larger than Francis's frugal one-bedroom Vatican apartment. Bertone later told an Italian journalist that, "I guarantee that the rooms are much smaller than those in some of the Vatican's other buildings. The pope was informed about everything, even the small secretary's office. He said to me, 'It's perfectly fine and you are entitled to it, seeing as you need to write your memoirs, given you have been witness to three papacies. . . .' " John Hooper, "Pope Said to Be Furious over Luxury Retirement Flat of Top Vatican Official," *The Guardian*, June 1, 2014; Bertone quoted in Andrea Purgatori, "Meet Cardinal Tarcisio Bertone, Pope Francis' Former Secretary of State," *Huffington Post*, February 18, 2015.

55 This write-off was part of the reason for the IOR's lower net profit of €2.9 million versus 2012's €86.6 million.

56 Cindy Wooden, "Vatican Denies Cardinal Bertone is Under Criminal Investigation," *Catholic Herald*, May 23, 2014.

57 Philip Pullella, "Pope Fires Entire Board of Vatican Financial Watchdog," Reuters, June 5, 2014.

58 Pope Francis quoted in Liam Moloney, "Pope Appoints Outside Experts to Oversee Vatican Finances," *The Wall Street Journal*, June 6, 2014, A7.

59 The new AIF directors include Juan C. Zarate, a Harvard law school professor and advisor at the Center for Strategic and International Studies, a Washington, DC, think tank; Marc Odendall, who administers philanthropic groups in Switzerland; Joseph Yuvaraj Pillay, a former managing director of Singapore's Monetary Authority; and Maria Bianca Farina, head of two Italian insurance companies.

60 Nicole Winfield, "Pope Francis Shakes Up Vatican Financial Watchdog," Associated Press, June 5, 2014.

61 Ibid.

62 Pope Francis quoted in Tully, "This Pope Means Business," *Fortune*.

63 Franssu was a director appointed the previous year to COSEA, one of Francis's financial advisory boards.

64 Glendon had been appointed to a less formal commission looking over the bank in 2013. Franssu had been one of the six financiers summoned to Rome in the summer of 2013 to brief Pope Francis on possible reforms.

65 Mark Thompson, "Vatican Turns to Wall Street to Fix Bank," CNN/Money, July 9, 2014.

66 Press Release for Financial Statement and Results, Istituto per le Opere di Religione, July 9, 2013. As of December 31, 2013, "The IOR had 17,419 customers (2012: approximately 18,900), of which 5,043 were Catholic institutions accounting for more than 80% of clients' assets and 12,376 individuals making up less than 20%. The recorded decrease in customers corresponds with a decrease in overall clients' assets of 5.9 %."

67 "Managing Mammon," *The Economist*, July 12, 2014.

68 Philip Pullella, "Vatican Bank To Be Scaled Back, Restructured: Sources," Vatican City, Reuters, July 7, 2014.

69 Pell quoted in Cindy Wooden, "Vatican Names New Bank President, Restructures Financial Offices," *National Catholic Reporter*, July 9, 2014. In March 2015, Francis passed a new round of statutes that further cemented his financial reforms.

70 Pell interviewed in John L. Allen Jr., "Finance czar aims to steer Vatican 'off the gossip pages,' " *The Boston Globe*, July 9, 2014. In November 2014, Pell distributed to all Vatican departments a 45-page manual on financial ethics and good behavior. It included new policies, emphasizing transparency and international accounting standards, all set to become effective January 1, 2015. Philip Pullela, "Vatican Issues Staff with Financial Ethics Guidebook," Reuters, Vatican City, November 6, 2014. In March 2015, Pell told a group of journalists: "Lay people are generally more expert than us when it comes to money. . . . [but] original sin is universal, lay people who manage finances are not a guarantee against difficulties arising." Pell quoted in Iacopo Scaramuzzi, "Pell: 'We Want a Jubilee That's Free from Economic Scandal,' " "Vatican Insider," *La Stampa*, March 31, 2015.

71 Some important details were buried in the agreement. The exchange of information extended back to 2009, possibly ensnaring some tax cheats who had not closed their IOR accounts until the past few years. And for the first time, Italians working inside the Vatican, as well as religious institutions based in Italy but banking with the IOR, would start paying taxes. But it also confirmed

the tax exemption of all buildings the Holy See owned in Italy, as well as reiterating the exemption for any basilicas or religious universities that had gotten extraterritorial status in the Lateran Pacts of 1929. See "Tax Agreement Between the Holy See and the Italian Republic," Vatican Information Service, Vatican City, April 1, 2015, at http://visnews-en.blogspot.com/2015/04/tax-agreement-between-holy-see-and.html; and the Announcement of Italy's Finance Ministry: *Italia e Santa Sede firmano un accordo in materia fiscal,* Comunicato Stampa N° 75 del 01/04/2015, at http://www.mef.gov.it/ufficio-stampa/comunicati/2015/comunicato_0075.html. See also Philip Pullella, "Italy, Vatican Sign Financial Information Exchange Deal," Reuters UK, April 1, 2015.

72 Frances D'Emilio, "Italy, Vatican Make Financial Pact, as Holy See Cleans House," Rome, Associated Press, April 1, 2015; Kay Aviles, "Vatican Bank: A Haven for Money Laundering & Tax Evasion No More," *International Business Times,* April 7, 2015; roundup of some Italian press comments in Marzia De Giuli, "Italian Media React Positively to Financial Transparency Accord with Vatican City," *Shanghai Daily,* April 3, 2015.

73 Gerald Posner, "The Vatican Bank: Are the Bad Old Days Finally Over?" Featured Perspective, *Tax Notes International* 77, no. 12, March 23, 2015, 1081–82. In June 2015 the Vatican and the U.S. also signed a tax sharing agreement.

74 Author interview with René Brülhart, Rome, September 23, 2013. Estimates from ranking cardinals advising Pope Francis about the reforms to Vatican finances is that they will not be complete until at least 2015. According to the NCR's John L. Allen Jr., all the financial changes are "revolutionary" and a "complete earthquake." But he notes, "The jury is still out on whether this reform will succeed." John L. Allen Jr., "If You Want More Evidence of the Francis Earthquake, Look at the Finances," *Crux,* November 6, 2014. See "Pope-C8 Meeting: Curia Reform Process Will Not Be Complete Until 2015," Iacopo Scaramuzzi, "Vatican Insider," *La Stampa,* April 29, 2014.

Index

Illustration Credits

Wikipedia Commons: 1, 3, 5, 6, 9, 11, 13, 22, 30, 37

Wikipedia Commons (Courtesy Museum of Fine Arts, Boston): 2

Museo Centrale del Risorgimento: 4

Library of Congress: 7, 17, 19

Wikipedia Commons (Courtesy of U.S. Department of the Interior): 8

German Federal Archives: 10, 14, 18, 20

Courtesy of Elan Steinberg: 12

Collezione Cartoline Albertomos: 15

AP Photo: 16, 28, 29, 31, 33

National Archives: 21, 35

© Bettmann/CORBIS: 23, 25, 26, 34, 36

© Corbis: 24

© Gianni Giansanti/Sygma/Corbis: 27

AP/Raul Fornezza: 32

© Andrzej Grygiel/epa/Corbis: 38

© KNA-Bild/dpa/Corbis: 39

© Gianni Giansanti/Immaginazione/Corbis: 40

Author photo of *Vanity Fair* cover: 41

© Stringer/Italy/Reuters/Corbis: 42

AP Photo/El Salvador School: 43

Author photo of *Time* cover: 44

© Alessandro Bianchi/Reuters/Corbis: 45